Blue Airguns
Eleventh Edition

by Dr. Robert D. Beeman & John B. Allen
Edited by S.P. Fjestad

$29.95
Publisher's Softcover
Suggested List Price

Publisher's Limited Edition
Hardcover Suggested List Price
$44.95 (limited quantities)

M000278218

Blue Book of Airguns™
Eleventh Edition

This book is the result of continual airgun research performed by attending shows and communicating with airgun dealers, collectors, company historians, contributing editors, and other knowledgeable industry professionals worldwide each year. This book represents an analysis of prices for which airguns have actually been selling during that period at an average retail level. Although every reasonable effort has been made to compile an accurate and reliable guide, airgun prices may vary significantly, depending on such factors as the locality of the sale, the number of sales we were able to consider, and economic conditions. Accordingly, no representation can be made that the airguns listed may be bought or sold at prices indicated, nor shall the author or publisher be responsible for any error made in compiling and recording such prices and related information.

All Rights Reserved
Copyright 2014
Blue Book Publications, Inc.
8009 34th Avenue South, Suite 250
Minneapolis, MN 55425 U.S.A.
Customer Service: 800-877-4867
Phone: 952-854-5229 (International)
Fax: 952-853-1486
Email: support@bluebookinc.com
Website: http://www.bluebookofgunvalues.com

Published and printed in the United States of America
ISBN 10: 1-936120-52-6
ISBN 13: 978-1-936120-52-9

Distributed in part to the book trade by Ingram Book Company and Baker & Taylor.
Distributed throughout Europe by:
Visier GmbH
Wipsch 1
Bad Ems, Germany D-56130
www.vsmedien.de

Deutsches Waffen Journal
Rudolf-Diesel-Strasse 46
Blaufelden, D-74572 Germany
Website: www.dwj.de

TABLE OF CONTENTS

ACKNOWLEDGEMENTS

Barry Abel	Mike Driskill	Yvette Hicks	Joe Murfin
Ingvar Alm	Fred Ehrlich	Matts Hammer	Dani Navickas
Dieter Anschütz	Laura Evans	Anders Hammerwall	Dave Nemanic
John Atkins	S.P. Fjestad	Larry Hannusch	Ed Niccum
Fredrik Axelsson	Dean Fletcher	Will Hartlep	Sue Piedmont
Dennis Baker	Kenth Friberg	Don Howard	Scott Pilkington
Geoffrey Baker	Bo Fred	Jon Jenkins	Wes Powers
Toshiko Beeman	Gregory Fuller	Denise Johnson	Don Raitzer
Larry Behling	Val Gamerman	Susan Johnston	Ron Sauls
Justin "JB" Biddle	Susan Gardner	John Knibbs	Tim Saunders
Randall Bimrose	Tom & Edith Gaylord	David Kosowski	David Swan
Adam Blalock	Peter Girardoni	Steve Loke	Joshua Ungier
George Brenzovich	Greg Glover	John McCaslin	Steve Upham
Gurney Brown	John Griffiths	Tim McMurry	Tod Utter
Robert Buchanan	John Groenewold	Paul Milkovich	John Walter

FALLEN COMRADES

Unfortunately, since the 10th Anniversary Edition *Blue Book of Airguns* was published, the airgun industry has lost some very significant collectors, shooters, and historians. They will be sorely missed.

Jim Coplen	Jack Haley
Big Bore Bob Dean	Mack McDonald
Jerry Franks	

ABOUT THE COVER & CREDITS

FRONT COVER:

The air rifle pictured comes to us from Daystate LTD located in Stone, Staffordshire, England. It's their new for 2014 Wolverine B Type PCP powered, bolt action, ten-shot repeating rifle with an ambidextrous walnut stock. The air pistol is an experimental model Daystate, originating from a joint venture with Harper Classic Guns in 2002. The Daystate Harper Classic Wolf is one of thirteen manufactured .22 caliber, PCP powered, eleven-shot repeating pistols with Electronic Firing System.

BACK COVER:

Photo courtesy S.P. Fjestad

Front cover images: Courtesy Daystate and Airguns of Arizona
Cover Design & Layout: Clint H. Schmidt & John B. Allen

11th Edition Credits:

Art Dept.: Clint H. Schmidt
Research & Contribution Coordinators: Dr. Robert Beeman & John B. Allen
Proofing/Copyediting: Lisa Beuning, Kelsey Fjestad, Cassandra Faulkner, and S.P. Fjestad
Background Textures by Brent C. Leimenstoll
Cover & Text Printing: Forms & Systems, Minnetonka, MN

While many of you have probably dealt with our company for years, it may be helpful for you to know a little bit more about our operation, including information on how to contact us regarding our various titles and other informational services.

Blue Book Publications, Inc.
8009 34th Avenue South, Suite 250
Minneapolis, MN 55425 USA
GPS Coordinates: N44° 51 28.44, W93° 13.1709
Phone No.: 952-854-5229 • Customer Service (domestic and Canada): 800-877-4867
Fax No.: 952-853-1486 (available 24 hours a day)
Web site: www.bluebookofgunvalues.com

General Email: support@bluebookinc.com - we check our email at 9am, 12pm, and 4pm M - F (excluding major U.S. holidays). Please refer to individual email addresses listed below with phone extension numbers.

To find out the latest information on our products, including availability and pricing, consumer related services, and up-to-date industry information (blogs, trade show recaps with photos/captions, upcoming events, feature articles, etc.), please check our website, as it is updated on a regular basis. Surf us - you'll have fun!

Since our phone system is equipped with voice mail, you may also wish to know extension numbers, which have been provided below:

Ext. 1000 - Beth Schreiber	(beths@bluebookinc.com)	Ext. 1800 - Tom Stock	(toms@bluebookinc.com)
Ext. 1300 - S.P. Fjestad	(stevef@bluebookinc.com)	Ext. 1900 - Cassandra Faulkner	(cassandraf@bluebookinc.com)
Ext. 1400 - Kelsey Fjestad	(kelseyf@bluebookinc.com)	Ext. 2000 - Adam Burt	(adamb@bluebookinc.com)
Ext. 1500 - Clint H. Schmidt	(clints@bluebookinc.com)	Ext. 2200 – Kate Steffenson	(kates@bluebookinc.com)
Ext. 1600 - John B. Allen	(johna@bluebookinc.com)		
Ext. 1700 - Zachary R. Fjestad	(zachf@bluebookinc.com)		

Office hours are: 8:30am - 5:00pm CST, Monday - Friday.

Additionally, an after-hours message service is available for ordering. All orders are processed within 24 hours of receiving them, assuming payment and order information is correct. Depending on the product, we typically ship Fed Ex, UPS, Media Mail, or Priority Mail. Expedited shipping services are also available domestically for an additional charge. Please contact us directly for an expedited shipping quotation.

All correspondence regarding technical information/values on guns or guitars is answered in a FIFO (first in, first out) system. That means that letters, faxes, and email are answered in the order in which they are received, even though some people think that their emails take preference over everything else.

Online subscriptions and informational services are available for the *Blue Book of Gun Values, Blue Book of Tactical Firearms Values, Blue Book of Modern Black Powder Arms, American Gunsmiths, Blue Book of Airguns, Ammo Encyclopedia, Blue Book of Pool Cues, Blue Book of Electric Guitars, Blue Book of Acoustic Guitars,* and the *Blue Book of Guitar Amplifiers.*

As this edition goes to press, the following titles/products are currently available, unless otherwise specified:

35th Anniversary Edition *Blue Book of Gun Values* by S.P. Fjestad

5th Edition *Blue Book of Tactical Firearms Values* by S.P. Fjestad

Blue Book Pocket Guide for Beretta Firearms & Values by S.P. Fjestad

Blue Book Pocket Guide for Browning/FN Firearms & Values 2nd Edition by S.P. Fjestad

Blue Book Pocket Guide for Colt Dates of Manufacture, 2nd Edition by R.L. Wilson

Blue Book Pocket Guide for Colt Firearms & Values 2nd Edition by S.P. Fjestad

Blue Book Pocket Guide for Remington Firearms & Values 2nd Edition by S.P. Fjestad

Blue Book Pocket Guide for Smith & Wesson Firearms & Values 2nd Edition by S.P. Fjestad

Blue Book Pocket Guide for Sturm Ruger Firearms & Values 2nd Edition by S.P. Fjestad

Blue Book Pocket Guide for Winchester Firearms & Values 2nd Edition by S.P. Fjestad

11th Edition *Blue Book of Airguns* by Dr. Robert D. Beeman & John B. Allen

8th Edition *Blue Book of Modern Black Powder Arms* by John Allen

Black Powder Revolvers - Reproductions & Replicas by Dennis Adler

Black Powder Long Arms & Pistols - Reproductions & Replicas by Dennis Adler

John Bianchi – An American Legend – 50 Years of Gunleather by Dennis Adler

3rd Edition *The Book of Colt Firearms* by R.L. Wilson

Book of Colt Paper 1834-2011 by John Ogle

L.C. Smith Production Records by Jim Stubbendieck

American Engravers – The 21st Century by C. Roger Bleile

Mario Terzi – Master Engraver by Elena Micheli-Lamboy & Stephen Lamboy

Firmo & Francesca Fracassi – Master Engravers by Elena Micheli-Lamboy & Stephen Lamboy

Giancarlo & Stefano Pedretti – Master Engravers by Elena Micheli-Lamboy & Stephen Lamboy

American Gunsmiths, 2nd Edition by Frank Sellers

Parker Gun Identification & Serialization, compiled by Charlie Price and edited by S.P. Fjestad

Blue Book of Electric Guitars, 14th Edition, by Zachary R. Fjestad

Blue Book of Acoustic Guitars, 14th Edition, by Zachary R. Fjestad

Blue Book of Guitar Amplifiers, 4th Edition, by Zachary R. Fjestad

Blue Book of Guitars 14th Edition DVD-ROM

Blue Book of Guitar Amplifiers 4th Edition CD-ROM

Gibson Flying V 2nd Edition by Larry Meiners & Zachary R. Fjestad

Gibson Amplifiers 1933-2008 – 75 Years of the Gold Tone by Wallace Marx Jr.

The Marshall Bluesbreaker – The Story of Marshall's First Combo by John R. Wiley

B.B. King's Lucille and the Loves Before Her by Eric E. Dahl

If you would like to get more information about any of the above publications/products, simply check our web sites: www.bluebookofgunvalues.com and www.bluebookofguitarvalues.com

We would like to thank all of you for your business in the past – you are the reason we are successful. Our goal remains the same – to give you the best products, the most accurate and up-to-date information for the money, and the highest level of customer service available in today's marketplace. If something's right, tell the world over time. If something's wrong, please tell us immediately – we'll make it right.

MEET THE STAFF

S.P. Fjestad
Editor/Publisher

Many of you may want to know what the person on the other end of the telephone/fax/email looks like, so here are the faces that go with the voices and emails.

John B. Allen
Co-Author & Associate Editor Arms Division

Lisa Beuning
Manuscript Editor

Cassandra Faulkner
Executive Editor

Adam Burt
President

Tom Stock
CFO

Clint H. Schmidt
Art Director

Kelsey Fjestad
Web Media Manager/Proofreader

Beth Schreiber
Operations Manager

Kate Steffenson
Operations

Katie Sandin
Operations

Zachary R. Fjestad
Author/Editor Guitar & Amp Division

HOW TO USE THIS BOOK

The prices listed in this edition of the *Blue Book of Airguns* are based on the national average retail prices a consumer can expect to pay for airguns that are mechanically and pneumatically functioning. This is not an airguns wholesale pricing guide (there is no such thing). More importantly, do not expect to walk into a gun/pawn shop or airgun/gun show and think that the proprietor/dealer should pay you the retail price listed within this text for your gun. Resale offers on most models could be anywhere from near retail to 50% less than the values listed. These prices paid will be depending upon locality, desirability, dealer inventory, and potential profitability. In other words, if you want to receive 100% of the price (retail value), then you have to do 100% of the work (become the retailer, which also includes assuming 100% of the risk).

Percentages of original finish, (condition factors with corresponding prices/values, if applicable) are listed between 20% and 100%.

Please refer to "Anatomy of an Airgun" to learn more about the various airgun parts and terminology. Also, you may want to check the Glossary and the Abbreviations for more detailed information about both nomenclature and airgun terminology.

A Trademark Index listing the current airgun manufacturers, importers, and distributors is provided. This includes the most recent email addresses, websites, and other pertinent contact information for these individuals and organizations. The Index is a handy way to find the make/model you're looking for in a hurry. To find an airgun in this text, first look under the name of the manufacturer, trademark, brand name, and in some cases, the importer (please consult the Index if necessary). Next, find the correct category name(s), typically Pistols, Rifles, and Shotguns.

Once you find the correct model or sub-model under its respective subheading, determine the specimen's percentage of original condition, and find the corresponding percentage column showing the price of a currently manufactured model or the value on a discontinued model.

Since this publication consists of 736 pages, you may want to take advantage of our Index as a speedy alternative to going through the pages, and our comprehensive Trademark Index and Importer/Distributor for a complete listing of airgun manufacturers, importers, and distributors. Don't forget to read the editorial "Gaylord Reports" by long time airgunner Tom Gaylord.

For the sake of simplicity, the following organizational framework has been adopted throughout this publication.

1 — **COMMANDO ARMS**
2 — **Current manufacturer located in Turkey. No U.S. importation.**
3 — Commando Arms manufactures air rifles in various configurations, as well as O/U, SxS, and semi-auto shotguns. For more information on their shotguns, please refer to the most recent edition of the *Blue Book of Gun Values*, or visit our website at www.bluebookofgunvalues.com.
4 — **RIFLES**
5 — Current models include AR-BS, AR-BV, AR-BA, AR-BC, T301, T201, 1000S, and 850S. Please contact the company directly for more information including options, pricing, and U.S. availability (see Trademark Index).

COMPASSECO, INC.
Previous importer/distributor located in Bardstown, KY beginning late-1980s. During 2010 Compasseco, Inc. joined business with Pyramyd Air International located in Solon, OH. Previously located in Warrensville Hts., OH. Dealer and

1. **Manufacturer Name or Trademark** - brand name, importer, or organization is listed alphabetically in uppercase bold face type.

2. **Manufacturer Status** - This information is listed directly beneath the trademark heading, providing current status and location along with importer information for foreign trademarks.

3. **Manufacturer Description** - These notes may appear next under individual heading descriptions and can be differentiated by the typeface. This will be specific information relating to the trademark or models.

4. **Category Name** - (normally, in alphabetical sequence) in upper case (inside a screened gray box), referring mostly to an airgun's configuration.

7 — **XL TACTICAL** – .177, .22, or .25 cal., BBC, SP, SS, 1000/730/700 FPS, 14.5 in. rifled steel barrel, blue finish, all-weather black synthetic stock and adj. two-stage trigger, high impact polymer compound stock is always warm to the touch, provides secure grip and remains warp-free in all climate conditions, full barrel noise dampener, vent. rubber recoil pad, raised cheek pad, rubber cushioned, anti-shock sight mounting rail, 37.5 in. OAL, 6.6 lbs. Mfg. 2007-current.

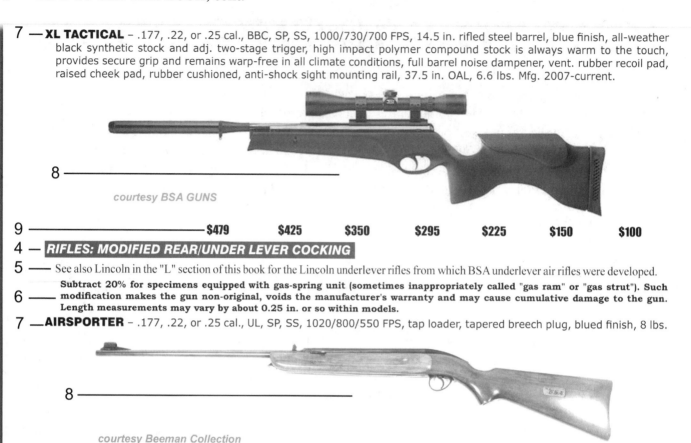

8 ————————————————————————

courtesy BSA GUNS

9 ———————————— **$479**   **$425**   **$350**   **$295**   **$225**   **$150**   **$100**

4 — **RIFLES: MODIFIED REAR/UNDER LEVER COCKING**

5 —— See also Lincoln in the "L" section of this book for the Lincoln underlever rifles from which BSA underlever air rifles were developed.

6 ——— **Subtract 20% for specimens equipped with gas-spring unit (sometimes inappropriately called "gas ram" or "gas strut"). Such modification makes the gun non-original, voids the manufacturer's warranty and may cause cumulative damage to the gun. Length measurements may vary by about 0.25 in. or so within models.**

7 — **AIRSPORTER** – .177, .22, or .25 cal., UL, SP, SS, 1020/800/550 FPS, tap loader, tapered breech plug, blued finish, 8 lbs.

8 ————————————————————————

courtesy Beeman Collection

13 — **Carbine versions with 14 in. barrels do not bring a premium.**

14 — This model was the first underlever to have a cocking lever hidden in the forearm.

---

5. **Category Note** - May follow a category name to help explain the category, and/or provide limited information on models and values.

6. **Category Price/Value Adjustment** - The last potential piece of information which may appear below a category name (above a model name) is a category price/value adjustment. These may be included here only if the adjustment applies to all models in the category.

7. **Model Name and Description** - appear flush left, are bold faced, and all upper-case letters, either in chronological order (normally) or alphabetical order (sometimes, the previous model name and/or close sub variation will appear at the end in parentheses) and are listed under the individual category names. These are followed by the model descriptions and usually include descriptive information about the model.

8. **Image** - Next in this long line of information an image of the model may appear, with a credit. A picture truly can say a thousand words.

9. **Price/Value line** - This information will either follow directly below the model name and description or, if there is an image, below the image. The information appears in descending order from left to right with the values corresponding to a condition factor shown in the Grading Line near the top of the page. 100% price on a currently manufactured airgun also assumes not previously sold at retail. In many cases, N/As (Not Applicable) are listed and indicate that the condition is not frequently encountered so the value is not predictable. On a currently manufactured airgun, the lower condition specimens will bottom out at a value, and a lesser condition airgun value will approximate the lowest value listed. An MSR automatically indicates the airgun is currently manufactured, and the MSR (Manufacturer's Suggested Retail) is shown left of the 100% column. Recently manufactured 100% specimens without boxes, warranties, etc., which are still currently manufactured must be discounted slightly (5%-20%, depending on the desirability of make and model). On vintage airguns, you may see N/As in the 100%-90% condition categories, as these original older guns are rarely encountered in 90%+ condition, and cannot be accurately priced. Higher condition factors may still exist, but if the only known sales have been of examples in 90% condition, a very desirable/collectible airgun may double or triple in value in the next higher condition range, so the value is not predictable. A currently manufactured airgun without a retail price published by the manufacturer/importer will appear as MSR N/A.

10 ——————————————————————————— **DAISY OUTDOOR PRODUCTS, cont. 281** **D**

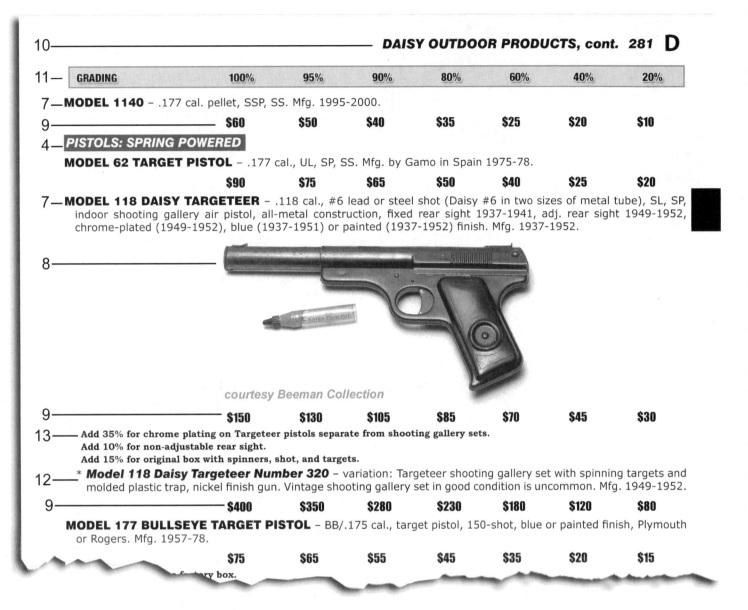

11 —

GRADING	100%	95%	90%	80%	60%	40%	20%

7 — **MODEL 1140** – .177 cal. pellet, SSP, SS. Mfg. 1995-2000.

9 ——————————————————— $60 $50 $40 $35 $25 $20 $10

4 — **PISTOLS: SPRING POWERED**

MODEL 62 TARGET PISTOL – .177 cal., UL, SP, SS. Mfg. by Gamo in Spain 1975-78.

$90 $75 $65 $50 $40 $25 $20

7 — **MODEL 118 DAISY TARGETEER** – .118 cal., #6 lead or steel shot (Daisy #6 in two sizes of metal tube), SL, SP, indoor shooting gallery air pistol, all-metal construction, fixed rear sight 1937-1941, adj. rear sight 1949-1952, chrome-plated (1949-1952), blue (1937-1951) or painted (1937-1952) finish. Mfg. 1937-1952.

8 —

courtesy Beeman Collection

9 ——————————————————— $150 $130 $105 $85 $70 $45 $30

13 —— Add 35% for chrome plating on Targeteer pistols separate from shooting gallery sets.
Add 10% for non-adjustable rear sight.
Add 15% for original box with spinners, shot, and targets.

12 — * **Model 118 Daisy Targeteer Number 320** – variation: Targeteer shooting gallery set with spinning targets and molded plastic trap, nickel finish gun. Vintage shooting gallery set in good condition is uncommon. Mfg. 1949-1952.

9 ——————————————————— $400 $350 $280 $230 $180 $120 $80

MODEL 177 BULLSEYE TARGET PISTOL – BB/.175 cal., target pistol, 150-shot, blue or painted finish, Plymouth or Rogers. Mfg. 1957-78.

$75 $65 $55 $45 $35 $20 $15

—— ...ory box.

---

10. **Alphabetical Section, Page Number, and Manufacturer Continued Heading** - Continued headings will aid the reader when looking at a manufacturer with several pages of model listings.

11. **Grading Line** - Grading lines will normally appear at or near the top of each page.

12. **Sub-model and Sub-Sub-model Name** - Variations within a model appear as sub-models, or sub-sub-models. They are differentiated from model names because they are preceded by a bullet, indented, and are in upper and lower case type, and are usually followed by a short description of that sub-model. These sub-model descriptions have the same typeface as the model descriptions.

13. **Model Price/Value Adjustments** - Extra cost features/special value orders and other value added/subtracted features are placed directly under individual price lines or in some cases,

category names. These individual lines appear bolder than other descriptive typeface. On many guns less than 15 years old, these add/subtract items will be the last factory MSRs (manufacturer's suggested retail price) for that option.

14. **Model Note** - Manufacturer and other notes/information appear in smaller type, and should be read since they contain both important and other critical, up-to-date information.

15. On many discontinued models/variations, a line may appear under the price line, indicating the last manufacturer's suggested retail price (MSR) or vintage era retail price (RP) flush right on the page.

FOREWORD

by S.P. Fjestad

Shown around the 5-Star Productions round-table set featured in *American Airgunner*, the entire production staff and "talent" finally take a small break before lunch. It remains the only television show dedicated to airgun shooting, hunting, collecting, and competing.

Welcome to the 11th Edition of the *Blue Book of Airguns*! Now expanded to 736 pages, it remains the largest single publication available today for up-to-date information and values on both currently manufactured and vintage airguns.

A lot has happened since the 10th Anniversary Edition was published two years ago. Today's advanced technology in manufacturing techniques combined with a very competitive airgun marketplace has resulted in a better selection of airguns. What this means is that today's airgun consumers willing to spend $150-$250 have never had more choices, regardless if the application is for simple target shooting, hunting, or even advanced competitive events.

I consider the current airgun marketplace to be composed of five segments based on the following price ranges:

- $35-$95 – These are typically BB guns that are used for plinking by beginning shooters. Most of these airguns do not have rifled barrels and represent a great value for a new young shooter. As such, they are the most important stepping stone to get kids involved in the shooting sports, and maybe take their next step up to firearms.

- $100-$250 – This price range offers more value to today's shooter than any other. For $200, a shooter can now buy a nice break barrel action capable of 700-950 FPS with surprisingly good accuracy. I remember paying $295 for my used Feinwerkbau 124 in the mid-1980s, and now many airguns in this price range have the same or better performance.

- $250-$500 – While unheard of a few years ago, this price range now includes some PCPs that give the shooter an outstanding value. This price point now also includes some of the less expensive target rifles and pistols.

- $500-$1,000 – These price points now represent a large segment of the advanced, adult airguns marketplace. These newest offerings are very sophisticated in terms of performance, features, and accuracy. Not only is their performance unequaled at this price level, but the look and eye appeal have never been greater.

- $1,000+ – This is definitely the top-end of the adult commercial airgun marketplace and includes such names as Air Arms, Anschütz, Daystate, FX, Feinwerkbau, Kalibrgun, Steyr, Walther, etc. These are the best of the best, and price points can easily go over $2,000.

Right before this 11th Edition went into production, I received an email from J.B. (Justin Biddle) inviting me to come down to Fort Smith, AR, and be part of the round-table segments of the TV series, *American Airgunner*, sponsored by Umarex USA.

Arriving at the round-table set inside of 5-Star Productions studio in downtown Fort Smith, Mike Hart and the rest of his talented crew got right down to business after the "talent" got powdered up – that included host Rossi Morreale, Tom Gaylord, Jim Chapman, Steve Criner, Rick Eutsler, and myself. We had a lot of fun during the segments I was involved with, and looking back, it was a great experience. I would certainly recommend to anyone interested in airgun shooting or hunting to watch *American Airgunner* on the Pursuit channel - you won't be disappointed.

As in the past, Tom Gaylord has contributed another great "Gaylord Reports" for this edition. Now referred to as "The Godfather of the Airgun Industry," Tom Gaylord remains the go-to guy for all information on today's newest crop of airguns and how they perform in real-world conditions. He's an old friend, and combined with his wife Edith, a seasoned editor/proofreader, they pack the best one-two punch of anyone currently writing about today's airgun industry.

Once again, John Allen is to be thanked for his commitment to this project. One of our local contributing editors who helps us out a lot is Ingvar Alm, who is not only very knowledgeable on vintage airguns, but also has a wealth of information on the operating systems of most airguns. This year, while Dr. Robert D. Beeman wasn't as active as he has been in the past updating the A-Z sections, he still remains extremely supportive in this project. Currently he is very busy trying to wrap up his new book entitled, *The Lewis & Clark Airgun - An Austrian Air Rifle Changed World History*. It should be out later this year, and I'm going to be one of the first to order a copy.

Don't forget this book is also available online and over 350 images have been added since the 10th Anniversary Edition was published two years ago!

I would like to thank our entire staff for doing an outstanding job on this publication over the years/editions including the publishing, editing, proofing, and operational support. It's a real team effort, and it shows. Last, but certainly not least, you, a valuable customer, are the real reason this publication continues to be successful – many thanks!

Sincerely,

S.P. Fjestad
Editor/Publisher – *Blue Book of Airguns*

INTRODUCTION

Co-author John B. Allen (L) with life-long friend and fellow Eagle Scout Eric Nerness elk hunting in southwest Montana's Beaverhead National Forest. We never pulled a trigger, but it was a great hunt.

When asked what's new in the Eleventh Edition *Blue Book of Airguns*, the short answer is we added 56 pages that are jammed full of new manufacturer listings, added existing manufacturers' new models, and increased the number of antique airgun listings. Over 350 new images have been added, and we also reviewed and/or updated the values of all existing models in the database. When asked what's new in the airgun industry for 2014, the short answer is to check out "Gaylord Reports" by Tom Gaylord for a hundred mile-an-hour view of where airguns are going. Tom outlines the newest airguns and innovations arriving on the scene for 2014. From the butt stock to grips, triggers to muzzles, Tom showcases several manufacturers and describes the latest models of pistols, rifles, and accessories to hit the market.

Many readers have asked how all of this information is assembled. Although we gather information year-round from manufacturers and industry trade/gun shows, this book would not be complete without our wonderful contributing editors. Most of them work in the airgun industry and come from a variety of different backgrounds, including dealers/collectors and major airgun manufacturers, as well as airgun product sales and marketing managers. Check out the Acknowledgements page for a list of the contributing editors who deserve a huge thanks for filling in very important pieces of this airgun "puzzle."

If you have an interest in airguns and want to get a leg up on your buddies before you go shopping, this book will help you. It doesn't matter if you are an airgun rookie or a seasoned veteran, some of the first sections you should visit are the Table of Contents and How to Use This Book. These sections will lead you to answers for questions on how this books is laid out, where to look for definitions of the new airgun terminology, and abbreviations used. They provide you with step-by-step descriptions along with pictures of sample pages to show you how the *Blue Book of Airguns* works. Combine this with the Photo Percentage Grading System and its color photos and descriptions to help understand condition rather than simply showing examples of what different conditions look like. The percentage of original finish on

an airgun (its condition) can be measured, but once the science of how to look at an airgun's condition is understood, the actual measuring part will become easier. The Glossary and Abbreviations sections are also expanded to include most of the definitions and explanations that are needed to properly use this book. We have updated and expanded both the Trademark Index and the Importers/Distributors Index with the latest contact information available including mailing addresses, phone and FAX numbers, websites, and email when available. Use these indexes to get all the contact information you need on each manufacturer's importer/distributor.

Once you know how to use this book, check out the expanded A-Z sections for all the latest information on new airgun manufacturers, new models, and updated prices. We have tried to include all the great information you need regarding descriptions and history for all current and vintage airgun manufacturers.

Here at Blue Book, we are doing our best to keep up with technological advancements. Similar to the Daystate air pistol on the front cover with an electronic trigger, our electronic/online products are moving forward. Don't miss our website (www.bluebookofgunvalues.com) to browse through the *Blue Book of Airguns* online subscription – yes, you can access the most up-to-date airgun information from any computer or mobile device - all you need is Internet access! Also included with our airgun/firearms online subscriptions is the inventory component ISP, which gives you the ability to inventory your entire collection online. Keep in mind that these online subscriptions are scheduled for monthly updates that include new model information and updated values that will reveal the information that our sources won't be able to release until much later. Please visit our website at www.bluebookofgunvalues.com for more information.

A project like this would never get finished without a great team effort, and I'm very proud of all the hard work done by everyone involved. Many thanks go to Beth, Katie, Kate, and Kelsey for their work year-round keeping our customers happy, our website fresh, products moving, and proofing. To Lisa and Cassandra, who help out with the manuscript content, research, and proofing. To Clint, our art director/production manager, who takes the work we've put into the database and turns it into a book. S.P. Fjestad, Author of the *Blue Book of Gun Values,* Editor for this project, and Publisher of all our projects; S.P. is the man behind the team who makes everything happen on time so we can move on to the next project. Thanks should also go to Tom and Adam, the guys behind the scenes that provide support in so many different ways. A very large thank you to all.

In closing, I'd like to thank you, our reader, for taking the time to pick up this latest Eleventh Edition. The *Blue Book of Airguns* is always a work-in-progress, and research is ongoing. Although we'll never claim to publish a perfect book, we are committed to making it the best we can. Please feel free to contact me with any corrections, additions, images, history, or information needed to make this a better title. This project would not be as successful without you – so Thank You!

John B. Allen
Co-author – *Blue Book of Airguns*

The Lewis & Clark Airgun
An Austrian Air Rifle Changed World History
by Dr. Robert D. Beeman

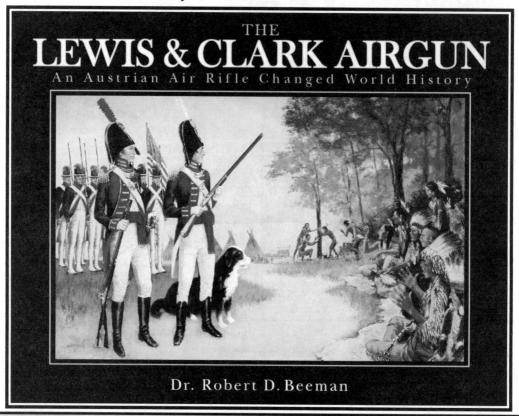

THE
LEWIS & CLARK AIRGUN
An Austrian Air Rifle Changed World History

Dr. Robert D. Beeman

Captain Lewis demonstrates his airgun to a large group of high ranking Yankton Sioux circa late August, 1804. Some of the Sioux's honor guard have run to the distant target tree and are incredulously reporting that numerous large lead balls had penetrated the bark and lodged into the wood.

Lewis and Clark revealed a rapid-fire, large-bore Girardoni repeating airgun on their famous expedition. Surely they were careful to never to let the natives see the gun charged or run out of balls or power. It apparently could fire infinitely without charging or loading and could easily do lethal damage without fire, smoke, or thunder. These explorers not only led the observers to believe they had many such guns (and perhaps other dreadful weapons) but also proclaimed loudly that they had far more power yet unrevealed. This amazing impression of the white man's incredible new generation of firepower may be why this vulnerable group of explorers was never attacked. These "firepower diplomacy" demonstrations were not casual entertainment, but rather the deterrent linchpin of a calculated power strategy that paid enormous dividends.

Publisher's Note: Dr. Robert D. Beeman has been very busy the last several years working on the definitive book on both the Lewis and Clark airgun, as well as Girardoni airguns. In this behalf, Dr. Beeman has traversed four continents to gather critical, in-depth information in addition to working with the top arms curators and gunsmiths in the closed-to-the public research labs in key arms museums such as the Heeresgeschichtliches Museum in Vienna, Austria, "ground-zero" for Girardoni research. Slated to be published and printed later this year, this new, deluxe, hard-bound publication will be a timeless story of how Lewis and Clark used a Girardoni repeating military air rifle as the "key" to the western expansion of the United States by providing for the safe return of these explorers in a very brief, critical time window. Without the firepower deterrent value of this incredible gun, the United States probably would still be a tiny group of colonies on the Atlantic seaboard, and it did this without ever firing a shot in anger or defense! For more information, including when the book will be available, please contact Dr. Beeman at BlueBookEdit@Beemans.net.

LIMITED EDITION - make a no-obligation reservation ASAP for an autographed copy.

Dr. Robert D. Beeman (left) and Peter Girardoni at the Girardoni family estate near Vienna, Austria. Peter is the present patriarch and historian of the family of the 18th century gunmaker Bartolomeo Girardoni. Peter and his wife, Pia Girardoni, graciously invited Robert and Toshiko Beeman to be their guests and to cooperate in studying the history of their ancestor, the family specimen of the Girardoni military repeating airgun, and specimens of battlefield and excavated Girardoni airguns at the Heeresgeschichtliches Museum in Vienna, Austria.

ANATOMY OF AN AIRGUN

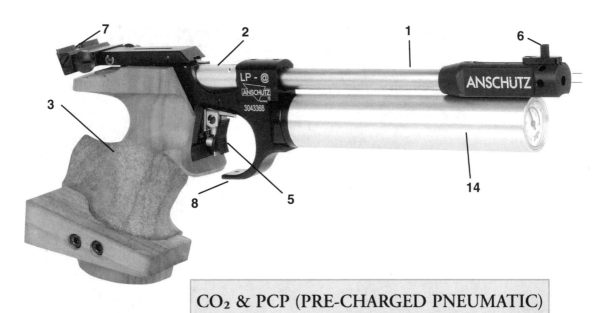

CO₂ & PCP (PRE-CHARGED PNEUMATIC)

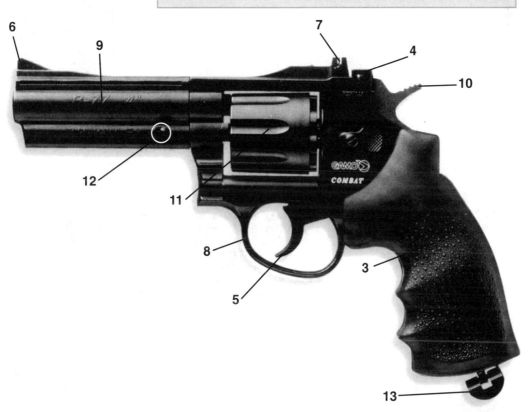

1. Barrel	6. Front Sight	11. Cylinder
2. Breech Area	7. Adjustable Rear Sight	12. Cylinder Base Pin Lock
3. Grip	8. Trigger Guard	13. CO₂ Cylinder Retaining Screw
4. Safety	9. Barrel Housing	14. Compressed Air Cylinder
5. Trigger	10. Hammer	

ANATOMY OF AN AIRGUN

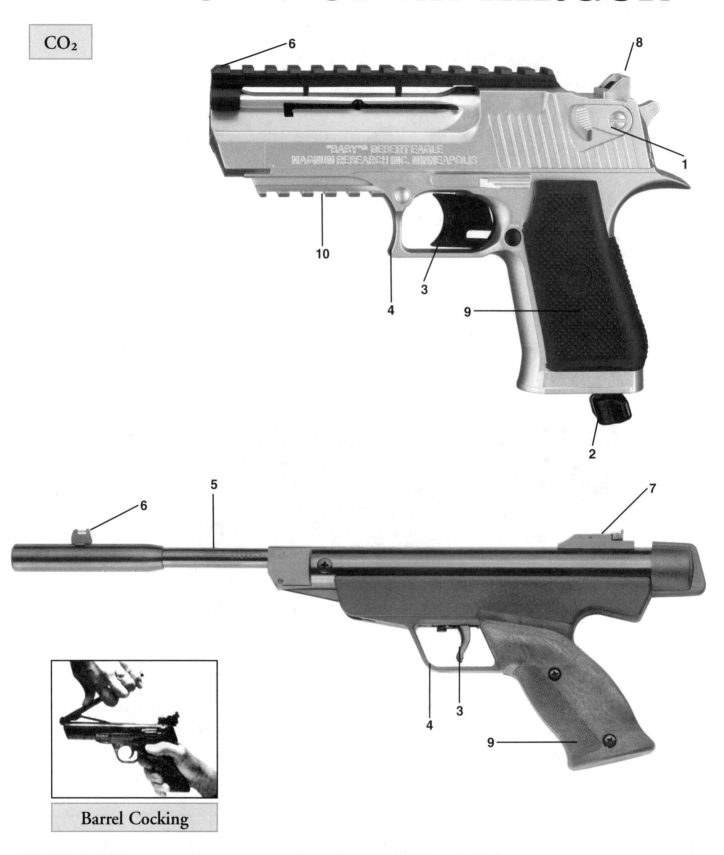

CO₂

Barrel Cocking

1. Safety	5. Barrel	9. Grip
2. CO₂ Cylinder Retaining Screw	6. Front Sight	10. Picatinny Rail (for mounting
3. Trigger	7. Adjustable Rear Sight	accessories)
4. Trigger Guard	8. Rear Sight	

ANATOMY OF AN AIRGUN

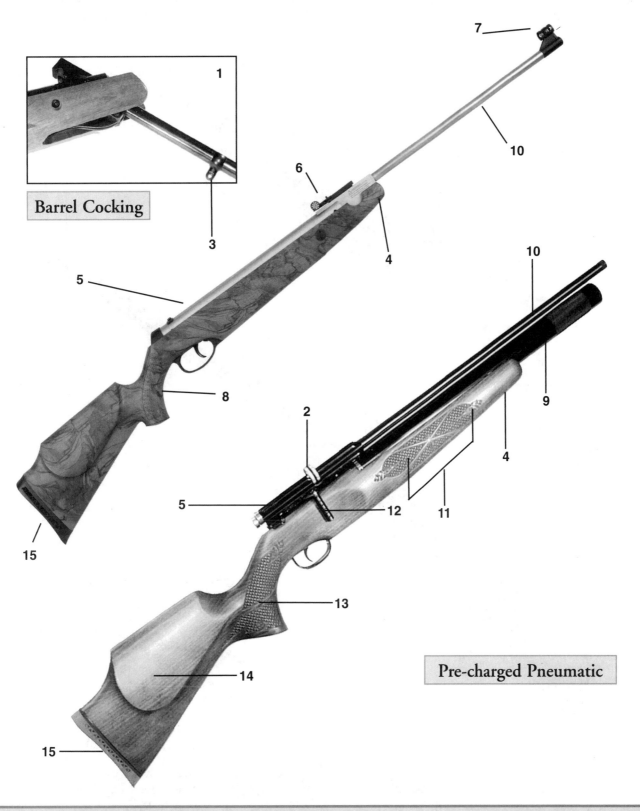

Barrel Cocking

Pre-charged Pneumatic

1. Barrel Cocking (barrel is pulled downward)
2. Rotary Magazine
3. Sling Swivel Studs
4. Forend
5. Grooved Receiver
6. Adjustable Rear Sight
7. Globe Front Sight
8. Semi-Pistol Grip
9. Cylindrical Air Reservoir
10. Barrel
11. Checkered Forearm
12. Bolt Handle
13. Full Pistol Grip
14. Monte Carlo Check Piece
15. Ventilated Recoil Pad

ANATOMY OF AN AIRGUN

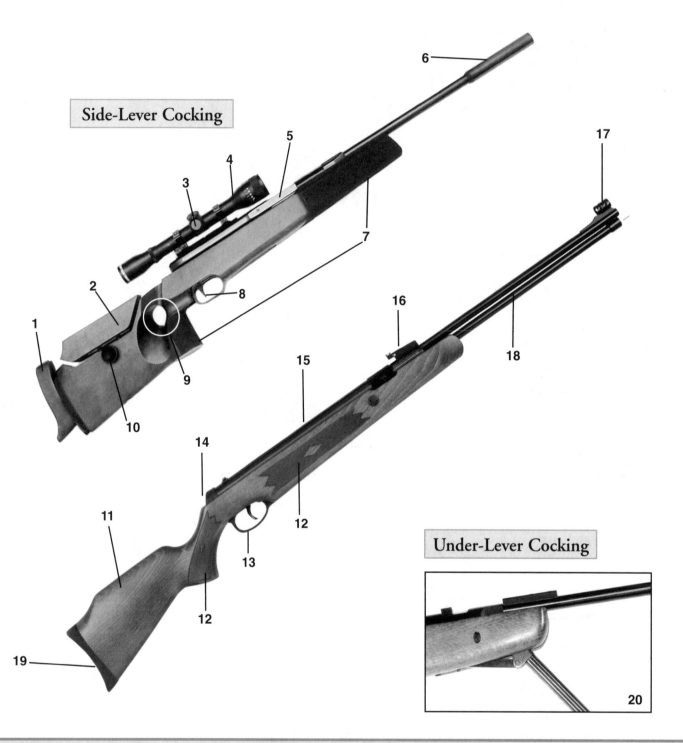

Side-Lever Cocking

Under-Lever Cocking

1. Adjustable Buttplate	7. Stippling	15. Grooved Receiver
2. Adjustable Cheekpiece	8. Trigger	16. Adj. Rear Sight
3. Vertical/Horizontal Scope Adjustments	9. Thumbhole Stock Design	17. Front Sight
4. Scope	10. Knob for Adjusting Cheekpiece	18. Under-Lever (for cocking)
5. Side-Lever For Cocking (lever is pulled out to the side)	11. Monte Carlo Cheekpiece	19. Recoil Pad
6. Muzzle Weight	12. Stock Checkering	20. Under-Lever Cocking (under-lever pivots downward)
	13. Trigger Guard	
	14. Safety	

GLOSSARY

ACTION

The working heart of an airgun; generally all of the working parts other than the stock, barrel, and sights (may or may not include the air compression or gas/air storage system).

AIRGUN

A gun that utilizes compressed air or other gas to launch the projectile.

AIRSOFT

Also called Soft Air, a different configuration than an airgun in that airsoft shoots round plastic 6mm or 8mm diameter balls and powered by spring-piston, electrically-driven spring piston (automatic electric gun), or low-pressure gasses like green gas and by CO_2. Many airsoft pistols and rifles are replicas of famous firearm makes and models. Used by competition shooters, including both target shooters and simulated war gamers, and purchased by collectors.

ANTI-DOUBLE PELLET FEED

A mechanism preventing more than one pellet loading into the barrel developed and patented by Hatsan.

ANTI-KNOCK SYSTEM

A system patented by Hatsan to prevent gas wastage when the rifle is knocked over or bounced.

APERTURE SIGHT

A rear sight consisting of a hole or aperture located in an adjustable assembly through which the front sight and target are aligned.

BB

"Air Rifle Shot" balls of lead or steel, which are used as projectiles in airguns. Generally 0.173 in. to 0.180 in. diameter.

BACK STRAP

The part of the revolver or pistol frame which is exposed at the rear of the grip.

BARREL

The steel tube through which a projectile is launched.

BARREL BAND

A metal band, either fixed or adjustable, around the forend of a gun which holds the barrel in the forearm stock.

BARREL COCKING

Also known as "break barrel cocking". The action of pivoting the barrel downward or upward compresses the mainspring of a spring-piston action into firing position.

BARREL SHROUD

An outer metal or synthetic tube which encloses the true barrel within it. Often used to conceal and protect the tube which is the real barrel in BB guns: More correctly known as the "shot tube". The barrel shroud is sometimes incorrectly referred to as the barrel.

BEAVERTAIL FOREND

A wider than normal forend.

BLUING

The chemical process of artificial oxidation (rusting) applied to gun parts so that the metal attains a dark blue or nearly black appearance.

BOLT ACTION

A breech closure which is in line with the bore at all times; manually reciprocated to load, unload and cock; and is locked in place by breech bolt lugs engaging abutments usually in the receiver. There are two principal types of bolt actions, i.e., the turn bolt and the straight pull type.

BORE

Internal dimensions of a barrel (smooth or rifled) which can be measured using the metric system (ie. millimeters), English system (i.e. inches), or by the gauge system (see gauge). On a rifled barrel, the bore is measured across the lands. Also, the traditional English term is used when referring to the diameter of a shotgun muzzle ("gauge" in U.S. measure).

BOTTLE-FED

A pre-charged pneumatic airgun with a removable gas/air cylinder.

BREAK-OPEN

A type of gun action which is cocked by "breaking open" the gun in the mid-line, generally just about over the trigger. In break-open BB guns, this moves internal rods which cock the piston.

BREECH

The opening to the chamber portion of the barrel.

BREECH SEAL

A seal which is designed to prevent propulsive gases from leaking out from behind the projectile. Usually an o-ring, circle of leather, or synthetic material. (Called a "barrel washer" in England.)

BULK FILL

The use of large capacity cylinders to fill CO_2 reservoirs.

BULL BARREL

A heavier than normal barrel with little or no taper.

BULL WHISPER TECHNOLOGY

Created by Gamo, this technology reduces the sound output of a Gamo air gun significantly due to the sound dampener housed within each bull barrel. When the pellet passes through the Bull Whisper sound dampener it dissipates the air around it making it extremely quiet without losing any velocity or performance.

BUTT

(Pistols) Bottom part of the grip. (Rifles) The end of a stock which rests against the shooter's shoulder.

BUTTPLATE

A protective plate attached to the butt of the buttstock. May be metal, plastic, or rubber. Sometimes airgun makers use a rubber recoil pad although its recoil dampening effect may not be needed.

BUTTSTOCK

Usually refers to the portion of a long gun that comes in contact with the shooter's shoulder.

CALIBER

The diameter of the bore (usually measured from land to land). It does not designate bullet diameter.

CHAMBER

The cavity at the breech end of the barrel bore that has been formed to accept and support a specific pellet.

CHECKERING

A functional decoration consisting of pointed pyramids cut into a stock's surface. Generally applied to the pistol grip and forend/forearm areas affording better handling and control.

CHEEK PIECE

A raised part of the comb of a shoulder-arm against which the shooter rests his face. Usually associated with a Monte Carlo-type stock. Its purpose is to raise the shooter's eye to the height necessary to maintain sight alignment.

COCKING INDICATOR

Any device which the act of cocking moves into a position where it may be seen or felt in order to notify the shooter that the gun is cocked.

COLOR CASE HARDENING

A method of hardening steel and iron while imparting colorful swirls as well as surface figure. Normally, the desired metal parts are put in a crucible packed with a mixture of charcoal and finely ground animal bone and heated to temperatures in the 800° C to 900° C range, after which they are slowly cooled, and then submerged into cold water.

COMB

The portion of the stock on which the shooter's cheek rests.

COMPENSATOR

A recoil-reducing device that mounts on the muzzle of a gun to deflect part of the propelling gases up and rearward. Also called a "muzzle brake."

COMPRESSED AIR

Air at greater than atmospheric pressure. Guns which use compressed air include hose-fed airguns, spring-piston airguns, pump pneumatics, and pre-charged pneumatics.

CONCENTRIC PISTON

An arrangement in spring piston airguns where the barrel serves as a guide for a compression piston which encircles the barrel.

CROWNING

The rounding or chamfering normally done to a barrel's muzzle to ensure that the mouth of the bore is square with the bore axis and that its edge is countersunk to protect it from impact damage. Traditionally, crowning was accomplished by spinning an abrasive-coated brass ball against the muzzle while moving it in a figure-eight pattern, until the abrasive had cut away any irregularities and produced a uniform and square mouth.

CYLINDER

In airguns, especially spring piston airguns, it is the cylinder-shaped main body or reciever. In such guns it is also known as the body tube or receiver.

DETENT

A spring-loaded cam which aids in holding an airgun mechanism, especially the barrel, in the closed position.

DIABOLO

A term referring to a pellet with a constricted waist.

DIOPTER

European term for aperture or peep sight. Usually refers to a target grade sight.

DOUBLE ACTION

The principle in a revolver or self-loading pistol wherein the hammer can be cocked and dropped by a single pull of the trigger. Most of these actions also allow for single-action fire.

DOUBLE ACTION ONLY

The principle in a revolver or self-loading pistol which can only be fired in double action mode.

DOUBLE-BARRELED

A gun consisting of two barrels joined either side by side or one over the other.

DOUBLE-SET TRIGGER

A device that consists of two triggers, one to cock the mechanism that spring-assists the other trigger, substantially lightening trigger pull.

DOVETAIL

A flaring machined or hand-cut slot that is also slightly tapered toward one end. Cut into the upper surface of barrels and sometimes actions, the dovetail accepts a corresponding part on which a sight is mounted. Dovetail slot blanks are used to cover the dovetail when the original sight has been removed or lost; this gives the barrel a more pleasing appearance and configuration.

DRY FIRING

Aiming and firing an airgun without a pellet in it. This is an excellent technique to improve marksmanship skills. Some manufacturers recommend not dry firing, so check with your airgun's instructions before trying it.

DUAL-STAGE NOISE REDUCTION SYSTEM

A system created by Stoeger and combines the functions of an internal air-regulator ring and baffles that work in tandem to reduce noise.

ENGLISH STOCK

A straight, slender-gripped stock.

ENGRAVING

The art of carving metal in decorative patterns. Scroll engraving is the most common type of hand engraving encountered. Much of today's factory engraving is rolled on, which is done mechanically. Hand engraving requires artistry and knowledge of metals and related materials.

ETCHING

A method of decorating metal gun parts, usually done by laser etching acid or photo engraving.

EYE RELIEF

The distance that the eye is positioned behind the ocular lens of the telescopic sight. A two-to three-inch distance is average. The shooter adjusts the eye relief to ensure a full field of view. This distance is also necessary to prevent the telescope from striking the shooter face during recoil in some rifles.

FAC

These letters are used in the United Kingdom as an abbreviation of Firearms Certificate, a licence granted by the police in order to own and use any air rifle capable of producing over 12 Ft/lbs of muzzle energy in the United Kingdom. The absolute power limit for pistols is 6 Ft/lbs and may not be legally exceeded.

FIXED SIGHTS

Non-adjustable sights.

FOREARM (FOREND)

Usually a separate piece of wood in front of the receiver and under the barrel used for hand placement when shooting.

FOREND (FOREARM)

Usually the forward portion of a one-piece rifle or shotgun stock, but can also refer to a separate piece of wood.

FRONT STRAP

That part of the pistol grip frame that faces forward and often joins with the trigger guard.

GAS-SPRING SYSTEM

The type of operating system in which the main spring is replaced by (and uses) a gas-filled cylinder with a piston to generate the energy to move a projectile through the barrel (inappropriately sometimes called "gas ram" or "gas strut").

GRAVITY FEED MECHANISM

A magazine which feeds projectiles, generally round balls or BBs, to the projectile feeding area by the simple, dependable action of gravity.

GRIP

The part of the frame used to hold a handgun, or the area of a stock directly behind and attached to the frame/receiver of a long gun.

GRIPS

Can be part of the frame or components attached to the frame used to assist in accuracy, handling, control, and safety of a handgun. Some currently manufactured handguns have grips that are molded with checkering as part of the synthetic frame.

GROOVE

The spiral cuts in the bore of a rifle or handgun barrel that give the bullet its spin or rotation as it moves down the barrel.

GROOVED RECEIVER

The straight cuts in the upper portion of the receiver used when attaching a scope.

HEEL

Back end of the upper edge of the buttstock at the upper edge of the buttplate or recoil pad.

HOODED SIGHT

A front sight that is equipped with a metal canopy. Designed to eliminate light reflections, as well as to protect the sight pillar.

INERT GAS TECHNOLOGY (IGT)

Created by Gamo, this technology consists of a pneumatic cylinder that replaces the traditional mainspring which increases velocity, reduces lock time, incurs less vibration, has a more consistent power level and requires less cocking effort than a traditional spring gun.

INERT GAS TECHNOLOGY - IGT™ MACH1 SYSTEM

The newest technological advancement developed by Gamo. The latest GAMO Power line of airguns are specifically designed to deliver maximum performance due to their on board 33mm air cylinders, but are further enhanced by the IGT™ Mach1 System which increases velocity by up to 20% when compared to the standard gas piston rifle. IGT™ Mach1 technology provides increased velocity and improved accuracy.

JOULES

A metric unit of energy used to measure the power of an airgun. A legal limit air rifle in the UK will be around 16 joules (12ft/lbs).

LAMINATED STOCK

A gunstock made of many layers of wood glued together under pressure. Together, the laminations become very strong, preventing damage from moisture, heat, and warping.

LANDS

Portions of the bore left between the grooves of the rifling in the bore of a firearm. In rifling, the grooves are usually twice the width of the land. Land diameter is measured across the bore, from land to land.

LENGTH OF PULL

The distance from the forward center of the trigger curve to the rear surface of the buttplate. A pull of about 13.5 inches is a typical adult size on rifles.

LOADING GATE

The area on an airgun which, when opened, allows for the insertion of the projectile.

LOADING TAP

An airgun mechanism into which single projectiles may be loaded and then moved into firing position. Varieties include: pop-up, turning (faucet), and swinging.

MAGAZINE (MAG.)

The container within or attached to an airgun which holds projectiles to be fed into the gun's chamber.

MAINSPRING

The spring which, when compressed and then released, generates the energy to move a projectile through the barrel.

MANNLICHER STOCK

A full-length slender stock with slender forend extending to the muzzle (full stock) affording better barrel protection.

MICROMETER SIGHT

A finely adjustable sight.

MODERATOR

A device designed to reduce muzzle report on an airgun by moderating the air released when firing. See Silencer.

MONTE CARLO STOCK

A stock with an elevated comb, used primarily for scoped rifles.

MUZZLE

The forward end of the barrel where the projectile exits.

MUZZLE BRAKE

A recoil-reducing device attached to the muzzle. Some "muzzle brakes" do not actually reduce recoil, but rather mainly are used as cocking aids.

MUZZLE ENERGY

The energy of a projectile as it departs from the muzzle of a gun. Derived from the formula: 0.5 x mass x velocity squared.

MUZZLE WEIGHT

A weight (usually adjustable) equalizing device attached at muzzle end of the barrel used to balance and stabilize the barrel.

NITRO PISTON 2

A completely new system created by Crosman with more speed, more power, and more range wrapped in a package that shoots smoother, is quieter than ever, and requires less effort to cock – up to a 10 pound reduction in cocking force. Also includes an upgraded precision trigger that breaks crisp and clean.

OPEN SIGHTS

Rear sight of traditional "leaf" type with open-topped V-notch or U-notch, as distinct from a scope or aperture (peep) sight.

PARALLAX

Occurs in telescopic sights when the primary image of the objective lens does not coincide with the reticle. In practice, parallax is detected in the scope when, as the viewing eye is moved laterally, the image and the reticle appear to move in relation to each other.

PARKERIZING

Matted rust-resistant oxide finish, usually matte or dull gray, or black in color, usually found on military guns.

PEEP SIGHT

Rear sight consisting of a hole or aperture through which the front sight and target are aligned.

PELLET

An airgun projectile that is not a ball. Available in many styles, including wadcutter (target and high impact), pointed (high penetration), round nose (general use), and hollow point (expands on impact).

PICATINNY RAIL

A serrated flat rail attached to a forward portion of pistols and rifles used to clamp (Weaver Style Mount) accessories on.

PNEUMATIC

A term referring to the use of air/gas pressure as an energy source. In airguns it propels the BB or pellet out of the barrel.

PRE-CHARGED PNEUMATIC SYSTEM

The type of operating system that uses an externally charged chamber (either integral or removable) of compressed air or gas to generate the energy to move a projectile through the barrel.

PUMP UP AIRGUN

Airgun powered by air compressed by a pump integral to the gun. Usually all of the compressed air is discharged when the gun is fired for a single shot per air charge.

QUATTRO TRIGGER

A two-stage fully adjustable match trigger mechanism developed and patented by Hatsan. It has a three point adjustment to control the trigger load, the position of the first and second stages of the firing cycle, and the length of trigger travel. It also features a drop safety interlock device which eliminates the possibility of the airgun accidentally firing if it is dropped (whether or not the safety is on).

REAXIS GAS PISTON

Developed by Umarex, the ReAxis Gas Piston is powered by nitrogen. Unlike other nitrogen-filled gas pistons, the ReAxis is reversed – meaning the gas strut is turned 180 degrees on its axis so that the larger mass of the strut pushes the piston instead of the rod. This generates more power, more velocity, and more impact than that provided by other gas pistons. The ReAxis gas piston provides a smooth and constant cocking effort, reduces felt recoil, lowers the air rifle's noise level, minimizes stock vibration, and provides a consistent powerful velocity over its lifetime.

RECEIVER

The central area of an airgun's mechanism which serves to house or connect some or all of these parts: trigger mechanism, power mechanism, barrel, stock. A round airgun receiver generally is referred to as the body tube, cylinder, compression tube, or receiver. In air pistols, it generally is referred to as the frame.

RECOILLESS

A mechanical design that allows an airgun to be shot with little or no felt recoil.

REGULATOR

Device fitted to higher quality pre-charged pneumatic airguns. It is designed to feed precisely metered amounts of air from the reservoir to the breech area in order to power each shot consistently. Capable of adding significantly to efficiency but also to cost.

REPEATER/REPEATING

A term used when referring to an airgun being capable of firing more than one shot without having to manually reload.

RESERVOIR

Storage area for airgun projectiles. Generally not connected to the projectile feeding area or magazine.

RIB

A raised sighting plane affixed to the top of a barrel.

RIFLING

The spirally cut grooves in the bore of a rifle or handgun. The rifling stabilizes the bullet in flight. Rifling may rotate to the left or the right, the higher parts of the bore being called lands, the cuts or lower parts being called the grooves. Most U.S.-made barrels have a right-hand twist, while British gun makers prefer a left-hand twist. In practice, there seems to be little difference in accuracy or barrel longevity.

SCHNABEL FOREND

The curved/carved flared end of the forend that resembles the beak of a bird (Schnabel in German). This type of forend is common on Austrian and German guns, and was popular in the U.S., but the popularity of the Schnabel forend/forearm comes and goes with the seasons.

SHOCK ABSORBING SYSTEM (SAS)

Developed and patented by Hatsan, a Shock Absorber System which reduces vibration.

SHOCK WAVE ABSORBER (SWA)

A new recoil pad developed by Gamo to improve the rate of absorption and the recoil distance. It features three removable inserts that have been incorporated in the butt pad so the shooter can adjust the recoil according to their own specific preference.

SIDE LEVER

The lever located on the side of an airgun used for cocking the mainspring into firing position.

SIDE-LEVER COCKING

The action of pivoting the side lever compresses the mainspring of a spring-piston action into firing position.

SILENCAIR TECHNOLOGY

The Umarex SilencAir is a 5-chamber noise dampener that's permanently affixed to the muzzle of an air rifle to reduce down-range muzzle noise. It reduces the decibel reading, or loudness, of the muzzle noise generated by the exiting of a pellet from an air rifle.

SILENCER

A device designed to slow and dissipate the sudden expansion of the gas that propels a projectile up the bore of a gun. Buyers of airguns equipped with a silencer (or any built-in or added device, which reduces discharge sound) are advised to obtain a federal permit for the silencer part ($200) and check their state and local laws very carefully. See warning at www.beemans.net.

SINGLE ACTION

A design which requires the hammer to be manually cocked for each shot.

SINGLE STAGE TRIGGER

Typical American hunting trigger that breaks upon application of pressure.

SKIRT

The flaring, thin area of diabolo-style pellets that engages the rifling in a barrel and acts as an air seal.

SLING SWIVELS

Metal loops affixed to the gun on which a carrying strap is attached.

SMOOTH ACTION TRIGGER (SAT)

Designed by Gamo, a custom made trigger which features a smooth trigger pull that provides a perfect transition from 1st to 2nd stage with little effort, increasing the rate of accuracy and provides a responsive, clean break when you need it most.

SOUND-LOC™ NOISE REDUCTION SYSTEM

AirForce has now improved sound reduction technology with the new Sound-Loc System designed specifically for AirForce's TalonSS and CondorSS air rifles. Sound-Loc incorporates asymmetrical deflection of air exiting the muzzle as the gun is fired. It also includes captured air expansion and reflexive air flow which combine to decelerate air velocity and minimize the report of the rifle.

SOUND MODERATOR ("SILENCER")

Device which reduces the discharge sound by one decibel or more. All versions, including built-in models, probably are illegal in the United States, unless accompanied by a $200 federal permit and, if required, a state permit. (See www.beemans.net.)

SPRING-FED MAGAZINE

A projectile storage area which is designed to feed the projectiles to the firing or loading area by means of a spring-loaded projectile follower.

SPRING-PISTON SYSTEM

Airgun operating system that uses a metal or gas mainspring to push a piston, which in turn uses a cushion of air to push the projectile through the barrel.

STIPPLING

The roughening of a surface (with the use of a special punch or tool) to provide the shooter with a better grip.

STOCKS

See GRIP.

SUPER SILENT TECHNOLOGY

A Walther innovation using zero-play fit in places like the barrel lock and cocking rod and an improved polyurethane seal and air cushion for the guided piston.

TAKEDOWN

A gun which can be easily taken apart in two sections for carrying or shipping.

TANG(S)

The extension straps of the receiver to which the stock is attached.

TARGET TURRETS

Raised adjuster knobs on a scope that can easily be turned by hand without use of tools.

TIROLERSCHAFT

Tyrolean style stock.

TOP LEVER

The lever located on the top of an airgun used for cocking the mainspring into firing position.

TOP-LEVER COCKING

The action of pivoting the top lever (generally found on air pistols) upward compresses the mainspring of a spring-piston action into firing position.

TRIOPAD BUTT SYSTEM

A recoil absorption system which provides added comfort and three stock spacers allow adjustments for appropriate length of pull.

TURBO STABILIZING SYSTEM™

The Turbo Stabilizing System™ is a technology designed to control the aggressiveness of the firing cycle by bringing the spring to a controlled stop within the chamber. TSS: more velocity than a standard spring air rifle, less vibration and reduced recoil.

TWO STAGE TRIGGER

A trigger mechanism that has two definite stages; a 'take-up' stage, and a 'release' stage. On a lot of two-stage triggers, the first stage is just the resistance offered by the trigger return spring, but on more expensive target airguns, some of the triggers total pull weight is loaded onto the first stage as well to make a smoother release. The benefit of a two-stage trigger over a single-stage trigger is that the shooter can take up the first stage, hold, then follow-through with the shot when the sight picture looks right.

UNDER LEVER

The lever located under an airgun used for cocking the mainspring into firing position.

UNDER-LEVER COCKING

The action of pivoting the under lever downward compresses the mainspring of a spring-piston action into firing position.

VELOCITY

The speed at which the ammunition is being propelled. Normally calculated as Feet-Per-Second (fps).

VIBRATION REDUCTION SYSTEM

Used by Walther, this system ensures better accuracy and smooth firing. It includes a piston with zero-play piston rings made of low-friction synthetic material. To gently brake the piston with an air cushion at the end of its travel, additional transfer holes for each energy level are drilled at optimum locations. This dampens the recoil and protects the rifle scope. The piston spring, made of specially tempered valve spring wire, has a long spring guide to keep vibration to a minimum.

YOUTH DIMENSIONS

Usually refers to shorter stock dimensions and/or lighter weight enabling youth/women to shoot and carry a lighter, shorter airgun.

WHISPER FUSION TECHNOLOGY

Noise and muzzle blast reduction technology. While the pellet passes through the end of the barrel, there is a first noise dampening technology using different air chambers and a second one that is reducing even more noise using several baffles.

WHISPER TECHNOLOGY

This technology from Gamo consists of a rifled steel barrel with a fluted polymer jacket and integrated with a sound moderator in the muzzle. This sound moderator compresses noise and prevents sound expansion by up to 52% compared to an ordinary muzzle.

WUNDHAMMER SWELL

A swelling of the pistol grip area of a rifle stock, intended to give support to the palm of the firing hand.

XRS - RECOIL REDUCTION SYSTEM

A recoil absorption system developed and patented by Hatsan where recoil is absorbed during the shot by the design of the sliding action.

British/American Translations of Airgun Terms

British	American	British	American
Horizontal Sight Adjustment	Windage	Anti-Clockwise	Counter Clockwise
Vertical Sight Adjustment	Elevation	Nought	Zero (the number)
Joint Washer, Barrel Washer	Breech Seal	Strip	Disassemble
Loading Lever	Cocking Arm	Fix (a design)	Finalize a Design
Fixing Screw	Lock Screw	Sort Out	Fix, figure out,
Kit	Equipment		Organize
Barrel Fixing Plunger, Barrel Latch	Detent	Knackered	Needs Repair
Cranked Spring	Spring w/Straight	One Off (on orders)	One On (on orders)
	Leg(s)	Brilliant	Excellent
Back Block	Receiver End Cap		Spot On
Bead	Front Sight		Absolutely
Receiver Sight	Peep Sight		Appropriate
Mains Line Tension	House Current	One Off	Unique
Fore-end	Forearm		
Cylinder, Body	Receiver, Body		
	Tube		
Grub Screw	Headless Screw		
Calibre	Caliber		
Arrestor Projections	Scope Stop		

ABBREVIATIONS

AA	*Addictive Airgunning*
AAG	*American Air Gunner*
adj.	Adjustable
AG	*Airgunnner*
AGNR	*Air Gun News & Report* Magazine
AH	*Airgun Hobby*
AL	*Airgun Letter*
ANIB	As New In Box
AO	Adjustable Objective
AR	*Airgun Revue* Magazine
AW	*Airgun World* Magazine
B	Blue
BA	Bolt Action
BACS	Brocock Air Cartridge System
BB	.175 cal. Air Rifle Shot
BBC	Break Barrel Cocking
BBL	Barrel
BC	Barrel Cocking
BF	Bulk Fill or Bottle Fed
BO	Break Open
BP	Buttplate
BT	Beavertail
ca.	Circa
cal.	Caliber
CBT	Clean Break Trigger
CC	Case Colors
CDT	Capacitive Discharge Technology, Harper patent
CH	Cross Hair
CO₂	Carbon Dioxide
COMP	Compensated/Competition
CP	Concentric Piston
CTC	Center to Center
CYL	Cylinder
DA	Double Action
DB	Double Barrel
DISC	Discontinued
DST	Double Set Triggers
DT	Double Triggers
DWJ	*Deutsches Waffen Journal*
EXC	Excellent
FA	Forearm
FAC	United Kingdom Firearms Certificate
FPS	Feet per Second
Ft/lbs	Foot pounds
FT	Field Target
g./ gm.	Gram
ga.	Gauge
GC	Grip Cocking
GD	Gun Digest
GOVT	Government
gr.	Grain
GR	*Guns Review*

GRT	Gas Ram Technology
GS	Gas Spring
HB	Heavy Barrel
HC	Hard Case
IGT	Inert Gas Technology
intro.	Introduced
ISSF	International Sport Shooting Federation
LA	Lever Action
LH, LHS	Left Hand, Left Hand Side
LOP	Length of Pull
LT	Light
Mag.	Extra Powerful; Magnum
mag.	Magazine or Clip
MC	Monte Carlo
ME	Muzzle Energy
MFC	Muzzle Flip Compensator
MFG/ mfg.	Manufactured/Manufacture
MK	Mark
MMC	Micro-Movement Cocking System
MPS	Meters Per Second
MSR	Manufacturer's Suggested Retail
MV	Muzzle Velocity
N	Nickel
N/A	Not Applicable or Not Available
NIB	New in Box
No.	Number
OA	Overall
OAL	Overall Length
OB	Octagon Barrel
OCT	Octagon
OD	Outside Diameter
OIR	Optic-illuminated Reticle
PBA	Gamo's Performance Ballistic Ammo
PCP	Pre-Charged Pneumatic
PG	Pistol Grip
POR/ P.O.R.	Price on Request
PSI/psi	Pounds per Square Inch
PIPS	Power Intensification Piston System
PP	Pump Pneumatic
PTFE	Synthetic nylon seal material
QB	Quackenbush
QD	Quick Detachable
RB	Round Barrel
RH	Right Hand
RHS	Right Hand Side
REC	Receiver
RPM	Rounds Per Minute
SA	Single Action
SAS	Shock Absorbing System
SAT	Smooth Action Trigger
SB	Smooth Bore

SG	Straight Grip
SL	Side Lever
S/N/SN	Serial Number
SP	Spring Piston
SPEC	Special
SPG	Semi-Pistol Grip
Spl.	Special
SR	Semi-recoilless
SS	Single Shot or Stainless Steel
SSP	Single Stroke Pneumatic
ST	Single Trigger
SWA	Shock Wave Absorber
TBD	To Be Determined
TD	Takedown
TGT	Target
TL	Top Lever
TSS	Turbo Stabilizing System (Gamo)
TT	Target Trigger /Target Turret
UIT	Union Internationale de Tir
UL	Under Lever
USA	United States of America or U.S. Airguns
VG	Very Good
V/Visier	*VISIER* magazine
w/	With
w/o	Without
WD	Wood
WFF	Watch For Fakes
WO	White Outline
WW	World War
XRS	Recoil Reduction System

CORRESPONDENCE/APPRAISALS/INFORMATION
AIRGUN QUESTIONS/APPRAISALS POLICY

Whether we wanted it or not, Blue Book Publications, Inc. has ended up in the driver's seat as the clearing house for airgun information. Because the volume of airgun questions now requires full-time attention, we have developed a standardized policy that will enable us to provide you with the service you have come to expect from Blue Book Publications, Inc. To that end, we have extended all of these services to our website (www.bluebookofgunvalues.com).

To ensure that the research department can answer every airgun question with an equal degree of thoroughness, a massive library of well over 1,300 reference books, thousands of both new and old factory brochures, price sheets, most major auction catalogs, and dealer inventory listings are maintained and constantly updated. It's a huge job, and we answer every question like we could go to court on it.

POLICY FOR AIRGUN QUESTIONS

The charge is $10 per airgun value question ($15 per if the airgun make and/or model needs to be identified first) payable by a major credit card. All airgun questions are answered on a first-come, first-served basis. All pricing requests will be given within a value range only. Airgun question telephone hours are 1:00 p.m. to 5:00 p.m., M-F, CST, no exceptions please. You must provide us with all the necessary airgun information if you want an accurate answer. Our goal is to answer most telephone airgun questions in less than 5 business days, unless we're away attending trade/gun shows.

APPRAISAL INFORMATION

Written appraisals will be performed only if the following criteria are met and when time is permitting:
We must have good quality high resolution images/photos with a complete description, including manufacturer's name, model, gauge or caliber, barrel length, and other pertinent information. On some airguns (depending on the trademark and model), a factory letter may be necessary. Our charge for a written appraisal is 2% of the appraised value with a minimum of $30 per airgun. For email appraisals, please refer to www.bluebookofgunvalues.com. Please allow 2-3 weeks response time per appraisal request.

ADDITIONAL SERVICES

Individuals requesting a photocopy of a particular page or section from any edition for insurance or reference purposes will be billed at $5 per page, up to 5 pages, and $3.50 per page thereafter. Please direct all airgun questions and appraisals to:

Blue Book Publications, Inc.
Attn: Research Dept.
8009 34th Ave. S., Suite 250
Minneapolis, MN 55425 USA
Phone: 952-854-5229, ext. 1600 • Fax: 952-853-1486 • www.bluebookofgunvalues.com
Email: guns@bluebookinc.com
Use "Airgun Inquiry" in the subject line or it may get deleted.

INTERESTED IN BUYING OR SELLING AIRGUNS?

Over the course of many editions, we have received many requests for, and provided referrals for buying, selling, or trading airguns. As Blue Book Publications, Inc. is a publisher, not a gun shop, this service is provided for the benefit of all concerned. There is no charge for this service, nor do we receive a commission (a thank you would be appreciated, however!). Our established international network of reliable dealers and collectors allows your particular buy or sell request to be referred to the most appropriate company/individual based on both your geographic location and area of collectibility. All replies are treated with strict confidentiality.

Correspondence and replies should be directed to:
Blue Book Publications, Inc.
Attn: John B. Allen
8009 34th Ave. So., Ste. 250 • Minneapolis, MN 55425 USA
Phone: 952-854-5229, ext. 1600 • Fax: 952-853-1486
Email: guns@bluebookinc.com
Use "Referral" in the subject line or it may get deleted.

AIRGUN GRADING CRITERIA

The following descriptions are provided to help evaluate condition factors for both vintage and currently/recently manufactured airguns. Please refer to the following eight-page color Photo Percentage Grading System (PPGS) to determine the correct grade for your airgun(s). Once the percentage of original condition has been determined, getting the correct value is as simple as finding the listing and selecting the correct condition factor. Also included are both the NRA Modern and Antique Condition Standards for firearms as a comparison, including a conversion chart for converting percentages to NRA Modern Standards. "N/As" throughout this book are used to indicate values that can't be accurately established because of rarity, lack of recorded sales, or other factors which may preclude realistic pricing within a condition factor.

100% - all original parts, 100% original finish, perfect condition in every respect, inside and out. On currently manufactured airguns, the 100% value assumes not previously sold at retail.

95% - all original parts, near new condition, very little use; minor scratches or handling dings on wood, metal bluing near perfect, except at muzzle or sharp edges.

90% - all original parts, perfect working condition, some minor wear on working surfaces, no corrosion or pitting, minor surface dents or scratches, sharp lettering, numerals and design on metal and wood; unmarred wood, fine bore.

80% - good working condition, minor wear on working surfaces, no broken or replacement parts, sharp lettering, numerals and design on metal and wood, some surface freckling/light rust (especially on vintage airguns).

60% - safe working condition, sharp lettering, numerals and design on metal and wood, some scratches, dings, and chips in wood, good bore, may have some corrosion and pitting.

40% - well-worn, perhaps requiring replacement of minor parts or adjustments, sharp lettering; numerals and design on metal and wood, on older airguns, major surface rust and pitting may be present, but do not render the airgun unsafe or inoperable.

20% - most of original finish is gone, metal may be seriously rusted or pitted, cleaned or reblued, principal lettering, numerals and design on metal still legible, wood may have serious scratches, dings, and may be refinished and/or cracked, both minor and major repairs may have been made.

NRA MODERN CONDITION DESCRIPTIONS

New - not previously sold at retail, in same condition as current factory production.

Perfect - in new condition in every respect.

Excellent - new condition, very little use, no noticeable marring of wood or metal, bluing near perfect (except at muzzle or sharp edges).

Very Good - in perfect working condition, no appreciable wear on working surfaces, no corrosion or pitting, only minor surface dents or scratches.

Good - in safe working condition, minor wear on working surfaces, no broken parts, no corrosion or pitting which will interfere with proper functioning.

Fair - in safe working condition, but well-worn, perhaps requiring replacement of minor parts or adjustments which should be indicated in advertisement, no rust, but may have corrosion pits which do not render article unsafe or inoperable.

CONVERTING TO NRA MODERN STANDARDS

When converting from NRA Modern Standards, the following rules generally apply:

New/Perfect - 100% with or without box. Not mint - new (i.e., no excuses). 100% on currently manufactured firearms assumes NIB condition and not sold previously at retail.

Excellent - 95%+ - 99% (typically).

Very Good - 80% - 95% (should be all original).

Good - 60% - 80% (should be all original).

Fair - 20% - 60% (may or may not be original, but must function properly and shoot).

Poor - under 20% (shooting not a factor).

NRA ANTIQUE CONDITION DESCRIPTIONS

Factory New - all original parts; 100% original finish; in perfect condition in every respect, inside and out.

Excellent - all original parts; over 80% original finish; sharp lettering, numerals and design on metal and wood; unmarred wood; fine bore.

Fine - all original parts; over 30% original finish; sharp lettering, numerals and design on metal and wood; minor marks in wood; good bore.

Very Good - all original parts; none to 30% original finish; original metal surfaces smooth with all edges sharp; clear lettering, numerals and design on metal; wood slightly scratched or bruised; bore disregarded for collectors airguns.

Good - some minor replacement parts; metal smoothly rusted or lightly pitted in places, cleaned or reblued; principal lettering, numerals and design on metal legible; wood refinished, scratched, bruised or minor cracks repaired; in good working order.

Fair - some major parts replaced; minor replacement parts may be required; metal rusted, may be lightly pitted all over, vigorously cleaned or reblued; rounded edges of metal and wood; principal lettering, numerals and design on metal partly obliterated; wood scratched, bruised, cracked or repaired where broken; in fair working order or can be easily repaired and placed in working order.

Poor - major and minor parts replaced; major replacement parts required and extensive restoration needed; metal deeply pitted; principal lettering, numerals and design obliterated, wood badly scratched, bruised, cracked, or broken; mechanically inoperative, generally undesirable as a collector's airguns.

Gaylord Reports

2014: What Are They Doing Now?
by Tom Gaylord

THE STATE OF THE AIRGUN INDUSTRY

I see some major changes to the industry in 2014. Among them are better triggers on guns at lower price points, better scope bases on spring guns, more attention to the customers' wishes in a lot of areas, and more innovation along multiple lines. In past years, the focus was on new products that were the old products with new skins. This year, there are fewer really new products, but those that exist are clearly new.

It seems the entire industry is listening to what customers say they want and trying to produce it. In the past, we saw the velocity wars between the major players, but that may have come to an end. The focus now seems to be on better powerplants, better triggers, and guns that have the performance that customers always assumed they should.

Also hot are several new lookalike airguns for those collectors who cannot own the firearms they desire. These have been with us in the past, but this year more companies are bringing them to market. Many are using the new BB-shooting models that are crossing over from companies that have an established background in airsoft guns.

I also see some ventures into areas that were considered experimental until now. The Benjamin Nitro Piston 2 is the most obvious example of this. This new airgun has several advanced tuning tricks that were previously used only by exclusive airgunsmiths. Buttoned pistons and debounce devices are new to the production world, and they're going to give the common man a taste for the exotic. I predict that Crosman will learn more from this venture than they have from their last five new products.

The other new venture is an experiment called the $100 precharged pneumatic air rifle. It's both a one-off proof of concept model and a limited production boutique conversion this year, but I see it expanding to a huge market in the years to come.

As always, there are a number of older guns with new names and new paint jobs. These aren't new in my book, nor am I interested in them. There are enough really new things that the warmed-up leftovers don't need to be included.

All things considered, 2014 is an exciting time to be an airgunner.

AIRFORCE AIRGUNS

The Escape (top), EscapeSS (middle), and EscapeUL (bottom) are three new powerful survival air rifles from AirForce Airguns.

Escape

The Escape survival rifle was developed by AirForce Airguns in cooperation with TV's Ton Jones of the popular series *Auction Hunters*. Jones wanted a powerful precharged air rifle he could take off the grid and asked AirForce if their TalonP pistol could work with a 24-inch .25-caliber barrel. They liked the idea and immediately went into development of a single-shot air rifle that gets up to 97.88 foot-pounds of muzzle energy when firing heavy 43.2-grain pellets.

The Escape rifle weighs just 5.3 lbs. and is 39 inches long, so it can be carried in the field without encumbrance. In these days of .22 rimfire ammunition shortages, it's nice to have an alternative in an air rifle whose pellets are always available. The Escape comes in either .22 or .25 caliber and has Ton Jones' logo on the frame.

The Escape survival rifle was developed for Ton Jones by AirForce Airguns.

One of Ton's requirements was that the Escape had to be easy to fill with a hand pump. All three models have the same 213cc air tank that fills quickly in the field with about five pump strokes per shot.

2014 STANDOUT!

The Escape rifle is a standout product for 2014.

EscapeUL

The EscapeUL is the ultralight version of the new rifle. It weighs just 4.25 lbs. and features a thinner 18-inch Lothar Walther barrel in either .22 or .25 caliber. The maximum power is less than the Escape's but still pumps out up to 79.46 foot-pounds of energy in .25 caliber. It's perfect for bush pilots, backpackers, guides, and everyone to whom ounces matter.

EscapeSS

As noted earlier, the Escape series is based on the TalonP pistol. It has a 12-inch Lothar Walther barrel, as does the EscapeSS rifle. So, the power is the same. The difference is the EscapeSS rifle has a baffled air chamber in front of the rifle's true muzzle and buried deep inside the tubular aluminum frame. This rifle's main feature is quieter operation. Not tiny suburban backyard quiet, mind you, for this is still a 55 foot-pound airgun, but quieter than one without the baffles. Think of it as a rifle with a noise signature far below that of a rimfire.

AIRGUNS OF ARIZONA

Daystate Wolverine B

The Wolverine is a .303-caliber air rifle that generates up to 100 foot-pounds. This year, Daystate has taken the same steel action and made it into .177 and .22 sporting rifles. The B in the name refers to the 500cc non-removable air tank (bottle), instead of an integral

reservoir. That gives enough air for up to 85 good shots per fill in .22 caliber from a rifle that delivers 30+ foot-pounds at the muzzle.

The Harper slingshot hammer stops any chance of hammer bounce on the valve, conserving air. Waste air is recycled to advance the 10-shot magazine, which prevents the double-loading of pellets.

A large-diameter shroud with integral suppressor quiets the report of the rifle to almost nothing, and a high-quality Lothar Walther barrel delivers pinpoint accuracy. Throw in an adjustable mechanical trigger, and you have a state-of-the-art precharged pneumatic rifle with old-school qualities.

Daystate has made the rifle reversible, so left-handed owners can reverse the bolt handle on their own. The Wolverine B is for all who wanted a smallbore version of the Wolverine.

FX Bobcat

What's the one thing about bullpups that sucks? The trigger! What if I told you that FX has solved that problem with its new Bobcat design, which puts rifle performance into a carbine? That was the first thing AoA owner Robert Buchanan told me about this airgun. There's a magnetic linkage in the trigger that solves the usual problems of slop and looseness.

FX Bobcat is a bullpup with a great trigger and a full-length barrel. Image courtesy: Airguns of Arizona

On top of that, the Bobcat has an 18.5-inch barrel, yet its total length is 29.50 inches! It packs a lot into a small space, as all bullpups do.

The rifle comes in .22, .25, and .30 calibers and features the FX smooth-twist barrel that is rifled only near the muzzle. An optional regulator is available for all three calibers.

Omega Super Charger compressor

The airgun world has been waiting for an affordable air compressor that can fill both guns and large storage tanks. Ideally, such a compressor would be able to fill large carbon

Daystate Wolverine B is an exciting new precharged rifle from Airguns of Arizona. Image courtesy: Airguns of Arizona

fiber tanks to 4,500 psi. I saw such a compressor in the AoA booth at the SHOT Show this year–the Omega Super Charger. It runs on 110 household current, fills 88 cubic-foot carbon fiber tanks to 4,500 psi, is water cooled, and is about as noisy as a quiet microwave oven. I saw it run in the booth and it didn't vibrate at all.

Omega Super Charger could change the face of airgunning by bringing high-pressure air into the home at a reasonable price. Image courtesy: Airguns of Arizona

This 60-lb. compressor is made by a Chinese medical equipment manufacturer, and the build quality is very high. The retail price is just $1,800, which is a little more than half of what other compressors with similar capability bring.

Some of the nice features are a set-and-forget capability. Turn this unit on and walk away–it does everything else. It fills to the preset pressure then stops. It can also be set to bleed moisture that has accumulated at various intervals, and the gauge on the front of the control panel is a large oil-filled unit that's easy to read.

2014 STANDOUT!

The Omega Super Charger is a standout product for 2014.

AIR VENTURI

Air Arms

Air Arms unveiled its S510 Ultimate Sporter at the SHOT Show in the Air Venturi booth this year. The Ultimate Sporter is a carbine with a fitted caliber-specific silencer, so the operation is quiet. The rifle is a 10-shot repeater with a sidelever bolt

action. It isn't regulated, but the valve is so well balanced that the rifle still gets an incredible number of shots. In the 12 foot-pound version made for the U.K., they're getting 90 good shots on one 2,600 psi fill.

Evanix Max-MN

The Max-MN from Evanix is a bullpup manual sidelever bolt-action repeater that comes in .22, .25, 9mm/.357, .45, and .50 calibers. The number of shots in the magazine varies with the caliber. This will be the first production bullpup in a big bore caliber.

Feinwerkbau (FWB)

This year, FWB will bring out a breakbarrel sporting air rifle–their first since the FWB 124 was discontinued in 1989. FWB doesn't come to the SHOT Show, so this was first seen at the German sporting arms show known as IWA.

Little is known about the rifle as this edition goes to press, but Feinwerkbau makes only top-quality airguns, so expect the new rifle to be good–and also expensive. When the 124 was sold, FWB had little competition; but in 2014, it'll go up against rifles like the TX200 Mark III and the Walther LGV family of sporting spring-piston rifles. So, this new offering will face stiff competition from the start.

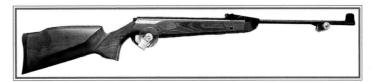

FWB sporter was revealed at the 2014 IWA show in Germany.

CROSMAN

Crosman Corporation has several different brands that will be addressed separately. The three airgun brands they make are Crosman, Benjamin, and Sheridan. The first news is that the Sheridan brand left the market in 2013. They had a long run from 1947 as Sheridan, then under the ownership of the Benjamin Air Rifle Company in the 1980s, and finally when Crosman acquired Benjamin in the late 1980s and also got Sheridan.

If there are airguns with the Sheridan name in the future, they'll be Crosman models. They may also come in calibers other than .20, which is the only airgun caliber Sheridan ever made.

Air Arms' Ultimate Sporter was shown at the 2014 SHOT Show. It shows a lot of promise for the airgun hunter.

Crosman also has an optics division known as CenterPoint Optics. They started several years ago with just a single supplier of quality optics and have branched out in recent years. CenterPoint makes scopes, dot sights, and accessories for airguns as well as the firearm market.

The company also produces Game Face airsoft. While I don't usually review airsoft and this book doesn't include it, there are some interesting new products this year that I'll be testing in my daily blog for Pyramyd Air.

Crosman 760 Powermaster

Crosman makes the baseline guns the company makes and sells. Of these, the Model 760 Powermaster (also called the Pumpmaster in several models) is their No. 1 product, selling tens of millions since it was first introduced in 1966. This year, it was redesigned with a longer pump handle for increased leverage and a strengthened pump rod and pump cup that make the mechanism more efficient.

Crosman Comrade AK

The Comrade AK is a semi-automatic CO_2-powered 22-shot BB gun. It produces velocities up to 600 f.p.s. and gets an astonishing 150 shots per cartridge. I guess the gas management is the big news there.

Crosman's Comrade AK is a 22-shot semi-automatic BB gun. Image courtesy: Crosman

The AK's banana magazine has storage for 150 additional BBs in the traditional Crosman style. The 4-lb. gun has a removable stock, which turns it into an AK pistol.

Benjamin NP2

The biggest news in the Crosman booth this year was also the biggest airgun news at the entire SHOT Show. The new Benjamin Nitro Piston 2 (NP2) is a completely redesigned gas piston unit that will have shooters talking for years.

I got to test it at Crosman's range during Media Day, when the industry allows gun writers to shoot all the new guns. The first thing they told me was that they had reduced the cocking effort by 10 lbs. So, I cocked the rifle and proved them…right! It cocked like a reduced-velocity gun, but the NP2 is full power.

Then, they told me the rifle was smooth and had a nice trigger, so I shot it…and, again, they were right. The trigger is two-stage and very light and crisp. If there's a complaint, it'll be that the first stage is long, but I don't mind that. No complaints from me. The shot was dead calm, without recoil or vibration. It felt as though the rifle was highly tuned. I told them after the first shot that they're going to sell a boatload of these air rifles, only I didn't

Benjamin's new NP2 rifle is going to set fire to the spring-piston world!

say *boat*. They had to edit what I said from the video they were shooting–I was that impressed. I told them that if the production guns shoot like the one I shot at the range, I'll buy the one they send me to test. That's how good it is.

2014 STANDOUT!

Remember the name. The Benjamin NP2 is **THE** standout product for 2014.

DAISY

Daisy Model 74

Daisy's Model 74 is a CO_2-powered semi-automatic BB gun. The velocity tops out at 350 f.p.s., which is brisk enough for plinking. It has a smoothbore barrel and a 15-shot magazine that's fed from an onboard 200-round reservoir. The sights are a conventional front blade and fully adjustable rear.

Daisy 74 looks like a new fun gun from Rogers, Arkansas. It's a semi-automatic 15-shot BB repeater that weighs less than two lbs. Image courtesy: Daisy

Daisy Model 415 pistol

Daisy's 415 BB pistol is a 21-shot CO_2-powered semi-automatic that pumps them out the spout at 500 f.p.s. That's extremely fast for a steel BB, so shooters have to take special care to avoid rebounds and ricochets. The fixed-sight 415 is light–weight, but definitely for adults because of the power.

Winchester 1400CS from Daisy

Winchester's 1400CS breakbarrel spring rifle by Daisy is a powerful magnum capable of 1,400 f.p.s. velocities with alloy pellets. It also has a sound suppressor on the muzzle that reduces the report by as much as 50 percent. The stock features a set of

Daisy 415 is a lightweight semi-automatic BB pistol with smashing power! Image courtesy: Daisy

Winchester 1400CS breakbarrel is a magnum spring rifle with Mossy Oak Break-Up Infinity camo and a built-in bipod. Image courtesy: Daisy

built-in bipod legs that swing down for support in the prone position. This rifle comes with a 3-9x32 scope and mount. The synthetic stock comes in Mossy Oak Break-Up Infinity camo.

Winchester MP4 from Daisy

The Winchester MP4 is a semi-automatic CO_2 air rifle that shoots both lead pellets and steel BBs. It uses two 12-gram cartridges to produce a maximum velocity of 700 f.p.s. The magazine has two 8-shot rotary clips at each end that can be loaded with any combination of BBs and pellets. The sights flip down, front, and rear, and an extended Picatinny rail on top permits the mounting of scopes.

Winchester MP4 by Daisy is a 16-shot semi-automatic rifle that shoots both BBs and pellets. Image courtesy: Daisy

GAMO

Buckmasters Squirrel Terminator

Gamo is heavily focused on hunting, and the Buckmasters Squirrel Terminator is an example of their latest breakbarrel hunting rifle. They rate it at 1,275 f.p.s. with alloy pellets in .177

Gamo Buckmasters Squirrel Terminator is a lightweight, purpose-built hunting spring rifle. Image courtesy: Gamo

caliber. It features a fluted polymer barrel jacket surrounding an inner steel barrel and their Turbo Stabilizing System, which is said to increase power by preventing piston bounce. This is a very light rifle, weighing just 6.1 lbs., and it comes without open sights but with a 4x32 scope and mount.

Whisper with Turbo Stabilizing System

The Whisper has been in Gamo's lineup for several years, and I've tested it with both a steel spring and a gas spring. Either way, I found it to be a lightweight winner. The latest Whisper incarnation has their Turbo Stabilization System with a steel spring. It should be interesting to see how this affects the performance, because the only complaint with the old Whisper was some buzziness from the spring.

MP-9 pellet pistol

The MP-9 is a semi-automatic submachine gun that shoots both BBs and pellets from the same magazine. It's configured in a machine pistol style with an extendable buttstock. Velocity of the CO_2 powerplant is up to 450 f.p.s.

P-900 IGT pistol

The Gamo P900 IGT pistol is the first breakbarrel spring-piston air pistol Gamo has made in a long time. It will have their IGT gas spring, fiberoptic sights, and a very ergonomic shape. It's available only in .177, with a rated velocity of 400 f.p.s.

The new Gamo P-900 IGT breakbarrel pistol is Gamo's first breakbarrel spring pistol in a long time. Image courtesy: Gamo

HATSAN

Hatsan TAC BOSS 250XT pistol

One BB pistol I'm really excited to see is Hatsan's new TAC BOSS 250XT. It's a Ruger Mark II lookalike, right down to the

Hatsan's 250XT BB pistol looks like a Ruger Mark II pistol and even disassembles the same way!

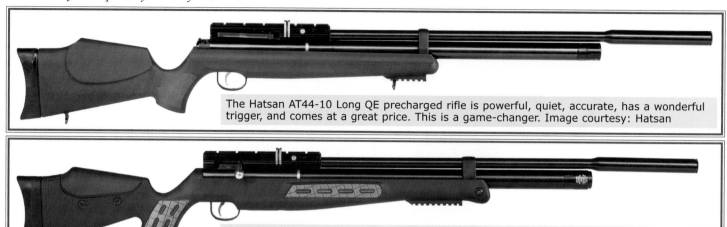

The Hatsan AT44-10 Long QE precharged rifle is powerful, quiet, accurate, has a wonderful trigger, and comes at a great price. This is a game-changer. Image courtesy: Hatsan

For greater power, Hatsan's BT-65 QE has all the benefits of the Quiet Energy series, with maximum horsepower! Comes in .177, .22, and the big .25. Image courtesy: Hatsan

quirky disassembly latch in the backstrap! The Mark II is a classic pistol, so this BB gun should be one as well. It's a 17-shot semi-automatic with a fiberoptic front sight and realistic all-metal construction.

Quiet Energy guns

I was treated to a video of the new Hatsan Quiet Energy rifles in the Hatsan booth, and I was amazed. At 50 yards, the group was close to a half-inch; even at 75 yards, it wasn't much over an inch! These guns are all repeaters, they all have fully shrouded barrels and integrated moderators (silencers) to quiet their powerful report, and they all have adjustable triggers that I am told adjust to a light, crisp release. Best of all, they come in all three popular calibers– .177, .22, and .25. No, strike that! Best of all, Hatsan is bringing them out at a very low price point. I think they'll bear much watching in the coming year. Quiet Energy features will be put in the Galatian QE, AT44-10 QE, AT44-10 Long QE, and the powerful BT-65 QE.

REMINGTON

Remington has been branding airguns for a long time through other companies. In 2013, they took over direct management of their entire airgun line and made their Express breakbarrel spring rifle the first product. It comes in both .177 and .22 calibers and a 4x32 scope plus mount is included. The Express also comes in various stock configurations and lengths. Velocities in .177 range from 750 to 1,150 f.p.s., depending on the model.

Remington's Express spring rifle is not new, but the company wisely chose it as their first internally managed product. Image courtesy: Remington

Remington will also bring out two gas-piston breakbarrel rifles– the ThunderCeptor and ThunderJet later in 2014. Both these rifles will be in the magnum class.

Remington 1911RAC BB pistol

Drawing on its firearm experience, Remington is bringing out a

semi-automatic BB pistol they call the 1911RAC. This realistic pistol resembles the Remington Model 1911 R1 more than a little and has a realistic blowback action to cock the single-action hammer.

The Remington 1911RAC is a realistic-looking 1911 BB pistol. Image courtesy: Remington

Field targets

Remington will also offer some new field targets this year. Some will be the conventional string-resettable type, while others are reset by shooting at a reset trigger on the target. The first offerings will be a crow, wild pig, and jackrabbit.

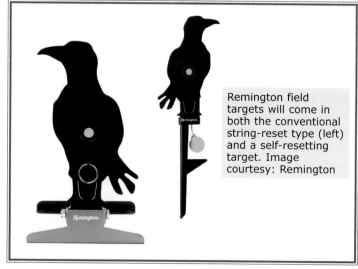

Remington field targets will come in both the conventional string-reset type (left) and a self-resetting target. Image courtesy: Remington

UMAREX USA

Umarex is a company that brings lots of new models to market every year. Let me start with the first one, which is a model most people will not be able to buy. It was sold as a 2014 SHOT Show special, and only 500 were available. It's a commemorative BB pistol model of the Colt M1911A1 pistol from WWII. Unlike most commemoratives, this one has been aged to look like it went through the War and bears the etched commemoration on the left side of the slide. All 500 pistols were sold by day three of the show, but I know that some dealers bought enough to resell. If you want one, the time to look is right now; and if you find one, act fast because the supplies are limited.

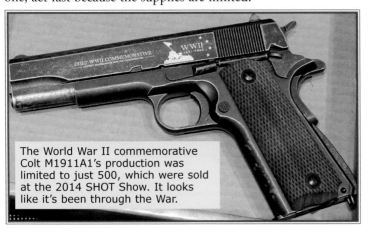

The World War II commemorative Colt M1911A1's production was limited to just 500, which were sold at the 2014 SHOT Show. It looks like it's been through the War.

Colt Commander pistol

The Commander BB pistol is a realistic all-metal Colt Commander-sized handgun with a 19-shot drop-free magazine. The skeleton trigger and hammer are both Commander firearm features reproduced in this pistol. It has a realistic blowback and a manual safety, just like the firearm.

Colt Python

Umarex is hot on their Legends-series of replica airguns, so watch for the release of the Colt Python– a very realistic BB revolver. It's finished in matte black, which no Python ever was, but the size and shape of the gun looks perfect! Plus it loads with realistic shells that contain the BBs.

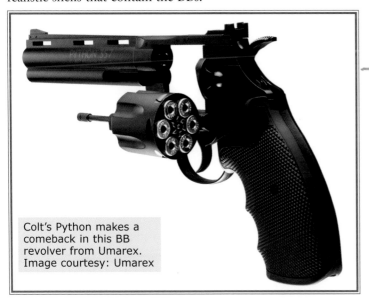

Colt's Python makes a comeback in this BB revolver from Umarex. Image courtesy: Umarex

Makarov Ultra

The Makarov BB pistol was one of the first Legends airguns from Umarex. It's realistic and wonderfully accurate, but you must cock it manually for every shot. Since the Makarov is a semi-automatic firearm, the market screamed for blowback on the BB pistol, as well, and in 2014, you get it.

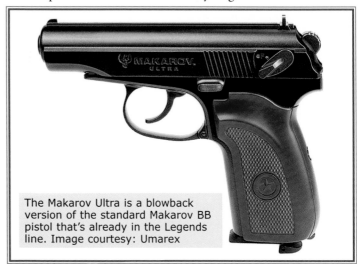

The Makarov Ultra is a blowback version of the standard Makarov BB pistol that's already in the Legends line. Image courtesy: Umarex

Umarex Fuel

The Fuel is a new breakbarrel that comes with a bipod built right into the stock. Powered by their Reaxis gas spring, this new .177 rifle gets up to 1,200 f.p.s. with lightweight alloy pellets. The SilencAir muzzlebrake with its five chambers ensures a quiet report.

The Fuel comes with a foldable bipod that swings down from both sides of the forearm. Image courtesy: Umarex

Walther PPS pistol

There's also a new Walther PPS BB pistol with blowback action. The pistol is metal, which adds realistic weight like the 9mm carry gun it mimics. The spring-loaded magazine holds 18 BBs, and the backstrap comes off to load the CO_2 cartridge.

Walther LGU

It wasn't shown at the SHOT Show, but Walther unveiled its new underlever LGU rifle at IWA, the German sporting arms show. The new rifle has the action parts of the successful new LGV line that was brought out in 2013, but it has an underlever with a sliding compression chamber. The piston is free to torque, which dampens the mainspring's vibration and rotational torque. With Walther quality equal to its new LGV line, this rifle should be received with interest in the U.S. Expect it to arrive in late 2014.

The Walther LGU wasn't shown at the 2014 SHOT Show, but only at Germany's IWA. It will compete with Air Arm's TX200 Mark III. Image courtesy: Umarex

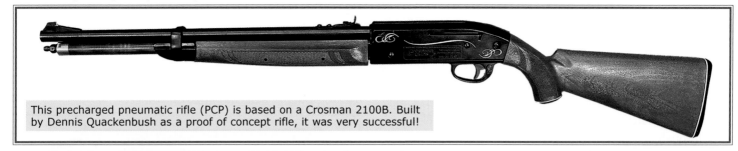

This precharged pneumatic rifle (PCP) is based on a Crosman 2100B. Built by Dennis Quackenbush as a proof of concept rifle, it was very successful!

THE $100 PRECHARGED PNEUMATIC (PCP) AIR RIFLE

For many years, I've had in my mind an idea to build a PCP air rifle that can retail for $100. When I worked with Crosman in 2006 on what became the Discovery air rifle, my thinking was to make the least expensive precharged air rifle possible and sell it in a package with a hand pump. The buyer would get everything needed to start shooting immediately.

They ran with that idea and produced the Discovery under the Benjamin brand, which is one of the all-time classic PCPs. They built it to sell at a very low price when all other precharged airguns were off the charts. That rifle got Crosman started as a producer of PCP airguns, but it didn't do everything I'd hoped. There were still holdouts who thought a rifle and hand pump selling for under $400 together was still too high.

Enter the $100 PCP. I knew that it could be built, but the mindset of the makers had to change. They had to embrace a 2,000 psi top pressure limit instead of overbuilding to offset liability. They had to accept plastic and diecast zinc parts on the gun, just as they do on many multi-pump pneumatics today. They had to accept a soda-straw steel barrel instead of one of full dimensions. In other words, they had a lot of rethinking to do.

To help them, I asked airgun maker Dennis Quackenbush to make a proof-of-concept gun. A gun that had minimal changes from what it started out as– which was a pump gun retailing for about $60.

He did. After testing it, I found that this is a product that ought to exist. It's accurate and powerful. Because it's based on a successful pump rifle, it has great lines from the start.

While Dennis and I were working on our rifle, another airgun dealer had ideas of his own. Mike Melick, owner of Flying Dragon Air Rifles, was making a $100 PCP of his own. Mike took the Chinese XS-60C CO_2 rifle and converted it to run on high-pressure air. His rifle is for sale, and he has sold about 100 of them as this went to press. After he uses up the last of his current rifles for conversions, the price will jump to $165 because the new rifles will cost him more.

Flying Dragon Air Rifles sells this converted XS-60C CO_2 rifle for $100. Image courtesy: Flying Dragon Air Rifles

CONCLUSION

The market is ready for a $100 precharged air rifle. Customers will accept fewer shots, simpler triggers, and open sights as long as they get a rifle that holds an air charge and operates as expected. I expect to see $100 PCP rifles from major manufacturers within the next 12 months.

What's needed is a way to fill these rifles. A hand pump is ideal. That's why the rifle Dennis built operates on 2,000 psi air. The hand pump needn't be as sophisticated as the 3,000 psi hand pumps, but it does have to be reliable, and it has to be priced to sell to the same buyers who purchase the rifle. ■

AIR PISTOLS

100% CONDITION

SMITH & WESSON MODEL 79G CO2 SINGLE SHOT AIR PISTOL, MFG. CIRCA 1971-1980.

This is an excellent example of an air pistol that is 100% new in every aspect. For currently manufactured airguns, the 100% value typically assumes not previously sold at retail. For older discontinued models like this, 100% means all the original finish must be as it was when shipped from the factory. A close inspection of the many edges and corners (exposed to possible wear from simple handling or deterioration from improper storage) reveals no visible wear or thinning of the finish. The checkered composition grips with right hand thumbrest are perfect. High desirability (value) is the result when the right combination of many factors (including trademark, condition, configuration, year of manufacture, total number produced, number of variations, etc.) comes together. In 1972, this pistol retailed for about $35, and today in 100% condition with the adjustable trigger, box, and paper work it will sell for about $235.

95% CONDITION

WINCHESTER MODEL 353 BREAK BARREL COCKING, SINGLE SHOT AIR PISTOL, MFG. BY DIANAWERK CIRCA 1969-1975.

This .22 caliber rifled barrel, BBC, SS, target air pistol has seen very little action. While the molded composition plastic stock with thumbrest and checkering is near mint, the small scratch below the front sight, the very slight edge wear on the muzzle, and the hinge pin area where the barrel and compression tube junction along with light freckling on the barrel and compression tube bring this pistol down out of the 100% condition factor. To find one in this condition with its box and paper work can be difficult and relatively speaking, expensive. Selling new in 1970 for about $30, this Winchester Model 353 in 95% condition with its box and paper work will cost you over $200 if you want to bring it home.

AIR PISTOLS

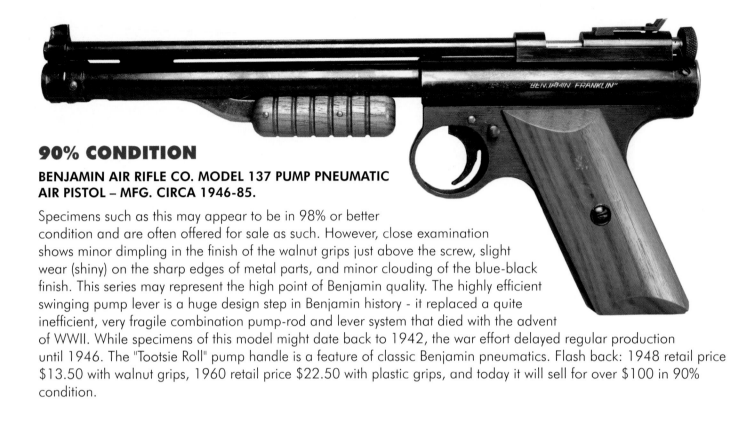

90% CONDITION

BENJAMIN AIR RIFLE CO. MODEL 137 PUMP PNEUMATIC AIR PISTOL – MFG. CIRCA 1946-85.

Specimens such as this may appear to be in 98% or better condition and are often offered for sale as such. However, close examination shows minor dimpling in the finish of the walnut grips just above the screw, slight wear (shiny) on the sharp edges of metal parts, and minor clouding of the blue-black finish. This series may represent the high point of Benjamin quality. The highly efficient swinging pump lever is a huge design step in Benjamin history - it replaced a quite inefficient, very fragile combination pump-rod and lever system that died with the advent of WWII. While specimens of this model might date back to 1942, the war effort delayed regular production until 1946. The "Tootsie Roll" pump handle is a feature of classic Benjamin pneumatics. Flash back: 1948 retail price $13.50 with walnut grips, 1960 retail price $22.50 with plastic grips, and today it will sell for over $100 in 90% condition.

80% CONDITION

CROSMAN CORP. MODEL 130 UNDER LEVER PUMP PNEUMATIC AIR PISTOL, MFG. CIRCA 1955-1970.

The original black finish shows considerable wear from finger contact above the grips and on the body tube where the pumping hand rubs the gun. Also note the surface blemishes on the aluminum breech and shiny edges on the front and rear grip straps and trigger guard. The wooden grips are very good with only minor nicks, but noticing the color difference would lead one to believe the grips were replaced affecting this pistol's overall eye appeal and dropping its desirability (value). Selling new in 1955 for about $10, in 80% overall condition today with the early aluminum breech and finger tip cocking it will sell in the $100 range.

AIR PISTOLS

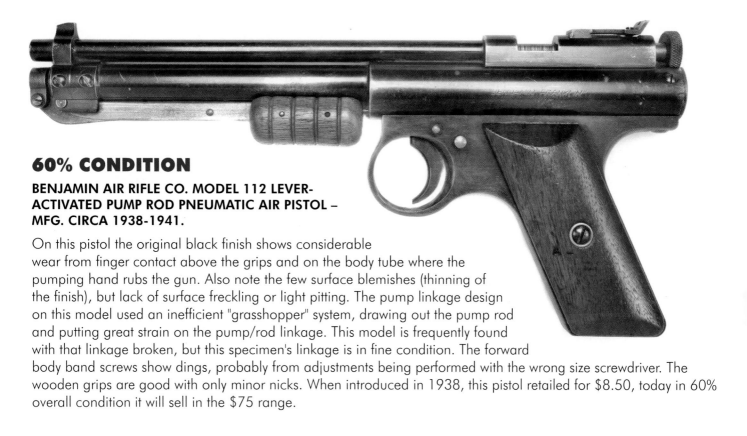

60% CONDITION

BENJAMIN AIR RIFLE CO. MODEL 112 LEVER-ACTIVATED PUMP ROD PNEUMATIC AIR PISTOL – MFG. CIRCA 1938-1941.

On this pistol the original black finish shows considerable wear from finger contact above the grips and on the body tube where the pumping hand rubs the gun. Also note the few surface blemishes (thinning of the finish), but lack of surface freckling or light pitting. The pump linkage design on this model used an inefficient "grasshopper" system, drawing out the pump rod and putting great strain on the pump/rod linkage. This model is frequently found with that linkage broken, but this specimen's linkage is in fine condition. The forward body band screws show dings, probably from adjustments being performed with the wrong size screwdriver. The wooden grips are good with only minor nicks. When introduced in 1938, this pistol retailed for $8.50, today in 60% overall condition it will sell in the $75 range.

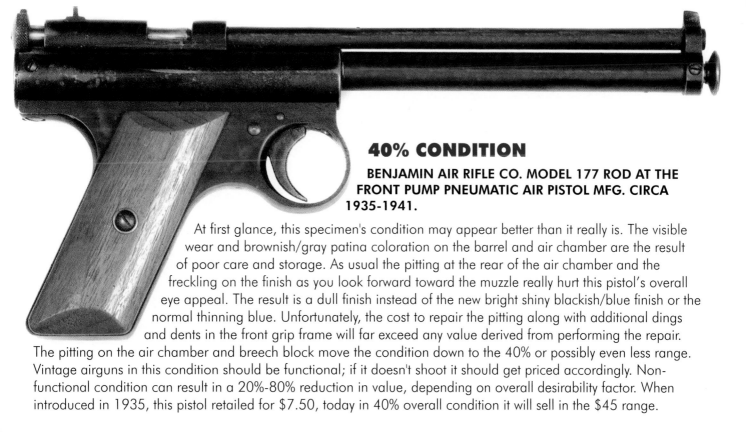

40% CONDITION

BENJAMIN AIR RIFLE CO. MODEL 177 ROD AT THE FRONT PUMP PNEUMATIC AIR PISTOL MFG. CIRCA 1935-1941.

At first glance, this specimen's condition may appear better than it really is. The visible wear and brownish/gray patina coloration on the barrel and air chamber are the result of poor care and storage. As usual the pitting at the rear of the air chamber and the freckling on the finish as you look forward toward the muzzle really hurt this pistol's overall eye appeal. The result is a dull finish instead of the new bright shiny blackish/blue finish or the normal thinning blue. Unfortunately, the cost to repair the pitting along with additional dings and dents in the front grip frame will far exceed any value derived from performing the repair. The pitting on the air chamber and breech block move the condition down to the 40% or possibly even less range. Vintage airguns in this condition should be functional; if it doesn't shoot it should get priced accordingly. Non-functional condition can result in a 20%-80% reduction in value, depending on overall desirability factor. When introduced in 1935, this pistol retailed for $7.50, today in 40% overall condition it will sell in the $45 range.

AIR PISTOLS

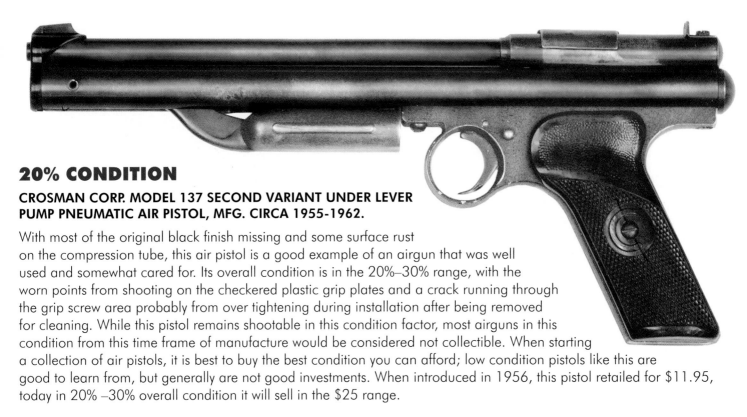

20% CONDITION

CROSMAN CORP. MODEL 137 SECOND VARIANT UNDER LEVER PUMP PNEUMATIC AIR PISTOL, MFG. CIRCA 1955-1962.

With most of the original black finish missing and some surface rust on the compression tube, this air pistol is a good example of an airgun that was well used and somewhat cared for. Its overall condition is in the 20%–30% range, with the worn points from shooting on the checkered plastic grip plates and a crack running through the grip screw area probably from over tightening during installation after being removed for cleaning. While this pistol remains shootable in this condition factor, most airguns in this condition from this time frame of manufacture would be considered not collectible. When starting a collection of air pistols, it is best to buy the best condition you can afford; low condition pistols like this are good to learn from, but generally are not good investments. When introduced in 1956, this pistol retailed for $11.95, today in 20% –30% overall condition it will sell in the $25 range.

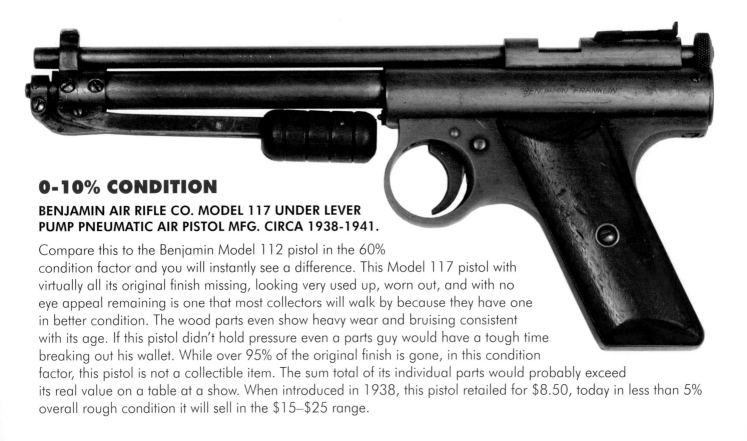

0-10% CONDITION

BENJAMIN AIR RIFLE CO. MODEL 117 UNDER LEVER PUMP PNEUMATIC AIR PISTOL MFG. CIRCA 1938-1941.

Compare this to the Benjamin Model 112 pistol in the 60% condition factor and you will instantly see a difference. This Model 117 pistol with virtually all its original finish missing, looking very used up, worn out, and with no eye appeal remaining is one that most collectors will walk by because they have one in better condition. The wood parts even show heavy wear and bruising consistent with its age. If this pistol didn't hold pressure even a parts guy would have a tough time breaking out his wallet. While over 95% of the original finish is gone, in this condition factor, this pistol is not a collectible item. The sum total of its individual parts would probably exceed its real value on a table at a show. When introduced in 1938, this pistol retailed for $8.50, today in less than 5% overall rough condition it will sell in the $15–$25 range.

AIR RIFLES

100% CONDITION

RWS MODEL 54 SIDE LEVER COCKING (SL) SPRING PISTON (SP) RECOILLESS RIFLE, MFG. BY DIANA CIRCA 1996-CURRENT.

This currently manufactured air rifle is perfect in every aspect, with no wear on either the metal or stock surfaces. When determining upper condition factors on airguns, always inspect the area(s) where wear will accumulate first due to use - in this case, the forward end and pivot point area of the side lever along with the stock forearm and barrel surface where the shooter will hold the rifle during cocking. Worn checkering on the wrist and forearm areas of the stock is also a good indicator of the amount of time in the field an airgun has seen. Also, check all edges or high spots, which could be subject to wear from handling or storage.

95% CONDITION

WALTHER LGR RUNNING BOAR MODEL SIDE LEVER COCKING (SL) SINGLE STROKE PNEUMATIC (SSP) RECOILLESS RIFLE, MFG. CIRCA 1974-1991.

Designed for competing in Olympic Running Boar matches, it is not uncommon to find these rifles heavily used. An experienced collector at a glance will determine this example has seen little usage. The stock shows some very minor handling marks while the metalwork has very limited discoloration (thinning of the blue finish) on its exposed edges. The presence of these condition factors on a mass produced common airgun can make them difficult to sell to a collector (reduces their value by 30%-50%). This condition factor (95% of all original finish intact) on a limited production run of high end target rifles that were used in specialized competitions, which required a lot of practice is uncommon. A limited supply of a collectible (desirable) airgun has a positive effect on its value. In 1989, this air rifle had an MSR of $975, today in 95% all original condition it has a retail value in the $1,250 range.

AIR RIFLES

90% CONDITION

RWS MODEL 24D BREAK BARREL COCKING (BBC) SPRING PISTON (SP) RIFLE, MFG. BY DIANA CIRCA 1984-2007.

This air rifle's overall condition factor is 90% plus, mostly due to visible wear on the trigger and guard, muzzle, light discoloration (duller finish with light freckling rather than shiny black when new) of metal bluing on the barrel and air chamber, and numerous handling marks on the stock. Wear (nicks, dings, and even light scratches) on the stock does not affect overall condition nearly as much as metal wear. This airgun shows normal wear and tear for its vintage and still operates perfectly, which is another key when trying to determine overall condition and value. If it doesn't shoot, how much will a potential buyer have to spend to make it shoot? This rifle had an MSR of $115 circa 1988, and today in 90% overall condition it still has a retail value in the $110 range.

80% CONDITION

DIANA MODEL 16 BREAK BARREL COCKING (BBC) SPRING PISTON (SP) RIFLE, MFG. CIRCA 1922-1944.

The blued metal of this specimen is beginning to turn a plum patina on the barrel, air chamber, and trigger guard, light freckling over most of its surfaces, and a few small scratches on the air chamber help to diminish this rifle's condition factor by 20%. The stock is in somewhat better condition (very few light handling marks) than the metal and when one part of the gun is better than another, it is necessary to consider whether any refinishing has taken place. Even excellent refinishing of either the metal or wood of an airgun can have a negative effect and will probably reduce the overall value. Careful examination of the stock edge varnish gives every indication that this finish is original, but the small chip missing at the toe of the butt works as an equalizer. This example is stamped 12.35 on back of the stock butt indicating a manufacturing date of December, 1935. When new it probably sold for about $8, and now in 80% overall condition it has a retail value in the $50 range.

AIR RIFLES

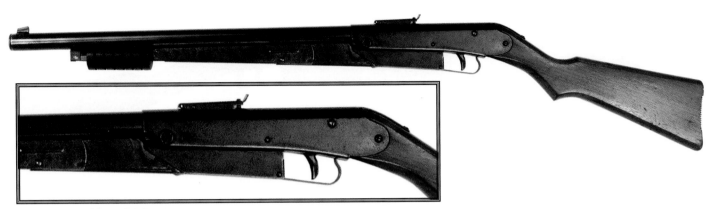

60% CONDITION

DAISY MODEL 25 VARIANT 5, LONG-LEVER ELBOW-SLIDE COCKING BB AIR RIFLE, MFG. CIRCA 1933-36.

The receiver finish edge deterioration (wear on the exposed edges reveling shiny metal) on this air rifle is a good example to show the new person on the block what we mean by edge wear. Plum patina with freckling on the barrel and frame along with dark pistol grip edges and butt stock scratches all add up to an overall condition of 60%. This gun was used quite a bit— notice the shiny replaced (new) screw in the welded barrel anchor near the muzzle, a high wear point on this slide action rifle. The case color finish on the pump lever is in good condition despite not being properly maintained. In most cases, a middle of the road (40%, 60%, and 80%) condition factor is far simpler to determine than high-end condition (95% or better). The middle of the road is also where the item's eye appeal can also affect the retail value as much as actual condition. The 1935 *Stoeger's Gun Catalog & Handbook No. 26* lists this Daisy Model 25 for $3.95, today in 60% overall condition, it has a retail value in the $175 range.

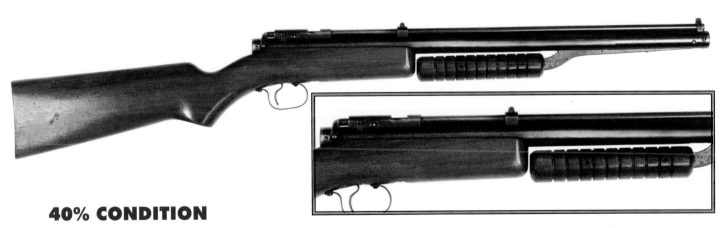

40% CONDITION

BENJAMIN MODEL 312 UNDER LEVER (UL) MULTI–PUMP PNEUMATIC AIR RIFLE, MFG. CIRCA 1940–1969.

This little rifle is one we all can relate to for one reason or another. The configuration of the barrel over air chamber set into a plain stock with a grooved wooden pump handle appears across many trademarks, and finish wear patterns are predictable. Note how the barrel and air chamber finish have turned a brownish patina because of wear and original bluing oxidation. The plain stock also has the normal handling marks with some dark spots that may clean off if attempted by a professional. These types of finish problems can drastically affect overall eye appeal and make a $50-$60 air rifle a tough sale at $40. Even though this air rifle is over half a century old, a buyer should not allow himself to be talked into spending more than what is fair. The 1950 *Stoeger's Gun Catalog & Handbook No. 41* lists this Benjamin Model 312 for $16.65; today in 40% overall condition it has a retail value in the $35 range.

AIR RIFLES

20% CONDITION

DAISY MODEL 25 VARIANT 4, LONG-LEVER ELBOW-SLIDE COCKING BB AIR RIFLE, MFG. CIRCA 1915–16.

The wear on the stock and metal of this gun is very consistent. There are considerable areas displaying original blue, but almost all are marked with small patches and/or freckling of rust. The stock finish obviously is original, but marked with some major blemishes, scratches, and even a small burn mark. It is interesting that the bluing does not seem to show much wear; its degradation seems to have been almost entirely due to poor storage conditions over the several decades of this gun's life. The total drop in condition from new is about 80%. Still a nice specimen in one of the most popular series Daisy ever produced. Over twenty million of the hard-hitting Model 25 airguns went through about 58 variants over 65 years - Daisy's longest lived model. In 20% overall condition this air rifle has a retail value in the $60 range.

0-10% CONDITION

BENJAMIN MODEL 310 SMOOTHBORE UNDER LEVER (UL) MULTI–PUMP PNEUMATIC AIR RIFLE, MFG. CIRCA 1940–1969.

This is an example of an all-too-common condition. Even to the novice this gun speaks volumes about its days (and probably nights) in the field chasing who knows what. Its black finish is virtually gone, and the underlying brass has a heavy patina. The barrel has been poorly brazed to the air tube and the rifle does not function. The stock may have been cleaned and refinished. If it was possible to have negative condition factors, this rifle would be a prime candidate. Very little original wood or metal finish and poor repairs attempted have earned this air gun a condition rating of less than 10%. Restoration generally is to be reserved for extreme cases, such as this, but must be done very carefully and generally the improved value does not cover the expense of restoration. In 20% overall condition this air rifle has a retail value in the $50 range.

A SECTION

ABT

Previous manufacturer located at 715-727 North Kedzie St., Chicago, IL circa 1925-1958. The company name is an acronym of the founders' names: Gus Adler, Jack Bechtol, and Walter Tratsch. ABT was a producer of carnival and shooting gallery BB pistols, BB rifles, and supplies. Developed Air-O-Matic airgun design, patented April 19, 1932, pat. no. 1854605 and Oct. 6, 1942, pat. no. 2297947. Other patents to 1949.

Most of the known ABT guns are pistols which were captive mounted in highly decorated wooden boxes serving as miniature, coin-operated firing ranges. These were used for entertainment and as covert/rigged games of chance. These game guns were manufactured from 1925 to about 1958. There are no production records from about 1941 to 1946 due to WWII. The shooting box part of the company's history is detailed at www.crowriver.com/abt.htm.

It is not clear when hose-fed compressed air ABT airguns were made, but the patents run from 1932 through 1949. ABT apparently applied for Arrow-Matic as a trademark, and so marked at least some guns, but were granted the Air-O-Matic trademark for semi-automatic airguns that are fed from a patented, pre-loaded filler tube of BBs that was inserted into a unique rear or top-feeding loading chute when the gun was opened by pulling back the top of the receiver or a side bolt. At least three versions of shoulder-fired, hose-fed pneumatic rifles and one similar pistol are known. Also known is a sliding pump action rifle, unmarked, but with exactly the same unusual, complex, loading chute.

Virtually all ABT specimens are well worn from hard shooting gallery use, but are very durable due to their rugged, excellent construction. Carnival airguns are now becoming more popular with airgun collectors, and values can be expected to rise accordingly.

GRADING	100%	95%	90%	80%	60%	40%	20%

PISTOLS

AIR-O-MATIC GALLERY PISTOL – .173 cal., hose pneumatic, semi-automatic repeater, pop-up loading chute loaded by insertion of pre-loaded filler tube of BBs, 7.1 in. smoothbore barrel, no safety, 12.7 in. OAL, 2.6 lbs. Probably mfg. 1930s to 1940s.

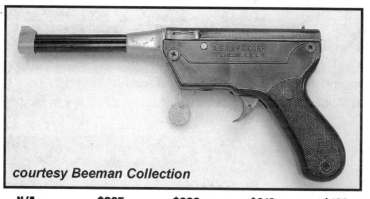

courtesy Beeman Collection

N/A	$325	$260	$210	$160	$115	$65

CAPTIVE SHOOTING BOX PISTOL – .40 cal., spring action, tube-fed repeater, 2.6 in. smoothbore blue barrel, no safety, 8.7 in. OAL, 2.9 lbs. Mfg. 1925-1958.

courtesy Beeman Collection

N/A	$225	$180	$145	$110	$80	$45

RIFLES

AIR-O-MATIC REAR LOADER – .173 cal., hose pneumatic, semi-auto repeater, loading chute in rear of receiver for

GRADING	100%	95%	90%	80%	60%	40%	20%

insertion of pre-loaded filler tube of BBs, approx. 16 in. smoothbore barrel within longer barrel shroud, stamped with 1932 patent date, model name cast in plastic buttplate, no safety, approx. 42 in. OAL, approx. 5 lbs.

* *Air-O-Matic Rear Loader Variant I* – large sheet metal receiver extends almost to bottom edge of the middle of the stock.

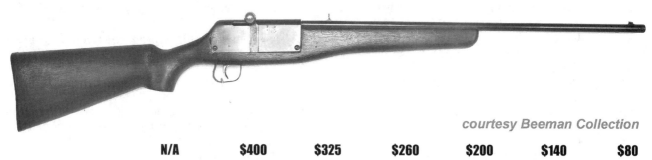

courtesy Beeman Collection

| N/A | $400 | $325 | $260 | $200 | $140 | $80 |

* *Air-O-Matic Rear Loader Variant II* – small receiver in line with barrel above one piece stock.

courtesy Beeman Collection

| N/A | $425 | $350 | $275 | $210 | $150 | $85 |

AIR-O-MATIC TOP LOADER – .173 cal. semi-auto repeater, hose pneumatic, approx. 23 in. smoothbore barrel within larger barrel shroud which is topped by a small full-length tube, metal box-like receiver divides stock into two pieces, no safety, approx. 42 in. OAL, approx. 5.6 lbs.

The loading chute is on top of the receiver for insertion of a pre-loaded filler tube of BBs, receiver is stamped with 1942 and 1949 patent dates, and the model name is cast in a plastic buttplate.

* *Air-O-Matic Top Loader Knob Variant* – short, straight-pull knob. Early mfg.

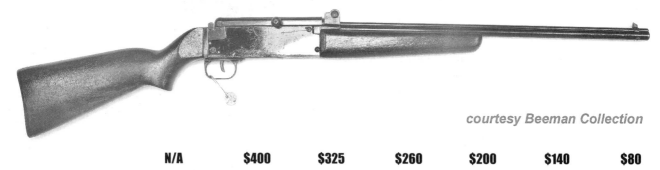

courtesy Beeman Collection

| N/A | $400 | $325 | $260 | $200 | $140 | $80 |

* *Air-O-Matic Top Loader Bolt Variant* – long bodied turning bolt. Later mfg.

courtesy Beeman Collection

| N/A | $400 | $325 | $260 | $200 | $140 | $80 |

AIR-O-MATIC SLIDE ACTION – .173 cal., hose pneumatic, repeater, 23 in. smoothbore barrel, no safety, 42.5 in.

GRADING	100%	95%	90%	80%	60%	40%	20%

OAL, 7.1 lbs. Probably mfg. 1940s.

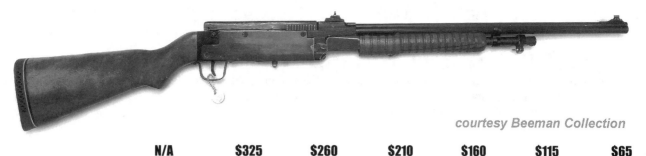

courtesy Beeman Collection

	N/A	$325	$260	$210	$160	$115	$65

This model is loaded by insertion of a pre-loaded filler tube of BBs in the loading chute, and has an unusual dual diameter sliding forearm. There are no markings on this gun.

ARS (AIR RIFLE SPECIALISTS)

Previous importer located in Pine City, NY. Dealer or consumer direct sales.

ARS previously imported airguns from Shin Sung, located in Korea, and Farco airguns from the Philippines. For information on Farco airguns, see the "F" section and for information on Shin Sung see the "S" section.

PISTOLS

For current information on the Hunting Master AR-6 see Evanix in the "E" section.

HUNTING MASTER AR-6 – .22 (.177 or .20 special order) cal., PCP, SS, 12 in. rifled steel barrel, 6-shot rotary mag., approx. twenty shots at 20 ft./lb. ME on one charge, 18.3 in. OAL, 3 lbs. Mfg. by Duk Il in Seoul, Korea. Disc.

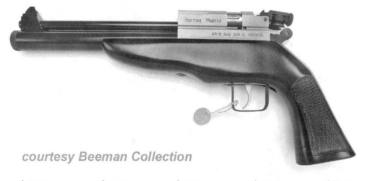

courtesy Beeman Collection

	$650	$550	$450	$375	$295	$195	$130

RIFLES

HUNTING MASTER 900 – 9mm cal., PCP, 26.8 in. barrel, 900 FPS, wood stock. Mfg. by Duk Il. Disc. 1999.

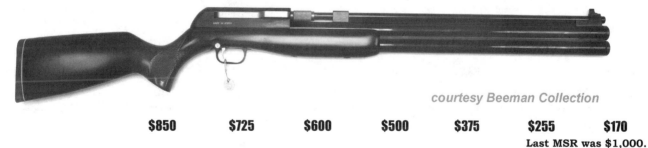

courtesy Beeman Collection

	$850	$725	$600	$500	$375	$255	$170

Last MSR was $1,000.

MAGNUM 6 – .22 cal., CO_2 or PCP, 6-shot, similar to the King Hunting Master. Mfg. in Korea, disc.

courtesy Howard Collection

	$400	$350	$300	$245	$190	$125	$85

Last MSR was $500.

GRADING	100%	95%	90%	80%	60%	40%	20%

QB 77 – .177 or .22 cal., CO_2, SS, 21.5 in. barrel, hardwood stock, 5.5 lbs. Mfg. in China. Disc. 2001.

	$165	$140	$115	$95	$75	$50	$35

Last MSR was $149.

ASG (ACTION SPORT GAMES A/S)

Current manufacturer of replica firearms and accessories located in Humlebaek, Denmark. Currently imported and distributed by Air Venturi/Pyramyd Air, located in Solon, OH. Previously located in Warrensville Hts., OH.

Founded in April 2003, ASG currently manufactures licensed airgun copies of Bersa, CZ, Dan Wesson, STI, and Steyr Mannlicher firearms.

PISTOLS

BERSA BP9CC – .177 cal., CO_2, blowback or non-blowback action, black frame with black metal slide, lower accessory rail, threaded barrel, fixed 3-dot sights, nylon/metal stippled grips, rear slide serrations, grooved front and rear gripstrap. New 2013.

courtesy ASG

MSR $120	$100	$90	$80	$65	$50	N/A	N/A

BERSA THUNDER 9 PRO – .177 cal., CO_2, non-blowback action, black frame with black metal slide, lower accessory rail, threaded barrel, fixed 3-dot sights, nylon/metal stippled grips, rear slide serrations, checkered front and rear gripstrap. New 2013.

courtesy ASG

MSR $76	$65	$55	$50	$40	$30	N/A	N/A

CZ 75D COMPACT – .177 cal., CO_2, 380 FPS, SA/DA, black frame with black or dual tone slide, 3.64 in. threaded barrel, checkered rubber grips, 17-shot mag., adj. rear sight, fixed front sight, Weaver accessory rail, manual safety, 1.46 lbs. New 2012.

courtesy ASG

MSR $90	$75	$70	$60	$50	$40	N/A	N/A

GRADING	100%	95%	90%	80%	60%	40%	20%

CZ 75 P-07 DUTY – .177 cal., CO_2, blowback or non-blowback action, black frame with black or dual tone metal slide, lower accessory rail, threaded barrel, nylon/metal stippled grips, rear slide serrations, checkered front and rear gripstrap. New 2012.

courtesy ASG

MSR $120	$100	$90	$80	$65	$50	N/A	N/A

STEYR M9-A1 – .177 cal., CO_2, non-blowback action, 449 FPS, black metal frame with black or dual-tone slide, ergonomic grips, illuminated fiber optic rear sight, lower accessory rail, 19-shot mag., textured polymer grips. New 2012.

courtesy ASG

MSR $111	$95	$85	$75	$60	$45	N/A	N/A

STI DUTY ONE – .177 cal., CO_2, blowback or non-blowback action, 383 FPS, 4.6 in. threaded barrel, 20-shot mag., Weaver accessory rail, black metal frame, front and rear slide serrations, fixed sights, manual safety, high rise beavertail grip, 1.82 lbs. New 2012.

courtesy ASG

MSR $120	$100	$90	$80	$65	$50	N/A	N/A

REVOLVERS

DAN WESSON REVOLVER – .177 cal., CO_2, 2 1/2, 4, 6, or 8 in. barrel, SA/DA, black or silver metal frame, 6-shot

courtesy ASG

GRADING	100%	95%	90%	80%	60%	40%	20%

mag., fixed front sight, adj. rear sight, textured polymer finger groove grips, manual safety, working ejector rod, includes detachable Weaver rail, speedloader, and 6 shells. New 2012.

MSR $150	$125	$100	$90	$75	$55	$35	$25

ABAS MAJOR

Previously manufactured by A.A. Brown & Sons located at 1 Snake Lane, Alvechurch, Birmingham, England, circa 1945-1946.

Albert Arthur Brown and his sons, Albert Henry Brown and Sydney Charles Brown, were co-patentees and partners in developing and producing the Abas Major air pistol. (ABAS = initials of A. Brown and Sons.)

PISTOLS

ABAS MAJOR – .177 cal., concentric piston SP action, tap loading, trigger guard and forward edge of grip frame swings forward under the 7.6 in. barrel to cock the mainspring, counterclockwise rifling, blue, black crinkled paint, or aluminum finish, no safety. Walnut Grip Variant: smooth walnut grips, blued, some with black crackle paint, earliest production with lever release button on bottom of grip. Smooth Plastic Grip Variant: smooth brown composition grips, blued, most common variant. Checkered Plastic Grip Variant: checkered brown plastic grips, 8.1 in. OAL, 2.7 lbs. Mfg. 1946-1949. Ref: AW: 1978, Apr. 1982.

courtesy Beeman Collection

	N/A	$800	$650	$525	$400	$280	$160

Add 10% for release button on bottom of grip.
Add 10% for black enamel.
Add 15% for Walnut Grip Variant.
Add 20%-50% for original factory box with Abas Major pellets (depending on condition).

Less than 1,870 of all variants known. Ref: AW: 1978, Apr. 1982.

ABBEY ALERT

For information on Abbey Alert airguns, see Produsit in the "P" section.

ACCLES & SHELVOKE LTD.

Previous manufacturer located at Talford Street Engineering Works, Birmingham, Warwickshire, England. Founded by James Accles and George Shelvoke in 1913.

Accles & Shelvoke originally produced humane cattle killers patented by James Accles and Charles Cash. Before WWII, the firm manufactured the Warrior, an air pistol developed and patented by Frank Clarke and Edwin Anson. They may have also produced the prototypes of the Titan air pistols for Frank Clarke. After WWII, the company produced the Acvoke air pistol, designed by John Arrowsmith. They were still recorded as making humane cattle killers in 2005. Air pistols were produced from 1931 to 1956. The authors and publisher wish to thank John Atkins for his valuable assistance with the following information in this edition of the *Blue Book of Airguns*.

PISTOLS

ACVOKE – .177 cal., SP, SS, concentric piston, cocked by pivoting grip forward with the aid of a lever which folds down

courtesy Beeman Collection

GRADING	100%	95%	90%	80%	60%	40%	20%

from grip backstrap, 8 in. rifled barrel, blue finish, vertically ribbed plastic grips marked "ACVOKE" in an oval logo, 8.6 in. OAL, 2 lbs. Mfg. circa 1946-1956.

	N/A	$450	$350	$295	$225	$160	$90

Add 20% for original factory box.
Add 10% for cork adapter.
Ref: GR Oct. '80.

WARRIOR – .177 or .22 cal., SL, SP, SS, 8 in. rifled barrel, blue or nickel finish. Concentric bbl. and piston. Chamfered Lever Variant: Outer front corner of cocking lever chamfered (mfg. 1930-33). Square Cocking Lever Variant: curved outer front corner of cocking lever is squarish, recurved trigger guard, serial numbered and marked "Accles & Shelvoke LTD", 8.6 in. OAL, 2.2 lbs. Mfg. 1933-1939.

courtesy Beeman Collection

	N/A	$600	$475	$400	$300	$210	$120

Add 25% for Chamfered Lever Variant.
Add 40% for nickel finish.
Add 30% for .22 cal.
Add 25% for Abercrombie and Fitch markings (MONOGRAM label stamped on LHS).
Add 20% for factory box.
Ref. GR Apr. 80 and AW Sept 81.

ACRO

For information on ACRO airguns, see Ampell in this section.

ACVOKE

For information on Acvoke, see Accles & Shelvoke Ltd. in this section.

ADAM & WESTLAKE COMPANY

Previous manufacturer of BB rifles located in Chicago, IL, circa 1892.

AERON CZ s.r.o.

Current manufacturer located in Brno, Czech Republic. Currently imported and/or distributed by Pomona Airguns, located in Hesperia, CA and Top Gun Air Guns Inc., located in Scottsdale, AZ. Previously imported and/or distributed by Airguns of Arizona/Precision Airgun Distribution located in Gilbert, AZ, Pilkington Competition Equipment LLC located in Monteagle, TN, Pyramyd Air, Inc. located in Warrensville Heights, OH, Euro-Imports, located in Pahrump, NV, Century International Arms, Inc., located in St. Albans, VT, and Bohemia Arms, located in Fountain Valley, CA.

Aeron was established in 1968 by "SVAZARM" - a Czech Army activity club. The company designed, manufactured, and serviced small airplanes. Since then it changed its activities several times and started to service and manufacture sports arms. Recently the company was acquired by a new team of people willing to keep the tradition and continue to develop and manufacture high precision air pistols and rifles for competition and junior shooting.

For information on TAU model pistols and rifles previously manufactured by Aeron, see TAU BRNO in the "T" section.

GRADING	100%	95%	90%	80%	60%	40%	20%

PISTOLS

MODEL ACZ101 SPIDER – .177 cal., PCP, SS, 10 in. Lothar Walther barrel, 443 FPS, adj. sights, adj. trigger, adj. barrel weight, adj. pistol grip, 2.4 lbs.

courtesy Aeron

MSR $1,300	$1,100	$975	$875	$725	$550	N/A	N/A

Add 5% for left-hand grip.

MODEL ACZ101 SPIDER JUNIOR – .177 cal., PCP, SS, 8 in. Lothar Walther barrel, 443 FPS, adj. sights, adj. trigger, adj. barrel weight, adj. pistol grip, 2.4 lbs.

courtesy Aeron

MSR $1,300	$1,100	$975	$875	$725	$550	N/A	N/A

Add 5% for left-hand grip.

MODEL B95 – .177 cal., CO_2 refillable from cylinder or 12-gram cylinder, SS, 8.3 in. Lothar Walther barrel, 425 FPS, adj. rear sight, adj. trigger, adj. barrel weight, adj. pistol grip, 2.4 lbs. Disc. 2004.

	$350	$300	$245	$205	$160	$105	$70

Add 5% for left-hand grip.

MODEL B96 – .177 cal., CO_2 bulk fill or 12-gram cylinder, 5-shot, 8.3-10 in. Lothar Walther barrel, 443 FPS, adj. rear sight, adj. trigger, adj. barrel weight, adj. pistol grip, 2.4 lbs. Disc. 2006.

courtesy Aeron CZ

	$575	$500	$400	$325	$260	$170	$115

Add 10% for left-hand model.

GRADING	100%	95%	90%	80%	60%	40%	20%

MODEL B97 CHAMELEON – .177 cal., CO_2, bulk fill or 12-gram cylinder, SS, 5-shot, 8.3-10 in. Lothar Walther barrel, 443 FPS, adj. rear sight, adj. trigger, adj. barrel weight, adj. pistol grip, 2.4 lbs. Disc. 2006.

courtesy Aeron CZ

	100%	95%	90%	80%	60%	40%	20%
	$375	$325	$265	$220	$170	$110	$75

MODEL B98 – .177 cal., PCP, 5-shot, 8.3 in. Lothar Walther barrel, 443 FPS, adj. sights, adj. trigger, adj. barrel weight, adj. pistol grip, 2.4 lbs. Disc. 2007.

courtesy Aeron

	100%	95%	90%	80%	60%	40%	20%
	$850	$725	$600	$500	$375	$255	$170

Add 5% for left-hand grip.

MODEL B99 – .177 cal., PCP, SS, 8.3 in. Lothar Walther barrel, 425 FPS, adj. rear sight, adj. trigger, adj. barrel weight, adj. pistol grip, 2.4 lbs. Disc. 2006.

	100%	95%	90%	80%	60%	40%	20%
	$700	$600	$475	$400	$300	$210	$140

Add 5% for left-hand grip.

MODEL B100 – .177 cal., PCP, SS, competition target pistol.

	100%	95%	90%	80%	60%	40%	20%
	$725	$625	$525	$425	$325	$220	$145

Add 5% for left-hand grip.

RIFLES

MODEL B40 – .177 cal., CO_2, 5-shot, 15.75 in. barrel, 476 FPS, UIT target model, adj. sight, adj. trigger, adj. cheek piece, adj. buttplate, wood stock, 9.5 lbs. Disc. 2005.

	100%	95%	90%	80%	60%	40%	20%
	$235	$200	$165	$135	$105	$70	$45

MODEL B40J – .177 cal., CO_2, 5-shot, 15.75 in. barrel, 476 FPS, UIT target model, adj. sight, adj. trigger, adj. cheek piece, adj. buttplate, wood stock, 9.5 lbs. Disc. 2005.

	100%	95%	90%	80%	60%	40%	20%
	$235	$200	$165	$135	$105	$70	$45

MODEL B41 – .177 cal., CO_2, SS, 15.75 in. barrel, 476 FPS, UIT target model, adj. sight, adj. trigger, adj. cheek piece, adj. buttplate, wood stock, 9.5 lbs. Disc. 2005.

	100%	95%	90%	80%	60%	40%	20%
	$235	$200	$165	$135	$105	$70	$45

MODEL B41-5 – .22 cal., CO_2, SS, 15.75 in. barrel, 410 FPS, UIT target model, adj. sight, adj. trigger, adj. cheek piece, adj. buttplate, wood stock, 9.5 lbs. Disc. 2005.

	100%	95%	90%	80%	60%	40%	20%
	$225	$190	$160	$130	$100	$65	$45

MODEL B41J – .177 cal., CO_2, SS, 15.75 in. barrel, 476 FPS, UIT target model, adj. sight, adj. trigger, adj. cheek piece, adj. buttplate, wood stock, 9.5 lbs. Disc. 2005.

	100%	95%	90%	80%	60%	40%	20%
	$235	$200	$165	$135	$105	$70	$45

GRADING	100%	95%	90%	80%	60%	40%	20%

MODEL B41J-5 – .22 cal., CO_2, SS, 15.75 in. barrel, 410 FPS, UIT target model, adj. sight, adj. trigger, adj. cheek piece, adj. buttplate, wood stock, 9.5 lbs. Disc. 2005.

	$225	$190	$160	$130	$100	$65	$45

AFTERMATH

Current trademark of air pistols imported and distributed by Air Venturi/Pyramyd Air, located in Solon, OH. Previously located in Warrensville Hts., OH.

PISTOLS

LADY SPORT TACTICAL – .177 cal., CO_2, semi-auto, 19 shot mag., 430 FPS, pink frame and hammer, black slide and trigger blade, fiber optic fixed sights, Weaver accessory rail, manual safety, 1.4 lbs. New 2012.

courtesy Aftermath

MSR $75	$65	$55	$50	$40	$30	N/A	N/A

MAYHEM SPORT TACTICAL – .177 cal., CO_2, semi-auto, 19 shot mag., 430 FPS, black frame, grips, and slide, fiber optic fixed sights, Weaver accessory rail, optics rail, manual safety, single stage trigger, 2.29 lbs. Imported 2012-13.

	$85	$70	$60	$50	$40	$25	$15

Last MSR was $100.

AIR ARMS

Current manufacturer located in East Sussex, England. Currently imported and distributed by Air Venturi/Pyramyd Air, located in Solon, OH. Previously located in Warrensville Hts., OH. Previously imported by Pomona Air Guns located in Hesperia, CA, Straight Shooters Precision Airguns located in St. Cloud, MN, Top Gun Air Guns, Inc., located in Scottsdale, AZ, and Dynamit Nobel-RWS, Inc. Dealer or consumer direct sales.

Air Arms is a division of its parent company NSP Engineering Ltd. and has been manufacturing airguns since the mid-1980s. The latest Air Arms models, S300, S310, S400, S410, and the Pro-Target (designed by three-time world champion Nick Jenkinson and gunsmith Ken Turner), are pre-charged pneumatics that can be filled from a SCUBA tank, allowing many shots to be fired from one charge. The remaining models, Pro-Sport, TX200 Mk III, TX200 HX, and Pro-Elite are spring piston rifles. All Air Arms models feature Walther barrels.

PISTOLS

ALFA – .177 cal., PCP, compressed air, 9.5 in. aqua blue barrel with slotted shroud, walnut grip, power regulator, anti-flip muzzle brake, mounting rail, adj. match grade trigger, fully adj. sights, dry fire practice facility, 16.75 in. OAL, 2 lbs. New 2012.

MSR $750	$625	$550	$500	$400	$325	N/A	N/A

PP1 EARLY (PRECHARGE PISTOL 1) – .177 cal., PCP, SS, breech loading, bright turn bolt finished action, 8 in. barrel, blue finish cylinder, 425 FPS, sliding adj. 2-stage trigger, anatomical wood grip, grooved action for optical sight, no safety.

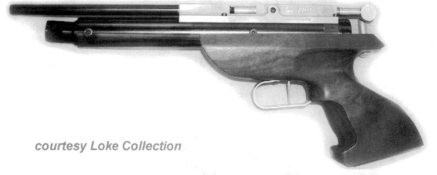

courtesy Loke Collection

	$1,250	$1,050	$875	$725	$550	$375	$250

GRADING	100%	95%	90%	80%	60%	40%	20%

PP1 LATE (PRECHARGE PISTOL 1) – .177 cal., PCP, SS, breech loading, blue straight pull bolt finished action, 8 in. barrel, blue finish cylinder, 425 FPS, sliding adj. 2-stage trigger, anatomical wood grip, grooved action for optical sight, no safety.

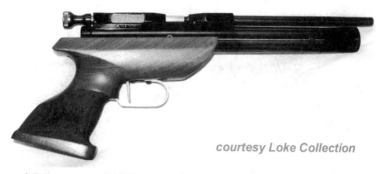

courtesy Loke Collection

	$1,250	$1,050	$875	$725	$550	$375	$250

RIFLES

BORA – .177 cal., SL, SP, 35-shot over barrel mag., 11 in. rifled steel barrel, blue finish, 625 FPS, two-stage adj. trigger, sling swivels, beech Monte Carlo stock with checkered PG and vent. recoil pad, 35.5 in. OAL, 7.7 lbs.

	$275	$235	$195	$160	$125	$80	$55

BORA AL – .22 cal., SL, SP, SS, 11 in. rifled steel barrel, blue finish, 625 FPS, two-stage adj. trigger, sling swivels, beech Monte Carlo stock with checkered PG and vent. recoil pad, 35.5 in. OAL, 7.7 lbs.

	$325	$275	$230	$190	$145	$95	$65

CAMARGUE – .177 cal., SL, SP, 35-shot over barrel mag., tap-loading, 15 in. rifled steel barrel, blue finish, 625 FPS, two-stage adj. trigger, sling swivels, walnut Tyrolean-style stock with checkered PG and vent. recoil pad, 39.8 in. OAL, 7.94 lbs.

	$450	$375	$325	$260	$205	$135	$90

CAMARGUE AL – .22 cal., SL, SP, SS, tap-loading, 15 in. rifled steel barrel, blue finish, 625 FPS, two-stage adj. trigger, sling swivels, walnut Tyrolean-style stock with checkered PG and vent. recoil pad, 39.8 in. OAL, 7.94 lbs.

	$550	$475	$375	$325	$250	$165	$110

EV2 – .177 cal., PCP, SS, side lever loading, 800 FPS, 16.15 in. rotary swaged barrel, red/nickel, black/nickel, or blue/nickel laminated competition stock, quick release charging connector, adj. trigger, silver color multi-adj. cheek piece, forearm, and buttplate, spirit level, wind indicator, approx. 40.5 in. OAL, 9.12 lbs. Mfg. 2004-2013.

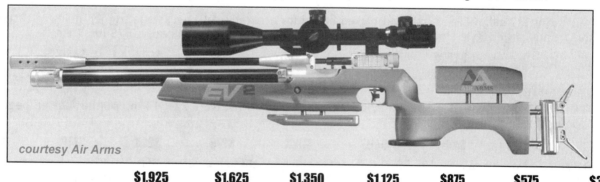

courtesy Air Arms

	$1,925	$1,625	$1,350	$1,125	$875	$575	$375

Last MSR was $2,270.

FTP 900 – .177 cal., PCP, SS, fully-regulated recoilless sidelever action, 19 in. fully floated and shrouded Lothar Walther match barrel with integral air stripper and muzzle-flip deflector, 800 FPS, two-stage adj. trigger, 203.5cc cylinder, integral manometer, fully adj. laminated competition stock, cheek piece, forearm, palm rest, and butt hook, swing out spirit level and windicator, accessory rail, approx. 41-42.1 in. OAL, 11 lbs. Mfg. 2013-current.

MSR $2,800	$2,375	$2,100	$1,900	$1,550	$1,175	N/A	N/A

KHAMSIN – .177 cal., SL, SP, 35-shot over barrel mag., tap-loading, 15 in. rifled steel barrel, specially polished blue finish, 625 FPS, two-stage adj. trigger, sling swivels, walnut thumbhole stock with checkered PG and vent. recoil pad, 39.8 in. OAL, 7.94 lbs.

	$400	$350	$280	$230	$180	$120	$80

GRADING	100%	95%	90%	80%	60%	40%	20%

KHAMSIN AL – .22 cal., SL, SP, SS, tap-loading, 15 in. rifled steel barrel, specially polished blue finish, 625 FPS, two-stage adj. trigger, sling swivels, walnut thumbhole stock with checkered PG and vent. recoil pad, 39.8 in. OAL, 7.94 lbs.

	$500	$425	$350	$290	$225	$150	$100

MISTRAL – .177 cal., SL, SP, 35-shot over barrel mag., 625 FPS, 15 in. rifled steel barrel, blue finish, two-stage adj. trigger, sling swivels, beech Monte Carlo stock with checkered PG and vent. recoil pad, 39.8 in. OAL, 7.94 lbs.

courtesy Beeman Collection

	$350	$300	$245	$205	$160	$105	$70

MISTRAL AL – .177 or .22 cal., SL, SP, SS, 625 FPS, 15 in. rifled steel barrel, blue finish, two-stage adj. trigger, sling swivels, beech Monte Carlo stock with checkered PG and vent. recoil pad, 39.8 in. OAL, 7.94 lbs.

	$425	$350	$300	$245	$190	$125	$85

MPR BIATHLON (S400 BIATHLON) – for model description and values please refer to S400 Biathlon in this category.

Beginning circa 2012 Air Arms adjusted model nomenclature and MPR (Multi-Positional-Rifle) became synonymous with S400.

MPR FIELD TARGET (S400 MPR FT) – for model description and values please refer to S400 MPR FT in this category.

Beginning circa 2012 Air Arms adjusted model nomenclature and MPR (Multi-Positional-Rifle) became synonymous with S400.

MPR 10mm PRECISION – .177 cal., PCP, BA, SS, 19.25 in. barrel with precision length muzzle end, ambidextrous fully adj. blonde poplar stock, full length barrel assembly, extended sight base, adj. buttpad with spacers to extend the length, adj. cheek piece, multi-adj. match trigger, external and internal accessory rail, built-in pressure gauge, competition diopter sights, removable cylinder, self-regulating firing valve, on-board air filter and air reserves, choice of black, blue, red, or yellow finish receiver, 41.75 in. OAL, 6.8 lbs. New 2012.

MSR $1,150	$975	$850	$775	$625	$475	N/A	N/A

MPR 10mm SPORTER (S400 MPR) – for model description and values please refer to S400 MPR in this category.

Beginning circa 2012 Air Arms adjusted model nomenclature and MPR (Multi-Positional-Rifle) became synonymous with S400.

NJR100 – .177 or .22 cal., PCP, 22 in. hand-picked barrel for accuracy, adj. two-stage trigger, quick release cylinder connector, walnut target-style stock with adj. cheek piece, forearm, and recoil pad, 10.75 lbs. Disc.

	$1,525	$1,300	$1,075	$875	$675	$450	$300

Last MSR was $2,600.

Add 5% for left-hand variation.

PRO-ELITE – .177 or .22 cal., BBC, SP, 18 ft/lbs. ME (.177), 22 ft/lbs. ME (.22), 14 in. Walther barrel, beech Monte Carlo stock with cheek piece, 9.3 lbs.

	$475	$400	$325	$270	$210	$140	$95

PRO-SPORT – .177 or .22 cal., SP, UL, SS, 9.5 in. Lothar Walther shrouded barrel, 950/750 FPS, gold plated multi-adj. two-stage trigger, internal baffle sound moderation, recessed aluminum under lever, ergonomically designed high comb

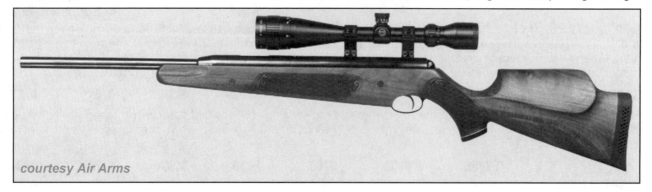

courtesy Air Arms

GRADING	100%	95%	90%	80%	60%	40%	20%

beech or walnut sporter stock with deep cut laser checkering for superb grip, ventilated buttpad, 42.25 in. OAL, 9 lbs.

MSR $800	$675	$600	$550	$450	$325	N/A	N/A

Add $150 for walnut stock.

PRO-TARGET – .177 cal., PCP, sliding bolt action, 12-groove 16 in. Walther barrel, multi-adj. trigger system, quick release charging connector, competition adj. cheek piece, wood grain laminate, or optional red or blue laminate stock with multi-adj. butt pad, 6.6 lbs. Disc. 2001.

	$850	$725	$600	$500	$375	$255	$170

Last MSR was $1,150.

Add 15% for optional laminate stock.

PRO-TARGET HUNTER – .22 cal., PCP, sliding bolt action, 12-groove 16 in. Walther barrel, multi-adj. trigger system, quick release charging connector, competition adj. cheek piece, wood grain laminate, or optional red or blue laminate stock with multi-adj. butt pad, 6.6 lbs. Disc. 2001.

	$850	$725	$600	$500	$375	$255	$170

Last MSR was $1,150.

Add 15% for optional laminate stock.

PRO-TARGET MK III – .177 cal., PCP, sliding bolt action, 12-groove 16 in. Walther free-floating barrel, multi-adj. trigger system, quick release charging connector, competition adj. cheek piece, wood grain laminate, or optional red or blue laminate stock with multi-adj. butt pad, 6.6 lbs. Disc. 2001.

	$975	$835	$700	$575	$450	$300	$200

Last MSR was $1,325.

SM100 – .177 or .22 cal., PCP, 22 in. barrel, adj. two-stage trigger, beech stock, 8.5 lbs. Disc. 1994.

	$700	$600	$500	$400	$325	$210	$140

Last MSR was $975.

Add 10% for left-hand variation.

S200 (SPORTER) – .177 or .22 cal., PCP, BA, SS, 800/581 FPS, built-in pressure gauge, 19.1 in. rotary swaged barrel, black finish, two-stage adj. trigger, ambidextrous beech stock and forearm, vent. recoil pad, removable cylinder, 35.7 in. OAL, 5.8 lbs. New 2004.

MSR $860	$725	$650	$575	$475	$350	N/A	N/A

Manufactured by CZ Brno. Distributed by Air Arms (UK).

S200FT (FIELD TARGET) – .177 cal., PCP, BA, SS, built-in pressure gauge, 19.1 in. rifled barrel, 800 FPS, black finish, two-stage adj. trigger, ambidextrous beech stock with adj. cheek piece and butt pad, beech forearm, 35.7 in. OAL, 6.17 lbs. New 2014.

MSR $650	$550	$475	$450	$350	$275	N/A	N/A

Manufactured by CZ Brno. Distributed by Air Arms (UK).

S200T (TARGET) – .177 cal., PCP, BA, SS, built-in pressure gauge, 19.1 in. rotary swaged barrel, black finish, adj. diopter rear and globe front sights, two-stage adj. trigger, ambidextrous beech stock with adj. cheek piece and butt pad, beech forearm, 36.25 in. OAL, 6.4 lbs. New 2004.

MSR $795	$675	$600	$550	$425	$325	N/A	N/A

Manufactured by CZ Brno. Distributed by Air Arms (UK).

S300 – .177 or .22 cal., PCP, bolt action, 12-groove 19.7 in. Walther barrel, multi-adj. two-stage trigger, quick release charging connector, beech or walnut stock with Monte Carlo-style cheek piece, 6.6 lbs. Disc. 2001.

	$400	$350	$280	$230	$180	$120	$80

Last MSR was $469.

Add 30% for optional deluxe thumbhole version and gold-plated trigger.

S310 – .177 or .22 cal., PCP, bolt action, 10-shot mag., 12-groove 19.7 in. Walther barrel, multi-adj. two-stage trigger, quick release charging connector, beech or walnut stock with Monte Carlo-style cheek piece, 6.6 lbs. Disc. 2001.

	$500	$425	$350	$290	$225	$150	$100

Last MSR was $569.

Add 30% for optional deluxe thumbhole version and gold-plated trigger.

GRADING	100%	95%	90%	80%	60%	40%	20%

S400 BIATHLON/MPR BIATHLON – .177 cal., 564 FPS, side lever action, PCP, 5-shot mag. repeater, 12 groove 19.25-20.5 in. rifled barrel, adj. match trigger, built-in pressure gauge, quick release charging connector, adj. diopter rear and globe front sights, white poplar stock with four magazine carriers built into forend, adj. cheek piece and butt pad, 38.5-41 in. OAL, approx. 6.99-7.2 lbs. New 2009.

MSR $1,600	$1,350	$1,200	$1,100	$875	$675	N/A	N/A

Beginning circa 2012 Air Arms adjusted model nomenclature and MPR (Multi-Positional-Rifle) became synonymous with S400.

S400 FAC (CARBINE) – .177 or .22 cal., PCP, side lever action, single shot, 920 FPS (.22 cal.), built-in pressure gauge, 12-groove 15.4 in. Walther barrel, multi-adj. two-stage trigger, quick-release charging connector, beech or walnut stock with Monte Carlo-style cheek piece, hand checkered forearm and pistol grip, 34.84 in. OAL, approx. 5.47 lbs. Mfg., 2001-2013.

	$800	$675	$550	$475	$350	$240	$160

Last MSR was $950.

Add 15% for LH stock.

S400H (CLASSIC) – .177 or .22 cal., PCP, BA, single shot, 581 FPS (.22 cal.), built-in pressure gauge, 12-groove 19.45 in. Walther barrel, multi-adj. two-stage trigger, quick-release charging connector, beech or walnut stock with Monte Carlo-style cheek piece, hand checkered forearm and pistol grip, 38.58 in. OAL, approx. 6 lbs. Mfg. 2001-2013.

	$725	$625	$500	$425	$325	$215	$145

Last MSR was $781.

S400 MPR/MPR 10mm SPORTER – .177 cal., PCP, BA, SS, built-in pressure gauge, 12-groove 18.63-19.25 in. rifled barrel, 540 FPS, adj. diopter rear with globe front sights, external accessory rail, black or nickel-plated finish, multi-adj. two-stage trigger, quick-release charging connector, lightweight ambidextrous white poplar, beech, or walnut stock with adj. butt pad, adj. cheek piece, 36.4-37.25 in. OAL, approx. 6.9 lbs. Imported 2007-current.

courtesy Air Arms

	$975	$825	$675	$575	$450	$290	$195

Last MSR was $1,150.

Beginning circa 2012 Air Arms adjusted model nomenclature and MPR (Multi-Positional-Rifle) became synonymous with S400.

S400 MPR FT/MPR FT (FIELD TARGET) – .177 cal., PCP, BA, SS, built-in manometer, 12-groove 18.63-19.25 in. semi-floating match grade Lothar Walther barrel with anti-flip muzzle brake, 800 FPS, black finish, multi-adj. two-stage trigger, accessory rail, quick-release charging connector, ambidextrous white poplar or beech stock with adj. Monte Carlo-style cheek piece, full match adj. buttplate with optional butt hook, 36.4-39.75 in. OAL, approx. 7.27-8.8 lbs. New 2007.

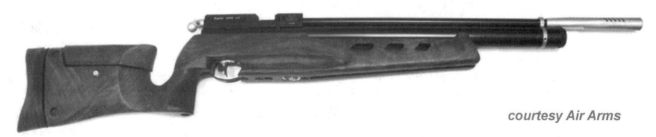

courtesy Air Arms

MSR $1,350	$1,150	$1,000	$925	$750	$575	N/A	N/A

Beginning circa 2012 Air Arms adjusted model nomenclature and MPR (Multi-Positional-Rifle) became synonymous with S400.

GRADING	100%	95%	90%	80%	60%	40%	20%

S400 MPR TARGET SPECIAL – .177 cal., PCP, side lever action, SS, built-in pressure gauge, 12-groove 18.63 in. barrel, 800 FPS, adj. diopter rear and globe front sights, black finish, multi-adj. match trigger, quick-release charging connector, ambidextrous walnut with adj. cheek piece and buttpad, 36.38 in. OAL, approx. 6.94 lbs. Mfg. 2009-2011.

	100%	95%	90%	80%	60%	40%	20%
	$975	$825	$675	$575	$450	$295	$195

S400 SIDELEVER (XTRA HI-POWER) – .177 or .22 cal., PCP, side lever action, single shot, built-in pressure gauge, 12-groove 19.45 in. Walther barrel, 1050 FPS (.22 cal.), multi-adj. two-stage trigger, quick-release charging connector, beech or walnut stock with Monte Carlo-style cheek piece, hand checkered forearm and pistol grip, ventilated rubber buttpad, 42.52 in. OAL, approx. 7.85 lbs. Mfg. 2001-2013.

	100%	95%	90%	80%	60%	40%	20%
	$925	$775	$650	$525	$425	$275	$185

Last MSR was $1,090.

Add 15% for walnut stock.

S410 (CARBINE) – .177 or .22 cal., PCP, side lever action, ten-shot mag. repeater, built-in pressure gauge, 12-groove 15.55 in. rifled Lothar Walther barrel, 920 FPS (.22 cal.), multi-adj. two-stage trigger, quick-release charging connector, checkered beech or walnut stock with Monte Carlo-style cheek piece or thumbhole and ventilated recoil pad, 38 in. OAL, approx. 5.47-6.6 lbs. Imported 2001-2010.

courtesy Air Arms

	100%	95%	90%	80%	60%	40%	20%
	$1,200	$1,025	$850	$700	$550	$350	$240

Add 15% for walnut stock.
Add 30% for optional deluxe thumbhole walnut stock.
Add 35% for optional deluxe LH thumbhole walnut stock.

S410 ERB – .177 or .22 cal., PCP, side lever action, ten-shot mag. repeater, built-in pressure gauge, adj. power level, 12-groove 15.55 in. rifled Lothar Walther barrel, 920 FPS (.22 cal.), multi-adj. two-stage trigger, quick-release charging connector, checkered beech or walnut stock with Monte Carlo-style cheek piece or thumbhole and ventilated recoil pad, 38 in. OAL, approx. 5.47-6.6 lbs. Mfg. 2005-2010.

courtesy Air Arms

	100%	95%	90%	80%	60%	40%	20%
	$950	$800	$675	$550	$425	$285	$190

Add 10% for walnut stock.
Add 20% for optional deluxe thumbhole walnut stock.

S410 SIDELEVER (XTRA HI-POWER) – .177 or .22 cal., PCP, side lever action, ten-shot mag. repeater, built-in pressure gauge, 12-groove 24 in. Lothar Walther barrel, 1050/920 FPS, multi-adj. two-stage trigger, quick-release charging connector, beech or walnut stock with Monte Carlo-style cheek piece, hand checkered forearm and pistol grip, ventilated recoil pad, 43.75 in. OAL, approx. 7.65 lbs. Mfg. 2001-2013.

	100%	95%	90%	80%	60%	40%	20%
	$1,225	$1,050	$850	$700	$550	$375	$245

Last MSR was $1,450.

Add 10% for optional deluxe thumbhole walnut stock.
Add 20% for optional deluxe LH thumbhole walnut stock.

GRADING	100%	95%	90%	80%	60%	40%	20%

S410 TDR (TAKE DOWN RIFLE) – .177 or .22 cal., PCP, side lever action, ten-shot mag. repeater, modular format with 15.5 in. 12 groove Lothar Walther barrel, 581 FPS, ambidextrous walnut takedown buttstock (no tools needed), two-stage adj. trigger, adj. butt pad, pressure gauge, trigger safety, and carrying case, 41.75 in. OAL, 6.25 lbs. New 2005.

MSR $1,150	$975	$850	$775	$625	$475	N/A	N/A

S500 EXTRA FAC SIDELEVER – .177 or .22 cal., PCP, side-lever action, SS, 1050/920 FPS (rifle), two-stage adjustable trigger, 15.5 (carbine) or 19.5 (rifle) in. Lothar Walther fully shrouded barrel, internal baffle sound moderation, blue finish, built-in air pressure gauge, checkered ambidextrous sporter or thumbhole walnut or poplar stock stained Hunter Green, ventilated rubber butt pad, 38-44.75 in. OAL, 5.9-6.2-7 lbs. New 2010.

MSR $1,000	$850	$750	$675	$550	$425	N/A	N/A

Add $50 for walnut stock.

S510 CARBINE – .177 or .22 cal., SL, 15.5 in. fully shrouded barrel, internal baffle sound moderation, trigger mounted safety, two-stage adj. trigger, 10-shot mag., beech, walnut, walnut with thumbhole, or ambidextrous superlite stock, Brown, Hunter Green, and High Gloss finish, 38.25 in. OAL, 6.4-7 lbs.

MSR $1,450	$1,225	$1,075	$975	$800	$600	N/A	N/A

S510 EXTRA FAC SIDELEVER – .177, .22, or .25 (new 2012) cal., PCP, side-lever cocking, 10-shot repeater, 1050/920 FPS, two-stage adjustable trigger, 15.5 (carbine) or 19.5 (rifle) in. Lothar Walther shrouded barrel, internal baffle sound moderation, blue finish, built-in air pressure gauge, beech, walnut, walnut with thumbhole, or ambidextrous superlite stock, available in traditional brown, hunter green, and high gloss finish, dual raised cheek pieces, checkered pistol grip and forearm, ventilated rubber butt pad, 38-44.75 in. OAL, 6.4-7.2 lbs. New 2010.

MSR $1,150	$975	$850	$775	$625	$475	N/A	N/A

Add $200 for walnut stock.

* **S510 Extra FAC Air Arms 30th Anniversary Limited Edition** – .177, .22, or .25 (new 2012) cal., PCP, side-lever cocking, 10-shot repeater, 1000/920/780 FPS, two-stage adjustable trigger, electroless nickel plated 19.5 in. Lothar Walther shrouded barrel with internal baffle sound moderation and 287cc cylinder, blue finish, built-in manometer, semi-gloss finished ambidextrous checkered walnut sporter stock with 30th Anniversary heel plate, high gloss finish, ventilated rubber butt pad, 44.75 in. OAL, 6.4 lbs. New 2013.

MSR $2,200	$1,875	$1,650	$1,500	$1,200	$925	N/A	N/A

Limited Edition includes key-lock aluminum foam-fitted hard case, 2 hex wrenches, fill adapter, extra magazine, .177 and .22 caliber rifles will include 500 pellets, and .25 caliber rifles will include 325 Air Arms pellets in commemorative tin, non-removable commemorative plaque, commemorative Air Arms 30th Anniversary pin and owner's manual.

S510 TC (TWICE) – .177 cal., PCP, SL, side by side twin cylinder (TC) action, 15.5 (carbine) or 19.5 (rifle) in. fully shrouded barrel, internal baffle sound moderation, 10-shot mag., ambidextrous sporter stock with dual raised cheek piece, Brown or Hunter Green finish, adj. two-stage trigger, built-in manometer, trigger mounted safety, 37.25-44.25 in. OAL, 7.7 lbs. New 2011.

courtesy Air Arms

MSR $1,500	$1,275	$1,125	$1,025	$825	$625	N/A	N/A

While "TWICE" is marked on the breech, the official model name from Air Arms is S510 TC (twin cylinders).

S510 TC EXTRA – .177, .22, or .25 cal., PCP, SL, side by side twin cylinder (TC) action, 15.5 (carbine) or 19.5 (rifle) in. fully shrouded barrel, 10-shot mag., built in power adjuster, ambidextrous sporter stock with dual raised cheek piece, Brown or Hunter Green finish, adj. two-stage trigger, built-in manometer, trigger mounted safety, 37.25-44.25 in. OAL, approx. 7 lbs. New 2012.

No current US importation, contact Air Arms (see Trademark Index) for price and availability.

GRADING	100%	95%	90%	80%	60%	40%	20%

T200 SPORTER – .177 cal., CO_2, semi-auto, BA, SS, 19 in. rifled barrel, ambidextrous brown wood stock, textured pistol grip, rubber buttplate, optics rail, two-stage adj. trigger, quick-release fill connector included, 35.5 in. OAL, 6.61 lbs. Mfg. 2011-current.

MSR $650	$550	$475	$450	$350	$275	N/A	N/A

TM100 – .177 or .22 cal., PCP, 22 in. barrel, adj. two-stage trigger, quick release cylinder connector, walnut target-style stock with adj. cheek piece and recoil pad, 8.75 lbs.

	$1,000	$850	$700	$575	$450	$300	$200

Last MSR was $1,650.

Add 5% for left-hand variation.

TX200 – .177 or .22 cal., UL, SP, 15.75 in. barrel, 913/800 FPS, 9.2 lbs.

	$450	$400	$325	$265	$205	$140	$90

Last MSR was $560.

Add 15% for walnut stock.
Add 10% for left-hand variation.

TX200SR (RECOILLESS) – .177 or .22 cal., UL, SP, 15.75 in. barrel, 913/800 FPS, 9.2 lbs.

	$525	$450	$375	$300	$235	$155	$105

Last MSR was $560.

Add 15% for walnut stock.
Add 10% for left-hand variation.
This model is recoilless.

* **TX200 HC (Hunter Carbine)** – .177 or .22 cal., UL, SP, SS, 9.53 in. rifled Lothar Walther barrel, 930-739 FPS, beech or walnut stock with Monte Carlo-style cheek piece, carbine version of TX200 MK III, 38.35 in. OAL, 8.5 lbs.

MSR $650	$550	$475	$450	$350	$275	N/A	N/A

Add $100 for walnut stock.

* **TX200 MK III** – .177 or .22 cal., UL, SP, SS, 13.19-14.1 in. rifled Lothar Walther shrouded barrel, 930/755 FPS, internal baffle sound moderation, beech or walnut stock with Monte Carlo-style cheek piece, automatic safety, 41.34 in. OAL, 9.25 lbs.

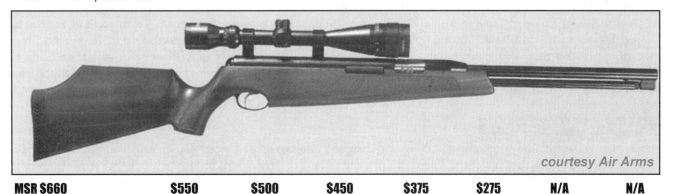

courtesy Air Arms

MSR $660	$550	$500	$450	$375	$275	N/A	N/A

Add $100 for walnut stock.
Add $150 for LH walnut stock.

XM100 – .177 or .22 cal., PCP, 22 in. barrel, adj. two-stage trigger, quick-release cylinder connector and walnut stock, 8 lbs. Disc. 1994.

	$800	$675	$550	$475	$350	$240	$160

Last MSR was $1,260.

Add 10% for left-hand variation.

AIRBOW

Previous trademark used by Robin Parks for a pneumatic rifle that fired special hollow arrows.

Research is ongoing with this trademark, and more information may be included both in future editions and online.

GRADING	100%	95%	90%	80%	60%	40%	20%

RIFLES

AIRBOW – .38 cal. arrow projectile, PCP, SS, shrouded barrel, black composition body, detachable buddy bottle, red plastic safety, Daisy spot sight, M16 carbine style extendable stock, 35 in. OAL with stock extended, 5 lbs.

courtesy Beeman Collection

$450	$375	$325	$260	$205	$135	$90

AIR CANES

As the name suggests, these are functional canes that also contain an airgun mechanism.

AIR CANE BACKGROUND

Air canes are a whole collecting field in themselves, but they form a delightful and key part of most quality airgun collections. Wolff's book (1958) has one of the few fairly good discussions regarding these intriguing guns. He points out that while cane firearms were novelty weapons of no great practical value, air canes were one of the pinnacles of airgun effectiveness and utility and certainly stand as some of the finest examples of wonderfully intricate and beautifully made airgun mechanisms. In most specimens, the gun function was concealed, but some bare trigger guards, shoulder stocks, or other obvious evidence as to their nature. Most apparently were designed for self-defense or as a method of carrying a hunting arm while out walking- in those days, the transition between town and country could come rather quickly.

The Golden Age of air canes came in the 1800s when English air canes dominated the field. Key makers of London and Birmingham included John Blanch, Edward Reilly, and James Townsend. An air cane was part of the attire of many a well-dressed English gentleman of the late 1800s. Most specimens were sold in wonderfully fitted cases with their pump and accessories. These accessories often included a rifle-style, buttstock-shaped air reservoir or skeleton wooden buttstock which could be carried in the huge pockets of a gentleman's "great coat" until extra air volume and/or steadiness of fire were needed when using an air cane.

AIR CANE CONFIGURATIONS

The mechanism almost always was pneumatic, usually charged by numerous strokes from a separate pump. A few had a self-contained pump and a few used pre-charged air cartridges, and extremely rare variants featured a spring-piston mechanism. The typical design consisted of two parts: the rear half of the gun was the tubular air reservoir and valve mechanism; the forward half contained the barrel and lock mechanism. These lock mechanisms were often jewel-like in their detail and operation.

Rather commonly, there were two barrels, a smooth bore in which a rifled barrel was nestled, or vice versa. The rifled barrels usually were brass, bearing an elegantly scalloped rifling of twenty-two or more shallow, low-friction grooves. A ramrod was housed within the nest of barrels, with its handle forming the screw-off base tip of the cane. The trigger was typically a simple button which protruded only when the gun was raised, aimed, and fired. Sights and even a trigger guard may be present externally. Weight varied from 1.5 to over 8 pounds; calibers generally were .30 to .36, but ranged from .177 to .75!

The projectiles of air canes generally were lead balls, cast from the molds included in cased outfits. However, imagination seemed to be the only limit as to what could be fired from these amazing guns. Shot, darts, arrows, bullets, harpoons, and multipronged fish and frog spears have been utilized!

AIR CANES RECENTLY MANUFACTURED

There was a small renaissance in air canes. In the 1980s, Harper produced some wonderful modern air canes in England. As these utilized the Brocock air cartridges instead of a built-in air reservoir, they could be made very slim and truly elegant. The handles sometimes were wonderfully carved dogs' heads or other figures. Fold-out triggers were virtually undetectable in the fine engraving. In the United States, also in the 1980s, the famed airgun maker Gary Barnes produced an amazingly intricate and functionally astonishing full automatic air cane!

AIR CANES CUE BALL TYPE

Cue Ball CO_2 Air Canes are configurations of air canes made to resemble a black metal cane with a billiard ball for its knob. These air canes fire a CO_2 cylinder as the projectile, with astonishing force and range. Firing causes the seal on the CO_2 cylinder to be pierced. Pressure builds until the cylinder itself is propelled from the muzzle. The cylinder, as a projectile, gathers additional velocity from jetting action. The inventor apparently wishes to remain anonymous because of the mistaken idea that these air canes would be considered as "destructive devices" by the BATFE as they are over .50 caliber. Actually, BATFE has no jurisdiction over these air canes because they are not firearms! John Caruth obtained six of these air canes and had twenty-five of them reproduced by Tom Allison in the 1990s. The original maker also made a few specimens which retain the CO_2 cylinder but fire a conventional .45 caliber lead ball. The original price for these Cue Ball CO_2 Air Canes was $350. Values now run from about $150 to $450 for the cylinder-shooting Cue Ball CO_2 air canes and about $200 to $500 for the ball-firing Cue Ball CO_2 air canes. The authors and publisher wish to thank Mr. John Caruth for assistance on Cue Ball Air Cane information in this section of the *Blue Book of Airguns*.

courtesy Beeman Collection

AIR CANE VALUES

Values of air canes vary greatly, but a typical British air cane in good condition generally will sell for $600 to $1,200. A cased air cane with accessories (original pump, bullet mold, cocking key, and disassembly tool) and in fine condition will sell in the $3,000 plus range.

A variety of air canes (top to bottom):
American aircane with built in pump, dogs head handle made of horn.
Giant British aircane with trigger guard.
British aircane with knobby branch surface - concealing nature of gun.
British aircane - slim, muzzle-loading version.
British breech loading aircane.
British muzzle-loading aircane - the most common aircane type.
Courtesy of Beeman Collection

AIRFORCE INTERNATIONAL (AIRFORCE AIRGUNS)

Current manufacturer and distributor located in Fort Worth, TX. Dealer and consumer direct sales.

The project to design and produce the AirForce Talon began in 1994. Shipping began in the U.S. during 1999. The Talon Series are pre-charged single shots with variable power. They were first marketed in England under the name Gun Power Stealth, and they are manufactured in Fort Worth, TX, by designer John McCaslin.

In 2012, the new Spin-Loc air tank attachment system was added allowing customers to use the standard Quick-

GRADING	100%	95%	90%	80%	60%	40%	20%

Detachable air tanks and the new Spin-Loc tanks with built-in pressure gauge and quick fill connection. This gives the shooter the ability to fill the new Spin-Loc tank directly from a standard quick disconnect without removing the air tank from the gun.

In 2013, Airforce Airguns joined forces with Airgun International and plans to import and distribute high quality airguns from around the world. AirForce International is negotiating with top airgun craftsmen in Europe to be able to bring those names to America.

PISTOLS

TALONP – .25 cal., 400-900 FPS, SS, PCP, external thumb-pressure-operated adj. power system, 12 in. Lothar Walther barrel, sights optional, two-stage adj. trigger, black anodized finish, aircraft-grade aluminum alloy and polymer construction with three integrated dovetail rails for accessories, choice of Quick-Detach or Spin-Loc (new 2012) air tanks, 24 in. OAL, 3.5 lbs. Mfg. 2011-current.

courtesy Airforce International

MSR $434	$375	$325	$295	$240	$180	N/A	N/A

Add $20 for Spin-Loc tank.
Add $23 for Airforce 1 inch scope rings.
Add $71 for Airforce fiber optic open sights or refill clamp w/gauge.
Add $132 for Airforce 3-9x40mm scope.
Add $164 for Airforce 4-16x50mm scope.

RIFLES

AirForce Airguns offers accessories for all models (too many to list). Contact AirForce Airguns (see Trademark Index) for price and availability. During 2008 Airforce Airguns introduced Tri-Power for the Condor, Talon, and Talon SS rifles. The standard high pressure cylinder was approved for use with air or nitrogen gas. A CO_2 adaptor for standard CO_2 paintball cylinder was also released. Velocity ranges listed are for rifles using original cylinder filled with air.

CONDOR – .177, .20 (new 2007), .22, or .25 (new 2011) cal., SS, PCP (490cc compressed air bottle doubles as shoulder stock), external thumb-pressure-operated adj. power system allows 600-1,300 FPS (depending on cal. and pellet weight), 24 in. Lothar Walther barrel (interchangeable for cal.), aircraft-grade aluminum alloy and polymer construction with three integrated dovetail rails for accessories, two-stage adj. trigger, available in red (new 2011), blue (new 2011), or black anodized finish, 38.75 in. OAL, 6.5 lbs. (gun and bottle). New 2004.

courtesy Airforce Airguns

MSR $690	$600	$500	$425	$350	$265	$175	$120

Add $20 for Spin-Loc tank.
Add $23 for Airforce 1 inch scope rings.
Add $71 for Airforce fiber optic open sights or refill clamp w/gauge.
Add $132 for Airforce 3-9x40mm scope.
Add $164 for Airforce 4-16x50mm scope.
Add $1,610-$1,630 for Ultimate Condor Combo.

GRADING	100%	95%	90%	80%	60%	40%	20%

* **Condor SS** – .177, .20, .22, or .25 cal., similar to Condor, except features 18 in. barrel and new sound technology, Black, Red, or Blue finish, 38.12 in. OAL, 6.1 lbs. New 2013.

courtesy Airforce International

	100%	95%	90%	80%	60%	40%	20%
MSR $717	$600	$500	$425	$350	$270	$180	$120

Add $20 for Spin-Loc tank.

CONDOR BOUNTY HUNTER – .22 cal., PCP, CO_2, SS, semi-auto, 24 in. Lothar Walther rifled barrel, removable 490cc air tank, gun is made of aircraft-grade aluminum and space age polymers, thumbhole stock and flash suppressor, no sights, two stage trigger, rubber buttplate, automatic safety, black, blue, or red anodized finish, 38.75 in. OAL, 6.5 lbs. New 2012.

courtesy Airforce International

	100%	95%	90%	80%	60%	40%	20%
MSR $763	$650	$550	$450	$375	$290	$195	$130

EDGE (3 POSITION SPORTER CLASS TARGET RIFLE) – .177 cal., PCP, SS, 500-575 FPS (depending on pellet weight), 3000 psi/206 bar (compressed air bottle doubles as shoulder stock), 12 in. Lothar Walther barrel in an extended shroud with muzzle capsound moderator system, ambidextrous cocking knob, regulated air system, position marks on all mounting rails, cheek piece and forearm with built-in acccessory rail, adj. TS1 Adaptive Target diopter rear sight and hooded front sight, adj. forend, aircraft-grade aluminum alloy and polymer construction with three integrated dovetail rails for accessories, two-stage adj. trigger, blue or red anodized finish, 35-40 in. OAL, 6.1 lbs. (gun and bottle). New 2009.

courtesy Airforce Airguns

	100%	95%	90%	80%	60%	40%	20%
MSR $680	$575	$500	$450	$375	$285	N/A	N/A

Subtract $134 for front sight only.

GRADING	100%	95%	90%	80%	60%	40%	20%

ESCAPE – .22 or .25 cal., PCP, SS, 24 in. Lothar Walther barrel, allows 800-1300 FPS, choice of Quick-Detach or Spin-Loc air tank, two-stage adj. trigger, open sights, Black finish, automatic safety, 34.5-39 in. OAL, 5.3 lbs. New 2014.

courtesy Airforce International

MSR $640	$550	$475	$375	$325	$245	$165	$110

Add $20 for Spin-Loc tank.

    Blue Book Publications selected this model as one of its Top 10 Industry Awards from all the new firearms at the 2014 SHOT Show.

ESCAPE SS – .22 or .25 cal., PCP, SS, small compact cylinder, 12 in. Lothar Walther barrel, allows 500-900 FPS, features new sound reduction technology, adj. power, lightweight, recoiless, choice of Quick-Detach or Spin-Loc air tank, two-stage adj. trigger, open sights, automatic safety, Black finish, 27.75-32.25 in. OAL, 4.3 lbs. New 2014.

courtesy Airforce International

MSR $630	$550	$450	$375	$325	$245	$160	$110

Add $20 for Spin-Loc tank.

    Blue Book Publications selected this model as one of its Top 10 Industry Awards from all the new firearms at the 2014 SHOT Show.

ESCAPE UL – .22 or .25 cal., PCP, SS, ultra lightweight with smaller air cylinder, 18 in. barrel, allows for 800-1200 FPS, choice of Quick-Detach or Spin-Loc air tanks, two-stage adj. trigger, automatic safety, open sights, Black finish, 28.5-33 in. OAL, 4.25 lbs. New 2014.

courtesy Airforce International

MSR $590	$500	$425	$350	$295	$230	$155	$100

Add $20 for Spin-Loc tank.

    Blue Book Publications selected this model as one of its Top 10 Industry Awards from all the new firearms at the 2014 SHOT Show.

TALON – .177, .20 (new 2008), .22, or .25 (new 2011) cal., SS, PCP (compressed air bottle doubles as shoulder stock), external thumb-pressure-operated adj. power system allows 400-1000 FPS (depending on cal. and pellet weight), 18 in. Lothar Walther barrel (interchangeable for cal.), aircraft-grade aluminum alloy and polymer construction with

GRADING	100%	95%	90%	80%	60%	40%	20%

three integrated dovetail rails for accessories, two-stage adj. trigger, black anodized finish, 32.6 in. OAL, 5.5 lbs. (gun and bottle). New 1998.

courtesy Airforce Airguns

MSR $562	$475	$400	$350	$280	$220	$145	$95

Add $20 for Spin-Loc tank.
Add $23 for Airforce 1 inch scope rings.
Add $71 for Airforce fiber optic open sights or refill clamp w/gauge.
Add $132 for Airforce 3-9x40mm scope.
Add $164 for Airforce 4-16x50mm scope.

TALON SS – .177, .20 (new 2008), .22, or .25 (new 2011) cal., SS, PCP (compressed air bottle doubles as shoulder stock), external thumb-pressure-operated adj. power system allows 400-1000 FPS (depending on cal. and pellet weight), 12 in. Lothar Walther barrel in an extended shroud with muzzle capsound moderator system, two-stage adj. trigger, aircraft-grade aluminum alloy and polymer construction with three integrated dovetail rails for accessories, choice of Quick-Detach or Spin-Loc air tanks, available in red (new 2011), blue (new 2011), or original black finish, 32.75 in. OAL, 5.25 lbs. (gun and bottle). New 2000.

courtesy Airforce Airguns

MSR $600	$525	$425	$350	$300	$230	$155	$105

Add $20 for Spin-Loc tank.
Add $23 for Airforce 1 inch scope rings.
Add $71 for Airforce fiber optic open sights or refill clamp w/gauge.
Add $132 for Airforce 3-9x40mm scope.
Add $164 for Airforce 4-16x50mm scope.

TALON BOUNTY HUNTER – .177 cal., PCP, CO_2, SS, semi-auto, 18 in. Lothar Walther rifled barrel, removable 490cc air tank, gun is made of aircraft-grade aluminum and space age polymers and includes thumbhole stock and flash suppressor, power adjustment wheel, no sights, two-stage trigger, rubber buttplate, auto safety, 32.6 in. OAL, 5.5 lbs. New 2012.

courtesy Airforce International

MSR $637	$550	$450	$375	$325	$245	$160	$110

GRADING	100%	95%	90%	80%	60%	40%	20%

AIRGUNAID

Previous manufacturer located in Chelmsford, Essex, Great Britain circa 1980-1982.

Research is ongoing with this trademark, and more information will be included both in future editions and online. Basically these are Scottish Diana rifles fitted with a .20 cal. barrel. It took the Brits a while to pick up on this caliber, which was introduced to precision spring piston airguns by the Beeman company in the 1970s. Average original condition specimens are typically priced in the $100 to $200 range.

AIRGUN EXPRESS, INC.

Previous importer with retail catalog sales located in Bedford Heights, OH. Previously located in Montezuma, IA. In July 2006, Airgun Express was sold to (and has been integrated with) Pyramyd Air in Warrensville Heights, OH.

Mail order and catalog sales of many major brand airguns including Beeman, Crosman, Daisy, Gamo, Mendoza (importer), RWS, and others.

AIR GUN INC.

Previous importer and distributor located in Houston, TX.

Air Gun Inc. previously imported Industry Brand airguns until 2006. Please refer to the "I" section of this book for information on these airguns.

AIR LOGIC

Previous manufacturer and distributor located in Forest Row, Sussex, England.

Air Logic had limited importation into the U.S.

RIFLES

GENESIS – .22 cal., SL, single-stroke pneumatic, 630 FPS, bolt-action sliding barrel by Lothar Walther, recoilless, adj. trigger, 9.5 lbs. Mfg. began in 1988. Disc.

	100%	95%	90%	80%	60%	40%	20%
	$575	$500	$400	$325	$260	$170	$115

Last MSR was $750.

AIR MATCH

Previous trademark manufactured in Italy circa 1980s. Previously imported by Kendall International located in Paris, KY.

PISTOLS

MODEL 400 – .177 cal., SL, single-stroke pneumatic, adj. trigger, UIT target model, 2 lbs.

	100%	95%	90%	80%	60%	40%	20%
	$350	$300	$245	$205	$160	$105	$70

MODEL 600 – .177 cal., SL, single-stroke pneumatic, adj. sights, adj. trigger, UIT target model, 2 lbs.

	100%	95%	90%	80%	60%	40%	20%
	$375	$325	$265	$220	$170	$110	$75

AIR ORDNANCE, LLC

Current manufacturer located in Fort Wayne, IN beginning 2011. Consumer direct sales.

RIFLES

SMG 22 – .22 cal., automatic belt fed system, CO_2, nitrogen or PCP (20 oz. CO_2 tank doubles as shoulder stock), two reusable 100 round pellet belt, rapid fire trigger up to 12 rounds per second, up to 600 FPS (depending on pellet weight), rifled steel barrel, cast aluminum receiver w/45 pistol grip style frame, rubber grips, composite forearm grip, lower Picatinny rail for accessories, dovetail adj. rear and fixed front sights, black anodized finish, 6.4 lbs. New 2011.

MSR $599	100%	95%	90%	80%	60%	40%	20%
	$600	$500	$425	$350	$270	$180	$120

AIRROW

Current registered trademark of Swivel Machine Works, Inc., currently located in Newtown, CT. Previously located in Milford, CT.

Swivel Machine Works, Inc. started manufacturing arrow-firing rifles and pistols in 1990, and has recently started manufacturing pellet-firing air rifles. Contact the manufacturer directly for information and prices on their arrow-firing models (see Trademark Index).

GRADING	100%	95%	90%	80%	60%	40%	20%

PISTOLS

AIRROW PISTOL ABS 013 – arrow firing, PCP, SS, take down design, watertight case (provided), 24.8 in. OAL, 5 lbs. Mfg. 1990-2005.

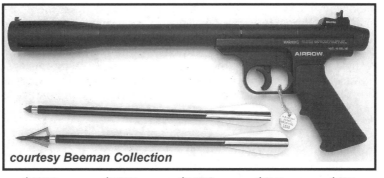

courtesy Beeman Collection

$1,500	$1,275	$1,050	$875	$675	$450	$300

RIFLES

AIRROW MODEL A-8SRB STEALTH – .177, .22, or .38/9mm cal., CO_2 or PCP, SS or nine-shot mag., 20 in. rifled barrel, 1100 FPS (in all calibers), scope rings included, 35 in. OAL, 7.5 lbs.

courtesy Airrow

MSR $2,299	$1,950	$1,725	$1,575	$1,275	$975	N/A	N/A

Add $549 for additional .177 or .22 cal. barrel.
Add $599 for additional .38/9mm cal. barrel.
Many options available.

AIRROW ARCHERY MODEL A-8S1P STEALTH – arrow firing, PCP, 7 oz. cylinder with valve, SS, 600 FPS, adj. air trigger, 16 in. barrel, M16 carbine style extendable stock, scope rings, take down design, watertight case (provided), 30.12 in. OAL, 3.5 lbs. Mfg. 1990-current.

courtesy Beeman Collection

MSR $1,699	$1,450	$1,275	$1,150	$925	$725	N/A	N/A

Add $149 for 1.5-5x20mm scope.
Performs to 2,000 PSIG above or below water level.

GRADING	100%	95%	90%	80%	60%	40%	20%

AIR SOFT

Term currently used to identify a configuration of gun copies primarily manufactured in Asia.

In the last two decades a new type of gun has appeared. The so-called Air Soft guns originally were designed to be a type of non-gun for customers whose local laws highly restricted or forbade the ownership of actual firearms. Generally, they are made in the styling (sometimes very exact styling) of well-known firearms. Models ranged from copies of famous handguns to heavy machine guns. They soon became popular with customers who wanted to collect, and even have the sensation of firing, guns which were too expensive, too highly regulated, or too dangerous for general ownership. Most fire relatively harmless 6 mm diameter light plastic balls at muzzle velocities below 300 FPS. Even those which fire at somewhat higher power generally are not capable of inflicting serious injury to humans or property. Balls filled with paint or made of aluminum sometimes are available but have not been very popular and may be difficult to buy locally. Many of the Air Soft guns are not designed to fire paintballs or metal balls and may be damaged or ruined by their use.

The classification of Air Soft guns has led to some interesting legal questions. Without a doubt, they are not firearms and are not dangerous or lethal weapons. In fact, they are not weapons in any sense unless one might use them as a club. They may use carbon dioxide, compressed air, or mechanical means, including electrical micro-motors to propel their projectiles - so some are not even truly airguns. Federal law requires the versions firing plastic balls to have at least their muzzle areas conspicuously marked with blaze orange color, but illegal unmarked imports often appear.

From a safety standpoint, by far the largest caution is to not brandish them where they might be mistaken for actual firearms. There have been cases where individuals used such guns in holdups or pointed them at police officers in dark alleys or where several teenagers wearing ski masks appeared with exact lookalikes of AK-47s, Thompson sub-machine guns, M16 rifles, etc. at their schools - distinctly unwise moves. But certainly over 99.9% are used and enjoyed harmlessly - often as enjoyable substitutes for real guns. Production of Air Soft guns, mainly in Asia, has become a huge market. They range from toy-like, almost insulting imitations to very sophisticated, expensive copies of heavy machine guns which may use well-made metal or even original parts from deactivated original automatic weapons. This is now a collecting field in itself and will not be covered in this guide unless a specimen has special historical significance. Values run from a couple of dollars for plastic specimens which only suggest their design origin to hundreds of dollars for those sophisticated specimens with well-made, or even original, metal parts. There is a great deal of information on Air Soft guns available on the web. Two examples are illustrated: Left (very realistic example): A Daisy copy of an Uzi sub-machine gun, with replica cartridges and magazine (produced before the requirement for blaze orange markings). Right (caricature, toy-like example): representation of AK-47 rifle. Note that the package of the projectiles is labeled: BB BULLET - but the contents are neither BBs nor bullets! Ref. 4th Edition *Blue Book of Airguns*.

courtesy Beeman Collection

AIR VENTURI

Current importer and distributor located in Solon, OH. Previously located in Warrensville Heights, OH and Bedford Heights, OH.

RIFLES

AVENGER 1100 – .177 or .22 cal., BBC, SS, 18.6 in. rifled steel barrel, 1030/700 FPS, two stage trigger, adj. sights, Monte Carlo style PG hardwood stock w/rubber buttplate, 45.25 in. OAL, 7.3 lbs. Mfg. 2010-2011.

courtesy Air Venturi

$170	$150	$135	$110	$85	N/A	N/A

Last MSR was $200.

GRADING	100%	95%	90%	80%	60%	40%	20%

BRONCO – .177 cal., SP, BBC, SS, 9 in. rifled steel barrel, 530 FPS, two-stage trigger, post globe front and adj. rear sights, SG hardwood stock with rubber buttplate, 40 in. OAL, 6.5 lbs. Mfg. 2010-current.

courtesy Air Venturi

MSR $150	$130	$115	$100	$85	$65	N/A	N/A

Add $40 for Bronco Target Pro Model.

HALESTORM – .177 or .22 cal., PCP, 1066/968 FPS, 10-shot mag. repeater, 19.5 in. rifled steel barrel, adj. two-stage trigger, adj. sights, checkered ambidextrous Monte Carlo style PG hardwood stock with adj. rubber butt pad, 39.4 in. OAL, 7.3 lbs. Mfg. 2010-2011.

courtesy Air Venturi

	$500	$450	$400	$325	$250	N/A	N/A

Last MSR was $600.

ALFA - PROJ spol. s.r.o.

Current manufacturer located in Brno, Czech Republic. Currently imported and/or distributed by Top Gun Air Guns Inc., located in Scottsdale, AZ. Previously by Pyramyd Air, Inc. located in Warrensville Heights, OH.

ALFA - PROJ spol. s r.o. was established in 1993 as a Czech limited company. The company enhanced its production with air arms in 2004. Currently these include air pistols and rifles for shooting sports.

PISTOLS

ALFA CO$_2$ SPORT – .177 cal., CO$_2$, SS, adj. sights, adj. trigger, 450 FPS. New 2006.

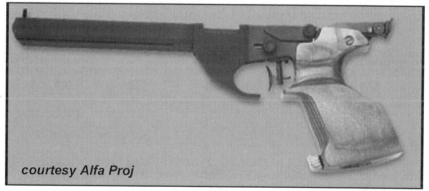

courtesy Alfa Proj

MSR $750	$625	$550	$500	$400	$325	N/A	N/A

RIFLES

ALFA CO$_2$ TARGET – .177 cal., CO$_2$, SS, adj. sights, adj. cheek piece, adj. buttplate. New 2006.

MSR $795	$675	$600	$550	$425	$325	N/A	N/A

ALROS

Previous manufacturer of CO$_2$ and PCP rifles located in Staffs, United Kingdom 1993-2009.

The authors and publisher wish to thank Mr. Tim Saunders for assistance with this information.

GRADING	100%	95%	90%	80%	60%	40%	20%

RIFLES

SHADOW – .177, .20, or .22 cal., PCP, SS or eight-shot mag., BA (RH or LH), blue finish, beech or walnut stock (with or without thumbhole). Sporting rifles variations (three with built-in air reservoir): M60 Hunter, M100 Carbine, M140 Standard, and the Shadow 400 with removable 400 cc buddy bottle, 39/40 in. OAL, 7-7.5 lbs. Mfg. beginning in 1997.

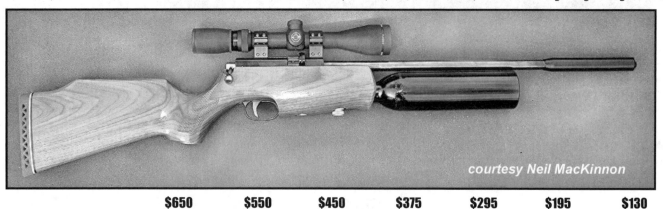

courtesy Neil MacKinnon

	$650	$550	$450	$375	$295	$195	$130

Add 10% for Shadow 400.
Add 20% for eight-shot magazine.
Add 10% for walnut stock.
Add 25% for thumbhole walnut stock.

STARFIRE – .177, .20, or .22 cal., two 12 gm CO_2 cylinders, SS or eight-shot mag., BA (RH or LH), blue finish, beech or walnut stock (with or without thumbhole), power level set at UK 12 ft/lbs ME limit, approx. forty shots per charge, 39-40 in. OAL, 7-7.5 lbs. Mfg. beginning in 1997.

	$400	$350	$280	$230	$180	$120	$80

TRAILSMAN – .177, .20, or .22 cal., PCP, SS, BA (RH or LH), 16mm Lothar Walther barrel, blue finish, adj. tubular stock, composition grips, takedown construction. Two variants: Trailsman Standard with built-in reservoir under barrel, 5 lbs.; Trailsman 400 with removable 400 cc buddy bottle reservoir, 6 lbs. New late 1990s.

	$530	$450	$375	$300	$225	$175	$125

Add 10% for Trailsman 400.

AMERICAN ARMS, INC.

Previous manufacturer and importer located in North Kansas City, MO until 2000.

Even though American Arms, Inc. imported Norica airguns, they are listed in this section because of their private label status. Importation began in late 1988 and was discontinued in 1989. For more information and current pricing on imported American Arms, Inc. firearms, please refer to the *Blue Book of Gun Values* by S.P. Fjestad (also available online).

PISTOLS

IDEAL – .177 cal., BBC, SP, 400 FPS, adj. sights, 3 lbs.

	$85	$70	$60	$50	$40	$25	$15

Last MSR was $105.

RIFLES

COMMANDO – .177 cal., BBC, SP, 540 FPS, adj. sights, 5 lbs.

	$95	$80	$65	$55	$45	$30	$20

Last MSR was $115.

JET RIFLE – .177 cal., BBC, SP, 855 FPS, adj. double-set triggers, hardwood stock, 7 lbs.

	$115	$100	$80	$65	$50	$35	$25

Last MSR was $160.

Subtract $35 for Junior Model.

AMERICAN GALLERY AIRGUNS

This is a group of fairly well-defined airguns which were produced by American gunsmiths just before and after the U.S. Civil War (1861-65).

Travel to the country was difficult for city folks at the time these guns were made. These airguns, typically provided by concessionaires in indoor ranges, provided a means of satisfying the desire to shoot. Again, Wolff (1958) has one of the few good discussions of these interesting airguns which had been unappreciated for a long time. Now they are becoming increasingly hard to acquire as demand and understanding has soared.

These airguns are highly stylized from European patterns, such as those made by Josef Rutte of Bohemia around 1830. All have a huge central spring cylinder ahead of the trigger guard, containing a double volute mainspring system. All have leather piston seals and smoothbore barrels. The two main cranking methods are by a crank handle ("Kurbelspanner") or by a lever pivoted at the buttplate and typically shaped into the trigger guard in the forward end ("Bügelspanner"). And while virtually all are breech loaders, the particular methods of loading and cocking are classified into several groups.

1. Primary New York: Apparently among the earliest of American gallery airguns, these seem to have developed from European forms which use a detachable crank handle to cock the mainspring. The European forms have a tip-up breech; the American forms developed an unusual breech which opened by twisting the receiver. Famous makers include David and Joseph Lurch, G. Fisher, and August Mock.

2. Secondary New York: A small group featuring the twist-breech loading of the Primary forms, but cocked by a cocking lever formed by a rearward extension of the trigger guard. A gun of this type by John Zuendorff has been credited as being used in the draft riots of the American Civil War.

3. Upstate New York: A small, special group. The main feature is a hand-operated revolving cylinder and barrel which is attached to the receiver with a pin, wedge, and bottom strap in a manner and styling very similar to an open-top Colt revolver. 12- or 13-shot cylinders are known. The only makers listed by Wolff are Charles Bunge and C. Werner.

4. St. Louis: The key characteristic is a long cocking lever with its forward end formed by the trigger guard and the remainder concealed in a groove in the under edge of the buttstock. The barrel tips up for breech loading. The stocks have separate buttstock and forearm sections. A large group; famous makers include Bandle, Blickensdoerfer, and Stein.

5. New England: The buttstock and forearm are one piece. A fixed, two-piece cocking lever along the forward side of the receiver swings up and back for cocking. The barrel tips up or twists to a loose open position for loading. Two known makers are Eggers and Tonks.

6. Top Lever Gallery Air Rifle: Cocks by pulling back on heavy lever inserted into comb of rifle. Illustration shows the lever partially up for clarity.

7. Pop Up: Loads via a pop-up breech block in the top of the receiver.

About 1870 the gallery gun design, so well-developed in America, migrated to Europe and was continued as the European "Bügelspanner" for almost a century by several makers, most notably Oscar Will of Zella-Mehlis, Germany. Will frequently marked his guns as "Original Will" to distinguish them from the many copies -- some of these copies, amusingly, were then marked as "Original". Unmarked copies are rather common.

Values of American Gallery Airguns will range from $500 to $2,000 depending on condition, and especially rare forms, such as Upstate New York models, bear asking prices of up to five thousand dollars. The later European "Bügelspanner" generally sells for $200 to $300, with the "Original Will" marking and better condition adding to the price.

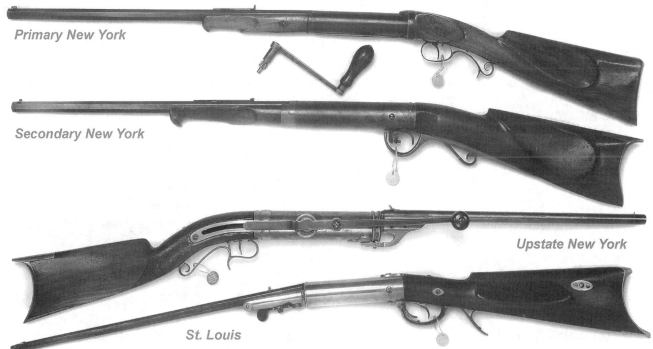

Primary New York

Secondary New York

Upstate New York

St. Louis

GRADING	100%	95%	90%	80%	60%	40%	20%

New England

Top Lever

courtesy Beeman Collection

AMERICAN LUGER

For information on American Luger airguns, see Schimel in the "S" section.

AMERICAN TOOL WORKS

Previous manufacturer of BB guns in Chicago, IL. This company purchased other BB gun makers and produced BB guns under American, Sterling, Upton, and Wyandotte trademarks.

The authors and publisher wish to thank Dennis Baker and John Groenewold for their valuable assistance with the following information in this section of the *Blue Book of Airguns*. Most guns by American Tool Works were typical SP, LA, BB rifles of rather plain appearance, except for the big 1000-shot repeaters with an octagonal barrel tube, walnut stock, and bright nickel plating. The factory tools, fixtures, and equipment went from buyer to buyer and finally ended up with Markham-King in 1929. Markham-King, which had been acquired by Daisy in 1916, destroyed American Tool Works' assets by dumping them in the Detroit River. Guns were made circa 1891-1928 (see Dunathan, 1971). Additional research is underway on this complex group. Information given here must be considered as tentative. Information and illustrations from other collectors is solicited at guns@bluebookinc.com.

RIFLES

AMERICAN DART RIFLE – BB/.174 cal., SP, LA, SS, loaded with feathered darts through a cover plate under the barrel, all sheet metal, barrel marked "American Dart Rifle, Upton Machine Company, St. Joseph, Michigan. Ca. 1912-20.

	N/A	$800	$650	$525	$400	$280	$160

STERLING SINGLE SHOT

There appear to be three variations. This model is under research, and more information will be made available in future editions.

STERLING MODEL D – BB/.174 cal., SP, LA, 1000 shot, octagon barrel tube, nickel or blue finish, 32.2 in. OAL, 2.4 lbs.

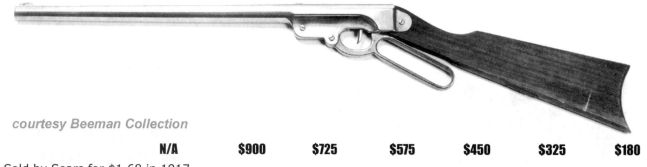

courtesy Beeman Collection

	N/A	$900	$725	$575	$450	$325	$180

Sold by Sears for $1.68 in 1917.

STERLING MODEL E – BB/.174 cal., SP, LA, 350 shot, octagon barrel tube, nickel or blue finish, 32.2 in. OAL, 2.4 lbs.

	N/A	$950	$750	$625	$475	$325	$190

GRADING	100%	95%	90%	80%	60%	40%	20%

STERLING MODEL G – BB/.174 cal., 1000 shot, SP, LA, octagon barrel tube, nickel or blue finish, barrel marked "American Tool Works". 36 in. OAL, 2.4 lbs.

courtesy Beeman Collection

	N/A	$900	$725	$575	$450	$325	$180

UPTON SPECIAL – BB/.174 cal., SP, LA, 500 shot repeater, SP, LA, octagon barrel tube, nickel or blue finish, barrel marked "Upton", 36 in. OAL, 2.4 lbs.

	N/A	$450	$350	$295	$225	$160	$90

Offered by Sears.

UPTON SINGLE SHOT – BB/.174 cal., similar to Sterling Single Shot, except marked "Upton".

	N/A	$250	$200	$165	$125	$90	$50

Offered by Sears in 1922 for $1.15.

UPTON MODEL 10 – BB/.174 cal., BBC, SS, ring trigger versions of Daisy 20 Variant 3 and Markham number 10 variant 3, 29.5 in. OAL.

	N/A	$900	$725	$575	$450	$325	$180

UPTON MODEL 20 – BB/.174 cal., SP, LA, SS, round barrel cover with distinctive humped ridge under barrel cover ahead of trigger guard, straight grip, slab sided stock, 32.3 in. OAL.

courtesy Beeman Collection

	N/A	$450	$350	$295	$225	$160	$90

This model was marked as made by Upton Machine Co. in St. Joseph, Michigan, with patents dated 1914 and 1923.

UPTON MODEL 30 (350 SHOT) – SP, LA, SS, round barrel cover with humped ridge under barrel cover ahead of trigger guard, straight grip, slab sided stock, 32.3 in. OAL.

Current values not yet determined.

This model marked as made by Upton Machine Co. in St. Joseph, Michigan, with a patent date of June 13, 1914 and other patents pending.

UPTON MODEL 40 – BB/.174 cal., SP, LA, SS, 1000 shot, round barrel cover with distinctive humped ridge under barrel cover ahead of trigger guard, straight grip, slab sided stock, 32.3 in. OAL.

	N/A	$500	$400	$325	$250	$175	$100

Sold by Sears in 1922 for $1.48.

This model was marked as made by Upton Machine Co. in St. Joseph, Michigan, with patents dated 1914 and 1923.

UPTON MODEL 50 (500 SHOT) – SP, LA, SS, round barrel cover with humped ridge under barrel cover ahead of trigger guard, straight grip, slab side stock, 32.3 in. OAL.

Current values not yet determined.

This model was marked as made by Upton Machine Co. in St. Joesph, Michigan with patents dated 1914 and 1923.

UPTON MODEL 1000 – BB/.174 cal. 1000 shot repeater, LA, 35.5 in. OAL.

	N/A	$625	$500	$400	$300	$220	$125

This model was similar in size, shape, and appearance to the Upton Model 40.

GRADING	100%	95%	90%	80%	60%	40%	20%

UPTON MODEL C – BB/.174 cal., SP, LA, very Daisy-like styling with pistol grip stock.

courtesy Beeman Collection

	N/A	$250	$200	$165	$125	$90	$50

UPTON MODEL D – BB/.174 cal. LA, SS, muzzle loader, 32.3 in. OAL.

	N/A	$575	$450	$375	$285	$200	$115

This model was similar in size, shape, and appearance to the Upton Model 50.

UPTON MODEL F (500 SHOT) – SP, LA, SS, 32.3 in. OAL.

Current values not yet determined.

WYANDOTTE – BB/.174 cal., SP, LA, SS, 1000 shot, round barrel cover with distinctive humped ridge under barrel cover ahead of trigger guard, straight grip, slab sided stock, 32.3 in. OAL.

	N/A	$450	$350	$295	$225	$160	$90

This model was marked "All Metal Products, Wyandotte, Michigan". It was also made under the Sears name as the Ranger Repeating Air Rifle.

AMPELL

Previous trade name of air and gas guns manufactured by Playtime Products located at 48 E. Main Street, Honeoye, NY, circa 1968-1975. Some production in Canada.

PISTOLS

ACRO 1/S-177/S-220 – BB/.175, .177 or .22 cal., CO_2, SS pellet or lead ball (S-177 or S-220) or 80-shot gravity feed mag. (BB/.175 cal. only), cocking gun also loads gun for each shot, all exposed parts cast metal with matte black finish, combination cocking knob/manual safety -- cannot be reset to safe after moving to fire position, 350 FPS, 11.5 in. OAL, 2.6 lbs.

courtesy Beeman Collection

	$85	$70	$60	$50	$40	$25	$15

Add 20% for BB/.175 cal. repeater pistols.
Add 20% for original factory kit with Ampell pellets, CO_2 cylinders, and papers.

RIFLES

BB MAGNUM M44 – BB/.174 cal., SSP, lead or steel BB, 48-shot gravity feed magazine, 350+ FPS, swinging forearm cocks, charges, and loads gun, wood stock, styled like Winchester M-1894 but without cocking lever, combination

courtesy Beeman Collection

GRADING	100%	95%	90%	80%	60%	40%	20%

cocking knob/manual safety -- cannot be reset to safe after moving to fire position, 38 in. OAL, 4.5 lbs.

| | $185 | $155 | $130 | $105 | $85 | $55 | $35 |

Add 15% for original factory box and papers.

ANICS GROUP

Current manufacturer established in 1990, and located in Moscow, Russia. No current U.S. importation. Previously imported by European American Armory Corp. located in Rockledge, FL, by Air Rifle Specialists located in Pine City, NY and Compasseco located in Bardstown, KY. Anics Group was originally an importer of Western-made airguns and firearms. In 1996, they began manufacturing their own line of CO_2 semi-autos and revolvers.

PISTOLS

MODEL A-101 – BB/.175 cal., CO_2, semi-auto, 15-shot mag., 450 FPS, checkered plastic grips, blue or silver finish, wooden checkered grips on silver models, adj. rear sight. Disc. 2006.

| | $100 | $85 | $70 | $60 | $45 | $30 | $20 |

MODEL A-101M (MAGNUM) – BB/.175 cal., CO_2, semi-auto, 15-shot mag., 490 FPS, compensator, checkered plastic grips, blue or silver finish, wooden checkered grips on silver models, adj. rear sight. Disc. 2006.

| | $100 | $85 | $70 | $60 | $45 | $30 | $20 |

MODEL A-111 – BB/.175 cal., CO_2, semi-auto, 15-shot mag., 450 FPS, contoured plastic grips, blue or silver finish, adj. rear sight. Disc. 2006.

| | $100 | $85 | $70 | $60 | $45 | $30 | $20 |

MODEL A-112 – BB/.175 cal., CO_2, semi-auto, 15-shot mag., 490 FPS, adj. rear sight, contoured plastic grips, blue or silver finish. Disc. 2006.

| | $100 | $85 | $70 | $60 | $45 | $30 | $20 |

MODEL A-112L (LASER) – BB/.175 cal., CO_2, semi-auto, 15-shot mag., 490 FPS, built-in laser housed in barrel lug automatically activated with slight pull of the trigger, contoured plastic grips, blue or silver finish. Disc. 2006.

| | $150 | $130 | $105 | $85 | $70 | $45 | $30 |

MODEL A-3000 SKIF – BB/.175 or .177 cal., CO_2, SA/DA, 28-shot rotary mag., 500 FPS, thumb-release safety, grooved trigger guard, ambidextrous mag. release, three-dot adj. target sights, fiberglass-reinforced polyamide frame and grip, matte black or matte black with silver finish slide, 1 lb. 9 oz. Mfg. 2001-Disc.

courtesy Howard Collection

| | $175 | $150 | $125 | $100 | $80 | $50 | $35 |

Last MSR was $167.

Add 10% for silver slide (Model A-3000 Silver).
Add 20% for long barrel (Model A-3000 LB).

This model also comes with a hard plastic carrying case, loading tool, and spare rotary magazine.

GRADING	100%	95%	90%	80%	60%	40%	20%

MODEL A9000S BERETTA – BB/.175 or .177 cal., CO_2, SA/DA, 22-shot rotary mag., 470 FPS, thumb-release safety, grooved trigger guard, ambidextrous mag. release, three-dot fixed sights, fiberglass-reinforced polyamide frame and grip, matte black, 1 lb. 9 oz. Mfg. 2007-Disc.

courtesy Anics Group

	100%	95%	90%	80%	60%	40%	20%
	$195	$165	$135	$115	$90	$60	$40

Last MSR was $178.

This model also comes with a hard plastic carrying case, loading tool, and spare rotary magazine.

REVOLVERS

MODEL A-201 – BB/.175 cal., CO_2, SA or DA, 30-shot, 410 FPS, loaded through cylinder (five BBs in each chamber), adj. rear sight, contoured plastic grips, CO_2 cartridge loads through base of grip, cylinder rotates when gun is fired, blue or silver finish. Disc.

	$120	$100	$85	$70	$55	$35	$25

MODEL A-201 MAGNUM – BB/.175 cal., CO_2, SA or DA, 30-shot, 460 FPS, loaded through cylinder (five BBs in each chamber), adj. rear sight, contoured plastic grips, CO_2 cartridge loads through base of grip, cylinder rotates when gun is fired, blue or silver finish.

	$125	$105	$90	$75	$55	$35	$25

ANSCHÜTZ

Current manufacturer (J. G. ANSCHÜTZ GmbH & Co. KG) established in 1856, and located in Ulm, Germany. Currently imported and/or distributed by Champion's Choice, located in LaVergne, TN, Champion's Shooter's Supply, located in Utica, OH, and Pilkington Competition Equipment LLC located in Monteagle, TN. Previously imported by Gunsmithing, Inc., located in Colorado Springs, CO, and International Shooters Service, located in Fort Worth, TX.

Models 2001 and 2002 were previously imported by Precision Sales Intl., Inc. Models 333, 335, and 380 were previously imported by Crosman from 1986 to 1988. Model 380 was also previously imported by Marksman. Research is ongoing with this trademark, and more information will be included both online and in future editions. For more information and current pricing on both new and used Anschütz firearms, please refer to the *Blue Book of Gun Values* by S.P. Fjestad (also available online).

PISTOLS

DOLLA MARK II – .177 cal., SP, SS, push-barrel cocking, may be stamped "KEENFIRE" or with "JGA" or "Dolla" medallion on wooden grips, no barrel shroud, mainspring visible around barrel when not cocked, nickel-plated finish, loaded by unscrewing plug at back end of barrel, 8.1 in. OAL (uncocked), 0.6 lbs. Mfg. 1929-1939.

courtesy Beeman Collection

	N/A	$195	$155	$125	$95	$70	$40

Add 30% for "KEENFIRE" marking (for American market only).

More primitive, but better materials, than JGA - sometimes with Dolla medallions.

GRADING	100%	95%	90%	80%	60%	40%	20%

JGA (MODEL 100) – .177 cal. darts, pellets, or shot, SP, SS, push-barrel cocking, mainspring covered by barrel shroud, black plastic body with JGA molded into brown plastic checkered grips, nickel plating on barrel shroud, trigger guard, and trigger, loaded by unscrewing plug at back end of barrel, 8.3 in. OAL uncocked, 0.5 lbs. Mfg. early 1950s to early 1960s.

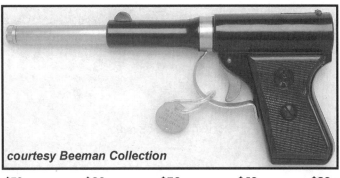

courtesy Beeman Collection

$70	$60	$50	$40	$30	$20	$15

Also known as IGA.

MODEL M5 JUNIOR – .177 cal., PCP, 492 FPS, 8 in. barrel with compensator, adj. trigger, sights and pistol grip, special dry firing mechanism, walnut grips. Mfg. by SAM in Switzerland 1997-1998.

$600	$500	$425	$350	$270	$180	$120

MODEL M10 – .177 cal., PCP, 492 FPS, 9.50 in. barrel with compensator, adj. trigger, sights and pistol grip, special dry firing mechanism, walnut grips. Mfg. by SAM in Switzerland 1997-1998.

$700	$600	$500	$400	N/A	N/A	N/A

Last MSR was $1,395.

MODEL LP@ ANSCHÜTZ – .177 cal., PCP, UIT match pistol, 8.93 in. barrel with compensator, internal stabilizer, adj. trigger, adj. sights, adj. Morini grip, 16.54 in. OAL, 2.47 lbs. Mfg. 2001-2009.

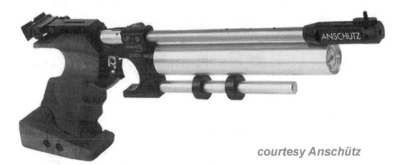

courtesy Anschütz

$1,450	$1,225	$1,025	$850	N/A	N/A	N/A

* **Model LP@ ANSCHÜTZ Junior** – .177 cal., PCP, UIT match pistol, 7.5 in. barrel with compensator, internal stabilizer, adj. trigger, adj. sights, adj. Morini grip, 13.98 in. OAL, 1.92 lbs. Mfg. 2004-2009.

$1,275	$1,100	$900	$750	N/A	N/A	N/A

* **Model LP@ ANSCHÜTZ Light** – .177 cal., PCP, UIT match pistol, 8.93 in. barrel with compensator, internal stabilizer, adj. trigger, adj. sights, adj. extra small Morini grip, 16.54 in. OAL, 2.05 lbs. Mfg. 2005-2009.

courtesy Anschütz

$1,275	$1,100	$900	$750	N/A	N/A	N/A

GRADING	100%	95%	90%	80%	60%	40%	20%

RIFLES

Note: Anschütz has issued a recall of some aluminum air cylinders for target air rifles manufactured prior to December 2005. This recall only refers to the aluminum air cylinders and not to the complete target air rifle. For more information go to the Anschütz website at www.anschuetz-sport.com.

During late 2007, Anschütz introduced the S2 version PCP target rifles. The S2 has improved air flow characteristics and needs about 50 % less impact energy to open the valve when firing the shot. Thus the air rifle's barreled action is subjected to almost no vibrations. This was accomplished by changing the following components:

1. Valve body and valve (the valve body is coated with gold).

2. Action head (coated with gold).

3. Improved cocking piston.

4. New stabilizer which has a higher mass and an extended adjusting range.

5. New spring box.

6. New pressure regulator.

HAKIM MILITARY TRAINING RIFLE – .22 cal., UL, SP, SS, rifled, tap-loading, full military style stock and sights, receiver ring marked with skull and Arabic markings for National Union Youth Movement, 10.5 lbs. Approx. 2,800 mfg. 1954.

courtesy Beeman Collection

N/A	$400	$325	$260	$200	$140	$80

This model was built in 1955 for the Egyptian Government, and was based on the Anschütz Model 1954 air rifle. Other Arabic markings for: "Training Airgun, Anschütz, Germany 1955". Ref: AR2 :27-29.

MODEL AIR-15 – .177 cal., PCP, PBA, SS, Model 8001 barrel and action and completion trigger, Bushmaster synthetic PG stock and forearm AR-15-A2 style with carry handle and adj. sights, 38.31 in. OAL, 9.4 lbs. Mfg. 2010-2013.

$2,550	$2,175	$1,775	$1,475	$1,150	$775	$500

Last MSR was $3,000.

MODEL 35 – .175 cal., BBC, SP, SS, 17.7 in. barrel, blue finish, adj. two-stage trigger, adj. rear and hooded ramp front sights, walnut stained checkered PG stock with rubber butt plate, 42.5 in. OAL, 7.4 lbs.

While advertised during 2008, this model was not imported.

MODEL 220 – .177 cal., SL, SP, SS, suppressed recoil system, twin metal piston rings, 18.5 in. barrel, no safety, precision match stock, aperture sight, 44.3 in. OAL, 10.4 lbs. Approx. 11,000 mfg. 1959-1967.

courtesy Beeman Collection

$475	$400	$325	$275	$215	$140	$95

GRADING	100%	95%	90%	80%	60%	40%	20%

MODEL 250 – .177 cal., SL, SP, SS, suppressed recoil system using unique oil pot designed by Hermann Wild, precision match stock, aperture sight, 18.5 in. barrel, 44.7 in. OAL, 10.9 lbs. Mfg. 1968 to the early 1980s.

courtesy Beeman Collection

	$450	$375	$325	$260	$205	$135	$90

MODEL 275 – .173 (4.4mm) No. 9 lead ball cal., Schmeisser system BA, six or twelve round removable box magazine, 17.3 in. barrel, Mauser-style swinging manual safety, 41.7 in. OAL, 5.9 lbs. Intro. mid-1950s.

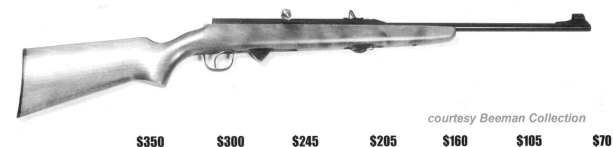

courtesy Beeman Collection

	$350	$300	$245	$205	$160	$105	$70

MODEL 275 REPEATING AIR RIFLE – .173 (4.4mm) No. 9 lead ball cal., BA, repeater, six or twelve round removable mag., 17.3 in. barrel, adj. rear and ramp front sights, two-stage trigger, walnut stained Monte Carlo style hardwood stock with BP, manual safety, 41.3 in. OAL, 5.7 lbs.

courtesy Anschütz

While advertised during 2008, this model was not imported.

MODEL 330 – .177 cal., BBC, SP, SS, Junior version of Model 335 sporter, 16.5 in. barrel, 40.6 in. OAL, 6.3 lbs.

	$150	$130	$105	$85	$70	$45	$30

MODEL 333 – .177 or .22 cal., BBC, SP, 700 FPS, adj. trigger, 18 in. barrel, 6.75 lbs.

	$180	$155	$125	$105	$80	$55	$35

Last MSR was $175.

MODEL 335 – .177 or .22 cal., BBC, SP, 700 FPS, adj. trigger, 18.5 in. barrel, 7.5 lbs. Disc. 2003.

courtesy Anschütz

	$275	$235	$195	$160	$125	$80	$55

Last MSR was $200.

Add $10 for Model 335 Mag. .22 cal.

GRADING	100%	95%	90%	80%	60%	40%	20%

MODEL 380 – .177 cal., UL, SP, 600-640 FPS, match model, removable cheek piece, adj. trigger, stippled walnut grips. Disc. 1994.

	$750	$625	$525	$425	$325	$225	$150

Last MSR was $1,250.

Subtract 10% for left-hand variation.
Add 10% for Moving Target Model.

MODEL 1954 – .22 cal., UL, SP, SS, tap-loading, receiver tapered forward of loading port, rifled barrel, sporter stock and sights.

	N/A	$500	$400	$325	$250	$175	$100

MODEL 2001 – .177 cal., SL, single stroke pneumatic, 10 lbs. 8 oz.

	$850	$725	$600	$500	$375	$255	$170

Last MSR was $1,800.

Subtract 10% for left-hand variation.
Add $80 for Running Target Model.

MODEL 2002 – .177 cal., PCP, 26 in. barrel, adj. buttplate and cheek piece, 10.5 lbs. Mfg. 1997-2006.

courtesy Anschütz

	$1,500	$1,275	$1,050	$875	$675	$450	$300

* **Model 2002 ALU** – .177 cal., PCP, SS, 25.2 in. barrel, easy-exchange 350-shot air cylinder with manometer, aluminum alloy stock with adj. laminate pistol grip and forearm, adj. alloy cheek piece, shoulder stock and buttplate attach to alloy frame, 42.5 in. OAL, 10.8 lbs. Mfg. 2000-2006.

	$1,600	$1,350	$1,125	$925	$725	$475	$325

* **Model 2002 Club** – .177 cal., PCP, SS, 25.2 in. barrel, walnut stock with adj. cheek piece and buttplate, 42.5 in. OAL, 10.8 lbs. Mfg. 2000-2005.

	$1,200	$1,025	$850	$700	$550	$350	$240

Last MSR was $1,065.

* **Model 2002 D-RT** – .177 cal., PCP, SS, 33.8 in. barrel, Running Target Model, 51.5 in. OAL, 9.2 lbs. Disc. 2006.

	$1,300	$1,100	$900	$750	$575	$400	$260

* **Model 2002 Junior** – .177 cal., PCP, SS, 20.8 in. barrel, adj. buttplate and cheek piece, 35 in. OAL, 7.9 lbs. Disc. 2005.

	$925	$775	$650	$525	$400	$275	$185

Last MSR was $1,065.

GRADING	100%	95%	90%	80%	60%	40%	20%

MODEL 2002 SUPERAIR – .177 cal., SL, SSP, SS, 25.2 in. barrel, aluminum alloy or color laminated wood stock with adj. buttplate and cheek piece, 42.5 in. OAL, 10.50 or 11 (aluminum) lbs. Mfg. 1992-2006.

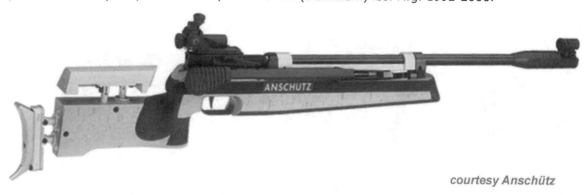

courtesy Anschütz

	$850	$725	$600	$500	$375	$255	$170

Add $200 for ALU stock.

MODEL 2020 FIELD – .177 cal., PCP, SS, 690 FPS, 25.2 in. barrel, easy-exchange 350-shot air cylinder with manometer, aluminum alloy stock with adj. laminate pistol grip and forearm, adj. alloy cheek piece, shoulder stock and buttplate attach to alloy frame, 42.5 in. OAL, 10.36 lbs. Disc. 2006.

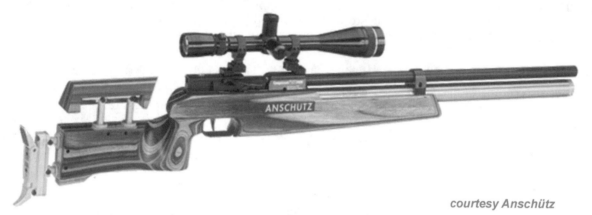

courtesy Anschütz

$1,350	$1,150	$950	$775	$600	$400	$270

MODEL 2025 FIELD – .177 cal., PCP, SS, 803 FPS, 25.2 in. barrel, easy-exchange 350-shot air cylinder with manometer, aluminum alloy stock with adj. laminate pistol grip and forearm, adj. alloy cheek piece, shoulder stock and buttplate attach to alloy frame, 42.5 in. OAL, 10.36 lbs. Disc. 2006.

courtesy Anschütz

$1,400	$1,175	$975	$800	$625	$425	$280

MODEL 2027 BIATHLON – .177 cal., PCP, 803 FPS, straight pull action, five-shot mag., 24 in. barrel, fully adj. sights, adj. match trigger, walnut stock with adj. cheek/buttplate and four mag. holder, 9 lbs. Mfg. 2003-2005.

$1,300	$1,100	$900	$750	$575	$400	$260

Last MSR was $1,400.

MODEL 8001 CLUB – .177 cal., PCP, BA, SS, 25.2 in. rifled barrel, non-stained lacquered walnut stock, adj. match

GRADING	100%	95%	90%	80%	60%	40%	20%

trigger, adj. cheek piece, adj. rubber buttpad, dry-fire capability, globe front and adj. diopter rear sights, 42.1-43.3 in. OAL, 8.38 lbs. Mfg. 2008-current.

courtesy Anschütz

MSR $2,000	$1,700	$1,500	$1,350	$1,100	$850	N/A	N/A

This model also comes with sight set 6834, compressed air cylinder, accessory box with filling adapter, air release screw, special grease, Allan key, safety discs, o-rings, barrel weight, manual, and test target.

MODEL 8001 JUNIOR – .177 cal., PCP, BA, SS, silver compressed air cylinder with manometer, 20.87 in. rifled barrel, laminated ambidextrous orange/blue stock, adj. match trigger, adj. cheek piece, aluminum adj. buttpad, dry-fire capability, globe front and adj. diopter rear sights, pressure regulator with air filter, 42.1-43.3 in. OAL, 7.94-10.14 lbs.

MSR $2,000	$1,700	$1,500	$1,350	$1,100	$850	N/A	N/A

This model also comes with sight set 6834, compressed air cylinder, accessory box with filling adapter, air release screw, special grease, Allan key, safety discs, o-rings, barrel weight, manual, and test targets.

MODEL 8002 – .177 cal., PCP, SS, easy-exchange 350-shot air cylinder with manometer, 25.2 in. barrel, color laminated wood stock with adj. laminated pistol grip and forearm, adj. alloy cheek piece, 42.5 in. OAL, 9.2 lbs. Mfg. 2005-2007.

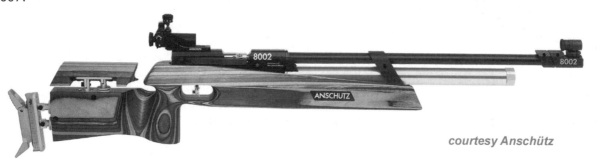

courtesy Anschütz

$1,800	$1,525	$1,250	$1,050	$800	$550	$350

* **Model 8002 Alu** – .177 cal., PCP, SS, easy-exchange 350-shot air cylinder with manometer, 25.2 in. barrel, aluminum alloy stock with adj. laminate pistol grip and laminate forearm, adj. alloy cheek piece, shoulder stock and buttplate attached to alloy frame, 42.5 in. OAL, 9.24 lbs. Mfg. 2005-2007.

courtesy Anschütz

$2,000	$1,700	$1,400	$1,150	$900	$600	$400

GRADING	100%	95%	90%	80%	60%	40%	20%

* **Model 8002 Alu Benchrest** – .177 cal., PCP, SS, easy-exchange 350-shot air cylinder with manometer, 25.2 in. barrel, aluminum alloy stock with adj. laminated pistol grip and forearm, adj. alloy cheek piece, shoulder stock and buttplate attached to alloy frame, 42.5 in. OAL, 9.92 lbs. Mfg. 2006-2007.

courtesy Anschütz

$1,850	$1,575	$1,300	$1,075	$825	$550	$375

* **Model 8002 Club** – .177 cal., PCP, SS, easy-exchange 350-shot air cylinder with manometer, 25.2 in. barrel, walnut stock with adj. pistol grip and forearm, adj. alloy cheek piece, 42.5 in. OAL, 8.8 lbs. Mfg. 2005-2007.

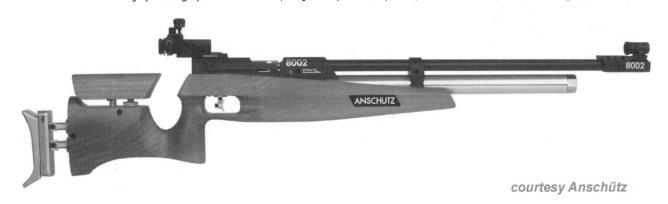

courtesy Anschütz

$1,600	$1,350	$1,125	$925	$725	$475	$325

* **Model 8002 Junior** – .177 cal., PCP, SS, easy-exchange 350-shot air cylinder with manometer, 25.2 in. barrel, color laminated wood stock with adj. laminated pistol grip and forearm, adj. alloy cheek piece, 37.4 in. OAL, 7.94 lbs. Mfg. 2006-2008.

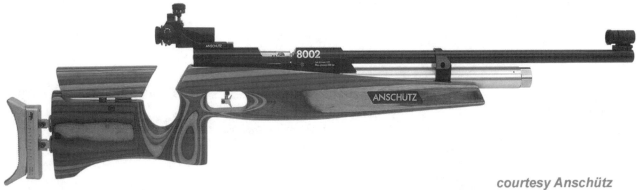

courtesy Anschütz

$1,600	$1,350	$1,125	$925	$725	$475	$325

MODEL 8002 S2 – .177 cal., PCP, BA, SS, 25.2 in. rifled match barrel, silver air cylinder, non-stained walnut benchrest stock with rubber buttplate, adj. match trigger, adj. forearm, air pressure regulator with air filter, removable air reservoir with integral manometer, globe front sight, adj. diopter rear sight, maintenance free stabilizer, 41.3-43.4 in. OAL, 9.04 lbs. Mfg. 2008-current.

MSR $2,620	$2,225	$1,975	$1,775	$1,450	$1,100	N/A	N/A

GRADING	100%	95%	90%	80%	60%	40%	20%

* **Model 8002 S2 Alu** – .177 cal., PCP, BA, SS, 25.2 in. rifled match barrel, blue air cylinder, silver aluminum stock with natural wood/blue grip or black Pro-Grip, adj. butt pad, adj. match trigger, adj. forearm, air pressure regulator with air filter, removable air reservoir with integral manometer, globe front sight, adj. diopter rear sight, maintenance free stabilizer, 42.1-43.3 in. OAL, 10.2 lbs. Mfg. 2008-current.

MSR $3,000	$2,550	$2,250	$2,050	$1,650	$1,250	N/A	N/A

This model also includes an accessory box, manual, and test target.

* **Model 8002 S2 Club** – .177 cal., PCP, SS, easy-exchange 350-shot air cylinder with manometer, 25.2 in. barrel, walnut stock with adj. pistol grip and forearm, adj. cheek piece, 42.5 in. OAL, 8.8 lbs. Mfg. 2007-current.

While advertised during 2008, this model was not imported.

* **Model 8002 S2 Junior** – .177 cal., PCP, SS, compressed air, easy-exchange 350-shot air cylinder with manometer, 25.2 in. barrel, color laminated wood stock,maintenance-free stabilizer, air filter, PRO-Grip equipment, 37.4 in. OAL, 7.94 lbs. Mfg. 2008.

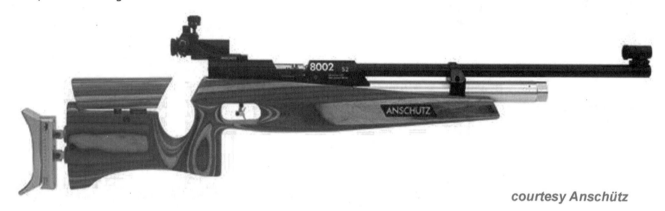

courtesy Anschütz

While advertised during 2008, this model was not imported.

* **Model 8002 S2 Walnut Benchrest** – .177 cal., PCP, cocking lever action, SS, easy-exchange 350-shot air cylinder with manometer, 25.2 in. barrel, adj. aperture rear with extension and hooded front sights, walnut stock with non-slip PG, extended benchrest cheek piece, adj. alloy buttplate, S2 up-grade, 41.34 in. OAL, 9.2 lbs. Mfg. 2008-current.

MSR $2,125	$1,800	$1,600	$1,450	$1,175	$900	N/A	N/A

» **Model 8002 S2 Benchrest Start** – .177 cal., PCP, cocking lever action, SS, easy-exchange 350-shot air cylinder with manometer, 25.2 in. barrel, adj. aperture rear with extension and hooded front sights, walnut stock with non-slip PG, extended benchrest cheek piece, non-slip rubber buttplate adj. for length, S2 up-grade, 41.34 in. OAL, 9.2 lbs. Mfg. 2008-current.

While advertised during 2008, this model was not imported.

MODEL 9003 PREMIUM – .177 cal., PCP, tension-free connection and vibration dampening of the barreled action in aluminum stock with Soft Link® shock absorber pads, adj. buttplate, adj. cheek piece, adj. forend, 9.9 lbs. Mfg. 2004-2007.

courtesy Anschütz

	$2,500	$2,125	$1,750	$1,450	$1,125	$750	$500

* **Model 9003 Premium 150th ANSCHÜTZ Anniversary** – .177 cal., PCP, SS, cocking lever action, compressed air cylinder, PRO-Grip equipment, rear sight knobs and front sight are in ANSCHÜTZ Royal Blue finish, 150 years

GRADING	100%	95%	90%	80%	60%	40%	20%

logo on stock and compressed air cylinder, with selected Limited Edition accessories. Mfg. 2007.

courtesy Anschütz

	$3,000	$2,550	$2,100	$1,725	$1,350	$900	$600

Accessories include rear sight 7002, the adj. front sight SWING PLUS, Model 6817 U1 rear sight elevator, black finish heavy steel columns, 3 plastic apertures in blue, 1 safety rod, 2 eye shields, 1 ANSCHÜTZ key pendant, 1 pellet box as well as various 150 years logos, pins and an anniversary certificate.

* **Model 9003 Premium Benchrest** – .177 cal., PCP, tension-free connection and vibration dampening of the barreled action in aluminum stock with Soft Link® shock absorber pads, adj. benchrest forend stock, rubber buttplate, seven stock decoration stickers and box with accessories, 9.9 lbs. Mfg. 2005-2007.

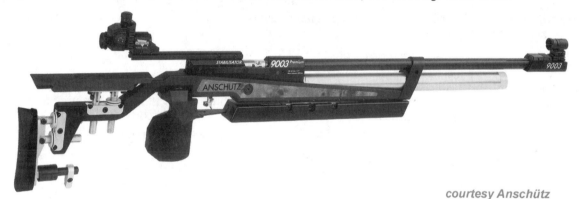

courtesy Anschütz

	$2,500	$2,125	$1,750	$1,450	$1,125	$750	$500

MODEL 9003 PREMIUM S2 – .177 cal., PCP, SS, silver compressed air cylinder with manometer, cocking lever action, 25.2 in. precision match black barrel, walnut or crossed aluminum black (new 2011) stock, adj. forend, PG, and cheek piece, Pro-Grip equipment, aluminum carrier, pressure regulator with air filter, aluminum buttplate, diopter rear sight, maintenance free stabilizer, dry firing safety, adj. trigger blade, 42.5-43.7 in. OAL, 9.78 lbs. Mfg. 2008-current.

courtesy Anschütz

MSR $3,900	$3,300	$2,950	$2,650	$2,150	$1,650	N/A	N/A

* **Model 9003 Premium S2 Alu** – .177 cal., PCP, SS, cocking lever action, compressed air, Pro-Grip equipment, aluminum carrier, pressure regulator with air filter, aluminum buttplate, aluminum adj. forend stock, PG, and cheek piece, maintenance free stabilizer, dry firing safety, adj. trigger blade, 42.5-43.7 in. OAL, 9.78 lbs. Mfg. 2008-current.

MSR $3,900	$3,300	$2,950	$2,650	$2,150	$1,650	N/A	N/A

GRADING	100%	95%	90%	80%	60%	40%	20%

* Model 9003 Premium S2 150th ANSCHÜTZ Anniversary – .177 cal., PCP, SS, cocking lever action, 25.2 in. precision match barrel, compressed air cylinder, PRO-Grip equipment, rear sight knobs and front sight are in ANSCHÜTZ Royal Blue finish, 150 years logo on stock and compressed air cylinder, and selected Limited Edition accessories, maintenance free stabilizer, pressure regulator with air filter, dry firing safety, adj. trigger blade. Mfg. 2008.

courtesy Anschütz

$3,500	$3,000	$2,450	$2,025	$1,575	$1,050	$700

Accessories include rear sight 7002, the adj. front sight SWING PLUS, Model 6817 U1 rear sight elevator, black finish heavy steel columns, 3 plastic apertures in blue, 1 safety rod, 2 eye shields, 1 ANSCHÜTZ key pendant, 1 pellet box as well as various 150 years logos, pins and an anniversary certificate.

* Model 9003 Premium S2 Benchrest – .177 cal., PCP, SS, cocking lever action, compressed air cylinder, precision match barrel, maintenance free stabilizer, aluminum carrier, PRO-Grip equipment, pressure regulator with air filter, adj. benchrest forend stock, rubber buttplate, seven stock decoration stickers and box with accessories, dry firing safety, adj. trigger blade, 9.9 lbs. Mfg. 2008-current.

MSR $3,900	$3,300	$2,950	$2,650	$2,150	$1,650	N/A	N/A

MODEL 9003 PREMIUM S2 PRECISE – .177 cal., PCP, SS, cocking lever action, compressed air cylinder with manometer, 25.2 in. black precision match barrel, Pro-Grip equipment, adj. match trigger, adj. trigger blade, maintenance free stabilizer, dry firing device, adj. forend, aluminum stock, adj. aluminum buttplate, pressure regulator with air filter, diopter rear sight, 41.7-43.7 in. OAL, 10 lbs. Mfg. 2011-current.

MSR $3,900	$3,300	$2,950	$2,650	$2,150	$1,650	N/A	N/A

This model also includes a plastic rifle case, sight set 6834, sight raiser block, covers for cheek piece and buttplate adjustment, accessory box with additional weights, filling adapter, air release screw, special grease, Allan key, original test target and service manual.

ANSON, E. & CO.

Previous manufacturer located in Birmingham, England circa 1890-1945.

Edwin Anson and Company was a gunsmithing business, previously active from about 1890 to 1945. Models produced were the Ansonia air rifle (apparently a copy of the MGR rifle of Mayer & Grammelspacher), Star air pistols, and small numbers of the Firefly air pistol. They designed, with Frank Clarke, but did not produce, the Westley Richards Highest Possible air pistols and the Accles & Shelvoke Warrior air pistol. Ref: AW-May 1984.

PISTOLS

FIREFLY – .177 cal., push-barrel cocking, SP, smoothbore, concentric mainsprings, wooden barrel cover, frame and grip are heavy cast iron, marked "O.K." on left side of trigger, "ANSON" on the right side, and "FIREFLY" on frame above trigger. Mfg. 1925-1933.

courtesy Beeman Collection

$350	$300	$245	$205	$160	$105	$70

Add 40% for factory box.

Distributed by the Midland Gun Company (later absorbed by Parker and Hale), Birmingham, England.

GRADING	100%	95%	90%	80%	60%	40%	20%

STAR – .177 cal., underlever, SS, SP, smoothbore, Vulcanite grips with "FC" monogram. Approx. 100 mfg. 1926-mid 1930s.

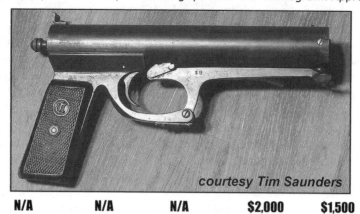

courtesy Tim Saunders

N/A	N/A	N/A	$2,000	$1,500	$1,000	$750

Add 20% for original box.

First variant: marked "The Star". Second Variant: unmarked or with "Anson Star". Ref. AGW March, 2003.

RIFLES

ANSONIA – .177 cal., BBC, SP, 17 in. octagonal barrel with nine-groove RH rifling, adj. sights, barrel screwed into barrel block, lever detent like MGR but two-piece barrel marked "The Ansonia", 41.5 in. OAL, 7.5 lbs. Mfg. 1905-1910.

courtesy Beeman Collection

$750	$625	$525	$425	$325	$225	$150

ANSONIA Mk. 2 – .177 cal., BBC, SP, 17 in. octagonal barrel and barrel block are one piece, fixed sight, 41.5 in. OAL. 7.5 lbs. Mfg. 1905-1910.

$450	$375	$325	$260	$205	$135	$90

APACHE (aka FIRE-BALL)

Previous trademark manufactured by Burhans and Associates of CA, or one of their subsidiaries, in 1948-1949.

APACHE BACKGROUND

The authors and publisher wish to thank Jon Jenkins and John Groenewold for their valuable assistance with the following information for this section of the *Blue Book of Airguns*.

The Apache rifle evidently is California's first publicly marketed airgun and is one of the shortest lived of all American airgun designs, apparently having been produced only in 1948 and 1949.

In 1949, the Apache tooling was acquired by Standard Interstate Machine Company (SIMCO) in Glendale, CA. By June of 1949, SIMCO had begun manufacturing an Apache-type model air rifle marked on the buttplate as the Texan. Apparently, the Apache tooling and parts were also used to produce the SIMCO rifles. These generally were marked "SIMCO" in an oval on the front left side of the receiver. Guns are known with both the SIMCO marking on the receiver and an Apache marking on the pump tube plug. Some SIMCO guns are not marked at all. Apparently, Apache parts were simply utilized until exhausted, but SIMCO guns generally are identifiable by their careful finishing. The final preparation of the metalwork is better and the finishing itself is of a greater consistency than the former Apache production. The stock lacquer is darker and more opaque than on Apache rifles and is more carefully applied. SIMCO rifles have a walnut stock with the word "Texan" on the buttplate. This buttplate marking appears to be the exception. Manufacturing of the Apache/Simco line seems to have ceased in 1949.

Pistol examples with SIMCO marked on end cap. The last address for SIMCO was on Hollywood Way in Burbank, CA. Ref: AGNR - Apr. 1986.

APACHE CONFIGURATION

Apache airguns were available in various design configurations, but there is some interesting confusion about which variations were actually produced. What was advertised does not always match what is actually seen in known specimens. The original

GRADING	100%	95%	90%	80%	60%	40%	20%

rifle was advertised as always having a .175 caliber insert barrel, but there are a number of specimens which do not have any threads at the muzzle. Such a lack makes it impossible to fix a sub-caliber barrel. They were also advertised as having a hollow space in the buttstock for a tube of ammunition, but apparently none were made with this feature. Eight-shot .175 caliber Fireball rifles were advertised in 1948, but none have been reported. A version called the SIMCO Texan was specified in 1949 dealer literature as taking regular .22 caliber pellets, but only .24 (No. 4 Buckshot) cal. specimens are known. And the pistols were promoted as coming in real wooden boxes, but rather fragile cardboard factory cartons seem to have been the reality. If you have clear evidence of the existence of previously unknown features or models, please contact Blue Book Publications or email: guns@bluebookinc.com.

Early production Apache rifles used a plastic stock and forearm. Plastic technology was only beginning at the time, and these plastic stocks were prone to frequent breakage. Production was switched to walnut stocks as early as March 1948. Since both were available at the same time, it is possible to find mismatched guns. Two buttstock attachment techniques were used with no clear definition between production runs. Attaching the buttstock with a bolt through the pistol grip is the least common variation. The standard, most common arrangement is a long bolt, hidden by the buttplate, running through the length of the buttstock. The steel barrel and pump tube on rifles were blued while the brass pump tube on pistols was chemically treated. On both the rifles and pistols only the .24 (No. 4 Buckshot) caliber barrel was rifled. Apache rifles are known with all possible combinations and variations of parts. Apparently, any parts handy at assembly time were used. Guns with various screws in the receiver, a plastic buttstock and a wooden forearm, completely unmarked, and/or with poor finishing of the metalwork were produced and should not be considered prototype efforts or mistakes.

It is clear that the first versions of the rifle were single shot. The second form of the rifle had a ten-shot magazine assembly. These rifles omit the .24 (No. 4 Buckshot) loading port on the top of the frame and can only be fired with .24 (No. 4 Buckshot) balls using the magazine. Some rifles were sold as .24 (No. 4 Buckshot) cal. repeaters only and some included the .175 cal. barrel. These seem to require muzzle loading in the early versions, but later versions could be loaded through a small hole in the top of the receiver. All non-repeater guns equipped with the .175 cal. barrel liner had to be muzzle-loaded when the liner was being used. Bolt handles on the non-repeater guns were fragile and specimens often have this item broken or missing. In the spring of 1948, a pistol was added to the Apache line. Available first as a single shot in .24(No. 4 Buckshot) cal., pistol was soon offered as a six-shot repeater with the same interchangeable caliber feature and spring-fed magazine as the rifles. The first production models of the pistols had heavy die-cast frames, similar to the rifles; later production featured an aluminum frame. These frames generally were polished to give the appearance of chrome plating, but some were painted black. Grips on the pistols were either wood (common), black, or ivory plastic (scarce). The .175 cal. insert for the pistol attached using the same type of threaded muzzle arrangement as the rifle. There are rare examples of the pistols with a friction fit, rather than a threaded arrangement, for the insert. The pump tube is thin-wall brass tubing prone to failure at the pivot points. The performance of the pistols was rather moderate in both calibers.

APACHE MARKINGS

Apache guns are marked on the forward pump tube plug (if at all) with "Burhans and Associates" or "National Cart Corporation", or just the word "Fire-ball", or "Apache". Some markings included an address with the word "Fire-ball" or "Apache" but not the company name. Charles Burhans operated the National Cart Corporation, so these various markings imply the same origin. Although not precision airguns, the genius of the Apache rifle was its larger .25 caliber barrel which allowed users to quickly change calibers.

PISTOLS

APACHE - FIRE-BALL PISTOL – BB/.175 and .24 (No. 4 Buckshot) cal. dual cal. variant, or .24 (No. 4 Buckshot) cal. only, UL multi-pump pneumatic, smooth or rifled (.24 - No. 4 Buckshot) barrel, walnut or plastic grips, die-cast zinc or aluminum frame, polished or all blue paint finish. Mfg. 1948-1949.

courtesy Beeman Collection

GRADING	100%	95%	90%	80%	60%	40%	20%

* **Apache - Fire-Ball Pistol First Variation** – usually .24 (No. 4 Buckshot) cal., SS only, 225 FPS, 8.25 in. rifled barrel, heavy cast zinc receiver (similar to rifle), 11.9 in. OAL, 1.9 lbs.

	$350	**$295**	**$250**	**$195**	**$150**	**$95**	**$65**

Add 25% for factory box and literature.
Add 10% for painted receiver.
Add 10% for ivory-colored grips.
Add 50% for press-fit inner barrel.

Subtract 10% for missing name.
Subtract 15% for missing .175 barrel insert on guns with threaded muzzle rings.

* **Apache - Fire-Ball Pistol Second Variation** – .24 (No. 4 Buckshot) cal., SS or repeater with six-round spring fed mag., aluminum receiver, polished or painted blue, 8.25 in. rifled barrel with removable smoothbore .175 cal. liner (may attach via screw threads in end of barrel or press-fit), wooden or plastic (ivory or black) grips. 1.3 lbs without barrel liner.

	$350	**$295**	**$250**	**$195**	**$150**	**$95**	**$65**

Add 25% for factory box and literature.
Add 10% for painted receiver.
Add 10% for ivory-colored grips.
Add 50% for press-fit inner barrel.

Subtract 10% for missing name.
Subtract 15% for missing .175 barrel insert on guns with threaded muzzle rings.

RIFLES

APACHE - FIRE-BALL - TEXAN – BB/.175 and .24 (No. 4 Buckshot) cal. dual cal. variant, or .24 (No. 4 Buckshot) cal. only, SS variant, UL multi-pump pneumatic, smooth or rifled (.24 - No. 4 Buckshot), 540 FPS, plastic and/or walnut stock and forearm, black finish, die-cast zinc or aluminum frame, 36.3 in. OAL, 5.5-6.5 lbs. Mfg. 1948-1949.

courtesy Beeman Collection

* **Apache - Fire-Ball - Texan First Variation** – .24 (No. 4 Buckshot) cal., SS, round loading port in top of receiver, may include .175 threaded barrel insert, plastic or walnut buttstock and forearm.

	$275	**$235**	**$195**	**$160**	**$125**	**$80**	**$55**

Add 25% for factory box and literature.
Add 20% for "Texan" with walnut stock and forearm, MSR was $14.95.
Add 10% for .24 (No. 4 Buckshot) cal. only.
Add 100% for chrome plating on all metalwork.
Subtract 25% for missing .175 barrel insert on guns with threaded muzzle rings.
Add 30% for "SIMCO" marked guns.

* **Apache - Fire-Ball - Texan Second Variation** – .175 or .24 (No. 4 Buckshot) cal., SS, .175 cal. threaded barrel insert loaded from the muzzle, later versions have a small round loading port in the top, or side of receiver, or six-shot repeater, walnut buttstock attached via a bolt through bottom of pistol grip.

courtesy Beeman Collection

	$275	**$235**	**$195**	**$160**	**$125**	**$80**	**$55**

Add 25% for factory box and literature.
Add 20% for "Texan" with walnut stock and forearm, MSR was $14.95.
Add 10% for .24 (No. 4 Buckshot) cal. only.
Add 100% for chrome plating on all metalwork.
Subtract 25% for missing .175 barrel insert on guns with threaded muzzle rings.
Add 30% for "SIMCO" marked guns.
Add 100% for bulk fill CO_2.

Transitional guns -- either buttstock or forearm of contrasting material (hardwood or plastic) priced as Variation Two or Three depending on method of buttstock attachment.

GRADING	100%	95%	90%	80%	60%	40%	20%

* **Apache - Fire-Ball - Texan Third Variation** – .175 or .24 (No. 4 Buckshot) cal., SS, .175 cal. threaded barrel insert loaded from the muzzle, later versions have a small round loading port in the top, or side of receiver, or six-shot repeater, walnut buttstock attached by long bolt running from under buttplate.

	$260	$220	$180	$150	$115	$80	$50

Add 25% for factory box and literature.
Add 20% for "Texan" with walnut buttstock and forearm, MSR was $14.95.
Add 10% for .25 cal. only.
Add 100% for chrome plating on all metalwork.
Subtract 25% for missing .175 barrel insert on guns with threaded muzzle rings.
Add 30% for "SIMCO" marked guns.

ARAL ARMS

Current manufacturer located in Turkey. No current U.S. importation.

Aral Arms manufactures high quality air rifles as well as blank pistols and shotguns. Please contact the company directly for more information on all their products including pricing and U.S. availability (see Trademark Index).

RIFLES

Please contact the company directly for more information on the following current models including options, pricing, and U.S. availability (see Trademark Index).

AR 450 – .177 cal., black pistol grip stock.

courtesy Aral Arms

AR 550 – .22 cal., camo pistol grip stock.

courtesy Aral Arms

AR 635 – .25 cal., camo pistol grip stock.

courtesy Aral Arms

ARES AIRGUNS

Current trademark manufactured by Doruk Silah Ltd. Sti., located in Konya, Turkey. No current U.S. importation.

Doruk Silah San Ltd. manufactures quality air rifles. Please contact the company directly for more information regarding U.S. availability and pricing (see Trademark Index).

ARMIGAS (ARMIGAS-COMEGA)

Previous manufacturer located at Via Valle Inzino, Brescia, Italy.

Associated with Atillio Zanoletti. Maker of gas-powered rifles, circa 1961 to early 1980s.

GRADING	100%	95%	90%	80%	60%	40%	20%

PISTOLS

OLIMPIC – 4.5mm lead round ball or pellet cal., semi-auto or SS self cocking pellet tap loader, bulk fill CO_2, 7 in. blue finish barrel, adj. rear and blade front sights, checkered wood grip.

courtesy Loke Collection

N/A	$950	$750	$625	$475	$325	$190

Add 20% for original box.

Add 20%-25% for original 10 oz. bulk fill CO_2 cylinder.

RECORD – 4.5mm lead round ball or pellet cal., SS self cocking pellet tap loader, bulk fill CO_2, 7 in. blue finish barrel, adj. rear and blade front sights, checkered wood grip.

courtesy Loke Collection

N/A	$800	$650	$525	$400	$280	$160

Add 20% for original box.

Add 20%-25% for original 10 oz. bulk fill CO_2 cylinder.

SPORT – 4.5mm lead round ball cal., SS, pellet tap loader, bulk fill CO_2, 7 in. blue finish barrel, adj. rear and blade front sights, checkered wood grip.

courtesy Loke Collection

N/A	$750	$600	$475	$375	$265	$150

Add 20% for original box.

Add 20%-25% for original 10 oz. bulk fill CO_2 cylinder.

RIFLES

ARTEMIA – 8mm cal., CO_2, BA.

No additional information or values available at this time.

GRADING	100%	95%	90%	80%	60%	40%	20%

OLIMPIC – .177 cal., CO_2, repeater, 80-shot spring-fed magazine removes for loading, tends to jam during operation, bulk feed CO_2 valve at muzzle end, 22 in. barrel, no safety, marked with Armigas brand, Olimpic name, and "BREV. INTERN" ("International Patent"), 4.5mm, 38 in. OAL, 5.5 lbs.

courtesy Beeman Collection

N/A	$600	$475	$400	$300	$210	$120

A tenuous and obscure relationship exists amongst the Olimpic and the TyRol COmatic rifle of Austria (see "T" section), the Ventyrini COmatic Rifle of Argentina (see "V" section), and the Fionda rifle of Brazil (see "F" section).

SHOTGUNS

HUNTER MOD. S66 – 8mm shot capsule (No. 11/12 birdshot) or 8mm lead ball, SS, two CO_2 cylinders provide about 20 shots, exterior hammer, 39 in. OAL, 6.4 lbs.

No other information or values available at time of printing.

ARMSCOR

Current trademark manufactured by Arms Corporation of the Philippines, located in Manila, Philippines. No current importation. Previously imported by Armscor Precision International, located in Las Vegas, NV. For more information and current pricing on both new and used Arms Corporation of the Philippines firearms, please refer to the *Blue Book of Gun Values* by S.P. Fjestad (also available online).

PISTOLS

ARMSCOR PISTOL – .22 cal., CO_2, SL, 7.5 in. barrel, 500 FPS, fixed sights, 2.2 lbs. Disc. 2002.

$175	$150	$125	$100	$80	$50	$35

Last MSR was $112.

SQUIRES BINGHAM MODEL – .22 cal., bulk fill CO_2, SL, 7.5 in. barrel, 500 FPS, fixed sights.

courtesy Loke Collection

N/A	$700	$550	$450	$350	$245	$140

RIFLES

ARMSCOR EXECUTIVE – .22 cal., CO_2, bolt action, 22 in. barrel, 700 FPS, leaf-type rear sight, hooded front sight, beech stock with checkered grip and forearm, manual safety, 5.75 lbs. Disc. 2002.

courtesy Howard Collection

$150	$130	$105	$85	$70	$45	$30

Last MSR was $120.

GRADING	100%	95%	90%	80%	60%	40%	20%

ARMSCOR RETRACTABLE – .22 cal., CO_2, bolt action, 22 in. barrel, 700 FPS, leaf-type rear sight, hooded front sight, composite pistol grip stock with collapsible buttstock, 6 lbs. Disc. 2002.

courtesy Howard Collection

	$175	$150	$125	$100	$80	$50	$35

Last MSR was $112.

ARMSCOR STANDARD – .22 cal., CO_2, bolt action, 22 in. barrel, 700 FPS, leaf-type rear sight, hooded front sight, beech stock, manual safety, 5.75 lbs. Disc. 2002.

	$145	$125	$100	$85	$65	$45	$30

Last MSR was $112.

ARROW

Previous trademark used by a few different manufacturers including Friedrich Langenham located in Zella - St. Blasii, Thüringen, Germany, the State Industry Factory located in Shanghai, China, and William Heilprin located in Philadelphia, PA.

These are completely unrelated makers. Please see the individual makers' information in this guide.

ARTES de ARCOS

Previous manufacturer of Setra air rifles located in Madrid and Barcelona, Spain. See SETRA in the "S" section.

ASAHI

Previous trademark manufactured by Kawaguchiya located in Japan circa 1948-1955.

Research is ongoing with this trademark, and more information will be included both online and in future editions. Copy of pre-WWII German "Millicia Style" rifles, e.g. Diana Model 27. Average original condition specimens are typically priced in the $100 range. The most recent specimens with a modern-looking half stock are rare and typically command an extra $50.

courtesy Beeman Collection

ATAMAN

Current trademark manufactured by Denyam LLC., located in Moscow, Russia. No current U.S. importation.

Ataman manufactures quality air rifles. Please contact the company directly for more information regarding U.S. availability and pricing (see Trademark Index).

ATAK SILAH SAN. TIC. LTD. STI.

For information see Zoraki in the "Z" section.

ATLAS AIR GUN MANUFACTURING CO.

Previous manufacturer located in Ilion, NY circa 1889.

See Atlas Gun Co. in this section.

ATLAS AIR RIFLE MANUFACTURING CO.

Previous manufacturer located in Ilion, NY circa 1953-1956.

Manufacturer of a pump-up pneumatic rifle. Research is ongoing with this trademark, and more information will be included both online and in future editions.

GRADING	100%	95%	90%	80%	60%	40%	20%

ATLAS GUN CO.

Previous manufacturer located in Ilion, NY circa 1886-1906.

The Atlas Gun Company of Ilion, New York is another of the links between key parts of the world airgun developmental picture. It was founded in 1886 by George P. Gunn of the Haviland & Gunn Company whose designs were the foundation of most modern production airguns. The Atlas company was then acquired by Daisy in 1906 as part of their aggressive program to eliminate competition.

The first Atlas gun was the 1886 model, a break-open BB gun using an unusual gravity repeater mechanism incorporating three iron rods as a BB raceway. Gunn was granted a patent for the design in 1895. The last of the Atlas BB guns have peculiar ring lever cocking arms which extend forward instead of back from the trigger and have a finger ring instead of the traditional loop. These guns typically have the name "ATLAS" cast into the frame, which also has a special shape. The combinations of these features are so distinctive that these models may be identified from quite far away. The Dandy BB gun that appeared in the 1897 Sears mail order catalog had these distinctive features, but is without the Atlas marking. It almost surely was produced by Atlas.

RIFLES

1886 ATLAS BREAK-OPEN REPEATER – .180 cal., BB, BC, SP, brass smoothbore barrel, break-open action, gravity-fed magazine, sheet metal frame and grip frame, wire trigger guard, nickel finish, walnut stock with deep crescent butt, stamped in a circle: "Atlas Gun Company, Pat. Mar. 9, 1886. USE B.B. SHOT. Ilion, New York, Patent applied for", no safety. Circa 1886-1890.

N/A	$1,500	$1,200	$975	$750	$525	$300

1899 VICTOR BREAK-OPEN REPEATER – .180 cal., BB, BC, SP, brass smoothbore barrel, break-open action, gravity-fed magazine, sheet metal frame and grip frame, wire trigger guard, nickel finish, walnut stock with deep crescent butt, stamped "VICTOR", no safety. Circa 1899-1906.

N/A	$1,200	$950	$775	$600	$425	$240

1900 ATLAS LEVER ACTION REPEATER – .180 cal., BB, BC, SP, brass smoothbore barrel, distinctive lever action with ring lever ahead of trigger, gravity-fed magazine, sheet metal barrel sheath, cast iron cocking lever, receiver frame and grip frame, walnut stock with crescent butt, lettering cast into grip frame: "ATLAS", no safety. First version circa 1900-1903.

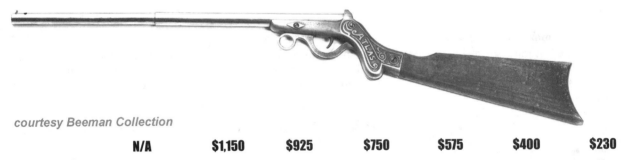

courtesy Beeman Collection

N/A	$1,150	$925	$750	$575	$400	$230

Add 20% for brass frame.
Subtract 20% for last version - simpler frame with Atlas name in script. Circa 1903-1906.

DANDY LEVER ACTION REPEATER – .180 cal. BB, BC, SP, brass smoothbore barrel, distinctive lever action with ring lever ahead of trigger, gravity-fed magazine, sheet metal barrel sheath, cast iron cocking lever, receiver frame and grip frame, walnut stock with crescent butt, no lettering on frame, no safety. Circa 1892.

N/A	$1,150	$925	$750	$575	$400	$230

Sears mail order version (Dandy evidently was a trade name for Sears and other sellers).

NEW DANDY – .180 cal. BB, BC, SP, brass smoothbore barrel, gravity-fed repeater, distinctive lever action with ring lever ahead of trigger, sheet metal barrel sheath, cast iron cocking lever, receiver frame, and grip frame, nickel finish. The only marking is on the RHS of the slab sided stock: "NEW DANDY MODEL 94". 32.2 in. OAL, 2.5 lbs. Mfg. circa 1894.

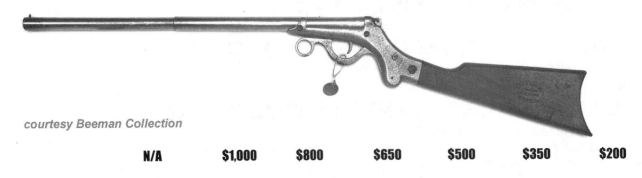

courtesy Beeman Collection

N/A	$1,000	$800	$650	$500	$350	$200

B SECTION

BAM (BEST AIRGUN MANUFACTURER IN CHINA)

Current trademark manufactured by Jiang Su Xin Su Machinery Manufacturing Co. Ltd. located in WuXi, JiangSu Province, China. Currently imported and distributed by Xisico USA, Inc. located in Houston, TX.

GRADING	100%	95%	90%	80%	60%	40%	20%

PISTOLS

XSP180 – .177 or .22 cal., BBC, SP, SS, anatomical polymer frame, 9.1 in. barrel with Picatinny rail under, 500/400 FPS, fixed fiber optic sights, 16.86 in. OAL, 2.5 lbs. Mfg. 2010-current.

MSR $145	$125	$110	$100	$80	$60	N/A	N/A

RIFLES

For current models listed within this section that do not have values, please contact the importer directly for pricing and availability (see Trademark Index).

MODEL B4-4 – .177 cal., UL, SP, 17.7 in. barrel, 40.94 in. OAL, 6.8 lbs. New 2010.

MODEL B19-14 – .177 cal., BBC, SP, 16.53 in. barrel, hardwood stock with pistol grip, adj. trigger, fiber optic sights, manual and auto cocking safety, 42.5 in. OAL, 6.39 lbs. New 2010.

MODEL B19-17 – .177 cal., BBC, SP, 16.53 in. barrel, hardwood thumbhole stock with pistol grip, adj. trigger, fiber optic sights, manual and auto cocking safety, 42.5 in. OAL, 6.39 lbs. New 2010.

MODEL B19-18 – .177 cal., BBC, SP, 16.53 in. barrel, checkered hardwood stock with pistol grip, adj. trigger, fiber optic sights, manual and auto cocking safety, 42.5 in. OAL, 6.39 lbs. New 2010.

MODEL B22 – .177 cal., BBC, SP, High Speed Series, 19.3 in. barrel, hardwood stock with pistol grip, recoil pad with ivory colored spacer, manual safety, 50 in. OAL, approx. 8 lbs. New 2010.

MODEL B22-1 – .177 cal., BBC, SP, High-Speed Series, 19.3 in. barrel, hardwood thumbhole stock with pistol grip, recoil pad with ivory colored spacer, manual safety, 50 in. OAL, approx. 8 lbs. New 2010.

MODEL B30-1 – .177 cal., SL, SP, 17.3 in. barrel, wood stock with pistol grip, recoil pad, manual and auto cocking safety, fiber optic sights, 44.5 in. OAL, 9.25 lbs. New 2010.

MODEL B41 – .177 cal., UL, SP, 13.2 in. barrel, wood stock with pistol grip, adj. trigger, manual safety, 41.3 in. OAL, 8.8 lbs. New 2010.

MODEL KL-3B – .177 or .22 cal., SL, SP, 15.5 in. barrel, 850/650 FPS, black parkerized finish, semi-pistol grip Monte Carlo wood stock with buttplate, hooded front and adj. rear sights, trigger safety, 6.8 lbs. Disc. 2007.

	$60	$50	$40	$35	$25	$20	$10

Last MSR was $70.

MODEL XS-B3-1 – .177 or .22 cal., SL, SP, 15 in. barrel, 540/410 FPS, black finish, metal collapsible buttstock, grooved pistol grip and forearm, hooded front and adj. rear sights, trigger safety, 7.15 lbs. Disc. 2009.

	$60	$50	$40	$35	$25	$20	$10

Last MSR was $70.

MODEL XS-B4-2 – .177 or .22 cal., UL, SP, 17.5 in. barrel, 630/480 FPS, black finish, semi-pistol grip wood stock with buttplate, hooded front and adj. rear sights, sling swivels, trigger safety, 7 lbs. Disc. 2009.

	$45	$40	$30	$25	$20	$15	$10

Last MSR was $50.

MODEL XS-B5-10 – .177 cal., multi-pump pneumatic, 15.3 in. barrel, 10 shot, 500 FPS, black finish, metal collapsible buttstock, pistol grip, hooded front and adj. rear sights, trigger safety, 20-30 in. OAL, 4.4 lbs. Mfg. 2007-2009.

	$100	$85	$70	$60	$45	$30	$20

Last MSR was $120.

MODEL XS-B7 – .177 or .22 cal., SL, SP, 15 in. barrel, 540/410 FPS, black finish, semi-pistol grip wood stock with buttplate, hooded front and adj. rear sights, scope rail, trigger safety, 7 lbs. Disc. 2006.

	$60	$50	$40	$35	$25	$20	$10

MODEL XS-B9-1 – .177 cal., SL, SP, 10 shot mag., 16.5 in. barrel, black polymer forend and pistol grip stock, take down design, black finish bbl., 4x32mm scope, trigger safety, 32 in. OAL, 6.2 lbs. Mfg. 2007-2009.

	$80	$70	$55	$45	$35	$25	$15

Last MSR was $95.

GRADING	100%	95%	90%	80%	60%	40%	20%

MODEL XS-B11 – .177 cal., BBC, SP, 16.38 in. barrel, 590 FPS, black finish, semi-pistol grip Monte Carlo wood stock, hooded front and adj. rear sights, trigger safety, 6 lbs. Mfg. 2006-2009.

	$100	$85	$70	$60	$45	$30	$20

Last MSR was $95.

MODEL XS-12 – .177 or .22 (new 2011) cal., BBC, SP, 16.5 in. barrel, 495/480 FPS, black finish, semi-pistol grip Monte-Carlo wood stock, hooded front and adj. rear sights, trigger safety, 40.5 in. OAL, 5.7 lbs.

MSR $75	$65	$55	$50	$40	$30	N/A	N/A

MODEL XS-B15 – .177 cal., BBC, SP, 14.4 in. barrel, 480 FPS, black finish, semi-pistol grip wood stock with buttplate, hooded front and adj. rear sights, trigger safety, 5.5 lbs. Disc. 2009.

	$80	$70	$55	$45	$35	$25	$15

Last MSR was $75.

MODEL XS-16 – .177 or .22 cal., BBC, SP, 16.5 in. black ABS finish barrel, 660/495 FPS, ambidextrous black ABS hardwood thumbhole pistol grip stock w/Shark-Fin cheek piece, grooved receiver, hooded front and adj. rear fiber optic sights, trigger safety, 40 in. OAL, 4.4 lbs. Mfg. 2009-current.

courtesy Xisico USA, Inc.

MSR $75	$65	$55	$50	$40	$30	N/A	N/A

MODEL XS-B18 – .177 or .22 cal., BBC, SP, 16.38 in. barrel, 850/650 FPS, black parkerized finish, semi-pistol grip Monte Carlo wood stock with buttplate, hooded front and adj. rear sights, trigger safety, 6.9 lbs. Disc. 2006.

	$90	$75	$65	$50	$40	$25	$20

MODEL XS-B20 – .177 cal., BBC, SP, 16 in. barrel, 930 FPS, blue finish, semi-pistol grip Monte Carlo wood stock with recoil pad, hooded front and adj. rear sights, Rekord trigger and auto-safety, 7.26 lbs. Disc. 2006.

	$135	$115	$95	$80	$60	$40	$25

MODEL XS-B21 – .177 or .22 cal., SL, SP, 19.5 in. barrel, 950/715 FPS, blue finish, semi-pistol grip Monte Carlo wood stock with recoil pad, adj. hooded front and adj. rear sights, double automatic trigger safety, 9.68 lbs.

MSR $175	$155	$135	$120	$100	$75	N/A	N/A

MODEL XS-25 – .177 or .22 cal., BBC, SP, 18.7 in. barrel, 1000/820 FPS, adj. trigger, black finish, sporter style PG hardwood stock, grooved receiver, adj. rear fiber optic sights, auto safety, 44.7 in. OAL, 7.3 lbs. Mfg. 2009-current.

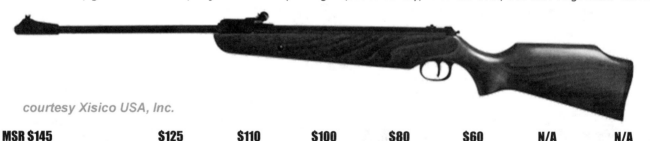

courtesy Xisico USA, Inc.

MSR $145	$125	$110	$100	$80	$60	N/A	N/A

* **Model XS-25S** – .177 or .22 cal., BBC, SP, 18.7 in. barrel, 1000/820 FPS, adj. trigger, black finish, sporter style PG synthetic stock, grooved receiver, adj. rear fiber optic sights, auto safety, 44.7 in. OAL, 7.3 lbs. Mfg. 2009-current.

courtesy Xisico USA, Inc.

MSR $145	$125	$110	$100	$80	$60	N/A	N/A

GRADING	100%	95%	90%	80%	60%	40%	20%

* **Model XS-25SF** – .177 or .22 cal., BBC, SP, upgraded sniper version of the XS-25, 18.7 in. barrel w/metal muzzle brake, 1000/820 FPS, adj. trigger, black finish, ambidextrous hardwood thumbhole pistol grip stock w/Shark-Fin cheek piece and vent. recoil pad, grooved receiver, auto safety, 45.1 in. OAL, 7.7 lbs. Mfg. 2009-current.

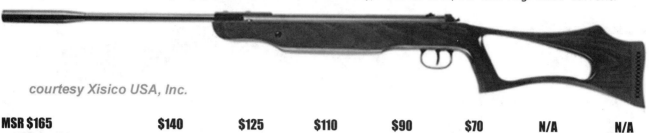

courtesy Xisico USA, Inc.

MSR $165	$140	$125	$110	$90	$70	N/A	N/A

* **Model XS-25SFB** – .177 or .22 cal., BBC, SP, upgraded sniper version of the XS-25, 18.7 in. barrel w/metal muzzle brake, 1000/820 FPS, adj. trigger, black finish, ambidextrous bamboo thumbhole pistol grip stock w/Shark-Fin cheek piece and vent. recoil pad, grooved receiver, auto safety, 45.1 in. OAL, 7.7 lbs. Mfg. 2009-current.

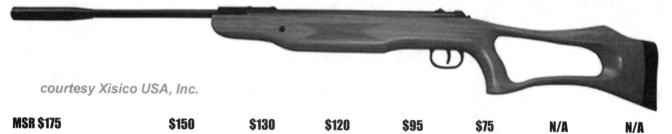

courtesy Xisico USA, Inc.

MSR $175	$150	$130	$120	$95	$75	N/A	N/A

MODEL XS-B26 – .177 cal., BBC, SP, 16 in. barrel, 880-1000 FPS, blue finish, semi-pistol grip Monte Carlo wood stock with recoil pad, hooded front and adj. rear sights, adj. trigger, auto-safety, 43 in. OAL, 7.3 lbs. Mfg. 2006-2009.

courtesy Xisico USA, Inc.

	$150	$130	$105	$85	$70	$45	$30

Last MSR was $175.

* **Model XS-B26-2** – .177 cal., BBC, SP, 16 in. barrel, 880-1000 FPS, blue finish, thumbhole hardwood stock with recoil pad, hooded front and adj. rear sights, adj. trigger and auto-safety, 43 in. OAL, 7.3 lbs. Mfg. 2006-2009.

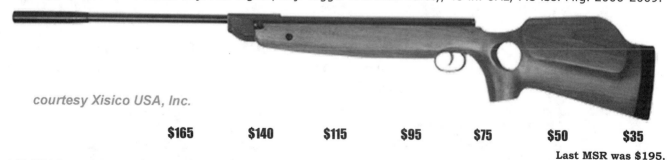

courtesy Xisico USA, Inc.

	$165	$140	$115	$95	$75	$50	$35

Last MSR was $195.

Add 25% for 4x32 AO Scope (Model XB-26-2C).

MODEL XS-26 – .177 or .22 cal., BBC, SP, 1000/820 FPS, based on the Legendary Beeman R9, 17.9 in. barrel, equipped with repeatable safety and a Rekord trigger, 44.9 in. OAL, 7.7 lbs. New 2012.

GRADING	100%	95%	90%	80%	60%	40%	20%

MODEL XS-28M – .177, .22, or .25 cal., BBC, 19.5 in. barrel, 1200/1000/720 FPS, Monte Carlo hardwood stock, raised cheek piece, checkering on grip and forearm, fixed front and adj. rear sights, grooved receiver, rubber recoil pad, 48 in. OAL, 8 lbs.

courtesy Xisico USA, Inc.

MODEL XS-B28 – .177 cal., BBC, SP, 19.5 in. barrel, 1000-1250 FPS, blue finish, semi-pistol grip Monte Carlo wood stock with recoil pad, hooded front and adj. rear sights, adj. trigger, auto-safety, 48 in. OAL, 8 lbs. New 2007.

	100%	95%	90%	80%	60%	40%	20%
MSR $195	$165	$145	$135	$105	$80	N/A	N/A

MODEL XS-B30 – .177 or .22 cal., SL, SP, 17.3 in. barrel, 1100/900 FPS, blue finish, semi-pistol grip Monte Carlo wood stock with recoil pad, adj. trigger, adj. hooded front and rear sights, double automatic trigger safety, 44.5 in. OAL, 9.4 lbs. Mfg. 2005-2010.

	100%	95%	90%	80%	60%	40%	20%
	$175	$150	$125	$100	$80	$50	$35

Last MSR was $195.

MODEL XS-B33 – .177 or .22 cal., SL, SP, SS, blue finish, semi-pistol grip stock, adj. trigger, adj. hooded front and adj. rear sights, automatic trigger safety. Mfg. 2008-2009.

	100%	95%	90%	80%	60%	40%	20%
	$110	$95	$75	$65	$50	$35	$20

Last MSR was $130.

MODEL XS-B40 – .177 or .22 cal., UL, SP, 14.1 in. barrel, 1050/850 FPS, black finish, adj. trigger, Monte Carlo semi-pistol grip wood stock with recoil pad, hooded front and adj. rear sights, sling swivels, trigger safety, 41.3 in. OAL, 9.3 lbs. Mfg. 2005-2010.

	100%	95%	90%	80%	60%	40%	20%
	$260	$220	$180	$150	$115	$80	$50

Last MSR was $305.

MODEL XS-46U – .177 or .22 cal., UL, SP, SS, 18.9 in. barrel, 1000/820 FPS, black finish, adj. trigger, Monte Carlo pistol grip wood stock with recoil pad, adj. rear fiber optic sights, sling swivels, trigger safety, 44.8 in. OAL, 8.6 lbs. Mfg. 2010-current.

courtesy Xisico USA, Inc.

	100%	95%	90%	80%	60%	40%	20%
MSR $230	$195	$175	$155	$125	$95	N/A	N/A

MODEL XS-B50 – .177 or .22 cal., PCP, 18.5 in. barrel, 1000 FPS, blue finish, semi-pistol grip or thumbhole Monte Carlo wood stock with recoil pad, manual safety. New 2003.

courtesy Xisico USA, Inc.

	100%	95%	90%	80%	60%	40%	20%
MSR $375	$325	$280	$255	$205	$160	N/A	N/A

Add $20 for .22 cal.

GRADING	100%	95%	90%	80%	60%	40%	20%

MODEL XS-B51 – .177 or .22 cal., PCP, 18.5 in. barrel, 1000 FPS, blue finish, thumbhole Monte Carlo wood stock with recoil pad, manual safety. New 2005.

courtesy Xisico USA, Inc.

MSR $425	$350	$325	$290	$235	$180	N/A	N/A

Add $25 for .22 cal.

MODEL XS-60C – .177 or .22 cal., CO$_2$, BA, SS, two 12 gram CO$_2$ cartridges or bulk fill, 21.4 in. barrel, 650/495 FPS, black finish, semi-pistol grip wood stock with rubber recoil pad, adj. rear fiber optic sights, 39.6 in. OAL, 5.3 lbs. Mfg. 2010-current.

courtesy Xisico USA, Inc.

MSR $120	$100	$90	$80	$65	$50	N/A	N/A

BBM

For information on BBM air pistols, see Steiner in the "S" section.

BRNO

See Aeron CZ s.r.o. listing in the "A" section.

BSA GUNS (U.K.), LTD.

Current manufacturer located in Birmingham, England. BSA Guns (UK), Ltd. was previously known as "The Birmingham Small Arms Co. Ltd." and "BSA GUNS Ltd." founded in 1861 in Birmingham, England. The original factory was destroyed by bombing during the period of August to November 1940. As a result they moved the operations to Marshall Lake Road, Shirley, Warwickshire from 1942 to 1964. From 1964 to 1967 it was located at Redditch, Worcestershire. In 1967 the factory was moved to its present address, Armory Road, Small Heath, Birmingham. Presently owned by Gamo of Spain. Currently imported/distributed by BSA GUNS USA (A division of Gamo Outdoor USA, Inc.) located in Ft. Lauderdale, FL. Previously imported by Precision Airgun Distribution/Airguns of Arizona located in Gilbert, AZ, Compasseco, Inc. located in Bardstown, KY, Precision Sales, located in Westfield, MA (1995-2002), Dynamit-Nobel/RWS, Ithaca Gun Co. (1975-1979), Marksman, Savage Arms, and others.

For information and current pricing on both new and used BSA firearms, please refer to the *Blue Book of Gun Values* by S.P. Fjestad (also available online).

For additional information on the origin of Lincoln Jeffries and BSA underlever air rifles, see "Lincoln" in the "L" section of this text.

BSA also manufactured firearms: military, sporting, and target rifles and shotguns. These are discussed in *The Golden Century* by John Knibbs.

BSA BACKGROUND

The history of BSA air rifles is based on the patents and the early marketing of airguns by Lincoln Jeffries. Therefore, reading the introduction to the Lincoln section of this book is a prerequisite to reading this section. The serious study of BSA airguns absolutely requires reference to the BSA books by John Knibbs. The authors and publisher wish to thank John Groenewold and John Knibbs for their assistance with the following information for this section of the *Blue Book of Airguns*.

The Lincoln Jeffries underlever air rifle made by BSA proved so successful that by 1906 BSA had begun marketing them under their own name and in several different models. The air rifles commonly referred to as "Lincoln Jeffries," "Lincoln patent," "Lincoln," "H," and "Light" models are actually stamped "H The Lincoln Air Rifle" or "L The Lincoln Air Rifle" and should be easy to identify. See Lincoln in the "L" section of this guide.

The bayonet type underlever cocking handle was the original Lincoln Jeffries design. The front end of this lever had a small handle, or "bayonet" dropping down from, but parallel to, the barrel. Original bayonet underlevers had a bend where they engaged the latch mechanism. Later ones were strengthened by additional metal bracing ("fillets or fences") on the sides of the bend area. The bayonet underlever was replaced by the much more reliable and less obtrusive side button underlever in 1911. Beginning in 1919, BSA started to replace side button underlevers with front button underlevers. Old-style underlevers were sometimes replaced with newer versions during repairs and modifications, and this may confuse present identification.

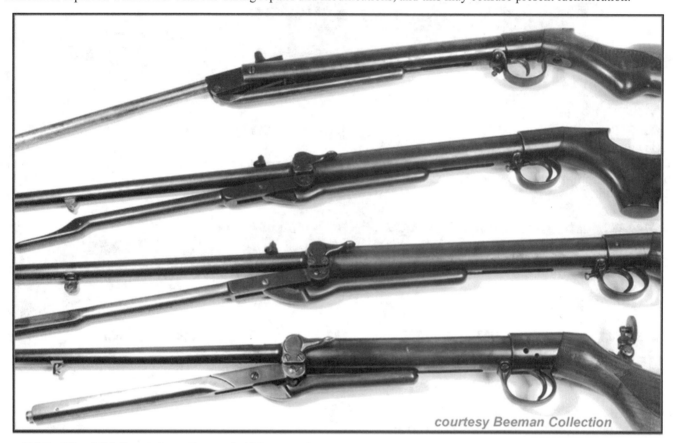

courtesy Beeman Collection

TOP: *"The BSA Breakdown Pattern" .177 cal., mfg. 1933-39.*
SECOND: *"The BSA Air Rifle Improved Model D", 2nd pattern showing cocking lever with side fences mfg. 1908-1921.*
THIRD: *"The BSA Air Rifle Standard Pattern" showing side button catch mfg. 1912-1914.*
BOTTOM: *"The BSA Standard Air Rifle" mfg. 1919-1939.*

BSA MODEL IDENTIFICATION

Although well-designed and well-built, the early BSA air guns can be difficult to identify. Early practice at the factory was to use up existing old parts wherever possible on new models. Hence numerous variations exist. Several duplicate names for different models of different sizes and configurations also exist.

The designations of Improved Model B and Improved Model D bring up the question: "Where are the Models A through D?" A great deal of study seems to rather conclusively show that there never were any such models, except perhaps as developmental steps in the minds and long-lost notes of BSA airgun designers. The existing models certainly represent improvements over developmental steps that never came into production. Furthermore, the BSA designers made additional improvements in their "Improved Models" B and D, without changing the public designations. They probably did this with the idea that they were avoiding confusion, but the result was that vendors, customers, and repair shops could not be sure of what parts they were ordering or what would be shipped to them. This type of confusion continued until new models were produced after WWII.

Serial numbers and their prefixes are very important as they designate the model variation of the gun, date of manufacture, sear mechanism, and/or the caliber. In mid-1914 BSA started to mark new air cylinders by photo etching. However, some air rifles were assembled from parts with stamped lettering long after that date. The photoetching process was not perfected then. Many guns which originally had photoetched markings now appear unmarked because the etching has been worn off or buffed off during refinishing. Additionally, many different models were assembled using old parts from stock; thus there are considerable variations, even within a single model. The serial number and its prefix generally will allow cross-referencing to factory records and published lists, but often caliber and physical measurements must also considered. Specimens may be up to almost 100 years old; many have been repaired or modified with parts that may not even resemble the original parts. Using the

GRADING	100%	95%	90%	80%	60%	40%	20%

information given here and some ingenuity, it should be possible to fairly well identify most BSA airguns. For serial number lists, production information, and a great deal of additional detail, one must consult the BSA references by John Knibbs. (His book sales partner in the USA is JG Airguns LLC.)

BSA MARKINGS

BSA airguns made prior to 1939 were marked with a single-digit "bore" size. These are not to be confused with model numbers. The bore size usually is marked on top of the gun near the piled arms symbol and loading port. Number 1 bore is .177 in. (4.5 mm). Number 2 is referred to as .22 in. (5.5 mm) but is actually 5.6 mm. Conventional 5.5 mm German and American .22 inch caliber pellets generally would not give optimal performance in Number 2 bore airguns. In the 1980s, Beeman Precision Airguns, then Webley's exclusive agent in the large USA market, insisted that Webley standardize their ".22 or No. 2 bores" to fit the German .22 in./5.5 mm precision pellets. Webley complied and BSA quietly followed suit soon after. Number 3 bore is .25 in. cal. (6.35 mm).

PISTOLS

240 MAGNUM – .177 or .22 cal., TL, SP, SS, 510/420 FPS, 6 in. barrel, two-stage adj. trigger, adj. rear sight, sights separate from barrel on up-swinging top receiver unit, integral scope rail, one-piece walnut grip, automatic safety, 9 in. OAL, 2 lbs. Mfg. 1994-2000.

courtesy Tim Saunders

$275	$235	$195	$160	$125	$80	$55

Last MSR was $259.

SCORPION – .177 or .22 cal., BBC, SP, SS, 7.9 in barrel, 510/380 FPS, automatic safety, 15.3 in. OAL, 3.4 lbs. Mfg. 1973-1993.

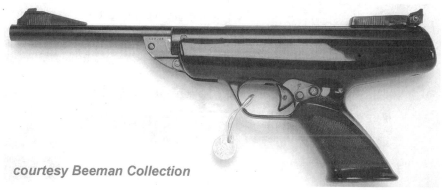

courtesy Beeman Collection

* **Scorpion MK I** – KEMATEL sights. Mfg. 1973-1977.

$235	$200	$165	$135	$105	$70	$45

Add 25% if boxed with all accessories.
Subtract 10% for missing cocking aid.
   Serial number codes; "P" for .177 cal. and "R" for .22 cal.

* **Scorpion MK II** – integral scope grooves, steel and plastic sights. Mfg. 1977-1993.

$265	$225	$185	$155	$120	$80	$55

Last MSR was $190.

Add 25% if boxed with all accessories.
Subtract 10% for missing cocking aid.
   Serial number prefix codes; "P" or "PB" for .177 cal. and "R" or "RB" for .22 cal. "B" was added to indicate shorter (less power) mainspring.

GRADING	100%	95%	90%	80%	60%	40%	20%

RIFLES: BARREL COCKING

Subtract 20% for specimens equipped with gas-spring unit (sometimes inappropriately called "gas ram" or "gas strut"). Such modification makes the gun non-original, voids the manufacturer's warranty, and may cause cumulative damage to the gun. Length measurements may vary by about 0.25 in. or so within models.

BREAKDOWN PATTERN – .177 cal., BBC, SP, SS, 18.5 in. barrel, marked "Breakdown Pattern", 41.5 in. OAL. Mfg. 1933-1939.

	N/A	$350	$280	$230	$175	$125	$70

This model is BSA's first barrel cocking air rifle. There was no serial number prefix from 1933 to 1936, a "B" prefix was used after 1936.

BUCCANEER – .177 or .22 cal., BBC, SP, SS, 18.5 in. rifled barrel, marked "BUCCANEER" on top of compression tube, black, brown, or camouflage composite thumbhole stock, integral scope grooves, steel and plastic sights, 35.5 in. OAL. Mfg. 1977-1983.

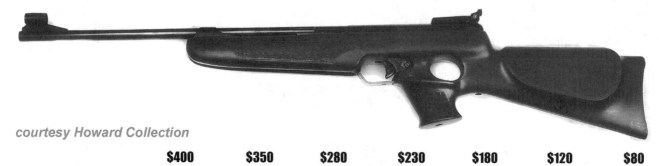

courtesy Howard Collection

	$400	$350	$280	$230	$180	$120	$80

Add 25% if boxed with all accessories.

CADET – .177 cal., BBC, SP, SS, rifled or smooth bore barrel, blue finish, 37.5 in. OAL, 4.75 lbs. Mfg. 1946-1959.

	$200	$170	$140	$115	$90	$60	$40

This model was manufactured for various export markets with "S.B." serial number suffix.

* **Cadet Major** – .177 cal., BBC, SP, SS, rifled or smooth bore barrel, blue finish, 42 in. OAL, 5.5 lbs. Mfg. 1947-1959.

	$200	$170	$140	$115	$90	$60	$40

This model was manufactured for various export markets with "S.B." serial number suffix.

COMET – .177 or .22 cal., BBC, SP, SS, 17.5 in. rifled barrel, blue finish, 825-570 FPS, adj. bridge style rear and fixed front sights (disc.) or fiber optic adj. sights (new 2012), scope grooves, anti-bear trap device, manual safety, black synthetic ambidextrous stock with vent. rubber buttpad and textured non-slip grip panels, checkered pistol grip and forend, two-stage adj. trigger, raised cheek pad, dovetails in cylinder, ABT safety system (disc.), 42.5 in. OAL, 5.9 lbs. Mfg. 2007-Disc. Re-introduced 2012.

courtesy BSA GUNS

MSR $400	$350	$295	$240	$200	$155	$105	$70

GRT LIGHTNING SE – .177, .22, or .25 cal., BBC, powered by a gas ram (GRT - gas ram technology) filled with pressurized nitrogen for consistent power, 1000/722/623 FPS, 14.5 in. steel carbine barrel, new ambidextrous beech stock with checkered pistol grip and forend, redesigned trigger mechanism, volumetric silencer and Maxi-Grip scope rail with recoil absorption system, vent. rubber buttpad, 38 in. OAL, 7 lbs. New 2012.

MSR $480	$400	$350	$325	$265	$200	N/A	N/A

GRT LIGHTNING XL SE – .177, .22, or .25 cal., BBC, powered by a gas ram (GRT - gas ram technology) filled with pressurized nitrogen for consistent power, 1000/722/623 FPS, 14.5 in. steel carbine barrel, new ambidextrous beech

GRADING	100%	95%	90%	80%	60%	40%	20%

or Grade 1 walnut stock with checkered pistol grip and forend, redesigned trigger mechanism, slim-line silencer and Maxi-Grip scope rail with recoil absorption system, vent. rubber buttpad, 38 in. OAL, 7 lbs. New 2012.

courtesy BSA GUNS

MSR $480	$400	$350	$325	$265	$200	N/A	N/A

GRT SUPERSPORT SE – .177, .22, or .25 cal., BBC, powered by a gas ram (GRT - gas ram technology) filled with pressurized nitrogen for consistent power, 1000/722/623 FPS, 18.5 in. steel barrel, new ambidextrous beech stock with checkered pistol grip and forend, redesigned trigger mechanism, adj. open sights, full length scope rail, vent. rubber buttpad, 43 in. OAL, 7 lbs. New 2012.

courtesy BSA GUNS

MSR $325	$275	$245	$220	$180	$135	N/A	N/A

LIGHTNING – .177 or .22 cal., BBC, SP, SS, 10 (British version) or 15 in. rifled barrel, blue finish, variation of the Supersport, 39.5 in. with Volumetric sound moderator or 33 in. w/o Volumetric sound moderator OAL, 6.1 lbs. Mfg. 1997-2007.

courtesy Precision Airgun Distribution

	$525	$425	$350	$300	$230	$155	$105

Last MSR was $540.

The British version with 10 in. barrel and BSA Volumetric sound moderator requires a $200 federal transfer tax in USA.

* ***Lightning XL*** – .177, .22, or .25 cal., BBC, SP, SS, 1000/730/700 FPS, 10 (British version) or 15 in. rifled steel barrel, blue finish, redesigned ambidextrous beech stock and adj. two-stage trigger, full barrel noise dampener, 37.5 in. OAL, 6.6 lbs. Mfg. 2005-current.

courtesy BSA GUNS

MSR N/A	$475	$400	$325	$280	$215	$145	$95

GRADING	100%	95%	90%	80%	60%	40%	20%

LIGHTNING SE – .177 or .22 cal., BBC, 1000/722 FPS, newly designed ambidextrous beech stock and completely redesigned trigger, 14.5 in. carbine barrel, checkered pistol grip and forend, volumetric silencer, full specification Maxi-Grip scope rail with recoil absorption system, no sights, vent. buttpad, two-stage adj. trigger, internally weighted, steel mainspring, 38 in. OAL, 7 lbs. New 2012.

MSR $400	$350	$300	$270	$220	$170	N/A	N/A

LIGHTNING XL SE – .177, .22, or .25 cal., BBC, 1000/722/623 FPS, ambidextrous deluxe beech or grade 1 oil-finished walnut stock, completely redesigned action, 14.5 in. carbine barrel, checkered pistol grip and forend, volumetric silencer, full specification Maxi-Grip scope rail with recoil absorption system, no sights, vent. buttpad, two-stage adj. trigger, internally weighted, steel mainspring, 38 in. OAL, 7 lbs. New 2012.

courtesy BSA GUNS

MSR $400	$350	$300	$270	$220	$170	N/A	N/A

MERCURY – .177 or .22 cal., BBC, SP, SS, 18.5 in. rifled barrel, blue finish, 700/550 FPS, serial number prefixes "W" and "Z," adj. rear and globe front sights, 43.5 in. OAL, 7.25 lbs. Mfg. 1972-1980.

courtesy Beeman Collection

	$180	$155	$125	$105	$80	$55	$35

* **Mercury S** – .177 or .22 cal., BBC, SP, SS, 18.5 in. rifled thicker barrel, blue finish, 825/600 FPS, adj. rear and globe front sights, oil finished and checkered walnut stock, 44.5 in. OAL, 7.25 lbs. Mfg. 1980-Disc.

	$230	$195	$160	$135	$105	$70	$45

MERCURY CHALLENGER – .177 or .22 cal., BBC, SP, SS, 850/625 FPS, 18.5 in. rifled barrel, blue finish, adj. rear and globe front sights, Maxi-Grip scope rail, redesigned stock, 43.5 in. OAL, 7.25 lbs. Mfg. 1983-1997.

	$250	$215	$175	$145	$115	$75	$50

Last MSR was $205.

MERCURY TARGET – .177 cal., BBC, SP, SS, 700 FPS, 18.5 in. rifled barrel, blue finish, ramp on trigger block for Anschutz aperture target rear sight, tunnel front sight, 43.5 in. OAL, 7.25 lbs. Approx. 2,000 mfg. 1975.

	$375	$325	$265	$220	$170	$110	$75

MERLIN MK I – .177 or .22 cal., BBC, SP, SS, 14.25 in. rifled barrel, blue finish, plastic pellet loading block, 36 in. OAL, 3.5 lbs. Mfg. 1962-1964.

	$250	$215	$175	$145	$115	$75	$50

* **Merlin MK II** – .177 or .22 cal., BBC, SP, SS, 14.25 in. rifled barrel, blue finish, metal pellet loading block, anti-bear trap device, 36 in. OAL, 3.5 lbs. Mfg. 1964-1968.

	$250	$215	$175	$145	$115	$75	$50

METEOR – .177 or .22 cal., BBC, SP, SS, 650/550 FPS, 18.5 in. rifled or smoothbore barrel, blue finish, adj. rear and fixed front sights, 6 lbs. New 1959.

* **Meteor MK I** – .177 or .22 cal., BBC, SP, SS, 650/500 FPS, 18 in. rifled or smoothbore barrel, blue finish, adj. rear and fixed front sights, 41 in. OAL, 5.25 lbs. Mfg. 1959-1962.

	$180	$155	$125	$105	$80	$55	$35

GRADING	100%	95%	90%	80%	60%	40%	20%

* ***Meteor MK II*** – .177 or .22 cal., BBC, SP, SS, 650/500 FPS, 18 in. rifled or smoothbore barrel, blue finish, more streamlined appearance, improved adj. rear and fixed front sights, first use of plastic rear body tube cap, 41 in. OAL, 5.25 lbs. Mfg. 1962-1968.

	$180	$155	$125	$105	$80	$55	$35

* ***Meteor MK III*** – .177 or .22 cal., BBC, SP, SS, 650/500 FPS, 18 in. rifled or smoothbore barrel, blue finish, more robust stock with squared-off forearm, adj. rear and fixed front sights, 41 in. OAL, 6 lbs. Mfg. 1969-1973.

	$180	$155	$125	$105	$80	$55	$35

* ***Meteor MK IV*** – .177 or .22 cal., BBC, SP, SS, 650/500 FPS, 18.5 in. rifled barrel, blue finish, adj. bridge style and fixed front sights, 41 in. OAL, 6 lbs. Mfg. 1973-1977.

	$180	$155	$125	$105	$80	$55	$35

* ***Meteor MK V*** – .177 or .22 cal., BBC, SP, SS, 650/500 FPS, 18.5 in. rifled barrel, blue finish, adj. bridge style and fixed front sights, 41 in. OAL, 6 lbs. Mfg. 1977-1994.

	$180	$155	$125	$105	$80	$55	$35

* ***Meteor MK 6*** – .177 or .22 cal., BBC, SP, SS, 760/580 FPS, 17.5 in. rifled barrel, blue finish, adj. trigger, adj. bridge style and fixed front sights, scope grooves, anti-bear trap device, manual safety, rubber buttpad, 42 in. OAL, 7.5 lbs. Mfg. 1993-2007.

courtesy BSA GUNS

	$325	$270	$225	$185	$145	$95	$65

Last MSR was $350.

» **Meteor MK 6 Carbine** – .177 or .22 cal., BBC, SP, SS, 760/580 FPS, 15 in. rifled barrel, blue finish, adj. trigger, adj. bridge style and fixed front sights, scope grooves, anti-bear trap device, manual safety, rubber buttpad, 39 in. OAL, 5.7 lbs. Mfg. 1993-2007.

	$350	$300	$245	$205	$160	$105	$70

Last MSR was $375.

Meteor MK 7 – .177 or .22 cal., BBC, SP, 825/570 FPS, 18.5 in. steel rifled barrel, fully checkered solid beech stock with vent. rubber recoil pad, two-stage adj. trigger, fiber optic adj. open sights, standard cheek pad, ABT Safety System, 43 in. OAL, 6.2 lbs. New 2010.

courtesy BSA GUNS

MSR $200	$170	$150	$135	$110	$85	N/A	N/A

* ***Meteor Super*** – .177 or .22 cal., BBC, SP, SS, 650/500 FPS, 19 in. rifled or smoothbore barrel, blue finish, Monte Carlo stock, adj. rear and fixed front sights, vent. recoil pad, 41 in. OAL, 6 lbs. Mfg. 1967-1973.

	$210	$180	$145	$120	$95	$65	$40

MODEL 635 MAGNUM – .25 cal., BBC, SP, SS, 850/625 FPS, rifled barrel, blue finish, 7.25 lbs.

	$300	$255	$210	$175	$135	$90	$60

GRADING	100%	95%	90%	80%	60%	40%	20%

POLARIS – .177 or .22 cal., BBC, SP, 1000/772 FPS, steel rifled fixed barrel with underlever, ambidextrous beechwood stock, raised cheek pad, vent. rubber recoil pad, checkered pistol grip, two-stage adj. trigger, fiber optic adj. sights, rotating breech, 45.6 in. OAL, 6.6 lbs. New 2009.

courtesy BSA GUNS

MSR $450	$375	$325	$270	$225	$175	$115	$75

SHADOW – .177 or .22 cal., BBC, SP, SS, rifled barrel, blue finish, black, brown, or camouflage (Trooper) thumbhole composite stock, marked "SHADOW" on compression tube, cocking aid, 27 in. OAL. Mfg. 1985-1986.

	$450	$375	$325	$260	$205	$135	$90

Add 25% if boxed with all accessories.

Add 25% for Trooper model.

SUPERSPORT – .177, .22, or .25 cal., BBC, SP, SS, 850/625/530 FPS, 18 in. rifled barrel, blue finish, Monte Carlo stock with vent. recoil pad, anti-bear trap, manual safety, 41 in. OAL, 6.6 lbs. New 1986.

* **Supersport America** – .177, .22, or .25 cal., BBC, SP, black finish, 850/625/530 FPS, black Monte Carlo composite stock with vent. recoil pad.

	$250	$215	$175	$145	$115	$75	$50

* **Supersport Custom** – .177 or .22 cal., BBC, SP, SS, 990/665 FPS, 18.5 in. rifled heavy barrel, blue finish, rotating breech for loading pellets, large diameter air cylinder, nylon parachute piston seal, checkered walnut stock with cheek piece and vent. recoil pad, Maxi-Grip sight rail, adj. metal two stage trigger, manual safety on RHS, 43.8 in. OAL, 7.8 lbs. Mfg. 1987-1992.

	$500	$425	$350	$290	$225	$150	$100

* **Supersport MK I** – .177, .22, or .25 cal., BBC, SP, rifled barrel, blue finish, 850/625/530 FPS. Mfg. 1986-1987.

	$230	$195	$160	$135	$105	$70	$45

Last MSR was $279.

* **Supersport MK I Carbine** – .177, .22, or .25 cal., BBC, SP, 14 in. rifled barrel, blue finish, 850/625/530 FPS. Mfg. 1986-1987.

	$255	$215	$180	$150	$115	$75	$50

Last MSR was $279.

* **Supersport MK2 E/E (Magnum)** – .177, .22, or .25 (disc.) cal., BBC, SP, 18.5 in. rifled barrel, blue finish, 950/750/600 FPS, 42 in. OAL, approx. 6.6 lbs. Mfg. 1987-2007.

	$400	$350	$285	$235	$180	$120	$80

Last MSR was $428.

* **Supersport MK2 SS Carbine E/E** – .177, .22 or .25 cal., BBC, SP, SS, 950/750/650 FPS, 15.5 in. barrel, 39 in. OAL, 6.2 lbs. Mfg. 1987-2007.

	$400	$350	$285	$235	$180	$120	$80

Last MSR was $428.

* **Supersport XL** – .177, .22, or .25 cal., BBC, SP, 18.5 in. rifled steel barrel, 900/650/600 FPS, adj. rear and ramp front sights, grooved for scope mounting, blue finish, adj. two-stage trigger, checkered hardwood Monte Carlo style

courtesy BSA GUNS

GRADING	100%	95%	90%	80%	60%	40%	20%

beech or Grade 1 oil finished walnut stock with rubber recoil pad, 42 in. OAL, approx. 6.6 lbs. Mfg. 2007-current.

MSR $300	$255	$225	$205	$165	$125	N/A	N/A

SUPERSPORT SE – .177 or .22 cal., BBC, SP, 1000/722 FPS, 18.5 in. steel barrel, newly styled ambidextrous beech stock, checkered pistol grip and forend, vent. rubber buttpad, two-stage adj. trigger, adj. sights, full length rail, internally weighted and powered by a high performance mainspring, optional scope arrestor block, manual safety, dovetails in cylinder for scope mounting, 43 in. OAL, 7 lbs. New 2012.

courtesy BSA GUNS

MSR $400	$350	$295	$240	$200	$155	$105	$70

SUPERSPORT TACTICAL – .177 or .22 cal., BBC, SP, SS, 1000/730 FPS, 18.5 in. rifled steel barrel, grey synthetic weatherproof stock, adj. two-stage trigger, checkered pistol grip and forend, vent. rubber recoil pad, raised cheek pad, fully adj. open sights, full length scope mounting grooves, optional scope arrestor block, 42 in. OAL, 6.6 lbs.

courtesy BSA GUNS

MSR $400	$350	$300	$270	$220	$170	N/A	N/A

XL TACTICAL – .177, .22, or .25 cal., BBC, SP, SS, 1000/730/700 FPS, 14.5 in. rifled steel barrel, blue finish, all-weather black synthetic stock and adj. two-stage trigger, high impact polymer compound stock is always warm to the touch, provides secure grip and remains warp-free in all climate conditions, full barrel noise dampener, vent. rubber recoil pad, raised cheek pad, rubber cushioned, anti-shock sight mounting rail, 37.5 in. OAL, 6.6 lbs. Mfg. 2007-current.

courtesy BSA GUNS

	$479	$425	$350	$295	$225	$150	$100

RIFLES: MODIFIED REAR/UNDER LEVER COCKING

See also Lincoln in the "L" section of this book for the Lincoln underlever rifles from which BSA underlever air rifles were developed.

Subtract 20% for specimens equipped with gas-spring unit (sometimes inappropriately called "gas ram" or "gas strut"). Such modification makes the gun non-original, voids the manufacturer's warranty and may cause cumulative damage to the gun. Length measurements may vary by about 0.25 in. or so within models.

AIRSPORTER – .177, .22, or .25 cal., UL, SP, SS, 1020/800/550 FPS, tap loader, tapered breech plug, blued finish, 8 lbs.

courtesy Beeman Collection

Carbine versions with 14 in. barrels do not bring a premium.

This model was the first underlever to have a cocking lever hidden in the forearm.

GRADING	100%	95%	90%	80%	60%	40%	20%

* ***Airsporter Club*** − .177 cal. only, 7.5 lbs. Mfg. 1948-1959.

	100%	95%	90%	80%	60%	40%	20%
	$300	$255	$210	$175	$135	$90	$60

* ***Airsporter MK I*** − .177 or .22 cal. Mfg. 1948-1959.

	$300	$255	$210	$175	$135	$90	$60

* ***Airsporter MK II*** − .177 or .22 cal. Mfg. 1959-1965.

	$300	$255	$210	$175	$135	$90	$60

* ***Airsporter MK III*** − .177 or .22 cal.. Mfg. began in 1965. Disc.

	$300	$255	$210	$175	$135	$90	$60

This model has serial number prefixes "EF", "EG", and "GE.

* ***Airsporter MK VII*** − .177 or .22 cal. Disc. 2001.

	$300	$255	$210	$175	$135	$90	$60

Last MSR was $375.

* ***Airsporter RB2 Magnum*** − .177, .22 or .25 cal., rotary breech replaced tap loading breech, 18 in. rifled barrel, 8.5 lbs. Mfg. 1991-2000.

	$300	$255	$210	$175	$135	$90	$60

Last MSR was $450.

Add 25% for Crown Grade RB2 with laminated wood stock.

» ***Airsporter RB2 Magnum Carbine*** − .177, .22 or .25 cal., rotary breech replaced tap loading breech, 18 in. rifled barrel, 8.5 lbs. Mfg. 1991-2000.

	$300	$255	$210	$175	$135	$90	$60

Last MSR was $450.

Add 25% for Crown Grade RB2 with laminated wood stock.

* ***Airsporter RB2 Stutzen*** − .177, .22 or .25 cal., mfg. began in 1992. Disc.

	$350	$300	$250	$210	$160	$110	$70

* ***Airsporter S*** − .177 or .22 cal., oil finish, checkered walnut stock, heavier barrel, 0.5 inch longer. Mfg. began in 1979. Disc.

	$350	$295	$250	$210	$160	$110	$70

* ***Airsporter Stutzen*** − .177 or .22 cal., full length stock. Mfg. 1985-1992.

	$350	$300	$250	$210	$160	$110	$70

Last MSR was $540.

AIRSPORTER S CENTENARY (COMMEMORATIVE) − .177 or .22 cal., SP, UL, SS, tap marked "BSA Piled Arms Centenary 1982 - One of One Thousand" on top of air chamber, blue finish, three-quarter length Stutzen-style checkered walnut stock with Schnabel forend (cocking lever contained in forend) and PG cap with trademark, Mk. X 4x40mm scope, QD sling swivels and leather sling, shooting kit, BSA patch, BSA gun case, and certificate numbered to rifle. Mfg. 1982 only.

	$1,000	$850	$700	$575	$450	$300	$200

Last MSR was $650.

Add 10% for gun case, accessories, and all literature.

Mfg. in 1982 to commemorate 100 years of BSA "Piled Arms" symbol (three Martini Henry .577 SS rifles stacked in military fashion).

BSA AIR RIFLE − .177 cal., UL (bayonet style), SP, SS, faucet tap loading, Marked: "THE BSA AIR RIFLE" (1905) or "THE BSA AIR RIFLE (Lincoln Jeffries Patent)" (1906-1907), 43.5 in. OAL. Mfg. 1905-1907.

	$500	$425	$350	$290	$225	$150	$100

BSA IMPROVED PATTERN − .177 cal., UL (bayonet style), SP, SS, tap loading, new patented breech plug retaining plate and larger chamber in the breech plug, breech plates marked "P. Par.," 43.5 in. OAL. Mfg. 1906-1907.

	$500	$425	$350	$290	$225	$150	$100

This model may have been what would have been called the Model C or D.

GRADING	100%	95%	90%	80%	60%	40%	20%

GOLDSTAR – .177 or .22 cal., UL, SP, 950/750 FPS, 10-shot rotary mag., 18.5 in. barrel, two-stage adj. trigger, hardwood stock, 8.5 lbs. Mfg. 1991-2001.

	100%	95%	90%	80%	60%	40%	20%
	$500	$425	$350	$290	$225	$150	$100

Last MSR was $847.

The Goldstar magazine was a development of the Model VS2000 magazine.

* ***Goldstar E/E (Magnum)*** – .177 or .22 cal., UL, SP, 1020/625 FPS, 17.5 in. barrel, two-stage adj. trigger, hardwood stock, ten-shot rotary magazine, 8.5 lbs. Disc. 2001.

	100%	95%	90%	80%	60%	40%	20%
	$450	$375	$325	$260	$205	$135	$90

Last MSR was $700.

E/E = "Export Extra"- power above 12 ft. lb. the British legal limit.

GUN LAYING TEACHER – .177 cal., UL (modified to rear), SP, SS, very special variation of Improved Model D underlever air rifle. Cocked by lever behind breech. Instead of a stock it had a system of heavy rails to allow function as a miniature artillery piece for teaching military artillery crews. Known as the Admiralty Pattern guns. Most were fired by pulling a lanyard attached to the firing mechanism, the later production models, had a solenoid-operated trigger mechanism. Second unmarked ("Improved Model" or "Inside Barrel Model") variation made in the early 1940s; were the ones with the Solenoid operated trigger. These were made for use in the Valentine Model tank used in New Zealand; used into the 1950s. It fits inside a tank's cannon barrel for training tank gunners. Mfg. 1911 - circa 1943. Ref. USA (Feb. 1995).

courtesy Beeman Collection

	100%	95%	90%	80%	60%	40%	20%
	N/A	$3,750	$3,000	$2,425	$1,875	$1,300	$750

This gun was designed in 1911, first delivered in June of 1915, and the last of only 212 produced was delivered in January of 1916. The entire period of production was only seven months.

IMPROVED MODEL B – .177 cal., UL (bayonet style), SP, SS, tap loading, marked with "Improved Model B", Standard version: 43.3 in. OAL. Light version: 39 in. OAL. Mfg. 1907-1908.

	100%	95%	90%	80%	60%	40%	20%
	$800	$675	$550	$475	$350	$240	$160

IMPROVED MODEL D – .177, .22, or .25 (1908-1918 only) cal., SP, SS, UL (bayonet, side button, end button styles), 1.125 (Juvenile) or 1.25 in. diameter air cylinder.

Approximately 600 total .25 cal. were mfg. in Ordinary and Light versions. Most .25 cal. models were sent to India where they saw rough use; very few exist today. There are five size variations (not marked as such) plus the Military models. Size may vary by about 0.25 in.

* ***Improved Model D (Junior)*** – .177 cal., 1.25 in. OD, 34.25 in. OAL. Approx. 1,097 mfg. 1912-1914.

	100%	95%	90%	80%	60%	40%	20%
	$800	$675	$550	$475	$350	$240	$160

* ***Improved Model D (Juvenile)*** – .177 cal., air cylinder 1.125 in. OD, folding leaf rear sight, 34.25 in. OAL. Approx. 600 mfg. 1913-1914.

	100%	95%	90%	80%	60%	40%	20%
	$1,000	$850	$700	$575	$450	$300	$200

GRADING	100%	95%	90%	80%	60%	40%	20%

* **Improved Model D (Light)** – .177 or .25 cal., 39 in. OAL. Mfg. 1908-1918.

courtesy Beeman Collection

	$500	$425	$350	$290	$225	$150	$100

Add 500% for original .25 cal. barrels.
  Less than 20 were mfg. in .25 cal.

* **Improved Model D (Military Model)** – .177 or .22 cal., UL, SP, SS, very special variation of Improved Model D for military training; duplicated size, balance, and sights of the Long Lee-Enfield Territorial Model .303 cal. military rifles. Variation one: .177 cal., simple bayonet cocking lever. Variation two: .177 or .22 cal., bayonet underlever cocking lever with side reinforcements ("fillets or fences") at bend point. Variation three: .22 (No. 2 bore) cal., side button cocking lever. Approx. 430 total of all variations mfg. 1907-1914.

courtesy Beeman Collection

	N/A	$3,500	$2,800	$2,275	$1,750	$1,225	$700

* **Improved Model D (Ordinary)** – .177, .22, or .25 (1908-1918) cal., 43.5 in. OAL.

	$500	$425	$350	$290	$225	$150	$100

Add 500% for original .25 cal. barrels.

* **Improved Model D (Sporting)** – .22 (No. 2 bore) cal., 45.5 in. OAL. Mfg. 1909-1917.

	$500	$425	$350	$290	$225	$150	$100

STANDARD – .177 or .22 (No. 2) cal., UL, SP, SS, marked "STANDARD". Mfg. 1919-1939.

  All air rifles made between WWI and WWII were marked "STANDARD".

* **Standard Variant 1** – "Giant" or "Long Tom" (common nicknames, not marked as such), S or T serial number prefixes, 45.5 in. OAL.

courtesy Beeman Collection

	$500	$425	$350	$290	$225	$150	$100

Add 25% for T serial number prefix.

* **Standard Variant 2** – Light (not marked as such) - L or A serial number prefixes.

courtesy Beeman Collection

	$500	$425	$350	$290	$225	$150	$100

Add 25% for A serial number prefix.

GRADING	100%	95%	90%	80%	60%	40%	20%

* **Standard Variant 3** – .177 cal. only, two verisons. Club No. 1 version: "CLUB" markings. 45.5 in. OAL. Mfg. 1922-1930. Club No. 4 version: "CLUB NO. 4" markings, C or CS serial number prefixes, 45.25 in. OAL. Mfg. 1930-1939.

courtesy Beeman Collection

	$500	$425	$350	$290	$225	$150	$100

Add 25% for C serial number prefix.

CLUB model designations and world wide patent details are photoetched on top of the compression tube.

STUTZEN MK 2 – .177, .22, or .25 cal., concealed UL, SP, rifled barrel, blue finish, 1020/800/675 FPS, 14 in. barrel, rotating breech, Monte Carlo stock with cheek piece and rosewood Schnabel forend cap, Maxi Grip scope rail, 6.25 lbs. Mfg. 1997-2000.

	$550	$475	$400	$325	$250	$170	$110

Last MSR was $700.

SUPERSTAR – .177, .22, or .25 cal., UL, SP, SS, 1020/800/675 FPS, 18.5 in. rifled barrel, blue finish, rotating breech for loading pellets, checkered beech stock, Maxi Grip scope rail, two-stage trigger, 43 in. OAL, 7.75 lbs. Mfg. 1992-1994.

	$425	$350	$295	$245	$190	$125	$85

Last MSR was $470.

* **Superstar Carbine** – .177, .22, or .25 cal., UL, SP, SS, 850/625/530 FPS, 14 in. rifled barrel, blue finish, rotating breech for loading pellets, checkered beech stock, Maxi Grip scope rail, two-stage trigger, 39.5 in. OAL. Mfg. 1992-1994.

	$425	$350	$295	$245	$190	$125	$85

Last MSR was $470.

SUPERSTAR MK2 E/E – .177, .22, or .25 cal., UL, SP, 18.5 in. rifled barrel, blue finish, 950/750/600 FPS, rotating breech for loading pellets, Monte Carlo stock, Maxi Grip scope rail, adj. two-stage trigger, 43 in. OAL, 8.5 lbs. Mfg. 1994-2001.

	$475	$400	$325	$280	$215	$145	$95

Last MSR was $350.

E/E = "Export Extra"- power above 12 ft. lb., the British legal limit.

* **Superstar MK2 Carbine E/E** – .177, .22, or .25 cal., UL, SP, SS, 950/750/600 FPS, 14 in. rifled barrel, blue finish, rotating breech for loading pellets, Monte Carlo stock, Maxi Grip scope rail, adj. two-stage trigger, approx. 8 lbs. Mfg. 1994-2001.

	$475	$400	$325	$280	$215	$145	$95

Last MSR was $350.

E/E = "Export Extra"- power above 12 ft. lb., the British legal limit.

* **Superstar MK2 Magnum** – .177, .22, or .25 cal., UL, SP, 18.5 in. rifled barrel, blue finish, 1020/800/675 FPS, rotating breech for loading pellets, Monte Carlo stock, Maxi Grip scope rail, adj. two-stage trigger, 43 in. OAL, 8.5 lbs. Mfg. 2001-2003.

	$475	$400	$325	$280	$215	$145	$95

Last MSR was $540.

RIFLES: PRECHARGED PNEUMATICS

FIREBIRD – .177 or .22 cal., PCP, UL, rotating breech action, SS, 1100/800 FPS, 17.5 in. barrel, adj. trigger and power level, beech Monte Carlo stock with vent. recoil pad, 42 in. OAL, 7.25 lbs. Mfg. 2001-2003.

	$325	$275	$230	$190	$145	$95	$65

$350.

* **Firebird Carbine** – .177 or .22 cal., PCP, UL rotating breech action, SS, 1100/800 FPS, 13 in. barrel, adj. trigger and power level, beech Monte Carlo stock with vent. recoil pad, 39 in. OAL, 7.5 lbs. Mfg. 2001-2003.

	$365	$300	$245	$205	$160	$105	$70

Last MSR was $395.

GRADING	100%	95%	90%	80%	60%	40%	20%

HORNET – .22 cal., PCP, SS, micro-movement cocking mechanism, SLC pressure regulator, 18.5 in. match grade free-floating barrel, 850 FPS, blue finish, adj. two-stage trigger, checkered beech Monte Carlo stock with vent. recoil pad, 37.5 in. OAL, 7.9 lbs. Mfg. 2003-2007.

	$875	$750	$600	$500	$400	$260	$175

Last MSR was $923.

HORNET CARBINE – .22 cal., PCP, SS or ten-shot mag. (new 2004), micro-movement cocking mechanism, pressure regulator, 15.75 in. match grade free-floating barrel, 850 FPS, blue finish, adj. two-stage trigger, checkered beech Monte Carlo stock with vent. recoil pad, 34 in. OAL, 7.5 lbs. Mfg. 2003-2007.

	$875	$750	$600	$500	$400	$260	$175

Last MSR was $923.

HORNET CARBINE MULTISHOT – .22 cal., PCP, ten-shot mag., micro-movement cocking mechanism, pressure regulator, 15.75 in. match grade free-floating barrel, 850 FPS, blue finish, adj. two-stage trigger, checkered beech Monte Carlo stock with vent. recoil pad, 34 in. OAL, 7.5 lbs. Mfg. 2004-2007.

	$950	$825	$675	$550	$425	$290	$190

Last MSR was $1,035.

HORNET MULTI SHOT – .22 cal., PCP, ten-shot mag., micro-movement cocking mechanism, SLC pressure regulator, 18.5 in. match grade free-floating barrel, 850 FPS, blue finish, adj. two-stage trigger, checkered beech Monte Carlo stock with vent. recoil pad, 37.5 in. OAL, 7.9 lbs. Mfg. 2004-2007.

	$950	$825	$675	$550	$425	$290	$190

Last MSR was $1,035.

LONE STAR – .22 or .25 cal., PCP, SS, MMC, 750 FPS (.25 cal.), 18.5 (.22 cal.) or 23 in. match grade BBL, beech Monte Carlo stock with vent. recoil pad, manual safety, BSA engraved trigger guard and stock, 37-41.5 in. OAL, 7.6-7.8 lbs. Mfg. 2008-2011.

	$600	$500	$425	$350	$270	$180	$120

R10 – .177 or .22 cal., PCP, BA, micro movement cocking, ten-shot rotary mag., 1050/935 FPS, 17.25 in. rifled shrouded free-floating match grade barrel, two-stage adj. match grade trigger, checkered walnut Monte Carlo stock with adj. recoil pad, aluminum scope rail, checkered grip and forend, 43 in. OAL, approx. 7.3 lbs. Mfg. 2010-2012.

courtesy BSA GUNS

	$1,025	$875	$725	$600	$450	$300	$205

Last MSR was $1,200.

R-10 MK2 – .177 or .22 cal., PCP, BA, 1055/935 FPS, 18.5 in. fully floating, match accurate shrouded steel barrel, threaded for a silencer and fitted with multi-port muzzle flip compensator, Grade 2 walnut stock with rosewood forend tip and grip cap, checkered grip and forend, adj. buttpad, Bowkett designed regulator and firing mechanism, supplied probe charger, 10-shot autoload system, multi-adj. two stage trigger, on-board air gauge, single shot adaptor, aluminum scope rail, 41 in. OAL, 7.3 lbs. New 2012.

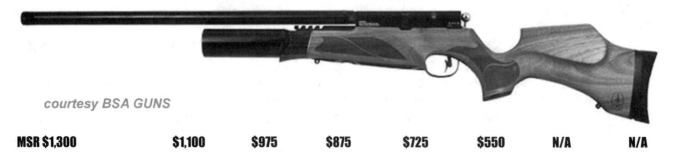

courtesy BSA GUNS

MSR $1,300	$1,100	$975	$875	$725	$550	N/A	N/A

GRADING	100%	95%	90%	80%	60%	40%	20%

SCORPION – .177 or .22 cal., PCP, SS, BA, 1000/860 FPS, 18.5 in. fully floating steel barrel with muzzle brake, fully checkered beech or walnut Monte Carlo stock or tactical version with synthetic stock and black bolt, vent. rubber recoil pad, two-stage adj. trigger, aluminum scope rail, self-regulating valve, 36.5 in. OAL, 7.7 lbs. New 2007.

courtesy BSA GUNS

MSR $900	$775	$675	$600	$500	$375	N/A	N/A

Add $150 for walnut stock.

SCORPION CARBINE – .177 or .22 cal., PCP, SS, BA, 988/815 FPS, 15 in. barrel, beech Monte Carlo stock with vent. recoil pad, 33.5 in. OAL, 6.8 lbs. Mfg. 2007-2012.

	$775	$650	$550	$450	$350	$230	$155

Last MSR was $900.

Add $150 for walnut stock.

SCORPION T-10 BULL BARREL – .177 or .22 cal., PCP, BA, ten-shot metal mag., 988/815 FPS, 18.5 in. fully shrouded barrel, adj. two-stage trigger, beech Monte Carlo or black synthetic (Tactical model) stock with vent. recoil pad, factory installed sling swivel studs, 44.5 in. OAL, 8 lbs. Mfg. 2008-2011.

	$900	$750	$625	$525	$400	$270	$180

SCORPION SE – .177, .22, or .25 cal., PCP, BA, 18.5 in. free floating steel barrel with muzzle brake, ambidextrous beech or walnut stock with stippled pistol grip and forend, or tactical version with synthetic stock and black bolt, new lightweight "fast strike" hammer system, pressure gauge, self-regulating valve, two stage adj. trigger, 10-shot mag., rubber buttpad, aluminum scope rail, 36.5 in. OAL, 7.7 lbs. New 2012.

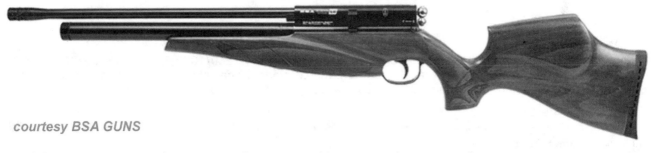

courtesy BSA GUNS

MSR $900	$775	$675	$600	$500	$375	N/A	N/A

Add $50 for beech stock.
Add $75 for walnut stock.

SPITFIRE – .177, .22 or .25 cal., PCP, BBC, SS, 1100/800 FPS, pellets are loaded at the rear of the 17.5 in. barrel similar to a spring gun, beech Monte Carlo stock with vent. recoil pad, 40.5 in. OAL, 7.2 lbs. Mfg. 1999-2006.

	$450	$375	$325	$260	$205	$135	$90

Last MSR was $465.

* ***Spitfire Carbine*** – .177 or .22 cal., PCP, SS, 1100/800 FPS, 14.5 in. barrel, beech Monte Carlo stock with vent. recoil pad, 39 in. OAL, 7.25 lbs. Mfg. 1999-2006.

	$500	$425	$350	$285	$225	$150	$100

Last MSR was $526.

* ***Bisley Spitfire*** – .177 or .22 cal., PCP, SS, similar to Spitfire except lower power designed for 10-Meter Match use with rear match aperture sight with an interchangeable front sight. Mfg. 2005-2006.

	$625	$525	$425	$350	$280	$185	$125

Last MSR was $641.

GRADING	100%	95%	90%	80%	60%	40%	20%

SPORTSMAN HV – .177 or .22 cal., PCP, SS, BA, 18.5 in. barrel, beech Monte Carlo stock with vent. recoil pad, 37 in. OAL, 7.8 lbs. Mfg. 2007-2009.

courtesy BSA GUNS

	$875	$750	$600	$500	$400	$260	$175

SUPERTEN – .177 or .22 cal., PCP, BA, 200cc bottle, ten-shot rotary mag., 1000/800 FPS, 17.25 in. rifled barrel, match grade trigger, beech or walnut Monte Carlo stock with adj. pad, 37.5 in. OAL, approx. 7.75 lbs. New 1996.

* **SuperTEN MK1** – .177 or .22 cal., PCP, BA, ten-shot rotary mag., 1000/800 FPS, 17.25 in. rifled barrel, match grade trigger, beech or walnut Monte Carlo stock with adj. pad, 37.5 in. OAL, approx. 7.75 lbs. Mfg. 1996-2001.

	$750	$625	$525	$425	$325	$225	$150

Last MSR was $880.

* **SuperTEN MK2** – .177 or .22 cal., PCP, BA, ten-shot rotary mag., 1250/1050 FPS, 17.25 in. rifled free-floating match grade barrel, adj. match grade trigger, checkered beech or walnut Monte Carlo stock with adj. recoil pad, 37.5 in. OAL, approx. 7.9 lbs. Mfg. 1999-2001.

	$950	$800	$675	$550	$425	$285	$190

Last MSR was $880.

Add 30% for walnut stock.

* **SuperTEN MK2 Carbine** – .177 or .22 cal., PCP, BA, ten-shot rotary mag., 1050/850 FPS, 13.25 in. rifled free-floating match grade barrel, adj. match grade trigger, checkered beech or walnut Monte Carlo stock with adj. pad, 33.5 in. OAL, approx. 6.6 lbs. Mfg. 1999-2001.

	$950	$800	$675	$550	$425	$285	$190

Last MSR was $880.

Add 30% for walnut stock.

* **SuperTEN MK3** – .177 or .22 cal., PCP, BA, ten-shot rotary mag., 1250/1050 FPS, 17.25 in. rifled standard or bull (new 2004) free-floating match grade barrel, adj. match grade trigger, checkered beech or walnut Monte Carlo stock with adj. recoil pad, removable 200cc buddy bottle, patented regulator, 37.5 in. OAL, approx. 7.9 lbs. Mfg. 2001-2012.

	$800	$675	$550	$450	$350	$240	$160

Add 30% for walnut stock.
Add 20% for Bull barrel.

* **SuperTEN MK3 Carbine** – .177 or .22 cal., PCP, BA, ten-shot rotary mag., 1050/850 FPS, 13.25 in. standard or bull (new 2004) rifled free-floating match grade barrel, adj. match grade trigger, checkered beech or walnut Monte Carlo stock with adj. pad, 33.5 in. OAL, approx. 6 lbs. Mfg. 2001-2007.

	$1,225	$1,050	$850	$700	$550	$375	$245

Last MSR was $1,277.

Add 30% for walnut stock.
Add 20% for Bull barrel.

TECH STAR – .22 cal., PCP, SS, 100cc reservoir, MMC, pressure regulator, 18.5 in. barrel, 1000 FPS, blue finish, adj. rear fixed front sights, adj. two-stage trigger, checkered beech Monte Carlo stock with vent. recoil pad, 37 in. OAL, 6.6 lbs. Mfg. 2004-2007.

	$650	$550	$450	$375	$295	$195	$130

Last MSR was $687.

ULTRA – .177 or .22 cal., PCP, SS, MMC, 825/706 FPS, 14 in. free floating match grade steel barrel with muzzle brake, fully checkered beech or walnut Monte Carlo ambidextrous stock or tactical version with synthetic stock and black

GRADING	100%	95%	90%	80%	60%	40%	20%

bolt, vent. rubber buttpad, two-stage adj. trigger, factory installed mini SAS moderator, BSA logos on grip cap and heel, includes a set of Scopemaster Professional mounts and silencer, manual safety, charging adaptor, spare seals and lubricant also included, 32 in. OAL, 5.7 lbs. Mfg. 2007-2012.

	$655	$550	$450	$375	$295	$195	$130

ULTRA MULTISHOT – .177 or .22 cal., PCP, 10 shot mag., MMC, 825/706 FPS, super compact design, 12 in. free floating steel barrel with muzzle brake, two-stage adj. trigger, fully checkered beech or Grade 2 walnut stock with BSA logo on grip cap and heel, vent. rubber recoil pad, self-regulating valve, quick-fit charging system, aluminum scope rail, charging adaptor, spare seals and lubricant included, 32 in. OAL, 5.9 lbs. Mfg. 2007-2012.

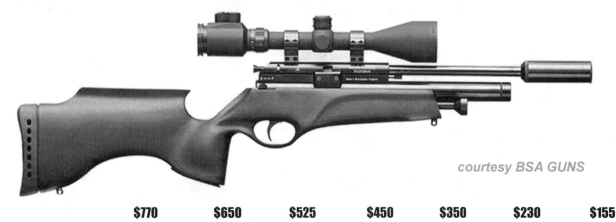

courtesy BSA GUNS

	$770	$650	$525	$450	$350	$230	$155

ULTRA TACTICAL – .177 or .22 cal., PCP, SS, MMC, 825/706 FPS, 14 in. free floating match grade steel barrel with muzzle brake, ambidextrous, black synthetic stock, vent. rubber buttpad, two-stage adj. trigger, self-regulating valve, BSA logos on grip cap and heel, includes a set of Scopemaster Professional mounts and silencer, manual safety, charging adaptor, spare seals and lubricant, 32 in. OAL, 5.7 lbs. New 2010.

courtesy BSA GUNS

	$650	$550	$450	$375	$295	$195	$130

ULTRA SE MULTISHOT – .177, .22, or .25 cal., PCP, 10 shot mag., MMC, 825/706 FPS, super compact design, 12 in. free floating steel barrel with muzzle brake, two-stage adj. trigger, fully checkered beech or walnut stock with BSA logo on grip cap and heel, vent. rubber recoil pad, self-regulating valve, quick-fit charging system, aluminum scope rail, charging adaptor, spare seals and lubricant included, 32 in. OAL, 5.9 lbs. Mfg. 2012-current.

MSR $950	$800	$700	$650	$525	$400	N/A	N/A

ULTRA SE MULTI-SHOT TACTICAL – .177, .22 or .25 cal., PCP, 10 shot mag., MMC, 825/706 FPS, super compact design, 11.8 in. free floating steel barrel with muzzle brake, two-stage adj. trigger, black synthetic stock, checkered grip and forend, BSA logo on grip cap and heel, vent. rubber recoil pad, self-regulating valve, quick-fit charging system, aluminum scope rail, charging adaptor, spare seals and lubricant included, 32 in. OAL, 5.7 lbs. New 2010.

MSR $900	$775	$675	$600	$500	$375	N/A	N/A

RIFLES: SIDE LEVER COCKING

VS 2000 – .177 or .22 cal., SL, SP, nine-shot repeater, rifled barrel, blue finish, 850/625 FPS, 9 lbs. Approx. ten were mfg. Disc. 1986.

	N/A	$3,000	$2,400	$1,950	$1,500	$1,050	$600

Last MSR was $330.

GRADING	100%	95%	90%	80%	60%	40%	20%

B.S.F. "BAYERISCHE SPORTWAFFENFABRIK"

Previous manufacturer located in Erlangen, Germany. Previously imported by Kendell International located in Paris, KY, and by Beeman Precision Arms under the Wischo label.

B.S.F. (Bayerische Sportwaffenfabrik) is the manufacturer for airguns marketed with B.S.F., Bavaria, and Wischo trade names. B.S.F. was founded in 1935 and produced a few airguns before the pressures of WWII took over. Production began again in 1948 and put an emphasis on solid, simple construction. The Model S54 remains as a classic example of solid, elegant construction for a sporter air rifle. B.S.F.'s own production was generally sold under the Bavaria label. The Wischo Company of Erlangen (founded by Egon Wilsker), one of Europe's leading gun distributors, distributed large numbers, especially to Beeman Precision Airguns in the USA, under the Wischo label. The collapse of their British agent, Norman May & Co, in 1980 resulted in the dismissal of most of the 130 workers. The Schütt family sold the business to Herbert Gayer, who reorganized the company and the production process. However, this was not enough to prevent further decline of the company. It was then purchased by the Hermann Weihrauch Company in nearby Mellrichstadt in the late 1980s. By incorporating some HW design and cosmetic features and parts, a surprisingly good line of upper economy level airguns was developed to supplement the top-of-the-line regular HW models. Weihrauch manufactures versions of B.S.F. models for Marksman (Marksman Models 28, 40, 55, 56, 58, 59, 70, 71, 72, and 75).

PISTOLS

B.S.F. (WISCHO) MODEL S-20 – .177 cal., BBC, 450 FPS, 2.5 lbs. Mfg. 1950-1985.

courtesy Beeman Collection

$125	$105	$90	$75	$55	$35	$25

Last MSR was $130.

Some Model S-20 pistols were assembled from components and sold by Weihrauch through 1988.

B.S.F. (WISCHO) MODEL CM – .177 cal., BBC, 450 FPS, target style, 2.5 lbs. Disc. in 1988.

courtesy Beeman Collection

$150	$130	$105	$85	$70	$45	$30

RIFLES

BAVARIA MODEL 35 – .177 cal., BBC, SP, 500 FPS, 4.5 lbs.

$150	$130	$105	$85	$70	$45	$30

Last MSR was $125.

BAVARIA MODEL 45 – .177 cal., BBC, SP, 700 FPS, 6 lbs.

$165	$140	$115	$95	$75	$50	$35

Last MSR was $125.

BAVARIA MODEL 50 – .177 cal., BBC, SP, 700 FPS, 6 lbs.

$175	$150	$125	$100	$80	$50	$35

GRADING	100%	95%	90%	80%	60%	40%	20%

BAVARIA MODEL S 54 – .177 or .22 cal., UL, SP, 685/500 FPS, 8 lbs.

courtesy Beeman Collection

	$235	$200	$165	$135	$105	$70	$45

Subtract 10% for Sport Model with plain stock (disc. 1986).
Add 10% for M Model.
Ref: ARG: 37-44.

* **Model S 54 Deluxe** – .177 or .22 cal., UL, SP, 19.1 in. rifled barrel (12 grooves RH), tap-loader, hand checkered walnut stock, cast aluminum buttplate, 46.8 in. OAL, 8.6 lbs., no safety.

courtesy Beeman Collection

	$500	$425	$350	$285	$225	$150	$100

Add 20% for pre-1980 hand checkered stock with rounded forearm.
Add 25% for diopter rear sight (S 54 Bayern).

BAVARIA MODEL S 55/55 N – .177 or .22 cal., BBC, SP, 16.1 in. rifled barrel (12 grooves, RH), 870/635 FPS, no safety, 40.6 in. OAL, 6.4 lbs. Disc. 1986.

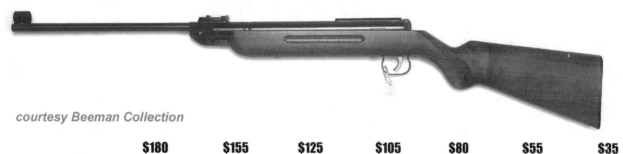

courtesy Beeman Collection

	$180	$155	$125	$105	$80	$55	$35

Add $15 for Deluxe Model.
Add $30 for Special Model 55 N (N = "Nussbaum," German for walnut).

BAVARIA MODEL S 60 – .177 or .22 cal., BBC, SP, 800/570 FPS, 6.5 lbs.

courtesy Beeman Collection

	$180	$155	$125	$105	$80	$55	$35

BAVARIA MODEL S 70 – .177 or .22 cal., BBC, SP, 19.1 in. barrel, 855/610 FPS, checkered Monte Carlo stock, ventilated rubber buttplate, 7 lbs.

	$265	$225	$185	$155	$120	$80	$55

GRADING	100%	95%	90%	80%	60%	40%	20%

BAVARIA MODEL S 80 – .177 or .22 cal., BBC, SP, 800/570 FPS, 8.25 lbs.

	100%	95%	90%	80%	60%	40%	20%
	$210	$180	$145	$120	$95	$65	$40

Last MSR was $185.

BAHCO

Previous manufacturer, Aktiebolaget Bahco (AB Bahco), has roots dating back to 1862 as a metal working business in Stockholm and Enköping, Sweden.

Due to a strange font used in the stamping of the name, BAHCO appears to read as "BAMCO" and is so listed in many places. Bahco was a brand name of Aktiebolaget Bahco (AB Bahco).

This Swedish firm has roots dating back to the founding of a steel works in 1862 by Göran Fredrik Göransson, and developed exceptional quality saws under the same Fish & Hook brand which their tools bear today. Their most famous products, based on 118 patents granted to Johan Johansson from 1888 to 1943, are the adjustable spanner wrench (Crescent wrench) and adjustable pipe wrench (monkey wrench). They have produced over 100 million examples of those world famous tools. According to Walter (2001) they also formerly specialized in bayonets and military equipment and produced gas-powered rifles under the Excellent brand from 1906 to 1915 with the patents of Ewerlöf and Blómen. Today the Bahco name can be found on garden and other tools in almost any large hardware or warehouse store, but no longer on airguns.

The Bahco Model No 1S air rifle is very similar to the Excellent BS air rifle. (See Excellent in the "E" section.)

RIFLES

MODEL NO 1R – 4.5mm or 5.5mm cal., SS, trombone-style slide action multi-pump pneumatic, steel rifled part octagonal and part round BBL, swing/twist breech block, nickel finish knurled pump handle, marked "BACHO Made in Sweden No 1R", no safety, SG walnut stock with cheek piece and steel buttplate, 38.38 OAL, 4.62 lbs. Mfg. circa 1908-1912.

N/A	$950	$750	$625	$475	$325	$190

This model is similar to the Excellent Model BR.

MODEL NO 1S – 4.5mm or 5.5mm cal., SS, trombone-style slide action multi-pump pneumatic, steel smoothbore part octagonal and part round BBL, swing/twist breech block, nickel finish knurled pump handle, marked "BACHO Made in Sweden No 1S", no safety, SG walnut stock with cheek piece and steel buttplate, 38.38 in. OAL, 4.62 lbs. Mfg. circa 1908-1912.

courtesy Beeman Collection

N/A	$950	$750	$625	$475	$325	$190

This model is similar to the Excellent Model BS.

BAIKAL

Current trademark of products manufactured by the Russian State Unitary Plant "Izhevsky Mekhanichesky Zavod" (SUP IMZ), located in Russia. Currently imported and/or distributed by Airguns of Arizona, located in Gilbert, AZ and Air Venturi/Pyramyd Air, located in Solon, OH (previously located in Warrensville Hts., OH). Previously imported by European American Armory Corp., located in Sharpes, FL, and Compasseco located in Bardstown, KY. Dealer sales. For more information and current pricing on both new and used Baikal firearms, please refer to the *Blue Book of Gun Values* by S.P. Fjestad (also available online).

First known to American airgunners after WWII via the Baikal IZh 22, a typical Russian simple, but fairly sturdy, break barrel .22 cal. air rifle. Baikal also manufactures many models which are not currently available in the American marketplace.

PISTOLS

IZH 46/46M/46M MATCH – .177 cal., CO_2, semi-auto, UL, SSP, SS, SA/DA, 410 FPS (IZh 46 disc.) or 460 FPS (IZh 46M with larger compressor), post front sight, micrometer fully adj. rear target sight, adj. international hardwood target grip, five-way adj. trigger, 11.2 in. hammer-forged rifled barrel, extra long cocking stroke, dry-fire mechanism,

GRADING	100%	95%	90%	80%	60%	40%	20%

includes cleaning rod, sight adjustment tool, drift punch tool and extra seals, 16.53 in. OAL, 2.86 lbs.

courtesy Baikal

MSR $596	$500	$425	$350	$295	$230	$155	$100

Add $54 for 46M configuration.
Add $80 for 46M with upgraded trigger.
Add $99 for Match Pistol combo with red dot sight.
Subtract 25% for IZh 46.

IZH 53 – .177 cal., BBC, SP, SS pistol, black plastic stock with thumb rest and finger grooves.

courtesy Beeman Collection

	$75	$65	$55	$45	$35	$20	$15

IZH 53M – .177 cal., BBC, SP, SS, 360 FPS, adj. rear sight, adj. trigger, rifled 8.8 in. barrel, black plastic target grip, 16.3 in. OAL, 2.4 lbs.

courtesy Baikal

MSR $95	$80	$70	$55	$45	$35	$25	$15

MP-651K – .177 cal., CO_2 semi-auto repeater, 8 or 12 g. cylinders, DA, 8-round mag., 5.9 in. BBL, 340 FPS, adj. rear blade and front sights, black finish, cast aluminum and synthetic construction, 9.45 in. OAL, 1.54 lbs. Imported 2007-2010.

courtesy Baikal

	$85	$70	$60	$50	$40	$25	$15

GRADING	100%	95%	90%	80%	60%	40%	20%

MP-654K (MAKAROV SEMI-AUTO) – .177 cal., CO_2 (capsule loads in magazine), single or double action, 13-shot, 3.8 in. barrel, 380 FPS, 1.6 lbs. Importation disc. 2003.

courtesy Baikal

$100	$85	$70	$60	$45	$30	$20

Last MSR was $120.

MP-655K – BB/.177 cal., CO_2 (capsule loads in magazine), double action, 100-shot, 3.75 in. barrel, 279 FPS, 7.87 in. OAL, 1.5 lbs. Imported 2009-2013.

$215	$190	$170	$140	$105	N/A	N/A

Last MSR was $250.

MP-672 – .177 cal., PCP, SS, micrometer fully adj. rear target sight, adj. target grip, adj. trigger, 10 in. hammer-forged rifled barrel, 2.6 lbs. Mfg. 2005-current.

courtesy Baikal

While advertised, this model has not been imported into the U.S.

MP-DROZD – BB/.177 cal., battery and 8 or 12 g. cylinder CO_2, electronic trigger rapid-fire (one, three, and six round rapid-fire bursts), 30 round mag., 10 in. rifled barrel, 330 FPS, two-stage trigger, black high-strength plastic construction, comes with detachable shoulder stock, scope rail, blade and ramp front sights, and a BB loader, 13.75 in. OAL, 3.5 lbs. Imported 2006-current.

courtesy Baikal

MSR $300	$245	$210	$170	$140	$110	$75	$50

Add $100 for 12 or 20 gram bulk fill CO_2 tank.
Add $100 for fake suppressor.

GRADING	100%	95%	90%	80%	60%	40%	20%

MP-DROZD 661K BLACKBIRD – .177 cal., one 88g CO_2 tank or three 12g CO_2 cartridges, semi-auto repeater, 8 in. rifled barrel, post front and adj. rear sights, Weaver mounts, platsic buttpad, Black finish, 28 in. OAL, 4.75 lbs.

courtesy Air Venturi

MSR $350	$295	$250	$205	$170	$135	$90	$60

RIFLES

IJ 22 – .177 cal., BBC, SP, SS, 17.9 in. rifled barrel, 410-498 FPS, vertical lever breech-lock on LHS of barrel, brass lined, rifled barrel, blued finish, trigger guard, grip cap and buttplate of dark red plastic, hardwood stock with unique shoulder up behind end cap, plastic insert marked "IJ 22", typically sold new with extra mainspring and seals, 40.8 in. OAL, 5.2 lbs. Mfg. in USSR circa 1970s.

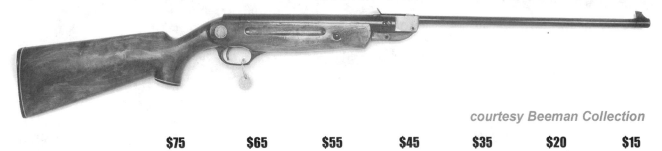

courtesy Beeman Collection

	$75	$65	$55	$45	$35	$20	$15

This model was also sold internationally as the Vostok, in Britain as the Milbro G530, and in the USA as the HyScore 870 Mark 3.

IZH 32BK – .177 cal., SL, SP, 541 FPS, integral rail for scope mount, adj. buttplate, adj. cheek piece, adj. trigger, walnut stock, 11.68 in. barrel, 12.13 lbs. Mfg. 1999-2002.

	$750	$625	$525	$425	$325	$225	$150

Last MSR was $1,100.

This model is designed for ten-meter running target competition.

IZH 38 – .177 cal., BBC, SP, SS, 410/498 FPS MV, very short pull, 40.8 in. OAL, 5.2 lbs.

Current values not yet determined.

IZH 60 – .177 cal., SL, SP, 460 FPS, 16.50 in. barrel, telescoping stock, 5 lbs. 6 oz.

courtesy Baikal

MSR $135	$110	$95	$75	$65	$50	$35	$20

Add $75 for IZH 60 Target Pro model with two stage adj. trigger.

GRADING	100%	95%	90%	80%	60%	40%	20%

IZH 61 – .177 cal., SL, SP, five-shot mag., 490 FPS, 17.80 in. barrel, polymer telescoping stock, 6.4 lbs.

courtesy Baikal

MSR $126	$105	$95	$85	$70	$55	N/A	N/A

IZH 61 MULTI-SHOT – .177 cal., SP, SS, sidelever action, 5 shot repeater, 18.5 in. barrel, 490 FPS, post globe front and adj. rear sight, dovetails, no safety, adj. synthetic stock, Black finish, 33 in. OAL, 4.3 lbs.

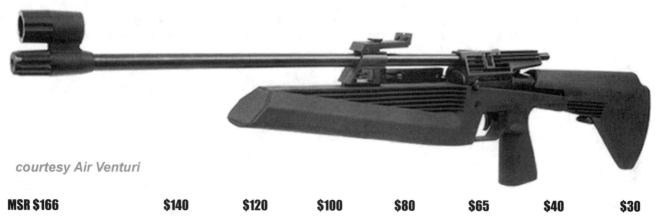

courtesy Air Venturi

MSR $166	$140	$120	$100	$80	$65	$40	$30

Add $44 for IZH 61 Target Pro model with hammer forged barrel and unmounted rear peep sight.

IZH DROZD – BB/.177 cal., battery and CO_2, rapid-fire (one, three, and six round rapid-fire busts), 330 FPS, 30 round mag., 10 in. barrel, adj. rear sight, black and yellow color high-strength plastic construction, detachable stock. Mfg. 2003-2006.

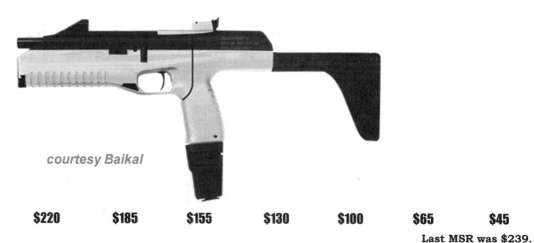

courtesy Baikal

	$220	$185	$155	$130	$100	$65	$45

Last MSR was $239.

This model became the MP-661K Drozd Blackbird circa 2007.

GRADING	100%	95%	90%	80%	60%	40%	20%

MP-512 – .177 cal., BBC, SP, SS, 490 FPS, integral rail for scope mount, adj. sights, polymer stock redesigned with grip enhancing inserts (new 2008), 17.7 in. barrel, 6.2 lbs. Imported 1999-2010.

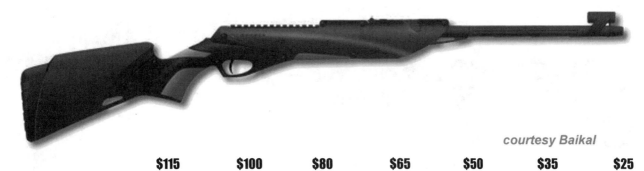

courtesy Baikal

	$115	$100	$80	$65	$50	$35	$25

MP-512M – .177 or .22 cal., BBC, SP, SS, 970/820 FPS, integral rail for scope mount, adj. sights, birch or polymer stock, 17.7 in. barrel, 6.2 lbs. Imported 2006-2010.

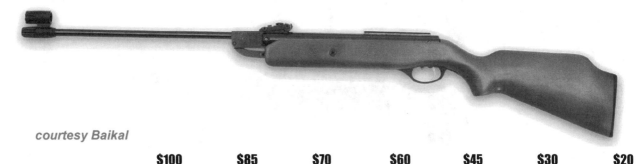

courtesy Baikal

	$100	$85	$70	$60	$45	$30	$20

MP-513/MP-513M – .177 or .22 (new 2006) cal., BBC, SP, SS, 1000 FPS, integral rail for scope mount, adj. sights, European wood stock, 17.7 in. barrel, 6.2 lbs. Imported 2003-current.

courtesy Baikal

MSR $250	$215	$190	$170	$140	$105	N/A	N/A

MP-514k – .177 cal., BC, SP, eight-shot mag., 558 FPS, 16.54 in. rifled BBL, adj. rear post front sights, polymer stock, auto-safety, 6.2 lbs., 25.6 in. OAL. Imported 2007-2011.

	$155	$135	$120	$100	$75	N/A	N/A

Last MSR was $180.

MP-532 – .177 cal., SL, SP, 15.75 in. rifled steel BBL, 427 FPS, adj. rear and hooded front sight, adj. butt pad, adj. trigger, 42 in. OAL, 9.26 lbs. Imported 1999-2007 and 2010-2011.

courtesy Baikal

	$500	$425	$350	$285	$225	$150	$100

Last MSR was $ 799.

GRADING	100%	95%	90%	80%	60%	40%	20%

MP-532T RUNNING BOAR – .177 cal., SL, SP, 15.75 in. rifled steel BBL, 427 FPS, scope rail, adj. butt pad, adj. trigger, 47.24 in. OAL, 11 lbs. Mfg. 2007-2011.

courtesy Baikal

Although manufactured from 2007-2011, this model was never imported into the U.S.

MP-571 BIATHLON – .177 cal., PCP, lever cocking repeater, includes four 5-shot mags., 15.75 in. rifled steel barrel, adj. rear and hooded front sights, adj. buttplate and cheek rest, adj. trigger, 41.7 in. OAL, 9.26 lbs. Mfg. 2008-2011.

courtesy Baikal

Although manufactured from 2008-2011, this model was never imported into the U.S.

MP-572 SPORTING – .177 cal., PCP, lever cocking SS, 17.75 in. rifled steel BBL, adj. rear and hooded front sights, adj. buttplate and cheek piece, adj. trigger, 46 in. OAL, 10.34 lbs. Mfg. 2008-2011.

courtesy Baikal

Although manufactured from 2008-2011, this model was never imported into the U.S.

MP-661K DROZD BLACKBIRD – BB/.177 BB cal., battery and 12 g and larger CO_2 or air cylinder, electronic trigger with switch allows SS or automatic fire (300, 450, or 600 rpm), 400 round mag., 8 in. rifled barrel, 330 FPS, post front sight, adj. rear sight, black high-strength plastic construction, includes scope rail, 28 in. OAL, 4.75 lbs. Imported 2007-current.

courtesy Baikal

MSR $350	$300	$265	$240	$195	$145	N/A	N/A

Add $10.50 for speed loader.

GRADING	100%	95%	90%	80%	60%	40%	20%

BAILEY

For information on Bailey airguns, see Columbian in the "C" section.

BALCO-SUB

Previous manufacturer of CO₂ spear pistols located in Greece.

PISTOL

BALCO PRO – CO$_2$, SS, heavy plastic, aluminum, and stainless steel construction. 22.9 in. OAL, 2.3 lbs.

courtesy Beeman Collection

$250	$225	$200	$150	$100	N/A	N/A

Add 10% for factory plastic sheath.

BALL RESERVOIR AIRGUNS

An easily recognized, but diverse group of antique, vintage or modern pneumatic airguns, characterized by a ball or otherwise rounded, detachable, external air reservoir.

Pneumatic airguns, that is "pump-up" airguns which employ pre-compressed air as their propulsive force, may go back to ancient times. Leonardo da Vinci considered pneumatic devices, but Arne Hoff, surely the dean of airgun history, notes (Hoff, 1972, 1977) that proof is lacking that da Vinci, or any other ancient artist/inventor ever invented an airgun. Hoff reported that the French gunmaker, Marin le Bourgeoys, made the first airgun with an air reservoir about 1605, only a decade or two after the very first known mechanical airguns (as contrasted to blowguns), powered by an internal bellows. These early pneumatic guns stored their compressed air in internal vessels. The earliest surviving pump-up airguns, from about 1640, employed a "barrel reservoir", a long tube concentrically sealed around the barrel. Others had an air reservoir built into the buttstock, sometimes in combination with a built-in air pump. These built-in reservoirs suffered from having two valves, one for air input from an internal or external pump, and one for air release at the moment of firing, as well as having the handicaps of difficult construction and lack of flexibility.

In the early 1670s, a young Frenchman, Denis Papin, experimented with using vacuum to drive a bullet, but his big contribution to airguns came about 1675 when he moved to London to work with Sir Robert Boyle. This was a detachable ball-shaped reservoir. His idea of using the barrel as both barrel and pump-cylinder (!) was impractical, but the ball reservoir opened a new century of airgun development. In 1686 John Evelyn demonstrated the first practical airgun utilizing a pre-charged ball reservoir, a gun apparently made in Amsterdam by an unknown maker (probably Andreas Dolep, a Dutchman who later worked in London), at the Royal Society in London. The ball reservoir required only one valve. Perhaps even more important, it could be instantly replaced by another ball with a fresh charge of air. A small supply of pre-charged balls added huge convenience to the field use of an airgun. A bonus was the instant replacement of the air valve. This freed the shooter from the sudden and acute problem of the failure of a valve buried within the gun. Airguns with built-in butt reservoirs and airguns with barrel reservoirs continued to be made into the 1700s but ball reservoir airguns, independently developed by several makers, came to dominate airgun design. Airguns with unscrewable butt-reservoirs that provided many more shots per reservoir, but whose reservoirs were heavier and more difficult to build, joined them.

Ball reservoir airguns did not develop in a clear evolutionary lineage, but rather represent several independent lines. A simplified classification is presented here.

BALL RESERVOIR AIRGUN VALUES

Ball reservoir rifle values for recently made examples or plain looking average condition specimens range from $700-$3,500. Average condition ball reservoir rifles of noted makers, have values in the $2,500-$5,500 range. Values for excellent condition noted makers examples, which are elaborately engraved with gold or silver inlays, have deluxe wood with original case and accessories range $5,500-$10,000. Ball reservoir pistol values will typically range 15%-25% more than Ball reservoir rifles. Unmarked specimens are less desirable, while noted markers marked airguns in excellent condition may bring premiums.

TOP AND SIDE BALL AIRGUNS

The very first ball airguns evidently were of the bottom ball configuration, but the earliest consistent ball pattern seems to have been to place the ball on top of the barrel ("top globe", "top ball", or "over globe"). While this may seem astonishing at first, the pattern probably developed because it allowed a simpler arrangement of internal lock parts. In all cases the ball was placed off center to avoid complete obstruction of the sights and target field. In any case, these guns understandably seem to have poor handling balance. Top ball air rifles are known from as early as 1750. Makers included Lieberkuhn, Gerlach, Saps, Hull, Wilson, Bate, and von der Fecht.

TOP BALL AIR RIFLE – .374 (9.5mm) cal., German mfg. circa 1760.

courtesy Beeman Collection

BOTTOM BALL AIRGUNS

By far the most common ball position is the "Bottom Ball" ("Bottom Globe" or "Under Globe"). The earliest balls were made of copper, which provided the safety advantage of tearing rather than shattering if the ball should fail. The most common pattern on the European mainland is what Wolff (1958) refers to as the "Berlin Bottom-Ball" system in which the ball is just forward of the trigger guard in the logical position directly below the lock mechanism. The ball is centrally hung, although two unmarked specimens have the ball hung from a side block. Makers of bottom ball airguns with the ball just ahead of the trigger guard include Sars, Angermann, Siegling, Fischer, Werner, and Kiobenhavn. British air rifles by Wallis, Houghton, and Lancaster with the ball in this position are known.

BERLIN BOTTOM BALL PATTERN – .407" (10.3mm) cal., German bar lock air rifle by Jo. Valetin Siegling of Frankfurt, cocked by lifting the finger hook on the barlock, marked 1753.

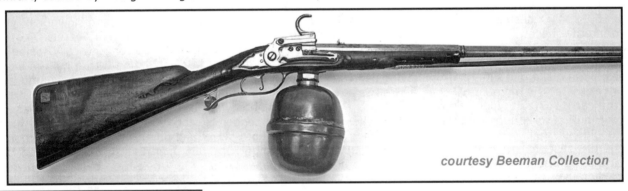

courtesy Beeman Collection

BRITISH BOTTOM BALL AIRGUNS

British Bottom Ball Airguns have the ball placed quite a bit forward of the trigger guard. While this adds complication to the air release parts linkage, it provides delightful gun balance and handling characteristics. One is reminded of a fine British double barrel shotgun when hefting and swinging one of these wonderful arms. Makers include the several Bates, Egg, Wilkinson, Bunney, Blunt, Bottomley, Martin, and Utting.

BRITISH PNEUMATIC BOTTOM BALL AIRGUN – .327" (8.32mm) cal., air rifle by George Wallis of Hull, England, mfg. circa 1860.

courtesy Beeman Collection

BOTTOM BALL AIR PISTOLS

It would be expected that some airgun makers would adapt the well-known bottom ball pattern to air pistols. While such pistols are very pleasing to handle, airguns of this pattern are extremely rare. An elegant long pistol of this pattern is known from the Bate shop of London.

BOTTOM BALL AIR PISTOL – .312" (7.92mm) cal., muzzle loading or unscrew barrel for loading, Liverpool, England, mfg. circa. 1820.

courtesy Beeman Collection

BALL IN THE BUTTSTOCK AIRGUNS

The most unexpected position of the air ball is the ball-in-the-buttstock airgun. The ball is fitted into a section of the buttstock that can be unscrewed and attached to a separate hand pump for charging. The sides of a normal-appearing air ball protrude on each side of the stock. The air passage and the air release rod are extremely long and probably quite inefficient.

BALL IN THE BUTTSTOCK AIRGUN – .368" (9.35mm) cal., marked Davaston.

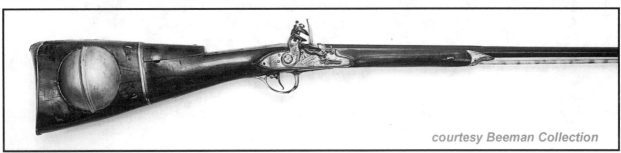

courtesy Beeman Collection

MODERN BALL RESERVOIR AIRGUN DERIVATIVES

While it may be stretching the ball reservoir category to include guns with removable air cylinders -- Wolff includes the modern Crosman bottom cylinder CO_2 rifles as "ball reservoir" guns. These guns are illustrated in the "C" section of this book. If we are to include these Crosman Model 121, 122, and 123 rifles then we must also include the O'Connell Gas Rifle in the "O" section and the Feinwerkbau Model C25 CO_2 pistol in the "F" section. We can then consider guns with such cylinders attached in a horizontal position as the evolutionary derivatives of this classification family. That would include early PCP guns such as the Beeman Gamekeeper in the "B" section, the Philippine Pampanga Shotgun in the "P" section and finally a wide variety of quite modern airguns with removable air or CO_2 cylinders.

BARNES PNEUMATIC

Current custom manufacturer located in New Windsor, MD.

Gary Barnes has over 30 years of experience, 22 as a master Bladesmith. Barnes applies unique artistic skill and design as well as mechanical creativity to his airguns. He specializes in large bore, high accuracy airguns, often with exotic styling and decoration of which all parts, including barrels are designed and manufactured in his shop. Various base models are listed on his website, but all are produced per-individual request. The following are examples of his craftsmanship. Contact Mr. Barnes directly (see Trademark Index) for price and availability.

AIRCANES

AUTOCANE – .27 in. cal., 800 psi traditionally configured PCP, full-automatic 500 rpm, 12 shot magazine, rosewood handle with gold lip pearl, sterling silver cap, acid etched body, deeply engraved top. 39.8 in. OAL, 4.7 lbs. Ref. USA (Nov-Dec 1997). Mfg. 1997.

courtesy Fred Liady

PISTOLS

HERITAGE CLASS 32 – .32 cal. (0 buckshot ball), SS, PCP, frictionless hammer, 2 stage match trigger, 11mm scope dovetail, high pressure breech, dueling style stock.

courtesy Gary Barnes

RIFLES

APPALOOSA – .32 cal. PCP with quick fill reservoir, SS, solid brass barrel shroud. Mfg. 2005.

courtesy Gary Barnes

FIRST MODEL – .45 cal., traditionally configured 500 psi PCP, magazine fed cross block repeater, adj. power, set trigger, deluxe walnut stock, acid-etched decoration, sterling silver shields, jeweled detail, 48 in. OAL, 10 lbs. Ref. USA (Jan. 1997). Mfg. 1996.

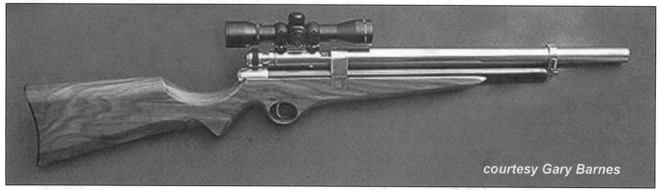

courtesy Fred Liady

HIGH PLAINS CARBINE – .375 cal., PCP, SS, LA, 850 FPS, "Shear Ring" breech sizes each round during loading, Claro walnut stock, brass rear sight, 36 in. OAL, 6.2 lbs. Mfg. 1997. Ref. AR 3: p.35.

courtesy Fred Liady

GRADING	100%	95%	90%	80%	60%	40%	20%

BARNETT INTERNATIONAL

Research continues with this trademark, and more information will be included both online and in future editions. Average original condition specimens on most common Barnett models are typically priced in the $150-$200 range.

BARON MANUFACTURING COMPANY

Previous manufacturer located in Burbank, CA, circa 1945-1949. Purchased by Healthways Corporation, Los Angeles, CA, in 1947 (distributed by Healthways as Sportsman, Jr. after 1947. Also private labeled as Wright Target Shot Jr. air pistol 1947-1949).

PISTOL

SPORTSMAN JR – .177 cal., SS, SP, 2.5 in. smoothbore bbl. unscrews for rear loading of BBs, darts, pellets, or removed for shooting corks, cocks by pulling knob at rear of compression tube, checkered grip panels, 8.1 in. OAL, 1 lb.

courtesy Beeman Collection

N/A	$100	$80	$60	$40	N/A	N/A

Last MSR was $3.49.

Add 20% for box and literature.

BARTHELMS, FRITZ (FB RECORD)

For information on Fritz Barthelms, please refer to FB Record in the "F" section.

BASCARAN, C. y T. SRC

Previous manufacturer located in Eibar, Guipuzcoa, Spain.

Bascaran, C. y T. SRC manufactured airguns under the Comento tradename. Research continues with this trademark, and more information will be included both in future editions and online. Average original condition specimens on most common Bascaran, C. y T. SRC models are typically priced in the $75-$125 range.

BAVARIA

For information on Bavaria airguns, see B.S.F. "Bayerische Sportwaffenfabrik" in this section.

BAYARD

Previously manufactured by Anciens Éstablissements Pieper in Herstal Liége, Belgium.

This company is best known for their semi-auto pistol manufacture. It produced a .177 cal., SP, BBC, SS air rifle for HyScore of New York, post-WWII. A mounted knight logo and "Bayard" may be stamped on the side of the body tube. Has a buttplate with cast letters "BELGIUM" in a vertical column. There are two known versions. One has a spring-loaded J-shaped pellet seating device on top of the breech. Very well made with hand checkered hardwood stock. Very good condition specimens sell in the $100-$200 range. Add $50 for pellet seating model.

courtesy Beeman Collection

BEC EUROLUX AIRGUNS

Previous trademark distributed by BEC Inc., located in Alhambra, CA.

GRADING	100%	95%	90%	80%	60%	40%	20%

RIFLES

MODEL BEC 15AG – .177 cal., BBC, SP, SS, 14.5 in. barrel, 500 FPS, black finish, walnut-tone hardwood stock, 5.5 lbs. Disc. 2006.

	$60	$50	$40	$35	$25	$20	$10

Last MSR was $69.

MODEL BEC 18AG – .177 or .22 cal., BBC, SP, SS, 16.5 in. barrel, 850/700 FPS, black finish, walnut-tone hardwood stock, 6.9 lbs. Disc. 2006.

	$85	$70	$60	$50	$40	$25	$15

Last MSR was $99.

MODEL BEC 21AG – .177 or .22 cal., BBC, SP, SS, 20 in. barrel, 1000/800 FPS, black finish, walnut-tone hardwood stock, 9.9 lbs. Disc. 2006.

	$160	$135	$110	$95	$70	$50	$30

Last MSR was $189.

BEDFORD

Previous maker and distributor of air pistols located at 45 High Street, Boston, Mass. Founded by American engineer, Augustus Bedford, about 1875.

Bedford evidently operated without a partner at first, manufacturing, or at least selling the Henry Quackenbush designed "Rifle Air Pistol". Bedford later developed airgun patent 172,376, issued January 18, 1876, covering moving the barrel more forward and loading an airgun with a cam sealing bolt action. He joined with George W. Walker who had patent 179,984, issued July 18, 1876, which further improved the bolt action, to form Bedford and Walker, to produce a new design airgun, known as the Bedford & Walker Eureka. Ref. Groenewold (2000).

PISTOL

BEDFORD RIFLE AIR PISTOL – .21 cal. smoothbore, SS, SP, cast iron frame nickel-plated or black finish, 12.75 in. OAL, 1.5 pounds. Barrel above compression tube. Cocked by pulling barrel forward. Loaded with dart when barrel is moved forward for cocking. Saw handle grip with embossed checkering. Rear edge of grip casting has a 5/16 in. hole for insertion of a wire shoulder stock. Marked: MANF'D BY A. BEDFORD. 45 HIGH ST. BOSTON. PATD. JUNE 6. DEC. 26, 1871. on LHS upper panel of frame. Stamped with SN on upper LHS of frame; production apparently low - this specimen is SN 11. Apparently identical to Quackenbush Rifle Air Pistol which bears these same patent dates. Mfg. 1878-1880.

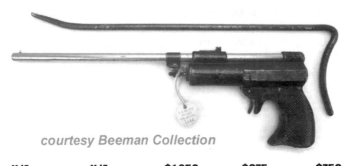

courtesy Beeman Collection

	N/A	N/A	$1,250	$975	$750	$525	$375

Add 10% for wire shoulder stock.
Add 20% for nickel finish.
Add 25% for original factory box and instructions.

BEDFORD & WALKER

Previous manufacturer located in Boston, MA circa 1880s.

Former gunmaking partnership of Augustus Bedford and George A. Walker located in Boston, MA. Manufactured the Eureka air pistol based on the Quackenbush push-barrel design with a loading bolt patented by Walker in 1876. Production started in Bedford's Eureka Manufacturing Co. circa 1876, then went to the Pope Brothers & Company plant, and finally transferred to the H.M. Quackenbush plant from the 1880s until 1893. Quackenbush featured the pistol in his catalogs and listed a sale of seventy-four Eureka air pistols in 1886. (Bedford worked in the Quackenbush factory for several years and he, Pope, Walker, and Quackenbush were close associates -- so there is a good deal of overlap and confusion about the origin, production, and sales of their designs). Last sales occurred circa 1893.

GRADING	100%	95%	90%	80%	60%	40%	20%

PISTOLS

EUREKA DELUXE – .21 cal., SP, SS push-plunger, nickel finish, rosewood inserts on flared grip, wire shoulder stock.

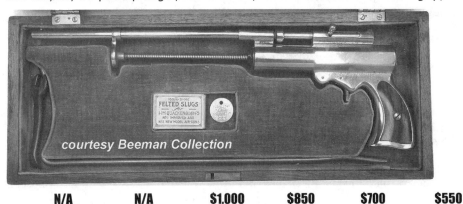

courtesy Beeman Collection

	N/A	N/A	$1,000	$850	$700	$550	$350

This model also includes a hardwood case with locking lid, wrench, and box of slugs or darts.

EUREKA STANDARD – .21 cal., SP, SS push-plunger, black or nickel finish.

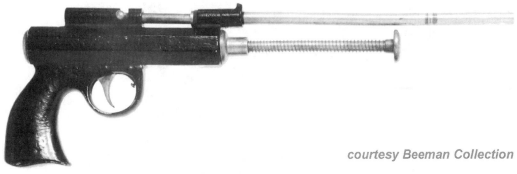

courtesy Beeman Collection

	$800	$675	$550	$450	$350	$240	$160

Add 10% for nickel finish.
Add 20% for wire shoulder stock.

BEEMAN PRECISION AIRGUNS

Current manufacturer and importer located in Santa Fe Springs, CA. Previously located in Huntington Beach, CA until 2010. Dealer and consumer direct sales.

The Beeman company was founded by Robert and Toshiko Beeman in 1972 in San Anselmo, CA. Originally named Beeman's Precision Airguns, the company began by importing airgun models and pellets from Weihrauch, Feinwerkbau, Webley, Dianawerk, Handler and Natermann, Hasuike, and other overseas companies. After moving to San Rafael, CA, circa 1975 the name of the company was changed to Beeman Precision Airguns, Inc. They began to design their own models of airguns and airgun pellets to be produced by Weihrauch, Webley, Norica, Handler and Natermann, and Hasuike. Among the many airgun items introduced by the Beemans were the first telescopic sights built especially for high power sporting air rifles and the first hollow point airgun pellets. By the late 1970s, the Beeman company was importing over 90% of the adult airguns brought into the USA.

Although several other companies, notably Winchester and Hy-Score, had previously attempted to introduce adult airguns to the American shooting market, Beeman is credited with the first successful, commercial development of the adult airgun market in the United States. Tom Gaylord, founder and former editor of *Airgun Letter*, *Airgun Revue*, and *Airgun Illustrated Magazine*, recorded in his book *The Beeman R1* that "the Beeman R1 is the rifle that brought America fully into the world of adult airguns." (Versions of the Beeman R1, generally lower in power or less deluxe, are marketed in other parts of the world as the Weihrauch HW 80.) Other models were produced for Beeman by Norica, Erma, FAS, Record, Sharp, Air Arms, Titan, Gamekeeper, and others. Circa 1987 Beeman moved to Santa Rosa and added certain precision firearms to its line and changed its name to Beeman Precision Arms, Inc. On April 3, 1993, Robert and Toshiko sold most of the assets of their company to S/R Industries of Maryland. S/R moved the company to Huntington Beach, CA to be near one of its other holdings, Marksman Industries, and restored the name of Beeman Precision Airguns. The company has continued to feature the very high quality airguns which had become synonymous with the Beeman name and added an economy line for mass marketers.

Beeman has exclusive rights to any airguns officially marketed in the U.S. under the names Beeman and Feinwerkbau, Beeman designed models manufactured by Weihrauch and others. Some models, marketed by Beeman in the late 1970s and early 1980s, were manufactured in Germany by Mayer & Grammelspacher (Dianawerk). Early production of those airguns used Diana model numbers under the Beeman's Original brand, but later shipments were marked

GRADING	100%	95%	90%	80%	60%	40%	20%

with the Beeman name and model numbers. Very small stampings on the Dianawerk receivers indicate the month and year of manufacture.

Beeman imported Feinwerkbau and Weihrauch Airguns, which appear under their respective headings in this section. Beeman/Webley airguns are incorporated into this section, as are economy airguns that are only promoted through chain stores under the Beeman name.

Additional material on the history of the Beeman company, the Beemans, the history of airguns, the development of the airgun market in the USA, and a wide range of other airgun information is available at www.Beemans.net .

At the end of 2009 the Beeman brand was split and sold. The Singapore Airgun Company bought all rights to the Marksman airguns and Beeman Precision Airguns, except the "Traditional Beeman Airguns". The precision models built for Beeman in Germany, were assigned to Richard Kazmaier and Mr. Kazmaier assigned the distribution of the Beeman "Traditional Models" to Pyramyd Airguns.

For more information and current values on used Beeman firearms, please refer to the *Blue Book of Gun Values* by S.P. Fjestad (also available online).

PISTOLS

For values and information on older Beeman/Weirauch Sport HW Model pistols see Weirauch Sport in the "W" section.

ADDER – .177, .20, .22, or .25 cal., 940/850/775/630 FPS, 14 to 20 ft. lbs. ME, PCP, SS, bolt action, grip, trigger guard, and forearm from one piece of select hardwood, smooth grips, scope grooves, blue receiver end cap, 10.5 in. barrel, 16.5 in. OAL, manual safety, 2.75 lbs. Mfg. by Titan in England with ten imported circa 1992.

courtesy Beeman Collection

N/A	$500	$400	$325	$250	$175	$100

Last MSR was $530.

Add 10% for .20 cal.

FAS 604

For information on the FAS 604 pistol, see FAS in the "F" section.

HURRICANE – .177 or .22 (disc.) cal., TL, SP, SS, 500 FPS, plastic grips with RH thumbrest, adj. rear sight supplied with adapter which replaced rear sight with scope mounting dovetail, hooded front sight, aluminum grip frame cast around steel body tube, RH manual safety, black epoxy finish, 8 in. button rifled barrel, 11.2 in. OAL, 2.4 lbs. Mfg. in England with importation beginning in 1990.

$235	$200	$165	$135	$105	$70	$45

Last MSR was $275.

Add 10% for wood grips.

Add 15% for finger groove Beeman "combat" wood grips.

Add 20% for Beeman factory markings with San Rafael address.

Add 10% for Beeman factory markings with Santa Rosa address.

Add 20% for large deluxe factory box with form-fitting depressions, including depression for mounted scope, in hard plastic shell with red flocked surface.

Add 10% for factory box with molded white foam support block.

Add 20% for Model 20 scope combo.

GRADING	100%	95%	90%	80%	60%	40%	20%

HW70A – .177 cal., BBC, SP, SS, 6 in. rifled barrel, post globe front sight, adj. rear sight, two-stage adj. trigger, auto safety, 12.8 in. OAL, 2.4 lbs.

courtesy Beeman Precision Airguns

MSR $335	$290	$245	$205	$170	$130	$85	$60

MODEL 700 – .177 cal., BBC, SP, 460 FPS, 7 in. barrel, 3.1 lbs. Disc. 1981.

courtesy Beeman Collection

	$125	$105	$90	$75	$55	$35	$25

Last MSR was $122.

Add 20% for left-hand grip.
Add 20% for Beeman walnut stock.
Add 50% for Beeman folding metal shoulder stock.
Add 10% if stamped "Beeman's Original".

Mfg. for Beeman in Germany by Mayer & Grammelspacher. First imports marked "Beeman's Original Model 5".

MODEL 800 – .177 cal., BBC, SP, SS, 460 FPS, 7 in. barrel, Giss patent double opposing piston recoilless mechanism, 3.2 lbs. Disc. 1982.

courtesy Beeman Collection

	$225	$190	$160	$130	$100	$65	$45

Last MSR was $191.

Add 10% if stamped "Beeman's Original".
Add 20% for left-hand grip.
Add 20% for Beeman walnut stock.
Add 50% for Beeman folding metal shoulder stock.

Mfg. for Beeman in Germany by Mayer & Grammelspacher. First imports marked "Beeman's Original Model 6".

GRADING	100%	95%	90%	80%	60%	40%	20%

MODEL 850 – .177 cal., BBC, SP, SS, 460 FPS, 7 in. barrel, Giss patent double opposing piston recoilless mechanism, rotating barrel shroud, 3.2 lbs. Disc. 1982.

courtesy Beeman Collection

	$295	$250	$205	$170	$135	$90	$60

Last MSR was $225.

Add 20% for left-hand grip or scope mount (shown in picture).
Add 20% for Beeman walnut grip (shown in picture).
Add 50% for Beeman metal wire shoulder stock (fitting shown in picture).
Add 10% if stamped "Beeman's Original".

Mfg. in Germany for Beeman by Mayer & Grammelspacher.

MODEL 900 – .177 cal., BBC, SP, 490 FPS, 7.1 in. barrel, double opposing piston recoilless mechanism, rotating barrel shroud, target model with adj. walnut match grips, match micrometer sights, 3.3 lbs. Disc. 1981.

	$375	$325	$265	$220	$170	$110	$75

Last MSR was $445.

Add 10% if stamped "Beeman's Original" or "Condor".
Add 10% for left-hand grip.
Add 20% for fitted factory case.

Mfg. in Germany for Beeman by Mayer & Grammelspacher. First imports marked "Beeman's Original Model 10".

P17 (MODEL 2004) – .177 cal., SSP, 410 FPS, black finish, finger groove grips, 9.25 in. OAL, 1.7 lbs. New 2010.

courtesy Beeman Precision Airguns

MSR $50	$40	$35	$30	$25	$20	N/A	N/A

Add $10 for Deluxe Pellet Pistol Kit, includes safety glasses and Wadcutter pellets (Model 2004K).
Add $20 for Deluxe Pellet Pistol w/Trap Kit, includes pellet trap and deluxe carry case (Model 2004DK, disc. 2012).

P17 Kit (MODEL 2006) – .177 cal., SSP, 410 FPS, black finish, finger groove grips, 9.25 in. OAL, red dot sight, 2 lbs. New 2010.

courtesy Beeman Precision Airguns

MSR $60	$50	$45	$35	$30	$25	N/A	N/A

GRADING	100%	95%	90%	80%	60%	40%	20%

MODEL 2008 – .177 cal., 12g CO_2 cartridge semi-auto, 400 FPS, includes 4 six-shot rotary clips, finger groove grips, black finish, 9.25 in. OAL, 2 lbs. New 2010.

courtesy Beeman Precision Airguns

MSR $90	$75	$70	$60	$50	$40	N/A	N/A

MODEL 2011 – BB/.177 cal., CO_2, 420 FPS, 18-shot mag., black finish, 9.25 in. OAL, 1.7 lbs. Mfg. 2010-2012.

	$35	$30	$25	$20	$15	N/A	N/A

Last MSR was $40.

NEMESIS – .177 or .22 cal., TL, SS, single-stroke pneumatic, 385/300 FPS, two-stage adj. trigger, black or brushed chrome finish, manual safety, adj. open sights, integral scope rail, 2.2 lbs. Mfg. in England. 1995-disc.

	$150	$130	$105	$85	$70	$45	$30

Last MSR was $200.

Add 10% for brushed chrome finish.

P1 MAGNUM – .177, .20, or .22 (disc.1995, reintroduced 2010) cal., TL, SP, SS, single (.22) or dual power action, 600/480 FPS in .177, 500/420 FPS in .20, two-stage trigger, scope groove, barrel and sights in same unit, walnut grips, Colt 1911A1 styling, accepts any custom grips designed for the 1911A1, 11 in. OAL, 2.56 lbs. Mfg. in Germany with importation beginning in 1983.

courtesy Beeman Collection

MSR $530	$450	$375	$325	$260	$205	$135	$90

Add $35 for .22 cal.
Add $70 for stainless steel variation.
Add 10% for Santa Rosa address.
Add 15% for grooved Combat grips (shown in picture).
Add 30% for Beeman shoulder stock (walnut) - designed by R. Beeman.
Add 100% for gold plating.
Add 30% for blue/stainless dual finish.
Add 100% for Commemorative Model, enameled 20th year logo inletted into deluxe rosewood grip (25 mfg. 1992 only).

Designed by Robert Beeman and engineered by H.W. Weihrauch Company. The P1 was the predecessor of the Weihrauch HW 45. 1983-1989 San Rafael markings; 1990-1995 Santa Rosa markings. 1996-2010: Huntington Beach markings (under S/R Industries ownership of Beeman company).

GRADING	100%	95%	90%	80%	60%	40%	20%

P2 – .177 or .20 (mfg. 1990-93) cal., TL, SSP, SS, 435/365 FPS, two-stage adj. trigger, walnut grips, scope groove, barrel and sights in same unit, Colt 1911A1 styling, 11 in. OAL, 2.56 lbs. Mfg. in Germany with importation 1990-2001.

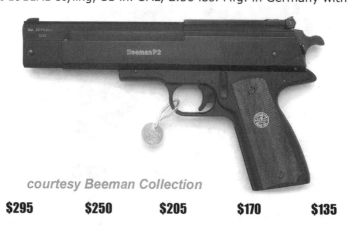

courtesy Beeman Collection

	$295	$250	$205	$170	$135	$90	$60

Last MSR was $385.

Add 20% for match grips.
Add 30% for .20 cal.
Add 10% for Santa Rosa address.

P3 – .177 cal., TL, SSP, SS, 410 FPS, cocking the hammer allows the top frame to swing up as a charging lever, automatic safety and bear trap prevention, adj. rear sight, rifled steel barrel, built-in muzzle brake, two-stage trigger, anatomical polymer composite grip, 1.7 lbs. Mfg. in Germany with importation beginning in 1999.

courtesy S.P. Fjestad

MSR $290	$235	$200	$165	$135	$105	$70	$45

Add 20% for Millennium Model with gold trigger, hammer, and safety.
Add 50% for P3 Combo with 5021 scope and accessories.

P11 – .177 cal., rifled barrel, single shot, overlever action, blade and ramp front sights, adj. rear sights, silver finish with black slide, grey laminated target grips with palmswell and thumbrest, two-stage adj. trigger. New 2012.

courtesy Beeman Precision Airguns

MSR $600	$525	$425	$350	$300	$230	$155	$105

GRADING	100%	95%	90%	80%	60%	40%	20%

TEMPEST – .177 or .22 (disc.) cal., TL, SP, SS, 500/400 FPS, plastic grips with RH thumb rest, adj. rear sight, aluminum grip frame cast around steel body tube, compact version of Hurricane (Tempest bodies produced by grinding off rear section of Hurricane castings), RH manual safety, 6.87 in. button rifled barrel, black epoxy finish, 9.2 in. OAL, 2 lbs. Mfg. in England 1981-Disc.

	$195	$165	$135	$115	$90	$60	$40

Last MSR was $235.

Add 10% for Beeman wood grips.
Add 15% for finger groove Beeman "combat" wood grips.
Add 20% for Beeman factory markings with San Rafael address.
Add 10% for Beeman factory markings with Santa Rosa address.

Add 20% for large factory box 11.6 x 8.6 inches, black with logo.
Add 10% for medium factory box 10.2 x 6.6 inches, black with logo.

WOLVERINE – .177 or .25 cal., PCP, SS, BA, 10.5 in. barrel, 940/630 FPS (14 to 20 ft. lbs. ME), 10.5 in. barrel, select walnut stippled grip, solid brass rear receiver cap, match trigger, scope grooves, manual safety, 16.5 in. OAL, 3 lbs. Mfg. by Titan in England with ten imported circa 1992.

courtesy Beeman Collection

	N/A	$500	$400	$325	$250	$175	$100

Last MSR was $700.

RIFLES

For values and information on older Beeman/Weirauch Sport HW Model rifles see Weirauch Sport in the "W" section.

CLASSIC MAGNUM – .20 or .25 cal., 910/680 FPS, BBC, GS, SS, 15 in. barrel, automatic lever safety, checkered walnut stock with angular forearm extending just forward of barrel base block, 44.5 in. OAL, 8.3 lbs. Mfg. in England 1992 only.

	$900	$750	$625	$525	$400	$265	$180

Last MSR was $895.

Add 5% for .20 cal.
Add 15% for power adjustment pump.

CROW MAGNUM I – .20 or .25 cal., 1060/815 FPS, BBC, GS, SS, 16 in. barrel, automatic safety (thin metal piece), smoothly curved trigger, built-in scope base, no sights, polished steel muzzle weight, 46 in. OAL, 8.6 lbs. Mfg. in England 1992-1993.

	$850	$725	$600	$500	$375	$255	$170

Add 5% for .20 cal.
Add 15% for power adjustment pump.

CROW MAGNUM II – .20 or .25 cal., 1060/815 FPS, BBC, GS, SS, 16 in. barrel, automatic safety (rugged metal strip), "beak shaped" trigger centered in guard, Dampa Mount scope rings provided for built-in scope rail, no sights, polished steel muzzle weight, 46 in. OAL, 8.6 lbs. Mfg. in England 1993-1995.

	$950	$800	$675	$550	$425	$285	$190

Last MSR was $1,220.

Add 15% for power adjustment pump.

CROW MAGNUM III – .20, .22, or .25 cal., BBC, GS, 1060/1035/815 FPS, 16 in. barrel, two stage adj. trigger, redesigned piston with steel face and O-rings, extended compression cylinder, deluxe hand checkered Hyedua ambidextrous stock, no sights, automatic safety (rugged metal strip), polished steel muzzle weight, 46 in. OAL, 8.6 lbs. Mfg. in England 1995-2001.

	$1,000	$850	$700	$575	$450	$300	$200

Last MSR was $1,220.

Add 15% for power adjustment pump.

GRADING	100%	95%	90%	80%	60%	40%	20%

CROW MAGNUM IV – .20, .22, or .25 cal., BBC, GS, 1060/1035/815 FPS, 16 in. barrel, deluxe hand checkered Hyedua ambidextrous stock, polished steel muzzle weight, redesigned piston with steel face and O-rings, extended compression cylinder, automatic safety with protective "bump" inside forward curve of trigger guard, trigger has straighter profile and is moved back in guard, 46 in. OAL, 8.6 lbs. Mfg. in England 2001-2004.

courtesy Beeman Collection

$1,150	$975	$800	$675	$525	$350	$230

Last MSR was $1,355.

ECLIPSE – for information on this model, see Webley & Scott, Ltd. in the "W" section.

FALCON 1 – .177 cal., BBC, SP, SS, 640 FPS, 43 in. OAL, 6.7 lbs. Mfg. in Spain 1981-1984.

courtesy Beeman Collection

$150	$130	$105	$85	$70	$45	$30

FALCON 2 – .177 cal., BBC, SP, SS, 580 FPS, 41 in. OAL, 5.9 lbs. Mfg. in Spain 1981-1984.

courtesy Beeman Collection

$120	$100	$85	$70	$55	$35	$25

Last MSR was $110.

FX 1 – .177 cal., BBC, SP, SS, 640 FPS, 43 in. OAL, 6.7 lbs. Mfg. in Spain 1985-1992.

$155	$130	$110	$90	$70	$45	$30

Last MSR was $140.

FX 2 – .177 cal., BBC, SP, SS, 580 FPS, 41 in. OAL, 5.9 lbs. Mfg. in Spain 1985-1992.

$125	$105	$90	$75	$55	$35	$25

LEWIS & CLARK COMMEMORATIVE (FWB 124) – .177 cal., BBC, SP, 780-830 FPS, etched silver plated receiver w/scene of Sacajawea pointing the way for Lewis and Clark superimposed on map (east and west are reversed) checkered Monte-Carlo stock, 7.2 lbs.

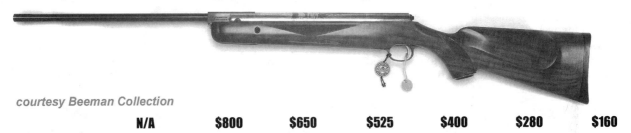

courtesy Beeman Collection

N/A	$800	$650	$525	$400	$280	$160

This model was available in three versions produced by Beeman on FWB 124 base. For information on the Feinwerkbau (FWB) Model 124, see Feinwerkbau in the "F" section.

GRADING	100%	95%	90%	80%	60%	40%	20%

MAKO – .177 cal., PCP, SS, BA, 930 FPS, hand cut checkered beech stock, adj. trigger, manual safety, 38.5 in. OAL, 7.3 lbs. Mfg. in England 1995-2002.

	$750	$625	$525	$425	$325	$225	$150

Last MSR was $1,000.

Add 50% for FT Model with checkered thumbhole stock.

MAKO MKII – .177 or .22 cal., PCP, SS, BA, 1000/860 FPS, checkered walnut stock, two stage adj. trigger, scope grooves, no sights, manual safety, 37 in. OAL, 5.5 lbs. Mfg. in England 2003-2006.

	$825	$700	$575	$475	$375	$245	$165

Last MSR was $999.

MANITOU FT – .177 cal. PCP, SS, 21 in. barrel, angular stock with adj. cheek piece, 36.3 in. OAL, 8.75 lbs. Mfg. in England 1992 only.

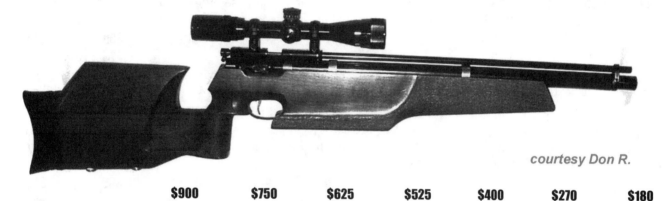

courtesy Don R.

	$900	$750	$625	$525	$400	$270	$180

Last MSR was $995.

Add 20% for left-hand variation.
Add 10% for charge adapter with gauge.
   A total of ten guns were imported into the U.S.

MODEL 100 – .177 cal., BBC, SP, 660 FPS, 18.7 in. barrel, 6 lbs. Disc. 1980.

	$125	$105	$90	$75	$55	$35	$25

Last MSR was $155.

Add 10% if stamped "Beeman's Original".
   Mfg. in Germany by Mayer & Grammelspacher. First imports marked "Beeman's Original Model 27".

MODEL 200 – .177 cal., BBC, SP, 700 FPS, 19 in. barrel, 7.1 lbs. Disc. 1979.

	$125	$105	$90	$75	$55	$35	$25

Last MSR was $197.

Add 10% if stamped "Beeman's Original".
   Less than 100 mfg. in Germany by Mayer & Grammelspacher. First imports marked "Beeman's Original Model 35".

MODEL 250 – .177, .20, or .22 cal., BBC, SP, 830/750/650 FPS, 20.5 in. barrel, 7.8 lbs. Disc. 1981.

courtesy Beeman Collection

	$275	$235	$195	$160	$125	$80	$55

Last MSR was $217.

Add 50% for Commemorative model (shown), Diana emblem in stock (approx. 20 Beeman 250s were so marked).
Add 30% for Long Safety version - safety bolt projects 1.225 in. (29 mm) from rear end of receiver and is not stamped "N". Such guns were recalled as a hazard and a shorter safety, stamped "N", installed.
Add 60% for .20 cal. version (approx. 40 were produced).
   Manufactured in Germany by Mayer & Grammelspacher.

GRADING	100%	95%	90%	80%	60%	40%	20%

MODEL 400 – .177 cal., SL, SP, 650 FPS, 19 in. barrel, target model with match micrometer aperture sight, 10.9 lbs. Disc. 1981.

	100%	95%	90%	80%	60%	40%	20%
	$800	$675	$550	$475	$350	$240	$160

Last MSR was $615.

Add 10% if stamped "Beeman's Original".
Add 15% for left-hand stock and lever.
Add 15% for Universal model (adj. cheekpiece).

Mfg. in Germany by Mayer & Grammelspacher. First imports marked "Beeman's Original Model 75".

MODEL GH500 COMBO – .177 cal., BBC, SP, SS, Belgium Matte finish, ported muzzle brake, 525 FPS, Monte Carlo sporter style composite stock, automatic safety, adj. 3-7x20 Beeman scope, 38.5 in. OAL, 5 lbs. Mfg. in USA 2004-2006.

	100%	95%	90%	80%	60%	40%	20%
	$75	$65	$55	$45	$35	$20	$15

Last MSR was $90.

MODEL GH650 – .177 cal., BBC, SP, 650 FPS, sporter trigger, automatic safety, walnut stained beech Monte Carlo stock with recoil pad, ported muzzle brake, 4x32mm Beeman scope, 41.5 in. OAL, 5.9 lbs. Mfg. 2003-2006.

	100%	95%	90%	80%	60%	40%	20%
	$165	$140	$115	$95	$75	$50	$35

Last MSR was $190.

MODEL GH1050 – .177 or .22 cal., BBC, SP, 812/1000 FPS, rifled steel barrel, fiber optic sights with fully adj. rear, two-stage adj. trigger, ambidextrous black synthetic stock with recoil pad, automatic safety, 45.67 in. OAL, 6.4 lbs. Mfg. 2005-2012.

	100%	95%	90%	80%	60%	40%	20%
	$195	$165	$135	$115	$90	$60	$40

MODEL GH1050 COMBO – .177 or .22 cal., BBC, SP, 812/1000 FPS, rifled steel barrel, fiber optic sights with fully adj. rear, 3-9x32mm scope with muzzle brake, two-stage adj. trigger, ambidextrous black synthetic stock with recoil pad, automatic safety, 45.67 in. OAL, 6.4 lbs. Mfg. 2005-2012.

	100%	95%	90%	80%	60%	40%	20%
	$225	$190	$160	$130	$100	$65	$45

MODEL GS700 – .177 cal., BBC, SP, 700 FPS, two-stage trigger, automatic safety, walnut stained beech stock, 6.9 lbs. Mfg. in Spain, disc. 2001.

	100%	95%	90%	80%	60%	40%	20%
	$100	$85	$70	$60	$45	$30	$20

Last MSR was $149.

MODEL GS950 – .177 or .22 cal., BBC, SP, 950/750 FPS, blue finish, adj. rear and fixed front fiber optic sights, two-stage trigger, automatic safety, walnut stained Monte Carlo stock, 46.25 in. OAL, 7.25 lbs. Mfg. in Spain 2001-2006.

	100%	95%	90%	80%	60%	40%	20%
	$210	$180	$145	$120	$95	$65	$40

Last MSR was $250.

* **Model GH950 Combo** – .177 or .22 cal., BBC, SP, 950/750 FPS, includes Model GS950 with ported muzzle brake, either 4x32mm or 3-9x32mm Beeman scope with adj. objective and target turrets with caps, and 250-count tin of hollow point pellets. Mfg. 2003-2006.

	100%	95%	90%	80%	60%	40%	20%
	$265	$225	$185	$155	$120	$80	$55

Last MSR was $320.

Add 10% for GH950 Combo with 3-9x32mm Beeman scope.

MODEL GS1000 – .177 or .22 cal., BBC, SP, 1000/765 FPS, micrometer adj. rear and blade front sights, two-stage adj. trigger, automatic safety, checkered European sporter style walnut stained stock with PG and recoil pad, 46.75 in. OAL, 7.5 lbs. Mfg. in Spain 2001-2006.

courtesy Beeman Collection

	100%	95%	90%	80%	60%	40%	20%
	$235	$200	$165	$135	$105	$70	$45

Last MSR was $280.

* **Model GH1000 Combo** – .177 or .22 cal., BBC, SP, 1000/765 FPS, includes Model GS1000 with ported muzzle brake, either 3-9x32mm or 3-12x40mm Beeman scope with adj. objective and target turrets with caps, and 250-count tin of hollow point pellets. Mfg. 2003-2006.

	100%	95%	90%	80%	60%	40%	20%
	$325	$285	$235	$195	$150	$100	$65

Last MSR was $420.

Add 5% for 3-12x40mm Beeman scope.

GRADING	100%	95%	90%	80%	60%	40%	20%

MODEL GT600 – .177 cal., BBC, SP, 600 FPS, sporter trigger, automatic safety, walnut stained beech stock, 5.9 lbs. Mfg. in Spain. Disc. 2001.

	$80	$70	$55	$45	$35	$25	$15

Last MSR was $119.

MODEL GT650 – .177 cal., BBC, SP, 600 FPS, sporter trigger, automatic safety, walnut stained beech stock, 5.9 lbs. Mfg. in Spain 2001-2002.

	$90	$75	$65	$50	$40	$25	$20

Last MSR was $135.

MODEL R1/R1-AW/R1 CARBINE – .177, .20, .22, or .25 (disc.) cal., BBC, SP, SS, 19.3 in. barrel, blue or nickel plated (R1-AW) finish, 1000/610 FPS, new design using some Weihrauch Model HW 35 parts with design changes to greatly increase power, speed, cocking ease and efficiency, beech Monte Carlo stock, hand cut checkered pistol grip with palm swell and white lined grip cap, forearm extends to front end of barrel block, white line rubber buttplate with molded BEEMAN lettering, solid steel receiver cap, 14.3 in. LOP, 45.2 in. OAL, 8.5 lbs. Mfg. in Germany 1981 to date.

courtesy Beeman Collection

MSR $760	$650	$550	$450	$375	$290	$195	$130

Add $10 for .20 cal. (Model R1).
Add $100 for left hand variation (.22 cal. only Model R1).
Add 10% for .25 cal.
Add 20% for Santa Rosa address.
Add 25% for San Rafael address.
Add 90% for custom grade.
Add 25% for Field Target Model.
Add 250% for Goudy/Beeman custom stock.
Add 125% for X fancy stock.
Add 10% for left-hand variation.
Add 25% for blue/silver finish.

Add 50% for Tyrolean stock (less than 25 mfg.).
Add 60% for commemorative model (50 mfg. 1992 only - 20th year commemorative medallion inlaid into stock, silver/blue metal finish, deluxe).
Add 20% for AW Model with electroless nickel finish and black Kevlar/graphite/fiberglass stock, available in .20 cal. carbine only, 9.7 lbs.
Subtract 20% for gas spring retrofit (inappropriately called gas ram or strut).
Chrome and gold-plated variations of the R1 with RDB prefix serialization may exceed retail values by 150%-300%.

This is the first spring piston airgun to reach 1000 FPS MV and first to extend forearm to cover barrel base block. Designed by Robert Beeman, stock design by Robert Beeman and Gary Goudy; engineered by H.W. Weihrauch. Predecessor of Weihrauch HW 80 and considered as first successful start of adult airgun market in USA. Ref: Gaylord, 1995, *The Beeman R1*.

MODEL R1 ELITE SERIES COMBO – .177, .22, or .20 cal., SP, BBC, SS, 1000/765/860 FPS, rifled barrel, two-stage adj. trigger, no sights, auto safety, hardwood stock and forearm, rubber buttpad, includes Bushnell 4-12x40 AO scope, 46.5 in. OAL, 10.2 lbs.

courtesy Beeman Precision Airguns

MSR $950	$825	$700	$575	$475	$375	$245	$165

Add $50 for .177 or .22 cal.

MODEL R1 LASER® – .177, 20, .22, or 25 cal., BBC, SP, SS, 19.3 in. barrel, blue finish, Laser® spring piston unit for up to an additional 200 FPS, laminated sporter stock inlaid with baked enamel Beeman Laser® logo, forearm extends to front end of barrel block, white line rubber buttplate with molded BEEMAN lettering, solid steel receiver cap, 14.3 in. LOP, 45.2 in. OAL, 8.5 lbs. Mfg. 1988-2001.

GRADING	100%	95%	90%	80%	60%	40%	20%

* *Model R1 Laser® MK I* – metal pistol grip cap replaced by rosewood in 1994. Mfg. 1988-1995.

	N/A	$1,200	$950	$775	$600	$425	$240

Add 25% for Mark 1 with Santa Rosa address.
Add 10% for metal grip cap.

* *Model R1 Laser® MK II* – similar to Model R1 Laser® MK I, except no pistol grip cap. .25 cal. disc. Mfg. 1995-1999.

	N/A	$1,000	$800	$650	$500	$350	$200

* *Model R1 Laser® MK III* – similar to Model R1 Laser® MK II, except gas spring version. Mfg. 1999-2001.

	N/A	$900	$725	$575	$450	$325	$180

MODEL R5 – .20 cal., BBC, SP, SS, similar to Feinwerkbau Model 124, except upgraded deluxe stock, receiver incorrectly factory stamped "Model 125, 5.mm/.22 cal." Four mfg. (two retained by factory) in Germany 1981.

courtesy Beeman Collection

Scarcity precludes accurate pricing.
Ref: Beeman (1998) AR3:61-62.

MODEL R6 – .177 cal., BBC, SP, SS, 815 FPS, two stage trigger, plain beech stock, rubber buttplate, automatic safety, 41.8 in. OAL, 7.1 lbs. Mfg. in Germany 1995-2001.

$225	$190	$160	$130	$100	$65	$45

Last MSR was $285.

Add 150% for custom grade.

MODEL R7 – .177 or .20 cal., BBC, SP, SS, 700/620 FPS, two-stage adj. trigger, beech stock with Monte Carlo comb, forearm extending to front end of barrel block, 14.3 in. LOP, scope grooves, hand checkered pistol grip, rubber buttplate with molded "BEEMAN", all metal sights, automatic safety, 40.2 in. OAL, 6.1 lbs. Mfg. in Germany 1983 to date. Ref: AA, (March 2003).

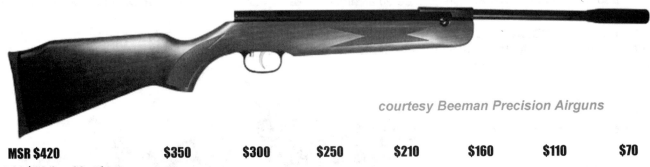

courtesy Beeman Precision Airguns

MSR $420	$350	$300	$250	$210	$160	$110	$70

Add $30 for .20 cal.
Add 20% for San Rafael or Santa Rosa address.
Add 10% for no safety (new 1986).
Add 20% for RDB versions, early production, soft rubber buttplate with Beeman name, cheekpiece with sharp edges and sweeping outline, greater detailing.

GRADING	100%	95%	90%	80%	60%	40%	20%

MODEL R7 ELITE SERIES COMBO – .177 or .20 cal., BBC, SP, SS, 700/620 FPS, 13.5 in. rifled barrel, two-stage trigger, auto safety, no sights, hardwood stock and forearm, rubber buttpad, 37 in. OAL, 7 lbs.

courtesy Beeman Precision Airguns

MSR $560	$475	$400	$350	$280	$220	$145	$95

Add $30 for .20 cal.

MODEL R8 – .177 cal., BBC, SP, SS, 720 FPS, two-stage adj. trigger, beech stock with sharply defined cheek piece, 14.3 in. LOP, solid steel receiver cap, hand checkered pistol grip, rubber buttplate, forearm extending to front end of barrel block, metal sights, scope grooves, automatic safety, 43 in. OAL, 7.1 lbs. Mfg. in Germany 1983-1997.

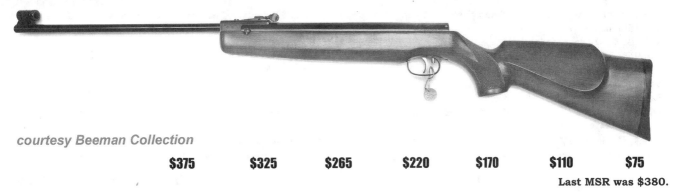

courtesy Beeman Collection

	$375	$325	$265	$220	$170	$110	$75

Last MSR was $380.

Add 20% for Santa Rosa address.
Add 20% for RDB versions, early production, soft rubber buttplate with Beeman name, cheekpiece with sharp edges and sweeping outline, greater detailing.

MODEL R9/R9 COMBO – .177, .20, or .22 cal., BBC, SP, SS, 1000/800 FPS, adj. trigger, automatic safety, beech stock, with or without (Model R9 Goldfinger) adj. rear and globe front sights, receiver cut for scope mounts, 4x32mm or 3-9x32mm (Model R9 Combo new 2003) Beeman scope, muzzle brake (Model R9 Goldfinger Combo new 2003), 43 in. OAL, 7.3 lbs. Mfg. in Germany. New 1995.

courtesy Beeman Collection

MSR $550	$475	$400	$325	$275	$215	$140	$95

Add $30 for .20 cal.
Add $80 for Model R9-Deluxe with hand checkered grip, white lined grip cap and buttplate.
Add 25% for laminate stock.
Add 5% for "Goldfinger" version with gold-plated trigger.
Add $70 for Model R9 Combo with 4x32mm Beeman adj. objective scope with target turrets with caps and tin of pellets (disc.).
Add $100 for Model R9 Combo with 3-9x32mm Beeman adj. objective scope with target turrets with caps and tin of pellets (disc.).
Add $100 for Model R9 Goldfinger Combo with 4-12x40mm Beeman adj. objective scope with target turrets and caps (disc.).

MODEL R9 ELITE SERIES COMBO – .177, .22, or .20 cal., BBC, SP, SS, 16.5 in. rifled barrel, 935/800 FPS, two-

GRADING	100%	95%	90%	80%	60%	40%	20%

stage adj. trigger, no sights, auto safety, hardwood stock and forearm, rubber buttpad, includes Bushnell 4-12x40 AO scope, 43.25 in. OAL, 8.5 lbs.

courtesy Beeman Precision Airguns

	100%	95%	90%	80%	60%	40%	20%
MSR $670	$575	$475	$400	$325	$255	$170	$115

Add $30 for .20 cal.

MODEL R10 – .177, .20, or .22 cal., BBC, SP, SS, 1000/750 FPS, smooth walnut finished beech stock, forearm ends at barrel pivot, solid steel machined receiver cap, automatic safety, 45.8 in. OAL, 7.5 lbs. Mfg. in Germany 1986-1995.

	$450	$375	$325	$260	$205	$135	$90

Last MSR was $400.

Add 25% for Model R10 Deluxe, hand checkered grip, white line grip cap and buttplate, forearm extends to forward end of barrel block.

Add 15% for .20 cal.

Add 100% for Laser Model (laminated stock).

Add 95% for custom grade walnut stock.

Add 100% for custom fancy walnut stock.

Add 110% for extra fancy walnut stock.

Subtract 5% for left-hand variation.

Add 20% for RDB versions, early production, soft rubber buttplate with Beeman name, cheekpiece with sharp edges and sweeping outline, greater detailing.

MODEL R11 – .177 cal., BBC, SP, SS, 925 FPS, 19.6 in. barrel with sleeve, adj. cheek piece and buttplate, adj. trigger, scope ramp on receiver, no sights, 43.5 in. OAL, 8.75 lbs. Mfg. in Germany 1994-1995.

	$675	$575	$475	$400	$300	$205	$135

Last MSR was $800.

* **Model R11 MK II** – .177 cal., BBC, SP, SS, 925 FPS, 19.6 in. barrel with sleeve, dovetailed receiver for scope mounting, improved trigger and end cap, adj. cheek piece and buttplate, adj. trigger, no sights, 43.5 in. OAL, 8.75 lbs. Mfg. in Germany with limited importation in 1995, re-introduced 2012.

courtesy Beeman Collection

	100%	95%	90%	80%	60%	40%	20%
MSR $770	$650	$550	$450	$375	$290	$195	$130

Add $30 for .22 cal.

MODEL RX – .177, .20, .22, or .25 cal., BBC, Theoben GS, SS, 1125/960/810/650 FPS, adj. velocity, deluxe Monte Carlo beech stock with cheek piece, forearm extends to forward end of barrel block, hand checkering and white-line PG cap, white-lined rubber buttplate with molded BEEMAN letters, all metal sights, scope grooves, automatic safety, 45.7 in. OAL, 8.7 lbs. Mfg. in Germany 1990-1992.

	$350	$300	$245	$205	$160	$105	$70

Last MSR was $470.

Add 15% for .20 and .25 cal.

Add 50% for Field Target version with adj. cheekpiece.

Add 10% for left-hand variation.

Add 25% for Power Adjustment Pump.

This model's GAS-SPRING piston system sometimes is inappropriately referred to as a "gas-ram" or "gas strut" system.

GRADING	100%	95%	90%	80%	60%	40%	20%

MODEL RX-1 – .177, .20, .22, or .25 cal., BBC, Theoben GS, SS, 1125/960/810/650 FPS, adj. velocity, deluxe Monte Carlo beech stock with cheek piece, forearm extends to forward end of barrel block, hand checkering and white-line PG cap, white-lined rubber buttplate with molded BEEMAN letters, all metal sights, scope grooves, automatic safety, adj. two-stage trigger and stamped with small "1" on rear of receiver. Mfg. in Germany 1992-2001.

courtesy Beeman Collection

	100%	95%	90%	80%	60%	40%	20%
	$475	$400	$325	$275	$215	$140	$95

Last MSR was $590.

Add 10% for left-hand variation.
Add 15% for Santa Rosa address.
Add 30% for hand checkered walnut "Luxury" stock.
Add 50% for Commemorative model with 20th Anniversary disc inlaid into stock.
Add 25% for Power Adjustment Pump.

MODEL RX-2 – .177, .20, .22, or .25 cal., BBC, Theoben GS, SS, 1125/960/810/650 FPS, adj. velocity, laminated beech stock with cheek piece, forearm extends to forward end of barrel block, hand checkering and white-line PG cap, all metal sights, scope grooves, automatic safety, improved non-adj. trigger, 9.8 lbs. Mfg. in Germany. New 2001.

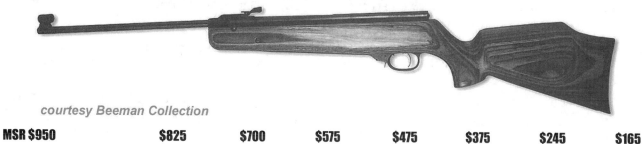

courtesy Beeman Collection

MSR $950	$825	$700	$575	$475	$375	$245	$165

Add $20 for .20 or $50 for .25 cal.

MODEL RX-2 ELITE SERIES COMBO – .177, .20, .22, or .25 cal., gas piston, BBC, SS, 1125/950/860/725 FPS, 19.63 in. rifled barrel with steel muzzle brake, two-stage trigger, no sights, laminated wood stock with raised cheekpiece and rubber buttpad, includes mounted Bushnell Trophy XLT 4-12x40 AO scope, 45.7 in. OAL, 11 lbs.

MSR $1,190	$1,025	$850	$700	$600	$450	$300	$205

Add $10 for .22 cal., $30 for .25 cal., or $110 for .20 cal.

MODEL S-1 – .177 cal., BBC, SP, SS, 900 FPS, two-stage adj. trigger, automatic safety, beech stock, 45.5 in. OAL, 7.1 lbs. Mfg. in Spain 1995-1999.

	$150	$130	$105	$85	$70	$45	$30

Last MSR was $210.

MODEL SLR-98 – .22 cal., GS, UL, 780 FPS, 12 in. barrel, blue finish, checkered walnut stock, seven-shot removable mag., automatic safety, 39 in. OAL, 7.9 lbs. Mfg. in Germany 2001-2004.

courtesy Beeman Collection

	$1,200	$1,025	$825	$700	$525	$350	$240

Last MSR was $1,385.

GRADING	100%	95%	90%	80%	60%	40%	20%

MODEL SS550 TARGET – .177 cal., BBC, SP, SS, Belgium Matte finish, 550 FPS, ambidextrous Monte Carlo sporter style composite stock with recoil pad, sporter grade trigger, automatic safety, diopter rear and hooded front sights, 36.5 in. OAL, 5 lbs. Mfg. 2005-2012.

	$55	$45	$40	$30	$25	$15	$10

MODEL SS550 HUNTER COMBO – .177 cal., BBC, SP, SS, 550 FPS, Belgium Matte finish, ambidextrous Monte Carlo sporter style composite stock with recoil pad, sporter grade trigger, automatic safety, 4x20 scope with ported muzzle brake, 38.5 in. OAL, 5 lbs. New 2005.

MSR N/A	$75	$65	$55	$45	$35	$20	$15

MODEL SS650/SH650 HUNTER COMBO – .177 cal., BBC, SP, SS, 700 FPS, sporter trigger, automatic safety, walnut stained beech stock with recoil pad, fiber optic sights or ported muzzle brake and 4x32mm Beeman scope (SH650 Hunter Combo), 39.5-41 in.OAL, 5.9-8.7 lbs. Mfg. 2005-2006.

	$85	$70	$60	$50	$40	$25	$15

Last MSR was $100.

Add 20% for SH650 Hunter Combo.

MODEL SS1000/SH1000 HUNTER COMBO – .177 or .22 cal., BBC, SP, 1000/800FPS, adj. fiber optic sights or 3-9x32mm AO/TT scope (SH1000 Combo), two-stage adj. trigger, automatic safety, sporter style walnut stained stock with PG and recoil pad, 44.5 in. OAL, 9-10 lbs. Mfg. 2005-2006.

	$145	$125	$100	$85	$65	$45	$30

Last MSR was $170.

Add 20% for SH1000 Combo Model.

MODEL SS1000H – .177 or .22 cal., BBC, SP, 1000/800FPS, 3-9x32mm scope, two-stage adj. trigger, automatic safety, sporter style walnut stained stock with PG and recoil pad, 46.5 in. OAL, 10 lbs. Mfg. 2007-2012.

	$145	$125	$100	$85	$65	$45	$30

MODEL SS1000T – .177 cal., BBC, SP, 1000 FPS, ported muzzle brake, 3-9x32mm AO/TT Beeman scope with adj. objective and target turrets with caps, hardwood Monte Carlo stock, adj. two-stage trigger, auto-safety, 47.25 in. OAL, 10.5 lbs. Mfg. 2007-2012.

	$175	$150	$125	$100	$80	$50	$35

MODEL UL-7 – .22 cal., UL, GS, 12 in. barrel, 780 FPS, manual safety, seven-shot rotary mag., checkered walnut stock, 39 in. OAL, 8.1 lbs. Mfg. in England 1992-1993.

	$1,200	$1,025	$825	$700	$525	$350	$240

Last MSR was $1,560.

Add 10% for power adjustment pump.

Approx. eight were imported to the U.S. 1992-1993.

AIR WOLF – .20, .22, or .25 cal., 940/822/660 FPS, PCP, SS, BA, light high comb walnut stock, hand checkered PG, white-lined rubber recoil pad, 20.8 in. barrel, blue finish, no sights, scope grooves, manual safety, 37 in. OAL, 5.6 lbs. Mfg. in England 1992 only.

	$950	$800	$675	$550	$425	$285	$190

Last MSR was $680.

Add 5% for .20 cal.

Add 10% for charging adapter with gauge.

Approx. 10-20 mfg.

BEAR CLAW – .177 or .22 cal. pellet, BBC, SP, 1000/830 FPS, all metal black bull barrel, thumbhole European hardwood stock with ambidextrous cheekpiece, RS3 two-stage adj. trigger, includes 3-9x32 scope and mounts, 45.5 in. OAL, 10 lbs. New 2010.

courtesy Beeman Precision Airguns

MSR $300	$245	$210	$170	$140	$110	$75	$50

GRADING	100%	95%	90%	80%	60%	40%	20%

BEAR CLAW X2 – .177 and .22 cal. interchangeable barrels, BBC, SP, 1000/830 FPS, European hardwood thumbhole stock with ambidextrous cheekpiece, ported muzzle brake, RS3 two-stage adj. trigger, includes 3-9x32 AO scope and mounts, 46.5 in. OAL, 10 lbs. New 2011.

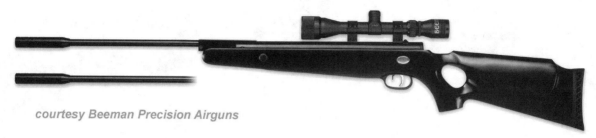

courtesy Beeman Precision Airguns

MSR $260	$220	$185	$155	$130	$100	$65	$45

CARNIVORE – .177 cal., BBC, SP, 1000 FPS, Next G1 camo synthetic stock, all metal black fluted barrel, RS2 two-stage adj. trigger, mounted 3-9x32 scope, 46.5 in. OAL, 9 lbs. Mfg. 2010-2012.

	$215	$190	$170	$140	$105	N/A	N/A

Last MSR was $250.

CARBINE C1 – field carbine with shotgun butt and straight grip.

courtesy Beeman Collection

For information on this model, see Webley & Scott, LTD. in the "W" section.

BEARCUB – for information on this model, see Webley & Scott, LTD. in the "W" section.

ELKHORN – .177 or .22 cal. pellet, BBC, SP, 1000/830 FPS, all metal black fluted barrel, checkered European hardwood stock, RS2 two-stage adj. trigger, includes 3-9x32 AO/TT scope and mounts, 46.5 in. OAL, 9 lbs. New 2010.

courtesy Beeman Precision Airguns

MSR $250	$210	$180	$145	$120	$95	$65	$40

ELITE X2 – .177 and .22 cal. interchangeable satin nickel plated barrels and receiver, BBC, SP, 1000/830 FPS, overmolded all-weather gray synthetic stock, ported muzzle brake, RS3 two-stage adj. trigger, 4-12x40 illuminated scope, includes carry case, 45.5 in. OAL, 10 lbs. Mfg. 2010-2012.

	$215	$190	$170	$140	$105	N/A	N/A

Last MSR was $250.

ELKHORN X2 – .177 and .22 cal. interchangeable barrels, BBC, SP, 1000/830 FPS, deluxe checkered European hardwood stock, ported muzzle brake, RS3 two-stage adj. trigger, includes 3-9x32 AO scope and mounts, 45.5 in. OAL, 10 lbs. New 2011.

courtesy Beeman Precision Airguns

MSR $240	$205	$175	$145	$120	$90	$60	$40

GRADING	100%	95%	90%	80%	60%	40%	20%

GRIZZLY X2 – .177 and .22 cal. interchangeable barrels, BBC, SP, 1000/830 FPS, European hardwood stock, fiber optic front and rear sights, RS2 two-stage adj. trigger, includes 4x32 scope and mounts, 45.5 in. OAL, 8.75 lbs. New 2010.

courtesy Beeman Precision Airguns

MSR $180	$155	$130	$110	$90	$70	$45	$30

Add $16 for carry case (Model 1072).

GAMEKEEPER – .25 cal., PCP, SS, quick-change air cylinder, 15 in. barrel, 680 FPS, steel receiver, composite detachable buttstock, stock, barrel, and air cylinder remove to pack gun into briefcase, steel barrel weight, no sights, scope grooves, manual lever safety, 36.3 in. OAL, 8.2 lbs. Mfg. in England by Cotchester 1992-1993.

courtesy Beeman Collection

Last MSR was $990.

Five were imported from England, value is in the $1,500-$2,500 range.

GUARDIAN – .177 cal., BBC, SP, 550 FPS, black rifled steel barrel, brown composite stock with ambidextrous cheekpiece, Sporter trigger with auto safety, mounted 4x20 scope, 37 in. OAL, 5.85 lbs. New 2010.

courtesy Beeman Precision Airguns

MSR $70	$55	$45	$40	$30	$25	N/A	N/A

HW97K BLUE LAMINATE – .177, .20, or .22 cal., SP, SS, underlever, 11.81 in. rifled barrel, no sights, auto safety, Rekord adj. trigger, Monte Carlo beech stock with raised cheekpiece and soft rubber recoil pad, hand checkering on pistol grip, includes 1 in. scope rings and medium profile vertical scope stop, 40.25 in. OAL, 9.2 lbs.

courtesy Beeman Precision Airguns

MSR $840	$725	$600	$500	$425	$325	$215	$145

Add $30 for .20 cal.

GRADING	100%	95%	90%	80%	60%	40%	20%

HW97K WOOD – .177, .20, or .22 cal., SP, SS, underlever, 11.81 in. rifled barrel, no sights, auto safety, Rekord adj. trigger, Monte Carlo beech stock with raised cheekpiece and soft rubber recoil pad, hand checkering on pistol grip, includes 1 in. scope rings and medium profile vertical scope stop, 40.25 in. OAL, 9.2 lbs.

courtesy Beeman Precision Airguns

MSR $740	$625	$525	$425	$350	$280	$185	$125

Add $10 for .20 cal. or $30 for .22 cal.

* *HW97K Wood Thumbhole* – .177, .20, or .22 cal., similar to HW97K Wood, except features ambidextrous Monte Carlo thumbhole stock with raised RH cheekpiece, adj. rubber buttpad, and stipling on grip and forearm.

courtesy Beeman Precision Airguns

MSR $890	$775	$650	$550	$450	$350	$230	$155

* *HW97K Wood Elite Series Combo* – .177, .20, or .22 cal., similar to HW97K Wood, except features mounted Bushnell Banner 4-12x40 scope.

courtesy Beeman Precision Airguns

MSR $850	$725	$625	$500	$425	$325	$215	$145

Add $40 for .20 cal.

HW97K SYNTHETIC THUMBHOLE – .177 or .22 cal., SP, SS, underlever, 11.8 in. rifled barrel with muzzle brake, auto safety, no sights, two-stage adj. trigger, sliding breech with anti-beartrap mechanism, Black synthetic thumbhole stock with dual raised cheekpieces and rubber recoil pad, 40.25 in. OAL, 9 lbs.

courtesy Beeman Precision Airguns

MSR $730	$625	$525	$425	$350	$280	$185	$125

GRADING	100%	95%	90%	80%	60%	40%	20%

* ***HW97K Synthetic Thumbhole Elite Series Combo*** – .177 or .22 cal., similar to HW97K Synthetic Thumbhole, except includes mounted Bushnell Banner 4-12x40AO scope.

courtesy Beeman Precision Airguns

MSR $820	$700	$600	$500	$400	$325	$210	$140

HW97K STAINLESS STEEL – .177 or .22 cal., SP, SS, underlever, 11.81 in. rifled barrel with muzzle brake, 2-stage adjustable Rekord match trigger, sliding breech with anti-beartrap mechanism, automatic safety, Black synthetic thumbhole stock with dual raised cheekpieces and rubber recoil pad, metal finished in stainless steel, includes 1 in. scope rings and hex wrenches, 40.25 in. OAL, 9 lbs.

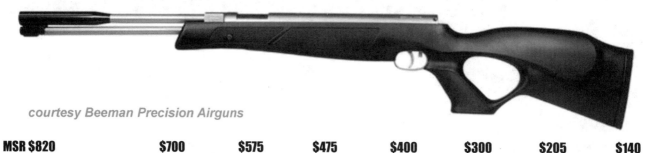

courtesy Beeman Precision Airguns

MSR $820	$700	$575	$475	$400	$300	$205	$140

* ***HW97K Stainless Elite Series*** – .177 or .22 cal., similar to HW97K Stainless, except includes mounted Bushnell Banner 4-12x40AO scope.

courtesy Beeman Precision Airguns

MSR $950	$825	$700	$575	$475	$375	$245	$165

HW100S FSB – .177, .20, or .22 cal., pre-charged pneumatic, sidelever repeater, 23.62 in. rifled shrouded barrel, 14 shot, quick disconnect fitting, integral manometer on tank, no sights, manual safety, 2-stage adjustable match trigger, checkered forearm and pistol grip, Monte Carlo stock with raised cheekpiece and rubber buttpad, 42.13 in. OAL, 8.6 lbs.

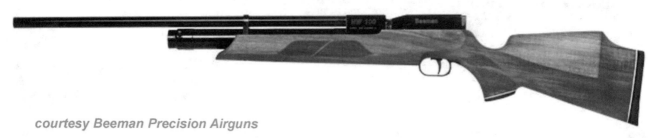

courtesy Beeman Precision Airguns

MSR $1,770	$1,450	$1,250	$1,025	$850	$650	$450	$290

Add $20 for .20 cal.

GRADING	100%	95%	90%	80%	60%	40%	20%

* **HW100T FSB** – .177, .20, or .22 cal., similar to HW100S FSB, except features Monte Carlo thumbhole stock.

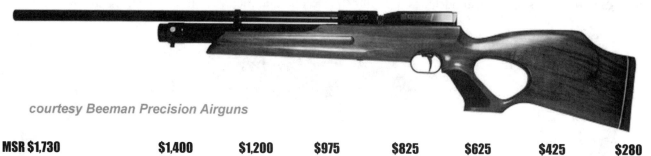

courtesy Beeman Precision Airguns

MSR $1,730	**$1,400**	**$1,200**	**$975**	**$825**	**$625**	**$425**	**$280**

Add $60 for .20 cal.

KODIAK – .22 or .25 cal., BBC, SP, 17.50 in. barrel, 865/775 FPS, deluxe Monte Carlo stock with cheek piece, grip cap and rubber buttplates with white line spacers, PTFE, muzzle threaded for Beeman Air Tamer or Webley Silencer, automatic safety, 45.6 in. OAL, 8.9 lbs. Mfg. in England. Mfg. 1993-disc.

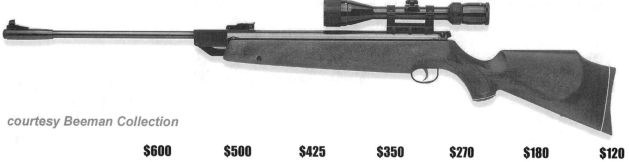

courtesy Beeman Collection

	$600	**$500**	**$425**	**$350**	**$270**	**$180**	**$120**

Add 10% for Air Tamer (muzzle unit without baffles).
Add 10% for Webley Silencer.

Since this model has a threaded muzzle (if a silencer is present), transfer to qualified buyer requires $200 federal tax in USA.

KODIAK X2 – .177 and .22 cal. interchangeable barrels, BBC, SP, 1000/830 FPS, all-weather black synthetic stock, ported muzzle brake, RS2 two-stage adj. trigger, includes 4x32 scope and mounts, 45.5 OAL, 8.75 lbs. New 2010.

courtesy Beeman Precision Airguns

MSR $180	**$155**	**$130**	**$110**	**$90**	**$70**	**$45**	**$30**

SILVER KODIAK X2 – .177 or .22 cal., BBC, SP, 1000/830 FPS, satin nickel plated barrel and receiver, ported muzzle brake, RS1 two-stage sporter trigger, all-weather black synthetic stock, includes 3-9x32 scope and mounts, 47.5 in. OAL, 8.75 lbs. New 2013.

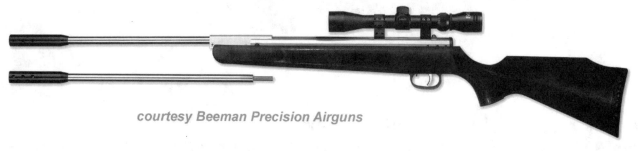

courtesy Beeman Precision Airguns

MSR $220	**$185**	**$155**	**$130**	**$105**	**$85**	**$55**	**$35**

This model is also available with 4x32 scope (Model 10774) or 4x32 scope and case (Model 1077sc).

GRADING	100%	95%	90%	80%	60%	40%	20%

MACH 12.5 – .177 or .22 cal. pellet, BBC, SP, 1250/1000 FPS, checkered European hardwood stock, ported muzzle brake, RS3 two-stage adj. trigger, includes 3-9x40 AO/TT scope and mounts, 46.5 in. OAL, 12 lbs. New 2010.

courtesy Beeman Precision Airguns

MSR $320	$265	$225	$185	$155	$120	$80	$55

OMEGA – for information on this model, see Webley & Scott, LTD. in the "W" section.

PANTHER – .177 or .22 cal., BBC, SP, 1000 FPS, all-weather black synthetic stock, ported muzzle brake, RS2 two-stage adj. trigger, includes 3-9x32 scope and mounts, 45.5 in. OAL, 8.75 lbs. New 2010.

courtesy Beeman Precision Airguns

MSR $200	$170	$145	$120	$100	$75	$50	$35

SILVER PANTHER – .177 or .22 cal., BBC, SP, 1000/830 FPS, satin nickel plated barrel and receiver, ported muzzle break, RS2 two-stage adj. trigger, all-weather Black synthetic stock, includes 4x32 scope and mounts, 47.5 in. OAL, 8.75 lbs. New 2013.

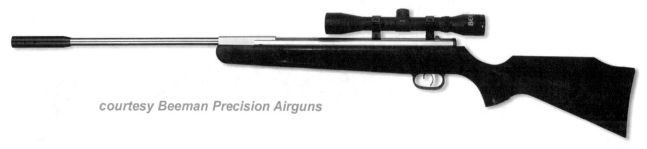

courtesy Beeman Precision Airguns

MSR $150	$125	$105	$90	$75	$55	$35	$25

PREDATOR – .177 or .22 (New 2013) cal., BBC, SP, 1000/830 FPS, Next G1 camo synthetic stock, fiber optic front and rear sights, automatic safety, RS2 two-stage adj. trigger, mounted 3-9x32 scope, 45.5 in. OAL, 8.75 lbs. New 2010.

courtesy Beeman Precision Airguns

MSR $220	$185	$155	$130	$105	$85	$55	$35

PREDATOR X2 – .177 or .22 cal., BBC, SP, 1000/830 FPS, interchangeable barrels, fiber optic sights, RS2 two-stage trigger, European hardwood stock with NEXT camo finish, 45.5 in. OAL, 8.5 lbs. New 2013.

While advertised during 2013, this model never went into production.

GRADING	100%	95%	90%	80%	60%	40%	20%

RS2 DUAL CALIBER – .177 and .22 cal. barrels, SP, BBC, SS, rifled barrel, fiber optic sights, two-stage non-adj. trigger, automatic safety, rubber buttpad, includes Beeman 4x32 scope and soft carrying case, 45.5 in. OAL, 6.9 lbs.

courtesy Beeman Precision Airguns

MSR $175	$150	$130	$105	$85	$70	$45	$30

R52 COMBO – .177 cal., BBC, 1000 FPS, blued rifled barrel, two-stage trigger, auto safety, wood stock, includes 3-9x32mm scope with ring mounts, 46.5 in. OAL, 10 lbs.

courtesy Beeman Precision Airguns

MSR $200	$170	$145	$120	$100	$75	$50	$35

RAM – .177 or .22 cal. pellet, BBC, SP, 1000/830 FPS, European hardwood stock, ported muzzle brake, RS2 two-stage adj. trigger, includes 3-9x32 scope and mounts, 46.5 in. OAL, 9 lbs. New 2010.

courtesy Beeman Precision Airguns

MSR $220	$185	$155	$130	$105	$85	$55	$35

RAM-XT – .177 or .22 cal. pellet, BBC, 1000/830 FPS, ported muzzle brake, RS2 two-stage trigger, European hardwood thumbhole stock with ambidextrous cheekpiece, includes 4x32 scope and mounts.

   While advertised during 2013, this model never went into production.

RAM DELUXE – .177 or .22 cal. pellet, BBC, 1000/830 FPS, ported muzzle brake, RS2 two-stage adj. trigger, checkered European hardwood stock, includes 4x32 scope and mounts.

   While advertised during 2013, this model never went into production.

RANGER – .177 cal., BBC, SP, 550 FPS, rifled steel barrel, nickel finish, black composite stock with ambidextrous cheekpiece, Sporter trigger with auto safety, mounted 4x20 scope, includes kit with four swinging silhouette targets

courtesy Beeman Precision Airguns

GRADING	100%	95%	90%	80%	60%	40%	20%

with hangers and 250 wadcutter pellets, 38.5 in. OAL, 5.85 lbs. New 2010.

MSR $100	$85	$70	$60	$50	$40	N/A	N/A

REBEL – .177 cal., BBC, SP, 550 FPS, black rifled steel barrel, lightweight skeletonized composite stock, mounted 4x20 scope, black finish, 37 in. OAL, 5.85 lbs. New 2010.

courtesy Beeman Precision Airguns

MSR $90	$75	$65	$55	$45	$35	N/A	N/A

SILVER BEAR COMBO (SB500) – .177 cal., BBC, SP, SS, Belgium Matte finish, muzzle brake, 500 FPS, Monte Carlo sporter style composite stock, vented recoil pad, automatic safety, 4x20mm Beeman scope, 37 in. OAL, 5 lbs. Mfg. in USA 2002-2006.

	$65	$55	$45	$40	$30	$20	$15

Last MSR was $72.

SCOUT – .177 cal., BBC, SP, 550 FPS, removable rifled steel barrel with nickel finish, black composite stock with ambidextrous cheek piece, Sporter trigger with auto safety, 4x20 scope, includes kit with 4 swinging silhouette targets with hangers, 250 wadcutter pellets, and carry case, 38.5 in. OAL, 5.85 lbs. Mfg. 2010-2011.

	$70	$60	$55	$45	$35	N/A	N/A

Last MSR was $83.

SUPER 7 – .22 or .25 (1994 only) cal., PCP, seven-shot mag., quick-change 280cc air cylinder (bottle), 19 in. barrel, 990 FPS (.22 cal.), checkered walnut stock, manual safety, 41 in. OAL, 7.25 lbs. Mfg. in England 1992-1994.

	$1,100	$925	$775	$650	$500	$325	$220

Last MSR was $1,575.

Add 5% for .25 cal.

SUPER 12 – .20, .22 or .25 cal., PCP, 12-shot mag., 850 FPS (.25 cal.), quick-change air cylinder (bottle), checkered walnut stock, manual safety, 41.7 in. OAL, 7.8 lbs. Mfg. in England 1994-2001.

courtesy Beeman Collection

	$1,400	$1,200	$975	$800	$625	$425	$280

Last MSR was $1,675.

Add 5% for .20 cal. or .25 cal.

SUPER 12 MKII – .20, .22 or .25 cal., PCP, 12-shot mag., 850 FPS (.25 cal.), match trigger assembly and new style stock, quick-change air cylinder (bottle), manual safety, 41.7 in. OAL, 7.8 lbs. Mfg. 2001-2004.

	$1,000	$850	$700	$575	$450	$300	$200

Last MSR was $2,015.

SUPER 17/17FT – .177 cal., PCP, 17-shot rotary mag., 1090 FPS, quick-change air cylinder (bottle), laminated target stock, adj. match trigger, adj. buttplate, optional adj. cheek piece. Mfg. in England 1998-2002.

	$1,400	$1,200	$975	$800	$625	$425	$280

Last MSR was $1,675.

Add 40% for Field Target model.

GRADING	100%	95%	90%	80%	60%	40%	20%

TETON – .177 or .22 (New 2013) cal. pellet, BBC, SP, SS, 1000/830 FPS, 18 in. rifled barrel, European hardwood stock with rubber buttpad, fiber optic front and rear sights, RS1 two-stage sporter (Model 1050) or RS2 two-stage adj. (Model 1051) trigger, with (Model 1051, became standard 2013) or without (Model 1050) 4x32 scope and mounts, 44.5 in. OAL, 8.5 lbs. New 2010.

courtesy Beeman Precision Airguns

MSR $230	$195	$165	$135	$115	$90	$60	$40

VULCAN I – for information on this model, see Webley & Scott, Ltd. in the "W" section.

VULCAN II – for information on this model, see Webley & Scott, Ltd. in the "W" section.

VULCAN III – for information on this model, see Webley & Scott, Ltd. in the "W" section.

WOLF PUP – .20, .22, or .25 cal., PCP, SS, BA, 13.5 in. barrel, 910/800/645 FPS, high comb walnut stock, hand checkered grip, white-line rubber recoil pad, no sights, scope grooves, manual safety, 31.5 in. OAL, 5 lbs. Approx. 10-20 mfg. in England by Titan 1992 only.

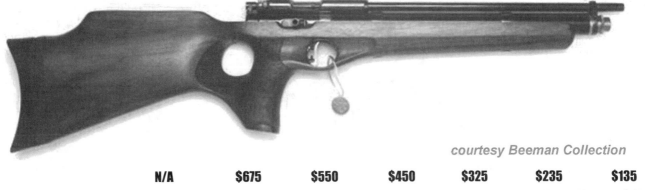

courtesy Beeman Collection

N/A	$675	$550	$450	$325	$235	$135

Last MSR was $680.

Add 5% for .20 cal.

Add 10% for charging adapter with gauge.

Add 25% for Deluxe Model with thumbhole stock and match trigger.

WOLVERINE CARBINE – .177 or .22 cal., BBC, SP, 1000 FPS, all-weather black synthetic stock, fiber optic front and rear sights, RS2 two-stage adj. trigger, includes 4x32 scope and mounts, 45.5 in. OAL, 8.75 lbs. New 2010.

courtesy Beeman Precision Airguns

MSR $150	$125	$105	$90	$75	$55	$35	$25

GRADING	100%	95%	90%	80%	60%	40%	20%

XCEL X2 – .177 and .22 cal. interchangeable barrels, BBC, SP, 1000/830 FPS, European hardwood stock, ported muzzle brake, RS3 two-stage adj. trigger, 3-9x32 AO scope, includes carry case, 45.5 in. OAL, 10 lbs.

courtesy Beeman Precision Airguns

MSR $240		$205	$180	$165	$130	$100	N/A	N/A

BELLOWS AIRGUNS

This is a quite well defined group of breech-loading spring-driven single-shot airguns generally made in the late 1700s to mid-1800s. They were made by craftsmen who often were not known gunmakers in a Germanic/Austrian region centered on Regensburg and roughly bounded by Nürnberg, Prague, Vienna, and Munich.

This design has a puzzling origin very suggestive of early wheellock firearms. Almost all specimens can be quickly identified as bellows airguns by their massive, heavy buttstocks that bear a large square cocking lug on the right hand side near the buttplate and by their lack of either a cocking lever (hammer)[1] or a pumping handle or threaded pump port in the buttplate. Their basic feature is a conical bellows hidden in the hollowed-out wooden buttstock. Turning the lug with a separate, large cocking handle (almost always missing) winds a short chain to compress one or two hidden V-shaped mainsprings and spreads the bellows. Pulling the double set trigger releases the mainspring(s) to suddenly force the bellows shut -- thus blowing a dart out of the barrel -- much as one could fire a wad of paper from a fireplace bellows. The projectiles usually are about .24 to .32 (6 to 8 mm) caliber darts, generally with a hair tail.

Releasing a latch on the side or underside of the forearm allows the breech to open for loading. The flexibility of the long wooden forearm acts as a barrel hinge. The power of these guns is very low; evidently they were intended for

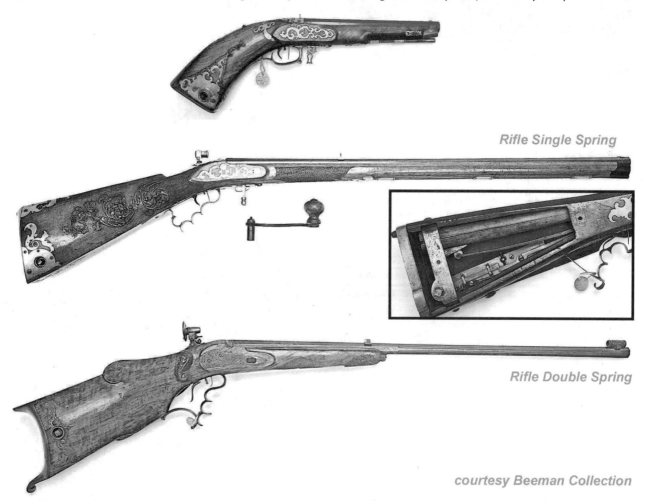

Rifle Single Spring

Rifle Double Spring

courtesy Beeman Collection

GRADING	100%	95%	90%	80%	60%	40%	20%

indoor recreational target shooting. Trigger guards commonly are similar to the huge, ornate, finger-grooved brass guards of wheellock firearms.

The stocks typically are full-length but some specimens, especially advanced late examples may have half stocks. The stocks may be plain or ornately carved and decorated. The upper side of the stock's wrist has a provision for an aperture sight (also usually missing) of greater than appropriate precision. Also like wheellock firearms, the barrel often is octagonal and "swamped", i.e. visibly narrower in its middle. The barrels are smoothbore, often with a brass bore liner.

The single-spring versions generally are distinguished by the cocking lug being near the toe of the buttplate while the double-spring versions have the lug between the toe and heel of the buttplate. The single-spring models apparently are the oldest and scarcest forms but the double-spring guns may sometimes be more valuable due to moderate to exquisite carving and elaborate brass decorations.

Makers include Christian Hintz in Prague, Ioh. Andrea Kuchenreiter (as inlaid on gun) (= Johann Andreas Kuchenreuter?), J. Adam Kuchenreuter, and Hornauer in Regensburg, Lachermeir and F.X. Wistaller in Munich, Sevcik in Laibaich, M. Dobner in Erding, Maringer, Mausch, Wenzel Spatzeirer, Rochus Wastl, Johann Planer, St. Jllichmann, and Peter Volkmann in Vienna, Dir in Reichenhall, Joh. Mond in Augsberg, Anton Pell in Linz, Anton Schreiber in Gratz, Wolf in Würzberg and Fran.Zelner in Salzburg, and K. Kiendlbacher.

At this time we know of two surviving bellows pistols, one in 8 mm caliber and the other in 7 mm. While unmarked, the pistols appear to be from the mid-1800s and possibly made by J. Adam Kuchenreuter, a top gunmaker in Regensburg, Germany. No bellows pistol (that we know of) has come to market in over 30 years, making it very difficult to establish values.

Plain rifle specimens of fair condition may sell for as little as $500; better condition, well-decorated specimens may go for well above $3,000. An original cocking handle or a container of darts is very scarce. Each will add 10% to 20% while an original aperture sight may add 15% to 25%. A fine specimen may be the most attractive item in your collection.

Little information is available on Bellows airguns. The best sources of additional information are Hoff (1972, updated 1977) and Wolff (1958). Some good details of the pistols are given by Griffiths (2008).

[1]A very few, early bellows airguns had fake flintlock hammers.

BEMMEN
Previous maker located in Indonesia circa 1960s - 1970s.

PISTOL

MODEL GRMH – .177 cal., CO_2, straight pull bolt action, 11 in. barrel, adj. rear and blade front sights, checkered and finger grooved hardwood stock, 18.75 in. OAL, 3.5 lbs.

courtesy Howard Collection

$425	$350	$300	$245	$190	$125	$85

BENELLI ARMI S.P.A.
Current manufacturer located in Urbino, Italy. Benelli air pistols are currently imported by Larry's Guns, located in Gray, ME. Benelli USA, located in Accokeek, MD, was established during late 1997 and is currently importing all Benelli shotguns.

For more information and current pricing on both new and used Benelli firearms, please refer to the *Blue Book of Gun Values* by S.P. Fjestad (also available online).

PISTOLS

KITE – .177 cal., PCP, match pistol, 9.45 in. barrel, 475 FPS, adj. trigger, adj. sights, adj. wood grip, 16.89 in. OAL, 2.36 lbs. New 2003.

MSR $1,319	$1,125	$1,000	$900	$725	$550	N/A	N/A

GRADING	100%	95%	90%	80%	60%	40%	20%

KITE YOUNG – .177 cal., PCP, match pistol, 7.48 in. barrel, 475 FPS, adj. sights, adj. wood grip 14.82 in. OAL, 2.13 lbs. New 2003.

MSR $1,119	$950	$850	$750	$625	$475	N/A	N/A

BENJAMIN AIR RIFLE COMPANY (BENJAMIN)

Current Benjamin trademark manufactured by Crosman Corp. located in Bloomfield, NY. Previous manufacturer located in Racine, WI. The Benjamin trademark was purchased in January 1992 by Crosman Air Guns, located in East Bloomfield, NY. Dealer and consumer direct sales.

BENJAMIN AIR RIFLE COMPANY BACKGROUND

The Benjamin Air Rifle Company has its roots in the St. Louis Air Rifle Company, founded by Walter Benjamin in 1899. The St. Louis Air Rifle Company produced several unique, but unreliable, air rifles until 1901. Because of low production, and the propensity of these guns to break and become unrepairable, very few specimens of St. Louis air rifles exist today. Sales of these air rifles are too infrequent to establish price levels. Some replicas were produced in the 1990s.

The Benjamin Air Rifle Company was formed in 1902 when Walter Benjamin purchased the patent rights from the defunct St. Louis Air Rifle Company. Production from 1902 to 1904 and from 1906 to 1986 was in St. Louis, MO (extremely limited production of the Single Valve Model "B" by the W.R. Benjamin Company from 1904 to 1906 was in Granite City, IL). Regular production facilities were not established until 1908 when the Benjamin Air Rifle and Manufacturing Company became a wholly owned subsidiary of the Wissler Instrument Co. In 1977, the Benjamin Air Rifle Company purchased Sheridan Products in Racine, WI, and moved production there from 1986 to 1994. In 1991, they started to merge the Benjamin and Sheridan pistol designs, as the pistol models shifted to a Sheridan-type design and were marketed as Benjamin/Sheridan.

CROSMAN PURCHASES BENJAMIN

Crosman Airguns purchased the combined companies in February 1992, and marketed the Benjamin CO_2 rifles as Benjamin/Sheridan 1993-1998, in addition to the Benjamin pump-up rifles 1994-98. During 1998-2000, the Crosman company began to again catalog and promote the .177 and .22 caliber guns under the Benjamin brand and the .20 caliber guns under the Sheridan name.

The only name to appear on some of the guns made during the interesting decade of the 1990s is in the required warning that cautions users to contact the "Benjamin Sheridan" offices in New York for an owner's manual. Many gun authorities would not consider such an address in a warning as a brand designation, any more than they would consider these guns to be Crosmans, because the Crosman Company is now using the Crosman name in the contact address.

Thus there is a period of about seven years, which to some degree continues to be unclear, where there is some confusion as to the names under which these various airguns were known. It is clear that the shooting public, and most dealers, continued their perception of these guns as Sheridans or Benjamins and never really accepted the Benjamin/Sheridan brand. As noted, Crosman recognized this brand perception and wisely began to again market the guns under the well-known separate Sheridan and Benjamin names. Now this guide is forced to consider all of the current models of these two lines under the poorly accepted name of Benjamin/Sheridan, even including such models as the Sheridan Blue and Silver Streak .20 caliber rifles, or to allow current shooters and dealers to find a particular model and learn its probable value by following each model series under their best known names. Since the concept of the Benjamin/Sheridan designation was a Benjamin idea, most models will be considered in the Benjamin section. Thus, this guide is following the designations used by the manufacturer's marketing department, the current catalogs, and virtually all shooters and dealers by considering the .177 and .22 caliber guns as Benjamins, and the .20 caliber guns as Sheridans. At this time, this really is only of academic interest because the guns produced since 1991 generally are purchased only as shooters; buyers of current models usually are not concerned with the nuances of name designations.

BENJAMIN AIR RIFLE COMPANY MARKINGS

There surely will come a time in the future, especially for the Sheridan PB and HB20 models, and the HB17 and HB22 pistols made in WI, where the manufacturing address and markings will be of importance in determining values. The marking of "Benjamin Franklin" (which began circa 1936) on some older models evidently has no significance, except as a marketing ploy.

From about 1935 until recently, Benjamin used a model numbering system for both its air rifles and pistols. Model numbers ending in 0 are smooth bore for lead or steel BBs and .177 caliber pellets or darts; model numbers ending in 7 are rifled for .177 caliber pellets or darts; model numbers ending in 2 are rifled for .22 caliber pellets or darts. To keep things interesting, it is apparent that the ever-frugal A.P. Spack and his son, who ran the company during most of its early history, might not have bothered to change stamping dies when they changed model numbers in their advertisements and bulletins. So a gun advertised and sold as a Model 107 might have come out of the factory stamped as Model 177, etc. Such situations evidently were confined to guns which actually were the same, but were under different model numbers, i.e. apparently no guns were stamped with incorrect numbers. Ref: AAG - July 1991.

GRADING	100%	95%	90%	80%	60%	40%	20%

BENJAMIN AIR RIFLE COMPANY VALUES

Values on Benjamin models are based on guns in good working order with no missing parts. Guns that have had their finish removed and the brass polished have their value reduced to one half or less of the 90% value.

PISTOLS

Although the Benjamin Air Rifle Company is best known for its pneumatic rifles, pneumatic pistols had been added to the line by 1935. There is mention of air pistols on Benjamin letterheads as early as 1908, but actual pistols probably were not introduced until about 1935 when *Popular Science Monthly* illustrated a Series 100 air pistol as a new high-power air "pistol." Evidently, Walter Benjamin did not invent the Benjamin air pistols. He certainly would have patented them, but no patents for the Benjamin air pistols have been uncovered. The air pistols may have come out of the efforts of Milhalyi and Spack to fill time during the Depression.

The Benjamin air pistols began with the simple pump rod-at-the-muzzle design. By 1938, an intriguing but mechanically weak hand lever mechanism had been added to some of the pistol models to operate the muzzle-based pump rod. Both of these rod-at-the-muzzle designs disappeared with the entry of the USA into WWII in 1941. Benjamin pneumatic air pistols reappeared in 1945 with the now familiar swinging arm pump handle mechanism. All single-shot pistols are bolt action and breech-loading.

MODEL 100 – BB/.175 cal., rod-at-the-muzzle pump-up pneumatic, SS, rifled or smoothbore barrel, black nickel finish, wood grips. Mfg. 1935-1941.

courtesy Beeman Collection

	N/A	$125	$100	$80	$60	$45	$25

Add 25% for box and instruction sheet.

MODEL 110 – BB/.175 cal., combination rod-at-the-muzzle/lever hand ("grass-hopper") pump-up pneumatic, SS, rifled or smoothbore barrel, black nickel finish, wood grips. Mfg. 1938-1941.

courtesy Beeman Collection

	N/A	$150	$120	$100	$75	$55	$30

Subtract 25%-75% for broken or incomplete pump/rod linkages.
Add 25% for box and instruction sheet.

MODEL 112 – .22 cal., combination rod-at-the-muzzle/lever hand ("grass-hopper") pump-up pneumatic, SS, rifled or smoothbore barrel, black nickel finish, wood grips. Mfg. 1938-1941.

	N/A	$150	$120	$100	$75	$55	$30

Subtract 25%-75% for broken or incomplete pump/rod linkages.
Add 25% for box and instruction sheet.

MODEL 117 – .177, combination rod-at-the-muzzle/lever hand ("grass-hopper") pump-up pneumatic, SS, rifled or smoothbore barrel, black nickel finish, wood grips. Mfg. 1938-1941.

	N/A	$150	$120	$100	$75	$55	$30

Subtract 25%-75% for broken or incomplete pump/rod linkages.
Add 25% for box and instruction sheet.

GRADING	100%	95%	90%	80%	60%	40%	20%

MODEL 122 – .22 cal., rod-at-the-muzzle pump-up pneumatic, SS, rifled or smoothbore barrel, black nickel finish, wood grips. Mfg. 1935-1941.

	N/A	$125	$100	$80	$60	$45	$25

Add 25% for box and instruction sheet.

When the Model 122 was introduced, the catalog designation of the Model 122 was changed to 102. However, apparently no guns were ever marked as 102.

MODEL 130 – BB/.175 cal., pump-up pneumatic, SS, rifled or smoothbore barrel, swinging lever hand pump, black nickel or matte finish, wood or plastic grips. Mfg. 1946-1985.

courtesy Beeman Collection

	N/A	$100	$80	$65	$50	$35	$20

Last MSR was $85.

Add 10% for wood grips.
Add 30% for black nickel.
Add 15% for box and instruction sheet of plastic grip versions.
Add 35% for box and instruction sheet of wood grip versions.

MODEL 132 – .22 cal., pump-up pneumatic, SS, rifled or smoothbore barrel, with swinging lever hand pump, black nickel or matte finish, wood or plastic grips. Mfg. 1946-1985.

	N/A	$100	$80	$65	$50	$35	$20

Last MSR was $85.

Add 10% for wood grips.
Add 30% for black nickel.
Add 15% for box and instruction sheet of plastic grip versions.
Add 35% for box and instruction sheet of wood grip versions.

MODEL 137 – .177 cal., pump-up pneumatic, SS, rifled or smoothbore barrel, with swinging lever hand pump, black nickel or matte finish, wood or plastic grips. Mfg. 1946-1985.

	N/A	$100	$80	$65	$50	$35	$20

Last MSR was $85.

Add 10% for wood grips.
Add 30% for black nickel.
Add 15% for box and instruction sheet of plastic grip versions.
Add 35% for box and instruction sheet of wood grip versions.

MODEL 150 – BB/.175 cal., pump-up pneumatic, smoothbore, repeating eight-shot, combination rod-at-the-muzzle/lever hand pump, black nickel finish, wood grips. Mfg. 1938-1941.

courtesy Beeman Collection

	N/A	$300	$240	$195	$150	$105	$60

Subtract 25%-75% for broken or incomplete pump/rod linkages.
Add 25% for box and instruction sheet.

GRADING	100%	95%	90%	80%	60%	40%	20%

MODEL 160 – BB/.175 cal., pump-up pneumatic, smoothbore, repeating 8-shot, swinging lever hand pump, black nickel finish, wood grips. Mfg. 1947-1960.

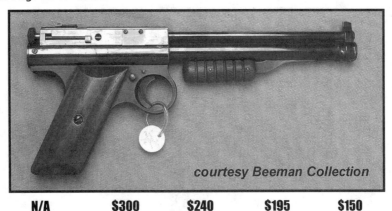

courtesy Beeman Collection

N/A	$300	$240	$195	$150	$105	$60

Add 25% for box and instruction sheet.

MODEL 177 – .177 cal., rod-at-the-muzzle pump-up pneumatic, SS, rifled or smoothbore barrel, black nickel finish, wood grips. Mfg. 1935-1941.

N/A	$125	$100	$80	$60	$45	$25

Add 25% for box and instruction sheet.

When the Model 177 was introduced, the catalog designation of the Model 177 was changed to 107. However, apparently no guns were ever marked as 107.

MODEL 232 – .22 cal., pump-up pneumatic, SS, BA, swinging lever hand pump, rifled barrel, black matte finish, plastic or wood grips. Mfg. 1985 only.

$115	$100	$80	$65	$50	$35	$25

Add 10% for wood grips.
Add 15% for box and instruction sheet.

MODEL 237 – .177 cal., pump-up pneumatic, SS, BA, swinging lever hand pump, rifled barrel, black matte finish, plastic or wood grips. Mfg. 1985 only.

$115	$100	$80	$65	$50	$35	$25

Add 10% for wood grips.
Add 15% for box and instruction sheet.

MODEL 242 – .22 cal., pump-up pneumatics, SS, BA, swinging lever hand pump, rifled barrel, black matte finish, wood or plastic grips. Mfg. 1986-1992.

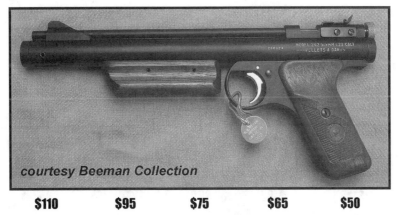

courtesy Beeman Collection

$110	$95	$75	$65	$50	$35	$20

Last MSR was $95.

Add 10% for wood grips.
Add 5% for box and instruction sheet.

MODEL 247 – .177 cal., pump-up pneumatic, SS, BA, swinging lever hand pump, rifled barrel, black matte finish, wood or plastic grips. Mfg. 1986-1992.

$110	$95	$75	$65	$50	$35	$20

Last MSR was $95.

Add 10% for wood grips.
Add 5% for box and instruction sheet.

GRADING	100%	95%	90%	80%	60%	40%	20%

MODEL 250 – BB/.175 smoothbore cal., 8-gram CO_2 cylinder, single-shot, rifled barrel, compact model, black nickel finish, wood grips. Mfg. 1952-1956.

courtesy Beeman Collection

	N/A	$130	$105	$85	$65	$45	$25

Add 10% for no serial number.

Add 35% for box and instruction sheet.

MODEL 252 – .22 cal., 8-gram CO_2 cylinder, single-shot, rifled barrel, compact model, black nickel finish, wood grips. Mfg. 1953-1956.

	N/A	$130	$105	$85	$65	$45	$25

Add 10% for no serial number.

Add 35% for box and instruction sheet.

MODEL 257 – .177 cal., 8-gram CO_2 cylinder, single-shot, rifled barrel, compact model, black nickel finish, wood grips. Mfg. 1953-1956.

	N/A	$150	$120	$100	$75	$55	$30

Add 10% for no serial number.

Add 35% for box and instruction sheet.

MODEL 260 "ROCKET" – BB/.175 smoothbore cal., 8-gram CO_2 cylinder, single-shot, rifled barrel, blue finish, plastic grips. Mfg. 1957-1964.

$250	$215	$175	$145	$115	$75	$50

Add 25% for box and instruction sheet.

Add 50% for Benjamin Target Practice Outfit and bell target.

MODEL 262 "ROCKET" – .177 cal., 8-gram CO_2 cylinder, single-shot, rifled barrel, blue finish, plastic grips. Mfg. 1956-1973.

courtesy Howard Collection

$125	$105	$90	$75	$55	$35	$25

Add 25% for box and instruction sheet.

Add 50% for Benjamin Target Practice Outfit and bell target.

MODEL 267 "ROCKET" – .177 cal., 8-gram CO_2 cylinder, single-shot, rifled barrel, blue finish, plastic grips. Mfg. 1956-1964.

$125	$105	$90	$75	$55	$35	$25

Add 25% for box and instruction sheet.

Add 50% for Benjamin Target Practice Outfit and bell target.

GRADING	100%	95%	90%	80%	60%	40%	20%

MODEL 422 – .22 cal., semi-auto, ten-shot, 8-gram CO_2 cylinder, black finish, plastic grips. Mfg. 1969-1973.

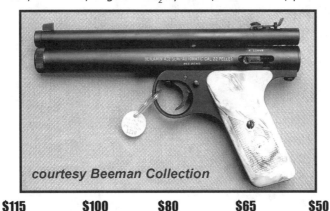

courtesy Beeman Collection

	$115	$100	$80	$65	$50	$35	$25

Add 25% for box and instruction sheet.

MODEL 1300 – BB/.175 cal., 50-shot, smoothbore barrel, pump-up pneumatic with swinging lever, black finish, plastic grips. Mfg. 1958-1964.

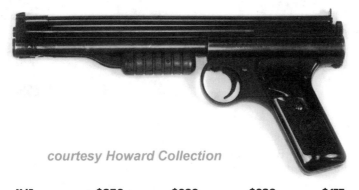

courtesy Howard Collection

	N/A	$350	$280	$230	$175	$125	$70

Add 30% for box and instruction sheet.

MODEL 1320 – .22 cal., 35-shot, rifled barrel, pump-up pneumatic with swinging lever, black finish, plastic grips. Mfg. 1959-1964.

	N/A	$450	$350	$295	$225	$160	$90

Add 30% for box and instruction sheet.

MODEL 2600 – BB/.175 cal., 8-gram CO_2 cylinder, thirty-five-shot, smoothbore barrel, blue finish, plastic grips. Mfg. 1958-1964.

courtesy Howard Collection

	N/A	$350	$280	$230	$175	$125	$70

Add 25% for box and instruction sheet.

MODEL 2620 – .22 cal., 8-gram CO_2 cylinder, thirty-five-shot, blue finish, plastic grips. Mfg. 1959-1964.

	N/A	$450	$350	$295	$225	$160	$90

Add 25% for box and instruction sheet.

GRADING	100%	95%	90%	80%	60%	40%	20%

MODEL E17 – .177 cal., CO_2, BA, single-shot, 6.38 in. rifled brass barrel, 500 FPS, bright nickel finish, walnut grips, 9 in. OAL, 1.75 lbs. Mfg. 1992-1998.

courtesy Benjamin

$100	$85	$70	$60	$45	$30	$20

Last MSR was $119.

Add 5% for box and instruction literature.

Add $20-$30 for factory holster in 95%+ condition.

This Series was marketed under the Benjamin/Sheridan name from 1992 to 1998. See Introduction to Benjamin section for information on guns produced during the 1990s. See also: SHERIDAN.

MODEL E20 – .20 cal., CO_2, BA, single-shot, 6.38 in. rifled brass barrel, 430 FPS, bright nickel finish, walnut grips, 9 in. OAL, 1.75 lbs. Mfg. 1992-1998.

$100	$85	$70	$60	$45	$30	$20

Last MSR was $119.

Add 5% for box and instruction literature.

Add $20-$30 for factory holster in 95%+ condition.

This model was marketed under the Benjamin/Sheridan name from 1992 to 1998. See Introduction to Benjamin section for information on guns produced during the 1990s. See also: SHERIDAN.

MODEL E22 – .22 cal., CO_2, BA, single-shot, 6.38 in. rifled brass barrel, 430 FPS, bright nickel finish, walnut grips, 9 in. OAL, 1.75 lbs. Mfg. 1992-1998.

$100	$85	$70	$60	$45	$30	$20

Last MSR was $119.

Add 5% for box and instruction literature.

Add $20-$30 for factory holster in 95%+ condition.

This model was marketed under the Benjamin/Sheridan name from 1992 to 1998. See Introduction to Benjamin section for information on guns produced during the 1990s. See also: SHERIDAN.

MODEL EB17 – .177 cal., CO_2, BA, single-shot, 6.38 in. rifled brass barrel, 500 FPS, matte black finish, walnut grips, 9 in. OAL, 1.75 lbs. New 1999-Disc.

$100	$85	$70	$60	$45	$30	$20

Last MSR was $105.

Add 5% for box and instruction literature.

Add $20-$30 for factory holster in 95%+ condition.

This model was manufactured and marketed under the Benjamin name by Crosman.

MODEL EB20 – .20 cal., CO_2, BA, single-shot, 6.38 in. rifled brass barrel, 430 FPS, matte black finish, walnut grips, 9 in. OAL, 1.75 lbs. New 1999-Disc.

$100	$85	$70	$60	$45	$30	$20

Last MSR was $105.

Add 5% for box and instruction literature.

Add $20-$30 for factory holster in 95%+ condition.

This model was manufactured and marketed under the Sheridan name by Crosman.

MODEL EB22 – .22 cal., CO_2, BA, SS, 6.38 in. rifled brass barrel, 430 FPS, matte black finish, walnut grips, fixed blade front and fully adj. rear sights, Crossbolt safety, 9 in. OAL, 1.75 lbs. New 1999-current.

MSR $119	$100	$90	$80	$65	$50	N/A	N/A

Add $20-$30 for factory holster in 95%+ condition.

GRADING	100%	95%	90%	80%	60%	40%	20%

MODEL H17 – .177 cal., single shot pump-up pneumatic, BA, 9.38 in. rifled brass barrel, 525 FPS, bright nickel finish, American walnut grips, 2.5 lbs. Mfg. 1991-1999.

courtesy Benjamin

$105	$90	$75	$60	$45	$30	$20

Last MSR was $120.

Add 10% for Wisconsin address. Add 5% for box and instruction literature.

The Model H17 Series replaced the Benjamin 242 Series, marketed under the Benjamin/Sheridan name from 1991 to 1998.

MODEL HB17 – .177 cal., single shot pump-up pneumatic, BA, 9.38 in. rifled brass barrel, 525 FPS, matte black finish, American walnut grip and forearm, high ramp blade front and open adj. rear sights, 12.25 in. OAL, 2.5 lbs. New 1999.

courtesy Crosman Corp.

MSR $155	$130	$115	$105	$85	$65	N/A	N/A

Add 10% for Wisconsin address.

This model is currently manufactured and marketed under the Benjamin name by Crosman.

MODEL HB20 – .20 cal., single shot pump-up pneumatic, BA, 9.38 in. rifled brass barrel, 460 FPS, matte black finish, American walnut grips, 2.5 lbs. Mfg. 1991-1998.

$105	$90	$75	$60	$45	$30	$20

Last MSR was $115.

Add 10% for Wisconsin address. Add 5% for box and instruction literature.

MODEL HB22 – .22 cal., single shot pump-up pneumatic, BA, 9.38 in. rifled brass barrel, 460 FPS, matte black finish, American walnut grip and forearm, high ramp blade front and open adj. rear sights, 2.5 lbs. New 1999.

courtesy Crosman Corp.

MSR $155	$130	$115	$105	$85	$65	N/A	N/A

Add 10% for Wisconsin address.

This model is currently manufactured and marketed under the Benjamin name by Crosman.

GRADING	100%	95%	90%	80%	60%	40%	20%

MARAUDER MODEL BP2220 – .22 cal. pellet, PCP, BA, 700 FPS, multi-shot self-indexing 8-shot rotary mag., 12 in. shrouded barrel, match-grade two-stage adj. trigger, includes stock extension to shoulder mount the gun, 18 in. OAL, 3.4 lbs. New 2010.

courtesy Benjamin

MSR $527	$450	$400	$350	$290	$220	N/A	N/A

MARAUDER WOODS WALKER MODEL BP2220-AP – .22 cal., PCP, multi-shot, bolt action, 700 FPS, rifled 12 in. shrouded barrel, 8-shot rotary mag., two-stage adj. trigger, shoulder stock included, CenterPoint Multi-Tac Quick Aim Sight allows for fast, accurate shots using the standard pistol grips or shoulder stock without having to adjust sight, Dovetail mounting rail, RealTree AP camo finish, 18 in. OAL, 2.7 lbs. New 2012.

courtesy Crosman Corp.

MSR $655	$550	$500	$450	$350	$275	N/A	N/A

MODEL NPB22 – .22 cal., BBC, Nitro Piston, SS, up to 700 FPS, features cocking aid and ergonomic ambidextrous finger groove grip, hooded front sight, adj. rear sight, 14.25 in. OAL, 2.75 lbs. New 2010.

While advertised during 2010, this model was never manufactured.

TRAIL NP PISTOL – .177 cal. pellet, BBC, Nitro Piston, SS, 5 1/2 in. rifled steel barrel, 525 FPS, tactical synthetic frame, fiber optic front and adj. rear sights, Dovetail mounting rail, includes removable cocking aid, Crossbolt safety, 16 in. OAL, 3.4 lbs. New 2012.

courtesy Crosman Corp.

MSR $101	$85	$75	$70	$55	$40	N/A	N/A

RIFLES

The designation of early Benjamin models is confusing, partly because Walter Benjamin tended to categorize his airguns by patents, rather than external features or appearance. Evidently, no guns are marked as models A, B, C, or D. The first appearance of any Benjamin letter model, in original Benjamin literature, was the model C.

Benjamin Models 300, 310, 312, 317, 360, 367, 700, 710, 720, 3030, 3100, 3120, 3600, and 3620 were recalled by Crosman in 1998.

GRADING	100%	95%	90%	80%	60%	40%	20%

ST. LOUIS 1899 – one of the predecessors to the Benjamin air rifles, made by the Walter Benjamin's St. Louis Air Rifle Company. Single-shot pneumatic, bicycle-type air pump under the barrel, muzzle loading. Octagonal barrel is blackened wood over a brass tube, smoothbore brass barrel liner. Simple trigger pinches shut a rubber tube serving as air reservoir. 35.8 in. OAL, 1.5 lbs.

> **Scarcity precludes accurate pricing.**

Russ Snyder made replicas of this model circa 1997. See Snyder in the "S" section.

ST. LOUIS 1900 – .22 cal., SS, SB, 17 3/8 in. barrel under body tube, incorporation of the hand pump incorporated into the body tube of the gun. A wooden rod, bearing a washer, has been inserted into the body tube over the barrel. Multiple in and out strokes of this rod charge the gun. This gun uses the same curved barrel found in the 1899 model and the same simple rubber air supply hose pinched shut by the trigger action. Marked on the LHS of slab sided buttstock "ST.LOUIS AIR RIFLE CO., ST. LOUIS, MO , PAT. JUNE 20 -1899. OTHER PATENTS PENDING." 32 5/8 in. OAL.

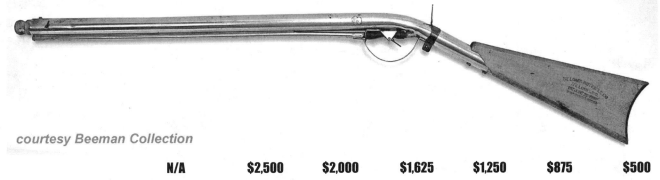

courtesy Beeman Collection

	N/A	$2,500	$2,000	$1,625	$1,250	$875	$500

Manufactured by Walter Benjamin's St. Louis Air Rifle Company, and is also known as Improved St. Louis or St. Louis No. 2.

Russ Snyder made replicas of this model circa 2002. See Snyder in the "S" section.

ST. LOUIS 1901 – Repeater. SB, Caliber not known. Wooden rod pump built into body tube above barrel, all metal, fixed buttstock air reservoir. See information on this complex model and image of replica from patent plans in Synder section of the "S" brand section of this book. Extremely rare or possibly not put into regular production. Ref. Fletcher (1999).

> **Scarcity precludes accurate pricing.**

Russ Snyder made replicas of this model circa 2002. See Snyder in the "S" section.

MODEL "A" (MODEL 1902) – BB/.175 cal. (smoothbore), barrel under the body tube, wooden pumping rod with operation instructions pasted onto it, receiver with a flat, vertical rear face, trigger guard cast as part of receiver, stock stamped: "Benjamin Air Rifle Company". Extremely rare.

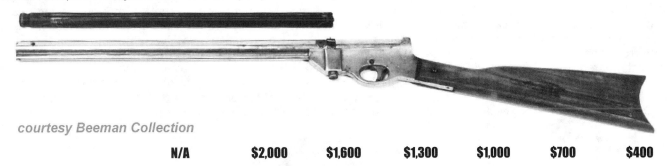

courtesy Beeman Collection

	N/A	$2,000	$1,600	$1,300	$1,000	$700	$400

This is the first Benjamin - referred to as "The Benjamin Air Rifle" by Walter Benjamin.

Evidently, there were at least three other very different appearing, unsuccessful variations of the Model "A" patent in the 1903-06 period. These were designated by Walter Benjamin as the Models 9 and 10, numbers which refer to design levels beginning in the St. Louis Air Rifle Company, and the "Benjamin Repeating Air Rifle." These variations use the same valve arrangement, and also have the barrel underneath the body tube, but have a gently sloping top surface behind the body tube. These variations presently are known only from Walter Benjamin's scrapbook.

GRADING	100%	95%	90%	80%	60%	40%	20%

MODEL "B" SINGLE VALVE MODEL – BB/.175 cal. (smoothbore), barrel above body tube, large conspicuous external figure-seven-shaped trigger lever. Extremely rare. Mfg. 1904-1908.

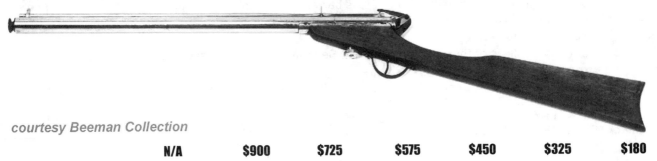

courtesy Beeman Collection

	N/A	$900	$725	$575	$450	$325	$180

Caution: the breech cap may fail explosively if these guns are charged. The 1904-06 variation, identifiable by a solid cast metal breech cap was produced by the W.R. Benjamin Co. The 1908 variation, mfg. by the reorganized Benjamin Air Rifle & Manufacturing Company, has a sheet metal breech cap.

MODEL C (1908) – BB/.175 cal. (smoothbore), same valve arrangement as the Model "B" but with a patented safety trigger to prevent dangerous bursting, gun can fire without the trigger being pulled, smaller trigger lever visible on top, but enclosed by receiver at back, breech cap stamped with "Benjamin Air Rifle & Manufacturing Co.", and 1899 to 1906 patents, not stamped with any model designation, sides of upper rear receiver unit without projections to side, short barrel version stops short of front end of body tube, very rare. Regular barrel version, rare.

courtesy Beeman Collection

	N/A	$300	$240	$195	$150	$105	$60

The above early Benjamins are single-shot (except for the unknown Repeater model), rod-at-the-muzzle, smoothbore, muzzle-loading, pump-up pneumatic air rifles with walnut quarter stocks. The reader is referred to *The St. Louis and Benjamin Air Rifle Companies,* D.T. Fletcher - Publisher, 1999, ISBN-1-929813-04-X. There apparently is no "Model D" Benjamin. An unsuccessful attempt to put a conical exhaust valve in a "Model C" may have represented the "Model D."

MODELS E AND F – BB/.175 cal. (smoothbore), rod-at-the-muzzle, pump-up pneumatics, muzzle-loading, walnut quarter stock, nearly identical to the Model C, but with a flat exhaust valve rather than a ball valve, Model E is the patent pending version, round turret-like unit projects to each side of upper rear receiver unit, rear sight about even with front end of one-piece stock, front sight is a triangular blade soldered to top of barrel, Model F was produced after the patent was issued, round turret-like unit projects to each side of upper receiver unit, rear sight about 1 in. back from front end of stock, front sight is a thin metal blade straddling each side of the barrel, Model E guns are the first Benjamins marked with a model letter; they use the Model C flat breech cap overstamped around the edge: "MODEL E PAT. PENDING", Model F breech cap is stamped as such and bears 1906-17 patent dates.

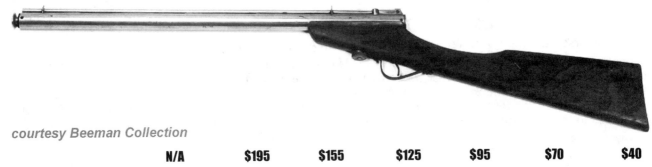

courtesy Beeman Collection

	N/A	$195	$155	$125	$95	$70	$40

Add 40% for box and instruction sheet.
Add 50% for Model E.

The Models E and F are the first really successful and reasonably safe production pneumatic air rifle models (by any manufacturer) and were extremely popular for 25 years, from 1910 to 1935.

GRADING	100%	95%	90%	80%	60%	40%	20%

MODEL G (MODEL 200) – similar to Models E and F, BB/.175 cal. smoothbore, muzzle loading, rod-at-the-muzzle, rear sight is a peep sight hole in a metal flange at rear end of receiver, walnut half stock, black nickel finish.

courtesy Howard Collection

	N/A	$190	$150	$125	$95	$65	$40

Add 40% for box and instruction sheet.

The single-shot Model 200 and the Benjamin Automatic (Model 600) repeater introduced the very different 1928 Mihalyi in-line valve design which is the basis for all later Benjamin valve systems. This is the first model to correct the accidental discharge problems of the Models C through F.

MODEL AUTOMATIC (MODEL 600) – BB/.175 cal., semi-auto, 25-shot, magazine-fed smoothbore for lead air rifle shot, rod-at-the-muzzle, similar valves as the single-shot Model 200, walnut half stock with pistol grip, black nickel finish, early versions are marked "Automatic" on the side plate.

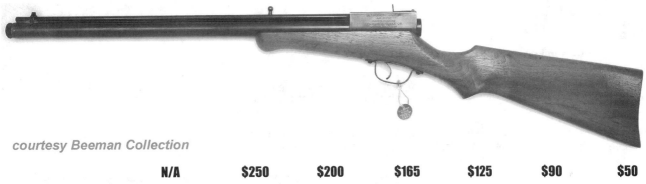

courtesy Beeman Collection

	N/A	$250	$200	$165	$125	$90	$50

Add 15% for "Automatic" marking.
Add 35% for box and instruction sheet.

MODEL 300 – BB/.175 (smoothbore) cal., single-shot, bolt action, pump-up pneumatics with rod-at-the-muzzle, rifled barrel, black finish, walnut stock. Mfg. 1934-1940.

	N/A	$195	$155	$125	$95	$70	$40

Add 100% for "one-piece bolt" variation, marked as "Model 300" on the side of the body tube (approx. 12 mfg.).
Add 30% for black nickel.
Add 25% for box and instruction sheet.

The Model 300 Series was the first Benjamin to use spring action triggers.

MODEL 317/307 – BB/.177 cal., single-shot, bolt action, pump-up pneumatics with muzzle pump rod, rifled barrel, black finish, later series walnut stock, spring action trigger. Mfg. 1934-1940.

	N/A	$195	$155	$125	$95	$70	$40

Add 30% for black nickel.
Add 25% for box and instruction sheet.

The Model 317 was later marketed, but not marked, as the Model 307, after a new Model 317, here known as the "317 PH" version, with a swinging pump handle. The "Model" 307 almost surely exists only as a catalog and owner's manual designation variation of guns marked as Model 317.

MODEL 322/302 – .22 cal., single-shot, bolt action, pump-up pneumatics with rod-at-the-muzzle, rifled barrel, black finish, walnut stock, spring action trigger. Mfg. 1934-1940.

	N/A	$195	$155	$125	$95	$70	$40

Add 30% for black nickel.
Add 25% for box and instruction sheet.

The Model 322 was later marketed as the 302. The "Model" 302 almost surely exists only as a catalog and owner's manual designation variation of guns marked as Model 322.

GRADING	100%	95%	90%	80%	60%	40%	20%

MODEL 310 – BB/.175 smoothbore, single-shot, bolt-action, breech-loading, pump-up pneumatic with swinging pump handle, rifled barrel, black nickel finish, walnut stock. Mfg. 1940-1969.

	N/A	$250	$200	$165	$125	$90	$50

Add 20% for CS versions with custom deluxe walnut stock.
Add 25% for box and instruction sheet.

MODEL 312 – .22 cal., single-shot, bolt-action, breech-loading, pump-up pneumatic with swinging pump handle, rifled barrel, black or nickel finish, walnut stock. Mfg. 1940-1969.

	N/A	$250	$200	$165	$125	$90	$50

Add 20% for CS versions with custom deluxe walnut stock.
Add 25% for box and instruction sheet.

MODEL 317 – .177 cal., single-shot, bolt-action, breech-loading, pump-up pneumatic with swinging pump handle, rifled barrel, black or nickel finish, walnut stock. Mfg. 1940-1969.

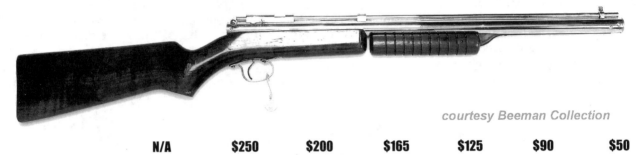

courtesy Beeman Collection

	N/A	$250	$200	$165	$125	$90	$50

Add 20% for CS versions with custom deluxe walnut stock.
Add 25% for box and instruction sheet.

This version of the Model 317, with its swinging pump handle, is known as the "317PH"; a different Model 317, with a pump rod at the muzzle, was marketed as the "307" but not marked "307", after this new version was introduced. Example shown is polished bright with no original black nickel finish remaining.

MODEL 340 – BB/.175 (smoothbore) cal., SS, BA, breech-loading, pump-up pneumatic, rifled barrel, centrally positioned tang safety, traditional grooved "corn-cob," checkered, or smooth walnut pump handle, black nickel finish. Mfg. 1969-1986.

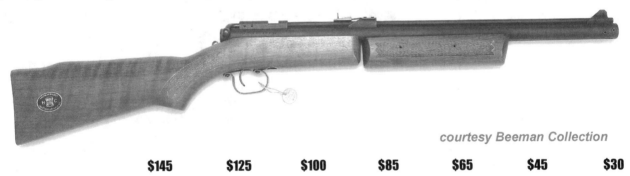

courtesy Beeman Collection

	$145	$125	$100	$85	$65	$45	$30

Last MSR was $110.

Add 15% for traditional grooved "corn-cob" pump handle.
Add 10% for 4x15mm scope.
Add 10% for box and instruction sheet.

MODEL 342 – .22 cal., SS, BA, breech-loading, pump-up pneumatic, rifled barrel, centrally positioned tang safety, traditional grooved "corn-cob," checkered, or smooth walnut pump handle. Mfg. 1969-1992.

$145	$125	$100	$85	$65	$45	$30

Last MSR was $110.

Add 15% for traditional grooved "corn-cob" pump handle.　　Add 10% for 4x15mm scope.
Add 10% for Williams peep sight.　　Add 10% for box and instruction sheet.

MODEL 347 – .177 cal., SS, rifled barrel, centrally positioned tang safety, traditional grooved "corn-cob," checkered, or smooth walnut pump handle. Mfg. 1969-1992.

$145	$125	$100	$85	$65	$45	$30

Last MSR was $110.

Add 15% for traditional grooved "corn-cob" pump handle.　　Add 10% for 4x15mm scope.
Add 10% for Williams peep sight.　　Add 10% for box and instruction sheet.

GRADING	100%	95%	90%	80%	60%	40%	20%

MODEL 352 – .22 cal., single shot, 8-gram CO_2 cylinder, bolt-action carbine, rifled barrel, rotating ring safety, black finish, walnut stock. Mfg. 1956-1957.

courtesy Beeman Collection

	$195	$165	$135	$115	$90	$60	$40

Add 35% for box and instruction sheet.

MODEL 360 – BB/.175 smoothbore cal., 8-gram CO_2 cylinder, SS, BA, rifled barrel, breech-loading, black finish, 21 in. walnut half stock, manual safety latch. Mfg. circa 1958-1959.

courtesy Beeman Collection

	$195	$165	$135	$115	$90	$60	$40

Add 20% for CS versions with 24.5 in. deluxe walnut custom stock.

Add 20% for rounded outer edge of muzzle, with recessed end of barrel liner (typical form is flat muzzle with slightly protruding brass barrel liner).

Add 25% for box and instruction sheet.

MODEL 362 – .22 cal., 8-gram CO_2 cylinder, SS, BA, rifled barrel, breech-loading, black finish, 21 in. walnut half stock, manual safety latch. New circa 1958-1959.

	$195	$165	$135	$115	$90	$60	$40

Add 20% for CS versions with 24.5 in. deluxe walnut custom stock.

Add 20% for rounded outer edge of muzzle, with recessed end of barrel liner (typical form is flat muzzle with slightly protruding brass barrel liner).

Add 25% for box and instruction sheet.

MODEL 367 – .177 cal., 8-gram CO_2 cylinder, SS, BA, rifled barrel, breech-loading, black finish, 21 in. walnut half stock, manual safety latch. Mfg. circa 1958-1959.

	$195	$165	$135	$115	$90	$60	$40

Add 20% for CS versions with 24.5 in. deluxe walnut custom stock.

Add 20% for rounded outer edge of muzzle, with recessed end of barrel liner (typical form is flat muzzle with slightly protruding brass barrel liner).

Add 25% for box and instruction sheet.

MODEL 392 – .22 cal., multi-pump pneumatic, bolt-action, single-shot, 19.38 in. rifled brass barrel, 700 FPS, black matte finish, fixed front sight, adj. rear sight, American hardwood Monte Carlo stock and forearm, Crossbolt safety, 36.75 in. OAL, 5.5 lbs. New 1992.

courtesy Benjamin

MSR $224	$190	$160	$135	$110	$85	$55	$40

Add 10% for Williams peep sight.

Add 15% for 4x15mm scope.

Add 5% for box and instruction sheet.

The Model 392 is marketed under the Benjamin name. (See Benjamin introduction section.)

GRADING	100%	95%	90%	80%	60%	40%	20%

MODEL S392 – .22 cal., multi-pump pneumatic, bolt-action, single-shot, 19.38 in. rifled brass barrel, 700 FPS, nickel finish, fixed front sight, adj. rear sight, American hardwood Monte Carlo stock and forearm, 36.75 in. OAL, 5.5 lbs. Mfg. 1992-1998.

	$120	$100	$85	$70	$55	$35	$25

Last MSR was $140.

Add 10% for Williams peep sight.
Add 15% for 4x15mm scope.
Add 5% for box and instruction sheet.

This model has a silver color finish. It was marketed under the Benjamin name 1994-1998. The Model S392 was discontinued and the Model 392 is marketed under the Benjamin name. (See Benjamin introduction section.)

MODEL AS392T – .22 cal., CO_2, 88g AirSource cylinder, SS, rifled steel barrel, 610 FPS, black finish, American hardwood stock, ramp front and adj. rear sights, 36.5 in. OAL, 5.25 lbs. Mfg. 2004-2007.

courtesy Benjamin

	$165	$140	$115	$95	$75	$50	$35

Last MSR was $180.

MODEL G392 – .22 cal., CO_2, bolt-action, single-shot, 19.38 in. brass rifled barrel, 500 FPS, black finish, American hardwood stock, adj. rear sight, 5 lbs. Mfg. 1991-1998.

	$155	$130	$110	$90	$70	$45	$30

Last MSR was $180.

Add 10% for Williams peep sight.
Add 15% for 4x15 scope.
Add 5% for box and instruction sheet.

Model G392 was marketed under the Benjamin name 1993-1998. A .20 cal. version, the Model F9, was marketed under the Sheridan name 1993-1998 (see Benjamin introduction and Sheridan Model F section).

MODEL GS392 – .22 cal., CO_2, bolt-action, single-shot, 19.38 in. brass rifled barrel, 500 FPS, nickel finish, American hardwood stock, adj. rear sight, 5 lbs. Mfg. 1991-1994.

	$175	$150	$125	$100	$80	$50	$35

Last MSR was $180.

Add 10% for Williams peep sight.
Add 15% for 4x15 scope.
Add 5% for box and instruction sheet.

The S prefix indicates silver finish.

MODEL 397 – .177 cal., multi-pump pneumatic, BA, SS, 19.38 in. rifled brass barrel, 750 FPS, black matte finish, adj. rear sight, fixed front sight, Monte Carlo American hardwood stock and forearm, Crossbolt safety, 36.75 in. OAL, 5.5 lbs. Mfg. 1992-current.

courtesy Howard Collection

MSR $224	$190	$160	$135	$110	$85	$55	$40

Add 10% for Williams peep sight.
Add 15% for 4x15 scope.
Add 5% for box and instruction sheet.

GRADING	100%	95%	90%	80%	60%	40%	20%

MODEL 397C – .177 cal., multi-pump pneumatic, bolt-action, single-shot, carbine, 16.38 in. rifled brass barrel, 750 FPS, black matte finish, adj. rear sight, American hardwood stock and forearm, rocker safety, 32.75 in. OAL, approx. 4.5 lbs. Mfg. 1992-1998.

	$120	$100	$85	$70	$55	$35	$25

Last MSR was $125.

Add 10% for Williams peep sight.
Add 15% for 4x15 scope.
Add 5% for box and instruction sheet.

This model was marketed under the Benjamin name from 1994-1998.

MODEL S397 – .177 cal., multi-pump pneumatic, bolt-action, single-shot, 19.38 in. rifled brass barrel, 750 FPS, nickel finish, adj. rear sight, American hardwood stock and forearm, 36.75 in. OAL, 5.5 lbs. Mfg. 1992-1994.

	$120	$100	$85	$70	$55	$35	$25

Last MSR was $144.

Add 10% for Williams peep sight.
Add 15% for 4x15 scope.
Add 5% for box and instruction sheet.

The S prefix denotes a silver color finish. This model was marketed under the Benjamin name from 1994-1998.

MODEL G397 – .177 cal., CO_2, bolt-action, single-shot, 19.38 in. brass rifled barrel, 600 FPS, black finish, American hardwood stock, adj. rear sight, 5 lbs. Mfg. 1991-1998.

	$155	$130	$110	$90	$70	$45	$30

Last MSR was $180.

Add 10% for Williams peep sight.
Add 15% for 4x15mm scope.
Add 5% for box and instruction sheet.

This model was marketed under the Benjamin name from 1993-1998. A .20 cal. version, the Model F9, was marketed under the Sheridan name 1993-1998 (see Benjamin introduction and Sheridan Model F section).

MODEL GS397 – .177 cal., CO_2, bolt-action, single-shot, 19.38 in. brass rifled barrel, 600 FPS, nickel finish, American hardwood stock, adj. rear sight, 5 lbs. Mfg. 1991-1994.

	$175	$150	$125	$100	$80	$50	$35

Last MSR was $180.

Add 10% for Williams peep sight.
Add 15% for 4x15mm scope.
Add 5% for box and instruction sheet.

The S prefix denotes silver finish.

MODEL 600 – see Model Automatic.

courtesy Howard Collection

MODEL 700 – BB/.175 cal. smoothbore, pump-up pneumatic with rod-at-the-muzzle pump, 25-shot magazine, black nickel finish, walnut stock. Disc. 1939.

courtesy Howard Collection

	N/A	$200	$160	$130	$100	$70	$40

Add 10% for early versions marked 700 on left side (later versions marked 700 on end cap).
Add 35% for box and instruction sheet.

GRADING	100%	95%	90%	80%	60%	40%	20%

MODEL 710 – BB/.175 cal. smoothbore, pump-up pneumatic with swinging pump handle, 25-five-shot magazine, black nickel finish, walnut stock. Mfg. 1940-1947.

	N/A	$165	$130	$105	$80	$60	$35

> Add 30% for extended air reservoir mounted under stock.
> Add 25% for box and instruction sheet.

MODEL 720 – BB/.175 cal. smoothbore, pump-up pneumatic with swinging pump handle, 25-shot magazine, black nickel finish, walnut stock. Mfg. 1947-1962.

courtesy Howard Collection

	N/A	$165	$130	$105	$80	$60	$35

> Add 25% for box and instruction sheet.

MODEL 3030 – BB/.175 cal. smoothbore, 8-gram CO_2 cylinder, breech-loading, bolt action, 30-shot, black finish, walnut half stock. Mfg. circa 1962-1976.

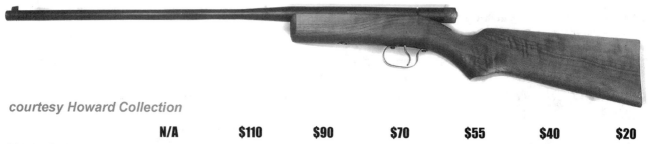

courtesy Howard Collection

	N/A	$110	$90	$70	$55	$40	$20

> Add 25% for box and instruction sheet.

MODEL 3100 – BB/.175 cal, pneumatic with swinging pump handles, smoothbore barrel, 100-shot. Mfg. 1958-1985.

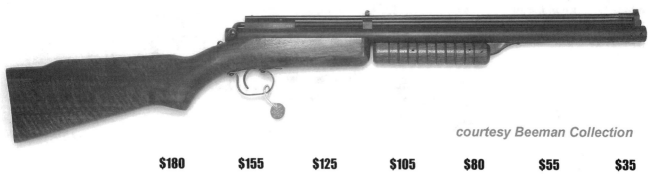

courtesy Beeman Collection

$180	$155	$125	$105	$80	$55	$35

> Add 20% for box and instructions.

The Model 3100 was first produced in 1958 followed by the 3120 in 1959. These dates seem to apply to all four of this type: 2600; 2620, 1300; 1320, 3100; 3120, and 3600; 3620. Benjamin offered .22 cal. lead balls, but the BB guns were much more popular, because BBs were more widely available.

MODEL 3120 – .22 cal. lead ball, rifled barrel, 85-shot, pneumatic with swinging pump handles. Mfg. 1959-1985.

$275	$235	$195	$160	$125	$80	$55

> Add 20% for box and instructions.

The Model 3100 was first produced in 1958 followed by the 3120 in 1959. These dates seem to apply to all four of this type: 2600; 2620, 1300; 1320, 3100; 3120, and 3600; 3620. Benjamin offered .22 cal. lead balls, but the BB guns were much more popular, because BBs were more widely available.

GRADING	100%	95%	90%	80%	60%	40%	20%

MODEL 3600 – BB/.175 cal., CO_2, 8-gram cylinder, smoothbore barrel, 100-shot. Mfg. 1958-1964.

courtesy Beeman Collection

	$250	$215	$175	$145	$115	$75	$50

Add 25% for box and instructions.
Add 30% for custom grade stock (24.5 in.).

MODEL 3620 – .22 cal. lead ball, CO_2, 8-gram cylinders, rifled barrel, 85-shot. Mfg. 1959-1964.

	$375	$325	$265	$220	$170	$110	$75

Add 25% for box and instructions.
Add 30% for custom grade stock (24.5 in.).

MODEL RM622 – .22 cal., BBC, SP, SS, rifled steel barrel, blue finish, 825 FPS, checkered Monte Carlo hardwood stock, swivel sling mounts, rubber butt pad, hooded front and adj. rear peep sights, 7.5 lbs. Mfg. 2002-2004.

	$200	$170	$140	$115	$90	$60	$40

MODEL RM777 – .177 cal., BBC, SP, SS, rifled steel barrel, blue finish, 1100 FPS, checkered Monte Carlo hardwood stock, swivel sling mounts, rubber butt pad, hooded front and adj. rear peep sights, 8.4 lbs. Mfg. 2002-2004.

	$200	$170	$140	$115	$90	$60	$40

DISCOVERY – .177 or .22 cal. pellet, BA, CO_2 or compressed air Duel Fuel PCP, SS, blue finished rifled steel barrel, 1000/900 FPS with lead free pellets, walnut PG stock with long steel breech and built-in pressure gauge, buttplate, Williams fiber optic front sights, fully adj. rear sights, cross bolt safety, 39 in. OAL, 5.1 lbs. Mfg. 2008-2011, reintroduced 2014.

courtesy Benjamin

MSR $321	$265	$225	$185	$155	$120	$80	$55

Last MSR in 2011 was $299.

DISCOVERY WITH PUMP – .177 or .22 cal. pellet, BA, CO_2 or compressed air Duel Fuel PCP, SS, 24 in. rifled steel barrel, blued finish, 1000/900 FPS, walnut PG stock with long steel breech and built-in pressure gauge, buttplate, Dovetail mounting rail, Williams fiber optic front sights, fully adj. rear sights, cross bolt safety, comes with three stage high pressure hand pump and 50 lead free pellets, 39 in. OAL, 5.1 lbs. Mfg. 2008-current.

MSR $560	$475	$400	$350	$280	$220	$145	$95

GENESIS – .22 cal., BBC, NP, SS, pellet, 800 FPS, rifled barrel, Picatinny rail, barrel integrated sound suppression system, adj. two-stage trigger, lever safety, black synthetic stock with overmolded inserts, adj. comb, recoil pad w/ Benjamin medallion, includes CenterPoint 3-9x32mm scope, 45.5 in. OAL, 6.7 lbs.

courtesy Crosman Corp.

MSR $240	$205	$175	$145	$120	$90	$60	$40

GRADING	100%	95%	90%	80%	60%	40%	20%

LEGACY 822 MODEL B8M22 – .22 cal., BBC, SP, SS, rifled steel barrel, blue finish, 800 FPS, checkered Monte Carlo style hardwood stock, vent. rubber butt pad, fiber optic front and adj. rear peep sights, 43 in. OAL, 6.5 lbs. Mfg. 2004-2007.

courtesy Benjamin

	100%	95%	90%	80%	60%	40%	20%
	$125	$105	$90	$75	$55	$35	$25

Last MSR was $140.

LEGACY 1000 MODEL B1K77 – .177 cal., BBC, SP, SS, rifled steel barrel, blue finish, 1000 FPS, checkered Monte Carlo style hardwood stock, vent. rubber butt pad, fiber optic front and adj. rear peep sights, 43 in. OAL, 6.5 lbs. Mfg. 2004-2007.

	100%	95%	90%	80%	60%	40%	20%
	$235	$200	$165	$135	$105	$70	$45

Last MSR was $260.

LEGACY 1000 MODEL B1K77X – .177 cal., BBC, SP, SS, rifled steel barrel, blue finish, 1000 FPS, checkered Monte Carlo style hardwood stock, vent. rubber butt pad, fiber optic front and adj. rear peep sights, 4x32mm scope, 43 in. OAL, 6.5 lbs. Mfg. 2004-2007.

courtesy Benjamin

	100%	95%	90%	80%	60%	40%	20%
	$250	$215	$175	$145	$115	$75	$50

Last MSR was $260.

LEGACY 1000 MODEL B1K77XRT – .177 cal., BBC, SP, SS, rifled steel barrel, blue finish, 1000 FPS, Realtree Hardwoods stock, vent. rubber butt pad, fiber optic front and adj. rear peep sights, 43 in. OAL, 6.5 lbs. Mfg. 2005-2007.

	100%	95%	90%	80%	60%	40%	20%
	$235	$200	$165	$135	$105	$70	$45

Last MSR was $260.

LEGACY 1000X MODEL B5M77X – .177 cal., BBC, SP, SS, rifled steel barrel, blue finish, 495 FPS, checkered Monte Carlo style hardwood stock, vented rubber butt pad, fiber optic front and adj. rear peep sights and 4x32mm scope, 43 in. OAL, 6.5 lbs. Mfg. 2004-2007.

	100%	95%	90%	80%	60%	40%	20%
	$125	$105	$90	$75	$55	$35	$25

Last MSR was $140.

LEGACY JIM SHOCKEY SIGNATURE SERIES – .177 or .22 cal. pellet, BBC, Nitro Piston, SS, 15 in. rifled steel barrel, 1000/800 FPS, adj. two-stage trigger, Picatinny mounting rail, Black synthetic ambidextrous stock with over molded inserts and adj. comb, CenterPoint 3-9x40mm AO scope, sling mounts, 43 in. OAL, 6.7 lbs. New 2013.

courtesy Crosman Corp.

	100%	95%	90%	80%	60%	40%	20%
MSR $296	$245	$210	$170	$140	$110	$75	$50

GRADING	100%	95%	90%	80%	60%	40%	20%

LEGACY JR. JIM SHOCKEY SIGNATURE SERIES – .177 cal., BBC, SP, SS, pellet, 12 1/2 in. rifled steel barrel, 720 FPS, Black synthetic lightweight stock sized for smaller shooters, Dovetail mounting rail, includes CenterPoint 4x32mm scope, fiber optic front and fully adj. rear sights, Crossbolt safety, 37 1/2 in. OAL, 4.9 lbs.

While advertised during 2013, this model never went into production.

MARAUDER (RECENT MFG.) – .177 (Model BP1763), .22 (Model BP2263), or .25 (Model BP2563, new 2011) cal., BA, CO_2 or compressed air Duel Fuel PCP, 1100/1000/900 FPS, 20 in. choked and internally shrouded rifled steel barrel, blued finish, hardwood PG stock with ambidextrous raised comb and custom checkering with a built-in pressure gauge, vent. recoil pad, two-stage adj. match-grade trigger, 8 (.25 cal.) or 10 shot round rotary mag., Dovetail mounting rail, lever safety, sling mounts, 43 in. OAL, 7.5 lbs. Mfg. 2009-2013.

courtesy Benjamin

| $525 | $425 | $350 | $300 | $230 | $155 | $105 |

Last MSR was $600.

MARAUDER (CURRENT MFG). – .177, .22, or .25 cal., PCP, CO_2, pellet, redesigned and featuring rifled and shrouded barrel with integrated resonance dampener, 10 shot round rotary mag., re-balanced all-weather black synthetic or classic wood stock, adj. raised comb cheekpiece, ambidextrous bolt handle, optimized trigger positioning, 42.8 in. OAL, 7.3 lbs. New 2014.

courtesy Crosman Corp.

| MSR $700 | $600 | $500 | $425 | $350 | $270 | $180 | $120 |

Add $50 for .25 cal.

MAV 77 UNDERLEVER AIR RIFLE – .177 cal. (Model UL77), SP, lever action, SS, pellet, 13 in. rifled steel barrel, 915 FPS, adj. two-stage trigger, underlever with ambidextrous hardwood stock, Dovetail mounting rail, automatic safety, includes a 3-9x32mm CenterPoint precision scope, 42 in. OAL, 8.9 lbs. Mfg. 2012-2013.

courtesy Benjamin Air Rifle Co.

| $325 | $295 | $265 | $215 | $165 | N/A | N/A |

Last MSR was $390.

GRADING	100%	95%	90%	80%	60%	40%	20%

NPS – .177 cal., BBC, NP, SS, pellet, 1000 FPS, rifled steel bull barrel with integrated shroud, adj. two-stage trigger, Dovetail mounting rail, all-weather ambidextrous thumbhole stock with adj. cheekpiece, carbon fiber finish, includes CenterPoint 3-9x40mm AO scope, 43.87 in. OAL, 6.9 lbs.

courtesy Crosman Corp.

MSR $300	$245	$210	$170	$140	$110	$75	$50

PROWLER – .177 cal. pellet, BBC, SS, Nitro Piston, 1000 FPS, rifled steel barrel, two-stage adj. trigger, lever safety, all weather black synthetic stock, includes CenterPoint 4x32mm scope, 45 in. OAL, 6.4 lbs. New 2014.

courtesy Crosman Corp.

MSR $156	$130	$110	$90	$75	$60	$40	$25

ROGUE MODEL BPE3571 – .357 cal., ePCP (electro pre-charged pneumatic), BA, multi-shot, compressed air, up to 700-1000 FPS, precision rifled and shrouded steel barrel, features the eVALVE system, EPiC (Electro-Pneumatic Intelligent Control), two-stage adj. electronic eTRIGGER, auto indexing 6 shot rotary mag., synthetic all-weather adj. stock with under barrel Picatinny accessory rail and 3/8 in. dovetail-style optics rail, LCD screen reports pressure and power settings, also offers quick disconnect Foster fittings for easy refilling, tan finish, 48 in. OAL, 9.8 lbs. New 2011.

courtesy Benjamin

MSR $1,500	$1,275	$1,125	$1,025	$825	$625	N/A	N/A

* ***Rogue Model BPE3571LE Limited Edition Package*** – .357 cal., ePCP (electro pre-charged pneumatic), BA, multi-shot, compressed air, up to 700-1000 FPS, precision rifled and shrouded steel barrel, features the eVALVE system, EPiC (Electro-Pneumatic Intelligent Control), two-stage adj. electronic eTRIGGER, auto indexing 6 shot rotary mag., synthetic all-weather adj. stock with under barrel Picatinny accessory rail and 3/8 in. dovetail-style optics rail, LCD screen reports pressure and power settings, also offers quick disconnect Foster fittings for easy refilling, tan finish, 48 in. OAL, 9.8 lbs. New 2012.

NO MSR	$1,500	$1,275	$1,050	$875	$675	$450	$300

The Rogue Limited Edition package also includes CenterPoint® Power Class 3-12x44mm optic, 3/8 dovetail optics mounting rings, Bipod with folding, height-adjustable legs, custom embroidered soft case and three year extended warranty.

* ***Rogue Model PROPICK002 Porkchop Pack*** – .357 cal., ePCP (electro pre-charged pneumatic), BA, multi-shot, compressed air, up to 700-1000 FPS, precision rifled and shrouded steel barrel, features the eVALVE system, EPiC (Electro-Pneumatic Intelligent Control), two-stage adj. electronic eTRIGGER, auto indexing 6 shot rotary mag., synthetic all-weather adj. stock with under barrel Picatinny accessory rail and 3/8 in. dovetail-style optics rail, LCD screen reports pressure and power settings, also offers quick disconnect Foster fittings for easy refilling, tan finish, 48 in. OAL, 9.8 lbs. New 2012.

NO MSR	$1,550	$1,325	$1,075	$900	$700	$475	$300

GRADING	100%	95%	90%	80%	60%	40%	20%

The Rogue Limited Edition package also includes CenterPoint® Power Class 3-12x44mm optic, 3/8 dovetail optics mounting rings, Bipod with folding, height-adjustable legs, custom embroidered soft case two boxes of Nosler Ballistic Tip bullets, one additional 8-round magazine, and authentic prostaff cap from Benjamin, and three year extended warranty.

SUPER STREAK MODEL B1122BTM – .22 cal., BBC, SP, SS, blue finished rifled steel barrel with fluted muzzle brake, up to 1500 FPS with lead free pellet, checkered thumbhole hardwood stock, vent. rubber butt pad, hooded front and micro adj. rear sight, 4-16x40mm AORG CenterPoint scope, manual safety, and 50 lead free pellets, 49.75 in. OAL, 8.5 lbs. Mfg. 2008-2010.

	$255	$215	$180	$150	$115	$75	$50

Last MSR was $300.

SUPER STREAK MODEL B1500BTM – .177 cal., BBC, SP, SS, blue finished rifled steel barrel with fluted muzzle brake, 1200 FPS with 7.9 grain pellet, up to 1500 FPS with lead free pellet, checkered thumbhole hardwood stock, vent. rubber butt pad, hooded front and micro adj. rear sight, 4-16x40mm AORG CenterPoint scope, manual safety, and 50 lead free pellets. 8.5 lbs., 49.75 in. OAL. Mfg. 2008-2010.

	$255	$215	$180	$150	$115	$75	$50

Last MSR was $300.

SUPER STREAK MODEL B1500STM – .177 cal., BBC, SP, SS, silver finished rifled steel barrel with fluted muzzle break, 1200 FPS with 7.9 grain pellet, up to 1500 FPS with lead free pellet, checkered thumbhole hardwood stock, vent. rubber butt pad, hooded front and micro adj. rear sight, 4-16x40mm AORG CenterPoint scope, manual safety, and 50 lead free pellets, 49.75 in. OAL, 8.5 lbs. Mfg. 2008-2010.

	$255	$215	$180	$150	$115	$75	$50

Last MSR was $300.

TITAN NP – .177 or .22 cal. pellet, Nitro Piston, BBC, SS, 1000/800 FPS, 15 in. rifled steel barrel, ambidextrous hardwood thumbhole stock, two-stage adj. trigger, vent. rubber recoil pad, lever safety, Dovetail mounting rail, includes Center Point 4x32mm scope, 44.5 in. OAL, 7.4 lbs. New 2012.

courtesy Crosman Corp.

MSR $195	$165	$140	$115	$95	$75	$50	$35

Add $16 for Titan Pest Pack (includes CenterPoint 10x50mm binoculars and tin of Destroyer pellets).

TRAIL NP ALL WEATHER BLACK – .177 (new 2011) or .22 cal. pellet, BBC, Nitro Piston, SS, 1000/800 FPS, 15 in. rifled steel bull barrel, durable all-weather black synthetic stock with thumbhole, features quick lock Weaver-style optic mounting rail system, integrated sling mount, vent. rubber recoil pad, 3-9x40mm CenterPoint scope, lever safety, 44.5 in. OAL, 8.6 lbs. Mfg. 2010-2013.

courtesy Crosman Corp.

	$195	$165	$135	$115	$90	$60	$40

Last MSR was $230.

Add $70 for .22 cal.

TRAIL NP ALL WEATHER CAMO – .22 cal. pellet, BBC, Nitro Piston, SS, 800 FPS, 15 in. rifled steel bull barrel, durable all-weather Realtree APG camo synthetic stock with thumbhole, features quick lock Weaver-style optic

GRADING	100%	95%	90%	80%	60%	40%	20%

mounting rail system, integrated sling mount, vent. rubber recoil pad, 3-9x40mm CenterPoint scope, lever safety, 44.5 in. OAL, 8.3 lbs. Mfg. 2011-2013.

courtesy Crosman Corp.

	$220	$185	$155	$130	$100	$65	$45

Last MSR was $260.

TRAIL NP HARDWOOD – .22 cal. pellet, BBC, Nitro Piston, SS, 800 FPS, 15 in. rifled steel barrel, checkered hardwood ambidextrous stock with thumbhole and checkering on grip and forearm, Picatinny mounting rail, features quick lock optic mounting system, integrated sling mount, vent. rubber recoil pad, 3-9x40mm CenterPoint scope, lever safety, 44.25 in. OAL, 7.1 lbs. Mfg. 2010-2013.

courtesy Crosman Corp.

	$195	$165	$135	$115	$90	$60	$40

Last MSR was $230.

Add $40 for laminated stock (Model BT9M22LNP, disc. 2012).

TRAIL NP XL MAGNUM – .177, .22, or .25 cal. pellet, BBC, Nitro Piston, SS, 1200/950/725/ FPS, 17 in. rifled steel barrel, checkered hardwood ambidextrous stock with thumbhole and checkering on grip and forearm, Picatinny mounting rail, integrated sling mount, vent. rubber recoil pad, 3-9x40mm CenterPoint scope, lever safety, 49 in. OAL, 8.5 lbs. New 2010.

courtesy Crosman Corp.

MSR $406	$350	$300	$245	$205	$160	$105	$70

Add $8 for .25 cal.

TRAIL NP2 SYNTHETIC – .177 or .22 cal. pellet, BBC, SS, features Nitro Piston 2 technology, 1100 FPS, precision rifled steel barrel, enhanced CBT (clean break trigger), Picatinny mounting rail, all weather black synthetic thumbhole stock with rubber recoil pad, lever safety, includes integrated sound suppression system and CenterPoint 3-9x32mm scope, 46.25 in. OAL, 8.3 lbs. New 2014.

courtesy Crosman Corp.

MSR $350	$295	$250	$205	$170	$135	$90	$60

Blue Book Publications selected this model as one of its Top 10 Industry Awards from all the new firearms at the 2014 SHOT Show.

GRADING	100%	95%	90%	80%	60%	40%	20%

* **Trail NP2 Camo** – .22 cal., similar to Trail NP2 Synthetic, except features Realtree Extra camo coverage on synthetic thumbhole stock and forend, 900 FPS. New 2014.

MSR $380	$325	$275	$230	$190	$145	$95	$65

Blue Book Publications selected this model as one of its Top 10 Industry Awards from all the new firearms at the 2014 SHOT Show.

* **Trail NP2 Wood** – .22 cal., similar to Trail NP2 Synthetic, except features hardwood thumbhole stock with rubber recoil pad and 900 FPS. New 2014.

courtesy Crosman Corp.

MSR $350	$295	$250	$205	$170	$135	$90	$60

Blue Book Publications selected this model as one of its Top 10 Industry Awards from all the new firearms at the 2014 SHOT Show.

TITAN XS NP – .177 cal. pellet, BBC, Nitro Piston, 1000 FPS, rifled barrel, two-stage adj. trigger, Picatinny mounting rail, ambidextrous all-weather black synthetic thumbhole stock, integrated sling mounts, includes CenterPoint 4x32mm scope. New 2014.

MSR $232	$195	$165	$135	$115	$90	$60	$40

VARMINT POWER PACK – .22 cal., BBC, SS, Nitro Piston, 800 FPS, precision rifled steel shrouded bull barrel, two-stage adj. trigger, Picatinny mounting rail, ambidextrous black synthetic stock with raised cheekpiece and rubber recoil pad, lever safety, includes 90 lumen LED flashlight with a red flip-up filter, red Class III fast acquisition laser with push on/off or remote tape switch, and CenterPoint 4x32mm scope, 44.5 in. OAL, 7.4 lbs. New 2014.

courtesy Crosman Corp.

MSR $250	$210	$180	$145	$120	$95	$65	$40

COMMEMORATIVE EDITION RIFLES

MODEL 87 (CENTENNIAL MODEL) – .177 or .22 cal., pump-up pneumatic, single-shot, breech loading, rifled barrel, polished brass finish, full-length walnut stock with inset bronze medallion. Approx. 400 mfg. 1987 only.

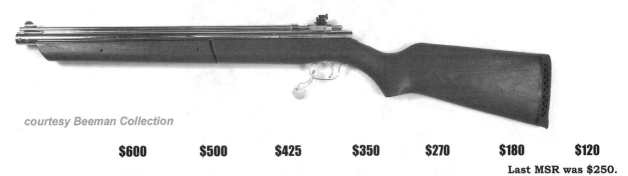

courtesy Beeman Collection

	$600	$500	$425	$350	$270	$180	$120

Last MSR was $250.

Add 40% for .177 cal.

Subtract 25% for missing factory soft side case marked "Benjamin" and manual.

Beware of "seconds" which have standard serial numbers instead of the special 00XXXX sequence. Offered during 1987 as a limited edition "Centennial" issue, the real Centennial for Benjamin was in 2002.

GRADING	100%	95%	90%	80%	60%	40%	20%

BENJAMIN

Previous marketing name used by the Benjamin Air Rifle Co. and Crosman Corp. from 1991 to about 1998.

See the introduction to the "Benjamin Air Rifle Company" section.

BENYAMIN

Unknown maker, possibly of the Philippines or the U.S., mid-20th century.

Not a copy of Benjamin features. Multiple stroke pump pneumatic with swinging metal pump lever. SS, faucet-style breech. Marked "Benyamin Super" with horse head figures. Full width receiver with slab sides bearing figure of rearing horse. Adult sized buttstock with Monte Carlo comb, cheekpiece, and checkering. Sling swivels on left side of gun. Extreme scarcity precludes accurate pricing on this model.

courtesy Beeman Collection

BERETTA, PIETRO

Current manufacturer located in Brescia, Italy. Currently imported and distributed by Umarex USA located in Fort Smith, AR beginning March, 2006. Previously imported by Beretta USA Corp., located in Accokeek, MD. Previously distributed by Crosman Corp. located in East Bloomfield, NY 2003-2006. Previously distributed by Beretta USA Corp., located in Accokeek, MD 2000-2003. Dealer sales.

Beretta USA Corp. was formed in 1977, and has been the exclusive importer of Beretta firearms since 1980. Beretta introduced a complete line of air pistols in 2000, which are identical in size, appearance, and model designation to the 9mm Model 92FS. Although the Model 92FS air pistol is identical in appearance to the Beretta 9mm semi-auto, it is not a semi-auto air pistol, but rather utilizes the traditional eight-shot rotary clip loaded at the breech and functions in the same way as a single or double action revolver. The barrel is recessed within a 9mm size muzzle, making this one of the most authentic-looking air pistols (firearm-copy) in production today. The slide is marked "Pietro Beretta Gardone V.T." on the left along with the PB logo, and marked "Carl Walther Alexandria/VA." on the right side. The airguns are manufactured for Beretta by Umarex Sportwaffen GmbH, the present owner of Walther. For more information and current pricing on both new and used Beretta firearms, please refer to the *Blue Book of Gun Values* by S.P. Fjestad (also available online).

PISTOLS

84FS – BB/.177 cal., CO_2, SA semi-auto repeater, blowback action, 360 FPS, 3.6 in. rifled steel barrel, 17 shot mag., black full metal replica, fixed sights, 7 in. OAL, 1.4 lbs. New 2014.

MSR $100	$85	$75	$70	$55	$40	N/A	N/A

90TWO – BB/.177 cal., CO_2, 375 FPS, SA/DA, 5 in. barrel, metal slide, polymer frame, blued, Black or Dark Ops finish, Picatinny rail and removable rail cover, 21-shot drop free magazine, 8.5 in. OAL, 1.1 lbs. Mfg. 2012-2013.

courtesy Beretta

$55	$45	$40	$30	$25	$15	$10

Last MSR was $68.

92FS – .177 cal., CO_2, SA/DA, 425 FPS, 4.5 in. rifled steel barrel, two 8-shot rotary mags., fixed front, interchangeable rear sight, ambidextrous safety, black plastic (disc.), synthetic, or optional checkered wood grips, available in blue

GRADING	100%	95%	90%	80%	60%	40%	20%

(disc.), black, satin nickel finish with black grips, or satin nickel with wood grips, comes in standard, match, and trophy (disc. 2003) versions, includes plastic carrying case w/foam lining, 8.5 in. OAL, 2.78 lbs. to 3 lbs. New 2000.

courtesy Umarex USA

MSR $157	$130	$110	$90	$75	$60	$40	$25

Add $70 for black finish with black grips.
Add $136 for nickel finish with wood grips.
Add $25 for Model 92FS Match with compensator (disc. 2008).
Add $243 ($265 in nickel) for Model 92FS Trophy with compensator, scope, and mount (disc. 2003).

92FS XX-TREME – .177 cal., CO_2, SA/DA, two 8-shot rotary mags., 4.5 in. rifled steel barrel, 425 FPS, tactical accessory mount, Walther top point sight and compensator, manual safety, black tactical finish, includes hard plastic carrying case, 12.6 in. OAL, 3.7 lbs. Mfg. 2008-2013.

courtesy Beretta

	$300	$260	$215	$175	$135	$90	$60

Last MSR was $361.

ELITE II – BB/.177 cal., CO_2, DA, semi-auto repeater, 410 FPS, 4.8 in. rifled steel barrel, 18 (disc. 2008) or 19 (new 2009) shot drop-free mag., fixed sights, manual ambidextrous safety, easy load system, integrated Weaver accessory rail, black plastic sporting replica, 8.5 in. OAL, 1.5 lbs. New 2007.

courtesy Umarex USA

MSR $52	$45	$35	$25	N/A	N/A	N/A	N/A

GRADING	100%	95%	90%	80%	60%	40%	20%

PX4 STORM – BB/.177 cal. or pellets, CO_2, SA/DA, dual-ended 16-shot mag., blowback action, 4.1 in. rifled steel barrel, metal slide, 380 FPS, fixed sights, integrated Weaver accessory rail, manual ambidextrous safety, black plastic replica, 7.6 in. OAL, 1.6 lbs. New 2007.

courtesy Umarex USA

MSR $105	$95	$75	$55	$45	$35	N/A	N/A

PX4 STORM RECON – BB/.177 cal. or pellets, CO_2, SA/DA, blowback action, dual-ended 16-shot mag., 4.1 in. rifled steel barrel, 380 FPS, Shot Dot point sights, ambidextrous safety, Dark Earth Brown finish, detachable compensator, tactical accessory rail mount, Walther tactical flashlight with cord switch, 11.64 in. OAL, 2.2 lbs. New 2008.

courtesy Umarex USA

MSR $186	$155	$130	$110	$90	$70	$45	$30

RIFLES

CX4 STORM – .177 cal., one 88g CO_2 cylinder, semi-auto blowback action, 30-shot mag., 17.5 in. barrel, 495-600 FPS, adj. front and rear sights, top integrated accessory rail, black synthetic stock, manual safety, two-stage trigger, 30.7 in. OAL, 4.5-5.6 lbs. Mfg. 2007-current.

courtesy Umarex USA

MSR $383	$325	$285	$260	$210	$160	N/A	N/A

GRADING	100%	95%	90%	80%	60%	40%	20%

CX4 STORM XT TACTICAL – .177 cal., one 88g CO_2 cylinder, semi-auto blowback action, 30-shot mag., 17.5 in. barrel, 495-600 FPS, adj. front and rear sights, top integrated accessory rail, black synthetic stock, BiPod, 4x32mm tactical scope and compensator, manual safety, two-stage trigger, 35.375 in. OAL, 5.6-7.35 lbs. Mfg. 2008-2013.

courtesy Umarex USA

$425	$350	$300	$245	$190	$125	$85

Last MSR was $500.

CX4 STORM COMMANDO II – .177 cal., one 88g CO_2 cylinder, 30-shot drop free mag., SA, ambidextrous black synthetic stock, adj. sights, dot sight included, Picatinny accessory rail, noise dampener, compensator, manual safety, 30.7 in. OAL, 6.3 lbs.

While advertised during 2012, this model did not go into production.

BIG CHIEF
Previous tradename used by unknown British maker for a folded metal BB gun believed to be pre-WWII.
For information on Big Chief airguns, see Produsit in the "P" section.

BIJOU
For information on Bijou airguns, see Plymouth Air Rifle Company in the "P" section.

BISLEY
For information on Bisley airguns, see Lincoln Jefferies in the "L" section.

BLACK MAJOR
For information on Black Major airguns, see Milbro in the "M" section.

BLOW
Previous trademark of airsoft and airguns manufactured by Ücyildiz Silah Sanayi Tic Ltd. Sti., located in Istanbul, Turkey. Previously distributed by Palco Sports, located in Maple Grove, MN and by KBI, located in Harrisburg, PA until early 2010.

BOBCAT
For information on Bobcat airguns, see Milbro in the "M" section.

BONEHILL, C.G.
See Britannia listing in this section.

BOONE
Previous trademark manufactured for a few years by Target Products Corp. located in Jackson, MI. beginning 1947.

GRADING	100%	95%	90%	80%	60%	40%	20%

PISTOLS

BOONE AIR PISTOL – .173 cal., SS, gravity-fed magazine, and a rearward-moving spring piston. Research is ongoing with this trademark, and more information will be included both online and in future editions.

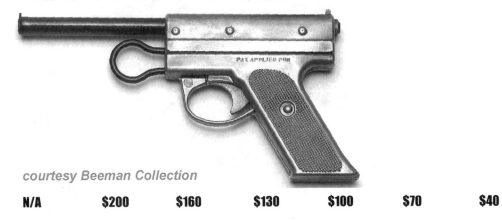

courtesy Beeman Collection

N/A	$200	$160	$130	$100	$70	$40

Add 20% for original box.

BOWKETT, JOHN

Current airgunsmith and designer located in England.

Beginning in the 1970s to date, John Bowkett has been one of Europe's leading airgun designers. He is famous for individual production of advanced design bulk filled CO_2 air pistols and rifles. Bowkett designed airguns for Titan in the 1990s.

PISTOLS

. 22 CAL. BULK FILL PISTOL – .22 cal., 650 FPS, SS, bulk fill CO_2, straight pull bolt action, 12 in. barrel, ramped blade front and adj. rear sights, anatomical walnut grip, 15.5 in. OAL, 3 lbs. Mfg. early 1980s.

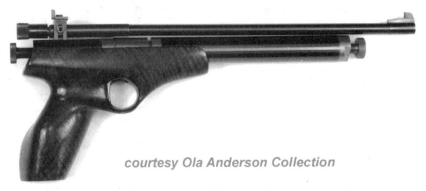

courtesy Ola Anderson Collection

$1,500	$1,275	$1,050	$875	$675	$450	$300

. 22 CAL. PCP PISTOL – .22 cal., 950 FPS, SS, PCP, bolt action, 9 in. barrel, grooved receiver for scope, anatomical walnut grip, 15 in. OAL, 3.25 lbs. Mfg. early 1980s.

courtesy Ola Anderson Collection

$1,500	$1,275	$1,050	$875	$675	$450	$300

GRADING	100%	95%	90%	80%	60%	40%	20%

. 25 CAL. BULK FILL PISTOL – .25 cal., 650 FPS, SS, bulk fill CO_2, bolt action, 5.5 in. barrel, adj. blade front and rear sights, anatomical walnut grip, 9.75 in. OAL, 1.5 lbs. Mfg. early 1980s.

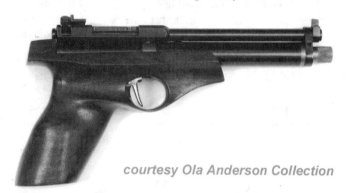

courtesy Ola Anderson Collection

	$1,750	$1,475	$1,225	$1,025	$775	$525	$350

. 30 CAL. BULK FILL PISTOL – .30 cal., 650 FPS, SS, bulk fill CO_2, straight pull bolt action, 8 in. barrel, adj. blade front and rear sights, anatomical walnut grip, 12.5 in. OAL, 3 lbs. Mfg. early 1980s.

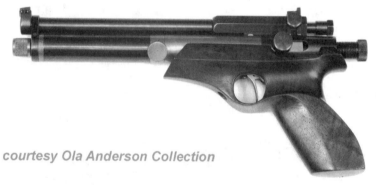

courtesy Ola Anderson Collection

	$1,500	$1,275	$1,050	$875	$675	$450	$300

RIFLES

BOLT ACTION 25 – .25 cal., 650 FPS, SS, CO_2, straight pull bolt action, 24 in. barrel, 44 in. OAL, 6.25 lbs. Mfg. early 1980s.

courtesy Ola Anderson Collection

	$1,750	$1,475	$1,225	$1,025	$775	$525	$350

BOLT ACTION 32 – .32 cal., 600 FPS, SS, PCP, bolt action, 42 in. OAL, 8.3 lbs. Mfg. early 1980s.

courtesy Tim Saunders

	$2,000	$1,700	$1,400	$1,150	$900	$600	$400

GRADING	100%	95%	90%	80%	60%	40%	20%

BRITANNIA

Previous trademark manufactured by C.G. Bonehill located in Birmingham, England circa 1903-1908.

The Britannia name has also been used for a small British push-barrel air pistol of unknown origin, probably made in the 1930s, having a value in the $75 range for gun only, or in the $150 range with original box.

RIFLES

Massive, heavily built airguns which could be considered as the ultimate development of the Gem line of airguns (See the "Gem" entry in the "G" section of this guide). Notable for a huge end plug on bottom end of the buttstock compression chamber.

BRITANNIA ANGLO-SURE SHOT MK I – .177, .22, or .25 cal., BBC, SP, SS air rifle with the SP located in the buttstock, 21 in. rifled BBL, dual power by moving the sear stop screw allows different levels of mainspring compression, first small production in Germany with variations in sights, breech latch, and power adjustments but total production probably less than 3500, 35.5 in. OAL, 6.5 lbs. Mfg. circa 1905-1908.

courtesy Beeman Collection

	N/A	$1,100	$800	$600	$450	$350	$250

Add 20% for .22 caliber.

IMPROVED BRITTANIA – .25 cal., BBC, SP, 13 in. barrel, barrel/receiver unit lifted from the frame for cocking, pellet loaded in curved chute with rotating cover, 44.5 in. OAL. Mfg. 1908-1909.

courtesy Beeman Collection

	N/A	$1,800	$1,550	$1,200	$850	$650	$450

BRITISH CHIEF

For information on British Chief airguns, see "Big Chief" in this section.

courtesy Beeman Collection

BRITISH CUB

For information on British Cub, see Dolla in the "D" section.

BRITON

Previous trademark ascribed to the T.J. Harrington Company of Walton, Surrey, England, or Edwin Anson or Frank Clark, both of Birmingham, England.

GRADING	100%	95%	90%	80%	60%	40%	20%

PISTOLS

BRITON AIR PISTOL – .177 cal., SS, telescoping barrel, spring-piston air pistol with smoothbore barrel, blue or nickel finish. Mfg. circa 1925.

courtesy Beeman Collection

N/A	$325	$260	$210	$160	$115	$65

Add 15% for spring tensioned pellet seater.
Add 50% for nickel finish.

BROCOCK

Current manufacturer/importer located in Redditch, Worcestershire, England with an engineering company located in Birmingham, England. Due to the legal issues in the UK with selling Air Cartridge System Rifles and Pistols, Brocock discontinued manufacture of ACS arms. Limited current importation and distribuiony by Airguns of Arizona located in Gilbert, AZ. Brocock was formed in 1989. Some of Brocock's airguns are manufactured (under contract to specifications) by other manufacturers including Cuno Melcher (ME Sportwaffen), Weihrauch Sport, A. Uberti & C., and Pietta. Dealer and consumer direct sales.

Beginning in 2010, Brocock Airguns started manufacturing the AimX line of precharged pistols and light rifles. The AimX line focuses on bringing top value in quality and price for an English made airgun. Models include the Atomic and Grand Prix Model PCP pistols and light hunting PCP rifles the Concept, Contour and Enigma Models. Brocock started (2008) working on design and manufacture of a PCP rifle named the Brocock Enigma Model and a BBC rifle named the Brocock Independent Model. All pre-2008 production Brocock air pistols and rifles use the dedicated BACS (Brocock Air Cartridge System). This unique system based on the .38 BAC uses a compressed air cartridge which contains a sophisticated valve system which when filled with air and loaded with a pellet, enables these airguns to feel, function, and look like real breech loading firearms.

Brocock was formed by the Silcock brothers (hence the name) to buy the liquidated Saxby and Palmer company in 1989. Brocock manufactured an air cartridge system whose roots go back to a British patent of 1872 used in a Giffard gas gun. The modern form, initially known as a 'TAC' (Tandem Air Cartridge, so called because of the twin sealing arrangement either end of the valve stem) later became 'BACS' (Brocock Air Cartridge System). An air cartridge is a manganese bronze, cartridge-like case that holds air pressure at around 2,700 psi. A spring loaded exhaust valve is opened by the gun's firing pin striking a button located where a primer would be found in a firearm cartridge. The valve opens and the escaping air propels a pellet from a screw-on nosecone.

Air cartridges can be individually charged with a 'Slim Jim' scissor pump. This rather strenuous step, requiring up to six or eight pumps per cartridge, can be avoided by using various devices to charge cartridges quickly and in bulk from SCUBA tanks.

Brocock manufactured the Safari, Predator and Fox rifles in Birmingham but also imported guns especially designed for air cartridges only from Cuno Melcher (ME Sportwaffen), Weihrauch Sport, Aldo Uberti, Pietta, and Armi San Marco. The latter three converted some of their replica antique firearm designs into air cartridge airguns.

All air cartridge guns were built so as to make conversion into a firearm very difficult. On early Saxby and Palmer revolvers this included pinning the barrel to prevent its exchange and deleting a portion of the forward end of the cylinder. Pinning the barrels became standard but, during the mid 1990s, the unattractive deletion of the forward end of the cylinders was replaced with machining the spaces between the individual chambers.

Despite the safeguards against conversion, there were a very limited number of cases where criminals using sophisticated machining equipment managed to turn some of these airguns into firearms. Such conversions often were dangerous and these criminals reportedly sometimes lost body parts or their lives when converted guns exploded.

American airgunners take warning! As of January 2004, the manufacture, importation, sale or transfer of all air cartridge guns was banned by the United Kingdom government. Existing UK owners were given three months in which to apply for a highly restricted Section 1 firearms certificate should they wish continue owning their guns, or to hand them to a police station for destruction without compensation. These guns can't be traded in the UK, or even exported, and thus have no commercial value in the UK.

Brocock is still selling their CO_2 and blank firing guns which were unaffected by the 2004 ban. Attempts are being made to have air cartridge guns manufactured outside of the UK and to import them directly into the USA, but development or continued success of such a program seems unlikely.

The authors and publisher wish to thank Mr. Tim Saunders for his assistance with this section of the *Blue Book of Airguns*.

GRADING	100%	95%	90%	80%	60%	40%	20%

PISTOLS

ATOMIC – .177 or .22 cal., PCP, BA, SS, 6-shot mag., similar to Grand Prix, except has 7.5 in. barrel, beech stock, 580/450 FPS, fiber optic sights, M10 internal moderator thread, 12.1 in. OAL, 2.6 lbs. Imported 2010-2013.

courtesy Airguns of Arizona

$425	$350	$300	$245	$190	$125	$85

Last MSR was $495.

GRAND PRIX – .177 or .22 cal., PCP, BA, SS, 6-shot mag., 11 in. rifled steel barrel, 687/543 FPS, with or without adj. sights, ambidextrous beech stock with checkered grip, 15.5 in. OAL, 2.8 lbs. Mfg. 2010-current.

courtesy Airguns of Arizona

MSR $700	$600	$525	$475	$375	$295	N/A	N/A

Add $54 for adj. sights.

MODEL PARA PPK 380 – .22 cal., BACS, 3 in. barrel, 300 FPS, seven-shot, blue or nickel finish, black composite or walnut grips, fixed sights, 1.45 lbs., Mfg. by ME Sportwaffen.

$185	$155	$130	$105	$85	$55	$35

Last MSR was $175.

Add $30 for nickel finish and walnut grips.

REVOLVERS

MODEL 1851 NAVY – .22 cal., BACS, SA, 5 or 7.5 in. barrel, 410 FPS, six-shot, blue with case color frame and brass grip strap or nickel finish, walnut grips, fixed sights, 2.4 lbs. Mfg. by Pietta.

courtesy Tim Saunders

$375	$300	$245	$205	$160	$105	$70

Last MSR was $343.

Subtract $40 for all-brass frame (Model 1851 Navy Sheriff).

GRADING	100%	95%	90%	80%	60%	40%	20%

MODEL 1858 REMINGTON ARMY – .22 cal., BACS, SA, 5.5 or 8 in. barrel, 410 FPS, six-shot, blue with case color frame and brass grip strap, walnut grips, fixed sights, 2.4 lbs. Mfg. by Pietta.

courtesy Tim Saunders

	$325	$270	$220	$185	$140	$95	$65

Last MSR was $286.

Add $55 for steel frame.

MODEL 1860 NM ARMY – .22 cal., BACS, SA, 6.5 or 8 in. barrel, 410 FPS, six-shot, blue with brass grip strap, walnut grips, fixed sights, 2.75 lbs. Mfg. by Pietta.

	$325	$270	$220	$185	$140	$95	$65

Last MSR was $286.

Add $55 for steel frame.

MODEL 1862 REB CONFEDERATE – .22 cal., BACS, SA, 5 in. barrel, 410 FPS, six-shot, blue with case color frame, brass grip strap and walnut grips, fixed sights, 2.4 lbs. Mfg. by Pietta.

	$325	$270	$220	$185	$140	$95	$65

Last MSR was $286.

MODEL 1873 CATTLEMAN SA – .22 cal., BACS, SA, 4.75, 5.5, or 7.5 in. barrel, 410 FPS, six-shot, blue with color case hardened frame or nickel finish, brass or steel grip strap, walnut, polymer pearlite, or polymer ivory grips, brass or steel grip frame, fixed sights, 2.6 lbs. Mfg. by Uberti.

	$550	$475	$375	$325	$250	$165	$110

Last MSR was $569.

Add $100 for polymer pearlite or ivory grips.

MODEL 1875 REMINGTON SA – .22 cal., BACS, SA, 5.5, or 7.5 in. barrel, 410 FPS, six-shot, blue with color case hardened frame finish, walnut grips, fixed sights, 2.6 lbs. Mfg. by Uberti.

	$550	$475	$375	$325	$250	$165	$110

MODEL 1877 THUNDERER SA – .22 cal., BACS, SA, 3, 3.5, 4, or 4.75 in. barrel, 410 FPS, six-shot, blue with color case hardened frame or nickel finish, walnut grips, fixed sights, 2.6 lbs. Mfg. by Uberti.

	$550	$475	$375	$325	$250	$165	$110

MODEL BISLEY SA REVOLVER – .22 cal., BACS, SA, 4.75, 5.5, or 7.5 in. barrel, 410 FPS, six-shot, blue with color case hardened frame, walnut grips, fixed sights, 2.6 lbs. Mfg. by Uberti.

	$600	$500	$425	$350	$270	$180	$120

MODEL BISLEY TARGET FLATTOP – .22 cal., BACS, SA, 4.75, 5.5, or 7.5 in. barrel, 410 FPS, six-shot, blue with color case hardened frame, walnut grips, adj. rear sight, 2.6 lbs. Mfg. by Uberti.

	$650	$550	$450	$375	$295	$195	$130

MODEL COMBAT – .22 cal., BACS, SA/DA, 2.5 in. barrel, 380 FPS, six-shot, blue finish, molded grips, fixed sights, 2 lbs. Mfg. by Weihrauch.

	$350	$300	$245	$205	$160	$105	$70

Last MSR was $319.

MODEL COMPACT – .22 cal., BACS, SA/DA, 2.25 in. barrel, 325 FPS, five-shot, blue or nickel finish, molded or walnut grips, fixed sights, 2.24 lbs. Mfg. by ME Sportwaffen.

	$215	$185	$150	$125	$95	$65	$45

Last MSR was $175.

Add $30 for nickel finish and walnut grips.

GRADING	100%	95%	90%	80%	60%	40%	20%

MODEL MAGNUM – .22 cal., BACS, SA/DA, 3 in. barrel, 350 FPS, five-shot, blue or nickel finish, molded or walnut grips, adj. rear sight, 1.38 lbs. Mfg. by ME Sportwaffen.

	$235	$200	$165	$135	$105	$70	$45

Last MSR was $143.

Add $40 for nickel finish and walnut grips.

MODEL ORION 3 – .22 cal., BACS, SA/DA, 3 in. barrel, 410 FPS, six-shot, blue finish, molded grips, adj. rear sight, 2 lbs. Mfg. by Weihrauch.

	$350	$300	$245	$205	$160	$105	$70

Last MSR was $319.

MODEL ORION 6 – .177 or .22 cal., BACS, SA/DA, 6 in. barrel, 550/410 FPS, six-shot, blue finish, molded grips, adj. rear sight, 2.3 lbs. Mfg. by Weihrauch.

	$350	$300	$245	$205	$160	$105	$70

Last MSR was $319.

Add 25% for Model Orion 66, chrome plated.

MODEL POCKET – .177 or .22 cal., BACS, SA/DA, 1.5 in. barrel, 300 FPS, five-shot, blue finish, molded grips, adj. rear sight, 1.2 lbs.

	$185	$155	$130	$105	$85	$55	$35

Last MSR was $143.

MODEL SPECIALIST – .22 cal., BACS, SA/DA, 4 in. barrel, 410 FPS, six-shot, blue finish, molded grips, adj. rear sight, 2.24 lbs. Mfg. by Weihrauch.

courtesy Beeman Collection

	$350	$300	$245	$205	$160	$105	$70

Last MSR was $319.

MODEL TEXAN – .177 or .22 cal., BACS, SA, 5.5 in. barrel, 550/410 FPS, six-shot, all blue or blue with case color frame and gold-plated trigger guard/grip straps finish, walnut grips, fixed sights, 2.86 lbs. Mfg. by Weihrauch.

	$350	$300	$245	$205	$160	$105	$70

Last MSR was $328.

Add $25 for case color frame and gold plating.

RIFLES

CONCEPT – .177 or .22 cal., BA, SS, 6-shot mag., American walnut or beech stock, double cheek piece, 36.75 in. OAL, 5 lbs. 8 oz. New 2011.

MSR $752	$650	$575	$500	$425	$325	N/A	N/A

CONTOUR – .177 or .22 cal., PCP, BA, SS, 12.75 in. rifled barrel, 661 FPS, American walnut or beech skeletonized

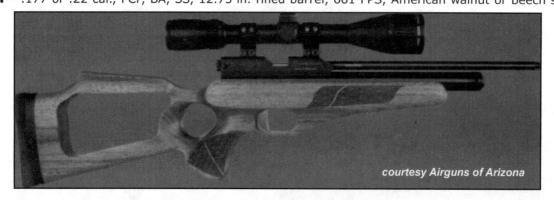

courtesy Airguns of Arizona

GRADING	100%	95%	90%	80%	60%	40%	20%

stock, checkered thumbhole pistol grip, two-stage adj. trigger, free floating barrel, 27.5 in. OAL, 4 lbs. Mfg. 2010.

| MSR $765 | $650 | $575 | $525 | $425 | $325 | N/A | N/A |

CONTOUR XL – .177 or .22 cal., PCP, BA, 15 in. rifled barrel, American walnut or beech skeletonized stock, checkered thumbhole pistol grip, two-stage adj. trigger, 29.7 in. OAL, 4 lbs. New 2012.

| MSR $695 | $600 | $525 | $475 | $375 | $290 | N/A | N/A |

ENIGMA – .177 or .22 cal., PCP, BA, nine-shot rotary magazine indexed and cocked by RHS cocking lever, 16 in. rifled BBL, checkered hardwood PG stock and forearm, two-stage adj. trigger, free floating barrel, 35 in. OAL, 6 lbs. Mfg. 2010.

courtesy Airguns of Arizona

| MSR $875 | $750 | $650 | $600 | $475 | $375 | N/A | N/A |

SPECIALIST – .177 or .22 cal., PCP, BA, 6-shot mag., integral bull barrel, open sights, black thumbhole stock, 29.7 in. OAL, 4 lbs. New 2012.

courtesy Airguns of Arizona

| MSR $695 | $600 | $525 | $475 | $375 | $290 | N/A | N/A |

MODEL 1866 YELLOWBOY CARBINE – .22 cal., BACS, six-shot, lever action, 19 in. barrel, 598 FPS, blue finish with brass receiver, walnut stock and forearm, blue forearm barrel band, adj. rear sight, 7.4 lbs. Mfg. by Uberti.

| | $750 | $625 | $500 | $425 | $325 | $215 | $145 |

MODEL 1866 SPORTING RIFLE – .22 cal., BACS, 12-shot, lever action, 24 in. barrel, 598 FPS, blue finish with brass receiver, walnut stock and forearm, brass forearm cap, adj. rear sight, 8.1 lbs. Mfg. by Uberti.

| | $750 | $625 | $500 | $425 | $325 | $215 | $145 |

MODEL 1871 ROLLING BLOCK RIFLE – .22 cal., BACS, SS, rolling block action, 17.7 barrel, 598 FPS, blue finish, walnut stock, adj. rear sight, 5.7 lbs. Mfg. by Uberti.

| | $850 | $725 | $600 | $500 | $375 | $255 | $170 |

Last MSR was $895.

MODEL 1873 CARBINE – .22 cal., BACS, six-shot, lever action, 19 in. barrel, 598 FPS, blue finish with color case hardened receiver, walnut stock and forearm, blue forearm barrel band adj. rear sight, 7.4 lbs. Mfg. by Uberti.

| | $850 | $725 | $600 | $500 | $375 | $255 | $170 |

Last MSR was $895.

MODEL 1873 PISTOL GRIP SPORTING RIFLE – .22 cal., BACS, 12-shot, lever action, 24 in. barrel, 598 FPS, blue finish with color case hardened or nickel receiver, checkered walnut pistol grip stock and forearm, blue forearm cap, adj. rear sight, 8.1 lbs. Mfg. by Uberti.

| | $1,100 | $925 | $775 | $650 | $500 | $325 | $220 |

MODEL FOX RIFLE – .22 cal., BACS, SS, 14.7 barrel, 598 FPS, blue finish, wire stock, folding trigger, 4x32mm scope included, 2.65 lbs. Mfg. by Brocock.

| | $325 | $275 | $230 | $190 | $145 | $95 | $65 |

Last MSR was $303.

GRADING	100%	95%	90%	80%	60%	40%	20%

MODEL REVOLVER CARBINE – .22 cal., BACS, six-shot, SA revolver action, 18 in. barrel, 520 FPS, blue finish, walnut stock, fixed sights, 4.4 lbs. Mfg. by Uberti.

	$650	$550	$450	$375	$295	$195	$130

MODEL HERALD RIFLE – .22 cal., BACS, bolt action. Mfg. by Brocock. Disc.

	$800	$675	$550	$475	$350	$240	$160

MODEL PREDATOR RIFLE – .22 cal., BACS, six-shot, bolt action, 17.7 in. barrel, 598 FPS, blue finish, checkered beech stock, two-stage adj. trigger, 5.7 lbs. Mfg. by Brocock.

	$495	$400	$325	$275	$215	$140	$95

Last MSR was $515.

MODEL SAFARI RIFLE – .22 cal., BACS, SS, bolt action, 17.7 in. barrel, 598 FPS, blue finish, checkered beech stock, two-stage adj. trigger, 6.5 lbs. Mfg. by Brocock.

	$425	$350	$300	$245	$190	$125	$85

Last MSR was $431.

BROLIN ARMS, INC.

Previous importer located in Pomona, CA 1997-99, and previously located in La Verne, CA 1995-97. For more information and current values on used Brolin Arms, Inc. firearms, please refer to the *Blue Book of Gun Values* by S.P. Fjestad (also available online).

RIFLES

SM 1000 – .177 or .22 cal., SL, SP, SS, 1100/900 FPS, adj. front and rear sights, match barrel, automatic safety, Monte Carlo beech stock, 9.125 lbs.

	$155	$130	$110	$90	$70	$45	$30

Last MSR was $200.

Add 10% for checkered stock.
Add 30% for adj. buttplate.

BROWN, A.A. & SONS

See Abas Major listing in the "A" section.

BROWN

Previously manufactured by O.H. Brown located in Davenport, IA.

PISTOLS

STANDARD MODEL BROWN PISTOL – .22 cal., multi-pump pneumatic, 7.5 in. rifled barrel, 17 in. overall, unique pump system behind the barrel compressed air on both push and pull strokes providing very high power, steel parts deep blue finished, select walnut grips, adj. rear sight, exceptionally well made, rare, featured only in 1939 Stoeger catalog, original instructions are an actual engineer's blueprint, 2.4 lbs.

courtesy Beeman Collection

	N/A	$3,000	$2,400	$1,950	$1,500	$1,050	$600

1939 retail price was $12.

Add 25% for original box and blueprint instructions.
Approximate retail for Colt Woodsman Sport Model in 1930 was $32.50.

GRADING	100%	95%	90%	80%	60%	40%	20%

DELUXE MODEL BROWN PISTOL – .22 cal., similar to Standard Model, except 10 in. barrel and checkered select walnut grips, very rare, 2.5 lb.

courtesy Beeman Collection

	N/A	$3,500	$2,800	$2,275	$1,750	$1,225	$700

1939 retail price was $20.

Add 25% for original box and blueprint instructions.

BROWNING

Current manufacturer with headquarters located in Morgan, UT.

Beginning 2009 Browning licensed Umarex USA to import and distribute airguns under the Browning trademark. The Browning Airstar was mfg. by Rutten Airguns SA, located in Herstal-Liege, Belgium. It is the first air rifle with a battery-powered electronic cocking system. Less than 400 examples were available for the U.S. market. For more information and current pricing on both new and used Browning firearms, please refer to the *Blue Book of Gun Values* by S.P. Fjestad (also available online).

HANDGUNS

800 EXPRESS – .177 or .22 cal., BBC, SP, 700/600 FPS, 8.25 in. rifled barrel, anti-recoil power system, ergonomic ambidextrous grip, grooved receiver, fiber optic sights, auto safety, cocking assist handle included, 18 in. OAL, 3.9 lbs. New 2012.

courtesy Umarex USA

MSR $168	$145	$125	$115	$90	$70	N/A	N/A

800 MAG – .177 or .22 (new 2010) cal., BBC, SP, SS, 9 in. rifled steel barrel, 700/600 FPS, blue finish, ambidextrous modeled synthetic black frame, adj. rear and fixed front fiber optic sights, automatic safety, 17.5 in. OAL, 7.5 lbs. Mfg. 2009-2012.

courtesy Umarex USA

	$145	$125	$115	$90	$70	N/A	N/A

Last MSR was $168.

GRADING	100%	95%	90%	80%	60%	40%	20%

BUCK MARK URX – .177 cal., BBC, SP, 320 FPS, 5.25 in. rifled barrel, ergonomic ambidextrous synthetic grip, integrated Weaver rail, fixed front blade sight, adj. rear sight, auto safety, 11.9 in. OAL, 1.5 lbs. New 2012.

courtesy Umarex USA

MSR $50	$40	$35	$30	$25	$20	$10	N/A

HI POWER MARK III – BB/.177 cal., 12g CO_2, DA, replica of the original Browning Hi Power Mark III, 410 FPS, 4.75 in. barrel, metal and synthetic construction, black finish, 18-shot drop free mag., fixed sights, manual safety, 8.1 in. OAL, approx. 1 lb. Mfg. 2012-2013.

courtesy Umarex USA

$50	$45	$35	$30	$25	N/A	N/A

Last MSR was $62.

RIFLES

BROWNING AIRSTAR – .177 cal., electronic cocking mechanism powered by rechargeable Ni-Cad battery (250 shots per charge), 780 FPS, flip-up loading port, warning light indicates when spring is compressed, electronic safety with warning light, 17.5 in. fixed barrel, hooded front sight with interchangeable sight inserts, adj. rear sight, frame grooved for scope mount, beech wood stock, came in Browning box, 9.3 lbs.

$650	$550	$450	$375	$295	$195	$130

Last MSR was $1,000.

This model was originally marketed in Europe through Browning dealers for $1,000 was available in the U.S., and marked with both the Browning and Rutten names, and Browning Trademark.

BROWNING GOLD (SYNTHETIC) – .177 or .22 cal., BBC, SP, 1000/800 FPS, 14 in. rifled barrel with blued receiver, black Monte Carlo synthetic stock with rubber inlays, fixed fiber optic front sight, adj. fiber optic rear sight, two-stage adj. trigger, contoured adj. rubber recoil pad, 3-9x40mm scope, raised ambidextrous cheekpiece, ambi. safety, 48.4 in. OAL, 8.4 lbs. Mfg. 2011-2013.

courtesy Umarex USA

$300	$255	$210	$175	$135	$90	$60

Last MSR was $355.

BROWNING GOLD (WOOD) – .177 or .22 cal., BBC, SP, 1000/800 FPS, 14 in. rifled barrel with blued receiver, Monte Carlo wood stock, fiber optic sights, contoured adj. rubber recoil pad, two-stage adj. trigger, ambidextrous safety,

GRADING	100%	95%	90%	80%	60%	40%	20%

3-9x40mm scope, 48.4 in. OAL, 8.4 lbs. Mfg. 2011-2012.

courtesy Umarex USA

		$350	**$300**	**$245**	**$205**	**$160**	**$105**	**$70**

Last MSR was $407.

BROWNING LEVERAGE – .177 or .22 cal., ULC, 1000/820 FPS, 18.9 in. rifled fixed barrel, blued finish, Monte Carlo wooden stock, adj. fiber optic rear, and fixed fiber optic front sights, two-stage adj. trigger, vent. rubber recoil pad, Picatinny scope rail, automatic ambidextrous safety, right-handed cheekpiece, 3-9x40mm scope, 44.8 in. OAL, 8.6 lbs. New 2011.

courtesy Umarex USA

MSR $229	**$195**	**$165**	**$135**	**$115**	**$90**	**$60**	**$40**

BROWNING PHOENIX – .177 cal., SP, BBC, ergonomically designed ambidextrous black synthetic stock with checkering pattern, soft grip on forend and pistol grip, vent. extendable rubber buttplate, adj. trigger, milled prism rail with an additional metal stop and two holes in receiver, fiber optic sights and foresight holder, auto safety, 45.3 in. OAL, 8.2 lbs.

While advertised during 2012, this model never went into production.

* ***Browning Phoenix Elite*** – .177 cal., SP, BBC, similar to the Browning Phoenix Elite, except comes with a noise dampener, 45.5 in. OAL, 8.2 lbs.

While advertised during 2012, this model never went into production.

BROWNING PHOENIX HUNTER – .177 cal., SP, BBC, slim ambidextrous wooden stock with checkering on the pistol grip, Browning logotypes on the forend and buttstock, vent. rubber buttplate, adj. trigger, fiber optic front sight, adj. rear sight, auto safety, permanently fitted noise dampener included, 45.5 in. OAL, 8 lbs.

While advertised during 2012, this model never went into production.

BULL DOG

Brand name of Bergmann's Industriewerke Establissement fur Neuheiten, Gaggenau, Germany.

The Bull Dog trademark appears on a very small spring piston single shot air pistol with cast metal frame, Birdshead checkered metal grip, and exposed trigger. The pistol is loaded by unscrewing a loading pin on back of frame and cocked by pulling a ring on the forward end of the pistol.

PISTOLS

BULL DOG – .177 cal., SP, SS, SB, die cast body and frame, 3.5" bbl, LHS above trigger: gnome-like figure of miner (a "Bergmann"). 5.5" OAL, 0.55 lb. Mfg. circa 1900-1910. Ref. Griffiths (2008).

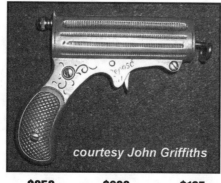

courtesy John Griffiths

N/A	**$250**	**$200**	**$165**	**$125**	**$90**	**$50**

BULLS EYE & SHARPSHOOTER

Previous trademark manufactured by Bull's Eye Pistol Co. located in Rawlins, WY circa 1928-1960s.

The Bulls Eye catapult air pistol was powered by elastic bands. An ingenious arrangement of a three-point traveling shot carrier produces fly-killing accuracy which has endeared these guns even to hard-core match shooters. ADD to refs: C.R. Suydam (1990) Amer. Soc. Arms Collectors 62: Spring. The Sharpshooter was introduced as a smaller version of the Bulls Eye circa 1938. The production of these models was moved to La Jolla, CA circa 1948, and the company name was changed to Bull's Eye Mfg. Co. Research is ongoing with this trademark, and more information will be included both online and in future editions. Average original condition specimens of most common Bulls Eye and Sharpshooter Models are typically priced in the $50-$100 range for unboxed models with short body, grip plates, and conventional-looking trigger guard. Early versions with a long body, sheet metal grip, and very thin trigger (which looks like a trigger guard) in original box sell in the $150-$200 range. Ref: AR 1 : 52-54, AR 2 : 54-57, AR4 : 31-39.

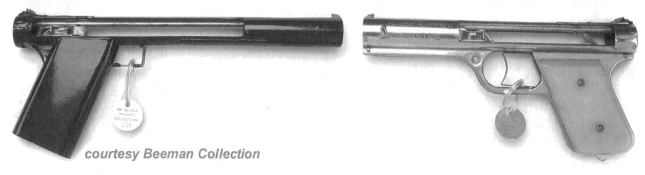

courtesy Beeman Collection

BULLS EYE

Previous trademark of Bulls Eye Air Rifle Company, former producer of sheet metal BB guns in Chicago from 1907 to an unknown date.

The company produced a lever, gravity feed BB repeater and a single shot break-open BB gun. Both models were well built; the lever cocking action used a lever system similar to that of a Colt Model 1860 revolver. The stocks are unusual in being fitted over the grip frames rather than into them. Ref. Dunathan (1957). Research is ongoing with this trademark, and more information will be included both in future editions and online.

BURGO

For information on Burgo, see Weihrauch Sport in the "W" section.

BUSSEY

Previous trademark of airguns previously manufactured by G.G. Bussey and Company located in London, England from 1870 to about 1914.

Based on a 1876 patent awarded to George Gibson Bussey for a simple airgun. The appearance is suggestive of a Quackenbush Model 1 air rifle, but there is almost no similarity in construction. Unusual spring piston action required removal of the barrel for cocking. An accessory plunger was inserted in the open action and used to push the piston backward until engaged by the sear. A pellet or dart was then placed in the breech and the barrel reinserted for firing. Extremely few specimens are known; one measured 29 in. long with a .21 caliber 9.5 in. smoothbore barrel. Research is ongoing with this trademark, and more information may be included both online and in future editions. Scarcity precludes accurate pricing at this time.

C SECTION

CZ (CESKA ZBROJOVKA)

Current manufacturer located in Uhersky Brod, Czech Republic, since 1936. Limited importation by Top Gun Airguns, located in Scottsdale, AZ. Previously imported by CZ-USA located in Kansas City, KS.

Research is ongoing with this trademark, and more information will be included both online and in future editions. For more information and current pricing on both new and used CZ firearms, please refer to the *Blue Book of Gun Values* by S.P. Fjestad (also available online).

GRADING	100%	95%	90%	80%	60%	40%	20%

PISTOLS

TEX MODEL 3 (CZ-3) – .177 cal., BBC, SP, 400 FPS, 7.50 in. barrel, adj. sights, plastic stock.

	100%	95%	90%	80%	60%	40%	20%
MSR N/A	$80	$70	$55	$45	$35	$25	$15

SLAVIA APP661 – 4.5mm round lead ball cal., CO_2, semi-auto repeater, vertical removable mag., Early Version: wood grips, 8 gm CO_2 cylinder, piercing pin in grip cap, Late Version: black plastic grips, 8 or 12 gm CO_2 cylinders, 7.8 in. OAL, 1.4 lbs. Mfg. circa 1960-1970.

courtesy Beeman Collection

100%	95%	90%	80%	60%	40%	20%
$125	$105	$90	$75	$55	$35	$25

Add 50% for early version.

SLAVIA ZVP (Vzduchová Pistole) – .177 cal., BBC, SP, SS, very solidly built, blued steel, hand checkered hardwood grips, 13.4 in. OAL, 2.4 lbs. Mfg. 1960-1972.

courtesy Beeman Collection

100%	95%	90%	80%	60%	40%	20%
$80	$70	$55	$45	$35	$25	$15

RIFLES

CZ MODEL Vz-24 – similar to CZ Model Vz-35, except no bayonet lug.

	100%	95%	90%	80%	60%	40%	20%
	N/A	$325	$260	$210	$160	$115	$65

CZ MODEL Vz-35 – 4.40mm lead ball, SP, rear bolt cocks action, gravity-fed magazine with trap lid, copy of Czech military rifle, with bayonet, 54.1 in. OAL (with bayonet), 9.7 lbs (with bayonet), approx. 9,850 mfg.

courtesy Beeman Collection

	100%	95%	90%	80%	60%	40%	20%
	N/A	$450	$350	$295	$225	$160	$90

Add 10% for bayonet.

GRADING	100%	95%	90%	80%	60%	40%	20%

CZ/STELLA MODEL Vz-36 – See Stella in the "S" section.

MILITARY AIRGUN Vz-47 (CZ-BB) – 4.50mm cal. lead balls, BA, Czech Army training rifle, most with military markings and SN but 40 made up late from factory parts do not have typical markings or SNs. 1947-1950.

	N/A	$350	$280	$230	$175	$125	$70

CZ 200 – .177 or .22 cal., PCP, BA, SS, 18.92 in. rifled barrel, black finish, beech stock and forearm, adj. trigger, mounting blocks for sight system of choice. New 2001.

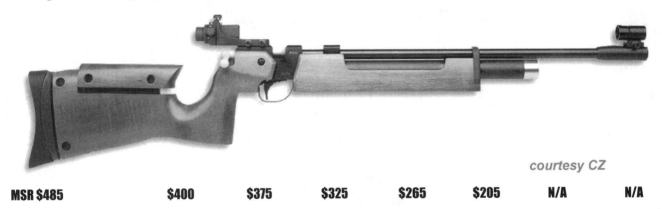

courtesy CZ

MSR $485	$400	$375	$325	$265	$205	N/A	N/A

CZ 200 S – .177 or .22 cal., similar to CZ 200, except 19 in. bbl., sport stock with recoil pad, 35.7 in. OAL, 6.17 lbs. New 2001.

courtesy CZ

MSR $630	$525	$475	$425	$350	$265	N/A	N/A

CZ 200 S FS – .177 or .22 cal., similar to the CZ 200 S, except is the full stock version, includes all features of the CZ 200 S complemented with more compact contours.

MSR $630	$525	$475	$425	$350	$265	N/A	N/A

CZ 200 T – .177 cal., similar to CZ 200, except competition (Target) stock with adj. cheek piece and buttplate, 19 in. barrel, 35.7 in. OAL, 6.4 lbs. New 2001.

courtesy CZ

MSR $645	$550	$475	$450	$350	$270	N/A	N/A

CZ 200 SCOUT – similar to CZ Model 200 T, except has high quality checkered Turkish walnut sporter stock. New 2012.

MSR $695	$600	$525	$475	$375	$290	N/A	N/A

GRADING	100%	95%	90%	80%	60%	40%	20%

SLAVIA 236 – .177 cal., BBC, SP, SS, hardwood stock with fluted forearm.

courtesy Beeman Collection

	$80	$70	$55	$45	$35	$25	$15

SLAVIA 612 – .177 in. cal., BBC, SP, SS, 12 in. rifled steel BBL, all metal except for buttstock, similar to Dianawerk Model 15, 32 in. OAL. Mfg. 1955-1965.

courtesy Beeman Collection

	$65	$55	$45	$40	$30	$20	$15

SLAVIA 618 – .177 cal., BBC, SP, SS, 14.5 in. rifled steel BBL, hardwood PG stock, 35.75 in. OAL. Mfg. 1970s.

	$65	$55	$45	$40	$30	$20	$15

SLAVIA 622 – .22 cal., BBC, SP, SS, 14.5 in. rifled steel BBL, hardwood PG stock, 35.75 in. OAL. Mfg. 1970s.

	$65	$55	$45	$40	$30	$20	$15

SLAVIA 625 – .177 cal., BBC, SP, 450 FPS, 15.75 in. barrel, adj. sights, wood stock, 4 lbs. Disc. 2003.

	$50	$45	$35	$30	$25	$15	$10

Last MSR was $60.

SLAVIA 630 (CZ 77) – .177 cal., BBC, SP, 700 FPS, 21 in. barrel, adj. sights, ambidextrous beechwood stock, automatic safety, adj. trigger, rubber buttplate, 45.6 in. OAL, 6.6 lbs.

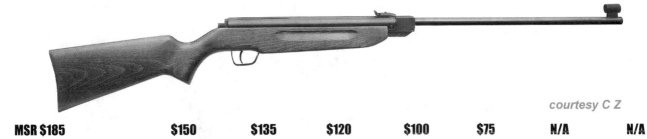

courtesy C Z

MSR $185	$150	$135	$120	$100	$75	N/A	N/A

SLAVIA 631 (CZ 77 LUX) – .177 cal., BBC, SP, 700 FPS, 21 in. fixed barrel, adj. sights, checkered beechwood or synthetic stock, adj. buttplate, automatic safety, 45.6 in. OAL, 6.8 lbs.

courtesy C Z

MSR $195	$160	$140	$130	$105	$80	N/A	N/A

CAP-CHUR EQUIPMENT

For information on CAP-CHUR Equipment tranquilizer guns, see Palmer Chemical & Equipment Co. in the "P" section.

GRADING	100%	95%	90%	80%	60%	40%	20%

CARBO-JET

For information on Carbo-Jet airguns, see Schimel in the "S" section.

CAROLUS

Previous trademark marketed by Hellstedt hardware store, located in Eskilstuna, Sweden.

PISTOL

CAROLUS – 4.5mm cal., UL, SP, SS, one-piece wood stock, marked with script CAROLUS on left hand side, blue finish, stamped with a shield design with a contained S. Mfg. 1941-1943.

courtesy Beeman Collection

$600	$500	$425	$350	$270	$180	$120

Add 30% for factory box.

Two styles of box observed, one is blue with white label with red and black printing one has embossed image, marked Hellsteds Eskilstuna Svensk kvalitéprodukt Refflad pipa, kaliber 4,5 Skottställd på 6 meter Utmärkt övningsvapen LUFTPISTOLEN Carolus ESKILSTUNAFABRIKAT PRIS KR. 19.

CASELMAN

Previous trademark manufactured by Jeff Caselman, located in Cameron, MO circa 1990 to 1994.

Only one or two .308 cal. and one .45 cal. were made. Five or six specimens of the 9mm variety are known. The Caselman airguns are fully automatic and are fed from a 3000 PSI bottle which serves as the buttstock. It is perhaps the first successful self-contained, fully automatic airgun. The 9mm guns have a .356 in. bore, and fire from a twenty-six-round vertical spring-fed magazine. Bullets are 122 grain flat point, soft lead, fired dry at about 750 FPS, and about 150 ft./lb. ME. Rate of fire about 600 RPM. The .45 cal. gun fires twenty rounds of 225 grain flat soft lead bullets at a somewhat higher rate of fire. Ad claims: Will saw off a 2x4 at 25 yards! The maker also sold plans and a video for a .30 cal. version. Caution: some units may have been built from plans by workers less skilled than this designer/maker. The authors and publisher wish to thank John Caruth for his valuable assistance with the following information in this edition of the *Blue Book of Airguns*. Ref. Behling (2006).

RIFLES: FULL AUTOMATIC

CASELMAN RIFLE – .308, 9mm, or .45 cal., extremely fine construction, 26 in. bench rest grade barrels and firing from a closed bolt allow great accuracy, 48 in. OAL, 16.5 lbs. Mfg. circa 1990-1994.

courtesy Beeman Collection

Scarcity precludes accurate pricing.

CENTERPOINT

For information on Centerpoint airguns, see Philippine Airguns in the "P" section.

CERTUS

Previous trademark manufactured by Cogswell & Harrison (Gunmakers) Ltd., located in London, England. Manufactured in Feltham, Middlesex, England.

Cogswell & Harrison is one of England's oldest and most prestigious gunmaking firms. Founded in 1770 by Benjamin Cogswell, the firm was very highly regarded for dueling pistols and military sidearms for officers. Edgar Harrison was granted British patent 330105 for an airgun in June 1930. Pistols relating to this patent were produced only in late 1929 and into 1930.

GRADING	100%	95%	90%	80%	60%	40%	20%

The Certus is a solid, barrel cocking, spring-piston air pistol with just a superficial resemblance to a Webley air pistol with its barrel running the length of the gun above the compression tube. The Certus has a quite complex mechanism with the barrel pivoting at the rear for cocking, opposite to the Webley front pivot. A 1929 factory catalog indicates both the standard air pistol and the long barrel target version with removable shoulder stock, available in .177 cal. only and rifled. It was all blued finish, except for select walnut grips. Three specimens were reported as known in an August 2002 *Airgun World* article by Tim Saunders, but a very few more do exist. Current retail value in the $2,500-$3,500 range depending on condition and whether original box or case is included. Add 25% for long barrel target version or original shoulder stock. Subtract 10% if missing rear sight. Ref. Griffiths (2008).

courtesy Beeman Collection

CHALLENGE

For information on Challenge airguns, see Plymouth Air Rifle Company in the "P" section.

CHALLENGER ARMS CORPORATION

Previous distributor of airguns under the Challenger brand located in Eagle Rock (annexed to City of Los Angeles), CA.

Many of these guns were made by Goodenow Manufacturing Company of Eric, PA about 1953-58 and will have fine walnut stocks. They included a pump pneumatic shotgun, a pump pneumatic and CO_2 rifle, a very solidly built pump pneumatic pistol and, finally, an equally well built CO_2 pistol. Construction and design was too good to be competitive at the time. Self-contained valve units, seals, and pump washers were designed for owner replacement.

There is considerable confusion about the Plainsman name. It was first applied to the solidly built guns distributed by Challenger Arms Corporation and later used by Healthways for these same guns and then by Healthways for an entirely different, more economical series of CO_2 rifles and pistols. (Healthways probably did not actually manufacture any of the Plainsman airguns listed below, but rather only sold acquired inventory and packaged, perhaps made, shot shells with the Plainsman name combined with the Healthways brand.) Even later, the brand of Plainsmaster was used by Marksman for their Model 1049 CO_2 pistol. Marksman also used the name Plainsman for a slide action BB rifle.

Dunathan's American BB Gun (1971) first reported two airgun models with the Challenger name. However, the gun he listed as an 1886 Challenger actually represents only a single patent model, perhaps made by the Plymouth Air Rifle Co., and is marked "Challenge". The second gun, listed as an 1887 Challenger, actually was made in small numbers, but its maker is not known (probably not Markham) and there seems to be no justification for referring to it under the Challenger name. The first verified use of the Challenger name for airguns seems to have been by the Challenger Arms Corporation. The Challenger name was again used in 1982-89 by Crosman for their versions of barrel cocking, spring-piston adult air rifles made by Dianawerk and Anschütz and, in 2000, on their own Model 2000 Challenger CO_2 bolt action rifle. Ref: AGNR - Jan. 1986.

For additional information on Plainsman Model airguns, see Healthways, Inc. in the "H" section.

PISTOLS

PLAINSMAN PNEUMATIC PISTOL – .177 or .22 cal., swinging arm pump pneumatic, SS, 300 FPS (.22 cal.) blue finish.

courtesy Beeman Collection

	N/A	$600	$475	$400	$300	$210	$120

Add 20% for .177 cal.

GRADING	100%	95%	90%	80%	60%	40%	20%

PLAINSMAN GAS PISTOL – .177 or .22 caliber, CO_2, SS, 380 FPS (.22 cal.), blue finish.

courtesy Beeman Collection

	N/A	$300	$240	$195	$150	$105	$60

Add 25% for .177 cal.

RIFLES

PLAINSMAN PNEUMATIC RIFLE – .177 or .22 cal., swinging forearm multiple pump pneumatic, bolt or knurled knob action, SS, hardwood or walnut pump handle/forearm and buttstock.

courtesy Beeman Collection

* *Plainsman Pneumatic Rifle Bolt Handle Variant* – .177 or .22 cal., cocking rod with bolt handle.

	N/A	$350	$280	$230	$175	$125	$70

Add 50% for .177 cal.
Add 15% for walnut.

* *Plainsman Pneumatic Rifle Knurled Knob Variant* – .177 or .22 cal., cocking rod with knurled knob handle.

	N/A	$350	$280	$230	$175	$125	$70

Add 10% for .177 cal.
Add 15% for walnut.

PLAINSMAN GAS RIFLE – .22 cal., CO_2, SS, 8 gram CO_2 cartridge, similar to Plainsman Pneumatic Rifle except, one piece hardwood or walnut stock.

* *Plainsman Gas Rifle Bolt Handle Variant* – .22 cal., CO_2, SS, cocking rod with bolt handle.

courtesy Beeman Collection

	N/A	$400	$325	$260	$200	$140	$80

Add 20% for bulk fill version.
Add 15% for walnut.

GRADING	100%	95%	90%	80%	60%	40%	20%

* Plainsman Gas Rifle Knurled Knob Variant – .22 cal., CO_2, SS, cocking rod with knurled knob handle.

courtesy Beeman Collection

	N/A	$400	$325	$260	$200	$140	$80

Add 20% for bulk fill version.
Add 15% for walnut.

SHOTGUNS

PLAINSMAN AIR SHOTGUN – .28 cal., swinging arm pump pneumatic, similar to Plainsman Pneumatic Rifle, except .28 cal. and marked "S" on RHS, forward side of receiver, uses special pre-packed cardboard shot tubes, hardwood or walnut pump handle/forearm and buttstock.

courtesy Beeman Collection

	N/A	$425	$350	$275	$210	$150	$85

Rumor has it five to ten pumps produced enough power to drive a small pattern of shot into a pine board at ten meters.

CHICAGO COIN MACHINE CO.

Previous manufacturer of coin operated air machine guns for high end shooting galleries. Division of Chicago Dynamic Industries, Inc., 1725 Diversey Blvd., Chicago, Il. Produced the Commando Air Machine Guns under patent No. 2,837,076 issued June 3, 1958, from about 1958 to the late 1970s.

Very well designed, complex, and extremely well built, the 1958 purchase cost of $995, adjusted for inflation to 2007 is about $6,900 each! Ref. Behling (2006).

MACHINE GUN

COMMANDO AIR MACHINE GUN – .219 in. steel balls, full-auto in 3 shot bursts, each use adjustable from 130 to 525 shots, 150 rpm. Self contained electric air compressor. 110 volt AC. 8000 round ball hopper. 250 FPS. 18 in. smoothbore bbl., 44.3 in. OAL, 74 lbs. Front post sight, rear circle-on-glass sight. Not marked with brand. Fired with two hands from a swiveling tripod. 1958 - late 1970s. 12 known specimens.

courtesy Beeman Collection

	N/A	$3,750	$3,000	$2,425	$1,875	$1,300	$750

Subtract 15% if without tripod.
Add 5 - 10% for wooden case.

GRADING	100%	95%	90%	80%	60%	40%	20%

CHINESE STATE FACTORIES

In 1987, John Walter wrote in the Fourth Edition of *The Airgun Book:* The Chinese products are usually crudely if sturdily made, and offer lower power and inferior accuracy than most of their Western European rivals. Some of these products are unauthorized copies of European designs such as the Chinese GLOBE, an imitation Feinwerkbau Model 65 air pistol, illustrated here. The value of this gun would be under $150 in 100% condition, but many of the new specimens are so roughly finished as to appear somewhat worn. While many of the airgun products from the Chinese State Factories have improved since then, the collector and shooter should carefully balance quality, backing, durability, ownership pride, and price.

courtesy Beeman Collection

CLASSIC

For information on Classic airguns, see Gun Toys SRL in the "G" section.

COGSWELL & HARRISON

For information on Cogswell & Harrison airguns, see Certus in this section.

For more information and current pricing on both new and used Cogswell & Harrison firearms, please refer to the *Blue Book of Gun Values* by S.P. Fjestad (also available online).

COLT'S MANUFACTURING COMPANY, INC.

Current manufacturer located in West Hartford, CT. Colt airguns are currently imported and serviced exclusively by Umarex USA located in Fort Smith, AR beginning 2007. Previously imported and serviced exclusively by Crosman Corp. located in East Bloomfield, NY 2003-2006 and by Daisy Manufacturing Company located in Rogers, AR.

Colt airguns are manufactured by Umarex, the current owner of Walther. Colt airguns are faithful copies with the size and weight of the original Model 1911 A1 and variants of it. Many of the same precision options offered for the cartridge pistols have been available for the airguns, including a barrel compensator, competition (tuning set with speed hammer, rapid release double thumb safety, beavertail grip safety, grip with thumb guard, backstrap, sights) features, and Colt Top Point (Red Dot) heads-up sighting scope. All models are pre-drilled for the Serendipity SL optical sight.

For more information and current pricing on both new and used Colt firearms, please refer to the *Blue Book of Gun Values* by S.P. Fjestad (also available online).

PISTOLS

COMMANDER – BB/.177 cal., CO_2, SA/DA, blowback action, 325 FPS, 4.5 in. barrel, all metal construction, 19 shot drop-free mag., fixed front and rear sights, manual safety, skeleton trigger and commander style hammer, CO_2 compartment in the grip, Black finish, 8.5 in. OAL, 2.1 lbs. New 2014.

MSR $114	$95	$80	$65	$55	$45	$30	$20

Add $36 for 19 shot drop free magazine.

DEFENDER – BB/.177 cal., CO_2, DA, 4.3 in. barrel, 16-shot mag., 440 FPS, black finish, all metal construction, spring

courtesy Umarex USA

GRADING	100%	95%	90%	80%	60%	40%	20%

powered grip release, adj. (disc. 2010) or fixed (new 2011) rear sight, fixed blade front sight, diamond cut black grips with silver Colt medallions, 6.75 in. OAL, 1.6 lbs. New 2010.

MSR $60	$50	$45	$35	$30	$25	N/A	N/A

GOVERNMENT MODEL 1911 A1 – .177 cal., CO_2, semi-auto, SA/DA, two eight-shot rotary magazines, 5 (disc. 2007) or 4.8 (new 2008) in. rifled steel barrel, 425 FPS, blade front/adj. rear sight, trigger safety, grip safety, blued, Dark Ops (new 2012), black or nickel/black (disc. 2011) finish, checkered black plastic or smooth wood grips, 8.6 in. OAL, 2.4 lbs.

courtesy Umarex USA

MSR $261	$220	$185	$155	$130	$100	$65	$45

Add $16 for nickel/black finish (disc. 2011).
Add $30-$50 for compensator (disc.).
Add $89 for wood grips (disc.).

MODEL 1911 · 100TH ANNIVERSARY – .177 cal., CO_2, DA, 395 FPS, 8-shot rotary mag., adj. rear sight, manual safety, polished black design, authentic double diamond wood grips, Rampant Colt logo, 8.6 in. OAL, 2.4 lbs. Limited edition. Limited mfg. 2012-2013.

Please contact the company directly for pricing on this model.

This anniversary model features the same lettering as the 1911 army model, and comes in authentic packaging of wax paper and stamped cardboard box.

MODEL 1911 A1 160TH ANNIVERSARY – .177 cal., CO_2, semi-auto, SA and DA, eight-shot cylinder magazine, 393 FPS, post front/adj. rear sight, trigger safety, grip safety, 5 in. rifled barrel, polished black finish with checkered white grips, slide marked with Colt 160th Anniversary banner, Colt logo, and floral scrollwork, 2.38 lbs. Disc. 2003.

	$195	$165	$135	$115	$90	$60	$40

Last MSR was $249.

MODEL 1911 A1 GOLD CUP – .177 cal., CO_2, semi-auto, SA/DA, eight-shot cylinder magazine, 393 FPS, post front/adj. rear sight, trigger safety, grip safety, 5 in. rifled barrel, standard black finish with checkered black plastic grips, 2.38 lbs. Disc. 2003.

	$225	$190	$160	$130	$100	$65	$45

Last MSR was $279.

Add $20 for nickel plated finish.

MODEL 1911 A1 TACTICAL – .177 cal., CO_2, semi-auto, SA and DA, eight-shot cylinder magazine, 5 in. BBL, 425 FPS, post front/adj. rear sight, trigger safety, grip safety, includes bridge mount, Top Point (red dot) sight, carrying case, and two rotary magazines, 13.75 in. OAL, 2.9 lbs. Mfg. 2007-2008.

courtesy Umarex USA

	$295	$250	$205	$170	$135	$90	$60

Last MSR was $330.

GRADING	100%	95%	90%	80%	60%	40%	20%

MODEL 1911 A1 TROPHY MATCH – .177 cal., CO_2, semi-auto, SA and DA, eight-shot cylinder magazine, 393 FPS, post front/adj. rear sight, trigger safety, grip safety, includes bridge mount, Top Point (red dot) sight, all competition accessories, carrying case and two rotary magazines. Disc. 2003.

	$550	$475	$400	$325	$250	$165	$110

Last MSR was $699.

Add $100 for nickel plated finish.

PYTHON – BB/.177 cal., CO_2, SA/DA, 400 FPS, 5 1/2 in. barrel, metal frame, swing-out cylinder, 6 shot, fixed front and adj. rear sights, CO_2 housed in the grip, removable casings, functioning casing ejector, Black finish, 11.25 in. OAL, 2.6 lbs. New 2014.

MSR $114	$95	$80	$65	$55	$45	$30	$20

Add $24 for 6 pack of spare casings and Speedloader.

SPECIAL COMBAT CLASSIC – .177 cal., CO_2, DA, heavy all-metal version of the legendary Colt classic, movable slide, stainless steel look, Picatinny rail, double action trigger, safety catch, blued, Dark Ops finish, 20-shot drop free mag., adj. rear sight, manual safety, 8.6 in. OAL, 2 lbs. Mfg. 2012 only.

Please contact the company directly for pricing on this model.

COLUMBIA

Probably made by the Adams & Westlake Company, Chicago, IL about 1905 to 1915.

One model, a simple push-barrel, single shot, sheet metal BB gun. Marked "COLUMBIA" with Adams & Westlake name and address in a circular logo.

Research is ongoing with this trademark, and more information will be included both online and in future editions.

RIFLES

COLUMBIA – .180 cal. BB, SS, SP. Only two or three examples known, an unusual push-barrel cocking system, sheet metal BB gun. To cock, entire upper body of gun is moved back to cocked position. Unusual tap-loading mechanism looks like an oil lamp part (Adams and Westlake were a large oil lamp manufacturer). Marked "COLUMBIA" in one-inch letters on the side of the buttstock. Stock also with circular logo: "MADE BY ADAMS & WESTLAKE CO. CHICAGO. PAT. APPLD." Nickel-plated metal; slab sided stock. 2.5 lbs., 8.5 in. smoothbore barrel, 33.3 in. OAL.

courtesy Beeman Collection

Good condition examples will retail in the $2,500 range.

Extremely rare, perhaps less than two or three specimens known (much more rare than 1st or 2nd model Daisy!).

COLUMBIAN & BAILEY AIRGUNS

This line of airguns began in 1892 with the Bailey BB guns produced by previous manufacturer E.E. Bailey Manufacturing Company in Philadelphia, PA.

The Bailey Company was not successful and only about a dozen Bailey specimens are known today. In 1893 a partnership of Elmer E. Bailey and William G. Smith began to produce airguns under the Columbian trademark. Upon Bailey's death in 1898, the partnership reverted to William Smith. Smith's company was taken over by William Heilprin in 1907 and continued producing airguns until the early 1920s. The airguns of these makers are often referred to as Heilprin airguns, but Heilprin was not involved with most of the Columbian models or most of their production. He produced only the last model of the elite cast iron models and then shifted into sheet medal models- most of those rather quickly expired. The break-open Models L and S, based on Heilprin's patents, were not successful; only a handful of specimens are known today.

Bailey's famous second patent, #507470, issued October 24, 1893, is the key to the Columbian airguns. The patent's key feature, having a reciprocating air chamber enclosed within the gun's frame casting, was central to the Columbian airguns. The 1000 shot design format was a standard of the BB gun industry for over 80 years.

The best known examples of the Columbian line are the heavy, cast metal BB rifles which not only weighed far more than any BB guns of the time but cost much more. When Daisy and other common BB guns were selling for $0.69 to $1.00, the Columbians were the elite airguns, selling for $1.95 to $3.50. Their solid construction, durability, and cost gave a boy who owned one tremendous neighborhood status.

GRADING	100%	95%	90%	80%	60%	40%	20%

William Johnson's 2002 book *Bailey and Columbian Air Rifles* is the absolute key to this complex line of airguns. We will follow his organization of the early, heavy, cast iron models into 11 types and the final sheet metal models into three lever action and two break open models. Not only must we stop referring to these guns as Heilprins, we must stop referring to some as the Squirrel Model, the Buffalo model, etc. The animal figures can help narrow down the choices, BUT there are three different squirrels in four different type groups for a grand total of nine "squirrel" models. There are two different stag's heads in two different type groups for a total of four models and two full buffalos in two different type groups. This section probably can lead to the identification of almost all models, but only Johnson's book and CD can confirm the ID and give you the known variations and the many details.

Most of the models do not trade often enough to clearly establish meaningful values. Johnson's rarity ratings have been translated here into estimated numbers of existing specimens per model.

courtesy Beeman Collection

CAST IRON RIFLES

Unless otherwise noted, all were genuine gravity-fed, 1000 shot, repeating BB rifles, large BB/.180 cal. w/ smoothbore brass barrels, Winchester-style cocking levers, nickel plated barrel shrouds, and heavy cast iron frames, painted black or nickeled, with ornate raised decorative designs. Johnson has classified the guns into 11 frame types - decorative designs, including the types of bird or mammal shown, within a type are identical except for dates cast in the date panels- unless otherwise noted. (Specifications given are for the Beeman Collection specimens illustrated - specifications of the same model may vary with bbl length, etc.)

TYPE I - BAILEY FIRST MODEL – Frame open at top, no decoration, 1000 shot. Perhaps made 1892-1895. No specimens known.

TYPE II - BAILEY SECOND MODEL – similar to First Model, but with embossed floral, animal designs, and checkering over entire frame. Large stag's head embossed just ahead of trigger. Barrel with shot tube often broken free of frame. Several variations. Usually marked: BAILEY 1000 SHOT AIR RIFLE, PAT'D NOV. 29,'92. Retail: $4.00 black paint, $5.00 nickel frame. Early variation - Rear sight cast into frame, bbl. usually 14", only nickel-plated. Late variation - Rear sight screws into frame, bbl. usually 12.6", nickel or black frames.

	N/A	$3,500	$2,750	$2,250	$1,750	$1,250	$750

TYPE III - COLUMBIAN MODEL 1893 – Frame closed along top (as are all future models). Plain frame w/o markings or embossed designs. 13" brass bbl.

	N/A	$2,500	$2,000	$1,625	$1,250	$875	$500

TYPE IV - COLUMBIAN MODEL 1894 – Sitting squirrel embossed above trigger. Date not cast on gun. First use of sliding loading sleeve cover.

	N/A	$2,500	$2,000	$1,625	$1,250	$875	$500

TYPE V - COLUMBIAN MODELS 1895 - 1899 – Sitting squirrel embossed above trigger. Date cast on LHS of iron forearm.

* **Model 1895** – 15-25 specimens known.

	N/A	$1,250	$1,000	$800	$625	$425	$250

* **Model 1896** – 25-50 known.

	N/A	$1,200	$950	$775	$600	$425	$240

* **Model 1897** – 8-10 known.

	N/A	$1,250	$1,000	$800	$625	$425	$250

GRADING	100%	95%	90%	80%	60%	40%	20%

* ***Model 1898*** – 25-50 known (including 500 shot carbine version stamped JUNIOR on stock), (specimen shown: 4.75 lbs., 34.9 in. OAL).

courtesy Beeman Collection

	N/A	$900	$700	$600	$500	$400	$200

* ***Model 1899*** – 10-15 known (including carbine version), rolled steel barrel.

TYPE VI · COLUMBIAN MODEL 1898 (BIG FRAME) – Running Buffalo (Bison) embossed above trigger LHS, standing buck on RHS. 1898 cast on forearm panel. Early production with heavy cast lever. About 10-15 black known, but nickel was offered. Original retail: $2.00 black, $2.50 nickel frame.

	N/A	$2,750	$2,200	$1,775	$1,375	$950	$550

TYPE VII · COLUMBIAN JUNIOR MODEL – Sitting squirrel embossed above trigger. Short barrel, 500 shot. Marked JUNIOR on LHS metal forearm. Distinctive cocking lever with ring loop at back end. About 6 specimens known. 1897-1898.

	N/A	$2,750	$2,200	$1,775	$1,375	$950	$550

TYPE VIII · COLUMBIAN CHAMPION MODEL – Decorations are raised embossing but markings "Champion" or "Junior" are incised. Rabbit and bird figures. Regular Version: Marked CHAMPION on LHS of iron forearm. Early versions with brass bbl., later with steel bbl. 25-50 specimens known. Retail = $1.75 black, $2.25 nickel. Junior Version: Marked JUNIOR on LHS of iron forearm, 1899 on RHS. Full size cocking lever loop. 30.5 in. OAL.

	N/A	$1,000	$800	$700	$600	$450	$250

Original retail was $1.50.

TYPE IX · BARTEN COLUMBIAN MODELS – Sitting squirrel embossed above trigger on both sides of receiver. Slim forearm. Unusual cocking lever with loop far behind trigger, 36 in. OAL. Only type produced by Joseph Barten under royalty from Cora Bailey after Elmer Bailey's death. Mfg. 1899-1902.

Original retail: $2.25 black, $2.50 nickel.

* ***Columbian Version*** – Embossed COLUMBIAN in large letters LHS of iron forearm. Rifle and carbine lengths. About 15-20 specimens known.

	N/A	$2,750	$2,200	$1,775	$1,375	$950	$550

* ***Model 99 Version*** – Identical to Columbian version except for name.

	N/A	$2,750	$2,200	$1,775	$1,375	$950	$550

TYPE X · COLUMBIAN MODELS 1900, 1906, 1908 – Only model with floral, bird, and snake designs embossed above trigger and tiny foxes and squirrel embossed on iron forearm. Only model with dates cast in LHS panel behind trigger. Rifles and carbines.

* ***Model 1900*** – perhaps over 200 known. (Shown: 4.25 lbs, 34.8 in. OAL).

	N/A	$600	$500	$400	$300	$200	$100

* ***Model 1906*** – COLUMBIAN cast on LHS of iron forearm. 15-25 known. (Specimen shown: 4 lbs. 30 in. OAL).

courtesy Beeman Collection

	N/A	$1,950	$1,550	$1,275	$975	$675	$400

GRADING	100%	95%	90%	80%	60%	40%	20%

* **Model 1908** – same as Model 1906 except for cast date. 50-200 known, (early version only with OCT. 23, '93 pat. date, later version adds DEC. 8, '08 pat. date).

	N/A	$600	$500	$400	$300	$200	$100

TYPE XI · COLUMBIAN MODEL 1902 – SS or Repeater, Running Buffalo (Bison) embossed on LHS and Deer on RHS above trigger, no checkering in metal, but the small frame is completely covered with embossed decoration, nickel finish, 27 1/2 in. OAL. Mfg. 1901-1903.

	N/A	$1,000	$800	$650	$500	$350	$200

SHEET METAL RIFLES

Sheet metal designs were introduced in 1907 when William Heilprin took over production from William Smith. Several unique features were added, most distinctive was a thumb operated "safety" which must be held down to fire the gun, a feature of dubious safety value which proved very unpopular in BB guns produced by other makers in the 20th century.

LEVER ACTION RIFLES

All marked HEILPRIN MFG. CO on RHS of receiver with 1893, 1908, and 1909 patent dates plus the model letter. All had Winchester style cocking lever, .173 in. BB repeaters, SP, nickel finish.

COLUMBIAN MODEL M – sheet metal cocking lever and trigger resulted in poor survival. Mfg. circa 1909-1911. 10-15 specimens known.

	N/A	$1,800	$1,450	$1,175	$900	$625	$350

COLUMBIAN MODEL E – Cast iron cocking lever and trigger, handsome design with large nickel plated, shiny areas, 34.6 in. OAL, 2.9 lbs. Mfg. 1912-1920s, perhaps over 50 specimens known.

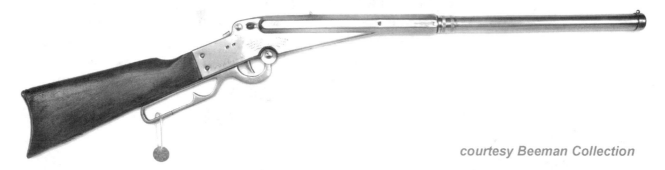

courtesy Beeman Collection

	N/A	$650	$525	$425	$325	$230	$130

COLUMBIAN MODEL J – similar to Model E, except 8 in. bbl and no buttplate. 4-5 known.

	N/A	$900	$725	$575	$450	$325	$180

BARREL-COCKING RIFLES

Barrel cocking design w/very touchy Heilprin hold-down safety. Cannot be uncocked. Mfg. 1913-1914.

COLUMBIAN MODEL L – Repeater with typical Columbian sliding cover sleeve for loading at rear of barrel. Trigger guard is the trigger. Shaped stock. Same metal buttplate as Model E. Nickel plated. Stamped on top of barrel shroud: COLUMBIAN MODEL L 350 SHOT HEILPRIN MFG. Co. PHILA. PA. U.S.A. PATS. PENDING. One specimen apparently w/o marking. 1.9 lbs., 32 in. OAL. Five known specimens.

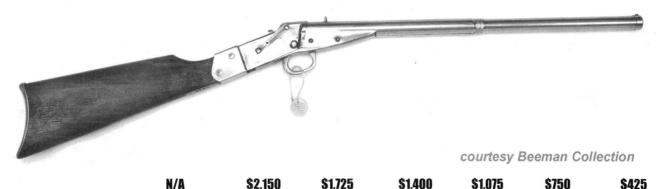

courtesy Beeman Collection

	N/A	$2,150	$1,725	$1,400	$1,075	$750	$425

Engraved inscription "W.R.A. 3-19-14" indicates specimen is from Winchester Repeating Arms Company airgun collection.

GRADING	100%	95%	90%	80%	60%	40%	20%

COLUMBIAN MODEL S – similar to Model L except, single shot, no buttplate. Four known.

	100%	95%	90%	80%	60%	40%	20%
	N/A	$3,100	$2,475	$2,025	$1,550	$1,075	$625

COMATIC

For information on Comatic airguns, see Venturini in the "V" section.

COMENTO

For information on Comento, see Bascaran in the "B" section.

COMET

For information on Comet airguns, see Milbro in the "M" section.

COMETA

Current manufacturer established in 1874 and located in Eibar, Spain. Currently imported and distributed by Airforce International, located in Fort Worth, TX beginning 2013.

Cometa manufactures a complete line of high quality air rifles and air pistols in a wide variety of configurations. Please contact the company directly for more information on their models, U.S. pricing, and availability (see Trademark Index).

PISTOLS

INDIAN – .177 cal., pellet, 500 FPS, fixed barrel over lever, adj. rear and fixed front sights, manual safety, Black or Nickel finish, 10.4 in. OAL, 2.42 lbs. Importation began 2013.

courtesy Airforce International

MSR $210	$175	$150	$125	$100	$80	$50	$35

Add $20 for nickel finish.

RIFLES

FENIX 400 – .177, .22, or .25 cal., SP, BBC, SS, up to 1100 FPS, Dovetail rails, automatic safety, wood stock, adj. trigger, adj. rear and fiber optic front sights, 44.9 in. OAL, 7.5 lbs. Importation began 2013.

courtesy Airforce International

MSR $310	$255	$215	$180	$150	$115	$75	$50

Add $10 for .25 cal.

* **Fenix 400 Premier Star** – .177, .22, or .25 cal., similar to Fenix 400, except features a walnut stock, checkered grip, and adj. cheekpiece. Importation began 2013.

courtesy Airforce International

MSR $373	$325	$270	$220	$185	$140	$95	$65

Add $16 for .25 cal.

GRADING	100%	95%	90%	80%	60%	40%	20%

FUSION – .177 or .22 cal., SP, BBC, SS, up to 1100 FPS, Dovetail rails, adj. trigger, wood stock, automatic safety, 44.9 in. OAL, 7.5 lbs. Importation began 2013.

courtesy Airforce International

MSR $352	$300	$255	$210	$175	$135	$90	$60

* ***Fusion Premier Star*** – .177 or .22 cal., similar to Fusion, except features walnut stock with checkered grip and adj. cheekpiece. Importation began 2013.

courtesy Airforce International

LYNX – .177 or .22 cal., PCP, slide lever, 1000/700 FPS, 18 1/2 in. precision hammer forged barrel with high efficiency barrel shroud, large air reservoir, regulated air system, adj. power, 13 (.177) or 17 (.22) shot rotary mag., Dovetail rails, adj. trigger, ambidextrous beech wood stock with raised cheekpiece and rubber butt pad, natural, blue, or black oil finish, modern checkering on grip and forearm, manual safety, 41.3 in. OAL, 7.8 lbs. Importation began 2013.

courtesy Airforce International

MSR $1,000	$850	$725	$600	$500	$375	$255	$170

COMMANDO ARMS

Current manufacturer located in Turkey. No U.S. importation.

Commando Arms manufactures air rifles in various configurations, as well as O/U, SxS, and semi-auto shotguns. For more information on their shotguns, please refer to the most recent edition of the *Blue Book of Gun Values*, or visit our website at www.bluebookofgunvalues.com.

RIFLES

Current models include AR-BS, AR-BV, AR-BA, AR-BC, T301, T201, 1000S, and 850S. Please contact the company directly for more information including options, pricing, and U.S. availability (see Trademark Index).

COMPASSECO, INC.

Previous importer/distributor located in Bardstown, KY beginning late-1980s. During 2010 Compasseco, Inc. joined business with Pyramyd Air International located in Solon, OH. Previously located in Warrensville Hts., OH. Dealer and consumer direct sales.

Compasseco was importing/distributing airguns from China since the late-1980s, when most were priced well under $100. Circa 2008, the Compasseco ecommerce website had been considerably improved and expanded, featuring airguns from some of the top trademarks world wide with price points for every level of consumer. Also available was virtually every airgun accessory usable. For information on Tech Force airguns, see Tech Force in the "T" section.

PISTOLS

For information on Tech Force air pistols, see Tech Force in the "T" section.

RIFLES

For information on Tech Force air rifles, see Tech Force in the "T" section.

RIFLES: CONTENDER SERIES

For information on Tech Force Contender Series air rifles, see Tech Force in the "T" section.

COUGAR

For information on Cougar airguns, see Milbro in the "M" section.

CROSMAN CORP.

Current manufacturer located in Bloomfield, NY.

CROSMAN BACKGROUND

The Crosman airgun line began with the production of the "First Model" Crosman pneumatic rifle by the Crosman Brothers Co. in June 1923. That rifle was based on a patent by William A. MacLean. In addition to being chauffeur to wealthy heavy construction contractor P.H. Murray, MacLean had developed a tiny business producing "Universal Pellets," .22 caliber diabolo-style pellets. These probably were for American owners of BSA air rifles whose supply of British pellets had been cut off by World War I. MacLean was intrigued by an airgun brought back from Europe by Murray, probably one of those BSA air rifles, and wished to "improve" upon its power source. Apparently he devised the idea of combining a highly accurate rifled barrel firing .22 caliber lead pellets with the then current American airgun pump rod system of the smoothbore Benjamin BB airguns. This pumping system had been well-known in America since the models of Bouron, Hawley (Kalamazoo), and Johnson and Bye in the late 1800s.

The oft-told tale that Murray's unidentified air rifle, which so impressed MacLean, was a French Giffard pneumatic rifle is controverted by the fact that MacLean was already involved with .22 caliber waisted pellets and that such Giffard guns had not been made for almost a half century. Murray, a pacifist and not at all interested in guns, almost surely would not have purchased a vintage Giffard. It is very probable that he would have brought back a BSA air rifle, then popular all over Europe but not common in America, because he knew that his chauffeur was interested in airguns and had a part-time business making pellets for such guns.

The Crosman Brothers Co., which made those first Crosman air rifles, was an offshoot of the then famous Crosman Brothers Seed Company located in Fairport, NY. Crosman Brothers became the Crosman Rifle Company in August 1923 and then the Crosman Arms Co. in 1925. The Crosman Arms Company later became Crosman Air Guns. The Crosman history has been traced, and its airguns discussed and illustrated, by Dean Fletcher in his excellent books, *The Crosman Rifle*, 1923-1950 (1996), *The Crosman Arms Handbooks* (1996), and *75 Years of Crosman Airguns* (1998).

As with many airguns, originality of parts may be hard to determine. The parts were not serial numbered. Newer parts were often placed, sometimes under company mandate, in older guns during repairs. In older Crosman airguns, the .177 caliber versions generally are much less common, while in the most recent models the .177 caliber is the most common.

Caution: Do not depend on older Crosman ads or catalogs to see detailed features. Their ad departments and agencies frequently used illustrations from previous periods.

CROSMAN TIMELINE

1923 - Crosman Brothers Company produces airgun pellets.

1924 - First pneumatic pump airgun debuts, revolutionalizing "power without powder".

1931 - Crosman CO_2 guns showcased at National Camp Perry Matches.

1940 - Crosman grows to six employees.

1966 - Model 760 Pumpmaster air rifle introduced, becoming the most enduring airgun model in history, with more than 16 million sold!

1991 - RepeatAir CO_2 powered, semi-automatic pistol introduced.

2003 - Crosman designs and manufactures first US-made break barrel air rifle.

2008 - Benjamin Discovery debuts as industry's first affordable pre-charged pneumatic air rifle.

2009 - CenterPoint Division established providing feature-rich shooting optics.

2010 - Nitro Piston break barrel technology introduced, reducing shot noise by 70%.

2011 - Benjamin Rogue .357 unveiled as first large caliber huntiing air rifle.

2012 - Crosman Undead Apocalypse Airsoft brand established to fan flames of zombie craze.

2013 - Crosman marks its first 90-years of shooting fun.

CROSMAN IN THE ADULT AIRGUN MARKET

Crosman expended heroic efforts to develop adult interest in airguns, but ended up a co-leader of the youth market instead. Ironically, it probably was the development of the Crosman pump rifle, and especially the development of mass production, low-cost versions of it, that pre-empted the significant introduction of adult-level spring-piston airguns into the United States. Crosman airguns became a product primarily of interest to, and eventually designed for, youthful shooters. Despite the past efforts of Crosman and others, the development of a significant American adult airgun market was delayed until the 1980s. Crosman's primary concern over the last few decades has been competition with the other leader of the American youth airgun market, Daisy. Crosman's adult precision airgun line consisted of the Models 6100-6500, from 1982-1989. During 2000, the company introduced the Challenger 2000 Series, a single shot, bolt action, CO_2 three position target rifle.

GRADING	100%	95%	90%	80%	60%	40%	20%

CROSMAN PRIVATE LABEL AND STOREBRAND AIRGUNS

Crosman produced some airguns under the name of their president, P.Y. Hahn, and under several private labels, such as J.C. Higgins and Ted Williams for Sears, Hawthorn for Montgomery Wards, and Revelation for Western Auto. While guns sold to the general public might come back to the factory one by one, private label models had the potential to come back en mass. Thus, the models sold to Sears and Wards usually represented the very best efforts and quality control that Crosman could muster. It is not possible to list all Crosman variations, and surely there are variations, even models, out there that even the factory does not know about. For information on Crosman airguns manufactured for other trademarks, see the Store Brand Cross-Over List at the back of this text.

CROSMAN CONVERSION KITS

MODEL 455 – .177 cal., CO_2, SS, pellet (Crosman/Blaser 45 conversion unit) converts Colt 45 Automatic firearm (series 70 or earlier) or clones to .177 cal. pellet use, CO_2, single shot. Mfg. in Germany 1987-1988.

	$175	$150	$125	$100	$80	$50	$35

Add 20% for original factory box w/instructions.

MODEL MAR177 – .177 cal., PCP, charge handle cocking repeater, ten shot rotary mag., 21 in. rifled steel barrel, 600 FPS, adj. flip peep rear in carry handle w/removable post front sights and Picatinny optics rail, match-grade trigger, matte black finish w/synthetic forend, 28.5 in. OAL, 7.6 lbs. Mfg. 2012-current.

MSR $650	$550	$475	$400	$325	$250	$165	$110

The MAR177 conversion kit replaces existing AR/M4 style upper and converts it into a PCP .177 caliber competition air rifle designed to meet 10-meter match air rifle competition requirements.

CROSMAN PRODUCTS NON-FACTORY ALTERED

For information on additional airgun models, see Palmer Chemical and Equipment Co. in the "P" section.

MODEL SSP-250 (ZZZ TRANQUILIZER DART PISTOL) – .50 cal., CO_2, single-shot dart gun, modified from Crosman Model SSP-250 air pistol by outside fabricator for ZZZ Dart of Cicero, IL.

	$250	$215	$175	$145	$115	$75	$50

MODEL 1300 (ZZZ TRANQUILIZER DART PISTOL) – .50 cal., pump pneumatic, single-shot dart gun, modified from Crosman Model 1300 air pistol by outside fabricator for ZZZ Dart of Cicero, IL.

	$250	$215	$175	$145	$115	$75	$50

MODEL 2100 (ZZZ TRANQUILIZER DART RIFLE) – .50 cal., pump pneumatic, single-shot dart gun, modified from Crosman Model 2100 air rifle by outside fabricator for ZZZ Dart of Cicero, IL.

	$250	$215	$175	$145	$115	$75	$50

MODEL 2200 (ZZZ TRANQUILIZER DART RIFLE) – .50 cal., pump pneumatic, single-shot dart gun, modified from Crosman Model 2200 air rifle by outside fabricator for ZZZ Dart of Cicero, IL.

	$250	$215	$175	$145	$115	$75	$50

JET LINE MODEL 101 (CONDUIT GUN) – CO_2 pistol which fires 12 gram CO_2 cylinder carrying wire-pulling fish line through large conduits for electric work (i.e. cylinder is the projectile!). Produced by Crosman Fabricators with Crosman parts, 10.5 in. OAL (gun only), 1.4 lbs.

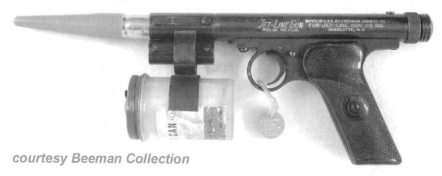

courtesy Beeman Collection

	$350	$300	$245	$205	$160	$105	$70

Add 20% for factory box. Add 50-100% for original accessories, holster, special spools of line, plastic projectile guides, funnels, box, etc.

GRADING	100%	95%	90%	80%	60%	40%	20%

* ***Jet Line Compact Model 101 (Conduit Gun)*** – compact version of Model 101 Jet Line pistol. Only marking is a large "C" on each of the orange plastic grip plates, light gray alloy body, 1.1 lbs., 7.1 in. OAL, gun only.

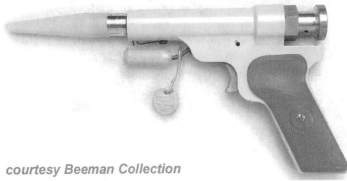

courtesy Beeman Collection

$175	$150	$125	$100	$80	$50	$35

Add 50-100% for original accessories, holster, special spools of line, plastic projectile guides, funnels, box, etc.

MODEL 1100 SLUG GUN – .380 bore, two CO_2 cylinders, SS, non-factory conversion.

courtesy Beeman Collection

This model is generally considered a novelty. The value will be directly related to the condition and the quality of the work performed.

HANDGUNS

MODEL 36 FRONTIER – BB/.175 cal., CO_2, one cylinder, SA, chambers hold 6 BBs; spring-fed tubular magazine holds 12 more. Full size, full weight replica of Colt Single Action revolver. Basically a continuation of the Hahn/Crosman Model 45, Series I - Mfg. 1970-1971, Series II - Mfg. 1972-1975.

courtesy Robert Lutter

N/A	$95	$75	$60	$45	$35	$20

Add 20% for original factory box.
Add $35-$75 for original Western-style holster (depending on condition).

GRADING	100%	95%	90%	80%	60%	40%	20%

MODEL 38C COMBAT – .177 or .22 cal., CO_2, one cylinder, SA or DA, six-shot revolving cylinder, 3.5 in. barrel, full size cast alloy metal replica of .38 cal. Smith & Wesson revolver, 350-400 FPS, .177 cal., 2.4 lbs. First Variant: metal rear sight and cylinder, mfg. 1964-1973. Second Variant: plastic rear sight and cylinder, Mfg. 1973-1976. Third Variant: .177 cal., mfg. 1976-1981.

courtesy Robert Lutter

$90	$75	$65	$50	$40	$25	$20

Add 20% for original factory box.
Add 200%-400% for chrome finish salesman sample.

MODEL 38T TARGET – .177 or .22 cal., similar to Model 38C Combat, except 6 in. barrel. First Variant: metal rear sight and cylinder, mfg. 1964-1973. Second Variant: plastic rear sight and cylinder, mfg. 1973-1976. Third Variant: .177 cal., mfg. 1976-1985.

courtesy Beeman Collection

$90	$75	$65	$50	$40	$25	$20

Add 20% for original factory box.
Add 200%-400% for chrome finish salesman sample.

MODEL 44 PEACEMAKER – .177 or .22 cal., CO_2, one cylinder, single action six-shot revolving pellet, Croswood grips, full size replica of Colt Peacemaker. Series I - mfg. 1970-1971, Series II - mfg. 1972-1975, Series III - mfg. 1976-1981.

courtesy Robert Lutter

N/A	$95	$75	$60	$45	$35	$20

Add 20% for original factory box.
Add $35-$75 for original Western-style holster (depending on condition).

GRADING	100%	95%	90%	80%	60%	40%	20%

MODEL 45 (HAHN "45") – BB/.175 cal., CO_2, one cylinder, SA, chambers hold 6 BBs, spring-fed tubular magazine holds 12 more. Full size, full weight replica of Colt Single Action Army revolver. Hahn 45 became Crosman Model 45, but casting dies were not changed, so Crosman Model 45 specimens are marked with the P.Y. Hahn Co. name. Became the Model "Frontier 36" in 1970. Mfg. 1958-1970. Variation: Sears (J.C. Higgins).

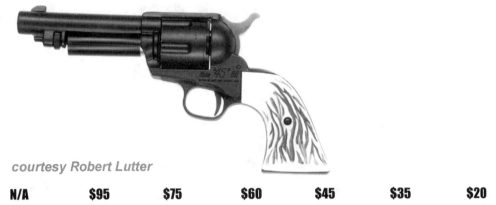

courtesy Robert Lutter

N/A	$95	$75	$60	$45	$35	$20

Add $65-$100 for original Western-style holster (depending on condition).
Add 20% for JC Higgins/Sears version.
Add 20% for original factory box.

MODEL 88 SKANAKER PISTOL – .177 cal., CO_2, 550 FPS, bulk fill cylinder, SS, target model. Mfg. 1987-1991.

courtesy Beeman Collection

$450	$375	$325	$260	$205	$135	$90

Last MSR was $795.

Add $65 for carrying case.

As of Dec. 31, 1991, Crosman liquidated its supply of Skanaker pistols due to expiration of Skanaker name use contract.

MODEL 105 (BULLSEYE) – .177 cal., pneumatic pump, pump lever with one or two open loops, SS, 8.4 in. rifled barrel, adj. rear sight, blue finish, checkered tenite grips, 31 oz. Mfg. 1947-1953.

courtesy Robert Lutter

N/A	$90	$70	$60	$45	$30	$20

Add 30% for original factory-marked box.

GRADING	100%	95%	90%	80%	60%	40%	20%

MODEL 106 (BULLSEYE) – .22 cal., similar to Model 105. Mfg. 1948-1953.

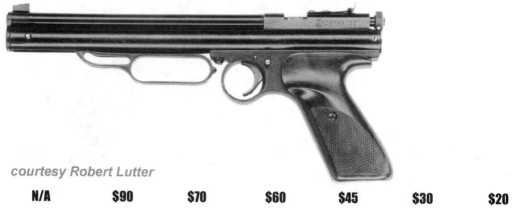

courtesy Robert Lutter

	N/A	$90	$70	$60	$45	$30	$20

Add 30% for original factory-marked box.

MODEL 111 – .177 cal., CO_2, 10 oz. separate gas cylinder, SS, 8 1/8 in. rifled barrel, adj. rear sight, blue finish, molded tenite grips, 2.5 lbs. Mfg. 1950-1954.

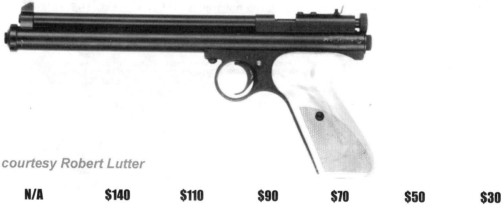

courtesy Robert Lutter

	N/A	$140	$110	$90	$70	$50	$30

Add 30% for original CO_2 cylinder.
Add 20% for original box.
Add 30% for "introduction year" box with gold-colored paper lining and insert cut to hold gun. (Models 111 and 112.)
Add 75% for gun with Model A306 dealer display case, cylinder, bell target, pellets. (Typical premium for such displays in other models.)

These are guns without hose or attached gas tank.

MODEL 112 – .22 cal., similar to Model 111. Mfg. 1950-1954.

courtesy Robert Lutter

	N/A	$125	$100	$80	$60	$45	$25

Add 30% for original CO_2 cylinder.
Add 20% for original box.
Add 30% for "introduction year" box with gold-colored paper lining and insert cut to hold gun. (Models 111 and 112.)
Add 75% for gun with Model A306 dealer display case, cylinder, bell target, pellets. (Typical premium for such displays in other models).

These are guns without hose or attached gas tank.

GRADING	100%	95%	90%	80%	60%	40%	20%

MODEL 115 – .177 cal., similar to Model 111, except has 6 in. barrel. Mfg. 1951-1954.

courtesy Robert Lutter

	N/A	$140	$110	$90	$70	$50	$30

Add 30% for original CO_2 cylinder.
Add 20% for original box.
Add 75% for gun with Model A306 dealer display case, cylinder, bell target, pellets. (Typical premium for such displays in other models.)

MODEL 116 – .22 cal., similar to Model 112, except has 6 in. barrel. Mfg. 1951-1954.

courtesy Robert Lutter

	N/A	$100	$80	$65	$50	$35	$20

Add 30% for original CO_2 cylinder.
Add 20% for original box.
Add 75% for gun with Model A306 dealer display case, cylinder, bell target, pellets. (Typical premium for such displays in other models.)

MODEL 130 – .22 cal., pneumatic pump, SS. First Variant: with walnut grips and pump handle. Mfg. 1953-1954. Second Variant: with formed metal pump handle. Mfg. 1955-1970.

courtesy Robert Lutter

$85	$70	$60	$50	$40	$25	$15

Add 20% for wood cocking handle.
Add 20% for original factory-marked box.
Add 30% for first variant box.

GRADING	100%	95%	90%	80%	60%	40%	20%

MODEL 137 – .177 cal., similar to Model 130. First Variant: with aluminum breech, and fingertip recocking. Mfg. 1954. Second Variant: .177 cal., with formed metal pump handle. Mfg. 1956-1962.

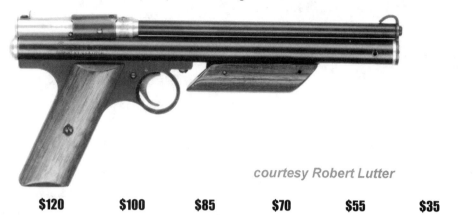

courtesy Robert Lutter

$120	$100	$85	$70	$55	$35	$25

Add 20% for wood cocking handle.
Add 20% for original factory-marked box.
Add 30% for first variant box.

MODEL 150 – .22 cal., 12.5 gm. CO_2 cylinder, SS, Type 1 - with two-piece barrel and breech assembly. First type 1 variation: rotating adj. power cocking knob. Second type 1 variation: non-adjustable power. Mfg. 1954-1956. Type 2 - with one-piece breech/barrel. Mfg. 1956-1967.

courtesy Robert Lutter

$110	$95	$75	$65	$50	$35	$20

Add 20% for Type 1 (except for special versions).
Add 150% for Type 1 Sears/J.C. Higgins Model 150 with grey-crinkle finish on frame and loading port.
Add 40% for SK (Shooting Kit) version.
Add 50% for Sears/Ted Williams version.
Add 50% for Wards Model 150.
Add 75% for Mexican version.
Add 100% for Canadian version.
Add 20%-40% for standard factory-marked box (five variations).

More than 20 variations are known, plus there are an unknown number of foreign models.

* **Model 150C Medalist** – .22 cal., similar to Model 150, except chrome plated and wood presentation box. Mfg. 1957-1961.

$250	$215	$175	$145	$115	$75	$50

Add 30% for presentation box.

* **Model 150PK** – .22 cal., similar to Model 150, except has portable metal target backstop. Mfg. 1959-1960.

$145	$125	$100	$85	$65	$45	$30

GRADING	100%	95%	90%	80%	60%	40%	20%

MODEL 157 – .177 cal., similar to Model 150. Type 1 - with two-piece barrel and breech assembly. First type 1 variation: rotating adj. power cocking knob. Second type 1 variation: non-adjustable power. Mfg. 1954-1956. Type 2 - with one-piece breech/barrel. Mfg. 1956-1967.

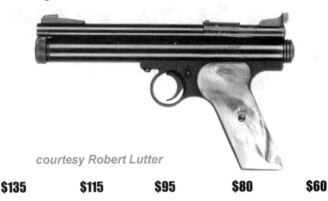

courtesy Robert Lutter

	$135	$115	$95	$80	$60	$40	$25

Add 75% for Type 1.
Add 40% for SK (Shooting Kit) version.
Add 30% for Sears/Ted Williams version.
Add 75% for Mexican version.
Add 100% for Canadian version.
Add 20%-40% for standard factory marked box (5 variations).

More than 20 variations are known, plus there are an unknown number of foreign models.

MODEL 338 – BB/.175 cal., CO_2, one cylinder, semi-auto replica of Walther P38 military pistol, 20-shot magazine, cast metal. Mfg. 1986-1991.

courtesy Robert Lutter

	$45	$40	$30	$25	$20	$15	N/A

Add 10% for original box.

MODEL 357 FOUR – .177 cal. pellets, CO_2, one cylinder, SA/DA revolver, replica of Colt Python firearm, ten-shot rotary clip, 4 in. rifled barrel, 350 FPS, black finish, adj. rear sight, 27 oz. Mfg. 1983-1997.

courtesy Robert Lutter

	$60	$50	$40	$35	$25	$20	$10

Add 10% for factory box.
Add 60% for silver finish.

* **Model 357 4GT** – .177 cal., similar to Model 357 Four, except gold color accents and black grips. Mfg. 1997. Disc.

	$60	$50	$40	$35	$25	$20	$10

Add 10% for factory box.
Add 60% for silver finish.

GRADING	100%	95%	90%	80%	60%	40%	20%

MODEL 3574W – .177 cal. pellets, CO_2, one cylinder, SA/DA revolver, ten-shot rotary clip, 4 in. rifled barrel, 435 FPS, black finish, adj. rear sight, 32 oz. Disc. 2004.

	$45	$40	$30	$25	$20	$15	N/A

Last MSR was $61.

* **Model 357GW** – .177 cal. pellets, similar to Model 3574W, except also includes extra 8 in. barrel, three ten-shot rotary clips, five paper targets, red dot sight and mounts, and hard case. Disc. 2004.

	$85	$70	$60	$50	$40	$25	$15

Last MSR was $100.

MODEL 357 SIX – .177 cal., similar to Model 357 Four, except has 6 in. barrel. Mfg. 1983-1997.

courtesy Robert Lutter

	$60	$50	$40	$35	$25	$20	$10

Add 10% for factory box.
Add 60% for silver finish.

* **Model 357 6GT** – .177 cal., similar to Model 357 Six, except had gold accents and black grips. Mfg. 1997. Disc.

	$60	$50	$40	$35	$25	$20	$10

Add 10% for factory box.
Add 60% for silver finish.

MODEL 3576W – .177 cal. pellets, CO_2, one 12g cylinder, SA/DA revolver, ten-shot rotary clip, 6 in. rifled steel barrel, 435 FPS, black finish, fixed blade front sight, adj. rear sight, synthetic finger molded grip, hammer block safety, 11.4 in. OAL, 2 lbs.

courtesy Crosman

MSR $60	$50	$45	$40	$35	$25	N/A	N/A

* **Model 357GW** – .177 cal. pellets, CO_2, one cylinder, SA/DA revolver, ten-shot rotary clip, 6 and 8 in. rifled barrel, 435 FPS, black finish, adj. rear and red dot sights, padded case, 2 lbs. Mfg. 2005-2007.

	$85	$70	$60	$50	$40	$25	$15

Last MSR was $100.

GRADING	100%	95%	90%	80%	60%	40%	20%

MODEL 357 EIGHT – .177 cal., similar to Model 357 Four, except has 8 in. barrel. Mfg. 1984-1996.

courtesy Robert Lutter

	$80	$70	$55	$45	$35	$25	$15

Add 10% for factory box.
Add 60% for scope or silver finish.

MODEL 380 ROCKET – CO_2, one cylinder, underwater speargun, one or two (early mfg.) piece grips. Mfg. 1959-1960.

courtesy Howard Collection

	$500	$425	$350	$290	$225	$150	$100

Add 10% for two-piece grips.

MODEL 451 – CO_2, one cylinder, semi-auto, six-shot, styled after Colt 45 Automatic. 4.75 in. barrel. Mfg. 1969-1970.

courtesy Beeman Collection

	N/A	$400	$325	$260	$200	$140	$80

Add 20% for original factory box.

MODEL 454 – BB/.175 cal., CO_2, one cylinder, semi-auto, styled after Colt Woodsman. 16-shot spring-fed magazine, adj. sights, brown Croswood grips. First variant: has coin slot piercing screw. Mfg. 1972-1977. Second variant (BB-Matic): has ring piercing screw lever. Mfg. 1978-1982.

courtesy Robert Lutter

	$50	$45	$35	$30	$25	$15	$10

Add 10% for first variant.
Add 20% for original factory box.

GRADING	100%	95%	90%	80%	60%	40%	20%

MODEL 600 – .22 cal., CO_2, one cylinder, semi-auto, sophisticated trigger design, ten-round spring-fed magazine, considered by many as the pinnacle of Crosman airgun development, often converted into custom airguns, original specimens are becoming scarce. Variations: three distinct variations based on CO_2 piercing caps. First variant: piercing cap. Second variant: internal piercing mechanism. Third variant: push button piercing. Sears variant: Sears markings. Mfg. 1960-1970.

courtesy Robert Lutter

	100%	95%	90%	80%	60%	40%	20%
	N/A	$275	$220	$180	$135	$95	$55

Add 75% for Sears variant.
Add 20% for original factory-marked box.
Add 20% for original holster.

MODEL 677 PLINK-O-MATIC – BB/.175 cal., CO_2, one cylinder, semi-auto, rare BB version of the Model 600. Mfg. 1961-1964.

	100%	95%	90%	80%	60%	40%	20%
	N/A	$600	$475	$400	$300	$210	$120

Add 25% for original factory box.

MODEL 971BF (BLACK FANG) – BB/.175 or .177 cal., spring piston, 17-shot mag. (BB), smooth steel barrel, 250 FPS (BB), black finish, synthetic grip/frame, fixed sights, 10 oz. Mfg. 1996-2002.

	100%	95%	90%	80%	60%	40%	20%
	$20	$15	$15	$10	N/A	N/A	N/A

MODEL 972BV (BLACK VENOM) – BB/.175 or .177 cal., spring piston, 17-shot mag. (BB), SS pellet/dart, smooth steel barrel, 270 FPS (BB), 245 FPS (.177 pellet), black finish, synthetic grip/frame, adj. sights, 15 oz. Mfg. 1996-2006.

	100%	95%	90%	80%	60%	40%	20%
	$25	$20	$20	$15	$10	N/A	N/A

Last MSR was $25.

MODEL 1008 (REPEATAIR) – .177 cal. pellet, CO_2, one cylinder, semi-auto, eight-shot mag., SA/DA action, 4.25 in. rifled barrel, 430 FPS, adj. rear sight, replica of Smith & Wesson pistol, 17 oz. Mfg. 1992-1997.

	100%	95%	90%	80%	60%	40%	20%
	$60	$50	$40	$35	$25	$20	$10

MODEL 1008B (REPEATAIR) – .177 cal. pellet, one CO_2 cylinder, eight-shot clip, M-1008B with black frame, 4.25 in. rifled barrel, 430 FPS, adj. rear sight, 17 oz. Mfg. 1997-2006.

	100%	95%	90%	80%	60%	40%	20%
	$55	$45	$40	$30	$25	$15	$10

Last MSR was $66.

* **Model 1008SB (Repeatair)** – .177 cal., similar to Model 1008B, except has silver frame. Mfg. 1997-2006.

	100%	95%	90%	80%	60%	40%	20%
	$55	$45	$40	$30	$25	$15	$10

Last MSR was $84.

* **Model 1008BRD (Repeatair)** – .177 cal., similar to Model 1008B, except has red dot sight. Mfg. 1997-2006.

	100%	95%	90%	80%	60%	40%	20%
	$65	$55	$45	$40	$30	$20	$15

Last MSR was $76.

* **Model 1008AK/1008SBAK (Repeatair Air Pistol Kit)** – .177 cal., kit includes Model 1008B or 1008SB pistol, red dot sight, shooting glasses, two CO_2 cylinders, 250-ct. package of pellets, and clamshell case. Disc. 2006.

	100%	95%	90%	80%	60%	40%	20%
	$65	$55	$45	$40	$30	$20	$15

Last MSR was $77.

Add $2 for Model 1008SBAK kit with Model 1008SB pistol.

* **MODEL 1078BG/1078SBG (Repeatair Pistol Kit)** – .177 cal., kit includes Model 1008B or 1008SB pistol, three eight-shot clips, three paper targets, three CO_2 cylinders, 250-ct. package of pellets, and clamshell case. Disc. 2006.

	100%	95%	90%	80%	60%	40%	20%
	$65	$55	$45	$40	$30	$20	$15

Last MSR was $77.

Add $2 for Model 1078SBG kit with Model 1008SB pistol.

GRADING	100%	95%	90%	80%	60%	40%	20%

MODEL 1088BG – BB/.175 and .177 cal. pellet, CO_2, one 12g cylinder, semi-automatic, eight-shot clip, black (Model 1088BG) or silver/black (Model 1088SB, disc.) synthetic frame, rifled steel barrel, 435-400 FPS, adj. rear sight, Weaver accessory rail under BBL., 7.75 in. OAL, 17 oz. Mfg. 2006-2011.

	100%	95%	90%	80%	60%	40%	20%
	$50	$45	$35	$30	$25	$15	$10

Last MSR was $60.

Add $10 for 1088 Kit, includes a silver 1088, 100 Crosman pellets, 100 Copperhead premium BBs, an ammo clip and shooting glasses (Model 1088BAK).

Add 15% for Model 1088AK, kit includes three 12g CO_2 cylinders, 250 pellets, and shooting glasses, mfg. 2006-2007.

Add 20% for Model 1088BKC, kit includes three 12g CO_2 cylinders, 250 pellets, three official airgun targets, four eight-shot rotary mags., shooting glasses, and hard sided case, mfg. 2007.

MODEL 1088BAK – .177 cal. BB or pellet, CO_2, semi-auto pistol, features easy to load 8 shot rotary clip and under barrel, Weaver style rail, 400-430 FPS, synthetic frame, rifled steel barrel, fixed blade front or adj. rear sight, crossbolt safety, includes a kit with shooting glasses, ammo clip, 100 BBs and 100 pellets, 7.75 in. OAL, 1.1 lbs.

courtesy Crosman Corp.

MSR $62	100%	95%	90%	80%	60%	40%	20%
	$55	$45	$40	$35	$25	N/A	N/A

MODEL 1088SBAK – BB/.175 and .177 cal. pellet, CO_2, one 12g cylinder, semi-automatic, eight-shot clip, silver/black synthetic frame, rifled steel barrel, 430-400 FPS, adj. rear sight, Weaver accessory rail under BBL., includes a silver 1088, two CO_2 cylinders, 100 Crosman pellets, 100 Copperhead premium BBs, an ammo clip and adult shooting glasses, 7.75 in. OAL, 17 oz. Mfg. 2006-2010.

courtesy Crosman

	100%	95%	90%	80%	60%	40%	20%
	$65	$55	$45	$40	$30	$20	$15

Last MSR was $75.

MODEL 1300 MEDALIST II – .22 cal., UL (forearm) pneumatic, SS, self-cocking, sliding breech cover, pump handle flared at forward end, 460 FPS, 11.75 in. OAL. Mfg. 1970-1976.

courtesy Robert Lutter

	100%	95%	90%	80%	60%	40%	20%
	$80	$70	$55	$45	$35	$25	$15

Add 20% for factory box.

GRADING	100%	95%	90%	80%	60%	40%	20%

MODEL 1322 MEDALIST – .22 cal., UL (forearm) pneumatic, SS, three-ring cocking knob, sliding breech cover, pump handle straight along bottom edge, 13.6 in. overall. First variant: manual cocking, has steel breech and cover. Mfg. 1977-1981. Second variant: has plastic breech and steel cover. Mfg. 1981-1996. Third variant: brass bolt action. Mfg. 1998-2000.

courtesy Robert Lutter

$65	$55	$45	$40	$30	$20	$15

Add 25% for first variant.

MODEL 1322C – .22 cal. pellet, PP, BA, SS, brass bolt, rifled steel barrel, ambidextrous black checkered grips, 460 FPS, fixed blade front and adj. peep or open rear sights, crossbolt safety, black synthetic frame, optional shoulder stock (Model 1399) also available, 13.6 in. OAL, 2 lbs. New 2012.

courtesy Crosman Corp.

MSR $78	$65	$60	$50	$40	$30	N/A	N/A

MODEL 1357 "SIX" – BB/.175 cal., CO_2, break-open, clip loading (six-shot), one cylinder, SA/DA, replica of .357 police revolver, 465 FPS, limited distribution may be Michigan only. Mfg. 1988-1996.

$55	$45	$40	$30	$25	$15	$10

MODEL 1377 AMERICAN CLASSIC – .177 cal., similar to Model 1322, pellet only, single shot, brass bolt action, 10.25 in. rifled barrel, 560 FPS, adj. rear sight, 32 oz. First variant: has manual cocking and steel breech. Mfg. 1977-1981. Second variant: has plastic breech. Mfg. 1981-1996. Also sold as Model 1388 "rifle" with shoulder stock. Mfg. 1982-1988.

courtesy Robert Lutter

$70	$60	$50	$40	$30	$20	$15

Add 20% with shoulder stock (Model 1388 "rifle").

GRADING	100%	95%	90%	80%	60%	40%	20%

* *Model 1377C American Classic* – .177 cal. pellet, UL (forearm) multi-pump pneumatic, single shot, brass bolt action, 10.25 in. rifled steel barrel, black finish, brown synthetic grip and forearm, 600 FPS, adj. rear peep or open sights, fixed blade front, 13.6 in. OAL, 2 lbs. Mfg. 1998-present.

courtesy Crosman Corp.

MSR $78	$65	$60	$50	$40	$30	N/A	N/A

MODEL 1600 POWERMATIC – BB/.175 cal., CO_2, one cylinder, semi-auto replica of Colt Woodsman, 17-shot spring-fed magazine, fixed sights, (economy version of Model 454). First variant: flathead gas filler cap screw. Second variant: barrel-shaped filler cap screw. Mfg. 1979-1990.

courtesy Robert Lutter

	$60	$50	$40	$35	$25	$20	$10

MODEL 1701P SILHOUETTE – .177 cal. pellet, PCP, BA, multi-shot, 450 FPS, 10.1 in. Lothar Walther rifled barrel, reversible bolt and two stage adj. trigger, adj. blade front sight and dovetail mounting rail, 14.75 in. OAL, 2.8 lbs. Mfg. 2010-current.

courtesy Crosman

MSR $478	$400	$350	$325	$265	$200	N/A	N/A

GRADING	100%	95%	90%	80%	60%	40%	20%

MODEL 1720T TARGET – .177 cal. pellet, PCP, SS, BA, 8.75 in. Lothar Walther choked shrouded barrel, two stage adj. trigger, Dovetail mounting rail, reversible bolt, 750 FPS, black synthetic frame and grip, rifled steel barrel, 14.75 in. OAL, 2.8 lbs. New 2012.

courtesy Crosman Corp.

MSR $608	$525	$450	$425	$325	$255	N/A	N/A

MODEL 1861 SHILOH – BB/.175 or .177 pellet cal., CO_2, one cylinder, SA revolver, patterned after U.S. Civil War Remington cap and ball revolver, 370 FPS, 1.9 lbs. Mfg. 1981-1983.

courtesy Robert Lutter

	$125	$105	$90	$75	$55	$35	$25

Add 20% for factory box.

MODEL 2210SB – .22 cal. pellet, CO_2, one cylinder, SS, 7.24 in. rifled barrel, 435 FPS, silver-colored finish, adj. rear sight, fiber optic front sight, 20 oz. Mfg. 1999-2003.

	$50	$45	$35	$30	$25	$15	$10

MODEL 2240 – .22 cal. pellet, CO_2, BA, SS, one 12g cylinder, SS, 7.25 in. rifled steel barrel, 460 FPS, black synthetic frame, black ambidextrous grip with checkering and thumb rest, fixed blade front sight, peep or open adj. rear sight, 11.12 in. OAL, 1.81 lbs. Mfg. 1999-present.

courtesy Crosman

MSR $80	$70	$60	$55	$45	$35	N/A	N/A

GRADING	100%	95%	90%	80%	60%	40%	20%

MODEL 2300S – .177 cal. pellet, CO_2, BA, one 12g cylinder, SS, 10.1 in. Lothar-Walther choked match BBL, single stage adj. trigger, stainless steel bolt, zinc alloy frame, adj. hammer spring for 440-520 FPS, post front sight, Williams adj. rear sight, Dovetail mounting rail, blue finish, 16 in. OAL, 2.7 lbs.

courtesy Crosman

MSR $344	$290	$260	$235	$190	$145	N/A	N/A

MODEL 2300T – .177 cal. pellet, CO_2, BA, SS, one 12g cylinder, SS, 10.1 in. Lothar Walther rifled steel barrel, single stage adj. trigger, 520 FPS, fixed blade front sight, LPA adj. rear sight, blue finish, 16 in. OAL, 2.6 lbs.

courtesy Crosman

MSR $219	$185	$165	$150	$120	$90	N/A	N/A

MODEL 3357 – .50 cal. version of the Model 357 CO_2 revolver, designed for firing paintballs.

courtesy Robert Lutter

	$80	$70	$55	$45	$35	$25	$15

MODEL AAII (Auto Air II) – BB/.175 cal. repeater, .177 pellet cal., SS, CO_2, one cylinder, 480 FPS (BB), 430 FPS (pellet), black finish, adj. rear sight. Mfg. 1991-1996.

	$25	$20	$20	$15	$10	N/A	N/A

Add 5% for factory box.

* **Model AAIIB (Auto Air II)** – BB/.175 cal. repeater, .177 pellet cal., SS, CO_2, one cylinder, smooth barrel, 480 FPS-BB, 430 FPS-pellet, black finish, adj. rear sight, 13 oz. Mfg. 1997-2005.

	$35	$30	$25	$20	$15	$10	N/A

Last MSR was $45.

* **Model AAIIB/AAIIBRD (Auto Air II)** – BB/.175 cal. repeater, .177 pellet cal., SS, CO_2, one cylinder, smooth barrel, 480 FPS (BB), 430 FPS (pellet), black finish, adj. rear sight, red dot sight, 13 oz. Mfg. 1997-2005.

	$50	$45	$35	$30	$25	$15	$10

Last MSR was $59.

GRADING	100%	95%	90%	80%	60%	40%	20%

MODEL C11 – BB/.177 cal., CO_2, one 12g cylinder, semi-automatic, removable 15-shot mag., black synthetic frame, smooth metal barrel, 480 FPS, Weaver accessory rail under barrel, fixed sights, 6.75 in. OAL, 1.1 lbs. Mfg. 2006-current.

courtesy Crosman

MSR $47	$40	$35	$30	$25	$20	N/A	N/A

The Model C11 was redesigned during 2006, adding a spring-activated BB mag. with push button release for 2007.

* ***Model C11 Tactical*** – BB/.177 cal., CO_2, one 12g cylinder, semi-automatic, tactical version of the Model C11, black synthetic frame, steel barrel, 550 FPS, compensator, four-sided accessory rail, fixed sights, laser, 6.75 in. OAL, 1.1 lbs. Mfg. 2008-current.

courtesy Crosman

MSR $89	$75	$65	$60	$50	$35	N/A	N/A

MODEL C11 SURVIVALIST – BB/4.5mm cal., CO_2, semi-auto, precision steel barrel, 20-shot quick release magazine, removable grip panel for easy replacement of CO_2, fixed front and fixed notched rear sights, accessory rail, slide safety, Black finish, 6.9 in. OAL, 1.1 lbs. New 2014.

courtesy Crosman Corp.

MSR $49	$40	$35	$35	$25	$20	N/A	N/A

GRADING	100%	95%	90%	80%	60%	40%	20%

MODEL C21 – BB/.177 cal., CO_2, one 12g cylinder, semi-automatic, removable 15-shot mag., black synthetic frame, metal barrel, 495 FPS, fixed sights, 6.75 in. OAL, 1.1 lbs. Mfg. 2008-2012.

courtesy Crosman

$55	$45	$40	$30	$25	$15	$10

Last MSR was $65.

MODEL C31 – BB/.177 cal., CO_2, one 12g cylinder, semi-automatic, removable 18-shot mag., black synthetic frame, smooth metal barrel, Weaver style rail under the barrel, 495 FPS, fiber optic sights, slide safety, includes belt holster, 6.75 in. OAL, 1.1 lbs. Mfg. 2008-2013.

courtesy Crosman

$50	$45	$35	$30	$25	$15	$10

Last MSR was $60.

MODEL C40 (CROSMAN 75TH ANNIVERSARY COMMEMORATIVE) – .177 cal., CO_2, eight-shot mag., 4.25 in. rifled barrel, 430 FPS, zinc alloy frame, silver finish, adj. rear sight, optional laser sight (C40 LS), new 1999, 40 oz. Mfg. 1998-2005.

$125	$105	$90	$75	$55	$35	$25

Last MSR was $138.

Add $45 for Model C40LS Kit with three mags., laser sight, and foam-padded case.

MODEL CB40 (CROSMAN 75TH ANNIVERSARY COMMEMORATIVE) – .177 cal., CO_2, eight-shot mag., 4.25 in. rifled barrel, 430 FPS, zinc alloy frame, black finish, adj. rear sight, optional laser sight CB40LS new 1999, 40 oz. Mfg. 1998-2003.

$95	$80	$65	$55	$45	$30	$20

Add $30 for CB40LS.

MODEL C41 – BB/.177 cal., CO_2, one 12g cylinder, medium sized semi-automatic German style pistol, removable 18-shot mag., black synthetic frame, brown ambidextrous grooved grip, metal barrel, 495 FPS, fixed sights, 8.5 in. OAL, 2 lbs., also available in Clam Package (Model C41-CL). Mfg. 2009-current.

courtesy Crosman

MSR $84	$70	$65	$55	$45	$35	N/A	N/A

Add $2 for clam metal frame (Model C41-CL).

GRADING	100%	95%	90%	80%	60%	40%	20%

MODEL C51 – BB/.177 cal., CO_2, one 12g cylinder, semi-automatic, gas blowback with genuine recoil action, 495 FPS, black polymer frame and grip, metal slide, 20 shot easy drop out mag., fixed sights, lever safety, 8.5 in. OAL, 2 lbs. Mfg. 2011-2013.

courtesy Crosman

	$70	$60	$50	$40	$30	$20	$15

Last MSR was $85.

MODEL CK92 – .177 cal., CO_2, eight-shot, 435 FPS, rifled steel barrel, solid die-cast zinc (frame, slide action release, safety), adj. rear sight, black or silver finish. Mfg. 2000-2003.

	$105	$90	$75	$60	$45	$30	$20

Add $20 for silver finish.

MODEL MARK I – .22 cal., CO_2, one cylinder, SS, rifled 7.25 in. barrel, 43 oz. First variant: adj. power. Mfg. 1966-1980. Second variant: non-adj. power. Mfg. 1981-1983.

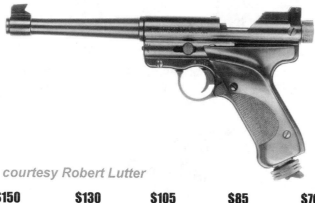

courtesy Robert Lutter

	$150	$130	$105	$85	$70	$45	$30

Subtract 20% for second variant.
Add 10% for factory box.

MODEL MARK II – BB/.175 cal., .177 cal. pellet, similar to Model Mark I. First variant: SS Mfg. 1966-1980. Second variant: without adjustable power. Mfg. 1981-1986.

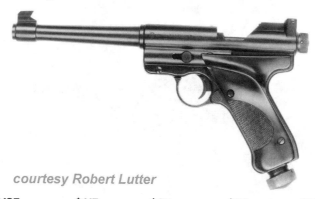

courtesy Robert Lutter

	$135	$115	$95	$80	$60	$40	$25

Subtract 20% for second variant.
Add 10% for factory box.

GRADING	100%	95%	90%	80%	60%	40%	20%

MODEL PC77B PUMPMASTER CLASSIC – .177 cal. pellet, UL (forearm) multi-pump pneumatic, single shot, brass bolt action, 10.25 in. rifled steel barrel, black finish, black synthetic grip and forearm, 600 FPS, adj. rear peep or open sights, fixed blade front, 13.6 in. OAL, 2 lbs. Mfg. 2011-current.

courtesy Crosman Corp.

MSR $78	$65	$60	$50	$40	$30	N/A	N/A

MODEL PRO77CS – BB/.175 cal., CO_2, one 12g cylinder, blowback semi-automatic action, spring-activated 17-shot mag., black synthetic frame with metal slide, rifled steel barrel, 325 FPS, fixed sights, Weaver accessory rail under barrel, hard sided case, 6.75 in. OAL, 1.3 lbs. Mfg. 2007-current.

courtesy Crosman

MSR $80	$70	$60	$55	$45	$35	N/A	N/A

* **Model PRO77KT** – BB/.175 cal., CO_2, compact semi-auto, gas blowback with genuine recoil action, Weaver accessory rail, 325 FPS, black synthetic frame with alloy slide, 17 shot mag., fixed sights, includes a kit with 350 Premium Copperhead BBs, two 12g CO_2 cylinders, and shooting glasses, 6.75 in. OAL, 1.31 lbs. Mfg. 2007-current.

courtesy Crosman

MSR $91	$75	$70	$60	$50	$40	N/A	N/A

MODEL SA 6 – .22 cal., CO_2, one cylinder, SA, six-shot, replica of Colt Peacemaker Single Action revolver. Mfg. 1959-1969.

courtesy Robert Lutter

	$120	$100	$85	$70	$55	$35	$25

Add 20% for factory box.
Add $35-$75 for original Western-style holster (depending on condition).

GRADING	100%	95%	90%	80%	60%	40%	20%

MODEL SSP 250 SILHOUETTE PISTOL – .177 cal., CO_2, one cylinder, SS, dual power settings, interchangeable .20 and .22 cal. rifled steel barrels available. Mfg. 1989-1995.

	$110	$95	$75	$65	$50	$35	$20

Add 25% for each additional caliber barrel.
Add 20% for factory box.

MODEL T4CS – BB/.177 cal. and pellet, CO_2, one 12g cylinder, semi-automatic, eight-shot rotary mag., black synthetic frame, soft ergonomic grip, rifled steel barrel, 450/430 FPS, fixed front sight, adj. rear sight, Weaver accessory rail under barrel, includes two ammo clips and hard shell protective case, 8.63 in. OAL, 1.32 lbs. Mfg. 2007-current.

courtesy Crosman

MSR $90	$75	$70	$60	$50	$40	N/A	N/A

* **Model T4KT** – BB/.177 cal. and pellet, same as Model T4CS, 400-430 FPS, except includes kit with two 12g CO_2 cylinders, 100 premium Copperhead BBs, 100 Crosman pellets, two ammo clips, and shooting glasses. Mfg. 2007-current.

courtesy Crosman

MSR $90	$75	$70	$60	$50	$40	N/A	N/A

* **Model T4OPTS** – BB/.177 cal. and tactical pellet, CO_2, one 12g cylinder, semi-automatic, eight-shot rotary mag., black synthetic frame, soft ergonomic grip, rifled steel barrel with compensator and four Weaver accessory rails, 430-450 FPS, red dot sight, tactical flashlight, two ammo clips, and hard sided case, 8.63 in. OAL, 1.32 lbs. Mfg. 2007-current.

courtesy Crosman

MSR $200	$170	$150	$135	$110	$85	N/A	N/A

MODEL UC-TT – BB/.175 cal., CO_2, semi-auto, styled after a WWII era Russian service handgun, heavyweight, metal frame with polymer grip, removable 18 shot mag., fixed sights, 400 FPS, slide safety, 8 in. OAL, 1.5 lbs. New 2012.

MSR $100	$85	$75	$70	$55	$40	N/A	N/A

GRADING	100%	95%	90%	80%	60%	40%	20%

MODEL V300 – BB/.175 cal., rear grip strap lever cocking, SP, SA, 23-shot spring-fed magazine. Mfg. 1963-1964.

courtesy Robert Lutter

	$150	$130	$105	$85	$70	$45	$30

Add 20% for factory box.

USMC MOS 5811 MILITARY POLICE – BB/4.5mm cal., CO_2, semi-auto, 480 FPS, precision steel barrel, polymer frame with checkered grips, removable grip panel for easy replacement of CO_2, Picatinny accessory rail, fixed blade front and fixed notch rear sights, convenient drop-out magazine for fast reloading holds 20 BBs, Crossbolt safety, Black/Tan finish, 7 7/8 in. OAL. New 2014.

courtesy Crosman Corp.

MSR $50	$45	$40	$35	$30	$20	N/A	N/A

The Marines Airgun series was created to spotlight and pay tribute to the achievements of our brothers and sisters in uniform. Proceeds help support Marines morale, welfare, and recreational activities.

VIGILANTE REVOLVER – BB/.177 cal. and pellet, CO_2, semi-automatic, 6 in. rifled steel barrel, 10 shot rotary mag., 435 FPS, fixed blade front and fully adj. rear sights, dual accessory rails, Black finish, 11.38 in. OAL, 2 lbs. New 2014.

courtesy Crosman Corp.

MSR $80	$70	$60	$55	$45	$35	N/A	N/A

GRADING	100%	95%	90%	80%	60%	40%	20%

P10 WILDCAT – BB/.177 cal., CO_2, semi-auto, precision steel barrel, 20 shot quick release mag., 480 FPS, Picatinny rail under barrel, front sight indicator, Pink polymer frame, Black grips, 8.1 in. OAL, 2 lbs. New 2014.

courtesy Crosman Corp.

MSR $50	$45	$40	$35	$30	$20	N/A	N/A

Z-77 UZI REPLICA – BB/.175 cal., CO_2, one cylinder, semi-auto, gravity-fed 20-shot magazine, with folding stock (but classed as pistol by Crosman). Mfg. 1987-1989.

	$175	$150	$125	$100	$80	$50	$35

Subtract 20% for missing sling.

Clamshell packaging on new gun.

1911BB – BB/4.5mm cal., CO_2, semi-auto, 480 FPS, 4.25 in. precision steel barrel, polymer frame with checkered grips, Picatinny accessory rail, fixed blade front and fixed notch rear sights, Crossbolt safety, 7 in. OAL, approx. 1 lb. New 2013.

courtesy Crosman Corp.

MSR $47	$40	$35	$30	$25	$20	N/A	N/A

TAC1911BB – BB/4.5mm cal., CO_2, semi-auto pistol, 550 FPS, 7.06 in. precision steel barrel, tactical polymer frame with mock compensator, Picatinny accessory rail, Class 2 Laser for fast target acquisition, mag. holds 20 BBs, convenient drop-out magazine for quick reloading, removable checkered grip panel easy replacement of CO_2, fixed blade front and fixed notch rear sights, slide safety, 12.2 in. OAL, 1.1 lbs. New 2013.

MSR $89	$75	$65	$60	$50	$35	N/A	N/A

GI MODEL 1911BBb – BB/4.5mm cal., CO_2, semi-auto blowback action, 450 FPS, 5.5 in. steel barrel, full metal construction, checkered polymer grips, full metal detachable magazine holds 20 BBs, innovative tool built into grip for easy replacement of CO_2, fixed blade front and fixed notch rear sights, slide safety, 8 in. OAL, 1.88 lbs. New 2013.

courtesy Crosman Corp.

MSR $105	$90	$80	$70	$60	$45	N/A	N/A

GRADING	100%	95%	90%	80%	60%	40%	20%

RIFLES

FIRST MODEL RIFLE ("1923 MODEL," HI-POWER, OR PLUNGER MODEL) – .22 cal., rifled barrel, bicycle-style plunger rod pump under the barrel, pneumatic, SS. First variant: peep sight mounted in dovetail slot forward of the pellet loading port of receiver; no elevation adjustment, machined steel receiver, steel compression tube. Second variant: peep sight, adjustable for elevation and windage, mounted on bridge-type bracket behind the pellet loading port, steel barrel and compression tube. Third variant: nickel-plated brass compression tube, die-cast receiver with logo: "Crosman Rochester, N.Y. Pat. April 23-23". Mfg. 1923-24.

courtesy Beeman Collection

	N/A	$1,500	$1,200	$975	$750	$525	$300

Add 50% for first variation.
Add 20% for third variation.
Subtract 50% for any cocking knob other than short knurled type on First, Second, or Third Model Crosman rifles.

Watch for refinished specimens and "made-up specimens" recently assembled from parts, usually combined with non-Crosman, recently made receivers - often with sharp edges and somewhat different shape and material (compare with specimen known to be authentic).

SECOND MODEL RIFLE (FIRST LEVER MODEL - "1924 MODEL") – .22 cal., rifled barrel, the first lever-action pump pneumatic, conspicuous "beer barrel" pump-lever handle protrudes under front of gun, single shot, no variations reported, extremely rare. Mfg. 1923-24.

courtesy Beeman Collection

	N/A	$2,900	$2,325	$1,875	$1,450	$1,025	$575

Sometimes refered to as the "1924 Model" but that can be confusing because production began in 1923 and many, much later, models carry the 1924 patent date - which leads collectors to refer them as 1924 Models.

THIRD MODEL RIFLE (SECOND LEVER MODEL) – .22 cal., rifled barrel, first swinging forearm pump pneumatic, SS, produced by both Crosman Rifle Co. (3-4 employees) and Crosman Arms Co. Rarest of the first three Crosman air rifle models. Mfg. 1924-25.

courtesy Beeman Collection

	N/A	$2,900	$2,325	$1,875	$1,450	$1,025	$575

GRADING	100%	95%	90%	80%	60%	40%	20%

MODEL 1 – .22 cal., swinging forearm pump pneumatic, SS, adj. Williams rear sight, wood stock/forearm, 10 pumps = 635 FPS. First variant: tapered steel barrel housing, mfg. 1981-82. Second variant: straight steel barrel housing, plastic sight sleeve, 5.1 lbs. Mfg. 1982-1985.

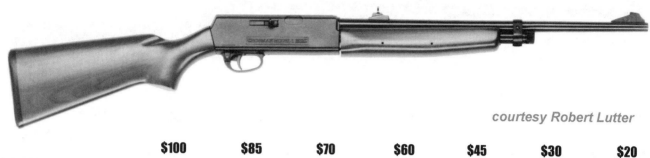

courtesy Robert Lutter

	$100	$85	$70	$60	$45	$30	$20

Subtract 20% for second variant.
Add 20% for factory box.

MODEL 66 POWERMASTER – BB/.175 cal., 18-shot mag. (plus 200 round reservoir) or .177 cal. pellet single shot, swinging forearm pump pneumatic. First variant: with zinc receiver. Mfg. 1983-1988. Second variant: with plastic receiver, 3.9 lbs. Mfg. began in 1988. Disc.

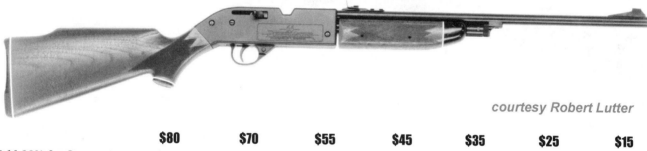

courtesy Robert Lutter

	$80	$70	$55	$45	$35	$25	$15

Add 20% for first variant.
Add 20% for factory box.

* **Model 66RT Powermaster** – similar to Model 66 Powermaster, except has camo stock and forearm. Mfg. 1993-1994.

	$100	$85	$70	$60	$45	$30	$20

* **Model 66BX Powermaster** – BB/.175 cal. 18-shot mag. (plus 200 round reservoir), or .177 cal. five-shot mag. pellet SS, swinging forearm pump pneumatic, bolt action, 680 FPS (BB), 645 FPS (pellet), 20.5 in. rifled steel barrel, black finish, brown checkered synthetic stock and forearm, fiber optic front and adj. rear sights, 2.9 lbs. Disc. 2005.

	$55	$45	$40	$30	$25	$15	$10

Last MSR was $63.

MODEL 66 POWERMASTER KIT – BB/.177 cal. or .177 cal. pellet, BA, short stroke high compression multi-stroke pump pneumatic, reservoir holds up to 200 BBs or use the 5-shot clip for pellets, 680/640 FPS, steel barrel, black synthetic frame, 18 shot mag., fiber optic front and fully adj. rear sights, Dovetail mounting rail, Crossbolt safety, includes 4x15mm scope, shooting glasses, 100 BBs, 100 pellets, and 5 paper targets, 37.5 in. OAL, 3.68 lbs. New 2012.

courtesy Crosman Corp.

MSR $59	$50	$45	$40	$35	$25	N/A	N/A

GRADING	100%	95%	90%	80%	60%	40%	20%

MODEL 70 – .177 cal., pellet, CO_2, BA, copy of Winchester Model 70, 650 FPS, full wood stock and forearm, 41 in. OAL, 5.8 lbs. Mfg. 1973-1980.

courtesy Howard Collection

	$120	$100	$85	$70	$55	$35	$25

Last MSR was $49.

Add 200%-300% for factory gold plating or Boy Scout versions. Add 300%-400% for factory walnut stock.

MODEL 73 SADDLE PAL – .175/BB cal., 16-shot repeater or .177 cal. pellet SS; CO_2, one cylinder, plastic stock, Winchester style lever, 3.2 lbs. First variant: Mfg. 1976-1977. Second variant: Mfg. 1977-1983.

courtesy Robert Lutter

	$50	$45	$35	$30	$25	$15	$10

Add 10% for factory box.

MODEL 84 CHALLENGER – .177 cal., CO_2, match rifle, 720 FPS, fully adj. sights, walnut stock, adj. cheek piece and buttplate, every Model 84 was "individually hand produced by Crosman model shop," not a "real production gun," 11 lbs. Mfg. 1985-1992.

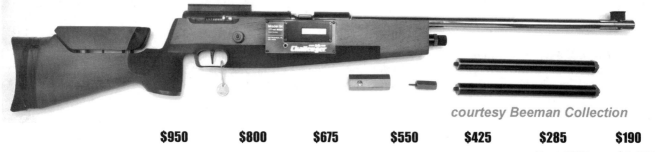

courtesy Beeman Collection

	$950	$800	$675	$550	$425	$285	$190

Last MSR was $1,295.

The Crosman Model 84 was the first U.S.-made air rifle designed to compete with established European models. Unlike its competitors, it is CO_2, with a digital gauge mounted on the forearm to show remaining pressure. Electronic trigger was a factory option.

MODEL 99 – .22 cal., CO_2, one cylinder, dual power selection, lever action, resembles Savage lever action big game rifle, 5.8 lbs. Mfg. 1965-1970.

courtesy Robert Lutter

	$140	$120	$100	$80	$65	$40	$30

Add 20% for factory box.

GRADING	100%	95%	90%	80%	60%	40%	20%

MODEL 100 – .177 cal. version of Model 101 (see Model 101). Mfg. 1940-1950.

courtesy Robert Lutter

N/A	$325	$260	$210	$160	$115	$65

The Barrel Problem: Some variations have brass barrels and brass body tubes, some have steel barrels with brass tubes, and in others both are steel. Dean Fletcher reports that from about 1925 to early 1927, barrels were rifled steel, probably made by nearby Remington Arms. From about 1927 to 1946, barrels were all bronze. From 1946 to 1947, barrels were either bronze or steel and in 1948 they were all bronze. Crosman preferred bronze for ease of tooling and because condensation which resulted from adiabatic cooling of discharge did not so easily corrode bronze.

MODEL 100 "CG" – .177 cal. version of Model 101 "CG" (see Model 101 "CG").

MODEL 101 ("1926 MODEL", SILENT .22 RIFLE) – .22 cal., pneumatic pump, SS, die-cast receiver with logo, pat. Oct. 28, 1924 Crosman Arms Co. Rochester, N.Y. This has been the standard Crosman air rifle for over 25 years. No model number markings, but may show serial numbers, numerous part variations are known: curved vs. straight bolt handles, short vs. medium knurled edge cocking knobs, round stamped aperture discs vs. hexagonal machined discs, various valve details, etc. For identifying post-WWII models see Fletcher's *The Crosman Arms Library*, Vol. 2 - Crosman Arms Model 101 & 121-GC Engineering Parts Drawings. Mfg. 1925-1950+.

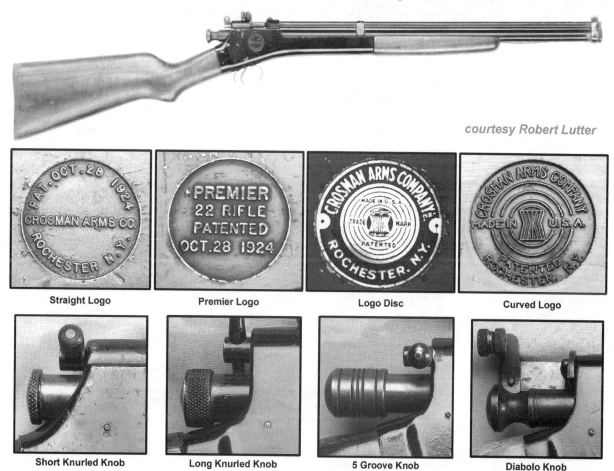

courtesy Robert Lutter

Straight Logo	Premier Logo	Logo Disc	Curved Logo
Short Knurled Knob	**Long Knurled Knob**	**5 Groove Knob**	**Diabolo Knob**

The Barrel Problem: Some variations have brass barrels and brass body tubes, some have steel barrels with brass tubes, and in others both are steel. Dean Fletcher reports that from about 1925 to early 1927, barrels were rifled steel, probably made by nearby Remington Arms. From about 1927 to 1946 barrels were all bronze. From 1946 to 1947 barrels were either bronze or steel and in 1948 they were all bronze. Crosman preferred bronze for ease of tooling and because condensation which resulted from adiabatic cooling of discharge did not so easily corrode bronze.

GRADING	100%	95%	90%	80%	60%	40%	20%

* **Model 101 Period One "Crosman Pneumatic Rifle"** – .22 cal. All variations: receiver area where barrel enters is octagonal, walnut stock and forearm, knurled cocking knob, rare in excellent condition. Mfg. late 1925-1929.

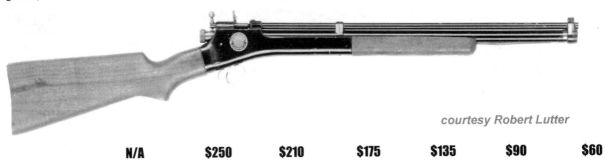

courtesy Robert Lutter

	N/A	$250	$210	$175	$135	$90	$60

Add 50% for original factory box.
Add 10% for high-comb stock or original checkering.
Add 20% for Model 100.

1925-1926 - production models have un-flared trigger and "Famous American manufactured" (Remington?) steel barrel. Circular logo cast into right side of receiver: "PAT. OCT. 28 1924, CROSMAN ARMS CO. ROCHESTER N.Y."

1927-1929 - production models have flared trigger, Crosman manufactured bronze barrel, long (1/2 inch) knurled cocking knobs. Disc logo version: on a stamped metal plate impressed into side of receiver - "CROSMAN ARMS COMPANY MADE IN U.S.A. TRADE (PELLET) MARK PATENTED ROCHESTER N.Y."

Note: the presence of a "diabolo pellet" cocking knob is an anomaly. "Diabolo pellet" cocking knobs are for the 121 "CG" series gas rifles (p/n. 121-15) only. However, the presence of this improved cocking knob enhances the look and functionality and, therefore, does not detract from value.

* **Model 101 Premier Brand Version** – logo cast on receiver reads: "PREMIER 22 RIFLE PATENTED OCT 28. 1924". Also known from specimens bearing a lettered disc (probably 1927-29). Not marked Crosman anywhere. Rare.

	N/A	$255	$210	$175	$135	$90	$60

Add 50% for original factory box.
Add 20% for Model 100.
Add 10% for high-comb stock or original checkering.

* **Model 101 Period Two "Crosman Silent Rifle"** – .22 cal. All variations: Receiver area is round where barrel enters, walnut stock, long knurled cocking knob, hexagonal rear sight disc., decal applied to forearm. Mfg. 1930-1940.

	N/A	$190	$160	$130	$100	$65	$45

Add 50% for original factory box.
Add 20% for Model 100.
Add 10% for high-comb stock or original checkering.

Note: the presence of a "diabolo pellet" cocking knob is an anomaly. "Diabolo pellet" cocking knobs are for the 121 "CG" series gas rifles (p/n. 121-15) only. However, the presence of this improved cocking knob enhances the look and functionality and, therefore, does not detract from value.

» **Model 101 Period Two "Crosman Silent Rifle" Clickless Variant** – "clickless" (hard rubber) forearm. Mfg. 1938-1939.

	N/A	$160	$135	$110	$85	$55	$40

Add 50% for original factory box.
Add 20% for Model 100.
Add 10% for high-comb stock or original checkering.

* **Model 101 Period Three** – .22 cal., all models: five-ring cocking knob, hardwood stock and forearm. Mfg. post-WWII (1946-1950+).

courtesy Robert Lutter

	N/A	$130	$105	$85	$70	$45	$30

GRADING	100%	95%	90%	80%	60%	40%	20%

Add 50% for original factory box.
Add 20% for Model 100.
Add 10-15% for high-comb, original checkering, or walnut stock.
Extreme scarcity precludes accurate pricing on this model.

Note: the presence of a "diabolo pellet" cocking knob is an anomaly. "Diabolo pellet" cocking knobs are for the 121 "CG" series gas rifles (p/n. 121-15) only. However, the presence of this improved cocking knob enhances the look and functionality and, therefore, does not detract from value.

»**Model 101 Period Three 1949 Variant** – knurled rear sight, large adjustment knob (same as on Model 107/108).

	N/A	$150	$125	$100	$80	$50	$35

Add 50% for original factory box.
Add 20% for Model 100.
Add 10-15% for high-comb, original checkering, or walnut stock.

»**Model 101 Period Three Sears Variant** – black crinkle finish paint, mfg. 1949-1950 and for some time beyond 1950.

	N/A	$155	$125	$105	$80	$55	$35

Add 50% for original factory box.
Add 20% for Model 100.
Add 10-15% for high-comb, original checkering, or walnut stock.

* *Model 101 "CG" Variation* – .22 cal., CO_2, 4.5 oz. cylinder vertically attached to gun, same rear sight assembly as found on standard Model 101, sold to public, circa 1948-1949, but only through Crosman authorized (ASA) shooting clubs.

	N/A	$350	$280	$230	$175	$125	$70

Subtract $75 for no CO_2 cylinder.

MODEL 102 – .22 cal., pump-lever pneumatic, ten-round mag., no model number markings, some specimens have pellet logo, others are plain, side of receiver may or may not be marked with "Crosman 22/Patented Oct. 28, 1924/ Other patents pending", early versions sometimes have simple checkering on forearm (mfg. 1929-1950) 1929-1940 models are distinguished by knurled cocking knob and walnut stocks, 1945-1950 models have a five-ring cocking knob. Clickless variant: "clickless" hard rubber forearm, mfg. only 1938-39. Mfg. 1929-1950.

courtesy Robert Lutter

	N/A	$250	$200	$165	$125	$90	$50

Add 20% for clickless variant.
Add 60% for original factory box.
Subtract 25% for 1945-1950 mfg.

* *Model 102 "OSS" Variant* – .22 cal., 15-shot pump pneumatic repeater for lead balls, round hole loading port, produced during WWII for the U.S. Office of Special Services.

Scarcity precludes accurate pricing.

Crosman states 2,000 were delivered. An invoice for 1,000 is known from contract #623. 957 specimens were inventoried in a U.S. government warehouse in Calcutta in January of 1945.

* *Model 102 "CG" Variant* – .22 cal., CO_2, ten-round magazine repeater, 4.5 oz. cylinder 47.5 degree or vertically attached to gun.

	N/A	$450	$350	$295	$225	$160	$90

GRADING	100%	95%	90%	80%	60%	40%	20%

MODEL 104 – .177 cal., pump-lever pneumatic, ten-shot mag., similar to Model 102, except for caliber. Mfg. 1949 only.

courtesy Robert Lutter

	N/A	$250	$200	$165	$125	$90	$50

Add 60% for original factory box.

* **Model 102 "Camp Perry" Variant** – .22 cal., first American CO_2 guns, introduced at 1931 Camp Perry matches. Commonly referred to as "hose guns," since CO_2 is supplied via a hose connected to a central cylinder. Sold only as part of shooting gallery.

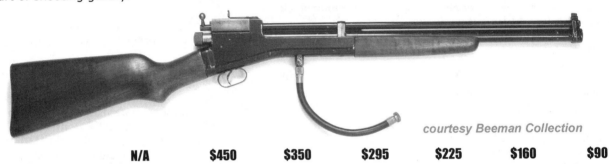

courtesy Beeman Collection

	N/A	$450	$350	$295	$225	$160	$90

MODEL 107 (TOWN & COUNTRY) – .177 cal., pump-lever pneumatic, SS, micro-precision rifling, heavy all wood stock/forearm, instant selection of front sights, 37.8 in. OAL, massive, extremely well built, 6.1 lbs. Mfg. 1949.

courtesy Robert Lutter

	N/A	$1,000	$800	$650	$500	$350	$200

Add 50% for original factory box.

MODEL 108 (TOWN & COUNTRY) – .22 cal., similar to Model 107. Mfg. 1949.

	N/A	$500	$400	$325	$250	$175	$100

Add 50% for original factory box.

MODEL 109 (TOWN & COUNTRY JR.) – .177 cal., pneumatic pump, SS. Mfg. 1949-1951.

courtesy Robert Lutter

	N/A	$195	$165	$120	$95	$60	$45

Add 40% for original factory box.

GRADING	100%	95%	90%	80%	60%	40%	20%

MODEL 110 (TOWN & COUNTRY JR.) – .22 cal., similar to Model 109. Mfg. 1949-1951.

	N/A	$160	$130	$105	$80	$55	$30

Add 40% for original factory box.

MODEL 113 – .177 cal., CO_2, 10 oz. charged from separate cylinder, SS, early Models 113 and 114 with fat, straight-line stock, later models with tapered, thin stock. Mfg. 1950-1955.

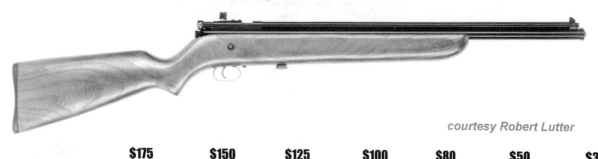

courtesy Robert Lutter

	$175	$150	$125	$100	$80	$50	$35

Add 30% for original CO_2 cylinder.
Add 20% for straight-line stock.
Add 60% for original factory box.

MODEL 114 – .22 cal., CO_2, 10 oz. separate cylinder, SS. Mfg. 1950-1955.

	$175	$150	$125	$100	$80	$50	$35

Add 15% for brass barrel.
Add 20% for straight-line stock.
Add 75% for early production with Crosman Arms logo buttplate as on Models 107-108.
Add 30% for original CO_2 cylinder.
Add 60% for original factory box.

MODEL 117 (SHOOT-A-SCORE) – .21 cal., CO_2, magazine repeater, 19 in. barrel, hose for connecting to central gas cylinder, one piece wood stock similar to Model 118, counter security chain attached at muzzle, 36 in. OAL. Mfg. 1947-1955.

Extreme scarcity precludes accurate pricing on this model.

MODEL 118 – .22 cal., CO_2, 10 oz. separate cylinder, magazine repeater. Mfg. 1952-1954.

courtesy Robert Lutter

	N/A	$450	$350	$295	$225	$160	$90

Add 60% for original factory box.
Subtract $50 for no CO_2 tank.

This magazine repeater is an adaptation of the Girardoni repeating airgun mechanism of 1780.

MODEL 120 – .22 cal., pneumatic pump, SS. Variant one: brass early. Variant two: steel. Mfg. 1952-1954.

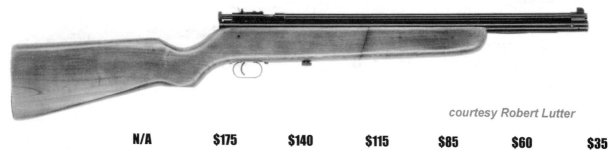

courtesy Robert Lutter

	N/A	$175	$140	$115	$85	$60	$35

Add 20% for variant one.
Add 10% for original white bead sight.
Add 30% for original factory box.

GRADING	100%	95%	90%	80%	60%	40%	20%

MODEL 121 "CG" (GALLERY RIFLES) – .210 cal., CO_2, repeater, 4.5 oz. cylinder, vertically attached to gun, adj. peep sight. Mfg. 1946-49.

courtesy Robert Lutter

	N/A	$500	$400	$325	$250	$175	$100

Subtract 20%-30% if missing CO_2 cylinder.

Add 10%-15% for Slant-cylinder variant, a small fitting added (circa 1949) to "CG" models to improve position of CO_2 cylinder.

Sold to commercial shooting galleries, shooting clubs, hospitals, and industrial companies for employee recreation. Ergonomic variations: various factory-added modifications intended to ease pellet loading, bolt operation, and cocking. Presumably intended for use by VA hospitals and others for rehabilitation. The complex of CG guns still needs study.

Note: .21 caliber intended to restrict supply of pellets to Crosman brand only. Original Crosman .210 pellet container, and some other sources, refer to this model as the Crosman Gas Carbine, Model 200.

MODEL 122 "CG" – .22 cal., CO_2, SS, 4.5 oz. cylinder vertically or 47.5 degree angle attached to gun, adj. peep sights.

	N/A	$450	$350	$295	$225	$160	$90

Subtract 20%-30% if missing CO_2 cylinder.

Add 10%-15% for Slant-cylinder variant, a small fitting added (circa 1949) to "CG" models to improve position of CO_2 cylinder.

MODEL 123 (100 CG, SHOOT-A-SCORE) – .177 cal., CO_2, SS, 4.5 oz. cylinder with 47.5 degree angle from stock, SS. Mfg. 1946-1950.

courtesy Beeman Collection

	N/A	$425	$350	$275	$210	$150	$85

Subtract 20%-30% if missing CO_2 cylinder.

MODEL 125 RAWHIDE – BB/.175 cal., single stroke swinging forearm pump pneumatic, repeater with thirty-five-shot magazine, 300 FPS, Crosman's first BB rifle and first single stroke pump pneumatic, 5 lbs. Mfg. 1973-1974. Recalled by factory.

courtesy Robert Lutter

$165	$140	$115	$95	$75	$50	$35

Add 20% for factory box.

GRADING	100%	95%	90%	80%	60%	40%	20%

MODEL 140 – .22 cal., pneumatic pump, swinging forearm, single shot, 4.8 lbs. First variant: spoon handle breech cover, aluminum breech, fingertip recocking, mfg. 1954. Second variant: spoon handle breech cover, aluminum breech, auto recocking, mfg. 1955-1957. Third variant: with automatic cocking, without spoon handle breech cover, steel breech. Mfg. 1956-1962. Fourth variant: die-cast trigger housing, mfg. 1961-1968.

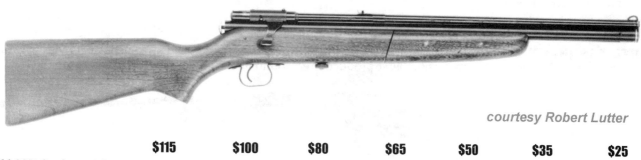

courtesy Robert Lutter

$115	$100	$80	$65	$50	$35	$25

Add 20% for first variant.
Add 20% for third variant.
Add 20% for factory box.

MODEL 147 – .177 cal., similar to Model 140. First variant: with spoon handle breech cover and aluminum breech, and auto recocking, mfg. 1955-1956. Second variant: with steel breech and without spoon handle breech cover, mfg. 1956-1962.

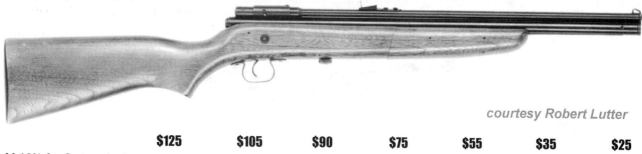

courtesy Robert Lutter

$125	$105	$90	$75	$55	$35	$25

Add 10% for first variant.
Add 20% for factory box.

MODEL 147 BP – BB/.175 cal. or .177 cal. pellet version of Model 147, has magnetic bolt tip for steel BBs, rifled barrel. Mfg. 1964-1966.

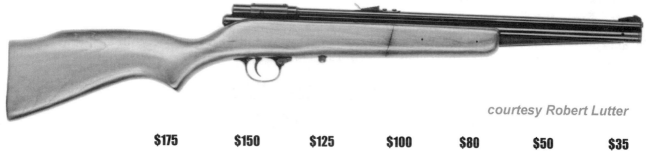

courtesy Robert Lutter

$175	$150	$125	$100	$80	$50	$35

Add 20% for factory box.

MODEL 160 – .22 cal., CO_2, two cylinders, BA, SS, steel or die cast automatic safety, full wood stock. First variant: steel automatic safety, without barrel band, mfg. 1955-1956. Second variant: barrel band, Model 360 peep sight, mfg. 1956-1959. Third variant: die cast trigger housing, Model S331 peep sight. Mfg. 1960-1971.

courtesy Robert Lutter

$225	$190	$160	$130	$100	$65	$45

GRADING	100%	95%	90%	80%	60%	40%	20%

Add 20% for Model 360 peep sight.
Add 30% for Model S331 peep sight.
Add 50% for Ted Williams version.
Add 40% for "Military" version with leather military sling (Model 160SP) or web sling and S331 peep sight.
Add 20% for factory box.
Add 20% for adj. trigger.

See Fletcher's (1998) book, *The Crosman Arms Model 160*, a must-have reference.

MODEL 166 (HAHN SUPER BB REPEATER) – BB/.175 cal., CO_2, one cylinder, Winchester-style lever action repeater, spring-fed thirty-shot magazine. First product of P.Y. Hahn Mfg. Co., Fairport, NY. Mfg. 1958-1971.

courtesy Robert Lutter

| | $125 | $105 | $90 | $75 | $55 | $35 | $25 |

Add 20% for factory box.

MODEL 167 – .177 cal., similar to Model 160. First variant: with steel or die cast automatic safety and without barrel band, mfg. 1956. Second variant: with barrel band and Model 360 peep sight, mfg. 1956-1959. Third variant: with die-cast trigger housing and Model S331 peep sight. Mfg. 1960-1966.

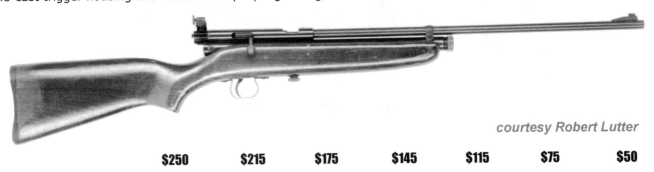

courtesy Robert Lutter

| | $250 | $215 | $175 | $145 | $115 | $75 | $50 |

Add 20% for Model 360 peep sight.
Add 40% for Model S331 peep sight.
Add 20% for adj. trigger.
Add 20% for factory box.

MODEL 180 – .22 cal., CO_2, one cylinder, BA, SS, full wood stock, 4 lbs. First variant: cross bolt safety, mfg. 1956-1959. Second variant: die-cast trigger housing. Mfg. 1962-1967.

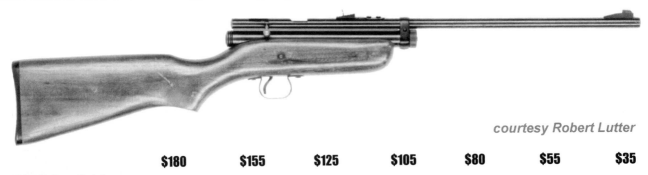

courtesy Robert Lutter

| | $180 | $155 | $125 | $105 | $80 | $55 | $35 |

Add 20% for adj. trigger.
Add 20% for factory box.
Add 50% for Sears variant.

GRADING	100%	95%	90%	80%	60%	40%	20%

MODEL 187 – .177 cal., similar to Model 180. First variant: has cross bolt safety. Mfg. 1956-1962. Second variant: with die-cast trigger housing. Mfg. 1962-1966.

courtesy Robert Lutter

	$145	$125	$100	$85	$65	$45	$30

Add 20% for adj. trigger.
Add 20% for factory box.
Add 50% for Sears variant.

MODEL 197 – 10 oz., CO_2 cylinder (not a gun). Excellent condition = $50 (caution: do not charge original cylinders, for firing use modern steel or aluminum cylinders only). Mfg. 1950-1970.

MODEL 200 – see Model 121 "CG."

MODEL 262 – .177 cal., CO_2, one cylinder, bolt action, SS, 38.25 in. OAL, 625 FPS, 4.8 lbs. Mfg. 1991-1993.

	$90	$75	$65	$50	$40	$25	$20

Add 10% for factory box.

* ***Model 262Y*** – youth version of Model 262, 33.75 in. OAL, 610 FPS, 4.7 lbs. Mfg. 1991-1993.

	$90	$75	$65	$50	$40	$25	$20

Add 10% for factory box.

MODEL 400 – .22 cal., CO_2, two cylinder, spring-fed, "swing feed" ten-round mag., full wood stock. First variant: cross bolt safety. Mfg. 1957-1962. Second variant: die-cast trigger housing. Mfg. 1962-1964.

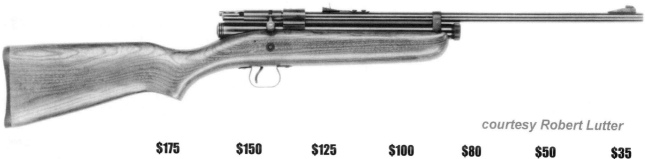

courtesy Robert Lutter

	$175	$150	$125	$100	$80	$50	$35

Add 20% for adj. trigger.
Add 20% for factory box.
Add 50% for Sears variant.

MODEL 500 POWERMATIC – BB/.175 cal., CO_2, one cylinder, semi-auto 50-shot, 350 FPS. Mfg. 1970-1979.

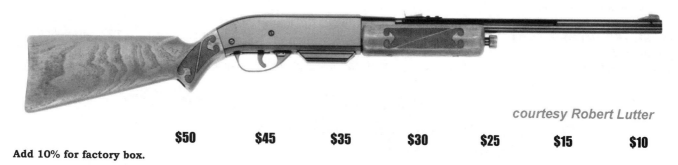

courtesy Robert Lutter

	$50	$45	$35	$30	$25	$15	$10

Add 10% for factory box.

GRADING	100%	95%	90%	80%	60%	40%	20%

MODEL 622 PELL-CLIP REPEATER – .22 cal., CO_2, one cylinder, slide action forearm, removable rotating six-shot clip, 450 FPS. Mfg. 1971-1978.

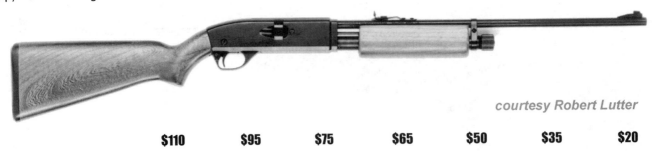

courtesy Robert Lutter

	$110	$95	$75	$65	$50	$35	$20

Add 20% for factory box.

Extended gas tube is an aftermarket addition, not factory original.

MODEL 664X – BB/.175 cal. 18-shot mag. (plus 200 round reservoir) or .177 cal. five-shot mag. pellet single shot, swinging forearm pump pneumatic, bolt action, 680 FPS (BB), 645 FPS (pellet), 20.5 in. rifled steel barrel, black finish, brown checkered synthetic stock and forearm, fiber optic front and adj. rear sights, four-power scope (M-0410) included, 2.9 lbs. Disc. 2004.

	$50	$45	$35	$30	$25	$15	$10

Last MSR was $60.

* **Model 664GT** – similar to Model 664X, except has black stock and forearm and gold accents. Mfg. 1997-2003.

	$65	$55	$45	$40	$30	$20	$15

* **Model 664SB** – similar to Model 664X, except has silver barrel and 4x15mm silver scope. Mfg. 1994-2009.

	$90	$75	$65	$50	$40	$25	$20

Last MSR was $106.

MODEL RM650 BB SCOUT – .177 cal., LA, SP, SS, smooth bore steel barrel, 300 FPS, black finish, checkered hardwood stock and forearm, 2.8 lbs. Mfg. 2002-2003.

	$40	$35	$30	$25	$20	$10	N/A

MODEL 700 – .22 cal., CO_2, one cylinder, SS, rotary tap loading. Mfg. 1967-1971.

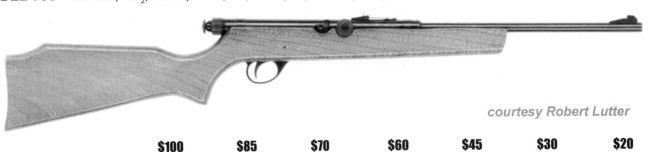

courtesy Robert Lutter

	$100	$85	$70	$60	$45	$30	$20

Add 20% for factory box.
Add 100% for Model S331 peep sight.

MODEL 707 – .177 cal., similar to Model 700. Mfg. 1967-1971.

	$140	$120	$100	$80	$65	$40	$30

Add 20% for factory box.
Add 100% for Model S331 peep sight.

MODEL 760 POWERMASTER – BB/.175 cal. repeater (180-shot gravity-fed magazine) and .177 cal. pellet SS, 10 pumps = 595 FPS (BB), BA, PP, 17 in. smoothbore steel BBL. First variant: wooden stock and forearm. Mfg. 1966-1970. Second variant: styrene stock/forearm, scope mount grooves. Mfg. 1971-1974. Third variant: self-cocking,

courtesy Robert Lutter

GRADING	100%	95%	90%	80%	60%	40%	20%

styrene stock, wood forearm. Mfg. 1974-1975. Fourth variant: ABS stock and forearm. Mfg. 1975-1977. Fifth variant: manual cocking. Mfg. 1977-1980. Sixth variant: plastic bolt. Mfg. 1980-1983. Seventh variant: plastic receiver, welded sights. Mfg. 1983-1991. Eighth variant: shortened barrel, pressed on sights. Mfg. began in 1991. Disc.

	100%	95%	90%	80%	60%	40%	20%
	$30	$25	$20	$15	$15	N/A	N/A

Subtract 10% for smoothbore (prior to 1981).
Add 300% for first variant.
Add 25% for factory scope.
Add 25% for wood stock (except first variant).
Add 5% for factory box.

The first short-stroke pump pneumatic, developed in Canada as "Canadian Boy" from Model 130 pistol covered later as Model Canadian Boy.

* **Model 760/20 (Model 760 20th Year Commemorative)** – BB/.175 cal. repeater or .177 cal. pellet single-shot pneumatic, similar to Model 760. Mfg. 1985.

courtesy Robert Lutter

	100%	95%	90%	80%	60%	40%	20%
	$65	$55	$45	$40	$30	$20	$15

Variation: Model 760/20-999. Special presentation commemoratives; individually engraved name plates and wall plaques. Special order by Crosman sales rep for key buyers and senior staff. Designed as a wall-mounted item, generally not used. Will bring a premium.

* **Model 760XL Powermaster** – BB/.175 cal. repeater or .177 cal., deluxe version of Model 760, brass-plated receiver, hooded front sight. Mfg. 1978-1980.

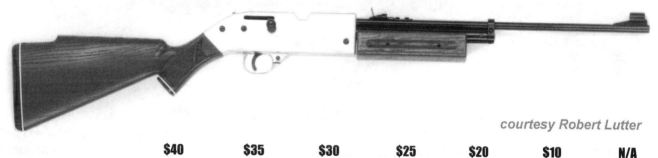

courtesy Robert Lutter

	100%	95%	90%	80%	60%	40%	20%
	$40	$35	$30	$25	$20	$10	N/A

MODEL 760AB PUMPMASTER – BB/.175 cal. repeater or .177 cal. SS pellet, pneumatic, similar to Model 760 with black stock and forearm. Mfg. began in 1997. Disc.

	100%	95%	90%	80%	60%	40%	20%
	$40	$35	$30	$25	$20	$10	N/A

* **Model 760B Pumpmaster** – BB/.177 cal. 18-shot mag. or .177 cal. 5-shot mag. pellet, multi-pump pneumatic, BA, 17 in. smooth bore steel barrel, 645/615 FPS, black finish, brown synthetic stock and forearm, fiber optic front and adj. rear sights, includes 5-shot Firepow'r pellet clip (new 2014), 33.5 in. OAL, 2.75 lbs. Mfg. 1997-present.

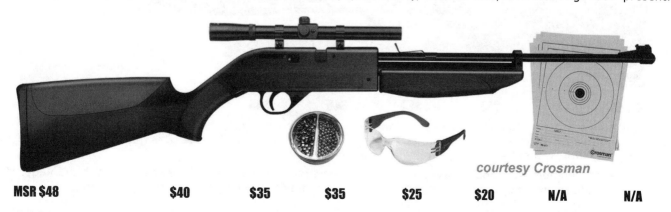

courtesy Crosman

	100%	95%	90%	80%	60%	40%	20%
MSR $48	$40	$35	$35	$25	$20	N/A	N/A

GRADING	100%	95%	90%	80%	60%	40%	20%

Add $190 for Pumpmaster Kit (Model 760BKT) which includes 4x15mm scope, 100 premium Copperhead BBs, 100 pellets, shooting glasses and 5 paper targets (new 2012).

In 2011, the Pumpmaster 760 underwent improvements in body styling and performance, including improved texture on forearm, checkering to the grip, and an ergonomically-styled cheek piece. This new design will also reduce the pumping effort without sacrificing performance or velocity.

In 2014, the Pumpmaster 760 received a state-of-the-art makeover while still staying true to its heritage. New features include sleek, integrated stock design, repositioned, gravity-fed BB port, and elongated forearm.

* **Model 760BRD Pumpmaster** – BB/.175 cal. 18-shot mag. or .177 cal. five-shot mag. pellet, similar to Model 760B, except includes red dot sight. Disc. 2005.

courtesy Crosman Corp.

$55	$45	$40	$30	$25	$15	$10

Last MSR was $62.

* **Model 760SK Pumpmaster Starter Kit** – BB/.177 cal. 18-shot mag. or .177 cal. five-shot mag. pellet, Model 760SK kit includes 100 Premium Copperhead BBs, 100 pellets, red dot sight, shooting glasses and five NRA targets. Disc. 2011.

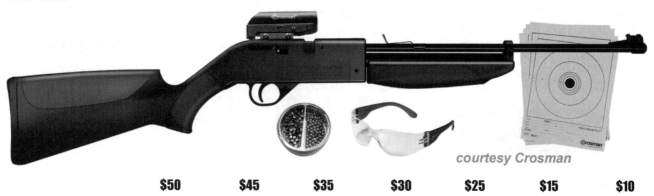

courtesy Crosman

$50	$45	$35	$30	$25	$15	$10

Last MSR was $60.

* **Model 760X Pumpmaster** – BB/.177 cal. 18-shot mag. or .177 cal. 5-shot mag. pellet, multi-pump pneumatic, BA, 17 in. smooth bore steel barrel, 645/615 FPS, black finish, brown synthetic stock and forearm, fiber optic front and adj. rear sights, 4x15mm scope, 33.5 in. OAL, 2.75 lbs. Mfg. 1997-present.

courtesy Crosman Corp.

MSR $64	$55	$50	$45	$35	$25	N/A	N/A

In 2011, the Pumpmaster 760 underwent improvements in body styling and performance, including improved texture on forearm, checkering to the grip, and an ergonomically-styled cheek piece. This new design will also reduce the pumping effort without sacrificing performance or velocity.

In 2014, the Pumpmaster 760 received a state-of-the-art makeover while still staying true to its heritage. New features include sleek, integrated stock design, repositioned, gravity-fed BB port, and elongated forearm.

GRADING	100%	95%	90%	80%	60%	40%	20%

* ***Model 760P Pumpmaster (Classic Pink)*** – BB/.177 cal. 18-shot mag. or .177 cal. 5-shot mag. pellet, multi-pump pneumatic, BA, 17 in. smooth bore steel barrel, 645/615 FPS, black finish, Pink or Granite Pink (New 2014) synthetic stock and forearm, fiber optic front and adj. rear sights. 33.5 in. OAL, 2.75 lbs. Mfg. 2007-present.

courtesy Crosman Corp.

MSR $50	$45	$40	$35	$30	$20	N/A	N/A

Add $19 for Pumpmaster kit that includes 4x15mm scope, 100 premium Copperhead BBs, 100 pellets, shooting glasses and 5 paper targets (Model 760PKT, new 2011).

Add $16 for Starter Kit that includes 100 premium Copperhead BBs, 100 pellets, red dot sight, shooting glasses and 5 paper targets (Model 760PSK, mfg. 2007-2011).

In 2011, the Pumpmaster 760 underwent improvements in body styling and performance, including improved texture on forearm, checkering to the grip, and an ergonomically-styled cheek piece. This new design will also reduce the pumping effort without sacrificing performance or velocity.

In 2014, the Pumpmaster 760 received a state-of-the-art makeover while still staying true to its heritage. New features include sleek, integrated stock design, repositioned, gravity-fed BB port, elongated forearm, and Granite Pink finish on stock and forearm.

MODEL 760 40TH ANNIVERSARY EDITION – .177 cal., deluxe version of Model 760, nickel-plated receiver, hooded front sight, hardwood stock and forearm, option for laser engraved name or message on receiver, 1,500 mfg. in 2006.

	$65	$55	$45	$40	$30	$20	$15

MODEL 760XLS – BB/.175 or .177 pellet cal., SS, multi-stroke pump pneumatic, adj. fiber optic sights, hardwood stock and forearm, rifled steel BBL, approx. 600 FPS, 33.5 in. OAL, 3.69 lbs. Mfg. 2007-2009.

	$85	$70	$60	$50	$40	$25	$15

Last MSR was $100.

MODEL 761XL – BB/.175 cal. repeater or .177 cal., deluxe version of Model 760, brass-plated receiver, hooded front sight, wood stock. First variant: mfg. 1972-1978. Second variant: manual cocking. Mfg. 1978-1981.

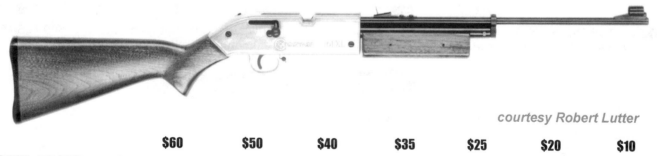

courtesy Robert Lutter

	$60	$50	$40	$35	$25	$20	$10

MODEL 764SB – BB/.177 cal. repeater or .177 cal. SS pellet, pneumatic, similar to Model 760B Pumpmaster with silver BBL, black stock and forearm, and 4x15mm scope. Mfg. 1994-present.

courtesy Crosman

MSR $78	$65	$60	$55	$45	$35	N/A	N/A

GRADING	100%	95%	90%	80%	60%	40%	20%

MODEL 766 AMERICAN CLASSIC – BB/.175 cal. repeater or .177 cal. pellet SS, multi-stroke pump pneumatic, 10 pumps = 710 FPS (BB), modeled after Remington autoloader firearm. First variant: tapered plastic BBL housing. Mfg. 1975-1981. Second variant: tapered steel barrel housing. Mfg. 1977-1983. Third variant: straight steel barrel housing. Mfg. 1981-1982.

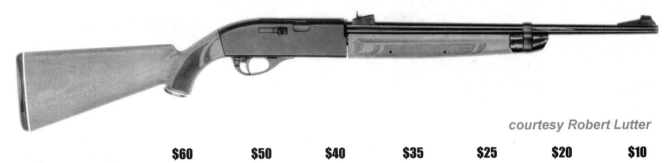

courtesy Robert Lutter

	$60	$50	$40	$35	$25	$20	$10

Add 10% for first variant.
Add 15% for second variant.
Add 10% for original box.
Add 50% for wood stock (pre-1983).

MODEL 781 – BB/.175 cal. repeater or .177 cal. pellet SS, single pump pneumatic, smoothbore, 450 FPS (BB), four-shot clip, 195 round reservoir, 2.9 lbs. Mfg. 1983-1995.

	$40	$35	$30	$25	$20	$10	N/A

* **Model 781AK Action Kit** – kit includes Model 7781 rifle, adj. 4x15mm scope, 250-count .177 cal. pellets, 350 BBs, five NRA targets, and shooting glasses. Mfg. 2002-2007.

	$75	$65	$55	$45	$35	$20	$15

Last MSR was $95.

* **Model 7781** – similar to Model 781, except has black stock and forearm. Mfg. 2002-2009.

	$65	$55	$45	$40	$30	$20	$15

Last MSR was $74.

MODEL 782 BLACK DIAMOND – BB/.175 cal. repeater or .177 cal. pellet SS, CO_2, one cylinder, five-shot mag. Mfg. began in 1990. Disc.

	$25	$20	$20	$15	$10	N/A	N/A

* **Model 782B** – .177 cal., CO_2, similar to Model 782 Black Diamond. Disc. 2002.

	$55	$45	$40	$30	$25	$15	$10

MODEL 788 BB SCOUT – BB/.175 cal., multi-pump pneumatic, gravity-fed 20-shot mag., 2.5 lbs., 500 FPS (BB). First variant: short pump stroke. Mfg. 1978-1979. Second variant: long pump stroke. Mfg. 1979-1990.

courtesy Robert Lutter

	$45	$40	$30	$25	$20	$15	N/A

Add 20% for short stroke variant.
Add 10% for factory box.

* **Model Black Fire** – variation of Model 788, black stock/forearm. Mfg. 1996-1997.

	$50	$45	$35	$30	$25	$15	$10

Add 20% for short stroke variant.
Add 10% for factory box.

MODEL 790 OUTBACKER – BB/.175 cal. repeater or .177 cal. pellet, single pump pneumatic, five-shot pellet mag., plastic stock with hidden canteen, 450 FPS (BB), 2.8 lbs. Mfg. 1990-1991.

	$60	$50	$40	$35	$25	$20	$10

Subtract 25% for missing canteen.

GRADING	100%	95%	90%	80%	60%	40%	20%

MODEL 795 SPRINGMASTER – .177 cal., BBC, SP, SS, 500 FPS, rifled steel barrel, hooded front adj. rear sights, black finish, checkered synthetic stock. Mfg. 1995-1997.

courtesy Crosman

	$75	$65	$55	$45	$35	$20	$15

* *Model 795 Springmaster* – .177 cal., similar to Model 795 Springmaster, except 600 FPS. Mfg. 1997-2007.

	$65	$55	$45	$40	$30	$20	$15

Last MSR was $80.

MODEL 1077 REPEATAIR – .177 cal. pellet, CO_2, one cylinder, 12-shot mag. repeater, semi-auto, 20.4 in. rifled steel barrel, 625 FPS, black finish, checkered black synthetic stock, fiber optic front and adj. rear sights, 36.8 in. OAL, 3.7 lbs. New 1994.

courtesy Crosman

MSR $97	$80	$75	$65	$55	$40	N/A	N/A

Add $45 for Pro Plinker Kit (Model Propick004) which includes CenterPoint red laser, 25 CO_2 cartridges, 1,250 pellets, three extra ammo clips, and Crosman official targets.

* *Model 1077CA Constant Air* – similar to Model 1077 RepeatAir, except bulk fill cylinder kit. Mfg. 1995.

	$180	$155	$125	$105	$80	$55	$35

* *Model 1077LB RepeatAir* – similar to Model 1077 RepeatAir, except black laminated hardwood stock. Mfg. 2002-2003.

	$85	$70	$60	$50	$40	$25	$15

* *Model 1077LG RepeatAir* – similar to Model 1077 RepeatAir, except green laminated hardwood stock. Mfg. 2002-2003.

	$85	$70	$60	$50	$40	$25	$15

* *Model 1077RD RepeatAir* – similar to Model 1077 RepeatAir, except red dot sight included. Disc. 2004.

	$85	$70	$60	$50	$40	$25	$15

Last MSR was $91.

* *Model 1077SB RepeatAir* – similar to Model 1077 RepeatAir, except has silver barrel. Mfg. 1995.

	$75	$65	$55	$45	$35	$20	$15

* *Model 1077W RepeatAir* – similar to Model 1077 RepeatAir, except has walnut stock. Mfg. 1997-2007.

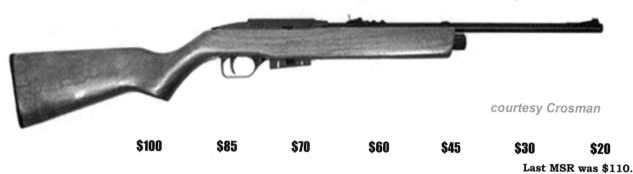

courtesy Crosman

	$100	$85	$70	$60	$45	$30	$20

Last MSR was $110.

GRADING	100%	95%	90%	80%	60%	40%	20%

* **Model 1077KT RepeatAir Action Kit** – .177 cal., CO_2, kit includes Model 1077 rifle, large-lens red dot sight, extra removable mag., three 12-shot rotary mags., 250-count .177 cal. pellets, three CO_2 cylinders, five NRA targets, and shooting glasses. Disc. 2006.

	$90	$75	$65	$50	$40	$25	$20

Last MSR was $97.

* **Model AS1077T AirSource** – .177 cal., CO_2, 88g AirSource cylinder, 12-shot rotary mag., semi-auto repeater, 20.4 in. rifled steel barrel, 625 FPS, black finish, checkered black synthetic stock, fiber optic front and adj. rear sights, 36.9 in. OAL, 3.7 lbs. Mfg. 2004-2010.

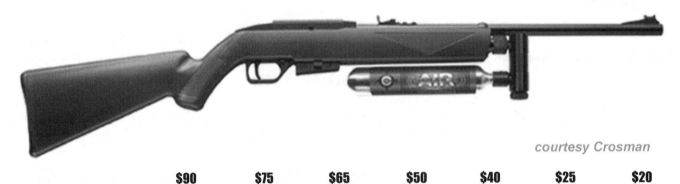

courtesy Crosman

	$90	$75	$65	$50	$40	$25	$20

Last MSR was $103.

Add $40 for Upgrade kit (Model AS1077AD) available for Model 1077 RepeatAir rifles manufactured since May 1999.

MODEL 1388 – BB/.175 cal. or .177 cal. pellet, pneumatic, SS, BA, 10.25 in. rifled barrel, 560 FPS, adj. rear sight, plastic breech, Model 1377 pistol with shoulder stock. Mfg. 1982-1988.

	$85	$70	$60	$50	$40	$25	$15

MODEL 1389 BACKPACKER – .177 cal., multi-pump pneumatic, SS, detachable stock, green, 10 pumps = 560 FPS, 3.3 lbs. Mfg. 1989-1998.

	$65	$55	$45	$40	$30	$20	$15

MODEL 1400 PUMPMASTER – .22 cal., multi-pump pneumatic, SS, 10 pumps = 580 FPS, 5.5 lbs., wood stock/forearm. Highly desired by shooters who have them upgraded and converted for current field use. As with certain other Crosman models sought by shooters, values are determined more by desirability of certain versions for shooting and conversion than scarcity. It is increasingly difficult for collectors to locate completely original specimens. First variant: has breech cover. Mfg. 1968-1972. Second variant: has bolt handle. Mfg. 1972-1973. Third variant: has bolt handle, slim-line stock. Mfg. 1973-1978.

courtesy Robert Lutter

	$125	$105	$90	$75	$55	$35	$25

Add 30% for second and third variants.
Add 10% for factory box.

MODEL 1760 – .177 cal., CO_2, one cylinder, BA, SA, one-piece walnut stock, 24 in. rifled steel barrel, black finish, hardwood stock, adj. rear sight, 600 FPS, 4.8 lbs. Mfg. 1999-2005.

	$80	$70	$55	$45	$35	$25	$15

Last MSR was $92.

MODEL 1894 – .177 cal., CO_2, LA, two 12g cylinders located in the buttstock, eight-shot rotary mag., 15 (carbine) or 18.9 (rifle) in. barrel, 610 FPS, blue finish, hardwood stock with plastic butt plate and forearm, hooded front and adj. rear sights, crossbolt safety, 7.5 lbs (rifle). Disc. 2002.

	$250	$215	$175	$145	$115	$75	$50

GRADING	100%	95%	90%	80%	60%	40%	20%

MODEL 2000 CHALLENGER – .177 cal., CO_2, BA, SS, 19 in. rifled steel BBL, 485 FPS, adj. rear target sight, hooded front sight with removable aperture, matte or gloss black, blue, dark blue, red, silver, or grey composite stock with adj. cheek piece and buttplate, 36.25 in. OAL, 7 lbs. Mfg. 2000-2001.

	100%	95%	90%	80%	60%	40%	20%
	$400	$350	$280	$230	$180	$120	$80

Add 20% for gloss black, blue, dark blue, red, silver, or grey stock.

* **Model CH2000 Challenger** – .177 cal., CO_2, BA, SS, 485 FPS, rifled barrel, adj. rear target sight, hooded front sight with removable aperture, matte black finish, black composite stock with adj. cheek piece and buttplate, 36.25 in. OAL, 6.95 lbs. Mfg. 2001-2009.

	100%	95%	90%	80%	60%	40%	20%
	$475	$400	$325	$275	$215	$140	$95

Last MSR was $500.

MODEL CH2009S CHALLENGER PCP – .177 cal., PCP/CO_2, ambi. BA, SS, 21.63 in. rifled steel Lothar Walther barrel, 530 FPS, with (Model CH2009S, new 2010 - became standard 2013) or without (Model CH2009, disc. 2012) adj. rear diopter and hooded front sight, two-stage adj. match-grade trigger, matte black, blue/grey composite stock with adj. cheek piece and buttplate, Crossbolt safety, 38.75-41.5 in. OAL, 7.1 lbs. Mfg. 2009-current.

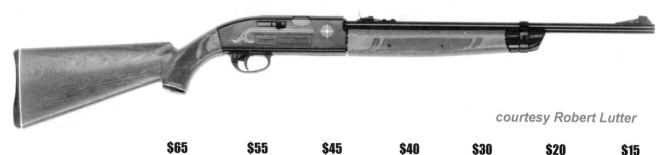

courtesy Crosman

MSR $934	100%	95%	90%	80%	60%	40%	20%
	$800	$700	$625	$525	$400	N/A	N/A

Subtract approx. $100 if without sights (Model CH2009, disc. 2012).

MODEL 2100 CLASSIC – BB/.175 cal. repeater or .177 cal. pellet SS, swinging forearm multi-stroke pump pneumatic, 10 pumps = 795 FPS (BB), 4.8 lbs. Similar to Model 766. Mfg. began in 1983. Disc.

courtesy Robert Lutter

	100%	95%	90%	80%	60%	40%	20%
	$65	$55	$45	$40	$30	$20	$15

* **Model 2100B** – BB/.177 cal. or .177 cal. pellet, SS, BA, multi-stroke pump pneumatic, 755/725 FPS, 20.14 in. rifled steel barrel, die cast receiver, Dovetail mounting rail, synthetic stock and forearm, fiber optic front and fully adj. rear sights, Crossbolt safety, 39.75 in. OAL, 4.8 lbs. Mfg. 1997-present.

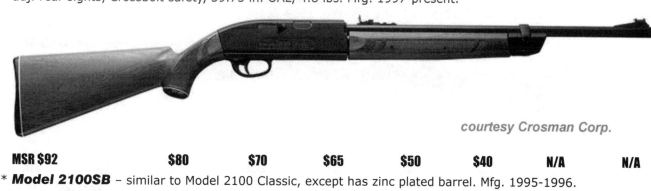

courtesy Crosman Corp.

MSR $92	100%	95%	90%	80%	60%	40%	20%
	$80	$70	$65	$50	$40	N/A	N/A

* **Model 2100SB** – similar to Model 2100 Classic, except has zinc plated barrel. Mfg. 1995-1996.

	100%	95%	90%	80%	60%	40%	20%
	$70	$60	$50	$40	$30	$20	$15

* **Model 2100W** – similar to Model 2100 Classic, except has walnut stock and forearm. Mfg. 1997-2003.

	100%	95%	90%	80%	60%	40%	20%
	$110	$95	$75	$65	$50	$35	$20

GRADING	100%	95%	90%	80%	60%	40%	20%

MODEL 2104GT – similar to Model 2100, except has gold accents and scope. Mfg. 1997-2003.

	$75	$65	$55	$45	$35	$20	$15

MODEL 2104X – similar to Model 2100, except with 4x15mm scope. Mfg. 2002-2011.

	$70	$60	$50	$40	$30	$20	$15

MODEL 2175W 75TH ANNIVERSARY COMMEMORATIVE – .177 cal., handcrafted American walnut stock and forearm with limited edition antique brass 75th anniversary medallion inlaid. Mfg. 1998 only.

	$125	$105	$90	$75	$55	$35	$25

MODEL 2200 MAGNUM – .22 cal., pneumatic, SS, similar to Model 2100, adj. rear sight, 4.8 lbs. First variant: with chrome-plated receiver. Mfg. 1978-1982. Second variant: with black receiver with silkscreen, straight steel barrel housing with plastic sight sleeve. Mfg. 1982-1983. Third variant: with brown stock and forearm. Mfg. 1983-1989.

courtesy Robert Lutter

	$65	$55	$45	$40	$30	$20	$15

Add 25% for first variant.
Add 10% for second variant.

* **Model 2200B** – .22 cal., similar to Model 2200 Magnum, except straight barrel housing. Mfg. 1989-2006.

	$70	$60	$50	$40	$30	$20	$15

Last MSR was $84.

* **Model 2200W** – similar to Model 2200 Magnum, except has walnut stock and forearm. Mfg. 1997-2003.

	$105	$90	$75	$60	$45	$30	$20

MODEL 2250B – .22 cal., CO_2, one cylinder, BA, SS, synthetic detachable skeleton stock, black finish, 14.6 in. rifled steel barrel, fiber optic front and adj. rear sights, 4X scope, 550 FPS, 3.3 lbs. Mfg. 1998-2008.

	$125	$105	$90	$75	$55	$35	$25

Last MSR was $134.

* **Model AS2250XT AirSource** – .22 cal., CO_2, 88g AirSource cylinder, BA, SS, synthetic detachable skeleton stock, black finish, 14.6 in. rifled steel barrel, fiber optic front and adj. rear sights, 4x32mm scope, 550 FPS, 30.25 in. OAL, 3.4 lbs. Mfg. 2004-2010.

	$130	$110	$90	$75	$60	$40	$25

Last MSR was $150.

MODEL 2260 – .22 cal., CO_2, one cylinder, BA, SS, one-piece hardwood walnut stock, 24 in. rifled steel barrel, black finish, adj. rear sight, 600 FPS, 39.63 in. OAL, 4.8 lbs. Mfg. 1999-2010.

courtesy Crosman

	$70	$60	$50	$40	$30	$20	$15

Last MSR was $83.

MODEL 2264X – .22 cal., similar to Model 2260, except 4x32mm scope (M-4032) included. Mfg. 1999-2002.

	$125	$105	$90	$75	$55	$35	$25

GRADING	100%	95%	90%	80%	60%	40%	20%

MODEL 2275W 75TH ANNIVERSARY COMMEMORATIVE – .22 cal., pneumatic pump-up, 595 FPS, handcrafted American walnut stock and forearm. Mfg. 1998 only.

	$125	$105	$90	$75	$55	$35	$25

MODEL 2289G BACKPACKER – .22 cal., swinging forearm pump pneumatic, BA, SS, detachable synthetic skeleton stock and forearm, 14.6 in. rifled steel barrel, black finish, fiber optic front and adj. rear sights, 525 FPS, 2.9 lbs. Mfg. 1998-2002.

	$60	$50	$40	$35	$25	$20	$10

MODEL 2576 (MODEL 760 25th YEAR COMMEMORATIVE) – BB/.175 cal., repeater or .177 cal. limited edition, similar to Model 760 original styling, except "Tootsie Roll" pump handle, etc. Mfg. 1991.

	$45	$40	$30	$25	$20	$15	N/A

MODEL 3100 – .177 cal., BBC, SP, SS, 600 FPS, one-piece hardwood stock, 6 lbs. Imported, Bascaran, Spain. Mfg. 1987-1990.

	$100	$85	$70	$60	$45	$30	$20

MODEL 3500 SLIDEMASTER – BB/.175 cal., push-barrel cocking, SP, 22-shot repeater, one-piece hardwood stock, updated version of Model V350. Mfg. 1970-1973.

	$120	$100	$85	$70	$55	$35	$25

Add 30% for factory box.

MODEL 6100 (DIANAWERK MODEL 45) – .177 cal., BBC, SP, 830 FPS, 20.50 in. barrel, 8.4 lbs. Mfg. 1982-1988.

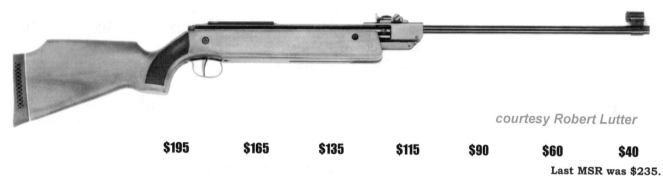

courtesy Robert Lutter

	$195	$165	$135	$115	$90	$60	$40

Last MSR was $235.

Basically, a Diana Model 45 with a modified Diana Model 35 stock.

MODEL 6300 (ANSCHÜTZ MODEL 333) – .177 cal., BBC, SP, 700 FPS, 18.5 in. barrel, 6.8 lbs. Mfg. 1986-1989.

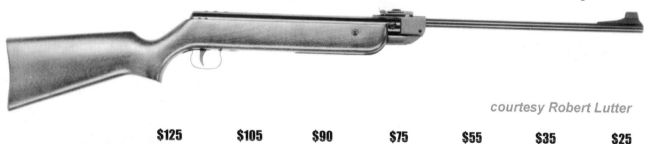

courtesy Robert Lutter

	$125	$105	$90	$75	$55	$35	$25

Last MSR was $175.

MODEL 6500 (ANSCHÜTZ MODEL 335) – .177 cal., BBC, SP, 700 FPS, 18.5 in. barrel, 7.7 lbs. Mfg. 1986-1988.

courtesy Robert Lutter

	$180	$155	$125	$105	$80	$55	$35

Last MSR was $200.

The three German air rifles (M-6100, M-6300, and M-6500) represented Crosman's 1980s "Challenger Line" excursion into adult precision air rifles. Fletcher's 1998 book notes that this line "caught between RWS on the low end and Beeman on the high end, never really had a chance."

GRADING	100%	95%	90%	80%	60%	40%	20%

MODEL 760/20-999 – see Model 760.

MODEL AIR-17 – BB/.175 cal. repeater or .177 cal., swinging forearm pump pneumatic, five-shot pellet clip, 21-round BB magazine, 195 round BB reservoir, replica of Colt AR-15 sporting high-power rifle. Mfg. 1985-1990.

courtesy Robert Lutter

	$150	$130	$105	$85	$70	$45	$30

MODEL BLACK FIRE – similar to Model 788, except has black stock and forearm. Mfg. 1996-1997.

	$50	$45	$35	$30	$25	$15	$10

MODEL BLACK LIGHTNING – BB/.175 cal., single stroke pump pneumatic, 20-shot magazine, 300 round reservoir, replica of Remington Model 1187 shotgun, 350 FPS, 150 round BB container shaped like shotgun shell. Mfg. began in 1997. Disc.

	$30	$25	$20	$15	$15	N/A	N/A

Subtract 10% for missing shotgun style BB container.

MODEL BLACK SERPENT – similar to Model 781, except has black stock and forearm. Mfg. 1996-2002.

	$45	$40	$30	$25	$20	$15	N/A

MODEL CANADIAN BOY – BB/.175 cal. repeater (180-shot gravity-fed magazine) and .177 cal. pellet SS, short-stroke pump pneumatic, 10 pumps = 595 FPS (BB), BA, PP, 17 in. smoothbore steel BBL, wood stock and forearm Mfg. 1964-66.

Canadian Boy
courtesy Howard Collection

	$275	$235	$195	$160	$125	$80	$55

Add 20%-25% for factory box.

The first short-stroke pump pneumatic, developed in Canada as "Canadian Boy" from Model 130 pistol.

MODEL M-1 CARBINE – BB/.175 cal., push-barrel, SP, smoothbore, 22-two-shot gravity-fed magazine, 180 round reservoir, basically a Model V350 styled as replica of US M1 .30 cal. carbine. First variant: wood stock, mfg. 1966-1967. Second variant: Croswood stock. Mfg. 1968-1976.

courtesy Robert Lutter

	$150	$130	$105	$85	$70	$45	$30

Add 60% for wood stock.
Add 20% for factory box.

GRADING	100%	95%	90%	80%	60%	40%	20%

MODEL M4-177 – BB/.177 cal. or .177 cal. pellet, multi-stroke pump pneumatic, BA, AR platform tactical appearance and feel, adj. stock, rifled steel barrel, textured polymer foregrip allows for easy pumping, 660/625 FPS, 18 shot mag., adj. front sight, dual aperture windage or adj. peep rear sight, Picatinny mounting rail, Crossbolt safety, removable magazine securely holds and stores a spare 5-shot pellet clip and front sight adjustment tool, Black or Tan (disc. 2013) finish, 34 in. OAL, 3.56 lbs. New 2012.

courtesy Crosman Corp.

	MSR $78	$65	$60	$55	$45	$35	N/A	N/A

Add $9 for M4-177 Kit (Model M4-177KT) which includes the M4-177 Black rifle, Premium Copperhead BBs, Crossman pellets, 5 paper targets, 3 Firepow'r clips, safety glasses, and a dual-aperture windage and elevation adj. carry handle (New 2014). New 2012.

Add $19 for M4-177 Tan Kit (Model M4-177 TKT) which includes M4-177 Desert Tan rifle, 100 BBs, 100 pellets, 5 paper targets, 3 Firpow'r clips, and safety glasses (mfg. 2012-2013).

Add $45 for Backyard Commando (Model Propick006) which includes Centerpoint red laser and 40mm enclosed reflex sight, 1,250 pellets, and 1,500 Copperhead BBs.

MODEL MK-177 – BB/.177 cal. or .177 pellet, BA, pump pneumatic, 750 FPS, 16 3/4 in. rifled steel barrel, 5-shot pellet clip or internal 300+ BB mag., large bolt handle, full Picatinny rail, fully adj. sights, accessory rails for flashlight or laser, tactical pistol grip, rugged all-weather construction, Black or Tan finish, Crossbolt safety, 33 in. OAL, 3.5 lbs. New 2013.

courtesy Crosman Corp.

	MSR $105	$90	$80	$70	$60	$45	N/A	N/A

Add $40 for MK-177 Kit which includes MK-177 rifle, soft carry case, CenterPoint red dot sight, 100 BBs, 100 pellets, shooting glasses, and two Firepow'r 5-shot pellet clips.

MODEL NS1200 NIGHT STALKER – .177 cal., CO_2, semi-automatic blowback action, one 88G AirSource cylinder, 12-shot rotary mag. repeater, 20.4 in. rifled steel barrel, 580 FPS, black finish, checkered black synthetic thumbhole stock, Mohawk adj. sight system, 30.5 in. OAL, 3.27 lbs. Mfg. 2005-2010.

courtesy Crosman

$85	$70	$60	$50	$40	$25	$15

Last MSR was $100.

GRADING	100%	95%	90%	80%	60%	40%	20%

MODEL NS1204A NIGHT STALKER TK – .177 cal., CO_2, semi-automatic blowback action, one 88G AirSource cylinder, 12-shot rotary mag. repeater, 20.4 in. rifled steel barrel, 580 FPS, black finish, checkered black synthetic thumbhole stock, Mohawk adj. sight system with dual illumination sight, tactical flashlight, collapsible bipod, 30.5 in. OAL, 3.27 lbs. Mfg. 2005-2007.

courtesy Crosman

	$185	$155	$130	$105	$85	$55	$35

Last MSR was $200.

MODEL RM177 – .177 cal., BBC, SP, SS, rifled steel barrel, blue finish, 825 FPS, checkered hardwood English style stock, rubber butt pad, sling mounts, hooded front and adj. apeture rear sights, 7.1 lbs. Mfg. 2002.

	$110	$95	$75	$65	$50	$35	$20

* **Model RM177** – .177 cal., similar to Model RM177, except 4x32mm (M-4032) scope included. Mfg. 2002.

	$125	$105	$90	$75	$55	$35	$25

MODEL RM277 – .177 cal., BBC, SP, SS, rifled steel barrel, blue finish, 825 FPS, hardwood Monte carlo style stock, rubber butt pad, hooded front and adj. rear sights, 7.1 lbs. Mfg. 2002-2003.

	$110	$95	$75	$65	$50	$35	$20

* **Model RM277X** – .177 cal., similar to Model RM177, except 4x32mm (M-4032) scope included. New 2002-2003.

	$125	$105	$90	$75	$55	$35	$25

MODEL RM422 – .22 cal., BBC, SP, SS, rifled steel barrel, blue finish, 825 FPS, hardwood Monte Carlo style stock, rubber butt pad, hooded front and adj. rear sights, 7.1 lbs. Mfg. 2003-2004.

	$115	$100	$80	$65	$50	$35	$25

Last MSR was $140.

MODEL RM522 – .22 cal., BBC, SP, SS, rifled steel barrel, blue finish, 825 FPS, hardwood Monte Carlo style stock, rubber butt pad, hooded front and adj. rear sights, 7.9 lbs. Mfg. 2002-2003.

	$150	$130	$105	$85	$70	$45	$30

MODEL RM577 – .177 cal., BBC, SP, SS, rifled steel barrel, blue finish, 1000 FPS, hardwood Monte Carlo style stock, rubber butt pad, hooded front and adj. rear sights, 7.9 lbs. Mfg. 2002-2003.

	$150	$130	$105	$85	$70	$45	$30

* **Model RM577X** – .177 cal., similar to Model RM177, except 4x32mm (M-4032) scope included. Mfg. 2002-2003.

	$175	$150	$125	$100	$80	$50	$35

MODEL RM677 – .177 cal., BBC, SP, SS, rifled steel barrel, blue finish, 1000 FPS, checkered hardwood thumbhole stock, rubber butt pad, hooded front and adj. rear apeture sights, 7.5 lbs. Mfg. 2002.

	$185	$155	$130	$105	$85	$55	$35

MODEL RM877 – .177 cal., BBC, SP, SS, rifled steel barrel, blue finish, 1100 FPS, checkered hardwood Monte Carlo style stock, rubber buttpad, hooded front and adj. rear apeture sights, 7.5 lbs. Mfg. 2002.

	$225	$190	$160	$130	$100	$65	$45

GRADING	100%	95%	90%	80%	60%	40%	20%

MODEL V350 – BB/.175 cal., push-barrel cocking, SP, 22 shot repeater, 350 FPS, 11 in. barrel, ramped blade front and adj. leaf rear sights, blue finish, hardwood stock, 35 in. OAL, 3.75 lbs. Mfg. 1961-1969.

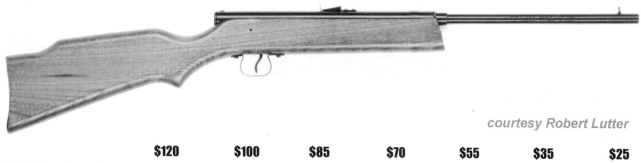

courtesy Robert Lutter

	$120	$100	$85	$70	$55	$35	$25

Add 20% for factory box.
Add 200% for factory gold-plated version.
Add 300-500% for Model V350M Military Trainer.

MODEL V350M (MILITARY TRAINER) – BB/.175 cal., push-barrel cocking, SP, 22 shot repeater, 350 FPS, 8 in. barrel w/knurled cocking and safety aid, on sights, blue finish, hardwood stock, 32.5 in. OAL, 3.75 lbs. Mfg. 1960's.

courtesy Howard Collection

	$600	$500	$425	$350	$270	$180	$120

Add 20% for factory box.

MODEL 1924 – See Second Model and notes about the designation of 1924 Model.

COMRADE AK – BB/4.5mm cal., CO_2, semi-auto, 600 FPS, 22-shot in visual magazine, 150 in reservoir, elevation and windage adj. rear sight, Picatinny mounting rail and removable stock, storage magazine holds BBs and extra CO_2 cartridge, slide safety, Black finish, 28.5 in. OAL, 4 lbs. New 2014.

courtesy Crosman Corp.

MSR $99	$85	$75	$65	$55	$40	N/A	N/A

DESERT ROSE MODEL PLA350 – BB/.177 cal., SP, lever action, SS, 350 FPS, features pink hardwood stock and forearm, all metal receiver and cocking lever, fixed blade front, adj. notch rear sights, Crossbolt safety, 35.5 in. OAL, 2.6 lbs. New 2012.

MSR $40	$35	$30	$25	$20	$15	N/A	N/A

GRADING	100%	95%	90%	80%	60%	40%	20%

FURY – .177 cal., BBC, SP, SS, pellet, 15 in. rifled steel barrel, 1200 FPS, Dovetail mounting rail, adj. two-stage trigger, all weather black synthetic stock, includes CenterPoint 4x32mm scope, 45 in. OAL, 6.4 lbs. New 2013.

courtesy Crosman Corp.

Please contact the company directly for pricing on this model.

* **Fury NP** – .177 cal., similar to Fury, except features Nitro Piston technology. New 2013.

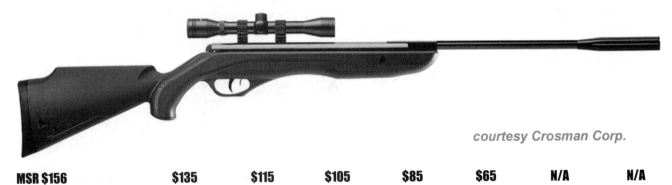

courtesy Crosman Corp.

MSR $156	$135	$115	$105	$85	$65	N/A	N/A

G1 EXTREME MODEL CS1K77KTBX – .177 cal., BBC, SP, SS, rifled steel (scope stop) barrel, black finish, muzzle brake, 1000 FPS, checkered ambidextrous black synthetic PG stock, two stage adj. trigger, rubber buttpad, CenterPoint 3-9x32mm Mil-Dot scope, 44.5 in. OAL, 6 lbs. Mfg. 2008.

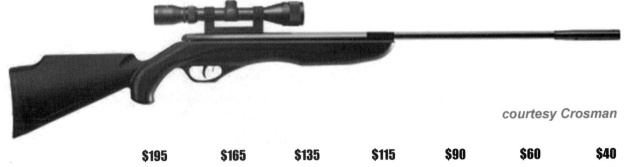

courtesy Crosman

	$195	$165	$135	$115	$90	$60	$40

Last MSR was $217.

NITRO VENOM HARDWOOD – .177 (Model CVW1K77NP) or .22 (Model CVW8M22NP) cal., BBC, Nitro Piston, SS, 1000/800 FPS, 15 in. rifled steel barrel with fluted muzzle brake, hardwood stock with checkering on grip and forearm, sculpted rubber recoil pad, 3-9x32mm CenterPoint scope, quick lock mounting system, ambidextrous raised cheek piece and modified beavertail forearm, 44.5 in. OAL, 7.4 lbs. New 2011.

courtesy Crosman

MSR $223	$190	$165	$150	$125	$95	N/A	N/A

GRADING	100%	95%	90%	80%	60%	40%	20%

NITRO VENOM DUSK – .177 (Model CD1K77NP) or .22 (Model CD8M22NP) cal. pellet, BBC, Nitro Piston, SS, 1000/800 FPS, 15 in. rifled barrel with fluted muzzle brake, black synthetic stock with sculpted grooves on grip and forearm, sculpted rubber recoil pad, 3-9x32mm CenterPoint scope, quick lock mounting system, ambidextrous raised cheek piece and modified beavertail forearm, 44.5 in. OAL, 7.4 lbs. New 2011.

courtesy Crosman

MSR $223	$190	$165	$150	$125	$95	N/A	N/A

OPTIMUS – .177 or .22 cal., SP, BBC, SS, pellet, 1000/800 FPS, 15 in. rifled steel barrel, ambidextrous hardwood stock, two-stage adj. trigger, fiber optic front sight, micro-adj. rear sight, lever safety, also available with 4x32mm CenterPoint scope, 43 in. OAL, 7.1 lbs. Mfg. 2011-current.

courtesy Crosman

MSR $125	$105	$95	$85	$70	$55	N/A	N/A

Add $31 for 4x32mm CenterPoint scope (Model CO1K77X).

PHANTOM – .177 or .22 (disc.) cal., BBC, SP, SS, pellet, 15 in. rifled steel (scope stop) barrel, blue finish, 1000 FPS, ambidextrous black synthetic PG stock, rubber butt pad, two-stage adj. trigger, hooded front and adj. rear fiber optic sights, lever safety, with or w/o 4x32mm CenterPoint scope, 45 in. OAL, 7 lbs. Mfg. 2006-current.

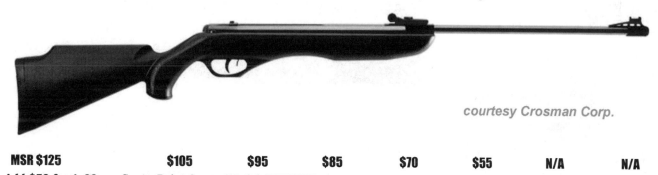

courtesy Crosman Corp.

MSR $125	$105	$95	$85	$70	$55	N/A	N/A

Add $50 for 4x32mm CenterPoint Scope (Model CS1K77X).

* ***Phantom Model Kit CS1K77KT*** – .177 or .22 cal., BBC, SP, SS, rifled steel (scope stop) barrel, nickel plated, muzzle break, 1000 FPS, ambidextrous black synthetic PG stock, rubber butt pad, hooded front and adj. rear fiber optic sights, CenterPoint Compact 6x32mm scope, 500 Premier pellets, gun sock, 25 official airgun targets, 45.5 in. OAL, 6 lbs. Mfg. 2007-2008.

	$185	$155	$130	$105	$85	$55	$35

Last MSR was $200.

QUEST 1000 MODEL C1K77 – .177 cal., BBC, SP, SS, rifled steel (scope stop) barrel, blue finish, 1000 FPS, hardwood Monte Carlo style stock, rubber butt pad, hooded front and adj. rear fiber optic sights, 45 in. OAL, 6 lbs. Mfg. 2004-2011.

	$85	$70	$60	$50	$40	$25	$15

Last MSR was $100.

GRADING	100%	95%	90%	80%	60%	40%	20%

* **Quest 1000X Model C1K77X** – .177 or .22 (Model C8M22X, new 2010) cal., similar to Model C1K77, except with 4x32mm fully adj. scope. Mfg. 2004-2011.

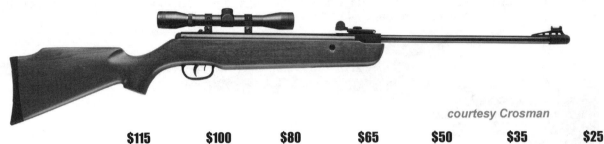

courtesy Crosman

	$115	$100	$80	$65	$50	$35	$25

Last MSR was $135.

QUEST MODEL C5M77 – .177 cal., BBC, SP, SS, rifled steel (scope stop) barrel, blue finish, 495 FPS, hardwood Monte Carlo style stock, rubber butt pad, hooded front and adj. rear fiber optic sights, 41.5 in. OAL, 5.5 lbs. Mfg. 2005-2007.

	$125	$105	$90	$75	$55	$35	$25

Last MSR was $150.

RAVEN MODEL CY6M77 – .177 cal. pellet, BBC, SP, SS, small frame, 600 FPS, 12 1/2 in. rifled steel barrel, black over molded finish, ambidextrous, all-weather black synthetic stock with ergonomic thumbhole grip, fully adj. fiber optic sights, crossbolt safety, also available with 4x32mm CenterPoint scope (Model CY6M77X, mfg. 2011-2012), 37.5 in. OAL, 4.9 lbs. Mfg. 2008-current.

courtesy Crosman

MSR $89		$75	$65	$60	$50	$35	N/A	N/A

Add $18 for 4x32mm CenterPoint scope (Model CY6M77X, mfg. 2011-2012).

RECRUIT – BB/.177 cal. 200-shot repeater or .177 cal. pellet 5-shot clip, BA, swinging forearm multi-stroke pump pneumatic, 680/645 FPS, 20.17 in. smooth bore bbl., adj. black synthetic stock, adj. fiber optic sights, Crossbolt safety, with (Model RCT525X) or w/o 4x15mm scope, scope became standard during 2012, 2.95 lbs. 36.75 in. OAL, 2.95 lbs. Mfg. 2009-current.

courtesy Crosman

MSR $68		$60	$50	$45	$35	$30	N/A	N/A

Add $31 for Recruit Kit (Model RCTYTHKT, New 2014) which includes Premium Copperhead BBs, Crosman pellets, shooting glasses, 4x scope, and five paper targets.

SIERRA PRO MODEL CW1K77XKT – .177 cal., BBC, SP, SS, rifled steel (scope stop) barrel, blue finish, 1000 FPS, checkered hardwood Monte Carlo style stock, rubber buttpad, hooded front and adj. rear fiber optic sights, 3-9x40mm Mil-Dot scope, OAL 45 in., 7.8 lbs. Mfg. 2008.

courtesy Crosman

	$185	$155	$130	$105	$85	$55	$35

Last MSR was $200.

GRADING	100%	95%	90%	80%	60%	40%	20%

STORM XT MODEL C1K773932 – .177 cal., BBC, SP, SS, rifled steel (scope stop) barrel, blue finish, 1000 FPS, hardwood Monte Carlo style stock, rubber buttpad, adj. rear and bead fiber optic sights, 3-9x32mm scope, 45 in. OAL, 6 lbs. Mfg. 2007-2010.

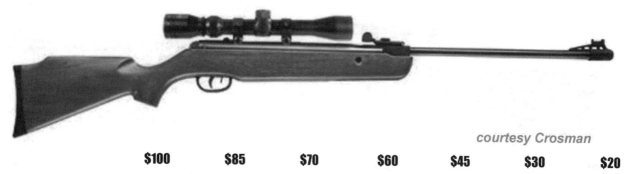

courtesy Crosman

$100	$85	$70	$60	$45	$30	$20

Last MSR was $115.

TAC 1 EXTREME MODEL CST8M22XKT – .22 cal., BBC, SP, SS, rifled steel (scope stop) barrel, nickel plated, muzzle brake, 800 FPS, ambidextrous black synthetic PG stock, two stage adj. trigger, rubber buttpad, hooded front and adj. rear fiber optic sights, CenterPoint 3-9x32mm scope, Flashlight, Bipod, Laser 45.5 in. OAL, 6 lbs. Mfg. 2007-2010.

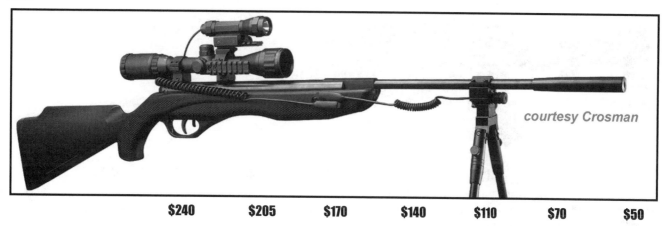

courtesy Crosman

$240	$205	$170	$140	$110	$70	$50

Last MSR was $280.

TAC 77 ELITE MODEL CT1K77XKT – .177 cal., BBC, SP, SS, rifled steel (scope stop) barrel, black finish, muzzle brake, 1000 FPS, ambidextrous black synthetic PG stock with padded adj. cheek piece, two stage adj. trigger, CenterPoint 3-9x32mm scope, flashlight, Bipod, Laser 45.5 in. OAL, 6 lbs. Mfg. 2008-2010.

courtesy Crosman

$300	$255	$210	$175	$135	$90	$60

Last MSR was $365.

GRADING	100%	95%	90%	80%	60%	40%	20%

TORRENT SX – BB/.177 cal. or .177 pellet cal., BA, pump pneumatic, 695/640 FPS, 14.15 in. rifled steel barrel, 5-shot clip, Dovetail mounting rail, fiber optic front and adj. rear sights, adj. synthetic stock with textured grip, Olive Drab Green finish, Crossbolt safety, 36.75 in. OAL, 2.9 lbs. New 2013.

courtesy Crosman Corp.

MSR $50	$45	$40	$35	$30	$20	N/A	N/A

TR77 – .177 cal. pellet, SP, BBC, SS, military styling and black all-weather tactical synthetic stock, rifled barrel, two stage adj. trigger, pistol grip, 1000 FPS, fiber optic front and adj. rear sights, Dovetail mounting rail, lever safety, includes CenterPoint 4x32mm scope. New 2012.

courtesy Crosman Corp.

MSR $150	$130	$115	$100	$85	$65	N/A	N/A

TR77 NPS – .177 cal., BBC, Nitro Piston, 12 in. overmolded rifled steel barrel, adj. two-stage trigger, 1000 FPS, Dovetail mounting rail, all-weather tactical synthetic stock, convenient storage behind recoil pad, Black finish, includes CenterPoint 4x32mm precision scope, 40 in. OAL, 5.5 lbs. New 2013.

courtesy Crosman Corp.

MSR $187	$160	$140	$125	$105	$80	N/A	N/A

USMC MOS 0311 RIFLEMAN – BB/.177 cal. or .177 cal. pellet, BA, pump pneumatic, 660/625 FPS, rifled steel barrel,

courtesy Crosman Corp.

GRADING	100%	95%	90%	80%	60%	40%	20%

5-shot Firepow'r pellet clip or internal 300+ BB mag., removable magazine stores pellet clip and sight adjustment tool, Picatinny accessory rails, adj. front and dual aperture flip rear sights, adj. stock with textured polymer foregrip, tactical pistol grip, Olive Drab Green/Black finish, Crossbolt safety, 34 in. OAL, 3.5 lbs. New 2014.

MSR $100	$85	$75	$70	$55	$40	N/A	N/A

The Marines Airgun series was created to spotlight and pay tribute to the achievements of our brothers and sisters in uniform. Proceeds help support Marines morale, welfare, and recreational activities.

MTR77 NP – .177 cal., BBC, Nitro Piston, 15 in. rifled steel barrel, 1000 FPS, adj. two-stage trigger, Picatinny mounting rail, all weather tactical synthetic stock, Black finish, sling mounts, includes removable carry handle with rear sight (Model 30062) or CenterPoint 4x32mm scope (Model 30060), storage in false magazine, 40 in. OAL, 5.9 lbs. New 2013.

courtesy Crosman Corp.

MSR $234	$200	$175	$160	$130	$100	N/A	N/A

VANTAGE – .177 cal., BBC, SS, SP, pellet, 15 in. rifled steel barrel, 1000 FPS, fiber optic front and adj. rear sight, dovetail mounting rail, hardwood stock, lever safety, includes CenterPoint 4x32mm scope, 45 in. OAL, 7.1 lbs. New 2013.

Please contact the company directly for pricing on this model.

* **Vantage NP** – .177 cal., similar to Vantage, except features Nitro Piston technology. New 2013.

courtesy Crosman Corp.

MSR $156	$135	$115	$105	$85	$65	N/A	N/A

SHOTGUN

MODEL 1100 TRAPMASTER – .380 bore, CO_2, two cylinders, SS, black chrome (early) or matte black painted finish. Mfg. 1968-1971.

courtesy Howard Collection

	$190	$160	$135	$110	$85	$55	$40

Add 20% for factory box.
Add 75% for complete trap set (trap, loading outfit, cases, etc.).
Add 200% for employee special gold-plated version.

SPECIAL/LIMITED EDITIONS

1760SE SPECIAL EDITION SPORTSMANS MODEL RIFLE – .177 cal., CO_2, one cylinder, BA, SA, 24 in. rifled steel barrel, 700 FPS, adj. rear blade front sights, CenterPoint 6x32mm scope and rings, black finish, American

GRADING	100%	95%	90%	80%	60%	40%	20%

hardwood PG stock, 39.75 in. OAL, 4.8 lbs. Mfg. 2008-2011.

courtesy Crosman

	$155	$135	$125	$100	$75	N/A	N/A

Last MSR was $182.

2260SE SPECIAL EDITION SPORTSMANS MODEL RIFLE – .22 cal., CO_2, one cylinder, BA, SS, 24 in. rifled steel barrel, 600 FPS, adj. rear blade front sights, CenterPoint 6x32mm scope and rings, black finish, American hardwood PG stock, 39.75 in. OAL, 4.8 lbs. Mfg. 2008-2011.

courtesy Crosman

	$155	$135	$125	$100	$75	N/A	N/A

Last MSR was $182.

MODEL 2300SLE LIMITED EDITION PISTOL – .177 cal., CO_2, one 12g cylinder, BA, SS, 10.1 in. Lothar-Walther choked match rifled BBL, adj. hammer spring for 440-520 FPS, single stage adj. trigger, Williams adj. rear sight, blue finish, pecan hardwood grips with fish scale laser etched design, silver muzzle break, silver trigger and silver trigger shoe, 16 in. OAL, 42.5 oz., hand crafted pecan wood case with rustic leather appointments, ten Crosman cylinders, ammo pouch, tin of Crosman Wadcutter pellets, and tube of Pellgunoil. Edition is limited to 100. Mfg. 2008-2011.

$425	$350	$295	$245	$190	$125	$85

MODEL 2300TLE LIMITED EDITION PISTOL – .177 cal., CO_2, one 12g cylinder, BA, SS, 10.1 in. Lothar-Walther choked match rifled BBL, adj. hammer spring for 440-520 FPS, single stage adj. trigger, Williams adj. rear sight, blue finish, pecan hardwood grips with fish scale laser etched design, silver muzzle brake, silver trigger and silver trigger shoe, 16 in. OAL, 42.5 oz., hand crafted pecan wood case with rustic leather appointments, ten Crosman cylinders, ammo pouch, tin of Crosman Wadcutter pellets, and tube of Pellgunoil. Edition is limited to 100. Mfg. 2008-2011.

$350	$300	$250	$210	$160	$110	$70

GRADING	100%	95%	90%	80%	60%	40%	20%

MODEL 2250XE OUTDOORSMAN – .22 cal., CO_2, one cylinder, BA, SS, long steel breech, 18 in. rifled steel barrel with muzzle break, 550 FPS, black finish, CenterPoint 3-9x32mm Mil-Dot scope, hand crafted pecan skeleton stock and forearm, 33 in. OAL, 3.3 lbs. Mfg. 2008-2011.

courtesy Crosman

$240	$210	$190	$155	$120	N/A	N/A

Last MSR was $280.

CROSS

Previous manufacturer located in Boston, MA, circa 1876.

PISTOL

CROSS PATENT PISTOL – .21 cal., SP, SS. Based on U.S. Patent no. 182,899 issued to Wm. C. Cross on Oct. 3, 1876. Standard Quackenbush/Bedford Rifle Air Pistol frame, unmarked, probably made by Quackenbush or Bedford. Stationary barrel. Instead of pulling the barrel to cock, a knob under the barrel is pulled to cock the gun. Brass chamber under the barrel bears the cocking knob. Swinging loading gate similar to that of the Quackenbush Type C air pistol at the rear of the gun. Black enamel finish. Retractable seating pin houses cocking knob return spring. Only one specimen known.

courtesy Stauff Collection

Scarcity precludes accurate pricing.

CUB

For information on Cub airguns, see Milbro in the "M" section and Langenhan in the "L" section.

CYBER GUN

International distributor of airguns located in Bondoufle, France.

CYCLOID/RAPID

Previous trade names previously manufactured by Cycloid Cycle Co. and Rapid Rifle Co., Grand Rapids, MI circa 1889-1900.

The Cycloid and Rapid BB guns are all metal and completely nickel plated. Any boy discovering one of these spectacular and most unusual air rifles under the Christmas tree surely would not be able resist immediately running out with it to show the entire neighborhood! There has been considerable confusion about the maker. Dunathan, in the classic *American BB Gun* book, indicates that A.K. Wheeler founded the Rapid Rifle Company in Grand Rapids, MI in 1898 to produce some version of these air rifles. He reports that they were known under the names Cycloid, Cyclone, and New Rapid. However, at least two versions are known. One version, almost surely the earliest, has a cast iron receiver with cast script letters reading "Cycloid" on the left side and "Cycloid Cycle Co., Grand Rapids,

GRADING	100%	95%	90%	80%	60%	40%	20%

Michigan" on the right. A more streamlined, simplified form, all sheet metal, is stamped, in simple block capitals, as the RAPID made by the RAPID RIFLE CO., GRAND RAPIDS, MICH. USA. It would appear that manufacture began under the name Cycloid as made by the Cycloid Cycle Co. and soon terminated under the name RAPID as made by the Rapid Rifle Co. Perhaps no specimens of the gun are known to be marked Cyclone and there doesn't seem to be any justification for the name "New" Rapid. Dunathan reports that the strange design was invented by Frank Simonds, Chauncey Fisher, and Hugh Ross, and that the company failed before the patent was issued in December 1901.

Aside from the all-metal construction, the most conspicuously strange aspect of the gun's design is an extremely long cocking lever, terminating in a Winchester-style cocking loop *behind* the base of the metal pistol grip. Internally, instead of the mainspring being coiled around or within the piston unit there is a rather long metal piston completely ahead of the forward end of the coiled mainspring. Two long, chain-like links attached to the hooked forward end of the exceptionally long cocking lever pull back the cocking assembly in a manner similar to a break action BB gun. The poor efficiency and high cost of such a design, in the face of considerable emerging competition, probably fated the design to a life of only a year or two, making these guns among the rarest, and most interesting, of American production airguns.

RIFLES

CYCLOID – .180/BB shot cal., muzzle-loading SS, SP, cast iron receiver and cocking lever, balance of parts sheet metal, nickel plated finish, cocking lever pivoted behind the trigger, with a Winchester-style hand loop behind the base of the pistol grip, "Cycloid" is cast in script on LHS of receiver, and "Cycloid Cycle Co, GRAND RAPIDS, MICH. PATD." is cast on RHS of receiver. 31.7 in. OAL, 2.7 lbs. Mfg. circa 1898.

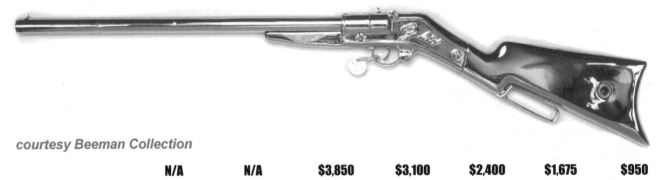

courtesy Beeman Collection

	N/A	N/A	$3,850	$3,100	$2,400	$1,675	$950

RAPID – .180/BB shot cal., muzzle-loading SS, SP, cast iron receiver and cocking lever, balance of parts sheet metal, nickel plated finish, cocking lever, pivoted behind the trigger, with a Winchester-style hand loop behind the base of the pistol grip, stamped in a circular logo on side of receiver "RAPID RIFLE CO. LTD. RAPID. PAT. APP. FOR, GRAND RAPIDS, MICH. USA", 31.5 in. OAL, 2.2 lbs. Mfg. circa 1900.

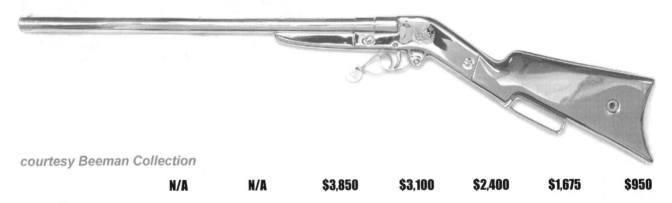

courtesy Beeman Collection

	N/A	N/A	$3,850	$3,100	$2,400	$1,675	$950

CYCLONE

For information on Cyclone, refer to the Cycloid/Rapid section above.

D SECTION
DAISY OUTDOOR PRODUCTS

Current manufacturer and distributor located in Rogers, AR established circa 1895. Previously located in Plymouth, MI 1895-1958. Dealer and consumer direct sales.

Daisy is one of the oldest and largest airgun manufacturers in the world, and for more than a century has produced some of the most coveted air rifles of all time. Vintage Daisy air rifles from the late 1880s can command prices up to $10,000. Daisy is also the maker of the famous Daisy Model 25 and Red Ryder lines. For vast numbers of young boys in rural America from the 1910s to the 1950s, and then in the developing suburbs of 1950 to about 1979, having an adult show you how to use a Daisy Model 25 slide action BB gun or a Red Ryder lever action BB gun was an integral part of growing up.

Until now there simply had been no "master" guide to Daisy airguns. The pioneering work, Dunathan's 1971 book, *The American BB Gun*, has long been somewhat of a "bible" to American BB gun collectors, but it was only moderately accurate even when it came out. Jim Thomas made a bit of an update of Dunathan's book in 1989, but we finally have a definitive guide to Daisy. We will be integrating data from Gary Garber's 2008 monumental treatise (see Lit. Guide) on the pre-Arkansas models as we verify and collate the immense amount of information there. At this time, this Blue Book can be used for most general Daisy information and as a value supplement to Griffiths' book -- for a level of details that are not appropriate here. In 2001, Neal Punchard, a long-time Daisy collector, published *Daisy Air Rifles & BB Guns -The First 100 Years,* a wonderfully illustrated general presentation of Daisy products over their first century of production. Finally, *An Encyclopedia of Daisy Plymouth Guns* (2007) produced by Gary Garber is a tremendous breakthrough concerning Daisy airgun information, at least for the models produced in Plymouth, MI from the late *1880s to 1958.* Daisy airguns are a large and complicated collecting group; this preliminary attempt at a model and value listing cannot be complete. Continual input from collectors and researchers will be necessary for greater and greater completeness and accuracy in future editions.

Unless otherwise noted, all Daisy airguns are spring piston designs in BB/.173 cal. The values quoted generally assume working condition. Many buyers will insist on a significant discount for lack of operation. Commemorative Model Warning: Surplus parts remaining after production of various post-1952 commemorative model airguns have found their way into the market. These parts have sometimes been used to construct or "enhance" regular production models. Sometimes the only way to detect such fraudulent specimens is to ask the Daisy company to compare the stamped registration number against their production records. For information on Daisy airguns manufactured for other trademarks, see the Store Brand Cross-Over List at the back of this text.

For more information and current pricing on both new and used Daisy firearms, please refer to the *Blue Book of Gun Values* by S.P. Fjestad (also available online).

DAISY IS BORN

Clarence Hamilton, known to firearm collectors as the manufacturer of Hamilton .22 caliber boys' firearms, invented the First Model all-metal Daisy air rifle while working at the Plymouth Iron Windmill Company in Plymouth, MI. The Plymouth Iron Windmill Company (founded in 1882) became the Daisy company in 1895 and continued operations in Plymouth until their move to their present location in Rogers, AR in 1958. The company has made a variety of products, but most of its production has been oriented towards BB guns and pellet rifles.

THE MODEL 25

The Model 25 slide action BB gun is often considered to be Daisy's most successful model, the model which was mainly responsible for Daisy's outstanding reputation. Made from 1914 to 1979, an amazing span of sixty-five years, the Model 25 is Daisy's longest running model. With approx. fifty-eight variants, total production of the Model 25 was over twenty million by 1979, more than all Ford Model T and Volkswagen "Bug" automobiles combined. The Model 25 probably also was the gun which gave Daisy the reputation of having the hardest hitting BB guns. With a bit of normal dieseling, many specimens could drive a steel BB out at speeds up to 450 FPS. Even that power was well exceeded by several lines of barrel cocking and side-lever air rifles, capable of velocities of 600 to 1000 FPS, which the company sold from the early 1960s to the present. And in the 1980s Daisy introduced a line of Daisy firearms - economical rifles using the potent (about thirty times the energy of a Daisy 880), but inexpensive, .22 long rifle ammunition.

THE POWERLINE AND SAFETY

Well over three decades ago, in 1972, Daisy started its own production of medium-powered pellet guns with the introduction of the "Powerline" Model 880. Contrasting quite completely with the one-cocking-stroke, lever and slide action BB guns, the Model 880 was their first swinging-arm, multiple-pump pneumatic pellet rifle. When fully pumped, these rifles can reach velocities of 680+ FPS. Although basically designed as accurate pellet rifles for field use, even sporting a scope sight or scope base, Daisy made it possible for users to shoot these new pellet rifles economically with BBs by providing them with amazing new rifling - dodecahedral flats in a helical pattern. This special rifling gave a stabilizing spin to even a steel projectile without cutting into the projectile or being injured by a hard steel projectile. The higher velocity of the Powerline guns gave the guns greater utility and greater effective accuracy in outdoor field shooting. The very name "Powerline" is a clear reference to high power, although these guns are by no means as strong as many other airguns now on the market.

While Daisy Powerline airguns were designed for use by shooters at least sixteen years old, Daisy has designated some of its BB guns, designed especially for youth over ten years old with adult supervision, as Youthline models. Mindful of the fact that

GRADING	100%	95%	90%	80%	60%	40%	20%

about 350 FPS is generally accepted as the minimum impact velocity at which a steel BB can perforate the human skin, the Youthline models are all designed to fire below that velocity at the muzzle. In addition to general public sales, these guns have been featured for well over a half-century in Daisy's huge shooting safety and education programs and events (see the Daisy "Take Aim at Safety" program at www.daisy.com).

COMPETITION AIRGUNS

Daisy made limited excursions into the field of high level competition airguns with their introductions of the German Feinwerkbau match airguns in the early 1970s and the Spanish El Gamo match airguns in the early 1990s. Because they were designed as match guns, they produced muzzle speeds in the 550-700 FPS range. Neither line was very strongly marketed and both were dropped rather soon. Much greater success was achieved with match-type guns of their own manufacture: the Model 753 and 853 rifles and the Model 747 and 777 pistols. Daisy now is presenting further expansion of their "Olympic-level" models. They also are marketing the Winchester QP "Quick Power" break-barrel air rifles (made in Turkey), which have the high power produced by the single stroke of barrel cocking airguns, and a popular new lever action Winchester Model 1894 replica.

CATEGORY INDEX

This Category Index is provided to help speed the process of locating a Daisy airgun in this text. The categories are in alphabetical order based on the configuration of the Daisy in question (i.e. pistol or rifle, type of action, cocking mechanism, or operating system).

DAISY COMMEMORATIVES

PISTOLS: CO_2 POWERED

PISTOLS: PNEUMATIC POWERED

PISTOLS: SPRING POWERED

RIFLES: BREAK ACTION, PRE-1900 (CAST METAL FRAME)

RIFLES: BREAK ACTION, POST-1900

RIFLES: BREAK BARREL COCKING

RIFLES: LEVER ACTION

RIFLES: LEVER ACTION, BUZZ BARTON SERIES

RIFLES: LEVER ACTION, DEFENDER SERIES

RIFLES: LEVER ACTION, DEMOULIN INITIATION SERIES

RIFLES: LEVER ACTION, RED RYDER SERIES

RIFLES: PNEUMATIC & CO_2 POWERED

RIFLES: PUMP/SLIDE ACTION

RIFLES: VL SERIES

DAISY COMMEMORATIVES

This grouping includes Commemorative airguns issued by Daisy that came in special packaging that directly affects their value. The graphics on these original boxes were specific to the issue, and if they are missing can reduce the value.

Subtract 40%-60% for missing box or any other related issue pieces.

MODEL 111-B AMERICAN YOUTH – BB/.175 cal., wood stock, die-cast cocking lever, stock laser engraved with the logo of a young boy proud to hold his first Daisy air rifle, production number stamped on the butt, gold silk screen words "American Youth" inscribed on the receiver, includes color print of an "American Youth" Bill of Rights. Approx. 1,000 mfg. 1998.

100%	95%	90%	80%	60%	40%	20%
$200	$170	$140	$115	$90	$60	$40

This is the lowest number of guns Daisy has ever produced in their collector series. Daisy discovered 1,000 die-cast cocking levers in an old warehouse, and used them to produce this limited edition. Prior to the "American Youth," Daisy had not made an air rifle with a die-cast cocking lever in twenty-five years.

MODEL 95 FIREFIGHTER – BB/.175 or .177 cal., similar to Model 95, except buttstock is laser engraved with an image of antique pumper wagon and "The Firefighter" with "going beyond the call" on the forearm, also included is a certificate of authenticity. Mfg. 2003-2004.

100%	95%	90%	80%	60%	40%	20%
$150	$130	$105	$85	$70	$45	$30

Last MSR was $60.

MODEL 1894 BUFFALO BILL 150TH ANNIVERSARY – BB/.175 cal., Winchester Model 94 style rifle, wood stock, wood forearm, gold style coin in stock. Approx. 2,500 mfg. 1996.

100%	95%	90%	80%	60%	40%	20%
$195	$165	$135	$115	$90	$60	$40

MODEL 1894 CARBINE SEARS VARIANT NUMBER 799.19052 – 1894 Commemorative, Winchester-style, octagon barrel, marked "Replica Centennial Rifle, Crafted by Daisy" or "Crafted by Daisy" on the barrel, gold paint finish, Sears. Mfg. 1969-1973.

100%	95%	90%	80%	60%	40%	20%
$250	$215	$175	$145	$115	$75	$50

MODEL 1894 CARBINE SEARS VARIANT NUMBER 799.19120 – regular 1894 Winchester-style, octagon barrel, gold paint or brass frame, Sears. Mfg. 1969-1973.

100%	95%	90%	80%	60%	40%	20%
$200	$170	$140	$115	$90	$60	$40

GRADING	100%	95%	90%	80%	60%	40%	20%

MODEL 3030 WESTERN CARBINE BUFFALO BILL SCOUT – forty-shot, saddle ring on forearm or receiver. Mfg. 1969-1973.

	$200	$170	$140	$115	$90	$60	$40

MODEL 5179 NRA COMMEMORATIVE – BB/.175 cal., spring catapult action, tubular, 12 shot tubular, spring-fed magazine. Mfg. 1971-1972.

	$150	$130	$105	$85	$70	$45	$30

MODEL 5179 NRA CENTENNIAL COMMEMORATIVE PISTOL/RIFLE SET – two guns, matching serial numbers, value given for pair. Mfg. 1971-1972.

	$400	$350	$280	$230	$180	$120	$80

MODEL 5694 TEXAS RANGERS COMMEMORATIVE RIFLE – mfg. 1973-1974.

	$600	$500	$425	$350	$270	$180	$120

MODEL 5894 NRA CENTENNIAL COMMEMORATIVE CARBINE – mfg. 1971-1972.

	$200	$170	$140	$115	$90	$60	$40

MODEL 5994 WELLS FARGO COMMEMORATIVE RIFLE – mfg. 1974-1975.

	$350	$300	$245	$205	$160	$105	$70

MODEL 1938 B CHRISTMAS STORY – BB/.175 cal., Red Ryder model manufactured due to interest in the 1983 film *A Christmas Story*, similar to standard "B" Model, but with large compass and sundial on left side of stock. Mfg. 1984.

	$450	$375	$325	$260	$205	$135	$90

Values equal with small compass.

A Christmas Story author Jean Sheperd invented this model, and Daisy followed his lead. An example in 100% condition must be unopened in original cellophane wrapped display box. To complete *A Christmas Story* set, collectors also need a movie poster, the movie (video tape or DVD), and the small cardboard stand-up display card.

Note: Due to the popularity of this model, there unfortunately are a handful of counterfeit Christmas Story BB guns in circulation. (These may be made up from regular Red Ryder guns by substituting factory stocks leftover from the production of true Christmas Story models.) Daisy had 9 to 10 different compass sources during the rush to provide this formerly non-existing model. "Daisy" may or may not be marked on the compass. Some are marked "Japan". Lot numbers on the side of the barrel indicate the year of manufacture. The beginning lot number 3 indicates 1983 and 4 indicates 1984. The letter "A" following the first digit indicates January, "B" indicates February, etc. The letter I was skipped. What no one seems to be able to counterfeit, however, is the original cellophane wrapper! According to a few collectors (who have them and will not part with them at any price), values are still on the conservative side.

MODEL 1938 B - LES KOUBA – BB/.175 cal., standard "B" model Red Ryder, but has extra fancy American walnut stock and forearm, gold forearm band, gold medallion on right side of stock showing a boy with his first Red Ryder. Stamped "Limited Edition", printing filled with gold paint, plastic lever, walnut-look wall rack in box, brass plaque. Includes Les C. Kouba print in cardboard tube marked with the same number as the air rifle. Mfg. 1986.

	$350	$300	$245	$205	$160	$105	$70

Add 50% for guns with artist's proofed and signed print.

Only 1,100 Les Kouba guns were produced. The print series numbers from 1 to 2500. The first 250 prints are artist proofed and hand signed on lower left side. There are counterfeit Les Kouba posters and guns which were not produced by Daisy. It is advised that you consult with a qualified expert before making a purchase.

NUMBER 1938 B 50TH ANNIVERSARY – Red Ryder, BB/.175 cal., similar to standard Model B, except has walnut stock and forearm, brass medallion on right side of stock, fifty-year warranty. Mfg. 1988.

	$125	$105	$90	$75	$55	$35	$25

MODEL 1938 B (MFG. 1995) – "It's A Daisy" Red Ryder Limited Edition. Mfg. 1995.

	$150	$130	$105	$85	$70	$45	$30

CHRISTMAS MORNING – BB/.175 or .177 cal., similar to Model 1938 Red Ryder, except gunstock is laser engraved with an image of Santa Claus placing a BB gun under a Christmas tree, also included in the full color package is a laser engraved wooden Christmas ornament (same image).

	$100	$85	$70	$60	$45	$30	$20

ROY ROGERS/TRIGGER COMMEMORATIVE – BB/.175 or .177 cal., similar to Model 1938 Red Ryder, first in series.

	$275	$235	$195	$160	$125	$80	$55

ROY/DALE LIMITED EDITION COMMEMMORATIVE – BB/.175 or .177 cal., similar to Model 1938 Red Ryder, except walnut stock has gold color medallion of Roy Rogers and Dale Evans inserted, forearm is laser engraved with their signatures and the gun's serial number, second rifle in the Roy Rogers Series, 2,500 to be mfg.

	$175	$150	$125	$100	$80	$50	$35

GRADING	100%	95%	90%	80%	60%	40%	20%

ROY ROGERS/GABBY HAYES COMMEMORATIVE – BB/.175 or .177 cal., similar to Model 1938 Red Ryder, except walnut stock has gold color medallion of Roy Rogers and Gabby Hayes inserted, forearm is laser engraved with Gabby's signature phrase "Yer durn tootin" and gun's serial number, third rifle in the Roy Rogers Series, 2,500 to be mfg.

	$175	$150	$125	$100	$80	$50	$35

ROY ROGERS/DUSTY COMMEMORATIVE – BB/.175 or .177 cal., similar to Model 1938 Red Ryder, except walnut stock has gold color medallion of Roy Rogers and Dusty inserted, forearm is laser engraved with Dusty's signature and gun's serial number, fourth rifle in the Roy Rogers Series, 2,500 to be mfg.

	$100	$85	$70	$60	$45	$30	$20

PISTOLS: CO$_2$ POWERED

MODEL 008 – BB/.175 or .177 cal., CO$_2$, semi-auto pistol, eight-shot rotary mag., rifled steel barrel, blade and ramp front and fixed rear sights, black finish, molded black checkered grips, rotary hammer block safety, 485 FPS, 7.1 in. OAL, 1 lb. New 2005.

courtesy Daisy

MSR $70	$60	$55	$50	$40	$30	N/A	N/A

* **Model 5008 Pistol Kit** – BB/.175 or .177 cal., CO$_2$, semi-auto pistol, kit includes shooting glasses, 500 count pellet tin, PrecisionMax 350 count BB tube, and three 12-gram CO$_2$ cylinders. New 2008.

courtesy Daisy

MSR $80	$70	$60	$55	$45	$35	N/A	N/A

MODEL 15XT – BB/.175 or .177 cal. pellet, CO$_2$, semi-auto pistol, 15-shot built-in mag., smoothbore steel barrel, blade and ramp front sight, fixed open rear sight, black finish, molded black checkered grips, manual trigger block safety, 480 FPS, 7.21 in. OAL, 1 lb. New 2002.

courtesy Daisy

MSR $40	$35	$30	$25	$20	$15	N/A	N/A

GRADING	100%	95%	90%	80%	60%	40%	20%

* ***Model 15XT Pistol Kit*** – BB/.175 or .177 cal. pellet, CO_2, semi-auto pistol, 15-shot built-in mag., smoothbore steel barrel, blade and ramp front sight, fixed open rear sight, black finish, molded black checkered grips, manual trigger block safety, kit includes shooting glasses, PrecisionMax 350 count BB tube, and three 12-gram CO_2 cylinders, 480 FPS, 7.21 in. OAL, 1 lb. New 2008.

courtesy Daisy

MSR $55	$45	$40	$35	$30	$25	N/A	N/A

MODEL 15XTP – BB/.175 or 177 cal., similar to Model 15XT, except has Max Speed electronic point sight. New 2002.

courtesy Daisy

MSR $55	$45	$40	$35	$30	$25	N/A	N/A

MODEL 15XK PISTOL KIT – BB/.175 or .177 cal., CO_2, semi-auto pistol, Model 15XT pistol kit including shooting glasses, NRA competition targets, 350 PrecisionMax BB tube, three PrecisionMax 12-gram CO_2 cylinders. New 2002.

courtesy Daisy

MSR $55	$45	$40	$35	$30	$25	N/A	N/A

MODEL 41 – .22 cal., CO_2, BA, replica of S&W Model 41, single shot, chrome plated. Mfg. circa 1984.

	$100	$85	$70	$60	$45	$30	$20

MODEL 44 (970) – .177 cal., CO_2, replica of S&W 44 Magnum revolver, six-shot swing-out cylinder. Mfg. 1984-2001.

	$100	$85	$70	$60	$45	$30	$20

MODEL 45 – .177 cal., CO_2, semi-auto pistol, 13-shot drop-in mag., rifled steel barrel, fiber optic fixed sights, black finish, molded black checkered grips, manual lever type trigger block safety, 400 FPS, 1.25 lb. Disc. 2002.

	$65	$55	$45	$40	$30	$20	$15

Last MSR was $70.

GRADING	100%	95%	90%	80%	60%	40%	20%

MODEL 45 GI – .177 cal., CO_2, 13-shot semi-auto. Colt 45 variant: replica of Colt 1911 .45 auto firearm. Smith & Wesson 45 variant: replica of Smith & Wesson .45 auto firearm. Mfg. 1992-97.

	$60	$50	$40	$35	$25	$20	$10

MODEL 45XT – .177 cal., CO_2, semi-auto pistol, 13-shot drop-in mag., rifled steel barrel, fiber optic fixed sights, black finish, molded black checkered grips, manual lever-type trigger block safety, 400 FPS, 1.25 lb.

	$45	$40	$30	$25	$20	$15	N/A

MODEL 91 – .177 cal., CO_2, SL, SS, wood grips, 10.25 in. barrel, 425 FPS, 2.4 lbs. Imported from Hungary 1991-1997.

	$425	$350	$290	$240	$185	$125	$85

This model was imported by Daisy as an entry level match target pistol.

MODEL 92 – .177 cal., semi-auto, styled like Beretta firearm pistol, ten-shot pellet feed. Mfg. in Japan, 1986-94.

	$75	$65	$55	$45	$35	$20	$15

MODEL 93 – BB/.175 or .177 cal., CO_2, semi-auto pistol, 15-shot drop-in mag., smooth bore steel barrel, fixed sights, black finish, molded brown checkered grips, manual trigger block safety, 400 FPS, 1.1 lb. Disc. 2004.

	$50	$45	$35	$30	$25	$15	$10

Last MSR was $60.

MODEL 100 – BB/.175 cal., CO_2, semi-auto pistol, 200-shot. Mfg. 1962.

	$45	$40	$30	$25	$20	$15	N/A

MODEL 200 – BB/.175 cal., CO_2, semi-auto, 200-shot. Mfg. 1963-1976.

courtesy Beeman Collection

	$40	$35	$30	$25	$20	$10	N/A

MODEL 400GX (DESERT EAGLE) – BB/.175 or .177 cal., CO_2, semi-auto pistol, 20-shot drop-in mag., smooth bore steel barrel, fixed sights, black (1994-97) or gold frame and black slide finish, molded black textured grips, manual lever safety, 420 FPS, 1.4 lb. Disc. 2002.

	$100	$85	$70	$60	$45	$30	$20

MODEL 454 – BB/.175 cal., CO_2, semi-auto, 20-shot. Mfg. 1994-1999.

	$45	$40	$30	$25	$20	$15	N/A

MODEL 500 RAVEN – .177 cal., CO_2, SS, 500 FPS. Mfg. 1994-98.

	$80	$70	$55	$45	$35	$25	$15

MODEL 617X – .177 cal. BB or pellet, CO_2, semi-auto pistol, six-shot rotary magazine holds pellets and BBs simultaneously, rifled steel barrel, TruGlo fiber optic fixed sights, black finish, molded black checkered grips, rotary hammer block safety, 485 FPS (BB) 425 FPS (Pellet), 8.5 in. OAL, 1.3 lbs. New 2004.

courtesy Daisy

MSR $70	$60	$55	$50	$40	$30	N/A	N/A

GRADING	100%	95%	90%	80%	60%	40%	20%

MODEL 622X – .22 cal., CO_2, semi-auto pistol, six-shot rotary mag., rifled steel barrel, fiber optic fixed sights, black finish, molded black checkered grips, rotary hammer block safety, 400 FPS, 1.3 lbs. Disc. 2004.

	$75	$65	$55	$45	$35	$20	$15

Last MSR was $80.

MODEL 645 – .177 cal., CO_2, semi-auto pistol, 13-shot drop-in mag., rifled steel barrel, fiber optic fixed sights, black and nickel finish, molded black checkered grips, manual trigger block safety. Colt 45 variant: styled like a Colt 1911 (1992-97). S&W 45 variant: styled like a S&W .45 auto, 400 FPS, 1.25 lbs. Disc. 2004.

	$75	$65	$55	$45	$35	$20	$15

Last MSR was $80.

MODEL 693 – BB/.177 cal., CO_2, semi-auto pistol, 449 FPS, 15-shot drop-in mag., smooth bore steel barrel, blade and ramp front, fixed open rear sights, black and nickel finish, lever safety and grip safety, 7.9 in. OAL, 1.1lbs.

courtesy Daisy

MSR $60	$50	$45	$40	$35	$25	N/A	N/A

* **Model 693 Pistol Kit** – BB/.175 or .177 cal., CO_2, semi-auto pistol kit including Model 693 pistol, shooting glasses, Official NRA competition targets (disc. 2011), PrecisionMax 350 BBs, pad of official airgun targets (disc.), and three 12-gram CO_2 cylinders.

courtesy Daisy

MSR $70	$60	$55	$50	$40	$30	N/A	N/A

MODEL 780 – .22 cal., CO_2, BA, SS, replica of S&W Model 41 firearm, blue paint finish, Daisy's continuation of S&W Model 78G CO_2 pistol. Mfg. 1982-1983.

	$125	$105	$90	$75	$55	$35	$25

MODEL 790 – .177 cal., CO_2, BA, SS, replica of S&W Model 41 firearm, blue paint finish, Daisy's continuation of S&W Model 79G CO_2 pistol. Mfg. 1982-1988.

	$125	$105	$90	$75	$55	$35	$25

GRADING	100%	95%	90%	80%	60%	40%	20%

MODEL 807 "CRITTER GITTER" – .38 cal., CO_2, BA, SS, 250 FPS, designed to shoot lead shot or patched ball with open ended cylinder as a cartridge (made in Germany by Umarex for Daisy, but Daisy decided not to continue production), very few went into the U.S. market, and some were sold in Germany. No box produced for U.S. market, 12.2 in. OAL, 2.2 lbs. Mfg. 1988 only.

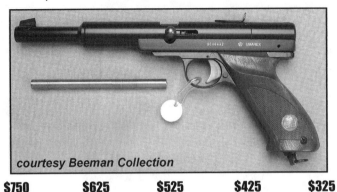

courtesy Beeman Collection

	$750	$625	$525	$425	$325	$225	$150

Add 20% for German box.
Add 15% for Daisy "Critter Gitter" shot cartridge tube with five cartridges.

MODEL 1200 – BB/.175 cal., CO_2, sixty-shot, plastic grips. Mfg. 1977-1989.

	$50	$45	$35	$30	$25	$15	$10

MODEL 1270 – .177 cal., CO_2, sixty-shot pump action repeater, molded polymer forend doubles as pump handle, molded black polymer grip, custom plated finish, 420 FPS, smooth bore steel barrel, adj. rear sight, cross bolt trigger block safety, 1.1 lbs. Disc. 2002.

	$40	$35	$30	$25	$20	$10	N/A

MODEL 1500 – BB/.175 cal., CO_2, similar to Model 1200, except chrome plated. Mfg. 1988 only.

	$40	$35	$30	$25	$20	$10	N/A

MODEL 1700 – .177 cal., CO_2, replica of Glock semi-auto firearm, uses Model 1200 valving. Mfg. 1991-1996.

courtesy Beeman Collection

	$40	$35	$30	$25	$20	$10	N/A

MODEL 2003 – .177 cal., CO_2, thirty-five-shot, helical clip, semi-automatic, plastic grips. Mfg. 1995-2001.

	$120	$100	$85	$70	$55	$35	$25

This model can be converted to full auto, and therefore dropped by Daisy.

MODEL 5170 – BB/.175 or .177 cal., CO_2, semi-auto pistol, 21-shot clip, smoothbore steel barrel with muzzle

courtesy Daisy

GRADING	100%	95%	90%	80%	60%	40%	20%

compensator and accessory rails, 520 FPS, blade and ramp front and open rear sights, black slide and bright frame finish, molded black grips, manual trigger block safety, 9.5 in. OAL, 1 lb. New 2008.

MSR $60	$50	$45	$40	$35	$25	N/A	N/A

* ***Model 5171 Pistol Kit*** – BB/.175 or .177 cal., CO_2, semi-auto pistol, kit includes Acculaser laser sight, Red Dot scope - LED light, 350 BBs, and three 12-gram CO_2 cylinders. New 2009.

courtesy Daisy

MSR $110	$95	$85	$75	$60	$45	N/A	N/A

MODEL 5501 – BB/.175 or .177 cal., CO_2, semi-auto blowback pistol, 15-shot clip, smoothbore steel barrel, 430 FPS, fixed sights, black slide and bright frame finish, molded black grips, manual trigger block safety, pressure release valve, 6.8 in. OAL, 1 lb. New 2008.

courtesy Daisy

MSR $90	$75	$70	$60	$50	$40	N/A	N/A

* ***Model 5502*** – BB/.175 or .177 cal., CO_2, semi-auto blowback pistol, 15-shot clip, smoothbore steel barrel with muzzle compensator and accessory rails, 430 FPS, blade and ramp front and open rear sights, black slide and bright frame finish, molded black grips, manual trigger block safety, 6.8 in. OAL, 1 lb. New 2009.

courtesy Daisy

MSR $100	$85	$75	$70	$55	$40	N/A	N/A

GRADING	100%	95%	90%	80%	60%	40%	20%

* ***Model 5503 Pistol Kit*** – BB/.175 or .177 cal., CO$_2$, semi-auto pistol, kit includes Acculaser laser sight, Red Dot scope - LED light, 350 PrecisionMax BBs (new 2012), and three 12-gram CO$_2$ cylinders. New 2009.

courtesy Daisy

MSR $190	$160	$145	$130	$105	$80	N/A	N/A

MODEL 415 – BB/.175 or .177 cal. pellet, CO$_2$, semi-auto pistol, 21-shot built-in mag., smoothbore steel barrel, fiber optic front sight, fixed open rear sight, black finish, molded black checkered grips, manual trigger block safety, 495 FPS, 8.6 in. OAL, .93 lb. Mfg. 2013-current.

MSR $40	$35	$30	$25	$20	$15	N/A	N/A

Add $10 for Model 415 Pistol Kit includes the 21-shot, semi-automatic, CO$_2$-powered BB repeater, shooting glasses, three 12 gram CO$_2$ cylinders and Daisy's famous 350 count BB tube.

PISTOLS: PNEUMATIC POWERED

MODEL 717 – .177 cal., side-lever cocking, single-stroke pneumatic, single shot, 432 FPS, rifled steel barrel, blade and ramp front and adj. rear sight, molded brown checkered grips with right-hand thumb rest, crossbolt trigger block safety, 13.5 in. OAL, 2.25 lbs.

courtesy Daisy

MSR $200	$170	$150	$135	$110	$85	N/A	N/A

MODEL 722 – .22 cal., similar to Model 717. Mfg. 1981-96.

	$100	$85	$70	$60	$45	$30	$20

MODEL 747 TARGET PISTOL – .177 cal., SL, SSP, SS, 360 FPS, Lothar Walther rifled barrel, adj. trigger, left or right-hand grips available, 3.1 lbs. New 1987.

courtesy Daisy

MSR $250	$215	$190	$170	$140	$105	N/A	N/A

MODEL 777 TARGET PISTOL – .177 cal., SL, SSP, SS, Lothar Walther rifled barrel, 360 FPS, wood target-style grips, 3.2 lbs. Mfg. 1990-97.

	$250	$215	$175	$145	$115	$75	$50

Last MSR was $200.

GRADING	100%	95%	90%	80%	60%	40%	20%

MODEL 1140 – .177 cal. pellet, SSP, SS. Mfg. 1995-2000.

	100%	95%	90%	80%	60%	40%	20%
	$60	$50	$40	$35	$25	$20	$10

PISTOLS: SPRING POWERED

MODEL 62 TARGET PISTOL – .177 cal., UL, SP, SS. Mfg. by Gamo in Spain 1975-78.

	100%	95%	90%	80%	60%	40%	20%
	$90	$75	$65	$50	$40	$25	$20

MODEL 118 DAISY TARGETEER – .118 cal., #6 lead or steel shot (Daisy #6 in two sizes of metal tube), SL, SP, indoor shooting gallery air pistol, all-metal construction, fixed rear sight 1937-1941, adj. rear sight 1949-1952, chrome-plated (1949-1952), blue (1937-1951) or painted (1937-1952) finish. Mfg. 1937-1952.

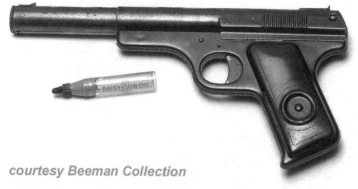

courtesy Beeman Collection

	100%	95%	90%	80%	60%	40%	20%
	$150	$130	$105	$85	$70	$45	$30

Add 35% for chrome plating on Targeteer pistols separate from shooting gallery sets.
Add 10% for non-adjustable rear sight.
Add 15% for original box with spinners, shot, and targets.

* ***Model 118 Daisy Targeteer Number 320*** – variation: Targeteer shooting gallery set with spinning targets and molded plastic trap, nickel finish gun. Vintage shooting gallery set in good condition is uncommon. Mfg. 1949-1952.

	100%	95%	90%	80%	60%	40%	20%
	$400	$350	$280	$230	$180	$120	$80

MODEL 177 BULLSEYE TARGET PISTOL – BB/.175 cal., target pistol, 150-shot, blue or painted finish, Plymouth or Rogers. Mfg. 1957-78.

	100%	95%	90%	80%	60%	40%	20%
	$75	$65	$55	$45	$35	$20	$15

Add 30% for Rogers factory box.
Add 50% for Plymouth factory box.
Add 50% for Family Fun Set with extra tube for shooting corks.

MODEL 179 PEACEMAKER REVOLVER – BB/.175 cal., spring catapult action, tubular, 12 shot tubular, spring-fed magazine. Mfg. 1960-81.

	100%	95%	90%	80%	60%	40%	20%
	$130	$110	$90	$75	$60	$40	$25

* ***Model 179 Peacemaker (Solid Brass Variant)*** – BB/.175 cal., variation mfg. of solid cast brass, very heavy, painted gray. Serial numbers to 34 are known, 10.5 in. OAL, No markings except SN stamped on butt, weighs 2.7 lbs!

courtesy Beeman Collection

	100%	95%	90%	80%	60%	40%	20%
	$2,000	$1,700	$1,400	$1,150	$900	$600	$400

MODEL 180 PEACEMAKER REVOLVER – BB/.175 cal., similar to Model 179, except boxed set with revolver with holster. Mfg. 1960-81.

	100%	95%	90%	80%	60%	40%	20%
	$250	$215	$175	$145	$115	$75	$50

GRADING	100%	95%	90%	80%	60%	40%	20%

MODEL 188 – BB/.175 cal., UL, SP, 24-four-shot. Mfg. 1979-89.

	100%	95%	90%	80%	60%	40%	20%
	$50	$45	$35	$30	$25	$15	$10

MODEL 201 – BB/.175 and .177 pellet cal., SP, 35-shot BB or SS pellet, smooth bore steel barrel, 230 FPS, blade and ramp front and fixed rear sights, trigger block safety, 9.25 in. OAL, 1 lbs. New 2008.

courtesy Daisy

MSR $25	$20	$18	$15	$13	$10	N/A	N/A

MODEL 288 – BB/.175 cal., UL, SP, 24-four-shot. Mfg. 1991-2001.

	$25	$20	$20	$15	$10	N/A	N/A

MODEL 340 – BB/.175 and .177 pellet cal., SP, 200-shot BB reservoir with 13-shot speedloader clip, black finish, smooth bore steel barrel, 240 FPS, blade and ramp front and fixed rear sights, molded black grip, trigger block safety, 8.5 in. OAL, 1 lbs. Mfg. 2013-current.

MSR $25	$20	$18	$15	$13	$10	N/A	N/A

MODEL 579 TEXAS RANGER – BB/.175 cal., Texas Rangers set of two matching guns similar to Model 197, each with grips imbedded with miniature Texas Rangers badges, barrels stamped "1823 - Texas Rangers - 1973", special box, booklet on Texas Ranger history. Mfg. 1973-1974.

	$500	$425	$350	$290	$225	$150	$100

RIFLES: BREAK ACTION, PRE-1900 (CAST METAL FRAME)

This grouping includes the early Daisy cast metal lever and break action BB guns, mfg. 1888-1900.

1ST MODEL – large BB/.180 cal., single-shot, muzzle-loading brass tubing barrel and air chamber, cast iron or brass frame, wire skeleton stock without wood, nickel plated, post front sight, V-notch rear sight integral with top cocking lever. Production quantities were very low, but unknown (despite previous claims). Mfg. by Plymouth Iron Windmill Co. 1889-95. Dates on variants unknown.

* **1ST Model Variant One** – cocking lever marked "Pat. Appl. For PIW", cast iron frame.

	N/A	N/A	$4,500	$3,200	$2,750	$2,125	$1,475

* **1ST Model Variant Two** – similar to variant one, but with brass frame. This may be the rarest of the Daisy First Models.

	N/A	N/A	$7,500	$6,500	$4,550	$3,500	$2,450

* **1ST Model Variant Three** – similar to variant two, brass frame with reinforcing rib where wire stock enters frame.

	N/A	N/A	$4,500	$3,200	$2,750	$2,125	$1,475

* **1ST Model Variant Four** – cocking lever marked "DAISY PAT. AUG. 1889 PLYMOUTH, MICH.", cast brass frame, no verifiable information on production quantities or mfg. dates.

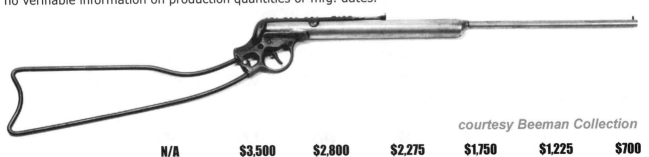

courtesy Beeman Collection

	N/A	$3,500	$2,800	$2,275	$1,750	$1,225	$700

GRADING	100%	95%	90%	80%	60%	40%	20%

* ***1ST Model Variant Five*** – similar to variant four, but with much more prominent, more highly raised cast lettering.

	N/A	$3,500	$2,800	$2,275	$1,750	$1,225	$700

Warning on Daisy First Models: reportedly there are fake specimens of some of the rarest versions of early cast metal Daisy airguns. Sometimes this takes the form of fake cocking levers on legitimate specimens of more common models. Careful measurements may be necessary to detect such fraudulent arrangements. It may be best to consult with a trusted Daisy expert before purchasing some of the most valuable specimens.

Replicas: For collectors who cannot locate some of the rarest models or are not willing to spend the large amounts necessary to obtain them, there are some legitimate replicas available.

2ND MODEL – large BB/.180 cal., break-open design, SS, brass tubing barrel and air chamber, cast iron frame, wire skeleton stock, nickel-plated post front sight, V-notch rear sight integral with breech, left frame marked "Daisy Imp'd Pat' May 6, 90", right frame marked "MFG. BY P.I.W. & CO. PLYMOUTH MICH." Quantities unknown, but far less than 1st Model. 31.5 in. OAL, 2.6 lbs. Mfg. by Plymouth Iron Windmill Co, 1890-91. Extremely rare.

courtesy Beeman Collection

	N/A	$7,000	$5,600	$4,550	$3,500	$2,450	$1,400

3RD MODEL – large BB/.180 cal., break open design, SS, brass tubing barrel and air chamber, cast iron frame, wire skeleton stock with or without wood insert, nickel plated, post front sight, V-notch rear sight, frame marked "Daisy Pat. May 6, 90, July 14, 91", 31.5 in. OAL, 2.3 lbs. Mfg. 1893-94. Rare.

* ***3RD Model "New Daisy" Variant*** – checkered frame, wire stock without wood insert, grip frame marked "NEW DAISY". Mfg. 1892-1895.

	N/A	$2,500	$2,000	$1,625	$1,250	$875	$500

* ***3RD Model "New Daisy" Variant*** – wire stock with wood insert, frame marked "NEW DAISY".

courtesy Beeman Collection

	N/A	$2,750	$2,200	$1,775	$1,375	$950	$550

* ***3RD Model "Raised Letter" Variant*** – wire stock without wood insert, patent dates on left side of grip frame. Garber (2007) recognizes 8 variations of the "RAISED LETTER" variant.

	N/A	$2,750	$2,200	$1,775	$1,375	$950	$550

* ***3RD Model "Raised Letter" Variant*** – wire stock with wood insert, patent dates on left side of grip frame.

	N/A	$2,750	$2,200	$1,775	$1,375	$950	$550

* ***3RD Model ("Model 96") Variant*** – marked "MODEL 96" and "DAISY", all wood stock. Mfg. 1896.

	N/A	$2,250	$1,800	$1,450	$1,125	$775	$450

* ***3RD Model "Model" Variant*** – marked "MODEL" only on right side of frame, marked "DAISY" on left side (possibly from modified Model 96 mold), all wood stock. Mfg. 1897.

courtesy Beeman Collection

	N/A	$2,250	$1,800	$1,450	$1,125	$775	$450

GRADING	100%	95%	90%	80%	60%	40%	20%

RIFLES: BREAK ACTION, POST-1900

This grouping starts with the 20th Century models mfg. beginning circa 1898.

20TH CENTURY CAST IRON FRAME SINGLE SHOT – BB/.180 cal., break action, SS, sheet metal barrel. Removable shot tube. Cast iron trigger, trigger guard, and frame (except as noted below), nickel finish, fixed sights, marked on the right side "20th CENTURY", on the left side marked "DAISY" between bullseyes. Slab-sided stocks. Stocks impressed on left side, "Daisy Mfg. Co., May 6, 90 July 14, 91". Mfg. 1898-1902.

* **20th Century Cast Iron Frame Single Shot First Variant** – wire stock without wood, checkered cast brass below barrel.

	N/A	$1,500	$1,200	$975	$750	$525	$300

* **20th Century Cast Iron Frame Single Shot Second Variant** – wood stock, checkered cast brass below barrel.

	N/A	$800	$650	$525	$400	$280	$160

* **20th Century Cast Iron Frame Single Shot Third Variant** – wire stock without wood, sheet metal wrap around base of barrel.

	N/A	$1,500	$1,200	$975	$750	$525	$300

* **20th Century Cast Iron Frame Single Shot Fourth Variant** – wood stock, sheet metal wrap around base of barrel.

	N/A	$800	$650	$525	$400	$280	$160

20TH CENTURY CAST IRON FRAME REPEATER – BB/.180 cal., break action, forty-shot, marked on right side "REPEATER", left side marked "DAISY". Mfg. 1898-1902.

* **20th Century Cast Iron Frame Repeater First Variant** – wood stock, checkered cast brass below barrel.

	N/A	$2,000	$1,600	$1,300	$1,000	$700	$400

* **20th Century Cast Iron Frame Repeater Second Variant** – wood stock, sheet metal wrap around base of barrel.

	N/A	$1,500	$1,200	$900	$700	$500	$300

Note: 20th Century models with checkered cast brass below the barrel sometimes are referred to as "Fourth Model" Daisys.

20TH CENTURY SHEET METAL FRAME SINGLE SHOT – BB/.180 cal., break action, sheet metal barrel and frame, cast iron trigger guard and trigger, removable shot tube, nickel finish, peep sight. Mfg. 1903-1910.

courtesy Beeman Collection

* **20th Century Sheet Metal Frame Single Shot First Variant** – two-step body tube (forward end of body tube steps down to barrel diameter in two steps), right side of frame with letters "PATENTED" plus patent numbers in indented rectangle, left side of frame is marked "DAISY" in indented rectangle, cast iron spring anchor (plate inside lower edge of body tube - open action to view). Slab-sided stock.

	N/A	$400	$325	$260	$200	$140	$80

* **20th Century Sheet Metal Frame Single Shot Second Variant** – similar to First Variant, except printing on right side of frame changed to just patent dates, slab-sided stock, most common of Sheet Metal 20th Century air rifles.

	N/A	$400	$325	$260	$200	$140	$80

* **20th Century Sheet Metal Frame Single Shot Third Variant** – similar to second variant, except stock is oval in profile, two-step barrel.

	N/A	$400	$325	$260	$200	$140	$80

GRADING	100%	95%	90%	80%	60%	40%	20%

* 20th Century Sheet Metal Frame Single Shot Fourth Variant – one-step body tube, cast iron spring anchor, long body tube (10.7 in.), 7 in. barrel.

	N/A	$400	$325	$260	$200	$140	$80

* 20th Century Sheet Metal Frame Single Shot Fifth Variant – similar to fourth variant, except shorter body tube (10 in.), 7.4 in. barrel.

	N/A	$400	$325	$260	$200	$140	$80

* 20th Century Sheet Metal Frame Single Shot Sixth Variant – similar to fourth variant (10.7 in. body tube, 7 in. barrel), except has sheet metal spring anchor.

	N/A	$400	$325	$260	$200	$140	$80

* 20th Century Sheet Metal Frame Single Shot Seventh Variant – indented rectangle on both side of frame stamped "DAISY" between two bullseyes.

	N/A	$600	$475	$400	$300	$210	$120

20TH CENTURY SHEET METAL FRAME REPEATER – BB/.180 cal., break action, sheet metal barrel and frame, cast iron trigger guard and trigger, shot tube and magazine tube remove together as a unit, magazine visible as small removable tube parallel under barrel housing from forward end of one-step body tube to muzzle (not really a repeater; unique forty-shot magazine must be moved to release each BB into firing position), nickel finish, peep sight. Mfg. 1903-1910.

* 20th Century Sheet Metal Frame Repeater First Variant – shot tube release is tiny latch behind front sight.

	N/A	$700	$550	$450	$350	$245	$140

* 20th Century Sheet Metal Frame Repeater Second Variant – shot tube release is a latch under the barrel with a magazine cover.

	N/A	$700	$550	$450	$350	$245	$140

* 20th Century Sheet Metal Frame Repeater Third Variant – shot tube release is a spring-loaded front sight which moves in an L-shaped slot to allow shot tube removal (Hough-style shot tube system).

courtesy Beeman Collection

	N/A	$750	$600	$475	$375	$265	$150

* 20th Century Sheet Metal Frame Repeater Fourth Variant – indented rectangle on both sides of the frame, stamped "DAISY" between two bullseyes.

	N/A	$800	$650	$525	$400	$280	$160

MODEL A REPEATER – BB/.180 cal., break action, 350-shot loading port behind blade front sight, repeater, nickel. Frame is marked "DAISY" between bullseyes, address and patents are on barrel top. Mfg. 1908-14.

	N/A	$3,500	$2,800	$2,275	$1,750	$1,225	$700

MODEL A SINGLE SHOT – BB/.180 cal., break action, SS, marked on barrel: "DAISY SINGLE SHOT MODEL A". Mfg. 1908-14.

	N/A	$3,500	$2,800	$2,275	$1,750	$1,225	$700

MODEL C NO. 1 REPEATER – BB/.175 cal., break action, 350-shot. Mfg. 1910-14.

courtesy Beeman Collection

	N/A	$500	$400	$325	$250	$175	$100

GRADING	100%	95%	90%	80%	60%	40%	20%

MODEL C NO. 2 SINGLE SHOT – BB/.175 cal., break action, SS, nickel finish. Mfg. 1911-1914.

	N/A	$400	$325	$260	$200	$140	$80

MODEL 20 "LITTLE DAISY" – BB/.175 cal., break action, Daisy's smallest BB rifle.

* *Model 20 "Little Daisy" Variant 1 (Frameless Model)* – nickel finish, no metal around grip. Mfg. 1908-11.

	N/A	$1,500	$1,200	$975	$750	$525	$300

* *Model 20 "Little Daisy" Variant 2 (Grip Frame Model)* – nickel finish, metal around grip (full grip frame), regular style cast iron trigger in trigger guard. Mfg. 1912-15.

	N/A	$700	$550	$450	$350	$245	$140

* *Model 20 "Little Daisy" Variant 3 (Ring Trigger Model)* – nickel or blue finish, cast iron ring trigger without guard, full grip frame. Mfg. 1915-37. Garber (2007) recognizes eight variations of this Model 20.

courtesy Beeman Collection

	N/A	$300	$240	$195	$150	$105	$60

MODEL 21 SIDE BY SIDE – BB/.175 cal., break action, ribbed barrel divider, dark and light brown plastic stock. Mfg. 1968-72.

	N/A	$800	$650	$525	$400	$280	$160

Last MSR was approximately $25.

* *Model 21 Sears Side by Side* – BB/.175 cal., break action, checkered barrel divider, wooden stock. Mfg. 1968 only.

	N/A	$1,400	$1,125	$900	$700	$500	$280

Add 30% for checkered rib.
Add 50-100% for the approx. 48 walnut stock sets mfg. by Reinhart Fajen, Inc. and Bishop Stock Co.

MODEL 104 SIDE BY SIDE – BB/.175 cal., break action, 96-shot spring-fed repeater, sheet metal, side-by-side barrel tubes with Model 25-type shot tubes, left and right shot tubes marked L and R, dummy sidelocks, blue, walnut stock, stamped designs of game birds, dogs, and scrolls. Approx. 45,000 mfg. 1938-40.

courtesy Beeman Collection

	N/A	$1,200	$1,000	$800	$600	$400	$200

MODEL 106 – BB/.175 cal., break action, 500-shot, painted finish, Plymouth or Rogers address. Mfg. 1957-1958.

	$150	$130	$105	$85	$70	$45	$30

Add 20% for Plymouth address.

MODEL 181 (JUNIOR SHOOTING OUTFIT) – BB/.177 cal., break action, boxed set, special target with gun. Mfg. 1949 only.

	$1,500	$1,275	$1,050	$875	$675	$450	$300

SENTINEL REPEATER – BB/.180 large cal., break action, 303-shot magazine. Sentinel models are not marked Daisy, but are shown in Daisy ads of the time. Mfg. 1900-1902. Ref: AR4.

* *Sentinel Repeater Variant 1* – 20th Century model frame, marked "SENTINEL" on grip frame. Made for A.F. Chaffee.

	N/A	$1,200	$950	$775	$600	$425	$240

GRADING	100%	95%	90%	80%	60%	40%	20%

* *Sentinel Repeater Variant 2* – marked "SENTINEL" on stock.

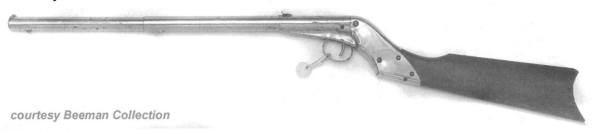

courtesy Beeman Collection

| | N/A | $1,350 | $1,075 | $875 | $675 | $475 | $270 |

SENTINEL SINGLE SHOT – large BB/.180 cal., break action. Mfg. circa 1908.

* *Sentinel Single Shot Variant 1* – marked "SENTINEL" on grip frame.

| | N/A | $900 | $725 | $575 | $450 | $325 | $180 |

* *Sentinel Single Shot Variant 2* – marked "SENTINEL" on stock.

| | N/A | $900 | $725 | $575 | $450 | $325 | $180 |

RIFLES: BREAK BARREL COCKING

MODEL 91 – .177 cal., BBC, SS, economy model made in Hungary by FEG.

| $50 | $45 | $35 | $30 | $25 | $15 | $10 |

MODEL 120 – .177 cal. pellet, BBC. Mfg. by El Gamo in Spain, 1984-85.

courtesy Howard Collection

| $75 | $65 | $55 | $45 | $35 | $20 | $15 |

MODEL 130 – .177 cal. pellet, BBC. Mfg. by Milbro in Scotland, 1983-85.

| $75 | $65 | $55 | $45 | $35 | $20 | $15 |

MODEL 130 EL GAMO – .177 cal. pellet, BBC, auto pellet feed, 800 FPS, adj. micrometer rear sight, 5.75 lbs. Mfg. by El Gamo in Spain 1986-1993.

| $85 | $70 | $60 | $50 | $40 | $25 | $15 |

Last MSR was $150.

MODEL 131 – .177 cal. pellet, BBC, 630 FPS, adj. micrometer rear sight, 5.4 lbs. Mfg. by El Gamo in Spain.

| $75 | $65 | $55 | $45 | $35 | $20 | $15 |

Last MSR was $120.

MODEL 160 – BB/.175 or .177 cal., pellet or dart, blue finish. Mfg. by Milbro in Scotland 1965-1974.

courtesy Beeman Collection

| $75 | $65 | $55 | $45 | $35 | $20 | $15 |

Note: This was a Diana brand airgun made by Milbro in Scotland, not to be confused with Diana brand airguns from Dianawerk in Rastatt, Germany. At the end of WWII, England was given the Diana brand and Dianawerk's (Mayer and Grammelspacher) factory machinery as war reparations. The defeated Germans had to install all new machinery and

GRADING	100%	95%	90%	80%	60%	40%	20%

temporarily use "Original" as a brand. Milbro, with the old German equipment, went out of business, and the Diana brand was restored to Dianawerk in Germany.

MODEL 220 – .177 cal. pellet, BBC, SP, blue finish. Mfg. by Milbro in Scotland (see note about Diana brand in Model 160 listing), 1965-70.

courtesy Beeman Collection

	$85	$70	$60	$50	$40	$25	$15

MODEL 225 – .177 cal. pellet, BBC, SP, blue finish. Mfg. by Milbro in Scotland, 1971-74.

	$100	$85	$70	$60	$45	$30	$20

MODEL 230 – .22 cal., BBC, SP, blue finish. Mfg. by Milbro in Scotland, 1965-74.

	$80	$70	$55	$45	$35	$25	$15

MODEL 250 – .22 cal., BBC, SP, blue finish. Mfg. by Milbro in Scotland, 1965-74.

	$125	$105	$90	$75	$55	$35	$25

MODEL 500 POWERLINE – .177 cal., BBC, SP, SS, 490 FPS, rifled steel barrel, stained solid wood stock, forearm, and grip, hooded front and adj. rear sights, 4x32 scope, 45.7 in. OAL, 6.6 lbs. Disc. 2011.

courtesy Daisy

	$125	$105	$90	$75	$55	$35	$25

Last MSR was $150.

MODEL 800 POWERLINE – .177 cal., BBC, SP, SS, 800 FPS, rifled steel barrel, Truglo fiber-optic front and micro-adj. rear sights, 4x32 scope, grooved receiver, auto-rear safety button, sporter-style black composite stock, 6.6 lbs., 46.7 in. OAL. Mfg. 2008-2011.

courtesy Daisy

	$100	$85	$70	$60	$45	$30	$20

Last MSR was $121.

MODEL 1000 POWERLINE – .177 cal., BBC, SP, SS, 1000 FPS, rifled steel barrel with solid steel shroud, Truglo fiber-optic front and micro-adj. rear sights, 4x32 scope, grooved receiver, auto-rear safety button, sporter-style

GRADING	100%	95%	90%	80%	60%	40%	20%

stained solid wood stock, 45.75 in. OAL, 6.6 lbs. Mfg. 2009-2011.

courtesy Daisy

	$125	$105	$90	$75	$55	$35	$25

Last MSR was $150.

MODEL 1000 – .177 cal., BBC, 1000 FPS, adj. rear with hooded front sight, hardwood Monte Carlo stock, 6.125 lbs. New 1997. Disc.

	$135	$115	$95	$80	$60	$40	$25

Last MSR was $175.

MODEL 1170 – .177 cal., BBC, 800 FPS, adj. micrometer rear sight, 5 1/2 lbs. Disc.

	$85	$70	$60	$50	$40	$25	$15

Last MSR was $110.

NO. 100 MODEL 38 – BB/.175 cal., BBC, SS, blue finish. Mfg. 1938-1941, and 1948-1952.

	$225	$190	$160	$130	$100	$65	$45

RIFLES: LEVER ACTION

This grouping includes models with a "Winchester-style" lever under the gun that is also a trigger guard.

MODEL B 1000 SHOT – BB/.175 cal., 1,000 shot. Mfg. 1910.

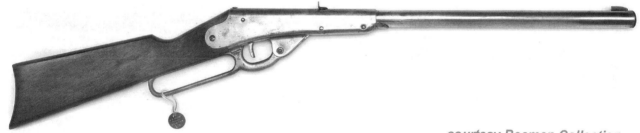

courtesy Beeman Collection

* ***Model B 1000 Shot Variant 1*** – nickel finish, cast iron rear sight, brass barrel, steel buttplate.

$400	$350	$280	$230	$180	$120	$80

* ***Model B 1000 Shot Variant 2*** – similar to Variant 1, except w/sheet metal barrel w/o buttplate.

$350	$300	$245	$205	$160	$105	$70

* ***Model B 1000 Shot Variant 3*** – similar to Variant 2, except w/sheet metal rear sight w/o buttplate.

$350	$300	$245	$205	$160	$105	$70

* ***Model B 1000 Shot Variant 4*** – similar to Variant 3, except blue finish.

$350	$300	$245	$205	$160	$105	$70

MODEL B 500 SHOT – BB/.175 cal., without steel buttplate. Mfg. 1910-23.

* ***Model B 500 Shot Variant 1*** – nickel finish, cast iron rear sight, brass barrel, steel buttplate.

$350	$300	$245	$205	$160	$105	$70

* ***Model B 500 Shot Variant 2*** – similar to Variant 1, except with sheet metal barrel.

$350	$300	$245	$205	$160	$105	$70

* ***Model B 500 Shot Variant 3*** – similar to Variant 2, except with sheet metal rear sight.

$350	$300	$245	$205	$160	$105	$70

* ***Model B 500 Shot Variant 4*** – similar to Variant 3, except has blue finish.

GRADING	100%	95%	90%	80%	60%	40%	20%

MODEL H SINGLE SHOT – BB/.175 cal., nickel finish mfg. 1913-20, blue finish mfg. 1921-23.

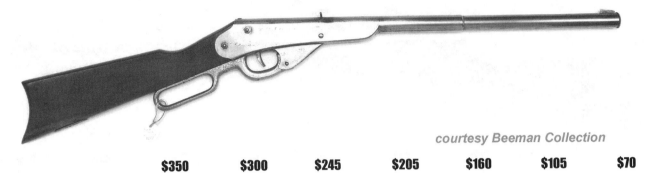

courtesy Beeman Collection

	$350	$300	$245	$205	$160	$105	$70

Add 20% for nickel finish.

Historical Note: This specimen, and several other illustrated BB rifles, engraved W.R.A. with date, were formerly in the Winchester Repeating Arms collection.

MODEL H REPEATER – BB/.175 cal., 500-shot nickel finish mfg. 1914-17, 350-shot nickel finish mfg. 1921-32, 350-shot blue finish mfg. 1918-20.

	$300	$255	$210	$175	$135	$90	$60

MODEL 3 SERIES B "DAISY SPECIAL" – BB/.175 cal., 1000-shot, black nickel finish, in lithograph box. Mfg. 1904-1908.

	$1,500	$1,275	$1,050	$875	$675	$450	$300

Add 10% for poor original box.
Add 20% for restored original box.
Add 100% or more for excellent original box.

MODEL 10 – BB/.177 cal., lever-cocking, spring air, 400-shot, smooth bore steel barrel and receiver, 350 FPS, stained wood stock and forearm, trigger block safety, leather thong and saddle ring, blade and ramp front and fixed open rear sights, 29.8 in. OAL. Mfg. 2010-current.

courtesy Daisy

MSR $35	$30	$25	$25	$20	$15	N/A	N/A

MODEL 27 (500 SHOT) – BB/.175 cal., 500-shot, blue finish. Mfg. 1927-32.

	$225	$190	$160	$130	$100	$65	$45

MODEL 27 (1000 SHOT) – BB/.175 cal., 1000-shot, nickel finish. Mfg. 1927-32.

	$300	$255	$210	$175	$135	$90	$60

MODEL 50 GOLDEN EAGLE – BB/.175 cal., commemorates 50th anniversary of Daisy, special copper-plated model, similar to No. 195 Buzz Barton, pistol grip stock and curved lever, easily identified by black painted stock with red, white, and blue federal eagle decal, and sight tube mounted on top of gun, hooded front sight. Mfg. 1936-1940. Very scarce.

	$400	$350	$280	$230	$180	$120	$80

Originally sold for $2.34 by Sears Roebuck & Co. in 1937.

MODEL 75 SCOUT RIFLE – BB/.175 cal., 500-shot, painted finish. Mfg. 1954-1958.

	$110	$95	$75	$65	$50	$35	$20

MODEL 80 – BB/.175 cal., 1000-shot repeater, with scope and canteen, painted. Mfg. 1954-1957.

	$300	$255	$210	$175	$135	$90	$60

* **Model 80/155** – over stamp. Mfg. 1955.

	$150	$130	$105	$85	$70	$45	$30

GRADING	100%	95%	90%	80%	60%	40%	20%

MODEL 83 – BB/.175 cal., 350-shot, scope. Mfg. 1961-1963.

	$300	$255	$210	$175	$135	$90	$60

MODEL 86 SERIES 70 SAFARI MARK 1 – BB/.175 cal., 240-shot repeater. Mfg. 1970-76.

	$130	$110	$90	$75	$60	$40	$25

Add 20% for factory box with large game poster.

MODEL 88 HUNTER – BB/.175 cal., 1000-shot, 2X scope, plastic stock, painted finish. Mfg. 1959-1960.

	$100	$85	$70	$60	$45	$30	$20

* **Sears Variant** – BB/.175 cal., Sears number 799.19920, Golden Hunter - J.C. Higgins. Mfg. 1957-1958.

	$125	$105	$90	$75	$55	$35	$25

MODEL 90 SPORTSTER – BB/.175 cal., 700-shot, safety, plastic stock, painted finish. Mfg. 1973-78.

	$75	$65	$55	$45	$35	$20	$15

MODEL 95 – BB/.175 cal., 700-shot, early versions: wood stock, plastic forearm; later version: wood/wood, painted finish. Mfg. 1962-76.

	$50	$45	$35	$30	$25	$15	$10

Quick Kill version - see Model 2299 Quick Kill listing.

* **Model 95A** – BB/.175 cal., 700-shot, plastic stock, painted finish. Mfg. 1979-80.

	$50	$45	$35	$30	$25	$15	$10

* **Model 95 Timberwolf** – BB/.175, .177 cal., LA, spring air, 325 FPS, 700-shot, black finish, stained wood stock, crossbolt trigger block safety, adj. rear sight, 2.4 lbs. Mfg. 2002-2004.

	$40	$35	$30	$25	$20	$10	N/A

* **Model 95 Pony Express** – similar to Timberwolf. Mfg. 1999.

	$150	$130	$105	$85	$70	$45	$30

* **Model 95 Gold Rush** – similar to Pony Express. Mfg. 1999.

	$150	$130	$105	$85	$70	$45	$30

MODEL 96 – BB/.175 cal., LA, 700-shot, painted finish. Mfg. 1963-73.

	$85	$70	$60	$50	$40	$25	$15

MODEL 97 SADDLE GUN – BB/.175 cal., LA, 650-shot, ricochet sound device, painted finish, plastic stock. Mfg. 1961 only.

	$180	$155	$125	$105	$80	$55	$35

MODEL 98 – BB/.175 cal., 700-shot, plastic or wood stock. Mfg. 1974 only.

	$85	$70	$60	$50	$40	$25	$15

Add 20% for wood stock.

MODEL 98 DAISY EAGLE – BB/.175 cal., 2X scope, plastic stock, painted finish, leather sling, Plymouth or Rogers addresses. Mfg. 1955-1960.

	$300	$255	$210	$175	$135	$90	$60

Add 20% for Plymouth address.

* **Model 98 Golden Eagle** – similar to Model 98 Daisy Eagle, with scope. 1957.

	$300	$255	$210	$175	$135	$90	$60

* **Model 98 Golden Hunter** – similar to Model 98 Daisy Eagle, with scope. 1958.

	$300	$255	$210	$175	$135	$90	$60

MODEL 99 TARGET SPECIAL – BB/.175 cal., painted finish, web sling.

* **Model 99 Target Special Variant 1** – gravity-fed magazine. Mfg. only 1959.

	$135	$115	$95	$80	$60	$40	$25

* **Model 99 Target Special Variant 2** – spring-fed magazine. Mfg. 1960-1979.

	$100	$85	$70	$60	$45	$30	$20

GRADING	100%	95%	90%	80%	60%	40%	20%

MODEL 99 CHAMPION – mfg. 1967.

	100%	95%	90%	80%	60%	40%	20%
	$100	$85	$70	$60	$45	$30	$20

Add 10% for peep sight.

MODEL 99 LUCKY MCDANIELS INSTINCT SHOOTER – BB/.175 cal., no sights. Mfg. 1960 only.

	$350	$300	$245	$205	$160	$105	$70

MODEL 102 CUB – BB/.175 cal., 350-shot, blue finish, wooden stock. Mfg. 1952-78.

	$85	$70	$60	$50	$40	$25	$15

MODEL 103 SCOUT – BB/.175 cal., plastic stock, painted finish. Mfg. 1964-1965 (disc. circa 1990).

	$75	$65	$55	$45	$35	$20	$15

MODEL 104 GOLDEN EAGLE – BB/.175 cal., 500-shot, plastic stock, peep sight, gold or black paint. Mfg. 1966-74.

	$125	$105	$90	$75	$55	$35	$25

MODEL 105 BUCK – BB/.177 cal., LA, SP, 275 FPS, 400-shot, smooth bore steel barrel, black finish, stained solid wood stock, crossbolt trigger block safety, TruGlo fiber optic fixed sights, 29.8 in. OAL, 1.6 lbs.

courtesy Daisy

MSR $30	$25	$25	$20	$15	$15	N/A	N/A

MODEL 105 CUB – BB/.175 cal., 350-shot, painted finish. Mfg. 1979-81, 1982-90.

courtesy Beeman Collection

	$45	$40	$30	$25	$20	$15	N/A

MODEL 108 SERIES 39 LONE SCOUT – BB/.175 cal., lightning loader, blue finish. Mfg. 1939 only.

	$500	$425	$350	$290	$225	$150	$100

*** Model 108 Series 39** – BB/.175 cal., lightning loader, adj. or fixed rear sight, blue finish. Mfg. 1939-42 and 1945.

	$200	$170	$140	$115	$90	$60	$40

MODEL 110 AIR FORCE ROCKET COMMAND – BB/.175 cal., LA. Mfg. 1959 only.

	$300	$255	$210	$175	$135	$90	$60

MODEL 111 WESTERN CARBINE – BB/.175 cal., 700-shot, plastic stock, curved cocking lever. Mfg. 1963-78.

courtesy Howard Collection

	$125	$105	$90	$75	$55	$35	$25

GRADING	100%	95%	90%	80%	60%	40%	20%

MODEL 155 – BB/.175 cal., repeater, blue finish (painted finish 1953), stamped "1000 shot", cast iron cocking lever 1946, aluminum lever 1947-1949. Reintroduced 1952-1953.

	$180	$155	$125	$105	$80	$55	$35

MODEL 299 – BB/.175 cal., 1000-shot, peep sight. Gravity-fed version of Model 99. Mfg. 1975-76.

	$100	$85	$70	$60	$45	$30	$20

MODEL 400 – BB/.175 cal., five-shot Roto-clip, .177 cal. pellet. Mfg. 1971-72.

	$100	$85	$70	$60	$45	$30	$20

MODEL 403 – BB/.175 cal., five-shot Roto-clip, .177 cal. pellet. Status of this model not clear. Mfg. 1973-76.

	$125	$105	$90	$75	$55	$35	$25

MODEL 404 – BB/.175 cal., five-shot Roto-clip, .177 cal. pellet. Mfg. 1974-76.

	$125	$105	$90	$75	$55	$35	$25

MODEL 450 – BB/.175 cal., five-shot Roto-clip, .177 cal. pellet. Mfg. 1972-73.

	$75	$65	$55	$45	$35	$20	$15

MODEL 452 – BB/.175 cal., five-shot Roto-clip, .177 cal. pellet. Mfg. 1973 only.

	$125	$105	$90	$75	$55	$35	$25

MODEL 453 – BB/.175 cal., five-shot Roto-clip, .177 cal. pellet. Mfg. 1974-76.

	$75	$65	$55	$45	$35	$20	$15

MODEL 454 – BB/.175 cal., five-shot Roto-clip, .177 cal. pellet. Mfg. 1974-76.

	$110	$95	$75	$65	$50	$35	$20

MODEL 499 – BB/.175 cal., target single shot, plastic or wood stock. Mfg. 1976-79.

	$125	$105	$90	$75	$55	$35	$25

AVANTI MODEL 499 CHAMPION – BB/.177 (4.5mm steel shot) cal., SP, SS muzzle loading, lever action smoothbore steel BBL, 240 FPS, hooded front with aperture inserts and adj. rear peep sights, Monte Carlo stained hardwood stock and forearm with weight compartments, 36.25 in. OAL, 3.1 lbs. New 2003.

courtesy Daisy

MSR $140	$120	$105	$95	$75	$60	N/A	N/A

MODEL 770 SUPER – .177 cal. pellet, UL, SP, single-stroke cocking. Mfg. 1978-80.

	$115	$100	$80	$65	$50	$35	$25

MODEL 1000 – BB/.175 cal., Western Auto. Mfg. 1957-1958.

	$90	$75	$65	$50	$40	$25	$20

MODEL 1105 – BB/.175 cal., 500-shot, safety. Mfg. 1975-79.

	$50	$45	$35	$30	$25	$15	$10

MODEL 1200 – BB/.175 cal., gold finish, blonde stock, Western Auto. Mfg. 1976-77.

	$125	$105	$90	$75	$55	$35	$25

MODEL 1205 – BB/.175 cal., economy version of Model 1200, sixty-shot. Mfg. 1979-81.

	$100	$85	$70	$60	$45	$30	$20

MODEL 1776 GOLDEN EAGLE – BB/.175 cal., 500-shot, peep sight, gold paint finish. Mfg. 1968-72.

	$200	$170	$140	$115	$90	$60	$40

GRADING	100%	95%	90%	80%	60%	40%	20%

MODEL 1894 WESTERN CARBINE – BB/.175 cal., forty-shot, grey painted finish, metal buttplate, plastic stock. Mfg. 1961-86.

	100%	95%	90%	80%	60%	40%	20%
	$125	$105	$90	$75	$55	$35	$25

Subtract 40% for missing factory box.

* ***Model 1894 Western Carbine And Pistol Set*** – BB/.175 cal., valued as a set. Mfg. 1970-80.

	100%	95%	90%	80%	60%	40%	20%
	$250	$215	$175	$145	$115	$75	$50

Subtract 40% for missing factory box.

* ***Model 1894 Buffalo Bill 150th Anniversary Model*** – see Daisy Commemorative section.

* ***Model 1894 Carbine Sears Variant Number 799.19052*** – see Daisy Commemorative section.

* ***Model 1894 Carbine Sears Variant Number 799.19120*** – see Daisy Commemorative section.

* ***Model 1894 Commemorative Wells Fargo Limited Edition*** – BB/.175 cal. Mfg. 1975-76.

	100%	95%	90%	80%	60%	40%	20%
	$300	$255	$210	$175	$135	$90	$60

Subtract 40% for missing factory box.

* ***Model 1894 Commemorative 1894-1994 Limited Edition*** – BB/.175 cal., octagon barrel. Mfg. 1994.

	100%	95%	90%	80%	60%	40%	20%
	$140	$120	$100	$80	$65	$40	$30

Subtract 40% for missing factory box.

* ***Model 1894 Cactus Carbine Sears Variant Number 799.19210*** – J.C. Higgins. Mfg. 1960-70.

	100%	95%	90%	80%	60%	40%	20%
	$100	$85	$70	$60	$45	$30	$20

* ***Daisy 1894 Carbine Sears Variant Number 799.19250*** – BB/.175 cal., J.C. Higgins. Mfg. 1952-1955.

	100%	95%	90%	80%	60%	40%	20%
	$100	$85	$70	$60	$45	$30	$20

MODEL 1998 PINK LEVER ACTION (SALUTING WOMEN IN THE OUTDOORS) – BB/.175 (disc.) or .177 cal., LA, SP, 350 FPS, 650-shot, smooth bore steel barrel, black finish, pink painted wood stock/forearm, crossbolt trigger block safety, blade and ramp front and adj. rear sights, saddle ring with pink leather saddle tie, 35.4 in. OAL, 2.2 lbs. New 2008.

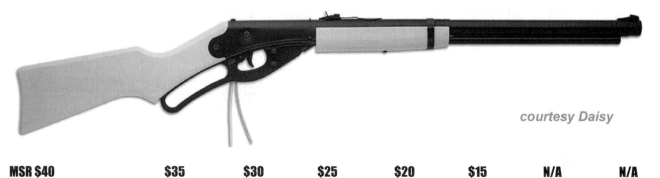

courtesy Daisy

MSR $40	100%	95%	90%	80%	60%	40%	20%
	$35	$30	$25	$20	$15	N/A	N/A

Add $5 for Model 4998 Lever Action Carbine Shooting Fun Starter Kit which includes the Pink Model 1998 BB gun, PrecisionMax 750 count BB tin, pink shooting glasses, and paper target fun pack.

MODEL 2299 QUICK KILL – civilian version of the U.S. Govt. Quick Kill, no sights, in box with safety glasses, aerial targets. Mfg. 1968-72.

	100%	95%	90%	80%	60%	40%	20%
	$200	$170	$140	$115	$90	$60	$40

Subtract 35% for missing box.

MODEL 2299 QUICK KILL U.S. GOVERNMENT ISSUE – no sights, used with fluorescent BBs to teach instinct shooting to troops in the Vietnam war, U.S. Govt. marking stamped into, or stenciled onto, stock. Mfg. 1968-70.

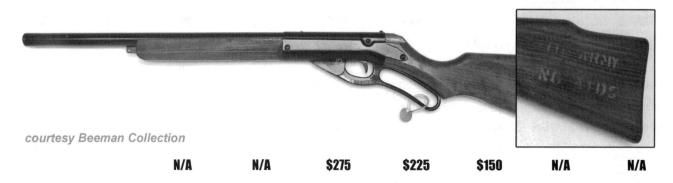

courtesy Beeman Collection

	100%	95%	90%	80%	60%	40%	20%
	N/A	N/A	$275	$225	$150	N/A	N/A

GRADING	100%	95%	90%	80%	60%	40%	20%

NO. 3 MODEL 24 – BB/.175 cal., thousand-shot, nickel plated. Mfg. 1924-26.

	$1,000	$850	$700	$575	$450	$300	$200

NO. 11 MODEL 24 – BB/.175 cal., 350-shot, nickel finish. Mfg. 1924-28.

	$225	$190	$160	$130	$100	$65	$45

NO. 11 MODEL 29 – BB/.175 cal., 350-shot, nickel finish. Mfg. 1929-32.

	$225	$190	$160	$130	$100	$65	$45

NO. 12 MODEL 24 – BB/.175 cal., single-shot, blue finish. Mfg. 1924-28.

	$225	$190	$160	$130	$100	$65	$45

NO. 12 MODEL 29 – BB/.175 cal., single-shot, blue finish. Mfg. 1929-1942.

	$225	$190	$160	$130	$100	$65	$45

NO. 30 MODEL 24 – BB/.175 cal., 500-shot, blue finish. Mfg. 1924-26.

	$1,200	$1,025	$850	$700	$550	$350	$240

NO. 101 MODEL 33 – BB/.175 cal., "Daisy for a Buck," SS, blue finish. Mfg. 1933-35.

	$130	$110	$90	$75	$60	$40	$25

NO. 102 MODEL 33 – BB/.175 cal., 500-shot, nickel finish, wooden stock. Mfg. 1933-35.

	$175	$150	$125	$100	$80	$50	$35

NO. 101 MODEL 36 – BB/.175 cal., SS, blue finish. Mfg. 1936-42.

	$150	$130	$105	$85	$70	$45	$30

NO. 102 MODEL 36 – BB/.175 cal., 500-shot, nickel (1936-40), blue (1941-42 and 1945-47), or painted (1953) finish, wood stock (plastic stock 1954), aluminum lever 1950 (none mfg. 1947-1949).

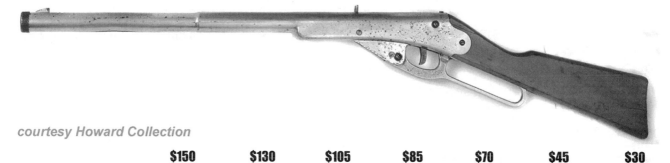

courtesy Howard Collection

	$150	$130	$105	$85	$70	$45	$30

NO. 103 MODEL 33 SUPER 1000 SHOT – BB/.175 cal., thousand-shot LA on Model 27 frame. Mfg. 1933 only.

Refer to No. 103 Model 33 Super 1000 Shot/ No. 103 Model 33 Super Buzz Barton Special listing in the Rifles: Lever Action, Buzz Barton Series category.

NO. 111 WESTERN CARBINE – BB/.175 cal., 700-shot, plastic stock, straight, uncurved cocking lever. Mfg. 1963-1978.

	$150	$130	$105	$85	$70	$45	$30

BENNETT 1000 SHOT – BB/.175 cal., thousand-shot, nickel. Mfg. 1903-1909.

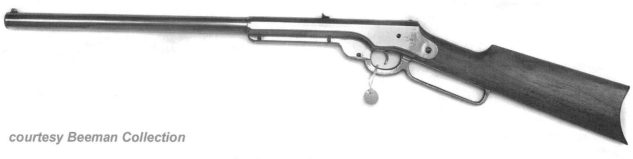

courtesy Beeman Collection

	N/A	$1,050	$875	$725	$550	$375	$250

GRADING	100%	95%	90%	80%	60%	40%	20%

BENNETT 500 SHOT – 500-shot. Mfg. 1905-1909.

	N/A	$1,525	$1,250	$1,050	$800	$550	$350

MODEL 111-B AMERICAN YOUTH – see Daisy Commemorative section.

RIFLES: LEVER ACTION, BUZZ BARTON SERIES

NO. 103 MODEL 33 SUPER 1000 SHOT/ NO. 103 MODEL 33 SUPER BUZZ BARTON SPECIAL – BB/.175 cal., thousand-shot LA on Model 27 frame bright nickel plate, easy to recognize Buzz Barton series by star-shaped "Buzz Barton" brand in stock. Mfg. 1933-37.

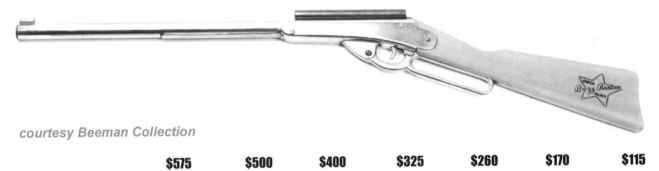

courtesy Beeman Collection

	$575	$500	$400	$325	$260	$170	$115

Add 10% for mahogany stock.

NO. 195 MODEL 32 BUZZ BARTON SPECIAL – BB/.175 cal., LA, thousand-shot, straight barrel and plunger housing with a patch shoulder underneath, blue, cast iron lever, rear sight tube, walnut stock with brand "Buzz Barton Special No. 195" inside lariat with two cowboys. Paper label 1932.

	$450	$375	$325	$260	$205	$135	$90

Add 50% for paper label.

This is a Markham/King design based upon the King No. 55.

* **No.195 Model 33** – BB/.175 cal., similar to Model 32 except has brand on stock, mfg. 1933-35.

	$450	$375	$325	$260	$205	$135	$90

Add 50% for paper label.

This is a Markham/King design based upon the King No. 55.

* **No. 195 Model 36** – BB/.175 cal., similar to Model 36 except has larger frame, mfg. 1936-41.

	$450	$375	$325	$260	$205	$135	$90

Add 50% for paper label.

This is a Markham/King design based upon the King No. 55.

RIFLES: LEVER ACTION, DEFENDER SERIES

NO. 40 MILITARY MODEL (WWI MILITARY MODEL) – full-length, one-piece wood stock, no bolt handle, 10 in. rubber-tipped metal bayonet, web sling.

* **No. 40 Military Model (WWI Military Model) Variant 1** – adj. front sight, extended shot tube with knurled end extends about .25 in. beyond muzzle. Mfg. 1916-18.

courtesy Beeman Collection

	N/A	$500	$400	$325	$250	$175	$100

Add $300-$500 for bayonet.
Add $100 for sling.

* **No. 40 Military Model (WWI Military Model) Variant 2** – fixed front sight, standard no. 25 shot tube. Mfg. 1919-32.

	N/A	$400	$325	$260	$200	$140	$80

Add $300-$500 for bayonet.
Add $100 for sling.

The metal bayonets were often taken away from children, and subsequently either lost or thrown away. Bayonet alone may sell for $300-$400.

GRADING	100%	95%	90%	80%	60%	40%	20%

NO. 140 DEFENDER ("WWII DEFENDER") – BB/.175 cal., military-style two-piece wooden stock with extended forearm, blue finish, bolt handle (acts as auto safety), gravity-fed, web sling, no bayonet. Very rare. Mfg. 1942 only.

| | N/A | $375 | $300 | $245 | $185 | $130 | $75 |

NO. 141 DEFENDER ("KOREAN WAR DEFENDER") – similar to No. 140, except with plastic stock and forearm, web sling, blue or painted finish, 50-shot spring-fed repeater. Mfg. 1951-1953.

| | N/A | $150 | $120 | $100 | $75 | $55 | $30 |

Add 50% for variation with wood stock.

NO. 142 DEFENDER MODEL – same military style, thousand-shot, gravity-fed, blue or painted finish. Mfg. 1954, painted, blue, mfg. 1957.

| | $250 | $215 | $175 | $145 | $115 | $75 | $50 |

RIFLES: LEVER ACTION, DEMOULIN INITIATION SERIES

MODEL B – first DeMoulin initiation guns have external water tubing on Daisy Bennett model and no markings on stock, rifles (pair). Mfg. 1910-1918.

| | $1,500 | $1,275 | $1,050 | $875 | $675 | $450 | $300 |

Special Daisy BB gun adapted to shoot water. Used as part of the Rough Masonic Initiation ceremony. Usually sold in pairs; one of the pair shot water forward; the other shot water backwards into the face and eyes of the shooter. (Contrary to previous reports, these guns were also sold individually). Stocks are stamped "DeMoulin Bros. & Co, Greenville, Illinois".

MODEL 3 SERIES 24 – (pair) mfg. 1924-26.

| | $2,000 | $1,700 | $1,400 | $1,150 | $900 | $600 | $400 |

Special Daisy BB gun adapted to shoot water. Used as part of the Rough Masonic Initiation ceremony. Usually sold in pairs; one of the pair shot water forward; the other shot water backwards into the face and eyes of the shooter. (Contrary to previous reports, these guns were also sold individually). Stocks are stamped "DeMoulin Bros. & Co, Greenville, Illinois".

MODEL 27 (WATER SHOOTER) – (pair) mfg. 1926-35.

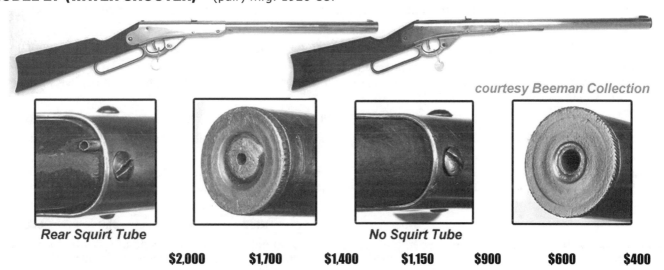

courtesy Beeman Collection

Rear Squirt Tube   **No Squirt Tube**

| | $2,000 | $1,700 | $1,400 | $1,150 | $900 | $600 | $400 |

Special Daisy BB gun adapted to shoot water. Used as part of the Rough Masonic Initiation ceremony. Usually sold in pairs; one of the pair shot water forward; the other shot water backwards into the face and eyes of the shooter. (Contrary to previous reports, these guns were also sold individually.) "Stocks are stamped: DeMoulin Bros. & Co, Greenville, Illinois".

RIFLES: LEVER ACTION, RED RYDER SERIES

This grouping contains the Red Ryder models manufactured beginning 1939-1940.

NO. 111 MODEL 40 RED RYDER VARIANT 1 – BB/.175 cal., thousand-shot, LA, copper plated forearm and barrel bands, front barrel band pinched into place, wood stock and forearm, saddle ring with leather thong, Red Ryder brand burned into left side of stock, cast iron lever, small screw through top of stock, adj. rear sight. Mfg. 1940-41.

| | N/A | $600 | $475 | $400 | $300 | $210 | $120 |

GRADING	100%	95%	90%	80%	60%	40%	20%

NO. 111 MODEL 40 ("1942" MODEL) VARIANT 2 – BB/.175 cal., barrel bands either prick-pinched or welded into place, wood stock and forearm, logo burned into left side of stock, cast iron lever (blue), small original size screw through the top of stock, fixed rear sight. Steel shortage due to WWII caused production to stop in early 1942. Mfg. 1941-42.

	N/A	$400	$325	$260	$200	$140	$80

NO. 111 MODEL 40 VARIANT 3 – BB/.175 cal., blue barrel bands, wood stock and forearm, Red Ryder logo silk screened onto stock with black paint on red background (because of temporary breakdown of regular stock marking equipment), fixed sights. About 1,000 mfg. The very rarest of all Red Ryder Models. Mfg. 1941.

Extreme scarcity precludes accurate pricing on this model.

NO. 111 MODEL 40 VARIANT 4 – BB/.175 cal., large screw through top of stock. Mfg. 1946.

	N/A	$375	$300	$245	$185	$130	$75

NO. 111 MODEL 40 VARIANT 5 – BB/.175 cal., wood stock, plastic forearm, logo stamped on left side of stock, black painted cast aluminum lever, fixed sights. Mfg. 1947.

	N/A	$350	$280	$230	$175	$125	$70

Note: Steel shortage of 1947 forced use of aluminum in cocking lever.

NO. 111 MODEL 40 VARIANT 6 – BB/.175 cal., wood stock, plastic forearm, logo stamped on left side of stock, black painted cast aluminum lever, fixed sights. Mfg. 1952.

	N/A	$350	$280	$230	$175	$125	$70

Plastic forearms on pre-1966 models had a tendency to warp.

NO. 111 MODEL 40 VARIANT 7 – BB/.175 cal., plastic stock and forearm, logo molded into left side of stock, blue painted finish, painted aluminum lever, fixed or adj. rear sight.

	N/A	$150	$120	$100	$75	$55	$30

First use of batch registration numbers in 1952.

NO. 111 MODEL 40 VARIANT 8 – BB/.175 cal., plastic stock, painted finish, white filled checkering on stock.

	$200	$170	$140	$115	$90	$60	$40

NO. 311 – Red Ryder set, gun similar to Number 111, except set with scope, bell target, cork firing tube, corks, etc., in large box. Mfg. 1947-1950.

	$650	$550	$450	$375	$295	$195	$130

MODEL 1938 – BB/.175 cal., Red Ryder similar to Number 111 Model 40, wood stock and forearm, logo stamped on left side of stock, narrow barrel bands, saddle ring staple does not go completely through side of receiver, blue paint finish, screws are slotted. Mfg. 1972-78.

	$150	$130	$105	$85	$70	$45	$30

Survival rate on these later models is very slim due to excessive use. Examples in 100% condition are extremely rare.

MODEL 1938 B DUCKS UNLIMITED – BB/.175 cal., special Red Ryder edition for Ducks Unlimited, walnut stock, right side of receiver stamped "Limited Edition", stamping lines filled with gold paint, walnut look rack with brass plaque. Mfg. 1975.

	$175	$150	$125	$100	$80	$50	$35

MODEL 1938 A-B – BB/.175 cal., Red Ryder, marked "1938 A-B" in gold paint on right side of receiver, loading gate on left side of barrel near muzzle, no muzzle band, plastic saddle ring staple, fake loading tube, plastic front sight and muzzle plug, trigger safety, hole in left side of receiver. Mfg. 1978.

	$150	$130	$105	$85	$70	$45	$30

MODEL 1938 B – BB/.175 cal., Red Ryder similar to Model 1938 A-B but with no hole on left side of receiver, stamped "1938-B". New 1979.

	$40	$35	$30	$25	$20	$10	N/A

MODEL 1938 B BUFFALO BILL – export model, plastic loading port, plain Red Ryder stock, gold stencil. Mfg. 1980-85.

	$125	$105	$90	$75	$55	$35	$25

MODEL 1938 "DIAMOND ANNIVERSARY" COMMEMORATIVE – BB/.175 cal., commemorates the 60th anniversary of the introduction of the Red Ryder BB gun, limited edition white scroll on the receiver, burnished forearm band, and special lariat logo in the stock. Mfg. 1998.

	$85	$70	$60	$50	$40	$25	$15

GRADING	100%	95%	90%	80%	60%	40%	20%

MODEL 1938 GOLD RUSH COMMEMORATIVE – BB/.175 cal., commemorates the 150th anniversary of the California Gold Rush, "Gold Rush" stamped on the top of the gold-painted barrel, natural finish walnut stock and forearm, countersunk in the stock is a 1-in. gold-colored medallion with a prospector panning for gold, forearm is laser engraved with the gun's production number. Approx. 2,500 mfg.

	$125	$105	$90	$75	$55	$35	$25

MODEL 1938 MILLENIUM EDITION COMMEMORATIVE – BB/.175 cal., commemorates the year 2000 with engraving on stock, natural finish walnut stock and forearm, barrels were numbered. Manufactured for one year in 2000.

	$65	$55	$45	$40	$30	$20	$15

MODEL 1938 "LAND OF BUFFALO BILL" RED RYDER MODEL – styled by Bill Cody, sold only from William Cody Museum, plastic stock. Mfg. about 1977.

	$150	$130	$105	$85	$70	$45	$30

MODEL 1938 RED RYDER – BB/.175 (disc.) or .177 cal., LA, SP, 280-350 FPS, 650-shot, smooth bore steel barrel with black finish, stained solid wood stock and forearm with lariat logo and burnished forearm band, crossbolt trigger block safety, blade and ramp front sight, adj. rear sight, saddle ring with leather thong, in 2011 a metal cocking lever became standard, 35.4 in. OAL, 2.2 lbs.

courtesy Daisy

MSR $40	$35	$30	$25	$20	$15	N/A	N/A

Add $5 for Model 1938-323 Red Ryder which includes 750 count BBs in Limited Edition Collector Tin (new 2008).

Add $10 for Model 4938 Red Ryder Shooting Fun Starter Kit with PrecisionMax 750 count BB tin, shooting glasses and target fun pack.

MODEL 1938 RED RYDER KIT – BB/.177 cal., LA, SP, kit includes Model 1938 Red Ryder rifle, shooting glasses, Red Ryder 750 count BB tin, eight ShatterBlast breakable clay targets and two target holders.

MSR $50	$45	$40	$35	$30	$20	N/A	N/A

MODEL 1938 RETRO RED RYDER – BB/.175 or .177 cal., LA, SP, 350 FPS, 650-shot, black finish, stained wood stock/forearm with lariat logo and gold tone forearm band, crossbolt trigger block safety, adj. rear sight, saddle ring with leather thong, 2.2 lbs., 35.4 OAL. Mfg. 2008-2010.

courtesy Daisy

	$50	$45	$35	$30	$25	$15	$10

Last MSR was $57.

MODEL 1938 (MFG. 1978) – BB/.175 cal., Red Ryder similar to Model 1938 but with logo on right side of stock, screws are Phillips type. Mfg. 1978.

	$150	$130	$105	$85	$70	$45	$30

MODEL 94 CARBINE – BB/.175 cal., 850-shot, plastic stock and forearm, gold (paint) embossed long horn and logo on left side of stock, dummy hammer on stock with leather boot, bright finish forearm band, high front sight, combo peep or open rear sight, blue paint finish, Plymouth and Rogers addresses. Mfg. 1955-1962.

	$250	$215	$175	$145	$115	$75	$50

Subtract 50% for missing boot or barrel band.

Add 20% for Plymouth address.

GRADING	100%	95%	90%	80%	60%	40%	20%

RED RYDER 70TH ANNIVERSARY EDITION – BB/.175, .177 cal., LA, SP, 350 FPS, 650-shot, smooth bore steel barrel, black finish, stained wood stock/forearm with lariat logo and gold tone forearm band, crossbolt trigger block safety, adj. rear sight, saddle ring with leather thong, blade and ramp front and adj. rear sights, featuring the 70th Anniversary inset medallion and matching forearm band, 2.2 lbs., 35.4 OAL. Mfg. 2010-2014.

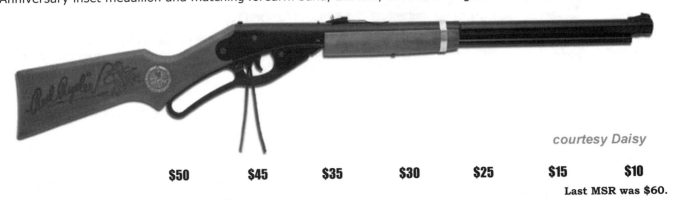

courtesy Daisy

	100%	95%	90%	80%	60%	40%	20%
	$50	$45	$35	$30	$25	$15	$10

Last MSR was $60.

RIFLES: PNEUMATIC & CO$_2$ POWERED

This grouping contains models powered by CO$_2$ or compressed air.

MODEL 22SG – .22 cal., multi-pump pneumatic, UL, SS, 550 FPS, die-cast metal receiver with dovetail scope mount, 4x32 scope, rifled steel barrel, black finish, solid hardwood stock and forearm, fiber optic front and adj. rear sights, crossbolt trigger block safety, 37 in. OAL, 4.5 lbs. Mfg. 2002-2007. Re-introduced 2010-2012.

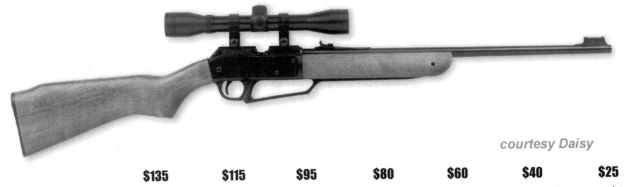

courtesy Daisy

	100%	95%	90%	80%	60%	40%	20%
	$135	$115	$95	$80	$60	$40	$25

Last MSR was $157.

MODEL 22X – .22 cal., multi-pump pnuematic, UL, SS, 550 FPS, die-cast metal receiver, rifled steel barrel, black finish, hardwood stock and forearm, fiber optic front and adj. rear sights, dovetail mount and 4x32 scope, 4.5 lbs. Disc. 2002.

	100%	95%	90%	80%	60%	40%	20%
	$95	$80	$65	$55	$45	$30	$20

MODEL 35 POWERLINE – BB/.177 or .177 cal. pellet, multi-pump pneumatic, 625 FPS, smooth bore steel barrel, 50-shot BB or SS pellet, black molded stock and forearm with checkering, blade and ramp front/adj. rear sights, crossbolt trigger block safety, 34.5 in. OAL, 3.1 lbs. New 2010.

courtesy Daisy

	100%	95%	90%	80%	60%	40%	20%
MSR $40	$35	$30	$25	$20	$15	N/A	N/A

MODEL 35 POWERLINE PINK CAMO – .177 cal. BB or pellet, multi-pump pneumatic, smooth bore steel barrel, 625 FPS, 50-shot BB or SS, molded stock and forearm with checkering featuring authentic Mossy Oak Pink camo, blade and ramp front/adj. rear sights, crossbolt trigger block safety, 34.5 in. OAL, 2.25 lbs. New 2013.

	100%	95%	90%	80%	60%	40%	20%
MSR $50	$45	$40	$35	$30	$20	N/A	N/A

GRADING	100%	95%	90%	80%	60%	40%	20%

MODEL 35C POWERLINE CAMO – .177 cal. BB or pellet, multi-pump pneumatic, smooth bore steel barrel, 625 FPS, 50-shot BB or SS, molded stock and forearm with checkering featuring authentic Mossy Oak Break-up Infinity camo, blade and ramp front/adj. rear sights, crossbolt trigger block safety, 34.5 in. OAL, 3.1 lbs. New 2011.

courtesy Daisy

MSR $50	$45	$40	$35	$30	$20	N/A	N/A

MODEL 35K POWERLINE – BB/.177 or .177 cal. pellet, multi-pump pneumatic, 625 FPS, smooth bore steel barrel, 50-shot BB or SS pellet, black molded stock and forearm with checkering, blade and ramp front/adj. rear sights, 4x15 scope, crossbolt trigger block safety, 34.5 in. OAL, 3.1 lbs. New 2013.

MSR $70	$60	$55	$50	$40	$30	N/A	N/A

The Model 35K kit also includes Daisy amber shooting glasses, a convenient Daisy Dial-A-Pellet container featuring flat, pointed and hollow-point pellets and a 750 count tin of Daisy BBs.

MODEL 74 – BB/.175 or .177 cal., CO_2, semi-auto repeater, 15-shot magazine, 200-round reservoir, smooth bore steel barrel, 350 FPS, black composite stock, adj. rear sight, crossbolt trigger block safety, 35.5 in. OAL, 1.98 lbs. Mfg. 2014-current.

MSR $60	$50	$45	$40	$35	$25	N/A	N/A

MODEL 126 EL GAMO – .177 cal., SSP, match style. Mfg. in Spain by El Gamo, 1984.

	$75	$65	$55	$45	$35	$20	$15

MODEL 126 EL GAMO SUPER MATCH TARGET RIFLE – .177 cal., SSP, 590 FPS, adj. sights, hardwood stock, match style, 10.6 lbs. Mfg. in Spain by El Gamo. Disc. 1994.

	$300	$255	$210	$175	$135	$90	$60

Last MSR was $765.

MODEL 128 GAMO OLYMPIC – .177 cal., similar to El Gamo 126 Super Match Target, except has adj. cheek piece and buttplate, high quality European diopter sight. Mfg. in Spain by El Gamo.

	$325	$275	$230	$190	$145	$95	$65

Last MSR was $735.

MODEL 177X – .177 cal., multi-pump, ULP, SS, 550 FPS, die-cast metal receiver, rifled steel barrel, black finish, hardwood stock and forearm, fiber optic front and adj. rear sights, 4.5 lbs. Mfg. 2003-2006.

courtesy Daisy

	$75	$65	$55	$45	$35	$20	$15

Last MSR was $80.

MODEL 300 – BB/.175 cal., CO_2 semi-auto, futuristic styling, plastic stock, five-shot repeater. Mfg. 1968-75.

	$85	$70	$60	$50	$40	$25	$15

* ***Model 300 Sears Variant*** – Sears number 799.19062 - similar to Model 300 except gold painted receiver and buttplate.

	$95	$80	$65	$55	$45	$30	$20

MODEL 822 – .22 cal., pneumatic, rifled barrel. Mfg. 1976-78.

	$75	$65	$55	$45	$35	$20	$15

MODEL 836 POWERLINE – BB/.175 or .177 cal. Mfg. 1984-85.

	$75	$65	$55	$45	$35	$20	$15

MODEL 840 – BB/.175 or .177 cal., SSP. Mfg. 1978-89.

	$75	$65	$55	$45	$35	$20	$15

GRADING	100%	95%	90%	80%	60%	40%	20%

MODEL 840 GRIZZLY/MODEL 840B GRIZZLY – BB/.175 or .177 cal. pellet, SSP, 350 FPS, smooth bore steel barrel, 350-shot (BB) or SS (pellet), black finish, molded woodgrain with checkering on stock and forearm, crossbolt trigger block safety, Truglo fiber optic front and adj. rear sights, 36.8 in. OAL, 2.25 lbs.

courtesy Daisy

	100%	95%	90%	80%	60%	40%	20%
MSR $45	$40	$35	$30	$25	$20	N/A	N/A

* **Model 840B Grizzly Kit** – BB/.175 or .177 cal., kit includes Model 840B Grizzly rifle, safety glasses, 4x15 scope, three PrecisionMax 750 count BB tin and PrecisionMax 250 count lead-free pellets tin, eight Shatterblast breakable clay targets and two target holders. New 2008.

	100%	95%	90%	80%	60%	40%	20%
MSR $90	$75	$70	$60	$50	$40	N/A	N/A

* **Model 840C Grizzly** – BB/.175 or .177 cal., similar to Model 840 Grizzly, except has Mossy Oak Break Up camouflage stock and forearm.

	100%	95%	90%	80%	60%	40%	20%
MSR $50	$45	$40	$35	$30	$20	N/A	N/A

Add $6 for Model 840C Grizzly Camo with 4x15 scope.

* **Model 840C Grizzly Camo Kit** – .177 cal. BB or pellet, SSP, kit includes Model 840C Grizzly Camo rifle, 4x15 scope, shooting glasses, PrecisionMax 750 count BB tin, PrecisionMax 250 count lead-free pellets tin, eight ShatterBlast breakable clay targets and two target holders.

	100%	95%	90%	80%	60%	40%	20%
MSR $90	$75	$70	$60	$50	$40	N/A	N/A

* **Model 840C Grizzly Kit** – BB/.175 or .177 cal., kit includes Model 840C Grizzly rifle, safety glasses, Truglo fiber optic sights, 350 BBs, 250 pellets, pad of targets, and Daisy's Right Start to Shooting Sports video. Disc. 2006.

	100%	95%	90%	80%	60%	40%	20%
	$65	$55	$45	$40	$30	$20	$15

Last MSR was $70.

MODEL 845 TARGET – similar to Model 840, except has peep sights. Mfg. 1980-89.

courtesy Daisy

	100%	95%	90%	80%	60%	40%	20%
	$75	$65	$55	$45	$35	$20	$15

GRADING	100%	95%	90%	80%	60%	40%	20%

MODEL 850 POWERLINE – BB/.175 or .177 cal., SSP, rifled barrel, black die-cast metal, adj. rear sight, hand-wiped checkered woodgrain finished stock, buttplate, BB 520 FPS, 4.3 lbs. Mfg. 1982-84.

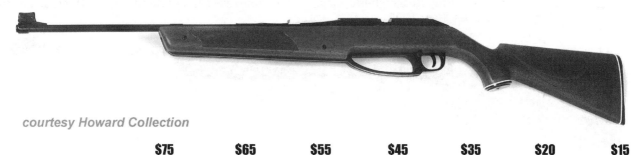

courtesy Howard Collection

	$75	$65	$55	$45	$35	$20	$15

MODEL 851 POWERLINE – BB/.175 or .177 cal., similar to Model 850 Powerline, except has select hardwood stock. Mfg. 1982-84.

	$110	$95	$75	$65	$50	$35	$20

MODEL 853 TARGET – .177 cal., SSP. Mfg. 1984.

	$250	$215	$175	$145	$115	$75	$50

MODEL 856 POWERLINE – .177 cal. (early versions .177 pellet SS/BB repeater combination), multi-pump pneumatic, SS, 670 FPS, rifled steel barrel, black finish, molded wood grain sporter style stock and forearm, crossbolt trigger block safety, adj. rear sight, 2.7 lbs.

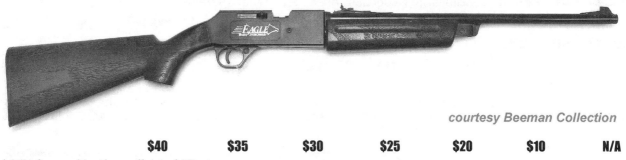

courtesy Beeman Collection

	$40	$35	$30	$25	$20	$10	N/A

Add 25% for combination pellet and BB gun.

* ***Model 856F Powerline*** – .177 cal., similar to Model 856 Powerline, except has fiber optic sights. Disc. 2004.

	$45	$40	$30	$25	$20	$15	N/A

Last MSR was $50.

Add 25% for Model 808 4x15 scope (Model 7856).

* ***Model 856C Powerline*** – .177 cal., similar to Model 856 Powerline, except has fiber optic sights and Mossy Oak Break Up Camo stock and forearm. Disc. 2004.

	$55	$45	$40	$30	$25	$15	$10

Last MSR was $60.

MODEL 860 POWERLINE – BB/.175 or .177 cal. Mfg. 1984-85.

	$75	$65	$55	$45	$35	$20	$15

MODEL 880 POWERLINE – BB/.175 or .177 cal., pellet, multi-stroke pump pneumatic. Mfg. 1972-89.

courtesy Howard Collection

	$65	$55	$45	$40	$30	$20	$15

**Add 100% for early models with metal receiver, metal pumping arm, no warnings printed on the guns - the "pure" original version.
Add 50% for metal receiver.**

GRADING	100%	95%	90%	80%	60%	40%	20%

MODEL 880 POWERLINE (CURRENT) – BB/.175 or .177 cal. pellet, UL, multi-pump pneumatic, 800 FPS, 50-shot (BB) or SS (pellet), dodecahedral rifling suited to pellet or steel BBs, rifled steel barrel, black finish, Monte Carlo-style molded woodgrain stock and forearm, TruGlo fiber optic front and adj. rear sights (standard 2008), crossbolt trigger block safety, 37.6 in. OAL, 3.1 lbs. New 1990.

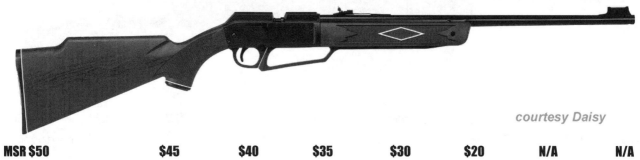

courtesy Daisy

MSR $50	$45	$40	$35	$30	$20	N/A	N/A

Add $5 for 4x15 scope (Model 880S) new 2008.

MODEL 880 POWERLINE KIT – .177 cal. BB or pellet, UL, multi-pump pneumatic, kit includes Model 880 Powerline rifle w/shooting glasses, 4x15 scope, PrecisionMax 750 count BB tin and PrecisionMax500 count pellet tin. New 2004.

MSR $80	$70	$60	$55	$45	$35	N/A	N/A

MODEL 881 POWERLINE – similar to Model 880, rifled barrel. Mfg. 1973-83.

	$75	$65	$55	$45	$35	$20	$15

MODEL 882 CENTENNIAL – similar to Model 880, rifled barrel. Mfg. 1975-76.

	$75	$65	$55	$45	$35	$20	$15

MODEL 900 SNAP SHOT – .177 cal., auto-fed, clip. Mfg. 1986.

	$95	$80	$65	$55	$45	$30	$20

MODEL 901 POWERLINE – .177 cal. BB or pellet, multi-pump pneumatic, 750 FPS (BB), 50-shot (BB) or SS (pellet), rifled steel barrel, black molded composite stock and forearm, advanced composite receiver with dovetail mount, Truglo fiber optic front and adj. rear sights, crossbolt trigger block safety, 37.5 in. OAL, 3.7 lbs. New 2005.

courtesy Daisy

MSR $70	$60	$55	$50	$40	$30	N/A	N/A

* *Model 901 Powerline Kit (Model 5901)* – .177 cal. BB or pellet, multi-pump pneumatic, 750 FPS (BB), 50-shot (BB) or SS (pellet), rifled steel barrel, black molded composite stock and forearm, advanced composite receiver with dovetail mount, Truglo fiber optic front and adj. rear sights, crossbolt trigger block safety, 37.5 in. OAL, 3.7 lbs. New 2005.

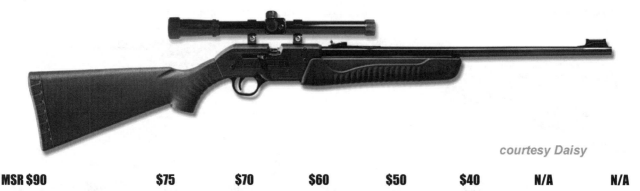

courtesy Daisy

MSR $90	$75	$70	$60	$50	$40	N/A	N/A

Kit which includes 4x15 air rifle scope, eight ShatterBlast breakable clay targets and two target holders, PrecisionMax 750 count BB tin, PrecisionMax 500 count pellet tin, and shooting glasses.

GRADING	100%	95%	90%	80%	60%	40%	20%

MODEL 917 – .177 cal., multi-stroke pneumatic, five-shot clip. Mfg. 1979-82.

	$95	$80	$65	$55	$45	$30	$20

MODEL 920 – multi-stroke pump pneumatic, similar to Model 922 except has wood stock and forearm, five-shot clip. Mfg. 1978-89.

	$130	$110	$90	$75	$60	$40	$25

MODEL 922 – pneumatic, multi-stroke, five-shot clip. Mfg. 1978-89.

	$95	$80	$65	$55	$45	$30	$20

MODEL 953 TARGETPRO POWERLINE – .177 cal. pellet, SSP, ULP, SS, 510 FPS, die-cast metal receiver with full cut loading port, high grade rifled steel barrel, black finish, full-length match style black composite stock and forearm, Truglo fiber optic front and Truglo micro-adj. fiber optic rear sights, manual crossbolt trigger block safety with red indicator, 5-shot indexing clip, 37.75 in. OAL, 6.4 lbs. New 2004.

courtesy Daisy

MSR $120	$100	$90	$80	$65	$50	N/A	N/A

MODEL 953 TARGETPRO KIT – .177 cal., SSP, ULP, SS, kit includes Model 953 TargetPro rifle w/shooting glasses, ShatterBlast targets and stakes (disc. 2007), Shoot-N-C targets, 4x15 scope (disc.), PrecisionMax 500 count pellet tin, eight ShatterBlast breakable clay targets and two target holders. Mfg. 2004-2011.

courtesy Daisy

	$160	$135	$110	$95	$70	$50	$30

Last MSR was $190.

MODEL 953 U.S. SHOOTING TEAM – .177 cal., single-stroke pneumatic. Mfg. 1984-85.

	$195	$165	$135	$115	$90	$60	$40

MODEL 977 – similar to Model 880, except has rifled barrel, peep sight. Mfg. 1980-83.

	$100	$85	$70	$60	$45	$30	$20

MODEL 990 – BB/.175 or .177 cal., 100 shot gravity feed BB magazine, SS pellet, combination multi-pump pneumatic and CO_2, rifled BBL, manual crossbolt safety, 630 FPS, 37.4 in. OAL, 4.1 lbs. Mfg. 1993-96 (listed until 2000).

	$150	$130	$105	$85	$70	$45	$30

MODEL 1880 POWERLINE – BB/.175 or .177 cal., pellet, multi-stroke pump pneumatic, similar to Model 880, except with scope. Mfg. 1978-80, reintroduced-Disc. 2007.

	$100	$85	$70	$60	$45	$30	$20

MODEL 1881 POWERLINE – BB/.175 or .177 cal., pneumatic pump. Mfg. 1978-80.

	$115	$100	$80	$65	$50	$35	$25

MODEL 1917 POWERLINE – .177 cal., five-shot clip, scope. Mfg. 1978-80.

	$115	$100	$80	$65	$50	$35	$25

GRADING	100%	95%	90%	80%	60%	40%	20%

MODEL 1922 POWERLINE – .22 cal., pneumatic, multi-stroke. Mfg. 1978-80.

	$75	$65	$55	$45	$35	$20	$15

MODEL 2880 POWERLINE – BB/.175 or .177 cal., pellet, multi-stroke pump pneumatic, similar to Model 880, except with 4x15 scope. Mfg. 2008-current.

courtesy Daisy

MSR $60	$50	$45	$40	$35	$25	N/A	N/A

MODEL 7840 BUCKMASTER – BB/.175 or .177 cal., SSP, 320 FPS (BB/.175 cal.), smooth bore steel barrel, 350 (BB/.175 cal.) or SS (.177 cal.), black finish, adj. rear sight and electronic point sight, molded woodgrain with checkering stock and forearm, crossbolt trigger block safety, 2.25 lbs. Mfg. 2003-2006.

	$50	$45	$35	$30	$25	$15	$10

Last MSR was $55.

AMERICAN SPIRIT – BB/.175 or .177 cal., CO_2 similar to Model 840 Grizzly, except stock and forearm are finished in stars and stripes design. Mfg. 2002.

	$50	$45	$35	$30	$25	$15	$10

AVANTI MODEL 753 ELITE – .177 cal., SSP, BA, SS, 510 FPS, competition sights, match-style hardwood stock with raised cheek piece and adj. length, adj. trigger, Lothar Walther rifled steel barrel, front globe and adj. rear sights, die-cast metal receiver with full cut loading port, adj. position sling, manual crossbolt trigger safety with red indicator, 39.75 in. OAL, 6.4 lbs.

courtesy Daisy

MSR $450	$375	$325	$300	$250	$190	N/A	N/A

AVANTI MODEL 845 MENTOR – .177 cal. BB or pellet, SSP, 350-shot BB, or SS pellet, 19 in. smooth bore steel shrouded barrel, sporter style molded woodgrain stock and forearm with checkered pistol grip, fluted comb, molded black finished receiver, hooded front and adj. rear sights, 36.8 in. OAL, 2.7 lbs. Mfg. 2012-2013.

	$100	$85	$70	$60	$45	$30	$20

Last MSR was $120.

This model was also available with the Mentor Kit which includes four Avanti Mentor BB training rifles, two bottles of 2,400 BBs, 400 Official NRA 5-meter paper targets, one set of instruction wall charts, two Official NRA 5-meter backstops, and one instructor's 10-Lesson Curriculum Guide.

GRADING	100%	95%	90%	80%	60%	40%	20%

AVANTI MODEL 853 LEGEND – .177 cal., SSP, BA, SS, 480 FPS, Lothar Walther rifled steel barrel, sporter-style hardwood stock, forearm and grip, adj. sights, manual crossbolt trigger block with red indicator safety, die-cast receiver with dovetail scope mount, adj. sling positioning, 38.5 in. OAL, 5.5 lbs.

courtesy Daisy

MSR $400	$350	$300	$270	$220	$170	N/A	N/A

AVANTI MODEL 853C LEGEND EX – .177 cal., similar to Model 853 Target, except has five-shot mag.

MSR $420	$375	$325	$295	$240	$180	N/A	N/A

AVANTI MODEL 853CM TARGET PRO – .177 cal. pellet, PSP, SS, Lothar Walther rifled high grade steel barrel, 510 FPS, full length match-style black composite stock, two muzzle weights and adj. nylon web sling, die-cast metal with full cut loading port, 5-pellet manual indexing clip, front globe sight, rear dipoter sight, manual crossbolt trigger block safety with red indicator, 39.75 in. OAL, 6.4 lbs. Mfg. 2012-current.

courtesy Daisy

MSR $432	$375	$325	$295	$240	$180	N/A	N/A

AVANTI MODEL 887 GOLD MEDALIST – .177 cal., CO_2 refillable 2.5 oz. cylinder, 500 FPS, SS, BA, Lothar Walther rifled steel target barrel, hooded front globe sight with changeable aperture inserts, micrometer adj. rear sight, laminate three-position sporter style hardwood stock, adj. trigger, 39.5 in. OAL, 7.3 lbs. New 2008.

courtesy Daisy

MSR $500	$425	$375	$350	$275	$210	N/A	N/A

AVANTI MODEL 888 MEDALIST – .177 cal., CO_2 2.5 oz. cylinder, BA, SS, 500 FPS, Lothar Walther rifled steel target barrel, hooded front sight with changeable aperture inserts, micrometer adj. rear sight, multi-color laminate three-position sporter style hardwood stock, adj. trigger, 38.5 in. OAL, 6.9 lbs. New 2001.

courtesy Daisy

MSR $470	$400	$350	$325	$260	$195	N/A	N/A

GRADING	100%	95%	90%	80%	60%	40%	20%

AVANTI PREMIO PRECISION MODEL XP 30 – .177 cal., CO_2, 580-600 FPS, built-in gauge in the cylinder, 19.8 in. Lothar Walther rifled steel barrel, Hämmerli precision target sights, hardwood laminate stock with adj. cheek piece and buttplate, fully adj. trigger, 8.5 lbs. Advertised 2001-2002.

> While advertised during 2001-2002, this model did not go into production.

AVANTI TROFEO PRECISION MODEL XT 10 – .177 cal., compressed air, 580-600 FPS, built-in gauge in the cylinder, 23.54 in. Lothar Walther rifled steel barrel, Anschütz precision target sights, hardwood laminate stock with carbon fiber finish, fully adj. cheek piece and buttplate, fully adj. trigger, 11.42 lbs. Advertised 2001-2002.

> While advertised during 2001-2002, this model did not go into production.

AVANTI VALIANT MODEL XS 40 – .177 cal., compressed air, 580-590 FPS, built-in gauge in the cylinder, 19 in. rifled steel target barrel, front globe sight with changeable aperture inserts, rear diopter sight with micrometer click adjustments for windage and elevation, hardwood stock with adj. cheek piece and buttplate, adj. trigger, 7 lbs. Mfg. 2001-2006.

$550	$475	$375	$325	$250	$165	$110

Last MSR was $881.

AVANTI VITTORIA PRECISION MODEL XV 20 – .177 cal., compressed air, 580-600 FPS, built-in gauge in the cylinder, 23.54 in. Lothar Walther rifled steel barrel, Anschütz precision target sights, fully adj. target stock with adj. cheek piece and buttplate, fully adj. trigger, 11.42 lbs. Advertised 2001-2002.

$1,200	$1,025	$850	$700	$550	$350	$240

> While advertised during 2001-2002, this model did not go into production.

RIFLES: PUMP/SLIDE ACTION

This grouping contains models that use a mechanical pump/slide action to cock the spring.

MODEL 25 SERIES – BB/.175 cal. elbow-slide pump action cocking, large takedown knurled-head bolt, MV to 450 FPS, internal spring-fed magazine, about 45 rounds, no safety. About 58 variants, 1914 to 1979.

* ***Model 25 Variant 1 ("1914")*** – short lever, slide handle with five grooves, straight stock, solder patch, adj. front sight (slides from side to side), black over nickel finish (never sold in bright nickel). Mfg. 1914 only.

N/A	$500	$400	$325	$250	$175	$100

* ***Model 25 Variant 2 ("1916")*** – similar to variation 1 except blue, adj. sights.

N/A	$350	$280	$230	$175	$125	$70

* ***Model 25 Variant 3*** – short lever, straight stock, fixed front sight. Mfg. date unknown.

courtesy Beeman Collection

N/A	$250	$200	$165	$125	$90	$50

* ***Model 25 Variant 4*** – long lever, five-grooved slide handle, straight stock, fixed front sight.

courtesy Beeman Collection

$300	$255	$210	$175	$135	$90	$60

* ***Model 25 Variant 5*** – pistol grip stock, small takedown screw.

$300	$255	$210	$175	$135	$90	$60

* ***Model 25 Variant 6 ("1932")*** – pistol grip stock, six-groove slide handle.

$300	$255	$210	$175	$135	$90	$60

GRADING	100%	95%	90%	80%	60%	40%	20%

* **Model 25 Variant 7 ("1936")** – pistol grip stock, stamped "engraving" with gold paint. Mfg. 1936-1942 and 1945-1951.

courtesy Beeman Collection

| | $350 | $300 | $245 | $205 | $160 | $105 | $70 |

* **Model 25 Variant 8 ("1952")** – pistol grip stock, factory Model 40 Daisy scope. Mfg. 1952 only.

| | $600 | $500 | $425 | $350 | $270 | $180 | $120 |

* **Model 25 Variant 9** – plastic stock, stamped engraving, electrostatic painted receiver. Mfg. 1952-1955.

| | $175 | $150 | $125 | $100 | $80 | $50 | $35 |

* **Model 25 Variant 10 ("1954")** – combination rear sight, mfg. 1954.

| | $150 | $130 | $105 | $85 | $70 | $45 | $30 |

* **Model 25 Variant 11 ("1955")** – added scope mounting holes and oil hole. Mfg. 1955.

| | $150 | $130 | $105 | $85 | $70 | $45 | $30 |

* **Model 25 Variant 12 ("1956")** – plastic PG, stenciled "engraving," Plymouth address. Mfg. 1956-1957.

| | $150 | $130 | $105 | $85 | $70 | $45 | $30 |

* **Model 25 Variant 12 Jr. NRA Commemorative Model** – Plymouth, MI. Mfg. 1956 only.

| | $300 | $255 | $210 | $175 | $135 | $90 | $60 |

* **Model 25 Variant 13 ("1958")** – plastic PG, stenciled engraving, Rogers address. Mfg. 1958-76.

| | $150 | $130 | $105 | $85 | $70 | $45 | $30 |

Add 20% for Preston Ontario-marked guns

* **Model 25 Variant 14 ("Bronze Blond")** – bronze finish, blond plastic stock. Mfg. 1958.

| | $150 | $130 | $105 | $85 | $70 | $45 | $30 |

* **Model 25 Sears Variant** – PG, plastic stock, marked Sears. Mfg. 1970-72.

| | $150 | $130 | $105 | $85 | $70 | $45 | $30 |

* **Model 25 Wards Variant** – PG, plastic stock, Montgomery Wards, Hawthorne brand. Mfg. 1970-72.

| | $150 | $130 | $105 | $85 | $70 | $45 | $30 |

* **Model 25 Variant 15 ("1977")** – plastic Monte Carlo stock. Mfg. 1977-79.

| | $150 | $130 | $105 | $85 | $70 | $45 | $30 |

* **Model 25 Centennial** – replica, straight wood stock. Mfg. 1986 only.

| | $275 | $235 | $195 | $160 | $125 | $80 | $55 |

* **Model 25 Current Mfg.** – BB/.177 cal. elbow-slide pump action cocking, MV to 350 FPS, stained solid wood pistol grip stock and forearm grip, steel construction, smooth bore steel barrel, decorative engraving on receiver, blade and ramp metal front and flip-up peep or open adj. rear sights, 50-shot internal spring-fed magazine, crossbolt trigger block safety, 36.5 in. OAL, 3 lbs. Mfg. 2010-current.

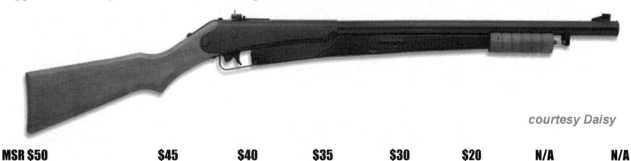

courtesy Daisy

| MSR $50 | $45 | $40 | $35 | $30 | $20 | N/A | N/A |

GRADING	100%	95%	90%	80%	60%	40%	20%

MODEL 26 FIELD MASTER – slide action, 45-shot. Mfg. 1964-1967.

	$125	$105	$90	$75	$55	$35	$25

MODEL 105 JUNIOR – slide action, blue finish. Mfg. 1932-34.

	$1,000	$850	$700	$575	$450	$300	$200

MODEL 105 RANGER – slide action, made for Sears & Roebuck. Mfg. 1932-34.

	$2,800	$2,375	$1,950	$1,625	$1,250	$850	$550

MODEL 107 BUCK JONES SPECIAL – slide action, blue finish, sundial markings on wooden stock, needle or floating compass, Daisy marked on compass dial, sixty-shot gravity-fed magazine. Mfg. 1934-42.

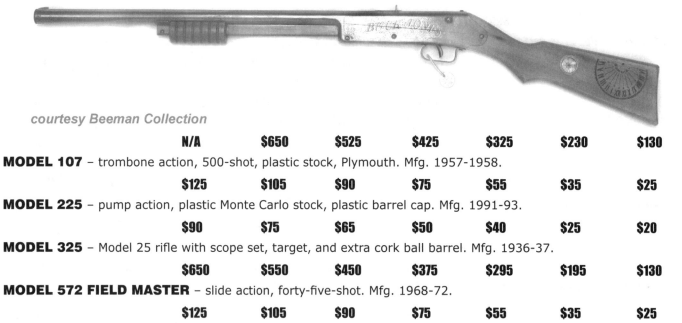

courtesy Beeman Collection

	N/A	$650	$525	$425	$325	$230	$130

MODEL 107 – trombone action, 500-shot, plastic stock, Plymouth. Mfg. 1957-1958.

	$125	$105	$90	$75	$55	$35	$25

MODEL 225 – pump action, plastic Monte Carlo stock, plastic barrel cap. Mfg. 1991-93.

	$90	$75	$65	$50	$40	$25	$20

MODEL 325 – Model 25 rifle with scope set, target, and extra cork ball barrel. Mfg. 1936-37.

	$650	$550	$450	$375	$295	$195	$130

MODEL 572 FIELD MASTER – slide action, forty-five-shot. Mfg. 1968-72.

	$125	$105	$90	$75	$55	$35	$25

MODEL 799 – There really aren't any "Model 799" guns. Rather, 799 is the prefix that Sears uses for all its Daisy airguns. Some of the Sears guns are listed as variations in the appropriate Daisy sections (i.e. 799.10275 is a Sears variation of the Daisy Model 25).

A crossover listing (see "Storebrand Cross-Over List") has been provided in the back of this text.

RIFLES: VL SERIES

MODEL VL – .22 cal., combination airgun/firearm rifle designed to use special Daisy VL caseless ammunition. Mfg. 1968-1969.

Clearly an underlever, spring-piston airgun, which will fire as just an airgun, but which is designed to have its typical airgun action supplemented by the ignition of a propellant mass molded on the base of special 29-grain bullets, i.e., caseless cartridges. Ignition is due to the high temperature normally developed by spring-piston airguns at the moment of firing (adiabatic compression)- not friction in the barrel as usually reported. MV is 1150 FPS.

Developed at Daisy by Jules van Langenhoven (= VL), but apparently the unique valve system, which seals the gun against the back pressure of ignition, was invented by M.R. Kovarik, and some other German engineers. Richard Daniel, former president of Daisy, reported that 25,000 guns had been made and were ready for a promotional launch just as U.S. Senator Robert Kennedy was assassinated. The public backlash against firearms was seen as a threat to Daisy's excellent public image, so the project was immediately dropped. When considering the question of whether this gun is an airgun or not, remember that power augmentation is not new in the airgun world. The Weihrauch Barakuda used ether to boost its power, and many airgunners, most notably the Brits, have been jacking up airgun power by dripping low flashpoint oil into their spring-piston guns for over a century.

The resulting diesel explosion can add real zest to the shot -- and real strain to the gun. This is why so many originally beautiful, originally tight, BSA and Webley airguns sound like a bag of bolts when you shake them. (Collectors and shooters beware.) In final analysis, the VL does not fit cleanly into any group; it definitely is both a firearm and an airgun!

* V/L Standard Rifle – .22 V/L cal. (caseless air-ignited cartridge), UL, SP airgun action, 1150 FPS, 18 in. barrel, plastic stock, not particularly accurate. Approx. 19,000 mfg. 1968-1969.

	$400	$350	$280	$230	$180	$120	$80

Add 50% for early version shown with checkered underlever, cheekpiece, Monte Carlo stock.

Note: The Daisy .22 V/L was discontinued because the BATFE ruled that the gun constituted a firearm, and since Daisy was not federally licensed to manufacture firearms, the factory decided to discontinue manufacture.

GRADING	100%	95%	90%	80%	60%	40%	20%

* **V/L Presentation** – .22 V/L cal., similar to Collector's Kit, except does not have brass plate on buttstock, walnut stock. 4,000 mfg. for dealers.

courtesy Beeman Collection

	$500	$425	$350	$285	$225	$150	$100

Last MSR was $125.

Note: The Daisy .22 V/L was discontinued because the BATFE ruled that the gun constituted a firearm, and since Daisy was not federally licensed to manufacture firearms, the factory decided to discontinue manufacture.

* **V/L Collector's Kit** – .22 V/L cal., Rifle comes with case, gun cradle, 300 rounds of ammo, walnut stock with brass plate with owner's name and serial number of gun. Approx. first 1,000 rifles mfg., available only by direct factory order.

courtesy Beeman Collection

	$700	$600	$500	$400	$325	$210	$140

Last MSR was $125

Note: The Daisy .22 V/L was discontinued because the BATFE ruled that the gun constituted a firearm, and since Daisy was not federally licensed to manufacture firearms, the factory decided to discontinue manufacture.

DART GUNS

A group of spring powered airguns manufactured in Europe circa mid to late 1800s.

HANDGUNS

MAGICIAN DART PISTOL – 8.5mm cal. dart, SS, SP, ML, steel small parts finished in the white, with or without reverse curved trigger guard flange, checkered walnut grip, two piece octagon smoothbore brass barrel with 4 in. bore and approx. 1.5 in. piston throw, adj. rear and pin front sights, 12 in. - 14.5 in. OAL.

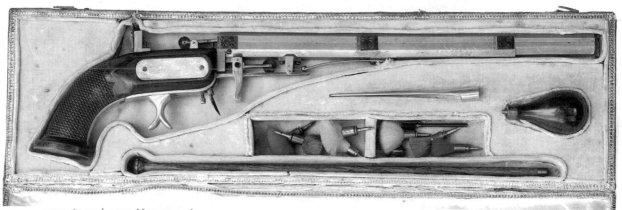

courtesy Larry Hannusch

	N/A	N/A	$2,400	$1,950	$1,500	$1,050	$600

Add 30%-50% for fitted hardwood case with accessories.

Makers unknown with construction more indicative of a watch maker than a gun maker. Possibly made for magic acts where a very low power pistol would be appropriate. Sometimes found in fitted hardwood case with several accessories. Refs: L. Hannusch, *Airgun Hobby*, Oct. 2007: pp.56-59. J. Griffiths, *The Encyclopedia of Spring Air Pistols*. Ashlea Publications, Leeds, England.

GRADING		100%	95%	90%	80%	60%	40%	20%

DAYSTATE LTD

Current manufacturer located in Stone, Staffordshire, England. Imported/distributed exclusively by Airguns of Arizona, located in Gilbert, AZ. Dealer and consumer sales. Founded 1973.

Although often reported as starting with captive bolt cattle killers, the company made only three specimens of such guns. Initially concentrating on tranquilizer guns, Daystate generally is now recognized as the founder of modern PCP airguns, producing PCP air rifles by 1973. By 1987, high precision PCP rifles had become their main line. The publisher and authors of the *Blue Book of Airguns* wish to thank Tony Belas, Sales Manager at Daystate, for assistance with this section.

PISTOLS

FIRST MODEL – PCP, SS, single stage trigger, no trigger guard, approx. 20 made to order circa 1980. Specs may vary as all were made to order, but these are not prototypes.

Value of well-worn specimens from animal control companies is in the $500-$700 range.

COMPETA – .177 or .22 cal., PCP, SS, based on Huntsman PCP rifle, breech loading, 8 in. barrel, 425 FPS in .177 cal., sliding 2-stage trigger, no safety, 14 in. OAL, 2.9 lbs. Mfg. 1980-1995.

courtesy Loke Collection

N/A	$1,100	$875	$725	$550	$375	$220

Last MSR was $730.

Add 20% for Midas Model with brass cylinder.

Most hand made with serial numbers standard after 1993.

RIFLES

AIR RANGER – .177 or .22 cal., PCP, BA, 400cc or 500cc bottle, ten-shot rotary mag., 16.8 in. fully shrouded and rifled BBL, factory tuned to 35 or 50 fp/lbs, matte black finish, adj. trigger, manual rotary safety, checkered thumbhole walnut stock, 35.5 in. OAL, approx. 7.8 lbs. Mfg. 2006-2013.

courtesy Precision Airgun Distribution

$1,825	$1,550	$1,275	$1,050	$825	$550	$375

Last MSR was $2,161.

GRADING	100%	95%	90%	80%	60%	40%	20%

* *Air Ranger Extreme (80 Ft/Lbs)* – .177 or .22 cal., PCP, BA, 400cc or 500cc bottle, ten-shot rotary mag., 24.25 in. rifled BBL, factory tuned to 80 Ft/lbs/lbs, matte black finish, adj. trigger, manual rotary safety, checkered thumbhole walnut stock, 42.75 in. OAL, approx. 9 lbs. Mfg. 2008-2013.

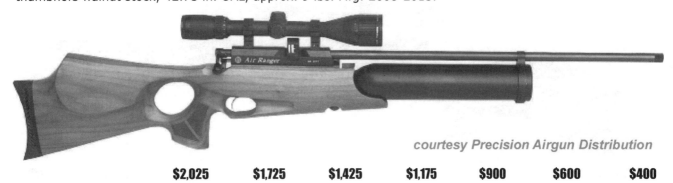

courtesy Precision Airgun Distribution

| $2,025 | $1,725 | $1,425 | $1,175 | $900 | $600 | $400 |

Last MSR was $2,598.

AIR WOLF – .177 or .22 cal., PCP, BA, 400cc or 500cc bottle, ten-shot rotary mag., 16.8 in. rifled BBL, matte black finish, Harper patent CDT electronic firing system, adj. trigger with electronic lock and MK3 CDT electronic rotary safety, keyed power switch in trigger guard, checkered thumbhole walnut stock, 41 in. OAL, approx. 8.1-8.6 lbs. Mfg. 2006-2011.

courtesy Daystate Collection

| $2,025 | $1,725 | $1,425 | $1,175 | $900 | $600 | $400 |

Last MSR was $2,395.

AIR WOLF MCT – .177, .20, .22, or .25 cal., 400 cc with 500 cc option, 10-shot rotary mag., 17 in. fully shrouded barrel, Turkish walnut ambidextrous thumbhole stock, includes Daystate's patented Map Compensated Technology (MCT), LCD information screen that displays shot counter, mag. counter, and remaining air pressure, battery power for the electrical system, Harper Patent valve system, threaded adaptor, Airstream IV carbon fibre reflex silencer, also available in full-length rifle model or high powered version, manual safety, electronic rotary lever with key-switch isolator, 40.5 in. OAL, 8 lbs. New 2011.

courtesy Precision Airgun Distribution

| MSR $2,598 | $2,200 | $1,950 | $1,775 | $1,425 | $1,100 | N/A | N/A |

GRADING	100%	95%	90%	80%	60%	40%	20%

AIR WOLF MCT TACTICAL – .177, .20, .22, or .25 cal., similar to Air Wolf MCT model, except has matte black finish with rubberized black coating on stock to make it weather resistant and give it a smooth grip feel, 8.6 lbs. New 2011.

courtesy Precision Airgun Distribution

MSR $2,598	$2,200	$1,950	$1,775	$1,425	$1,100	N/A	N/A

CR 94 – all steel action, specialized Field Target rifle, no safety, 60 guns mfg. 1994-1996.

	$1,950	$1,650	$1,375	$1,125	$875	$575	$400

Successor to Model 2000.

CR 97 – similar to CR 94 except has improved and restyled breech block, cocking bolt and lighter alloy cylinder, improved regulator, no safety. Mfg. 1996-1998.

courtesy Beeman Collection

	$1,850	$1,575	$1,300	$1,075	$825	$550	$375

Last MSR was $1,750.

* **CR 97 Special Edition** – special Silver gun production with improved regulator and new, highly adjustable match trigger, no safety. 50 mfg. 1998-1999.

	$2,100	$1,775	$1,475	$1,225	$950	$625	$425

Last MSR was $1,900.

CR-MM – a special version of the CR-X. Made of pure titanium.

Scarcity precludes accurate pricing.

CR-X – .177, .20, or .22 cal., PCP, BA, SS, 20.5 in. barrel, blue-black matte finish, two-stage adj. trigger, improved breechblock and other refinements, field target competition wood stock with adj. cheek piece and butt, no safety, 43 in. OAL, 9.6 lbs. Mfg. 1999-2003.

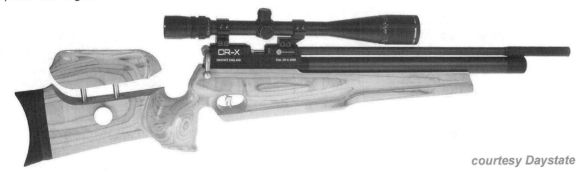

courtesy Daystate

	$1,800	$1,525	$1,250	$1,050	$800	$550	$350

Last MSR was $2,055.

Add 10% for .20 or .25 cal.

Several stock options available. Harrier-style blue-black matte finish (last ten rifles with gloss finish).

GRADING	100%	95%	90%	80%	60%	40%	20%

CR-X ST – .177, .20, or .22 cal., PCP, BA, SS, similar to CR-X, except all steel action, improved breechblock and other refinements, no safety 9.6 lbs. Mfg. 1999-2003.

| | $2,150 | $1,825 | $1,500 | $1,250 | $975 | $650 | $425 |

Last MSR was $2,055.

Add 10% for .20 or .25 cal.

All-steel action version of Model CR-X manufactured for USA only.

FIREFLY – similar to Mirage, except has manual rocker safety, 36 in. OAL, 6 lbs. 50 rifles mfg. March to Dec. 2002.

courtesy Beeman Collection

| | $850 | $725 | $600 | $500 | $375 | $255 | $170 |

Last MSR was $930.

FIRST PELLET RIFLE – .22 cal., SS, PCP, no safety, SN 1-42. Mfg. 1975-78.

Scarcity precludes accurate pricing.

These were Daystate's first pellet rifles, made while "still on the farm" by applying 42 surplus .22 cal. barrels which had been removed from Brno .22 rifles when they modified those firearms to 13 mm tranquilizer firearms.

GRAND PRIX – .177 or .22 cal., PCP, BA, SS, 17 in. rifled BBL, 950 FPS (.177 cal.), matte black finish, computer controlled electronic firing system, MVT digital regulator, built-in chronograph, adj. trigger with electronic lock and CDT electronic rotary safety, keyed power switch in trigger guard, fully adj. laminated thumbhole walnut stock, 41 in. OAL, approx. 9.6 lbs. Mfg. 2010-2011.

courtesy Precision Airgun Distribution

| | $2,900 | $2,475 | $2,025 | $1,675 | $1,300 | $875 | $575 |

Last MSR was $3,395.

HARRIER – .177, .20, .22, or .25 cal., PCP, BA, SS, 16 in. barrel, alloy breech block, matte black finish, adj. trigger, ambidextrous beech or walnut stock, manual rocker safety, Extra Short (XS) variant (for Spanish market where most cylinders will be hand filled), silencer, 35 in. OAL, 7 lbs. Mfg. 1997-2002.

courtesy Daystate

| | $625 | $525 | $425 | $350 | $280 | $185 | $125 |

Last MSR was $855.

GRADING	100%	95%	90%	80%	60%	40%	20%

Add 10% for .20 or .25 cal.

Add 5% for walnut stock.

Add 15% for XS variant.

Add 10% for thumbhole walnut stock.

Basically a Huntsman shortened by two inches with a new alloy breech block.

* ***Harrier SE*** – .177, .20, .22, or .25 cal., PCP, similar to Harrier, except has satin chrome finish on steel parts, Gary Cane handmade walnut stock, manual rocker safety, 38 in. OAL, 8.6 lbs. Mfg. 1997-2002.

	100%	95%	90%	80%	60%	40%	20%
	$900	$750	$625	$525	$400	$265	$180

Last MSR was $900.

Add 10% for .20 or .25 cal.

* ***Harrier PH6*** – .177, .20, .22, or .25 cal., PCP, similar to Harrier, except has stainless steel six-shot rotary mag., Muzzle Flip Compensator (MFC), cylinder rotates counter-clockwise away from loading point, manual rocker safety. 38 in. OAL, 8.4 lbs. Mfg. 1998-2002.

	100%	95%	90%	80%	60%	40%	20%
	$1,025	$850	$700	$600	$450	$300	$205

Last MSR was $1,050.

Add 10% for .20 or .25 cal.

Add 50% for SE version (like Harrier SE).

Designed with Paul Hogarth. Several stock and finish options were available.

* ***Harrier PH6 SE*** – .177, .20, .22, or .25 cal., PCP, similar to Harrier SE, except has stainless steel six-shot rotary mag. and is fitted with MFC. 8.6 lbs. Mfg. 2003.

	100%	95%	90%	80%	60%	40%	20%
	$1,150	$975	$800	$675	$525	$350	$230

Last MSR was $1,260.

* ***Harrier X*** – .177 or .22 cal., PCP, BA, ten-shot rotary mag., 15.8 in. BBL, MFC, matte black finish, adj. two-stage trigger, rotary manual safety, 35 in. OAL, 7.5 lbs. Mfg. 2003-2004.

courtesy Daystate

	100%	95%	90%	80%	60%	40%	20%
	$825	$700	$575	$475	$375	$250	$165

Last MSR was $835.

Add 10% for walnut stock.

Add 25% for thumbhole walnut stock.

HUNTSMAN BUCKMASTER LIMITED EDITION – .177 or .22 cal., PCP, BA, ten-shot rotary mag., 15.75 in. fully shrouded and rifled BBL, 790/850 FPS, satin black finish, adj. trigger, manual rotary safety, deluxe checkered PG walnut stock, 38 in. OAL, approx. 6 lbs. Limited edition of 100 Mfg. 2009-2011.

courtesy Precision Airgun Distribution

	100%	95%	90%	80%	60%	40%	20%
	$1,600	$1,350	$1,125	$925	$725	$475	$325

Last MSR was $1,895.

GRADING	100%	95%	90%	80%	60%	40%	20%

HUNTSMAN CLASSIC – .177 or .22 cal., PCP, BA, ten-shot rotary mag., 15.75 in. fully shrouded and rifled match grade barrel, solid breech block, two stage mechanical release trigger, 790/850 FPS, satin black finish, adj. trigger, manual rotary safety, checkered PG walnut stock, 38 in. OAL, approx. 6 lbs. Mfg. 2009-2013.

$1,275	$1,075	$900	$750	$575	$375	$255

Last MSR was $1,495.

HUNTSMAN CLASSIC XL – .177 or .22 cal., PCP, 10-shot mag., built on Huntsman Classic platform, lightweight design, integral barrel shroud, pressure gauge, safety catch, extended air cylinder, Harper MK4 "sling-shot" valve, manual safety, 38 in. OAL, 6.2 lbs. Mfg. 2010-13.

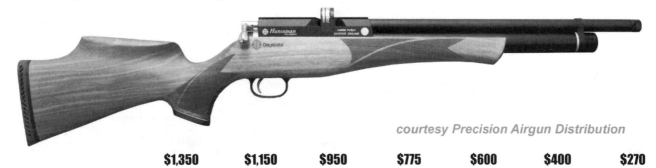

courtesy Precision Airgun Distribution

$1,350	$1,150	$950	$775	$600	$400	$270

Last MSR was $1,595.

HUNTSMAN MIDAS – .22 cal., PCP, SS, two-piece cylinder, square breechblock, pressed steel, single- or two-stage trigger designed by Barry McGraw, manual cross-bolt safety, Midas Mk2 variant -- HM prefix on SN and rocker safety. Mfg. 1983-1992.

$900	$750	$625	$525	$400	$265	$180

Last MSR was $900.

Add 5% for brass body tube or two-stage trigger.
Add 15% for stainless steel body tube.
Add 10% for Huntsman Midas Mk2 variant.

Very early guns made for animal control companies have stainless steel body tube. Later versions with brass body tube gave rise to the Midas name which is still used for blued models. High power versions prefix SN with HH (Huntsman High) prefix, low power version with HL prefix.

HUNTSMAN MK I – .22 cal., PCP, SS, round tubular breechblock - early versions with loading port as scallop on right side, later versions with loading port cut completely across, higher pressure valve intro. April 1994. Final version with square breechblock, single stage trigger, manual rocker safety, barrels by BSA. Mfg. 1988-1995.

courtesy Daystate

$625	$525	$425	$350	$280	$185	$125

Less expensive version of Midas, designed by Rob Thompson.

HUNTSMAN MK II – .177, .20, .22, or .25 cal., PCP, bolt action, SS, new version of Mk I, MK II engraved on breech,

courtesy Beeman Collection

GRADING	100%	95%	90%	80%	60%	40%	20%

lighter body tube reduced wt. 2 lbs., adj. two-stage trigger, beech or walnut stock, several finish options, manual rocker safety. Three versions: 1. Heavy Air Tube Variant - used Mk 1 air tube, figure of dart protrudes from engraved logo. 2. BSA Barrel Variant - deeply concave muzzle crown, unchoked, early. 3. Walther Barrel Variant - Lothar Walther choked barrel - later. 8.4 lbs. Mfg. 1995 -2002.

	$800	$675	$550	$475	$350	$240	$160

Last MSR was $810.

Add 10% for walnut stock.
Add 10% for "TH" (thumbhole version).
Add 10% for .20 or .25 cal.
Add 250% for solid brass construction, two manufactured in .22 cal., 10.3 lbs.

* ***Huntsman MK II PH6*** – .177, .20, .22, or .25 cal., similar to Huntsman MK II, except has stainless steel six-shot rotary mag., 8.4 lbs. Disc. 2003.

courtesy Beeman Collection

	$1,025	$850	$700	$600	$450	$300	$205

Last MSR was $1,040.

Add 10% for .20 or .25 cal.
Several stock and finish options were available.

HUNTSMAN REGAL XL – .177 or .22 cal., PCP, BA, ten-shot repeater, blue finish aircraft grade aluminium receiver, adj. two-stage mechanical trigger, blue finish, 17 in. Lother Walther barrel with integral sound suppression, sporter walnut stock, 162cc cylinder, 36.5 in. OAL, 6.17 lbs. New 2013.

MSR $1,742	$1,475	$1,300	$1,175	$950	$725	N/A	N/A

HUNTSMAN SCOUT LIMITED EDITION – .22 cal., PCP, BA, ten-shot rotary mag., 15.75 in. fully shrouded and rifled BBL, titanium-alloy finish with laser engraving, adj. trigger, manual rotary safety, deluxe checkered black and gray laminate PG stock, 44.25 in. OAL, approx. 7.95 lbs. Limited edition of 50 mfg. 2014.

MSR $2,195	$1,875	$1,650	$1,500	$1,200	$925	N/A	N/A

HUNTSMAN WINGMASTER LIMITED EDITION – .177, .20, or .22 cal., PCP, 10-shot mag., built on Huntsman Classic platform, engraved breech in Titanium finish with Wingmaster logos in gold inlay, integral barrel shroud, pressure gauge, safety catch, extended air cylinder, Harper MK4 "sling-shot" valve, hand oiled selected Turkish Walnut stock, 38 in. OAL, 6.2 lbs. Disc. 2011.

	$1,950	$1,650	$1,375	$1,125	$875	$575	$400

Last MSR was $2,295.

LR90 (LIGHT RIFLE 1990) – .177 cal., PCP, SS, BA, 930 FPS, similar to Huntsman except has one-inch diameter body tube, smooth or hand checkered stock, adj. trigger, manual safety, 7.3 lbs., 38.5 in. OAL. Mfg. 1995-99.

	$825	$700	$575	$475	$375	$245	$165

Last MSR was $900.

Add 50% for FT model with checkered thumbhole stock.
This model is the same as the Beeman Mako.

MIRAGE MK2 – .177 or .22 cal., PCP, SS, BA, improved version of Mirage with steel LR90 air cylinder, more robust breech block, new valve design, scope grooves, no sights, manual rocker safety, 1000/860 FPS, 37 in. OAL, 5.5 lbs. Mfg. 2002-2004.

	$825	$700	$575	$475	$375	$245	$165

Last MSR was $895.

This model is the same as the Beeman Mako 2.

GRADING	100%	95%	90%	80%	60%	40%	20%

MIRAGE XLR (EXTRA LIGHT RIFLE) – .177, .20, .22, or .25 cal., PCP, bolt action, SS, 16 in. BBL, aircraft aluminum cylinder, matte blue finish, adj. trigger, beech or walnut stock, 36 in. OAL, 4.2 lbs. Mfg. 1999-2002.

courtesy Daystate

$850	$725	$600	$500	$375	$255	$170

Last MSR was $895.

Add 5% for walnut stock.
Add 10% for .20 or .25 cal.
Several stock and finish options available.

MK3 FT-R – .177 or .22 cal., PCP, BA, ten-shot rotary mag., 16.25 in. fully shrouded and rifled BBL with threaded end, MFC, matte black finish, Harper patent CDT electronic firing system, adj. trigger with electronic lock and MK3 CDT electronic rotary safety, keyed power switch in trigger guard, pneumatic regulator, checkered walnut thumbhole with adj. cheek piece and buttplate stock, 37.5 in. OAL, 8 lbs. Mfg. 2003-2009.

courtesy Daystate Collection

$2,200	$1,875	$1,525	$1,275	$975	$650	$450

Early A type: "on" light in stock behind action, brass trigger blade, UK only. Current B type: "on" light in the action, alloy trigger blade.

MK3 S (SPORT) – .177 or .22 cal., PCP, BA, ten-shot rotary mag., 16.25 in. shrouded and rifled BBL with threaded end, matte black finish, Harper patent CDT electronic firing system, adj. trigger with electronic lock and MK3 CDT electronic rotary safety, keyed power switch in trigger guard, pneumatic regulator, checkered pistol grip walnut stock, 37.5 in. OAL, 8 lbs. Mfg. 2003-2009.

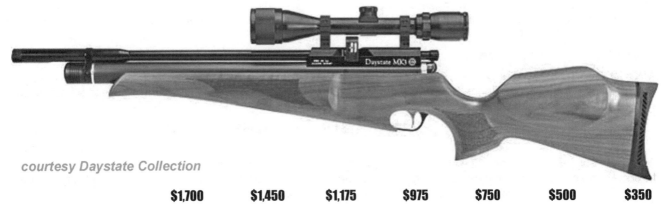

courtesy Daystate Collection

$1,700	$1,450	$1,175	$975	$750	$500	$350

Early A type: "on" light in stock behind action, brass trigger blade, UK only. Current B type: "on" light in the action, alloy trigger blade.

GRADING	100%	95%	90%	80%	60%	40%	20%

MK3 ST (SPORT THUMBHOLE) – .177 or .22 cal., PCP, BA, ten-shot rotary mag., 16.25 in. shrouded and rifled BBL with threaded end, matte black finish, Harper patent CDT electronic firing system, adj. trigger with electronic lock and MK3 CDT electronic rotary safety, keyed power switch in trigger guard, pneumatic regulator, checkered thumbhole walnut stock, 37.5 in. OAL, 8 lbs. Mfg. 2003-2009.

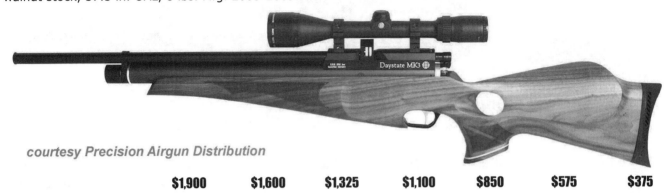

courtesy Precision Airgun Distribution

$1,900	$1,600	$1,325	$1,100	$850	$575	$375

Early A type: "on" light in stock behind action, brass trigger blade, UK only. Current B type: "on" light in the action, alloy trigger blade.

MK4 PLATINUM LIMITED EDITION – .177 or .22 cal., PCP, BA, SS, 17 in. rifled BBL, 950 FPS (.177 cal.), satin platinum finish, computer controlled electronic firing system, MVT digital regulator, built-in chronograph, adj. trigger with electronic lock and CDT electronic rotary safety, keyed power switch in trigger guard, fully adj. laminated thumbhole walnut stock, 41 in. OAL, approx. 9.6 lbs. Limited edition. Mfg. 2011 only.

courtesy Precision Airgun Distribution

$2,900	$2,475	$2,025	$1,675	$1,300	$875	$575

Last MSR was $3,395.

MK4 iS SPORT – .177 or .22 cal., PCP, BA, SS, 17 in. rifled and shrouded BBL, 790/880 FPS, satin black finish, MCT electronic firing system, adj. trigger with electronic lock and electronic rotary safety, keyed power switch in trigger guard, anatomical PG walnut stock with ventilated recoil pad, 36.5 in. OAL, approx. 7.5 lbs. New 2009.

MSR $1,997	$1,700	$1,500	$1,350	$1,100	$850	N/A	N/A

* **MK4 iS Thumbhole** – .177 or .22 cal., PCP, BA, 10-shot rotary mag., 17 in. rifled and shrouded BBL, 790/880 FPS, satin black finish, MCT electronic firing system, adj. trigger with electronic lock and electronic rotary safety, keyed power switch in trigger guard, anatomical thumbhole walnut stock with ventilated recoil pad, 36.5 in. OAL, approx. 7.5 lbs. New 2009.

MSR $2,288	$1,950	$1,725	$1,550	$1,250	$950	N/A	N/A

* **MK4 iS Panther** – .177 or .22 cal., PCP, 17 in. barrel with moderated muzzle, 10 shot rotary mag., LCD information screen, electronic release trigger, black ambidextrous "Soft Touch" rubber over wood adj. thumbhole stock, Sill air muzzle compensator, 36.5 in. OAL, 9.5 lbs. Mfg. 2012 only.

$2,250	$1,900	$1,575	$1,300	$1,000	$675	$450

Last MSR was $2,646.

* **MK4 iS Target** – .177 or .22 cal., PCP, BA, 17 in. barrel with moderated muzzle, 10 shot rotary mag., LCD information screen, electronic release trigger, black ambidextrous "Soft Touch" rubber over wood adj. thumbhole stock, Sill air muzzle compensator, 36.5 in. OAL, 9.5 lbs. New 2013.

MSR $2,889	$2,450	$2,175	$1,975	$1,600	$1,225	N/A	N/A

GRADING	100%	95%	90%	80%	60%	40%	20%

MODEL 2000 – .177 or .22 cal., PCP, SS, similar to Huntsman with added regulator, manual rocker safety, 41 in. OAL, 9 3/4 lbs. Mfg. 1990-1994.

Last MSR was $1,400.

Current values not yet determined.

Regulators for 12 ft./lb. British versions did not work, but rifle could fire at a reduced force. Most specimens now have an aftermarket regulator or have removed the regulator.

QC (QUICK CHANGE) – .22 cal., PCP with removable 16 in. air cylinder. Mfg. 1997-1998.

Current values not yet determined.

* **QC 2** – improved version of QC w/alloy air cylinder. Mfg. 1992-1996.

Last MSR was $875.

Current values not yet determined.

SABLE – .177 or .22 cal., PCP, BA, SS, 790/880 FPS, 15.75 in. rifled and shrouded barrel, satin black finish, MCT electronic firing system, adj. trigger, thumbhole walnut stock with ventilated recoil pad, 38 in. OAL, approx. 7.5 lbs. Disc. 2011.

courtesy Precision Airgun Distribution

	100%	95%	90%	80%	60%	40%	20%
	$2,125	$1,800	$1,475	$1,225	$950	$625	$425

Last MSR was $2,495.

SPORTSMAN – .22 cal., SS, UL, multi-pump pneumatic, Monte Carlo stock w/o cheek piece, manual safety. FAC models fire to 855 FPS on 9-10 pumps. Non-FAC multi-pump models require six strokes. 38.5 in. OAL, 7.9 lbs. Mfg. 1980-86.

	100%	95%	90%	80%	60%	40%	20%
	$1,000	$850	$700	$575	$450	$300	$200

Last MSR was $375.

SPORTSMAN MK II – .22 cal. SS, side-lever SSP for British market, two-stroke pneumatic for unrestricted markets, no safety. Mfg. 1996-98.

Last MSR was $570.

Current values not yet determined.

TRANQUILIZER AIRGUN – .50 (13mm) cal., SS, PCP, Daystate's first airguns, PCP tranquilizer gun. Mfg. 1973-1978.

Current values not yet determined.

WOLVERINE 303 – .303 cal., PCP, ambidextrous BA, five-shot repeater, bright finish aircraft grade aluminium receiver, adj. two-stage mechanical trigger, blue finish 23 in. Lother Walther barrel with integral sound suppression, ambidextrous walnut stock, 300cc cylinder, 44 in. OAL, 9.5 lbs. New 2012.

MSR $2,803	$2,375	$2,100	$1,900	$1,550	$1,175	N/A	N/A

* **Wolverine B-Type** – .177 or .22 cal., PCP, ambidextrous BA, ten-shot repeater, blue finished aircraft grade aluminium receiver, adj. two-stage mechanical trigger, blue finish 17 in. Lother Walther barrel with integral sound suppression, ambidextrous walnut stock, 400cc (12 ft/lbs) or 500cc (31 ft/lbs) cylinder, 42 in. OAL, 7.4 lbs. Mfg. 2014-current.

MSR $1,995	$1,700	$1,500	$1,350	$1,100	$825	N/A	N/A

* **Wolverine HP (Hi-Power)** – .22 cal., PCP, ambidextrous BA, ten-shot repeater, bright finish aircraft aluminium grade receiver, adj. two-stage mechanical trigger, blue finish 23 in. Lother Walther barrel with integral sound suppression, ambidextrous walnut stock, 300cc cylinder, 44 in. OAL, 9.5 lbs. Mfg. 2014-current.

MSR $2,803	$2,375	$2,100	$1,900	$1,550	$1,175	N/A	N/A

GRADING	100%	95%	90%	80%	60%	40%	20%

X2 AMBI/X2 SPORTS/X2 PRESTIGE – .177 or .22 cal., PCP, BA, SS, 15.75 in. fully shrouded and rifled BBL with threaded end (New 2008), alloy breech block, satin finish, adj. trigger, ambidextrous beech (X2 Ambi Disc. 2006), RH or LH synthetic (Disc. 2006) or walnut (X2 Sports, new 2006), or thumbhole extra grade American walnut (X2 Prestige Disc. 2006) stock, manual rocker safety, 38 in. OAL, 7.5 lbs. Mfg. 2004-2009.

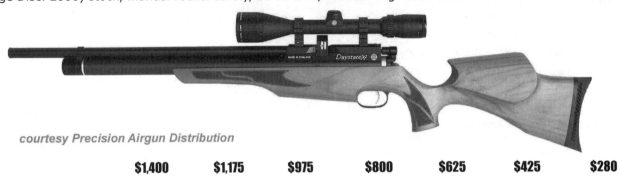

courtesy Precision Airgun Distribution

$1,400	$1,175	$975	$800	$625	$425	$280

> **Add 20% for regulated versions, less desirable in USA.**
> **Add 35% for Prestige variant with Gary Cane stock (Disc. 2006).**

Most are marked "Daystate X2", a few early guns are marked "Harrier X2". Sports Variant: black synthetic stock, black bolt handle (also, in British market regulated version, chrome bolt handle, limited to 25 ft./lb. ME).

X2 MERLYN – .177 or .22 cal., PCP, BA, SS, 15.75 in. fully shrouded and rifled BBL with threaded end (new 2008), MFC, alloy breech block, regulator, satin finish, adj. trigger, walnut thumbhole stock with rosewood cap, manual rocker safety, 38 in. OAL, 7.5 lbs. Mfg. 2003-2009.

courtesy Precision Airgun Distribution

$1,800	$1,525	$1,250	$1,050	$800	$550	$350

X2 SPORTS REGULATED – .177 or .22 cal., PCP, BA, SS, 15.75 in. BBL, alloy breech block, regulator, satin finish, adj. trigger, walnut PG stock, manual rocker safety, 36 in. OAL, 7.5 lbs. Mfg. 2006-2009.

$1,600	$1,350	$1,125	$925	$725	$475	$325

SHOTGUNS

SHOTGUN – .38 or .50 cal., smoothbore, SS, PCP, 24.3 in. barrel, designed for controlling pests, such as small birds and rats in grain storage, without lead or powder. Fired hard, silver-colored, BB-shaped, candy cake decorations (in UK = "Dragees" or "Rainbow Pearls") from tubular brass case. Basically a tranquillizer barrel built onto a Huntsman air rifle, 45 in. OAL, 8.3 lbs. Approx. 17 mfg. 1987.

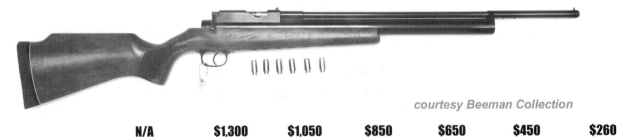

courtesy Beeman Collection

N/A	$1,300	$1,050	$850	$650	$450	$260

DECKER

Previous trademark of Decker Manufacturing Company located in Detroit, Michigan from about 1898 to 1991.

Decker Manufacturing Company, formerly produced sheet metal BB guns. Decker produced some cast iron guns under the Decker name around 1898. Charles Decker and his brother, Frederick Decker, and associate Frank Trowbridge, formed the Hexagon Air Rifle Company which produced the Hexagon air rifles about 1900-1901. These

BB guns featured a hexagon shaped barrel cover and an unusual BB reservoir (not properly called a magazine) in the buttstock. Despite a cast iron grip, the Hexagon rifles did not stand up and are rarely found. Prices of the Hexagon airguns now may run from about $300 to over $1000 depending on model and condition. Additional details about the guns and their values are subject to further study and information for future editions of the *Blue Book of Airguns*. Ref. Dunathan (1957).

DERYA ARMS INDUSTRY

Current manufacturer established in 2000, and located in Konya, Turkey. No current U.S. importation.

Derya Arms Industry currently manufactures air rifles and tactical accessories, as well as semi-auto, slide action, and single shot shotguns in various configurations. Please contact the factory directly for more information, values, and availability (see Trademark Index).

RIFLES

LION – .177 or .22 cal., hardwood or plastic stock, 5 lbs. 15 oz.

courtesy Derya Arms Industry

Please contact the company directly for more information including pricing and U.S. availability for this model.

DIANA (DIANAWERK) MAYER & GRAMMELSPACHER GmbH & CO. KG

Current trademark manufactured by Mayer & Grammelspacher GmbH & Co. KG located in Rastatt, Germany. Currently imported exclusively by Umarex USA located in Fort Smith, AR begining 2006. Previously imported by Dynamit Nobel RWS Inc., located in Closter, NJ. Dynamit Nobel RWS Inc. is a division of RUAG AmmoTec GmbH, located in Furth, Germany. Dealer and consumer direct sales.

Dynamit Nobel RWS, Inc. also imports airguns manufactured by Air Arms, BSA, Gamo, and Shinsung/Career. Please refer to their respective listings for pricing.

The authors and publisher wish to thank Ulrich Eichstädt, Mike Driskill, and John Atkins, for their valuable assistance with the following information in this edition of the *Blue Book of Airguns*. Because of the destruction of records in two World Wars, it was not possible to verify all information. Additional information and corrections will be made in future editions. Such information is actively solicted. Please send inputs directly to guns@bluebookinc.com.

This section covers only the real Dianawerk airguns, made by Mayer & Grammelspacher of Rastatt, Germany. It DOES NOT INCLUDE British "Diana" airguns. For British made "Diana" airguns, see the Millard Brothers section.

DIANAWERK BACKGROUND

Despite the company's 119 year history, the trademark of the hunting goddess Diana has become more famous than the official name of its company: "Mayer & Grammelspacher Dianawerk GmbH & Co. KG." One of the founders, Jakob Mayer, born in 1866, worked as a toolmaker at the Eisenwerke ("Ironworks") Gaggenau, in Gaggenau, Germany before he left to start his new company in 1890 in nearby Rastatt on the German/French border.

Mayer was the technical director of the new company; his friend, Josef Grammelspacher, financed it. Almost nothing is known of Josef Grammelspacher. He seems to have left the company by 1901 and the Grammelspacher family died out about 80 years ago. All documents concerning the family were lost during the two World Wars.

DIANAWERK 1892-1932: BIRTH OF THE TRADEMARK

Around 1892, Mayer presented his first air pistol, which showed a great resemblance to a Gaggenau patent taken on the Haviland & Gunn patent design of 1872. Composed chiefly of a single piece of cast iron, it housed its mainspring in the grip and was marked only with the cast letters "MGR". The MGR trademark, representing Mayer & Grammelspacher in Rastatt, apparently was first used with the MG over the R and later was combined, at least in printed materials, with a target and a smiling boy's face. It is not known exactly when the famous Diana trademark, showing the hunting goddess Diana holding her air rifle aloft while standing on her discarded bow and arrows, was first used.

One of Mayer's many patents was issued in 1901 for a spring-loaded wedge mechanism to serve as a detent lock on barrel-cocking airguns. This mechanism, which has appeared on millions of airguns, is still in common use. Production of a number of models of airguns and toy guns developed rapidly during the 1890 to 1910 period, but, again, wars have destroyed most of the records. The toy guns, shooting corks and suction cup darts, were produced under the trademark "Eureka."

Trying to look back through the mists of time, what we do seem to see of the period around the start of the 20th century is a company that did not seem to have a focus. Like so many other airgun makers, they were adding, without particular distinction, to the seemingly endless flow of GEM airguns and toy guns. The advent of the solid MGR "First Model" pistols and rifles, both incorporating superb patent features of Jakob Mayer, seems to been the developmental and economic base, for the future of the company. However, the rapidly growing success of Dianawerk probably was due, as with contemporary Daisy, and even recent airgun company success stories, to aggressive marketing efforts and skills of a visionary, in this case, Jakob Mayer. The creation of the Diana name and logo was the first major step in this marketing.

In the "roaring twenties" the demand of military air rifle trainers was replaced by airgun shooting as a new family game and leisure-time sport. The quality and performance of these first Diana "adult air rifles," like the models 25 and 27, was increased. In 1930, a Model 25 was offered for 25 Marks, while the extra high quality LG 58 was available for 90 Marks. A tin of the newly invented "diabolo" pellets sold for 3.40 Marks. Unfortunately, the catalogs of that period did not mention velocities of the airguns and most of the specimens in collections are not capable of their original power, so we don't know the potential of those "adult airguns."

DIANAWERK 1933-1949: LOSS OF THE TRADEMARK

By 1933, the emerging Nazi government had had a bad effect on Dianawerk. Decreasing sales forced withdrawal from the Leipzig trade fair and export to 28 countries was forbidden for political reasons. By 1936, Rastatt had become a center for housing troops and in 1940 all civilian production was halted when the company was forced to produce gun parts for the Mauser factory in Oberndorf (Dianawerk's military production was marked with the secret code "lxr"). This military activity resulted in extremely heavy bombing of Rastatt by the British. In 1945, the French occupied the area and Dianawerk was completely dismantled. As production of air rifles was then subject to a death penalty, the French were glad, to sell, at a donative price (in the spirit of war reparations), all of the company, including its machinery, old parts, and Diana trademark, to London-based Millard Bros. Ltd. With the abbreviated name "Milbro," the operation was moved to Motherwell in Scotland. The first Scottish "Dianas" were produced in 1949.

DIANAWERK 1950-1984: REGAINING THE TRADEMARK

The Allied Control Council again allowed production of airguns in 1950. By September, the Mayers began production of airguns in their old factory in Rastatt. The loss of their world-famous "Diana" trademark hit them very hard. Within Germany the air rifles were sold as "Original." To commonwealth countries Diana exported "GECADO" models; "Condor," "Firebird," or "Original Diana" was used for Dianawerk guns in England. Many large foreign companies contracted for Diana models, or special variations including different cosmetics and features, under the names of Winchester, Condor, Hy-Score, Beeman, Peerless, etc. By 1982, despite the advantage of the trademark, Milbro, using Dianawerk's old machinery and materials, had gone out of business. Dianawerk repurchased their trademark in 1984.

DIANAWERK MATCH AIRGUNS AND RESTRICTIONS

Although Dianawerk never became a major force in the growing market of match airgun production like Walther and Feinwerkbau, they had a major effect on that market. Kurt Giss, the chief designer in Rastatt, invented the double piston system at the end of 1950s. This design used two pistons, connected and synchronized by a gear rod. The forward piston compressed the air for pellet propulsion. The second piston moved backward and eliminated recoil. The Giss System resulted in the production of the first recoilless match-guns: the LP 6 air pistol in 1960 and then in 1963 the LG 60 air rifle. The introduction of recoilless airguns caused a revolution in the design of match airguns and established Germany as the leader in this field.

A complete family of airguns with the double piston system followed. However, production of the numerous parts was very expensive and maintenance was very difficult. In the mid-1960s, Dianawerk, like many gun companies, began to simplify the construction and materials of their guns. By the mid-1970s competitors Feinwerkbau, Anschütz, and Walther had eclipsed Dianawerk. Dianawerk continued to concentrate on the production of economy-level, leisure-time models and on reducing production and material costs. A few attempts to get back into the "match market," with the LG 100 (a single-stroke pneumatic rifle), and match grade smallbore rifles, failed. A 1972 German gun law severely restricted air rifles with power over 7.5 joules; only about 5.5 ft./lb. or 575 FPS in .177 caliber! The British limit is 12 ft./lb. This led to a deepening crisis within the company. The 1979 to 1982 discontinuance of key Diana airgun models by Beeman Precision Airguns in the USA, one of their largest potential markets, may also have had a further disastrous effect. However, as of April 1, 2002, the German airgunners have a new lease on life: they now can have air rifles (over 60 cm) up to 16.3 joules (12 ft./lb.) for field target competition and even more powerful ones on a hunting license permit.

DIANAWERK TODAY

So at the beginning of the 1990s, directors Peter Mayer, the last descendant of the Diana founder, and Hans-Günther Frey faced serious decisions. More than five hundred employees had worked in the huge halls at Karlstraße, but now the halls were empty, and rumors went out that M & G desperately needed a buyer to keep the last hundred employees. No competitor, who was interested in the still successful Diana line, wanted to take the high risk of also buying the buildings. So Dianawerk began to rescue itself. Several production processes were outsourced. Retiring employees were no longer replaced. Models were slightly altered to use standard, plastic, and interchangeable parts. Stock making was discontinued. And a large browning/blueing machine was purchased, which, by drawing work from other companies, could profitably be used to full capacity.

German airgun shooting received a huge boost from the introduction of field target shooting. Firms like Diana, Weihrauch,

GRADING	100%	95%	90%	80%	60%	40%	20%

Dynamit Nobel, and Haendler & Natermann cooperated to help form the first clubs and establish rules which considered the special German situations. Development of separate classes for air rifles above and below the 7.5 joule limit and also for precharged and spring-piston air rifles helped the shooters who had to document a need for high power air rifles. Now many different kinds of airguns and shooters could find shooting opportunities ranging from local fun to serious international competition.

Despite rumors to the contrary, the firm entered 2003 owned 100% by the Frey family (with relatives left from the Mayer and Dorf clans). Now with ninety employees and seven apprentices, Dianawerk was back in the black, beginning its 111th year without old headaches, looking forward to what the future might bring.

DIANAWERK COLLECTING

At the current time, Dianawerk airguns present a good collecting opportunity and challenge. These guns generally are under appreciated and under valued. There is a great deal yet to be learned about Dianawerk airguns. Certainly a major matter is how to designate the many different guns which bear the same factory model number!

Numbering of Diana models is somewhat confusing. Not only were model numbers not issued in chronological order, but sometimes the same model number has been issued to very different guns at different historical periods. Letters shown ahead of and after the model numbers generally do not appear on the guns themselves. Production dates may be stamped on gun in very small type - the date may be the key to the model variation. American collectors should note that all RWS airguns are not made by Dianawerk; those models will not be listed here.

DIANAWERK COMPARABLE MODEL NUMBERS

For information on Diana airguns manufactured for other trademarks, see the Dianawerk Comparable Model Numbers chart in the Store Brand Cross-Over List at the back of this text.

Important note: Comparable models often have very different values due to different demand by collectors, different levels of scarcity, and because distributors of private label guns often specified different power levels (for different markets, and not just mainspring differences), stock design, stock material and quality, calibers, sights, trigger mechanisms, etc., which may be different from the basic manufacturer's model. Beeman and pre-1970 Winchester-marked guns generally sell for a premium. Early models of the same number may differ from more recent models.

HANDGUNS

MGR FIRST MODEL – .177 cal., SP, slugs, pellets, or darts, 6.7 in.BBL, frame, sights, barrel, and grip of single piece are cast iron, spring piston in grip cocked by attaching intergrated "T" bar handel to pull action bar, loaded via screw-in breech plug with leather seal, adjustable trigger, no trigger guard, black lacquer or completely nickel-plated finish, integrally cast floral design on sides of frame with cast letters MG over R, for Mayer & Grammelspacher in Rastatt, the company's early trademark, smoothbore barrel, later versions with brass liner, 1.3 lbs., 7.9in. OAL, Mfg.circa 1892-1914. Ref: Gilbart, *Guns Review*, Nov. 1988, Atkins, *Airgunner*, July 1976.

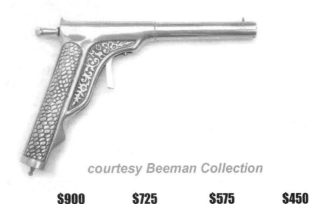

courtesy Beeman Collection

	N/A	$900	$725	$575	$450	$325	$180

Add 20% for nickel-plated version.
Add 20% for early version with original separate cocking tool.
Add 30% for original wood box with papers and accessories.

Probably Dianawerk's first air pistols. Sold as the Tahiti by A.W. Gamage Ltd. of England, but this name should not be applied to this model in general. Evidently Dianawerk also provided Gamage, circa 1909-1911, with a large BC, SP air pistol, like a cut-down Diana 20 air rifle, under the private label of Holborn.

GRADING	100%	95%	90%	80%	60%	40%	20%

MODEL 1 – .177 cal., 5 3/4 in. barrel, similar to MGR First Model, except economy version with pressed sheet metal, tubular brass barrel in sheet metal housing, spring piston in grip, several minor variations. Mfg. 1924-1935.

courtesy Beeman Collection

	N/A	$170	$140	$115	$90	$60	$40

MODEL 2 (PRE-WWII MODEL) – .177 cal., push-barrel cocking, with shaped sheet steel frame, nickel finish, 7.9 in. smoothbore telescopic two-part steel barrel, removable knurled knob at back end of receiver for loading pellets or darts, marked "DIANA" on grip (1930-33), "Model 2" marked on barrel, post 1933 with huntress on top of cylinder (not on grips) fixed sight, 10.6 oz. Pre-WWII variant, approx. 100,000 mfg. 1933-1940.

courtesy Beeman Collection

$135	$115	$95	$80	$60	$40	$25

* ***Model 2 Improved*** – similar to Model 2, except has adj. sights and riveted wooden grips. Mfg. 1955-1985.

courtesy Beeman Collection

$75	$65	$55	$45	$35	$20	$15

MODEL 3 – .177 cal., BBC, 7.1 in. rifled barrel, blue finish, plastic grips, adj. rear sight, 325 FPS, 2.4 lbs. New 1991- disc.

courtesy Diana

$85	$70	$60	$50	$40	$25	$15

Last MSR was $97.

GRADING	100%	95%	90%	80%	60%	40%	20%

MODEL 4 (IV) – .177 cal., BBC, more information in future editions.

   No other information or values available at time of printing.

MODEL 5 (V) – .177 cal., BBC, SP, rifled or smoothbore 7.5 in. barrel, hand checkered wood grip, 13.3 in. OAL. Mfg. 1931-1940.

N/A	$170	$140	$115	$90	$60	$40

   Probably the only Dianawerk airgun with circle "D" trademark. Not related to post-WWII Model 5 listed below.

MODEL 5 – .177 or .22 cal., BBC, 7.3 in. tapered barrel, 450/300 FPS, metal trigger guard, adj. rear sight, hooded front sight, adj. trigger and wood grip until 1960, light gray plastic grip in early 1970s, later dark brown, safety, 15.75 in. OAL, 2.4 lbs. Mfg. 1958-1978.

courtesy Beeman Collection

$125	$105	$90	$75	$55	$35	$25

   Add 40% for wooden grip versions with tapered barrel.
   Add 5% for gray grips.
   Add 10% for "Beeman's Original" markings -- the rarest version.

* ***Model 5FO*** – fiber optic sight inserts.

$150	$125	$100	$85	$65	$45	$30

* ***Model 5G/GS*** – .177 or .22 cal., BBC, 450/300 FPS, 7 in. barrel, improved version of Model 5, precision-cast alloy frame, smaller plastic grip (right/left-handed) with grip angle of 125°, receiver with plastic end cap, two-stage adj. trigger, GS Model equipped with factory scope, 16.5 in. OAL, 2.5 lbs. Mfg. beginning in 1978. Disc.

courtesy Diana

$175	$145	$120	$100	$75	$50	$35

                                                                Last MSR was $260.

   Add 20% for GS.
   Add 20% for GN with matte nickel plating.

GRADING	100%	95%	90%	80%	60%	40%	20%

* **Model 5GM (Magnum)** – .177 cal., BBC, SP, SS, 700 FPS, blue finish, molded black grips, adj. rear sight, adj. trigger. Marked Umarex USA beginning 2006. Mfg. 2003-2008.

courtesy Diana

	$190	$170	$140	$115	$90	$60	$40

Last MSR was $246.

* **Model P5 Magnum** – .177 or .22 cal., BBC, SP, SS, 568/422 FPS, 9 in. BBL, blue finish, molded black grip, fiber optic adj. rear sight, 2.64 lbs. Mfg. 2001-2003.

	$190	$170	$140	$115	$90	$60	$40

Last MSR was $250.

MODEL 6 – .177 cal., BBC, similar to Model 5, recoilless Giss double contra-piston system, 7.1 in. tapered barrel, wood grip, adj. trigger, 16.5 in. OAL, 2.9 lbs. Mfg. 1960-1978.

courtesy Beeman Collection

	$190	$170	$140	$115	$90	$60	$40

This model can sometimes be misread as the "Model 8."

* **Model 6G** – .177 cal., BBC, Giss recoilless, 450 FPS, 7 in. barrel (professional target), alloy frame, separate plastic grip similar to Model 5. Mfg. 1978-2000.

	$325	$275	$230	$190	$145	$95	$65

Add 5% for gray grips.

Add 20% for "Beeman's Original" markings - the rarest version.

* **MODEL 6GS** – .177 cal., BBC, 450 FPS, 7 in. barrel (professional target), equipped with factory scope and scope rail, muzzle weight, plastic sport or wooden palm rest grip, 3 lbs. Importation disc. 1995.

	$375	$300	$250	$210	$160	$110	$70

Last MSR was $445.

Add 15% for palm rest grips.

* **Model 6M** – .177 cal., BBC, 450 FPS, 7 in. barrel (professional target), match style, plastic sport or wooden palm rest grip, rotating barrel-shroud from Model 10 without sight hood. Mfg. 1978-1999.

	$425	$350	$280	$230	$180	$120	$80

Last MSR was $620.

Add 15% for palm rest grips.

GRADING	100%	95%	90%	80%	60%	40%	20%

MODEL 8 – .177 in. cal., SS, SP, BC, 20 in. OAL, 2.4 lbs. Walnut 1 pc. grip and forearm. Mfg. 1907-1914.

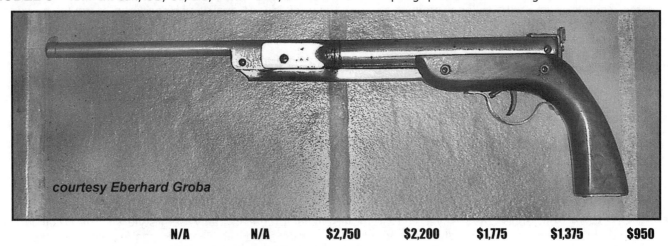

courtesy Eberhard Groba

		N/A	N/A	$2,750	$2,200	$1,775	$1,375	$950

There are very few surviving specimens.

MODEL 10 – .177 cal., BBC, recoilless Giss double contra-piston system, 7.1 in. barrel, 450 FPS, adj. trigger and rear sight, open front sight with adj. width 0.1 in. to 0.2 in., rotating barrel shroud covered front sight during cocking and carried a special designed additional weight, matte phosphate finish, adj. wooden grip, eccentric rotating plastic sleeve around rear of receiver to secure shooting hand on early variant, 7 in. barrel, 16.1 in. OAL, 2.5 lbs. Mfg. 1974-1989.

courtesy Beeman Collection

$550	$475	$375	$325	$250	$165	$110

Last MSR was $670.

Add 15% for cased model.
Add 10% for left-hand variation.
Add 10% for eccentric rotating plastic sleeve.

MODEL P8 – .177 or .22 cal., BBC, SP, SS, 568/422 FPS, 9 in. BBL, blue finish, molded black grip, fiber optic adj. rear sight, 2.64 lbs. Mfg. 2001-2003.

$225	$190	$160	$130	$100	$65	$45

Last MSR was $250.

RIFLES

MGR FIRST MODEL – These airguns are probably Dianawerk's first airguns. They are marked M&G over R, for Mayer & Grammelspacher, Rastatt, instead of Diana. All are very rare. Ref: Larry Hannusch, *US Airgun* Oct. 1995, or in *Pneumatic Reflections* by Larry Hannusch, 2001.

* ***MGR First Model 1901 Variant*** – .177 cal., BC, SP, 19 in. smoothbore octagonal blued barrel, rest of gun is nickel plated, complex cast spring cylinder projects straight ahead of trigger, guard, fixed rear sight, side-barrel latch, quarter length straight grip buttstock with cheek piece, 41.3 in. OAL, 5.3 lbs. M&G German Sept. 1901 patent no. 135599. Mfg. 1901-1904/05.

	N/A	$2,000	$1,600	$1,300	$1,000	$700	$400

GRADING	100%	95%	90%	80%	60%	40%	20%

* ***MGR First Model 1904 Variant*** – .177 cal., BC, SP, 18.9 in. rifled octagonal blued barrel, rest of gun is nickel plated, complex cast spring cylinder projects straight ahead of trigger, guard, side-mounted barrel latch, wedge-shaped detent, quarter length straight grip buttstock with cheek piece, 42.6 in. OAL, 7.1 lbs. M&G German Aug. 1904 patent no. 163094. Mfg. 1904-1905.

courtesy Beeman Collection

N/A	$1,750	$1,400	$1,125	$875	$600	$350

GEM MODELS – from about 1895 Mayer and Grammelspacher produced many Gem-style air rifles (copied from Haviland and Gunn designs), reportedly including a "Ladies" model and MGR "Patent Repeating Air Gun," capable of 100 shots per loading, around end of 19th century. (See Gem in the "G" section.)

MODEL 10DL – .177 cal., SL, SP, blue finish, revmovable smoothbore barrel for darts, balls, and pellets, fires corks with barrel removed, wood halfstock, fixed sights, 29.5 in. OAL, 1.5 lbs. Mfg. 1950-1952.

courtesy Beeman Collection

$400	$350	$280	$230	$180	$120	$80

MODEL 1 (JUNIOR) – .177 cal., BBC, SP, blue finish, tinplate construction, wooden buttstock, Diana goddess trademark above the trigger, fixed sights, loaded via removable rifled barrel (darts or balls), 31.5 in. OAL, 2 lbs. Mfg. 1913-1940.

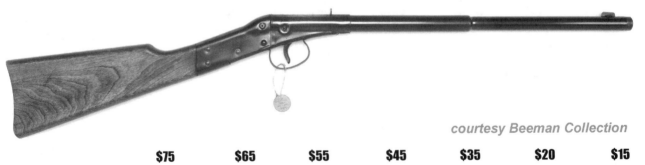

courtesy Beeman Collection

$75	$65	$55	$45	$35	$20	$15

While identical to a model sold by Bonehill about 1898, this may be Mayer & Grammelspacher 's first offering of a barrel-cocking air rifle. But the maker is unknown.

* ***Model LG 1 Improved*** – .177 cal., BBC, SP, blue finish, an unspecified major improvement was made, per factory newsletter, after March 1, 1933. Readers determining the improvement should advise *Blue Book of Airguns*. Reported about 60,000 made per year from Nov. 1952 to 1960s, often with various private brand marks.

$50	$45	$35	$30	$25	$15	$10

MODEL 2 – .177 cal., UL, SP, nickel finish, fixed sights, rotating loading tap. Mfg. circa 1910-1940.

$90	$75	$65	$50	$40	$25	$20

GRADING	100%	95%	90%	80%	60%	40%	20%

MODEL 3 – .177 cal., blue finish, gallery-type trigger-guard cocking lever ("Bügelspanner"), break barrel to load, fixed sights, 35.4 in. OAL, 5.3 lbs. Mfg. 1913-1940.

courtesy Beeman Collection

	$135	$115	$95	$80	$60	$40	$25

* **Model 3L** – .177 cal., blue finish, 34.6 in. OAL, 4.4 lbs.

	$135	$115	$95	$80	$60	$40	$25

MODEL 3 (MFG. 1927-1940) – .177 or .22 cal., BBC, SP, blue finish, smoothbore or rifled barrel, developed as training rifle for smallbore rifle shooters, two-stage trigger (special order: set trigger), beech stock with pistol grip, finger grooves in forearm, screw-in rear sight, bead front sight, 43.3 in. OAL, 6.6 lbs. Mfg. 1927-1940.

	$225	$190	$160	$130	$100	$65	$45

MODEL 6 – .177 cal., BBC, SP, blue finish, less powerful version of Model 3, fixed sights, octagon steel barrel, cylinder and trigger guard nickel plated, walnut stock, 33.5 in. OAL, 4 lbs.

	$110	$95	$75	$65	$50	$35	$20

MODEL 10 – .177 cal., BBC, SP, blue finish, 29.9 in. OAL, 2 lbs. Mfg. 1950-1952.

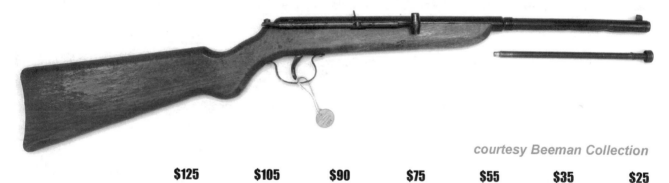

courtesy Beeman Collection

	$125	$105	$90	$75	$55	$35	$25

MODEL 14 – .177 cal., bolt-action-style cocking, SP, blue finish, fixed sights, 38.2 in. OAL, 3.5 lbs. Mfg. 1913-1940.

courtesy Beeman Collection

	$150	$130	$105	$85	$70	$45	$30

* **Model 14A** – .177 cal., military style full stock, contained a cleaning rod which looks like a bayonet.

	$300	$255	$210	$175	$135	$90	$60

GRADING	100%	95%	90%	80%	60%	40%	20%

MODEL 15 (MFG. 1930-1940) – .177 cal., BBC, SP, smoothbore, blue finish, tinplate design, lighter and shorter child's version of Model 16, without forestock. Mfg. circa 1930-1940.

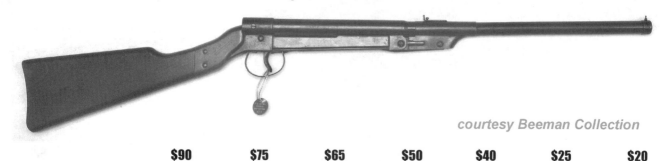

courtesy Beeman Collection

	$90	$75	$65	$50	$40	$25	$20

MODEL 15 (MFG. 1951-1980) – .177 cal., BBC, SP, blue finish, tinplate, stamped construction, beech buttstock, 12 in. rifled barrel inside sheet steel body tube, two-stage trigger, bead front sight, adj. rear sight, 32.5 in. OAL, 2.4 lbs. Mfg. 1951-1980.

	$50	$45	$35	$30	$25	$15	$10

MODEL 16 (MFG. 1922-1940) – .177 cal., BBC, SP, 12 in. smoothbore barrel, blue finish, all other metal parts blue or nickel plated, beech buttstock and forearm, rear sight adj. for elevation, no safety, 37.8 in. OAL, 4.4 lbs. Approx. 25,000 per year mfg. 1922-1940.

	$90	$75	$65	$50	$40	$25	$20

* **Model 16 Special Order Variation** – completely blued, matte oiled stock.

	$145	$125	$100	$85	$65	$45	$30

* **Model 16 (Mfg. 1950-1985)** – .177 cal., BBC, SP, blue finish, similar to pre-WWII Model 16, stamped until 1984 with "Original Diana 16", 33 in. OAL, 2.7 lbs. Mfg. 1950-1985.

	$45	$40	$30	$25	$20	$15	N/A

MODEL 17 – .177 cal., BBC, SP, blue finish, similar to Model 16, except 41 in. OAL, 5.5 lbs. Mfg. 1922-1940.

	$75	$65	$55	$45	$35	$20	$15

* **Model 17P** – .177 cal., BBC, SP, blue finish, similar to Model 17, except has pistol grip.

	$110	$95	$75	$65	$50	$35	$20

MODEL 18 – .177 cal., BBC, SP, blue finish, similar to Model 16, except 41.3 in. OAL, 6.6 lbs. Mfg. 1922-1940.

	$75	$65	$55	$45	$35	$20	$15

* **Model 18P** – .177 cal., BBC, SP, blue finish, similar to Model 18, except has pistol grip.

	$95	$80	$65	$55	$45	$30	$20

MODEL 19 – .177 cal., BBC, SP, blue finish octagon barrel, all other metal parts nickel plated, beech buttstock, adj. rear sight, 37.4 in. OAL, 6.6 lbs. Mfg. 1922-1940.

	$95	$80	$65	$55	$45	$30	$20

* **Model 19 Special Order Variation** – similar to Model 19, except completely blued, matte oiled walnut stock.

	$125	$105	$90	$75	$55	$35	$25

* **Model 19P** – similar to Model 19, except with pistol grip.

	$110	$95	$75	$65	$50	$35	$20

* **Model 19S** – similar to Model 19, except with safety.

	$110	$95	$75	$65	$50	$35	$20

* **Model 19PS** – .177 or .22 cal., BBC, SP, blue finish, 14 in. barrel, 36 in. OAL, 3.75 lbs. Mfg. 1953-1985. Similar to Model 19, except with both pistol grip and safety.

	$120	$100	$85	$70	$55	$35	$25

MODEL 20 (MFG. 1907-1911) – .177 cal., UL, tinplate construction, 12.6 in. smoothbore brass barrel, all metal parts nickel plated, beech buttstock, 20 in. OAL, 2.7 lbs. Mfg. circa 1907-1911.

	$170	$145	$120	$100	$75	$50	$35

The 1907-1911 Model 20, Model 20 Youth, and Model 20 Adult are not related to each other.

GRADING	100%	95%	90%	80%	60%	40%	20%

MODEL 20 YOUTH – .177 cal., BBC, SP, youth model, all-metal parts are nickel plated, walnut buttstock, date of mfg. stamped on heel, 35 in. OAL, 2.7 lbs. Tens of thousands mfg. 1912-1940.

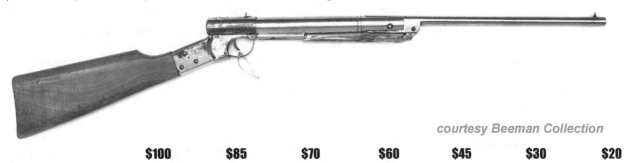

courtesy Beeman Collection

	$100	$85	$70	$60	$45	$30	$20

Add 10% for early versions with simple rear sight mounted on receiver tube.
Add 20% for stamping "Foreign" instead of "Made in Germany" (just prior to WWII).
Add 20% for specimens w/o model markings but marked "Diana Luft-Gewehr Schutzenmarke".
Add 50% for original box.

The 1910-1911 Model 20, Model 20 Youth, and Model 20 Adult are not related to each other. Circa 1930 the rear sight was moved to the barrel block and changed to adjustable.

MODEL 20 ADULT – .177 cal., BBC, SP, 480 FPS, 17 in. barrel, black finish, hardwood stock, hooded front and adj. rear sights, 5.5 lbs. Mfg. 1991-2003.

courtesy Diana

	$95	$80	$65	$55	$45	$30	$20

Last MSR was $120.

The 1910-1911 Model 20, Model 20 Youth, and Model 20 Adult are not related to each other.

MODEL 21 – .177 cal., BBC, 460 FPS, 16.5 in. barrel, black finish, black composite stock, Truglo adj. sights, 5.8 lbs. Mfg. 2005-2006.

	$130	$110	$90	$75	$60	$40	$25

MODEL 22 (MFG. 1927-1940) – .177 cal., BBC, SP, blue finish, youth model, walnut stock, brass barrel either smooth or rifled in sheet steel body tube, adj. rear sight, 35.8 in. OAL. Mfg. 1927-1940.

courtesy Beeman Collection

	$115	$100	$80	$65	$50	$35	$25

The 1927-1940 and 1953-1985 Model 22 air rifles appear somewhat similar, but they are completely unrelated with virtually no common parts.

MODEL 22 (MFG. 1953-1985)

	$65	$55	$45	$40	$30	$20	$15

The 1927-1940 and 1953-1985 Model 22 air rifles appear somewhat similar, but they are completely unrelated with virtually no common parts.

MODEL 23 (DISC. 1940) – .177 cal., BBC, SP, blue finish, smoothbore or rifled barrel, 35.8 in. OAL. 4.2 lbs. Disc. 1940.

	$115	$100	$80	$65	$50	$35	$25

The Disc. 1940 and 1951-1983 Model 23 air rifles appear somewhat similar, but they are completely unrelated with virtually no common parts.

GRADING	100%	95%	90%	80%	60%	40%	20%

MODEL 23 (MFG. 1951-1983) – .177 or .22 cal., BBC, SP, blue finish, 14 in. smoothbore or rifled barrel, bead front and adj. spring-leaf rear sights, 36 in. OAL, 4.25 lbs. Mfg. 1951-1983.

	$65	$55	$45	$40	$30	$20	$15

Subtract 20% for post-1965 versions with thicker stocks without forearm grooves, with stamped checkering, shallow cheekpieces, front sights as screwed-on ramps or clamped-on tunnels, plastic rear sights.

The Disc. 1940 and 1951-1983 Model 23 air rifles appear somewhat similar, but they are completely unrelated with virtually no common parts.

MODEL 24/24C – .177 or .22 cal., BBC, 700/400 FPS, 13.5 (Model LG 24C) or 17 in. barrel, black finish, hardwood stock, hooded front and adj. rear sights, 5.6 lbs. Mfg. 1984-2007.

courtesy Diana

	$160	$135	$110	$95	$70	$50	$30

Last MSR was $187.

This model has had a number of changes to it and such the customer must specify the model and change number in order to get the proper support. The "change number" ie T0X is marked on the receiver just after the model number. To add to the confusion, the Models 24D, 24 T01 and T02 have the same piston seal, mainspring, mainspring guide and cocking lever. However these same parts for the Models 24 T03 and T04 are completely different.

* *Model 24D* – .177 or .22 cal., BBC, similar to Model 24 except, has 3 ball sear.

	$160	$135	$110	$95	$70	$50	$30

* *Model 24 TO1* – similar to LG 24 except with metal trigger like older Diana Models 22 and 33, no safety.

	$170	$145	$120	$100	$75	$50	$35

* *Model 24 TO2 "Diana Star"* – similar to Model 24, except has colored stocks without model number.

	$120	$100	$85	$70	$55	$35	$25

* *Model 24 TO3* – similar to Model 24, except with different trigger than previous Model 24s.

	$170	$145	$120	$100	$75	$50	$35

* *Model 24 TO4* – similar to Model 24, except with different trigger than previous Model 24s.

	$170	$145	$120	$100	$75	$50	$35

MODEL 25A – .177 cal., BBC, SP, blue finish, solid steel parts, walnut stock with finger grooves in forearm, adj. rear sight, no safety, 38.5 in. OAL. Mfg. 1925-1934.

	$115	$100	$80	$65	$50	$35	$25

The Model 25A, 25 Improved, 25D, and 25DS air rifles appear somewhat similar, but they are completely unrelated with virtually no common parts.

* *Model 25 Improved* – .177 or .22 cal., BBC, SP, blue finish, smoothbore or rifled barrel, slightly longer forestock, metal rear sight, 39.7 in. OAL. Mfg. 1933-1940 and 1950-1986.

	$65	$55	$45	$40	$30	$20	$15

Add 30% for pre-WWII version.

Subtract 20% for post-1965 versions with thicker stocks without forearm grooves, with stamped checkering, shallow cheekpieces, front sights as screwed-on ramps or clamped-on tunnels, plastic rear sights.

The Model 25A, 25 Improved, 25D, and 25DS air rifles appear somewhat similar, but they are completely unrelated with virtually no common parts.

GRADING	100%	95%	90%	80%	60%	40%	20%

MODEL 25D – .177 or .22 cal., BBC, ball trigger sear 525/380 FPS, 15.75 in. smooth or rifled barrel, 5.75 lbs. Disc. 1986.

courtesy Beeman Collection

	$120	$100	$85	$70	$55	$35	$25

Last MSR was $120.

The Model 25A, 25 Improved, 25D, and 25DS air rifles appear somewhat similar, but they are completely unrelated with virtually no common parts.

* **Model 25DS** – .177 or .22 cal., similar to Model 25D, except has two-piece cocking lever, trigger block manual safety, angular stock styling. Disc. 1986.

	$150	$130	$105	$85	$70	$45	$30

Subtract 20% for post-1965 versions with thicker stocks without forearm grooves, with stamped checkering, shallow cheekpieces, front sights as screwed-on ramps or clamped-on tunnels, plastic rear sights.

Approx. ten million Model LG 25 have been sold; this model group is one of the world's most successful air rifles.

The Model 25A, 25 Improved, 25D, and 25DS air rifles appear somewhat similar, but they are completely unrelated with virtually no common parts.

MODEL 26 YOUTH – .177 cal., BBC, SP, blue finish, youth model, no safety. Mfg. 1913-1933.

courtesy Beeman Collection

	$350	$300	$245	$205	$160	$105	$70

The Model 26 Youth, 26U, and 26 air rifles are not related to each other.

MODEL 26U – similar to Model 26 Youth, except UL cocking and loading tap, 38.2 in. OAL, 5 lbs. Mfg. 1933-1940.

	$300	$255	$210	$175	$135	$90	$60

The Model 26 Youth, 26U, and 26 air rifles are not related to each other.

MODEL 26 – .177 or .22 cal., BBC, SP, 750/500 FPS, 17.25 in. barrel, 6 lbs. Importation 1984-1992.

	$150	$130	$105	$85	$70	$45	$30

Last MSR was $195.

This model has had a number of changes to it and such the customer must specify the model and change number in order to get the proper support. The "change number" ie T0X is marked on the receiver just after the model number. To add to the confusion, the Models 26 T01 and T02 have the same piston seal, mainspring, mainspring guide and cocking lever. However these same parts for the Models 26 T03 and T04 are completely different.

The Model 26 Youth, 26U, and 26 air rifles are not related to each other.

MODEL 27L – .177 cal., BBC, SP, blue finish, 18.5 in. smoothbore or rifled barrel, beech stock with metal buttplate, adj. trigger, no safety, 42.5 in. OAL. Tens of thousands mfg. 1910-1936.

	$110	$95	$75	$65	$50	$35	$20

Add 20% for pre-1923 version with octagonal to round barrel.

One of the most successful barrel cocking adult air rifles of all time.

The Model 27L, 27A, 27E, 27S, and 27 air rifles appear somewhat similar, but they are completely unrelated with virtually no common parts.

GRADING	100%	95%	90%	80%	60%	40%	20%

MODEL 27A – .177 or .22 cal., BBC, SP, blue finish, 17.5 in. smoothbore or rifled barrel, two-stage trigger, adj. rear sight, triangular front sight, wooden half stock, 41.3 in. OAL, 6.2 lbs. Mfg. 1936-1940.

	$135	$115	$95	$80	$60	$40	$25

Add 20% for smoothbore.

The Model 27L, 27A, 27E, 27S, and 27 air rifles appear somewhat similar, but they are completely unrelated with virtually no common parts.

MODEL 27E – .177 or .22 cal., BBC, SP, blue finish, checkered beech stock with pistol grip.

	$245	$210	$170	$140	$110	$75	$50

The Model 27L, 27A, 27E, 27S, and 27 air rifles appear somewhat similar, but they are completely unrelated with virtually no common parts.

MODEL 27S – .177 or .22 cal., BBC, SP, blue finish, two-piece cocking lever, trigger block safety, angular stock styling.

	$190	$160	$135	$110	$85	$55	$40

The Model 27L, 27A, 27E, 27S, and 27 air rifles appear somewhat similar, but they are completely unrelated with virtually no common parts.

MODEL 27 – .177 or .22 cal., BBC, SP, 550/415 FPS, 17.25 in. smoothbore or rifled barrel, pre-1965 version with ball trigger sear, 6 lbs. Disc. 1987.

courtesy Beeman Collection

	$125	$105	$90	$75	$55	$35	$25

Last MSR was $150.

Subtract 20% for post-1965 versions with thicker stocks without forearm grooves, with stamped checkering, shallow cheekpieces, front sights as screwed-on ramps or clamped-on tunnels, plastic rear sights.

The Model 27L, 27A, 27E, 27S, and 27 air rifles appear somewhat similar, but they are completely unrelated with virtually no common parts.

MODEL 28 (MFG. 1913-1940) – .177 cal., BBC, SP, blue finish, adj. rear sight, smoothbore or rifled barrel, no safety, 46.5 in. OAL, 7 lbs. Mfg. 1913-1940.

	$225	$190	$160	$130	$100	$65	$45

* **Model 28 Improved** – .177 cal., BBC, SP, blue finish, improved version after 1923, sight moved to base of barrel and made adjustable.

	$185	$155	$130	$105	$85	$55	$35

* **Model 28 (Mfg. 1985-1992)** – .177 or .22 cal., BBC, SP, 15.75 in. barrel, 750/500 FPS, automatic safety, 6.75 lbs. Importation 1985-1992.

courtesy Diana

	$185	$155	$130	$105	$85	$55	$35

Last MSR was $205.

This model has had a number of changes to it and such the customer must specify the model and change number in order to get the proper support. The "change number" ie T0X is marked on the receiver just after the model number. To add to the confusion, the Models 28 T01 and T02 have the same piston seal, mainspring, mainspring guide and cocking lever. However these same parts for the Models 28 T03 and T04 are completely different.

GRADING	100%	95%	90%	80%	60%	40%	20%

MODEL 30B (BUGELSPANNER) – .25 cal., gallery-type with trigger-guard cocking system ("Bügelspanner"), beech buttstock with cheek piece, octagon blued barrel, nickel finish, adj. rear sight, no safety, 41.7 in. OAL, 6.2 lbs. Mfg. 1913-1935.

	$850	$725	$600	$500	$375	$255	$170

The Model 30B, 30M, and 30R air rifles are not related to each other. The suffix letters have been added to distinguish these models; these letters do not appear on the guns.

MODEL 30M (MILITARY) – .177 cal., UL, cocking lever hidden in forearm, military-style full stock with top hand guard, fixed barrel with loading tap, two-stage trigger, wing safety, front and rear sights similar to the Mauser 98k carbine, 41.7 in. OAL, 5.5 lbs. Mfg. 1935-1940.

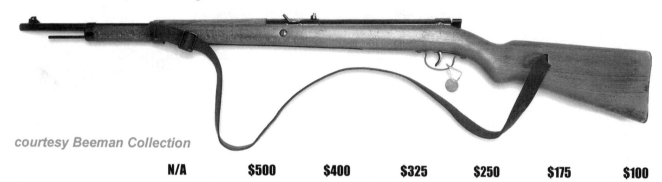

courtesy Beeman Collection

	N/A	$500	$400	$325	$250	$175	$100

The Model 30B, 30M, and 30R air rifles are not related to each other. The suffix letters have been added to distinguish these models; these letters do not appear on the guns.

MODEL 30R (REPEATER) – 4.4mm (RWS #7) round ball cal., bolt-action cocking system, ball shot repeater, fixed barrel, 16.9 in., mechanical shot-counter in left side of forearm for gallery use, capacity 125 balls, beech stock with rubber buttplate, two-stage trigger, manual safety, adj. rear sight, triangular front sight, 43.3 in. OAL, 7.25 lbs. Limited mfg. 1972-2000.

courtesy Beeman Collection

	N/A	$450	$350	$295	$225	$160	$90

Last MSR was $1,025.

Special orders were still possible through 2003.

The Model 30B, 30M, and 30R air rifles are not related to each other. The suffix letters have been added to distinguish these models; these letters do not appear on the guns.

MODEL 31 PANTHER PRO COMPACT – .177 or .22 cal., BBC, SP, SS, 15.6 in. rifled steel barrel, 1000/740 FPS, blue finish, 11mm optics dovetail, ambidextrous synthetic stock with ridged texturing on forearm and pistol grip, rubber butt pad, two-stage adj. metal T06 match trigger, automatic safety, 42 in. OAL, approx. 7.9 lbs. Mfg. 2014-current.

MSR $430	$375	$325	$290	$235	$180	N/A	N/A

MODEL 32 – .177 cal., BBC, SP, blue finish, similar to Model LG 27, except with more power, 42.5 in. OAL, 6.6 lbs. Mfg. 1936-1940.

	$225	$190	$160	$130	$100	$65	$45

MODEL 33 – .177 cal., BBC, SP, blue finish, checkered wood stock with pistol grip, 42.9 in. OAL, 6.6 lbs. Mfg. 1928-1940.

	$250	$215	$175	$145	$115	$75	$50

GRADING	100%	95%	90%	80%	60%	40%	20%

MODEL 34 (MFG. 1928-1940) – .177 cal., BBC, SP, blue finish, similar to LG 33, except with British market style stock and pistol grip. Mfg. 1928-1940.

	100%	95%	90%	80%	60%	40%	20%
	$250	$215	$175	$145	$115	$75	$50

The 1928-1940 Model 34 and later Model 34 air rifles are not related to each other.

MODEL 34/34BC/34C/34N – .177, .20 (disc.) or .22 cal., BBC, blue, matte nickel (Model 34N disc.), or matte black finish, 1000 (.177 cal.) or 800 (.22 cal.) FPS, hardwood stock or black epoxy finish stock (Model 34BC disc.), 15.5 (compact, Model 34C disc.) or 19.75 in. barrel, open rear sight, fixed fiber optic front sight, rubber recoil pad, two-stage adj. trigger, 46 in. OAL, approx. 7 lbs. New 1984.

courtesy Diana

	100%	95%	90%	80%	60%	40%	20%
	$220	$195	$175	$140	$110	N/A	N/A

Last MSR was $259.

Add $51 for 4x32 scope with lockdown mount.
Add 5% for the hundred-year Diana Commemorative Model (new 1990).
Add 25% for .20 cal. model (Disc.).
Add 15% for Model 34N matte nickel finish (Disc.).
Add 20% for compact with 4x32 airgun scope and C-Mount (Disc.).
Add 100% for black epoxy finish stock and 4x32 airgun scope (Disc.).
Add 15% for "Sport Mfg." without model number.

The 1928-1940 Model 34 and later Model 34 air rifles are not related to each other.

MODEL 34 PREMIUM (CURRENT MFG.) – .177 or .22 cal., BBC, SP, SS, 19.5 in. rifled steel barrel, 1000/740 FPS, blue finish, globe front and fully adj. micrometer rear sights, deluxe Monte Carlo beech stock with checkered pistol grip and forearm, ventilated rubber recoil pad, two-stage adj. metal T06 match trigger, automatic safety, 46 in. OAL, approx. 7.5 lbs. Mfg. 2014-current.

MSR $480	$400	$350	$325	$265	$200	N/A	N/A

MODEL 35 (MFG. 1953-1964) – .177 or .22 cal., BBC, SP, 665/540 FPS, 19 in. barrel, Monte Carlo stock with shallow cheek piece, stamped checkering, globe front sight, plastic or metal click adj. rear sight with four-notch insert, plastic or stamped trigger blade, ball sear, 8 lbs. Mfg. circa 1953-1964.

courtesy Beeman Collection

* ***Model 35 Standard Variant 1*** – sporting stock, alloy trigger blade, fixed post front sight, simple rear sight in transverse dovetail.

	100%	95%	90%	80%	60%	40%	20%
	$225	$190	$160	$130	$100	$65	$45

* ***Model 35A Variant 2*** – like Model 35 Standard except has hooded front sight with four posts on rotating star, click adj. rear sight with four-notch insert, extra dovetail on rear of receiver.

	100%	95%	90%	80%	60%	40%	20%
	$250	$215	$175	$145	$115	$75	$50

* ***Model 35B Variant 3*** – like 35A except aperture attachment replaces rear sight notch assembly, allowing rear sight to mount on receiver dovetail for match shooting.

	100%	95%	90%	80%	60%	40%	20%
	$275	$235	$195	$160	$125	$80	$55

* ***Model 35M Variant 4*** – like 35B except has match stock with cut checkering.

	100%	95%	90%	80%	60%	40%	20%
	$275	$235	$195	$160	$125	$80	$55

About 1964 these were replaced with a simpler version with three variations in addition to standard model.

GRADING	100%	95%	90%	80%	60%	40%	20%

MODEL 35 (MFG. 1965-1987) – .177 or .22 cal., BBC, SP, 665/540 FPS, 19 in. barrel, 8 lbs. Mfg. 1965-1987.

	100%	95%	90%	80%	60%	40%	20%
	$120	$100	$85	$70	$55	$35	$25

Last MSR was $160.

Add 10% for metal rear sight or solid alloy trigger blade.

Subtract 20% for post-1965 versions with thicker stocks without forearm grooves, with stamped checkering, shallow cheekpieces, front sights as screwed-on ramps or clamped-on tunnels, plastic rear sights.

* **Model 35 Centennial** – commemorative model.

	100%	95%	90%	80%	60%	40%	20%
	$160	$135	$110	$95	$70	$50	$30

* **Model 35M** – target stocked version. Mfg. 1958-1964.

	100%	95%	90%	80%	60%	40%	20%
	$150	$130	$105	$85	$70	$45	$30

Add 10% for metal rear sight or solid alloy trigger blade.

Subtract 20% for post-1965 versions with thicker stocks without forearm grooves, with stamped checkering, shallow cheekpieces, front sights as screwed-on ramps or clamped-on tunnels, plastic rear sights.

* **Model 35S** – two-piece cocking lever, trigger block safety, angular stock styling.

	100%	95%	90%	80%	60%	40%	20%
	$150	$130	$105	$85	$70	$45	$30

Add 10% for metal rear sight or solid alloy trigger blade.

Subtract 20% for post-1965 versions with thicker stocks without forearm grooves, with stamped checkering, shallow cheekpieces, front sights as screwed-on ramps or clamped-on tunnels, plastic rear sights.

MODEL 36/36C/36S – .177 or .22 cal., BBC, SP, 1000/800 FPS, 15.5 (Model 36C) or 19.5 in. barrel, 8 lbs.

courtesy Diana

	100%	95%	90%	80%	60%	40%	20%
	$300	$255	$210	$175	$135	$90	$60

Last MSR was $350.

Add $40 for 36S Model with scope.

Subtract $10 for muzzle brake model without factory sights.

MODEL 37 – .177 cal., BBC, SP, blue finish, beech buttstock without forearm, simple rear sight, bead front sight, no safety, 42.9 in. OAL, 6 lbs. Mfg. 1922-1940.

	100%	95%	90%	80%	60%	40%	20%
	$250	$215	$175	$145	$115	$75	$50

* **Model LG 37E** – British market-style stock.

	100%	95%	90%	80%	60%	40%	20%
	$300	$255	$210	$175	$135	$90	$60

MODEL 38 (MFG. 1922-1940) – .177 cal., BBC, SP, Deluxe version of the Model 36, similar to Model 37, except 7 lbs. Mfg. 1922-1940.

	100%	95%	90%	80%	60%	40%	20%
	$200	$170	$140	$115	$90	$60	$40

The 1922-1940, 38E, and disc. 1998 Model 38 air rifles are not related to each other.

MODEL 38E – British market-style stock.

	100%	95%	90%	80%	60%	40%	20%
	$250	$215	$175	$145	$115	$75	$50

The 1922-1940, 38E, and disc. 1998 Model 38 air rifles are not related to each other.

GRADING	100%	95%	90%	80%	60%	40%	20%

MODEL 38 (MFG. DISC. 1998) – .177 or .22 cal., BBC, 919/689 FPS, 19.5 in. barrel, beech stock, 34.53 in. OAL, 8 lbs. Importation Disc. 1998.

courtesy Diana

	100%	95%	90%	80%	60%	40%	20%
	$275	$235	$195	$160	$125	$80	$55

Last MSR was $345.

The 1922-1940, 38E, and disc. 1998 Model 38 air rifles are not related to each other.

MODEL 40 – .177 or .22 cal., BBC, SP, 950/780 FPS, 19 in. rifled barrel with muzzle brake, blue finish, hardwood stock with buttpad, adj. trigger, 7.5 lbs. Mfg. 2002-2008.

	$245	$210	$170	$140	$110	$75	$50

Last MSR was $282.

MODEL 42 – .177 or .22 cal., UL, SP, blue finish, similar to Model 27, except 19.1 in. fixed barrel, adj. rear sight, bead front sight, adj. trigger, 40.9 in. OAL, 6.8 lbs. Mfg. 1927-1940.

	$250	$215	$175	$145	$115	$75	$50

* **Model 42E** – British market-style stock.

	$275	$235	$195	$160	$125	$80	$55

MODEL 43 – .177 or .22 cal., UL, SP, blue finish, similar to Model 42, except has additional checkering, pistol grip, and manual safety. Mfg. 1928-1940.

	$275	$235	$195	$160	$125	$80	$55

MODEL 44 – .177 or .22 cal., UL, SP, blue finish, similar to Model 48, except 43.7 in. OAL, 7 lbs. Mfg. 1928-1940.

	$235	$200	$165	$135	$105	$70	$45

MODEL 45U – .177 or .22 cal., UL, SP, blue finish, loading tap, similar to Model 26 (and simpler version of the later Model LG 58), 40.2 in. OAL, 7 lbs. Mfg. 1927-1940.

	$295	$250	$205	$170	$135	$90	$60

MODEL 45/45S DELUXE (MFG. 1978-1988) – .177, .20, or .22 cal., BBC, SP, 790/550 FPS, 19. in. barrel, blue finish, two-stage adj. trigger, adj. rear sight, front sight with inserts, hardwood stock with rubber butt pad, 8 lbs. Mfg. 1978-1988.

courtesy Beeman Collection

	$220	$185	$155	$130	$100	$65	$45

Add 15% for Deluxe version.

Add 25% for .20 caliber.

Add 20% for LG 45S Model with scope and sling.

Add 10% for original long safety (recalled), within metal flap below, not marked (use guns with original safety with caution).

Subtract 20% for RWS 45 or Crosman Challenger 6100 markings, less desirable sight and stock systems; inferior handling to standard Diana 45. Ref: Walther, *The Airgun Book*.

* **Model 45 Jubilaums Model** – commemorative model with special Rastatt factory plates in stock.

	$295	$250	$205	$170	$135	$90	$60

GRADING	100%	95%	90%	80%	60%	40%	20%

MODEL 45/45S DELUXE/45 TO1 (RECENT MFG.) – .177, .20, or .22 cal., BBC, SP, basically a restocked Model 34, 1000/800 FPS, 19. in. barrel, blue finish, two-stage adj. trigger, adj. rear sight, front sight with inserts, hardwood stock with rubber butt pad, 8 lbs. Mfg. 1988-2004.

courtesy Diana

$220	$185	$155	$130	$100	$65	$45

Last MSR was $350.

Add 20% for Deluxe version.

Add 35% for Model 45S with scope and sling.

The post-WWII Model 45 is not related to the pre-WWII Model 45 and the post-WWII model 45 was replaced, still using the Model 45 designation, about 1988 with a restocked Model 34!

MODEL 46 – .177 or .22 cal., UL, SP, 950/780 FPS, 18 in. barrel, blue finish, auto-safety, adj. trigger, extended scope rail, Monte Carlo stock with checkered forearm and grip (Model 46), recoil pad, 8.2 lbs. Mfg. 1998-disc.

courtesy Diana

$350	$295	$240	$200	$155	$105	$70

Last MSR was $387.

* **Model 46C** – .177 or .22 cal., UL, SP, similar to Model 46, except shorter. Mfg. 1998-2008.

courtesy Diana

$350	$295	$240	$200	$155	$105	$70

Last MSR was $387.

* **Model 46E** – .177 or .22 cal., UL, SP, similar to Model 46, except different barrel, receiver and stock configurations.

$350	$295	$240	$200	$155	$105	$70

* **Model 46 Stutzen** – .177 or .22 cal., UL, SP, similar to Model 46, except full length Mannlicher-style stock. Mfg. 1998-2010.

courtesy Diana

$525	$450	$425	$325	$255	N/A	N/A

Last MSR was $611.

GRADING	100%	95%	90%	80%	60%	40%	20%

* **Model 46 Stutzen Luxus** – .177 or .22 cal., UL, SP, similar to Model 46 Stutzen, except has deluxe stock. Mfg. 1998-disc.

courtesy Diana

	$900	$750	$625	$525	$400	$270	$180

Last MSR was $975.

* **Model 46 Stutzen Prestige** – .177 or .22 cal., UL, SP, similar to Model 46, except engraved. Mfg. 1998-disc.

courtesy Diana

	$1,750	$1,475	$1,225	$1,025	$775	$525	$350

Last MSR was $2,000.

The Model 46 combines under-lever cocking with a flip-up loading port that provides easy loading, and allows the pellet to be inserted directly into the rifled barrel for pinpoint accuracy.

MODEL 48U – .177 or .22 cal., UL, SP, unlicensed copy of the British Jeffries pattern air rifle, adj. rear sight, 46 in. OAL, 7.5 lbs. Mfg. circa 1920-1940.

	$350	$300	$245	$205	$160	$105	$70

* **Model 48E** – English-style stock.

	$350	$300	$245	$205	$160	$105	$70

MODEL 48/48A/48B/48SL – .177, .20 (disc. 2006), .22, or .25 (mfg. 1994-2006) cal., SL, SP, SS, 950/575 FPS, 17 in. rifled barrel, adj. cheek piece (Model 48SL), 42.5 in. OAL, 8.5 lbs. Disc. 2007.

courtesy Diana

	$375	$300	$255	$210	$165	$110	$75

Last MSR was $410.

Add 10% for .25 cal.
Add 15% for .20 cal.
Add 5% for Model 48B with black matte finish stock (new 1995).
Add 20% for Model 48A.
Add 10% for combo with 4x32 compact scope and mount (new 2006).

GRADING	100%	95%	90%	80%	60%	40%	20%

MODEL 50 – .177 or .22 cal., UL, SP, two-piece cocking lever, angular stock styling, trigger block safety introduced about two years after the introduction of angular stock styling. Mfg. 1952-1965.

courtesy Beeman Collection

* *Model 50 Standard Variant 1* – sporting stock, alloy trigger blade, fixed post front sight, simple rear sight in transverse dovetail.

	$200	$170	$140	$115	$90	$60	$40

* *Model 50A Variant 2* – similar to Model 50 Standard, except hooded front sight with four posts on rotating star, click adj. rear sight with four-notch insert, extra dovetail on rear of receiver.

	$220	$185	$155	$130	$100	$65	$45

* *Model 50B Variant 3* – similar to Model 50A, except with match aperture sight mounted on receiver dovetail for match shooting, 45.3 in. OAL, 8.38 lbs.

	$245	$210	$170	$140	$110	$75	$50

* *Model 50M Variant 4* – similar to Model 50B, except multi-purpose rear sight, match stock with cheek piece and deep rubber buttplate 45.3 in. OAL, 10.6 lbs.

	$255	$215	$180	$150	$115	$75	$50

MODEL 50S – replaced regular Model 50 about 1965 with a simplified version without the ball sear trigger.

	$175	$150	$125	$100	$80	$50	$35

MODEL 50T/T01 – .177, .22, or .25 cal., UL, SP, 745/600 FPS, 18.5 in. barrel, ball trigger sear, 8 lbs. Mfg. 1952-1987.

* *Model 50T/T01 Variant 1* – standard with sporting stock, blued finish, sporting front sight with interchangeable posts.

	$285	$240	$200	$165	$130	$85	$55

Add 10% for .25 cal.

Add 25% for T01 Model.

Subtract 20% for post-1965 versions with thicker stocks without forearm grooves, with stamped checkering, shallow cheekpieces, front sights as screwed-on ramps or clamped-on tunnels, plastic rear sights.

* *Model 50T/T01 Variant 2* – military with parkerized finish, military front sight with fixed post and protective wings.

	$260	$220	$180	$150	$115	$80	$50

Last MSR was $210.

Add 10% for .25 cal.

Add 25% for T01 Model.

Subtract 20% for post-1965 versions with thicker stocks without forearm grooves, with stamped checkering, shallow cheekpieces, front sights as screwed-on ramps or clamped-on tunnels, plastic rear sights.

MODEL 52/52 DELUXE – .177, .22, or .25 (disc. 2006) cal., SL, SP, 950/550 FPS, 17 in. barrel, walnut-stained beech Monte Carlo stock, checkering on forend and pistol grip, ventilated rubber butt pad, 43.75 in. OAL, 8.5 lbs. Disc. 2007.

courtesy Diana

	$450	$375	$325	$260	$205	$135	$90

Last MSR was $481.

Add 10% for .25 cal.

Add 55% for Deluxe version with handcrafted walnut stock, patterned checkering on forend and pistol grip, ornamental black wood insert in forend and base of pistol grip.

Add 8% for combo with 4x32 scope and mount (new 2006).

GRADING	100%	95%	90%	80%	60%	40%	20%

MODEL 52 (CURRENT MFG) – .177, .22 or .25 cal., SL, SP, SS, sliding breech action, 17.3 in. rifled steel barrel, 1150/850/610 FPS, blue finish, fixed blade ramp front and fully adj. rear sights, 11mm optics dovetail, checkered beech Monty Carlo style stock with rubber buttpad, two-stage adj. metal T06 match trigger, automatic safety, 43 in. OAL, approx. 8.8 lbs. Mfg. 2014-current.

MSR $596	$500	$450	$400	$325	$250	N/A	N/A

Add $54 for .25 cal.

MODEL 56TH TARGET HUNTER (CURRENT MFG) – .177, .22 or .25 cal., SL, SP, SS, sliding breech action, 17.3 in. rifled steel barrel, 1100/890/610 FPS, blue finish, 11mm optics dovetail, ambidextrous carved beech thumbhole stock with adj. rubber butt pad, two-stage adj. metal T06 match trigger, automatic safety, 44 in. OAL, approx. 11.1 lbs. Mfg. 2014-current.

MSR $970	$825	$725	$650	$525	$400	N/A	N/A

Add $87 for .25 cal.

MODEL 58 – .177 or .22 cal., UL, SP, three main variations, "Dianawerk's pre-WWII flagship model." Mfg. 1915-1940.

courtesy Beeman Collection

This model is considered one of the most classic of the Dianawerk guns, with very heavy, unusually solid construction.

* ***Model 58/1915 First Variant*** – .177 or .22, cal., UL, SP, 625/500 FPS, set trigger, steel turn bolt, walnut buttstock with PG, steel buttplate. 45.25 in. OAL, 8.25 lbs. Mfg. 1915-16.

	N/A	$1,400	$1,125	$900	$700	$500	$280

* ***Model 58/2 Second Variant*** – .177 or .22, cal., UL, SP, 641 FPS (.177), different design: turn bolt replaced by knurled knob at the end of the receiver, checkered pistol grip stock with finger groove forearm, $70 in Stoeger's 1937 catalog, when the Winchester Model 12 shotgun was $42.50, 47.25 in. OAL, 8.8 lbs. Mfg. early 1920s-1935.

	N/A	$1,300	$1,050	$850	$650	$450	$260

* ***Model 58/3 Third Variant*** – .177 or .22, cal., UL, SP, adj. trigger, no outer trigger cocking device, 45.25 in. OAL, 7.9 lbs. Mfg. circa 1936-1940.

	N/A	$900	$725	$575	$450	$325	$180

MODEL 60/60T – .177 cal., Giss double contra-SP system, 17.9 in. barrel, beech, Tyrolean (Model LG 60T) or walnut stock with rubber buttplate, match diopter rear and tunnel front sight with inserts, adj. trigger, optional barrel weight (tube), 42.7 in. OAL, 9.9 lbs. Mfg. 1963 to circa 1982 (Tyrolean stocks were discontinued by 1980).

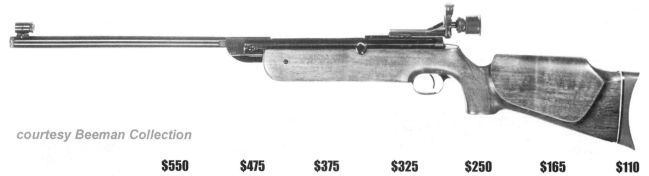

courtesy Beeman Collection

	$550	$475	$375	$325	$250	$165	$110

Add 30% for Model 60T.

MODEL 64 – .177 cal., records not yet clear about this model - if it existed, it probably was only a restocked Model 34. Mfg. circa 1986-1989.

GRADING	100%	95%	90%	80%	60%	40%	20%

MODEL 65/65T – .177 cal., BBC, Giss double contra-SP system with radial lock lever, beech, Tyrolean (Model 65T), or walnut stock with rounded forearm, rubber butt pad, automatic safety, match diopter rear and tunnel front sight with inserts, adj. trigger, 43.3 in. OAL, 10.6 lbs. Mfg. 1968-1989 (Tyrolean stocks gone by 1980).

courtesy Beeman Collection

	$500	$425	$350	$290	$225	$150	$100

Add 35% for Model 65T.

MODEL 66/66M – .177 cal., BBC, similar to Model 65, except squared and deeper forestock, modified pistol grip and vertically adjustable rubber buttplate. Mfg. 1974-1983.

	$425	$350	$300	$245	$190	$125	$85

MODEL LG 68 – variant of Models 34/36/38 action with different stock.

No other information or values were available at time of printing.

MODEL 70 – .177 cal., BBC, 450 FPS, 13.5 in. barrel, youth dimensions. Mfg. 1979-1994.

	$130	$110	$90	$75	$60	$40	$25

Last MSR was $190.

MODEL 72 – .177 cal., similar to Model 70, except with Giss recoilless action. A rifle version of Model 6 pistol. Mfg. 1979-1993.

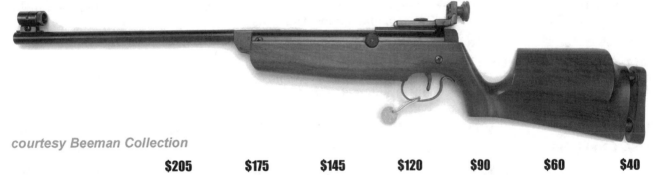

courtesy Beeman Collection

	$205	$175	$145	$120	$90	$60	$40

Last MSR was $340.

MODEL 75/75HV/75K/75S/75U/75TO1 MATCH MODEL – .177 cal., SL, 580 FPS, 19 in. barrel, micrometer-adj. rear sights, adj. cheek piece, adj. recoil pad, 43.3 in. OAL, 11 lbs.

courtesy Howard Collection

	$850	$725	$600	$500	$375	$255	$170

Last MSR was $1,745.

Subtract 10% for left-hand variation.
Premiums may exist for variations of Model 75 mfg. 1977-1983, Model 75B mfg. 1988-1994, Model 75HV and Model 75TO1 mfg. 1983-1988, Model 75K was disc. in 1990, Model 75S mfg. beginning in 1999, now disc., Model 75U mfg. 1982-1986.

GRADING	100%	95%	90%	80%	60%	40%	20%

MODEL 100 – .177 cal., SSP, 580 FPS, 18.9 in. barrel, adj. cheek piece, target model, 42.9 in. OAL, 11 lbs. Mfg. 1989-1998.

	$1,000	$850	$700	$575	$450	$300	$200

Last MSR was $1,950.

MODEL 300 – .177 or .22 cal., UL, SP, 900/700 FPS, 11 in. barrel, blue finish, adj. rear sight, auto-safety, Monte Carlo stock with checkered forearm and grip (Model 46), recoil pad, 45.31 in. OAL, 7.9 lbs. New 2005.

courtesy Diana

	$475	$400	$350	$280	$220	$145	$95

Last MSR was $537.

MODEL 350 MAGNUM CLASSIC PRO – .177 or .22 cal., BBC, SP, SS, 19.5 in. rifled steel barrel, 1250/910 FPS, blue finish, 11mm optics dovetail, ambidextrous beech stock, rubber butt pad, two-stage adj. metal T06 match trigger, automatic safety, 48 in. OAL, approx. 8.8 lbs. Mfg. 2014-current.

MSR $550	$475	$400	$375	$300	$230	N/A	N/A

MODEL 430 – .177 or .22 cal., UL, SP, SS, sliding breech action, 15.4 in. rifled steel barrel, 870/670 FPS, blue finish, fixed blade ramp front and fully adj. rear sights, 11mm optics dovetail, checkered beech stock with rubber butt pad, two-stage adj. metal T06 match trigger, automatic safety, 41 in. OAL, approx. 7.9 lbs. Mfg. 2014-current.

MSR $650	$550	$475	$450	$350	$275	N/A	N/A

MODEL 430 STUTZEN – .177 or .22 cal., UL, SP, SS, sliding breech action, 15.4 in. rifled steel barrel, 870/670 FPS, blue finish, fixed blade ramp front and fully adj. rear sights, 11mm optics dovetail, Mannlicher beech stock with fish scale checkering framed by carved oak leaves on forearm and pistol grip, rubber butt pad, two-stage adj. metal T06 match trigger, automatic safety, 41 in. OAL, approx. 8.2 lbs. Mfg. 2014-current.

MSR $750	$625	$550	$500	$400	$325	N/A	N/A

MODEL 470TH TARGET HUNTER – .177 or .22 cal., UL, SP, SS, sliding breech action, 18 in. rifled steel barrel with muzzlebrake, 1120/890 FPS, blue finish, 11mm optics dovetail, checkered ambidextrous beech thumbhole stock with adj. rubber buttpad, two-stage adj. metal T06 match trigger, automatic safety, 45 in. OAL, approx. 9.4 lbs. Mfg. 2014-current.

MSR $725	$625	$550	$500	$400	$300	N/A	N/A

MODEL 1000 – .177 cal., BBC, colored plastic stocks (black, red, blue, white, and yellow). Disc. 1991.

	$150	$130	$105	$85	$70	$45	$30

Last MSR was $215.

The Model 1000 was the sport model of the standard Model 34.

MODEL P1000 – .177 or .22 cal., PCP, 1150/950 FPS, 14-shot mag., single shot adapter, 17.5 in. barrel, two-piece hunting stock, 300 bar steel air cylinder, TO6 metal trigger, 11mm top rail, automatic safety, 38 in. OAL, 7.9 lbs. New 2011.

MSR $1,500	$1,275	$1,125	$1,025	$825	$625	N/A	N/A

MODEL P1000TH – .177 or .22 cal., PCP, 1150/950 FPS, 14-shot mag., single shot adapter, 17.5 in. barrel, ergonomic thumbhole stock and adj. rubber pad, 300 bar steel air cylinder, TO6 metal trigger, 11mm top rail, automatic safety, 38 in. OAL, 7.9 lbs. New 2011.

MSR $1,596	$1,350	$1,200	$1,075	$875	$675	N/A	N/A

DOLLA

The Dolla name appeared about 1927 as a general designation for a number of push barrel air pistols with a cast one-piece grip and frame of distinctive shape but typically with no maker's name.

Most apparently were produced in Germany between WWI and WWII and may have been produced by several makers. They were especially promoted by Darlow of Bedford, England and Midland Gun Company of Birmingham, England. All are very solid and have very low power. The name came from the fact that the guns were priced at about

GRADING	100%	95%	90%	80%	60%	40%	20%

the equivalent of an American dollar at the time of their introduction (SP, SS, .l77 cal.).

Noted European airgun historian, John Atkins, indicates that the term Dolla, strictly speaking, should be applied only to models produced after 1927. Earlier, similar appearing pistols, perhaps first produced about the 1895 by the Langenhan and Eisenwerke Gaggenau factories in Zella Mehlis, Germany, never had this name appliedto them while they were in production. Typical specimens bear cast letter names such as "BRITISH CUB" or "CUB". The recent Dolla pistols typically have a trigger guard with a completely rounded opening while the similar, older, pre-Dolla versions typically had the upper rear area of the trigger guard opening with a distinct right angle profile. The pre-Dolla versions are worth significantly more.

Push barrel air pistols with sheet metal trigger guards, as made by Anschütz, and perhaps others, as early as 1930, had graduated to the designation of Dolla Mark II.

Dolla values range from about $100 to $500 depending on model, condition, and case. Ref: AG Jan. 2005.

courtesy Beeman Collection

DONG KI

Current manufacturing/marketing group in Seoul, Korea whose products include airguns.

RIFLES

MODEL DK G 3030 – .22 cal., PCP, SS, 21.5 in. barrel, blue finish, wood stock.

courtesy Howard Collection

	$1,000	$850	$700	$575	$450	$300	$200

M1 CARBINE MODEL 106 – .177 cal., SP, SL, full-scale replica air rifle of the U.S. Model M1 Carbine complete with military sling stock slots and bayonet base.

courtesy Beeman Collection

	$1,500	$1,300	$1,100	$900	$800	N/A	N/A

DREIBUND

For information on Dreibund airguns, see Philippine Airguns in the "P" section.

DRULOV

Current manufacturer located in Litomysl, Czech Republic. Currently imported and distributed by Top Gun Air Guns Inc. located in Scottsdale, AZ.

GRADING	100%	95%	90%	80%	60%	40%	20%

PISTOLS

DRULOV DU-10 CONDOR – .177 cal., CO_2, five-shot mag., 7 in. barrel, adj. sights, blue finish, dovetail scope rail, walnut wood grip.

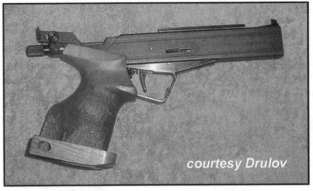

courtesy Drulov

MSR $635	$550	$475	$425	$350	$265	N/A	N/A

DRULOV LOV-21 – .177 cal., CO_2, SS, black plastic frame, 6 in. rifled steel BBL, 420 FPS, adj. sights, 11.3 in. OAL. Mfg. 2004-2009.

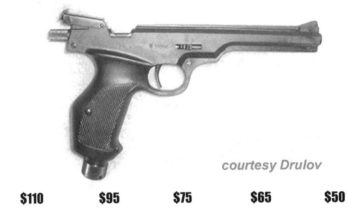

courtesy Drulov

$110	$95	$75	$65	$50	$35	$20

Last MSR was $119.

DRULOV RADA PISTOL – 9mm cal., CO_2, SS, adj. sights, rifled steel BBL, 210 FPS, blue finish, wood grip and forend, detachable wire shoulder stock. New 2004.

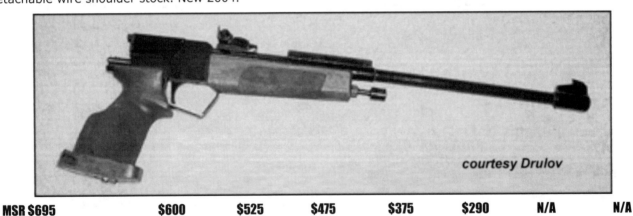

courtesy Drulov

MSR $695	$600	$525	$475	$375	$290	N/A	N/A

Add 10% for Rada Convertible with longer BBL.

GRADING	100%	95%	90%	80%	60%	40%	20%

RIFLES

DRULOV 10 EAGLE – .177 cal., CO_2, five-shot mag., 525 FPS, 15.75, 19.7, or 21 in. barrel, adj. sights, blue finish, wood stock with adj. cheek piece and buttplate.

courtesy Drulov

MSR $635	$550	$475	$425	$350	$265	N/A	N/A

DRULOV 10 SOKOL – .375 or 9mm cal., CO_2, SS, adj. sights, blue finish, wood stock.

courtesy Howard Collection

MSR $695	$600	$525	$475	$375	$290	N/A	N/A

DRUMMEN CUSTOM GUNS

Current custom manufacturer located in the Netherlands. No current U.S. importation.

RIFLES

DZ SINNER – multiple calibers, PCP, only 3 screws to change caliber, standard walnut stock with short pressure tube, newest design mfg. in Holland.

Please contact the company directly for pricing and U.S. availability for this model.

DUK IL

Manufacturing group located in Pusan, South Korea. Previously located in Seoul, Korea. Products include pre-charged pneumatic airguns. Previously imported/distributed in USA by Air Rifle Specialists.

For information on Duk Il airguns, see ARS in the "A" section.

As a member, you will receive these benefits:

★ 24/7 defense of your firearm freedoms
★ Choice of an award-winning magazine
★ $2,500 in ArmsCare® firearms insurance
★ $5,000 Life & Accidental Insurance ($10,000 for Life Members)
★ Access to NRA's hunting, shooting, and safety programs

JOIN NRA TODAY!

Join online at www.NRA.org/BlueBook

E SECTION

EASTERN ENGINEERING CO.

Previous manufacturer located in Syracuse, NY.

GRADING	100%	95%	90%	80%	60%	40%	20%

PISTOLS

GAMESTER – .177 or .25 cal., SP, SS, push-barrel action similar to the Hubertus air pistol of Germany. Bronze frame, blued steel body tube, silver colored thin barrel. No marks on gun but fitted cardboard factory box with illustrated information inside cover, 5.5 in. BBL, 11 in. OAL, 2.1 lbs.

courtesy Beeman Collection

N/A	$1,750	$1,400	$1,125	$875	$600	$350

Factory information indicates that .177 cal. barrel and supplied mainspring was for "semi-harmless use" while an optional .25 cal. barrel and stronger mainspring was available for pest control.

EDGUN

Current manufacturer established in 2002, and located in Russia. No current U.S. importation.

Current models include the Lelya, Matador, Matador R3M, Morana, and Veles. Please contact the company directly for more information including pricing, options, and U.S. availability (see Trademark Index).

EDISON GENERAL ELECTRIC

Previously manufactured by Edison General Electric Appliance Co., Chicago, IL.

These are large airguns which simulated heavy machine guns for training gunners during WWII. Used in simulated combat with back projected images of enemy planes flying at different speeds and angles. Edison General Electric Appliance became General Electric after WWII. "Hotpoint" was their appliance brand. Mfg. circa 1943-1945. Ref. Behling (2006), Handbook of Description, Armament Training Devices, T.O. 11-65-12, January 25, 1944.

TRAINER MACHINE GUNS

Gunnery trainer machine guns -- fully automatic, powered via hose from air compressor. .375 cal. bakelite ball ammo, magazine tube above and parallel to shorter true barrel, magazine loaded by unscrewing cap at muzzle end and attaching loader which mates with projectile exit opening below. 100 round loader filled from separate projectile hopper. 115v/60 cycle firing mechanism, painted black. There are three known models.

ANTI-AIRCRAFT MACHINE GUN MODEL M9 – .375 cal., ground to air gunnery trainer, 500 rpm, dual hand grips, massive steel plate pivoting/swiveling base, barrel sleeve about 4 3/4 in. diameter to simulate water-cooled barrel jacket of .50 cal. machine gun; marked with Edison General Electric Appliance Company name but without Hotpoint brand marking, 67 in. OAL, 78 lbs.

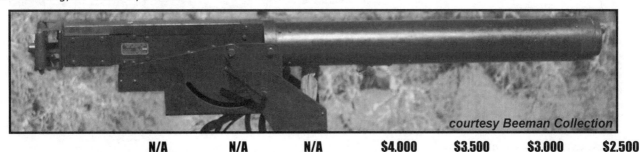

courtesy Beeman Collection

N/A	N/A	N/A	$4,000	$3,500	$3,000	$2,500

Add 10% for loading funnel, hopper.
Original shipping box, operating manual, and bags of ammo typically have retail values in the $25-$50 range for each item.

GRADING	100%	95%	90%	80%	60%	40%	20%

AERIAL GUNNERY MACHINE GUN MODEL E10 – .375 cal., remote control version of Model E11, no hand grips; probably mounted in pairs in remote gun turrets, marked with Hotpoint brand and Edison General Electric Appliance Company name, 110 volts, 60 cycles, 300 watts, 48 in. OAL, 24 lbs.

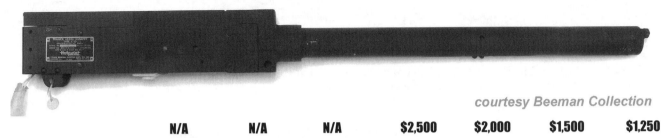

courtesy Beeman Collection

	N/A	N/A	N/A	$2,500	$2,000	$1,500	$1,250

Add 10% for loading funnel, hopper.

AERIAL GUNNERY MACHINE GUN MODEL E11 – .375 cal., side gunner version for training gunners in U.S. bombers, dual hand grips; barrel sleeve simulates barrel sleeve of air-cooled machine guns, small steel pin support base, marked with Hotpoint brand and Edison General Electric Appliance Company name, 110 volts, 60 cycles, 400 watts, 57.5 in. OAL, 41 lbs.

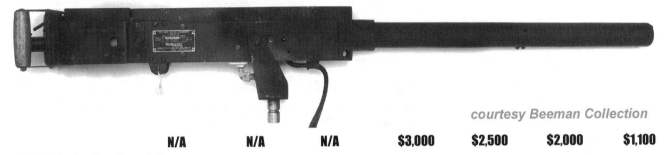

courtesy Beeman Collection

	N/A	N/A	N/A	$3,000	$2,500	$2,000	$1,100

Add 10% for loading funnel, hopper.

EISENWERKE GAGGENAU (GAGGENAU IRONWORKS)

As noted in the Gaggenau Ironworks listing, there is NO such brand as "Eisenwerk". That word simply means "iron works" or "factory". See Gaggenau Ironworks in the "G" section.

EL GAMO

For information on El Gamo airguns, see Gamo in the "G" section.

ELMEK

Previous trademark manufactured by Electro Mechanical located in Oslo, Norway, circa 1948-1950.

The Elmek air rifle was designed by Mr. Jan Emil Raastad.

RIFLES

ELMEK RIFLE – .25 cal., smoothbore, SP, UL, SS, 21.5 in. BBL, blue/nickel finish, iron cocking lever behind trigger with unique attached wooden pistol grip, downswing of underlever causes breech block, which contains the mainspring and piston to move back as a unit - exposing barrel breech for direct loading - upswing causes compression chamber tube only to move forward, leaving piston cocked, and closing breech - similar to the complex, fully opening breech system in the Feinwerkbau 300 and 65 airguns, receiver body is brass with nickel plating, hexagon containing the word "ELMEK" is stamped on lower edge of receiver.

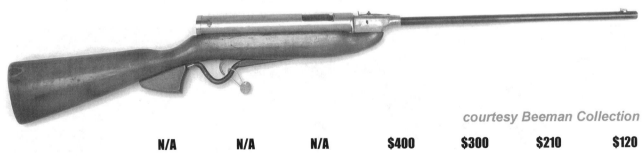

courtesy Beeman Collection

	N/A	N/A	N/A	$400	$300	$210	$120

At least two model variants mfg.

GRADING	100%	95%	90%	80%	60%	40%	20%

EM-GE

Previous trademark manufactured by Moritz & Gerstenberger located in Zella-Mehlis, Thüringen, Germany circa 1922-1940, for airguns, starting pistols, blank-firing guns, and flare pistols. Re-established as Gerstensberger & Eberwein located in Gerstetten-Gussenstadt, Germany about 1950. Company seems to have vanished circa 1997.

Moritz & Gerstenberger apparently produced products for the German military program during WWII under the code "ghk". Now known mainly for rather low grade airpistols, teargas and blank-firing pistols; some of their pre-WWII products, such as the very interesting top-lever Zenit air pistol (SP) were quite good. Among their older products is a BBC, SP pistol, without model markings, which is very similar to a pre-WWII Diana Model 5 (probably an early version of the EmGe LP3A). Ref: AR2: 16-20.

PISTOLS

HERKULES – .177 cal., BC, SS, fixed sights, 325 FPS, fixed sights, blue finish, wood grips, no safety. Mfg. 1933-1940.

courtesy Beeman Collection

	N/A	$300	$240	$195	$150	$105	$60

MODEL 3 – .22 cal., BC, SS, fixed sights, 7.4 in. stepped, rifled steel barrel, all steel receiver, blue finish, checkered wood grips, no safety, 15.5 in. OAL, 2.6 lbs. Mfg. pre-WWII.

	$275	$235	$195	$160	$125	$80	$55

Rear sight at back end of receiver.

MODEL LP 3 – .177 or .22 cal. BC, SS, 5.8 in. rifled steel BBL, adj. trigger, adj. sights, no safety, checkered brown plastic grips, anodized blue finish on zinc barrel cover, receiver, and other zinc die-cast metal parts, 12.4 in. OAL, 2.7 lbs. Mfg. circa 1957-1975.

	$175	$150	$125	$100	$80	$50	$35

Subtract 25% for LP3A (top of receiver and BBL ribbed). Ref: GR, Aug. 76. Ca. 1975-1980.

Branded as HyScore 822T in USA. Ref: GR Dec. 74.

MODEL 100 – No other information or values available at this time.

ZENIT – .177 cal., TL, SS or 10-shot repeater, fixed sights, smoothbore or rifled steel BBL, 325 FPS, blue finish, wood grip, (marked "gez") translates to rifled, no safety. Mfg. circa 1936-1940. Ref: AR2:16-20.

courtesy Beeman Collection

	N/A	$195	$155	$125	$95	$70	$40

Add 300% for ten-shot repeater (if with mag.).
Add 40% for black Bakelite grip.

GRADING	100%	95%	90%	80%	60%	40%	20%

RIFLES

EM-GE KRONE – 4.5mm cal., BBC, SS or 15-shot repeater, 15.75 in. rifled steel BBL, 560 FPS, adj. rear and blade front sights, walnut stock with PG, 38.5 in. OAL, 5.1 lbs. Mfg. circa 1935-1940.

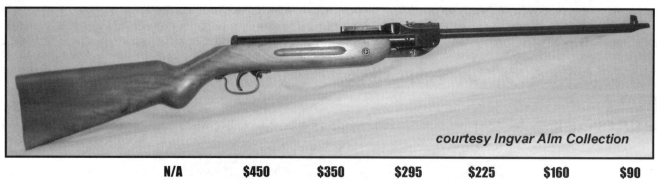

courtesy Ingvar Alm Collection

	N/A	$450	$350	$295	$225	$160	$90

Add 250% for 15-shot repeater, marked "KRONE M" w/original mag.

ENSIGN ARMS CO., LTD.

Previous international distributors for Saxby Palmer Airguns located in Newbury, England. Previously imported until 1988 by Marksman Products, located in Huntington Beach, CA.

Ensign Arms previously distributed the Saxby Palmer line of airguns into the U.S. Please refer to the Saxby Palmer section for these guns. Ensign-designated models were trademarked by Ensign Arms Co., Ltd.

ERIE IRON WORKS

Previous manufacturer originally located in St. Thomas, Ontario, Canada, later moved to Toronto, Canada. Manufactured circa 1940-1955.

RIFLES

BISLEY SHARPSHOOTEER – BB/.174 cal., trigger guard UL, SP, 1000 shot similar to Erie Target rifle with yellow and black decal with model name on side of stock above trigger.

	$300	$255	$210	$175	$135	$90	$60

ERIE TARGET RIFLE – BB/.174 cal., trigger guard UL, SP, 1000 shot, flat sided hardwood stock, manual safety at rear of receiver, unique trigger guard cocking lever w/no metal on inner side, early versions w/hooded front sight and cast iron levers, later versions with aluminum lever and plain blade front sight, diamond shape yellow and black decal on LHS forearm, 36 in. OAL, approx. 3 lbs.

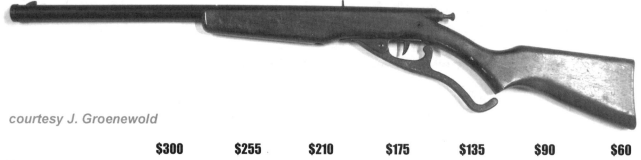

courtesy J. Groenewold

	$300	$255	$210	$175	$135	$90	$60

Add 10% for cast iron cocking lever.

ERMA

Previously manufactured by Erma-Werke GmbH, located in München-Dachau, Germany.

Erma produced their only airgun, the ELG 10, in 1981, which was discontinued in the 1990s. Apparently related to pre-WWII Erfurter Maschinenfabrik. Erma (= Erma Maschinenfabrik) was relocated from Erfurt to Bavaria after WWII like the other companies (which mostly went to the Baden-Wurtemmberg region, Ulm, etc.). Having the same origin in the 1990s, Erma went back to Suhl (after near insolvency and a management buyout). In 1998, the company was officially closed. Some models and spare parts were bought and distributed by Frankonia Jagd, Würzburg (wholesaler).

Makers of blowback copies of the Luger-style firearms, such as the Beeman P-08 and MP-08 in .22 LR and .380 ACP, respectively, and copies of the U.S. M1 carbine in .22 LR (and in .22 WMR, famous as the "Jungle Carbine" in banana republics). They also produced some very little-known electro-optical shooting guns, including a version of the ELG 10, known as the EG 80 Ermatronic, and an Ermatronic copy of a Colt revolver.

GRADING	100%	95%	90%	80%	60%	40%	20%

For more information and current values on Erma-Werke firearms, please refer to the *Blue Book of Gun Values* by S.P. Fjestad (also available online).

RIFLES

ELG 10 – .177 cal., SP, SS, LA, manual safety, copy of the Winchester 1894, 38 in. OAL, 6.4 lbs.

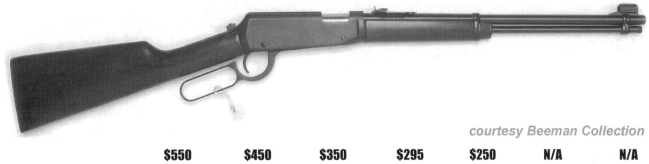

courtesy Beeman Collection

	$550	$450	$350	$295	$250	N/A	N/A

Add 10% for Webley "Ranger" marking.

EUN JIN

Current manufacturer located in Korea. Currently imported and distributed by Air Venturi/Pyramyd Air located in Solon, OH. Previously located in Warrensville Hts, OH.

RIFLES

SUMATRA 2500 CARBINE – .177, .20, .22, or .25 cal., adj. power PCP, lever action, six shot mag. repeater, 16 in. rifled steel barrel, 1000/950/910 FPS, blue finish (coin finish receiver with adj. cheek piece), engraved receiver, adj. sights, adj. two stage trigger, checkered PG hardwood stock and forearm w/rubber buttpad, manual safety, 35.50 in. OAL, 6 lbs. Mfg. 2010-current.

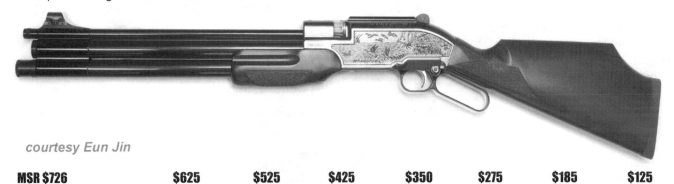

courtesy Eun Jin

MSR $726	$625	$525	$425	$350	$275	$185	$125

SUMATRA 2500 RIFLE – .177, .22, or .25 cal., adj. power PCP, lever action, six shot mag. repeater, 24 in. rifled steel barrel, 1200/1100/1000 FPS, blue finish (coin finish receiver with adj. cheek piece), engraved receiver, adj. sights, adj. two stage trigger, checkered PG hardwood stock and forearm w/rubber buttpad, manual safety, 43 in. OAL, 8 lbs. Mfg. 2010-current.

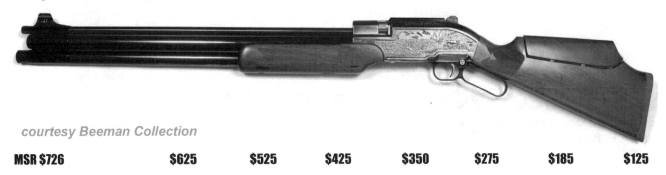

courtesy Beeman Collection

MSR $726	$625	$525	$425	$350	$275	$185	$125

GRADING	100%	95%	90%	80%	60%	40%	20%

SUMATRA 2500 RIFLE (500CC RESERVOIR) – .22 or .25 cal., adj. power PCP, lever action, six shot mag. repeater, 24 in. rifled steel barrel, 1260/1000 FPS, blue finish, engraved receiver, adj. sights, adj. two stage trigger, checkered PG hardwood stock and forearm w/adj. cheek piece and rubber buttpad, manual safety, 43 in. OAL, 8 lbs. Mfg. 2010-current.

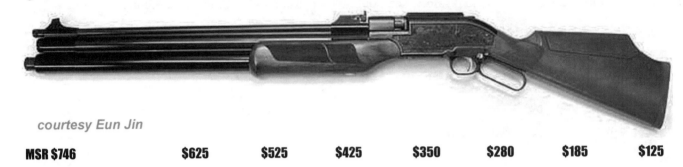

courtesy Eun Jin

MSR $746	$625	$525	$425	$350	$280	$185	$125

EUSTA

Previous trademark used by Alpina-Werk M&M Vorwerk GmbH & Co., KG, 8950 Kaufbeuren, Germany on inexpensive sheet metal air pistols.

The authors and publisher wish to thank Dr. Trevor Adams for his valuable assistance with the following information for this section of the *Blue Book of Airguns*. Trademark registered in Germany on October 13, 1965. Gun design was invented by Walter Ussfeller, A. Weber, and H. Witteler. Most notable for the concentric piston design. Distributed by Eckhard G. Damaschke, Weickartshain, Germany, 1968-1976.

PISTOLS

LP 100 – .177 cal., SP, TL, SS, sheet metal frame with plastic grips, concentric piston, 6.3 in. rifled steel barrel, 8 in. OAL, 1.5 lbs. Mfg. 1965-1968.

	$350	$300	$250	$200	$150	$100	$50

Add 20% for factory box and papers.

This model was patented in Germany by Walter Ussfeller on Sept. 24, 1969.

LP 210 – .177 cal., SP, TL, SS, similar to LP 100, except for a modified top lever catch, breech-end of cylinder sloped forward, and two-piece trigger. Mfg. 1968-1971.

courtesy Trevor Adams

N/A	$175	$125	$75	$50	$30	$20

Add 20% for factory box and papers.

This model was based on Alpina Werk patent of Nov. 5, 1970.

EVANIX (MECA EVANIX CORPORATION)

Current manufacturer located in Seoul, Korea. Currently imported and distributed by Air Venturi/Pyramyd Air located in Solon, OH. Previously located in Warrensville Heights, OH.

EVANIX is a Korean manufacturer of high quality air rifles, gun stocks and tactical shooting goods.

GRADING	100%	95%	90%	80%	60%	40%	20%

PISTOLS

HUNTING MASTER AR6 – .22 cal., PCP, six shot rotary mag. repeater, thumb hammer cocking, 10 in. rifled steel barrel, 1000 FPS, anatomical finger grooved hardwood grip, 17.3 in. OAL, 3 lbs.

courtesy Evanix

MSR $660	$550	$500	$450	$375	$275	N/A	N/A

HUNTING MASTER P – .177 cal., PCP, 6-shot mag., 10 in. rifled barrel, single action trigger, manual safety, no sights, brown finger grooved hardwood grip, 17.3 in. OAL, 3.05 lbs. New 2012.

> This model is not currently imported, please contact Evanix (see Trademark Index) directly for pricing and availability.

RIFLES

AVALANCHE – .177, .20, .22, .25, or .357 cal., PCP, semi-full auto, repeater, 10-shot mag., 19 in. rifled barrel, hardwood or black synthetic stock, two stage trigger, manual safety, 42 in. OAL, 8.8 lbs. New 2012.

> This model is not currently imported, please contact Evanix (see Trademark Index) directly for pricing and availability.

BLACK LEOPARD – .177, .20 (new 2012), .22, .25 (new 2012), or .357 (new 2012) cal., PCP, has air tube in front, air bottle in rear, side-lever, 10-round repeater, 19.76 in. barrel, ambidextrous walnut thumbhole stock with adj. buttpad, or black thumbhole stock, two-stage adj. trigger, manual safety, 40.16 in. OAL, 8.6 lbs. New 2010.

courtesy Air Venturi

MSR $1,751	$1,500	$1,325	$1,200	$975	$725	N/A	N/A

BLIZZARD S10 – .177 or .22 cal., PCP, side lever cocking, new compact design (2012), 10-shot rotary mag. repeater, 20.87 (new 2012) or 27 (disc. 2011) in. rifled barrel, 1300/1175 FPS, blue finish, two stage trigger, grooved receiver, checkered Monte Carlo hardwood stock, adj. rubber butt pad, quick disconnect fill system, 40.55 (new 2012) or 47.75 (disc. 2011) in. OAL, 8.75 lbs.

courtesy Evanix

MSR N/A	$650	$550	$450	$375	$295	$200	$130

Add $100 for thumbhole stock.

This model is also available with a rear bolt action (RB), or a side bolt action (SB).

GRADING	100%	95%	90%	80%	60%	40%	20%

CONQUEST – .177, .20, .22, .25, or .357 cal., PCP, semi-auto, 13 (.177 cal.), 11 (.22 cal.), 10 (.25 cal.), or 7 (.357 cal.) shot mag., 17 in. rifled barrel, built-in manometer, 400cc cylinder, hardwood thumbhole stock, two stage trigger, manual safety, 40 in. OAL, 8.4 lbs. New 2012.

courtesy Air Venturi

	100%	95%	90%	80%	60%	40%	20%
MSR $1,850	$1,575	$1,375	$1,250	$1,025	$775	N/A	N/A

Add $50 for .177 cal.
Add $80 for .25 cal.
Add $350 for .357 cal.

GIANT – .177, .20, .22, .25, or .357 cal., PCP, semi or full (disc. 2013) auto action, dual 480cc composite cylinders, compact and ergonomic, 13 (.177 cal.), 11 (.22 cal.), 10 (.25 cal.), or 10 (.357 cal.) shot mag., 19 in. rifled barrel, hardwood or black synthetic stock, two stage trigger, 40.35 in. OAL, 8.4 lbs. New 2012.

courtesy Air Venturi

	100%	95%	90%	80%	60%	40%	20%
MSR $2,250	$1,900	$1,675	$1,525	$1,225	$950	N/A	N/A

Add $200 for .25 cal.
Add $200 for hardwood stock.
Add $500 for .357 cal. with synthetic or hardwood stock.

GIANTx2 – .25 or .357 cal., PCP, semi-auto action, dual 480cc composite cylinders, 10 (.25 cal.), or 7 (.357 cal.) shot mag., 19 in. rifled barrel, military style vented alloy forearm with black synthetic PG and butt stock, two-stage trigger, 40.35 in. OAL, 8.4 lbs. New 2013.

	100%	95%	90%	80%	60%	40%	20%
MSR $2,546	$2,175	$1,900	$1,725	$1,400	$1,075	N/A	N/A

Add $200 for .357 cal.

GTK290 – .177, .22, .25, or .357 cal., PCP, semi-auto action, 13 (.177 cal.), 11 (.22 cal.), or 10 (.25, .357 cal.) shot rotary mag. repeater, 17.13 in. shrouded barrel with threaded muzzle, 1310/1150/910/730 FPS, 288cc cylinder, built-in manometer, blue and tan finish, two-stage adj. trigger, ambidextrous metal stock with adj. forearm, rubber buttpad and Weaver accessory/optics rail, manual safety, 36.02 in. OAL, 8.89 lbs. Mfg. 2014-current.

courtesy Air Venturi

	100%	95%	90%	80%	60%	40%	20%
MSR $1,866	$1,575	$1,400	$1,275	$1,025	$775	N/A	N/A

Add $30 for .25 cal.
Add $185 for .357 cal.

GRADING	100%	95%	90%	80%	60%	40%	20%

HUNTING MASTER AR4 – .177 cal., PCP, SA, exposed cocking hammer, six-shot rotary mag. repeater, 23.2 in. rifled barrel, 1450 FPS, blue finish, adj. single stage trigger, grooved receiver, checkered Monte Carlo hardwood stock, rubber butt pad, 38.25 in. OAL, 6.82 lbs. Disc. 2013.

	100%	95%	90%	80%	60%	40%	20%
	$600	$500	$425	$350	$270	$180	$120

Last MSR was $700.

Add $200 for 24 in. shrouded barrel (new 2010).

HUNTING MASTER AR6 – .177, 20 (disc.) or .22 cal., PCP, SA, 1450/1200 FPS, exposed cocking hammer, six-shot rotary mag. repeater, 23.2 in. rifled barrel, blue finish, adj. single stage trigger, grooved receiver, built-in manometer, checkered Monte Carlo hardwood stock, rubber butt pad, 38.25 in. OAL, 6.82 lbs.

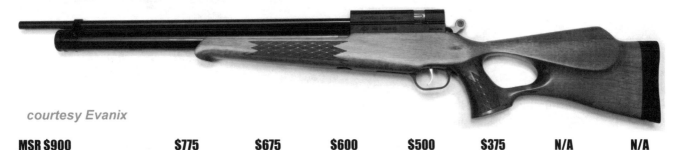

courtesy Evanix

MSR $900	$775	$675	$600	$500	$375	N/A	N/A

Add $200 for 24 in. shrouded barrel (new 2010).
Add $191 for thumbhole stock.

HUNTING MASTER AR6 MAGNUM – .22 cal., PCP, six-shot rotary mag., 22.75 in. blue finish barrel, alloy receiver with gold burnish finish, 1000 FPS, adj. rear sight, checkered walnut stock and forearm, 6.75 lbs. Mfg. in Korea, disc.

	$425	$350	$300	$245	$190	$125	$85

Last MSR was $580.

Add $20 for extra six-shot cylinder.
Add $50 for charging unit.

HUNTING MASTER K550 – .177, .20, or .22 cal., PCP, 6-shot mag., 13.62 in. barrel, walnut with adj. buttpad or sepatia thumbhole stock, single stage trigger, quick-disconnect fitting, manual safety, 40.94 in. OAL, 8.16 lbs. New 2012.

This model is not currently imported, please contact Evanix (see Trademark Index) directly for pricing and availability.

KING HUNTING MASTER – .22 cal., PCP, five-shot rotary mag. Mfg. in Korea, disc.

	$425	$350	$300	$245	$190	$125	$85

Last MSR was $580.

MAX – .177, .20, .22, or .25 cal., PCP, CO_2, full auto, bullpup design, 13 (.177 cal.), 11 (.22 cal.), 10 (.25 and .357 cal.) shot mag., repeater, 19 in. shrouded rifled barrel, ambidextrous walnut thumbhole stock, checkered pistol grip with finger grooves, rubber recoil pad, built-in manometer, two-stage trigger, manual safety, 29.3 in. OAL, 8.6 lbs. New 2012.

courtesy Air Venturi

MSR $1,850	$1,575	$1,375	$1,250	$1,025	$775	N/A	N/A

Add $80 for .25 cal.
Add $650 for .357 cal.

GRADING	100%	95%	90%	80%	60%	40%	20%

MONSTER – .177, .20 (new 2012), .22, .25 (new 2012), or .357 (new 2012) cal., PCP, 1200/995 FPS, 10-shot mag., side lever, 19.76 in. barrel, two-stage adj. trigger, manual safety, walnut with adj. buttpad, or black thumbhole stock, includes two buddy air bottles in rear and front, 40.16 in. OAL, 8.6 lbs. Mfg. 2010-current.

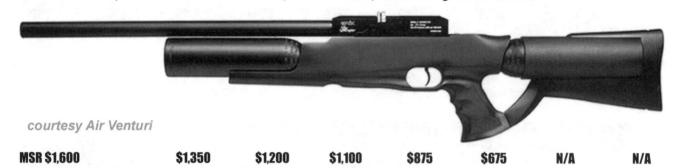

courtesy Air Venturi

MSR $1,600	$1,350	$1,200	$1,100	$875	$675	N/A	N/A

RAINSTORM – .177 or .22 cal., PCP, side lever cocking, compact carbine, ten shot rotary mag. repeater, 19 in. barrel with threaded muzzle, 1300/1176 FPS, blue finish, two stage adj. trigger, grooved receiver, checkered Monte Carlo walnut or Sepatia thumbhole or Sporter stock, lasercut checkering, adj. rubber butt pad, manual safety, in 2012 a new cycling system and new magazine were added, 37.5 in. OAL, 6.75 lbs. Disc. 2013.

courtesy Evanix

	$650	$550	$450	$375	$295	$195	$130

Last MSR was $760.

Add $100 for thumbhole stock.

This model is also available with a traditional rear bolt action with a buffalo horn ball (Rainstorm RB), or a side bolt action with a buffalo horn ball (Rainstorm SB).

RAINSTORM II – .177, .22, .25, or .357 cal., PCP, side lever cocking, 13 (.177 cal.), 11 (.22 cal.), 10 (.25 cal.) or 7 (.357 cal.) shot rotary mag. repeater, 17 in. barrel with threaded muzzle, 1300/1176/910/800 FPS, blue finish, two stage adj. trigger, grooved receiver, checkered ambidextrous sporter stock, adj. rubber butt pad, manual safety, 39 in. OAL, 7.2 lbs. Mfg. 2014-current.

courtesy Air Venturi

MSR $850	$725	$625	$575	$475	$350	N/A	N/A

Add $50 for .25 cal.
Add $300 for .357 cal.

GRADING	100%	95%	90%	80%	60%	40%	20%

RAINSTORM 3D BULLPUP – .177, .22, .25, or .357 cal., PCP, side lever cocking, 13 (.177 cal.), 11 (.22 cal.), 10 (.25 cal.) or 7 (.357 cal.) shot rotary mag. repeater, 17 in. barrel with threaded muzzle, 1300/1176/910/800 FPS, built-in manometer, blue and tan finish, two stage adj. trigger, ambidextrous bullpup style stock with rubber butt pad and Weaver accessory/optics rail, manual safety, 27 in. OAL, 7.8 lbs. Mfg. 2014-current.

courtesy Air Venturi

MSR $946	$800	$700	$650	$525	$400	N/A	N/A

Add $50 for .25 cal.
Add $150 for .357 cal.

RENEGADE CARBINE – .177 or .22 cal., PCP, exposed cocking hammer, SA or DA, six shot rotary mag. repeater, 16.75 in. barrel, 1065/1023 FPS, blue finish, two stage trigger, grooved receiver, checkered Monte Carlo walnut stock, adj. rubber butt pad, 37.50 in. OAL, 6.75 lbs. Disc.

courtesy Evanix

$675	$575	$475	$400	$300	$200	$135

Last MSR was $800.

RENEGADE RIFLE – .177 or .22 cal., PCP, exposed cocking hammer, SA or DA, six shot rotary mag. repeater, 23.2 in. barrel, 1065/1023 FPS, blue finish, two stage trigger, grooved receiver, checkered Monte Carlo walnut stock, adj. rubber butt pad, 41 in. OAL, 6.82 lbs. Disc. 2011.

courtesy Evanix

$675	$575	$475	$400	$300	$200	$135

Last MSR was $800.

Add $100 for thumbhole stock.

GRADING	100%	95%	90%	80%	60%	40%	20%

RENEGADE TDR (TAKE DOWN RIFLE) – .22 cal., PCP, exposed cocking hammer, SA or DA, six shot rotary mag. repeater, 10 in. barrel, 841 FPS, blue finish, two stage trigger, grooved receiver, checkered Monte Carlo PG walnut take down stock, rubber butt pad, 17.30 in. OAL, 3 lbs. Disc.

courtesy Evanix

	100%	95%	90%	80%	60%	40%	20%
	$575	$500	$400	$325	$260	$170	$115

Last MSR was $680.

SPEED – .177, .20, .22, or .25 cal., PCP, semi-full auto, 19 in. rifled barrel, 10-shot mag., repeater, hardwood stock with checkering on grip and forend, two stage trigger, manual safety, 42 in. OAL, 8.6 lbs. New 2012.

courtesy Air Venturi

MSR $1,600	$1,350	$1,200	$1,100	$875	$675	N/A	N/A

Add $80 for .25 cal.

TACTICAL SNIPER – .22, .25, .357, or .45 cal., PCP, side lever cocking, 11 (.22 cal.), 10 (.25 cal.), 7 (.357 cal.) or 6 (.45 cal.) shot rotary mag. repeater, 18.5 in. shrouded barrel with threaded muzzle, 1200/910/800/720 FPS, 290cc cylinder, built-in manometer, blue finish, two-stage adj. trigger, ambidextrous metal stock with finger grooves and textured pistol grip, adj. butt stock, cheekpiece and forearm, and Weaver accessory/optics rail, manual safety, 46 in. OAL, 8.4 lbs. Mfg. 2014-current.

courtesy Air Venturi

MSR $1,200	$1,025	$900	$825	$650	$500	N/A	N/A

Add $100 for .25 cal.
Add $200 for .357 cal.
Add $290 for .45 cal.

WINDY CITY – .177 or .22 cal., PCP, side-lever action, new compact design (2012), 13 (.177 cal.) or 11 (.22 cal.) shot mag., 480cc removable cylinder, 1200/995 FPS, 18.5 in. barrel, walnut or Sepatia hardwood thumbhole stock, 37.5 in. OAL, 6 lbs. 12 oz. Mfg. 2010-2013.

	$1,025	$875	$725	$600	$450	$300	$205

Last MSR was $1,200.

This model is also available with a traditional rear bolt action with a buffalo horn ball (Windy City RB), or a side bolt action with a buffalo horn ball (Windy City SB).

GRADING	100%	95%	90%	80%	60%	40%	20%

WINDY CITY II – .177, .22, .25, or .357 cal., PCP, side-lever action, 13 (.177 cal.), 11 (.22 cal.), 10 (.25 cal.) or 7 (.357 cal.) shot mag., 17.25 in. barrel, 1200/995/940/730 FPS, 480cc removable cylinder, built-in manometer, ambidextrous Sepatia hardwood thumbhole stock, 41.75 in. OAL, 7.85 lbs. Mfg. 2014-current.

courtesy Air Venturi

MSR $1,395	$1,175	$1,050	$950	$775	$575	N/A	N/A

Add $100 for .25 cal.
Add $255 for .357 cal.

EXCELLENT

Previous manufacturer, AB Vapenfabriken Exellent of Stockholm, Sweden was formed by A.L. Blomen, P.S. Everlöf and G.S. Appequist in the early 1900s. The authors and publisher wish to thank several Swedish collectors for providing the following information that was organized by Mr. Ingvar Alm.

The patent on their first pneumatic rifle was granted circa 1904 and their patent on the CO_2 rifle was granted circa 1908. In 1941 AB Vapenfabriken Exellent was acquired by Adolf M. Arnnheim (name changed to Excellent Geväret AB) and was sold in 1963 to Peter Odendfeldt. Manufacturing ended circa 1970 after approximately 38,000 total rifles and 8,700 pistols were produced. Some dates and production numbers are difficult to establish due to the lack of surviving historical data, and in these cases they have been approximated. Approximate pistol production 1946-1959 was 8,700, approximate rifle production was as follows; 1905-1943 - 8,000 rifles, 1943-1945 - 5,000 rifles, 1945-1970 - 25,000 rifles.

Note: Roman numeral markings were started after 1941 and lasted until the end of production. Additional research is underway concerning this group, and any updates will be available through online subscriptions and in future editions.

PISTOLS

EXCELLENT AIRPISTOL MODEL – 4.5mm pellet cal., TL, concentric SP, SS, 8.1 in. rifled steel barrel marked "EXCELLENT pat. Made in Sweden", blue finish, adj. trigger, no safety, press checkered wood grip, 8.5 in. OAL, 2 lbs. Approx. 3,900 mfg. circa 1946-1959. Ref: AGNR Apr. 1989.

courtesy Beeman Collection

N/A	$450	$350	$295	$225	$160	$90

Add 30% for factory box.

Marketed as the Model 1950 circa 1950-1959. Three different boxes noted; 1946-1949 brown w/printing, 1950 red w/printing, and 1950-1959 green w/decal.

GRADING	100%	95%	90%	80%	60%	40%	20%

PHANTOM MODEL – .173 (4.4mm) steel balls cal., UL, concentric SP, ten shot mag. repeater, smoothbore barrel, zinc metal die-cast frame, marked "Phantom Repeater 4.4 Excellent Geväret AB Stockholm", adj. trigger, checkered plastic grips, no safety, 7.1 in. OAL, 1.5 lbs. Approx. 4,800 mfg. 1953-1959.

courtesy Höger Collection

	N/A	$650	$525	$425	$325	$230	$130

Add 50% for factory box.

Design flaw resulted in very low survival rate.

RIFLES

MODEL AE – .22 cal., multi-stroke pneumatic, in-line pump, rifled bore, swing breech, folded/rolled metal barrel jacket w/brass insert, marked AE w/serial number on breech and Fabrik Excellent Patent on barrel, SG hardwood stock w/metal butt plate, adj. rear sight, 34.84 in. OAL, 2.5 lbs. Mfg. 1905-1912.

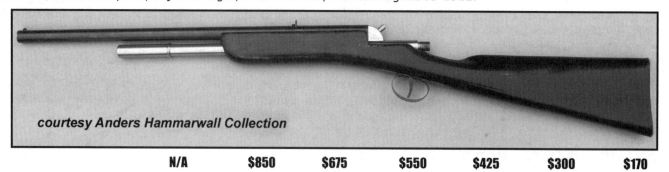

courtesy Anders Hammarwall Collection

	N/A	$850	$675	$550	$425	$300	$170

MODEL AS – .22 cal., multi-stroke pneumatic, in-line pump, smooth bore, swing breech, folded/rolled metal barrel jacket w/brass insert, marked AS w/serial number on breech and Fabrik Excellent Patent on barrel, SG hardwood stock w/metal butt plate, adj. rear sight, 34.84 in. OAL, 2.5 lbs. Mfg. 1905-1912.

	N/A	$850	$675	$550	$425	$300	$170

The physical appearance of this model is identical to Model AE.

MODEL BR – 5.5mm (for 5.4mm lead balls only) cal., multi-stroke pneumatic, in-line pump w/knurled nickel pump handle, paragon rifled bore, swing breech, detent screw, solid blue steel barrel, part octagon and part round, marked AB Vapenfabrik Excellent Stockholm BR on barrel, SG hardwood stock w/cheek piece and metal butt plate, adj. rear sight, 38.38 in. OAL, 2.6 lbs. Mfg. 1908-1912.

courtesy Beeman Collection

	N/A	$600	$475	$400	$300	$210	$120

This model is similar to BACHO marked rifles produced circa 1909.

GRADING	100%	95%	90%	80%	60%	40%	20%

MODEL BO – 5.5mm (for 5.4mm lead balls or darts) cal., multi stroke pneumatic, in-line pump w/knurled nickel pump handle, smooth bore, swing breech, detent screw, solid blue steel barrel, part octagon and part round, marked AB Vapenfabrik Excellent Stockholm BO on barrel, SG hardwood stock w/cheek piece and metal butt plate, adj. rear sight, 38.38 in. OAL, 2.6 lbs. Mfg. 1908-1912.

	N/A	$600	$475	$400	$300	$210	$120

The physical appearance of this model is identical to Model BR.

MODEL C1 – 5.5mm (for 5.4mm lead balls or darts) cal., multi stroke pneumatic, in-line pump w/knurled nickel (1912-1916) or grooved wood (1916-1941) pump handle, smooth bore, swing breech, detent screw, solid blue steel barrel, part octagon and part round, marked Excellent Made in Sweden and C1 on barrel, SG walnut stock with (1912-1916) or without (1916-1941) cheek piece and metal butt plate, adj. rear sight, 38.94 in. OAL, 4.6 lbs. Mfg. 1912-1941.

	N/A	$600	$475	$400	$300	$210	$120

The physical appearance of this model is identical to the Model BR.

MODEL C2 – 5.5mm (for 5.4mm lead balls only) cal., multi stroke pneumatic, in-line pump w/knurled nickel (1912-1916) or grooved wood (1916-1941) pump handle, paragon rifled bore, swing breech, detent screw, solid blue steel barrel, part octagon and part round, marked Excellent Made in Sweden and C2 on barrel, SG walnut stock with (1912-1916) or without (1916-1941) cheek piece and metal butt plate, adj. rear sight, 38.94 in. OAL, 4.6 lbs. Mfg. 1912-1941.

	N/A	$600	$475	$400	$300	$210	$120

Add 20% for early version with checkered metal slide handle.

The physical appearance of this model is identical to the Model BR.

MODEL C3 – 5.5mm (for 5.4mm lead balls only) cal., multi stroke pneumatic, in-line pump w/knurled nickel pump handle, paragon rifled bore, Mauser type bolt breech with safety, detent screw, solid blue steel barrel, part octagon and part round, marked Excellent Made in Sweden and C3 on barrel, SG walnut stock with cheek piece and metal butt plate, adj. rear sight, 43.30 in. OAL, 5.7 lbs. Mfg. 1907-1912.

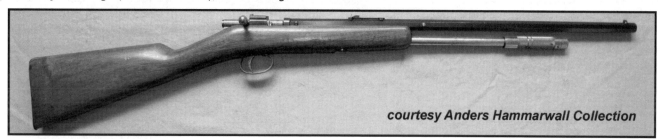

courtesy Anders Hammarwall Collection

Scarcity precludes accurate pricing.

MODEL C4 – 6.5mm (for darts) cal., CO_2, twist breech, smooth bore octagon barrel, adj. sights, SG walnut stock with cheek piece and steel butt plate, 43.3 in. OAL, 5.5 lbs. Mfg. circa 1908-1915.

Scarcity precludes accurate pricing.

This model was manufactured for traveling shooting galleries.

MODEL C5 – 5.5mm (for 5.4mm lead balls only) cal., CO_2, twist breech, paragon rifled octagon steel barrel w/detent screw, SG walnut stock w/cheek piece, 43.30 in. OAL, 5.5 lbs. Mfg. circa 1910-1915.

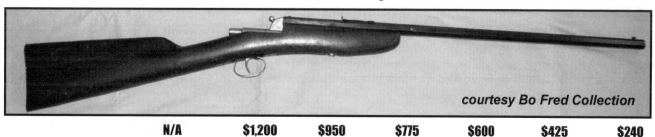

courtesy Bo Fred Collection

	N/A	$1,200	$950	$775	$600	$425	$240

This model was manufactured for indoor shooting galleries and clubs.

GRADING	100%	95%	90%	80%	60%	40%	20%

MODEL C6 – 5.5mm (for 5.4mm lead balls only) cal., CO_2, Mauser type bolt breech w/safety, paragon rifled octagon steel barrel w/detent screw, SG walnut stock w/cheek piece, 43.30 in. OAL, 5.5 lbs. Mfg. circa 1910-1915.

courtesy Anders Hammarwall Collection

Scarcity precludes accurate pricing.

MODEL CF (EARLY PRODUCTION) – 4.5mm cal., BBC, SP, SS, rifled steel BBL, very small pistol grip hardwood stock w/steel butt plate, 2 in. tang extending from compression tube into stock, marked Excellent Mod CF on compression tube, 38.18 in. OAL, 4.62 lbs. Mfg. 1933-1949.

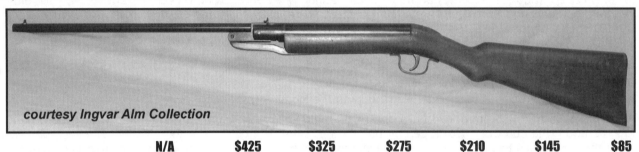

courtesy Ingvar Alm Collection

	N/A	$425	$325	$275	$210	$145	$85

MODEL CF R (LATE PRODUCTION) – 4.5mm cal., BBC, SP, SS, rifled steel BBL, PG hardwood stock w/steel butt plate, marked Excellent Mod CF R on barrel, Excellent decal on LH side of stock, 37.79 in. OAL, 4.95 lbs. Mfg. 1949-1959.

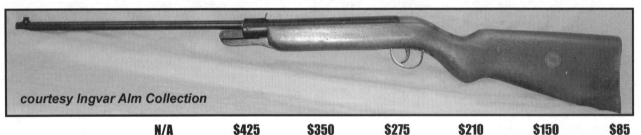

courtesy Ingvar Alm Collection

	N/A	$425	$350	$275	$210	$150	$85

MODEL CF S (LATE PRODUCTION) – 4.5mm cal., BBC, SP, SS, rifled steel BBL, PG hardwood stock w/steel butt plate, marked Excellent Mod CF S on barrel, Excellent decal on LH side of stock, 37.79 in. OAL, 4.95 lbs. Mfg. 1949-1959.

	N/A	$425	$350	$275	$210	$150	$85

The physical appearance of this model is identical to the Model CF R (Late Production).

MODEL CG – 4.5mm cal., BBC, SP, SS, rifled steel BBL, PG hardwood stock, marked Carl Gustaf Stads Gevärsfactori Sweden & Royal Crown, Excellent decal on stock, 38.77 in. OAL, 4.95 lbs. Mfg. 1962-1970.

	N/A	$300	$240	$195	$150	$105	$60

MODEL CI – 5.4mm (for 5.4mm round balls or darts (1967-1971)) cal., multi-pump pneumatic, swing breech, smoothbore round step down in diameter barrel, blue finish, adj. rear sights, PG beech stock, multi-grooved pump handle, marked Excellent Geväret Mod I, yellow w/blue print decal on stock, 38.2 in. OAL, 4.73 lbs. Mfg. 1946-1971.

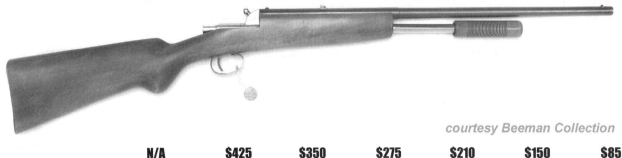

courtesy Beeman Collection

	N/A	$425	$350	$275	$210	$150	$85

GRADING	100%	95%	90%	80%	60%	40%	20%

MODEL CII – 5.4mm (for 5.4mm lead balls only) cal., multi-pump pneumatic, swing breech, paragon rifled barrel, round step down in diameter barrel, blue finish, adj. rear sights, PG beech stock, multi-grooved pump handle, marked Excellent Gevӓret Mod II, yellow w/blue print decal on stock, 38.2 in. OAL, 4.73 lbs. Mfg. 1946-1966.

	N/A	$425	$350	$275	$210	$150	$85

The physical appearance of this model is identical to Model CI.

MODEL CII K – 5.4mm (for 5.4mm lead balls only) cal., multi-pump pneumatic, rotating tap loader, paragon rifled barrel, round step down in diameter barrel, blue finish, adj. rear sights, PG beech stock, multi-grooved pump handle, marked Excellent Gevӓret Mod CII K, yellow w/blue print decal on stock, 38.2 in. OAL, 4.73 lbs. Mfg. 1953-1967.

courtesy Ingvar Alm Collection

	N/A	$425	$350	$275	$210	$150	$85

This model was also produced with match stock and trigger guard cocking.

MODEL F1 – 4.5mm cal., TL, SP, SS, twist and slide barrel breech, smoothbore steel barrel, blue finish, marked F1 Excellent Made in Sweden, patent on barrel, hardwood stock w/steel butt plate, 38.1 in., 4.73 lbs. Mfg. circa 1920-22.

	N/A	$950	$750	$625	$475	$325	$190

MODEL F2 (TRIGGERGUARD COCKING) – 4.5mm cal., UL (trigger gaurd cocking), SP, SS, twist and slide barrel breech, smoothbore steel barrel, blue finish, marked F2 Excellent Made in Sweden, Patent on barrel, hardwood stock, 38.77 in. OAL, 4.62 lbs. Mfg. circa 1922.

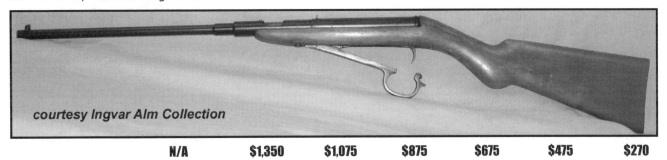

courtesy Ingvar Alm Collection

	N/A	$1,350	$1,075	$875	$675	$475	$270

MODEL F2-TL (TOPLEVER COCKING) – 4.5mm cal., TL, SP, SS, twist and slide barrel breech w/locking ring, smoothbore steel barrel, blue finish, marked F2 Excellent Made in Sweden, patent on barrel, hardwood stock w/steel butt plate, 39.56 in. OAL, 4.73 lbs. Mfg. circa 1922-1924.

courtesy Beeman Collection

	N/A	$850	$675	$550	$425	$300	$170

Early production was similar to the Model F1, later production has breech with bolt handle.

GRADING	100%	95%	90%	80%	60%	40%	20%

MODEL F3 – 4.5mm cal., SS, SP, TL, tap loading, smoothbore steel barrel, blue or nickel finish, hardwood stock w/ steel butt plate, 38.97 in. OAL, 4.62 lbs. Mfg. circa 1925-1926.

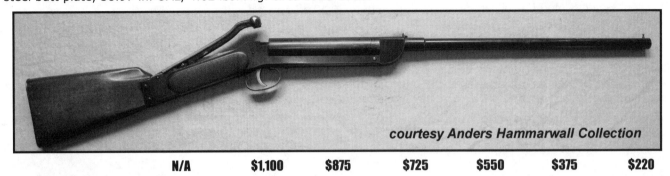

courtesy Anders Hammarwall Collection

N/A	$1,100	$875	$725	$550	$375	$220

MODEL MATCH – 5.4mm (for 5.4mm lead balls only) cal., multi-pump pneumatic, trigger guard cocking action, repeater, rotary tap loading from 10-shot magazine, paragon rifled barrel, round barrel, blue finish, adj. rear sights, scope rail, PG beech stock, flat sided pump handle, marked Excellent Match on top of scope rail, Excellent decal on stock, 38.2 in. OAL, 5.83 lbs. Mfg. 1966-1970.

courtesy Beeman Collection

N/A	$600	$475	$400	$300	$210	$120

F SECTION

FARAC (FABRICA ARGENTINA DE RIFLER DE AIR COMPRIMIDO)

Previous manufacturer of spring piston airguns located in Buenos Aires, Argentina circa 1990s.

GRADING	100%	95%	90%	80%	60%	40%	20%

RIFLES

SUPER VALIANT – .22 lead ball cal., SP, UL, vertical loading tap with tubular magazine, blue finish, hardwood stock, 42.6 in. OAL, 9.6 lbs.

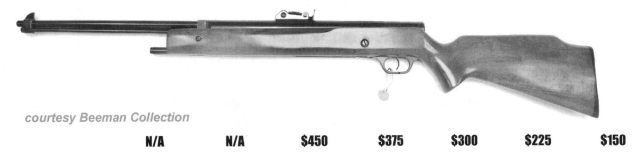

courtesy Beeman Collection

	100%	95%	90%	80%	60%	40%	20%
	N/A	N/A	$450	$375	$300	$225	$150

FAS

Current manufacturer located in Milan, Italy. Currently imported by Airguns of Arizona, located in Gilbert, AZ. Previously imported by Beeman, then located in Santa Rosa, CA, by Nygord Products, located in Prescott, AZ, and by Top Gun Air Guns Inc., located in Scottsdale, AZ.

For more information and current pricing on both new and used FAS firearms, please refer to the *Blue Book of Gun Values* by S.P. Fjestad (also available online).

PISTOLS

FAS 400 – .177 cal., TL, SSP, similar to Model 604, except without dry fire feature.

	100%	95%	90%	80%	60%	40%	20%
	$195	$165	$135	$115	$90	$60	$40

Add 20% for factory box and manual.

FAS 604 (STANDARD) – .177 cal., TL, SSP, adj. trigger, adj. sights, target model.

courtesy Beeman Collection

	100%	95%	90%	80%	60%	40%	20%
MSR $795	$675	$600	$550	$425	$325	N/A	N/A

FAS 604 (MATCH) – .177 cal., TL, SSP, adj. trigger, adj. sights, target model.

	100%	95%	90%	80%	60%	40%	20%
MSR $895	$750	$675	$600	$500	$375	N/A	N/A

Add $75 for left hand grip.

FAS 606 – .177 cal., TL, SSP, 7.5 in. barrel, adj. trigger, adj. sights, UIT target model, walnut grips, 2 lbs. 3 oz. Disc. 1994.

	100%	95%	90%	80%	60%	40%	20%
	$400	$325	$275	$230	$180	$120	$80

Add 20% for factory box and manual.

FAS 609 – .177 cal., PCP, 7.5 in. barrel, adj. trigger, adj. sights, UIT target model, adj. walnut grips. New 1997.

	100%	95%	90%	80%	60%	40%	20%
MSR $1,295	$1,100	$975	$875	$700	$550	N/A	N/A

Add $75 for left hand grip.

GRADING	100%	95%	90%	80%	60%	40%	20%

FB RECORD (BARTHELMS, FRITZ)

Current manufacturer located in Heidenheim-Oggenhausen, Germany.

Founded by Fritz Barthelms in 1948 and now owned by his son, Martin Barthelms. Production of airguns began in the late 1960s. The specialty of the company is producing economical air pistols using alloy and plastic casting methods that have minimal labor involvement. Annual production in the mid-1980s was about 40,000 air pistols, produced by only twenty workers.

In the 1980s, the Record brand began to include more substantial and interesting air pistols. The little, strangely named Jumbo features one of the most interesting mechanisms in the airgun field, a very compact concentric piston design. The extremely unexpected oval profile of the piston forces perfect piston alignment.

PISTOLS

FB RECORD LP 1 – .177 cal., smoothbore, SP, BBC, SS, fixed sights, brown plastic grips with RH thumbrest, no safety, 10.9 in. OAL, 1.6 lbs.

	100%	95%	90%	80%	60%	40%	20%
	$40	$35	$30	$25	$20	$15	$10

FB RECORD LP 2 – .177 cal., rifled, SP, BBC, SS, adj. sights, white plastic grips with RH thumbrest, no safety, 11.5 in. OAL, 1.7 lbs.

courtesy Beeman Collection

	100%	95%	90%	80%	60%	40%	20%
	$50	$45	$40	$35	$30	$25	$20

FB RECORD LP 3 – .177 cal., rifled, SP, BBC, SS, adj. sights, brown plastic grips with RH thumbrest, no safety, 11.5 in. OAL, 1.9 lbs.

	100%	95%	90%	80%	60%	40%	20%
	$60	$55	$45	$40	$35	$30	$25

FB RECORD 68 – .177 cal., rifled, SP, BBC, SS, adj. sights, brown plastic grips with RH thumbrest, no safety, 14.6 in. OAL, 3.1 lbs.

	100%	95%	90%	80%	60%	40%	20%
	$90	$80	$70	$55	$50	$30	$25

FB RECORD 77 – .177 cal., rifled, SP, BBC, SS, adj. sights, tan plastic grip with RH thumbrest, trigger guard and bar molded in front of grip, ventilated rib on barrel, anti-bear trap, no safety, 12.4 in. OAL, 2.1 lbs.

courtesy Beeman Collection

	100%	95%	90%	80%	60%	40%	20%
	$65	$60	$50	$45	$40	$30	$25

GRADING	100%	95%	90%	80%	60%	40%	20%

FB RECORD CHAMPION – .177 cal., SP, TL, SS, styling like Beeman P1 or BSA 240, blue finish, hardwood grips, 6 in. round barrel. Mfg. 2001-Disc.

courtesy Beeman Collection

N/A	$200	$150	$95	$65	$55	$45

FB RECORD JUMBO – .177 cal., 260 FPS, rifled, TL, SS, oval-shaped concentric piston, fixed sights, contoured walnut grips, may be marked with "Mauser U90/U91", 7.3 in. OAL, 1.9 lbs. Mfg. 1982-1997.

courtesy Beeman Collection

$150	$125	$100	$75	$60	$50	$35

Add 10% for Target model, adj. sights (new 1983).
Add 10% for Deluxe model with oakleaf carving on walnut grips.

This air pistol is very compact, well balanced, may be marked with "Mauser U90/U91" (not made by Mauser). Previously imported by Beeman Precision Airguns, then located in San Rafael, CA.

FEG

Current manufacturer located in Hungary (FEG stands for Fegyver es Gepgyar) since circa 1900. Previously imported by K.B.I. Inc. (formerly Kassnar Imports). Dealer sales.

Research is ongoing with this trademark, and more information will be included both in future editions and online. For more information and current pricing on both new and used FEG firearms, please refer to the *Blue Book of Gun Values* by S.P. Fjestad (also available online).

PISTOLS

MODEL GPM-01 – .177 cal., CO_2 cartridge or bulk fill, 425 FPS, 10.25 in. barrel, 2 lbs. 7 oz.

MSR $525	$450	$400	$350	$290	$220	N/A	N/A

The Model GPM-01 has been imported as the Daisy Model 91.

RIFLES

CLG-62 – .177 cal., match rifle. Disc.

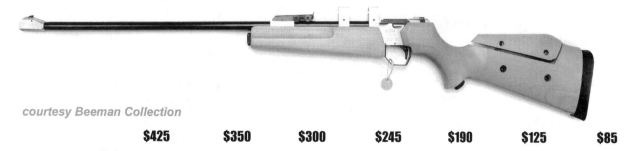

courtesy Beeman Collection

$425	$350	$300	$245	$190	$125	$85

GRADING	100%	95%	90%	80%	60%	40%	20%

CLG-462 – .177 or .22 cal., CO_2 cartridge or cylinder charge, 490/410 FPS, 16.5 or 24 (.22 cal. only) in. barrel, 5 lbs. 8 oz.

	$400	$350	$280	$230	$180	$120	$80

Last MSR was $550.

CLG-468 – .177 or .22 cal., CO_2 cartridge or cylinder charge, 705/525 FPS, 26.75 in. barrel, 5 lbs. 12 oz.

	$450	$375	$325	$260	$205	$135	$90

Last MSR was $600.

F.I.E.

Previous importer (F.I.E. is the acronym for Firearms Import & Export) located in Hialeah, FL until 1990.

For more information and current pricing on F.I.E. firearms, please refer to the *Blue Book of Gun Values* by S.P. Fjestad (also available online).

PISTOLS

TIGER – .177 cal., BBC, SP, SS, black enamel finish, black plastic grip frame, marked "Made in Italy" (believed by Gun Toys), 12.6 in. OAL, 1.7 lbs.

courtesy Beeman Collection

	$50	$45	$40	$35	$30	N/A	N/A

Add 10% for factory box with new targets.

Factory box bears the letters "MAM" in raised foam, thus probably eliminating Mondial as the maker, as their initials are MMM.

FLZ

For information on FLZ air pistols, see Langenhan in the "L" section.

FX AIRGUNS AB

Current manufacturer located in Hova, Sweden. Currently imported and distributed by Airguns of Arizona located in Gilbert, AZ. Previously located in Mesa, AZ. Dealer and consumer direct sales.

PISTOLS

RANCHERO – .177 or .22 cal., PCP, biathlon style BA, removable 8-shot rotary mag., 8.5 in. Lothar Walther match grade free floating barrel, blue finish, two-stage adj. trigger, walnut stock and grip or black synthetic stock with soft touch panels (new 2012), side lever hammer (new 2012), grooved receiver for scope mounting, adj. power, built-in pressure gauge, removable air cylinder, quick charge system, straight pull cocking system with thumb return, also includes hard plastic carrying case (new 2012), 18 in. OAL, 3.3 lbs. Mfg. 2006-current.

courtesy Precision Airgun Distribution

GRADING	100%	95%	90%	80%	60%	40%	20%
MSR $1,289	$1,100	$925	$775	$625	$500	N/A	N/A

RIFLES

For information on the FX2000, see Webley & Scott, Ltd. in the "W" section.

BIATHLON – .177 or .22 cal., side lever straight pull cocking system, SS, 19.7 in. FX smooth twist barrel, fully adj. black synthetic stock, fully adj. rubber recoil pad, adj. cheek piece, built-in pressure gauge, scope rail, front compensator and diopter sight option, adj. match grade trigger, thumb return safety, 39.8-40.7 in. OAL, 7.2 lbs.

> While advertised during 2012, this model was never imported into the U.S. Please contact the company directly for pricing and availability on this model.

BOBCAT – .177, .22, .25, or .30 cal., sidelever cocking action, 18 1/2 (.22 cal) or 24 in. shrouded barrel, full shroud muzzle, removable airtube, power adjustor wheel, 9, 11, 12, or 16 shot built-in magazine holder, quick fill adaptor, sound suppressing system, high strength synthetic thumbhole stock with large pressure gauge, adj. cheekpiece, extended scope rail, black finish, 29.5-37 in. OAL, 7.8-8 lbs. New 2014.

courtesy Airguns of Arizona

MSR $1,795	$1,500	$1,275	$1,050	$875	$675	$450	$300

BOSS – .30 cal., SS, sidelever cocking, 24 in. smooth twist barrel with shrouded muzzle, removable 9 shot mag., walnut or black synthetic thumbhole stock with adj. recoil pad, pressure regulated system, 500cc air capacity, manual safety, adj. match trigger, quick charge system, 47.5 in. OAL, 7.15 lbs. New 2013.

courtesy Airguns of Arizona

MSR $1,995	$1,700	$1,425	$1,175	$975	$750	$500	$350

Add $200 for walnut stock.

CUTLAS (SUPER SWIFT) – .177 or .22 cal., PCP, self-closing Biathlon style action, removable eight-shot rotary mag., 19.7 in. Lothar Walther match grade rifled, choked, free floating barrel, blue finish, two-stage adj. trigger, walnut thumbhole stock with adj. recoil pad, or black synthetic thumbhole stock with Weaver accessory rail, grooved receiver for scope mounting, external power adjuster, built-in pressure gauge, removable air cylinder, adj. recoil pad, forend Weaver-style accessory rail, built-in mag. holder, 40.5 in. OAL, 5.3 lbs. New 2004.

courtesy Airguns of Arizona

MSR $1,387	$1,175	$1,050	$950	$750	$575	N/A	N/A

Add $320 for walnut stock.

GRADING	100%	95%	90%	80%	60%	40%	20%

CYCLONE – .177 or .22 cal., PCP, biathlon style BA, removable eight-shot rotary mag., 19.7 in. Lothar Walther match grade choked free floating barrel, blue finish, two-stage adj. trigger, walnut stock with adj. recoil pad, or ambidextrous black synthetic stock with soft grip, grooved receiver for scope mounting, adj. power, built-in pressure gauge, removable air cylinder, adj. rubber recoil pad, straight pull cocking system with thumb return, 6.6 lbs.

courtesy Airguns of Arizona

MSR $1,395	$1,175	$1,000	$825	$675	$525	$350	$235

Add $154 for walnut stock.

GLADIATOR – .177 or .22 cal., PCP, dual air cylinders (butt stock and forearm) self-closing Biathlon style action, removable eight-shot rotary mag., 19.7 in. Lothar Walther match grade rifled free floating barrel, adj. power level, blue finish, two-stage adj. trigger, black pistol grip synthetic stock, adj. recoil pad, grooved receiver for scope mounting, external power adjuster, built-in pressure gauge, adj. bottle cover, 41.5 in. OAL, 7.8 lbs. Mfg. 2006-2013.

courtesy Precision Airgun Distribution

	$1,225	$1,100	$1,000	$800	$600	N/A	N/A

Last MSR was $1,455.

GLADIATOR MKII – .177, .22, or .25 cal., PCP, SL, SS, similar to the Gladiator, except has a new stock design making it comfortable for both left and right hand shooters, 11.8 in. FX smooth twist barrel, flat muzzle, whisper quiet shroud, black synthetic stock with ambidextrous adj. recoil pad, adj. bottle cover and cheek piece, removable 12-shot mag., adj. LOP, adj. two stage match trigger, removable front air cylinder, manual safety, 44.25 in. OAL, 8.5 lbs. Mfg. 2012-current.

courtesy Airguns of Arizona

MSR $1,695	$1,375	$1,175	$950	$800	$625	$400	$275

GRADING	100%	95%	90%	80%	60%	40%	20%

GLADIATOR TACTICAL – .22 cal., PCP, dual air cylinders (butt stock and forearm) self-closing Biathlon style action, eight-shot rotary mag., 19.7 in. Lothar Walther match grade free floating barrel with permanently affixed sound moderator, adj. power level, blue finish, two-stage adj. trigger, black pistol grip synthetic stock, grooved receiver for scope mounting, external power adjuster, built-in pressure gauge, 41.5 in. OAL, 7.8 lbs. Mfg. 2011-2013.

courtesy Precision Airgun Distribution

	$1,225	$1,100	$1,000	$800	$600	N/A	N/A

Last MSR was $1,455.

INDEPENDENCE (ROYALE INDEPENDENT) – .177, .22, or .25 cal., PCP with built-in high pressure pump, SL, 11, (.25 cal.), 12 (.22 cal.), or 16 (.177 cal.) shot mag., 19.5 in. smooth twist barrel, black synthetic thumbhole stock, adj. recoil pad, molded grooves on grip, large pressure gauge, adj. trigger, 43.5 in. OAL, approx. 8 lbs. Mfg. 2010-current.

courtesy Precision Airgun Distribution

MSR $1,799		$1,500	$1,275	$1,050	$875	$675	$450	$300

INDY – .22, .25, or .30 cal., sidelever cocking, hybrid bullpup action, Quick charge MKII system or build in pump, 18 1/2 (.22 cal.) or 24 in. barrel, 11, 12, or 16 shot removable mag., black synthetic stock with adj. cheekpiece, adj. recoil pad, high performance pressure gauge, manual safety, can also be fitted with the extreme arrow shooting system, 29.5-37 in. OAL, 8.7-9 lbs.

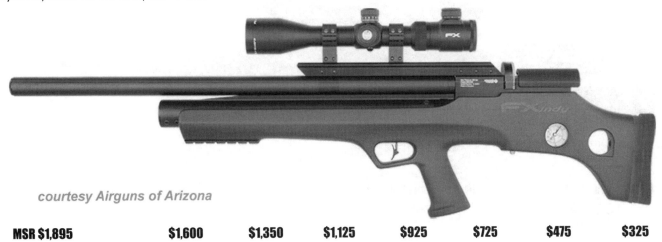

courtesy Airguns of Arizona

MSR $1,895		$1,600	$1,350	$1,125	$925	$725	$475	$325

GRADING	100%	95%	90%	80%	60%	40%	20%

MONSOON – .177 or .22 cal., PCP, semi-auto repeater, removable spring tensioned 12 shot mag., 19.7 in. Lothar-Walther Match grade fully shrouded barrel, blue finish, walnut or black synthetic thumbhole stock, adj. ventilated recoil pad, grooved receiver for scope mounting, disabling safety catch, adj. rubber recoil pad, manual bolt lever, 43 in. OAL, 6.6 lbs. Mfg. 2006-current.

courtesy Airguns of Arizona

MSR $1,595	$1,325	$1,125	$925	$775	$600	$400	$265

Add $200 for walnut stock.

RANCHERO CARBINE – .177 or .22 cal., PCP, biathlon style BA, eight-shot rotary mag., 8.5 in. Lothar Walther match grade barrel, blue finish, two-stage adj. trigger, ambidextrous walnut PG thumbhole stock, grooved receiver for scope mounting, adj. power, built-in pressure gauge, removable air cylinder, 27 in. OAL, 4.8 lbs. Mfg. 2009-current.

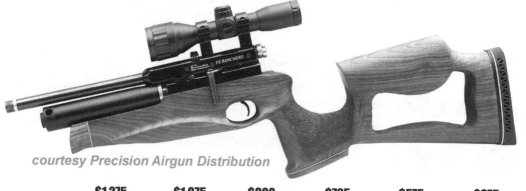

courtesy Precision Airgun Distribution

MSR $1,495	$1,275	$1,075	$900	$725	$575	$375	$255

REVOLUTION – .22 cal., PCP, semi-auto repeater, spring tensioned 12 shot mag., 19.25 in. Lothar Walther match grade rifled choked barrel, blue finish, black ambidextrous synthetic stock, grooved receiver for scope mounting, manual bolt lever, disabling safety catch, adj. bottle cover/cheek piece, adj. rubber recoil pad, removable air cylinder, 39.75 in. OAL, 7.7 lbs. Mfg. 2006-current.

courtesy Precision Airgun Distribution

MSR $1,895	$1,600	$1,350	$1,125	$925	$725	$475	$325

GRADING	100%	95%	90%	80%	60%	40%	20%

ROYALE 200 – .177, .22, or .25 cal., PCP, SL, 11, 12, or 16 shot removable mag. (depending on cal.), 19.68 in. FX smooth twist match-grade fully shrouded barrel, black ambidextrous synthetic stock, adj. recoil pad, removable cylinder, manual safety, 43.3 in. OAL, 7.3 lbs. New 2011.

courtesy Airguns of Arizona

MSR $1,585	$1,325	$1,125	$925	$775	$600	$400	$265

The Elite series which uses the Royale breech block with a single shot, direct barrel loading system is also available for this model. This loading platform allows the shooter to insert the pellet directly into the barrel.

ROYALE 200 FT – .177 or .22 cal., PCP, Field Target version of the Royale 200, 19 1/2 in. barrel, new fully adj. match trigger system, fully adj. alloy target stock with grip, cheek, butt, forend, and LOP adjustment allowing the shooter to fit the rifle to their style, precision regulator, multi-shot mag., Royale power wheel, sound moderator, and pressure gauge are standard, 41.75-45.75 in. OAL, 10.45 lbs. New 2013.

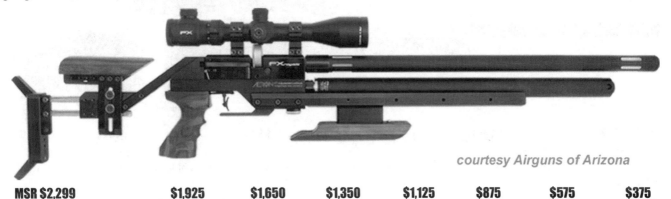

courtesy Airguns of Arizona

MSR $2,299	$1,925	$1,650	$1,350	$1,125	$875	$575	$375

ROYALE 400 – .177, .22, or .25 (new 2012) cal., PCP, BA, SL, 12 (.22 cal.) or 16 shot mag., 400 cc air bottle, 19.5 in. Lothar-Walther match grade rifled free floating barrel, shrouded muzzle, blue finish, checkered walnut or high quality black synthetic thumbhole stock, adj. recoil pad, grooved receiver for scope mounting, two-stage adj. match trigger, built-in pressure gauge and quick fill connector, removable air cylinder, 40.25 in. OAL, 6.5 (walnut stock) lbs. Mfg. 2010-current.

courtesy Airguns of Arizona

MSR $1,647	$1,350	$1,150	$950	$800	$600	$400	$270

Add $206 for walnut stock.
Add $452 for Royale 400 Sport model.

The Elite series which uses the Royale breech block with a single shot, direct barrel loading system is also available for this model. This loading platform allows the shooter to insert the pellet directly into the barrel.

GRADING	100%	95%	90%	80%	60%	40%	20%

ROYALE 400 FT – .177 or .22 cal., PCP, Field Target version of the Royale 400, 19 1/2 in. barrel, new fully adj. match trigger system, fully adj. alloy target stock with grip, cheek, butt, forend, and LOP adjustment allowing the shooter to fit the rifle to their style, precision regulator, multi-shot mag., Royale power wheel, sound moderator, and pressure gauge are standard, 38-42 in. OAL, 9.55 lbs. New 2013.

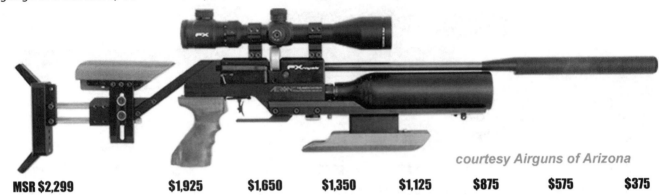

courtesy Airguns of Arizona

MSR $2,299	$1,925	$1,650	$1,350	$1,125	$875	$575	$375

ROYALE 500 – .25 cal., SL, PCP, BA, removable 11 shot mag., FX smooth twist match-grade barrel, 500 cc air bottle, shrouded muzzle, walnut or black synthetic thumbhole stock, adj. recoil pad, built-in pressure gauge and quick fill connector, adj. match-grade trigger, includes plastic case, 47 in. OAL. New 2011.

courtesy Airguns of Arizona

MSR $1,719	$1,400	$1,200	$975	$825	$625	$425	$280

Add $130 for walnut stock.

The Elite series which uses the Royale breech block with a single shot, direct barrel loading system is also available for this model. This loading platform allows the shooter to insert the pellet directly into the barrel.

ROYALE 500 FT – .25 cal., PCP, Field Target version of the Royale 500, side lever cocking action, 25.5 in. barrel, 3-step power adjustor, self-cycling magazine, new fully adj. match trigger system, fully adj. alloy target stock with grip, cheek, butt, forend, and LOP adjustment allowing the shooter to fit the rifle to their style, precision regulator, multi-shot mag., Royale power wheel, sound moderator, and pressure gauge are standard, 44.5-48.5 in. OAL, 10.3 lbs. New 2013.

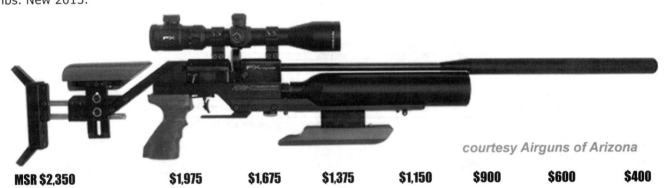

courtesy Airguns of Arizona

MSR $2,350	$1,975	$1,675	$1,375	$1,150	$900	$600	$400

TARANTULA (EXCALIBRE) – .177 or .22 cal., PCP, BA, eight-shot rotary mag., 19.7 in. Lothar Walther match grade barrel with threaded muzzle weight, blue finish, two-stage adj. trigger, checkered grade three hand rubbed oil finished Turkish Circassian walnut (Tarantula) stock, ventilated recoil pad, grooved receiver for scope mounting, adj. power, built-in pressure gauge, 39.5 in. OAL, 6 lbs. Disc. 2007.

	$1,200	$1,025	$825	$700	$525	$350	$240

Last MSR was $946.

Add 15% for grade four walnut stock.

GRADING	100%	95%	90%	80%	60%	40%	20%

TARANTULA SPORT – .177 or .22 cal., PCP, BA, eight-shot rotary mag., 19.7 in. Lothar Walther match grade barrel with threaded muzzle weight, blue finish, two-stage adj. trigger, grade two English (Webley) walnut or synthetic stock, ventilated recoil pad, grooved receiver for scope mounting, adj. power, built-in pressure gauge, 39.5 in. OAL. 6 lbs. Disc. 2006.

	$950	$800	$675	$550	$425	$285	$190

Last MSR was $815.

TIMBERWOLF – .22 cal., PCP, bolt action, two-shot mag., 19.7 in. Lothar Walther match grade barrel, blue finish, two-stage adj. trigger, checkered beech or grade two walnut stock, ventilated recoil pad, grooved receiver for scope mounting, adj. power, built-in pressure gauge, 6.5 lbs. Disc. 2005.

	$700	$600	$475	$400	$300	$210	$140

Last MSR was $578.

Add 30% for walnut stock.

TYPHOON – .177, .22, or .25 (new 2012) cal., PCP, BA, SS, 19.7 in. Lothar Walther match grade free-floating fully shrouded barrel, blue finish, lightweight black synthetic sporter or ambidextrous walnut stock, fully adj. rubber recoil pad, adj. cheek piece, adj. match trigger, grooved receiver for scope mounting, 41 in. OAL, 6.1-7.1 (walnut stock) lbs. Imported 2006-2013.

courtesy Precision Airgun Distribution

	$675	$600	$550	$425	$325	N/A	N/A

Last MSR was $795.

Add $194 for walnut stock.

T12 TYPHOON – .177, .22, or .25 (new 2012) cal., PCP, BA, 12 shot mag., 19.7 in. Lothar-Walther Match grade fully shrouded barrel, blue finish, black ambidextrous sporter lightweight synthetic or walnut stock, fully adj. ventilated rubber recoil pad, grooved receiver for scope mounting, two-stage adj. match trigger, 41 in. OAL, 6.1-7.1 (walnut stock) lbs. Imported 2006-2013.

	$725	$625	$525	$425	$325	$220	$145

Last MSR was $859.

Add $230 for walnut stock.

T12 WHISPER – .177, .22, or .25 (new 2012) cal., PCP, BA, 12 shot mag., 19.7 in. Lothar-Walther match-grade fully shrouded barrel, whispering barrel shroud, blue finish, ambidextrous thumbhole black synthetic or walnut stock, adj. ventilated rubber recoil pad, grooved receiver for scope mounting, two-stage adj. match trigger, built with highly restrained noise level for non-disturbing shooting, spring tensioned removable anodized aluminum magazine, 43 in. OAL, 6.2 (walnut stock) lbs. Mfg. 2010-current.

courtesy Precision Airgun Distribution

MSR $915	$775	$675	$550	$450	$350	$235	$155

Add $174 for walnut stock.

GRADING	100%	95%	90%	80%	60%	40%	20%

T12 400 – .177 or .22 cal., BA, 19 1/2 in. free-floating smooth twist barrel, 12 shot, built-in pressure gauge, MKII quick connector, two stage trigger, soft touch metallic surface, 400cc air capacity, removable air cylinder, ergonomic synthetic stock with ambidextrous cheekpiece, black finish, 39.75 in. OAL, 6.5 lbs. New 2013.

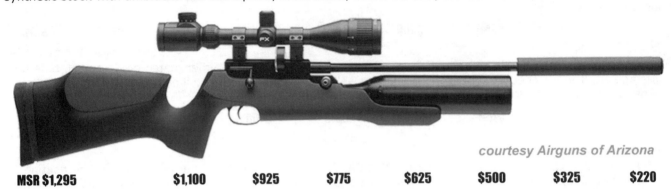

courtesy Airguns of Arizona

MSR $1,295	$1,100	$925	$775	$625	$500	$325	$220

ULTIMATE – .177 or .22 cal., PCP, pistol grip pump action, eight-shot rotary mag., 19.7 in. Lothar Walther match grade barrel, blue finish, two-stage adj. trigger, synthetic stock, grooved receiver for scope mounting, built-in pressure gauge, 6.6 lbs. Disc. 2007.

	$800	$675	$550	$450	$350	$240	$160

Last MSR was $729.

VERMINATOR – .177 or .22 cal., PCP, forearm pump action, removable 8-shot rotary mag., 8.27 in. FX smooth twist match grade free floating barrel, blue finish, two-stage adj. trigger, black pistol grip synthetic stock, grooved receiver for scope mounting, built-in pressure gauge, adj. bottle cover/cheek piece, muzzle thread for silencer, removable air bottle, includes compact hard case, 25.2-28.4 in. OAL, 5.3 lbs. Imported 2010-2013.

	$1,225	$1,100	$1,000	$800	$600	N/A	N/A

Last MSR was $1,455.

Add $150 for pistol adaptor.

VERMINATOR MKII – .177 or .22 cal., SL, takedown style rifle, 11.8 in. FX smooth twist match grade fully shrouded choked barrel with threaded muzzle, adj. match grade trigger, black synthetic stock with adj. ambidextrous recoil pad, adj. bottle cover and cheek piece, removable 12-shot mag., 400 cc air cylinder, super efficient valve system, 3-step power adjuster, includes compact hard case, 29.5-31.5 in. OAL, 6.4 lbs. New 2012.

courtesy Airguns of Arizona

MSR $1,699	$1,400	$1,175	$975	$800	$625	$425	$280

GRADING	100%	95%	90%	80%	60%	40%	20%

VERMINATOR MK II EXTREME – .177 or .22 cal., side lever cocking, quick charge system, 11.8 and 19.7 in. FX smooth twist barrel with threaded muzzle and shroud extension, allowing the shooter to switch between short and long barrels with no tools required, pressure gauge, adj. match trigger, 400 cc removable air cylinder, black synthetic stock with adj. recoil pad, power adjuster, removable 12-shot magazine, manual safety, also includes compact hard case, FX scope mounted with quick change mounts, bipod and mount, torch and mount, a special barrel that will shoot arrows, target and hunting arrows with a special arrow for line shooting or spear fishing, and a fishing reel and mount, 21.5-31.5 in. OAL (depending on barrel), 6.4 lbs. Mfg. 2012-current.

courtesy Airguns of Arizona

MSR $2,495	$2,125	$1,800	$1,475	$1,225	$950	$625	$425

XTERMINATOR – .177 or .22 cal., PCP, forearm pump action, eight-shot rotary mag., 19.7 in. Lothar Walther match grade barrel, blue finish, two-stage adj. trigger, synthetic stock, grooved receiver for scope mounting, built-in pressure gauge, 4.4 lbs. Mfg. 2007-2010.

courtesy Precision Airgun Distribution

$1,275	$1,075	$900	$750	$575	N/A	N/A

Last MSR was $1,505.

FALCON AIRGUNS

Current trademark manufactured by NSP Developments and Manufacturing Ltd. located in East Sussex, England. Previously manufactured by Falcon Pneumatic Systems Limited located in East Sussex, England and previously located in Birmingham, England. No current U.S. importation. Previously imported 2011-2013 by Air Venturi, located in Warrensville Hts., OH. Previously imported and distributed until 2011 by Airhog Inc. located in Cedar Crest, NM. Dealer and consumer direct sales.

Falcon Airguns was bought by NSP Developments and Manufacturing Ltd. in 2005. Falcon Pneumatic Systems had been manufacturing air guns since 1993, when it took over air gun production from Titan Enterprises. NSP is an engineering company who have been trading for some 30 plus years and have vast experience in the manufacture of air rifles as Air-Arms. The Falcon name was also used by Beeman for economy-level Spanish air rifles. See Beeman in the "B" section.

PISTOLS

HAWK PISTOL MODEL FN6-PGH – .177 or .22 cal., PCP, 8-shot mag., 6 in. Walther rifled barrel, grooved receiver for adj. rear sight or scope, high gloss blue finish, checkered hardwood grip, 12-15 in. OAL, 2.9-3.3 lbs. Importation disc. 2004.

$575	$500	$400	$325	$260	$170	$115

Last MSR was $650.

Add $30 for left-hand variation.
Add 10% for open front and adj. rear sights.

GRADING	100%	95%	90%	80%	60%	40%	20%

HAWK PISTOL MODEL FN6-WGH – .177 or .22 cal., PCP, 8-shot mag., 6 in. Walther rifled barrel, grooved receiver for adj. rear sight or scope, high gloss blue finish, walnut with stippled palm swell grip, 12-15 in. OAL, 2.9-3.3 lbs. Importation disc. 2004.

	100%	95%	90%	80%	60%	40%	20%
	$675	$575	$475	$400	$300	$200	$135

Last MSR was $767.

Add $30 for left-hand variation.
Add 10% for open front and adj. rear sights.

HAWK PISTOL MODEL FN8-PGH – .177 or .22 cal., PCP, eight-shot mag., 8 in. Walther rifled barrel, grooved receiver for adj. rear sight or scope, high gloss blue finish, checkered hardwood grip, 12-15 in. OAL, 2.9-3.3 lbs. Importation disc. 2011.

	100%	95%	90%	80%	60%	40%	20%
	$575	$500	$400	$325	$260	$170	$115

Last MSR was $650.

Add $30 for left-hand variation.
Add 10% for open front and adj. rear sights.

HAWK PISTOL MODEL FN8-WGH – .177 or .22 cal., PCP, eight-shot mag., 8 in. Walther rifled barrel, grooved receiver for adj. rear sight or scope, high gloss blue finish, walnut with stippled palm swell grip, 12-15 in. OAL, 2.9-3.3 lbs. Importation disc. 2011.

	100%	95%	90%	80%	60%	40%	20%
	$675	$575	$475	$400	$300	$200	$135

Last MSR was $767.

Add $30 for left-hand variation.
Add 10% for open front and adj. rear sights.

RAPTOR PISTOL MODEL FN6-PGR – .177 or .22 cal., PCP, eight-shot mag., 6 in. Walther rifled barrel, grooved receiver for adj. rear sight or scope, high gloss blue finish, checkered hardwood grip, 12-15 in. OAL, 2.9-3.3 lbs. Importation disc. 2004.

	100%	95%	90%	80%	60%	40%	20%
	$600	$500	$425	$350	$270	$180	$120

Last MSR was $664.

Add $30 for left-hand variation.
Add 10% for open front and adj. rear sights.

RAPTOR PISTOL MODEL FN6-WGR – .177 or .22 cal., PCP, eight-shot mag., 6 in. Walther rifled barrel, grooved receiver for adj. rear sight or scope, high gloss blue finish, walnut with stippled palm swell grip, 12-15 in. OAL, 2.9-3.3 lbs. Importation disc. 2004.

	100%	95%	90%	80%	60%	40%	20%
	$700	$600	$500	$400	$325	$210	$140

Last MSR was $787.

Add $30 for left-hand variation.
Add 10% for open front and adj. rear sights.

RAPTOR PISTOL MODEL FN8-PGR – .177 or .22 cal., PCP, eight-shot mag., 8 in. Walther rifled barrel, grooved receiver for adj. rear sight or scope, high gloss blue finish, walnut with stippled palm swell grip, 12-15 in. OAL, 2.9-3.3 lbs. Importation disc. 2011.

	100%	95%	90%	80%	60%	40%	20%
	$600	$500	$425	$350	$270	$180	$120

Last MSR was $664.

Add $30 for left-hand variation.
Add 10% for open front and adj. rear sights.

RAPTOR PISTOL MODEL FN8-WGR – .177 or .22 cal., PCP, eight-shot mag., 8 in. Walther rifled barrel, grooved receiver for adj. rear sight or scope, high gloss blue finish, walnut with stippled palm swell grip, 12-15 in. OAL, 2.9-3.3 lbs. Importation disc. 2011.

	100%	95%	90%	80%	60%	40%	20%
	$700	$600	$500	$400	$325	$210	$140

Last MSR was $787.

Add $30 for left-hand variation.
Add 10% for open front and adj. rear sights.

SINGLE SHOT PISTOL MODEL FN6-PG – .177, .20, or .22 cal., PCP, SS, 6 in. Walther rifled barrel, grooved receiver for adj. rear sight or scope, high gloss blue finish, checkered hardwood grip, 12-15.5 in. OAL, 2.7-3.1 lbs. Importation disc. 2004.

	100%	95%	90%	80%	60%	40%	20%
	$500	$425	$350	$290	$225	$150	$100

Last MSR was $554.

Add $30 for left-hand variation.
Add 10% for open front and adj. rear sights.

GRADING	100%	95%	90%	80%	60%	40%	20%

SINGLE SHOT PISTOL MODEL FN6-WG – .177, .20, or .22 cal., PCP, SS, 6 in. Walther rifled barrel, grooved receiver for adj. rear sight or scope, high gloss blue finish, walnut with stippled palm swell grip, 12-15.5 in. OAL, 2.7-3.1 lbs. Importation disc. 2004.

	$600	$500	$425	$350	$270	$180	$120

Last MSR was $672.

Add $30 for left-hand variation.
Add 10% for open front and adj. rear sights.

SINGLE SHOT PISTOL MODEL FN8-PG – .177, .20, or .22 cal., PCP, SS, 8 in. Walther rifled barrel, grooved receiver for adj. rear sight or scope, high gloss blue finish, checkered hardwood grip, 12-15.5 in. OAL, 2.7-3.1 lbs. Importation disc. 2011.

	$500	$425	$350	$290	$225	$150	$100

Last MSR was $554.

Add $30 for left-hand variation.
Add 10% for open front and adj. rear sights.

SINGLE SHOT PISTOL MODEL FN8-WG – .177, .20, or .22 cal., PCP, SS, 8 in. Walther rifled barrel, grooved receiver for adj. rear sight or scope, high gloss blue finish, walnut with stippled palm swell grip, 12-15.5 in. OAL, 2.7-3.1 lbs. Importation disc. 2011.

courtesy Loke Collection

	$600	$500	$425	$350	$270	$180	$120

Last MSR was $672.

Add $30 for left-hand variation.
Add 10% for open front and adj. rear sights.

RIFLES

CLASSIC FALCON SINGLE SHOT CARBINE MODEL FN12-LS – .177, .20, .22, or .25 cal., PCP, SS, 12 in. Walther rifled barrel, grooved receiver for adj. rear sight or scope, high gloss blue finish, laminate target with adj. cheek piece and adj. butt pad, 30-38 in. OAL, 4.8-5.1 lbs. Importation disc. 2011.

	$775	$650	$550	$450	$350	$230	$155

Last MSR was $924.

Add $30 for left-hand variation.
Add 10% for open front and adj. rear sights.

CLASSIC FALCON SINGLE SHOT CARBINE MODEL FN12-SB – .177, .20, .22, or .25 cal., PCP, SS, 12 in. Walther rifled barrel, grooved receiver for adj. rear sight or scope, high gloss blue finish, beech pistol grip sporter stock with checkered grip and forearm, ventilated butt pad, 30-38 in. OAL, 4.8-5.1 lbs. Importation disc. 2011.

	$575	$500	$400	$325	$260	$170	$115

Last MSR was $665.

Add $30 for left-hand variation.
Add 10% for open front and adj. rear sights.

CLASSIC FALCON SINGLE SHOT CARBINE MODEL FN12-SL – .177, .20, .22, or .25 cal., PCP, SS, 12 in. Walther rifled barrel, grooved receiver for adj. rear sight or scope, high gloss blue finish, laminate sporter stock, adj. butt pad, 30-38 in. OAL, 4.8-5.1 lbs. Importation disc. 2011.

	$700	$600	$500	$400	$325	$210	$140

Last MSR was $815.

Add $30 for left-hand variation.
Add 10% for open front and adj. rear sights.

GRADING	100%	95%	90%	80%	60%	40%	20%

CLASSIC FALCON SINGLE SHOT CARBINE MODEL FN12-SW – .177, .20, .22, or .25 cal., PCP, SS, 12 in. Walther rifled barrel, grooved receiver for adj. rear sight or scope, high gloss blue finish, walnut sporter stock with checkered grip and forearm, ventilated butt pad, 30-38 in. OAL, 4.8-5.1 lbs. Importation disc. 2011.

	100%	95%	90%	80%	60%	40%	20%
	$625	$525	$425	$350	$280	$185	$125

Last MSR was $748.

Add $30 for left-hand variation.
Add 10% for open front and adj. rear sights.

CLASSIC FALCON SINGLE SHOT CARBINE MODEL FN12-TW – .177, .20, .22, or .25 cal., PCP, SS, 12 in. Walther rifled barrel, grooved receiver for adj. rear sight or scope, high gloss blue finish, walnut thumbhole with stippled palm swell and forend, adj. butt pad, 30-38 in. OAL, 4.8-5.1 lbs. Importation disc. 2011.

	100%	95%	90%	80%	60%	40%	20%
	$725	$625	$500	$425	$325	$215	$145

Last MSR was $868.

Add $30 for left-hand variation.
Add 10% for open front and adj. rear sights.

CLASSIC FALCON SINGLE SHOT CARBINE MODEL LIGHTHUNTER 8L – .177, .20, .22, or .25 cal., PCP, SS, 8 in. Walther rifled barrel, grooved receiver for adj. rear sight or scope, high gloss blue finish, laminate beech skeleton pistol grip stock with adj. butt pad, 26.5 in. OAL, 4.5-4.8 lbs. Importation disc. 2011.

	100%	95%	90%	80%	60%	40%	20%
	$775	$650	$550	$450	$350	$230	$155

Last MSR was $924.

Add $30 for left-hand variation.
Add 10% for open front and adj. rear sights.

CLASSIC FALCON SINGLE SHOT CARBINE MODEL LIGHTHUNTER 12L – .177, .20, .22, or .25 cal., PCP, SS, 12 in. Walther rifled barrel, grooved receiver for adj. rear sight or scope, high gloss blue finish, laminate skeleton stock with adj. butt pad, 30-38 in. OAL, 4.8-5.1 lbs. Importation disc. 2011.

	100%	95%	90%	80%	60%	40%	20%
	$775	$650	$550	$450	$350	$230	$155

Last MSR was $924.

Add $30 for left-hand variation.
Add 10% for open front and adj. rear sights.

CLASSIC FALCON SINGLE SHOT CARBINE MODEL LIGHTHUNTER 8W – .177, .20, .22, or .25 cal., PCP, SS, 8 in. Walther rifled barrel, grooved receiver for adj. rear sight or scope, high gloss blue finish, checkered walnut beech skeleton pistol grip stock with adj. butt pad, 26.5 in. OAL, 4.5-4.8 lbs. Importation disc. 2011.

	100%	95%	90%	80%	60%	40%	20%
	$775	$650	$550	$450	$350	$230	$155

Last MSR was $894.

Add $30 for left-hand variation.
Add 10% for open front and adj. rear sights.

CLASSIC FALCON SINGLE SHOT CARBINE MODEL LIGHTHUNTER 12W – .177, .20, .22, or .25 cal., PCP, SS, 12 in. Walther rifled barrel, grooved receiver for adj. rear sight or scope, high gloss blue finish, walnut skeleton stock with adj. butt pad, 30-38 in. OAL, 4.8-5.1 lbs. Importation disc. 2011.

	100%	95%	90%	80%	60%	40%	20%
	$750	$625	$525	$425	$325	$225	$150

Last MSR was $894.

Add $30 for left-hand variation.
Add 10% for open front and adj. rear sights.

CLASSIC FALCON SINGLE SHOT RIFLE MODEL FN19-LS – .177, .20, .22, or .25 cal., PCP, SS, 19 in. Walther rifled barrel, grooved receiver for adj. rear sight or scope, high gloss blue finish, laminate skeleton stock with adj. butt pad, approx. 37.5 in. OAL, 5.8-6.5 lbs. Importation disc. 2011.

	100%	95%	90%	80%	60%	40%	20%
	$775	$650	$550	$450	$350	$230	$155

Last MSR was $924.

Add $30 for left-hand variation.
Add 10% for open front and adj. rear sights.

CLASSIC FALCON SINGLE SHOT RIFLE MODEL FN19-SB – .177, .20, .22, or .25 cal., PCP, SS, 19 in. Walther rifled barrel, grooved receiver for adj. rear sight or scope, high gloss blue finish, checkered beech pistol grip sporter stock, ventilated butt pad, approx. 37.5 in. OAL, 5.8-6.5 lbs. Importation disc. 2011.

	100%	95%	90%	80%	60%	40%	20%
	$575	$500	$400	$325	$260	$170	$115

Last MSR was $665.

Add $30 for left-hand variation.
Add 10% for open front and adj. rear sights.

GRADING	100%	95%	90%	80%	60%	40%	20%

CLASSIC FALCON SINGLE SHOT RIFLE MODEL FN19-SL – .177, .20, .22, or .25 cal., PCP, SS, 19 in. Walther rifled barrel, grooved receiver for adj. rear sight or scope, high gloss blue finish, laminate sporter stock, adj. butt pad, approx. 37.5 in. OAL, 5.8-6.5 lbs. Importation disc. 2011.

	100%	95%	90%	80%	60%	40%	20%
	$700	$600	$500	$400	$325	$210	$140

Last MSR was $815.

Add $30 for left-hand variation.
Add 10% for open front and adj. rear sights.

CLASSIC FALCON SINGLE SHOT RIFLE MODEL FN19-SW – .177, .20, .22, or .25 cal., PCP, SS, 19 in. Walther rifled barrel, grooved receiver for adj. rear sight or scope, high gloss blue finish, checkered walnut sporter pistol grip stock, ventilated butt pad, approx. 37.5 in. OAL, 5.8-6.5 lbs. Importation disc. 2011.

courtesy Howard Collection

	100%	95%	90%	80%	60%	40%	20%
	$625	$525	$425	$350	$280	$185	$125

Last MSR was $748.

Add $30 for left-hand variation.
Add 10% for open front and adj. rear sights.

CLASSIC FALCON SINGLE SHOT RIFLE MODEL FN19-TW – .177, .20, .22, or .25 cal., PCP, SS, 19 in. Walther rifled barrel, grooved receiver for adj. rear sight or scope, high gloss blue finish, walnut thumbhole stock with stippled palm swell and forend, adj. butt pad, approx. 37.5 in. OAL, 5.8-6.5 lbs. Importation disc. 2011.

	100%	95%	90%	80%	60%	40%	20%
	$725	$625	$500	$425	$325	$215	$145

Last MSR was $868.

Add $30 for left-hand variation.
Add 10% for open front and adj. rear sights.

CLASSIC FALCON SINGLE SHOT RIFLE MODEL FN19-WS – .177, .20, .22, or .25 cal., PCP, SS, 19 in. Walther rifled barrel, grooved receiver for adj. rear sight or scope, high gloss blue finish, walnut skeleton stock, adj. butt pad, approx. 37.5 in. OAL, 5.8-6.5 lbs. Importation disc. 2011.

	100%	95%	90%	80%	60%	40%	20%
	$750	$625	$525	$425	$325	$225	$150

Last MSR was $894.

Add $30 for left-hand variation.
Add 10% for open front and adj. rear sights.

HAWK CARBINE MODEL FN12-HB – .177, .20, .22, or .25 cal., PCP, 8-shot mag., 12 in. barrel, beech pistol grip sporter stock with checkered grip and forearm, vent. butt pad, grooved receiver for adj. rear sight or scope, high gloss blue finish, 30.5 in. OAL, 5.5-6.3 lbs. Disc. 2010.

	100%	95%	90%	80%	60%	40%	20%
	$675	$575	$475	$400	$300	$200	$135

Last MSR was $786.

Add 5% for left-hand variation.
Add 5% for open front and adj. rear sights.

HAWK CARBINE MODEL FN12-HL – .177, .20, .22, or .25 cal., PCP, 8-shot mag., 12 in. barrel, laminate skeleton stock, adj. butt pad, grooved receiver for adj. rear sight or scope, high gloss blue finish, 30.5 in. OAL, 5.5-6.3 lbs. Disc. 2010.

	100%	95%	90%	80%	60%	40%	20%
	$825	$700	$575	$475	$375	$245	$165

Last MSR was $982.

Add 5% for left-hand variation.
Add 5% for open front and adj. rear sights.

HAWK CARBINE MODEL FN12-HS – .177, .20, .22, or .25 cal., PCP, 8-shot mag., 12 in. barrel, walnut skeleton stock, grooved receiver for adj. rear sight or scope, high gloss blue finish, 30.5 in. OAL, 5.5-6.3 lbs. Disc. 2010.

	100%	95%	90%	80%	60%	40%	20%
	$775	$650	$550	$450	$350	$230	$155

Last MSR was $904.

Add 5% for left-hand variation.
Add 5% for open front and adj. rear sights.

GRADING	100%	95%	90%	80%	60%	40%	20%

HAWK CARBINE MODEL FN12-HT – .177, .20, .22, or .25 cal., PCP, 8-shot mag., 12 in. barrel, walnut thumbhole stock, adj. butt pad, grooved receiver for adj. rear sight or scope, high gloss blue finish, 30.5 in. OAL, 5.5-6.3 lbs. Disc. 2010.

	$800	$675	$550	$475	$350	$240	$160

Last MSR was $943.

Add 5% for left-hand variation.
Add 5% for open front and adj. rear sights.

HAWK CARBINE MODEL FN12-HW – .177, .20, .22, or .25 cal., PCP, 8-shot mag., 12 in. barrel, walnut sporter stock, adj. butt pad, grooved receiver for adj. rear sight or scope, high gloss blue finish, 30.5 in. OAL, 5.5-6.3 lbs. Disc. 2010.

	$725	$625	$500	$425	$325	$215	$145

Last MSR was $865.

Add 5% for left-hand variation.
Add 5% for open front and adj. rear sights.

HAWK RIFLE MODEL FN19-HB – .177, .20, .22, or .25 cal., PCP, 8-shot mag., 19 in. barrel, grooved receiver for adj. rear sight or scope, high gloss blue finish, checkered beech pistol grip sporter stock, ventilated butt pad, 37.5 in. OAL, 5.8-6.6 lbs. Disc. 2010.

	$675	$575	$475	$400	$300	$200	$135

Last MSR was $786.

Add 5% for left-hand variation.
Add 5% for open front and adj. rear sights.

HAWK RIFLE MODEL FN19-HL – .177, .20, .22, or .25 cal., PCP, 8-shot mag., 19 in. barrel, grooved receiver for adj. rear sight or scope, high gloss blue finish, laminate skeleton stock, adj. butt pad, 37.5 in. OAL, 5.8-6.6 lbs. Disc. 2010.

	$825	$700	$575	$475	$375	$245	$165

Last MSR was $982.

Add 5% for left-hand variation.
Add 5% for open front and adj. rear sights.

HAWK RIFLE MODEL FN19-HS – .177, .20, .22, or .25 cal., PCP, 8-shot, 19 in. barrel, walnut skeleton stock, adj. butt pad, high gloss blue finish, grooved receiver, 37.5 in. OAL, 5.8-6.6 lbs. Disc. 2010.

	$775	$650	$550	$450	$350	$230	$155

Last MSR was $904.

Add 5% for left-hand variation.
Add 5% for open front and adj. rear sights.

HAWK RIFLE MODEL FN19-HT – .177, .20, .22, or .25 cal., PCP, 8-shot mag., 19 in. barrel, walnut thumbhole stock, adj. butt pad, grooved receiver, high gloss blue finish, 37.5 in. OAL, 5.8-6.6 lbs. Disc. 2010.

	$800	$675	$550	$475	$350	$240	$160

Last MSR was $943.

Add 5% for left-hand variation.
Add 5% for open front and adj. rear sights.

HAWK RIFLE MODEL FN19-HW – .177, .20, .22, or .25 cal., PCP, 8-shot mag., 19 in. barrel, walnut sporter stock, vent. butt pad, high gloss blue finish, grooved receiver, 37.5 in. OAL, 5.8-6.6 lbs. Disc. 2010.

	$725	$625	$500	$425	$325	$215	$145

Last MSR was $863.

Add 5% for left-hand variation.
Add 5% for open front and adj. rear sights.

PRAIRIE FALCON MULTI-SHOT CARBINE MODEL PF18-MB – .177 or .22 cal., PCP, 8 or 16 shot mag., 18 in. Walther rifled barrel, air cylinder, pressure gauge, quikfill system and moderator, checkered beech pistol grip sporter

courtesy Falcon

GRADING	100%	95%	90%	80%	60%	40%	20%

stock, ventilated butt pad, approx. 37.75 in. OAL, approx. 6.1 lbs. Imported 2006-2011.

| | $725 | $625 | $500 | $425 | $325 | $215 | $145 |

Last MSR was $858.

PRAIRIE FALCON MULTI-SHOT CARBINE MODEL PF18-MP – .177 or .22 cal., PCP, 8 or 16 shot mag., 18 in. Walther rifled barrel, air cylinder, pressure gauge, quikfill system and moderator, walnut profile thumbhole stock with checkered palm swell and forend, ventilated butt pad, approx. 37.75 in. OAL, approx. 6.1 lbs. Imported 2006-2011.

| | $975 | $825 | $675 | $575 | $450 | $290 | $195 |

Last MSR was $1,158.

PRAIRIE FALCON MULTI-SHOT CARBINE MODEL PF18-MW – .177 or .22 cal., PCP, 8 or 16 shot mag., 18 in. Walther rifled barrel, air cylinder, pressure gauge, quikfill system and moderator, checkered walnut pistol grip sporter stock, ventilated butt pad, approx. 37.75 in. OAL, approx. 6.1 lbs. Imported 2006-2011.

| | $875 | $750 | $600 | $500 | $400 | $260 | $175 |

Last MSR was $1,030.

PRAIRIE FALCON MULTI-SHOT RIFLE MODEL PF25-MB – .177 or .22 cal., PCP, 8 or 16 shot mag., 25 in. Walther rifled barrel, air cylinder, pressure gauge, quikfill system and moderator, checkered beech pistol grip sporter stock, ventilated butt pad, approx. 44.75 in. OAL, approx. 6.5 lbs. Imported 2006-2011.

| | $750 | $625 | $525 | $425 | $325 | $225 | $150 |

Last MSR was $880.

PRAIRIE FALCON MULTI-SHOT RIFLE MODEL PF25-MP – .177 or .22 cal., PCP, 8 or 16 shot mag., 25 in. Walther rifled barrel, air cylinder, pressure gauge, quikfill system and moderator, walnut profile thumbhole stock with checkered palm swell and forend, ventilated butt pad, approx. 44.75 in. OAL, approx. 6.5 lbs. Imported 2006-2011.

| | $1,000 | $850 | $700 | $575 | $450 | $300 | $200 |

Last MSR was $1,188.

PRAIRIE FALCON MULTI-SHOT RIFLE MODEL PF25-MW – .177 or .22 cal., PCP, 8 or 16 shot mag., 25 in. Walther rifled barrel, air cylinder, pressure gauge, quikfill system and moderator, checkered walnut pistol grip sporter stock, ventilated butt pad, approx. 44.75 in. OAL, approx. 6.5 lbs. Imported 2006-2011.

| | $900 | $775 | $625 | $525 | $400 | $270 | $180 |

Last MSR was $1,056.

PRAIRIE FALCON SINGLE SHOT CARBINE MODEL PF18-SB – .177 or .22 cal., PCP, SS, 18 in. Walther rifled barrel, air cylinder, pressure gauge, quikfill system, and moderator, checkered beech pistol grip sporter stock, ventilated butt pad, approx. 37.75 in. OAL, approx. 6.25 lbs. Imported 2006-2011.

courtesy Falcon

| | $625 | $525 | $425 | $350 | $280 | $185 | $125 |

Last MSR was $739.

PRAIRIE FALCON SINGLE SHOT CARBINE MODEL PF18-SP – .177 or .22 cal., PCP, SS, 18 in. Walther rifled barrel, air cylinder, pressure gauge, quikfill system, and moderator, walnut profile thumbhole stock with checkered palm swell and forend, ventilated butt pad, approx. 37.75 in. OAL, approx. 6.25 lbs. Imported 2006-2011.

| | $850 | $725 | $600 | $500 | $375 | $255 | $170 |

Last MSR was $998.

PRAIRIE FALCON SINGLE SHOT CARBINE MODEL PF18-SW – .177 or .22 cal., PCP, SS, 18 in. Walther rifled barrel, larger air cylinder, pressure gauge, quikfill system, and moderator, checkered walnut pistol grip sporter stock, ventilated butt pad, approx. 37.75 in. OAL, approx. 6.25 lbs. Imported 2006-2011.

| | $775 | $650 | $550 | $450 | $350 | $230 | $155 |

Last MSR was $924.

GRADING	100%	95%	90%	80%	60%	40%	20%

PRAIRIE FALCON SINGLE SHOT RIFLE MODEL PF25-SB – .177 or .22 cal., PCP, SS, 25 in. Walther rifled barrel, air cylinder, pressure gauge, quikfill system and moderator, checkered beech pistol grip sporter stock, ventilated butt pad, approx. 44.5 in. OAL, approx. 6.25 lbs. Imported 2006-2011.

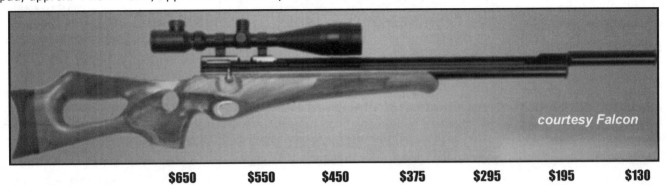

courtesy Falcon

	$650	$550	$450	$375	$295	$195	$130

Last MSR was $771.

PRAIRIE FALCON SINGLE SHOT RIFLE MODEL PF25-SP – .177 or .22 cal., PCP, SS, 25 in. Walther rifled barrel, air cylinder, pressure gauge, quikfill system and moderator, walnut profile thumbhole stock with checkered palm swell and forend, ventilated butt pad, approx. 44.5 in. OAL, approx. 6.25 lbs. Imported 2006-2011.

$875	$750	$600	$500	$400	$260	$175

Last MSR was $1,041.

PRAIRIE FALCON SINGLE SHOT RIFLE MODEL PF25-SW – .177 or .22 cal., PCP, SS, 25 in. Walther rifled barrel, air cylinder, pressure gauge, quikfill system and moderator, checkered walnut pistol grip sporter stock, ventilated butt pad, approx. 44.5 in. OAL, approx. 6.25 lbs. Imported 2006-2011.

$775	$650	$550	$450	$350	$230	$155

Last MSR was $925.

PRAIRIE FALCON B (BULL BARREL) MULTI-SHOT CARBINE MODEL PF18B-MW – .177 or .22 cal., PCP, 8 or 16 shot mag., 18 in. Walther rifled full shrouded barrel, checkered walnut pistol grip sporter stock, ventilated butt pad, air cylinder, pressure gauge, quikfill system and moderator, approx. 35.5 in. OAL, approx. 7.5 lbs. Imported 2006-2011.

courtesy Falcon

$875	$750	$600	$500	$400	$260	$175

Last MSR was $1,021.

PRAIRIE FALCON B (BULL BARREL) MULTI-SHOT CARBINE MODEL PF18B-MP – .177 or .22 cal., PCP, 8 or 16 shot mag., 18 in. Walther rifled fully shrouded barrel, walnut profile thumbhole stock with checkered palm swell and forend, ventilated butt pad, air cylinder, pressure gauge, quikfill system and moderator, approx. 35.5 in. OAL, approx. 7.5 lbs. Imported 2006-2011.

$1,000	$850	$700	$575	$450	$300	$200

Last MSR was $1,174.

GRADING	100%	95%	90%	80%	60%	40%	20%

PRAIRIE FALCON B (BULL BARREL) MULTI-SHOT RIFLE MODEL PF25B-MW – .177 or .22 cal., PCP, 8 or 16 shot mag., 25 in. Walther rifled fully shrouded barrel, checkered walnut pistol grip sporter stock, ventilated butt pad, air cylinder, pressure gauge, quikfill system and moderator, approx. 42.5 in. OAL, approx. 7.75 lbs. Imported 2006-2011.

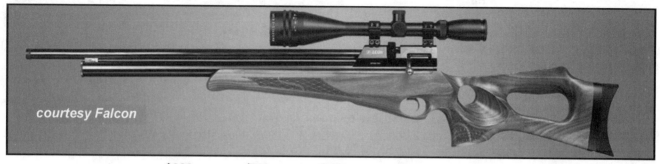

courtesy Falcon

$900	$775	$625	$525	$400	$270	$180

Last MSR was $1,045.

PRAIRIE FALCON B (BULL BARREL) MULTI-SHOT RIFLE MODEL PF25B-MP – .177 or .22 cal., PCP, 8 or 16 shot mag., 25 in. Walther rifled fully shrouded barrel, walnut profile thumbhole stock with checkered palm swell and forend, ventilated butt pad, air cylinder, pressure gauge, quikfill system and moderator, approx. 42.5 in. OAL, approx. 7.75 lbs. Imported 2006-2011.

$1,025	$875	$725	$600	$450	$300	$205

Last MSR was $1,202.

RAPTOR CARBINE MODEL FN12-RB – .177 or .22 cal., PCP, SS, eight-shot mag., 12 in. Walther rifled barrel, grooved receiver for adj. rear sight or scope, high gloss blue finish, beech sporter stock with checkered grip and forearm, approx. 30.5 in. OAL, 5.8-5.9 lbs. Importation disc. 2011.

$675	$575	$475	$400	$300	$200	$135

Last MSR was $806.

Add $30 for left-hand variation.   *Add 5% for open front and adj. rear sights.*

RAPTOR CARBINE MODEL FN12-RL – .177 or .22 cal., PCP, SS, eight-shot mag., 12 in. Walther rifled barrel, grooved receiver for adj. rear sight or scope, high gloss blue finish, laminate sporter stock, approx. 30.5 in. OAL, 5.8-5.9 lbs. Importation disc. 2011.

$800	$675	$550	$475	$350	$240	$160

Last MSR was $955.

Add $30 for left-hand variation.   *Add 5% for open front and adj. rear sights.*

RAPTOR CARBINE MODEL FN12-RLS – .177 or .22 cal., PCP, SS, eight-shot mag., 12 in. Walther rifled barrel, grooved receiver for adj. rear sight or scope, high gloss blue finish, laminate skeleton stock with adj. butt pad, approx. 30.5 in. OAL, 5.8-5.9 lbs. Importation disc. 2011.

$950	$800	$675	$550	$425	$285	$190

Last MSR was $1,116.

Add $30 for left-hand variation.   *Add 5% for open front and adj. rear sights.*

RAPTOR CARBINE MODEL FN12-RTW – .177 or .22 cal., PCP, SS, eight-shot mag., 12 in. Walther rifled barrel, grooved receiver for adj. rear sight or scope, high gloss blue finish, walnut thumbhole stock with palm swell and foregrip, approx. 30.5 in. OAL, 5.8-5.9 lbs. Importation disc. 2011.

$850	$725	$600	$500	$375	$255	$170

Last MSR was $1,006.

Add $30 for left-hand variation.   *Add 5% for open front and adj. rear sights.*

RAPTOR CARBINE MODEL FN12-RW – .177 or .22 cal., PCP, SS, eight-shot mag., 12 in. Walther rifled barrel, grooved receiver for adj. rear sight or scope, high gloss blue finish, walnut sporter stock with checkered grip and forearm, approx. 30.5 in. OAL, 5.8-5.9 lbs. Importation disc. 2011.

$750	$625	$525	$425	$325	$225	$150

Last MSR was $888.

Add $30 for left-hand variation.   *Add 5% for open front and adj. rear sights.*

RAPTOR CARBINE MODEL FN12-RWS – .177 or .22 cal., PCP, SS, eight-shot mag., 12 in. Walther rifled barrel, grooved receiver for adj. rear sight or scope, high gloss blue finish, walnut skeleton stock with adj. butt pad, approx. 30.5 in. OAL, 5.8-5.9 lbs. Importation disc. 2011.

$875	$750	$600	$500	$400	$260	$175

Last MSR was $1,019.

Add $30 for left-hand variation.   *Add 5% for open front and adj. rear sights.*

GRADING	100%	95%	90%	80%	60%	40%	20%

RAPTOR RIFLE MODEL FN19-RB – .177 or .22 cal., PCP, SS, 19 in. blue steel with Walther barrel and eight-shot mag., beech sporter stock with checkered grip and forearm, 37-37.5 in. OAL, 6.1-6.5 lbs. Importation disc. 2011.

	$675	$575	$475	$400	$300	$200	$135

Last MSR was $806.

Add $30 for left-hand variation.   Add 5% for open front and adj. rear sights.

RAPTOR RIFLE MODEL FN19-RL – .177 or .22 cal., PCP, SS, 19 in. blue steel with Walther barrel and eight-shot mag., laminate sporter stock, 37-37.5 in. OAL, 6.1-6.5 lbs. Importation disc. 2011.

	$800	$675	$550	$475	$350	$240	$160

Last MSR was $955.

Add $30 for left-hand variation.   Add 5% for open front and adj. rear sights.

RAPTOR RIFLE MODEL FN19-RLS – .177 or .22 cal., PCP, SS, 19 in. blue steel with Walther barrel and eight-shot mag., laminate skeleton stock with adj. butt pad, 37-37.5 in. OAL, 6.1-6.5 lbs. Importation disc. 2011.

	$950	$800	$675	$550	$425	$285	$190

Last MSR was $1,116.

Add $30 for left-hand variation.   Add 5% for open front and adj. rear sights.

RAPTOR RIFLE MODEL FN19-RTW – .177 or .22 cal., PCP, SS, 19 in. blue steel with Walther barrel and eight-shot mag., walnut thumbhole stock with stippled palm swell and fore grip with adj. butt pad, 37-37.5 in. OAL, 6.1-6.5 lbs. Importation disc. 2011.

	$850	$725	$600	$500	$375	$255	$170

Last MSR was $1,006.

Add $30 for left-hand variation.   Add 5% for open front and adj. rear sights.

RAPTOR RIFLE MODEL FN19-RW – .177 or .22 cal., PCP, SS, 19 in. blue steel with Walther barrel and eight-shot mag., walnut sporter stock with checkered grip and forearm, 37-37.5 in. OAL, 6.1-6.5 lbs. Importation disc. 2011.

	$750	$625	$525	$425	$325	$225	$150

Last MSR was $888.

Add $30 for left-hand variation.   Add 5% for open front and adj. rear sights.

RAPTOR RIFLE MODEL FN19-RWS – .177 or .22 cal., PCP, SS, 19 in. blue steel with Walther barrel and eight-shot mag., walnut skeleton stock with adj. butt pad, 37-37.5 in. OAL, 6.1-6.5 lbs. Importation disc. 2011.

	$875	$750	$600	$500	$400	$260	$175

Last MSR was $1,109.

Add $30 for left-hand variation.   Add 5% for open front and adj. rear sights.

TARGET RIFLE MODEL FN19-FSJ – .177 or .22 cal., PCP, SS, 19 in. Walther rifled barrel, grooved receiver for adj. rear sight or scope, high gloss blue finish, beech target stock with adj. cheek piece and butt pad, adj. match trigger, 35.5-38 in. OAL, 6.3-8.7 lbs. Disc. 2010.

	$700	$600	$500	$400	$325	$210	$140

Last MSR was $819.

Add 5% for left-hand variation.   Add 5% for open front and adj. rear sights.

TARGET RIFLE MODELS FN19-FLP/FN19-FSPL – .177 or .22 cal., PCP, SS, 19 in. Walther rifled barrel, grooved receiver for adj. rear sight or scope, high gloss blue finish, walnut (Model FN19-FLP) or laminate (Model FN19-FSPL) target stock with adj. cheek piece and butt pad, adj. match trigger, 35.5-38 in. OAL, 6.3-8.7 lbs. Disc. 2010.

	$875	$750	$600	$500	$400	$260	$175

Last MSR was $1,024.

Add 5% for left-hand variation.
Add 5% for open front and adj. rear sights.
Add 10% for laminate target stock (Model FN19-FSPL).

TARGET RIFLE MODELS FN19-TR/FN19-TRL – .177 or .22 cal., PCP, SS, 19 in. Walther rifled barrel, grooved receiver for adj. rear sight or scope, high gloss blue finish, walnut (Model FN19-TR) or laminate (Model FN19-TRL) target stock with adj. cheek piece and butt pad, adj. match trigger, 35.5-38 in. OAL, 6.3-8.7 lbs. Disc. 2010.

	$875	$750	$600	$500	$400	$260	$175

Last MSR was $1,024.

Add 5% for left-hand variation.
Add 5% for open front and adj. rear sights.
Add 10% for laminate target stock (Model FN19-TRL).

GRADING	100%	95%	90%	80%	60%	40%	20%

TARGET RIFLE MODELS FN19-PTB/FN19-PTL – .177 or .22 cal., PCP, SS, 19 in. Walther rifled barrel, grooved receiver for adj. rear sight or scope, high gloss blue finish, beech (Model FN19-PTB) or laminate (Model FN19-PTL) target stock with adj. cheek piece and butt pad, adj. match trigger, 35.5-38 in. OAL, 6.3-8.7 lbs. Disc. 2010.

	$950	$800	$675	$550	$425	$285	$190

Last MSR was $1,106.

Add 5% for left-hand variation.
Add 5% for open front and adj. rear sights.
Add 10% for laminated target stock (Model FN19-PTL).

PRAIRIE FALCON BULL BARREL – .177, .22., or .25 cal., 21 in. shrouded bull barrel, 8 shot mag., raised right hand cheek piece, two-stage adj. trigger, manual safety, vent. rubber buttplate, walnut or beech checkered pistol grip stock, 6.8 lbs. Importation began 2012.

MSR $1,200	$1,025	$900	$825	$650	$500	N/A	N/A

Add $200 for walnut stock.

This model is also available in Carbine Sporter (not imported), Lighthunter B (not imported), or Profile configuration.

PRAIRIE FALCON CLASSIC C – .177 or .22 cal., 21 in. shrouded bull barrel, 8 shot mag., raised right hand cheek piece, two-stage adj. trigger, manual safety, vent. rubber buttplate, walnut or beech checkered pistol grip stock, 6.8 lbs. Importation began 2012.

MSR $1,120	$950	$850	$750	$625	$475	N/A	N/A

Add $130 for walnut stock.

This model is also available in Profile Classic (not imported), Lighthunter C (not imported), or Walnut Sporter configuration.

FALKE AIRGUN

Previous manufacturer located in Wennigsen, Germany 1951-1958.

The authors and publisher wish to thank Mr. Trevor Adams for assistance with the following information for this section of the *Blue Book of Airguns*.

In February 1949, Albert Föhrenbach founded the engineering firm of Falkewerke in Wennigsen near Hanover, Germany. It provided maintenance for conveyer belt machines, a service vital to the industrial recovery of post-WWII Germany. Very soon their conveyer belt expertise was extended to making shooting arcade games. By mid-1951 it started production of a variety of air rifles and one air pistol under the brand of Falke (German for Falcon). The rifles were superior copies of guns made by Dianawerk, Haenel, BSA, and Will. The one air pistol, the Falke 33, apparently was a Falke original. Despite the excellence of Falke products, the firm failed to prosper. The advertising and marketing strengths of larger manufacturers such as Mayer & Grammelspacher, BSA, and Webley prevented Falke from becoming a well-known brand. Financial difficulties led to the cessation of production in 1958, and in 1961 Falkewerke went into airgun history. Due to their very limited production run during only seven years and their special quality of manufacture, Falke airguns now are of considerable interest to both collectors and shooters.

The production period of each model isn't known. An early 1953 catalog describes all models and *Smith's Encyclopedia of Air Gas & Spring Guns*, published in 1957, notes the full range of models as available - just one year before the end of production. Special Reference: *John Walter, Guns Review* April 1988.

PISTOLS

MODEL 33 – .177 cal., trigger guard swings forward to cock, SP, rifled barrel, beech grip with Falcon badge on each side, 11.25 in. OAL, 1.75 lbs. Mfg. 1951-1958.

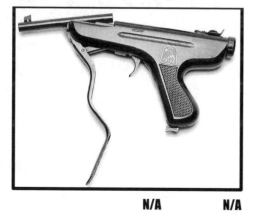

courtesy Beeman Collection

	N/A	N/A	$250	$200	$175	$150	$100

GRADING	100%	95%	90%	80%	60%	40%	20%

RIFLES

MODEL 10 – .177 cal., BBC, SP, tinplate, smoothbore, wood buttstock, 30.5 in. OAL.

	N/A	N/A	N/A	$60	$50	$40	$30

MODEL 20 – .177 cal., BBC, SP, similar to Model 10, except has checkered wood forearm.

	N/A	N/A	N/A	$100	$80	$60	$50

MODEL 30 – .177 cal., BBC, SP, tinplate, smoothbore, 32 in. OAL.

	N/A	N/A	N/A	$70	$60	$50	$40

MODEL 40 – .177 cal., BBC, SP, tinplate, smoothbore, simple post front sight, 35 in. OAL.

	N/A	N/A	N/A	$70	$60	$50	$40

MODEL 50 – similar to Model 40, except has seamless tube steel smooth or rifled barrel, ramp rear and blade front sight, 36 in. OAL.

	N/A	N/A	N/A	$100	$80	$60	$50

MODEL 60 – .177 or .22 cal., BBC, SP, solid steel, rifled, adj. trigger, some mfg. with breech lock, 38 in. OAL.

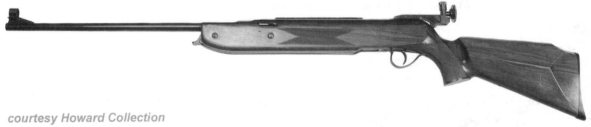

courtesy Beeman Collection

	N/A	N/A	N/A	$100	$80	$60	$50

MODEL 70 – .177 or .22 cal., BBC, SP, adj. trigger, breech lock device, 42.5 in. OAL, 6.6 lbs.

	N/A	N/A	N/A	$140	$115	$90	$70

This is the most frequently encountered Falke rifle.

MODEL 80 – .177 or .22 cal., UL, SP, auto. opening loading tap, micrometer rear sight, interchangeable insert front sight, elm stock, 44.5 in. OAL, 8.25 lbs. Approx. 400 mfg.

	N/A	N/A	N/A	$425	$350	$275	$200

Add 10% for diopter sight.

MODEL 90 – .177 or .22 cal., UL, SP, similar to Model 80, except has walnut stock, micrometer and diopter rear and interchangeable insert front sight, sling swivels, 44.5 in. OAL, 9.5 lbs., approx. 200 mfg.

courtesy Howard Collection

	N/A	N/A	N/A	$550	$425	$350	$275

MODEL 100 – .177, .22, or .25 cal., trigger guard cocking gallery gun, blue finish with nickel action, barrel drops for loading, 42 in. OAL, 7 lbs.

	N/A	N/A	N/A	$350	$275	$200	$150

FAMAS

Current manufacturer located in Gardone, Italy. Previously imported by Century International Arms, Inc., located in St. Albans, VT.

RIFLES

FAMAS MODEL – .177 cal., CO_2, semi-auto, copy of French-made MAS .223, used for military training, clip-fed.

	$395	$350	$285	$195	$125	N/A	N/A

GRADING	100%	95%	90%	80%	60%	40%	20%

FARCO

Current manufacturer located in the Philippines. Previously imported by ARS located in Pine City, NY. Dealer or consumer direct sales. Ref: AR 2:10.

PISTOLS

MODEL 1733 – .22 cal., bulk fill CO_2, SS, top lever cocking, 7.5 in. barrel, fixed rear and blade front sights, black finish, ambidextrous anatomical hardwood grips, 11.5 in. OAL, 2.75 lbs.

courtesy Howard Collection

$450	$375	$325	$260	$205	$135	$90

MODEL 1832 – .22 cal., bulk fill CO_2, SS, top lever cocking, 5 in. barrel, fixed rear and blade front sights, black finish, ambidextrous anatomical hardwood grips, 9 in. OAL, 2.5 lbs.

courtesy Howard Collection

$450	$375	$325	$260	$205	$135	$90

RIFLES

FARCO FP SURVIVAL – .22 or .25 cal., footpump action multi-pump pneumatic, SS, 22.75 in. barrel, nickel finish, hardwood stock, fixed sights, 5.75 lbs. Disc. 2001.

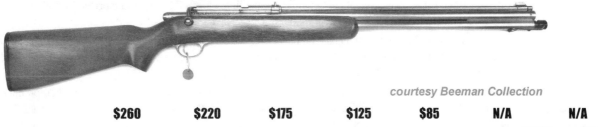

courtesy Beeman Collection

$260	$220	$175	$125	$85	N/A	N/A

Last MSR was $295.

FARCO SHORT CYLINDER RIFLE – .22 or .25 cal., CO_2, charged from bulk fill 10 oz. cylinder, stainless steel, adj. rear sight, Monte Carlo hardwood stock, hard rubber buttplate, approx. 7 lbs. Disc. 2001.

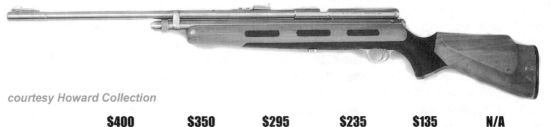

courtesy Howard Collection

$400	$350	$295	$235	$135	N/A	N/A

Last MSR was $460.

GRADING		100%	95%	90%	80%	60%	40%	20%

LONG CYLINDER RIFLE – .22 or .25 cal., CO_2, similar to Short Cylinder Rifle except gas cylinder extends to end of barrel. Approx. 25 mfg. Disc. 2001.

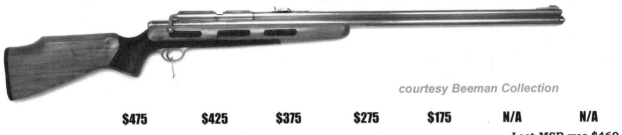

courtesy Beeman Collection

		$475	$425	$375	$275	$175	N/A	N/A

Last MSR was $460.

SHOTGUNS

FARCO SHOTGUN – 28 ga., CO_2, 30 in. barrel, charged from bulk fill 10 oz. cylinder, hardwood stock, 7 lbs. Imported 1988-2001.

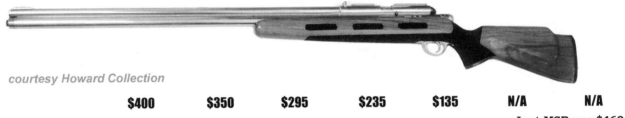

courtesy Howard Collection

		$400	$350	$295	$235	$135	N/A	N/A

Last MSR was $460.

Add $20 for extra CO_2 cylinder. (Caution, use only recently mfg. stainless steel cylinders!)
Add $1 for extra brass shells (12 included with gun).

FEINWERKBAU WESTINGER & ALTENBURGER GmbH

Current manufacturer established circa 1951, and located in Oberndorf, Germany. Currently imported and distributed by Brenzovich Firearms & Training Center located in Ft. Hancock, TX, Champion's Choice located in LaVergne, TN, and Air Venturi/Pyramyd Air located in Solon, OH. Previously imported by Airguns of Arizona located in Gilbert, AZ, Marksman (marked Beeman), located in Santa Fe Springs, CA, and Pilkington Competition Equipment LLC located in Monteagle, TN. Dealer and consumer direct sales.

FWB COMPANY OVERVIEW

The authors and publisher wish to thank Mr. Ulrich Eichstädt for his valuable assistance with the following information for this section of the *Blue Book of Airguns*.

Feinwerkbau, an airgun industry leader, has been responsible for developing many of the current technical innovations used in fabricating target air pistols and rifles. In 1992, Feinwerkbau swept the Olympic competition. Feinwerkbau guns are prized by both match shooters and those who just enjoy fine guns - especially ones they can shoot indoors!

"Feinwerkbau" means "fine work factory" and was just a brand name. For many years it was only a prefix to the actual company name (named for its founders): Westinger & Altenburger. Gradually, the word Feinwerkbau (and the abbreviation FWB) came to be an equivalent term for this airgun maker and their products. So, you find this text under "F" instead of "W" in this book.

Although the Westinger & Altenburger company never used big advertising campaigns or sponsored top shooters, their products are on top: the first recoilless match air rifle with a fixed barrel was the Feinwerkbau Model 150. Introduced in 1961, it soon forced the UIT (Union Internationale de Tir, now known as the International Shooting Sports Federation or ISSF) to reduce the size of their targets. This success was repeated in 1965 with the introduction of the FWB Model 65 Match air pistol. This pistol was in production and pretty much ruled air pistol competition for more than three decades. The Feinwerkbau 600 series have simply owned this title since 1984. The pre-charged successor to the FWB 600 series, the FWB P 70, wins one title after another (including the world record with the maximum score of 600 out of 600 points).

The firm was founded by two engineers, Ernst Altenburger and Karl Westinger. They both worked in the famous Mauser factory in Oberndorf/Neckar, which has been the leading gun manufacturing city in Germany since 1870. After WWII, the factory fell into the French occupation zone. The French authorities ordered the disassembly of all Mauser's machines. Metal processing was forbidden, and the two engineers desperately sought a new way to use their technical knowledge. In 1948, they were allowed to establish a small workshop in Dettingen. It was not far away, but because the French military authority had poor maps, they did not realize that they had allowed the establishment of a shop across the line in the adjoining Hohenzollern territory, which was not under French control.

With the help of a small punch machine they produced wooden wheels for children's scooters, wooden casings for pencils, and even wooden spoons. Stealthily, in the attic of what is now Oberndorf College, they designed their first prototype of an electro-mechanical calculator. In

1948, after the Allies again allowed metal processing companies in that region, Feinwerkbau Westinger & Altenburger became a registered company. Their new calculator went into production at the Olympia-Werke in Wilhelmshaven, Germany. Thousands of their machines were sold internationally. Later they produced textile mandrels, counters, and for IBM, a small device to cut letters out of paper punchcards. Today, a part of the company manufactures vital, but undisclosed, parts for "Formula-One" race cars.

The Feinwerkbau Westinger & Altenburger factory is still located in Oberndorf at the headwaters of the Neckar River in Germany's Black Forest, and has about two hundred employees. The company is managed by two sons of the founders: Jörg Altenburger and Rolf Westinger, while two other sons, Reiner Altenburger and Gerhard Westinger, respectively, oversee the sales and purchasing departments. Note: Do not depend on dates in importer catalogs for model production dates.

FWB HISTORY: 1951-1979

In 1951, the German Shooting Federation was re-established. Starting in 1952, the production of rifled barrels was again allowed. The 1950s was the decade of the Carl Walther Company in Ulm. Their barrel-cocking air rifles Model 53, and later Model 55, were used by almost every competitive European air rifle shooter. However, many of the top marksmen believed that wear at the hinge point in these barrel-cocking guns caused reduced accuracy.

In 1961, Walter Gehmann, one of the top marksmen in Germany before WWII and also a famous inventor, came to visit his old friend Ernst Altenburger, with whom he had worked in the legendary Mauser R & D department. (Together they had invented the Mauser "Olympia" smallbore rifle, which was the predecessor of all modern .22 match rifles.) Soon the company started to design air rifles with the barrel rigidly fixed to the receiver.

Anschütz also presented a fixed barrel air rifle, their side-lever Model 220. Feinwerkbau replied with their Model 100. It was immediately successful. Helmut Schlenker, the reigning German shooting champion, took the German championship with this gun in 1961 - this is especially significant because that was the year of the German Shooting Federation's centennial.

Feinwerkbau exceeded that success with the Model 150. This gun featured an elegantly simple, very effective recoil-elimination device which made Feinwerkbau rifles almost unbeatable during the next decade: When the trigger was released, the entire rigid, upper action and barrel was released to ride on concealed steel rails and thus absorb the recoil. The basic mechanism was based on a recoil control mechanism that Westinger and Altenburger had developed, when working for Mauser, for controlling machine gun recoil. All the succeeding FWB spring-piston match airguns used this mechanism. It was covered by patent 1,140 489, awarded in February of 1961 to Westinger and Altenburger and their chief engineer, Edwin Wöhrstein. Walter Gehmann was honored for his input with a gift of the Model 150 with serial number "000001."

The 1966 World Shooting Championship in Wiesbaden, Germany was a turning point for air rifle shooting. Here the world was introduced to precision match air rifles. While the first world championship was won by Gerd Kuemmet with a non-production, prototype Anschütz Model 250, Feinwerkbau would come into its glory with world championships by Gottfried Kustermann (1970), Oswald Schlipf (1978), Walter Hillenbrand (1979), Hans Riederer (1986 and 1990), and Sonja Pfeilschifter (1994).

Feinwerkbau extended their very successful recoilless sledge mechanism to an air pistol in 1965; the FWB Model LP 65. It had special arrangements to block the recoil compensating mechanism and to switch the trigger pull from 500 to 1360 grams. This allowed this air pistol to be used for simulated firearm pistol training. It was produced in several minor variations until 1998. Although other models, such as the LP 80 and the LP 90 (the first air pistol with an electronic trigger), were introduced during that period, the Model 65 reigned supreme. Air pistol shooting became an official international sport in 1969 and Feinwerkbau had come to virtually "own" that field of competition. Model 65 air pistols also had become very popular with non-match shooters, especially in the USA.

FWB HISTORY: 1980-CURRENT

At the beginning of the 1980s, two Austrian technicians, Emil Senfter and Viktor Idl revived the century-old French patent by Paul Giffard for a CO_2 pistol with a tubular gas cylinder under the barrel. The first "Senfter" pistols were very successful in competition and could be shot like a free pistol. Their advantage over the spring-piston air pistols was a lack of movement from a piston during firing and a quicker shot release. When Senfter and Idl parted company, Senfter offered the system to Walther and Idl went to Feinwerkbau. As a result, the first two CO_2 pistols of both companies, the Walther CP 1 and FWB Model 2, respectively, appear to be almost identical. (Some years later a lawsuit awarded the patent and system to Senfter.)

Feinwerkbau took an excursion into producing sporting air rifles in the early 1970s. This was the "Sport" series under the model numbers 120 to 127. These were slim, highly efficient barrel-cocking, spring-piston air rifles. The primary market was the United States where the high power versions were known as the Model 124 in 4.5 mm (.177) caliber and the much less popular Model 127 in 5.5mm (.22) caliber. A lower powered version of the 5.5mm caliber model was fairly popular in Great Britain. Limited numbers of the lowest powered version, the Model 121, were made for countries like Germany where there were very strict airgun power limits. Feinwerkbau began a joint effort with Beeman Precision Airguns to develop a 5mm version, with a special stock to Beeman specifications, to be known as the Beeman R5. Regular production was not possible because Feinwerkbau was not able to find suitable 5 mm barrels in the numbers projected for first sales. The Model R5 is now one of the rarest of collectors' items. Production of the Sport series was halted in the 1980s because Feinwerkbau's technicians were so tuned to produce limited quantities of match guns with extremely close fitting and quality control that they could not seem to produce such production level items at a reasonable cost! Now much sought after by both shooters and collectors, its slender profile and trigger placement make it a favorite for restocking with premium quality custom stocks.

In the USA, Beeman Precision Airguns, Feinwerkbau's American partner, had taken an unusual step. They created a larger market for match air rifles among America's quality conscious non-match gun buyers than had existed for America's much lower concentration of match shooters. So, in America, the sales of FWB match guns continued to exceed those of all other match airguns combined.

In 1973, Walther introduced a new type of recoilless air rifle, the Walther LGR, a single-stroke pneumatic. It had a shorter shot release time than the spring-piston air rifles and was soon adopted, at least in Europe, by most of the top competitive air rifle shooters.

In 1984, Feinwerkbau struck back, from its factory deep in the German Black Forest, with their own single stroke pneumatic rifle, the FWB 600 (named after the 600-point maximum possible score in the new 60-shot international competitions). This rifle featured a reverse cocking lever which closed towards the body, a much easier motion, and had a shorter barrel of only 420mm (16.5 in.), which reduced the shot release time even more. Feinwerkbau again dominated the world of match air rifles. Scores of 600 became so common that the international shooting authorities again had to reduce the size of the ten ring, from one to one/half millimeter (2/100") diameter! However, the FWB 600 shooters soon began to crowd even that incredibly small bullseye with all of their shots. The models FWB 601, 602, and 603, introduced during the 1990s, were only slight modifications of FWB's basic single-stroke pneumatic system.

In air pistol competitions, only a few shooters preferred pneumatic pistols instead of CO_2 models (and later PCP), but the air rifle shooters were more reluctant in choosing the easy-to-shoot carbon dioxide systems: They didn't want to rely on uncertain CO_2 supplies during competitions in foreign countries and therefore had to tolerate the heavier cocking effort of the single-stroke pneumatic rifles.

That changed again in 1997, when the key manufacturers of precision airguns introduced their pre-charged pneumatic (PCP) match air rifles. These guns did not depend on local supplies of CO_2 and did not have the physical limitations of CO_2 guns. They simply were charged from easily portable cylinder of compressed air. Despite the keen competition of Anschütz, Walther, Steyr-Mannlicher, and Hämmerli, the FWB Model P70 PCP match air rifle has maintained the lead in air rifle competition. Using the FWB P70, Gaby Bühlmann from Switzerland fired the first ever maximum of 400, followed by the first 600 score by Tavarit Majchacheep from Thailand.

Today's leading airguns are the Feinwerkbau P34 PCP air pistol and the Model 603 single-stroke pneumatic and P70 PCP air rifles. These models use a special "Absorber" feature which reduces even the tiny recoil produced by the pellet itself during its acceleration. A five-shot version of the PCP air pistol, known as the P55, was developed for the new ISSF "Falling Targets" event. And, a five-shot PCP rifle, the Model P75, is used in the summer biathlon competitions. Several smaller and lighter versions of these models are designed for young shooters and smaller adults.

Feinwerkbau now also produces some very successful match firearms: The FWB smallbore rifle earned the Olympic gold medal in 1992, the FWB semi-auto .22 caliber pistol, and the AW 93 (based on a Russian patent).

PISTOLS

MODEL 2 – .177 cal., CO_2, 425-525 FPS, adj. trigger, adj. sights, UIT target model, 2.5 lbs. Disc. 1989.

$450	$375	$325	$260	$205	$135	$90

Last MSR was $780.

Feinwerkbau manufactured three helical barrels (twisted around the gas cylinder), and yes, they shoot accurately.

MODEL C5 – .177 cal., CO_2, five-shot, 7.33 in. barrel, 510 FPS, 2.4 lbs. Disc. approx. 1993.

$650	$550	$450	$375	$295	$195	$130

Last MSR was $1,350.

Add 10% for left-hand variation.

MODEL C10 – .177 cal., CO_2, 510 FPS, adj. trigger, adj. sights, UIT target model, 2.5 lbs. Disc. 1990.

courtesy Beeman Collection

$500	$425	$350	$290	$225	$150	$100

Last MSR was $965.

Add 10% for left-hand variation.

MODEL C20 – .177 cal., CO_2, 510 FPS, adj. trigger, adj. sights, UIT target model, 2.5 lbs. Mfg. 1991-95.

$600	$500	$425	$350	$270	$180	$120

Last MSR was $1,160.

Add 10% for left-hand variation.

This model was intended as a replacement for the Model C2 and the Model C10.

GRADING	100%	95%	90%	80%	60%	40%	20%

MODEL C25 – .177 cal., CO_2, 510 FPS, CO_2 flask placed directly below action, adj. trigger, adj. sights, UIT target model, 2.5 lbs.

	$700	$600	$500	$400	$325	$210	$140

Last MSR was $1,325.

Add 10% for left-hand variation.

MODEL C55 – .177 cal., CO_2, SS or five-shot, 510 FPS, CO_2 flask placed directly below action for vertical CO_2 feed, up to 225 shots/fill, 2.5 lbs. Mfg. 1994-2001.

	$800	$675	$550	$475	$350	$240	$160

Last MSR was $1,460.

Add 10% for left-hand variation.

* **Model C55P** – .177 cal., compressed air, five-shot, 8.75 in. barrel, 510 FPS, adj. rear and interchangeable front sights, adj. trigger, swiveling anatomical grip, compressed air cylinder is fitted with integrated manometer, 2.4 lbs. Mfg. 2001-2004.

	$1,425	$1,200	$1,000	$825	$650	$425	$285

Last MSR was $1,570.

Add 5% for left-hand variation.

MODEL P11 – .177 cal., compressed air, SS, 7.2 in. barrel, black ambidextrous grip that adjusts three dimensionally, ergonomically shaped metallic trigger shoe, rear sight blade exchangeable, block-type front and adj. rear sights, red frame, 13.6 in. OAL, 1.6 lbs. Mfg. 2012-current.

MSR $1,500	$1,275	$1,125	$1,025	$825	$625	N/A	N/A

MODEL P11 PICCOLO – .177 cal., CO_2, 6 in. barrel, front sight, black beechwood grip, adj. trigger, 12.4 in. OAL, 1.5 lbs. New 2011.

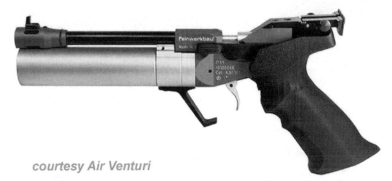

courtesy Air Venturi

MSR $1,500	$1,275	$1,125	$1,025	$825	$625	N/A	N/A

MODEL P30 – .177 cal., PCP, 515 FPS, adj. match trigger, adj. sights, UIT target model, stippled walnut match grip, 2.4 lbs. Disc.

	$1,000	$850	$700	$575	$450	$300	$200

Last MSR was $1,275.

Add 10% for left-hand variation.

MODEL P34 – .177 cal., PCP, 515 FPS, adj. match trigger, adj. sights, UIT target model, 7.2 or 9.2 in. (standard) barrel, blue or red air cylinder, stippled walnut match grip, revised version of the P30 with contoured barrel shroud, sliding barrel weight system, valve housing reduced in size, and removable trigger guard, 2.4 lbs. Mfg. 1999-2004.

courtesy Beeman Collection

	$1,100	$925	$775	$650	$500	$325	$220

Last MSR was $1,640.

Add 5% for left-hand variation.
Add 10% for Morini walnut grip and interchangeable trigger unit.

GRADING	100%	95%	90%	80%	60%	40%	20%

MODEL P40 – .177 cal., PCP, 515 FPS, adj. match trigger, adj. sights, UIT target model, 5.9 in. barrel, two air cylinders with integrated manometer, fully adj. multi-color Morini laminated grip, sliding barrel weight system, cased, 16.1 in. OAL, 2.5 lbs. Mfg. 2004-2007.

	100%	95%	90%	80%	60%	40%	20%
	$1,550	$1,325	$1,075	$900	$700	$475	$300

Last MSR was $1,574.

Add 5% for left-hand variation.

* ***Model P40 Basic*** – .177 cal., PCP, similar to Model P40, except has anatomical adj. Morini walnut grip, no weight system, 16.1 in. OAL, 2.3 lbs. Mfg. 2004-2007.

	100%	95%	90%	80%	60%	40%	20%
	$1,300	$1,100	$900	$750	$575	$400	$260

Last MSR was $1,314.

Add 5% for left-hand variation.

MODEL P44 – .177 cal., PCP, 515 FPS, adj. match trigger, adj. sights, UIT target model, 9 in. barrel, two air cylinders with integrated manometer, fully adj. multi-color Morini laminated grip, sliding barrel weight system, 16.3 in. OAL, 2.1 lbs., cased. Mfg. 2008-current.

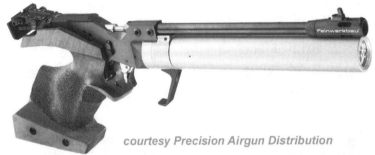

courtesy Precision Airgun Distribution

MSR $2,000	100%	95%	90%	80%	60%	40%	20%
	$1,700	$1,500	$1,350	$1,100	$850	N/A	N/A

Add $100 for left-hand configuration.

* ***Model P44 Short*** – .177 cal., PCP, 515 FPS, adj. match trigger, adj. sights, UIT target model, 7.2 in. barrel, two air cylinders with integrated manometer, fully adj. multi-color Morini laminated grip, sliding barrel weight system, 14.37 in. OAL, 1.9 lbs., cased. Mfg. 2008-current.

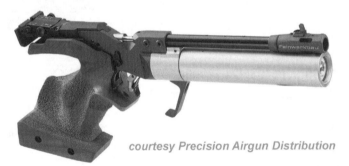

courtesy Precision Airgun Distribution

MSR $2,000	100%	95%	90%	80%	60%	40%	20%
	$1,700	$1,500	$1,350	$1,100	$850	N/A	N/A

Add $100 for left-hand variation.

MODEL P56 – .177 cal., compressed air, five-shot, 8.75 in. barrel, 510 FPS, adj. rear and interchangeable front sights, adj. trigger, swiveling anatomical grip, compressed air cylinder is fitted with integrated manometer, 2.4 lbs. Mfg. 2006-2008.

	100%	95%	90%	80%	60%	40%	20%
	$1,600	$1,350	$1,125	$925	$725	$475	$325

Last MSR was $1,890.

Add 5% for left-hand variation.

MODEL P58 – .177 cal., compressed air, five-shot, 8 in. barrel, 510 FPS, adj. rear and interchangeable front sights,

courtesy Precision Airgun Distribution

GRADING	100%	95%	90%	80%	60%	40%	20%

adj. trigger, adj. Morini anatomical walnut grip, compressed air cylinder is fitted with integrated manometer, adj. barrel weights, 16.5 in. OAL, 2.9 lbs. Mfg. 2010-current.

| MSR $2,140 | $1,825 | $1,600 | $1,450 | $1,175 | $900 | N/A | N/A |

Add $68 for left-hand variation.

MODEL 65 MK I AND II – .177 cal., SL, SP, 525 FPS, recoil compensating mechanism may be locked, adj. trigger pull may be instantly switched from 500 to 1360 grams, adj. sights, UIT target model, 2.6-2.9 lbs., MKII Model has shorter barrel. M-65 MK I. Approx. 145,000 mfg. 1965-2001.

| | $550 | $475 | $375 | $325 | $250 | $165 | $110 |

Last MSR was $1,070.

Add 10% for left-hand variation. Add 7% for adj. grips.

MODEL 80 – .177 cal., SL, SP, 475-525 FPS, similar to Model 65, except has stacking barrel weights and fine mechanical trigger, adj. sights, UIT target model, 2.8-3.2 lbs. Approx. 48,000 mfg. 1977-1983.

| | $600 | $500 | $425 | $350 | $270 | $180 | $120 |

Last MSR was $625.

Add 100% for factory gold plating.

MODEL 90 – similar to Model 80, except has electronic trigger. Approx. 20,000 mfg. 1982-1992.

| | $500 | $425 | $350 | $290 | $225 | $150 | $100 |

Last MSR was $1,155.

Add 5% for short barrel.
Subtract 10% for left-hand variation.

MODEL 100 – .177 cal., pneumatic action, adj. trigger, adj. sights, UIT target model, 460 FPS, 2.5 lbs. Disc. 1992.

| | $600 | $500 | $425 | $350 | $270 | $180 | $120 |

Last MSR was $1,100.

Add 10% for left-hand variation.

MODEL 102 – similar to Model 100, except has two cocking levers. Mfg. 1992.

| | $850 | $725 | $600 | $500 | $375 | $255 | $170 |

Last MSR was $1,555.

Add 10% for left-hand variation.

MODEL 103 – .177 cal., detachable UL, pneumatic, 6.38 in. BBL, 475-508 FPS, adj. trigger, adj. sights, adj. Morini grip (new 2005), 10.5 in. OAL, 3 lbs. Disc. 2008.

courtesy Beeman Collection

| | $1,200 | $1,025 | $850 | $700 | $550 | $350 | $240 |

Last MSR was $1,555.

Add 5% for left-hand variation.

RIFLES

MODEL 110 – .177 cal., SP, SL, SS, similar to Model 150, but no recoil-compensating mechanism, less than 200 made March 1962-March 1964. Extremely rare, esp. in good condition.

| | $1,800 | $1,400 | $1,000 | $800 | $600 | N/A | N/A |

Most existing specimens were heavily used by individuals or shooting club members.

GRADING	100%	95%	90%	80%	60%	40%	20%

MODEL 121 – .177 or .22 cal., basic European low power version of the Models 124 and 127, 465mm barrel, plain beechwood stock without buttplate or high comb. 7.2 lbs.

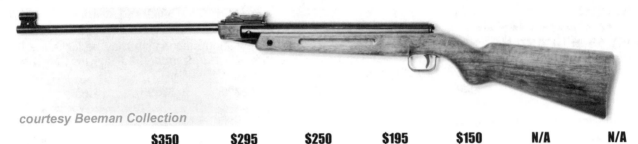

courtesy Beeman Collection

	$350	$295	$250	$195	$150	N/A	N/A

Add 30% for Deluxe version with checkered beechwood stock, buttplate, high comb.

This low-velocity model was not distributed in the USA.

MODEL 124 – .177 cal., BBC, SP, 780-830 FPS, early version with plastic trigger, rear sight marked 50m, 7.2 lbs. Disc. 1989. Ref: AR3: 61-62.

courtesy Beeman Collection

	N/A	$400	$395	$295	$195	N/A	N/A

Last MSR was $490.

Add 5% for San Rafael address. Add 10% for San Anselmo address.
Add 35% for factory deluxe with walnut stock.
Add 10% for left-hand deluxe version (rare).
Add 100% for custom select or fancy.
Add 110% for custom extra fancy.
Subtract 10% for no Wundhammer palm swell on Deluxe models.

MODEL 127 – .22 cal., BBC, SP, 620-680 FPS, rear sight marked 40m, 6 -7 lbs. Disc. 1989.

	N/A	$450	$395	$295	$195	N/A	N/A

Last MSR was $490.

Add 5% for San Rafael address. Add 10% for San Anselmo address.
Add 35% for factory deluxe with walnut stock.
Add 10% for left-hand deluxe version (rare).
Add 100% for custom select or fancy.
Add 110% for custom extra fancy.

MODEL 150 – .177 cal., SL, SP, first FWB airgun with the patented recoil-compensation sledge system, 20 in. (510mm) barrel, 450 FPS. Mfg. 1961-1968.

	$800	$600	$500	$475	$300	N/A	N/A

Add 60% for Tyrolean stock.

Most existing specimens were heavily used by individuals or shooting club members.

MODEL 200 – similar to Model 300, but without recoil-compensation mechanism.

	$400	$350	$280	$230	$180	$120	$80

MODEL 300 – .177 cal., SP long SL, recoil-compensation system, 460 FPS, rubber buttplate, rounded forearm, match aperture sight. Disc. 1972.

	N/A	$500	$500	$400	$250	N/A	N/A

GRADING	100%	95%	90%	80%	60%	40%	20%

* **Model 300S** – .177 cal., SP, SL, 640 FPS, 8.8-10.8 lbs. Disc. circa 1996.

courtesy Beeman Collection

	$950	$650	$525	$425	$325	N/A	N/A

Last MSR was $1,235.

Add 50% for Tyrolean stock.
Add 100% for Running Boar stock configuration or Universal Model with adj. cheek piece.
Add 20% for Match L Model, similar to Universal Model w/o adj. cheek piece.
Add 10% for figured walnut.
Subtract 10% for left-hand variation (all styles).
Add 10% for junior stock.

MODEL 500 – .177 cal., PCP, SS, match model, 10.8 in. barrel, 570 FPS, beech stock with fully adj. cheek piece, grip, and buttplate, adj. match trigger, 43.3-46.25 in. OAL, 10.8 lbs. Mfg. 2009-current.

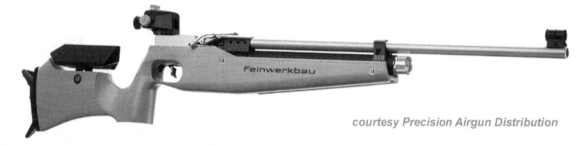

courtesy Precision Airgun Distribution

MSR $1,650	$1,375	$1,150	$950	$800	$625	$400	$275

MODEL 600 – .177 cal., SL, SSP, recoilless top-of-the-line match rifle with aperture sights, unique hardwood laminate stock, 585 FPS, 10.5 lbs. Disc. 1988.

	$800	$600	$500	$450	$300	N/A	N/A

Last MSR was $900.

Subtract 10% for left-hand variation.

This model was also available in a Running Boar variation with an extra-long barrel cover that unscrewed for transporting.

MODEL 601 – .177 cal., SL, SSP, 10.5 lbs.

	$850	$750	$650	$600	$400	N/A	N/A

Last MSR was $1,750.

Add 5% for 5454 diopter sight.
Subtract 10% for left-hand variation.
Add 25% for Running Target Model.

This model replaced the Model 600.

MODEL 602 – .177 cal., SL, SSP.

	$900	$800	$700	$650	$450	N/A	N/A

Last MSR was $1,875.

Subtract 10% for left-hand variation.

This model replaced the Model 601.

GRADING	100%	95%	90%	80%	60%	40%	20%

MODEL 603/603 JUNIOR – .177 cal., SL, SSP, recoilless top-of-the-line match rifle with aperture sights, unique hardwood laminate stock, 570 FPS, 43 in. OAL, 10. lbs. Disc. 2008.

courtesy Beeman Collection

	100%	95%	90%	80%	60%	40%	20%
	$2,150	$1,500	$1,300	$900	$795	N/A	N/A

Last MSR was $2,445.

Add 5% for left-hand variation.
Add 10% for multi-colored laminated stock.
Add 15% for left-hand multi-colored laminated stock.
Subtract 20% for FWB 603 Junior.

This model replaced the Model 602.

MODEL C60 – .177 cal., CO$_2$, 570 FPS, similar to Model 600, 9.2-10.6 lbs.

	100%	95%	90%	80%	60%	40%	20%
	$600	$525	$475	$375	NA	N/A	N/A

Last MSR was $1,675.

A Running Target Model was also available.

MODEL C60 MINI – .177 cal., CO$_2$, quick change cylinder (bottle), mini-version of Model C60, 7.75 lbs. Mfg. beginning in 1991. Disc.

	100%	95%	90%	80%	60%	40%	20%
	$650	$550	$475	$375	N/A	N/A	N/A

Last MSR was $1,675.

MODEL C62 – .177 cal., CO$_2$, similar to Model C60.

	100%	95%	90%	80%	60%	40%	20%
	$650	$550	$475	$375	N/A	N/A	N/A

Last MSR was $1,750.

MODEL P70 – .177 cal., PCP, lever cocking, match model, 17 in. barrel, adj. trigger, 570 FPS, laminated wood or multi-color stock with fully adj. cheek piece and buttplate, 10.6 lbs. New 1998.

courtesy Beeman Collection

	100%	95%	90%	80%	60%	40%	20%
	$1,800	$1,525	$1,250	$1,050	N/A	N/A	N/A

Add 5% for left-hand variation.
Add 10% for multi-colored stock.
Add 45% for right-hand P70 variation with aluminum stock (Field Target).
Add 50% for left-hand P70 variation with aluminum stock.
Subtract 10% for right-hand Running Target model with laminated wood stock.
Add 5% for left-hand Running Target model with laminated wood stock.

* **Model P70 Junior** – .177 cal., similar to Model P70, except has youth dimensions. Mfg. 1998-2006.

	100%	95%	90%	80%	60%	40%	20%
	$1,150	$1,000	$895	$750	$650	N/A	N/A

Last MSR was $1,595.

GRADING	100%	95%	90%	80%	60%	40%	20%

MODEL P75 BIATHLON – .177 cal., PCP, five-shot mag., match model, 17 in. barrel, repeat lever trigger system cocks trigger and transports magazine simultaneously, 570 FPS, laminated wood stock with fully adj. cheek piece and buttplate. New 2000.

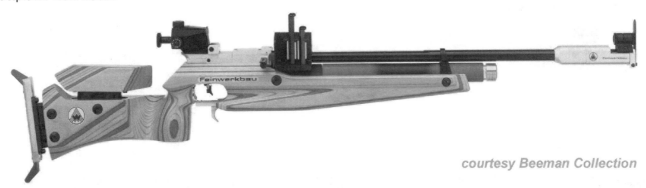

courtesy Beeman Collection

MSR $3,255	$2,850	$2,425	$2,000	$1,650	$1,275	$850	$575

MODEL 700 BENCHREST – .177 cal., CO_2, SP, 610-910 FPS, 16.73 in. barrel, colored laminated wood or anodized aluminum stock, available in silver/black, silver/blue, or silver/red, high precision adj. sighting system, anatomical adj. grips, adj. buttplate, adj. cheek piece, slender, sleek front stock design, adj. aluminum hand rest, 43.3-46.2 in. OAL. Disc. 2011.

courtesy Precision Airgun Distribution

	$2,375	$2,025	$1,650	$1,375	$1,075	$700	$475

Last MSR was $2,800.

MODEL 700 BENCHREST BASIC – .177 cal., CO_2, 780-815 FPS, 16.73 in. barrel, high quality beechwood in right or left-hand variation, adj. cheek piece and buttplate, interior absorber, Feinwerkbau precision diopter, front sight, silver compressed air cylinder with integrated manometer, adj. trigger, 43.7 in. OAL, 9.04 lbs.

courtesy Precision Airgun Distribution

MSR $2,000	$1,700	$1,450	$1,175	$975	$750	$500	$350

MODEL 700 JUNIOR – .177 cal., similar to Model 700, except has 700-740 FPS, 39.4-43.3 in. OAL. Mfg. 2007-current.

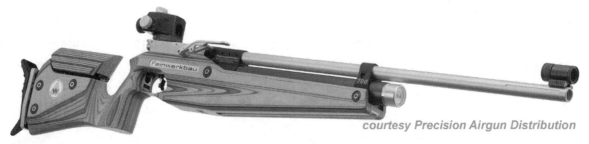

courtesy Precision Airgun Distribution

MSR $1,996	$1,700	$1,425	$1,175	$975	$750	$500	$350

GRADING	100%	95%	90%	80%	60%	40%	20%

MODEL 700 ALUMINUM BLUE – .177 cal., PCP, BA, SS, 16.73 in. rifled barrel, 557-574 FPS, globe front and diopter rear adj. sights, 5-way adj. match trigger, right or left-hand configuration, removable air reservoir with integral manometer (air pressure gauge), Blue anodized aluminum frame with blue laminated wood grip and adj. cheekpiece, adj. buttpad, inner absorber eliminates shooting impulse, 46.26 in. OAL, 10.58 lbs.

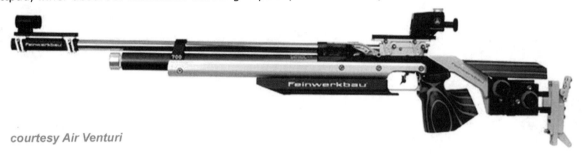

courtesy Air Venturi

MSR $3,350	$2,850	$2,425	$2,000	$1,650	$1,275	$850	$575

MODEL P700 ALUMINUM – .177 cal., PCP, SS, match model, 16.73 in. barrel, interior vibration absorber, 570 FPS, Silver/Black or Silver/Red aluminum stock with fully adj. cheek piece, grip, and buttplate, adj. match trigger, 43.3-46.25 in. OAL, 10.8 lbs. Mfg. 2004-current.

courtesy Precision Airgun Distribution

MSR $3,396	$2,900	$2,475	$2,025	$1,675	$1,300	$875	$575

Add $130 for left-hand variation.

* **Model 700 Aluminum Junior** – .177 cal., PCP, SS, match model, 10.8 in. barrel, interior vibration absorber, 570 FPS, aluminum stock with fully adj. cheek piece, grip, and buttplate, adj. match trigger, 39.4-43.3 in. OAL, 9.7 lbs. Mfg. 2004-2010.

	$2,250	$2,095	$1,750	$1,450	$1,150	N/A	N/A

Last MSR was $2,385.

MODEL P700 EVOLUTION – .177 cal., PCP, SS, match model, 16.73 in. barrel, 570 FPS, aluminum stock with fully adj. cheek piece, grip, and buttplate, adj. match trigger, universal right or left-hand ergonomic grip, adj. hand rest, available in green, blue, red, or yellow, 39.4-40.9 in. OAL, 7.94 lbs. Mfg. 2009-2011.

courtesy Precision Airgun Distribution

	$2,350	$2,195	$1,850	$1,550	$1,250	N/A	N/A

Last MSR was $2,800.

GRADING	100%	95%	90%	80%	60%	40%	20%

MODEL 700 EVOLUTION TOP – .177 cal., similar to the Model 700 Evolution, except has additional options, 39.8-43.7 in. OAL, 8.8 lbs. Mfg. 2009-2011.

courtesy Precision Airgun Distribution

	$1,875	$1,575	$1,300	$1,075	$850	$550	$375

Last MSR was $2,200.

MODEL P700 UNIVERSAL – .177 cal., PCP, SS, match model, 16.73 in. barrel, interior vibration absorber, 570 FPS, warp free white laminated wood stock with fully adj. cheek piece, grip, and buttplate, adj. match trigger, 43.3-44.9 in. OAL, 9.9 lbs. New 2004.

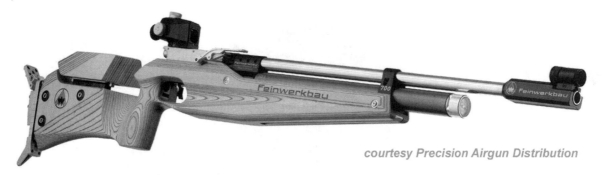

courtesy Precision Airgun Distribution

MSR $2,535	$2,150	$1,825	$1,500	$1,250	$975	$650	$425

Add $102 for left-hand variation.

MODEL 800 ALU – 177 cal., PCP, SS, 16.73 in. rifled barrel, Vario 4x4 adj. rear sight, laterally adj. globe front sight, anatomical beech wood grip, removable air cylinder with integral manometer (air pressure gauge), 557 to 574 FPS, Silver/Black or Silver/Red anodized aluminum, adj. hand rest, adj. buttplate (can be screwed in two positions) and cheekpiece, inner absorber eliminates shooting impulse, right or left-hand configuration, 41.93-46.65 in. OAL, 10.36 lbs.

MSR $2,885	$2,425	$2,075	$1,700	$1,400	$1,100	$725	$475

Add $75 for left-hand configuration.

MODEL 800 UNIVERSAL – .177 cal., PCP, rifled barrel, laminated wood stock with ergonomical grip, right or left-hand configuration, rail for mounting of a shooting sling, pressure reducer with optimized feedback control, full adj. buttplate, cheekpiece pivoted and height adjustable.

MSR $2,110	$1,800	$1,525	$1,250	$1,050	$800	$550	$350

MODEL 800 X – .177 cal., PCP, SS, 16.73 in. rifled barrel, Vario 4x4 adj. rear sight, laterally adj. globe front sight, match trigger with trigger stop, anatomical beech wood grip, removable air cylinder with integral manometer (air pressure gauge), 557 to 574 FPS, revolutionary front stock with optimum damping behavior, Silver/Black or Silver/Red anodized aluminum, adj. hand rest, height and length adj. buttplate and cheekpiece, inner absorber eliminates shooting impulse, right or left-hand configuration, 41.93-46.65 in. OAL, 10.36 lbs.

courtesy Air Venturi

MSR $3,100	$2,650	$2,250	$1,850	$1,525	$1,175	$800	$525

Add $50 for left-hand configuration.

GRADING	100%	95%	90%	80%	60%	40%	20%

FELTMAN PRODUCTS

Previous manufacturer of arcade and military training air machine guns. Founded by Chas. Feltman in Coney Island, NY in 1939. Sold to Wm. Meinch in early 1960s - for a short time Meinch added his name to the Feltman nameplates. Moved to Scotch Pines, NJ in 1978 and then to Center Moriches, N.Y. in 1986. Sold to Vintage Pneumatics in Sheboygan, WI in 1994 and then to Air Force Airguns in Fort Worth, Texas in 2003, where the last 50 Vintage Starfire guns were sold.

Fred Andreae Jr., former factory head of Feltmans, opened Shooting Star Inc. in NJ in 1986 to make high quality near-clones of the original Feltman Tommyguns (NOT available to collectors) under the Shooting Star brand and to repair the originals. Ref. Behling (2006).

MILITARY TRAINERS AND GALLERY AUTOMATICS

FELTMAN "CONEY ISLAND" PNEUMATIC MACHINE GUN – Feltman's first product. .174 in. cal. steel BBs, hose pneumatic, 110 AC, full auto 600 rpm @ 300 FPS, 200 shot convoluted tubular magazine, very similar appearance to Browning Water-Cooled Machine Gun, "Water Jacket" painted orange, receiver painted blue-black or blue, very sturdy, heavy construction of cast aluminum, steel, copper, and brass, heavy metal spade handles and massive swiveling tripod. Patent 2,238,384 issued June 1, 1939, improved with Patent 2,312,244 issued April 15, 1941. Used at Coney Island Amusement Park in N.Y. and 1939 World's Fair in San Francisco. 22 in. smoothbore bbl, 35 in. OAL, 24 lbs. Highest observed SN is 97; 10 specimens known.

courtesy Beeman Collection

	100%	95%	90%	80%	60%	40%	20%
	N/A	N/A	$3,500	$2,750	$2,000	$1,250	$750

Add 20% for original tripod.

Add 5% for use counter in window under "water jacket" barrel shroud.

FELTMAN "AIR-COOLED" PNEUMATIC MACHINE GUN – .160 in. cal. (No. 1 lead shot), full auto 1200 rpm @ 280 FPS, (Feltman Second Model) 101 shot convoluted tubular magazine, hose pneumatic, very similar appearance to Browning Air-Cooled .30 cal. Machine Gun, metal spade grips, ball-bearing 2 axis mount, ring rear sight with cross-wires, front post, same int. mechanism as Feltman Tommygun. About 1945-1950s.

* ***Feltman Second Model First Variation*** – welded steel plate receiver, 21 in. smoothbore barrel, 38.8 in. OAL, 16.1 lbs. 5 known.

courtesy Beeman Collection

	100%	95%	90%	80%	60%	40%	20%
	N/A	N/A	$3,500	$2,750	$2,000	$1,250	$750

GRADING	100%	95%	90%	80%	60%	40%	20%

* Feltman Second Model Second Variation – cast aluminum receiver, 20 in. smoothbore bbl., 37.1 in. OAL, 14.9 lbs. 1 specimen known.

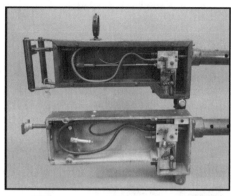

First Variation

Second Variation

courtesy Beeman Collection

	N/A	N/A	$3,500	$2,750	$2,000	$1,250	$750

Subtract 10% for missing mount.

FELTMAN "TOMMYGUN" PNEUMATIC MACHINE GUN

FELTMAN "TOMMYGUN" PNEUMATIC MACHINE GUN – .160 in. cal. (No. 1 lead shot), Hose pneumatic, full auto 1200 rpm @ 280 FPS, 101 shot convoluted tubular magazine, very similar appearance to Thompson Sub-Machine Gun with double grip handles, distinctive buttstock, walnut grip plates and stock, the infamous "Shoot Out the Star" target, designed by Wm. Meinch was all the harder to shoot out because some operators reused the lead shot! Point of impact adj. internally by moving the bbl. 12 in. smoothbore barrel, 35.5 in. OAL, 6.4 lbs. 5,700 mfg. 1941-1994.

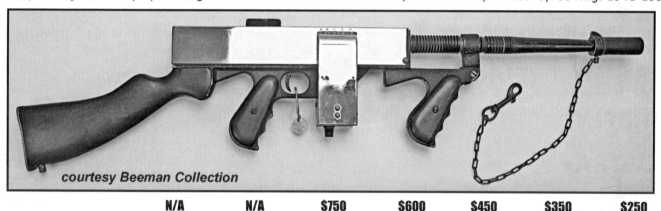

courtesy Beeman Collection

	N/A	N/A	$750	$600	$450	$350	$250

SHOOTING STAR COMMERCIAL GALLERY MACHINE GUNS

SHOOTING STAR COMMERCIAL GALLERY MACHINE GUNS – excellent current copies of Feltman Tommyguns sold by unrelated Shooting Star Inc. (See Feltman introduction) in kits of 2-6 guns for amusement parks only - so all are used. Regular Shooting Star (800+ made as of Jan. 2006) and Shooting Star Combat (3000+ made as of Jan. 2006) - both sell used for about $750 per gun. Ref. Behling (2006).

VINTAGE PNEUMATICS STARFIRE

VINTAGE PNEUMATICS STARFIRE – .160 in. cal. (No. 1 lead shot). Hose pneumatic, 125 psi, full auto 800 rpm @ 280 fps, 113 shot loading tube. Basically a very high quality copy of the Feltman Tommygun. 12 in. smoothbore bbl, 36 in. OAL, 6 lbs. 1994-2003.

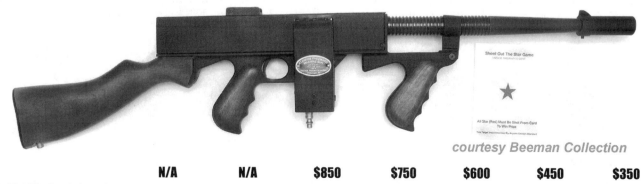

courtesy Beeman Collection

	N/A	N/A	$850	$750	$600	$450	$350

Add 30% for deluxe kit set from Air Force Airguns.

MSR $575 (1995) with 5 loading tubes, glasses, 25 Starfire targets, oil, rod. Production under 200, last 50 sold by Air Force Airguns in deluxe kits for $1,000 each with above items plus 25 lbs. #1 shot and a walnut display plaque made by Tom Gaylord. Mfg. 2003 only.

GRADING	100%	95%	90%	80%	60%	40%	20%

FIONDA

Trademark of previous line of CO_2 guns from Ind. Brasileira of Brazil. Production closed about 1990 due to governmental suppression of civilian arms.

RIFLES

FIONDA MODEL 63 – .177 in. balls, CO_2 filled from bulk cylinder, semi-automatic, began in Europe as the Italian ArmiGas Olimpic or the Austrian Tyrol C-O-Matic CO_2 rifle, then copied as the Venturini Golondrina C-O-Matic rifle and pistol in Argentina. Key feature is the removable, spring-fed 80 shot 21.3 in. tubular magazine along the RHS of barrel. Marked LHS: MOD. 63, PAT. PROV. NO. 129,028. RHS: FIONDA, IND. BRASILEIRA. One piece hardwood butt stock and forearm. Cross bolt manual safety. Metal black or black and silver, 22.2 in. rifled barrel, 39.4 in. OAL, 4.5 lbs.

courtesy Beeman Collection

$800	$675	$550	$450	$350	$240	$160

Add 10% for original bulk fill CO_2 tank.

This model is now rare in Brazil due to ban by and destruction of the Brazilian government; only a few outside of Brazil.

FIRE BALL (FIREBALL)

For information on Fire Ball (Fireball) airguns, see Apache in the "A" section.

FIREFLY

For information on Firefly air pistols, see Anson, E. & Co. in the "A" section.

FLECHA

Previous trade name of unknown Spanish manufacturer on air rifles. Research is ongoing.

FLÜRSCHEIM

For information on Flürscheim, see Gaggenau in the "G" section.

FOOTE, H.S.

Previous manufacturer of unknown location, probably U.S.A. 1904.

PISTOL

TROMBONE PISTOL – .21 in. cal., SS, SP, 6 in. cocked by using two fingers of off hand on lateral prongs to pull cocking tube back, brass cover slides open to breech load thin, brass, smoothbore 6 in. barrel, brass frame and receiver, walnut inset grips. Marked on top of receiver: H.S. FOOTE, MAKER, 1904. 14.3 in. OAL, 1.4 lbs.

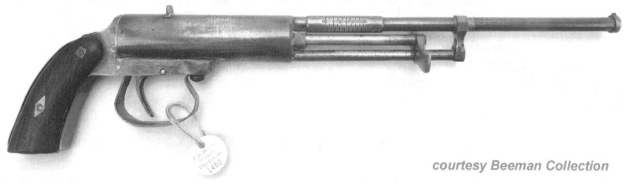

courtesy Beeman Collection

Scarcity precludes accurate pricing.

G SECTION

GAGGENAU IRONWORKS (EISENWERKE GAGGENAU)

Previous airgun manufacturer located in Gaggenau, Germany circa 1879-1900. (See also Dianawerk, Gem, Haviland & Gunn and Lincoln sections in this text.)

The authors and publisher wish to thank Mr. Ulrich Eichstädt for much of the following information in this section of the *Blue Book of Airguns*.

The Gaggenau Ironworks (Eisenwerke Gaggenau) was noted as a "very old company" in a letter dated 1680. Gaggenau is a small town near Rastatt in the middle of the German Black Forest, an area traditionally famous for gunmaking (Feinwerkbau, Dianawerk, Heckler & Koch, and Mauser). The ironworks were not very successful during the 17th century. Although they had cheap power from the nearby Murg-creek, the distance to iron ore forced them to use scrap metal as raw material. Their fortunes were changed in the mid-1800s with the addition of a new casting furnace and especially by their connection, via the Murgtal railroad, to Rastatt and the modern rail system spreading across Europe. By the end of the century, they were producing structural steel, bridges, railings, gas regulators, crushing and paint mills, enamel advertising signs, and bicycles. In 1873, Michael Flürscheim (1844-1912) purchased the works with its forty workers. Flürscheim added a joiners' shop, a tool shop, metal-plating equipment, and a wood processing division to produce rifle stocks. The staff grew to 390 in 1882 and 1,041 in 1889.

Theodor Bergmann (later famous with Louis Schmeisser as a designer of self-loading cartridge pistols) joined Flürscheim as managing partner in 1879. One year earlier Flürscheim had been granted a patent for an air pistol, and in 1879, he patented two air pistol improvements. Thus, the company's first air pistol, sometimes known as the Bergmann Air Pistol is more properly the Flürscheim air pistol. The Flürscheim air pistol may be Germany's oldest production air pistol. Actually, this pistol, right down to the detail of its disassembly/cocking tool, seems to be a clear copy of the Haviland and Gunn pistol patented in the USA in 1872. At that time, companies outside of the USA were more interested in local monopoly than they were worried about overseas lawsuits.

Jakob Mayer worked in the Gaggenau Ironworks before he founded Dianawerk in nearby Rastatt in 1890. It comes as no surprise that he used the same basic design for his first MGR air pistol (see Dianawerk section). Around 1905, the same design again appeared in Belgium, marked "Brevet" (French for Patent!). Possibly the same unknown maker also made the virtually identical "Dare Devil Dinkum" air pistol which later appeared on the British market based on George Gunn's 1872 invention in far-off Ilion, New York. As noted in the Lincoln section of this book, the same design led to the Lincoln air pistols and the famous Walther LP 53.

By 1891, the "gun division" in Gaggenau produced hunting and military rifles, air rifles and air pistols, gun barrels, reloading tools, and clay-target traps. Production of airguns had become significant, especially of Gem-style air rifles. Pellets and darts were made by automatic machines at about 20,000 pellets per hour.

From 1885 to 1898, the official brand of Gaggenau was two crossed Flürscheim air pistols, usually with the letter "E" above and "G" below. Apparently, many guns made by Gaggenau were not marked, probably so that they could be sold under other trade names.

Two other Flürscheim patents for airguns are known: Patent no. 399962 covers a combination air rifle/.22 firearm apparently derived from George Gunn's combination airgun/rimfire rifle or its derivatives, the Quackenbush Model 5 and Gem air rifles. The second patent, no. 42091 from June 5, 1887, covers a repeating air rifle with a spring-fed magazine for pointed pellets.

Production of Gaggenau airguns apparently ceased about 1900. However, some airguns bearing the Bergmann name or Th.B. may date from 1880 to as late as 1920. Today the Gaggenau company is one of the largest manufacturers of built-in kitchen appliances in Germany and sells to fifty countries on all five continents. The former question as to whether the company should be called Eisenwerke, which simply means Iron Works in German (no more descriptive than Manufacturing Works or just Factory), or Gaggenau, has been resolved by the company which calls itself Gaggenau. Refs: Atkins, AG July 1990; Hannusch, AAG Jan-May 1992.

PISTOLS

FLUERSCHEIM – several calibers including .181 cal., smooth bore for darts, SP, mainspring in grip, barrel and grip of gray cast iron, outer parts nickel plated, deeper parts of raised floral patterns and checkering painted black, separate cocking device has two small hooks which grip protruding piston shaft knob during cocking, two prongs at other end of this tool serve as a spanner wrench for removing mainspring retainer ring, later version of the pistol has large T-shaped handle at the end of the piston shaft to allow cocking without a separate tool, fitted wooden cases. Mfg.

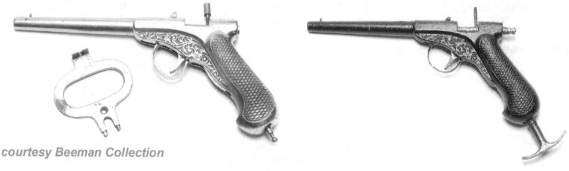

courtesy Beeman Collection

GRADING	100%	95%	90%	80%	60%	40%	20%

circa 1881- early 1900s.

	$1,500	$1,275	$1,050	$875	$675	$450	$300

The wooden cases almost surely were also made by Gaggenau. The company had a box factory producing nearly 300,000 special wooden boxes per year for tools, guns, cigars, etc.

Reference: Dr. Bruno Brukner

PEERLESS – .21 cal., SP, rear cocking "T"-shaped handle, one-piece wood grip and forearm, nickel plated. Mfg. 1885-1895.

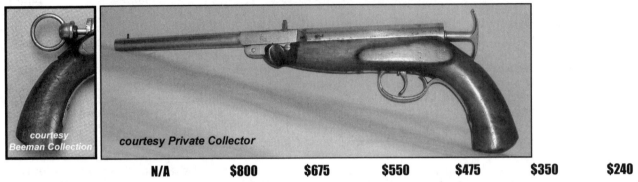

courtesy Beeman Collection

courtesy Private Collector

	N/A	$800	$675	$550	$475	$350	$240

A Ring is a replacement for the original "T" handle.

CONTRACT MODELS – evidently a variety of cast iron push-barrel air pistols were made under other brands or without brand markings.

Values generally run from about $50 to $300.

PP TARGET PISTOL ("PATENT-PRÄCISIONS") – .180 cal., SP, BBC, SS, small, LHS "push-lever" lock barrel release lever assembly, one-piece hardwood grip and forearm, carved flutes on grip, Schnabel forearm, complex cocking leverage system, cocking plunger exposed under barrel, marked "PATENT" and with Gaggenau crossed-pistols logo on barrel, similar to mechanism and styling as Gaggenau rifles marked "COLUMBIA". Nickel-plated/blued, 8.7 in. smoothbore, octagonal BBL, 18.3 in. OAL, 2.8 lbs. Mfg. circa 1880s-1890.

courtesy Beeman Collection

	N/A	$2,950	$2,450	$1,950	$1,600	$1,225	$850

RIFLES

MODEL 1 GALLERY RIFLE – .25 in. cal., SP, UL, SS, 23.5 in. smoothbore blued BBL, nickel-plated metal work, the forward end of the cocking lever has a very distinctive, trigger-guard-like loop just behind the real trigger guard loop. 42.5 in. OAL, 6 lbs. Circa 1881-87. Ref: AAG - Jan. 1992.

No current values available at this time.

Ref: Hannusch AAG Jan-March 1992.

MODEL 2 COLUMBIA – .21 cal., SP, BBC, SS, rear sight slides as barrel release, smoothbore octagonal barrel, one-piece hardwood buttstock, sweeping cheek piece, and Schnabel forearm, complex cocking leverage system, cocking plunger exposed under barrel, marked "PATENT" and with Gaggenau crossed-pistols logo and "COLUMBIA" on barrel (some not marked "COLUMBIA"). Nickel-plated/blued, 18.7 in. smoothbore, octagonal BBL. Circa 1880s.

courtesy Beeman Collection

	N/A	$2,250	$1,800	$1,450	$1,125	$775	$450

GRADING	100%	95%	90%	80%	60%	40%	20%

MODEL 3 GEM – (see Gem section) especially the distinction between combo rimfire firearm/airgun and airgun-only models (see figures here and in the Gem section).

courtesy Beeman Collection

LH insert shows Gaggenau logo stamped on the barrel. It depicts a crossed pair of Flürscheim air pistols.
Upper gun in RH insert is a combination rimfire and air gun. Note the side wings of the cartridge case extractor.

GALWAY

Previous trademark of Galway Arms Co. located in Leicestershire, England, founded in 1964.

The Galway Arms Co. manufactured high grade firearm silencers and introduced the first airgun silencers (requiring a $200 transfer tax in USA). In 1983, the company developed and produced in limited numbers the Fieldmaster Mark 2 PCP rifle with adjustable power levels and easily interchanged barrels in .177, .20, or .22 cal.

Excellent condition specimens sell in the $2,000 range.

GAMO PRECISION AIRGUNS (INDUSTRIAS EL GAMO, S.A.U.)

Current trademark manufactured by Industrias El Gamo, located in Barcelona, Spain. Currently imported by Gamo Outdoor USA, Inc., located in Ft. Lauderdale, FL. Previously imported by Stoeger Industries, located in Wayne, NJ, and by Dynamit Nobel, RWS, Inc., located in Closter, NJ. Dealer sales.

One of the oldest manufacturers of lead products in Europe, Gamo was founded during the late 1880s in Barcelona, Spain, as Antonio Casas, S.A. Sixty years ago, the company changed its name to Industrias El Gamo, and expanded into the manufacturing of high-quality airgun pellets and precision airguns. Today, Gamo is one of the largest airgun manufacturers in Europe. Some models were also sold by Daisy.

HANDGUNS

AF-10 – .177 cal. pellets or BBs (new 2012), pneumatic, non-blowback action, 430 FPS, 7 in. barrel, full metal slide, 1 1/4 lbs. Importation disc. 1993. Re-introduced 2012.

MSR N/A	$90	$75	$65	$50	$40	$25	$20

Last MSR in 1993 was $115.

AUTO 45 – .177 cal., CO_2, DA, 12 BB magazine or SS with pellets, 410 FPS, 4.3 in. rifled steel BBL, manual safety, 1.1 lbs. Mfg. 1999-2004.

	$75	$65	$55	$45	$35	$20	$15

Last MSR was $100.

C-15 BLOWBACK – BB/.177 cal., 12g CO_2, semi-auto blowback, 480 FPS, compact design, smooth steel barrel, 15 shot mag., manual safety, fixed sights with reflective white dots. New 2013.

courtesy GAMO Outdoor USA

MSR $100	$85	$75	$70	$55	$40	N/A	N/A

GRADING	100%	95%	90%	80%	60%	40%	20%

CENTER – .177 cal., UL, SP, 400-435 FPS, 14 in. barrel, 2 lbs. 8 oz. Mfg. 1973-1994.

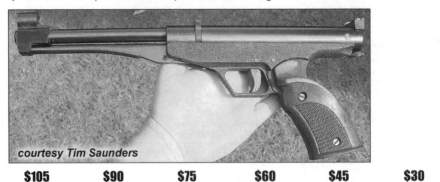

courtesy Tim Saunders

$105	$90	$75	$60	$45	$30	$20

COMPACT TARGET – .177 cal., SSP, 400 FPS, 9 1/4 in. rifled steel barrel, adj. match trigger, fully adj. rear sight, anatomical walnut grip with heavy stippling and adj. palm shelf, 1.94 lbs. Disc. 2010. Re-introduced 2012.

courtesy Gamo Collection

MSR N/A	$245	$210	$170	$140	$110	$75	$50

Last MSR in 2010 was $290.

FALCON – .177 cal., UL, SP, 430 FPS, 7 in. barrel, ABS plastic grips, 2 7/8 lbs. Importation disc. 1993.

$80	$70	$55	$45	$35	$25	$15

Last MSR was $105.

K1 DOUG KOENIG – .177 cal., CO_2, non-blowback action, full metal black slide, black grips, tan finish. New 2012.

Please contact the importer directly for pricing and availability on this model.

MP9 BLOWBACK – BB/.177 cal. or pellet, 12g CO_2, SA/DA, semi-auto blowback, 458 FPS, precision rifled steel barrel, manual safety, 21 in. OAL. New 2013.

courtesy GAMO Outdoor USA

MSR $150	$130	$115	$100	$85	$65	N/A	N/A

This model is also available in a tactical version (MP9 Blowback Tactical, New 2014). Please contact the importer directly for more information, pricing, and availability for this model.

P-23 – .177 cal., CO_2, DA, 12 BB magazine or SS with pellets, 410 FPS, 4.25 in. rifled steel barrel, manual safety, 1 lbs. Disc. 2010.

courtesy Gamo Collection

$75	$65	$55	$45	$35	$20	$15

Last MSR was $90.

GRADING	100%	95%	90%	80%	60%	40%	20%

* ***P-23 Combat*** – BB/.177 cal., CO$_2$, DA, 10 BB magazine or SS with pellets, 410 FPS, 4.25 in. rifled steel barrel, adj. rear sight, black color with ergonomic rubber grip, manual safety, 7.5 in. OAL, 1 lb. Mfg. 2009-current.

MSR $70	$60	$55	$50	$40	$30	N/A	N/A

* ***P-23 Combo Laser*** – .177 cal., CO$_2$, DA, 12 BB magazine or SS with pellets, 410 FPS, 4.25 in. rifled steel barrel, 650Nm laser sight mounted under frame, manual safety, 1.1 lbs. Disc. 2010.

courtesy Gamo Collection

	$120	$100	$85	$70	$55	$35	$25

Last MSR was $140.

P-25 BLOWBACK – .177 cal., CO$_2$, semi-auto blowback system, SA/DA, 16-shot rotary magazine, 4.25 in. rifled steel barrel, 450 FPS (with PBA Platinum ammo, new 2011), manual safety, fixed sights with reflective white dots, 3-dot position aiming, black finish with checkered and textured grip, 7.72 in. OAL, 1.5 lbs. Mfg. 2010-current.

MSR $105	$90	$80	$70	$60	$45	N/A	N/A

P-25 BLOWBACK TACTICAL – .177 cal., CO$_2$, semi-auto blowback system, SA/DA, 16-shot rotary magazine, 4.25 in. compensator rifled steel barrel, 500 FPS, or 560 FPS (with PBA Platinum ammo, new 2011), black metal full action blowback slide, textured grip, manual safety, adj. fixed sights with reflective white dots, quad rail with 80 Lumen tactical light and 20mm RGB dot sight, push button and momentary pressure switches, includes 50 rds. PBA Platinum ammo, 14.96 in. OAL, 2.8 lbs. Mfg. 2010-current.

MSR $190	$160	$145	$130	$105	$80	N/A	N/A

P-900 – .177 cal., SP, non-blowback action, black finish, textured grips. New 2012.

Please contact the importer directly for pricing and availability on this model.

This model is also available as a P-900 Gun Set which includes flat catch pellets, targets, 80 Lumen tactical flashlight, RGB red dot 30mm, and 65mm laser.

P-900 IGT – .177 cal., IGT, TruGlo sights, black finish. New 2014.

As this edition went to press, pricing and model specs could not be ascertained for this model.

PR-45 – .177 cal., pneumatic, 9 1/4 in. barrel, 1 lb. 9 oz.

	$115	$100	$80	$65	$50	$35	$25

Last MSR was $135.

PT-80 – .177 cal., CO$_2$, semi-auto, SA/DA, 410 FPS, tilt-up barrel for quick loading of the 8-shot rotary magazine, 4.25 in. rifled steel barrel, black finish, manual safety, adj. three-dot sights, 4.2 in. OAL, 1.2 lbs. New 2001.

courtesy Gamo Collection

MSR $80	$70	$60	$55	$45	$35	N/A	N/A

Add $10 for wood grips (new 2002).

GRADING	100%	95%	90%	80%	60%	40%	20%

PT-80 LASER – .177 cal., CO_2, semi-auto, SA/DA, 410 FPS, tilt-up barrel for quick loading of the eight-shot rotary magazine, 4.25 in. rifled steel barrel, manual safety, adj. three-dot sights, 650nm laser sight mounted under frame, 7.2 in. OAL, 1.2 lbs. Mfg. 2001-2010. Re-introduced 2012.

courtesy Gamo Collection

MSR N/A	$135	$115	$95	$80	$60	$40	$25

PT-80 TACTICAL – .177 cal., CO_2, semi-auto, SA/DA, tilt-up barrel for quick loading of the eight-shot rotary magazine, 4.25 in. rifled steel fixed bull barrel, 410 FPS, manual safety, adj. three-dot sights, muzzle blast suppressor, tactical scope rail with Quick Shot illuminated red point scope, and tactical 35 lumens flashlight with pressure pad, 7.2 in. OAL, 1.8 lbs. New 2006.

courtesy Gamo Precision Airguns

MSR N/A	$130	$110	$90	$75	$60	$40	$25

Add $10 for wood grips (new 2002).

PT-85 BLOWBACK – .177 cal., CO_2, semi-auto blowback system, SA/DA, 16-shot magazine, 4.25 in. rifled steel barrel, 450 FPS (with PBA Platinum ammo, new 2011), black metal, Desert (new 2012), or Olive (New 2014) finish, full action blowback slide, textured grip, manual safety, fixed sights, 11.02 in. OAL, 1.5 lbs. Mfg. 2010-current.

MSR $115	$100	$85	$80	$65	$50	N/A	N/A

PT-85 BLOWBACK TACTICAL – .177 cal., CO_2, semi-auto blowback action, SA/DA, 16-shot magazine, 4.25 in. compensator rifled steel barrel, 450 FPS or 560 FPS (with PBA Platinum ammo, new 2011), black metal, full action blowback slide, manual safety, includes quad rail, 650nm laser sight, 80 Lumen tactical light, pressure switch on grip, and 50 rds. PBA Platinum ammo, 30mm RGB dot adj. sights, 15.11 in. OAL, 3.3 lbs. Mfg. 2010-current.

MSR $270	$230	$205	$185	$150	$115	N/A	N/A

PT-85 BLOWBACK SOCOM – .177 cal., CO_2, semi-auto blowback action, SA/DA, 16-shot mag., compensator rifled steel barrel, 500 FPS or 560 FPS (with PBA Platinum ammo, new 2011), black metal, full action blowback slide, manual safety, quad rail, includes 50 rds. PBA Platinum ammo, 15.11 in. OAL, 2.32 lbs. Mfg. 2010-current.

MSR $140	$120	$105	$95	$75	$60	N/A	N/A

PT-90 – .177 cal., CO_2, semi-auto, SA/DA, 410 FPS, tilt-up barrel for quick loading of the eight-shot rotary magazine, 4.25 in. rifled steel BBL, blue or chrome finish, manual safety, adj. three-dot sights, 1.2 lbs. Mfg. 2002-2006.

	$80	$70	$55	$45	$35	$25	$15

Last MSR was $115.

Add $5 for chrome finish.

GRADING	100%	95%	90%	80%	60%	40%	20%

PX-107 – .177 cal., CO_2, semi-auto, non-blowback action, 15-shot BB magazine also holds CO_2 cylinder in grip, 425 FPS, rifled steel barrel, black or chrome finish, adj. rear three-dot sight, manual safety, 7.9 in. OAL, 0.8 lbs. Mfg. 2005-2010. Re-introduced 2012.

courtesy Gamo Precision Airguns

MSR N/A	$75	$65	$55	$45	$35	$20	$15

Last MSR in 2010 was $90.

Add $10 for chrome finish.

PX-107 LASER – .177 cal., CO_2, semi-auto, 15-shot BB magazine also holds CO_2 cylinder in grip, 425 FPS, rifled steel barrel, black or chrome finish, adj. rear three-dot sight, 650Nm laser sight mounted under frame, manual safety, 7.9 in. OAL, 0.8 lbs. Mfg. 2005-2007.

courtesy Gamo Collection

	$125	$105	$90	$75	$55	$35	$25

Last MSR was $140.

Add $10 for chrome finish.

R 357 – .177 cal., CO_2, SA/DA revolver, 5.7 in. Lothar Walther barrel, target-style front sight, adj. rear sight, plastic grips. Mfg. 1997-2001.

	$115	$100	$80	$65	$50	$35	$25

Last MSR was $130.

R-77 CLASSIC/COMBAT 2.5/COMBAT 4 – .177 cal., SA/DA revolver, CO_2 (12-gram cartridge in grip housing), checkered walnut (Classic) or Santoprene (Combat) grips, swing-out cylinder holds eight pellets, 2.5 (R-77 2.5), 4 (Combat) or 6 in. rifled steel barrel, 400 FPS, adj. rear sights, cross-bolt hammer block safety, 8-11.6 in. OAL, 1.5 lbs. Disc. 2006.

	$70	$60	$50	$40	$30	$20	$15

Last MSR was $100.

Add $20 for R-77 Classic.

R-77 COMBAT LASER – .177 cal., SA/DA revolver, CO_2 (12-gram cartridge in grip housing), checkered walnut (Classic) or Santoprene (Combat) grips, swing-out cylinder holds eight pellets, 2.5 (R-77 2.5), 4 (Combat) or 6 in. rifled steel BBL, 400 FPS, adj. rear sights, cross-bolt hammer block safety, R77 Laser has built-in grip-pressure activated 650 Nm laser mounted in barrel shroud. Disc. 2006.

	$125	$105	$90	$75	$55	$35	$25

Last MSR was $200.

TAC 82X – .177 cal., CO_2, non-blowback action, full metal black slide, black grips, military green finish, tactical rail. New 2012.

Please contact the importer directly for pricing and availability on this model.

GRADING	100%	95%	90%	80%	60%	40%	20%

V-3 – BB/.177 cal., CO_2, semi-auto, DA, 15-shot BB magazine also holds CO_2 cylinder in grip, 425 FPS, 4.25 in. rifled steel barrel, full metal slide, black or chrome finish, adj. rear three-dot sight, manual safety, skeletonized trigger, 7.6 in. OAL, 1.1 lbs.

courtesy Gamo Collection

MSR $80	$70	$60	$55	$45	$35	N/A	N/A

Add $10 for chrome finish.

V-3 LASER – .177 cal., CO_2, semi-auto, 15-shot BB magazine also holds CO_2 cylinder in grip, 425 FPS, rifled steel barrel, black or chrome (disc. 2010) finish, adj. rear three-dot sight, 650Nm laser sight mounted under frame, manual safety, skeletonized trigger, 7.6 in. OAL, 1.1 lbs.

courtesy Gamo Collection

MSR $150	$130	$115	$100	$85	$65	N/A	N/A

Add $10 for chrome finish (disc. 2010).

RIFLES

RECALL NOTICE: December 6, 2006 GAMO USA Corp., of Fort Lauderdale, FL issued a recall for the following GAMO models: Hunter Pro, Hunter Sport, Shadow Sport, and F1200. These models bare the serial numbers 04-IC-415577-06 through 04-IC-579918-06. The model and serial numbers can be found on the left side of the barrel just above the front left side of the stock. Models Shadow Sport and F1200 look identical. Sold by: Sporting goods stores and gun shops nationwide from June 2006 to September 2006. Contact GAMO USA Corp. directly or on their website (see Trademark Index) for additional information.

Note: Integrated dampener (built in noise reduction device) see Silencer in the Glossary.

ANTONIO CASAS BB Gun – BB/.173 cal., SP, 6.2 in. barrel, Winchester-style lever action, decal on RHS has Casas' initials around a deer and an ad for El Gamo lead "Diabolo" pellets. Mfg. circa 1930.

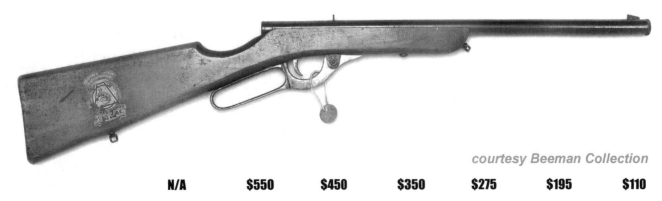

courtesy Beeman Collection

N/A	$550	$450	$350	$275	$195	$110

GRADING	100%	95%	90%	80%	60%	40%	20%

BARRICADE – .177 or .22 cal., steel barrel, green synthetic stock with ergonomic design, SWA recoil pad, 5.1 lbs. New 2012.

  Please contact the importer directly for pricing and availability on this model.

BIG CAT – .22 cal., BBC, SP, 975 FPS (with PBA ammo), 18 in. fluted rifled steel barrel, all-weather black synthetic stock with twin cheek pads, SWA recoil pad, non-slip checkering on grip and forearm, includes 25 rds. PBA ammo, 4x32 scope and rings, 43.3 in. OAL, 6.1 lbs. New 2012.

MSR $200	$170	$150	$135	$110	$85	N/A	N/A

BIG CAT (BIG CAT 1200) – .177 or .22 (disc. 2011) cal., BBC, SP, 1250 FPS (with PBA Platinum ammo), 950 FPS (.22 cal., disc.), 18 in. fluted polymer and rifled steel barrel, two-stage adj. trigger, cocking and trigger safeties, 4x32mm scope with rings, all-weather black Monte Carlo-style synthetic stock with twin cheek pads, non-slip checkering on grip and forearm, ventilated rubber (disc. 2011) or SWA (new 2012) recoil pad, two-piece solid mount, includes 50 rds. PBA Platinum ammo, 43.3 in. OAL, 6.1 lbs. Mfg. 2010-current.

courtesy GAMO Outdoor USA

MSR $200	$170	$150	$135	$110	$85	N/A	N/A

BIG CAT 1400 – .177 cal., BBC, SP, 1400 FPS (Platinum PBA), 18 in. fluted polymer jacketed rifled steel barrel, SAT, all-weather black stock with twin cheek pads, rubberized grips, SWA recoil pad, SAT, manual safety, includes 4x32 scope and 59 rounds PBA ammo, 44.7 in. OAL, 6.61 lbs. New 2013.

courtesy GAMO Outdoor USA

MSR $230	$195	$175	$155	$125	$95	N/A	N/A

LITTLE CAT – .177 cal., BBC, SP, 525 FPS, metal steel barrel, fiber optic sights, Beechwood stock designed for young shooters, 33.3 in. OAL, 5.5 lbs. New 2013.

MSR $130	$110	$100	$90	$70	$55	N/A	N/A

BLACK BULL – .177 or .22 cal., SP, 33mm cylinder, 420 FPS, Bull Whisper technology, SAT, black synthetic ambidextrous stock with SWA recoil pad, includes 4x32WR scope.

  Please contact the importer directly for pricing and availability on this model.

BLACK BULL IGT MACH1 – .177 or .22 cal., IGT Mach1, 33mm cylinder, 420 FPS, Bull Whisper technology, SAT, black synthetic ambidextrous stock with SWA recoil pad, SAT, includes 3-9x40 scope. New 2014.

  Please contact the importer directly for pricing and availability on this model.

BLACK KNIGHT – .177 or .22 cal., BBC, SP, 1100 FPS, black synthetic stock with SWA recoil pad, SAT trigger, 6.6 lbs.

  Please contact the importer directly for pricing and availability on this model.

BLACK KNIGHT IGT MACH1 – .177 or .22 cal., IGT Mach1, 33mm cylinder, 420 FPS, black synthetic ambidextrous stock with SWA recoil pad, SAT, TruGlo fiber optic sights, includes 3-9x40WR scope. New 2014.

  Please contact the importer directly for pricing and availability on this model.

BLACK FUSION – .177 or .22 cal., BBC, SP, 340/255 FPS, barrel with Whisper Fusion noise and muzzle blast dampener, SAT trigger, black synthetic stock with SWA recoil pad, 6.6 lbs. New 2012.

  Please contact the importer directly for pricing and availability on this model.

GRADING	100%	95%	90%	80%	60%	40%	20%

BLACK FUSION IGT MACH 1 – .177 or .22 cal., IGT Mach1, 33mm cylinder, 420 FPS, Whisper Fusion technology, SAT, TruGlo fiber optic sights, black synthetic ambidextrous stock, SWA recoil pad. New 2014.

Please contact the importer directly for pricing and availability on this model.

BLACK SHADOW – .177 or .22 cal., steel barrel, black synthetic stock with ergonomic design, SWA recoil pad, 5.1 lbs. New 2012.

Please contact the company directly for pricing and availability on this model.

BLACK SHADOW IGT – .177 or .22 cal., IGT, 200/160 FPS, rifled steel barrel, SAT trigger, black synthetic ergonomic stock with SWA recoil pad, non-slip checkering on grip and forearm, 5.3 lbs. New 2012.

Please contact the company directly for pricing and availability on this model.

BONE COLLECTOR – .177 or .22 cal., BBC, SP, SS, 1250/950 (with PBA Platinum ammo) FPS, 18 in. fluted polymer and rifled steel BBL, two-stage adj. trigger, cocking and trigger safeties, 3-9x40 scope, all-weather green synthetic stock with dark gray rubber grips and twin cheek pads, ventilated rubber butt pad, 46 in. OAL, 5.28 lbs. Mfg. 2010-2011.

courtesy GAMO Outdoor USA

	$325	$275	$230	$190	$145	$95	$65

Last MSR was $370.

BONE COLLECTOR BULL WHISPER – .177 or .22 cal., IGT, BBC, 1250/950 FPS (with PBA ammo), 19.2 in. Bull Whisper noise dampener, fluted, steel barrel, all-weather green synthetic stock, rubber grips, twin cheek pads, non-slip checkering on grip and forearm, SWA recoil pad, SAT two-stage trigger, fiber optic sights, one-piece solid mount, includes 4x32 scope and PBA Platinum ammo, 44.6 in. OAL, 5.28 lbs. New 2012.

courtesy GAMO Outdoor USA

MSR $290	$245	$220	$195	$160	$120	N/A	N/A

BULL WHISPER – .177 or .22 cal., BBC, SP, 305/220 FPS, Bull Whisper barrel, SAT trigger, black synthetic thumbhole stock with SWA recoil pad, includes 4x32 scope, 6.2 lbs. New 2012.

Please contact the company directly for pricing and availability on this model.

BULL WHISPER EXTREME – .177 or .22 cal., BBC, SP, 1400/1000 FPS (with PBA ammo), 19.2 in. bull barrel with Whisper integrated noise dampener, all-weather black synthetic stock with twin cheek pads, non-slip checkering on grip and forearm, one-piece solid mount, SWA recoil pad, SAT two-stage adj. trigger, manual safety, 3-9x40AO scope, PBA ammo included, 45.9 in. OAL, 6.61 lbs. New 2012.

courtesy GAMO Outdoor USA

MSR $320	$270	$240	$220	$175	$135	N/A	N/A

GRADING	100%	95%	90%	80%	60%	40%	20%

CADET – .177 cal., BBC, SP, 570 FPS, beechwood stock, 5 lbs.

	$70	$60	$50	$40	$30	$20	$15

CAMO ROCKET IGT – .177 cal., IGT, BBC, 1250 FPS (with PBA ammo), 18 in. fluted rifled steel barrel, all-weather Real Tree synthetic stock with twin cheek pads, vent. rubber recoil pad, non-slip checkering on grip and forearm, SAT two-stage adj. trigger, manual safety, 4x32 scope with rings, includes 50 rds. PBA Platinum ammo, 43 in. OAL, 6.1 lbs. New 2012.

MSR $240	$205	$180	$165	$130	$100	N/A	N/A

CARBINE SPORT – .177 cal., BBC, SP, 640/880 (with PBA ammo) FPS, rifled steel BBL, adj. trigger, cocking and trigger safeties, 4x32 scope, Monte Carlo-style synthetic stock with soft forearm insert, ventilated rubber butt pad, 41.75 in. OAL, 5.3 lbs. Mfg. 2006-2010.

courtesy Gamo Collection

	$160	$135	$110	$95	$70	$50	$30

Last MSR was $190.

CF 20 – .177 or .22 cal., UL, SP, 790-625 FPS, 17.75 in. barrel, checkered stock, 6 lbs. 6 oz. Importation disc. 1993.

	$155	$130	$110	$90	$70	$45	$30

Last MSR was $190.

CF-30 – .177 cal., UL, SP, 950 FPS, rifled steel barrel with scope mount rail, micrometer rear sight with four-position interchangeable windage plate, two-stage trigger, manual cocking and trigger safeties, Monte Carlo-style walnut stained beech stock with checkered grip, ventilated rubber butt pad, 6.4 lbs. Disc. 2001.

	$215	$185	$150	$125	$95	$65	$45

Last MSR was $270.

CFR – .177 or .22 cal., SP, black synthetic thumbhole stock with rubber grips, SWA recoil pad, adj. cheekpiece, TruGlo fiber optic sights, 6.8 lbs. New 2012.

> **Please contact the importer directly for pricing and availabity on this model.**

CFR IGT – .177 or .22 cal., IGT, 280/210 FPS, fixed barrel, SAT trigger, adj. cheek piece, black synthetic thumbhole stock with SWA recoil pad, non-slip checkering on grip and forearm, 6.6 lbs. New 2012.

> **Please contact the importer directly for pricing and availability on this model.**

CFR WHISPER – .177 or .22 cal., BBC, SP, 280/210 FPS, fluted rifled steel fixed barrel with Whisper sound moderator in the muzzle, adj. cheekpiece, black synthetic thumbhole stock with SWA recoil pad, non-slip checkering on grip and forearm, TruGlo fiber optic sights, 7.7 lbs. New 2012.

> **Please contact the importer directly for pricing and availability on this model.**

CFR WHISPER IGT – .177 or .22 cal., IGT, 280/210 FPS, fluted rifled steel fixed barrel with Whisper sound moderator in the muzzle, SAT, adj. cheekpiece, black synthetic thumbhole stock with SWA recoil pad, non-slip checkering on grip and forearm, TruGlo fiber optic sights, 7.7 lbs. New 2012.

> **Please contact the importer directly for pricing and availability on this model.**

CFR WHISPER ROYAL – .177 or .22 cal., BBC, SP, 280/210 FPS, fluted rifled steel fixed barrel with Whisper sound moderator in the muzzle, hardwood stock with SWA recoil pad, SAT trigger, 6.6 lbs. New 2012.

> **Please contact the importer directly for pricing and availability on this model.**

GRADING	100%	95%	90%	80%	60%	40%	20%

CFX – .177 cal., UL, SP, 1000/1200 (with PBA ammo) FPS, rifled steel barrel with scope mount rail, Truglo adj. rear sight, two-stage trigger, manual cocking and trigger safeties, synthetic stock, ventilated rubber butt pad, 44 in. OAL, 6.6 lbs. Mfg. 2003-2010.

courtesy Gamo Collection

	$220	$185	$155	$130	$100	$65	$45

Last MSR was $260.

CFX COMBO – .177 cal., UL, SP, 1000/1200 (with PBA ammo) FPS, similar to CFX Model, except with BSA 2-7x32mm or 4x32mm scope. Mfg. 2004-2010.

courtesy Gamo Collection

	$245	$210	$170	$140	$110	$75	$50

Last MSR was $290.

CFX ROYAL – .177 cal., UL, SP, 1000 FPS, rifled steel barrel with scope mount rail, Truglo adj. rear sight, two-stage trigger, manual cocking and trigger safeties, deluxe wood stock, ventilated rubber butt pad, 44 in. OAL, 6.6 lbs. Mfg. 2004-2006.

courtesy Gamo Collection

	$250	$215	$175	$145	$115	$75	$50

Last MSR was $300.

CONTEST – .177 cal., SL, SP, 543 FPS, beechwood stock, 10.1 lbs.

	$100	$85	$70	$60	$45	$30	$20

CUSTOM 600 – .177 or .22 cal., BBC, SP, 690 FPS, 17.75 in. barrel, two-stage adj. trigger, checkered stock, 6 lbs. 3 oz.

	$130	$110	$90	$75	$60	$40	$25

Last MSR was $170.

DELTA – .177 cal., BBC, SP, 525 FPS, 15.75 in. barrel, two-stage trigger, automatic safety, adj. sights, plastic stock, 5 lbs. 5 oz. Disc. 2006.

	$65	$55	$45	$40	$30	$20	$15

Last MSR was $90.

Add $25 for 4x15 scope, rings, and 1000 rounds ammo (Delta Combo).

DELTA FOREST – .177 cal., SP, ambidextrous hardwood stock, TruGlo fiber optic sights, 5.1 lbs. New 2012.

Please contact the importer directly for pricing and availability on this model.

DELTA FOX WHISPER – .177 cal., rifled steel barrel with Whisper noise moderator in the muzzle, black synthetic thumbhole stock, 4.9 lbs. New 2012.

Please contact the company directly for pricing and availability for this model.

DYNAMAX – .177 or .22 cal., PCP, 1000 FPS (with PBA Platinum ammo), fingertip cocking repeater, 10-shot rotary mag., 20.5 in. match quality fully floated and rifled steel BBL, two-stage adj. trigger, manual safety, 3-9x50 RGB Dot scope, all-weather black synthetic tactical stock with ventilated rubber butt pad, non-slip checkering on grip and forearm, 38.25 in. OAL, 8.75 lbs. Mfg. 2010-2011.

	$600	$500	$425	$350	$270	$180	$120

Last MSR was $700.

GRADING	100%	95%	90%	80%	60%	40%	20%

EUROPIA – .177 cal., SL, SP, 625 FPS, adj. sights, Monte Carlo stock.

	$165	$140	$115	$95	$75	$50	$35

EXPO – .177 or .22 cal., BBC, SP, 625 FPS, adj. trigger, special sights, 5 lbs. 8 oz. Disc. 1994.

	$80	$70	$55	$45	$35	$25	$15

Last MSR was $130.

EXPO 24 – .177 cal., BBC, SP, 560 FPS, 15.7 in. rifled steel BBL with non-glare polymer coating, two-stage trigger, automatic anti-bear trap safety, manual trigger safety, adj. rear sight, hardwood beech stock with black ABS buttplate, 4.2 lbs.

courtesy Gamo Precision Airguns

	$70	$60	$50	$40	$30	$20	$15

Last MSR was $120.

EXPOMATIC – .177 cal., BBC, SP, repeater, 575 FPS, adj. trigger, 5 lbs. 5 oz. Disc. 1997.

	$120	$100	$85	$70	$55	$35	$25

Last MSR was $170.

EXPO 2000 – .177 cal., BBC, SP, 625 FPS, 17 in. barrel, Monte Carlo-style stock, 5 1/2 lbs. Mfg. 1992-1994.

	$90	$75	$65	$50	$40	$25	$20

Last MSR was $135.

EXTREME CO$_2$ – .177 (disc. 2010), or .22 cal., CO$_2$, SS, pump action repeater, 10-shot rotary mag., 88g cylinder, 22.6 in. fluted and rifled steel bull barrel with integral fiber optic sights, manual trigger safeties, 3-9x40 scope with one-piece mount, all-weather black Monte Carlo-style synthetic stock with twin cheek pads and ventilated rubber butt pad, also includes 200 rds. of TS-22 ammo, 43.31 in. OAL, 8 lbs. Mfg. 2008-2011.

	$325	$275	$230	$190	$145	$95	$65

Last MSR was $370.

FOREST – .177 or .22 cal., hardwood stock, ambidextrous cheek piece, 5.4 lbs. New 2012.

Please contact the importer directly for pricing and availability on this model.

GAMO 68 – .177 or .22 cal., BBC, SP, 600 FPS, 6 lbs. 8 oz.

	$80	$70	$55	$45	$35	$25	$15

GAMATIC 85 – .177 cal., BBC, SP, 560 FPS, 17.75 in. BBL, two-stage trigger, pistol grip stock, 6 lbs. 3 oz.

	$75	$65	$55	$45	$35	$20	$15

Last MSR was $160.

G-1200 – .177 cal., CO$_2$ cylinder, 560 FPS, 17.75 in. barrel, 6 lbs. 6 oz.

courtesy Gamo Precision Airguns

	$165	$140	$115	$95	$75	$50	$35

Last MSR was $185.

GRADING	100%	95%	90%	80%	60%	40%	20%

G-1200M (MAGNUM) – .177 cal., larger CO_2 cylinder, 560 FPS, 17.75 in. barrel, 6 lbs. 6 oz.

	$250	$215	$175	$145	$115	$75	$50

HORNET – .177 cal., BBC, SS, 1000 FPS, 18 in. barrel, two-stage trigger, manual trigger safety, all-weather molded black synthetic stock with ventilated rubber pad, twin cheek pads, non-slip texture on grip and forearm, includes 4x32 scope with rings, 43.3 in. OAL, 6.1 lbs.

courtesy GAMO Outdoor USA

MSR $140	$120	$105	$95	$75	$60	N/A	N/A

HUNTER 220/220 COMBO – .177 or .22 cal., BBC, SP, 1000 FPS, rifled steel barrel, adj. barrel-mounted rear sight or BSA 4x32 scope (Hunter 220 Combo), hooded front sight, manual cocking and trigger safeties, matte finish beechwood stock, black buttplate, 6.2 lbs. Disc. 2006.

	$140	$120	$100	$80	$65	$40	$30

Last MSR was $190.

Add $20 for Hunter 220 Combo.

HUNTER 440/440 COMBO – .177 or .22 cal., BBC, SP, 1000/750 FPS, 18 in. rifled steel BBL, two-stage adj. trigger, fully adj. rear sight or BSA 4x32 scope (Hunter 440 Combo), wood Monte Carlo-style stock with checkered grip, rubber ventilated butt pad, 6.6 lbs. Disc. 2006.

courtesy Gamo Precision Airguns

	$185	$155	$130	$105	$85	$55	$35

Last MSR was $230.

Add $20 for .22 cal.
Add $50 for Hunter 440 Combo.

HUNTER 890S – .177 or .22 cal., BBC, SP, 1000/750 FPS, 18 in. rifled steel BBL with muzzle brake, two-stage adj. trigger, manual safety and automatic anti-bear trap safety, walnut-stained beech Monte Carlo-style stock with checkered grip, rubber ventilated butt pad, includes BSA 3-12x44mm air rifle scope, 7.5 lbs. Disc. 2006.

courtesy Gamo Precision Airguns

	$275	$235	$195	$160	$125	$80	$55

Last MSR was $300.

HUNTER 1250 HURRICANE – .177 cal., BBC, SP, 1250 FPS, rifled steel BBL with muzzle brake, two-stage adj. trigger, hand-finished walnut stained beech Monte Carlo-style stock, checkered grip, ventilated rubber butt pad, 7.5 lbs. Mfg. 1999-2006.

	$325	$270	$225	$185	$145	$95	$65

Last MSR was $400.

GRADING	100%	95%	90%	80%	60%	40%	20%

HUNTER DX – .177, .22, or .25 cal., hardwood stock with water varnish treatment, SWA recoil pad, adj. cheek piece, 6.6 lbs. New 2012.

Please contact the importer directly for pricing and availability on this model.

HUNTER ELITE – .177 cal., BBC, SP, 1000/1200 (with PBA ammo) FPS, polymer and rifled steel bull BBL, adj. trigger, cocking and trigger safeties, 3-9x50 OIR scope, checkered Monte Carlo-style hardwood stock, ventilated rubber butt pad, 43.25 in. OAL, 8 lbs. Mfg. 2006-2008.

courtesy Gamo Collection

$295	$250	$205	$170	$135	$90	$60

Last MSR was $320.

HUNTER EXTREME – .177, (.22, or .25 new 2009) cal., BBC, SP, 1250/1600 (with PBA ammo) FPS, polymer and rifled steel bull BBL, adj. trigger, cocking and trigger safeties, 3-9x50 OIR scope, full size checkered Monte Carlo-style select beech stock, ventilated rubber butt pad, 48.5 in. OAL, 10.5 lbs. Mfg. 2006-2010.

courtesy Gamo Collection

$450	$375	$325	$260	$205	$135	$90

Last MSR was $530.

HUNTER EXTREME SE – .177 cal., BBC, SP, SS, 18 in. jacketed steel bull barrel, two-stage adj. trigger, manual safety, completely redesigned beechwood stock with raised Monte Carlo cheekpiece and SWA recoil pad, laser engraved checkering, 3-9x50 illuminated reticle scope, 45.8 in. OAL, 9 lbs. New 2013.

courtesy GAMO Outdoor USA

MSR $500	$425	$375	$350	$275	$210	N/A	N/A

HUNTER IGT – .177 or .22 cal., IGT, SAT trigger, adj. cheek piece, hardwood stock with SWA recoil pad. New 2012.

Please contact the importer directly for pricing and availability on this model.

GRADING	100%	95%	90%	80%	60%	40%	20%

HUNTER PRO – .177 cal., BBC, SP, 1000/1200 (with PBA ammo) FPS, fluted polymer and rifled steel BBL, adj. trigger, cocking and trigger safeties, 3-9x40 OIR scope, checkered Monte Carlo-style hardwood stock, ventilated rubber butt pad, 43.25 in. OAL, 7 lbs. Mfg. 2006-2008.

courtesy Gamo Collection

	$275	$235	$195	$160	$125	$80	$55

Last MSR was $300.

See recall notice.

HUNTER REALTREE/REALTREE COMBO – .177 cal., BBC, SP, 1000 FPS, 18 in. rifled steel barrel, two-stage adj. trigger, fully adj. rear sight or BSA 4x32 scope (Hunter Realtree Combo), Realtree impregnated wood Monte Carlo-style stock with checkered grip, rubber ventilated butt pad, 6.6 lbs. Disc. 2004.

	$225	$190	$160	$130	$100	$65	$45

Last MSR was $250.

Add $30 for Hunter Realtree Combo.

HUNTER SPORT – .177 cal., BBC, SP, 1000/1200 (with PBA ammo) FPS, fluted polymer and rifled steel BBL, adj. trigger, cocking and trigger safeties, 3-9x40 scope, Monte Carlo-style hardwood stock, ventilated rubber butt pad, 43.25 in. OAL, 6.5 lbs. Mfg. 2006-2010.

courtesy Gamo Collection

	$205	$175	$145	$120	$90	$60	$40

Last MSR was $240.

See recall notice.

HUNTER SUPERSPORT – .177 cal., BBC, SP, 1250 FPS (with PBA ammo), 18 in. rifled steel barrel, all-weather black synthetic stock with twin cheek pads, non-slip checkering finish on grip and forearm, SWA recoil pad, SAT two-stage adj. trigger, one-piece solid mount, 3-9x40 AO scope included, also includes one tube of Red Fire and PBA Platinum ammo, 45 in. OAL, 6.1 lbs. New 2012.

courtesy GAMO Outdoor USA

MSR $250	$215	$190	$170	$140	$105	N/A	N/A

MAGNUM 2000 – .177 or .22 cal., BBC, SP, 820-660 FPS, 17.75 in. barrel, adj. two-stage trigger, checkered stock, 7 lbs. 2 oz.

	$165	$140	$115	$95	$75	$50	$35

Last MSR was $200.

GRADING	100%	95%	90%	80%	60%	40%	20%

MAXIMA – .177 cal., BBC, SP, 1000 FPS, rifled steel BBL with muzzle brake, manual safety and automatic anti-bear trap safety, walnut-stained beech Monte Carlo-style stock with checkered grip, rubber ventilated butt pad, includes BSA 3-12x40mm air rifle scope, 46.3 in. OAL, 6.8 lbs. Mfg. 2005-2006.

courtesy Gamo Collection

	$255	$215	$180	$150	$115	$75	$50

Last MSR was $280.

MAXIMA COMBO – .177 cal., BBC, SP, 1000 FPS, similar to Maxima except includes BSA 3-12x40mm air rifle scope, 46.3 in. OAL, 6.8 lbs. Mfg. 2005-2006.

$295	$250	$205	$170	$135	$90	$60

Last MSR was $320.

MAXIMA RX – .177, .22, or .25 cal., BBC, SP, 305/220/190 FPS, hardwood stock, adj. cheek piece, 6.8 lbs. New 2012.

Please contact the company directly for pricing and availability on this model.

MODEL 126 EL GAMO

For information on the Model 126 El Gamo, see Daisy in the "D" section.

MODEL 126 EL GAMO SUPER MATCH TARGET RIFLE

For information on the Model 126 El Gamo Super Match Target Rifle, see Daisy in the "D" section.

MODEL 128 EL GAMO OLYMPIC

For information on the Model 128 El Gamo Olympic, see Daisy in the "D" section.

MODEL 130 EL GAMO

For information on the Model 130 El Gamo Olympic, see Daisy in the "D" section.

MODEL F1200 – .177 cal., BBC, SP, 1000/1200 (with PBA ammo) FPS, fluted polymer and rifled steel BBL, adj. trigger, cocking and trigger safeties, 3-9x40 scope, Monte Carlo-style synthetic stock, ventilated rubber butt pad, 43.5 in. OAL, 6.25 lbs. Disc. 2009.

$195	$165	$135	$115	$90	$60	$40

See recall notice. The Model F1200 looks identical to the Shadow Sport and was sold exclusively at Wal-Mart stores.

MRA SHOWSTOPPER SHAWN MICHAELS – .177 cal., 33mm cylinder, BBC, SP, SS, 1400 FPS (with PBA ammo), 18 in. fluted polymer jacketed steel barrel, all-weather black synthetic stock with twin cheek pads, SWA recoil pad, rubberized grips, SAT, includes 4x32 scope, 45 in. OAL, 8 lbs. New 2013.

courtesy GAMO Outdoor USA

MSR $250	$215	$190	$170	$140	$105	N/A	N/A

MULTISHOT – .177 cal., BBC, SP, eight-shot rotary mag., 750 FPS, rifled steel BBL with polymer-coated finish, adj. rear sight, hooded front sight, dovetail grooves for scope, adj. trigger, cocking and trigger safeties, beech stock, hard rubber butt pad, 6.4 lbs. Mfg. 2001-04.

$170	$145	$120	$100	$75	$50	$35

Last MSR was $190.

GRADING	100%	95%	90%	80%	60%	40%	20%

NITRO 17 – .177 cal., BBC, SP, 850/1050 (with PBA ammo) FPS, fluted polymer and rifled steel BBL, adj. trigger, cocking and trigger safeties, 3-9x40 scope, Monte Carlo-style synthetic stock with soft forearm insert, ventilated rubber butt pad, 43.5 in. OAL, 6.25 lbs. Mfg. 2006-2010.

courtesy Gamo Collection

	$180	$155	$125	$105	$80	$55	$35

Last MSR was $210.

RECON – .177 cal., BBC, SP, 525 or 750 (with PBA Platinum ammo) FPS, 16 in. rifled polymer and steel fluted barrel with Whisper integrated noice dampener (new 2012), 4x20 scope, two-stage adj. trigger, all-weather black molded synthetic thumbhole stock with twin cheek pads, ventilated rubber butt pad, manual cocking and trigger safeties, non-slip checkering on grip and forearm, 43.3 in. OAL, 4.63 lbs. New 2006.

courtesy Gamo Collection

MSR $120	$100	$90	$80	$65	$50	N/A	N/A

* **Lady Recon** – .177 cal., BBC, SP, SS, 525 FPS, 16 in. rifled polymer and steel barrel, adj. rear and fixed front sights, two-stage trigger, manual cocking and trigger safeties, all-weather molded pink synthetic thumbhole stock with twin cheek pads, ventilated rubber butt pad, 37.2 in. OAL, 4.63 lbs. New 2009.

courtesy GAMO Outdoor USA

MSR $140	$120	$105	$95	$75	$60	N/A	N/A

RECON WHISPER – .177 cal., BBC, SP, SS, 19.25 in. rifled barrel, ND52 noise dampener at the muzzle, fiber optic sights, two-stage adj. trigger, black synthetic thumbhole Monte Carlo stock with dual raised cheekpiece, ventilated rubber buttpad, manual safety, includes 4x20 scope, 40.5 in. OAL, 4.45 lbs.

courtesy GAMO Outdoor USA

MSR $120	$100	$90	$80	$65	$50	N/A	N/A

GRADING	100%	95%	90%	80%	60%	40%	20%

ROCKET – .177 cal., BBC, SP, SS, 1250 (with PBA Platinum ammo) FPS, 18 in. fluted polymer and rifled steel BBL, two-stage adj. trigger, cocking and trigger safeties, 4x32 scope with rings, all-weather OD green synthetic stock with twin cheek pads, ventilated rubber butt pad, non-slip checkering on grip and forearm, includes 50 rds. PBA Platinum ammo, 43 in. OAL, 6.1 lbs. Mfg. 2010-2011.

courtesy GAMO Outdoor USA

$170	$145	$120	$100	$75	$50	$35

Last MSR was $200.

* **Rocket Camo** – .177 cal., similar to Rocket model, except has RealTree camo finish. Mfg. 2010-2011.

courtesy GAMO Outdoor USA

$185	$155	$130	$105	$85	$55	$35

Last MSR was $220.

* **Rocket DX** – .177 cal., similar to Rocket model, except has all-weather black synthetic stock and black rubber grips, 5.28 lbs. Mfg. 2010-2011.

courtesy GAMO Outdoor USA

$205	$175	$145	$120	$90	$60	$40

Last MSR was $240.

SHADOW 1000/HUNTER BLACK/SILVER/SILVER SUPREME/COMBO – .177 or .22 cal., BBC, SP, SS, 1000/722 FPS, rifled steel BBL with black polymer-coated or nickel (Silver/Silver Supreme) finish, adj. rear fiber optic sight, BSA 4x32 scope (Shadow/Silver Combo) BSA 30mm red dot scope (Hunter Black), or BSA 3-12x50 scope (Silver Supreme), dovetail grooves for scope, adj. trigger, cocking and trigger safeties, synthetic stock, hard rubber butt pad, 6.6 lbs. Mfg. 2002-06.

$170	$145	$120	$100	$75	$50	$35

Last MSR was $190.

Add $40 for Silver Shadow (new 2003).
Add $30 for Shadow Combo (new 2003).
Add $60 for Silver Shadow Combo (new 2003).
Add $150 for Silver Shadow Supreme (new 2003).
Add $50 for Shadow Hunter Black (new 2003).

GRADING	100%	95%	90%	80%	60%	40%	20%

SHADOW 640 – .177 cal., BBC, SP, 640 FPS, rifled barrel, two-stage trigger, automatic safety, Truglo adj. sights, synthetic stock, 41 in. OAL, 5.3 lbs. Mfg. 2003-04.

courtesy Gamo Precision Airguns

	$115	$100	$80	$65	$50	$35	$25

Last MSR was $140.

SHADOW DX – .177, .22, or .25 cal., steel barrel, black synthetic stock with non-slip inserted grips, SWA recoil pad. New 2012.

Please contact the importer directly for pricing and availability on this model.

This model is also available in different variations: Shadow DX Barricade (has a green stock), Shadow DX Tactical, Shadow DX RSV, and Shadow DX Express. All mfg. 2012.

SHADOW FOX – .177 cal., BBC, SP, 1200 FPS with PBA ammo, fluted and rifled steel bull barrel with 3-9x40mm scope and one-piece mount, two-stage trigger, manual cocking and trigger safeties, synthetic thumbhole stock, ventilated rubber recoil pad, 43.5 in. OAL, 5.28 lbs. Mfg. 2008-2010.

courtesy GAMO Outdoor USA

	$220	$185	$155	$130	$100	$65	$45

Last MSR was $260.

SHADOW IGT – .177, .22, or .25 cal., IGT, 305/220/190 FPS, SAT trigger, black synthetic stock with SWA recoil pad, 6.6 lbs. New 2012.

As this edition went to press, prices had yet to be established on this model.

SHADOW SPORT – .177 cal., BBC, SP, 1000/1200 (with PBA ammo) FPS, 18 in. fluted polymer and rifled steel BBL, two-stage adj. trigger, cocking and trigger safeties, 3-9x40 scope, all-weather black Monte Carlo-style synthetic stock with twin cheek pads, ventilated rubber butt pad, non-slip checkering on grip and forearm, 43 in. OAL, 6.25 lbs. Mfg. 2006-2011.

courtesy Gamo Collection

	$215	$185	$150	$125	$95	$65	$45

Last MSR was $250.

See recall notice at the beginning of this section.

SILENT CAT – .177 or .22 (mfg. 2010-2011) cal., BBC, SP, SS, 1200/950 (with PBA ammo) FPS, 18 in. fluted and rifled steel bull barrel with Whisper non-removable noise dampener, adj. fiber optic sights, two-stage adj. trigger, cocking and trigger safeties, 4x32 scope with one-piece mount, all-weather black thumbhole synthetic stock with twin

GRADING	100%	95%	90%	80%	60%	40%	20%

cheek pads, ventilated rubber recoil pad, includes 50 rds. PBA ammo (.177 cal.), or 25 rds. PBA Platinum ammo (.22 cal.), 46 in. OAL, 5.28 lbs. Mfg. 2009-current.

courtesy Gamo Precision Airguns

MSR $270	$230	$205	$185	$150	$115	N/A	N/A

SILENT STALKER – .177 or .22 cal., IGT, BBC, 1300/975 FPS (with PBA ammo), 18 in. fluted steel barrel, all-weather black synthetic stock with twin cheek pads, SWA recoil pad, non-slip checkering finish on grip and forearm, SAT two-stage adj. trigger, manual safety, one-piece solid mount, Gamo 4x32 scope and one tube of ammo included, 43.3 in. OAL, 6.1 lbs. New 2012.

courtesy GAMO Outdoor USA

MSR $255	$215	$190	$175	$140	$105	N/A	N/A

SILENT STALKER WHISPER – .177 or .22 cal., IGT, BBC, 1300/975 FPS (with PBA ammo), 18 in. Whisper noise dampener, fluted, steel barrel, all-weather black synthetic stock with twin cheek pads, non-slip checkering finish on grip and forearm, one-piece solid mount, SAT two-stage adj. trigger, SWA recoil pad, Gamo 3-9x40 scope and one tube of PBA ammo included, 46 in. OAL, 6.1 lbs. New 2012.

courtesy GAMO Outdoor USA

MSR $300	$255	$225	$205	$165	$125	N/A	N/A

SOCOM 1000 – .177 or .22 cal., BBC, SP, 305/220 FPS, black synthetic stock, tactical design, adj. cheekpiece, TruGlo fiber optic sights, 6 lbs. New 2012.

Please contact the importer directly for pricing and availability on this model.

SOCOM 1000 IGT – .177 or .22 cal., IGT, 305/220 FPS, steel barrel, SAT trigger, adj. cheek piece, black synthetic stock with SWA recoil pad, tactical design, 7.7 lbs. New 2012.

Please contact the importer directly for pricing and availability on this model.

GRADING	100%	95%	90%	80%	60%	40%	20%

SOCOM EXTREME – .177, .22, or .25 (new 2011) cal., BBC, SP, 1650/1300/1000 (with PBA ammo) FPS, 18 in. steel bull barrel, two-stage adj. trigger, cocking and trigger safeties, Gamo 3-9x50 RGBD scope with one-piece solid mount, all-weather black Monte Carlo-style synthetic stock with twin cheek pads and ventilated rubber recoil pad, non-slip checkering on grip and forearm, includes 50 (.177 cal.), 25 (.22 cal.), or 18 (.25 cal.) rds. PBA Platinum ammo, 43.5 in. OAL, 9.5 lbs. Mfg. 2010-current.

courtesy GAMO Outdoor USA

MSR $420	$350	$325	$285	$230	$175	N/A	N/A

SOCOM TACTICAL – .177 or .22 (new 2012) cal., BBC, SP, 305/220 FPS or 1200 (.177 cal. with PBA ammo) FPS, 18 in. fluted polymer and rifled bull barrel with Whisper noise dampener in the muzzle, adj. cheek piece, adj. fiber optic sights, two-stage adj. trigger, cocking and trigger safeties, 3-9x40 scope with one-piece mount, laser and light, all-weather black Monte Carlo-style synthetic stock with ventilated rubber recoil pad and adj. cheek piece, non-slip checkering on grip and forearm, includes 50 rds. PBA ammo, 46 in. OAL, 6.6 lbs. New 2010.

courtesy GAMO Outdoor USA

MSR $370	$325	$280	$250	$205	$155	N/A	N/A

SPORTER – .177 cal., BBC, SP, 760 FPS, rifled steel BBL with polymer coated finish, adj. rear sight, hooded front sight, adj. trigger, cocking and trigger safeties, Monte Carlo-style beech stock, ventilated rubber butt pad, 5.5 lbs. Disc. 2004.

	$120	$100	$85	$70	$55	$35	$25

Last MSR was $160.

STINGER – .177 cal., BBC, SP, eight-shot mag., 750 FPS, rifled steel barrel, fully adj. rear sight, cocking and trigger safeties, Monte Carlo-style beech stock, hard rubber butt pad, 6.4 lbs. Disc. 2001.

	$145	$125	$100	$85	$65	$45	$30

Last MSR was $190.

STUTZEN – .177 cal., UL, SP, 950 FPS, micrometer rear sight with a four-position interchangeable windage plate, rifled steel BBL, one-piece, full-length hardwood Mannlicher stock, hand-carved cheek piece, and ventilated rubber butt pad. Mfg. 2000-2011.

courtesy Gamo Collection

	$400	$350	$280	$230	$180	$120	$80

SUPER – .177 cal., SL, SP, 593 FPS, 10 lbs. 8 oz.

	$145	$125	$100	$85	$65	$45	$30

GRADING	100%	95%	90%	80%	60%	40%	20%

TROOPER RD CARBINE – .177 cal., BBC, SP, 560 FPS, rifled steel BBL with polymer coated finish, muzzle brake, two-stage trigger, manual safety, automatic anti-bear trap safety, Gamo red dot sight, black synthetic stock with cheek piece and checkered grip, 5.3 lbs.

	$90	$75	$65	$50	$40	$25	$20

Last MSR was $120.

TWIN – .177 or .22 cal., BBC, SP, 675 FPS, adj. sights, barrel insert tubes to change from .177 to .22 cal., hardwood stock.

	$140	$120	$100	$80	$65	$40	$30

Last MSR was $165.

VARMINT HUNTER – .177 cal., BBC, SP, SS, 1000/1200 (with PBA ammo) FPS, rifled steel BBL with black polymer coated finish, 4x32 scope, laser, flashlight, dovetail grooves for mounting all three on special bracket, cocking and trigger safeties, ambidextrous synthetic stock, deluxe recoil pad, 43.8 in. OAL, 6.2 lbs. Mfg. 2005-2011.

courtesy Gamo Collection

	$240	$205	$170	$140	$110	$70	$50

Last MSR was $280.

VARMINT HUNTER HP – .177 or .22 cal., BBC, SP, 1400/1000 FPS (with PBA Platinum ammo), 18 in. fluted rifled steel barrel, all-weather molded synthetic stock with twin cheek pads, SWA (new 2012) vent. rubber recoil pad, SAT (new 2012) two-stage adj. trigger, cocking and trigger safeties, non-slip checkering on grip and forearm, 4x32 scope with laser, light, and one-piece mount, includes 50 (.177 cal.), or 25 (.22 cal.) rds. PBA Platinum ammo, 43.78 in. OAL, 6.61 lbs. New 2011.

courtesy GAMO Outdoor USA

MSR $300	$255	$225	$205	$165	$125	N/A	N/A

VARMINT HUNTER STALKER – .177 cal., BBC, SP, 1250 FPS (with PBA Platinum ammo), 19.2 in. Bull Whisper fluted steel bull barrel with integrated noise dampener, all-weather black synthetic stock with twin cheek pads, non-slip checkering on grip and forearm, SWA recoil pad (new 2012), SAT (new 2012) two-stage adj. trigger, automatic safety, 4x32 scope with laser and light, includes 50 rds. PBA Platinum ammo, 44.6 in. OAL, 6.1 lbs. New 2011.

courtesy GAMO Outdoor USA

MSR $270	$230	$205	$185	$150	$115	N/A	N/A

GRADING	100%	95%	90%	80%	60%	40%	20%

VARMINT STALKER – .177 cal., BBC, SP, 1250 FPS (with PBA Platinum ammo), 19.2 in. Bull Whisper fluted steel bull barrel with integrated noise dampener, all-weather black synthetic stock with twin cheek pads, non-slip checkering on grip and forearm, two-piece solid mount, SAT (new 2012) two-stage adj. trigger, SWA recoil pad (new 2012), 4x32 scope with rings, includes 50 rds. PBA Platinum ammo, 44.6 in. OAL, 6.1 lbs. New 2011.

courtesy GAMO Outdoor USA

MSR $240	$205	$180	$165	$130	$100	N/A	N/A

* **Varmint Stalker Deluxe** – .177 cal., BBC, SP, 1250 FPS (with PBA Platinum ammo), 19.2 in. Bull Whisper fluted steel bull barrel with integrated noise dampener, all-weather black sythnetic stock, SWA recoil pad (new 2012), non-slip checkering on grip and forearm, SAT (new 2012) two-stage trigger, automatic safety, 4x32 scope with rings, includes 50 rds. PBA Platinum ammo, 44.6 in. OAL, 6.1 lbs. New 2011.

MSR $250	$215	$190	$170	$140	$105	N/A	N/A

VIPER – .177 cal., BBC, SP, 1000/1200 (with PBA ammo) FPS, polymer and steel rifled bull BBL, adj. trigger, cocking and trigger safeties, 3-9x40 OIR scope, ambidextrous Monte Carlo-style synthetic stock with soft forearm and pistol grip inserts, ventilated rubber butt pad, 43.5 in. OAL, 7.25 lbs. Mfg. 2006-2010.

courtesy Gamo Collection

	$290	$245	$205	$170	$130	$85	$60

Last MSR was $340.

WHISPER – .177 or .22 cal., BBC, SP, 1200/950 (with PBA ammo) FPS, 18 in. fluted and rifled steel barrel with Whisper non-removable noise dampener, adj. fiber optic sights, adj. trigger, cocking and trigger safeties, 3-9x40 scope with one-piece mount, all-weather black synthetic stock with twin cheek pads, ventilated rubber recoil pad, non-slip checkering on grip and forearm, includes 25 rds. PBA ammo, 46 in. OAL, 6.1 lbs. Mfg. 2008-current.

courtesy Gamo Precision Airguns

MSR $270	$230	$205	$185	$150	$115	N/A	N/A

GRADING	100%	95%	90%	80%	60%	40%	20%

WHISPER CFR – .177 cal., UL, 20 in. steel fixed barrel, 1100 FPS (with PBA Platinum ammo), 3-9x40AO scope, all-weather black synthetic stock with thumbhole and adj. cheek pads, SWA (new 2012) vent. rubber recoil pad, manual safety, SAT (new 2012) two-stage adj. trigger, non-removable noise dampener, rotating breech loading system, includes 50 rds. PBA Platinum ammo, 46.85 in. OAL, 8 lbs. New 2011.

courtesy GAMO Outdoor USA

MSR $350	$300	$265	$240	$195	$145	N/A	N/A

* **Whisper Classic** – .177 cal., BBC, SP, SS, 1200 (with PBA ammo) FPS, 18 in. fluted polymer jacketed and rifled steel bull barrel with non-removable noise dampener, adj. fiber optic sights, adj. trigger, cocking and trigger safeties, 3-9x40 scope, European beech stock with right-hand cheek piece, ventilated rubber recoil pad, 46 in. OAL, 5.28 lbs. Mfg. 2010-2011.

courtesy Gamo Precision Airguns

$255	$215	$180	$150	$115	$75	$50

Last MSR was $300.

* **Whisper Deluxe** – .177 cal., BBC, SP, 1200 (with PBA ammo) FPS, 18 in. fluted and rifled steel bull BBL with non-removable noise dampener, adj. fiber optic sights, adj. trigger, cocking and trigger safeties, 3-9x40 scope with one-piece mount, Deluxe Monte Carlo-style all-weather black synthetic stock, rubber grips, and twin cheek pads, ventilated rubber recoil pad, non-slip checkering on grip and forearm, includes 50 rds. PBA ammo, 46 in. OAL, 5.28 lbs. Mfg. 2008-2011.

courtesy Gamo Precision Airguns

$300	$255	$210	$175	$135	$90	$60

Last MSR was $350.

WHISPER FUSION – .177 cal., IGT, 1300 FPS (Platinum PBA), 18 in. fluted polymer jacketed rifled steel barrel with Whisper Fusion noise and muzzle blast dampener, SAT two-stage adj. trigger, all-weather black stock with adj. cheekpiece, rubberized grips, SWA recoil pad, fiber optic sights, 3-9x40 scope, 44.7 in. OAL, 6.6 lbs. New 2013.

courtesy GAMO Outdoor USA

MSR $310	$265	$235	$210	$170	$130	N/A	N/A

GRADING	100%	95%	90%	80%	60%	40%	20%

WHISPER FUSION PRO – .177 cal., BBC, SP, 1400 FPS (Platinum PBA), 18 in. fluted, polymer jacketed rifled steel barrel with Whisper Fusion dual noise dampening technology, manual safety, all-weather black stock with twin cheek pads, rubberized grips, SWA recoil pad, fiber optic sights, SAT, includes 3-9x40 AO scope, 50 rounds Platinum and 30 rounds Lethal pellets, 44.7 in. OAL, 6.6 lbs. New 2013.

courtesy GAMO Outdoor USA

MSR $330	$280	$250	$225	$180	$140	N/A	N/A

WHISPER G2 – .177 or .22 cal., SS, BBC, 1000 FPS, 18 in. fluted polymer jacketed steel barrel with Whisper G2 Turbo Stabilizing System, SAT, black synthetic thumbhole stock with SWA recoil pad, adj. cheekpiece, rubberized grips, non-slip texture on grip and forearm, fiber optic sights, 4x32 scope, manual safety, 43 in. OAL, 8 lbs. New 2014.

courtesy GAMO Outdoor USA

MSR $270	$230	$205	$185	$150	$115	N/A	N/A

WHISPER IGT – .177 or .22 cal., IGT, 305/220 FPS, fluted rifled steel barrel with Whisper sound moderator in the muzzle, SAT trigger, black synthetic thumbhole stock, 6.6 lbs. New 2012.

Please contact the importer directly for pricing and availability on this model.

* ***Whisper Royal*** – .177 cal., BBC, SP, SS, 1250 (with PBA ammo) FPS, 18 in. fluted polymer jacketed and rifled steel BBL with non-removable noise dampener, adj. trigger, cocking and trigger safeties, 3-9x40 scope, checkered European beech stock with right-hand cheek piece, fine cut checkering with semi-gloss varnish finish, ventilated rubber recoil pad, 46 in. OAL, 5.28 lbs. Mfg. 2010-2011.

courtesy Gamo Precision Airguns

$255	$215	$180	$150	$115	$75	$50

Last MSR was $300.

GRADING	100%	95%	90%	80%	60%	40%	20%

* **Whisper VH** – .177 cal., BBC, SP, 1200 (with PBA ammo) FPS, 18 in. fluted and rifled steel bull BBL with non-removable noise dampener, adj. fiber optic sights, adj. trigger, cocking and trigger safeties, 3-9x40 scope with one-piece solid mount, flashlight and laser, all-weather black Monte Carlo-style synthetic stock with thumbhole and twin cheek pads, ventilated rubber recoil pad, includes 50 rds. PBA ammo, 46 in. OAL, 5.28 lbs. Mfg. 2008-2011.

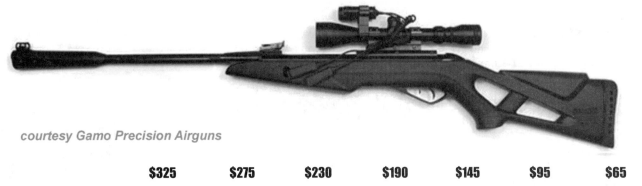

courtesy Gamo Precision Airguns

	$325	$275	$230	$190	$145	$95	$65

Last MSR was $370.

WHISPER X – .177 or .22 cal., BBC, SP, 305/230 FPS, fluted rifled steel barrel with Whisper sound moderator in the muzzle, black synthetic thumbhole stock, SAT trigger, 6.6 lbs. New 2012.

Please contact the importer directly for pricing and availabiliy on this model.

YOUNG HUNTER/COMBO – .177 cal., BBC, SP, 640 FPS, 17.7 in. rifled steel BBL, adj. rear sight, hooded front sight, two-stage adj. trigger, manual trigger safety, automatic anti-bear trap safety, Monte Carlo-style beech stock, ventilated rubber butt pad. Disc. 2005.

courtesy Gamo Precision Airguns

	$85	$70	$60	$50	$40	$25	$15

Last MSR was $130.

Add $40 for Young Hunter Combo with 4x32 scope.

ZOMBIE – .177 cal., BBC, SS, 1000 FPS, 18 in. fluted polymer jacketed rifled steel barrel, all-weather molded black synthetic stock with twin cheek pads, ventilated rubber butt pad, non-slip texture on grip and forearm, includes 4x32 scope and 35 Zombie pellets, 43.3 in. OAL, 6.1 lbs. New 2013.

courtesy GAMO Outdoor USA

MSR $200	$170	$150	$135	$110	$85	N/A	N/A

560 CARBINE – .177 cal., BBC, SP, 560 FPS, rifled steel barrel with muzzle brake, blue finish, ambidextrous black synthetic stock, two-stage trigger, automatic safety, 4x20 scope with mounts, 42.1 in. OAL, 5.2 lbs. Mfg. 2005-2006.

	$65	$55	$45	$40	$30	$20	$15

Last MSR was $90.

640 CARBINE – .177 cal., BBC, SP, 640 FPS, rifled steel barrel with muzzle brake, blue finish, ambidextrous black synthetic stock, two-stage trigger, automatic safety, 4x28 scope with mounts, 42.1 in. OAL, 5.3 lbs. Mfg. 2005-2006.

	$95	$80	$65	$55	$45	$30	$20

Last MSR was $100.

GRADING	100%	95%	90%	80%	60%	40%	20%

850 CARBINE – .177 cal., BBC, SP, 850 FPS, rifled steel barrel with muzzle brake, blue finish, ambidextrous black synthetic stock, two-stage trigger, automatic safety, 4x32 scope with mounts, 43.1 in. OAL, 5.3 lbs. Mfg. 2005-06.

	$100	$85	$70	$55	$45	$30	$20

Last MSR was $120.

SHOTGUNS

SHADOW EXPRESS – .22 cal. shotshell or .22 cal. pellet with chamber adapter, BBC, SP, ventilated rib steel rifled BBL, adj. trigger, cocking and trigger safeties, bead front sight, ambidextrous Monte Carlo-style synthetic stock, ventilated rubber butt pad, 43.3 in. OAL, 5.5 lbs. Mfg. 2008-2010.

courtesy Gamo Precision Airguns

	$185	$155	$130	$105	$85	$55	$35

Last MSR was $220.

VIPER EXPRESS – .22 cal. shotshell or .22 cal. pellet with chamber adapter, BBC, SP, ventilated rib steel rifled BBL, adj. trigger, cocking and trigger safeties, bead front sight, ambidextrous Monte Carlo-style synthetic stock with soft forearm and pistol grip inserts, ventilated rubber buttpad, 43.5 in. OAL, 5.5 lbs. Mfg. 2006-2010.

courtesy Gamo Collection

	$220	$185	$155	$130	$100	$65	$45

Last MSR was $260.

GAMESTER
For information on Gamester, see Eastern Engineering Co. in the "E" section.

GARCO
For information on Garco airguns, see Philippine Airguns in the "P" section.

GAT
Previous trademark of T. J. Harrington & Son located in Walton, Surrey, England.

For information on GAT airguns, see Harrington in the "H" section.

GECADO
Previous tradename used on sporting goods made by Mayer and Grammelspacher (Dianawerk).

Gecado was used by G.C. Dornheim of Suhl, Germany until 1940 and was used in certain German and other markets for guns made by Mayer and Grammelspacher. For more information see Dianawerk in the "D" section of this book.

GECO
Previous tradename used on sporting goods by Gustav Genschow & Co. located in Berlin prior to 1959.

This company was purchased by Dynamit Nobel in 1959, the present owners of Mayer and Grammelspacher. For more information see Dianawerk in the "D" section of this book.

GEM
A general term sometimes used like a brand name. See also Haviland & Gunn, Gaggenau Ironworks, and Dianawerk (Mayer & Grammelspacher).

The term "Gem" has been used to refer to an enormous number of spring piston air rifles. Although a great variety of airguns fall into this category, they have a general similarity in appearance characterized by having the compression

GRADING	100%	95%	90%	80%	60%	40%	20%

chamber in the slanted wrist of the gun rather than ahead of the trigger, and a one-piece wooden buttstock behind the compression chamber. Apparently all are derived from a USA patent issued to George Gunn on April 18, 1871 as modified by a USA patent issued to Asa Pettengill on May 28, 1878. The original Gunn patent is the basis for the drop-barrel cocking mechanism so popular among spring piston airguns throughout the world for over a century. George Peck Gunn combined the wrist-cylinder with the drop-barrel mechanism in his USA patent of March 9, 1886.

Patents properly licensed to Henry Quackenbush in the United States were further licensed to Gaggenau Ironworks in Europe, where production of European Gems began in the 1880s. Other early makers, eager for monopoly control of their own markets and simply ignoring prior foreign patents, often copied the basic Gunn and Pettengill patterns or added minor features. Most guns so produced are airguns, but some are combination firearm/airgun designs derived from the Haviland & Gunn designs which became the Quackenbush Model 5.

Gem-type guns were made by many manufacturers from circa 1885 until the 1930s and were at least distributed from many countries and companies, esp. Gaggenau Ironworks, Langenham, and Mayer & Grammelspacher (Dianawerk) in Germany, Jean Marck, a Belgian gunmaker (using an encircled "M" as a mark), Arbebz, Sugg, Lane Bros, Baker & Marsh in England, and Coirier of France. They range from crude to excellent in quality and often are "notoriously difficult to classify." Ref: GR March 1974.

Most Gems are small to medium size with octagonal, smoothbore barrels ranging from .177/4.5mm to .25/6.35mm caliber. Current values typically run from about $60 to $120 with few exceeding $350.

Gem Air Rifle - typical shape and design with angled body tube which serves as mainspring/piston housing and pistol grip. This Jewel Model by Lane of England is special for its "Lane-style" barrel latch and because it is a .177 cal. smoothbore shotgun, designed to fire Lane's Patent Shot Cartridges, filled with No. 7 or No. 9 lead birdshot.

courtesy Beeman Collection

GERMAN SPORT GUNS GmbH (GSG)

Current manufacturer and distributor located in Ense-Höingen, Germany. Currently imported beginning 2012 by Air Venturi, located in Solon, OH. Previously located in Warrensville Hts., OH.

PISTOLS

GSG 92 – BB/.177 cal., CO_2, semi-auto blowback action, 20 shot mag., full metal construction, blade and ramp front sights, fixed rear sight, manual safety, black finish, lower accessory rail, 8.54 in. OAL, 2.42 lbs. Imported 2012-2013.

$125	$100	$90	$75	$55	$35	$25

Last MSR was $150.

GIFFARD

Previous trade name of airguns manufactured in succession, by Rivolier & Fils and Sociéte d'Stephanoise d'Armes, and Manufacture Française d'Armes et Cycles located in St. Étienne, France. Paul Giffard (1837-1897) was the designer of pump pneumatic and CO_2 air rifles and pistols.

Giffard's 1862 patent for a pump pneumatic with an in-line pump built under the barrel is often credited with being the basis of virtually all pump pneumatics of the present time. The basic design quickly appeared (1869) in far-off America as Hawley's Kalamazoo air pistol.

The first production CO_2 guns were patented by Giffard in 1873. Giffard, and many military experts of the time, predicted that the CO_2 guns would produce a major revolution in warfare; perhaps even lead to an end of warfare! Very small quantities of a hammerless CO_2 rifle were made by International Giffard Gun Company Ltd. in London. Giffard also patented (1872) and produced an air cartridge rifle which is similar to the Saxby-Palmer air cartridge system introduced in England in the 1980s.

GRADING	100%	95%	90%	80%	60%	40%	20%

PISTOLS

PNEUMATIC PISTOL – .177 cal., in-line pneumatic pump along underside of 8 in. barrel, Faucet loading tap with RH oval turning tab, walnut forearm and grip continuous, grip fluted, floral carving on forearm, moderate engraving on all metal parts except barrel and pump, blue finish, no safety, 16.3 in. OAL, 1.8 lbs. Mfg. 1860s.

courtesy Beeman Collection

	N/A	$5,000	$4,000	$3,250	$2,500	$1,750	$1,000

GAS PISTOL – 4.5mm, 6mm or 8mm cal., CO_2 with removable gas cylinder affixed horizontally under the 10 in. round barrel of single diameter or steeped midway to smaller diameter, SS, rotating bolt tap-loading, exposed hammer rests on power adjustment wheel, arched walnut grip with fine checkering and ornate blued steel grip cap, deep blue finish, no safety, 17.9 in. OAL, 3 lbs. Mfg. late 1870s.

courtesy Beeman Collection

	N/A	$4,000	$3,200	$2,600	$2,000	$1,400	$800

Add 20% for 8mm cal.

GAS DUELING PISTOL – 8mm cal., wax bullets only, CO_2 with removable gas cylinder, similar to Gas Pistol, except has hand guard and fixed rear sight, came standard in cased set of two pistols with accessories. Mfg. late 1870s.

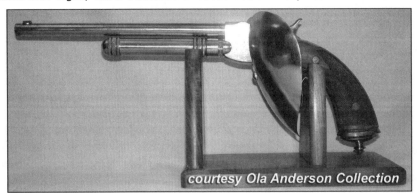

courtesy Ola Anderson Collection

Scarcity precludes accurate pricing. However, a complete cased set including a matched pair of dueling pistols and all accessories in excellent condition will sell in the low five digits.

RIFLES

PUMP PNEUMATIC RIFLE – 4.5mm, 6mm, 8mm or 10mm cal., in-line pneumatic pump along underside of 19.3-20.3 in. barrel, SS, faucet-loading tap with RH folding or rigid bi-lobed turning tab, external hammer, walnut forearm with deep floral engraving or smooth raised panels and English grip finely checkered or smooth, plain or deeply

GRADING	100%	95%	90%	80%	60%	40%	20%

engraved on all metal parts except barrel and pump, blue or blue with German Silver on receiver and steel buttplate finish, "Giffard-style" guard. No safety, 36.3-38 in. OAL, 4.1-4.6 lbs. Mfg. 1870s.

courtesy Beeman Collection

	N/A	$4,000	$3,200	$2,600	$2,000	$1,400	$800

Add 50% to 100% for engraving, German silver, stock carving, etc. (depending on condition).

GAS RIFLE (EXTERNAL HAMMER MODEL) – 4.5mm, 6mm or 8mm cal., CO_2 removable and rechargeable gas cylinder with decorative knurled rings affixed horizontally under the 24.4-24.9 in. round barrel, SS, exposed hammer rests on power wheel, rotating bolt tap loading, operated by bolt or small lever on surface of receiver which exposes rectangular or round loading port, engraved receiver, Swiss rear sight, slim walnut stock, English grip with fine checkering, Giffard name and maker's name may be stamped or inlaid in gold, deep blue finish, simple or ornate "Giffard style" trigger guard and butt plate, no safety, 41.6-42.6 in. OAL, 5.4 lbs. Mfg. late 1870s.

courtesy Beeman Collection

	N/A	$2,500	$2,000	$1,625	$1,250	$875	$500

Add 30% for 4.5mm cal.   Add 100% for first CO_2 models with transverse loading tap.

This model is also known in a pneumatic version with hand pump - may not be original.

GAS RIFLE (HAMMERLESS MODEL) – .22, .25 (special order), or .295 (standard) cal. conical lead projectile, CO_2 with removable 10.2 in. rechargeable gas cylinder affixed horizontally under the round barrel, SS, gas cylinder with flats for removal, top-loading tap operated by trigger guard acting as a cocking lever, LHS receiver marked "The Giffard Gun Company Limited London", advertised by maker as "A gun shooting three hundred shots without reloading," with or w/o white-face shot counter (to 200), English-style walnut stock with fine checkering, tang manual safety, light engraving, blue steel parts. Mfg. late 1880s to early 1890s.

courtesy Beeman Collection

	N/A	$2,500	$2,000	$1,625	$1,250	$875	$500

Add 5% for shot counter.

SHOTGUNS

GAS SHOTGUN – 8mm cal., CO_2, rotating bolt tap loading, similar to Gas Rifle, except has small brass pin front sight, double flip up "V" rear sight, rectangle loading port.

courtesy Howard Collection

	N/A	$2,500	$2,000	$1,625	$1,250	$875	$500

GIRARDONI/AUSTRIAN AND SIMILAR AIR GUN SYSTEMS

Girardoni was a previous manufacturer located in Austria, circa 1780-1799.

Girardoni-system air guns have a horizontal transverse bar action with a gravity-fed magazine alongside the barrel.

PISTOLS

AUSTRIAN REPEATING AIR PISTOL – 9.5mm cal., PCP, 11-shot tubular gravity-fed ball magazine, horizontal transverse bar action, 6.2 in. rifled wrought-iron barrel, 12 groove rifling, leather-covered removable air reservoir grip, air by-pass button on upper left receiver, blued finish, 13 in. OAL, 3.9 lbs. Circa 1810-1820.

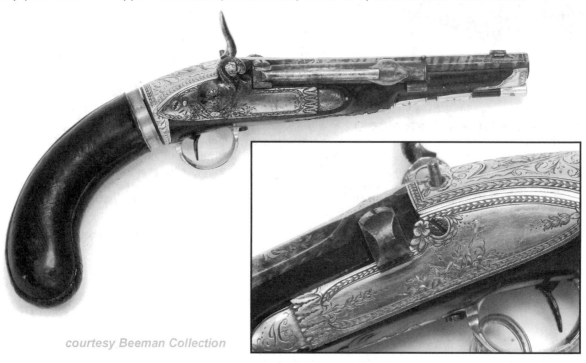

courtesy Beeman Collection

Scarcity precludes accurate pricing.

The gold-plated engraved bronze receiver on example is marked "JC" on LH sidepate and "in Wien" (in Vienna) RH lockplate.

GIRARDONI PISTOL – 9.5mm cal., PCP, 6.9 in. rifled barrel, 12 groove rifling, 13 ball tubular gravity-fed magazine, leather-

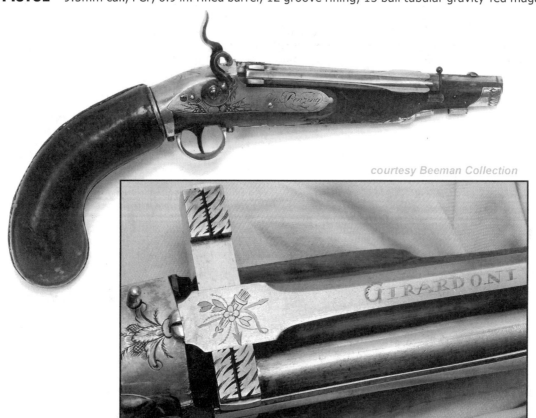

courtesy Beeman Collection

covered removable air reservoir as grip, air by-pass button on upper left receiver, 14.5 in. OAL, 3.9 lbs. Mfg. circa 1799.

Scarcity precludes accurate pricing.

This example has silver inlay on barrel marked "GIRARDONI", gold-plated, engraved and inlaid bronze receiver, manufactured in Penzing, Austria with RH sideplate engraved "in Penzing".

RIFLES

1780 MODEL AUSTRIAN MILITARY REPEATING AIR RIFLE – .462 (11.79mm) cal., PCP, horizontal transverse bar action, 21-shot mag., 32.7 in. oct. tapered wrought iron barrel, 12 groove rifling, blued finish, no air by-pass control, removable conical butt-reservoir, tubular gravity-fed magazine, walnut stock extends from trigger guard to muzzle, 48.5 in. OAL, 9.2 lbs. Approx. 1,500 mfg. in Penzing, Austria circa 1787-1799.

courtesy Beeman Collection

There is strong evidence in the Lewis and Clark expedition journals suggesting that this specimen is[1] the air rifle carried on the Lewis and Clark Expedition. Many arms and historical experts consider the Lewis Airgun, ca. 1790, as the world's most important and most valuable airgun.

[1] In 2004 by Ernest Cowan and Rick Keller in the Beeman Collection. See Beeman (2005) *The Lewis and Clark Air Rifle-A Preliminary Note on New Evidence*, Fifth Edition *Blue Book of Airguns* and Beeman (2007) *Air Power Diplomacy: Lewis's Assault Rifle*, Sixth Edtion *Blue Book of Airguns*.

courtesy Beeman Collection

Operational museum copy of Lewis Airgun made in 2006 by Ernest Cowan and Rick Keller.

See the Tenth Edition *Blue Book of Airguns* cover for original SN 1356 of the Austrian Army Repeating Air Rifle with accessories.

Scarcity precludes accurate pricing. Every example should be individually assessed.
Original leather accessory pouch for butt reservoir, hand pump, speedloaders, and additional accessories will bring substantial premiums.

Less than 25 original specimens are known.

ECKARD DOUBLE BARRELED AIR RIFLE – 9.5mm cal., PCP, horizontal transverse bar action, 29.4 in. O/U barrels, one with 12 groove rifling, one smoothbore, tubular gravity-fed ball magazine, conical leather covered removable air reservoir as buttstock, 45.7 in. OAL, 9.9 lbs. Mfg. in Bamberg, Germany circa 1810.

A double barrel Girardoni-system air rifle by Eckard of Bamberg, ca. 1810. Slide selects F (Flinte) for shotgun or B (Büchse) for rifle barrel.

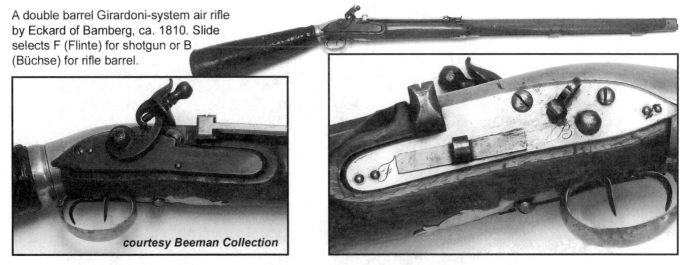

courtesy Beeman Collection

Scarcity precludes accurate pricing. Every example should be individually assessed.

MORTIMER REPEATING AIR RIFLE – 11.5mm cal., PCP, horizontal transverse bar action, 12 groove 32 in. rifled barrel, tubular gravity-fed ball magazine, leather-covered, conical removable air reservoir as buttstock, engraved, air by-pass, fitted wooden case, 48 in. OAL, 10.1 lbs. Mfg. circa 1815.

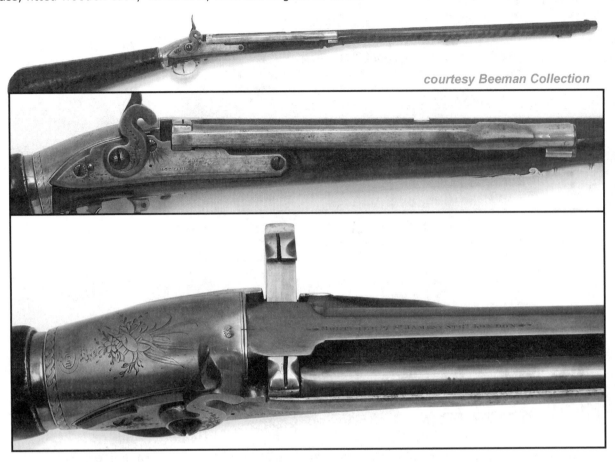

courtesy Beeman Collection

Scarcity precludes accurate pricing. Every example should be individually assessed.

This example was probably manufactured by Jackson Mortimer, of London, England.

STORMER DUAL-CALIBER RIFLE/SHOTGUN – 10mm cal., PCP, horizontal transverse bar action, eight groove 26.6 in. rifled barrel plus 8mm cal. 27.1 in. smoothbore barrel, tubular gravity-fed ball magazine serves rifled barrel,

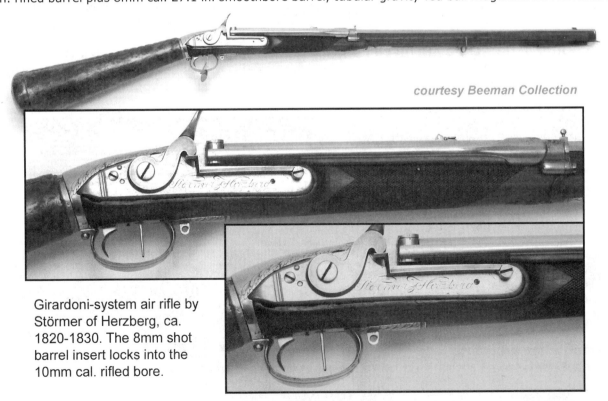

courtesy Beeman Collection

Girardoni-system air rifle by Störmer of Herzberg, ca. 1820-1830. The 8mm shot barrel insert locks into the 10mm cal. rifled bore.

leather-covered, conical, removable air reservoir buttstock, 42.1-42.7 in. OAL, 8.25 lbs. Mfg. in Herzberg, Germany circa 1820-1830.

Scaricity precludes accurate pricing.

GIRARDONI OR GIRANDONI?

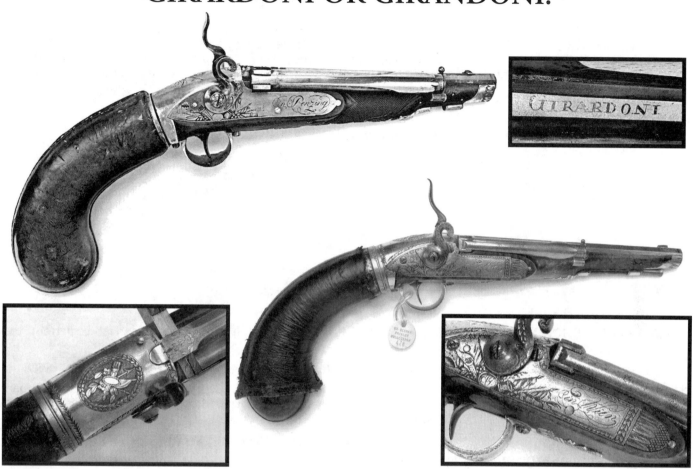

When we first illustrated the upper air pistol in the Eighth Edition of the *Blue Book of Airguns*, almost all references to the maker of this gun used GIRANDONI as the spelling of his name. So although the gun is clearly marked GIRARDONI in large capital letter silver inlays, we commented that spelling was not important in that period and continued to use the well-established convention of spelling his name GIRANDONI. Since then, Peter Girardoni, the present patriarch and historian of this gunmaker's family, invited Mrs. Beeman and myself to an extended stay at the family's estate near Vienna. We examined the very detailed family records and actual copies of letters and contracts signed by the gunmaker that were in the Austrian State Archives. These original documents, even multi-language ones, bore the gunmaker's actual signature as BARTOLOMEO GIRARDONI. In a very few cases, he had used a common signature flourish of presenting the final "i" as a "y", but he never used an "n" for the fifth letter. Research into the linguistic origins of the name showed that it probably had been derived from Girard, a solid Italian name, but that a base name of Girand simply didn't exist in the local languages. The maker's own marks on our two air pistols: GIRARDONI and GIRARDONY clinched the matter. The gunmaker recognized himself as GIRARDONI and so should we.

Only two Girardoni air pistols are known to us. The upper image shows the "GIRARDONI in Penzing" pistol. (Penzing was a tiny town attached to Vienna.) Multiple lead balls are manually fed by gravity from the 13 ball tubular magazine to a firing socket in the sliding loading bar—just as in the Lewis and Clark air rifle. The air reservoir is the leather-covered pistol grip. It is unscrewed from the receiver for charging with a separate pump. The 12-groove rifled barrel is .374 (9.5 mm) caliber. This gun probably was made shortly before Bartolomeo died in 1799.

The lower image shows a superbly-made, gold-plated, silver inlaid, deeply engraved pistol on the Girardoni system but with Contriner styling. Its elegant construction suggests an important, perhaps royal, customer. Caliber is about .38" (9 mm). Originally we thought that the barrel was signed "Girandony" but closer examination reveals the fifth letter as an "r", not at all like the "n" at the end of the name. The lock on this gun clearly shows a "JG". One of Bartolomeo Girardoni's sons was named Johann Girardoni. This suggests, as was previously not known, that Johann, described as especially talented and trained by his father in technical skills, may have been involved in the production of Girardoni repeating airguns—perhaps in the Contriner shop in Vienna, after his father's death in 1799. This very specimen is shown on pg. 93 of Wolff (1958). *Both guns courtesy of Beeman collection.*

GRADING	100%	95%	90%	80%	60%	40%	20%

GLOBE

Trade name of BB rifles previously manufactured by J.A. Dubuar Manufacturing Company of Northville, MI circa 1890-1908.

The Globe airguns were invented by Merritt F. Stanley, a former Markham Air Rifle Company employee. Stanley set up a small machine shop in the second story of the Ely Dowell Manufacturing Company in Northville, MI. Apparently unable to make a go of machine work by himself, he moved into a larger shop in the J.A. Dubuar Manufacturing Company and apparently began making the first Globe air rifles in 1890. Stanley had three BB gun patents issued to him; one for a lever action gun which evidently was never produced. Stanley's patents went to Daisy Manufacturing Company in 1908 as Daisy closed down the production of another competitor.

courtesy Beeman Collection

RIFLES

All rifles have smoothbore barrels and are without safeties.

FIRST MODEL - (IRON LATTICE MODEL) – .180 large BB cal., BO, SP, SS, frame and diamond lattice pattern stock of cast iron, nickel finish, brass smoothbore barrel, globe design at body hinge. Circa 1890-1891.

	N/A	$3,000	$2,400	$1,950	$1,500	$1,050	$600

SECOND MODEL – .180 large BB cal., BO, SP, SS, similar to First Model, except has wood stock with metal parts marked "GLOBE, Pats. Jan. 28, 1890" on both sides, nickel finish, brass smoothbore barrel, globe design at body hinge, peep sight, post front sight. Circa 1892-1897.

	N/A	$2,800	$2,250	$1,825	$1,400	$975	$550

THIRD MODEL ("G" MODEL) – .180 large BB cal., BO, SP, SS. Similar to First Model, cast iron frame, more ornate than First Model, pine wood stock with oval containing "J.A. Dubuar" and address, nickel finish, sheet metal smoothbore barrel with full length external patch, grip frame marked "GLOBE" and large "G". Circa 1894.

	N/A	$2,500	$2,000	$1,625	$1,250	$875	$500

GENERAL CUSTER – no known specimens.

MICHIGAN – no known specimens.

SPECIAL (PUSH BARREL MODEL) – .180 large BB cal., SP, SS, push-barrel cocking, cast iron frame, sheet metal plunger housing, plunger housing marked "GLOBE SPECIAL", wood stock with oval containing "J.A. Dubuar" and address, deep crescent butt, nickel finish, brass tube smoothbore barrel, grip frame with checkered pattern. Circa 1897-99.

	N/A	$1,100	$875	$725	$550	$375	$220

WARRIOR – .180 large BB cal., BO, SP, SS, sheet metal frame, barrel shroud, sights, pine wood stock without stamping, nickel finish, sheet metal smoothbore barrel, grip frame marked "GLOBE" and J.A. Dubuar address. Circa 1900-1908.

	N/A	$700	$550	$450	$350	$245	$140

* **Warrior Barrel Lug Version** – .180 cal., similar to Warrior, except with lug under barrel near muzzle. Circa 1908.

	N/A	$650	$525	$425	$325	$230	$130

* **Warrior Buster Brown Version** – .180 cal., similar to Warrior, except has Dubuar oval logo on buttstock with "BUSTER BROWN SHOES". Spring loaded shot cup under barrel. Circa 1908.

	N/A	$750	$600	$475	$375	$265	$150

* **Warrior Embossed Version** – .180 cal., similar to Warrior, except sides with embossed design. Dubuar stock stamp. Circa 1901.

	N/A	$675	$550	$450	$325	$235	$135

GRADING	100%	95%	90%	80%	60%	40%	20%

* *Warrior Repeater Version* – .180 cal., similar to Warrior, except repeater. Mfg. circa 1908.

	N/A	$850	$675	$550	$425	$300	$170

Subtract 25% if not complete.
These models are usually missing parts.

MODEL 99 – .180 large BB cal., BO, SP, SS, similar to Third Model with cast iron frame, no "J.A. Dubuar" marking, 16.75 in. smoothbore barrel, nickel finish grip frame marked "99 GLOBE", 31.3 in. OAL.

	N/A	$2,250	$1,800	$1,450	$1,125	$775	$450

GLOBE RESERVOIR AIRGUNS

For information on Globe Reservoir Airguns, see Ball Reservoir Airguns in the "B" section.

GOLONDRINA

For information on Golondrina airguns, see Venturini in the "V" section.

GREENER, W.W., LIMITED

Previous manufacturer located in Birmingham, England, since 1829.

Producers of many guns from sub-machine guns to fine shotguns and a unique spring piston air rifle. The rifle was based on British patent 411,520, issued 8 June 1934, to Charles Edward Greener, for a cam mechanism to tightly seal the breech area.

For more information and current pricing on Greener firearms, please refer to the *Blue Book of Gun Values* by S. P. Fjestad (also available online).

RIFLES

GREENER – .177 or .22 cal., BBC, SP, SS, usually distinguished by a large cam lever on the left forward end of the compression tube, this lever swings forward to cause the barrel to move forward of the breech block for opening and loading the breech, moving it back cams the barrel tightly shut, buttstock similar to BSA designs with top ridge for the shooting hand's web, no wood forward of trigger, 43 in. OAL, 7.5 lbs. Mfg. 1934 to 1960s.

courtesy Beeman Collection

	N/A	$500	$400	$325	$250	$175	$100

GUNPOWER LIMITED

Current manufacturer located in Kent, U.K. No current U.S. importation.

GUNPOWER HISTORY

In 1994, Geoff Darvill came up with the idea of using the air cylinder of a pre-charged rifle as the stock instead of placing in front of the rifle. This meant the balance of the rifle was better becase the weight was to the rear and gave the possibility of greater efficiency because the tank was in-line with the barrel. He teamed up with John McCaslin based in Texas to design and improve the idea.

In December 1997 the GunPower Stealth was born. At the time it was unique, a pre-charged pneumatic air rifle giving over 500 shots per fill in .22 (5.5mm), with no wood on the rifle it was incredibly light and when launched was the least expensive pre-charged air rifle in the world. Since then the design has been continually improved with the launch of the Stealth 2000 - the safety was improved, together with the introduction of Lothar Walther precision match grade barrels in all the guns. The Shadow was introduced for the American market having an integral silencer, and AirForce Airguns was set up to supply the U.S. market. Later the Storm and then the SSS (at the time the world's most powerful airgun at 60 ft/lbs.) were added and in the last decade the Edge Target rifle was launched. In 2013, the XS, an integrally silenced SSS and the Hellcat, the U.K's first 12 ft/lb. pistol (50 ft/lb for export) were also launched.

RIFLES

Gunpower manufactures high quality tactical, hunting, and target air rifles. A wide variety of options and configurations are available. Current models include Edge ($1,160), Hellcat ($790), SSS ($1,160), Shadow ($870), Stealth ($790), Storm ($870), and XS ($1,200). Please contact the company directly for more information, options, and U.S. availability (see Trademark Index).

GRADING	100%	95%	90%	80%	60%	40%	20%

GUN POWER STEALTH

Current trademark manufactured in conjunction with AirForce International (previously AirForce Airguns), located in Ft. Worth, TX.

See listing for AirForce International in the "A" section.

GUN TOYS SRL

Current manufacturer of inexpensive barrel cocking air pistols and pistol/carbines located in Miliano, Italy beginning about early 1970. No current U.S. importation.

Gun Toys SRL also privately labeled airguns for Scalemead and Sussex Armory of Britain.

PISTOLS/CARBINES

RO-71 – .177 cal., SP, BBC, SS, die-cast metal and plastic parts, black plastic buttstock, about 250 FPS, 13.3 in. OAL, 2.1 lbs. Mfg. circa 1973.

courtesy Beeman Collection

	100%	95%	90%	80%	60%	40%	20%
	$50	$40	$35	$30	$20	$10	N/A

This model was sold under the names Scalemead Hotshot Standard, Sussex Armory Panther, Classic, IGI202, and Bullseye, and is also known as IGI 202 (IGI became FAS about 1980). Ref: AW Dec. 2004.

RO-72 – .177 cal., SP, BBC, SS, similar to RO71, except has one-piece black plastic buttstock, 300 FPS, 14.2 in. OAL, 2.3 lbs.

	100%	95%	90%	80%	60%	40%	20%
	$55	$45	$40	$35	$25	$15	N/A

This model was also sold under the names Scalemead Hotshot Deluxe, Sussex Armory Panther Deluxe, Classic Deluxe, and IGI203.

RO-76 – .177 cal., SP, BBC, SS, similar to RO-72, except has hardwood buttstock and separate pistol grip.

	100%	95%	90%	80%	60%	40%	20%
	$55	$45	$40	$35	$25	$15	N/A

RO-77 – .177 cal., SP, BBC, SS, similar to RO-76, except has longer barrel and shoulder stock rod screwed directly into end cap of receiver.

	100%	95%	90%	80%	60%	40%	20%
	$55	$45	$40	$35	$25	$15	N/A

RO-80 – .177 cal., SP, BBC, SS, similar to RO-72, except has plain receiver end cap and grey buttstock.

	100%	95%	90%	80%	60%	40%	20%
	$55	$45	$40	$35	$25	$15	N/A

H SECTION

HS (HERBERT SCHMIDT)

Previous trademark of Herbert Schmidt located in Ostheim an der Röhn, Germany. Manufacturers of cartridge and blank firing pistols and air pistols including the HS 71A, a side lever BB repeater, and the HS 9A, a push barrel model of the type known to the British as a "Gat."

GRADING	100%	95%	90%	80%	60%	40%	20%

PISTOLS

HS 9A – .177 cal., push-barrel cocking, SP, screw-in breech plug for loading, smoothbore barrel, port in right side of frame to allow lubrication of mainspring and piston seal, hard plastic coated frame, approx. 250 FPS, no safety, 5-7.8 in. OAL, 0.5 lbs. Mfg. 1975-1995.

courtesy Beeman Collection

	$40	$35	$30	$25	$20	N/A	N/A

Earlier versions are known.

HS 71A – .177 cal. lead balls, SL, SP, spring-fed hundred-shot magazine, composition or wood grips, 6 in. BBL. Mfg. 1971-1990s.

courtesy Beeman Collection

	$250	$200	$175	$150	$125	$100	N/A

Add 20% for factory box and accessories.

HAENEL

Previous manufacturer located in Suhl, Germany. Previously imported by Pilkington Competition Equipment LLC located in Monteagle, TN, Cape Outfitters, located in Cape Girardeau, MO, and G.S.I., located in Trussville, AL.

The Haenel Company was founded in 1840 by Carl Gottlieb Haenel. The company originally produced military weapons, then sporting guns and later airguns. The company was sold around 1890 and the Haenel brand name has changed hands many times since then. Haenel airguns were most recently made by Suhler Jagd-und Sportwaffen GmbH, in Suhl, Germany. Waffentechnik in Suhl currently has control. Identity of the company itself and all of the records were lost when the firm was integrated into the communist state-run firearms industry in the late 1940s. Therefore, accurately dating and identifying every Haenel airgun is not always possible.

Haenel guns are all stamped with the Haenel name and model number. The 1926 catalog only lists the Models I, II, III, and IV air rifles and no air pistols. The 1937 catalog lists the Model 10 and IV ER and VR, and four air pistols including the 28R and 50.

The Luger-style Model 28 air pistol and the Model 33 air rifle are Haenel's most famous models. Designed by Hugo Schmeisser, of sub-machine gun fame, the Model 33 was the basis for the later Haenel 49, 310, 400, 510, LP55R and the Anschütz 275. The Schmiesser brothers worked at the factory for about twenty years.

Haenel had been noted for exceptionally high quality, but standards seemed to almost vanish under the state-owned operation. Quality improved some after the unification of Germany.

The key reference on post-WWII Haenel airguns was compiled by Ernst Dieter (a pseudonym) (2002), a former top

GRADING	100%	95%	90%	80%	60%	40%	20%

engineer at Haenel: *Luftgewehre und Luftpistolen nach 1945 aus Suhl und Zella-Mehlis*.

Spare parts and repairs for some discontinued Haenel air rifles may be available at: WTS Waffentechnik in Suhl, Germany. Please see the Trademark Index for more information.

For more information and current pricing on used Haenel firearms, please refer to the *Blue Book of Gun Values* by S.P. Fjestad (also available online).

PISTOLS

MODEL 26 – .177 cal. pellets, SP, SS, smoothbore or rifled barrel, GC cocks by lifting receiver tube up from trigger guard and grip frame, loaded by tipping breech open, black enamel finish, ribbed black plastic or hardwood grips with straight line checkering, no safety, 10 in. OAL, 1.5 lbs. Circa 1926-late 1930s.

courtesy Beeman Collection

N/A	$225	$175	$145	$105	$85	$50

Add 30% for factory box.

MODEL 28 – .177 or .22 cal. pellets, SP, SS, smoothbore or rifled barrel (rifled barrel indicated by asterisk after caliber marking), GC cocks by lifting receiver tube up from trigger guard and grip frame, loaded by tipping breech open, blue finish, synthetic or wood grips with brass Haenel or Super medallion, no safety, 10 in. OAL, 2.5 lbs.

courtesy Beeman Collection

N/A	$240	$190	$155	$120	$85	$50

Add 30% for factory box.
Add 30% for Super 28 markings.

Pistols marked "Heanel Air Pistol" mfg. 1928-1930, marked "Haenel Model 28" mfg. 1930-1940.

MODEL 28R – .177 or .22 cal. pellets, GC, SP, similar to Model 28, except repeating mechanism, twenty rounds of .177 or fifteen rounds of .22, rifled barrel, manual safety, 10.5 in. OAL, 2.6 lbs. Mfg. 1930-1940s.

courtesy Beeman Collection

N/A	$400	$325	$260	$200	$140	$80

Add 30% for factory box.

Magazine knob projection from rear of receiver immediately identifies this gun.

GRADING	100%	95%	90%	80%	60%	40%	20%

MODEL 50/51 – .174 cal. (4.4mm lead balls), SP, repeater, 50-shot gravity-fed magazine (Model 51 - lighter, SS), smoothbore barrel, nickel finish, hardwood grips with or without Haenel brass medallion, no safety, 8.8 in. OAL, 2.6 lbs. Shorter version was also available. Mfg. 1930-1934.

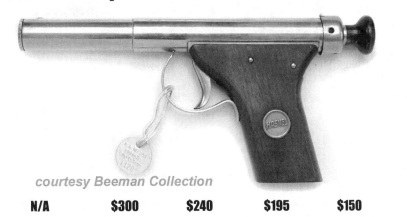

courtesy Beeman Collection

	N/A	$300	$240	$195	$150	$105	$60

Add 30% for factory box.

MODEL 100 – .174 cal. (4.4mm lead balls), SP, cocked by pulling ring on base of grip to release grip-backstrap cocking lever, 50-shot gravity-fed magazine, smoothbore barrel, nickel or blued finish, no safety. Mfg. 1932-1940.

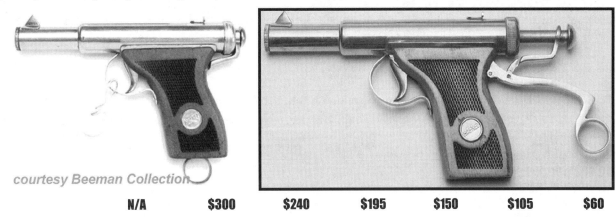

courtesy Beeman Collection

	N/A	$300	$240	$195	$150	$105	$60

Add 30% for factory box.

RIFLES

MODEL 1 – .177 or .22 cal., SS, BBC, SP, smoothbore or rifled barrel, beech stock, small pistol grip, blue finish, no safety, 38.3 in. OAL, 4.6 lbs. Mfg. 1925-1939. (Listed in 1939 Stoeger Catalog as their Model 3100).

courtesy Beeman Collection

$130	$110	$90	$75	$60	$40	$25

Add 30% for factory box.
Add 20% for Stoeger markings.

MODEL 1-53 – .177 cal., SS, BBC, SP, rifled barrel with lock similar to Haenel II and III, beech stock, small pistol grip, manual safety, blue finish, 38.3 in. OAL, 4.6 lbs. Mfg. 1949-1969.

$150	$130	$105	$85	$70	$45	$30

Add 30% for factory box.

GRADING	100%	95%	90%	80%	60%	40%	20%

MODEL II/MODEL III – .177 or .22 cal. pellets, rifled (eight grooves) or smoothbore, SS, BBC, SP, barrel release lever LHS of breech, 43.3 in. OAL, sight radius 17.7 in., 6.6 lbs. Circa 1925 to 1939.

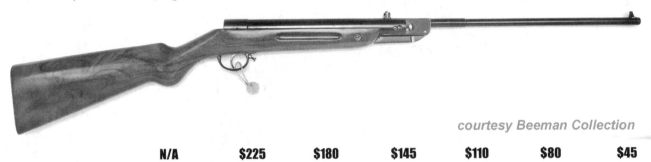

courtesy Beeman Collection

	N/A	$225	$180	$145	$110	$80	$45

Add 30% for factory box.

Numbers stamped under barrel may be manufacturing date and serial number. Model II with only wood buttstock. Model III with full stock with integral finger-grooved forearm.

MODEL III-53/III-56/III-60/III-284/3.014 – .177 or .22 cal. pellets, SS, BBC, SP, five variations of Model III made from 1950 to 1993, 568 FPS (173 MPS) for .177 cal., 400 FPS (122 MPS) for .22 cal., 19 in. barrel with 12-groove rifling, walnut finish beech or laminated stock, open or micrometer sights, 43.3-44.3 in. OAL, 6.8 to 7.7 lbs.

East German quality problems and very limited distribution outside of East Germany preclude determination of market values at this time (estimated $50 to $150).

MODEL IV – .177 or .22 cal. pellet, SS, SP, UL, wood buttstock behind trigger guard (Millita-style), sight radius 17.7 inches, 43.3 in. OAL, 6.6 lbs. Circa 1927-1939.

	N/A	$300	$240	$195	$150	$105	$60

Add 30% for factory box.
Add 150% for Repeater.

The Model IV-E repeater has the drum magazine on top of breech.

MODEL IV/M – .177 cal. pellet, SP, SS, TL, match rifle, characteristic top cocking bolt pivots at rear sight, 43 in. OAL, 6.75 lbs.

	N/A	$275	$220	$180	$135	$95	$55

Add 30% for factory box.
Add 100% for Repeater.

This model was available in 1958 and 1959, and became the Model IV/M in 1960.

MODEL VIII – .177 or .22 cal. pellets, UL, SP, smoothbore or rifled, wood buttstock behind grip, blued, sight radius 17.3 in., 42.9 in. OAL, 5.7 lbs. Mfg. circa 1925-1939.

$130	$110	$90	$75	$60	$40	$25

Add 30% for factory box.

MODEL 10 (X) – .177 cal. smoothbore, SP, SS, BO, slab-sided wood buttstock behind grip area, sheet metal "tinplate construction" (may have been made by Dianawerk; this model is not listed in Dieter's book), nickel-plated, 1.3 lbs., 31 in. OAL.

	N/A	$225	$180	$135	$105	$80	$55

Add 50% for German variation.

Date stamp on under edge of stock. German variation: stamped rippling on air chamber, stamped "MADE IN GERMANY", blued finish. Mfg. circa mid-1930s-1939.

MODEL 15 (XV) – .177 cal., BBC, SP, SS, smoothbore barrel, loaded by removing brass inner barrel from sheet metal barrel shroud, sheet metal/tinplate construction, beech buttstock behind grip area, blued or nickel, 32.5 in. OAL, 2 lbs. 7 oz.

Model XV
courtesy Beeman Collection

$225	$190	$160	$130	$100	$65	$45

Add 30% for factory box.
Add 30% for Model XV/VA.

Model XV (Model VA) similar but with wood forearm side slabs, more complex barrel lock, 2.75 lbs. Mfg. 1929 to late 1930s.

GRADING	100%	95%	90%	80%	60%	40%	20%

MODEL 20 (XX) – .177 cal. smoothbore, similar to Model 15, except direct breech loading, thin inner barrel within sheet metal barrel shroud, early versions with round Haenel logo; later with typical Haenel arrow logo, late 1930s rear sight moved from body tube to barrel, nickel or blued finish, 34.5 in. OAL, 3.2 lbs. Mfg. circa mid-1920s-1930s.

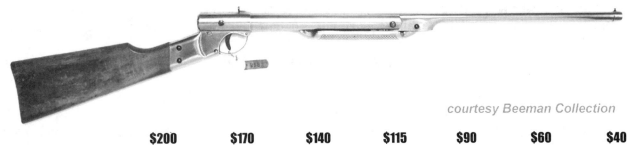

courtesy Beeman Collection

	$200	$170	$140	$115	$90	$60	$40

Add 20% for round Haenel logo.
Subtract 10% for rear sight on barrel.
Add 30% for factory box.

MODEL 30 (XXX) – .177 cal., similar to Model 20, except rifled or smoothbore, full stock with pistol grip and grooved forearm, no buttplate, no safety, 34.5 in. OAL, 3.1 lbs.

	$200	$170	$140	$115	$90	$60	$40

MODEL 33/33 JUNIOR – .174 cal. (4.45mm lead balls), SP, bolt lever cocking, paramilitary-style with bayonet lug and stock slot for sling, detachable spring-fed 8 or 12 (Model 33) or 6 or 12 (Model 33 Junior) round box magazines, Mauser type wing manual safety, 44 in. OAL, 7.5 lbs. (Model 33), 40 in. OAL, 5.3 lbs (Model 33 Junior). Model 33 sling on side of stock. 33 Junior sling on bottom of stock. Ca. 1933-early 1940s.

courtesy Beeman Collection

	N/A	$375	$300	$245	$185	$130	$75

Add 30% for factory box.

Production may have been resumed in 1950s. Schmeisser's Patent.

MODEL 40 – .177 cal., SP, BBC, SS, similar to Model 30 (XXX), except solid 14.8 in. barrel, pistol grip stock with finger grooved forearm, no buttplate, no safety, 35.5 in. OAL, 3.75 lbs. Mfg. 1930s to 1939.

	$150	$130	$105	$85	$70	$45	$30

MODEL 45 – .177 cal. only, SP, BBC, SS, solid steel rifled or smoothbore barrel, straight grip stock with no forearm, 35 in. OAL, 3.6 lbs. Mfg. 1930s to 1939.

	$150	$130	$105	$85	$70	$45	$30

MODEL 49/MODEL 49a – .174 cal. (4.4mm lead balls), SP, rocking-bolt lever cocking, Sporter version of Model 33, detachable spring-fed six, eight, or 12-shot round ball box magazines, Mauser-type wing manual safety, date stamp on steel buttplate. Model 49 sight radius: 16.2 in., 41.5 in. OAL, Model 49a sight radius: 18.5 in. 41.75 in. OAL, 5.9 lbs. Mfg. circa 1949-1960.

courtesy Beeman Collection

	N/A	$425	$350	$275	$210	$150	$85

Add 30% for factory box.

GRADING	100%	95%	90%	80%	60%	40%	20%

MODEL 85 (KI 1) – .177 cal. Importation disc. 1993.

	100%	95%	90%	80%	60%	40%	20%
	$100	$85	$70	$60	$45	$30	$20

Last MSR was $130.

MODEL B96 BIATHLON TRAINER – .177 cal., PCP, SS or five-shot repeater using one-round and five-round magazines, Fortner-type action, adj. match trigger, adj. sights, competition stock with adj. cheek piece, 39.4 in. OAL, 9.6 lbs.

	100%	95%	90%	80%	60%	40%	20%
	$1,425	$1,225	$1,000	$825	$650	$425	$285

Last MSR was $1,595.

Add 10% for semi-auto conversion.

This model is designed as a trainer for Biathlon rifle disciplines.

MODEL 100/MODEL 510 – .177 cal., SS, BBC, small pistol grip, blue finish, 38.3 in. OAL, 4.6 lbs. Model 510 mfg. 1989-1991. Model 100 mfg. 1991-1993.

	100%	95%	90%	80%	60%	40%	20%
	$150	$130	$105	$85	$70	$45	$30

Number change for Model 300.

MODEL 110/MODEL 520 – .177 cal. pellets, Model 110 mfg.1992-1993. Model 520 mfg.1991-1993.

	100%	95%	90%	80%	60%	40%	20%
	$125	$105	$90	$75	$55	$35	$25

Improved deluxe versions of Model 303.

MODEL 300 – .177 cal., SS, BBC, small pistol grip, blue finish, 38.3 in. OAL, 4.6 lbs. Mfg. 1969-1989.

	100%	95%	90%	80%	60%	40%	20%
	$150	$130	$105	$85	$70	$45	$30

Became Model 510 in 1989. Became Model 100 in 1991.

MODEL 302 – .177 or .22 cal., SS, BBC, larger version of Model 300, several versions with minor changes. Production began in 1966.

	100%	95%	90%	80%	60%	40%	20%
	$150	$130	$105	$85	$70	$45	$30

MODEL 303 (KI)/MODEL 303-8 SUPER – .177 or .22 cal., similar to Model 302 with minor improvements. Production began 1969. Presumably replaced Model 302. USA importation discontinued ca. 1993. Unusual variation: Model 303-8 Super with target stock and aperture sights.

	100%	95%	90%	80%	60%	40%	20%
	$125	$105	$90	$75	$55	$35	$25

Last MSR was $190.

Add 75% for 303-8 Super.

MODEL 304 – similar to Model 303, except with plastic stock. Mfg. after 1976.

	100%	95%	90%	80%	60%	40%	20%
	$125	$105	$90	$75	$55	$35	$25

MODEL 308-8 – .177 cal., SP, SS. Importation disc. 1993.

	100%	95%	90%	80%	60%	40%	20%
	$225	$190	$160	$130	$100	$65	$45

Last MSR was $300.

Not well known outside of former Soviet bloc countries.

MODEL 310 (KI 104) – 4.4mm round lead ball, SP, rocking-bolt lever cocking, sportier version of Model 49/49a, detachable, spring-fed six, eight, or 12-shot round ball box magazines, push pull safety at rear of compression tube, numerous versions differ mainly in sights and stock, fifth version (4.5 [.177] cal.) has horizontal seven-shot drum repeating mechanism mounted horizontally over top of breech. Mfg. 1960-1989.

	100%	95%	90%	80%	60%	40%	20%
	$175	$150	$125	$100	$80	$50	$35

Last MSR was $200.

Add 100% for repeater version Model 310-5.

MODEL 311 (KI 102) – .177 cal. pellets, SS, SP, top action bolt cocking handle, tap loader, open or aperture sight, 43.75 in. OAL, 7.2 lbs. Mfg. 1964-1992.

	100%	95%	90%	80%	60%	40%	20%
	N/A	$225	$180	$145	$110	$80	$45

Last MSR was $395.

Numerous variations mainly are minor stock changes.

GRADING	100%	95%	90%	80%	60%	40%	20%

MODEL 312 – .177 cal., SL, SP, multiple spring/rubber buffer recoil-reduction system, tap-loading, 42.5 in. OAL, 10.8 lbs. Mfg. early 1970s-1990s.

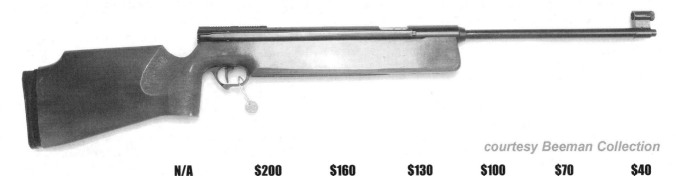

courtesy Beeman Collection

	N/A	$200	$160	$130	$100	$70	$40

MODEL 400/MODEL 570 – upgrades of Model 310, Model 570 is 1989 model number change for Model 310, Model 400 is 1991 model number change for Model 570, detachable spring-fed six, eight, or 12-round box magazines for 4.4mm round lead balls.

	$175	$150	$125	$100	$80	$50	$35

MODEL 410/MODEL 580 – 4.4mm lead balls, SP, unique lever action repeater, same magazine system as Models 400 and 570, dummy in-line magazine below barrel resembles tubular .22 cal. rimfire magazine.

	$175	$150	$125	$100	$80	$50	$35

MODEL 600 – .177 or .22 cal., SP, SS, SL, match rifle, open or aperture sights, adj. buttplate, 42.13 in. OAL, 8.8 lbs.

	$250	$215	$175	$145	$115	$75	$50

Replaced Model 312.

MLG 550 (KI 101) – .177 cal., SP, SS, tap-loading, SS top lever mechanism, 25.6 in. BBL, recoilless match rifle, the MLG (Meisterschafts-Luftgewehr) approx. 500 FPS, match trigger, 42.8 in. OAL, 10.8 lbs. USA importation disc. 1993.

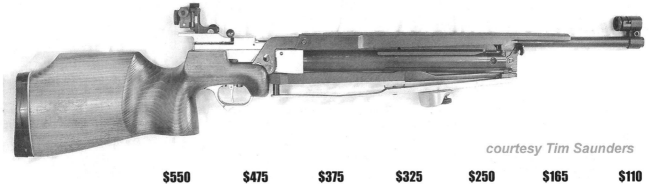

courtesy Tim Saunders

	$550	$475	$375	$325	$250	$165	$110

Last MSR was $695.

Small numbers were made for Soviet bloc international match competitors.

MODEL 800 – .177 cal., SS, SP, match rifle, characteristic top-cocking bolt pivots at rear sight. Mfg. ca. 1990-1992.

	$450	$375	$325	$260	$205	$135	$90

Replaced Model 550-1.

HAKIM

For information on this Egyptian military training air rifle, please refer to Anschütz in the "A" section.

HÄMMERLI AG

Current trademark purchased during 2006 by Walther, and firearms are currently manufactured in Ulm/Donau, Germany beginning 2008. Current airgun manufacturer located in Lenzburg, Switzerland, with most manufacturing actually done in Schaffhausen in the old SIG factory. They are now separate from SIG. Current match/target airguns imported by Larry's Guns, located in Gray, ME, and Air Venturi/Pyramyd Air located in Solon, OH. Current sport airguns imported by Umarex USA located in Fort Smith, AR beginning 2006. Previously imported until 1995 by Champion's Choice, located in LaVergne, TN, Gunsmithing, Inc., located in Colorado Springs, CO, 10 Ring Service Inc. located in Jacksonville, FL, George Brenzovich located in Fort Hancock, TX and Wade Anderson (Hämmerli Pistols USA), located in Groveland,

GRADING	100%	95%	90%	80%	60%	40%	20%

CA. Dealer and consumer direct sales. In late 2000, SIG Arms AG, the firearms portion of SIG, was purchased by two Germans named Michael Lüke and Thomas Ortmeier, who have a background in textiles. Today the Lüke & Ortmeier group includes independently operational companies such as Blaser Jadgwaffen GmbH, Mauser Jagdwaffen GmbH, J.P. Sauer & Sohn GmbH, SIG-Sauer Inc., SIG-Sauer GmbH and SAN Swiss Arms AG.

The Hämmerli CO_2 rifles and pistols were the first true precision CO_2 guns in the world. This is only a partial listing of models, with preliminary information. Additional research is underway and more information will be presented about Hämmerli airguns in future editions of this guide.

A devastating fire in 1977 destroyed the production lines for precision CO_2 guns. Some recent airguns bearing the Hämmerli name have been built to much more economical standards than the pre-1977 models. Hämmerli recently has served as a distributor of BSA and El Gamo airguns, but the claims that any of the Hämmerli brand airguns were made by other companies evidently is not true.

Beginning in 2007, Umarex USA took over the importation and marketing of a new Hämmerli sport airgun product line with some models not manufactured in Switzerland. These sport airguns will be marked Umarex USA. As of 2007, all Hämmerli match/target airguns are still being manufactured in Switzerland.

For more information and current pricing on both new and used Hämmerli AG firearms, please refer to the *Blue Book of Gun Values* by S.P. Fjestad (also available online).

PISTOLS

Add 20% for original factory box.
Add 30% for factory fitted case.

DUELL – .177 cal., CO_2 cylinder, five-shot manual, spring-fed magazine horizontal on top of receiver feeds pop-up loading block, black crinkle and blued finish, composition checkered RH thumbrest grip, 16.1 in. OAL, 2.6 lbs. Mfg. 1967-1970.

courtesy Beeman Collection

N/A	$850	$700	$575	$450	$300	$200

FIREHORNET – .177 cal., BBC, 575 FPS, black synthetic stock, adj. trigger, spring mounted front sight, adj. rear sight, manual safety, permanently floating action, shock absorber buttplate, cocking aid also included, 14.8 in. OAL, 3.04 lbs. New 2012.

Please contact the company directly for pricing and availability on this model.

MASTER – .177 cal., CO_2 (bulk fill or capsules), adj. sights and trigger, UIT target model, no safety, 15.9 in. OAL, 2.4 lbs. Mfg. 1964-1979.

courtesy Beeman Collection

N/A	$400	$325	$275	$215	$140	$95

Add 15% for wood grips.

This model won the German National Championships in 1965, 1966, and 1967.

GRADING	100%	95%	90%	80%	60%	40%	20%

PRINZ – .177 cal., CO$_2$ cylinder, five-shot manual, spring-fed, vertical magazine replaces pop-up loading block, black crinkle and blued finish, composition checkered RH thumbrest grip, not marked Hammerli (identified by box), the only marking is "MOD 5/1", 11.8 in. OAL, 2.2 lbs. Mfg. 1967-1970.

courtesy Beeman Collection

N/A	$700	$550	$450	$350	$245	$140

RAPID – BB/.174 lead ball cal., CO$_2$, five-shot semi-auto, adj. sights and trigger, training pistol for UIT rapid fire, 13 in. OAL, 3.4 lbs. Mfg. 1966-69.

courtesy Beeman Collection

N/A	$600	$475	$400	$300	$210	$120

Add 10% for wood grips.

SINGLE – .177 cal., CO$_2$, (bulk fill or capsules), adj. sights and trigger, pop-up breech loading plug, no safety, 13.8 in. OAL, 2.2 lbs. Mfg. 1961-1970s.

courtesy Beeman Collection

N/A	$400	$325	$255	$195	$140	$80

Add 10% for wood grips.

Declining velocity is prevented by two measures: 1. Constant pressure metering sytem. 2. Pressure vented to atmosphere when a set low pressure level is reached. Junior Target Model 2nd Variant has the same grip frame and trigger as Master Model so that 12 gm CO$_2$ cylinders may be used.

GRADING	100%	95%	90%	80%	60%	40%	20%

SPARKLER – .175/BB and .177 cal., CO_2 "Sparkler" cartridge, manual repeater five-shot magazine, Two versions: R and RD. The RD can fire lead balls as a repeater and pellets as a SS, 13.7 in. OAL, 2.7 lbs. Mfg. 1958-1960.

courtesy Beeman Collection

	N/A	$295	$235	$190	$145	$105	$60

Add 10% for wood grips.
Add 25% for RD version.
Add 15% for fitted factory case.

MODEL 480 – .177 cal., CO_2 or PCP, fixed cylinder, adj. grips, UIT target model, adj. sights, adj. trigger, adj. grip, up to 320 shots per full compressed air cylinder, approx. 2.25 lbs. Mfg. 1994-99.

	$500	$425	$350	$290	$225	$150	$100

Last MSR was $1,355.

Add $145 for walnut grips.

MODEL 480K – .177 cal., CO_2 or PCP, similar to Model 480, except has detachable cylinders.

	$650	$550	$450	$375	$295	$195	$130

Add $145 for walnut grips.

MODEL 480K2 – .177 cal., CO_2 or PCP, similar to Model 480, except has detachable cylinders. Mfg. 1998-2000.

	$800	$675	$550	$475	$350	$240	$160

Add $145 for walnut grips.

MODEL AP20 – .177 cal., PCP, SS, BA, 492 FPS, rifled steel Hämmerli match barrel, removable PRO-line aluminum air reservoir, adj. post front sight, fully adj. rear sight, all-in-one grip has switchable, removable palm shelf and thumbrest for right- or left-handed shooters, polymer grip, 2-stage adj. match trigger, no safety, includes DIN fill adapter, separate pressure gauge (manometer), safety cord, Allen wrenches, triggerguard, 6 total barrel jackets (black, orange, blue, silver, green and pink), plastic pistol case and owner's manual.

courtesy Umarex USA

MSR $1,100	$925	$775	$650	$525	$425	$275	$185

MODEL AP40 BALANCE – .177 cal., CO_2, 9.8 in. high precision steel barrel with gas ports, aluminum cylinder with anodized scratch-proof finish and pressure gauge, two-stage and dry firing trigger, 3D grip adjustment, integral front sight in three widths, front sight mount with compensator, universal setting options, supplied in plastic case with filler and tool, 2.1 lbs. Mfg. in Switzerland. New 2011.

Please contact the company directly for pricing and availability on this model.

* **Model AP40 Balance Junior** – .177 cal., CO_2, similar to Model AP40 Balance, except has shortened cylinder, 1.9 lbs. Mfg. in Switzerland. New 2011.

Please contact the company directly for pricing and availability on this model.

MODEL AP 40 MATCH – .177 cal., PCP (cylinder with integral pressure gauge), adj. rear target sights, integral front sight with three different sight widths, fully adj. trigger system, optional adj. "Hi-Grip," blue or gold breech and cylinder, 9.85 in. aluminum barrel, includes case and replacement cylinder, 2.2 lbs. Mfg. in Switzerland. Mfg. 2001-disc.

	$1,150	$1,000	$925	$750	$575	N/A	N/A

Last MSR was $1,350.

Add 6% for ported steel BBL (Model AP40 Pro new 2005).

GRADING	100%	95%	90%	80%	60%	40%	20%

* ***Model AP 40 Junior*** – .177 cal., PCP (cylinder with integral pressure gauge), adj. rear target sights, integral front sight with three different sight widths, fully adj. trigger system, optional adj. "Hi-Grip," blue breech and cylinder, includes case and replacement cylinder, 14.82 in. OAL, 1.9 lbs. Mfg. in Switzerland.

	$975	$825	$675	$575	$450	$290	$195

Add 5% for adj. "Hi-Grip".

MODEL P26 – .177 cal., CO_2, DA, 8-shot rotary mag., 385 FPS, power cocking system, full metal construction, blued, adj. rear sight, 7.3 in. OAL, 2.3 lbs. New 2012.

Please contact the company directly for pricing and availability on this model.

RIFLES

AIR GUN TRAINER – 4.4mm cal. precision lead balls, SP, SS, SL, A side-lever, spring piston powered insert designed to instantly replace the bolt in the Swiss Kar. 31 service rifle, with its own barrel which fits into the firearm barrel. Uses the frame, stock, trigger mechanism, and sights of the host rifle; its cocking action mimics that of this straight pull bolt action rifle, developed in circa late 1950s; machined and blued. Ref.: Smith (1957, pp. 155-166, 168). 28 in. OAL (fits into K31 rifle w/OAL of 43 in.), 1 lbs., 250 FPS. Marked Hammerli Trainer, SN, and model of host firearm. A 6 shot, gravity fed, CO_2 version definitely was also patented and developed for the German Kar. 98 service rifle, but actual production may not have been commenced; SN 10 is the highest number reported to Blue Book as of March 2005. A number of experimental and prototype versions apparently were made for other rifles and even pistols such as the German P38. Evidently produced only for the Mauser 98 and the Swiss Kar. 31 firearms, extremely scarce, most specimens surviving WWII reportedly were lost in a fire. Ref: W.H.B Smith (1957).

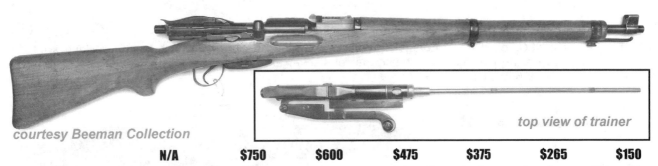

courtesy Beeman Collection

top view of trainer

N/A	$750	$600	$475	$375	$265	$150

Subtract 20% for trainer w/o equal or better condition K31 rifle. Note that the rifle with airgun trainer insert still is subject to USA firearm regulations because the firearm receiver is intact. Values of versions other than K31: TBD.

CADET REPEATER (MEHRLADER) – .174/BB cal., CO_2 cylinder, BA, spring-fed eighty-shot magazine, derived from a previous SS Cadet Model, no safety, 41.5 in. OAL, 6 lbs. Mfg. 1968-69.

courtesy Beeman Collection

N/A	$400	$325	$260	$200	$140	$80

Add 20% for older Cadet SS model.

FIREFOX 500 – .177 cal., BBC, SP, 575 FPS, blued, black synthetic stock and grip with checkering, fixed compensator, Picatinny rail, auto safety above the grip, adj. rear sight, 6.3 lbs. New 2012.

Please contact the company directly for pricing and availability on this model.

This model is also available with the Firefox 500 Kit which includes 3-7x20 scope.

HUNTER FORCE 600 COMBO – .177 cal., BBC, SP, 575 FPS, blued, beech stock with checkering on grip and forearm, auto safety, adj. rear sight, includes 4x32 scope, 43.3 in. OAL, 7.1 lbs. New 2012.

Please contact the company directly for pricing and availability on this model.

HUNTER FORCE 750 COMBO – .177 cal., BBC, SP, 820 FPS, blued, carved beech stock with checkering and vent. rubber cap, adj. trigger, auto safety, fiber optic front sight, adj. rear sight, includes 4x32 scope, 43.2 in. OAL, 7.4 lbs. New 2012.

Please contact the company directly for pricing and availability on this model.

GRADING	100%	95%	90%	80%	60%	40%	20%

HUNTER FORCE 900 COMBO – .177 cal., SP, UL, 820 FPS, blued, carved beech stock with checkering on grip and forearm, auto safety inside trigger guard, fiber optic front sight, adj. rear sight, includes 6x42 rifle scope, 45.3 in. OAL, 8.9 lbs. New 2012.

Please contact the company directly for pricing and availability on this model.

HUNTER FORCE 1000 COMBO – .177 cal., BBC, SP, 1000 FPS, blued, beech stock with checkering, rubber recoil pad, three stage trigger, auto safety, includes 6x42 scope, 46.1 in. OAL, 8.6 lbs. New 2012.

Please contact the company directly for pricing and availability on this model.

JUNIOR – similar to the Match, except uses disposable CO_2 cartridges, does not have a rubber buttplate or barrel sleeve, and is scaled down in size, no safety, aperture sight/base swing forward for charging, 41.5 in. OAL, 6 lbs. Mfg. 1962-1970.

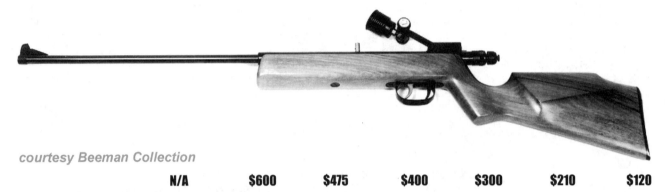

courtesy Beeman Collection

	N/A	$600	$475	$400	$300	$210	$120

MATCH – .177 cal., CO_2 filled from storage cylinder, SS, cocking the gun by pushing the cocking knob forward automatically pops up the loading block, heavy barrel sleeve, extremely angular stock lines and cheek piece, no safety, 41.5 in. OAL, 9.6 lbs. Mfg. 1962-67.

courtesy Beeman Collection

	N/A	$700	$550	$450	$350	$245	$140

MODEL 3 (OR PUMA 496) – .177, SL, SP, SS, rotary tap, intended for match shooting, but provided with fixed sights, barrel-like weight under barrel, no safety, w/o barrel wgt., 44.3 in. OAL, 7.5 lbs. Mfg. 1971-74.

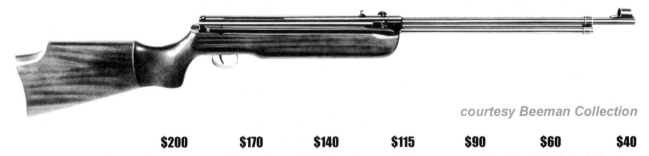

courtesy Beeman Collection

$200	$170	$140	$115	$90	$60	$40

Side lever may be very dangerous as it has sharp edges and no anti-beartrap mechanism (Models 1, 2, 4, and 10 are similar rifles in the Puma 490 series with different sights, barrel weights, etc.), all the 490 series were replaced by a 400 series circa 1974 which has an anti-bear trap mechanism and manual safety. The 490 series included Models 401, 402, 403 and the strange military-style 420 with a greenish plastic stock with pistol grip handle and dummy cartridge magazine.

MODEL 403 – .177 cal., SL, SP, 700 FPS, adj. sight target model, 9.25 lbs.

$325	$275	$230	$190	$145	$95	$65

Last MSR was $400.

GRADING	100%	95%	90%	80%	60%	40%	20%

MODEL 420 – .177 cal., SL, SP, 700 FPS, plastic stock, 7.5 lbs.

	$225	$190	$160	$130	$100	$65	$45

Last MSR was $300.

MODEL 450 – .177 cal., TL, SP, adj. target sight and cheek piece, target model. Imported 1994-2001.

	$1,225	$1,050	$850	$725	$550	$375	$245

Last MSR was $1,400.

Add $40 for walnut stock.

MODEL AR 20 – .177 cal., PCP, Field Target or Competition models, 560 (disc.) or 780 (new 2012) FPS, 19.7 in. Lothar Walther match barrel, fully adj. rear precision peep sight, standard foresight holder, hooded front sight, adj. trigger system, T-rail for 3-position competitions, four-piece all aluminum fully adj. stock in Deep Blue, Hot Red, or Silver finish, anatomical ambidextrous pistol grip, ambidextrous cocking piece with release lever, adj. cheek piece, adj. recoil pad, 39.7 in. OAL, 8.75 lbs. (Competition) or 12.41 (Field Target) lbs. New 2009.

courtesy Umarex USA

MSR $1,177	$1,000	$850	$700	$575	$450	$300	$200

MODEL AR 30 – .177 cal., PCP, fully adj. rear precision peep sight, hooded front sight, polygon rifling, adj. trigger system, aluminum adj. stock in silver finish, interchangeable pistol grips, 8.6 lbs. New 2005.

	$925	$775	$650	$525	$425	$275	$185

Add 30% for Model AR 30 Pro with Hämmerli Precision sight and MEC buttplate and weights (new 2006).

MODEL AR 50 – .177 cal., PCP, fully adj. rear precision peep sight, hooded front sight, 19.5 in. polygon rifling, adj. trigger system, laminated wood or four-piece all aluminum fully adj. (Model AR 50 Alum Pro) stock in blue or silver finish, interchangeable pistol grips (aluminum stock), adj. pistol grip and cheek piece, 10.5 lbs. New 2001.

	$1,075	$925	$750	$625	$475	$325	$215

Add 40% for AR 50 Alu.
Add 50% for AR 50 Alu Pro with IRC (new 2006).
Add 60% for AR 50 Alu Bench Rest with IRC (new 2006).
Subtract 10% for AR 50 Junior with beech stock and curved rubber butt plate.

MODEL CR20 S – .177 cal., CO_2, 19.7 in. barrel with muzzle brake, 800 FPS, blued, aluminum stock, adj. cheek piece, adj. MIL-SPEC 1913 Picatinny rail on forearm, adj. match trigger, adj. rubber recoil pad, ambi. adj. grip, includes a 3-9x44 sniper scope w/MilDot reticle (new 2012) and bipod (new 2012), 43-45 in. OAL, 10.6 lbs. New 2011.

courtesy Umarex USA

MSR $1,093	$925	$775	$650	$525	$425	$275	$185

GRADING	100%	95%	90%	80%	60%	40%	20%

MODEL 490 EXPRESS – .177 cal., BBC, SP, 18.75 in. barrel, 490 FPS, adj. rear and fixed hooded front fiber optic sights, automatic safety, semi-Monte Carlo dark hardwood stock with rubber recoil pad, right-handed cheek piece, 42.75 in. OAL, 6 lbs. Mfg. 2007-2012.

courtesy Umarex USA Collection

	$80	$70	$65	$50	$40	N/A	N/A

Last MSR was $94.

Add $24 for combo with 4x32 scope.

MODEL 850 AIR MAGNUM – .177 or .22 cal., CO$_2$, 88g cylinder, BA repeater with 8-shot rotary mag., 23.5 in. BBL, 760/655 FPS, checkered black polymer ambidextrous Monte Carlo stock, checkered grips and forearm, hooded fiber optic front sight, adj. rear fiber optic sights, automatic safety, two-stage adj. trigger, butt pad, ambi. cheek pieces, also available with 6x42 scope (.177 cal. only, disc. 2012), 41 in. OAL, 5.8 lbs. Mfg. 2007-current.

courtesy Umarex USA Collection

MSR $351	$295	$250	$205	$170	$135	$90	$60

Add $92 for combo with 6x42 scope (disc. 2012).

This model is also available with an 850 Air Magnum Target Kit which includes an additional Walther rifle 6x42 scope, a silencer, and an adapter tank with one-way valve for two 12g CO$_2$ capsules (mfg. 2012 only).

MODEL 850 AIR MAGNUM CLASSIC – .177 cal., CO$_2$, BA, 8-shot rotary mag., 820 FPS, ambidextrous wood stock, blued, vent. rubber recoil pad, includes adapter tank for two 12g CO$_2$ capsules which can be easily removed without pressure loss due to its one-way valve, fiber optic front sight, adj. rear sight, automatic safety, three-stage adj. trigger, 40.9 in. OAL, 7.5 lbs. New 2012.

Please contact the company directly for pricing and availability on this model.

MODEL 850 AIR MAGNUM HUNTER – .177 cal., CO$_2$, 88g cylinder, BA, 8-shot rotary mag., 820 FPS, elegant ambidextrous beech stock with fine checkering and vent. rubber recoil pad, also features the newly designed swiveling capsule holder which allows the 88g CO$_2$ capsule to be changed quickly and easily, checkered grip and forearm, fiber optic front sight, adj. rear sights, automatic safety, three-stage adj. trigger, 40.9 in. OAL, 6.8 lbs. New 2012.

Please contact the company directly for pricing and availability on this model.

MODEL 850 AIR MAGNUM XT – .177 cal., CO$_2$, 88g cylinder, BA repeater with 8-shot rotary mag., 23.5 in. BBL, 820 FPS, checkered black polymer ambidextrous Monte Carlo stock, checkered grip and forearm, fiber optic front sight, adj. rear sights, automatic safety, three-stage adj. trigger, includes a 6x42 Walther rifle scope, adj. bipod, and silencer, 45.7 in. OAL, 9.7 lbs. New 2012.

Please contact the company directly for pricing and availability on this model.

MODEL X2 – .177 and .22 cal., BBC, SP, 18.5 in. interchangable two-barrel system, 1000/900 FPS, adj. rear and fixed hooded front fiber optic sights, automatic safety, Monte Carlo wood stock w/butt pad, 44 in. OAL, 7.37 lbs. Mfg. 2007-2010.

courtesy Umarex USA Collection

	$215	$185	$150	$125	$95	$65	$45

Last MSR was $253.

Add 20% for X2 Combo.

GRADING	100%	95%	90%	80%	60%	40%	20%

NOVA – .177 cal., UL, SS, 18 in. BBL, 1000 FPS, adj. rear fiber optic sights, automatic safety, checkered vaporized beech wood competition stock, butt pad, 45.5 in. OAL, 7.8 lbs. Mfg. 2007-2009.

courtesy Umarex USA Collection

	$300	$260	$215	$175	$135	$90	$60

Last MSR was $342.

PNEUMA – .177 or .22 cal., PCP, SS, BA, 19 in. BBL, 1200/1050 FPS, adj. rear and front fiber optic sights, automatic safety, checkered black polymer ambidextrous thumbhole stock, adj. butt pad, 39 in. OAL, 7.3 lbs. Mfg. 2009-2010.

	$475	$400	$325	$275	$215	$140	$95

Last MSR was $556.

PNEUMA ELITE 10 – .177 or .22 cal., PCP, 1070/970 FPS, 19.4 in. rifled barrel, 10-shot, ambi. thumbhole stock, adj. fiber optic front and rear sights, automatic safety, two-stage adj. trigger, adj. recoil pad, checkered grip, integrated accessory rail, 39.4 in. OAL, 7.9 lbs. Mfg. 2011-2012.

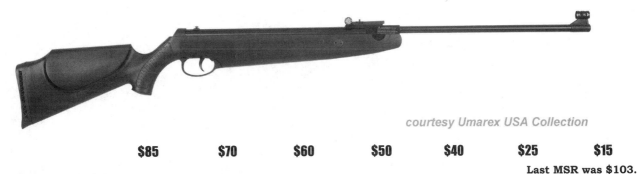

courtesy Umarex USA

	$350	$300	$270	$220	$170	N/A	N/A

Last MSR was $399.

Add $127 for an additional Pneuma Air Cylinder.

QUICK – .177 cal., BBC, SP, 18.25 in. barrel, 623 FPS, adj. rear sight, automatic safety, black synthetic stock with butt pad, 41 in. OAL, 5.5 lbs. Mfg. 2007.

courtesy Umarex USA Collection

	$85	$70	$60	$50	$40	$25	$15

Last MSR was $103.

Add 40% for combo with 4x32 compact scope.

RAZOR – .177 or .22 cal., BBC, SS, 19 in. BBL, 1000/820 FPS, adj. rear fiber optic sights, automatic safety, checkered vaporized beech wood Monte Carlo stock, butt pad, 45.5 in. OAL, 7.5 lbs. Mfg. 2007.

courtesy Umarex USA Collection

	$285	$240	$200	$165	$130	$85	$55

Last MSR was $310.

GRADING	100%	95%	90%	80%	60%	40%	20%

STORM – .177 or .22 cal., BBC, SS, 19.5 in. BBL, 1000/820 FPS, adj. rear fiber optic sights, automatic safety, checkered black polymer ambidextrous Monte Carlo stock, butt pad, 45.5 in. OAL, 6.5 lbs. Mfg. 2007.

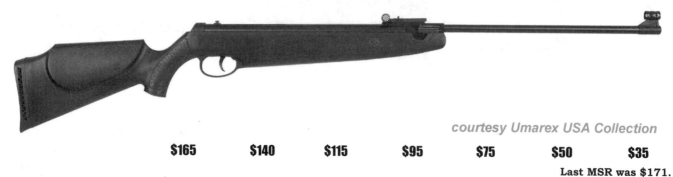

courtesy Umarex USA Collection

$165	$140	$115	$95	$75	$50	$35

Last MSR was $171.

Add 15% for combo with 4x32 scope.

STORM ELITE – .177 cal., BBC, SS, 19.5 in. nickel plated BBL, 1000/820 FPS, adj. rear fiber optic sights, automatic safety, checkered burled wood look polymer ambidextrous Monte Carlo stock, butt pad, 45.5 in. OAL, 6 lbs. Mfg. 2007.

courtesy Umarex USA Collection

$195	$165	$135	$115	$90	$60	$40

Last MSR was $223.

STUTZEN – Hämmerli marked Stutzen-style long forearm SP air rifle. Apparently a private brand production by BSA of their Stutzen model.

For more information on this air rifle, see BSA in the "B" section of this text.

TITAN – .177 cal., BBC, SP, 1000 FPS, adj. rear sight and 4x32 scope, automatic safety, Monte Carlo wood stock with butt pad. Mfg. 2007-2009.

courtesy Umarex USA Collection

$125	$105	$90	$75	$55	$35	$25

Last MSR was $145.

HAMMOND, KEN

Current custom airgun maker located in Ontario, Canada. Direct sales only.

Ken Hammond makes custom airguns with a military look, even using military spec M-16 parts to mimic the firearm. His airguns feature a spool valve of his own design which doubles as the intermediate air reservoir. The back of the valve is at atmospheric pressure and thus requires very little force to open. This allows for a simple trigger design with a low trigger release pressure.

GRADING	100%	95%	90%	80%	60%	40%	20%

RIFLES

HAMMOND WASP – 9mm cal., PCP or CO_2 up to 3000 PSI, 850 FPS, SS with interchangeable barrels of any caliber. Uses a "cartridge" which holds a standard bullet and acts as connector between valve and barrel, 44 in. OAL, 10 lbs.

courtesy Fred Liady

$2,500	$2,125	$1,750	$1,450	$1,125	$750	$500

HANSON

Three previous gun makers could be referred to as "Hanson of Huddersfield": George Hanson (1809) and two Charles Hansons (1833, 1839-45). A John Hanson (1860-1868) filed a British patent that seems to match the pistol below.

Very little is known about back action airguns. The name derives from the cocking lever being pushed forward to cock the gun. Two other specimens of this action are air rifles, one in America marked Conway. The Conway rifles and the Hanson air pistol have identical action areas, even sharing the same very strange trigger guard configuration. Rifle probably by Thomas Conway, Manchester, England 1804-1855. Ref. Wolff (1958), Hoff (1972).

PISTOLS

HANSON BACK ACTION AIR PISTOL – .335 cal., tap loading SS, 10.5 in. octagon barrel rifled with about 30 microgrooves, gold-plated, heavy brass air reservoir forms the pistol's grip, unscrews for charging with separate air pump, receiver and reservoir grip engraved with English scroll designs, receiver with case hardened finish, barrel browned with faux Damascus pattern, top of barrel engraved: "Hanson Huddersfield", 17.6 in. OAL.

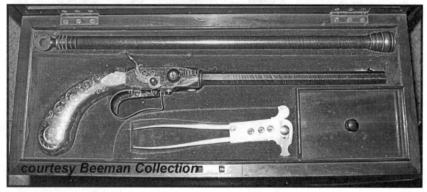

courtesy Beeman Collection

Scarcity precludes accurate pricing.

HARLIE

For information on Harlie airguns, see Philippine Airguns in the "P" section.

HARPER CLASSIC GUNS

Previous manufacturer located in Buckingham, England. Previously imported by Beeman Precision Airguns, Santa Rosa, CA. Introduced circa 1985.

Products included air canes and pistols. Some Harper pneumatics, based on the Saxby-Palmer rechargeable air cartridges. More recent airguns, including electronic trigger guns, will be considered in future editions of this guide. See Brocock introduction in the "B" section of this guide for information on the U.K. 2004 ban on production and sale of air cartridge airguns.

GRADING	100%	95%	90%	80%	60%	40%	20%

PISTOLS

CLASSIC MICRO PISTOL – .177 cal., air cartridge forms the body of the gun, SS, manual firing block, includes separate 9.6 in. air pump which uses a special chamber to fill the air cartridge without connecting to the cartridge, 2.3 in. OAL, 0.8 oz.

courtesy Beeman Collection

MSR N/A	$350	$300	$245	$205	$160	$105	$70

Subtract 40% for missing pump.

This model was created to be the world's smallest air pistol and, unlike true miniatures, it is a full size caliber. Brass collection ID tag in illustration is 7/8 inches in diameter. Under their anti-airgun-cartridge law, this gun is now illegal in the U.K. as a dangerous weapon!

CLASSIC PISTOL – .22 or .25 cal., Harper Air Cane rifle action, walnut handle, brass barrel, concealed fold-out trigger, 300 FPS, 6.5 in. OAL, 4 oz. Mfg. 1989 only.

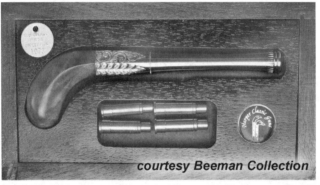

courtesy Beeman Collection

	$600	$500	$425	$350	$270	$180	$120

Last MSR for a cased pair was $700.

Add 50% if cased.
Add 10% for .25 cal.

Add 10% for deluxe.
Add 50%-75% for rare specimens of air pistols in the form of smoking pipes, ball-point pens, etc.

Only six were imported into the U.S. Under the anti-airgun-cartridge law, this gun is now illegal in the U.K. as a dangerous weapon!

CLASSIC PEPPERBOX – .22 cal., PCP, similar to Beeman/Harper Classic Pistol, 9.8 oz. Mfg. 1989 only.

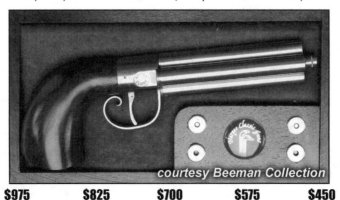

courtesy Beeman Collection

	$975	$825	$700	$575	$450	$295	$195

Last MSR was $575.

Only three were imported into the U.S. Under the anti-airgun-cartridge law, this gun is now illegal in the U.K. as a dangerous weapon!

GRADING	100%	95%	90%	80%	60%	40%	20%

AIR CANES

CLASSIC AIR CANE – .22 or .25 cal., pneumatic (reusable gas cartridge), 650 FPS, reproduction of 19th century Walking Cane Gun, 1 lb. Mfg. circa 1980s.

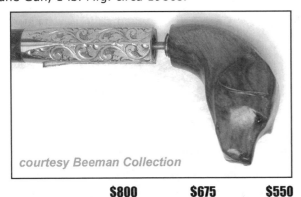

courtesy Beeman Collection

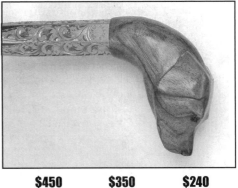

$800	$675	$550	$450	$350	$240	$160

Last MSR was $595.

Add $55 for decorative head piece.

Only ten of these models were imported into the U.S. Under the anti-airgun-cartridge law, this gun is now illegal in the U.K. as a dangerous weapon!

RIFLES

CLASSIC WOLF – .22 cal. 11 shot repeater, PCP, 3000 psi, removable skeleton stock, 16.5 in. barrel, electronic trigger in grip.

$1,050	$900	$725	$600	$475	$325	$210

HARRINGTON

Current trade name of T.J. Harrington & Sons Ltd. of Walton, Surrey, England. About one million spring-piston, push-barrel airguns (based on the 1877 H.M. Quackenbush patent) mfg. from 1937 to 1940 and 1947 to 2000. Sold to Marksman Products of Huntington Beach, CA circa 2000 with production continuing.

The GAT is a low cost, mostly cast alloy, pop-out type pistol. This gun enjoyed enormous popularity for decades. In fact, most airgunners outside of the USA probably cut their teeth on a GAT. It was first introduced in 1937, production ceased during the war but recommenced postwar and still carries on. The design of the GAT drew heavily upon an H. M. Quackenbush patent of 1877. All GATs have a smoothbore .177 barrel. Many are also fitted with a muzzle device that enables corks, as well as pellets and darts, to be fired.

The GAT design has undergone few variations; the most significant one would be the addition of a safety catch in 1982, to make the gun acceptable on the U.S. market.

In 1987 a smoothbore long gun version of the GAT was produced and marketed with little success.

The authors and publisher wish to thank Trevor Adams and John Atkins for their valuable assistance with the following information in this section of the *Blue Book of Airguns*.

PISTOLS

GAT – .177 darts, slugs, waisted pellets, or corks, SP, SS, push-barrel cocking, cast alloy and (later) plastic, smoothbore barrel, muzzle nut for shooting corks, safety added in 1982 for USA market, initially black or bright chrome finish, then black paint or polished (buffed bare metal) and finally black paint only.

courtesy Beeman Collection

$40	$30	$20	$10	N/A	N/A	N/A

Add 25% for bright nickel finish. Add 50% for original green factory box. Add 20% for other factory boxes.

RIFLES

GAT RIFLE – .177 cal. darts, balls, or pellets, SP, SS, push-barrel cocking similar to Gat Pistol, except long gun version. Mfg. 1987.

Current retail values in the $50 to $75 range depending on condition.

GRADING	100%	95%	90%	80%	60%	40%	20%

HATSAN ARMS CO.

Current manufacturer located in Izmir, Turkey beginning 1976. Hatsan air rifles are currently imported and distributed by Hatsan USA located in Bentonville, AR beginning 2011.

Hatsan manufactures quality air pistols and air rifles. Please contact the company directly for more information regarding U.S. availability and pricing (see Trademark Index).

PISTOLS

MODEL AT-P1 – .177, .22, or .25 cal., PCP, side lever action, 810/750/680 FPS, detachable 10-shot rotary mag., 10.4 in. barrel, ergonomic black synthetic grip, blued finish, black anodized receiver, built-in pressure gauge, manual and automatic safety, scope mount rail, Truglo adj. fiber optic sights, gold plated metal Quattro trigger, includes one additional magazine, detachable aluminum air cylinder tube, a quick-fill nozzle and air cylinder discharging cap, and plastic case, 16.3 in. OAL, 4.5 lbs. New 2012.

MSR $550	$475	$400	$375	$300	$230	N/A	N/A

This model also features the Anti-knock system and Anti-double pellet feed mechanism.

MODEL AT-P2 – .177, .22, or .25 cal., PCP, side lever action, 870/780/710 FPS, detachable 10 or 9 (.25 cal.) shot rotary mag., 10.4 in. barrel, ergonomic black synthetic grip, blued finish, black anodized receiver, 50cc cylinder, built-in manometer, manual and automatic safety, scope mount rail, Truglo adj. fiber optic sights, gold plated metal Quattro trigger, includes one additional magazine, detachable aluminum air cylinder tube, a quick-fill nozzle and air cylinder discharging cap, detachable telescopic rifle stock, and plastic case, 29.1 in. OAL, 6.4 lbs. New 2013.

MSR $600	$500	$450	$400	$325	$250	N/A	N/A

This model also features the Anti-knock system and Anti-double pellet feed mechanism.

MODEL 25 – .177 or .22 cal., BBC, SS, 500/400 FPS, 6.3 in. rifled steel barrel (outside covered with synthetic), ergonomic rugged and compact Black or Luxurious walnut woodgrain camo synthetic pistol grip stock, manual safety, anti-bear trap safety, Truglo fiber optic micro adj. rear and hooded front sights, 14.5 in. OAL, 2.7 lbs.

courtesy Hatsan Arms Co.

$75	$70	$60	$50	$40	N/A	N/A

Last MSR was $90.

This model also includes a pellet catcher, paper targets, and a box of pellets.

MODEL 25 SUPERCHARGER – .177 or .22 cal., BBC, SS, 700/600 FPS, 11.2 in. rifled steel barrel with threaded muzzle and fitted muzzle cap, ergonomic rugged synthetic grip with checkering, Quattro trigger, gold plated metal trigger blade, manual and automatic safety, anti-bear trap safety, Truglo fiber optic micro adj. rear and front sights, XRS recoil reduction system, also includes aluminum cocking aid, 20 in. OAL, 3.9 lbs. New 2012.

courtesy Hatsan Arms Co.

MSR $160	$135	$120	$110	$90	$65	N/A	N/A

GRADING	100%	95%	90%	80%	60%	40%	20%

MODEL 250XT TAC-BOSS – .177/BB cal., CO_2, 12 gram cylinder, semi-auto repeater, 17 shot mag., 6.75 in. smooth bore barrel, 430 FPS, ambidextrous ergonomic design, black metal finish frame with plastic grips, fixed fiber optic front and notch rear sights, 9.75 in. OAL, 1.75 lbs. Mfg. 2013-current.

MSR $100	$85	$75	$70	$55	$40	N/A	N/A

RIFLES

AT44 – .177, .22, or .25 cal., PCP, side lever action, SS, 1070/970/870 FPS, 19.3 in. rifled and choked barrel, blued finish, black anodized receiver, ambidextrous black synthetic, Mossy Oak New Break Up camo (AT44 Camo), or luxurious walnut woodgrain camouflage (AT44 MW) thumbhole stock, Monte Carlo cheek piece, adj. rubber butt pad, built-in pressure gauge, manual and automatic safety, Truglo adj. fiber optic sights, Quattro trigger, gold plated metal trigger and metal trigger guard, also includes a detachable air cylinder tube, and quick-fill nozzle and air cylinder discharging cap, 39 in. OAL, 6.8 lbs.

courtesy Hatsan Arms Co.

$300	$255	$210	$175	$135	$90	$60

This model is also available in a long version (AT44 Long) with 23 in. barrel, and 7.7 lbs. The AT44X model is equipped with a fixed sound moderator and no sights. All variations of the AT44 utilize the Anti-knock system and Anti-double pellet feed mechanism.

AT44 S – .177, .22, or .25 cal., PCP, side lever action, SS, 1070/970/870 FPS, 19.3 in. rifled and choked barrel, blued finish, black anodized receiver, ergonomic ambidextrous black synthetic, Mossy Oak New Break Up camo (AT44S Camo), or luxurious walnut woodgrain camouflage (AT44S MW) stock, Monte Carlo cheek piece, adj. rubber butt pad, built-in pressure gauge, manual and automatic safety, Truglo adj. fiber optic sights, Quattro trigger, gold plated trigger, also includes a detachable air cylinder tube, and quick-fill nozzle and air cylinder discharging cap, 39 in. OAL, 6.6 lbs.

courtesy Hatsan Arms Co.

$300	$255	$210	$175	$135	$90	$60

This model is also available in a long version (AT44S Long) with 23 in. barrel, and 7.5 lbs. The AT44SX model is equipped with a fixed sound moderator and no sights. All variations of the AT44S utilize the Anti-knock system and Anti-double pellet feed mechanism.

AT44-10 – .177, .22, or .25 cal., PCP, side lever action, 1070/970/870 FPS, detachable 10-shot rotary mag., 19.3 in. rifled and choked barrel, blued finish, black anodized receiver, ambidextrous black synthetic, Mossy Oak New Break Up camo (AT44-10 Camo), or luxurious walnut woodgrain camouflage (AT44-10 MW) thumbhole stock, Monte Carlo cheek piece, adj. rubber butt pad, built-in pressure gauge, manual and automatic safety, Truglo adj. fiber optic sights, Quattro trigger, gold plated metal trigger and metal trigger guard, also includes one additional magazine, detachable air cylinder tube, and quick-fill nozzle and air cylinder discharging cap, 39.4 in. OAL, 7.3 lbs.

courtesy Hatsan Arms Co.

$400	$350	$280	$230	$180	$120	$80

This model is also available in a long version (AT44-10 Long) with 23 in. barrel, and 8.1 lbs. The AT44X-10 model is equipped with a fixed sound moderator and no sights. All variations of the AT44-10 utilize the Anti-knock system and Anti-double pellet feed mechanism.

GRADING	100%	95%	90%	80%	60%	40%	20%

AT44-10 TACT – .177, .22, or .25 cal., PCP, side lever action, detachable 10 (.177 and .22 cal) or 9 (.25 cal.) shot rotary mag., 19.4 in. rifled barrel, 1070/970/870 FPS, blued finish, black anodized receiver, detachable and telescopic ambidextrous black synthetic stock with adj. comb, textured PG and forearm, rubber butt pad, manual and automatic safety, adj. Truglo fiber optic sights, two stage adjustable Quattro gold plated metal trigger and metal trigger guard, also includes one additional magazine, 180cc detachable air cylinder, built-in manometer, and quick-fill nozzle and air cylinder discharging cap, 34.8-38.8 in. OAL, 8.6 lbs. Mfg. 2013-current.

MSR $625	$525	$475	$425	$350	$265	N/A	N/A

AT44S-10 – .177, .22, or .25 cal., PCP, side lever action, 1070/970/870 FPS, detachable 10-shot rotary mag., 19.3 in. rifled and choked barrel, blued finish, black anodized receiver, ergonomic ambidextrous black synthetic, Mossy Oak New Break Up camo (AT44S-10 Camo), or luxurious walnut woodgrain camouflage (AT44S-10 MW) stock, Monte Carlo cheek piece, adj. rubber butt pad, built-in pressure gauge, manual and automatic safety, Truglo adj. fiber optic sights, Quattro trigger, gold plated metal trigger and metal trigger guard, also includes an extra magazine, detachable air cylinder tube, and quick-fill nozzle and air cylinder discharging cap, 39 in. OAL, 7 lbs.

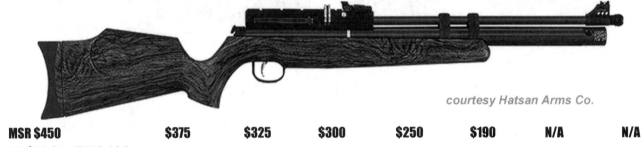

courtesy Hatsan Arms Co.

MSR $450	$375	$325	$300	$250	$190	N/A	N/A

Add $70 for AT44S-10 Long.

This model is available in a long version (AT44S-10 Long) with 22.8 in. barrel, and 7.9 lbs. The AT44SX-10 model is equipped with a fixed sound moderator and no sights. All variations of the AT44S-10 utilize the Anti-knock system and Anti-double pellet feed mechanism.

AT44W-10 – .177, .22, or .25 cal., PCP, side lever action, 1070/970/870 FPS, detachable 10-shot rotary mag., 19.4 in. rifled and choked barrel, blued finish, black anodized receiver, Turkish walnut ambidextrous stock, Monte Carlo cheek piece, adj. butt pad, built-in pressure gauge, manual and automatic safety, Truglo adj. fiber optic sights, Quattro trigger, gold plated metal trigger and metal trigger guard, also includes an extra magazine, detachable air cylinder tube, and quick-fill nozzle and air cylinder discharging cap, 39 in. OAL, 7.9 lbs.

courtesy Hatsan Arms Co.

MSR $496	$425	$375	$325	$275	$210	N/A	N/A

This model is also available in a long version (AT44W-10 Long) with 23 in. barrel, and 8.8 lbs. The AT44WX-10 model is equipped with a fixed sound moderator and no sights. All variations of the AT44W-10 utilize the Anti-knock system and Anti-double pellet feed mechanism.

AT44 PA – .177, .22, or .25 cal., PCP, pump action, 1070/970/870 FPS, detachable 10-shot rotary mag., 19.3 in. rifled and choked barrel, blued finish, black anodized receiver, ambidextrous black synthetic thumbhole stock, Monte Carlo cheek piece, adj. rubber butt pad, built-in pressure gauge, manual safety, Truglo adj. fiber optic sights, Quattro trigger, gold plated metal trigger and metal trigger guard, also includes an extra magazine, detachable air cylinder tube, and quick-fill nozzle and air cylinder discharging cap, 39 in. OAL, 8.4 lbs.

courtesy Hatsan Arms Co.

MSR $450	$375	$325	$300	$250	$190	N/A	N/A

Add $70 for AT44PA Long.

GRADING	100%	95%	90%	80%	60%	40%	20%

This model is also available in a long version (AT44PA Long) with 23 in. barrel, and 9.7 lbs. The AT44PAX model is equipped with a fixed sound moderator and no sights. All variations of the AT44 PA utilize the Anti-knock system and Anti-double pellet feed mechanism.

AT44 W – .177, .22, or .25 cal., PCP, side lever action, SS, 1070/970/870 FPS, 19.4 in. rifled and choked barrel, blued finish, black anodized receiver, Turkish walnut ambidextrous stock, Monte Carlo cheek piece, adj. rubber butt pad, built-in pressure gauge, manual and automatic safety, Truglo adj. fiber optic sights, Quattro trigger, gold plated trigger, also includes a detachable air cylinder tube, and quick-fill nozzle and air cylinder discharging cap, 39 in. OAL, 7.5 lbs.

	$300	$255	$210	$175	$135	$90	$60

This model is also available in a long version (AT44W Long) with 23 in. barrel, and 8.3 lbs. The AT44WX model is equipped with a fixed sound moderator and no sights. All variations of the AT44 W utilize the Anti-knock system and Anti-double pellet feed mechanism.

BT65 RB – .177, .22, or .25 cal., PCP, rear bolt action, 1250/1180/1090 FPS, detachable 10-shot rotary mag., 23 in. rifled and choked barrel, blued finish, black anodized receiver, ambidextrous and ergonomic black synthetic or Mossy Oak New Break Up camo (BT65 RB-camo) stock, Monte Carlo cheek piece, integrated Picatinny rail beneath the forearm, soft rubber inlays on grip and forearm, adj. rubber butt pad, adj. comb, detachable aluminum air cylinder tube, built-in pressure gauge, manual and automatic safety, Quattro trigger, gold plated trigger, fitted sling swivels, Truglo adj. front and rear fiber optic sights, includes bipod and sling, one additional magazine, and a quick-fill nozzle and air cylinder discharging cap, 42.5 in. OAL, 9 lbs. New 2011.

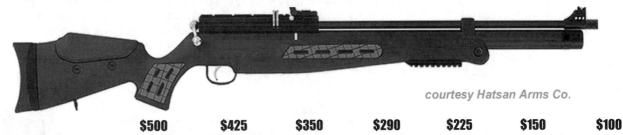

courtesy Hatsan Arms Co.

	$500	$425	$350	$290	$225	$150	$100

This model also features the Anti-knock system and Anti-double pellet feed mechanism.

BT65 RB-W – .177, .22, or .25 cal., PCP, rear bolt action, 1250/1180/1090 FPS, detachable 10-shot rotary mag., 23 in. rifled and choked barrel, blued finish, black anodized receiver, Turkish walnut or luxurious walnut woodgrain (BT65 RB-MW) stock, Monte Carlo cheek piece, adj. butt pad, adj. comb, Quattro trigger, gold plated metal trigger and metal trigger guard, fitted sling swivels, detachable aluminum air cylinder tube, built-in pressure gauge, Truglo adj. front and rear fiber optic sights, manual and automatic safety, includes one additional magazine, a quick-fill nozzle and air cylinder discharging cap, and a sling, 42.5 in. OAL, 9.4 lbs. New 2011.

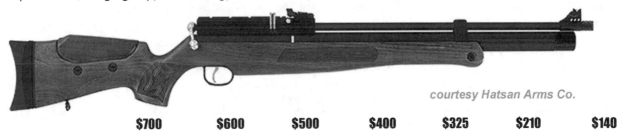

courtesy Hatsan Arms Co.

	$700	$600	$500	$400	$325	$210	$140

This model also features the Anti-knock system and Anti-double pellet feed mechanism.

BT65 RB ELITE – .177, .22, or .25 cal., PCP, rear bolt action, 1250/1180/1090 FPS, detachable 10-shot rotary mag., 23 in. rifled and choked barrel, blued finish, black anodized receiver, ambidextrous and ergonomic black synthetic thumbhole stock with magazine carrying slot for two spare mags., Monte Carlo cheek piece, three Picatinny rails beneath and on the sides of forearm, soft rubber inlays on forearm, checkering on grip, adj. rubber butt pad, adj. comb, detachable aluminum air cylinder tube, built-in pressure gauge, manual safety, Quattro trigger, gold plated metal trigger and metal trigger guard, fitted sling swivels, Truglo adj. front and rear fiber optic sights, includes hard plastic case, bipod, sling, flashlight, Optima 3-12x44AOE scope, three magazines, and a quick-fill nozzle and air cylinder discharging cap, 42.5 in. OAL, 9.3 lbs. New 2012.

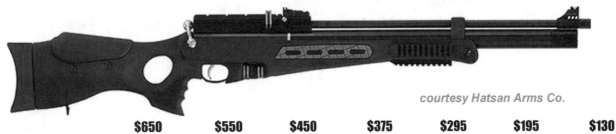

courtesy Hatsan Arms Co.

	$650	$550	$450	$375	$295	$195	$130

This model also features the Anti-knock system and Anti-double pellet feed mechanism.

GRADING	100%	95%	90%	80%	60%	40%	20%

BT65 SB – .177, .22, or .25 cal., PCP, side bolt action, 1250/1180/1090 FPS, detachable 10-shot rotary mag., 23 in. rifled and choked barrel, blued finish, black anodized receiver, ambidextrous and ergonomic black synthetic or Mossy Oak Break Up camo (BT65 SB Camo) stock, integrated Picatinny rail beneath the forearm, soft rubber inlays on grip and forearm, adj. rubber butt pad, adj. comb, detachable aluminum air cylinder tube, built-in pressure gauge, manual safety, Quattro trigger, gold plated metal trigger and metal trigger guard, fitted sling swivels, Truglo adj. front and rear fiber optic sights, includes bipod and sling, one additional magazine, and a quick-fill nozzle and air cylinder discharging cap, 42.5 in. OAL, 9 lbs. New 2011.

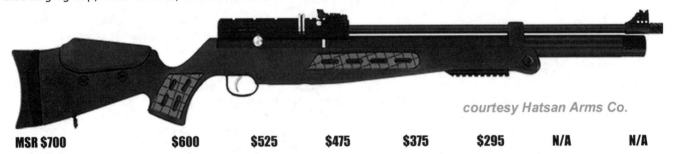

courtesy Hatsan Arms Co.

MSR $700	$600	$525	$475	$375	$295	N/A	N/A

This model also features the Anti-knock system and Anti-double pellet feed mechanism.

BT65 SB-W – .177, .22, or .25 cal., PCP, side bolt action, 1250/1180/1090 FPS, detachable 10-shot rotary mag., 23 in. rifled and choked barrel, blued finish, black anodized receiver, Turkish walnut or luxurious walnut woodgrain (BT65 SB-MW) stock, Monte Carlo cheek piece, adj. butt pad, adj. comb, Quattro trigger, gold plated metal trigger and metal trigger guard, fitted sling swivels, detachable aluminum (disc. 2011) or steel (new 2012) air cylinder tube, built-in pressure gauge, Truglo adj. front and rear fiber optic sights, manual safety, fitted sling swivels, includes one additional magazine, a quick-fill nozzle and air cylinder discharging cap, and comes in its box with a sling, 42.5 in. OAL, 9.4 lbs. New 2011.

courtesy Hatsan Arms Co.

MSR $850	$725	$625	$575	$475	$350	N/A	N/A

This model also features the Anti-knock system and Anti-double pellet feed mechanism.

BT65 SB ELITE – .177, .22, or .25 cal., PCP, side bolt action, 1250/1180/1090 FPS, detachable 10-shot rotary mag., 23 in. rifled and choked barrel, blued finish, black anodized receiver, ambidextrous and ergonomic black synthetic thumbhole stock with a spare magazine carrying slot for two spare mags., Monte Carlo cheek piece, three Picatinny rails beneath and on sides of forearm, soft rubber inlays on forearm, checkering on grip, adj. rubber butt pad, adj. comb, detachable aluminum air cylinder tube, built-in pressure gauge, manual safety, gold plated Quattro trigger, fitted sling swivels, Truglo adj. front and rear fiber optic sights, includes hard case, bipod, sling, flashlight, Optima 3-12x44AE scope, three magazines, and a quick-fill nozzle and air cylinder discharging cap, 42.5 in. OAL, 9.3 lbs. New 2012.

courtesy Hatsan Arms Co.

MSR $750	$625	$550	$500	$400	$325	N/A	N/A

This model also features the Anti-knock system and Anti-double pellet feed mechanism.

GRADING	100%	95%	90%	80%	60%	40%	20%

DOMINATOR 200S – .177, .22, or .25 cal., UL, break open loading port, 1000/800/650 FPS, 17.7 in. rifled steel fixed barrel with large muzzle brake, ergonomic and ambidextrous black synthetic stock, adj. comb, adj. buttpad, soft rubber inlays on grip and forearm, scope mount rail and shock absorber scope stop, Truglo fiber optic sights, manual and automatic safety, anti-bear trap cocking safety, Quattro trigger and SAS (Shock Absorber System), gold plated trigger blade, includes three stock spacers to extend stock length, a bipod, and a sling, 45.5 in. OAL, 9.9 lbs.

courtesy Hatsan Arms Co.

MSR $429	$375	$325	$290	$235	$180	N/A	N/A

DOMINATOR 200S CARBINE – .177, .22, or .25 cal., UL, break open loading port, 1000/800/650 FPS, 15.7 in. rifled steel fixed barrel with threaded muzzle for sound moderator and fitted muzzle cap, ergonomic and ambidextrous black synthetic stock, adj. comb, adj. buttpad, soft rubber inlays on grip and forearm, scope mount rail and shock absorber scope stop, no sights, manual and automatic safety, anti-bear trap cocking safety, Quattro trigger and SAS (Shock Absorber System), gold plated trigger blade, includes three stock spacers to extend stock length, a bipod, and a sling, 43.2 in. OAL, 9.7 lbs.

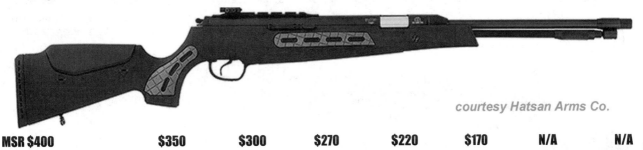

courtesy Hatsan Arms Co.

MSR $400	$350	$300	$270	$220	$170	N/A	N/A

DOMINATOR 200W – .177, .22, or .25 cal., UL, break open loading port, 1000/800/650 FPS, 17.7 in. rifled steel fixed barrel with large muzzle brake, Turkish walnut ambidextrous stock, adj. comb, adj. buttpad, checkering on grip and forearm, scope mount rail and shock absorber scope stop, Truglo fiber optic sights, manual and automatic safety, anti-bear trap cocking safety, Quattro trigger and SAS (Shock Absorber System), includes three stock spacers to extend stock length, a bipod, and a sling, 45.5 in. OAL, 9.9 lbs.

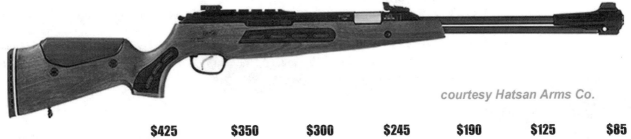

courtesy Hatsan Arms Co.

	$425	$350	$300	$245	$190	$125	$85

DOMINATOR 200W CARBINE – .177, .22, or .25 cal., UL, break open loading port, 1000/800/650 FPS, 15.7 in. rifled steel fixed barrel with threaded muzzle for sound moderator and fitted muzzle cap, Turkish walnut ambidextrous stock, adj. comb, adj. buttpad, checkering on grip and forearm, scope mount rail and shock absorber scope stop, no sights, manual and automatic safety, anti-bear trap cocking safety, Quattro trigger and SAS (Shock Absorber System), gold plated trigger blade, includes three stock spacers to extend stock length, a bipod, and a sling, 43.2 in. OAL, 9.7 lbs.

courtesy Hatsan Arms Co.

	$400	$350	$280	$230	$180	$120	$80

GRADING	100%	95%	90%	80%	60%	40%	20%

GALATIAN – .177, .22, or .25 cal., PCP, side lever action, detachable 16 (.177 CAL.), 14 (.22 cal) or 13 (.25 cal.) shot rotary mag., 23 in. rifled barrel, 1190/1100/1000 FPS, blued finish, ambidextrous black synthetic stock with adj. comb and rubber butt pad, manual and automatic safety, adj. Truglo fiber optic sights, two stage adjustable Quattro gold plated metal trigger and metal trigger guard, also includes one additional magazine, 255cc detachable air cylinder, built-in manometer, and quick-fill nozzle and air cylinder discharging cap, 42.3 in. OAL, 9.10 lbs. Mfg. 2013-current.

MSR $821	$700	$625	$550	$450	$350	N/A	N/A

Add $130 for walnut stock and forearm.

MODEL 33 – .177 cal., BBC, SS, 650 FPS, 17.7 in. rifled steel barrel, ergonomic black synthetic, Mossy Oak Break-Up camo, Mossy Oak Break-Up Pink Camo, or Luxurious walnut woodgrain camo stock with cheek piece, rubber butt pad, adj. trigger pull, checkering on grip, manual safety and automatic cocking safety, anti-bear trap safety, micro adj. rear sight and hooded front sight, 41 in. OAL, 6.4 lbs.

courtesy Hatsan Arms Co.

This model is not currently imported, please contact Hatsan (see Trademark Index) directly for pricing and availability.

MODEL 35S – .177 cal., BBC, SS, 650 FPS, 17.7 in. rifled steel barrel, English style wood stock, plastic butt pad, manual safety and automatic cocking safety, anti-bear trap safety, adj. trigger pull, micro adj. rear sight and hooded front sight, 41 in. OAL, 6.6 lbs.

courtesy Hatsan Arms Co.

This model is not currently imported, please contact Hatsan (see Trademark Index) directly for pricing and availability.

MODEL 55S – .177 or .25 cal., BBC, SS, 1000/650 FPS, 17.7 in. rifled steel barrel, ergonomic wooded stock with raised comb, checkering on grip and forearm, rubber vent. buttpad, Quattro trigger and SAS, manual safety and automatic cocking safety, anti-bear trap safety, metal trigger blade, micro adj. rear sight and hooded front sight, 45 in. OAL, 7.5 lbs.

courtesy Hatsan Arms Co.

This model is not currently imported, please contact Hatsan (see Trademark Index) directly for pricing and availability.

MODEL 60S – .22 cal., BBC, SS, 800 FPS, 17.7 in. rifled steel barrel, ergonomic wooded stock with raised comb, checkering on grip and forearm, rubber vent. buttpad, Quattro trigger and SAS, manual safety and automatic cocking safety, anti-bear trap safety, metal trigger blade, micro adj. rear sight and hooded front sight, 45 in. OAL, 7.5 lbs.

courtesy Hatsan Arms Co.

This model is not currently imported, please contact Hatsan (see Trademark Index) directly for pricing and availability.

GRADING	100%	95%	90%	80%	60%	40%	20%

MODEL 70 – .177, .22, or .25 cal., BBC, SS, 1000/800/650 FPS, 17.7 in. rifled steel barrel, ergonomic black, Mossy Oak Break Up camo, or Luxurious walnut woodgrain camo stock with Monte Carlo cheek piece, checkering on grip, rubber buttpad, Quattro trigger and SAS, manual safety and automatic cocking safety, anti-bear trap safety, metal trigger blade, micro adj. rear sight and hooded front sight, 44.5 in. OAL, 7 lbs.

courtesy Hatsan Arms Co.

This model is not currently imported, please contact Hatsan (see Trademark Index) directly for pricing and availability.

MODEL 80 – .177, .22, or .25 cal., BBC, SS, 1000/800/650 FPS, 17.7 in. rifled steel barrel, ergonomic black, Mossy Oak Break Up camo, or Luxurious walnut woodgrain camo stock with Monte Carlo cheek piece, canals on grip and forearm, rubber buttpad, Quattro trigger and SAS, manual safety and automatic cocking safety, anti-bear trap safety, metal trigger blade, micro adj. rear sight and hooded front sight, 44 in. OAL, 7.2 lbs.

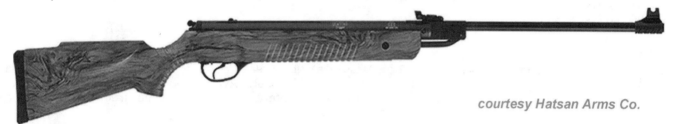

courtesy Hatsan Arms Co.

This model is not currently imported, please contact Hatsan (see Trademark Index) directly for pricing and availability.

MODEL 85 – .177, .22, or .25 cal., BBC, SS, 1000/800/650 FPS, 17.7 in. rifled steel barrel, ergonomic Dark Grey, Mossy Oak New Break-Up Camo, or Luxurious walnut woodgrain camo synthetic stock with Monte Carlo cheek piece and raised forearm grip, canals on grip and forearm, Triopad butt system, grooved cylinder, Quattro trigger and SAS, manual safety and automatic cocking safety, anti-bear trap safety, metal trigger blade, Truglo fiber optic micro adj. rear sight and Truglo open front sight, includes three Triopad stock spacers, 44 in. OAL, 7.2 lbs.

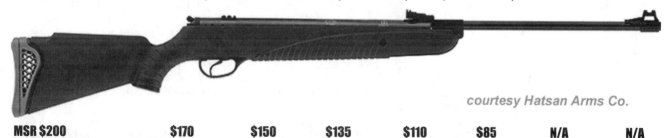

courtesy Hatsan Arms Co.

MSR $200	$170	$150	$135	$110	$85	N/A	N/A

MODEL 85X – .177, .22, or .25 cal., BBC, SS, 1000/800/650 FPS, 17.7 in. rifled steel barrel, aluminum sound moderator on the muzzle, ergonomic Dark Grey, Mossy Oak New Break-Up Camo, or Luxurious walnut woodgrain camo synthetic stock with Monte Carlo cheek piece and raised forearm grip, canals on grip and forearm, Triopad butt system, grooved cylinder, Quattro trigger and SAS, manual safety and automatic cocking safety, anti-bear trap safety, metal trigger blade, includes three Triopad stock spacers, and an Optima 3-9x32 scope, 44 in. OAL, 7.2 lbs.

courtesy Hatsan Arms Co.

MSR $200	$170	$150	$135	$110	$85	N/A	N/A

GRADING	100%	95%	90%	80%	60%	40%	20%

MODEL 85 SNIPER – .177, .22, or .25 cal., BBC, SS, 1000/800/650 FPS, 18.1 in. rifled steel barrel with integrated sound moderator inside the muzzle brake, ergonomic black, Mossy Oak Break Up camo, or Luxurious walnut woodgrain synthetic stock with Monte Carlo cheek piece and raised forearm grip, canals on grip and forearm, Triopad butt system, Quattro trigger, SAS, scope mount rail and mounted scope stop, includes 3-9x32 Optima scope, Truglo fiber optic micro adj. rear and open front sights, sling swivels, manual and automatic safety, anti-bear trap safety, 44.7 in. OAL, 7.2 lbs. New 2012.

courtesy Hatsan Arms Co.

MSR $220	$185	$165	$150	$120	$90	N/A	N/A

Add $30 for Mossy Oak Break Up camo.
Add $60 for gas piston.

This model also includes a bipod, sling, and three Triopad stock spacers.

MODEL 88 – .177, .22, or .25 cal., BBC, SS, barrel lock system, 1000/800/650 FPS, 17.7 in. rifled steel barrel with threaded muzzle, ergonomic and slim design Grey, Mossy Oak New Break-Up Camo, or Luxurious walnut woodgrain camo synthetic stock with checkering on grip and forearm, rubber buttpad, grooved cylinder, Quattro trigger and SAS, manual safety and automatic cocking safety, anti-bear trap safety, metal trigger blade, Truglo fiber optic micro adj. rear sight and Truglo hooded front sight, 44 in. OAL, 6.8 lbs. New 2010.

courtesy Hatsan Arms Co.

This model is not currently imported, please contact Hatsan (see Trademark Index) directly for pricing and availability.

MODEL 88TH – .177, .22, or .25 cal., BBC, SS, barrel lock system, 1000/800/650 FPS, 17.7 in. rifled steel barrel with large muzzle brake, ergonomic Grey, Mossy Oak New Break-Up Camo, or Luxurious walnut woodgrain camo synthetic thumbhole stock with checkering on grip and forearm, rubber buttpad, grooved cylinder, Quattro trigger and SAS, manual safety and automatic cocking safety, anti-bear trap safety, metal trigger blade, Truglo fiber optic micro adj. rear sight and Truglo open front sight, 44 in. OAL, 7.7 lbs. New 2010.

courtesy Hatsan Arms Co.

This model is not currently imported, please contact Hatsan (see Trademark Index) directly for pricing and availability.

MODEL 90 – .177, .22, or .25 cal., BBC, SS, 1000/800/650 FPS, 17.7 in. rifled steel barrel, ergonomic black, Mossy Oak Break Up camo, or Luxurious walnut woodgrain camo stock with Monte Carlo cheek piece, checkering on grip, rubber buttpad, Quattro trigger and SAS, manual safety and automatic cocking safety, anti-bear trap safety, metal trigger blade, micro adj. rear sight and hooded front sight, 44.6 in. OAL, 7 lbs.

courtesy Hatsan Arms Co.

This model is not currently imported, please contact Hatsan (see Trademark Index) directly for pricing and availability.

GRADING	100%	95%	90%	80%	60%	40%	20%

MODEL 95 – .177, .22, or .25 cal., BBC, SS, 1000/800/650 FPS, 17.7 in. rifled steel barrel with large muzzle brake, ergonomic, ambidextrous hunting style Turkish walnut stock, checkering on grip and forearm, rubber buttpad, Quattro trigger and SAS, manual safety and automatic cocking safety, anti-bear trap safety, scope mount rail, gold plated trigger blade, Truglo fiber optic micro adj. rear sight and Truglo open front sight, 44.3 in. OAL, 8.4 lbs.

courtesy Hatsan Arms Co.

MSR $190	$160	$145	$130	$105	$80	N/A	N/A

This model is also available as a Combo which includes a 3-9x32 scope and mount.

MODEL 99 – .177, .22, or .25 cal., BBC, SS, barrel lock system, 1000/800/650 FPS, 17.7 in. rifled steel barrel with large muzzle brake, ergonomic, ambidextrous hunting style Turkish walnut stock with Monte Carlo cheek piece, checkering on grip and forearm, rubber vent. buttpad, Quattro trigger and SAS, manual safety and automatic cocking safety, anti-bear trap safety, scope mount rail, gold plated trigger blade, Truglo fiber optic micro adj. rear sight and Truglo open front sight, 45 in. OAL, 8.4 lbs. New 2010.

courtesy Hatsan Arms Co.

This model is not currently imported, please contact Hatsan (see Trademark Index) directly for pricing and availability.

MODEL 125 – .177, .22, or .25 cal., BBC, SS, 1250/1000/750 FPS, 19.6 in. rifled steel fixed barrel with large muzzle brake, ergonomic black, OD Green, Mossy Oak New Break Up camo, or Luxurious walnut woodgrain camo synthetic stock with Monte Carlo cheek piece, checkering on grip and forearm, Triopad butt system, Quattro trigger and SAS, manual safety and automatic cocking safety, anti-bear trap safety, scope mount rail and shock absorber scope stop, metal trigger blade, Truglo fiber optic micro adj. rear sight and Truglo open front sight, includes three Triopad stock spacers, 48.8 in. OAL, 8.4 lbs.

courtesy Hatsan Arms Co.

MSR $250	$215	$190	$170	$140	$105	N/A	N/A

Add $45 for Mossy Oak New Break Up camo. Add $100 for gas piston.

MODEL 125 SNIPER – .177, .22, or .25 cal., BBC, SS, 1250/1000/750 FPS, 19.6 in. rifled steel barrel with integrated sound moderator inside the muzzle brake, ambidextrous ergonomic black, Mossy Oak Break Up camo, or Luxurious walnut woodgrain synthetic stock with Monte Carlo cheek piece and raised forearm grip, soft rubber inlays on grip and forearm, fully adj. elevated comb, Triopad butt system, Quattro trigger, SAS, scope mount rail and mounted scope stop, includes 3-9x32 Optima scope, Truglo fiber optic micro adj. rear and open front sights, sling swivels, manual and automatic safety, anti-bear trap safety, 48.8 in. OAL, 9 lbs. New 2012.

MSR $320	$270	$240	$220	$175	$135	N/A	N/A

Add $50 for Mossy Oak Break-Up camo finish. Add $110 for gas piston.

This model also includes a bipod, sling, and three Triopad stock spacers.

GRADING	100%	95%	90%	80%	60%	40%	20%

MODEL 125TH – .177, .22, or .25 cal., BBC, SS, 1250/1000/750 FPS, 19.6 in. rifled steel barrel with large muzzle brake, ergonomic black, OD Green, Mossy Oak New Break-Up Camo, or Luxurious walnut woodgrain camo synthetic thumbhole stock with Monte Carlo cheek piece, Triopad butt system, Quattro trigger and SAS, manual safety and automatic cocking safety, anti-bear trap safety, scope mount rail and mounted scope stop, metal trigger blade, Truglo fiber optic micro adj. rear sight and Truglo open front sight, includes three Triopad stock spacers, 47.4 in. OAL, 9 lbs.

courtesy Hatsan Arms Co.

MSR $250	$215	$190	$170	$140	$105	N/A	N/A

Add $20 for Mossy Oak Break-Up camo finish.
Add $100 for gas piston.

MODEL 135 – .177, .22, or .25 cal., BBC, SS, 1250/1000/750 FPS, 17.7 in. rifled steel barrel, ergonomic hunting style Turkish walnut stock with Monte Carlo cheek piece, checkering on grip and forearm, Triopad butt system, Quattro trigger and SAS, manual safety and automatic cocking safety, anti-bear trap safety, scope mount rail and shock absorber scope stop, gold plated trigger blade, Truglo fiber optic micro adj. rear sight and Truglo open front sight, includes three Triopad stock spacers, 47.2 in. OAL, 9.2 lbs.

courtesy Hatsan Arms Co.

MSR $290	$245	$220	$195	$160	$120	N/A	N/A

This model is also available equipped with an Optima 1x40 red dot sight and sound moderator (Model 135 XRD), and a model equipped with an Optima 3-9x32 scope and ported muzzle brake (Model 135 SP).

STRIKER 1000S COMBO – .177, .22, or .25 cal., BBC, SS, 1000/800/650 FPS, 17.7 in. rifled steel barrel, ambidextrous stylish black or Mossy Oak Break-Up camo synthetic stock with Monte Carlo cheek piece on both sides, soft rubber inlays on grip and forearm available in Dark Grey, Orange, or Yellow, rubber butt pad, adj. trigger pull and trigger travel, metal trigger blade, manual safety and automatic cocking safety, anti-bear trap safety, Truglo fiber optic micro adj. rear sight, 3-9x32 Optima scope, large muzzle brake with integrated Truglo fiber optic hooded front sight, 43 in. OAL, 6.4 lbs.

MSR $150	$130	$115	$100	$85	$65	N/A	N/A

STRIKER 1000X – .177, .22, or .25 cal., BBC, SS, 1000/800/650 FPS, 17.7 in. rifled steel barrel, ambidextrous stylish wood stock with Monte Carlo cheek piece on both sides, checkering on grip and forearm, rubber vent. butt pad, adj. trigger pull and trigger travel, metal trigger blade, manual safety and automatic cocking safety, anti-bear trap safety, Truglo fiber optic micro adj. rear sight, large muzzle brake with integrated Truglo fiber optic hooded front sight, 43 in. OAL, 6.4 lbs.

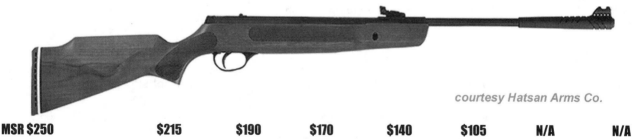

courtesy Hatsan Arms Co.

MSR $250	$215	$190	$170	$140	$105	N/A	N/A

STRIKER EDGE – .177, .22, or .25 cal., BBC, SS, 17.7 in. rifled steel barrel, 1000/800/650 FPS, ambidextrous black synthetic thumbhole stock with Monte Carlo cheek piece and textured pistol grip and forearm, rubber butt pad, adj. trigger, manual safety and automatic cocking safety, anti-bear trap safety, Truglo fiber optic micro adj. rear sight, 3-9x32 Optima scope, large muzzle brake with integrated Truglo fiber optic hooded front sight, 43.3 in. OAL, 6.6 lbs. Mfg. 2013-current.

MSR $140	$120	$105	$95	$75	$60	N/A	N/A

Add $21 for Harvest Moon camo stock.
Add $30 for Mossy Oak Break-Up camo stock.

GRADING	100%	95%	90%	80%	60%	40%	20%

STRIKER JUNIOR – .177 or .22 cal., BBC, SS, 15.6 in. rifled steel barrel, ambidextrous short size black, Mossy Oak Break Up camo, or Luxurious walnut woodgrain synthetic stock with Monte Carlo cheek piece, checkering on grip and forearm, rubber butt pad, adj. trigger pull and trigger travel, metal trigger blade, manual safety and automatic cocking safety, anti-bear trap safety, Truglo fiber optic micro adj. rear sight and hooded front sight, 37.8 in. OAL, 5.3 lbs. New 2012.

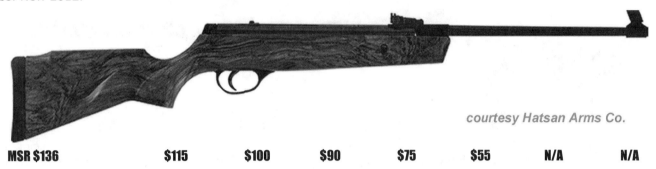

courtesy Hatsan Arms Co.

MSR $136	$115	$100	$90	$75	$55	N/A	N/A

This model also includes a pellet catcher, paper targets, and a box of pellets.

TORPEDO 100X – .177, .22, or .25 cal., UL, BA, 1000/800/650 FPS, 17 in. rifled steel fixed barrel, ergonomic hunting style Turkish walnut stock with Monte Carlo cheek piece, checkering on grip and forearm, rubber buttpad, Quattro trigger and SAS, manual and automatic cocking safety, anti-bear trap safety, scope mount rail and shock absorber scope stop, gold plated trigger blade, Truglo fiber optic micro adj. rear sight and Truglo open front sight, includes a bipod, 47.2 in. OAL, 9.2 lbs.

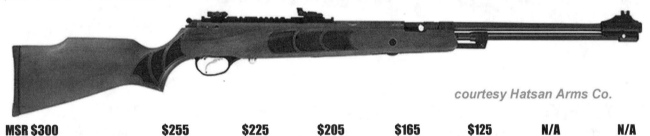

courtesy Hatsan Arms Co.

MSR $300	$255	$225	$205	$165	$125	N/A	N/A

TORPEDO 105X – .177, .22, or .25 cal., UL, BA, 1000/800/650 FPS, 17 in. rifled steel fixed barrel, ergonomic black, Mossy Oak New Break Up camo, or Luxurious walnut woodgrain camo synthetic stock with Monte Carlo cheek piece, checkering on grip and forearm, rubber buttpad, Quattro trigger and SAS, manual and automatic cocking safety, anti-bear trap safety, scope mount rail and shock absorber scope stop, metal trigger blade, Truglo fiber optic micro adj. rear sight and Truglo open front sight, includes a bipod, 47.2 in. OAL, 8.6 lbs.

courtesy Hatsan Arms Co.

MSR $260	$220	$195	$175	$145	$110	N/A	N/A

Add $40 for Mossy Oak New Break Up camo finish.

TORPEDO 150 – .177, .22, or .25 cal., UL, BA, 1250/1000/750 FPS, 17 in. rifled steel fixed barrel, ergonomic black, OD Green, Mossy Oak New Break-Up Camo, or luxurious walnut woodgrain camo synthetic stock with Monte Carlo cheek piece, checkering on grip and forearm, Triopad butt system, Quattro trigger and SAS, manual and automatic cocking safety, anti-bear trap safety, scope mount rail and shock absorber scope stop, metal trigger blade, Truglo fiber optic micro adj. rear sight and Truglo open front sight, includes a bipod and three Triopad stock spacers, 47.6 in. OAL, 9.4 lbs.

courtesy Hatsan Arms Co.

MSR $350	$300	$265	$240	$195	$145	N/A	N/A

GRADING	100%	95%	90%	80%	60%	40%	20%

TORPEDO 150TH – .177, .22, or .25 cal., UL, BA, 1250/1000/750 FPS, 17 in. rifled steel fixed barrel, ergonomic black, OD Green, Mossy Oak New Break-Up Camo, or Luxurious walnut woodgrain camo synthetic thumbhole stock with Monte Carlo cheek piece, Triopad butt system, Quattro trigger and SAS, manual and automatic cocking safety, anti-bear trap safety, scope mount rail and shock absorber scope stop, metal trigger blade, Truglo fiber optic micro adj. rear sight and Truglo open front sight, includes a bipod and three Triopad stock spacers, 46 in. OAL, 10 lbs.

courtesy Hatsan Arms Co.

MSR $350		$300	$265	$240	$195	$145	N/A	N/A

TORPEDO 155 – .177, .22, or .25 cal., UL, BA, 1250/1000/750 FPS, 17 in. rifled steel fixed barrel, ergonomic hunting style Turkish walnut stock with Monte Carlo cheek piece, checkering on grip and forearm, Triopad butt system, Quattro trigger and SAS, manual and automatic cocking safety, anti-bear trap safety, scope mount rail and shock absorber scope stop, gold plated trigger blade, Truglo fiber optic adj. rear sight and open front sight, includes a bipod and three Triopad stock spacers, 47.6 in. OAL, 11 lbs.

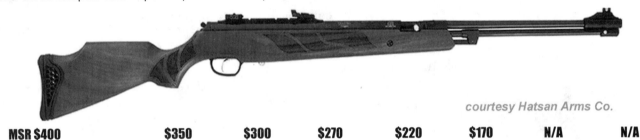

courtesy Hatsan Arms Co.

MSR $400		$350	$300	$270	$220	$170	N/A	N/A

HAVILAND AND GUNN (G.P. GUNN COMPANY)

Previous airgun designers and manufacturers located in Ilion, NY circa 1871-1882. Then the company was purchased by H.M. Quackenbush. (See also Gem and Quackenbush sections).

The authors and publisher wish to thank Mr. John Groenwold for the following information in this section of the *Blue Book of Airguns*.

GEORGE GUNN

The airgun designs of George Gunn have had enormous impact on the development of modern airguns. Patent number 113766, dated April 18, 1871, registered to Benjamin Haviland and George Gunn, was the basis for not only the Haviland & Gunn barrel-cocking air rifles and the resulting wonderful H.M. Quackenbush Model 5 rifles, but led to the great variety of air rifles known as the Gem airguns in Europe and indeed most of the amazing number and variety of barrel-cocking air rifles and pistols which have been developed since then! Patent number 126954, dated May 21, 1872, also registered to Haviland and Gunn, for an air pistol with the mainspring within the grip, is the basis for another more than century-long parade of airguns, including some early Gaggenau air pistols, the MGR air pistols, the Lincoln air pistols, and even the Walther LP 53 made famous by James Bond!

George P. Gunn was born in Tioga County, PA in 1827. He was a gunsmith in North Ilion, NY. He first marketed an airgun under his own name while working for Remington Arms Company and then another after leaving their employ. These guns, based on his first patents, were marked "G. P. GUNN, ILION, NY, PAT. APR. 18, 1871".

BENJAMIN HAVILAND JOINS GEORGE GUNN

About the time of Gunn's first patent, he joined with Benjamin Haviland to form the firm of Haviland and Gunn. Benjamin Haviland (1823-1920) had been involved with the grocery, commission, and freighting fields. His position as senior partner in the new firm evidently resulted from bringing essential marketing skills and financial backing. Throughout the 1870s the firm of Haviland and Gunn was engaged in the manufacture of airguns at the Ilion Depot, on the New York Central Railroad, in Ilion, NY.

HAVILAND AND GUNN HISTORY

Most of the rifles produced by Gunn or Haviland & Gunn were combination guns which could function as either an air rifle or as a .22 rimfire firearm. Some models were strictly air rifles and some may have been strictly rimfire. A "patch box" in the buttstock of the combination guns stored the firing pin and/or breech seal. When used as a rimfire gun, the firing pin was installed in the air transfer port on the front of the cylinder face. When the trigger was pulled, the piston moved forward, without significant air compression, and struck the firing pin which in turn crushed and detonated the primer of the rimfire cartridge. The patch box on the Haviland and Gunn rifles underwent several changes in shape, style, lid type functioning, and location, finally ending up as

GRADING	100%	95%	90%	80%	60%	40%	20%

round on the right side of the stock.

A traditional "tee bar" breech latch is found on most Haviland and Gunn air rifles and combination rifles. A side swinging breech latch on smooth bore air rifles probably was an earlier design.

Haviland & Gunn developed numerous "improved" modifications of their various models during the 1870s. They produced their last catalog in 1881. In 1882, H.M. Quackenbush purchased at least part of the Haviland and Gunn Company, including patent rights, machinery, existing stock, and equipment related to gun and slug manufacture. George Gunn agreed to work for H.M. Quackenbush but Benjamin Haviland did not.

QUACKENBUSH TAKES OVER

In 1884, Quackenbush offered exactly the same gun as the Haviland and Gunn "Improved 1880" as the Quackenbush Model 5. The parts were the same but not all were interchangeable. Quackenbush soon began offering it with an increased number of options. The stronger marketing by Quackenbush contributed to a much increased success of the Number 5 Rifle.

While working for H. M. Quackenbush, George Gunn considered a repeating version of the combination rifle known as the Hurricane. Apparently it exists only in the papers of patent number 337,395 of March 9, 1886. That Henry Marcus Quackenbush's name does not appear on this patent, filed August 12, 1885, may be related to George Gunn leaving the Quackenbush firm in that year.

A mechanical target, as produced by Haviland and Gunn for many years, was improved with several Quackenbush patents and became an important item in the Quackenbush line. A reversible "iron face" plate with a hole in the center created the "bullseye." When the shooter struck the bullseye, a figure popped up on the top of the target and/or a bell sounded. These targets are known only unmarked or with Quackenbush markings.

George Gunn also invented the felted airgun slug, patenting the process for manufacturing them on December 18, 1883. Quackenbush was granted United States patent 358,984, on March 8, 1887, for improvements in their manufacturing process. The felted slug was so superior to the burred slug that its sales immediately surpassed those of the burred slug, but Quackenbush continued selling the burred slugs until 1947.

Entries in H.M Quackenbush's personal diary indicate that George Gunn was ill, on and off, for quite some time after joining the Quackenbush Company. The last record of his employment by Quackenbush was August 12, 1885, at which time he was working on the Quackenbush Safety Rifle.

ATLAS GUN CO.

After leaving Quackenbush, George Gunn invented another airgun and in 1886, started the Atlas Gun Company, in Ilion, NY to market it. He died on March 2, 1906 when he was hit by a train while walking home from the Central Depot in Ilion, NY. Atlas Gun Co. was then acquired by Daisy.

PISTOLS

1872 MODEL – .177 cal., SP, SS, breech loading, mainspring within grip. It is cocked by inserting the breech block hook into a hole in the piston rod projecting from the base of the grip, has cast iron body with smooth surface or cast checkered grip, stamped metal trigger blade with round wire trigger guard, smoothbore, unmarked except for patent date of May 21, 1872 stamped onto surface of mainspring ring retainer. This design was also apparently licensed for Morse patent improved air pistol.

courtesy Beeman Collection

N/A	$1,500	$1,200	$975	$750	$525	$300

Subtract 20% for missing breech block with cocking hook.

RIFLES

All models are breech-loading airguns with walnut buttstocks and no forearms unless otherwise noted. Smoothbore models had a brass-lined barrel to fire darts, slugs, or shot. Rifled barrels were designed for burred or felted slugs. A tee bar breech latch is found on most guns; a side swinging latch is less common, presumably an earlier style. Except for the Parlor rifle, the H&G guns were finished in nickel plating or browning.

GRADING	100%	95%	90%	80%	60%	40%	20%

STRAIGHT LINE MODEL – .22 cal., BBC, SP, SS, receiver/spring chamber in straight line with barrel, metal stock wrist does not contain mainspring, receiver nickel plated, barrel brown finish.

	N/A	$3,500	$2,800	$2,275	$1,750	$1,225	$700

NEW MODEL – combination air rifle/.22 rimfire gun, "patch box" of various shapes in buttplate holds firing pin or breech seal when other is in use, spring chamber angled down from barrel to form wrist of stock above trigger.

courtesy Beeman Collection

	N/A	$3,000	$2,400	$1,950	$1,500	$1,050	$600

Add 10% for browned finish.
Add 25% for side swinging breech latch.

NEW IMPROVED 1880 MODEL – .22 cal., combination air rifle/rimfire rifled gun (rare version: smoothbore air rifle only), predecessor to the Quackenbush Model 5, spring chamber angled down from barrel to form wrist of stock above trigger, patch box for firing pin only in lower edge of buttstock, serial number stamped on rear of barrel, under barrel latch, trigger. Barrel base only under lower half of barrel.

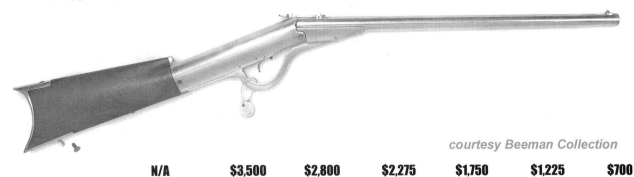

courtesy Beeman Collection

	N/A	$3,500	$2,800	$2,275	$1,750	$1,225	$700

Add 10% for browned finish.
Add 20% for nickel finish.
Add 25% for smoothbore airgun only.

IMPROVED JUNIOR MODEL – .22 cal., BBC, SP, SS, spring chamber angled down from barrel to form wrist of stock above trigger, rifled or smoothbore barrel. Minor differences in barrel lengths and patch box locations, airgun action only so "patch box" served no real purpose.

	N/A	$3,000	$2,400	$1,950	$1,500	$1,050	$600

Add 10% for browned finish.
Add 25% for smoothbore airgun only.

PARLOR MODEL – .22 cal., piston cocked by pulling plunger ring within metal frame skeleton stock, 17.8 in. smoothbore barrel, heavy cast iron receiver, black and gilt (black enamel and bright nickel) finish, other colors are known but have no factory documentation.

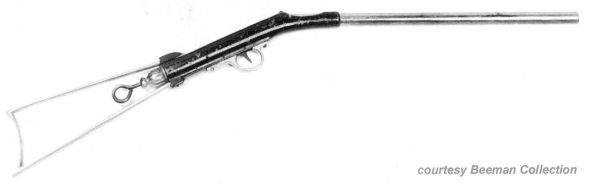

courtesy Beeman Collection

	N/A	$4,000	$3,200	$2,600	$2,000	$1,400	$800

GRADING	100%	95%	90%	80%	60%	40%	20%

HAWLEY

Previous maker of the "Kalamazoo" air pistol, located in Kalamazoo, MI about 1870.

Probably should be called the "Hawley" after Edwin H. Hawley, its inventor and maker, but it has been affectionally known by the delightfully sounding name of "Kalamazoo". That refers to the location of manufacture, but actually neither name, nor any other markings, appear on the pistol itself! In addition to being delightful both in name and design, this gun has special historical significance: Evidently this is America's first commercial pneumatic pistol. (Lukens and Kunz made pneumatic rifles in the Philadelphia area circa 1800-1815 but evidently did not make pistols). Based on patent #90,749, issued June 1, 1869 to Hawley but built to design advertised in 1870, covered by improved patent #118,886, issued to Edwin Hawley and George Snow on Sept. 12, 1871. A butt-reservoir pneumatic with straight pump affixed under barrel. Hammer suggestive of flintlock hammer with sear mechanism fully visible on bottom curve.

Improved patent including making front sight by merely turning up section of front barrel band. Sight arrangement strikingly strange: valve release pin protrudes from top center of receiver, thus rear sight groove has been displaced to right. To sight gun one must tip it about 45 degrees to left (this may be half-way precursor to flat-on-its-side "gangsta" firing stance of 20th century!).

Cast iron receiver contains air reservoir in the butt and firing mechanism in forward part. Three large casting holes sealed by pewter/lead or brass plugs. Brass plug just ahead of trigger allows access to install and repair exhaust valve.

PISTOLS

HAWLEY KALAMAZOO – .22, .26, or .28 cal., possibly other cals., smoothbore BBLs. about 4.5-5 in., one known to 10.5 in., SS, PP, breech-loading, black enamel finish on grip, nickel finish on bbl. and pump. Longitudinal pump with forward ring may have used a simple rod as pumping handle. Ref. AW (Nov. 1979), USA (July 1995), Hannusch (2001). Two variants:

* ***Early Version (Lead Plug)*** – receiver holes closed with large, somewhat crude, slotted pewter/lead plugs, knurled sliding breech-loading cover, flat (smooth) sided hammer, grip frame casting has smooth side in front of trigger, around exhaust valve, and on bottom of grip around air chamber access plug, trigger sear pin hole bored through grip frame casting.

courtesy Beeman Collection

N/A	$2,250	$1,800	$1,450	$1,125	$775	$450

Add 15% for nickel finish.
Add 30% for unusual purple original box.
Add 30% for original instruction sheet and target.

Flat side hammer and knurled loading cover illustrated in June 1970 *Scientific American* ad and in 1871 patent drawing. Early factory literature offered brass replacement plugs and they were sold as spare parts. Specimens observed with 1 or 2 brass plugs probably represent repairs - even the maker would find it difficult to replace a removed lead plug. Forward access hole most likely to have substitute brass plug.

GRADING	100%	95%	90%	80%	60%	40%	20%

* ***Late Version (Brass Plug)*** – similar to earlier version except grooved side on hammer, most receiver plugs still lead until very late models had neatly machined from brass w/standard groove, side of grip frame casting is contoured (bulged) in front of trigger around exhaust valve to proved move room (better access)during assembly, bottom of grip has a groove around air chamber access plug, trigger sear pin hole not bored through left hand side of grip frame casting.

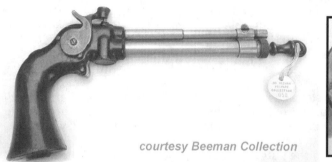

courtesy Beeman Collection

N/A	$1,800	$1,450	$1,175	$900	$625	$350

Add 15% for nickel finish.
Add 30% for unusual triangular shaped original box.
Add 30% for original instruction sheet and target.

HAWTHORNE

Previous Store Brand name used by Montgomery Wards.

For the original manufacturer and model name/number of Hawthorne Brand airguns see the Store Brand Cross-Over List at the back of this text.

HEALTHWAYS, INC.

Previous trademark manufactured and distributed by Healthways, Inc., located in Compton, CA into the 1970s. Healthways purchased Baron Mfg. Co. in 1947 and discontinued Baron air pistols. CO_2 versions designed by Richard Kline and Kenneth Pitcher in 1955-56; patented in late 1950s. Healthways was purchased by Marksman.

For additional information on Plainsman Model airguns, see Challenger Arms Corp. in the "C" section.

PISTOLS

PLAINSMAN MODEL 9400 – BB/.175 cal. steel only, CO_2 (8 gm. CO_2 cylinders inserted in grip) semi-auto with coin-slotted, 350 FPS, 5.9 in. rifled barrel, three-position power screw, hundred-shot gravity-fed mag., manual thumb safety, black plastic (later Marksman production had simulated woodgrain) grips, black epoxy finish, 1.72 lbs.

$90	$75	$65	$55	$45	$35	$25

1977 retail was approx. $30.

Add 25% for box, accessories, and factory papers.

PLAINSMAN MODEL 9401 – BB/.175 cal., similar to Model 9400, except smoothbore.

$90	$75	$65	$55	$45	$35	$25

1977 retail was approx $30.

Add 25% for box, accessories, and factory papers.

GRADING	100%	95%	90%	80%	60%	40%	20%

PLAINSMAN MODEL 9404 "SHORTY" – .22 cal. for lead-coated steel round balls, CO_2 (8 gm or 12 gm), 40-shot magazine, similar to Model 9400, except has 3.9 in. barrel, 1.65 lbs.

courtesy Beeman Collection

N/A	$100	$85	$75	$55	$45	$35

1977 retail was approx $35.

Add 30% for box, accessories, and factory papers.

PLAINSMASTER MODEL 9405 – BB/.175 cal., CO_2, 9.4 in. rifled barrel, black epoxy finish, detachable walnut wood-grain plastic thumbrest grip and forend, adj. rear sight, thumb safety, three-position power switch, hundred-round capacity, approx. 2.54 lbs.

$90	$75	$65	$55	$45	$35	$25

1977 retail was approx $45.

Add 25% for box, accessories, and factory papers.
Subtract 75% for missing forearm and hand grip.

PLAINSMASTER MODEL 9406 – .22 cal. for lead-coated steel round balls, similar to Model 9405, except smoothbore.

courtesy Beeman Collection

N/A	$90	$75	$65	$55	$45	$35

1977 retail was approx $45.

Add 25% for box, accessories, and factory papers.
Subtract 75% for missing forearm and hand grip.

PLAINSMAN MODEL MA 22 – .22 cal. lead covered steel balls, CO_2, approx. 350 FPS, gravity-fed fifty-shot mag., manual safety, similar to the Colt Woodsman. Mfg. 1969-1980.

courtesy Beeman Collection

$40	$35	$30	$25	$20	$10	N/A

GRADING	100%	95%	90%	80%	60%	40%	20%

PLAINSMAN MODEL ML 175 – BB/.175 cal., CO_2, approx. 350 FPS, gravity-fed 50-shot mag., 6 in. barrel, manual safety, metal grips, styled like Colt Woodsman, black finish, plastic grips, 9.3 in. OAL, 1.9 lbs. Mfg. 1969-1980.

	100%	95%	90%	80%	60%	40%	20%
	$40	$35	$30	$25	$20	$10	N/A

Add 25% for chrome finish.

PLAINSMAN WESTERN – BB/.175 cal., CO_2 or SP, spring-fed magazine (approx. fifteen shots), no safety, styled like Colt Peacemaker SA revolver, 11.5 in. OAL, 2.1 lbs.

courtesy Beeman Collection

	100%	95%	90%	80%	60%	40%	20%
	$175	$150	$125	$100	$80	$50	$35

Add 20% for spring version, barrel sleeve will remove to shoot corks or darts.

TOPSCORE MODEL 9100 – BB/.175 cal., lifting-barrel spring air action, 6.5 in. smoothbore barrel, approx. 200 FPS, fifty-shot gravity-fed mag., manual thumb safety, die-cast one-piece grip/frame, 1.7 lbs.

	100%	95%	90%	80%	60%	40%	20%
	$75	$60	$50	$45	$40	$30	$25

1977 retail was approx $20.

Add 25% for box, accessories, and factory papers.

PLAINSMAN TOPSCORE 175 – BB/.177 cal., CO_2, repeater, 10.5 in. OAL, 2.2 lbs.

courtesy Beeman Collection

	100%	95%	90%	80%	60%	40%	20%
	$75	$60	$50	$45	$40	$30	$25

PLAINSMAN SHARP SHOOTER 175 – BB/.177 cal., CO_2, repeater.

Values and dates not available at the time of publication.

RIFLES

PLAINSMAN MODEL MX175 – BB/.175 cal., CO_2 12 gm, 20 in. barrel, scope rail cast in top, low power, beech stock, 4 lbs.

courtesy Beeman Collection

	100%	95%	90%	80%	60%	40%	20%
	$65	$55	$50	$40	$35	$30	$20

Add 20% for box, accessories, and factory papers.

PLAINSMAN MODEL MC22 – .22 cal., lead coated steel round balls, similar to Model MX175.

	100%	95%	90%	80%	60%	40%	20%
	$75	$65	$55	$50	$40	$35	$30

Add 20% for box, accessories, and factory papers.

GRADING	100%	95%	90%	80%	60%	40%	20%

HECKLER & KOCH GmbH

Current manufacturer established in 1949, and located in Oberndorf/Neckar, Germany. Currently imported and distributed beginning 2009 by Umarex USA, located in Fort Smith, AR, and beginning 2012 by Air Venturi/Pyramyd Air, located in Solon, OH. Previously located in Warrensville Hts., OH. Previously imported by H & K USA, located in Columbus, GA, Merkel USA, located in Trussville, AL, and by Heckler & Koch, Inc. located in Sterling, VA (previously located in Chantilly, VA). During 2004, H & K built a new plant in Columbus, GA, primarily to manufacture guns for American military and law enforcement. In early 1991, H & K was absorbed by Royal Ordnance, a division of British Aerospace (BAE Systems) located in England. During December 2002, BAE Systems sold Heckler & Koch to a group of European investors. Heckler & Koch, Inc. and HKJS GmbH are wholly owned subsidiaries of Suhler Jag und Sportwaffen Holding GmbH and the sole licensees of Heckler & Koch commercial firearms technology. During 2009 a licensed partnership was formed with Umarex USA Inc. located in Fort Smith, AR to manufacture and market airguns under the Heckler & Koch trademark.

For more information and current pricing on both new and used Heckler & Koch firearms, please refer to the *Blue Book of Gun Values* by S.P. Fjestad (now online).

CARBINES

MP5 K-PDW – BB/.177 cal., one 12g CO_2 cylinder, semi-auto, DA, blowback action, 40-shot, 400 FPS, 6 (new 2013), 7 (mfg. 2012-2013) or 9.75 (disc.) in. barrel, black finish, foldable stock, vertical forearm grip, Picatinny rail, removable compensator with bayonet lock, 24.5 in. OAL, 2.4-3.71 lbs. New 2010.

courtesy Umarex USA

MSR $123	$100	$85	$70	$60	$45	$30	$20

PISTOLS

P30 – BB/.175 cal. (disc. 2012) or .177 cal., CO_2, SA/DA, 3.3 in. rifled barrel, blued, polymer frame, full metal slide, ambi. mag. release, 360 FPS, drop out 15 (BB) and rotary 8 (pellet) shot mag., black finish, adj. sights, textured finger groove grips, integrated accessory rail, 7.1 in. OAL, 1.7 lbs. Mfg. 2009-current.

courtesy Umarex USA

MSR $239	$205	$175	$145	$120	$90	$60	$40

GRADING	100%	95%	90%	80%	60%	40%	20%

USP – BB/.177 cal., CO_2, DA, 4 (disc. 2010, reintroduced 2012) or 4.5 (new 2011) in. barrel, blued, polymer frame, 400 FPS, 22-shot mag., ambi. mag. release, black finish, fixed sights, integrated accessory rail, realistic hammer movement, 7.5 in. OAL, 1.8 lbs. Mfg. 2009-current.

courtesy Umarex USA

MSR $50	$40	$35	$30	$25	$20	$10	N/A

Add $34 for 22-shot drop-free magazine.

HEGMANS, THEO

Current craftsman located in Kerken, Germany.

Theo Hegmans is a German who can only be described as a craftsman genius - although he is a graduate economist and computer specialist, he retreats to an old-fashioned shop in his barn to make too many things to describe, but all wonderful. These creations include the most unusual firearms and astonishing airguns. His inventions include a version of the old large bore German airguns, or Windbüchsen. This Windbüchsen is most unusual in that it uses a percussion cap to open the air valve to a charge of stored air and push a 200-grain, .45 caliber lead bullet out at great velocity. Ref: VISIER, March 2005.

PISTOLS

HEGMANS MCAIRROW CLASSIC – soda straw cal., the only Hegmans airgun ever made in quantity. The straw projectiles are fitted with a rubber tip and some fins cut from other straws. The projectile is shoved over the concealed barrel - the missile is around the barrel rather than in it! Two to twelve pumps power the gun. On full power it fires up to 230 FPS to a range of 30 or 40 yards!

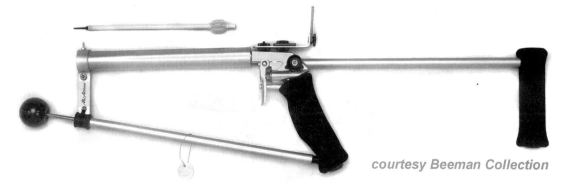

courtesy Beeman Collection

Original retail price equaled about $125. Scarcity precludes accurate pricing.

In 1999, this started out as a toy for his then nine-year-old nephew, made from a bicycle tire pump, a grease gun, and garden soaker hose! As projectiles, he used plastic drinking straws from an international fast food firm whose name may be suggested by the name of this gun. The fast food firm was not pleased and he was pressured to stop production after only exactly fifty specimens had been made over three years.

GRADING	100%	95%	90%	80%	60%	40%	20%

RIFLES

AIR TWIN – .177 or .22 cal., SxS double-barrel, SP, SS, mainsprings around the barrels, 18.5/33.4 ft./lb. ME, 41.3 in. OAL, 8.8 lbs.

courtesy Theo Hegmans

Scarcity precludes accurate pricing.
   Each barrel holds 10mm group ctc at 25 yds, together 20mm ctc.

CHIP MUNK – .22 cal., SS, PCP, real barrel hidden under false barrel air reservoir, 25 shots per charge, 52 ft./lb. ME, 41.3 in. OAL, 7 lbs.

courtesy Theo Hegmans

Scarcity precludes accurate pricing.

GO WEST – .177 cal., PCP, real BBL hidden under false barrel air reservoir, eight-shot repeater with lever activated cylinder, 32 shots @ 14.8 ft./lb. ME, 16 shots @ 11.4 ft./lb. ME, 40.6 in. OAL, 9.3 lbs.

courtesy Theo Hegmans

Scarcity precludes accurate pricing.

GRANDPA – .45 cal., PCP, muzzle loader, walnut stock, 297 ft./lb. ME at 3000 PSI with 250 gr. bullet, 900 PSI, 89 ft./lb. ME, 47.2 in. OAL, 9.7 lbs.

courtesy Theo Hegmans

Scarcity precludes accurate pricing.

GRADING	100%	95%	90%	80%	60%	40%	20%

HOW STUFF WORKS – .177 cal., BBC, SP, SS, butt reservoir, all operating elements on the outside of the gun, 40 shots per charge @ 18 ft./lb. ME. 43.3 in. OAL, 6.2 lbs.

courtesy Beeman Collection

Scarcity precludes accurate pricing.

HEILPRIN MANUFACTURING CO.

For information on Heilprin Manufacturing Co. airguns, see Columbian in the "C" section.

HEIRINKAN

Previous trade name of Heirinkan Co. located in Tokyo, Japan.

Heirinkan airguns were designed by the company's founder, the late Ueda Shoji (1918-1981). Former producer of high powered pneumatic air rifles. These rifles were made only in small numbers and for a very short time in the 1970s. Reportedly most of the rifles remaining in Japan were destroyed by the government and ownership was forbidden without a special need - such as professional pest control. Collecting as such is not allowed. Much sought after by collectors and shooters because of their high power, accuracy, and high quality. Reportedly in production 1953-1981, information not confirmed. Research is ongoing with this trademark, and more information will be included both in future editions and online.

RIFLES

MODEL A – .177 or .22 cal., swinging arm, multi-pump pneumatic, sporter model, 36.6 in. OAL, 6.6 lbs.

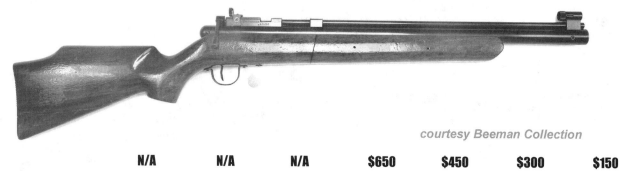

courtesy Beeman Collection

	N/A	N/A	N/A	$650	$450	$300	$150

MODEL SS – .177 or .22 cal., swinging arm, multi-pump pneumatic, sporter model with telescopic sight, 36.6 in. OAL, 6.6 lbs.

Scarcity precludes accurate pricing.

MODEL Z – no information at this time.

Scarcity precludes accurate pricing.

MODEL 120 – .177 or .22 cal., swinging arm, multi-pump pneumatic, thumbhole stock and adj. aperture target sight, 36.6 in. OAL, 6.6 lbs.

Scarcity precludes accurate pricing.

BREAK BARREL MODEL – no information or values available at this time.

HEXAGON

For information on Hexagon airguns, see Decker in the "D" section.

HEYM AG

Current manufacturer established in 1865 and located in Gleichamberg, Germany since 1995. Made airguns from 1949-1952. Currently firearms are imported beginning 2006 by Double Gun Imports LLC, located in Dallas, TX. Limited importation 1999-2005 by New England Custom Gun Service, Ltd., located in Plainfield, NH.

During 1998, Heym underwent a management change. The company name was changed from Heym Waffenfabrik AG to Heym AG during mid-2007. Previously manufactured in Muennerstadt, Germany circa 1952-1995 and Suhl, Germany between 1865 and 1945. Originally founded in 1865 by F.W. Heym. Previously imported by JagerSport, Ltd. located in Cranston, RI 1993-94 only, Heckler & Koch, Inc. (until 1993) located in Sterling, VA, Heym America, Inc. (subsidiary of F.W. Heym of W. Germany) located in Fort Wayne, IN, and originally by Paul Jaeger, Inc. 1970-1986.

For more information and current pricing on both new and used Heym firearms, please refer to the *Blue Book of Gun Values* by S.P. Fjestad (also available online).

PISTOLS

LP 103 – .177 cal., SP, SS, push-barrel Gat-style air pistol, white plastic checkered grips, 7.8 in. OAL, 12 oz.

courtesy Beeman Collection

Estimated value in average condition about $35.

RIFLES

Research is ongoing for this rifles section, and more information will be included both in future editions and online. Three models are known: LG 100 (about 3000 produced), LG 101 (repeater version of LG 100), and LG 103 (junior version of LG 100).

HILL & WILLIAMS

Previous manufacturer located in Staffordshire, England, circa 1905-1911.

The Hill & Williams air rifle in .22 cal. is a barrel-cocking, spring-piston design cocked by pushing forward a barrel latch at the breech and then pivoting the barrel downward. British patent number 25222/'05 was issued to Arthur Henry Hill and Walter F. Williams on 16 July 1908 for the design. Hill's address was 28 Leyton Road, Handsworth, Staffordshire, England. Walter notes that the gun may not have been made by Hill and Williams until about 1908. It was probably too complicated and expensive to compete with the Lincoln Jeffries design underlever rifles from BSA. Production ended by 1911. Apparently about two hundred guns were produced.

This gun evidently was one of the pioneer production designs, along with the somewhat similar MGR First Model Rifle, developed at the very beginning of the 20th century. Specimens in good condition should have a retail value in the $2,600 range. Refs: *Airgunner* April 1986, Dec. 1986, and *Guns Review*, Aug. 1978.

courtesy Beeman Collection

HOLBORN

For information on Holborn airguns, see Dianawerk in the "D" section.

HORNET

For information on Hornet airguns, see Plymouth Air Rifle Company in the "P" section.

HOTSHOT

For information on Hotshot airguns, see Gun Toys SRL in the "G" section.

HOWA

Current manufacturer located in Tokyo, Japan. Previously located in Nagoya, Japan. No current U.S. importation.

Howa Machinery Limited manufactures Japanese defense force assault rifles, Weatherby Vanguard rifle actions, and rifles and shotguns for Smith & Wesson. Also produced small numbers of extremely high grade CO_2 rifles (styled like the Weatherby Mark V semi-auto rifle, reportedly to induce Weatherby to distribute them in the USA) in the mid-1970s.

For more information and current pricing on both new and used Howa firearms, please refer to the *Blue Book of Gun Values* by S.P. Fjestad (also available online).

GRADING	100%	95%	90%	80%	60%	40%	20%

RIFLES

MODEL 55G – .177 cal., two CO_2 cylinders back-to-back, BA feeds five pellets from spring-fed magazine, blue finish, highly polished steel parts with highly finished and detailed hardwood or synthetic stocks, 38.7 in. OAL, 6 lbs. Mfg. 1975-current.

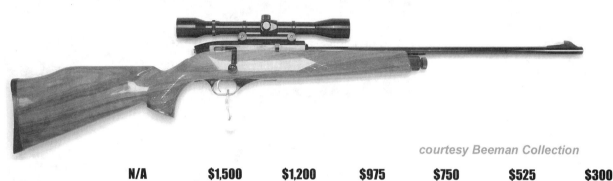

courtesy Beeman Collection

	N/A	$1,500	$1,200	$975	$750	$525	$300

Add 30% for first variant.
Add 25% for Deluxe variant.
Add 20% for Howa scope.

This model is very rarely seen anywhere in the world, especially outside of Japan.

User's note and warning: bolt will not close after magazine delivers its last pellet until the charging rod is retracted.

HUBERTUS

Previously manufactured by Jagdwaffenfabrik, in Suhl, Germany. (Other addresses may include Molin, Germany.)

PISTOLS

HUBERTUS – .177 or .22 cal., push-barrel, spring-piston action, single shot (barrel must be pulled back out before loading and firing), blue steel receiver, plain barrel, both front and rear sights on receiver, marked "D.R.G.M. Deutsches Reichs-Gebrauch-Muster" (a low level patent notice). Small frame variant: smoothbore, 8.5 in. OAL, early production. Large frame variant: rifled, forward breech ring ribbed, 10.5 in. OAL, about 1.5 lbs., patented 1925, mfg. 1925-1935. See *Guns Review*, May, 1973 and Dec. 1975.

small frame

large frame

courtesy Beeman Collection

	N/A	$250	$175	$135	$100	$75	$50

Add 40% for factory box and papers.
Add 40% for cocking aid and pellet tin.
Add 40% for spare barrel.
Add 100% for small frame version.
Add 25% for .22 caliber.

The large version was distributed as the Snider Air Pistol for a short time in the USA by E.K. Tryon & Co, Philadelphia, PA.

RIFLES

MODEL 53 – .177 cal. (may be for shot cartridges), BB, SS, SP, breech-opening lever. Marked DRGM for "Deutsches Reich Gebrauchs Muster" (German Government Registered Design - a weak patent level.)

No other information or values are available at this time.

HYDE

Previous trademark manufactured by Floyd Hyde located in South California.

PISTOLS

HYDE PISTOL – BB/.174 cal., CO_2, semi-auto repeater, similar to Daisy Model 100. April 1959.

	N/A	N/A	$150	$125	$100	$65	$40

HY-SCORE ARMS CORPORATION
Previous distributor and importer located in Brooklyn, NY.

The American Hy-Score CP (Concentric Piston) air pistols are well-made airguns by a unique American company. As spring piston airguns, especially with their unusual concentric piston design, they stand in bold contrast to the pump and CO_2 guns that were the standard in the USA. Steven E. Laszlo founded the S.E. Laszlo House of Imports of Brooklyn, NY in 1933. The company imported many items, including airguns, ammunition, black powder firearms, binoculars, telescopes, magnetic compasses, and movie camera lenses. The S.E. Laszlo House of Imports served as the umbrella company for the Hy-Score Arms Corporation, whose main claim to fame was their development and manufacture of a unique series of concentric piston spring air pistols. The company originally was located at 25 Lafayette St. in Brooklyn, NY. In October 1965, the firm moved to 200 Tillary Street, Brooklyn, NY, where it remained until Steve Laszlo's death in 1980.

In 1970, Hy-Score discontinued marketing of the Hy-Score CP air pistols, perhaps due to increased legal and political pressure for a safety mechanism. He had started to import other airguns as early as 1950. From 1970 until his death in 1980, he concentrated on selling airguns made by overseas factories.

The American Hy-Score CP air pistols were produced for only about twenty-five years, but they form one of the most interesting groups of airguns for collectors who appreciate their unique nature.

In 1989, the Hy-Score concentric-piston design returned full circle to England when the Hy-Score brand became British. Richard Marriot-Smith purchased the trademark, plans, and what remained of the long idle Hy-Score factory machinery and Hy-Score pistol parts. Operating under the name of the Phoenix Arms Co., in Kent, England, he began production of the "New Hy-Score" Single-Shot pistol using original Hy-Score machinery and many original American parts. The general appearance was that of the Model 803 Sportster with the muzzle threaded for a moderator. It was a rather expensive, unfamiliar style for the English market and regular exports to the USA were precluded by the lack of a safety mechanism. Production was extremely limited; almost as soon as Phoenix Arms had arisen from the ashes of Marriot-Smith's other gun enterprises, it disappeared, having created instant collectibles.

HY-SCORE PISTOL DESIGN

Steve Laszlo was an expert marketer, but he was not a designer. About 1940, he asked his brother, Andrew Lawrence (nee Laszlo), an engineer in applied mechanics, to develop a compact, modern high-powered air pistol. See Ref: Lawrence (1969).

Andrew designed the gun to be produced without the forgings and leather seals typical of contemporary air pistols, to have a light, good trigger action, and to look like a firearm. A desire for easy cocking, no pumping, and reliability dictated a spring piston powerplant. His Stanford University research paper, which outlined the development of this pistol, discussed the pros and cons of the Zenit, Webley, Diana, and Haenel spring piston airguns. He settled on the concentric piston design found in the English Acvoke, Warrior, Westley Richards, and Abas-Major air pistols. These pistols are conspicuous by their lack of any mention in Andrew's paper and he dismissed consideration of English patents as "too costly."

Concentric piston airguns use the barrel as a guide for a piston snugly fitted around it. The concentric powerplant allowed for a very long, powerful mainspring and a long barrel, conducive to both high power and accuracy, in a rather compact pistol. World War II delayed production until about 1946. Hy-Score advertised their new pistols as the world's most powerful airguns, with the accuracy of an air rifle, and the looks and feel of a Luger.

Andrew was skilled in automotive engineering; so instead of the conventional leather seals, the first Hy-Score CP pistols used automotive-type steel piston rings made by the Perfect Circle Co., expected to be good for a lifetime of normal use. (The seals were later changed to o-rings when the steel piston rings proved to be a maintenance problem.) The solid, durable grips were made of Tenite, a new plastic from General Electric. Steel blocks cast into the grip provided excellent heft and balance.

The trigger system is unique and deserves special mention. Rather than having the full pressure of the mainspring bear on the seal, Lawrence designed a special "servo-mechanism" to enable the shooter to apply relatively little pressure to very smoothly release the shot. A "dry practice" feature allowed the shooter to slightly open the gun, without cocking the mainspring, to set the trigger for practice trigger pulls.

Lawrence's genius is revealed by the loading mechanism. The loading gate is a very ingenious camera-shutter system, which, in the repeater version, is coupled with one of the cleverest projectile feeding mechanisms in the world of gun design. When the breech cap is turned by the shooter, six little steel cylinders cam their way around, like bumper cars at a carnival, to each feed their contained pellet into the firing chamber. This mechanism apparently has never been duplicated in any other gun.

The body tube is a very sturdy, drawn steel tube which, in the later models, is smoothly tapered down to form the barrel profile. The frame is a smooth stamping. Engraving-style, stamped scroll markings were added to the frame at approximately serial number 850,000. An excellent blue finish was standard. Chrome plating was an extra cost option and is rarely seen.

The various Hy-Score CP air pistol models all used the same basic mechanism and frame. The key differences were in single vs. repeater mechanism, finish, grip color, barrel style, and barrel length. The 700 and 800 model series appear to be fixed long-barrel single-shots, although what appears to be the visible barrel in the Model 700 is just a large-bore tube extending forward from the frame which contains a short barrel. The 802 is a fixed long-barrel repeater. The 803 Sportster is a short interchangeable-barrel single-shot. The 804 is a short fixed-barrel repeater. An "R" on the repeaters or an "S" on the Sportster models precedes serial numbers in the 800,000 range. Serial numbers over 900,000 are without the prefixes.

HY-SCORE COMPARATIVE MODEL NUMBERS

Most of Hy-Score's airgun imports were made by Dianawerk of Rastatt, Germany. (See the comparative model chart in the Dianawerk section.) Various other airguns were made for Hy-Score by BSF, Hämmerli, Anschütz, Baikal, Em-Ge, Slavia, and

GRADING	100%	95%	90%	80%	60%	40%	20%

FN. Important note: Comparable models often have different values due to varying degrees of scarcity, different demand by collectors, and because distributors of private label guns often specified different power levels (for different markets, not just mainspring differences), stocks, calibers, sights, trigger mechanisms, etc. from the basic manufacturer's model. Early models of the same number may differ from more recent models.

Hy-Score imports not made by Dianawerk:

Hy-Score 822T Pistol - Made by Em-Ge in Germany.

Hy-Score 821, 833SM, 894 sidelever rifle - Made by Hämmerli of Germany.

Hy-Score 824M Pistol - Hämmerli "Master" CO_2.

Hy-Score 823M Pistol - Hämmerli "Single" CO_2.

Hy-Score 817M Pistol - BSF (Wischo) CM w/o front sight hood.

Hy-Score 818 Pistol - toy-like pistol from Anschütz, etc. (8 3/4 ounces).

Hy-Score 833 - Hämmerli Model 10 (Puma Model 497).

Hy-Score 870 Mark III - Izhevsk Vostok IZh022 (Baikal).

Hy-Score 894 or 894 Sport - Hämmerli Model 4 (Puma Model 490).

PISTOLS

All models feature no safety.

MODEL 700 TARGET SINGLE SHOT – .177 or .22 cal., GC, rifled short barrel within the frame, 350 FPS (.22 cal.), what appears to be the visible barrel is only a tube for cosmetic purposes, angular step where false barrel base is pinned to the separate compression tube, rear sight attached with screw, Tenite grips (walnut, petrified wood, ivory, or onyx), blue finish. Not marked with model number but all Model 700 serial numbers begin with a seven. Approx. 2500 mfg. 1947 only.

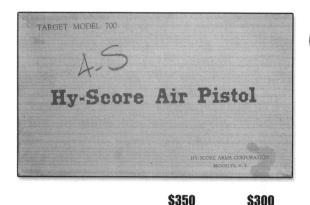

courtesy Beeman Collection

$350	$300	$245	$205	$160	$105	$70

Add 10% for grip colors other than walnut.
Add 50%-60% for box and instruction sheet (box must say "700" on it).
Subtract 5% for missing rear sight riser.

MODEL 800 TARGET SINGLE SHOT – BB/.175 smoothbore, .177 or .22 rifled cal., GC, 10.25 in. barrel, 350 FPS (.22 cal.), barrel cover and compression chamber a single smoothly tapered unit, dovetailed rear sight, Tenite grips (walnut, petrified wood, ivory, or onyx), blue or chrome finish. Mfg. 1948-1970.

courtesy Beeman Collection

$150	$130	$105	$85	$70	$45	$30

Add 75% for chrome finish ("C").
Add 10% for grip colors other than walnut.
Add 30%-50% for box and instruction sheet.
Add 10% for BB smoothbore barrel (Model 800BB).
Add 25%-30% for Hy-Score holster.
Subtract 5% for missing rear sight riser.

GRADING	100%	95%	90%	80%	60%	40%	20%

MODEL 802 TARGET REPEATER – BB/.175 smoothbore, .177 or .22 rifled cal., GC, 10.25 in. barrel, 350 FPS (.22 cal.), six-shot, cammed rotation magazine, barrel cover and compression chamber a single smoothly tapered unit, dovetailed rear sight, Tenite grips (walnut, petrified wood, ivory, or onyx), blue or chrome finish. Mfg. 1949-1970.

courtesy Beeman Collection

$200	$170	$140	$115	$90	$60	$40

Add 80% for chrome finish ("C").
Add 10% for grip colors other than walnut.
Add 30%-50% for box and instruction sheet.
Add 10% for BB smoothbore barrel (Model 802BB).
Add 25%-30% for Hy-Score holster.
Subtract 5% for missing rear sight riser.

MODEL 803 SPORTSTER SINGLE SHOT – BB/.175 smoothbore, .177 and .22 rifled cal., GC, interchangeable 7.75 in. barrels, 300 FPS (.22 cal.), short design, dovetailed rear sight, blue or chrome finish. Mfg. 1952-1954.

courtesy Beeman Collection

$225	$190	$160	$130	$100	$65	$45

Add 60% for chrome finish ("C").
Add 25%-40% for box and instruction sheet.
Add 10%-15% for each extra barrel.
Add 70% for five-in-one gun kit, blue, two extra barrels, ammo, and accessory tin (Model 803 SB).
Add 100% for five-in-one gun kit, chromed, two extra barrels, ammo, and accessory tin (Model 803 SC).
Subtract 5% for missing rear sight riser.

MODEL 804 SPORTSTER REPEATER – BB/.175 smoothbore, .177 or .22 rifled cal., GC, fixed 7.75 in. barrel, 300 FPS (.22 cal.), short design, six-shot cammed rotation magazine, dovetailed rear sight, blue or chrome finish. Mfg. 1953-1954.

courtesy Beeman Collection

$300	$255	$210	$175	$135	$90	$60

Add 35% for chrome finish ("C").
Add 30%-50% for box and instruction sheet.
Add 10% for BB only smoothbore barrel.
Subtract 5% for missing rear sight riser.

GRADING	100%	95%	90%	80%	60%	40%	20%

MODEL 805 SPORTSTER SINGLE SHOT – .177 cal, GC, SP, SS, 7.75 in. rifled barrel, 300 FPS (.22 cal.), similar to Model 803, except the barrel is permanently fixed.

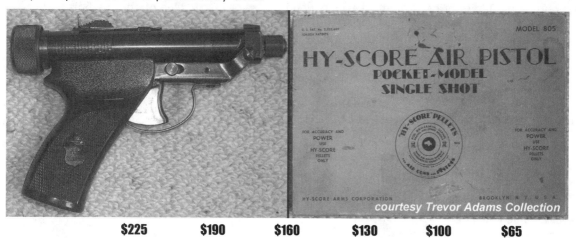

courtesy Trevor Adams Collection

$225	$190	$160	$130	$100	$65	$45

Add 25%-40% for box and instruction sheet.

MODEL 814 JUNIOR SINGLE SHOT – .177 cal., pellets or darts, push-barrel cocking, with shaped sheet steel frame, nickel finish, 7.9 in. smoothbore telescopic two-part steel barrel, removable knurled knob at back end of receiver for loading, adj. sights and riveted wooden grips, 10.6 oz.

courtesy Beeman Collection

$45	$40	$30	$25	$20	$15	N/A

NEW HY-SCORE SPORTER SINGLE SHOT – .177 cal., SP, GC, SS or repeater (intro. 1991), rifled barrel, semi-compact design with flat sided fixed barrel, threaded at the muzzle for moderator, rear sight adjustable for windage only or fully adjustable, blue finish. Made by Phoenix Arms Co., England. Mfg. 1989-1994.

courtesy Beeman Collection

N/A	$350	$280	$230	$175	$125	$70

Add 10% for fully adjustable rear sight (Mk II Model).

Add 20% for factory box and literature.

Add 10% for extra interchangeable barrel (modified original Hy-Score 803 barrels).

Add 25% for repeater.

Add 50% for chrome finish and white grips.

Add 20% for Fake Moderator (apparently a non-functional expansion chamber).

Add 100% or more for functional silencer/moderator with transferable $200 federal permit (required in U.S.).

RIFLES

Hy-Score imported many models of airguns, air rifles and pistols, private branded as Hy-Score by overseas makers, especially Dianawerk in Germany, some from Hämmerli in Switzerland and Baikal in Russia, and very few from Fabrique Nationale in Belgium. Some bear the maker's name and even date of manufacture.

I SECTION

IAR, INC.

Previous importer and distributor of Chinese air rifles, located in San Juan Capistrano, CA, and purchased by EMF during 2009.

GRADING	100%	95%	90%	80%	60%	40%	20%

RIFLES

MODEL B-19 – .177 cal., BBC, SP, SS, rifled steel barrel, 900 FPS, blue finish, hardwood Monte Carlo-style stock with recoil pad, hooded front and adj. rear sight, push/pull safety, 5.5 lbs.

100%	95%	90%	80%	60%	40%	20%
$90	$75	$65	$50	$40	$25	$20

MODEL B-21 – .177 cal., SL, SP, SS, rifled steel barrel, 1000 FPS, blue finish, hardwood Monte Carlo-style stock with recoil pad, hooded front and adj. rear sight, dovetail scope base, push/pull safety, 9.9 lbs.

100%	95%	90%	80%	60%	40%	20%
$150	$130	$105	$85	$70	$45	$30

MODEL B-22 – .22 cal., SL, SP, SS, rifled steel barrel, 800 FPS, blue finish, hardwood Monte Carlo-style stock with recoil pad, hooded front and adj. rear sight, dovetail scope base, push/pull safety, 9.9 lbs.

100%	95%	90%	80%	60%	40%	20%
$150	$130	$105	$85	$70	$45	$30

IGA

For information on IGA airguns, see Anschütz in the "A" section.

IGI

For information on IGI airguns, see Gun Toys SRL in the "G" section.

IMPERIAL AIR RIFLE CO.

Previous manufacturer of the Double Express, a double barrel airgun manufactured by Mike Childs in the UK, who subsequently produced the Skan airguns.

Many components were produced by Helston Gunsmiths in Helston, Cornwall, England.

RIFLES

DOUBLE EXPRESS – .177, .22, or .25 cal., O/U double barrel, multiple-pump pneumatic DT, flip-open breech block loading, blue finish, walnut stocks, 10 ft./lb. ME, no sights, scope rail on valve housing, 40.5 in. OAL, 7.4 lbs. Mfg. 1987.

courtesy Vic Thompson

100%	95%	90%	80%	60%	40%	20%
$1,500	$1,250	$1,000	N/A	N/A	N/A	N/A

Add 10% for mixed calibers.

Seventeen guns were produced with approximately fourteen sold, most were .22 cal.

IN KWANG

Previous manufacturing or marketing group in Seoul, Korea whose products included pre-charged pneumatic airguns.

GRADING	100%	95%	90%	80%	60%	40%	20%

RIFLES

MIRACLE GLS – .22 cal., PCP, six-shot revolving cylinder, 42.4 in. OAL, 8.3 lbs. Disc.

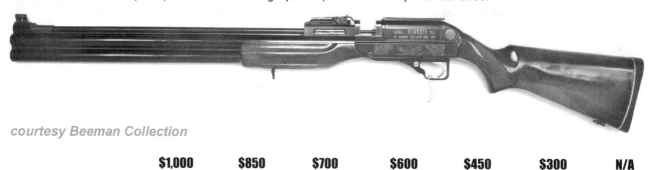

courtesy Beeman Collection

	$1,000	$850	$700	$600	$450	$300	N/A

INDUSTRY BRAND

Current trademark manufactured by Shanghai located in Shanghai, China. No current U.S. importation. Previously imported by Compasseco, located in Bardstown, KY, and Air Gun Inc. located in Houston, TX.

See Compasseco listing in the "C" section.

ISAAC

For information on Isaac airguns, see Philippine Airguns in the "P" section.

ISRAEL WEAPON INDUSTRIES (I.W.I.)

Current manufacturer established circa 2009, and located in Israel. Currently imported and distributed by Air Venturi/Pyramyd Air, located in Solon, OH. Previously located in Warrensville Hts., OH.

Israel Weapon Industries (I.W.I.) is part of a group of companies specializing in development, manufacturing, and marketing a variety of products for the international and national military and law enforcement. In early 2011, Carl Walther from Ulm, Germany indicated that it had reached a licensing agreement with I.W.I. Ltd. to manufacture a series of Uzi pistols in .22 LR cal., as well as air pistols.

PISTOLS

JERICHO 941 – .177 cal., CO_2, 22 shot mag., ambidextrous safety, copy of the Baby Eagle, black finish, 443 FPS, includes BB speedloader, Allen wrench, and one box of .177 cal. steel BBs. New 2012.

MSR $90	$75	$65	$55	$45	$35	$20	$15

ISW

Previous maker of air rifles and pistols in Calcutta, India. Generally produced copies of other airguns. About circa 1980s.

PISTOLS

SENIOR – .22 cal., SP, SS, barrel-lift cocking, copy of Webley Senior air pistol.

courtesy UK collector

$95	$80	$65	$55	$45	$30	$20

IZH

For information on IZH airguns, see Baikal in the "B" section.

J SECTION

JBC

For information on JBC airguns, see Philippine Airguns in the "P" section.

JAGUAR ARMS

Previous trademark manufactured in the mid-1970s by Jaguar Arms of Batavia, NY.

Tiny, compact CO_2 pistols, described as "the smallest CO_2 gun ever made." Very low power, inaccurate, and the finish was not durable. Thus, only a small number were sold and survived.

GRADING	100%	95%	90%	80%	60%	40%	20%

PISTOLS

CUB – .177 or .22 cal., use 8-gram CO_2 cylinders, black painted finish, brown or white grips.

courtesy Beeman Collection

courtesy Beeman Collection

	100%	95%	90%	80%	60%	40%	20%
	$225	$150	$125	$100	$75	$55	$45

Add 30% for box and papers.
Add 60% for .22 cal.

BICENTENNIAL CUB – .177 or .22 cal., 8-gram CO_2 cylinders, chrome-plated finish, brown or white grips.

courtesy Beeman Collection

	100%	95%	90%	80%	60%	40%	20%
	$300	$225	$185	$150	$100	$80	$65

Add 30% for box and papers.
Add 60% for .22 cal.

JAPANESE MILITARY TRAINER

Previously produced by unknown maker or makers in Osaka, Japan during WWII.

RIFLES

MILITARY TRAINER – .177 cal., SS, SP, straight-pull action, blue finished 19.8 in. smoothbore barrel, bolt, trigger guard, barrel bands, nickeled buttplate, bayonet lug, fake cleaning rod, 38.2 in. OAL, 13.1 in. LOP, 4.8 lbs.

courtesy Beeman Collection

	100%	95%	90%	80%	60%	40%	20%
	N/A	N/A	N/A	$975	$750	$525	$300

Original ammo not known, but fired pellets well, air powered version of Japanese service rifles. Marked with various

GRADING	100%	95%	90%	80%	60%	40%	20%

Japanese characters (inc. Osaka address), JAPAN OSAKA, bomb symbol containing letters HA, and stamped with large AFC under sunburst on forward receiver ring. SN of specimen shown: L93497. 38.2 in. OAL, 13.1 in. stock pull, ca. 8 lb. trigger pull, 4.8 lbs. Very rare; Japanese wartime production efforts desperately had to turn to production of only actual firearms. Very heavy wear is to be expected of military trainers.

JELLY

For information about Jelly trademarked airguns, see Relum Limited in the "R" section.

JIFRA

Current manufacturer located in Guadalajara, Jalisco, Mexico beginning about 1980.

RIFLES

MODEL 700 – BB/.174 cal., SP, LA, repeating BB gun of classic Daisy styling, finished in bright color paints or nickel plated, may have fake telescope tube, riveted tinplate construction, 32.8 in. OAL.

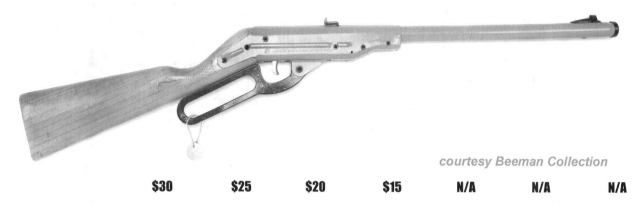

courtesy Beeman Collection

	100%	95%	90%	80%	60%	40%	20%
	$30	$25	$20	$15	N/A	N/A	N/A

JOHNSON & BYE

Previous trade name of airguns manufactured by Johnson & Bye Co. located in Worchester, MA.

Iver Johnson was the co-patentee, with Martin Bye, on U.S. patents 176,003 and 176,004 of April 11, 1876. These two Norwegian immigrants had developed an air pistol in which the barrel rotates to form a T-shaped cocking handle. Iver Johnson started his small gunsmithing shop about 1867 and then joined with Bye to form Johnson and Bye about 1875. In 1883 the company became Iver Johnson & Company and soon changed to Iver Johnson Arms & Cycle Works which became famous for inexpensive revolvers.

As noted elsewhere, Johnson, Bye, Bedford, Walker, and Quackenbush all were close associates. Their production, distribution, and ownership is confusing at times: H.M. Quackenbush recorded selling 69 Champion air pistols in 1884. It is not clear who made those 69, or how the total production of Champion air pistols was divided. And Albert Pope of Boston apparently was the main seller of Champion air pistols and also marketed air pistols, made by Quackenbush, under the Pope name. The Bedford & Walker air pistol production started in the Pope plant, then went to the Bedford & Walker plant, and finally transferred to the H.M. Quackenbush factory.

For more information and current pricing on Iver Johnson firearms, please refer to the *Blue Book of Gun Values* by S.P. Fjestad (also available online).

PISTOLS/RIFLES

CHAMPION – .21 cal., SP, SS, barrel turns to form cocking handle, 8.3 in. smoothbore barrel, black lacquer or nickel plated finish, cast iron or hardwood grips, only markings: PAT. MAR, 7. APR. 11. 76 ENG. JULY 1, 75, MAY 20, 76,15.5 in. OAL, 1.6 lbs. Mfg. 1875-1883, with advertising until 1893.

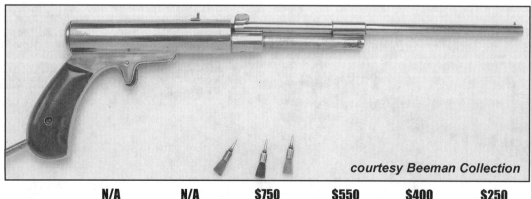

courtesy Beeman Collection

	100%	95%	90%	80%	60%	40%	20%
	N/A	N/A	$750	$550	$400	$250	$100

GRADING	100%	95%	90%	80%	60%	40%	20%

Add 10% for nickel plating.
Add 10% for wire shoulder stock.
Add 20% for deluxe model with nickel plating and hardwood grip plates.
Add 20% for original fitted wood case with some accessories.

An optional feature was a fitted wooden case with a wire shoulder stock, slugs, targets, a dart pulling claw, and a wrench.

JOHNSON AUTOMATICS, INC.

Previous manufacturer located in Providence, RI. Johnson Automatics, Inc. moved many times during its history, often with slight name changes. Also produced the Johnson Indoor Target gun until at least 1949. M.M. Johnson, Jr. died in 1965, and the company continued production at 104 Audubon Street in New Haven, CT as Johnson Arms, Inc. mostly specializing in sporter semi-auto rifles in .270 Win. or .30-06 cal. For more information and current pricing on Johnson Automatics firearms, please refer to the *Blue Book of Gun Values* by S.P. Fjestad (also available online).

RIFLES

INDOOR TARGET GUN – BB/.174 cal., catapult rifle, hundred-shot, spring-fed magazine, 100 FPS, brown bakelite stock, 28.7 in. OAL.

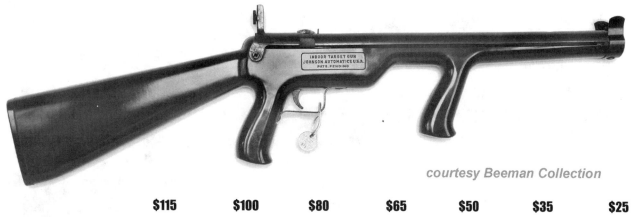

courtesy Beeman Collection

$115	$100	$80	$65	$50	$35	$25

Add 25% for original factory shooting range box.

This model was originally available with shooting gallery setup in factory cardboard box retailing for $15.

Johnson "Micro-Match Pellets" were precision made BB sized, ground ball bearings.

JONES, TIM

Current custom airgun maker located in Hawley, PA.

Designs typically include modern sporting rifles with Monte Carlo or thumbhole stocks or eighteenth century traditional ball reservoir guns. These Tim Jones rifles will usually retail in the $3,000-$6,000 range. Tim Jones air rifles are stamped "ETJ" on back of the action under the stock.

PISTOLS

.50 BALL RESERVOIR – .50 cal., PCP, SS.

courtesy Loke Collection

RIFLES

.20 CUSTOM – .20 cal., PCP, SS.

.22 CUSTOM – .22 cal., PCP, SS.

courtesy Howard Collection

.357 SPORTER – .357 cal., PCP, SS.

courtesy Howard Collection

.395 LONG RIFLE – .395 cal., PCP (3000 PSI), SS, 850 FPS, tiger maple Kentucky-styled stock, steel barrel and cylinder, cast brass furniture, 7.2 lbs. New circa 2000.

courtesy Fred Liady

.44 BALL RESERVOIR – .44 cal., ball reservoir, SS, octagon barrel, fixed sights, left hand full stock.

10MM SPORTER – 10mm cal., PCP, SS.

JONISKEIT

Current manufacturer Detlef Joniskeit located in Allmersbach im Tal, near Stuttgart., Germany.

Developed the Waffentechnik Joniskeit sidelever match air pistol in 1983.

PISTOLS

WAFFENTECHNIK JONISKEIT – .177 cal., SP, SL, SS, match grips, left-hand cocking lever lifts barrel for loading. A slightly improved version; the "Joniskeit Hurrican" was introduced in 1990. Special international distribution included Beeman Precision Airguns in USA ceased in the 1980s, but the pistol is still made to order. Experiments with the very low 120 m/s velocity of this pistol revealed that differences in lock time between low and high velocity pistols are far below the human reaction time, which is around 15 milliseconds.

Value is about $2,000.

JONISKEIT FINALE – .177 cal., SS, PCP and/or CO_2, many variations: Finale PCP, Finale CO_2, and Finale Super (hybrid) in various barrel lengths, compensators, etc. Works at 300 bar pressure.

Value from about $500 to $650, plus shipping and duty.

This model is a modified and vented version of the Tau 7 air pistol from Aeron, a daughter company of CZ in Czech Republic introduced in 1991. This model had a test review in 1991 VISIER magazine.

K SECTION

KWC (KIEN WELL TOY INDUSTRIAL CO. Ltd)

Current airgun and airsoft manufacturer located in Tainan, Taiwan. Currently imported and/or distributed by Palco Sports located in Maple Grove, MN and Air Venturi/Pyramyd Air, located in Solon, OH. Previously located in Warrensville Heights, OH.

KWC currently manufactures licensed copies of several trademarks including Sig Sauer pistols listed in the "S" section.

KAFEMA

GRADING	100%	95%	90%	80%	60%	40%	20%

Previous trademark of Industria Argentina, Buenos Aires, Argentina circa pre-WWII.

Research is ongoing with this trademark, and more information will be included both online and in future editions.

RIFLES

KAFEMA – .177 cal., BBC, SS, SP, hardwood stock with fluted forearm, no buttplate.

courtesy Beeman Collection

	100%	95%	90%	80%	60%	40%	20%
	$200	$175	$150	$115	$85	$50	N/A

KALAMAZOO

For information on Kalamazoo airguns, see Hawley in the "H" section.

KALIBRGUN

Current manufacturer located in Prague, Czech Republic. Currently imported by Airguns of Arizona, located in Gilbert, AZ and Top Gun-Airguns, Inc. located in Scottsdale, AZ.

KalibrGun manufactures a complete line of good quality pre-charged bullpup style air rifles with a wide variety of options. Configurations include hunting, sporting, and target. Please contact the company directly for more information, including pricing and U.S. availability (see Trademark Index).

RIFLES

CRICKET STANDARD BULLPUP – .177 or .22 cal., PCP, side lever action, 14-shot repeater, bullpup design, 17.5 in. shrouded barrel, blue finish, 30 ft./lbs., checkered walnut or black synthetic stock w/cheek piece and 4 magazine magnetic holder in stock, includes 2 magazines, 27 in. OAL, 7.75 lbs. Mfg. 2014-current.

MSR $1,549	$1,325	$1,150	$1,050	$850	$650	N/A	N/A

Add $300 for walnut stock.

CRICKET COMPACT BULLPUP – .177 or .22 cal., PCP, side lever action, 14-shot repeater, bullpup design, 15 in. shrouded barrel, blue finish, 30 ft./lbs., checkered walnut or black synthetic stock w/cheek piece and 4 magazine magnetic holder in stock, includes 2 magazines, 24.5 in. OAL, approx. 5.8 lbs. Mfg. 2014-current.

MSR $1,549	$1,325	$1,150	$1,050	$850	$650	N/A	N/A

Add $300 for walnut stock.

CRICKET .25 CAL. BULLPUP – .25 cal., PCP, side lever action, 12-shot repeater, bullpup design, 23.5 in. shrouded barrel, 47 ft./lbs., blue finsih, checkered hard wood stock w/cheek piece and 4 magazine magnetic holder in stock, includes 2 magazines, 33 in. OAL, 7.65 lbs. Mfg. 2014-current.

MSR $1,895	$1,600	$1,425	$1,300	$1,050	$800	N/A	N/A

CRICKET RIFLE – .22 cal., PCP, side lever action, 14-shot repeater, 20.5 in. barrel w/sound moderator, 32 ft./lbs., blue finish, ambidextrous walnut stock w/adj. cheek piece and butt plate, includes 2 magazines, 42 in. OAL, approx. 7 lbs. Mfg. 2014-current.

MSR $1,450	$1,225	$1,075	$975	$800	$600	N/A	N/A

KEENFIRE

For information on Keenfire airguns, see Anschütz in the "A" section.

KENDALL INTERNATIONAL

Previous importer and distributor located in Paris, KY. Kendall International previously imported Air Match air pistols. Information on firearms imported by Kendall International can be found in the *Blue Book of Gun Values* **by S.P. Fjestad (also online).**

For information on airguns imported by Kendall International, see Air Match in the "A" section.

KESSLER

Previous trade name of Kessler Rifle Company, located in Buffalo, Rochester, and Silver Creek, NY, circa 1948-1950.

Ref: AR 1: pp 18-21.

RIFLES

ONE-PIECE STOCK MODEL – .22 cal., swinging arm pump pneumatic, BA, SS, distinctive ball exhaust valve apparently descended from the Rochester airgun which in turn apparently derived from the Sheridan Super Grade, 36 in. OAL.

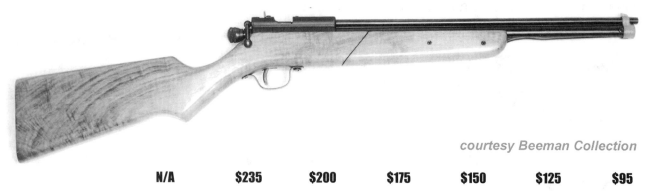

courtesy Beeman Collection

	N/A	$235	$200	$175	$150	$125	$95

Variation 1: Small Stock Version - black barrel, body tube, and cocking knob.

Variation 2: Large Stock Version - chromed barrel, body tube, and cocking knob. Large walnut stock with cheek piece; stock styled like Sheridan Super Grade.

TWO-PIECE STOCK MODEL – .177 cal., swinging arm pump pneumatic, BA, SS, same as Rochester air rifle with two piece stock (see Rochester in the "R" section), except stamped "KESSLER" on the barrel.

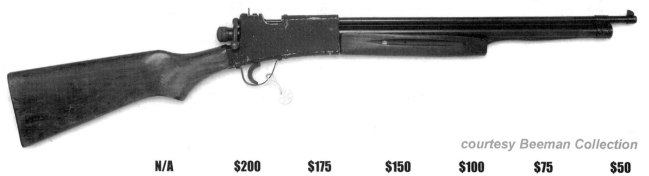

courtesy Beeman Collection

	N/A	$200	$175	$150	$100	$75	$50

Airgun smith and historian John Groenewold investigated the Rochester/Kessler arrangement in his local New York area. He reports that the Rochester Airgun Company was formed by a few ex-Crosman employees. The Rochester company and all of its assets, including parts and patent rights, were purchased by Kessler Gun Co. Kessler proceeded to use up the Rochester parts making Rochester-style airguns and marking some of the barrels with the Kessler name. Some of these guns have the Rochester name on a hidden part of the barrel, and the name Kessler, evidently stamped later, on the exposed part. There are legitimate Rochester airguns and legitimate Kessler airguns of identical design and appearance. Numrich Arms purchased Kessler when they went out of business and may still have some parts for sale (including some of the earlier Rochester parts).

KING

For information on King airguns, see Markham-King in the "M" section.

KOFFMANZ

For information on Koffmanz airguns, see Philippine Airguns in the "P" section.

GRADING	100%	95%	90%	80%	60%	40%	20%

KRAL

Current manufacturer located in Konya, Turkey. No current U.S. importation.

Kral Av Sanayi manufactures a line of air rifles. Please contact the company directly for more information on their models, U.S. pricing, and availability (see Trademark Index).

KRICO

Current trademark manufactured by Kriegeskorte Handels GmbH Co, located in Pyrbaum, Germany. Previously located in Stuttgart-Hedelfingen, Germany.

Manufacturers of spring piston air rifles after WWII and quality firearms since the mid-1950s. Krico firearms previously were imported by Beeman Precision Arms Inc., located in Santa Rosa, CA in the 1980s. Only one basic model of airgun was made circa 1946-1953.

For more information and current pricing on both new and used Krico firearms, please refer to the *Blue Book of Gun Values* by S.P. Fjestad (also available online).

RIFLES

MODEL LG 1 – .177 or .22 cal., BBC, SP, SS, rifled barrel, grooved forearm, no buttplate.

courtesy Beeman Collection

	N/A	$300	$250	$200	$150	$100	$75

MODEL LG 1S – .177 or .22 cal., BBC, SP, SS, rifled barrel, buttplate, checkered pistol grip and grooved forearm.

	N/A	$350	$300	$250	$200	$150	$100

MODEL LG 1 LUXUS – .177 cal. only, BBC, SP, SS, rifled barrel, buttplate, checkered pistol grip, heavily checkered grooved forearm, heavy stock, sights.

	N/A	$400	$350	$300	$250	$200	$150

KÜNG (KUENG) AIRGUNS

Current tradename of Dan Küng (Kueng) located in Basel, Switzerland. No current U.S. importation.

Working in Switzerland, Dan Kueng builds high-end, side-lever, spring-piston, recoilless magnum air rifles and is in the final stages of developing a spring piston air pistol that will produce over 10 ft./lb. ME. His website, at www.blueline-studios.com/kuengairguns.com, gives a great deal of technical airgun information and illustrates the products. Production is based almost entirely on components made in-house, thus production is still very limited. Costs up to $6,000 for guns like those illustrated on the website are expected to be considerably reduced.

KYNOCH LIMITED

Current ammunition manufacturer located in Witton, Brimingham, Warwickshire England, founded in 1862.

Manufacturers of sporting rifle and shotgun cartridges, previously produced the Swift air rifle. Also produced the Mitre airgun slug and the Lion, Match, and Witton diabolo airgun pellets.

RIFLE

SWIFT – .177 or .25 cal., BBC, SP, SS, snap hook on each side of the breech, plain walnut buttstock. Circa 1908.

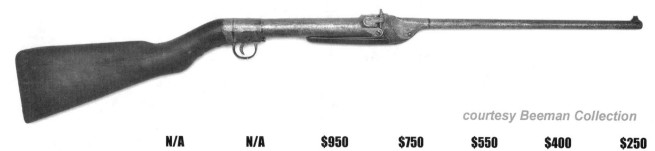

courtesy Beeman Collection

	N/A	N/A	$950	$750	$550	$400	$250

This model was based on the 1906 patents of George Hookham and Edward Jones.

Go to **NRASTANDANDFIGHT.COM** to hear the story that the media ignores and join the NRA to strengthen the voice of all gun owners.

WWW.NRASTANDANDFIGHT.COM

L SECTION

LD AIRGUNS

Previous manufacturer located in Mandaluyong City, Manila, Philippines 1968-2001.

As discussed in the Philippine Airguns section of this guide, the unexpected development of powerful, bulk-fill CO_2 guns for hunting primarily was due to one man, president/dictator Ferdinand Edralin Marcos, who declared martial law and outlawed civilian firearms in the Philippines in 1972.

There had been a few airgun makers around before martial law hit, but one soon came to the foreground. That was the shop of Eldyfonso Cardoniga which had opened in 1968 in Mandaluyong City, a part of metropolitan Manila.

Values have yet to be established for many LD airguns, but in the Philippines it is said that excellent specimens sell for about triple their original cost. Good specimens are about double and poor specimens go for about their original cost.

We felt that it was important to chronicle this amazing line of airguns before the information faded away. Having jumped in and made this first listing, we recognized that much of this information needs improvement and augmentation. This must not be considered as a complete nor final list. We actively solicit your positive input at guns@bluebookinc.com.

The authors and the publisher wish to thank Guillermo Sylianteng Jr. and Mandy Cardoniga for their assistance with this section.

LD HISTORY

Eldyfonso Cardoniga (or "Eldy" or just "LD") was born in 1930 in Navotas, Rizal, then a fishing port north of Manila. Reportedly, he made his first airgun at eight years of age by welding together various worn out guns. He studied architecture at the excellent Mapua University in Manila and worked as an architectural assistant for a while, and then as a skilled mechanic and welder. He started the LD airgun factory in 1968 from a design that he had developed. This was the LD 380, a combo rifle/shotgun. The key features were the multi-caliber barrel system, a breech block that swings to the side for loading, and an external hammer for releasing the exhaust valve. This breech system, now known as the "hammer swing action," has been basic to perhaps most of the Philippine airguns. To overcome the power limits of the Crosman hammer-valve system, the LD designs used a larger valve and valve stem activated by a stronger and heavier hammer arrangement. The result was exactly what the market needed: a dependable airgun that was economical to produce and use and of unprecedented POWER! [1]

Of the Philippine airguns, those made by LD certainly are the best known and among the very best quality. The innovation represented by the LD airguns is well demonstrated by the "Rancher" version of the LD 380S. This .50 caliber air rifle is provided with insert barrels of several calibers for pellets, balls, darts, arrows, spears, and shot charges. Some versions of this model were equipped with spinning reels, from the fishing equipment trade, to provide for retrieval of arrows and spears. The .50 caliber barrel could fire large tranquilizer syringes or even fearful "torpedoes" consisting of finned brass projectiles containing a shaped charge of TNT! When Eldy visited the Beemans in California in the 1980s he told us that these torpedoes were very effective, but presented the problem of sometimes "blowing away one quarter of the water buffalo!" (Times have changed - note: he had some of these loaded torpedoes with him, carried on the plane in his coat pocket!)

The factory grew rapidly and Eldy brought in his son Mandy as an apprentice and then as a partner. As his skill grew, Mandy developed the MC TOPGUN line of precision match guns and moved to a nearby separate shop to concentrate on these models. However, this market was too limited due to the high cost of the guns and the diminished ranks of match shooters. He returned to work with his father on the powerful hunting guns and inherited the shop when Eldy passed away in September 1998. During those thirty years, Eldy is credited with at least thirty airgun designs, including several full auto ball shooters. The LD airguns developed and maintained a reputation as dependable, innovative, and powerful. The quality of the rifling in LD guns is believed to be due to the barrels being imported from a precision barrel manufacturer in Japan.

Mandy Cardoniga, now a master gunmaker in his own right, continued to produce LD airguns until sometime in 2001 when the tooling was changed to produce stainless steel industrial accessories, especially equipment for the baking industry. The LD airguns became history.

[1] Eldy reported that one tuned specimen fired a single charge of three .380 cal. steel balls, combined wgt 180+ grains of 800 FPS MV. Three groups of three balls all punched through both sides of a 55 gallon steel drum (18 ga.) at 5 meters. Used with #4 or #6 lead shot for duck hunting.

AIRGUN PRODUCTION

All Philippine hunting airguns are relatively scarce. Production ran from an average of less than one hundred guns per month for LD, evidently the largest maker, down to a few guns a month from a custom maker such as JBC. Perhaps 70% to 99% of most production runs stayed in the Philippines. Most American and European airgun factories, and large importers, figure on several thousand or tens of thousands of guns per month.

GRADING	100%	95%	90%	80%	60%	40%	20%

PISTOLS

LD M45 – .22 cal., CO_2 bulk fill, SS, 4.3 in. rifled brass barrel, slide action and manual safety, Narra wood grips, black nickel or satin nickel finish, adj. sights, 8 in. OAL, 2.5 lbs. Mfg. 1987.

courtesy Howard Collection

	$295	$250	$205	$170	$135	$90	$60

Add 20% for Colt 80 Mark V markings.

This model is a close replica of the M1911A1 Colt U.S. military pistol.

LD M45 REPEATER – .25 cal., CO_2 bulk fill, 4.3 in. rifled brass barrel, slide action and manual safety, spring-fed magazine in slide for 6-8 .25 in. ball bearings or #3 lead buck shot balls, manual repeating action, Narra wood grips, black nickel or satin nickel finish, adj. sights, 8 in. OAL, 2.5 lbs. Mfg. circa 1990s.

	$400	$325	$275	$230	$180	$120	$80

This model is a close replica of the M1911A1 Colt U.S. military pistol.

LD BERETTA 9M – .22 cal., CO_2 bulk fill, SS, slide action and manual safety, 4.3 in. rifled brass barrel, Narra wood grips, black nickel or satin nickel finish, adj. sights, 8 in. OAL, 2.7 lbs. Mfg. circa 1990s. Approx. 200 mfg.

courtesy Howard Collection

	$350	$300	$245	$205	$160	$105	$70

This model is a close replica of the Beretta 92SB-F U.S. military pistol.

LD GLOCK – .22 cal., CO_2 bulk fill, SS, close replica of Glock Model 19 semi-auto pistol, slide action like original firearm, blued steel slide, polymer frame, rifled brass BBL, exact copy of Glock logo on LHS grip, shipped in actual Glock plastic case, 7.4 in. OAL, 2.2 lbs. Mfg. circa 1990s. Approx. 30 mfg.

courtesy Howard Collection

	$295	$250	$205	$170	$135	$90	$60

Subtract 15% for "politically correct" specimens with Glock logo not legible.

GRADING	100%	95%	90%	80%	60%	40%	20%

LD LONG PISTOL (REPEATER) – .22/.380 cal. combo, CO_2 bulk fill, hammer swing action, adj. trigger, deluxe Narra grip with forearm, dark wood grip cap, black nickel finish, smoothbore .380 shot barrel with rifled brass barrel .22 cal. insert, (fires pellets, lead or steel balls, shot cartridges, short arrows, and spears, etc.), threaded muzzle ring for suppressor and/or barrel retaining insert, spring-fed tubular magazine LHS for about ten .22 cal. lead balls, see-through scope mounts, 21.1 in. OAL, 3.6 lbs.

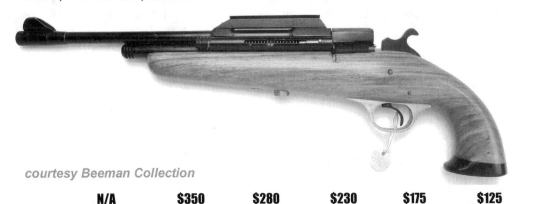

courtesy Beeman Collection

	N/A	$350	$280	$230	$175	$125	$70

LD LONG PISTOL (SINGLE SHOT) – .177/.380 cal. combo, CO_2 bulk fill, hammer swing action, SS, adj. trigger, deluxe Narra grip with forearm, dark grip cap, black nickel finish, smoothbore .380 shot barrel rifled brass barrel .177 cal. insert (fires pellets, lead or steel balls, shot cartridges, short arrows, and spears, etc.), threaded muzzle ring for suppressor and/or barrel retaining insert, regular scope base, 20 in. OAL, 2.7 lbs.

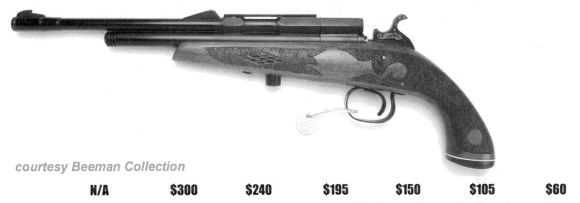

courtesy Beeman Collection

	N/A	$300	$240	$195	$150	$105	$60

LD M100 – .22/.380 cal. combo, CO_2 bulk fill, hammer swing action, SS, adj. trigger, deluxe Narra grip with forearm, dark grip cap, black nickel finish, smoothbore .380 shot rifled brass barrel, .22 cal. friction-fit insert (fires pellets, lead or steel balls, shot cartridges, short arrows, and spears, etc.), no scope base, extended gas tube under barrel gives over/under appearance, heavy aluminum trigger guard, nickel satin finish, 17.1 in. OAL, 2.6 lbs.

courtesy Beeman Collection

	N/A	$275	$220	$180	$135	$95	$55

LD MC 87 – target pistol, 700 mfg.

No other information or values available at this time.

RIFLES

Note: Some of the guns listed below may be combination (combo) calibers, but this could not be determined at time of writing.
Degrees of metal engraving, stock shaping, stock decorations, and special features will affect pricing from 10% to 100%.

GRADING	100%	95%	90%	80%	60%	40%	20%

LD LC 3000 – .22 cal., CO_2 bulk fill, SS, hammer swing action, two-stage trigger, double cock hammer, deluxe Narra Monte Carlo stock, ambidextrous cheek pieces, rubber buttplate, black nickel or satin nickel finish, 27 in. rifled brass barrel, 42 in. OAL.

 No other information or values available at time of printing.

LD M 300 M – .22/.380 cal. combo, CO_2 bulk fill, SS, hammer swing action, two-stage trigger, double cock hammer, gas tube extended to end of barrel, deluxe Narra Monte Carlo stock, thumbhole grip (for RH only), ambidextrous cheek pieces, rubber buttplate, smoothbore .380 shot barrel rifled brass barrel .22 cal. insert (fires pellets, lead or steel balls, shot cartridges, short arrows and spears, etc.), threaded muzzle ring for suppressor and/or barrel retaining insert, black nickel or satin nickel finish, 42.8 in. OAL, 5.8 lbs.

	N/A	$1,000	$800	$650	$500	$350	$200

LD 500 – hunting rifle.

 No other information or values available at time of printing.

LD STINGER – .22 cal., CO_2 bulk fill, SS, SL action, adj. power, exotic carbine-style Narra stock like a pistol with shoulder stock, separate Narra forearm, adj. open sights and scope grooves, 19 in. rifled brass barrel, gold, black nickel, or satin nickel finish, 42 in. OAL, 11 lbs. 300 mfg.

 No other information or values available at time of printing.

LD MATCH – .177 cal., CO_2 bulk fill, SS, hammer swing or SL action, micrometer aperture sights, Narra match stock with adj. high cheek piece and buttplate, 27 in. rifled brass barrel, 42 in. OAL, 11 lbs.

 No other information or values available at time of printing.

LD 600 SPORTER – .177 or .22 cal., CO_2 bulk fill, SS, hammer swing action, adj. two-stage trigger, adj. power, deluxe Narra Monte Carlo stock, rubber buttplate, black nickel or satin nickel finish, 27 in. rifled brass barrel, 44 in. OAL.

 No other information or values available at time of printing.

LD SPORTER – .22 cal., CO_2 bulk fill, SS, hammer swing or SL action, adj. trigger, deluxe Narra Monte Carlo stock, rubber buttplate, black nickel finish, 24 in. rifled brass barrel, 42 in. OAL, 5.5 lbs.

 No other information or values available at time of printing.

LD 380/380S (SPECIAL) – evidently all variations had these features in common: multiple caliber barrel inserts, CO_2 bulk fill, SS, hammer swing action, two-stage trigger, double cock hammer, deluxe Narra Monte Carlo stock with rubber buttplate and sling swivels, black nickel or satin nickel finish, rifled brass barrel insert, threaded muzzle ring for suppressor and/or barrel retaining insert.

courtesy Beeman Collection

 This was Eldy's first and highest production model. During the thirty years of production from 1966 to 1996, 17,500 guns were produced. This model probably had more variations and custom features than any other model. Two of the many variations suggest the range of features, calibers, size, and weights possible.

* ***LD 380/380S (Special) Rancher*** – four caliber combo: .50 smoothbore, .380 smoothbore insert, .22 rifled insert, .177 rifled insert cal., laminated two-tone Narra stock with RH cheek piece and RH Wundhammer swell grip, standard scope mount base, 44.6 in. OAL, 9 lbs.

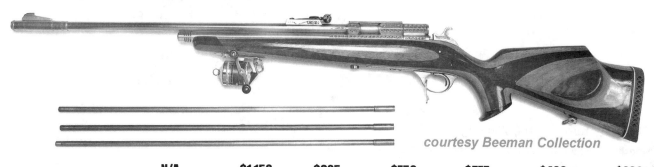

courtesy Beeman Collection

	N/A	$1,150	$925	$750	$575	$400	$230

Add 20% for thumbhole stock.
Subtract 20% if stock is not laminated.
Add 50% for .50 caliber (less than one hundred were made).

GRADING	100%	95%	90%	80%	60%	40%	20%

This caliber range gave the Rancher amazing flexibility: it could project .177 or .22 cal. pellets, .38 cal. shot charges, .38 cal. bullets or lead or steel balls, arrows without fletching, expanding tip spears, multi-prong spears, .50 in. tranquilizer darts, and even shaped TNT charges in brass "torpedoes." A spinning reel mounted under the forearm enhanced fishing and frog hunting. (Perhaps less than five hundred of this Special variation were produced. Many were elaborately engraved and given special stock checkering and treatment.)

* ***LD 380/380S (Special) Barbarella*** – three caliber combo: .380 smoothbore, .22 cal. rifled insert, .177 cal. rifled insert. Could fire: .177 or .22 cal. pellets, .38 cal. shot charges, .38 cal. bullets or lead balls, arrows w/o fletching, expanding tip spears, and multi-prong spears, SS, ambidextrous checkered Narra stock with both cheek pieces and thumbhole grip (top of the stock has a saddle-like appearance), metal engraving, blackened design areas on the stock, see-through scope mount base, 41.5 in. OAL, 6.8 lbs.

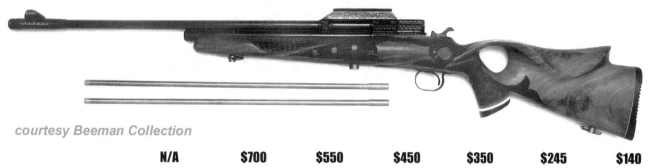

courtesy Beeman Collection

	N/A	$700	$550	$450	$350	$245	$140

Subtract 30% for single caliber (.22, .25, or .380).
Subtract 20% for no thumbhole.
Add 30% for retractable wire stock.

LD 300 SS PHANTOM – hunting rifle. 2,500 mfg.

No other information or values available at time of printing.

LD 380 SS PHANTOM – .22 cal., CO_2 bulk fill, SS, hammer swing action, 22 in. rifled barrel, two-stage trigger, double cock hammer, Narra cruiser-style stock ends at pistol grip, retractable stainless steel folding wire shoulder stock, sling swivels, black nickel or satin nickel finish, see-through scope base, muzzle ring covers suppressor threads, 27 in. OAL, retracted. 5,000 mfg.

courtesy Howard Collection

	N/A	$600	$475	$400	$300	$210	$120

LD 700 – .32 or .40 (10 mm) cal., CO_2 bulk fill, BA, SS, styled after Remington Model 700 big bore rifle, rifled, deluxe Narra stock with semi-ambidextrous cheek piece, threaded for suppressor, satin nickel finish, manual safety, 39.3 in. OAL, 6.6 lbs. 24 units made (17 RH 10mm, 4 LH 10mm, 1 RH .32, 2 LH .32) - all to order, may not be marked LD.

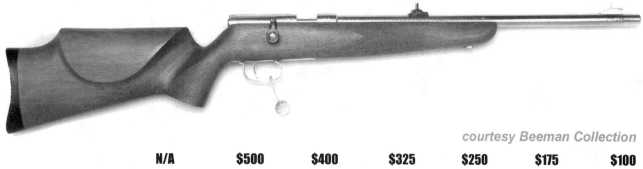

courtesy Beeman Collection

	N/A	$500	$400	$325	$250	$175	$100

Add 25% for highly engraved.
Add 50% for PCP (only one was made).

Suppressor requires $200 Federal Transfer Tax in USA.

GRADING	100%	95%	90%	80%	60%	40%	20%

LD MC 2400 – bolt action sporter rifle. 320 mfg.

   No other information or values available at time of printing.

LD MC 2800 – lever action sporter rifle. 180 mfg.

   No other information or values available at time of printing.

LD HOME DEFENSE REPEATER – .380/.22 cal. combo., CO_2 bulk fill, SS, hammer swing action, probably seven-shot, 24 in. barrel with .22 cal. rifled insert, .380 steel ball smoothbore manual repeater, spring-fed, tubular magazine attached along left side of barrel, not marked, Cruiser-style stock with pistol grip and extendable heavy wire shoulder stock, machined trigger guard, threaded muzzle cap, light engraving plus recessed panels of unique engraving designs, open sights, no scope grooves, 41.1 in. OAL (32.8 in. retracted), 6.7 lbs.

courtesy Beeman Collection

	N/A	$700	$550	$450	$350	$245	$140

   Costs 45% more than standard LD 380.

   This model has been confirmed by Mandy Cardoniga as the work of Eldy Cardoniga.

LD SLIDE ACTION REPEATER – .22 (and .25 and .380?) cal. ball repeater, CO_2 bulk fill, slide action, 22.5 in. barrel, spring-fed, fixed tubular magazine cal. 10 balls, two-stage trigger, double cock hammer, Narra Monte Carlo stock with ambidextrous cheek pieces, rubber buttplate, sling swivels on Narra wood buttstock and separate wood cocking slide, satin nickel finish, scope grooves, cast aluminum trigger guard, light engraving plus recessed panels of unique engraving designs, 39.5 in. OAL, 6.1 lbs. Rare, less than 1,500 total mfg. Most models stayed in the Philippines. Circa 1980s.

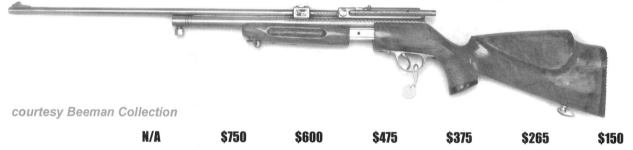

courtesy Beeman Collection

	N/A	$750	$600	$475	$375	$265	$150

   While not marked, this model has been confirmed by Mandy Cardoniga as work of Eldy Cardoniga.

SHOTGUNS

   See also Rifles - the .380 and .50 cal. models served as both shotguns and rifles.

LD 20 GAUGE – 20 ga., CO_2 bulk fill, SB shotgun, 29.8 in. barrel, block hammer action, scope rails, nickel black finish, uses 1.8 in. aluminum tubes with wad in each end to hold shot, Narra stock with skip checkering, Wundhammer swell RHS pistol grip, 46 in. OAL, approx. 7 lbs.

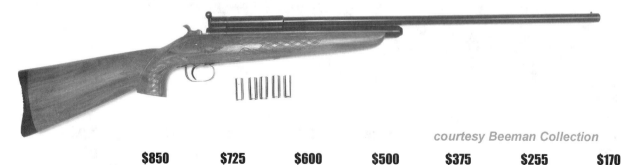

courtesy Beeman Collection

$850	$725	$600	$500	$375	$255	$170

   Add 50% for double barrels (only four were made).
   Add 10% for rifled barrel inserts (.22, .32, .38, and .40 cal.).

   Only 18 made, plus four double barrel specimens. All special order, therefore not marked with LD mark.

GRADING	100%	95%	90%	80%	60%	40%	20%

LANGENHAN

Previous manufacturer of firearms and airguns. Founded by Valentin Friedrich Langenhan in Zella Mehlis, Germany in 1842. Moved to adjacent Zella St. Blasii in 1855.

About 1900, Langenhan started production of airguns, apparently making huge numbers of them under a wide variety of its own and private labels. The most definitive mark is FLZ (i.e. Friedrich Langenhan in Zella-Mehlis) with the letters in a three-segmented circle. Other labels include Ace, Favorit, and FL. Among the most commonly encountered Langenhan airguns are the militia-style air rifles (commonly imported into England from Germany by Martin Pulverman & Company of London circa 1900) and the rifle-like break-barrel, spring-piston FLZ pistols, made MFG. 1927-1940, 2nd variation (pictured) 1937-1940. Langenhan finally succumbed to competition from Mayer und Grammelspacher, Weihrauch, Haenel, etc.

The FLZ pistols generally sell in the $200 range; more for excellent specimens. (The FLZ air pistols range from about 1.6 to 1.9 lbs, and from about 16.7-18.0 in. OAL). The British Cub, which may have been made by another maker for Langenhan, will have a retail value in the $150 range for very good specimens. Ref: AGNR - Oct. 1985.

courtesy Beeman Collection

LARC

Previous trade name of LARC International located in Miami, FL.

Previous manufacturer of freon-charged, fully automatic BB sub-machine guns designed by LARC president Russell Clifford circa 1974-1980.

RIFLES

MODEL 19A – BB/.174 cal., powered from removable can of freon gas, fully automatic, 3000-round gravity-fed magazine, rate of fire approx. 2500 RPM, 350 FPS, approx. range 120 yards, plastic body, aluminum smoothbore barrel black with white or red/brown insert plates, early models may have heavy wire shoulder stock, fake suppressor, later models with plastic shoulder stock bar, 23.5-33 in. OAL, approx. 1 lb.

courtesy Beeman Collection

$70	$60	$50	$40	$30	N/A	N/A

Add 150% for early Model 19 with pressure hose and hose for BB magazine.
Add 100% for metal body.
Add 20% for fitted case.

LINCOLN JEFFRIES

Previous designer and gunmaker located in Birmingham, England circa 1873-1930s.

The authors and publisher wish to thank Mr. John Groenwold and John Atkins for valuable assistance with the following information in this section of the *Blue Book of Airguns*. Lincoln Jeffries was born in Norfolk, England in 1847. By 1873 he had established a well regarded gun business in Birmingham producing shotguns and breech loading and muzzle loading air canes. The firm also put their name on a variety of imported break barrel, smoothbore air rifles - generally Gem-style copies of Haviland & Gunn designs and rifled militia-style (not military!) airguns. In 1904, he patented a fixed-barrel, under-lever, tap-loading, rifled air rifle which was the forerunner of the enormously successful

GRADING	100%	95%	90%	80%	60%	40%	20%

BSA underlever air rifles. These rifles were manufactured for Jeffries by the Birmingham Small Arms factory. They were branded Lincoln Jeffries and later as BSA. These airguns are discussed and listed in the BSA section.

The Lincoln Jeffries firm continued to market the Lincoln Jeffries air rifles until the line of models came completely under the BSA label. By 1921, Lincoln Jeffries, Jr. had been issued a patent for a Lincoln air pistol with the mainspring housed in the gun's grip. Two versions of this unusual, all-metal air pistol were produced in very small numbers during the 1920s, with a few special pistols being individually made by Lincoln Jeffries, Jr. until circa 1927. The first version had a lever in the back of the grip which was pulled down to compress the mainspring and cock the gun. The second type was a barrel cocking air pistol which used the forward part of the trigger guard as a link to compress the mainspring. This was based on the American Haviland and Gunn patent. The Walther LP52 and LP53 air pistols were clearly derived from this gun. The all-metal Lincoln differed from the Walther mainly by not having grip plates and in having an exposed slot in the forward part of the grip which could take flesh samples from a shooter unlucky enough to have his fingertips in that groove when the piston head rushed upward during firing.

The grandsons of Lincoln Jeffries, Messrs. A.H. Jeffries, and L.G. Jeffries were still operating the company in the 1990s, but now only to produce Marksman brand airgun pellets. Ref: *Guns Review*, Dec. 87.

PISTOLS

BISLEY BACKSTRAP COCKING MODEL – .177 cal., SP, SS, all-metal construction, fixed trigger guard, lever along backstrap of grip for cocking mainspring in the grip, blue or nickle finish, rotary or side latch for locking cocking lever. Approx. 150 mfg. 1911 to the early 1920s. Ref: AG. Small and Large size variants.

courtesy Beeman Collection

N/A	$3,000	$2,400	$1,950	$1,500	$1,050	$600

Add 20% for rotary lock variant.

A handful of other variations exist. These may be experimental, special order, or prototypes. SN 3 has grip safety on forward side of grip and dull nickel finish. A larger specimen based on the 1910-11 patents, with top loading tap, brass frame, and walnut grip plates, is known. Values of these special forms cannot be estimated at this time.

BARREL-COCKING MODEL – .177 cal. (one known in .22 cal.), BBC, SP, SS, all-metal construction, trigger guard is cocking link between barrel and piston assembly in grip. Standard version: .177 cal., large knurled screw head on take-down screw linking barrel block and cocking arm, receiver steps up in thickness just above trigger, spring chamber cap top at angle to barrel, thick trigger, crowded trigger guard area, point on inside of trigger guard ahead of trigger. Grip cylinder typically about 5.5 in., but several specimens with extended cylinders known. Rare. Large version: .177 cal., receiver uniform in thickness, spring chamber cap top in line with axis of barrel, thin trigger, uncrowded trigger guard area, trigger guard/cocking lever with only smooth curves, grip cylinder over 5.5 in. long, max. (diagonal) OAL about 14.9 in. Small head on takedown screw. Very rare. Giant version: .177 and .22 cal., larger diameter grip cylinder, 15.5 in. max. OAL. Extremely rare, only two known in .22 cal. approx. 1,500 mfg. circa 1921-1930. Ref: AG.

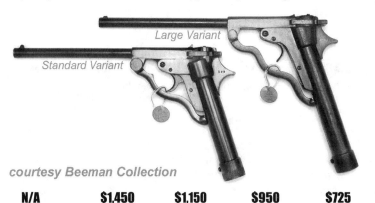

Large Variant

Standard Variant

courtesy Beeman Collection

N/A	$1,450	$1,150	$950	$725	$500	$290

Add 30% for standard versions with extended grip cylinder.
Add 30% for large version.

Other experimental and special order versions are known. Values are unestimated.

GRADING	100%	95%	90%	80%	60%	40%	20%

SCOUT MODEL – .177 cal., push barrel cocking, smooth bore, blue or nickel finish, rubber grips. Mfg. 1922-26.

courtesy Loke Collection

N/A	$500	$400	$325	$250	$175	$100

Add 20% for nickel finish.

RIFLES

All rifles sold by Lincoln Jeffries were rifled and stamped "H THE AIR RIFLE" or "L THE LINCOLN AIR RIFLE". The meaning of the "H" and "L" letters has yet to be clearly determined. The guns stamped "H" are larger than the guns stamped "L", but the theory that these letters refer to "Heavy" and "Light" is not strong. All are single shot.

GEM STYLE - H THE AIR RIFLE/L THE LINCOLN AIR RIFLE – various cals., SS, BBC, SP, mainspring in grip similar to Haviland and Gunn air rifle design, from various European makers, sizes varied. Mfg. late 1800s-very early 1900s.

	$300	$250	$200	$160	$120	$90	$60

MILITIA STYLE - H THE AIR RIFLE/L THE LINCOLN AIR RIFLE – various cals., BBC, SS, SP, from various European makers, sizes varied. Mfg. late 1800s and first few years of 1900s.

courtesy Beeman Collection

	$300	$250	$200	$160	$120	$90	$50

Although Militia actually was a Langenhan/Pulvermann air rifle brand or model, "Militia" is commonly used to represent a barrel cocking type of air rifle that does not have wood forward of the grip area), sizes varied. Mfg. late 1800s and first few years of 1900s.

UNDERLEVERS - H THE AIR RIFLE/L THE LINCOLN AIR RIFLE – various cals., SS, SP, UL (bayonet style), made on the Lincoln Jeffries 1904 Patent by BSA and sold as Lincoln Jeffries air rifles (as sold by BSA as The BSA Air Rifle - see BSA in the "B" section), faucet tap loading. The bayonet type underlever was the original Lincoln Jeffries design. The front end of this lever bears a small handle, or "bayonet" dropping down from, but parallel to the barrel. Original bayonet underlevers just had a bend where they engaged the latch mechanism. Variation H: The Air Rifle model, marked "H", 43.5 in. OAL. Mfg. 1904-1908. Variation L: The Lincoln Air Rifle, 39 in. OAL, marked "L", sometimes referred to as the "Ladies" or "Light" version. Mfg. 1906-1908.

courtesy Beeman Collection

	$500	$450	$400	$325	$275	$200	$100

LINDNER

Previous manufacturer of a uniquely designed American air pistol, probably Lindner & Molo, New York, N.Y. Based on U.S Patent No. 37,173 issued to E. Lindner on Dec. 16, 1862.

GRADING	100%	95%	90%	80%	60%	40%	20%

PISTOL

LINDNER – .23 cal., SS, SP, system cocked by a unique, internally hinged cocking lever which wraps all around the back, bottom, and front of the pistol grip, brass receiver, tip up smoothbore brass 5.4 in. octagonal barrel, fine wood grips, no markings, 13 in. OAL.

courtesy Beeman Collection

Scarcity precludes accurate pricing.

LOGUN

Previous manufacturer located in Willenhall, West Midlands, UK beginning 1998-circa 2012. Previously distributed by Pyramyd Air Inc. located in Warrensville Hts, OH, Straight Shooters Precision Airguns located in St. Cloud, MN, and Crosman Corporation located in Bloomfield, NY.

RIFLES

AXSOR – .177 or .22 cal., PCP, Supa Glide BA, 1000 FPS, 8-shot rotary magazine, 19.5 in. rifled steel barrel, equipped for scope mounts, two-stage adj. trigger, blue finish, English gloss walnut Monte Carlo stock, checkered grip and forearm (with pressure gauge), rubber recoil pad, 40 in. OAL, 6.8 lbs. Mfg. 2004-disc.

	100%	95%	90%	80%	60%	40%	20%
	$850	$695	$550	N/A	N/A	N/A	N/A

While first advertised during 2001, this model was first imported into the USA during 2004.

DOMIN8OR – .177 or .22 cal., PCP, Side Speed side lever action, 8-shot rotary mag., 19.7 in. rifled steel barrel, two-stage adj. trigger, equipped for scope mounts, blue finish, checkered synthetic thumbhole stock, rubber recoil pad, 490cc Buddy Bottle encased in butt stock, 40.5 in. OAL, 5.3 lbs. Mfg. 2004-disc.

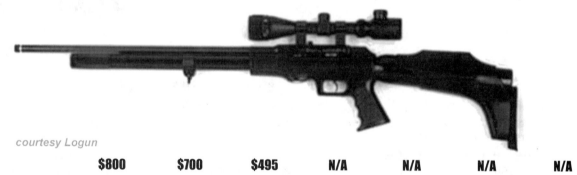

courtesy Logun

	100%	95%	90%	80%	60%	40%	20%
	$800	$700	$495	N/A	N/A	N/A	N/A

EAGLE – .177 or .22 cal., PCP, ambidextrous Versa Glide action, SS or eight-shot manual mag., two-stage adj. trigger, equipped for scope mounts, 17.5 in. rifled steel barrel, blue finish, molded synthetic thumbhole PG stock, rubber recoil pad, 36 in. OAL, 5.6 lbs. Mfg. 2005-disc.

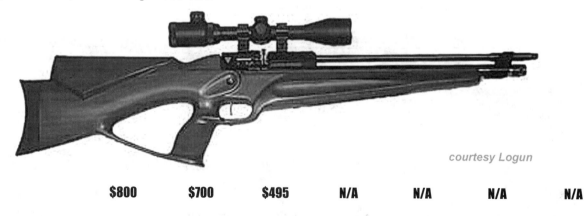

courtesy Logun

	100%	95%	90%	80%	60%	40%	20%
	$800	$700	$495	N/A	N/A	N/A	N/A

GRADING	100%	95%	90%	80%	60%	40%	20%

GEMINI – .177 or .22 cal., PCP, BA, multi-shot magazine (two shots: .177 or .22), equipped for scope mounts, English gloss walnut Monte Carlo stock, checkered grip and forearm, rubber recoil pad, 37.75 in. OAL, 7.1 lbs.

	$695	$595	$495	N/A	N/A	N/A	N/A

GLADI8OR – .177 or .22 cal., PCP, Side Speed side lever action, 8-shot rotary mag., 19.7 in. rifled steel barrel, two-stage adj. trigger, equipped for scope mounts, blue finish, checkered pistol grip, rubber recoil pad, 490cc Buddy Bottle, 41.5 in. OAL, 7.8 lbs. New 2004.

courtesy Logun

	$950	$850	$595	N/A	N/A	N/A	N/A

LG-MKII PROFESSIONAL – .177 or .22 cal., PCP, Supa Glide BA, 1050 FPS, 9-shot inline magazine, 21 1/4 in. rifled steel barrel, blue finish, equipped for scope mounts, English gloss walnut Monte Carlo stock, checkered grip and forearm (with pressure gauge), rubber recoil pad, 45 in. OAL, 8.25 lbs. Mfg. 2004-disc.

courtesy Logun

	$1,425	$1,225	$995	N/A	N/A	N/A	N/A

While first advertised during 2001, this model was first imported into the USA during 2004.

S-16s (SWEET SIXTEEN) – .22 cal., PCP, Supa-Speed BA, 400cc buddy bottle, 16-shot (two eight-shot rotary) mag., 14.5 in. rifled steel shrouded barrel, equipped for scope mounts, two-stage adj. trigger, blue finish, checkered synthetic grip and forearm (with pressure gauge), cross over safety, 34.5-38 in. OAL, 8.5 lbs. Mfg. 2004-disc.

	$800	$725	$575	N/A	N/A	N/A	N/A

SOLO – .177 or .22 cal., SS or 8-shot manual mag., PCP, BA, equipped for scope mounts, checkered English gloss walnut Monte Carlo stock, rubber recoil pad, 41 in. OAL, 6.1 lbs.

	$575	$495	$395	N/A	N/A	N/A	N/A

LUCZNIK

Previous tradename probably used by the Polish state firearms company, Zaklady Metalowe Lucznik.

As with most Iron Curtain guns, the construction is more sturdy than precise. The guns are infamous for unavailability of parts. Formerly imported into UK by Viking Arms Company, although dates are not known.

PISTOLS

PREDOM-LUCZNIK 170 – .177 cal., BBC, SP, SS, 12.2 in. OAL, 2.6 lbs. Mfg. circa 1975-1985.

	N/A	$125	$100	$80	$60	$45	$25

Add 10% for factory box with test target.

This model is a copy of the Walther LP 53.

GRADING	100%	95%	90%	80%	60%	40%	20%

RIFLES

MODEL 87 – .177 cal., BBC, SP, SS, simple hardwood stock with fluted forearm.

courtesy Beeman Collection

	$100	$85	$70	$60	$45	$30	$20

MODEL 141 – .177 cal., BBC, SP, SS, 14.5 in. rifled steel barrel, adj. rear sight, hardwood stock with fluted forearm, 36.5 in. OAL. Mfg. 1970s.

	$80	$70	$55	$45	$35	$25	$15

MODEL 188 – .177 cal., BBC, SP, SS, large hardwood stock with cheek piece and grooved forearm.

	$220	$185	$155	$130	$100	$65	$45

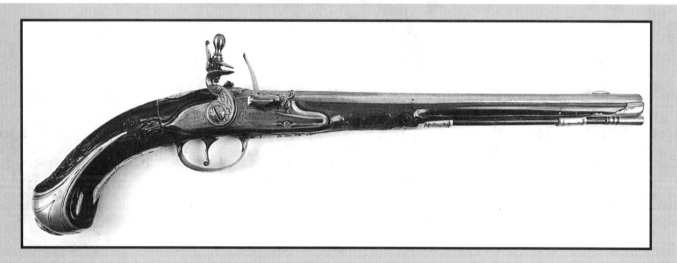

An elegant pneumatic pistol for a wealthy or royal Czech gentleman of the 1690 to 1730 period. This is a pistol version of a butt reservoir air rifle; the pistol grip is the air reservoir. It unscrews to attach it to a separate air pump. Note the flintlock mechanism complete except for the lack of a touchhole into the barrel. Marked: "**Frantz Heinz In Sternberg**." Muzzle-loading smoothbore barrel is 9 mm caliber. Overall length: 20.2"(51 cm).

M SECTION
MAS (MANUFACTURE D'ARMES DE ST. ETIENNE)

Previous brand designation of Manufacture (National) D'Armes de St. Etienne, of St. Etienne, France.

This company produced an air pistol modeled after the French Model 1950 automatic 9mm pistol for troop training and made only for the military, with a few sold by the French government to civilians in 1959.

PISTOLS

MAS 50 (MODEL 1950 MILITARY) – .177 cal., SP, SS, bbl rifled with 4 grooves, extended cocking lever, forms trigger guard, cocks gun and draws action open for loading, 8-8.5 in. OAL. Ref. Hannusch (2001 or U.S. Airgun magazine, July 1997 and P.J. Godfrey, Guns Review).

courtesy Mike Godfrey

Values TBD.

MC

For information on MC airguns, see Philippine Airguns in the "P" section.

MG

Previous trademark of Industrias Martinez in Spain circa 1970.

SHOTGUNS

MG AIR SHOTGUN – 10mm, SB, SS, bolt action, less than 200 mfg.

No other information or values available at this time.

This model fired shot from plastic cartridges that were packed 50 to the box.

MGR

For information on MGR, see Dianawerk in the "D" section.

MMM - MONDIAL

Previous tradename of Modesto Molgora located in Milano, Italy circa 1950s to 1990s.

Most Molgora products are toys and blank-firing guns, but there are several youth/adult airguns. Research is ongoing with this trademark, and more information will be included both online and in future editions.

GRADING	100%	95%	90%	80%	60%	40%	20%

PISTOLS

OKLAHOMA – .177 cal., BBC, SP, SS, 6.3 in. rifled BBL, 200 FPS, fixed sights, with only minor variations, resembles the Steiner air pistol, black or nickel finish, plastic or hardwood grips, no safety, 12.3 in. OAL, 1.9 lbs. Mfg. 1960s-1988.

	100%	95%	90%	80%	60%	40%	20%
	$45	$40	$35	$30	$25	$20	$15

ROGER – .173/BB cal., CO_2, semi-auto, styled after Colt Woodsman, smoothbore BBL, adj. sights, DA trigger, hundred-shot gravity-fed magazine, manual safety, black finish, die-cast parts, 10.9 in. OAL, 2.3 lbs.

courtesy Beeman Collection

	100%	95%	90%	80%	60%	40%	20%
	$50	$45	$40	$30	$25	$20	$15

Add 100% for gun in factory shooting kit.

GRADING	100%	95%	90%	80%	60%	40%	20%

MACGLASHAN AIR MACHINE GUN CO.

Previous manufacturer located in Long Beach, CA and later at 4615 Hampton St., Los Angeles, CA.

The MacGlashan Air Machine Gun Company formed July 22, 1939, closed Nov. 12, 1943. They began production in early 1937 with a single shot BB air rifle. During WWII, they produced two models of the now famous air machine gun trainer, used to train gunners in U.S. bombers. In 1945, they returned to making airguns for arcades with a pump action .24 cal. rifle. In 1947, they produced a .24 cal. semi-automatic carbine, followed by an improved and lighter version in 1951. MacGlashan Gallery Pistol known only from a magazine ad for concessionaires. Apparently SP (knob at back end of receiver may be a cocking knob) and SS, no trigger guard, 12 in. OAL, 17 oz. For further info contact www.macglashanbbgun.com. Ref. Behling (2006).

RIFLES: SEMI-AUTO

SEMI-AUTOMATIC CARBINE ARCADE GUN – .24 cal. round lead shot, 25-shot semi-auto, magazine parallel to barrel, wood stock, cross-bolt feed, 600 FPS at 1500 PSI. First Model: fiber fore grip, 35.75 in. overall, 6 lbs. Improved Model: wood fore grip, 37.5 in. OAL, 5 lbs.

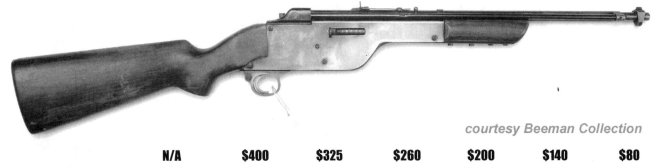

courtesy Beeman Collection

N/A	$400	$325	$260	$200	$140	$80

Add 10% for First Model.

RIFLES: SLIDE ACTION

"DRICE" SLIDE ACTION RIFLE – .24 cal. round lead shot, pump action 25-shot magazine parallel to barrel, 750 FPS at 1500 PSI (can operate at CO_2 pressures also), rifled barrel, blue finish, walnut stock and "tootsie roll" slide, designed to compete with .22 cal. firearms in arcades, 40.5 in. OAL, 6.6 lbs.

courtesy Beeman Collection

N/A	$550	$450	$350	$275	$195	$110

RIFLES: TRAINER/ARCADE AUTOMATIC

MODEL E-3 AERIAL GUNNERY TRAINER – .174 cal. steel BB cal., 15 in. smoothbore barrel full automatic 300-500 rpm @ 500-600 FPS, simulates .30 cal. Browning M1919A4 machine gun with dual wood spade grips, button trigger, steel cylinder parallel to top is a 1100 round magazine concentric with an inner cavity for a E-5 telescope sight (no telescope sight specimens known). Traditional blued steel finish. Requires hose fed compressed air (or CO_2) @ 180-200 psi and 24 volts DC, solenoid operated air valve, racheted BB feed disc. Used in WWII to train gunners with Model 2000N target carrier with pivoting arms on top of 18 ft. high spinner shaft, carrying 10" airplane models in target plane circle of 30 ft. Gun is 30.75 in. OAL, l6 lbs. About 1941-45. Ref. Behling (2006).

Voltages: 6, 12, or 24 volts. Model E-3 Army Air Force Variant, introduced at AAF Aerial Gunnery School in 1941. Model E-3N: Navy Variant: 30 in. OAL, 7 lbs. Navy purchased 424 guns.

GRADING	100%	95%	90%	80%	60%	40%	20%

* **Model E-3: Army Air Force Variant** – may have post front sight but generally without ring rear sight with cross wires and without ventilated barrel shroud. Approx. 50+ known specimens.

courtesy Beeman Collection

	N/A	$2,500	$2,000	$1,625	$1,250	$875	$500

Add 15% for Ring rear sight with cross wires (as illustrated).
Add 5% for USAAF inspection tag.

* **Model E-3N: Navy Variant** – ring rear sight with cross wires, ventilated barrel shroud, different arrangement of internal trigger and breech block travel assembly switches. Perhaps 10+ known specimens.

	N/A	$3,000	$2,400	$1,950	$1,500	$1,050	$600

MODEL E-13 REMOTE CONTROL AERIAL GUNNERY TRAINER – same specifications as E-3 models but designed to be used in remote control machine gun turrets, no sights, magazine is a 6 in. tall vertical cylinder with rubber top plug, 15 in. smoothbore barrel, 30 in. OAL, 14 lbs. Approx. 50 known specimens.

courtesy Beeman Collection

	N/A	$2,000	$1,600	$1,300	$1,000	$700	$400

Various modified versions of the above models are known. Deductions are appropriate in proportion to lack of authentic original condition.

MACGLASHAN "TOMMYGUN" - SUB-MACHINE ARCADE GUN – .174 in. steel BB cal., full automatic, version of E-3 solenoid air valve system, requires compressed air (or CO_2) probably @ 180-200 psi and 24 volts DC. Spring-loaded 100 shot tubular magazine under barrel. Dual grips and buttstock of hardwood. Heavily built. Cooling louvers on receiver sides. Cast aluminum buttplate with stamped serial number and in raised print: MACGLASHAN AIR MACHINE GUN CO. LONG BEACH CALIF PAT PEND (No MacGlashan patents are known.) Installed in Frontierland Shooting Gallery at original Disneyland in California from opening in 1955 until mid-1960s. Smoothbore 16 in. barrel with traditional cooling ribs, 40.6 in. OAL, 9.6 lbs. Seven specimens known. Ref. Behling (2006).

courtesy Beeman Collection

Scarcity precludes accurate pricing.

This gun was illustrated on the MacGlashan Air Machine Gun Co. letterhead in 1942 - indicating that it was a regular model.

GRADING	100%	95%	90%	80%	60%	40%	20%

MAC-1 AIRGUN DISTRIBUTORS

Current manufacturer and importer located in Gardena, CA. Dealers and consumer direct sales. Started in 1932 as Les McMurray's Fin Fur & Feather. The name changed to McMurray and Son in 1959, then to Custom Airguns by McMurray & Son in 1978, and is now known as Mac-1 Airgun Distributors.

Mac-1 celebrated their 80th anniversary in the airgun business in 2012. Present owner Tim McMurray has spent a lifetime challenging himself, and others, to find the last bit of accuracy and power from standard production airguns. In 2004 he and associate, Larry Durham, conceived the idea that became the first purpose-built field target gun to be manufactured in the United States. In 2005 Mac-1 started shipping their United States Field Target (US FT) Model rifle and in 2006 produced and shipped the US FT "Hunter Model" configuration of the gun. 2010 brought the addition of the US FT "Hunter BR" (BenchRest) model. Tim McMurray is continuing the practice of small-shop produced, high quality airguns in the tradition of makers going back centuries. Mac-1 can be reached at www.mac1airgun.com.

PISTOLS

MODEL "LD" SILHOUETTE TARGET PISTOL – .20 or .22 cal., SS, CO_2, 3 lbs. (without bulk CO_2 system), rifled 10 and 12.5 in. barrel (15mm Lothar Walther until 1989), or 10, 12, or 14 in. 15mm barrel (custom manufactured for MAC-1 by HW). Using a Crosman Mark I or Mark II frame as the base MAC-1 builds a competition-level target pistol. Caliber is determined by barrel and not by the original Crosman frame markings. (The name "LD" is from the initials of the barrel and cylinder concept creator.) All guns are delivered black with original Crosman grips. The LD Pistol was designed both for airgun Silhouette competition, and as an accurate hunting weapon. All LD Pistols have straight (non-tapered) barrels. Limited Edition ("LE") model added in 2010 to celebrate manufacture of 1,000th LD. Other makers long-barreled pistols based on the Crosman MK I and II frames exist. Contact MAC-1 directly to authenticate. Many custom options available.

MSR $550	$475	$400	$375	$300	$230	N/A	N/A

Add 10% for original steel or aluminum Venom full-shroud (1994-2004).
Add $50 for LE model (Mac-1 logo engraved and numbered 901-1000, stainless steel bolt knob).
Add $10 for .20 cal.
Add $75 for Millet rear sight.
Add $20 for front sight.
Add $40 for 17" bbl.
Add $35 for Ralph Brown oiled walnut grips.
Subtract $35 for each missing external "hangy tank" CO_2 cylinder.
Subtract $40 for missing cylinder adapter.
Subtract $60 for no muzzle brake.
Other options or customizations: Contact Mac-1 directly for values.

MSR pricing is based on a standard gun with muzzle brake, 12 gram piercing cap, bulk cylinder adapter, scope grooves, and two 3.5 oz. CO_2 cylinders, or one high-pressure air (HPA) cylinder.

RIFLES

UNITED STATES FIELD TARGET (US FT) MODEL – .177 cal., PCP, SS, 25 in. rifled bbl., color or clear anodizing per customer choice, machined aluminum and steel construction throughout with pistol grip, Mac-1 markings on breech, standard equipment includes: Lothar-Walther (new 2010) or Weihrauch (disc. 2010) barrel, Walnut thigh rest, forearm and cheek piece, butt hook, Weaver scope base, Colt Model 1911A style grip panels, pressure gauge, no sights, 40 in. OAL, 12 lbs. New 2005.

MSR $2,300	$1,950	$1,725	$1,575	$1,275	$975	N/A	N/A

Add $100 for HPA system (high pressure air) with Mac-1 regulator, removable 3,000 psi cylinder (new 2011).

Available options include: Left hand, carbine length, lightweight, upright (non-canted scope position), and .22 cal. barrels.

UNITED STATES FIELD TARGET (US FT) HUNTER MODEL – .22 cal., PCP, SS, 20 in. rifled bbl., 800 FPS, similar to US FT Model, except standard with upright (non-canted scope position), no butt hook, no thigh rest, black and clear anodized only, 36 in. OAL, 8.5-10 lbs.

MSR $1,500	$1,275	$1,125	$1,025	$825	$625	N/A	N/A

Add $100 for HPA system (high pressure air) with Mac-1 regulator, removable 3,000 psi cylinder (new for 2011).
Similar options as US FT Model.

UNITED STATES FIELD TARGET (US FT) HUNTER "BR" MODEL – .22 cal., PCP, SS, 800 FPS, similar to US FT Hunter Model, except Bench Rest version with 20 in. custom heavy stainless steel rifled bbl., buttplate and bottom rail, 36 in. OAL, 9.5 lbs. Mfg. 2011-current.

MSR $1,900	$1,625	$1,425	$1,300	$1,050	$800	N/A	N/A

Add $100 for HPA system (high pressure air) with Mac-1 regulator, removable 3,000 psi cylinder.
Similar options as US FT Model.

GRADING	100%	95%	90%	80%	60%	40%	20%

MAGIC

For information on Magic airguns, see Plymouth Air Rifle Company in the "P" section.

MAGNUM RESEARCH, INC.

Current trademark of pistols and rifles currently imported and distributed by Umarex·USA located in Fort Smith, AR begining 2006.

Centerfire pistols (Desert Eagle Series) are manufactured beginning 1998 by IMI, located in Israel. Previously mfg. by Saco Defense located in Saco, ME during 1995-1998, and by TAAS/IMI (Israeli Military Industries) 1986-1995. .22 Rimfire semi-auto pistols (Mountain Eagle) were previously manufactured by Ram-Line. Single shot pistols (Lone Eagle) were manufactured by Magnum Research sub-contractors. For more information and current pricing on both new and used Magnum Research, Inc. firearms, please refer to the *Blue Book of Gun Values* by S.P. Fjestad (also available online).

PISTOLS

DESERT EAGLE – .177 cal. pellets, CO_2, SA/DA, blowback action, eight-shot rotary mag., 5.7 in. rifled steel barrel, 425 FPS, adj. rear sight, Picatinny rails (top and bottom), ambidextrous safety, plastic grips, black finish, 10.8 in. OAL, 2.5 lbs. Mfg. 2007-current.

courtesy Magnum Research

MSR $239	$200	$170	$140	$115	$90	$60	$40

BABY DESERT EAGLE – BB/.177 cal., CO_2, DA, 15-shot mag., 4.25 in. rifled steel barrel, 410 FPS, fixed sights, Picatinny rail bottom and bonus top-side Picatinny rail, ambidextrous safety, plastic grips, black or silver (disc. 2011) finish, 8.25 in. OAL, 1 lb. Mfg. 2007-current.

courtesy Magnum Research

MSR $40	$35	$30	$25	$20	$15	N/A	N/A

Add $10 for Baby Desert Eagle Kit which includes the Baby Desert Eagle pistol (black), two 12g CO_2 capsules, 5 targets, shooting glasses, and 250 steel BBs.

MAGTECH

Current trademark manufactured by CBC, located in Ribeirão Pires, Sao Paolo, Brazil. No current U.S. importation.

CBC has been a well-known manufacturer of ammunition, as well as shotguns, rifles, and air guns, since 1960. CBC offers a complete line of good quality air rifles and spring air pistols in a variety of configurations including sporting, hunting, and tactical. Please contact the company directly for more information including pricing, options, and U.S. availability (see Trademark Index).

RIFLES

N2 – .177 or .22 cal., nitrogen piston gas ram system, 1000/800 FPS, brushed chrome finish, dovetail, automatic safety device, hardwood or synthetic stock, checkered grip, rubber buttpad, 43.5 in. OAL.

Please contact the company directly for pricing and U.S. availability on this model.

GRADING	100%	95%	90%	80%	60%	40%	20%

N2 ADVENTURE – .177 or .22 cal., compressed nitrogen gas piston (gas ram system), 1200/980 FPS, automatic safety, enhanced trigger system with two point adjustments, ergonomic grip, fiber optic sights, black synthetic thumbhole stuck with tube rubber buttpad.

> **Please contact the company directly for pricing and U.S. availability for this model.**

N2 EXTREME AIR RIFLE – .177 or .22 cal., nitrogen piston gas ram system, 1300/1000 FPS, muzzle brake, fiber optic sights, ambidextrous black synthetic thumbhole stock with tube rubber buttpad, ergonomic grip, additional safety trigger, automatic safety device, 47 in. OAL.

> **Please contact the company directly for pricing and U.S. availability on this model.**

MAHELY

Previous trademark of Giachetti Gonzales & Cia., circa 1950s-1990s and located in Buenos Aires, Argentina. Not regularly exported.

PISTOLS

MAHELY 51 – .177 cal., SP, SS, BBC, 8.2 in. rifled barrel, plastic or wooden vertically grooved grips, 2.3 lbs. Mfg. 1950s. Ref: Hiller (1993).

courtesy Beeman Collection

	N/A	$550	$450	$350	$275	$195	$110

RIFLES

MAHELY 1951 – .177 cal., SP, UL, SS, wood handle on underlever looks like a pump action handle, 39.4 in. OAL, 7.2 lbs. Disc. circa 1950s.

courtesy Beeman Collection

	N/A	$450	$350	$295	$225	$160	$90

MAHELY R 0.1 – .177 cal., SP, BBC, SS, thumbhole stock. Disc. late 1990s.

courtesy Beeman Collection

	N/A	$375	$300	$245	$185	$130	$75

GRADING	100%	95%	90%	80%	60%	40%	20%

MAKAROV

Current trademark manufactured beginning 2010 by Umarex Sportwaffen GmbH & Co. KG, located in Arnsberg, Germany, and imported by Umarex USA, located in Fort Smith, AR.

PISTOLS

C96 – BB/.177 cal., SA, CO_2, semi-auto repeater, German replica, 5.5 in. barrel, 19 shot mag., 380 FPS, adj. rear sight, fixed front sight, manual safety, Black finish, Brown grip, 11.5 in. OAL, 1.75 lbs. New 2014.

MSR $102	$85	$70	$60	$50	$40	$25	$15

MAKAROV – BB/.177 cal., one 12g CO_2, 380 FPS, SA/DA, 18-shot mag., 3.75 in. barrel, full metal frame with movable slide, replica of the original Makarov design, fixed front and rear sights, checkered brown plastic grips, black finish, 6.25 in. OAL, 1.5 lbs. New 2010.

courtesy Umarex USA

MSR $65	$55	$50	$45	$35	$25	N/A	N/A

MAKAROV ULTRA – BB/.177 cal., CO_2, SA semi-auto, blowback action, famous Russian replica, 3.5 in. barrel, 16 shot mag., all metal frame, 350 FPS, fixed sights, manual safety, Gray finish with Brown grips, 6.37 in. OAL, 1.4 lbs. New 2014.

MSR $91	$75	$65	$55	$45	$35	$20	$15

P.08 – BB/.177 cal., CO_2, DA, 410 FPS, famous German replica, 21 shot drop-free metal mag., 4.6 in. metal barrel, fixed sights, all metal parts, manual safety, black finish, 8.5 in. OAL, 1.8 lbs. New 2013.

courtesy Umarex USA

MSR $69	$50	$45	$35	$30	$25	N/A	N/A

MÄNNEL SPORT SHOOTING GmbH

Current manufacturer located in Kronstorf, Austria since 2008. No current U.S. importation.

Männel Sport Shooting GmbH manufactures a line of air pistols. Current models include the AP One, and the AP One Expert. Please contact the company directly for more information on these and other models, U.S. pricing, and availabilty (see Trademark Index).

MANU-ARMS

Previous French trademark of confusing origin and association. ManuArm is a French company formed in 2000, but both of the airguns below are from the 1980s. An association with Manufacture Française d'Armes et de Cycles de Saint Etienne, a.k.a. Manufrance, has been suggested. The original company was the producer of Paul Giffard's famous CO_2 guns in the 1880s and Manufrance was a household name in France, selling almost every form of consumer hard goods until the firm closed in 1986.

GRADING	100%	95%	90%	80%	60%	40%	20%

PISTOLS

MANU-ARMS AIR PISTOL – .177 cal., BBC, SP, SS, very similar to the Dianawerk Model 5, black or brightly colored paint finish, receiver is marked "MANU ARMS", 14.3 in. OAL, 2.7 lbs.

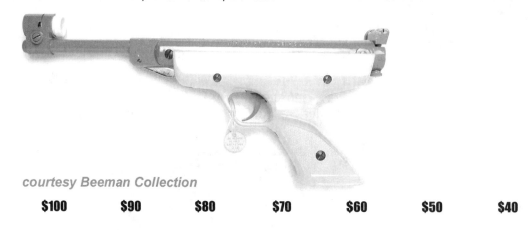

courtesy Beeman Collection

$100	$90	$80	$70	$60	$50	$40

RIFLES

MANU-ARMS AIR RIFLE – .177 cal., BBC, SP, SS, wood stock, beavertail forearm.

courtesy Beeman Collection

$60	$50	$40	$30	$20	N/A	N/A

MARKHAM-KING

Previous manufacturer located in Plymouth, MI. Circa 1887-1941. Owned and operated by Daisy Manufacturing Company from 1916.

The Markham Air Rifle Company has been credited with the development of the first commercially successful toy BB airgun. Dunathan's *American BB Gun* (1971) reported two BB rifles with the Challenger name as the first models made by Markham. However, the gun listed there as an 1886 Challenger actually represents only a single patent model without any markings and almost surely not made by Markham. The second gun, listed as an 1887 Challenger, actually was marked "Challenge" and was made in small numbers, but, again, probably not by Markham. There seems to be no justification for referring to either one under the Challenger name or as Markhams. The Chicago model, which appeared about 1887, made mainly of wood, probably was Markham's first real model.

The story of how the company grew to producing over 3,000 guns per day in 1916 is one of the great stories of airgun development and production. However, the company did little promotion and eventually was absorbed into the emerging airgun giant, Daisy. The history and models of Markham-King and Daisy became inseparably intertwined for a quarter of a century. Although Daisy ownership began in 1916, the Markham King models continued for decades and the sub-company gradually became known as King. In 1928, Daisy officially changed the company name to King. The advent of WWII probably caused Daisy to issue the last King price list on Jan. 1, 1942. Much of the model information in Dunathan's book has now been superseded, but this pioneering work absolutely is still required reading.

There are many variations of the early Markham air rifles. All minor variations cannot be covered in this guide. Variations may include changes in type or location of sights, location and text of markings, muzzle cap design, etc.

The authors and publishers wish to thank Robert Spielvogel and Dennis Baker for assistance with this section of the *Blue Book of Airguns*.

RIFLES: NO ALPHA-NUMERIC MARKINGS

All models have smoothbore barrels and are without safety.

CHICAGO – .180 large BB cal., darts, BC, SP, SS, exterior all maple wood with rosewood stain, double cocking rods pass through the stock. Stock stamped: "Chicago Air Rifle - Markham's Patent" on two lines. 9.8 in. brass barrel liner. 32 in. OAL. Circa 1887-1910. Patch Box Variation: Wooden "Patch Box" (dart storage?), 2.4 in. diameter, on LH side of stock. Stock stamped on left side with logo printed "Markham Air Company, Plymouth, Michigan, Chicago, patented" or

GRADING	100%	95%	90%	80%	60%	40%	20%

"CHICAGO AIR RIFLE, MARKHAM'S PATENT". Considered by some to be the oldest version. Circle Logo Variation: slight change in stock shape, stock stamped "Markham Air Rifle Co. - Plymouth Mich." and "CHICAGO - Patented" in circle.

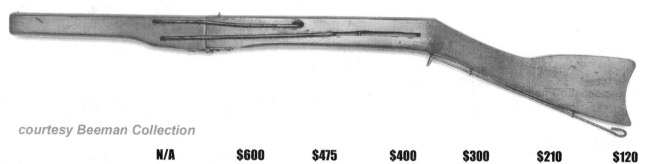

courtesy Beeman Collection

	N/A	$600	$475	$400	$300	$210	$120

Add 10% for BB clearing rod.
Add 15% for patch box variation.
Subtract 10% for circle logo variation.
Subtract 15% for cracked stock (common fault).

1890 KING – .180 large BB cal., darts, BC, SP, SS, cast iron frame, brass barrel, screw-on muzzle cap, button barrel release on side of receiver, nickel finish. "KING" cast in grip frame. 31 in. OAL. Mfg. circa 1890-1893.

	N/A	$2,500	$2,000	$1,625	$1,250	$875	$500

1892 KING – .180 large BB cal., darts, BC, SP, SS, sheet metal frame, brass barrel, screw-on muzzle cap, barrel release button on side of receiver, flat sided stock with oval King logo, 31 in. OAL. Mfg. circa 1892.

	N/A	$1,500	$1,200	$975	$750	$525	$300

1896 NEW KING SINGLE SHOT – .180 large BB cal., darts, BC, SP, SS, sheet metal frame, sheet metal barrel shroud, metal patch soldered over seam under shroud, muzzle cap over barrel shroud. Red stained stock stamped: "New King Patent Number 483159" in oval logo on slab sided stock. 31 in. OAL. Mfg. circa 1896-1905.

courtesy Beeman Collection

	N/A	$2,500	$2,000	$1,625	$1,250	$875	$500

1896 NEW KING REPEATER – .180 large BB cal., BC, SP, sheet metal frame, 150-shot magazine, domed muzzle cap lever allows BBs to be fed one by one from magazine to shot tube. Barrel release button on top of frame. Soldered patch under full length of barrel shroud. Shaped stock (oval in cross section) with logo. Later versions with flush muzzle cap and slab-sided stock. Variation: foreign patent numbers on stock. 31 in. OAL. Mfg. circa 1896-1904.

	N/A	$2,750	$2,200	$1,775	$1,375	$950	$550

Add 20% for shaped stock.
Subtract 10% for flush muzzle cap.

1900 NEW KING SINGLE SHOT – .180 large BB cal., darts, BC, SP, SS, first use of "friction latch barrel": a section of rear frame snaps over raised part of trigger guard part of frame - holding gun together by friction; this replaced barrel release button of previous King air rifles. Fixed muzzle cap over outside of barrel shroud. (Variations: rounded muzzle cap.) Slab-sided stock stamped "New King" on one side and patent dates on other side. Nickel plated. 31 in. OAL. Mfg. circa 1900-1904.

	N/A	$1,500	$1,200	$975	$750	$525	$300

There may have been a repeater version.

1900 PRINCE SINGLE SHOT – .180 large BB cal., darts, BC, SP, SS, sheet metal frame, sheet metal barrel shroud, friction barrel latch, marked "Prince", nickel finish, no trigger guard, walnut stock with oval profile, crescent butt. Ref: AR4. (Sears Roebuck advertised a New Rival version, but no specimens are known.) Mfg. circa 1900-07. Variation: "Dandy," made by Markham for private label sales, marked "DANDY" with Markham patent dates (not marked "Markham"), not sold directly by Markham.

	N/A	$2,500	$2,000	$1,625	$1,250	$875	$500

Add 100% for Dandy variation.

GRADING	100%	95%	90%	80%	60%	40%	20%

1900 PRINCE REPEATER – similar to Prince Single Shot but with 150-shot magazine, BB release button on muzzle cap. Not a true repeater. Mfg. circa 1900-07.

	N/A	$2,750	$2,200	$1,775	$1,375	$950	$550

1900 PRINCE (TRIGGER GUARD MODEL) – .180 large BB cal., darts, BC, SP, SS, sheet metal frame wraps completely around wrist, sheet metal barrel shroud, separate sheet metal trigger guard. Variant: Marked "Boy's Own", premium gun. Mfg. circa 1900-07.

No other information or values available at time of printing.

1900 QUEEN – .180 large BB cal., darts, BBC, SP, SS, removable pins were substituted for rivets to allow gun to be taken down to three pieces, no trigger guard, similar to 1900 Prince Single Shot, circular markings on wrist: "Markham Air Rifle Co. Plymouth, Mich" plus two patent numbers, advertised as the "Queen Take Down," but not marked "Queen", nickel finish, 33 in. OAL. Mfg. 1900-07.

	N/A	$1,500	$1,200	$975	$750	$525	$300

1903 NEW KING SINGLE SHOT – .180 large BB cal., darts, BC, SP, SS, friction barrel latch, fixed muzzle cap within barrel shroud, stamped "New King" on one side and patent dates on other of slab sided stock, nickel plated, 31 in. OAL. Mfg. circa 1903-1904.

	N/A	$1,500	$1,200	$975	$750	$525	$300

1904 SINGLE SHOT – .180 in large BB cal., BBC, SP, SS, friction barrel latch, domed muzzle cap with sight. Patch under barrel shroud. Slab sided stock marked "King Markham Air Rifle Co." Later versions with oval shaped stocks, without markings. Early versions had name stamping on small area on top of receiver; later name stamping was on barrel shroud. Mfg. circa 1904.

courtesy Beeman Collection

	N/A	$800	$600	$500	$400	$300	$150

1904 REPEATER – .180 large BB cal., BBC, SP, friction barrel latch, spring release at muzzle like 1896 New King Repeater. Later versions had oval-shaped stocks without markings. Mfg. circa 1904.

courtesy Beeman Collection

	N/A	$950	$750	$625	$475	$325	$190

RIFLES: WITH ALPHA-NUMERIC MARKINGS

MODEL C (REPEATER) – BB/.180 or .177 in. lead air rifle shot cal., SP, BC, gravity-fed 500-shot storage. Smooth contour Polley patent sheet metal frame wraps around wrist, barrel shroud with step, nickel finish, walnut stock with oval profile and deep crescent butt, stock stamped "King 500 Shot Repeater". Not a true repeater, 33 in. OAL. Mfg. circa 1906-09.

	N/A	$700	$550	$450	$350	$245	$140

GRADING	100%	95%	90%	80%	60%	40%	20%

MODEL C (SINGLE SHOT) – BB/.180 or .177 lead air rifle shot cal., SP, BC, SS, smooth contour Polley patent sheet metal frame wraps around wrist, barrel shroud with step, nickel finish, walnut stock with oval profile and deep crescent butt, domed muzzle cap allows a BB to be shaken from BBs stored in barrel shroud into the shot tube (true barrel). Not a true repeater, oval stock, 32 in. OAL. Mfg. 1905-09.

	N/A	$600	$475	$400	$300	$210	$120

MODEL D (REPEATER) – BB/.180 or .177 in. lead air rifle shot cal., SP, BC, 350-shot gravity-fed magazine, barrel tube removes to load, shot tube with oval cap, smooth contour Polley patent sheet metal frame wraps around wrist, barrel shroud with step, marked "KING MODEL D, THE MARKHAM AIR RIFLE CO., PLYMOUTH, MICH., U.S.A.", nickel finish, walnut stock with oval profile and deep crescent butt, 9.5 in barrel, 31 in. OAL. Mfg. circa 1907-09.

	N/A	$700	$550	$450	$350	$245	$140

MODEL D (SINGLE SHOT) – BB/.180 caliber or .177 in. lead air rifle shot cal., SP, BC, muzzle loading SS, 9.5 in. barrel, barrel tube retained by spring clip, muzzle cap not removable, smooth contour Polley patent sheet metal frame wraps around wrist, barrel shroud with step, marked "KING MODEL D, THE MARKHAM AIR RIFLE CO., PLYMOUTH, MICH., U.S.A.", nickel finish, walnut stock with oval profile and deep crescent butt, 31 in. OAL. Mfg. circa 1907-1909.

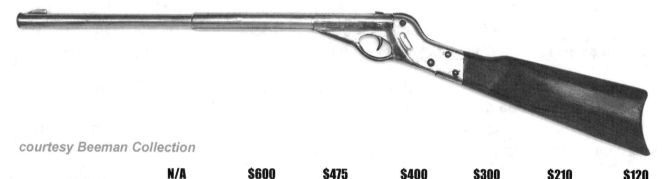

courtesy Beeman Collection

	N/A	$600	$475	$400	$300	$210	$120

MODEL E (REPEATER) – .180 large BB cal., darts, BC, SP, Model D frame with straight (no step down) Prince type barrel, muzzle lever repeater, gravity-fed, smooth profile (Polley Patent) sheet metal frame, sheet metal barrel shroud, full length solder patch, walnut stock with oval profile, deep crescent butt, nickel finish, 32 in. OAL. Dates not known.

	N/A	$750	$600	$475	$375	$265	$150

NUMBER 1 – .180 large BB cal., darts, BC, SP, SS, similar to Model D, removable shot tube, barrel marked "KING NO. 1", 31 in. OAL. Mfg. 1910-14.

	N/A	$600	$475	$400	$300	$210	$120

NUMBER 2 – .180 large BB cal., darts, BC, SP, 350-shot repeater, loading port below front sight, side of grip stamped "KING 350 SHOT NO. 2", 31 in. OAL. Mfg. 1910-14.

	N/A	$900	$725	$575	$450	$325	$180

NUMBER 4 – .177 lead air rifle shot cal., SP, lever action, gravity-fed 500-shot magazine, one-piece sheet metal frame and half-round, half-octagonal barrel shroud, frame with scroll stamping "King 500 Shot" with Markham address and patent dates, nickel finish, walnut stock with deep crescent butt, 34 in. OAL. Mfg. circa 1908-1915. Smooth variation: no scroll stamping on frame. Mfg. 1910-14. Blued finish mfg. 1914-1922.

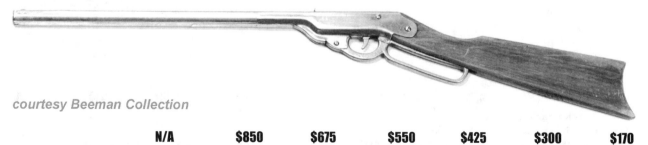

courtesy Beeman Collection

	N/A	$850	$675	$550	$425	$300	$170

Add 5% for smooth variation.
Subtract 15% for blued finish.
Markham's first lever action repeater.

GRADING	100%	95%	90%	80%	60%	40%	20%

NUMBER 5 LEVER ACTION – .177 lead air rifle shot cal., SP, LA, gravity-fed 1000-shot magazine, one-piece sheet metal frame and half-round, half-octagonal barrel shroud, blue or nickel finish, walnut stock with deep crescent butt, 36 in. OAL, 2.5 lbs. Mfg. circa 1908-1922.

	N/A	$850	$675	$550	$425	$300	$170

* ***Number 5 Lever Action Scroll Side Variant*** – frame with scroll stamping "King 1000 Shot" with Markham address and patent dates, nickel finish, walnut stock with deep crescent butt. Mfg. circa 1908-1922.

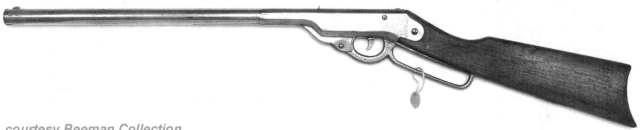

courtesy Beeman Collection

	N/A	$950	$750	$625	$475	$325	$190

* ***Number 5 Lever Action Plain Side Variant*** – markings on top, no scroll stampings on side, nickel finish, mfg. 1910-14.

	N/A	$1,000	$800	$650	$500	$350	$200

* ***Number 5 Lever Action Blued Variant*** – blue finish, mfg. 1914-1922.

	N/A	$825	$650	$525	$400	$290	$165

NUMBER 5B SPECIAL LEVER ACTION – .177 lead air rifle shot cal., SP, lever action, gravity-fed magazine, one-piece sheet metal frame and half-round, half-octagonal barrel shroud, frame with scroll stamping "King 1000 Shot" with Markham address and patent dates, special black nickel finish on metal, special finish on walnut stock with deep crescent butt. Hinged gift box with color lithographing, 36 in. OAL. Mfg. circa 1908-1916.

	N/A	$1,150	$925	$750	$575	$400	$230

Deduct 25% if w/o gift box.

NUMBER 5 SLIDE ACTION – .177 lead air rifle shot cal., SP, sixty-shot gravity-fed magazine, six-groove wooden cocking slide, pistol grip stock, 36 in. OAL (same design used by Daisy for Daisy No. 105 Junior Pump Gun and Daisy No. 107 Buck Jones Special). Mfg. 1932-36.

	N/A	$550	$450	$350	$275	$195	$110

NUMBER 10 JUNIOR – .177 air rifle shot cal., SP, BC, SS, sheet metal frame, flat sided walnut stock with crescent butt. Cast iron trigger guard (E.S. Roe patent) extends into wrist and provides cocking action fulcrum. Nickel or blued finish. 29 in. OAL. Variation 1: cast iron trigger guard and conventional trigger. One-piece barrel. Nickel finish. Variation 2: cast iron trigger guard and conventional trigger. Stepped barrel. Blued finish. Variation 3: ring trigger, one-piece barrel, blue finish. Variation 4: stepped barrel, blue finish. Mfg. 1909-1941.

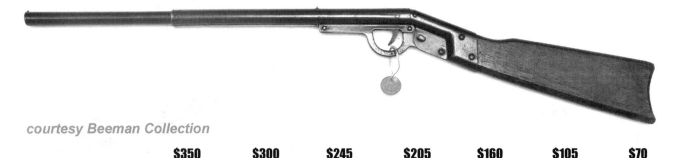

courtesy Beeman Collection

$350	$300	$245	$205	$160	$105	$70

Subtract 25% for variation two.
Subtract 50% for variations three and four.

NUMBER 11 JUNIOR (THREE IN ONE GUN) – .177 air rifle shot or darts cal., or corks fired with shot tube removed, SP, BC, SS, sheet metal frame and straight one-piece barrel shroud, flat-sided walnut stock with crescent butt, cast iron trigger guard (E.S. Roe patent) extends into wrist and provides cocking action fulcrum, nickel finish, 29 in. OAL. Mfg. 1910-16.

	N/A	$550	$450	$350	$275	$195	$110

GRADING	100%	95%	90%	80%	60%	40%	20%

NUMBER 17 BREECH LOADER – .177 lead air rifle shot or darts cal., SP, SS, sheet metal frame and barrel shroud, blued finish, BC action with two external cocking rods similar to Chicago Model, 12 in. BBL, 31 in. OAL. Mfg. circa 1917-1932.

	N/A	$450	$350	$295	$225	$160	$90

Add 20% for ammo box variant.

Ammo box variant - small ammo storage chamber below barrel pivot. Bears June 13, 1922 patent date.

NUMBER 21 SINGLE SHOT – .177 lead air rifle shot or darts cal., SP, SS, removable shot tube, lever action, cast iron lever, sheet metal frame and barrel shroud, blue or nickel finish. "NO. 21, KING MANUFACTURING Co., PLYMOUTH, MICH., SINGLE SHOT" plus patent dates marked on gun. 31 in. OAL. Mfg. circa 1913-1932. Variation one: earlier production with scroll stamped receiver marked "KING SINGLE SHOT No. 21, THE MARKHAM AIR RIFLE CO." with 1907 to 1913 patent dates. Variation two: blued finish, plain receiver. Variation Three: nickel finish, plain receiver.

	N/A	$275	$220	$180	$135	$95	$55

Add 50% for variation one.

Note: The dash in the following four-digit model numbers does not appear on the guns themselves - but is added here to highlight the two-digit date of introduction which is added to the basic two-digit model number (i.e. Number 2123 is shown as Number 21-33 to indicate that it is a variation of No. 21 introduced in 1933).

MODEL 21-33 SINGLE SHOT – .177 lead air rifle shot or darts cal., SP, SS, removable shot tube, lever action, cast iron lever, sheet metal frame and barrel shroud, blue finish. Barrel marked "KING MFG. CO" and with Markham address, 31 in. OAL. Mfg. circa 1933-35.

	N/A	$275	$220	$180	$135	$95	$55

NUMBER 21-36 SINGLE SHOT – .177 air rifle shot cal., SP, SS, cast iron cocking lever, sheet metal frame and barrel shroud, removable shot tube, blued finish, straight grip stock, 32 in. OAL. Mfg. circa 1936-1941.

courtesy Beeman Collection

	N/A	$275	$220	$180	$135	$95	$55

NUMBER 22 REPEATER – .177 inch air rifle shot cal., SP, same as Number 21 gun but with 500-shot gravity-fed magazine repeater, lever action, cast iron lever, sheet metal frame and barrel shroud, blue or nickel finish, Markham address on barrel, loading port below front sight, 31 in. OAL. Mfg. circa 1916-1932.

	N/A	$295	$235	$190	$145	$105	$60

NUMBER 22-33 REPEATER – .177 air rifle shot cal., SP, 500-shot gravity-fed magazine repeater, lever action, cast iron lever, sheet metal frame and barrel shroud, blue finish. Marked "King". Markham address on barrel, loading port on RH side, 32 in. OAL. Mfg. circa 1933-1935.

	N/A	$250	$200	$165	$125	$90	$50

NUMBER 22-36 500 SHOT REPEATER – .177 lead air rifle shot cal., SP, lever action, gravity-fed magazine, one-piece sheet metal frame and barrel shroud, cast iron lever, blued finish, straight grip wood stock. Daisy design influence, replaced King Number 22-33. 32 in. OAL. Mfg. circa 1936-1941.

$125	$105	$90	$75	$55	$35	$25

NUMBER 23 KADET ARMY – .177 air rifle shot cal., SP, gravity-fed 500-shot magazine repeater, lever action, cast iron lever, sheet metal frame and barrel shroud, nickel finish, frame marked "King Kadet", Markham address on barrel, military type rear sight, rubber tipped bayonet, web sling, 31 in. OAL (38 in. with bayonet). Mfg. circa 1915-16.

	N/A	$800	$650	$525	$400	$280	$160

Subtract 30% for missing bayonet.
Subtract 10% for missing sling.

GRADING	100%	95%	90%	80%	60%	40%	20%

NUMBER 24 NEW CHICAGO – .177 lead air rifle shot or darts cal., SP, SS, BC. Barrel marked "New Chicago Number 24" and Markham address. Bolt action locking device. Blued finish. 36 in. OAL. Mfg. 1917 only. Ref: AR 2.

courtesy Beeman Collection

	N/A	$1,200	$950	$775	$600	$425	$240

NUMBER 55 REPEATER – .177 lead air rifle shot or .174 in. steel BB cal., SP, lever action, gravity-fed 1000-shot magazine, one-piece sheet metal frame and barrel shroud, cast iron lever, blued finish. Markham address on top of barrel. Variation one: straight walnut stock. Variation two: pistol grip model with curved lever. 35 in. OAL. Mfg. 1923-1931.

	N/A	$225	$180	$145	$110	$80	$45

Add 30% for variation two.

NUMBER 55-32 SINGLE SHOT – .177 lead air rifle shot or 174 in. steel BB cal., SP, lever action, one piece sheet metal frame and barrel shroud, cast iron lever, blued finish, pistol grip wood stock, used Number 55 frame, loading port LH side, 35 in. OAL. Mfg. 1932 only.

$100	$85	$70	$60	$45	$30	$20

NUMBER 55-33 1000 SHOT REPEATER – .174 steel BB cal., SP, lever action, 1,000 shot gravity feed magazine, new frame with Daisy-type spring anchor and rear sight, straight grip stock, blued finish, 35 in. OAL. Mfg. 1933-35.

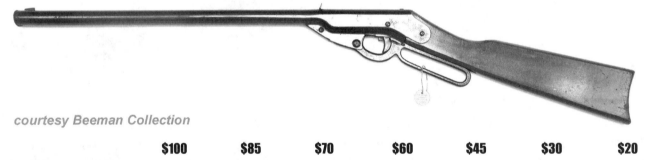

courtesy Beeman Collection

$100	$85	$70	$60	$45	$30	$20

Add 5% for peep sight.

NUMBER 55-36 1000 SHOT REPEATER – BB/.174 cal., SP, lever action gravity-fed magazine, one-piece sheet metal frame and barrel shroud, cast iron lever, blued finish, pistol grip wood stock, Daisy design influence, similar to Daisy Red Ryder and Number 155, 36 in. OAL. Mfg. circa 1936-1941.

$125	$105	$90	$75	$55	$35	$25

Add 5% for peep sight.

MARKSMAN PRODUCTS

Current manufacturer and importer located in Santa Fe Springs, CA. Previously located in Huntington Beach, CA until 2010. Marksman is a division of S/R Industries. Dealers and consumer direct sales.

Morton Harris, operating as Morton H. Harris Inc. in Beverly Hills and then Los Angeles, CA, developed a simple spring piston pistol during 1955-1957. The firm continued as Marksman Products in Torrance, CA with airguns and expanded to slingshots and accessories. They later acquired Healthways, the manufacturer of some of the airguns sold under the Plainsman label. They also formerly imported Milbro Diana from Scotland, BSA from England, Weihrauch/BSF, and Anschütz spring piston air rifles from Germany. Most of these imports were not special Marksman models and many were not marked with the Marksman name and thus generally are not covered here. Marksman produced the Model 1010 air pistol under private labeling via Milbro of Scotland.

PISTOLS

MODEL MP (MARKSMAN PISTOL) – BB/.175 or .177 cal. pellet or dart, SS, SP, one-stroke cocking by sliding top of receiver, 2.5 in. smoothbore BBL, black paint or chrome finish, die-cast body, Morton Harris markings. Variation one:

GRADING	100%	95%	90%	80%	60%	40%	20%

rotating cover in left grip over an ammunition storage area; marked "Beverly Hills, Calif." Apparently produced only in 1955 in very limited numbers. Variation two: without ammunition storage area; marked "Los Angeles, Calif." 1.5 lbs., 8.75 in. OAL. Mfg. 1955-1957.

courtesy Beeman Collection

	100%	95%	90%	80%	60%	40%	20%
	$75	$65	$55	$45	$35	$20	$15

MSR was $8.95 for black, $12.95 for chrome.

Add 100% for factory box, ammo samples, and literature.
Subtract 50% for variation two.
Add 100% for chrome finish.
Add 200% for Dillingham Industries, Los Angeles, Calif. markings.

MODEL MPR (MARKSMAN PISTOL REPEATER) – BB/.175 or .177 cal. pellet or dart, SP-slide cocking, smoothbore 2.5 in. BBL, die-cast, twenty-shot spring-fed BB magazine, forerunner of nearly identical Model 1010, black paint or chrome finish, early production marked "Los Angeles 25", later ones may be marked "Torrance, Calif." Sears Model 1914 with "Sears" cast into sideplate instead of "Marksman". Styrofoam box base appeared in 1967. 1.7 lbs, 8.75 in. OAL. Mfg. 1958-1977.

	100%	95%	90%	80%	60%	40%	20%
	$15	$15	$10	N/A	N/A	N/A	N/A

MSR was $8.95 for black, $12.95 for chrome.

Add 10% for Los Angeles address.
Add 50% for box, ammo samples, and paperwork.
Add 35% for chrome finish.
Add 100% for Sears markings.

MODEL 1010/1010C/1010H/1010HC – BB/.175 or .177 cal. pellet or dart, slide action cocking, SP, smoothbore, 200 FPS, die-cast, 20-shot spring-fed BB magazine, black paint, brass, or chrome finish (Model 1010C), fixed sights, and holster (Model 1010H). Mfg. 1977-present.

courtesy Beeman Precision Airguns

MSR $30	100%	95%	90%	80%	60%	40%	20%
	$25	$25	$20	$15	$15	N/A	N/A

Add 20% for models other than basic 1010.
Add 50% for box and literature (later versions had clamshell packaging, no premium).
Add 50% for chrome.
Add 200% for gold color plating, presentation box.
Add 100% for original presentation case.

Model 1015 Special Edition - "combat" styling. Model 1300 with "Shootin' Darts" set. Model 1320 "Shootin' Triangles" with self-contained target box.

MODEL 1010X – similar to Model 1010, except has full nickel plating and black plastic grip panels with inlaid silver colored Marksman logos.

	100%	95%	90%	80%	60%	40%	20%
	$20	$15	$15	$10	N/A	N/A	N/A

GRADING	100%	95%	90%	80%	60%	40%	20%

MODEL 1015 – similar to Model 1010, except has full nickel plating and brown plastic grip panels with inlaid silver colored Marksman logos.

	100%	95%	90%	80%	60%	40%	20%
	$20	$15	$15	$10	N/A	N/A	N/A

MODEL 1020 – BB/.175 cal., slide action, SP, black finish, 18-shot reservoir (BB), 200 FPS, fixed sights.

	100%	95%	90%	80%	60%	40%	20%
	$20	$15	$15	$10	N/A	N/A	N/A

Last MSR was $21.

MODEL 1049 (PLAINSMAN) – BB/.174 cal., CO_2 (12 gram), repeater, hundred-shot BB gravity-fed reservoir, adj. 300-400 FPS.

	100%	95%	90%	80%	60%	40%	20%
	$40	$35	$30	$25	$20	$10	N/A

Discontinued in 1990s. See Healthways in the "H" section of this guide.

MODEL 1399 – BB/.175 cal. and .177 pellet, darts, or bolts, slide action, SP, silver chrome finish, gravity-fed 24-shot BB reservoir, 230 FPS, fiber optic front sight, extended barrel, includes dartboard and twelve darts. Disc. 2012.

	100%	95%	90%	80%	60%	40%	20%
	$25	$20	$20	$15	$10	N/A	N/A

Last MSR was $26.

MODEL 2000 – BB/.175 cal., slide action, SP, 200 FPS similar to Model 1010C, except has silver chrome finish and squared trigger guard. Disc. 2012.

	100%	95%	90%	80%	60%	40%	20%
	$30	$25	$20	$15	$15	N/A	N/A

Last MSR was $35.

MODEL 2000K – BB/.177 cal., single-stroke SP, 230 FPS, BB repeater shoots BBs through 18 shot reservoir, also shoots pellets, darts, and bolt single shot, silver chrome finish, kit includes holster, high impact shooting glasses, BB speed loader with 300 BBs, 50 count Wadcutter pellets, and six mohair darts, 9 in. OAL, 1 lb.

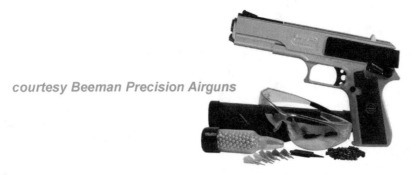

courtesy Beeman Precision Airguns

MSR $45	100%	95%	90%	80%	60%	40%	20%
	$40	$35	$30	$25	$20	N/A	N/A

MODEL 2002 – BB/.177 cal. or .177 cal. pellets, darts, or bolts, single-stroke SP, extended barrel with fiber optic sight, BB repeater shoots BBs through 18-shot reservoir, black finish, includes speed loader with 300 BBs, 11 in. OAL, 1 lb. Mfg. 2010-current.

MSR $26	100%	95%	90%	80%	60%	40%	20%
	$20	$20	$20	$15	$10	N/A	N/A

MODEL 2002Z ZOMBIE PISTOL – BB/.177 cal., single stroke SP, repeater, also shoots pellets, darts, and bolts single shot, 230 FPS, extended barrel with fiber optic sight, includes 2095Z paper targets with cardboard stand, 9 in. OAL, 1 lb. New 2013.

courtesy Beeman Precision Airguns

MSR $25	100%	95%	90%	80%	60%	40%	20%
	$20	$20	$15	$15	$10	N/A	N/A

GRADING	100%	95%	90%	80%	60%	40%	20%

MODEL 2004 DELUXE – .177 cal. pellet, SSP, over-cocking, polymer frame with finger grooves and cast aluminum slide, black finish, 410 FPS, adj. rear sight, squared trigger guard, automatic trigger safety, 9.5 in. OAL, 1.7 lbs. Mfg. 2005-2006.

	$40	$35	$30	$25	$20	$10	N/A

Last MSR was $45.

MODEL 2005 – BB/.175 cal. and .177 pellet, darts, or ballistic bolt, slide action, SP, silver chrome finish, 24-shot BB reservoir, 260 FPS, "Laserhawk" fiber optic front sight, extended barrel, squared trigger guard.

	$25	$20	$20	$15	$10	N/A	N/A

Last MSR was $26.

MODEL 2010 – BB/.175 cal., slide action, SP, 230 FPS, black composite frame and silver chrome finish slide. Mfg. 2006-2011.

	$25	$20	$20	$15	$10	N/A	N/A

Last MSR was $25.

RIFLES

JUNIOR MODEL 28 – .177 cal., BBC, SP, 600 FPS, 16.75 in. barrel, blue finish, 6 lbs. Mfg. for Marksman by Weihrauch.

	$135	$115	$95	$80	$60	$40	$25

Last MSR was $225.

MODEL 29/30 – .177 or .22 cal., BBC, SP, 800/625 FPS, 18.5 in. barrel, blue finish, 6 lbs. Mfg. for Marksman by BSA. Disc. 1991.

	$135	$115	$95	$80	$60	$40	$25

Last MSR was $200.

MODEL 40 – .177 cal., BBC, SP, 720 FPS, 18.4 in. barrel, blue finish, 7 lbs. 5 oz.

	$145	$125	$100	$85	$65	$45	$30

Last MSR was $250.

MODEL 45 – .177 cal., BBC, SP, 900-930 FPS, 19.2 in. barrel, blue finish, 7.15 lbs. New 1993.

	$125	$105	$90	$75	$55	$35	$25

Last MSR was $195.

MODEL 55 (RIFLE) & 59 CARBINE – .177 cal., BBC, SP, 925 FPS, 19.75 (rifle) or 14 (carbine) in. barrel, blue finish, 7.5 lbs.

	$195	$165	$135	$115	$90	$60	$40

Last MSR was $300.

Manufactured for Marksman by Weihrauch, using B.S.F. tooling.

MODEL 56/56K – .177 cal., BBC, SP, 925 FPS, 19.6 in. barrel, blue finish, adj. cheek piece and trigger, 8.7 lbs.

	$300	$255	$210	$175	$135	$90	$60

Add 50% for 56K Model with Marksman Model 6941 scope.

Manufactured for Marksman by Weihrauch, using B.S.F. tooling.

MODEL 58/58K – .177 cal., BBC, SP, 925 FPS, 16 in. heavy bull barrel, blue finish, adj. trigger, designed for silhouette shooting, 8 lbs. 8 oz. Importation disc. 1993.

	$250	$215	$175	$145	$115	$75	$50

Last MSR was $390.

Add 50% for 58K Model with Marksman Model 6941 scope.

Manufactured for Marksman by Weihrauch, using B.S.F. tooling.

MODEL 60/61 CARBINE – .177 cal., UL, SP, blue finish, 810-840 FPS, 8 lbs. 12 oz.

	$300	$255	$210	$175	$135	$90	$60

Last MSR was $490.

This model is a modified version of HW77 by Weihrauch manufactured for Marksman using B.S.F. tooling.

MODEL 70 – .177, .20, or .22 cal., BBC, SP, 19.75 in. barrel, blue finish, 925/760 FPS, 8 lbs.

	$235	$200	$165	$135	$105	$70	$45

Last MSR was $355.

Add 10% for .20 cal.

Manufactured for Marksman by Weihrauch, using B.S.F. tooling.

GRADING	100%	95%	90%	80%	60%	40%	20%

MODEL 72 – .177, .20, or .22 cal., BBC, SP, similar to Model 70.

	100%	95%	90%	80%	60%	40%	20%
	$235	$200	$165	$135	$105	$70	$45

Last MSR was $355.

Add 10% for .20 cal.

Manufactured for Marksman by Weihrauch, using B.S.F. tooling.

MODEL 746 – .177 cal., BBC, SP, SS, rifled barrel, 580 FPS, 42 in. OAL.

	100%	95%	90%	80%	60%	40%	20%
	$125	$105	$90	$75	$55	$35	$25

Marksman private branding of Diana Milbro G79 from Scotland.

MODEL 1700 – BB/.177 cal., pump action cocking, SP, 275 FPS, 20-shot spring-fed mag., blue finish.

	100%	95%	90%	80%	60%	40%	20%
	N/A	$20	$15	$10	N/A	N/A	N/A

MODEL 1702 – BB/.177 cal., pump action cocking, SP, 275 FPS, 20-shot spring-fed mag., blue finish, adj. rear and fiber optic front sights.

	100%	95%	90%	80%	60%	40%	20%
	$25	$20	$15	$15	$10	N/A	N/A

Last MSR was $26.

MODEL 1705 – BB/.177 cal., similar to Model 1702, except has three-position length adj. stock.

	100%	95%	90%	80%	60%	40%	20%
	$25	$25	$20	$15	$10	N/A	N/A

Last MSR was $30.

MODEL 1710 (PLAINSMAN) – BB/.177 cal., pump action cocking, SP, 275 FPS, 20-shot spring-fed mag., blue finish.

	100%	95%	90%	80%	60%	40%	20%
	$20	$15	$15	$10	N/A	N/A	N/A

MODEL 1740 – BB/.177 cal., BBC, SP, 450 FPS, 18-shot reservoir, blued finish.

	100%	95%	90%	80%	60%	40%	20%
	N/A	$35	$30	$25	$15	$10	N/A

MODEL 1745 – BB/.177 cal., BBC, SP, 450 FPS, 18-shot reservoir, blued finish, ambidextrous Monte Carlo plastic stock.

	100%	95%	90%	80%	60%	40%	20%
	N/A	$25	$20	$20	$15	N/A	N/A

Add 20% for Model 1745S with factory installed Marksman 1804 scope.

MODEL 1750 – BB/.177 cal., BBC, SP, similar to Model 1740, except skeletonized.

	100%	95%	90%	80%	60%	40%	20%
	N/A	$30	$25	$20	$15	$10	N/A

MODEL 1780 – BB/.177 cal., BBC, SP, 450 FPS, single shot version of Model 1740.

	100%	95%	90%	80%	60%	40%	20%
	N/A	$30	$25	$20	$15	$10	N/A

MODEL 1790 (BIATHLON TRAINER) – BB/.177 cal., BBC, SP, 450 FPS, plastic stock.

	100%	95%	90%	80%	60%	40%	20%
	N/A	$60	$50	$40	$30	$20	$10

MODEL 1792 – .177 cal., BBC, SP, 450 FPS, similar to Model 1790.

	100%	95%	90%	80%	60%	40%	20%
	N/A	$45	$35	$30	$20	$15	N/A

MODEL 1795 – BB/.177 cal., UL, SP, bolt action loading, 450/500 FPS, ten-round spring-fed magazine.

	100%	95%	90%	80%	60%	40%	20%
	N/A	$50	$40	$35	$25	$20	$10

Add 10% for Model 1795S with factory installed Marksman 1804 scope.

MODEL 1798 – .177 cal., BBC, SP, similar to Model 1790 Biathlon Trainer, except has "Laserhawk" sighting system.

	100%	95%	90%	80%	60%	40%	20%
	N/A	$50	$40	$35	$25	$20	$10

MODEL 2015/2015K – BB/.177 cal., similar to Model 1705, except has "Laserhawk" sighting system, BB speed loader, and targets (Model 2015K only).

	100%	95%	90%	80%	60%	40%	20%
	$40	$35	$25	$25	$20	$10	N/A

Last MSR was $42.

Add 10% for Model 2015K with all accessories.

MODEL 2020 – BB/.177 cal., SP, single-stroke pump action cocking, 300 FPS, 20 shot mag., fiber optic front sight, adj. rear sight, black composite stock and finish, automatic safety, 33.5 in. OAL, 2 lbs. Mfg. 2005-2011.

	100%	95%	90%	80%	60%	40%	20%
	$20	$20	$15	$15	N/A	N/A	N/A

Last MSR was $25.

GRADING	100%	95%	90%	80%	60%	40%	20%

MODEL 2021 – BB/.177 cal., single-stroke pump action cocking, 300 FPS, lightweight black composite design, fiber optic front sight, automatic safety, 20-shot mag., 33.5 in. OAL, 2 lbs. New 2010.

courtesy Beeman Precision Airguns

MSR $36	$30	$25	$25	$20	$15	N/A	N/A

MODEL 2021Z ZOMBIE RIFLE – BB/.177 cal., single stroke pump action, 300 FPS, spring loaded positive feed 20 shot mag., fiber optic front sight, automatic safety, durable and lightweight composite design, includes 2095Z paper targets with cardboard stand, 33.5 in. OAL, 2 lbs. New 2012.

courtesy Beeman Precision Airguns

MSR $46	$40	$35	$30	$25	$20	N/A	N/A

MODEL 2025 – BB/.177 cal., SP, single-stroke pump action cocking, 300 FPS, 20 shot mag., fiber optic front sight, adj. rear sight, mounted 4x20 scope, black composite stock and finish, automatic safety, 33.5 in. OAL, 2.5 lbs. Mfg. 2005-2011.

	$30	$25	$20	$20	$15	N/A	N/A

Last MSR was $35.

MODEL 2026 – BB/.177 cal., single-stroke pump action cocking, lightweight black composite design, fiber optic front sight, automatic safety, 20-shot mag., mounted 4x20 scope, 33.5 in. OAL, 2.5 lbs. New 2010.

courtesy Beeman Precision Airguns

MSR $46	$40	$35	$30	$25	$20	N/A	N/A

MODEL 2030 – BB/.177 cal., SP, single-stroke pump action cocking, 300 FPS, 20 shot mag., fiber optic front sight, adj. rear sight, black composite stock, zinc finish, automatic safety, 33.5 in. OAL, 2.5 lbs. Mfg. 2007-2011.

	$35	$30	$25	$20	$15	$10	N/A

Last MSR was $40.

GRADING	100%	95%	90%	80%	60%	40%	20%

MODEL 2040 – BB/.177 cal., SP, single-stroke pump action cocking, 300 FPS, 20 shot mag., all metal receiver and barrel assembly, fiber optic front sight, mounted 4x20 scope, black composite stock, zinc finish, automatic safety, 33.5 in. OAL, 4 lbs. New 2007.

courtesy Beeman Precision Airguns

MSR $60	$50	$45	$40	$35	$25	N/A	N/A

MARLIN

Current trademark with headquarters located in Madison, NC beginning 2010. Currently manufactured by Remington in Ilion, NY beginning early 2011. Previous manufacturer located in North Haven, CT (1969-2010), and in New Haven, CT (1870-1969). The Marlin company manufactured firearms between 1870-2010. Distributor sales only.

On Nov. 10th, 2000, Marlin Firearms Company purchased H&R 1871, Inc. This includes the brand names Harrington & Richardson, New England Firearms, and Wesson & Harrington.

During 2005, Marlin Firearms Company once again started manufacturing an L.C. Smith line of both SxS and O/U shotguns.

In late Jan. of 2008, Remington acquired the Marlin Firearms Company, including the H&R, New England Firearms (NEF), and L.C. Smith brands, and plans to continue with production of these trademarks.

Marlin Firearms Company had been a family-owned and operated business since 1921 until 2007.

Beginning 2010 Marlin licensed Crosman to use the Marlin Trademark.

For more information and current pricing on both new and used Marlin firearms, please refer to the *Blue Book of Gun Values* by S.P. Fjestad (also available online).

RIFLES

COWBOY – BB/.177 cal., lever action, SS, 350 FPS, all metal receiver, hardwood stock and forearm, front blade fiber optic sight, adj. notched rear sight, 35.5 in. OAL, 2.75 lbs. Mfg. 2010-current.

courtesy Crosman

MSR $45	$40	$35	$30	$25	$20	N/A	N/A

MAROCCHI

Current trademark established in 1922, and currently manufactured by CD Europe SRL, located in Sarezzo, Italy. Currently imported/distributed beginning 2010 exclusively by Precision Airgun Distribution/Airguns of Arizona located in Gilbert, AZ. Dealer and consumer sales.

RIFLES

SM45 HP – BB/.177 cal., CO_2, semi-auto repeater, 88 gram CO_2 bottle, 14 in. barrel, 439 FPS, adj. sights, black or wood finished synthetic sporter stock. Mfg. 2010-current.

courtesy Precision Airgun Distribution

MSR $229	$190	$160	$135	$110	$85	$55	$40

Add $20 for wood finished synthetic stock.

GRADING	100%	95%	90%	80%	60%	40%	20%

MARS

Previous trademark manufactured by Venus Waffenfabrik located in Thüringen, Germany.

The Mars military-style air rifles were listed with many models of Tell airguns in old Venus Waffenfabrik factory catalogs. It presently is assumed that VWF were the makers. For more information on Mars airguns, see Tell in the "T" section.

MARTIN

Previous trade name on air pistol by unknown maker.

Air pistol is in .177 cal. with ivory color grips. Patent approved for R.S. Martin in 1954. No other information or values are available at this time.

MATCHGUNS srl

Current air pistol manufacturer located in Parma, Italy. No current U.S. importation. Previously imported and distributed by Nygord Precision Products, located in Prescott, AZ.

Cesare Morini of Matchguns srl manufactures a complete line of high quality air pistols in target and free pistol configurations. Please contact him directly for more information, including pricing, current models, and U.S. availability (see Trademark Index).

For more information and current pricing on Matchguns srl firearms, please refer to the *Blue Book of Gun Values* by S.P. Fjestad (also available online).

PISTOLS

MODEL MG I – .177 cal., PCP, SS, 9.36 in. barrel, black finish, 625 FPS, adj. anatomical wood grip, adj. electronic trigger, fully adj. sights, adj. stabilizer, 10.7 in. OAL, 2.42 lbs.

No MSR	$825	$750	$695	N/A	N/A	N/A	N/A

MODEL MG I LIGHT – .177 cal., PCP, SS, similar to Model MG 1, except standard grip and no stabilizers, 10.7 in. OAL, 2.42 lbs.

courtesy Matchguns srl

Please contact the company directly for pricing and availablity on this model.

MATCHLESS

Previous trade name of BB rifles manufactured by Henry C. Hart Company located in Detroit, MI, circa 1890 to 1900.

These were spring piston BB rifles using a top lever for cocking; similar in this function to the First Model Daisy introduced in 1889. Cast iron parts made them more substantial and heavier than contemporary BB rifles. Promoted as the only repeating BB guns on the market, they actually were single shots, which, like some of the early Daisy "repeaters," could be fed BBs one at a time from a built-in magazine.

RIFLES

FIRST MODEL – .180/large BB cal., SP, TL, sixty-five-shot gravity-fed magazine, cast iron frame with black paint finish, blued steel barrel, marked "MATCHLESS" in a curving line on the side of the grip frame, top cocking lever w/o knob, no safety, 35.5 in. OAL, 2.5 lbs. Mfg. 1890-95.

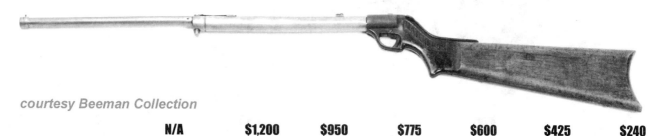

courtesy Beeman Collection

N/A	$1,200	$950	$775	$600	$425	$240

Commonly the rear sight, magazine latch, and/or loading gate at the muzzle have been lost.

GRADING	100%	95%	90%	80%	60%	40%	20%

SECOND MODEL – similar to First Model, except "MATCHLESS" name is much smaller and in a straight line on the side of the breech area of the receiver, seamless brass nickel-plated barrel, top cocking lever with false-hammer knob. Mfg. 1895-1900.

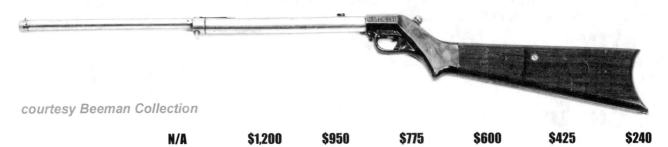

courtesy Beeman Collection

	N/A	$1,200	$950	$775	$600	$425	$240

CHAMPION

No information available at the time of publishing, research is ongoing.

MAUSER

Current trademark manufactured in Europe by various subcontractors. No current U.S. importation. Mauser airguns are not manufactured by Mauser-Werke. Previously imported and distributed by Beeman Precision Airguns located in San Rafael, CA, and Marksman, located in Huntington Beach, CA.

For more information and current pricing on both new and used Mauser firearms, please refer to the Blue *Book of Gun Values* by S.P. Fjestad (also available online).

PISTOLS

U90/U91 JUMBO AIR PISTOLS – for information on this model, see FB Record (Fritz Barthelms) in the "F" section.

RIFLES

MATCH 300SL/SLC – .177 cal., UL, SP, 550/450 FPS, adj. sights and hardwood stock, 8 lbs. 8 oz.

	$200	$165	$120	$85	$55	N/A	N/A

Last MSR was $330.

Add 25% for SLC Model with diopter sights.

This model was manufactured in Hungary.

MAXIM

Previous trade name of airguns produced by Industrias Irus S.L., located in Spain.

MAYER AND GRAMMELSPACHER

For information on Mayer and Grammelspacher airguns, see Dianawerk in the "D" section.

MEIER

Previous marking on custom pistol made by Jeff Meier of Miami, FL.

PISTOLS

MEIER PISTOL – .38 cal. smoothbore for round ball/slugs or .380 Crosman shot shells, built on Crosman 2240 frame, 18.5 in. OAL. Circa 1998.

courtesy Beeman Collection

	N/A	$250	$200	$165	$125	$90	$50

MENALDI

Current tradename of Menaldi Armas Neumaticas located in Cordoba, Argentina. No current U.S. importation.

In 2004 Luis Menaldi started development of a line of CO_2 rifles of high end quality for both target and hunting. At time of printing only a few handmade samples had been made and digital illustrations were not available. Additional information on this line will be provided in future issues of this guide. Best current source of information is the Menaldi website at www.menaldi.com.ar.

MENDOZA S.A. de C.V.

Current manufacturer Productas Mendoza, S.A. located in Xochimilco, Mexico. Currently imported and distributed under the Benjamin and Crosman names by Crosman Corp., located in Bloomfield, NY and by Air Venturi/Pyramyd Air located in Solon, OH (previously located in Warrensville Heights, OH). Previously distributed by Airgun Express, Inc. located in Montezuma, IA, and by Compasseco located in Bardstown, KY.

For information on Models RM622 and RM777, see Benjamin Air Rifle Co. in the "B" section. For information on Models RM177, RM277, RM522, RM577, RM677, RM877, and RM 650 BB Scout, see Crosman Corp. in the "C" section.

The Mendoza brand has an exotic history, beginning in 1911 when engineer Rafael Mendoza established the company to develop a unique 7mm two-barrel machine gun and then an improved Mauser-type bolt action rifle. Mendoza produced machine guns and hand grenades, 35 and 37mm field artillery cannons, and field heliographs for General Francisco Villa (Pancho Villa) during the Mexican Revolution. In 1934, the Mendoza 1934 C model rifle/machine gun was selected as standard ordnance for the Mexican Army and Navy.

In the 1950s, Mendoza began production of an interesting variety of BB guns including the Model 50 double barrel BB gun - a gun considerably rarer than the Daisy double barrel BB guns. In 1971, still owned by the family, the Mendoza Company moved from exclusive production of guns to six different product lines, including sophisticated pellet guns such as the RM 2003 with its quick change calibers and dual component safety trigger (RM, in case you hadn't guessed, stands for Rafael Mendoza).

A wide variety of airguns has been produced by Mendoza. This is a first, preliminary model list. There presently is confusion regarding the designation, specifications, and dates for several models. Additional research is being done on this brand and results will appear in future editions of this guide and on the web. Information is actively solicited from Mendoza collectors. Please contact Blue Book Publications, send inputs to guns@bluebookinc.com.

The authors and publisher of *Blue Book of Airguns* wish to express their appreciation to Ralph Heize Flamand of the Mendoza Company for his assistance with this section.

PISTOLS

MODEL M-56 – tinplate copy of Colt Single Action Army revolver.

No other information or values available at time of printing. Please submit info. to guns@bluebookinc.com.

RIFLES

MODEL 4 – .177 or .22 cal., SP, UL, SS, mahogany or habillo wood stock, rubber buttplate.

courtesy Mendoza

No other information or values available at time of printing.

MODEL 5 – deluxe version of Model 4.

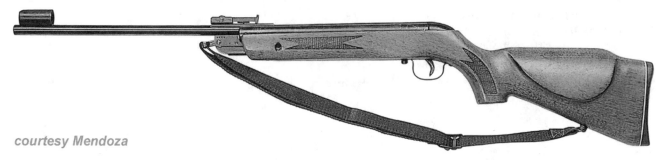

courtesy Mendoza

No other information or values available at time of printing.

GRADING	100%	95%	90%	80%	60%	40%	20%

MODEL 25 – BB/.177 cal., BBC, tinplate construction, nickel plated. Mfg. circa 1950.

courtesy Mendoza

No other information or values available at time of printing.

Mendoza's first airgun.

MODEL 50 DOUBLE BARREL BB GUN – double barrel version of Model 25; extremely rare. Mfg. circa 1954.

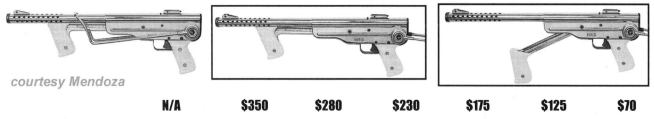

courtesy Beeman Collection

	N/A	N/A	N/A	$1,500	$1,400	$1,300	$1,000

MODEL 50 LEVER ACTION BB GUN – BB/.174 cal., SP, Winchester-style cocking lever, tinplate BB gun-type construction. Separate wood buttstock and forearm.

No other information or values available at time of printing.

MODEL 85 LEVER ACTION BB GUN – BB/.174 cal., SP, Winchester-style cocking lever, tinplate BB gun-type construction. Separate wood buttstock and forearm.

No other information or values available at time of printing.

MODEL COMPETITION – BB, SP, SS, mahogany or habillo wood Monte Carlo stock, checkered grip and forearm, buttplate with white line spacer, sling swivels, rear body tube cap styled like Webley Airsporter, blued finish, pellet holder at base of barrel. Circa 1980s.

No other information or values available at time of printing.

MODEL HM-3 – BB/.177 cal., SP, UL, 35-shot spring-fed magazine, folding metal stock, nickel plated. Mfg. 1957-1960.

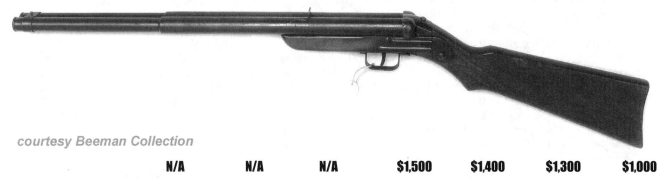

courtesy Mendoza

	N/A	$350	$280	$230	$175	$125	$70

MODEL LARGO

No other information or values available at time of printing.

MODEL MAGNUM – BB, SP, SS, "high velocity," mahogany or habillo wood Monte Carlo stock, checkered grip and forearm, buttplate with white line spacer, sling swivels, rear body tube cap styled like Webley Airsporter, blued finish, pellet holder at base of BBL. Circa 1980s.

No other information or values available at time of printing.

GRADING	100%	95%	90%	80%	60%	40%	20%

MODEL RM 10 – .22 cal., SP, BBC, SS, 14.2 in. BBL, 450 FPS, mahogany or habillo wood Monte Carlo stock, sling, 35.4 in. OAL, 5.94 lbs. New 1986.

courtesy Mendoza

MSR N/A	$125	$110	$90	$75	$55	$40	$25

MODEL RM 65 – BB/.174 cal., SP, Winchester-style cocking lever, 11.8 in. BBL, 250 FPS, tinplate BB gun-type construction, separate Monte Carlo-style wood buttstock and forearm, blue finish, 35.83 in. OAL, 3.08 lbs. New 1986.

courtesy Mendoza

No other information or values available at time of printing.

* **Model RM 650** – similar to RM 65, except with 500-shot magazine.

No other information or values available at time of printing.

MODEL RM 100 – .177 or .22 cal., SP, BBC, SS, 19 in. BBL, 750/675 FPS, mahogany or habillo wood Monte Carlo stock, sling, 41 in. OAL, 6.6 lbs. New 1986.

courtesy Mendoza

No other information or values available at time of printing.

MODEL RM 200 – .177 or .22 cal., BBC, SP, SS, 19 in. BBL, mahogany or habillo wood Monte Carlo stock, RH cheek piece, swivels and sling, 41 in. OAL, 6.6 lbs.

MSR N/A	$160	$140	$115	$95	$75	$50	$30

Add $51 for Model RM-200 Combo with 4x32mm scope.

MODEL RM 450C/450L – .177 cal., BBC, SP, SS, 18.5 in. BBL, 600 FPS, mahogany or habillo wood Monte Carlo stock, RH cheek piece, deep belly forearm, swivels and sling, 40.16-42.5 in. OAL, 6.82 lbs.

MSR $200	$170	$145	$120	$100	$75	$50	$35

MODEL RN 600 – .22 cal., BBC, SP, SS, 18.5 in. BBL, 900 FPS, mahogany or habillo wood Monte Carlo stock, RH cheek piece, swivels and sling, 45.28 in. OAL, 7.7 lbs.

MSR N/A	$200	$170	$140	$115	$90	$60	$40

Add $49 for Model RM-600 Combo with 4x32mm scope.
Add $75 for Model RM-600 Combo with 3-9x32mm scope.

MODEL RM 800 – .177 or .22 cal., SP, BBC, SS, 18.5 in. BBL, 1050/900 FPS, laminated wood thumbhole stock, nylon sling, rubber pellet holder on barrel, manual safety, blue finish, 20.5 in. round barrel, 45.28 in. OAL, 7.92 lbs. New 1986.

	$350	$300	$245	$205	$160	$105	$70

MODEL RM 1000 – .22 cal., SP, BBC, seven-shot repeater, 19 in. BBL, 650 FPS, mahogany or habillo wood Monte Carlo stock, 45.28 in. OAL, 7.7 lbs. New 1986.

No other information or values available at time of printing.

GRADING	100%	95%	90%	80%	60%	40%	20%

MODEL RM 2000 – .22 cal., BBC, SP, SS, 18.5 in. BBL, 850 FPS, mahogany or habillo wood Monte Carlo stock, RH cheek piece, swivels and sling, 45.28 in. OAL, 7.7 lbs.

MSR N/A	$240	$205	$170	$140	$110	$70	$50

Add $47 for Model RM-2000 Combo with 4x32mm scope.

MODEL RM 2003 ADVANCE – .177 or .22 cal., SP, BBC, SS, 18.5 in. BBL, 1200/1000 FPS, mahogany or habillo wood Monte Carlo stock, instant change barrels with dual caliber muzzle brake, double blade safety trigger, 45 in. OAL, 7.7 lbs. New 2003.

courtesy Mendoza

MSR N/A	$270	$230	$190	$155	$120	$80	$55

Add $45 for Model RM-600 Combo with 4x32mm scope.
Add $86 for Model RM-600 Combo with 3-9x32mm scope.

MODEL 2800 – .22 cal., BBC, SP, SS, 1150/950 FPS, 18.5 in. barrel, mahogany or habillo wood Monte Carlo thumbhole stock, RH cheek piece, swivels and sling, 45.28 in. OAL, 7.7 lbs.

No other information or values available at time of printing.

MODEL SHORT M6 – BB, SP, SS, mahogany or habillo wood Monte Carlo stock, buttplate with white line spacer, sling swivels, rear body tube cap styled like Webley Airsporter, blued finish, pellet holder at base of BBL. Mfg. circa 1980s.

No other information or values available at time of printing.

MODEL SUPER V-57 – BB/.177 cal., gravity-fed magazine, Daisy-style lever action cocking, tinplate construction, nickel plated.

courtesy Mendoza

No other information or values available at time of printing.

MODEL TI MEN – BB/.177 cal., gravity-fed magazine, Daisy-style lever action cocking, tinplate construction, blued.

courtesy Mendoza

No other information or values available at time of printing.

MODEL VAQUERO – appears to be a copy of Beeman C1 hunting carbine, BB, SP, SS, mahogany or habillo wood straight shotgun-style stock without pistol grip, buttplate with white line spacer, rear body tube cap styled like Webley Airsporter, blued finish. Mfg. circa 1980s.

No other information or values available at time of printing.

MILBRO

Previous trade name of Millard Brothers located in Motherwell, Lanarkshire, Scotland.

The name Milbro is derived from "Millard Brothers," a family owned business founded in 1887; apparently the senior figure was David W. Millard.

GRADING	100%	95%	90%	80%	60%	40%	20%

Milbro began producing airguns in 1949, using machinery and equipment taken as WWII war reparations from the Mayer and Grammelspacher Company (DIANAWERK) in Rastatt, Germany in 1945. Milbro also received the brand name DIANA and even the Diana logo showing the goddess of hunting, Diana, discarding her bow and arrow in favor of an airgun, held high above her head. This resulted in today's collectors having both German and British airguns bearing the Diana name and logo! In 1950, DIANAWERK again began the production of airguns in their old factory in Rastatt. They were forced to use names other than "Diana." Within Germany the Dianawerk airguns were sold as "Original." The brand "Original Diana" was used for Dianawerk guns in England. Dianawerk repurchased their trademark in 1984 after Milbro ceased airgun production. After 1984 all Diana airguns were again made in Rastatt, Germany (see Dianawerk section). For greater detail on this aspect, see DIANAWERK in the D section of this book.

Milbro produced airguns under both their own name and the acquired Diana brand. Most of these guns were close copies of the German pre-war models; many bore the same model number as their German pre-war siblings. Meanwhile Dianawerk in Germany had resumed production of some of the same models under the same model numbers (but under the Original or Original Diana labels); some with modifications or improvements! Milbro made airguns for other firms in the shooting trade including Umarex in Germany, Daisy in the USA, and Webley & Scott and Phoenix Arms in England. The Webley Jaguar was manufactured by Milbro and the virtually identical Webley Junior may also have been a Milbro product. Some of the Milbro airguns did not bear the Diana name, but were marked "Milbro Foreign" which indicates that they may have been made for Milbro of Scotland by Dianawerk in Germany in the pre-WWII period when German markings were not in favor in England.

Milbro was sold in 1970 to Grampian Holdings who also owned businesses making fishing tackle, golf clubs, and other items. During the mid-1970s Milbro sold airguns to mail order catalog retailers. By 1982, despite the advantage of the famous old Diana trademark, Milbro, using Dianawerk's old machinery and materials, had ceased making airguns. The machinery was sold to El Gamo. Some remaining guns were sold to a Swiss firm for mail order sales.

Milbro began making airgun pellets in 1950. The pellet business was sold to former Milbro employee Jim Mark. Milbro pellets, under the names of Caledonian, Jet, Rhino, Clipper, Match and TR are still made in Motherwell, Scotland.

The authors and publisher wish to thank Tim Saunders and Jim Mark for their valuable assistance with the following information in this section of the *Blue Book of Airguns*. Ref.: Dennis Hiller's British based *The Collectors' Guide to Air Rifles* and *The Collectors' Guide to Air Pistols*. Much of the following is based on those books. Additional information is actively sought from readers; direct info to guns@bluebookinc.com.

PISTOLS

DIANA G2 – .177 cal., pellets or darts, SP, SS, derived from German Diana Model 2, except has black or nickel finish, 2 pc. black plastic grips, "Gat" style push-barrel cocking. Mfg. 1965-1982.

courtesy Beeman Collection

| $55 | $45 | $40 | $30 | $25 | $15 | $10 |

Add 50% for factory box.
Add 20% for nickel finish.

DIANA MODEL 2 – .177 cal., pellets or darts, SP, SS, "Gat" style push-barrel cocking, black or nickel finish, similar to German Diana Model 2 push-barrel pistol, except with wood grips. Mfg. 1949-1965.

courtesy Beeman Collection

| $55 | $45 | $40 | $30 | $25 | $15 | $10 |

Add 50% for factory box.
Add 20% for nickel finish.

GRADING	100%	95%	90%	80%	60%	40%	20%

MILBRO MK II – .177 cal., SP, TL, SS, based on 1937 patent of German Em-Ge Zenit, single stage trigger, one piece wooden stock, 11 in. OAL, 1.5 lbs.

	100%	95%	90%	80%	60%	40%	20%
	$160	$135	$110	$95	$70	$50	$30

Add 60% for original six sided box.

Add 30% for original four sided box.

DIANA MK II (G4) – .177 cal., SP, TL, SS, based on 1937 patent of German Em-Ge Zenit, single stage trigger, one piece wooden stock with medallion of Diana logo or Diana name, 11 in. OAL, 1.5 lbs.

	100%	95%	90%	80%	60%	40%	20%
	$150	$130	$105	$85	$70	$45	$30

Add 25% for factory box.

MILBRO CUB – 2.41mm lead balls (No.7 lead birdshot) cal., fired by a quick squeeze on the rubber bulb in the grip, gravity feed 500 shot magazine, one piece cast alloy construction; no moving parts, purple anodized finish or polished zinc alloy. Mfg. began during late 1940s.

courtesy Beeman Collection

	100%	95%	90%	80%	60%	40%	20%
	$300	$255	$210	$175	$135	$90	$60

Add 50% for factory box.

"World's Weakest Air Pistol". Shot sold by Milbro in packets marked "Spare charges". Patented in France during 1948 and also produced in France in an all plastic version.

MILBRO G10 – .177 cal., SP, slide pulls to load and cock, 20 shot repeater with BBs, SS with pellets or darts, may be various finishes, markings, and accessories. Mfg. 1952-1982.

	100%	95%	90%	80%	60%	40%	20%
	$35	$30	$25	$20	$15	$10	N/A

A private branding of Marksman 1010 air pistol from California.

DIANA SP50 – .177 cal., SP, SS, push barrel design, 400 FPS, styled like an automatic pistol, cast alloy frame, darts or pellets loaded at the rear, sold in polystyrene cartons complete with packets of .177 darts and pellets. Mfg. 1970s-1982. 7 in. OAL, 1.6 lbs.

courtesy Beeman Collection

	100%	95%	90%	80%	60%	40%	20%
	$55	$45	$40	$30	$25	$15	$10

Add 5% for factory box.

Identical pistol marketed by Phoenix Arms Company, Eastbourne, East Sussex, England as G50 until at least 1989. Also sold as Perfecta SP50.

MILBRO COUGAR – .177 or .22 cal., SP, BBC, SS, similar to BSA Scorpion, grips and barrel pivot cover plates of simulated wood, blue steel body tube and barrel, black finished cast metal receiver, 18.5 in. OAL. Mfg. 1978-1982.

	100%	95%	90%	80%	60%	40%	20%
	$175	$150	$125	$100	$80	$50	$35

Add 20% for box with shoulder stock, sight blades, scope ramp, and pellets.

GRADING	100%	95%	90%	80%	60%	40%	20%

MILBRO BLACK MAJOR – .177 or .22 cal., SP, BBC, SS, similar to Milbro Cougar, except skeletal shoulder stock, reflector sight system. Mfg. 1981-82.

	$200	$170	$140	$115	$90	$60	$40

MILBRO TYPHOON – .177 cal., push-barrel, aluminum pistol, similar to Harrington "GAT", beech grip, 6.8 in. OAL. Mfg. 1950s.

Current values not yet determined.

Name conflict with Webley Typhoon air pistol and Relum Typhoon air rifle.

RIFLES

Early models may have date stamp on the lower edge of the stock.

DIANA MODEL 1 – .177 cal., BBC, SP, SS, similar to pre-WWII German Diana Model 1, removable smoothbore barrel, tinplate construction. Mfg. circa 1949-1959.

	$75	$65	$55	$45	$35	$20	$15

DIANA MODEL 15 – .177 cal., BBC, SP, SS, similar to pre-WW2 German Diana Model 1, tinplate construction, smoothbore barrel. Mfg. 1950s-1980.

	$90	$75	$65	$50	$40	$25	$20

DIANA MODEL 16 – .177 cal., BBC, SP, SS, similar to pre-WW2 German Diana Model 16, tinplate construction, smoothbore barrel, later models with scope ramp spot welded to body cylinder. Mfg. late 1940s -1974.

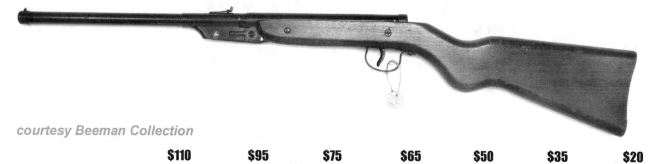

courtesy Beeman Collection

	$110	$95	$75	$65	$50	$35	$20

Also sold in USA as the Winchester 416, HyScore 805, and Daisy 160.

DIANA MODEL 22 – 177 cal., BBC, SP, SS, similar to pre-WW2 German Diana Model 22, tinplate construction, smoothbore barrel. Mfg. late 1940s- early 1970s.

courtesy Beeman Collection

	$125	$105	$90	$75	$55	$35	$25

MILBRO MODEL 22 – .177 cal., BBC, SP, SS, similar to English Diana Model 22, tinplate construction, smoothbore barrel, recognizable by sweeping curve of stock up behind rear of cylinder. Mfg. late 1940s to early 1970s.

	$125	$105	$90	$75	$55	$35	$25

Add 10% for box.

Gave rise to Webley Jaguar and Junior.

DIANA MODEL 23 – .177 cal., BBC, SP, SS, similar to pre-WWII German Diana Model 23, solid barrel version of Model 22, 37 in. OAL. Mfg. late 1940s to approx. 1960.

	$150	$130	$105	$85	$70	$45	$30

Became Milbro G23.

MILBRO G23 – .177 cal., BBC, SP, SS, similar to English Diana Model 23, 37 in. OAL, 3.5 lbs. Mfg. circa 1970s.

	$150	$130	$105	$85	$70	$45	$30

GRADING	100%	95%	90%	80%	60%	40%	20%

DIANA 25 – .177 or .22 cal., BBC, SP, SS, similar to pre-WWII German Diana Model 25, rifled or smoothbore, 38.3 in. OAL, 5 lbs.

	100%	95%	90%	80%	60%	40%	20%
	$120	$100	$85	$70	$55	$35	$25

DIANA COMET – .177 or .22 cal., BBC, SP, SS, kit version, similar to pre-WW2 German Diana Model 25. Mfg. early 1960s-1963.

	$250	$215	$175	$145	$115	$75	$50

DIANA G25 – .177 or .22 cal., BBC, SP, SS, similar to English Diana Model 25, 38 in. OAL, 5 lbs. Mfg. 1963-66.

	$130	$110	$90	$75	$60	$40	$25

DIANA 27 – .177 or .22 cal., BBC, SP, SS, similar to pre-WWII German Diana Model 27, smoothbore or rifled BBL, 5.8 lbs. Mfg. circa 1950s-1963.

	$120	$100	$85	$70	$55	$35	$25

DIANA G27 – .177 cal., smoothbore/rifled BBL, .22 rifled cal., similar to English Diana 27, except with manual safety (early production may lack safety), 41.5 in. OAL, 5.9 lbs. Mfg. circa 1963-67.

	$125	$105	$90	$75	$55	$35	$25

DIANA G36 – .177 or .22 cal. BBC, SP, SS, manual safety, 41.5 in. OAL, Mfg. 1966-early 1970s.

	$120	$100	$85	$70	$55	$35	$25

DIANA G44 (TARGETMASTER) – .177 or .22 cal., BBC, SP, SS, similar to British Diana Model 25, rifled or smoothbore, manual safety, aperture sight, 42 in. OAL, 6.3 lbs. Mfg. circa 1967-early 1970s.

	$250	$215	$175	$145	$115	$75	$50

DIANA G46 (TARGETMASTER) – .177 or .22 cal., BBC, SP, SS, similar to British Diana Model 27, rifled or smoothbore in .177 cal., rifled only in .22 cal., aperture sight, manual safety. Mfg. circa 1967-early 1970s.

	$250	$215	$175	$145	$115	$75	$50

DIANA 55/G55 – .177 or .22 cal., UL, SP, SS, similar to German Original Model 50, faucet tap loading, 42 in. OAL, 7.2 lbs. Mfg. circa late 1950s-early 1960s.

	$375	$325	$265	$220	$170	$110	$75

DIANA SERIES 70 – .177 or .22 cal., BBC, SP, SS. Mfg. circa 1971-1980s.

* **Model 71** – .177 cal., BBC, SP, SS, rear manual safety, deluxe Monte Carlo stock with white line buttpad, checkering, BBL with outer sleeve, 42.8 in. OAL. Mfg. circa 1971-1982.

	$225	$190	$160	$130	$100	$65	$45

* **Model 74 (G74)** – .177 cal., BBC, SP, SS, similar to German Original Model 16 except improved stock, tinplate construction, smoothbore barrel, 32.5 in. OAL, 3 lbs. Mfg. early 1970s-late 1970s.

	$50	$45	$35	$30	$25	$15	$10

* **Model 75** – .177 cal., BBC, SP, SS, similar to Diana Series 70, Model 74 except rifled barrel, tinplate construction, 32.5 in. OAL, 3 lbs. Mfg. circa 1980-1982.

	$60	$50	$40	$35	$25	$20	$10

* **Model 76** – .177 or .22 cal., BBC, SP, SS, semi-tinplate construction, rifled barrel, 400/300 FPS, 37 in. OAL, 5.3 lbs. Mfg. circa 1972-1980s.

	$120	$100	$85	$70	$55	$35	$25

* **Model 77** – .177 or .22 cal., BBC, SP, SS, rifled barrel, 400/300 FPS, 38.5 in. OAL, 6 lbs. Mfg. circa 1972-1980s.

	$120	$100	$85	$70	$55	$35	$25

* **Model 78 (Standard)/Model 79 (Deluxe)** – .177 cal. BBC, SP, SS, manual safety on side, 38.5 in. OAL. Mfg. circa 1978-1980s.

	$120	$100	$85	$70	$55	$35	$25

DIANA G80 – .177 or .22 cal., BBC, SP, SS, 625/500 FPS, sloping forearm as of 1980, 42 in. OAL, 6.8 lbs. Mfg. early 1977-1982.

	$150	$130	$105	$85	$70	$45	$30

DIANA G85 (BOBCAT) – .177 cal., BBC, SP, SS, smoothbore barrel, 33 in. OAL, 3.8 lbs. Mfg. circa 1978-1982.

	$120	$100	$85	$70	$55	$35	$25

Similar to Diana Series 70, Model 74 (G74), an updated version of Model 16.

GRADING	100%	95%	90%	80%	60%	40%	20%

MILBRO SCOUT – .177 cal., BBC, SP, SS, similar to pre-WWII German Diana Model 1 except 2 ball detents to hold barrel shut.

	$35	$30	$25	$20	$15	$10	N/A

MILLARD BROTHERS

For information on Millard Brothers airguns, see Milbro in this section.

MOLOT

Current manufacturer located in Russia. No current U.S. importation.

Molot manufactures the Recruit model air rifle. Please contact the company directly for more information on this model, U.S. pricing, and availability (see Trademark Index).

MONDIAL

For information on Mondial airguns, see MMM - Mondial in this section.

LA MONDIALE

Previous trade name of air rifle made by Martin Bilak Ft. d'armes, in Liege, Belgium.

Little is known of this gun. It is in .177 cal., barrel-cocking with straight, non-twisting 4 groove rifling, heavily-built.

MONOGRAM

For information on Monogram, see Accles & Shelvoke Ltd. in the "A" section.

MONTGOMERY WARD

Catalog sales/retailer which subcontracted various domestic and international manufacturers to private label various brand names under the Montgomery Ward conglomerate.

Montgomery Ward airguns have appeared under various labels and endorsers, including Western Field and others. Most of these models were manufactured through subcontracts with both domestic and international firms. Typically, they were "spec." airguns made to sell at a specific price to undersell the competition. Most of these models were derivatives of existing factory models with less expensive wood and perhaps missing the features found on those models from which they were derived. Please refer to the Store Brand Crossover Section in the back of this book under Montgomery Ward for converting models to the respective manufacturer.

To date, there has been limited interest in collecting Montgomery Ward airguns, regardless of scarcity. Rather than list Montgomery Ward models, a general guideline is that values generally are under those of their "first generation relatives." As a result, prices are ascertained by the shooting value of the airgun, rather than its collector value.

MORINI COMPETITION ARM SA

Current manufacturer located in Bedano, Switzerland. Currently imported and distributed by Pilkington Competition Equipment, located in Monteagle, TN, and by Champion's Choice, located in LaVergne, TN. Previously imported 1993-2004 by Nygord Precision Products, located in Prescott, AZ.

For more information and current pricing on both new and used Morini Competition Arm SA firearms, please refer to the *Blue Book of Gun Values* by S.P. Fjestad (also available online).

PISTOLS

MODEL 162E – .177 cal., PCP, UIT pistol with fixed cylinder, electronic trigger, adj. sights, adj. grips.

	$800	$675	$550	$450	$350	$240	$160

Last MSR was $1,000.

MODEL 162EI/162EI SHORT – .177 cal., PCP, SS, match pistol, 7.41 (Short) or 9.36 in. Lothar Walther barrel, two detachable cylinders, black finish, Morini anatomical adj. wood grip, adj. electronic trigger, adj. sights, 2.2 lbs.

courtesy Morini

MSR $1,755	$1,450	$1,225	$1,025	$850	$650	$425	$290

Add $25 for Model 162EI Short.

GRADING		100%	95%	90%	80%	60%	40%	20%

MODEL 162MI/162MI SHORT – .177 cal., similar to Model 162EI, except has mechanical trigger.

courtesy Morini

MSR $1,725		$1,425	$1,200	$1,000	$825	$650	$425	$285

N/O SECTION

NANTONG UNIVERSAL OPTICAL INSTRUMENT CO., LTD

For information on Nantong Universal Optical Instument Co., Ltd. airguns, see ZOS in the "Z" section.

NATIONAL (KOREA)

Current status is unknown. Beeman Precision Airguns imported examples of one model in the mid-1970s.

GRADING	100%	95%	90%	80%	60%	40%	20%

RIFLES

NATIONAL VOLCANIC – .25 cal., SS, swinging lever pump pneumatic, with sliding loading port system identical to Yewha 3B air shotguns, requires same plastic shot tube, no markings, blued rifled barrel and body tube, parkerized trigger guard, 37 in. OAL, 6.6 lbs. Extremely rare in USA. Ref: AA Oct. 1987 (reprinted as Hannusch, 2001).

courtesy Beeman Collection

N/A	N/A	$1,200	$900	$600	$400	$250

NATIONAL RIFLES LTD. (INDIA)

Current manufacturer located in Ahmedabad, India. Distributed by Indian Hume Pipe Co. Ltd., located in Mumbai (formerly Bombay), India. No current U.S. importation.

National Rifles Ltd. is India's leading airgun manufacturer, and production based on German machinery and airgun designs. Walter (1984) reported that National produced a National Cadet CO_2 bulb rifle version of the Hammerli Cadet CO_2 rifle under a 1968 license from Hammerli and the National 25, as a simpler version of the Dianawerk Model 25.

NELSON PAINT COMPANY

Paint company and previous manufacturer of paintball markers located in Iron Mountain, MI, and founded in 1940.

Nelson marketed the first paintball guns (invented by James C. Hale of Daisy, U.S. patent 3,788,298, Jan 29, 1974), and originally marketed to ranchers and foresters for marking cattle and trees. Undoubtedly, one day, a cowboy or ranger was holding a Nelson marking gun when he saw his partner, not too far away, bend over to pick something up. At that moment, the paintball combat game market was born! The first organized paintball game in 1981 used Nelson 007 pistols. The first paintball game gun was the Splatmaster (U.S. patent 4,531,503, Robert G Shepherd, July 30, 1985), also rather collectible, values $25 to $40.

Paintball markers are now a huge specialized field onto themselves and thus will not be covered in this guide except where the models have historical connections with the regular airgun field. Nelson tree markers today are specialized paint spraying devices, but the company continues to produce paintballs.

PISTOLS

NEL-SPOT 007 – .68 cal. paintball, 12g CO_2 cylinder, bolt action, 8-shot gravity fed (10-shot with threaded ball tube), steel and brass construction, black paint finish, 11 in. OAL, 3 lbs. Mfg. by Daisy beginning 1974. Disc.

courtesy Beeman Collection

$200	$150	$100	$75	$50	N/A	N/A

Add 5% for holster.
Add 100% for early versions without removable barrel sleeve, magazine tube threaded inside to accept threaded aluminum paint ball tubes. Plastic pellet stop snapped into magazine center holes.

GRADING	100%	95%	90%	80%	60%	40%	20%

NEL-SPOT 707 – .68 cal. paintball, CO_2, six-ball gravity-fed magazine along LHS of receiver, blue finish, 11.6 in. OAL, 3.2 lbs. unloaded. Disc.

courtesy Beeman Collection

	100%	95%	90%	80%	60%	40%	20%
	$400	$325	$250	$175	$100	N/A	N/A

Add 5% for holster.

This model was briefly made by Crosman, apparently before the NEL-SPOT 007.

NORICA FARMI S.A.L.

Current trademark manufactured by Norica-Farmi, S.A.L., located in Eibar, Spain. No current U.S. importation. Previously imported by Beeman Precision Airguns in Santa Fe Springs, CA, (previously located in San Rafael and Santa Rosa, CA), American Arms, Inc., located in North Kansas City, MO, K.B.I., located in Harrisburg, PA, and by S.A.E., located in Miami, FL.

Norica produces several economy level private label airguns. Norica airguns imported by American Arms, Inc. will appear under the American Arms, Inc. heading.

PISTOLS

SINGLE SHOT PISTOL – 4.5mm cal., SS, CO_2, one or two 8.5 gram CO_2 cylinders, 5.5 or 8 in. barrel, blue finish, fixed sights, white plastic grips, similar to Crosman Model 150.

courtesy Loke Collection

	100%	95%	90%	80%	60%	40%	20%
	N/A	$200	$160	$130	$100	$70	$40

Add 20% for 8 in. barrel.

RIFLES

BLACK WIDOW – .177 or .22 cal., BBC, SP, 500/450 FPS, black plastic stock, 5 lbs.

	100%	95%	90%	80%	60%	40%	20%
	$120	$100	$85	$70	$55	$35	$25

INTREPID SILVER – .177 or .22 cal., BBC, SP, 17.87 in. rifled barrel, ambidextrous silver synthetic stock with textured grip and forearm, vent. rubber buttpad, dual raised cheek piece, auto safety, fiber optic sights, 46.46 in. OAL, 6.39 lbs.

MSR $310	$265	$235	$210	$170	$130	N/A	N/A

MASSIMO – .177 or .22 cal., BBC, SP, vaporized beech stock with checkered grip and forearm, 17.87 in. rifled barrel, fiber optic sights, auto safety, 47 in. OAL, 7.5 lbs.

MSR $390	$325	$295	$265	$215	$165	N/A	N/A

MODEL 47 – .177 cal., SL, SP, 600 FPS, black pistol grip, 5.5 lbs.

	100%	95%	90%	80%	60%	40%	20%
	$120	$100	$85	$70	$55	$35	$25

GRADING	100%	95%	90%	80%	60%	40%	20%

MODEL 56 BASIC – .177 cal., BBC, SP, 15.91 in. rifled barrel, vaporized beech stock, auto safety, 37.56 in. OAL, 5.07 lbs.

MSR $120	$100	$90	$80	$65	$50	N/A	N/A

MODEL 61C – .177 cal., BBC, SP, 600 FPS, 5.5 lbs.

	$85	$70	$60	$50	$40	$25	$15

MODEL 73 – .177 or .22 cal., BBC, SP, 580/525 FPS, 6 lbs. 4 oz.

	$110	$95	$75	$65	$50	$35	$20

MODEL 80G – .177 or .22 cal., BBC, SP, 635/570 FPS, 7 lbs. 2 oz.

	$140	$120	$100	$80	$65	$40	$30

MODEL 90 – .177 cal., BBC, SP, 650 FPS, rifled barrel with muzzlebrake, includes scope. Made in Spain.

MSR $150	$130	$115	$100	$85	$65	N/A	N/A

MODEL 92 – .177 cal., SL, SP, 650 FPS, 5.75 lbs.

	$125	$105	$90	$75	$55	$35	$25

NORICA QUICK – .177 or .22 cal., UL, pump action, 17.87 in. rifled barrel, checkered beech stock with dual raised cheek piece, vent. rubber buttpad, fiber optic sights, auto safety, 45.79 in. OAL, 8.16 lbs.

MSR $350	$300	$265	$240	$195	$145	N/A	N/A

NORICA YOUNG – .177 cal., BBC, SP, 600 FPS, colored stock.

	$85	$70	$60	$50	$40	$25	$15

TRIBAL BASIC – .177 or .22 cal., BBC, 19 in. rifled barrel, beech stock with raised cheek piece and decorative texture on forearm, rubber buttpad, fiber optic sights, 46.5 in. OAL.

MSR $300	$255	$225	$205	$165	$125	N/A	N/A

O SECTION

O'CONNELL GAS RIFLE

Previous trade name manufactured by the George Robinson Co. located in Rochester, NY circa 1947-1949.
See George Robinson Co. in the "R" section.

courtesy Beeman Collection

OKLAHOMA

For information on Oklahoma airguns, see MMM - Mondial in the "M" section.

OTTOMANGUNS

Current manufacturer located in Istanbul, Turkey. No current U.S. importation.

Ottomanguns manufactures air rifles. Please contact the company directly for more information regarding U.S. availability and pricing (see Trademark Index). For more information and current pricing on both new and used Ottomanguns firearms, please refer to the *Blue Book of Gun Values* by S.P. Fjestad (now online also).

Your support has its rewards

The Buffalo Bill Center of the West in Cody, Wyoming, holds the surviving original factory records from the Winchester, Marlin, and L.C. Smith firearms companies. As a Firearms Member, enjoy free serial number searches on individual firearms and special rates on factory letters.

ANNUAL FIREARMS MEMBERSHIP BENEFITS

- Free serial number searches.
- Discounts on factory letters.
- Factory search and letter package offers.
- Subscription to *Points West* magazine and Cody Firearms Record newsletter.
- Many additional benefits such as free admission to the Buffalo Bill Center of the West and other partner museums across the country, special mailings, and discounts.

MEMBERSHIP LEVELS

- $150 Wild West Circle: 5 serial number searches.
- $250 Bison Circle: 10 serial number searches, 2 factory letters, 10% discount on package offers.
- $500 Stagecoach Circle: 15 serial number searches, 5 factory letters, 20% discount on package offers.
- $1,000 1–of–1000 Circle: 20 serial number searches, 10 factory letters, 40% discount on package offers.
- $2,500 Pahaska Circle: 25 serial number searches, 15 factory letters, 50% discount on package offers.

Winchester Model 1866 Deluxe Sporting Rifle- This Model 1866 rifle is perhaps one of the finest Winchester examples of semi-relief engraving. Signed by master artisan Conrad F. Ulrich, it features an unusual decorative border at the wrist using Grecian key pattern. Also unusual is the rare depiction, on the right panel, of Diana, goddess of the hunt. Other panels depict elk, deer, bear, buffalo and rabbit. **Gift of Olin Corporation, Winchester Arms Collection 1988.8.3283**

BUFFALO BILL CENTER OF THE WEST

For a Membership,
307–578–4008
support.centerofthewest.org/firearms/join

Cody Firearms Museum Records Office

720 Sheridan Avenue, Cody, WY 82414 | 307–578–4031 FAX: 307–578–4079
EMAIL: *cfmrecords@centerofthewest.org*
ONLINE: *centerofthewest.org/explore/firearms/firearms-records/*
HOURS: Monday thru Friday – 8 a.m. to 4 p.m. and the occasional Saturday

P SECTION

PAFF

Previous tradename used by the merchant Henry Schuermans located in Liege, Belgium.

In 1890, Henry Schuermans registered the bow and arrow trademark, with the letters "PAFF", found on the airgun discussed here. Schuermans was the producer and/or distributor for the Paff air rifle patented by L. Poilvache of Leige under Belgian patents- number 76743 (March 1887), 79663 (November, 1887), and 84461 (December, 1888). Ref: John Atkins, AG, Feb. 2003.

PISTOLS

PAFF PISTOL – .177 cal., SB 10.5 in. bbl, BC, 21 in. OAL, "Patentiert" is only mark.

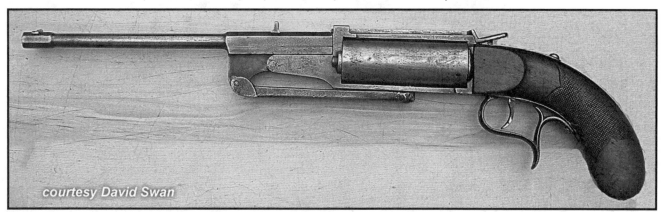

courtesy David Swan

Scarcity precludes accurate pricing.

RIFLES

GRADING	100%	95%	90%	80%	60%	40%	20%

PAFT RIFLE – .177 cal., BBC, SP, 3.5 in. long air chamber contains three concentric mainsprings which power a hollow piston, 37.7 in. OAL, 5.1 lbs.

courtesy Beeman Collection

100%	95%	90%	80%	60%	40%	20%
N/A	N/A	$1,400	$1,125	$875	$600	$350

PAINTBALL

For information on Paintball, see Nelson in the "N" section.

PALCO SPORTS

Current importer and/or distributor of licensed airgun and airsoft copies of major firearms trademarks, including Sig Sauer located in Maple Grove, MN.

Information on Sig Sauer airguns is located in the "S" section.

PALMER

Previous trade name used by Frank D. Palmer Inc., located in Chicago, IL.

Frank D. Palmer Inc., was a maker of carnival machine guns. Research on this brand is ongoing and additional material will be published in this guide and online as available. Ref. Behling (2006).

MACHINE GUN

PALMER MACHINE GUN – .174 BB cal., not known if steel or lead, or both, 9 in. smoothbore BBL, electrically driven horizontally rotating feeding disc which is gravity fed from top 2000 BB hopper, approximately one hundred balls, dual spade handle grips with RH trigger built-in. 69 in. tall, 20 in. wide, 1/6 HP AC motor for built-in compressor, about

GRADING	100%	95%	90%	80%	60%	40%	20%

300 pounds on original steel stand, black paint finish, marked with eagle shaped logo plate bearing the Palmer name.

courtesy Beeman Collection

Value in good condition about $3,000.

PALMER CHEMICAL AND EQUIPMENT CO.

Current manufacturer of tranquilizer guns located in Douglasville, GA.

Manufacturers of Palmer CapChur tranquilizer guns, generally based on CO_2 models of Crosman airguns. Generally use a small explosive charge in the syringe dart to force out the contents into the target, but the guns themselves are not firearms. Please contact the company directly for more information and prices of current products (see Trademark Index listing).

PISTOLS

STANDARD CAPCHUR PISTOL – .50 cal. tranquilizer darts, SS, CO_2, bolt action, small explosive charge for injecting the contents of the syringe dart into the animal to be subdued.

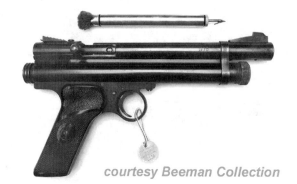

courtesy Beeman Collection

	100%	95%	90%	80%	60%	40%	20%
	$250	$200	$150	$100	$75	N/A	N/A

VEWT 4X CAPCHUR PISTOL – more recent version of Standard CapChur pistol.

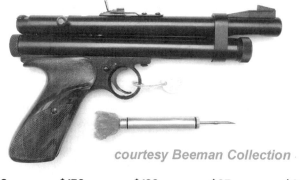

courtesy Beeman Collection

	100%	95%	90%	80%	60%	40%	20%
	$200	$150	$100	$85	$65	N/A	N/A

GRADING	100%	95%	90%	80%	60%	40%	20%

RIFLES

RED'S SPECIAL – .50 cal. tranquilizer darts, SS, CO_2, bolt action, small explosive charge for injecting the contents of the syringe dart into the animal to be subdued.

courtesy Beeman Collection

	$350	$300	$250	$200	$150	N/A	N/A

Add 20% for adj. trigger.

PAMPANGA

For information on Pampanga airguns, see Philippine Airguns in this "P" section.

PANTHER

For information on Panther airguns, see Gun Toys SRL in the "G" section.

PARDINI, ARMI S.r.l.

Current manufacturer located in Lido di Camaiore, Italy. Currently imported by Pardini USA LLC., located in Tampa, FL beginning 2012. Previously imported by Larry's Guns, located in Gray, ME, previously located in Portland, ME, by Nygord Precision Products, located in Prescott, AZ, and by MCS, Inc.

For more information and current pricing on both new and used Pardini firearms, please refer to the *Blue Book of Gun Values* by S.P. Fjestad (also available online).

PISTOLS

MODEL K-2 – .177 cal., CO_2, (250-shot capacity), UIT model, 9.1 in. barrel, adj. trigger, adj. walnut grip, 16 in. OAL, 2.6 lbs. Disc. 2008.

	$925	$775	$650	$525	$425	$275	$185

Last MSR was $919.

MODEL K-2 JUNIOR – .177 cal., CO_2, (250-shot capacity), UIT model, similar to Model K-2, except has 7.6 in. barrel. Disc. 2008.

	$925	$775	$650	$525	$425	$275	$185

Last MSR was $919.

MODEL K-2 LIGHT – .177 cal., CO_2, (250-shot capacity), UIT model, similar to Model K-2, except 2.3 lbs. Disc. 2008.

	$925	$775	$650	$525	$425	$275	$185

Last MSR was $919.

MODEL K-2S – .177 cal., PCP, (250-shot capacity), UIT model, 9.1 in. barrel, adj. trigger, adj. walnut grip, 16 in. OAL, 2.6 lbs. Importation disc. 2011.

	$1,350	$1,175	$1,075	$875	$650	N/A	N/A

Last MSR was $1,577.

MODEL K-2S JUNIOR – .177 cal., PCP, (250-shot capacity), UIT model, similar to Model K-2S, except has 7.6 in. barrel. Importation disc. 2011.

	$1,350	$1,175	$1,075	$875	$650	N/A	N/A

Last MSR was $1,577.

MODEL K-2S LIGHT – .177 cal., PCP, (250-shot capacity), UIT model, similar to Model K-2S, except 2.3 lbs. Disc. 2008.

	$950	$800	$675	$550	$425	$285	$190

Last MSR was $999.

GRADING	100%	95%	90%	80%	60%	40%	20%

MODEL K10 – .177 cal., PCP, UIT model, 9.1 in. barrel, adj. trigger, adj. walnut grip, 16 in. OAL, 2.6 lbs. Mfg. 2008-current.

courtesy of Pardini USA, LLC

MSR $1,699	$1,400	$1,200	$975	$800	$625	$425	$280

MODEL K10 JUNIOR – .177 cal., PCP, UIT model, similar to Model K-2S, except has 7.6 in. barrel. Mfg. 2008-current.

courtesy of Pardini USA, LLC

MSR $1,699	$1,400	$1,200	$975	$800	$625	$425	$280

MODEL K12 ABSORBER – .177 cal., SS, 9 in. compensated steel barrel, detachable cylinder for compressed air, innovative shot recoil system, two-stage trigger, interchangeable front sights, anatomical, adj. walnut grip, side readable pressure gauge, 16 in. OAL, 2 lbs. 2.9 oz. Mfg. 2012-current.

courtesy of Pardini USA, LLC

MSR $1,899	$1,600	$1,350	$1,125	$925	$725	$475	$325

* **Model K12 Junior** – .177 cal., similar to K12, except has 8 in. barrel, 14 in. OAL, 2 lbs. Mfg. 2012-current.

courtesy of Pardini USA, LLC

MSR $1,899	$1,600	$1,350	$1,125	$925	$725	$475	$325

GRADING	100%	95%	90%	80%	60%	40%	20%

MODEL K58 – .177 cal., UL, 9 in. barrel, UIT model, 2 lbs. 6 oz. Disc. 2008.

	$650	$550	$450	$375	$295	$195	$130

Last MSR was $819.

MODEL K60 – .177 cal., CO_2, 9.5 in. barrel, 2 lbs. 4 oz. Disc. 1997.

	$425	$350	$300	$245	$190	$125	$85

Last MSR was $795.

Add 20% for pre-charged pneumatic.

MODEL K90 – .177 cal., CO_2, youth model, 7.25 in. barrel, 1.85 lbs.

	$425	$350	$300	$245	$190	$125	$85

Last MSR was $580.

MODEL KID – .177 cal., SS, based on K-10 frame, 7 7/8 in. barrel, ambidextrous adj. wood grips, lightweight, adj. rear sight and two-stage trigger, designed for young shooters, parts are interchangeable with the K10 model, so the shooter can grow up with the gun, approx. 13 in. OAL. New 2012.

courtesy of Pardini USA, LLC

MSR $1,199	$1,025	$875	$725	$600	$450	$300	$205

MODEL P10 – .177 cal., UL, 7.75 in. barrel, 2 lbs. 3 oz. Disc. 1990.

	$400	$350	$280	$230	$180	$120	$80

Last MSR was $560.

PARDUS

Current manufacturer located in Istanbul, Turkey. No current U.S. importation.

Pardus manufactures a complete line of good quality air rifles in hunting, sporting, and tactical configurations. Please contact the company directly for more information, including pricing and U.S. availability (see Trademark Index).

PARK RIFLE COMPANY

Current manufacturer located in Kent, England. No current U.S. importation.

RIFLES

RH93/93W/93-800 – .177 or .22 cal., UL, 12ft./lb. energy, 37 or 38 (Model 93-800) in. barrel. 9 lbs. 10 oz.

	$400	$350	$275	$200	$135	N/A	N/A

Add $100 for thumbhole walnut stock.

PARKER-HALE

Parker was the previous tradename of the A.G. Parker Company located in Birmingham, England, which was formed from a gun-making business founded in 1890 by Alfred Gray Parker. The company became the Parker-Hale company in 1936, and was purchased by John Rothery Wholesale about circa 2000.

This firm made an air pistol designed by Alfred Hale and Ernest Harris and also made Lee-Enfield sporter firearm rifles. For more information and current pricing on Parker-Hale firearms, please refer to the *Blue Book of Gun Values* by S.P. Fjestad (also available online).

GRADING	100%	95%	90%	80%	60%	40%	20%

PISTOLS

PARKER PATENT PRECISION AIR PISTOL – .177 cal., SP, SS, fixed rifled 9.6 in. BBL, piston moves rearward during firing. Cocked by turning a large crank on the RHS 3.5 turns; crank remains attached to gun at all times but disengages internally for firing; blued finish. Loaded by unscrewing a large knurled screw on the breech block and swinging the loading gate downward. A built-in pellet seater could help swage the pellet into place. Later production had a two-diameter compression cylinder/body tube, there was a larger diameter area between the barrel support and about the middle of the wooden grip. Serial numbers known to 215. 10.6 in. OAL, 3.3 lbs. Ref: John Atkins, AG, April 1992: 65.

courtesy Beeman Collection

	N/A	N/A	$1,950	$1,500	$1,000	$750	$500

Add 10% for first version with single-diameter body tube.

These guns are often referred to as the "Parker-Hale" air pistols. However, this is not correct, as these pistols were made about 1921 and the Parker-Hale Company did not come into existence until 1936.

RIFLES

PHOENIX MK 1 – .177 or .22 cal., PCP, detachable air cylinder in buttstock, ten-shot BSA Superten magazine, lever action cocking, beech stock. Mfg. circa 1998-1999.

   Current values not yet determined.
   Designed by Graham Bluck.

PHOENIX MK 2 – .22 cal., PCP, detachable air cylinder in buttstock, new repeater magazine, other design improvements, deluxe walnut stock. Intro. 2004.

courtesy Tim Saunders

   Current values not yet determined.

DRAGON – .177 or .22 cal., SSP, SS, walnut sporter stock (about twelve with large FT stocks). Mk1 and Mk 2 variants: identical except for hardened valve in Mk 2, 40 in. OAL. Made circa 1994.

	$400	$350	$275	$195	$150	N/A	N/A

Designed by Graham Bluck.

PARRIS MANUFACTURING COMPANY

Previous manufacturer located in Savannah, TN.

This company began in Iowa in 1943 making toy guns (pop guns, cork guns, Kadet training rifles, etc). They also made a few bolt action military training firearm rifles during WWII. They moved to Savannah, TN circa 1953. BB guns manufactured circa 1960-1970 when the company became a Division of Gayla Industries. All BB rifles with decal, on RHS buttstock, usually marked Kadet or Trainer but w/o model number. Additional research is underway on this complex group. Information given here must be considered as tentative. The authors and publisher wish to thank John Groenewold for his valuable assistance with the following information in this section of the *Blue Book of Airguns*.

PISTOLS

KADET 507 – .174 cal., SP, SS, BB or Cork, 11 in. OAL.

	$150	$140	$120	$100	$80	$60	$40

GRADING	100%	95%	90%	80%	60%	40%	20%

RIFLES

KADET 500 – .l74 cal., SP, LA, "Selector Loader" mechanism at muzzle holds 50 BBs, twisting it releases 1 to 6 BBs to be fired together at one time, magnetic shot retainer holds BBs until fired, one piece wood stock, 30 in. OAL, 2.6 lbs.

courtesy Beeman Collection

	100%	95%	90%	80%	60%	40%	20%
	$150	$140	$120	$100	$80	$60	$40

KADET 501 – .174 cal. BB or cork, SS, SP, LA, 32 in. OAL, 2.6 lbs.

	$150	$140	$120	$100	$80	$60	$40

Add 40% for shooting kit Model 501WT.

KADET 502 – .l74 cal., SP, LA, "Selector Loader" mechanism at muzzle holds 50 BBs, twisting it releases 1 to 6 BBs to be fired together at one time, magnetic shot retainer holds BBs until fired, one piece wood stock, 37.5 in. OAL, 3.2 lbs.

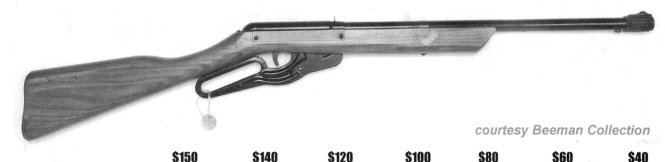

courtesy Beeman Collection

	$150	$140	$120	$100	$80	$60	$40

Add 40% for shooting kit Model 502WT.

KADET 504 – similar to Kadet 502, except has army style stock and 1 inch sling.

	$200	$175	$150	$125	$100	$75	$50

Add 40% for shooting kit Model 504WT.

KADET "X" (MODEL NO. UNKNOWN) – .174 cal., SP, LA, plastic muzzle piece and rectangular assembly under the barrel near muzzle houses safety, 37 in. OAL, 2.9 lbs. Mfg. circa 1969-1970.

courtesy Beeman Collection

	$250	$225	$200	$175	$150	$125	$100

This model was probably the last BB gun configuration made by Parris Manufacturing Company.

PAUL

Previous trademark manufactured by William Paul located in Beecher, IL.

Pump pneumatic SS shotgun with bicycle-type pump under barrel. To charge, fold out the foot pedal on the forward end of pump rod held to ground, and gun moved up and down for about seventy strokes. Additional strokes needed between shots. See *Airgun Journal* 4(1) - 1983, AGNR - Apr. 1987.

SHOTGUNS

MODEL 420 – .410 cal., smoothbore barrel slides forward for breech loading, nickel plated brass receiver, barrel, and pump; cast aluminum buttplate and trigger guard; 43 in. overall, walnut stock, shotshells are brass tubes with wad at each end, cardboard shotshells illustrated on cover of cartridge box, each shell contains about 32 pellets number

GRADING	100%	95%	90%	80%	60%	40%	20%

6 birdshot (1/6 oz.). Jan. 1924 patent shows cocking rod in pistol grip (apparently never produced). Production followed Sept. 1924 patent with cocking rod projecting from forearm. Two variants (with small variations within each type): 6.5 lbs., approx. 1,000 mfg. mid-1920s to mid-1930s.

* ***Model 420 Banded Variant*** – .410 cal., barrel and pump tube connected by soldered bands, barrel flat spring clamped to body tube.

courtesy Beeman Collection

	N/A	$1,000	$900	$850	$750	$700	$600

Add 25% for original shotshell loading kit.
Add $95 for excellent condition original full carton of 25 Paul shot shells.

* ***Model 420 Ringed Variant*** – .410 cal., barrel and pump tube connected by soldered rings, barrel flat spring soldered to body tube.

courtesy Beeman Collection

	N/A	$1,250	$995	$895	$795	$650	$400

Add 25% for original shot shell loading kit.
Add $95 for excellent condition original full carton of 25 Paul shot shells.

MODEL 420 REPLICA

See Dennis Quackenbush in the "Q" section of this book.

PEERLESS

Previous tradename used pre-WWII by Stoeger Arms of New York for airguns imported from Germany, probably all from Dianawerk, using original Dianawerk model numbers.

For information on Peerless airguns, see Dianawerk in the "D" section.

PENNEY, J.C.

Catalog sales/retailer that has subcontracted manufacturers to private label airguns.

To date, there has been limited interest in collecting J.C. Penney airguns, regardless of scarcity. Rather than list models, a general guideline is that values generally are under those of their "first generation relatives." As a result, prices have been ascertained by the shooting value of the airgun, rather than its collector value. See "Store Brand Crossover List" located in the back of this text.

PERFECTA

Trademark used on a copy of the Milbro Diana SP50 air pistol.

Perfecta was a brand name for spring piston airguns made by Oskar Will of Zella Mehlis, Germany in the 1920s for the Midland Gun Company of Birmingham, England, so it may have been resurrected by Midland Gun Company, or another company, for use on this pistol which was made in the British Diana form from the mid-1970s to 1982.

GRADING	100%	95%	90%	80%	60%	40%	20%

PISTOL

PERFECTA SP50 – .177 cal., darts or pellets, push barrel SP, SS, die-cast body, black paint finish.

courtesy Beeman Collection

	$25	$20	$15	$10	N/A	N/A	N/A

Same as the Milbro Diana SP50.

PHILIPPINE AIRGUNS

Previous and current manufacturers located in the Philippines.

There has been a thriving production of airguns in the Philippines since the 1970s. The reason for this and why the spring piston airgun revolution largely bypassed the Philippines basically was due to one man: President/Dictator Ferdinand Edralin Marcos. In 1972 [1], Marcos declared martial law and all gun importations were stopped, including importation of airguns. All firearms were confiscated except for those belonging to people who were able to get a special license only for pistols under 9mm, .22 rimfire rifles, and shotguns. Even those guns became hard to get because of the ban on importation. Local supplies of American airguns, like the popular Crosman 114 and 160, and precision European airguns, quickly dried up. The Squires Bingham Company tried to resurrect the Crosman 160, but this failed and, in any case, that gun was not up to the hunting standards of Philippine shooters. Airgun clubs dedicated to the precision shooting sports closed because of the halt in the importation of precision airguns; there were no precision airguns produced locally. Philippine shooters suddenly needed airguns, but mainly they wanted power for hunting. Spring piston airguns and guns using soda pop cartridges were not up to their needs, and PCP guns were not a viable choice due to the difficult filling requirements. Bulk fill CO_2 was the answer for this new hunter-driven market. Bulk fill CO_2 guns were light and easy to fill from a 10 oz. cylinder on the shooter's belt and the cylinders could be filled easily and cheaply at many places. So the Philippines became a hunter's airgun market, not a precision airgun market!

The most interesting things about Philippine airguns are their power, freewheeling designs, and their variety. Separate sections of this guide now give an introduction to some of the main Philippine brands found in the USA: Some of the best known makers are LD, Farco, MC Topgun, Valesquez, Valiente, Rogunz, Koffmanz, JBC, Harlie, Isaac, Garco, Centerpoint, Trident, Dreibund, Armscor (SB), and Spitfire. Some especially interesting guns are the beautifully made side lever Pampanga-type CO_2 guns.

It is reported that the majority of the Philippine airguns that have come into the USA were brought via service men who purchased them in the Philippines. This was especially true of the LD airguns; apparently about 20% to 25% of their production came in via that route. Several models of Philippine airguns also have been imported into the USA by Air Rifle Specialties in New York and Bryan and Associates in South Carolina. (Dave Schwesinger, owner of Air Rifle Specialties in New York, used to live in the Philippines and spent a lot of time in the LD airgun shop.)

All Philippine hunting airguns are relatively scarce. Production ran from an average of less than one hundred guns per month for LD, evidently the largest maker, down to a few guns a month from a custom maker such as JBC. Perhaps 70% to 99% of most production runs stayed in the Philippines. Most American and European airgun factories, and large importers, figure on several thousand or tens of thousands of guns per month. Thus Philippine hunting airguns are very desirable from an airgun hunter's or collector's standpoint.

[1] By interesting coincidence, this was just about the time that the adult airgun market in the USA got its first significant commercial start, based primarily on spring-piston airguns. (See www.beemans.net/adult_airguns_in_america.htm.)

A sampling of Philippine airguns is given below. See the "L" section for LD airguns and the "F" section for Farco airguns.

JBC/LD/PAMPANGA/ROGUNZ/VALESQUEZ/UNKNOWN MAKERS

Selected brands (all are CO_2 bulk fill and in calibers .177 to .25 as specified by buyer):

JBC – High end, small maker. Valve body and stem aluminum or brass. 12-groove rifling.

GRADING	100%	95%	90%	80%	60%	40%	20%

* **Monkey Gun** – .22 cal., SS, BA rifle, thumbhole stock, approx. 725 FPS, 33.9 in. OAL, 6.3 lbs.

courtesy Beeman Collection

	N/A	$1,000	$800	$650	$500	$350	$200

Monkey Gun is a name used on Philippine made air rifles which typically have shorter barrels and thumbhole stocks.

LD – For more info and other LD models, see LD Airguns in the "L" section of this guide.

* **LD 380 (Rancher)** – four caliber combo: .50 in. smoothbore, .380 smoothbore insert, .22 cal. rifled insert, .177 cal. rifled insert. This caliber range gave the Rancher amazing flexibility: it could project .177 or .22 cal. pellets, .38 cal. shot charges, .38 cal. bullets or lead balls, arrows w/o fletching, expanding tip spears, multi-prong spears, .50 in. tranquilizer darts, and even shaped TNT charges in brass "torpedoes." A spinning reel mounted under the forearm enhanced fishing and frog hunting. Laminated two-tone Narra stock.

PAMPANGA – This is not a brand, but a geographical group of guns made in the central Luzon section of the Philippines in the region of the former U.S. Clark Air Force Base. This area was turned into hundreds of square miles of desert by the massive Pinatubo volcanic explosion. The Pampanga guns are especially designed for hunting the wild dogs and ducks which now abound there. The identifying characteristics are: 1) extensive use of red Narra wood (very decorative, but too heavy according to some); 2) finely made stainless steel parts; brass or stainless steel valve parts; 3) removable CO_2 reservoirs extended under the barrel; 4) straight-pull bolt action or a modified LD-type hammer swing action. 5) unusually good fitting of parts; 6) lack of an expansion chamber so that these guns may dump CO_2 as fast as possible for maximum power; 7) twelve-groove rifling. There are very few shops in the Pampanga area, especially in the City of San Fernando, that specialize in acquiring these guns from very small makers (two or three-man operations) who do not produce more than five or six guns a month. Pampanga airguns are the most expensive airguns in the Philippines, but generally are the finest and most desired of all Philippine airguns. Values begin circa $1250.

Not all Pampanga guns have the above features. Some are high end copies of LD, JBC, Rogunz, and other brands. The best way to identify unmarked Philippine bulk fill CO_2 guns is to count the rifling grooves; the Pampanga guns almost always have twelve grooves while most of the main line Philippine guns have seven or eight-groove rifling. Also, Pampanga guns have brass or stainless steel valves, while others have only brass valve bodies (or brass or aluminum, in the case of JBC guns) with Teflon valve stems (white for LD, colored for Rogunz). Because they are made for the retailers, they generally do not bear any conspicuous sign of the maker. However, close examination of the reservoir and areas hidden by the stock often reveals small identification marks of the actual maker.

* **Pampanga Rifle** – .22 cal., 47.3 in. OAL, straight pull bolt action.

courtesy Beeman Collection

* **Pamapanga Shotgun** – 20 ga., 57.4 in. OAL, straight pull bolt action, almost entirely stainless steel.

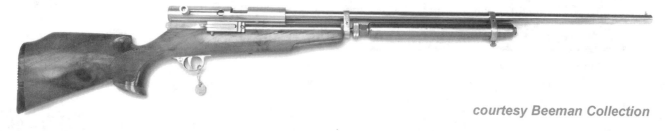

courtesy Beeman Collection

ROGUNZ – Major maker, seven or eight-groove rifling, valve body of Tiger brass, valve stem of Teflon, lock ring (bolt retaining ring) is always knurled, expansion chambers.

* ***Falcon 1-132*** – SS, hammer swing match rifle.

courtesy Beeman Collection

Value about $750 in new condition.

* ***Match Model*** – .22 cal., turning bolt, robust match stock with decorative panels cut in forearm, lateral easy-feed magazine on RHS. Expansion chamber.

UNKNOWN MAKERS – Perhaps as a result of subcontracting gun construction, many of the Philippine airguns are not marked. An example is this well made, bulk fill, long range pistol, made in .22 and .25 calibers, hand checkered black ebony wood grips, no maker's name, two specimens marked only "1" and "2" on hidden grip frame area, 14.6 in. OAL.

courtesy Beeman Collection

Value estimated at $295 in new condition.

VALESQUEZ – seven or eight-groove rifling, valve body of Tiger brass, valve stem of Teflon, expansion chambers.

* ***Brass Beauty*** – .22 in. cal., SS, bolt action, barrel and most metal parts are brass.

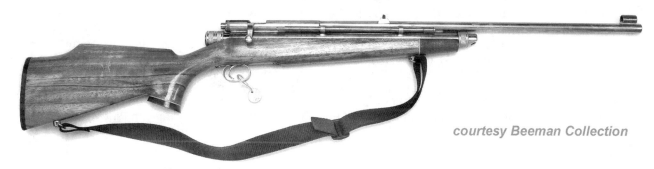

courtesy Beeman Collection

Value about $850.

* ***Bolt Action Match Rifle***

courtesy Beeman Collection

Value about $700.

GRADING	100%	95%	90%	80%	60%	40%	20%

PIPER

Current manufacturer located in Lampasas, TX. Founded by Paul Piper, manufacturing started in 1999. Huge variety of air machine guns. Most are high end products designed around rotating barrel Gatling Gun design of the American Civil War - a system adopted for ultra-high rate of fire U.S. military air borne weapons. Most air machine guns run out of ammo very quickly. Piper's designs have projectile capacities from 1200 to 24,000 BBs! Models operate on standard screw-on CO_2 bottles, high pressure compressed air (HPA), or 80 to 150 psi pressure from shop-type air compressors. Distributed by Xcaliber Tactical, located in Round Rock, TX. The great, wonderful variety of high and middle cost guns cannot be covered here. See www.xcalibertactical.com and excellent coverage and illustrations in Behling (2006).

Research is ongoing with this trademark, and more information will be included both online and in future editions.

RIFLES: AUTOMATIC

MINI-VULCAN – .174/steel BB cal., CO_2, portable 12 oz. cylinder mounted in center axis of six rotating barrels, laser sight, powered by onboard DC motor, 1200 rounds per minute, portable gun fired from arm sling, machined aluminum and steel, some optional features, 24 in. OAL, 22 lbs. 20 mfg. Ref: AR4: 75-76, Behling (2006).

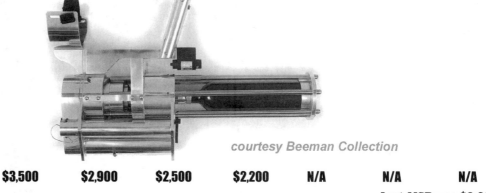

courtesy Beeman Collection

$3,500	$2,900	$2,500	$2,200	N/A	N/A	N/A

Last MSR was $2,800.

Subtract $300-$400 if not updated with steel cam and barrel sleeves.

PLAINSMAN

For information on Plainsman airguns, see Challenger in the "C" section.

PLYMOUTH AIR RIFLE COMPANY

Previous manufacturer of iron and wooden BB guns, located in Plymouth, MI from 1888-1894.

Daisy was not the first company to produce BB rifles for boys! Markham produced an all-wood BB rifle in 1886, but the Plymouth Air Rifle Company produced the first conventional BB rifle (invented by Clarence Hamilton in 1887) with an iron barrel and wooden stock. (The Daisy all-metal BB rifle was introduced in 1889.) Founded by Cyrus Pinckney and Clarence Hamilton (who founded the Plymouth Iron Windmill Company in 1882 and invented the Daisy BB gun and a line of .22 rimfire rifles for boys). Previous references have confused the history of the Plymouth Air Rifle Company with that of the Decker Air Rifle Company. To clear up the confusion: The Plymouth Air Rifle Company produced the Plymouth, Challenge, Bijou, and Magic airguns. Ref.: Wesley Powers, American Rifleman (Feb. '88) and U.S. Airgun (May/June 1998).

RIFLES

PLYMOUTH – .180 large BB cal., SS, SP, cocking lever snaps under screw in stock on lower edge of buttstock, breech loading, barrel slides fwd to receive BB on underside, s/b bbl angles up to muzzle, blue or nickel finish, flat walnut buttstock, invented 1887, patn'd 2 October 1888, intro. 1888.

courtesy Beeman Collection

N/A	$2,500	$2,000	$1,625	$1,250	$875	$500

1888 MSR was $2.35.

GRADING	100%	95%	90%	80%	60%	40%	20%

First Version - straight, blued bbl, no markings.

Second Version - nickel plated, brass bbl with step, date OCT 2, 88 on left side of anchor casting.

Third Version - trigger guard part of 2-pc frame, screw holding anchor casting to stock is perpendicular, pat. date OCT 2, 88 stamped on anchor frame.

Fourth Version - 2 step barrel, nickeled, sep. 1-pc trigger guard, frame straddles stock w/screw on each side, pat. date OCT 2, 88 straddling left rear of frame, 32 in. OAL, s/b bbl 9.25 in. (Copied exactly in Australia as the Hornet air rifle.)

CHALLENGE – .180 large BB cal., SP, almost all wood gun produced to compete with Markham CHICAGO. Iron cocking lever foreward of trigger guard, sheet metal trigger guard, "CHALLENGE" recess cast into iron spring anchor, solid one piece yellow maple stock w/o center hinge (listed as unmarked Challenger under Markham-King brand by Dunathan's American BB Gun book).

1890 MSR was $1.

Extreme scarcity precludes pricing, estimate values over $2,500, more for a repeater.

Single Shot Version (Pat.#390,311 Oct. 2, 1888).

Repeater Version (Pat. # 477,385, June 21, 1892, George Sage).

MAGIC – .180 large BB cal., SP, LA under bbl, cast iron frame, receiver, and lever, all metal nickeled, walnut stock, ring on fwd. end of cocking lever, marked MAGIC on grip frame. Rare. Circa 1891.

First Version - SS, BC, black painted frame, "MAGIC" recess cast in cartouche.

Second Version - same as 1st but repeater, black painted frame.

Third Version - same as 2nd, nickel plated.

Fourth Version - same as 3rd, with round tang on half of frame for improved stock connection.

BIJOU – .180 large BB cal., SS, SP, BC, nickel plated metal. Circa 1893-1895.

First Version - 10.25 in. frame, "BIJOU" recess cast in grip frame, wooden stock.

Second Version - 9 in. sheet metal frame, area of BIJOU casting as a plaque with rays and dots. Wooden stock.

Third Version - cast iron skeleton stock, action with spring-loaded detent. (Perhaps actually the 1st model?).

PNEU-DART, INC.

Current marketers of tranquilizer guns located in Williamsport, PA.

Pneu-Dart, Inc. also supply firearm dart projectors and tranquilizer supplies. Guns and parts made on Benjamin/Crosman. Crosman parts diagrams and Crosman parts numbers. Evidently, repeating air projectors are no longer available. Please contact the company directly for more information on their products (see Trademark Index).

PISTOLS

MODEL 179B – .50 cal., CO_2, BA, 9 in. smooth bore bbl., adj. rear and blade front sights, black finish, hard wood grips, 13.5 in. OAL, 2 lbs.

courtesy Pneu-Dart Inc.

MSR $220	$185	$155	$130	$105	$85	$55	$35

GRADING	100%	95%	90%	80%	60%	40%	20%

MODEL 190B – .50 cal., PP, BA, 9 in. smooth bore bbl., adj. rear and blade front sights, black finish, hard wood grips, 13.5 in. OAL, 2.4 lbs.

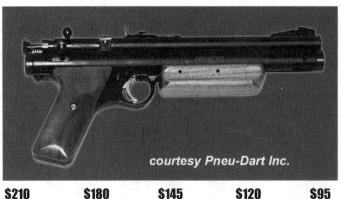

courtesy Pneu-Dart Inc.

MSR $250		$210	$180	$145	$120	$95	$65	$40

RIFLES

MODEL 167J – .50 cal., CO_2, three-shot sliding magazine repeater, blue steel finish, hardwood stock, 37.2 in. OAL, 6.6 lbs.

courtesy Beeman Collection

	N/A	$700	$550	$450	$350	$245	$140

MODEL 176B – .50 cal., CO_2, SS, 20 in. smooth bore bbl., adj. rear and blade front sights, blue steel finish, hardwood stock, 41 in. OAL, 4.75 lbs.

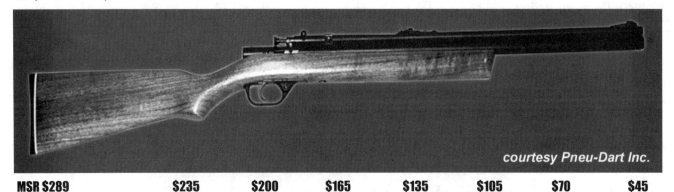

courtesy Pneu-Dart Inc.

MSR $289		$235	$200	$165	$135	$105	$70	$45

MODEL 178B – .50 cal., PP, SS, 20 in. smooth bore bbl., adj. rear and blade front sights, blue steel finish, hardwood stock, 41 in. OAL, 5.68 lbs.

courtesy Pneu-Dart Inc.

MSR $315		$260	$220	$180	$150	$115	$80	$50

GRADING	100%	95%	90%	80%	60%	40%	20%

PODIUM

Previous trademark of Sportil S.A. Portal De Gamarra, located in Vitoria, Spain.

From 1983 to 1987, Sportil manufactured and distributed three CO_2 powered guns. Each bore an uncanny resemblance to an obsolete Crosman model, but this firm says that Sportil did not manufacture under license. Although they were well made and very reliable, Podium gas guns had a very limited international distribution. The authors and publisher wish to thank Trevor Adams for his valuable assistance with the following information in this edition of the *Blue Book of Airguns*.

PISTOLS

MODEL 284 – BB cal., CO_2, repeating pistol and a clone of the Crosman Model 454.

	100%	95%	90%	80%	60%	40%	20%
	$80	$55	$40	$30	N/A	N/A	N/A

RIFLES

MODEL 186 – BB cal., CO_2, BA, fires a single pellet or BBs from a magazine, outwardly resembling the Crosman 766 pneumatic rifle, cylinder concealed beneath the forearm.

	100%	95%	90%	80%	60%	40%	20%
	$100	$80	$65	$50	$35	N/A	N/A

MODEL 286 – BB cal., CO_2, BA, similar to Crosman Model 70, fires either a single lead pellet or BBs from an eight-shot mag., cylinder lies in the forearm, knurled ring, halfway along the plastic barrel shroud, helps prevent barrel warp in the noonday sun (maybe).

	100%	95%	90%	80%	60%	40%	20%
	$120	$95	$80	$65	$50	N/A	N/A

POPE

Previous tradename of Pope Brothers located in Boston, MA.

At least part-time producers and sellers of a spring piston air pistol invented by H.M. Quackenbush. Patented in 1874, this was not Quackenbush's first air pistol, as sometimes reported, but it was the basis for the Bedford, Bedford & Walker, Johnson and Bye, and later Quackenbush air pistols and other airguns. Produced from at least 1871. Pope received the rights to the gun in 1874, but abandoned the original Quackenbush design later, allowing Quackenbush to have the patent reissued to him. Quackenbush reported sales of seventy-four Eureka air pistols in 1884. Some of the never-to-be-completely-unraveled features of the relationship of Pope and other makers of this time and place in America are summarized in the Johnson & Bye listing in the "J" section of this guide.

PISTOLS/RIFLES

POPE AIR PISTOL – .210 cal., SP, SS, pull-barrel cocking and loading, black enamel or nickel finish, hole in base of "Birds Head" grip for wire shoulder stock, 12 in. OAL. Mfg. circa 1874-1878.

courtesy Beeman Collection

	100%	95%	90%	80%	60%	40%	20%
	N/A	$600	$475	$400	$300	$210	$120

Add 10% for nickel finish.
Add 10% for wire shoulder stock.
Add 10%-40% for factory fitted wooden case with accessories.

POWERLINE

For information on Powerline, see Daisy in the "D" section.

GRADING	100%	95%	90%	80%	60%	40%	20%

PRECHARGE AB

Previous manufacturer located in Hova, Sweden.

During 2002 PRECharge AB changed its name to FX Airguns AB. PRECharge AB airguns were previously imported and/or distributed by ARS, Airguns of Arizona, RWS, and Webley & Scott. For current information on FX Airguns AB airguns, see listing in the "F" section.

RIFLES

FX EXCALIBRE – .177 or .22 cal., PCP, bolt action, eight-shot rotary mag., 21 in. choked Lothar Walther rifled barrel, high gloss blue finish, checkered walnut Monte-Carlo style stock with Schnabel forend and recoil pad, adj. trigger, receiver grooved for scope, 7 lbs.

$1,250	$1,050	$875	$725	$550	$375	$250

Add 20% for deluxe Turkish walnut stock.

PREDOM

For information on Predom airguns, see Lucznik in the "L" section.

PRODUSIT

Previous manufacturer located in Birmingham, England.

Produsit Ltd., previous makers of a concentric piston air pistol very similar to the Tell II in design, but somewhat larger.

PISTOLS

THUNDERBOLT JUNIOR – .177 cal., SP, SS, concentric piston design, cocked with lever which includes the backstrap, rear loading cover, brown plastic grips marked with "THUNDERBOLT JUNIOR", a lightning bolt, and "MADE IN ENGLAND", 6.7 in. OAL. Approx. 8,000 mfg. circa 1947-1949.

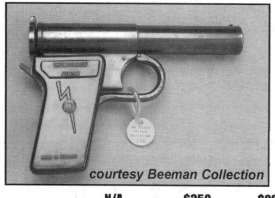

courtesy Beeman Collection

N/A	$350	$280	$230	$175	$125	$70

This model was also marked "Big Chief".

RIFLES

BIG CHIEF – BB/.174 cal., SS, SP, break action, folded metal construction, slab sided hardwood stock with colored decal: "BIG CHIEF AIR GUN BRITISH MADE". No other markings. Patented Feb.13, 1952, blue steel finish, 31.7 in. OAL, 2.5 lbs. Ref: Trevor Adams, Dec. 1991, New Zealand Guns Magazine. (Also known with Abbey Alert decal on stock and "Prov Pat 33207" on frame. May have been a premium gun and may appear with other labels.) Circa 1950s.

courtesy Beeman Collection

$250	$200	$150	$100	$65	N/A	N/A

GRADING	100%	95%	90%	80%	60%	40%	20%

PULSE-MATIC

Previous trademark manufactured by Pulse Manufacturing Inc., located in Pittsburg, Pennsylvania. Produced three production models of full automatic CO_2 rifles based on pat. no. 5,054,464, issued Oct. 8. 1991 to William Young. Manufactured 1987-1992. William Young died Oct. 2005. Ref. Behling (2006).

Pulse-Matic model rifles do not show any markings of any kind! The authors and publisher wish to thank Mr. Will Hartlep for his assistance in this edition of the *Blue Book of Airguns*.

RIFLES

MODEL A – .22 pellet or round lead ball cal., three 12 gm CO_2 cylinders, 6, 7.5, or 12 in. rifled under barrel, flat walnut, 2 pc. stock, tubular 30-50 round magazine, loaded from muzzle, 1800-2000 rpm, 550 FPS, adj. rear sight, black finish, manual bolt safety, 36.5 in. OAL, 10 lbs. Approx. 60 mfg.

courtesy Beeman Collection

$1,250	$1,050	$875	$725	$550	$375	$250

Last MSR was $500.

MODEL B – .22 pellet or round lead ball cal., three 12g CO_2 cylinders over bbl., 75 round tubular mag., 13 in. rifled under barrel, 1800-2000 rpm, 550 FPS, adj. rear sight, black finish, flat walnut forend with skeleton butt stock, 42 in. OAL, 9.5 lbs. Approx. 25 mfg.

courtesy Beeman Collection

$1,750	$1,475	$1,225	$1,025	$775	$525	$350

Last MSR was $600.

MODEL C – .22 pellet or round lead ball cal., bulk fill CO_2 on frame, 75 round tubular mag., 12 in. rifled under barrel, 1800-2000 rpm, 550 FPS, adj. rear sight, black finish, flat walnut forend with skeleton butt stock, 36 in. OAL, 9 lbs. with CO_2 bottle. Approx. 10 mfg.

courtesy Beeman Collection

$2,150	$1,825	$1,500	$1,250	$975	$650	$425

PYRAMYD AIR INTERNATIONAL

Current importer and distributor located in Solon, OH. Previously located in Warrensville Heights, OH.

Pyramyd Air International imports and markets the largest caliber air rifle in mass production, the Big Bore 909, manufactured in Korea by Sam Yang.

Pyramyd Air International also imports ASG, Aftermath, Air Arms, BSA, Beretta, Blackwater, CZ, China Shanghai, Dan Wesson, Diana, Eun Jin, Evanix, Feinwerkbau-FWB, Gamo, Hämmerli, Hatsan, Heckler, IZH-Baikal, KWC, Legends, Magnum Research, Mendoza, RWS, Remington, Ruger, Sig Sauer, Sam Yang, Sheridan, Smith & Wesson, Steyr, Stoeger Arms, Swiss Arms, Tanfoglio, Tau Brno, Tech Force, Umarex, Walther, Webley & Scott Ltd./Venom, Weihrauch and Winchester airguns. Please refer to these individual listings in this text.

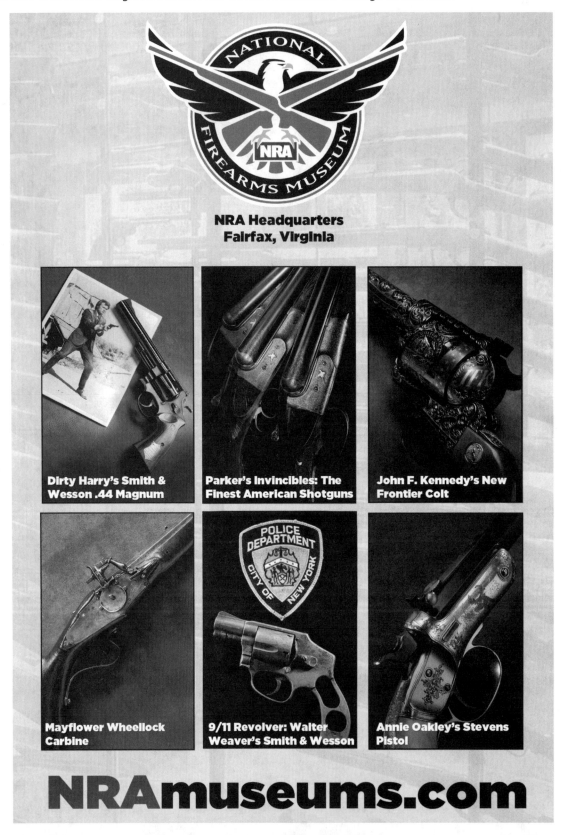

NRA Headquarters
Fairfax, Virginia

Dirty Harry's Smith & Wesson .44 Magnum

Parker's Invincibles: The Finest American Shotguns

John F. Kennedy's New Frontier Colt

Mayflower Wheellock Carbine

9/11 Revolver: Walter Weaver's Smith & Wesson

Annie Oakley's Stevens Pistol

NRAmuseums.com

Q SECTION

QUACKENBUSH, DENNIS

Current manufacturer located in Urbana, MO beginning in 1992.

In addition to the models listed, Dennis Quackenbush has also produced a wide variety of single order items and some excellent replicas of antique airguns, such as External Lock (Liege Lock) Air Rifles and Paul Air Shotguns (see Paul in the "P" section). See a wider range and notice of current products at www.quackenbushairguns.com.

GRADING	100%	95%	90%	80%	60%	40%	20%

PISTOLS

These pistols were custom manufactured action and barrel conversions for the Crosman Models SSP 250 and 2240 pistols. Production through 2006 of complete pistols is as follows: Crosman 250 frame: .375 smoothbore cal. 144 mfg., .375 rifled round ball cal. 36 mfg., 9mm cal. 4 mfg. Crosman 2240 frame .25 cal., round breach 144 mfg., square breech 327 mfg., 9mm 90 mfg. Crosman 2440 steel breech 850 mfg.

PISTOL – .20, .25, 9mm, or .375 cal., CO_2 or PCP, SS, BA, 8-11 in. rifled barrel, blue finish, adj. rear sight. Approx. 450 mfg. Disc.

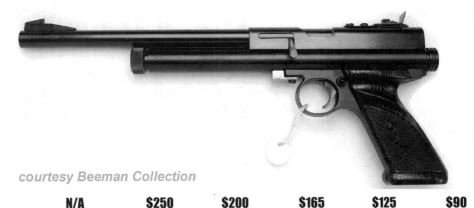

courtesy Beeman Collection

N/A	$250	$200	$165	$125	$90	$50

Subtract 50% for guns built from top-end kits (conversion units) not serial numbered.
Add 100% for 9mm with "A", "B", "C", and "D" (on "D" pistols S/N is the month and year of mfg.) serialization.
Add 50% for rifled .375 and .25 cal. pistols sold by the maker as completed guns (not kits).

Manufactured as a custom barreled action conversion for the Crosman SSP 250 and 2240 pistols. The .375 CO_2 smoothbore shot version (utilizing Crosman 1100 shotshells as ammunition and breech seal). Early guns have round breeches (sold as complete guns), later versions are square-section (many sold as kits meant to use a customer's existing gun).

OUTLAW – .25, .308, 9mm, .45, or .50 (limited) cal., PCP, SS, BA, 10-14 in. rifled barrel, approx. 1000/500 FPS (depending on caliber), blue finish, no sights. Mfg. beginning 2004.

courtesy Loke Collection

N/A	$800	$650	$525	$400	$280	$160

Subtract 20% for .25 cal.
Add 5% for carbine buttstock.

GRADING	100%	95%	90%	80%	60%	40%	20%

RIFLES: EARLY MFG.

AMARANTH (OUTSIDE/LEIGE LOCK) – .375 or .43 cal. (optional .445 barrel available), PCP (20 mfg. 1995-1999), SS, removable reservoir, tap-loading 24-36 in. rifled steel barrel, 600-800 FPS, blue finish, leather covered butt-reservoir, 41 in. OAL. Mfg. 1996-1999.

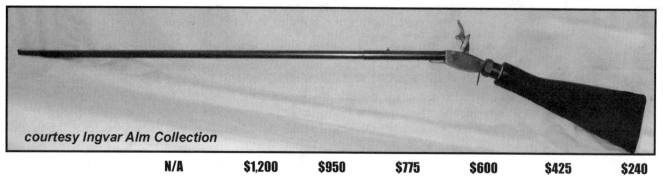

courtesy Ingvar Alm Collection

	N/A	$1,200	$950	$775	$600	$425	$240

Subtract 25% for smoothbore muzzle-loading versions.

LIADY SPECIAL – .22 cal., uses Brocock-type air cartridges (large style, about size of 20 ga. Shotgun cartridge), BA, SS, no open sights, grooved for scope, no markings, 41.8 in. OAL, 5.3 lbs. with scope. One specimen known. Mfg. circa 1997.

courtesy Beeman Collection

Scarcity precludes accurate pricing.

LIGHT SPORTER – .22 or .25 cal., CO_2 or PCP, SS, fixed reservoir, Lothar Walther barrel, 650-850 FPS, blue finish, walnut stock, 35 in. OAL, 6.75-7 lbs. Mfg. circa 1995-1996.

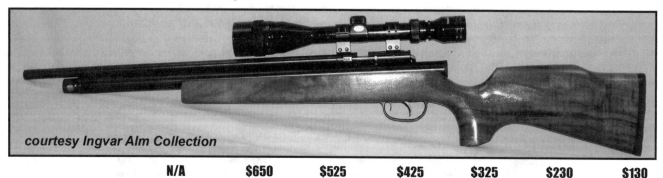

courtesy Ingvar Alm Collection

	N/A	$650	$525	$425	$325	$230	$130

XL – .22 cal., CO_2 or PCP, SS, removable bottle, Lothar Walther barrel, 650-850 FPS, blue finish, walnut stock, 35 in. OAL, 6.75-7 lbs. Mfg. beginning in 1994. Disc.

	N/A	$650	$525	$425	$325	$230	$130

RIFLES: OUTLAW SERIES

Production of the Outlaw Series Rifles through 2013 is in excess of 1,400 rifles. Production quantities of discontinued models by caliber: Brigand .375 cal., CO_2 total of 84 rifles mfg., Brigand .375 cal., PCP total of 9 rifles mfg., Rogue .44 cal., total of 28 rifle mfg., Knave .25 cal., total of 10 rifles mfg. Total production of all (including both current and discontinued model rifles) in the Outlaw Series to date is over 1,600 rifles.

50%-100% (depending on condition) premiums are being paid for current production and used rifles by individuals that cannot wait for production to catch up to demand.

GRADING	100%	95%	90%	80%	60%	40%	20%

BANDIT – .50 cal., PCP, SS, fixed reservoir, 26 in. rifled steel barrel, 780 (.50 cal.) FPS, blue finish, American walnut or laminate stock, 43 in. OAL, 7.25 lbs. Mfg. 2000-current.

courtesy Beeman Collection

MSR $595	N/A	$600	$475	$375	$295	$210	$120

Add $80 for Standard grade with deluxe blue.
Add $130 for Select grade with deluxe blue and select stock.
Add $310 for Superior grade with deluxe stock or master blue.
Add $165 for laminate stock.
Add $85 for stock checkering.

The Bandit .50 caliber bore size is .495 in.

BRIGAND – .375 cal., CO_2 or PCP, SS, fixed reservoir, rifled steel barrel, 600-800 FPS, blue finish, walnut stock, 41 in. OAL, 7.25 lbs. Mfg. 1996-1999.

courtesy Beeman Collection

	N/A	$700	$550	$450	$350	$245	$140

Add 20% for PCP.

EXILE – .308 cal., PCP, SS, fixed reservoir, 26 in. rifled steel barrel, 850 (130 gr.) FPS, blue finish, American walnut stock, 43 in. OAL, 7.25 lbs. New 2000.

MSR $595	N/A	$600	$475	$375	$295	$210	$120

Add $80 for Standard grade with deluxe blue.
Add $130 for Select grade with deluxe blue and select stock.
Add $310 for Superior grade with deluxe stock or master blue.
Add $165 for laminate stock.
Add $85 for stock checkering.

KNAVE – .25 cal., PCP, SS, fixed reservoir, 26 in. rifled steel barrel, 900 FPS, blue finish, American walnut stock, 43 in. OAL, 7.25 lbs. Disc. 2000.

	N/A	$800	$650	$525	$400	$280	$160

Last MSR was $495.

Add 5% for Standard grade with deluxe blue.
Add 15% for Select grade with deluxe blue and select stock.
Add 30% for superior grade with deluxe stock or master blue.

LA (LONG ACTION) – .458 cal., PCP, SS, fixed reservoir, 25 in. rifled steel barrel (30 in. optional), 730 FPS, blue finish, walnut stock, 44 in. OAL, 8.25 lbs. Mfg. 2005-Present.

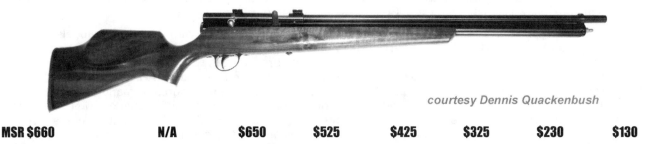

courtesy Dennis Quackenbush

MSR $660	N/A	$650	$525	$425	$325	$230	$130

Add $85 for Standard grade with deluxe blue.
Add $140 for Select grade with deluxe blue and select stock.
Add $340 for Superior grade with deluxe stock or master blue.
Add $165 for laminate stock.
Add $85 for stock checkering.

GRADING	100%	95%	90%	80%	60%	40%	20%

ROGUE – .44 cal., PCP, SS, fixed reservoir, rifled steel barrel, 800 FPS, blue finish, walnut stock, 41 in. OAL, 7.25 lbs. Approx. 40 mfg. in 1999 only.

	N/A	$750	$600	$475	$375	$265	$150

SHOTGUNS

MODEL 420 REPLICA – .410 cal., smoothbore barrel slides forward for breech loading, nickel plated brass receiver, barrel, and pump, cast aluminum buttplate and trigger guard, walnut stock, replica of Paul Model 420, 43 in. OAL.

	N/A	$950	$750	$625	$475	$325	$190

QUACKENBUSH, H.M.

Previous manufacturer located in Herkimer, NY from 1871 to 1943.

The first airguns made by Henry M. Quackenbush were air pistols. (See Bedford & Walker, Johnson & Bye, and Pope sections of this guide.)

The authors and publisher wish to thank Mr. John Groenewold for his valuable assistance with the following information in this section of the *Blue Book of Airguns*.

The H.M. Quackenbush factory began air rifle production in 1876. The airguns sold from 1929 to 1943 were assembled from parts on hand. During that time no parts manufacturing occurred, only airgun assembly. Some airguns made after 1903 had two-part serial numbers, separated by a hyphen. The number to the left of the hyphen is the model number. These guns were available in several different types of boxes. The Model 1 came with a combination wrench and a cast iron dart removal tool. The other airguns came with a steel dart removal tool. Airguns with these accessories will command significantly more than the listed prices.

H.M. Quackenbush also produced airgun ammunition, rimfire rifles, and targets. For precise identification of all models and more information on the guns and accessories manufactured by H.M. Quackenbush, see the book *Quackenbush Guns*, by John Groenewold. Price adjustments for "original bluing" below mean factory bluing or browning applied instead of nickel plating before the gun left the factory. Reblued or replated guns are substantially lower in value.

For more information and current pricing on used Quackenbush firearms, please refer to the *Blue Book of Gun Values* by S.P. Fjestad (also available online).

Square loading port detail

Spoon shape loading port detail

Round loading port detail

Model 9/10 muzzle cap detail

courtesy Beeman Collection

PISTOLS

Made from 1871 to about the late 1890s. Identifying QB air pistols is a special problem. They are covered here in hope of unearthing additional specimens. Henry Quackenbush, Iver Johnson, Martin Bye, Albert Pope, Augustus Bedford, and George Walker were close associates; there seems to have been a great deal of sharing of designs, production (with QB doing most of it), and even sales. Evidently huge numbers of QB design guns, and related designs, were produced without the maker's name on the gun and/or were made under private labels. There must be many old specimens of QB pistols that we presently cannot identify as having been made by QB. Overuse of punctuation by Henry QB may be a clue to his production of guns stamped with other makers' names. Pistols which may have been made by QB, but which were made to patents issued to others, such as Pope, Johnson & Bye, Bedford, Bedford & Walker, Cross, and others are listed under the company name which held the patent for that design, even if QB may have retailed such models or listed them in QB ads. QB records reveal that QB sold 74 "Eureka" brand pistols and 69 "Champion" air pistols in 1871.

SIX TYPES OF QB AIR PISTOLS – The types are lettered to avoid confusion with QB air rifle models and because each type may contain several models and variations of the same basic design. Some of these types and sub-models apparently were made only as prototypes. Henry QB's grandson, Bronson QB, who worked in the QB firm from before 1928 to 1986 and was President from 1968, had a collection of the full range of air pistols using Henry's various QB patented and unpatented ideas. Bronson, and Henry QB's scrapbooks, are the source of many of the details of this QB chapter. When Bronson died in 1996, he left a collection of prototype air pistols, all marked H.M. Quackenbush. For additional information, patent details and illustrations see Groenewold (2000). The patent numbers given below are only those granted to Henry Quackenbush. Values will be established as specimens are located and sold.

* **Type A - Target Air Pistol** – .22 cal., darts, SS, SP, cast iron body and grip, saw handle grip with embossed coarse checkering, frame hexagonal for rear half, forward frame cylindrical, cocking knob around muzzle, cocked by pulling muzzle knob forward, loaded by pushing barrel back for loading at rear of gun, side-swinging gate to close rear end of barrel after loading, rear-firing piston, blade trigger w/o guard, trigger sear mid-gun, projectile storage

GRADING	100%	95%	90%	80%	60%	40%	20%

compartment with sliding door at bottom of grip, 5 in. barrel concentric around piston, 12 oz. Patent 115,638 granted June 6, 1871. Combined features from patent number 122,193, granted Dec. 26, 1871. Sometimes compared to the "Gat" air pistols, but Gats have a forward firing piston, their trigger sear is at the very rear, and lack many of the Target Air Pistol features.

This was H.M. QB's first gun. It was featured in his two page circular of 1872 which Bronson QB said was "laboriously composed after a great deal of mental effort while sitting under an apple tree adjacent to his first factory". Specimens beyond the prototypes have not been identified, but must exist as unmarked pistols. The above distinctive features should enable collectors to locate strong suspects.

* **Type B - Improved Target Pistol** – basically the same as the Target Pistol, but with an improved device to receive the dart when the gun is loaded from behind, combined with a groove, to align the barrel and close its rear end when the barrel is moved forward as to be flush with the back of the gun, ready for firing. QB's flyer for 1872 may illustrate this patent's design, leading us to wonder if the basic Target Pistol was ever produced in quantity for sale. Patent 122,193 issued Dec. 26, 1871.

* **Type C- Transitional Pistol** – barrel is above compression tube and no longer concentric with piston - as in Type D- Rifle Air Pistols. Basically still based on Patent 115,638 with a flip-to-the-right side-swinging loading gate as shown in that patent. Major change was a cocking knob that pulled out to cock the gun's mainspring. The knob and its plunger stayed out until firing caused it to travel into the gun as the piston rushed to the rear compressing air to force the projectile out of the barrel. This is so similar to the 1876 Cross patent (see the "C" section of this guide) that the two designs may be related.

* **Type D - Rifle Air Pistol** – .22 in. cal., s/b, SS, SP, cast iron frame nickel-plated or black finish, 12.75 in. OAL, 1.5 pounds. Barrel above compression tube. Cocked by pulling barrel forward. Loaded with dart when barrel is moved forward for cocking. Saw handle grip with embossed checkering. Blued, browned, or nickel finish. Marked H.M. Quackenbush on LHS upper panel of frame. Based on patent 156,890 issued Nov. 17, 1874, earlier patents, and others into 1876. Quackenbush's most successful air pistol.

»**Type D - Rifle Air Pistol Variant 1** – PATCH BOX PISTOL - functions only as a pistol; stamped: MFGD. BY H.M. QUACKENBUSH. HERKIMER. N.Y. PATD. JUNE.6.DEC.26.1871. No provision for shoulder stock wire, base of grip with sliding brass door which opens to store projectiles inside hollow grip, head of brass screw or dimple which secures door not visible from side. Approx. 2mm dia. hole in upper rear edge of grip. Non-adj. trigger, no safety.

courtesy Beeman Collection

	N/A	$5,500	$4,400	$3,600	$2,750	$1,925	$1,100

Add 25% for original box and literature.

Subtract 10% if wire shoulder stock is missing.

»**Type D - Rifle Air Pistol Variant 2** – rifle air pistol - early version. Marked: MFGD. BY H.M. QUACKENBUSH. HERKIMER. N.Y. PATD. JUNE.6.DEC.26.1871; grip with small screw holes in butt for attaching wire shoulder stock (this version shown in QB flyers and stationery).

Add 30% for proper wire shoulder stock with flattened forward end with holes for screw attachment to gun.

GRADING	100%	95%	90%	80%	60%	40%	20%

»**Type D - Rifle Air Pistol Variant 3** – rifle air pistol - late version. Marked: MFGD. BY H.M. QUACKENBUSH. HERKIMER. N.Y. PATD. JUNE.6.DEC.26.1871. Iron screw runs up from butt to secure wire shoulder stock in 5/16 in. hole in rear edge of grip; screw head visible from side. Non-adj. trigger, no safety.

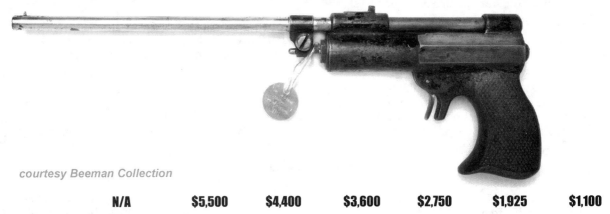

courtesy Beeman Collection

	N/A	$5,500	$4,400	$3,600	$2,750	$1,925	$1,100

Add 25% for original box and literature.
Subtract 10% if wire shoulder stock is missing.
Add 10% for proper wire shoulder stock (20% for early versions with flat on lower side of angled front end - to receive securement screw pressure).

This version gave rise to the Bedford Rifle Air Pistols, with saw-handle grip and the Pope air pistols which all have a "bird's head" cast iron grip. This "saw handle" version may have been the one sold by H.M. QB after he took back this design from Pope, due to non-payment, after Pat. No. 158,890 was reissued to him as re-issue patent no. 6973 on March 7, 1876. A saw handle version was also sold under the name Creedmoor by Peck & Synder in New York. (Note that the "Eureka" name, a generic term at that time, has been applied to both the QB "Rifle Air Pistol" and to Bedford and Walker's push plunger air pistol - probably it should best be restricted to the Bedford and Walker design, just as QB apparently did.)

* **Type E- Push Barrel Pistol** – .22 cal., SS, SP. Pushing in barrel cocks forward-firing piston. Barrel, concentric with piston, must be pulled forward before firing. Pat. no. 178,327 issued June 6, 1876. No specimens known, but this design was basic to the QB Rifle No. 1 which revolutionized the air rifle market.

* **Type F - Gat Style Pistol** – .22 cal., SS, SP., very simple, inexpensive design, at rest the mainspring is visible wrapped around fwd part of barrel, pushing in barrel cocks piston, barrel is attached to piston, both move forward at firing, simple sear hook retains cocked piston at very rear of pistol, QB marked pistols of this design were made with frames of cast alloy or iron. Patent No. 188,028 (issued March 6, 1877) drawings show a birds-head shaped grip. While not very successful for QB, this design has been made by others in enormous numbers for well over a century.

RIFLES

MODEL EXCELSIOR – .21 cal., spring powered, SS, smooth bore, nickel-plated, walnut stock, action is very similar to the Johnson and Bye Champion pistol (see the Johnson and Bye section of this book), very low powered, sequential serial number is usually found on the bottom rear of the compression tube, some not serial numbered, 35 in. OAL, 3.5 lbs. Approx. less than 1,000 mfg. circa 1887-1891.

	N/A	$4,500	$3,600	$2,950	$2,250	$1,575	$900

Many parts are interchangeable with the Champion and other Quackenbush air guns.

MODEL 0 (LIGHTNING) – .21 cal., smooth bore rubber band powered SS, nickel-plated, walnut stock, 32 in. OAL, 4 lbs. Mfg. 1884 only.

courtesy Beeman Collection

	N/A	$4,500	$3,600	$2,950	$2,250	$1,575	$900

Add 50% for original box and literature.

This model was the only rubber band powered air rifle made by H.M. Quackenbush.

GRADING	100%	95%	90%	80%	60%	40%	20%

MODEL 1 – .21 cal., push-barrel, SP, SS, smooth bore, nickel finish, walnut stock. Designed to shoot round shot, felted slugs, burred slugs, or darts. Loads through rectangular loading port in front part of receiver. Easily identified by the two-part receiver and simple, single loop trigger guard. Eleven variations of the Model 1 are distinguished by various features. The serial number can be used to approximate these variations. Later versions not listed below can be valued by listed prices unless special circumstances exist. Mfg. 1876-1938.

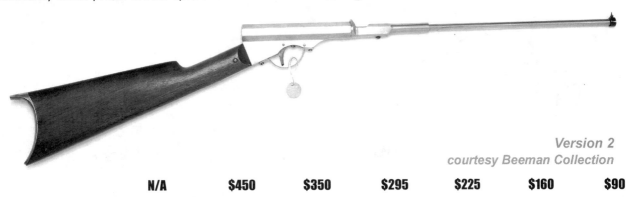

Version 2
courtesy Beeman Collection

	N/A	$450	$350	$295	$225	$160	$90

Add 10% for original bluing.
Add 50% for original wood box and literature.
Add 25% for original cardboard box and literature.
Add 100% for Version 1, no serial number, round receiver, and no name.
Add 60% for Version 2, serial number 1 to 300 or w/o number, octagon receiver.
Add 40% for Version 3, serial number 301 to 1000.
Add 20% for Version 4, serial number 1001 to 7500.
Add 10 % for Version 5, serial number 7501 to 12484.
   Versions 6 to 11, serial number 12485 to 36850 - use prices listed above.

MODEL 2 – .21 cal., push-barrel, SP, SS, smooth bore, nickel finish, walnut stock, distinguished from Model 1 by much heavier, one-piece receiver. Versions 1 and 2 with rectangular loading port ahead of rear sight, other versions with spoon shaped loading port behind rear sight. Version 1 with single loop, simple trigger guard, later versions with forward end of trigger guard much extended and with another loop. Designed to shoot round shot, felted slugs, burred slugs, or darts. Five versions distinguished by various features. The serial number can be used to approximate these variations. Mfg. 1879-1918.

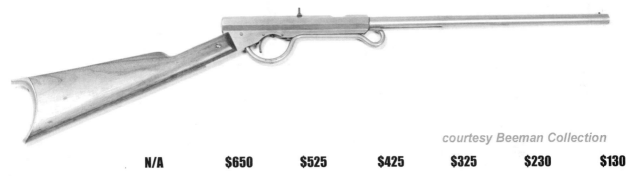

courtesy Beeman Collection

	N/A	$650	$525	$425	$325	$230	$130

Add 10% for original bluing.
Add 35% for original cardboard box and literature.
Add 35% for Version 1, serial number 1 to 5500.
Add 30% for Version 2, serial number 5501 to 20000.
Add 25% for Version 3, Model 83, serial number 1 to 8000 (number sequence started over).
Add 10% for Version 4, serial number 1 to 8000 (number sequence started over).
   Version 5 serial number 8001 to 16823.

MODEL 3 – .21 cal., round ball, push-barrel, SP, SS, smooth bore, nickel finish, walnut stock. Round loading port/hole in top of receiver behind rear sight. Five versions are distinguishable by various features. The serial number can be used to approximate these variations. Values for Version 5 are listed. Mfg. 1881-1919.

	N/A	$750	$600	$475	$375	$265	$150

Add 10% for original bluing.
Add 50% for original box and literature.
Add 35% for Version 1, serial number 1 to 1300.
Add 30% for Version 2, serial number 1300 to 2600.
Add 25% for Version 3, serial number 2600 to 8000.
Add 10% for Version 4, serial number 8000 to 88700.

GRADING	100%	95%	90%	80%	60%	40%	20%

MODEL 4 – .21 cal., round ball, push-barrel, SP, smooth bore, nickel finish, walnut stock, gravity-fed in-line magazine repeater. Three variations distinguished by various features. The serial number can be used to approximate these variations. Version 3 values are listed. Mfg. 1882-1910.

courtesy Beeman Collection

	N/A	$900	$725	$575	$450	$325	$180

Add 10% for original bluing.
Add 50% for original box and literature.
Add 10% for Version 1, serial number 1 to 1000.
Add 5% for Version 2, serial number 1001 to 1425.

MODEL 5 (COMBINATION GUN) – .22 cal., BBC, SP, smooth bore, blue or nickel finish, walnut stock. The smooth bore version did not have an extractor and operated only as an airgun. Designed to shoot round shot, felted slugs, burred slugs, or darts. Another version, rifled and with an extractor, could operate as an air rifle or fire .22 caliber rimfire ammunition. A removable firing pin was stored in a "patch box" on the right side of the buttstock. To function as a firearm, the firing pin was installed in place of the breech seal. (Replacement firing pins are available from John Groenewold.) Four variations are distinguished by various features. The serial number can be used to approximate these variations. Prices below are for the 22-inch barrel version. Mfg. 1884-1913.

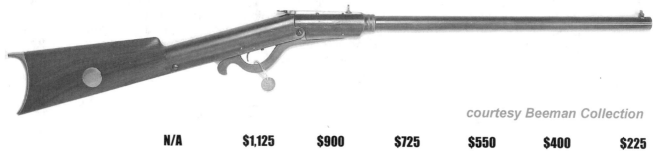

courtesy Beeman Collection

	N/A	$1,125	$900	$725	$550	$400	$225

Subtract 20% for rifled barrel.
Subtract $50.00 for missing firing pin.
Add 10% for 18-inch barrel.
Add 20% for original bluing.
Add 20% for optional hooded front sight and flip-up rear aperture sight.
Add 35% for original cardboard box and literature.
Add 50% for original wood box and literature.
Add 15% for Version 1, serial number 1 to 100.
Add 10% for Version 2, serial number 101 to 1350.
Add 5% for Version 3, serial number 1351 to 2850.

MODEL 6 – BB/.175 cal., push-barrel, SP, smooth bore, blue finish, one-piece walnut buttstock/forearm, breech loading SS, sheet metal barrel housing, almost same general appearance as Number 7 except for round cocking stud in "2" slot under barrel instead of flat rectangular lug. Early versions with Z-shaped slot for cocking stud. Later versions with J shaped slot. No serial numbers. Mfg. 1907 to approximately 1911.

courtesy Beeman Collection

	N/A	$2,000	$1,600	$1,300	$1,000	$700	$400

Add 50% for original box and literature.

GRADING	100%	95%	90%	80%	60%	40%	20%

MODEL 7 – BB/.175 cal., push-barrel, SP, breech loading SS, smooth bore, blue finish, one-piece walnut buttstock/forearm, sheet metal barrel housing, flat, rectangular cocking lug in slot running almost full length of underside of barrel shroud (housing). No serial numbers. Mfg. 1912-1936.

courtesy Beeman Collection

	N/A	$400	$325	$260	$200	$140	$80

Add 35% for original box and literature.

MODEL 8 – BB/.175 cal., push-barrel, SP, SS, muzzle loader, smooth bore, blue finish, walnut stock, similar to Models 6 and 7, except no cocking lug/stud or open slot on underside of barrel housing. Sheet metal barrel housing. No serial numbers. Mfg. 1918-1920.

	N/A	$2,750	$2,200	$1,775	$1,375	$950	$550

Add 50% for original box and literature.

Beware of recently assembled Model 8 from Model 7 parts being sold as originals.

MODEL 9 – BB/.175 cal., push-barrel, spring piston, smooth bore, felted slugs and darts, nickel-plated finish, walnut stock. Similar to Model 2 (with spoon shaped loading port), except for .175 caliber and a sheet metal barrel shroud with knurled muzzle piece to support shot tube at muzzle. Two-part serial numbers, e.g., 9-16620. Sold from 1920-1941.

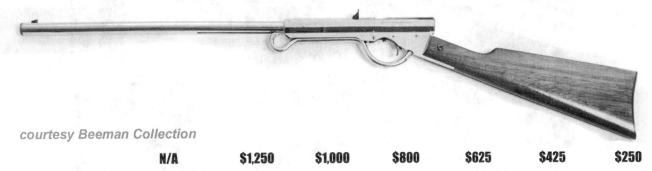

courtesy Beeman Collection

	N/A	$1,250	$1,000	$800	$625	$425	$250

Add 10% for original factory blue finish.
Add 35% for original box and literature.

MODEL 10 – BB/.175 cal., push-barrel, spring piston, smooth bore, nickel plated finish, walnut stock, similar to Model 3 (with round loading port), except for .175 caliber and sheet metal barrel shroud with knurled muzzle piece to support shot tube at muzzle. Two-part serial numbers, e.g., 10-16000. Sold from 1919-1943.

	N/A	$2,950	$2,350	$1,925	$1,475	$1,025	$600

Add 10% for original factory blue finish.
Add 35% for original box and literature.

MODEL 83 – see Model 2, version 3.

R SECTION

RWS PRECISION PRODUCTS

Current trademark currently imported and distributed by Umarex USA Inc. located in Fort Smith, AR beginning 2006. Previously imported and distributed by Dynamit Nobel-RWS (Rheinisch Westfalische Sprengstoff-Fabriken) Inc. located in Closter, NJ. RWS is a division of RUAG AmmoTec GmbH, located in Furth, Germany. Dealer sales only.

The RWS trademark appears on airguns manufactured by Dianawerk, Mayer and Grammelspacher. These models are listed in the "D" section of this book.

For more information and current pricing on both new and used RWS firearms, please refer to the *Blue Book of Gun Values* by S.P. Fjestad (also available online).

GRADING	100%	95%	90%	80%	60%	40%	20%

PISTOLS

MODEL 9B/9N – .177 cal., SL, SP, SS, 550 FPS, black or nickel finish, molded black grips, adj. rear sight. Mfg. 2002-2004.

	100%	95%	90%	80%	60%	40%	20%
	$115	$100	$80	$65	$50	$35	$25

Last MSR was $157.

MODEL C-225 – .177 cal., CO_2, semi-auto, SA or DA, 385 FPS, 4 or 6 in. barrel, eight-shot rotary clip, styled after a modern handgun, interchangeable 4 or 6 in. barrels, adj. rear sight, black or nickel finish. Disc. 2001.

	100%	95%	90%	80%	60%	40%	20%
	$175	$150	$125	$100	$80	$50	$35

Last MSR was $210.

Add $10 for nickel finish. Add $10 for 6 in. barrel, $25 for nickel model.

MODEL C-357 – .177 cal., CO_2 revolver, 380 FPS, eight-shot cylinder, 6 in. rifled barrel. Mfg. 1998-99.

	100%	95%	90%	80%	60%	40%	20%
	$115	$100	$80	$65	$50	$35	$25

Last MSR was $170.

MODEL CP-7 – .177 cal., match/sport SS, CO_2 refillable from cylinder or 12-gram cylinder, 425 FPS, adj. rear sight, adj. trigger, adj. counter weight, 8.27 in. barrel, includes hard case and accessories, 2.23 lbs. Mfg. 1999-2001.

	100%	95%	90%	80%	60%	40%	20%
	$350	$295	$240	$200	$155	$105	$70

Last MSR was $450.

Subtract $50 for left-hand variation.

MODEL CP95 – .177 and .22 cal. match grade SS, CO_2 refillable from cylinder or 12-gram cylinder, 425 FPS, adj. rear sight, adj. trigger, adj. barrel weight, adj. pistol grip, 10.24 in. Lothar Walther barrel, 2.31 lbs. Disc. 2001.

	100%	95%	90%	80%	60%	40%	20%
	$400	$350	$285	$235	$180	$120	$80

Last MSR was $525.

This model includes UIT regulations for international match shooting.

MODEL CP96 – .177 cal. match grade five-shot, CO_2 refillable from cylinder or 12-gram cylinder, 425 FPS, adj. rear sight, adj. trigger, adj. barrel weight, adj. pistol grip, 10.24 in. Lothar Walther barrel, 2.23 lbs. Mfg. 1999-2001.

	100%	95%	90%	80%	60%	40%	20%
	$500	$425	$350	$285	$220	$145	$100

Last MSR was $635.

Subtract $100 for left-hand variation.

This model includes UIT regulations for international match shooting.

MODEL LP8 MAGNUM – .177 cal., BBC, SP, SS, 7 in. barrel with muzzle brake, 700 FPS, blue finish, molded black synthetic frame, two-stage adj. trigger, adj. rear and fixed front fiber optic sights, automatic safety, marked Umarex USA, 18 in. OAL, 3.2 lbs. New 2008.

courtesy Umarex USA

MSR $316	100%	95%	90%	80%	60%	40%	20%
MSR $316	$270	$235	$215	$175	$135	N/A	N/A

GRADING	100%	95%	90%	80%	60%	40%	20%

RIFLES

MODEL 34 – .177 or .22 cal., BBC, blue finish, 1000/800 FPS, 19.75 in. barrel, adj. open rear sight, fixed fiber optic front sight, classic straight hardwood stock with rubber recoil pad, two-stage adj. trigger, scope rail, 46 in. OAL, 7.5 lbs. New 2006.

MSR $343	$290	$255	$235	$190	$145	N/A	N/A

Add $53 for 4x32 scope with lockdown mount.

* **Model 34 Panther** – .177 or .22 cal., BBC, 1000/800 FPS, 19.75 in. barrel, blue finish, black composite all-weather stock, Truglo adj. sights, two-stage adj. trigger, rubber recoil pad, 46 in. OAL, 7.7 lbs. Mfg. 2007-current.

courtesy Umarex USA Collection

MSR $300	$255	$225	$205	$165	$125	N/A	N/A

Add $50 for Combo with 4x32 compact scope and mount.

* **Model 34 Panther Pro** – .177 cal., BBC, SP, SS, 1000 FPS, 19.75 in. rifled BBL with weight, black finish, ambidextrous black composite stock with rubber recoil pad, two-stage adj. trigger, 3-9x40mm scope, 46 in. OAL, 8.5 lbs. Mfg. 2008-2009.

courtesy Umarex USA

	$275	$235	$195	$160	$125	$80	$55

Last MSR was $318.

The barrel weight on this model aids in the balance of the rifle and provides the shooter with a robust handle for easier cocking.

* **Model 34 Panther Pro Compact** – .177 cal., BBC, SP, SS, 1000 FPS, 15.75 in. rifled BBL with weight, black finish, ambidextrous black composite stock with rubber recoil pad, two-stage adj. trigger, 3-9x40mm scope, 42.12 in. OAL, 8 lbs. Mfg. 2008-current.

courtesy Umarex USA

MSR $366	$300	$275	$250	$200	$155	N/A	N/A

MODEL 34 MEISTERSCHÜTZE PRO – .177 cal., BBC, SP, SS, rifled 19 in. BBL with weight, 1000 FPS, matte black finish, classic ambidextrous hardwood straight stock with PG and rubber recoil pad, two-stage adj. trigger, auto-safety, 3-9x40mm scope with "C" mount, 46.12 in. OAL, 8 lbs. Mfg. 2008-2009.

courtesy Umarex USA

	$325	$275	$230	$190	$145	$95	$65

Last MSR was $365.

GRADING	100%	95%	90%	80%	60%	40%	20%

MODEL 34 MEISTERSCHÜTZE PRO COMPACT – .177 cal., BBC, SP, SS, rifled 15.75 in. barrel with weight, 1000 FPS, matte black finish, classic ambidextrous hardwood straight stock with PG and rubber recoil pad, two-stage adj. trigger, auto-safety, 3-9x40mm scope with "C" mount, 42.25 in. OAL, 7.75 lbs. Mfg. 2008-current.

courtesy Umarex USA

MSR $396	$325	$295	$270	$220	$165	N/A	N/A

MODEL 48 – .177 or .22 cal., SL, SP, sliding-breech SS, 1100/900 FPS, 17 in. fixed rifled barrel, blued finish, adj. rear and front sights, two-stage adj. trigger, auto-safety, classic ambidextrous wood stock with contoured rubber recoil pad, also available with black stock (Model 48 Black, disc. 2012), or with matte glass bead blasted metal black stock with sporty design (Model 48 Black Pro, disc. 2012), 42.5 in. OAL, 9 lbs. Mfg. 2008-current.

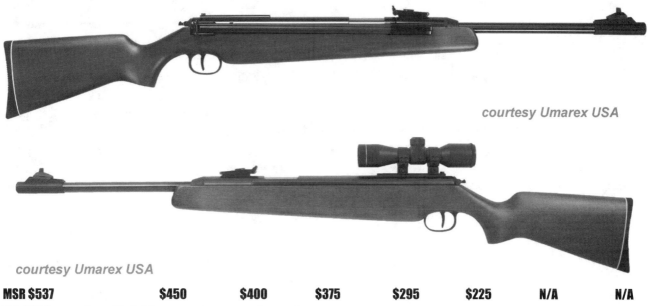

courtesy Umarex USA

courtesy Umarex USA

MSR $537	$450	$400	$375	$295	$225	N/A	N/A

Add $57 for combo with 4x32 compact scope and mount.

MODEL 52 – .177 or .22 cal., SL, SP, sliding breech loading SS, rifled 17 in. BBL, adj. rear and front sights, two-stage adj. trigger, checkered walnut colored hardwood Monte Carlo stock with contoured rubber butt pad and fine cut checkering on pistol grip and forend, 43.75 in. OAL, 9 lbs. Mfg. 2008-2012.

	$450	$375	$325	$260	$205	$135	$90

Add $43 for combo with 4x32 scope and mount.

* ***Model 52 Luxus*** – .177 or .22 cal., SL, SP, sliding breech loading SS, rifled 17.5 in. BBL, 1000/900 FPS, adj. rear and front sights, two-stage adj. trigger, checkered Walnut Monte Carlo stock with ventilated rubber butt pad and Ebony forend tip/PG cap, 44.12 in. OAL, 8.75 lbs. Mfg. 2008.

courtesy Umarex USA

	$600	$500	$425	$350	$270	$180	$120

Last MSR was $677.

GRADING	100%	95%	90%	80%	60%	40%	20%

MODEL 54 – .177 or .22 cal., SL, SP, recoilless floating action, 950/780 FPS or 1100/900 FPS (new 2008), 17 in. fixed barrel, blued finish, two-stage adj. trigger, match type trigger safety catch with additional cocking guard, adj. front and rear sights, beechwood Monte Carlo stock with contoured rubber butt pad, right-handed sculpted cheekpiece, hand-checkered forend and pistol grip, 44 in. OAL, 9-10 lbs.

courtesy Diana

MSR $750	$625	$550	$500	$400	$325	N/A	N/A

Add $45 for combo with 4x32 scope and mount (new 2006).

MODEL 92 – .177 cal., BBC, SP, SS, 700 FPS, black finish, beech stock, grooved receiver for scope, rifled barrel, adj. rear sight, automatic safety. Mfg. in Spain 2002-2004.

	$95	$80	$65	$55	$45	$30	$20

Last MSR was $122.

MODEL 93 – .177 or .22 cal., BBC, 850 FPS (.177 cal.), beech stock, adj. trigger, grooved receiver for scope, rifled barrel, adj. rear sight, hooded front sight, manual safety. Mfg. in Spain 2001-2004.

	$160	$135	$110	$95	$70	$50	$30

Last MSR was $172.

MODEL 94 – .177 or .22 cal., BBC, SP, 1000 FPS (.177 cal.), beech stock, adj. trigger, grooved receiver for scope, rifled barrel, adj. rear sight, hooded front sight with interchangable inserts, automatic safety. Mfg. in Spain 2001-2004.

	$195	$165	$135	$115	$90	$60	$40

Last MSR was $227.

MODEL 312 – .177 cal., BBC, SP, SS, 900 FPS, black finish, beech stock, hooded front and adj. rear sights, automatic safety. Mfg. 2002-2004.

	$70	$60	$50	$40	$30	$20	$15

Last MSR was $87.

MODEL 320 – .177 cal., BBC, SP, SS, 1000 FPS, black finish, beech stock, hooded front and adj. rear sights, manual safety. Mfg. 2002-2011.

	$130	$110	$90	$75	$60	$40	$25

Last MSR was $152.

MODEL 350 MAGNUM – .177 or .22 cal., BBC, SP, SS, 1250/1000 FPS, 19.5 in. barrel, hooded front sight, adj. rear sight, checkered Monte Carlo beech stock with sculpted right-hand cheekpiece, ventilated rubber recoil pad, grip and forearm checkering, blued finish, fixed front sight, adj. rear sight, vent. rubber recoil pad, two-stage adj. trigger, scope rail, 48 in. OAL, 8.5 lbs. New 2001.

courtesy Diana

MSR $500	$425	$375	$350	$275	$210	N/A	N/A

Add $55 for combo with 4x32 scope and mount.

GRADING	100%	95%	90%	80%	60%	40%	20%

MODEL 350 P MAGNUM – .177 or .22 cal., BBC, SP, SS, 1250/1000 FPS, 19.5 in. barrel, blued finish, adj. rear and hooded front TruGlo fiber optic sights, ambidextrous black all-weather stock w/textured grip and forearm, ambidextrous cheekpiece, two-stage adj. trigger, 48 in. OAL, 8.5 lbs. New 2009.

courtesy Umarex USA

MSR $420	$350	$325	$285	$230	$175	N/A	N/A

Add $55 for combo with 4x32 scope and mount.

MODEL 350 FEUERKRAFT – .177 or .22 cal., SL, SP, sliding-breech SS, rifled 19.62 in. BBL, 1250/1000 FPS, adj. rear and front fiber optic sights, classic ambidextrous wood stock with rubber recoil pad, two-stage adj. trigger, auto-safety, 48.37 in. OAL, 8 lbs. Mfg. 2008-2009.

	$375	$325	$265	$220	$170	$110	$75

Last MSR was $431.

Add $40 for combo with 4x32 compact scope and mount.

* *Model 350 Feuerkraft Pro Compact* – .177 or .22 cal., BBC, SL, SP, sliding-breech SS, 15.75 in. rifled barrel with weight, 1250/1000 FPS, 3-9x40mm scope with RWS Lock Down mount, classic ambidextrous wood stock with rubber recoil pad, two-stage adj. trigger, auto-safety, 44.25 in. OAL, 8.5 lbs. Mfg. 2008-2013.

courtesy Umarex USA

	$425	$350	$300	$245	$190	$125	$85

Last MSR was $514.

MODEL 460 MAGNUM – .177 or .22 cal., ULC, SP, 1350/1150 (1200/1000 FPS beginning 2009) FPS, 18.5 in. barrel, fixed front sight, adj. rear sight, checkered wood Monte Carlo Sporter stock with cheekpiece, pistol grip and forearm checkering, vent. rubber recoil pad, two-stage adj. trigger, scope rail, 45 in. OAL, 8.3 lbs. New 2007.

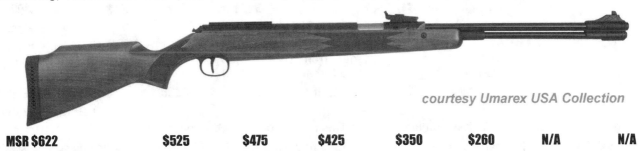

courtesy Umarex USA Collection

MSR $622	$525	$475	$425	$350	$260	N/A	N/A

Add $73 for combo with 4x32 scope and mount.

MODEL 512 – .177 cal., BBC, SP, SS, 490 FPS, 17.7 in. barrel, black finish, synthetic stock, hooded front and adj. rear sights, scope rail, automatic safety, 6.2 lbs. Mfg. 2002-2004.

	$80	$70	$55	$45	$35	$25	$15

Last MSR was $97.

MODEL 514 – .177 cal., SLC, SP, SS, 490 FPS, five-shot mag., 17.8 in. barrel, black finish, adj. black synthetic pistol grip stock, hooded front and adj. rear sights, automatic safety, 6.4 lbs. Mfg. 2002-2004.

	$90	$75	$65	$50	$40	$25	$20

Last MSR was $106.

GRADING	100%	95%	90%	80%	60%	40%	20%

MODEL 516 – .177 cal., BBC, SP, SS, 1000 FPS, 17.7 in. barrel, black finish, synthetic stock, hooded front and adj. rear sights, scope rail, automatic safety, 6.2 lbs. Mfg. 2002-2004.

	100%	95%	90%	80%	60%	40%	20%
	$115	$100	$80	$65	$50	$35	$25

Last MSR was $147.

MODEL CA 100 – .177 cal., PCP, 22 in. barrel, diopter sight, match trigger, adj. laminated stock, 11 lbs. 6 oz. Disc. 1998.

	100%	95%	90%	80%	60%	40%	20%
	$1,000	$850	$700	$575	$450	$300	$200

Last MSR was $2,200.

MODEL CA 200 TARGET – .177 cal., PCP, 22 in. barrel, adj. rear sight, hooded front sight, match trigger, laminated stock with adj. cheek piece, adj. recoil pad, available in right or left-hand variation, 11 lbs. 6 oz.

	100%	95%	90%	80%	60%	40%	20%
	$350	$300	$245	$205	$160	$105	$70

Last MSR was $570.

This model was also listed as CR 200 in some catalogs.

MODEL CA-707 – .22, .25, or 9mm cal., PCP, LA, eight-shot repeater or side-loading single shot, 1200 FPS at high-power setting, three-position power setting, built-in pressure gauge to monitor remaining shots, 16 (carbine) or 23 in. barrel, Western-style straight heel stock, high-gloss blue finish, Indonesian walnut stock with checkered forearm and hand grip, 7.75 lbs. Mfg. 1999-2011.

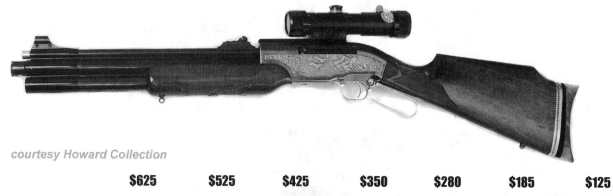

courtesy Howard Collection

	100%	95%	90%	80%	60%	40%	20%
	$625	$525	$425	$350	$280	$185	$125

Last MSR was $730.

MODEL CA-710T – .22 or .25 cal., PCP, LA, eight-shot repeater or side-loading single shot, similar to Model CA-707, except has interchangeable cylinder, 16 (carbine) or 19 in. barrel, Western-style straight heel stock, high-gloss blue finish, Indonesian walnut stock with checkered forearm and hand grip, 7 lbs. Mfg. 2000-2011.

	100%	95%	90%	80%	60%	40%	20%
	$725	$625	$500	$425	$325	$215	$145

Last MSR was $850.

MODEL CA-715 – .22 cal., CO_2 refillable from cylinder or 12-gram cylinder, BA, SS, 1200 FPS, 20 in. barrel, open rear sight fully adj., hooded front sight with post, Indonesian walnut stock with rubber buttplate, raised cheek piece, hand checkered hand grip, includes ten rechargeable cylinder, pellet seater, cylinder holder to refill cylinder with air, optional adaptor for scuba tank or pump, 6.5 lbs. Mfg. 1999-2000.

	100%	95%	90%	80%	60%	40%	20%
	$500	$425	$350	$290	$225	$150	$100

Last MSR was $685.

MODEL RA-800 BREAKBARREL (BY THEOBEN) – .177, .20, or .22 cal., 1110-1150 FPS, 12.25 in. barrel with integral extended muzzle brake, two-stage adj. trigger (from 1.75 to 3.25 lbs.), Deluxe African Hyedua stock with high cheek piece and fine checkering on pistol grip and forearm. Mfg. 2000-2001.

	100%	95%	90%	80%	60%	40%	20%
	$1,000	$850	$700	$575	$450	$300	$200

Last MSR was $1,400.

This gas-spring model was built in conjunction with Theoben, and featured a match grade Anschütz barrel.

MODEL SCHÜTZE (YOUTH) – .177 cal., BBC, SP, SS, rifled 16.5 in. BBL, 580 FPS, black finish, classic straight hardwood PG stock with rubber recoil pad, Truglo adj. sights, auto-safety, 41 in. OAL, 5 lbs. Mfg. 2008-current.

courtesy Umarex USA

MSR $208	100%	95%	90%	80%	60%	40%	20%
	$175	$155	$140	$115	$85	N/A	N/A

GRADING	100%	95%	90%	80%	60%	40%	20%

RADCLIFFE

Previously manufactured by C.H. Radcliffe, located in Chicago, IL.

RADCLIFFE – appears to be a .25 cal. air rifle, but it is designed to shoot water back into the eyes of the shooter, 20.5 in. barrel, walnut buttstock with heavy steel buttplate, marked "Patd. June 17, 1902. No. 702478". For Masonic initiation rites; it predates the light (2.8 lbs.), little Daisy "back squirters," 38.5 in. OAL, 5.8 lbs.

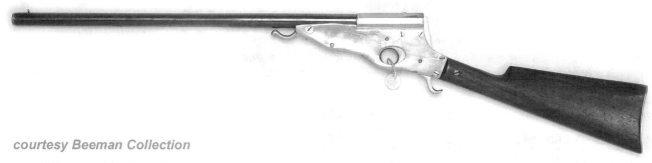

courtesy Beeman Collection

Value over $1,000.

RANCO

For information on Ranco, see "Targ-Aire" in the "T" section.

courtesy Beeman Collection

RANDALL BROTHERS

Previous trademark manufactured by Myron Randall located in Waupaca, WI, circa 1924-1929 under U.S. patent #1,509,257 (9/23/24).

Randall Brothers manufactured high quality air rifles of unique design. Estimated production 20-25 guns. Ref: AI, Oct. 2002.

RANDALL REPEATER AIR RIFLE – .22 cal., SP, LA moves sliding breech block, tapered steel barrel, tubular magazine under barrel for ten diabolo pellets, blue finish, walnut quarter stock with steel buttplate, walnut forearm, unmarked except for serial number stamped in several places, 38 in. OAL, 6 lbs.

courtesy Hannusch Collection

Current retail values are in the $1,000-$2,000+ range.

RANDALL SINGLE SHOT AIR RIFLE – similar to repeater, except without magazine.

courtesy Hannusch Collection

Current retail values are in the $1,000-$2,000+ range.

RANGER

Previous tradename of American Tool Works located in Chicago, IL.

For information on Ranger, see American Tool Works in the "A" section.
Also used as a tradename for Erma ELG-10 lever action air rifles sold under the Webley brand, circa 1980s.

RAPID

For information on Rapid, refer to Cycloid/Rapid in the "C" section.

RAPID AIR WEAPONS LLC (RAW)

Current manufacturer and supplier of precision air rifle accessories/components and their HM1000 PCP air rifle located in Minor Hill, TN.

Please contact the company directly for more information, including pricing and availability (see Trademark Index).

RAPIDE

For information on Rapide airguns, see Relum Limited in this section.

REAMES, MIKE

Current custom airgun maker located in Lima, OH.

Mike Reams typically designs and builds CO_2 and PCP single shot and repeater ball reservoir pistols. Most examples come in a custom fitted wood case with accessories. Prices range from $600 to $2,500 depending on complexity of the design.

courtesy Mike Reames

RECORD

For information on Record, refer to FB Record in the "F" section.

RELUM LIMITED

Previous London distributor of several lines of Hungarian products including airguns, founded by George Muller in 1954.

Relum is a reverse version of the name Muller. Brands included Relum, Jelly, FEG Telly (sometimes misread as Jelly), Rapide, Taurus, and Super Tornado. Most are heavily built economy line air rifles with .177 MV in the 500 FPS area. Relum Limited was still in business as of 1980. Resale values are generally well under $100.

REMINGTON ARMS COMPANY, INC.

Current manufacturer and trademark established in 1816, with factories currently located in Ilion, NY, and Mayfield, KY. Founded by Eliphalet Remington II and originally located in Litchfield, Herkimer County, NY circa 1816-1828. Remington established a factory in Ilion, NY next to the Erie Canal in 1828, and together with his sons Philo, Samuel, and Eliphalet III pioneered many improvements in firearms manufacture. Corporate offices were moved to Madison, NC in 1996. DuPont owned a controlling interest in Remington from 1933-1993, when the company was sold to Clayton, Dubilier & Rice, a New York City based finance company. The Mayfield, KY plant opened in 1997. On May 31st, 2007, a controlling interest in the company was sold to Cerberus Capital. Currently, Remington employs 2,500 workers in the U.S., including 1,000 in its Ilion, NY plant alone.

Remington licensed Crosman to use the Remington Trademark on airguns 2003-2014. Spring of 2014 Remington announced the arrival of the all new Remington Airguns family. For more information and current pricing on both new and used Remington firearms, please refer to the *Blue Book of Gun Values* by S.P. Fjestad (also available online).

GRADING	100%	95%	90%	80%	60%	40%	20%

PISTOLS

MODEL 1911 RAC – - BB/.177 cal., CO2, 12g cylinder, semi-auto repeater, blowback action, 18-shot BB mag., 345 FPS, smoothbore barrel, manual safety, black finish, fixed sights, 2 lbs. Mfg. 2014-current.

MSR $140	$120	$105	$95	$75	$60	N/A	N/A

Add $10 for Model 1911 RAC Pistol Kit including case.

RIFLES

AIRMASTER MODEL AM77 – BB/.177 cal., pump pneumatic, 20.8 in. rifled barrel, 725 FPS, fiber optic front sight, adj. rear sight, brushed nickel barrel and black receiver finish, black synthetic pistol grip buttstock, 4x20mm scope, kit also includes 100 pellets, 100 BBs, shooting glasses, and five official airgun targets, imported, 39.75 in. OAL, 4.8 lbs. Mfg. 2003-2013.

courtesy Remington

	$95	$80	$65	$55	$45	$30	$20

Last MSR was $111.

EXPRESS – .177 cal., BBC, SP, SS, 19 in. rifled steel barrel, up to 1000 FPS, two-stage adj. trigger, fiber optic front and fully adj. rear sights, 4x32mm scope, blue finish, checkered hardwood PG stock, rubber butt pad, automatic safety, 45 in. OAL, 8 lbs. Mfg. 2014-current.

MSR $200	$170	$150	$135	$110	$85	N/A	N/A

EXPRESS XP – .177 cal., BBC, SP, SS, 19 in. rifled steel barrel, up to 1000 FPS, two-stage adj. trigger, fiber optic front and fully adj. rear sights, 4x32mm scope, blue finish, checkered hardwood PG stock, rubber butt pad, automatic safety, 45 in. OAL, 8 lbs. Mfg. 2014-current.

MSR $200	$170	$150	$135	$110	$85	N/A	N/A

GENESIS 1000 MODEL R1K77PG – .177 cal., BBC, SP, SS, rifled steel barrel, two stage adj. trigger, 1000 FPS, adj. rear sight, 3-9x40mm scope (Model R1K77PGX new 2005), blue finish, ergonomic soft synthetic pistol grip stock, vented recoil pad. Mfg. 2004-2009.

	$195	$165	$135	$115	$90	$60	$40

Last MSR was $221.

* Genesis 1000 Model R1K77PGX – .177 cal., BBC, SP, SS, rifled steel barrel, two-stage adj. trigger, 1000 FPS, adj. rear sight, 3-9x40mm scope, blue finish, ergonomic soft synthetic pistol grip stock, vented recoil pad. Mfg. 2005-2010, reintroduced 2012-13.

	$255	$215	$180	$150	$115	$75	$50

Last MSR was $300.

MODEL 26 REPEATING AIR RIFLE – .177 cal. for lead shot (early) or steel, SS pump action, spring air rifle with unique geared system, 21 1/8 in. barrel, adj. rear sight, blue (early) or black painted finish, plain varnished walnut pistol grip buttstock, ten-groove forearm, 4 lbs. Approx. 19,646 total mfg. by Remington circa 1928-1930.

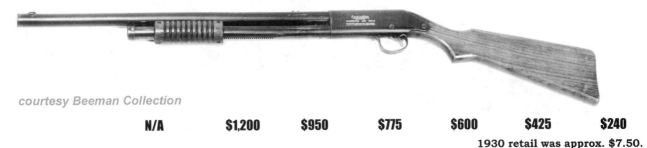

courtesy Beeman Collection

	N/A	$1,200	$950	$775	$600	$425	$240

1930 retail was approx. $7.50.

Add 15% for first model with blue finish.

GRADING	100%	95%	90%	80%	60%	40%	20%

NPSS MODEL RNP77 – .177 cal., BBC, Nitro Piston, SS, rifled steel bull barrel, 1200 FPS, two-stage adj. trigger, adj. sculpted cheek piece and built-in pistol grip, fiber optic sights, carbon fiber look finish, Monte Carlo style thumbhole synthetic stock, vent. recoil pad, 3-9x40mm CenterPoint scope, 43 in. OAL, 6 lbs 15 oz. Mfg. 2010-2013.

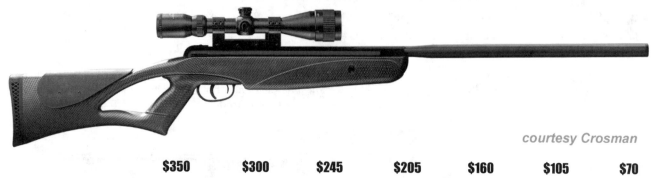

courtesy Crosman

	$350	$300	$245	$205	$160	$105	$70

Last MSR was $400.

NPSS MODEL RNP77DC – .177 cal., BBC, Nitro Piston, SS, 14.8 in. rifled steel bull barrel, 1200 FPS, two-stage adj. trigger, adj. sculpted cheek piece and built-in pistol grip, fiber optic sights, digital camo finish, Monte Carlo style thumbhole synthetic stock, vent. recoil pad, 3-9x40mm CenterPoint scope, 43 in. OAL, 6 lbs 15 oz. Mfg. 2010-2013.

	$350	$300	$245	$205	$160	$105	$70

Last MSR was $400.

NPSS MODEL RNP22 – .22 cal., BBC, Nitro Piston, SS, rifled steel bull barrel, 1000 FPS, two-stage adj. trigger, adj. sculpted cheek piece and built-in pistol grip, fiber optic sights, carbon fiber look finish, Monte Carlo style thumbhole synthetic stock, vent. recoil pad, 3-9x40mm CenterPoint scope, 43 in. OAL, 6 lbs. 15 oz. Mfg. 2010-2013.

	$350	$300	$245	$205	$160	$105	$70

Last MSR was $400.

NPSS MODEL RNP22DC – .22 cal., BBC, Nitro Piston, SS, rifled steel bull barrel, 1000 FPS, two-stage adj. trigger, adj. sculpted cheek piece and built-in pistol grip, fiber optic sights, digital camo finish, Monte Carlo style thumbhole synthetic stock, vent. recoil pad, 3-9x40mm CenterPoint scope, 43 in. OAL, 6 lbs. 15 oz. Mfg. 2010-2014.

courtesy Crosman

	$350	$300	$245	$205	$160	$105	$70

Last MSR was $400.

SUMMIT MODEL RW1K77X – .177 cal., BBC, SP, SS, rifled steel barrel, up to 1000 FPS, two-stage adj. trigger, 3-9x40mm CenterPoint scope, blue finish, checkered high-gloss walnut finish Monte Carlo style stock, vented rubber butt pad, 45 in. OAL, 7.8 lbs. Mfg. 2006-2014.

courtesy Remington

	$245	$210	$170	$140	$110	$75	$50

Last MSR was $290.

GRADING	100%	95%	90%	80%	60%	40%	20%

SUMMIT MODEL RW8M22X – .22 cal., similar to Summit Model RW8M22X, except up to 1200 FPS. Mfg. 2010-2014.

	$245	$210	$170	$140	$110	$75	$50

Last MSR was $290.

VANTAGE MODEL RW1K77X2 – .177 cal., BBC, SP, SS, rifled steel barrel with blue finish, 1200 FPS, two-stage adj. trigger, fiber optic sights, 4x32mm CenterPoint scope, satin finish Monte Carlo style hardwood stock with pistol grip, recoil pad, 44.5 in. OAL, 6 lbs. Mfg. 2009-2014.

courtesy Crosman

$145	$125	$100	$85	$65	$45	$30

Last MSR was $170.

REN GUN COMPANY

Previous manufacturer located at PO Box 454, Richmond VA, circa 1946-1950.

PISTOL

SERG'T REN – BB gun, SS, cardboard tubing with wood grip, operates by sliding one end of the tubing over the other, 16.5 in. OAL. Rare in good condition.

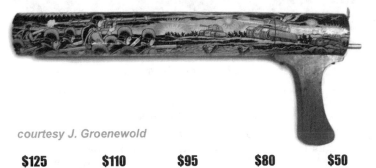

courtesy J. Groenewold

$125	$110	$95	$80	$50	$30	N/A

RETAY ARMS CORP.

Current manufacturer located in Konya, Turkey. No current U.S. importation.

Retay Arms Corp. currently manufactures a complete line of good quality air rifles, as well as an air pistol. Please contact the company directly for more information on models, U.S. pricing, and availability (see Trademark Index).

RIPLEY AIR RIFLES

Current trademark of PCP rifles manufactured by Hogan Firearms Limited located in Leicestershire, United Kingdom. Currently imported/distributed exclusively by Precision Airgun Distribution/Airguns of Arizona located in Gilbert, AZ. Dealer and consumer sales.

Hogan Firearms Limited was established in 2008 and is a joint collaboration between Highland Outdoors Limited and Jim Hogan. Hogan Firearms Limited have also developed a joint agreement between itself and Ripley Air Rifles to bring the consumer a 100% British made Air Rifle.

RIFLES

RIPLEY ELITE SPORTER – .177 or .22 cal., PCP, BA, SS, 1250/1100 FPS, match grade choked Lothar Walther rifled barrel, adj. two-stage trigger, checkered sporter walnut stock, 41 in. OAL, 7.6 lbs. Mfg. 2010-current.

MSR $1,279	$1,075	$950	$875	$700	$525	N/A	N/A

RIPLEY ELITE THUMBHOLE – .177 or .22 cal., PCP, BA, SS, 1250/1100 FPS, match grade choked Lothar Walther rifled barrel, adj. trigger, checkered thumbhole walnut stock, 41 in. OAL, 7.2 lbs. Mfg. 2010-current.

MSR $1,349	$1,150	$1,000	$925	$750	$575	N/A	N/A

RIPLEY ELITE SPORT CARBINE – .177 or .22 cal., PCP, 1050/900 FPS, Lothar Walther barrel, adj. two-stage trigger, no safety, wood stock with raised cheekpiece, checkering on grip and forearm, 35 in. OAL, 7 lbs.

MSR $1,195	$1,025	$875	$725	$600	$450	$300	$205

GRADING	100%	95%	90%	80%	60%	40%	20%

RIPLEY ELITE THUMBHOLE CARBINE – .177 or .22 cal., PCP, 1050/900 FPS, Lothar Walther barrel, no safety, two-stage adj. trigger, hardwood thumbhole stock with raised cheekpiece, checkering on grip and forearm, 35 in. OAL, 6.6 lbs.

MSR $1,265	$1,075	$925	$750	$625	$475	$325	$215

RIPLEY RIFLES

Current manufacturer of PCP rifles, located in Derbyshire, United Kingdom.

The authors and publisher wish to thank Tim Saunders for his valuable assistance with the following information in this section of the *Blue Book of Airguns*. Owned and operated by Steve Wilkins, son of the late Joe Wilkins, who manufactured the Predator rifle and had a significant role in developing the modern PCP. High end regulated PCP rifles, mainly FT. Sporting rifles were available as XL series, .22 cal. SS or with nine-shot rotary magazine (XL9) or twenty-five-shot version (XL25) with spring-loaded linear magazine feeding the rotary magazine.

Most production is custom; all typical airgun calibers. Many actions fitted with very high end stocks from Paul Wilson and other custom stockmakers. Finishes include blue, nickel, colored, and camo. These air rifles typically will retail in the $1,500-$2,000 range.

courtesy Neil MacKinnon

RO

For information on RO airguns, see Gun Toys SRL in the "G" section.

ROBINSON, GEORGE CO.

Previous manufacturer of the O'Connell Gas Rifle located in Rochester, NY circa 1947-49.

During WWII, the Robinson Co. produced munitions for the U.S. Government. Shortly after the company turned to the production of toy tools, an engineer by the name of O'Connell approached George Robinson with a design for a single shot CO_2 rifle. At about the same time, Crosman Arms Corporation was promoting their CG (Compressed Gas) series rifles via indoor shooting leagues, one of which was in East Rochester, NY. It is probably no coincidence that the O'Connell rifle so closely resembles a Crosman CG rifle that collectors who have seen one of these very rare rifles often think that it a prototype or a version of the Crosman CG rifles. The complete lack of any markings on the O'Connell rifles helps promote this error. However, the internal design is considerably different and the quality is higher.

RIFLES

O'CONNELL GAS RIFLE – .22 cal., CO_2, SS, rifled barrel, with removable, vertically attached 4 oz. CO_2 cylinder (cylinder are not interchangeable with Crosman CG guns), aperture rear sight only, safety gas by-pass lever on right side of receiver, breech loading by pulling a knob at the rear of the receiver, valve similar to a Schimel gas pistol, approx. 540 FPS, dark stained hardwood stock, machined steel parts, 41.5 in. OAL, 6 lbs. Approx. 100-200 mfg. 1947-1949.

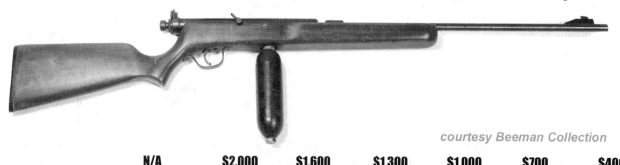

courtesy Beeman Collection

	N/A	$2,000	$1,600	$1,300	$1,000	$700	$400

ROCHESTER

Previous tradename of air rifles manufactured by the Monroe Gasket and Manufacturing Company located in Rochester, NY circa 1948.

The Rochester Air Rifle is the only model, a swinging air pump pneumatic, BA, SS, two-piece wooden stock, with a black crackled paint finish. Probably the direct ancestor of the Kessler Two Piece Stock Model (see Kessler in the

GRADING	100%	95%	90%	80%	60%	40%	20%

"K" section) with which it is identical except for the names stamped on the barrel. Research is ongoing with this trademark, and more information will be included both online and in future editions. Average original condition specimens are typically priced in the $100-$300 range. MSR was $10.

courtesy Beeman Collection

ROGER

For information on Roger airguns, see MMM - Mondial in the "M" section.

ROGUNZ

For information on Rogunz airguns, see Philippine Airguns in the "P" section.

RÖHM GmbH

Current trademark picked up by Umarex during late 2010. Current manufacturer located in Sontheim an der Benz, Germany and Fort Smith, AR. Currently imported by Airguns of Arizona/Precision Airgun Distribution, located in Gilbert, AZ, and Umarex USA located in Fort Smith, AR.

For more information and current pricing on both new and used Röhm firearms, please refer to the *Blue Book of Gun Values* by S.P. Fjestad (also available online).

PISTOLS

TWINMASTER ACTION CO₂ MODEL – .177 cal., CO_2, eight-shot mag. repeater, 8.58 in. rifled Walther barrel, black frame with brushed barrel finish, molded grip, adj. trigger, adj. rear sight, trigger safety, 1.96 lbs.

courtesy Röhm

MSR N/A	$450	$400	$325	$270	$210	$140	$90

TWINMASTER ALLROUNDER MODEL – .177 cal., PCP, eight-shot mag. repeater, 8.58 in. rifled steel Walther barrel, black frame with brushed barrel finish, molded grip, adj. trigger, adj. rear sight, trigger safety, built-in gauge, 2 lbs.

courtesy Röhm

MSR N/A	$650	$550	$450	$375	$290	$195	$130

TWINMASTER COMBAT TRAINER CO₂ MODEL – .177 cal., CO_2, eight-shot mag. repeater, 8.58 in. rifled Walther barrel, black frame with brushed barrel finish, universal contoured grip, adj. trigger, adj. rear sight, trigger safety, 11 in. OAL, 2.4 lbs. New 2005.

MSR N/A	$575	$475	$400	$325	$255	$170	$115

GRADING	100%	95%	90%	80%	60%	40%	20%

TWINMASTER MATCH MODEL – .177 cal., PCP, SS, 8.58 in. rifled steel Walther barrel, black frame and barrel finish, adj. walnut grip, adj. trigger, adj. rear sight with extra blades, trigger safety, built-in gauge, balance weights, tool kit, hard case, 2 lbs. New 2005.

courtesy Röhm

MSR N/A	$1,075	$900	$750	$625	$475	$325	$210

TWINMASTER MATCH TRAINER CO$_2$ MODEL – .177 cal., CO$_2$, eight-shot mag. repeater, 8.58 in. rifled Walther barrel, black frame with brushed barrel finish, adj. laminate grip, adj. trigger, adj. rear sight, trigger safety, 11 in. OAL, 2.4 lbs. New 2005.

courtesy Röhm

MSR N/A	$650	$550	$450	$375	$295	$195	$130

TWINMASTER SPORT MODEL – .177 cal., PCP, SS, 8.58 in. rifled steel Walther barrel, black frame and barrel finish, adj. molded grip, adj. trigger, adj. rear sight with extra blades, trigger safety, built-in gauge, balance weights, tool kit, hard case, 2 lbs.

courtesy Röhm

MSR N/A	$950	$800	$675	$550	$425	$285	$190

TWINMASTER TOP MODEL – .177 cal., PCP, eight-shot mag. repeater, 8.58 in. rifled steel Walther barrel, black frame with brushed barrel finish, adj. wood grip, adj. trigger, adj. rear sight, trigger safety, built-in gauge, 2 lbs.

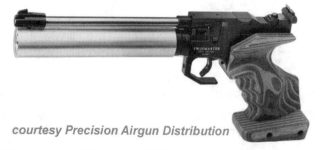

courtesy Precision Airgun Distribution

MSR N/A	$750	$650	$525	$450	$350	$230	$150

GRADING	100%	95%	90%	80%	60%	40%	20%

* *Twinmaster Action CO₂ Model* – .177 cal., CO_2, DA, eight-shot mag. repeater, 8.58 in. rifled black finish Walther barrel, frame, molded grip and tank, adj. trigger, adj. rear sight, trigger safety, 12.8 in. OAL, approx. 2 lbs.

	100%	95%	90%	80%	60%	40%	20%
MSR N/A	$450	$400	$325	$270	$210	$140	$90

TWINMASTER COMPETITOR MODEL – .177 cal., PCP, DA, eight-shot mag. repeater, 8.58 in. rifled steel Walther barrel, black frame and barrel finish, molded finger grooved grip, adj. trigger, adj. rear sight, trigger safety, built-in gauge, 13.4 in. OAL, 2.3 lbs.

	100%	95%	90%	80%	60%	40%	20%
MSR N/A	$750	$650	$525	$450	$350	$230	$150

RUBI

For information on Rubi airguns, see Venturini in the "V" section.

RUTTEN AIRGUNS SA

Current manufacturer located in Herstal-Liege, Belgium. Previously imported on a limited basis by Pyramyd Air, then located in Pepper Pike, OH. Previously imported by Cherry's Fine Guns, located in Greensboro, NC, and by Compasseco, located in Bardstown, KY.

The Browning Airstar, built by Rutten, was the first air rifle with a battery-powered electronic cocking system. Less than 800 were manufactured. Please refer to Browning in the "B" section for more information. Rutten also builds three other models sold through selected Rutten dealers.

For more information and current pricing on both new and used Rutten firearms, please refer to the *Blue Book of Gun Values* by S.P. Fjestad (also available online).

PISTOLS

J&L RUTTEN WINDSTAR HS550 TARGET PISTOL – .177 cal., BBC, SP, SS, 550 FPS, automatic safety, fully adj. rear sight, checkered beech grips, 2.35 lbs. Disc. 2002.

	100%	95%	90%	80%	60%	40%	20%
	N/A	$500	$400	$325	$250	$175	$100

Last MSR was $235.

RIFLES

AIRSTAR – .177 cal., electronic cocking mechanism powered by rechargeable Ni-Cad battery (250 shots per charge), 780 FPS, flip-up loading port, warning light indicates when spring is compressed, electronic safety with warning light, 17.5 in. fixed barrel, hooded front sight with interchangeable sight inserts, adj. rear sight, frame grooved for scope mount, beechwood stock, 9.3 lbs.

	100%	95%	90%	80%	60%	40%	20%
MSR $490	$425	$375	$325	$270	$205	N/A	N/A

BROWNING AIRSTAR – please refer to the Browning section.

J&L RUTTEN WINDSTAR MACH 1 D.E. – .177 cal., UL, SP, SS, 870 FPS, safety integrated with cocking lever, 18 in. barrel, hooded front sight with interchangeable inserts, fully adj. rear sight, frame grooved for scope mount, beechwood stock, 9.7 lbs. Disc. 2002.

	100%	95%	90%	80%	60%	40%	20%
	$450	$375	$325	$260	$205	$135	$90

Last MSR was $525.

J&L RUTTEN WINDSTAR PRO 2000 D.E. TARGET – .177 cal., UL, SP, SS, 570 FPS, safety integrated with cocking lever, 18 in. barrel, hooded front sight with interchangeable inserts, fully adj. rear peep sight, frame grooved for scope mount, beechwood target stock with adj. buttplate, 10 lbs.

	100%	95%	90%	80%	60%	40%	20%
MSR $510	$425	$375	$350	$280	$215	N/A	N/A

RUGER

For information on Ruger airguns, see Sturm, Ruger & Co., Inc. in the "S" section.

Blue Book Supports
New Hunting Heritage Trust
Firearms Consignment Program

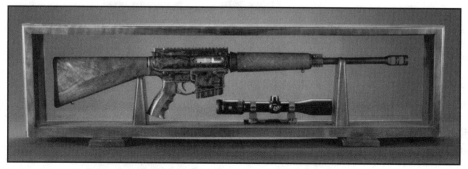

This Turnbull TAR-10 auctioned for $136,024 on the
Hunting Heritage Trust's Treasures & Traditions auction in 2013.

For several years, the Hunting Heritage Trust has administered its "Treasures & Traditions" charity auction on GunBroker.com., auctioning firearms to generate funding for pro-shooting programs.

In 2014, the Trust has expanded the "Treasures & Traditions" auction by inviting individuals to consign firearms for auction on the popular GunBroker.com site. The Trust will assist with the auction and retain a commission of 15% to support its programs.

S.P. Fjestad, author of the *Blue Book of Gun Values*, is impressed by the potential of program, saying, "The Hunting Heritage Trust is a respected organization and I know its Treasures & Traditions auction attracts very competitive prices."

The Hunting Heritage Trust supports many groups working in support of our firearms heritage including USA Shooting, the Youth Shooting Sports Alliance, IHEA, PVA and many others.

HUNTING HERITAGE TRUST

Contact the Hunting Heritage Trust for additional information.
428 Spalding Lake Circle, Aiken, SC 29803
803-641-1030, fax– 803-641-1070, huntingheritagetrust@earthlink.net

S SECTION

SAG (SHANGHAI AIR GUN FACTORY)

Current manufacturer of Industry Brand airguns located in Shanghai, China. No current U.S. importation. Previously imported by Compasseco Inc. located in Bardstown, KY.

S G S (SPORTING GUNS SELECTION)

Previous trademark imported by Kendell International.

GRADING	100%	95%	90%	80%	60%	40%	20%

RIFLES

DUO 300AP – .177 or .22 cal., TL, SP, 455/430 FPS.

	100%	95%	90%	80%	60%	40%	20%
	$135	$115	$70	$50	$40	N/A	N/A

DUO 300AR – .177 or .22 cal., TL, SP, 455/430 FPS, with extra stock and barrel assembly to create a three-in-one gun.

	100%	95%	90%	80%	60%	40%	20%
	$195	$135	$85	$65	$50	N/A	N/A

SAINT LOUIS

For information on Saint Louis airguns, see Benjamin in the "B" section.

SAM YANG PRECISION IND. CO.

Current manufacturer located in Korea. Currently imported and distributed by Air Venturi/Pyramyd Air located in Solon, OH. Previously located in Warrensville Heights, OH.

RIFLES

DRAGON CLAW – .50 cal., PCP, CO_2, semi-auto, SS, BA, single tank, 21.6 in. rifled barrel, hardwood Monte Carlo stock with checkered forearm and grip, raised cheek piece, blade and ramp front and adj. rear sights, two-stage trigger, rubber buttplate, 42.1 in. OAL, 7.65 lbs. Mfg. 2012-current.

MSR $700	$600	$525	$475	$375	$295	N/A	N/A

Add $30 for Dragon Claw rifle with a dual tank.

MODEL 909 BIG BORE 44 LIGHT HUNTER – .45 cal., PCP, SS, pull bolt cocking, 21.65 in. rifled barrel, 700 FPS, engraved coin finished receiver, blue finish, adj. sights, single stage trigger, checkered PG walnut stock w/rubber butt pad, 42.1 in. OAL, 7.1 lbs. Mfg. 2000-current.

courtesy Sam Yang

MSR $730	$625	$550	$500	$400	$300	N/A	N/A

MODEL 909S BIG BORE 45 – .45 cal., PCP, BA, SS, pull bolt cocking, 21.65 in. rifled barrel, 730 FPS, engraved coin finished receiver, blue finish, adj. sights, two stage trigger, checkered PG walnut stock w/rubber butt pad, 42.1 in. OAL, 7.5 lbs. Mfg. 2005-current.

courtesy Sam Yang

MSR $700	$600	$525	$475	$375	$295	N/A	N/A

GRADING	100%	95%	90%	80%	60%	40%	20%

RECLUSE – .357 cal., PCP, CO_2, semi-auto, SS, BA, single tank, 21.6 in. rifled barrel, hardwood Monte Carlo stock with checkered forearm and grip, raised cheek piece, two-stage trigger, rubber buttplate, built-in air pressure gauge, manual safety, 42.1 in. OAL, 8.35 lbs. Mfg. 2012-current.

MSR $700	$600	$525	$475	$375	$295	N/A	N/A

Add $30 for Recluse Model with dual air tank.

SAULS, RON

Current custom airgun maker and dealer located in Anderson, SC. Ron Sauls occasionally imports airguns from the Republic of the Philippines.

Ron Sauls, in his spare time makes a variety of unique and unusual design air rifles and pistols. Mr. Sauls also produces a wide variety of aftermarket accessories and spare parts for current and discontinued airguns. Contact Mr. Sauls directly for pricing and availability (see Trademark Index).

PISTOLS

B & A REPEATING PISTOL – .22 cal., CO_2 bulk fill or cylinder, 24-shot repeater.

courtesy Ron Sauls

RIFLES

B & A REPEATERE RIFLE – .22 cal., CO_2 bulk fill, 24-shot gravity feed repeater.

courtesy Ron Sauls

BALL RESERVOIR RIFLE – .375 cone head darts cal., CO_2, ball reservoir, tap loader, SS, 24 in. smoothbore BBL, 41.75 in. OAL, 5 lbs.

courtesy Ron Sauls

GRADING	100%	95%	90%	80%	60%	40%	20%

BUTT RESERVOIR RIFLE – .38 cal. round ball or pellet, CO_2 or 2200 psi compressed air, butt reservoir, tap loader, SS, 31.87 in. half octagon/half round rifled barrel, 46.75 in. OAL, 8.5 lbs.

courtesy Ron Sauls

SAVAGE ARMS

Current manufacturer and importer located in Westfield, MA.

A century-old manufacturer of rifles and shotguns (more than two hundred different models since 1895), Savage brought its expertise to air rifles in 1999 with five imported sporting models in .177 caliber.

For more information and current pricing on both new and used Savage Arms firearms, please refer to the *Blue Book of Gun Values* by S.P. Fjestad (also available online).

RIFLES

PLAY RIFLE – .38 cal., SP, pump action, sheet metal construction, spring-fed tubular magazine, fixed sights, marked "SAVAGE" in large letters on RHS of receiver, with SVG in circle, barrel stamped: "SAVAGE PLAY RIFLE MANUF. BY SAVAGE ARMS CORP, UTICA, N.Y. PAT. APPLIED FOR", black finish, 34.1 in. OAL, 3 lbs. Mfg. circa 1920-1930s, may be up to three variations.

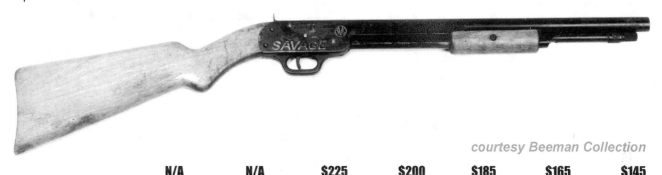

courtesy Beeman Collection

	N/A	N/A	$225	$200	$185	$165	$145

MODEL 560F – .177 cal., BBC, SP, two-stage trigger with manual safety, adj. rear sight, grooved receiver, 18 in. rifled steel barrel, velocity 560 FPS, black polymer stock with metallic finish, 5.5 lbs. Mfg. 1999-2001.

	$73	$62	$50	$35	$25	N/A	N/A

Last MSR was $93.

MODEL 600F – .177 cal., similar to Model 600FXP, except without scope and rings, 6 lbs. Mfg. 1999-2001.

	$100	$85	$70	$45	$30	N/A	N/A

Last MSR was $128.

MODEL 600FXP – .177 cal., BBC, SP with twenty-five-shot mag., two-stage trigger with manual safety, adj. rear sight, hooded front sight, grooved receiver, includes 2.5x20 scope and rings, 18 in. rifled steel barrel, 600 FPS, black polymer stock with lacquer finish and rubber recoil pad, 6.5 lbs. Mfg. 1999-2001.

	$105	$90	$70	$50	$35	N/A	N/A

Last MSR was $135.

MODEL 1000G – .177 cal., similar to Model 1000GXP, except without scope and rings, 7.1 lbs. Mfg. 1999-2001.

	$145	$125	$100	$85	$65	N/A	N/A

Last MSR was $186.

MODEL 1000GXP – .177 cal., BBC, SP with anti-bear trap mechanism, two-stage adj. trigger with manual safety, adj. rear sight, hooded front sight, grooved receiver, includes 4x32 scope and rings, 18 in. barrel, 1000 FPS, walnut stained hardwood stock with vent. rubber recoil pad, 7.5 lbs. Mfg. 1999-2001.

	$169	$144	$119	$95	$70	N/A	N/A

Last MSR was $216.

GRADING	100%	95%	90%	80%	60%	40%	20%

SAXBY PALMER

Previous manufacturer located in Stratford-Upon-Avon, England. Previously imported/distributed by Marksman Products, located in Huntington Beach, CA.

Saxby Palmer developed a cartridge loading air rifle. This is not a CO_2 or other type of compressed gas gun. The cartridges are pressurized (2250 PSI) and reusable, facilitating speed of loading and much greater velocities. Rifles were supplied with the table pump (for reloading brass or plastic cartridges) and ten cartridges. These accessories are necessary in order to operate air rifles or pistols. See Brocock introduction in the "B" section for information on the British 2004 ban on production and sale of air cartridge airguns.

REVOLVERS

Subtract 50% if without accessories.

ORION AIR REVOLVER – .177 cal., six-shot, compressed air cartridges (reusable), 550 FPS, 6 in. barrel, 2.2 lbs. Disc. 1988.

courtesy Beeman Collection

N/A	$550	$450	$350	$275	$195	$110

Add 20% for chrome finish.

This model was manufactured by Weihrauch of Germany and included a Slim Jim pump and twelve reusable cartridges. It also came with a 30 grain .38 cal. zinc pellet to allow cartridges to be used in a .38 Special pistol for practice.

MODEL 54 – .177 cal., five-shot, compressed air cartridges (reusable), 4 in. barrel, 1.35 lb. Disc. 1988.

courtesy Beeman Collection

N/A	$195	$155	$125	$95	$70	$40

This model was manufactured by Weihrauch of Germany and included a Slim Jim pump and twelve reusable cartridges.

WESTERN 66 – .177 or .22 cal., compressed air cartridge, styled after Colt SAA (Peacemaker), blue finish, 11.6 in. OAL, 2.4 lbs.

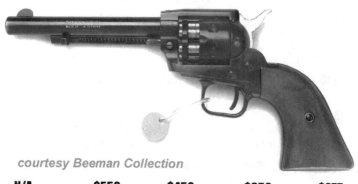

courtesy Beeman Collection

N/A	$550	$450	$350	$275	$195	$110

GRADING	100%	95%	90%	80%	60%	40%	20%

RIFLES

Subtract 50% if without accessories.

ENSIGN ELITE – .177 or .22 cal., compressed air cartridge, BA, 1000/800 FPS automatic safety.

	$275	$235	$195	$160	$125	$80	$55

Last MSR was $175.

ENSIGN ROYAL – .177 or .22 cal., compressed air cartridge, BA, 1000/800 FPS automatic safety, walnut stock.

	$250	$215	$175	$145	$115	$75	$50

Last MSR was $275.

GALAXY – .177 or .22 cal., compressed air cartridge, BA, 1000/800 FPS, automatic safety, walnut stained hardwood stock, 6.5 lbs.

	$225	$190	$160	$130	$100	$65	$45

SATURN – .177 or .22 cal., compressed air cartridge, BA, 1000/800 FPS, automatic safety, black polymer stock, 6.5 lbs. Disc. 1987.

	$275	$235	$195	$160	$125	$80	$55

Last MSR was $175.

SBS

For information on SBS, see Shark Manufacturing Co. in this section.

SCALEMEAD

For information on Scalemead airguns, see Gun Toys SRL in the "G" section.

SCHIMEL

Previous trademark manufactured by Schimel Arms Company located in California circa 1952-54, and A.C. Swanson located in Sun Valley, CA, circa 1956-58.

The Schimel was the first of a series of pistols made from the same general design by Orville Schimel. Due to undercapitalization and a number of design flaws in the Schimel, the small company went bankrupt. In 1955, the manufacturing fixtures were acquired by the American Weapons Corporation, headed by Hy Hunter. The unsatisfactory seals were replaced by a one-seal unit and an ingenious eight-shot magazine for .22 cal. lead balls was added. The improved design was marketed as the "American Luger". Stoeger Arms had U.S. ownership of the Luger trademark and quickly forced these "American Lugers" from the market, making them very rare pistols.

PISTOLS

Smith (1957) heralds these as the first American-made CO_2 production pistol and the first to use disposable CO_2 cylinders.

MODEL GP-22 – .22 cal., CO_2, SS, close copy of the German Luger, toggle action, 6 in. barrel, 380 FPS, die-cast body, blue finish, 9.3 in. OAL, 2.5 lbs. Ref.: Ronald Kurihara (1986) Airgun News & Report 1:3- June.

courtesy Beeman Collection

	$225	$195	$160	$125	$100	$60	$40

Add 15% for factory box.
Add 10% for Model P-22 marking.

A pneumatic version, the Model AP-22 was presented in catalogs but no specimens are known.

GRADING	100%	95%	90%	80%	60%	40%	20%

AMERICAN LUGER – .22 cal., CO_2, similar to Model GP-22, except is an eight-shot repeater. Ref: AGNR - Jan. 1989.

courtesy Beeman Collection

	N/A	$900	$725	$575	$450	$325	$180

Add 15% for factory box.
Add 25% for Swanson variable power version.
Add 20% for single shot variant.

Information sheet included in box with "American Luger" guns may refer to Model V822 and Model HV822, however the guns are marked "American Luger" on the LHS and have the "AL" logo on each grip.

CARBO JET – Smith (1957) and others have reported a repeating CO_2 pistol, supposedly related to the American Luger. Smith illustrates a Schimel and an American Luger as the Carbo Jet. Despite almost a half century of looking, no verified specimens of the Carbo Jet are known.

SCOUT

For information on Scout airguns, see Milbro in the "M" section.

SEARS ROEBUCK AND CO.

Catalog merchandiser that, in addition to selling major trademark firearms, also private labeled many configurations of airguns and firearms (mostly longarms) under a variety of trademarks and logos (i.e. J.C. Higgins, Ted Williams, Ranger, etc.). Sears discontinued the sale of all firearms circa 1980, and the Ted Williams trademark was stopped circa 1978.

A general guideline for Sears Roebuck and related labels (most are marked "Sears, Roebuck and Co." on left side of barrel) is that values are generally lower than those of the major factory models from which they were derived. Remember, 99% of Sears Roebuck and related label airguns get priced by their shootability factor in today's competitive marketplace, not collectibility. A crossover listing (see "Storebrand Cross-Over List") has been provided in the back of this text for linking up the various Sears Roebuck models to the original manufacturer with respective "crossover" model numbers.

SELECTOR

Previous trademark used by SGL Industries of Rockville, MD (formerly GL Industries in Westville, NJ) for Special Purpose CO_2 pistols. Circa 1969-1970.

PISTOL

SELECTOR – .68 cal., CO_2, 6 shot semi-automatic, fires special purpose projectiles, mainly for law enforcement work. Projectiles include: Stinger, noise/confusion, CN tear gas, CS tear gas, and fluorescent dye.

courtesy Beeman Collection

	$125	$100	$90	$80	N/A	N/A	N/A

Add 20% for SGL factory box.
Add 30% for GL factory box.

GRADING	100%	95%	90%	80%	60%	40%	20%

SETRA

Previous trademark of Artés de Arcós, S.A., Corcega 371, Barcelona, Spain. Founded by Jose Artés de Arcós in 1934.

Thanks to Jose Manuel for information on Setra and other Spanish airguns. For additional information contact Jose Manuel at giuliaman@terra.es.

RIFLES

AS 1000 – .177 or .22 cal., pump pneumatic, SS, similar in design to Sheridan Model C, 800/550 FPS, checkered pump handle and pistol grip, 37.3 in. OAL, 5.5 lbs. Approx. 16,000 mfg. 1965-1985.

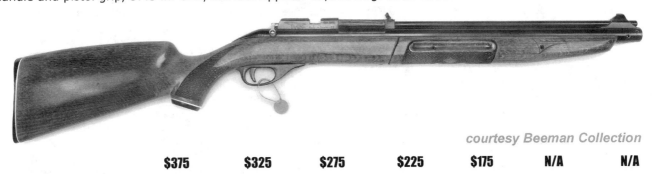

courtesy Beeman Collection

	$375	$325	$275	$225	$175	N/A	N/A

Add 50%-75% for original chrome finish.

Less than 200 imported into England after WWII and few of these went to New Zealand. No USA importation.

AS 2000 – .177 or .22 cal., bulk fill CO_2 or cartridge, SS, 550 FPS, all metal part bronze, 36.63 in. OAL, 4.62 lbs. Approx. 3,600 mfg. 1965-1985.

	$375	$325	$275	$225	$175	N/A	N/A

AS 2000 LUXURY – .177 cal., bulk fill CO_2 or cartridge, SS, 550 FPS, all metal part bronze, deluxe wood with schnabel forearm, 36.63 in. OAL, 4.62 lbs. Approx. 300-400 mfg.

No other information or values available at time of printing.

AS 3000 – .177 or .22 cal., CO_2 two 12g. cartridge, SS, BA, 550 FPS, all metal part black finish, 36.63 in. OAL, 4.62 lbs. Mfg. circa 1965-1985.

courtesy Howard Collection

	$375	$325	$275	$225	$175	N/A	N/A

SETRA REPEATER – .177 cal., slide action, at least 5 mfg. circa 1966.

No other information or values available at time of printing.

SETTER

Previous trademark for 28 gauge pneumatic shotgun made by Armibrescia, Italy circa 1935-1947. Ref: Hannusch (2001).

There may be a pneumatic rifle version. Additional information is solicited from readers, please contact guns@bluebookinc.com. Late 1930s.

SHAKIR CORPORATION

Previous airgun factory located at Karim Pora Rd, Sialkot, Pakistan which made airguns under the Shakir name since 1971.

Shakir Corporation also made large numbers of copies of other models including Diana 25, 27, 35, 65, China 55, G-3, Commando folding airgun, and airgun dummies. No specimens have been examined.

SHARK MANUFACTURING CO.

Current manufacturer located in Buenos Aires, Argentina. Previously imported by Sunshine Airguns located in Miami, FL. No current U.S. importer.

The authors and publisher wish to thank Mr. Eduardo Poloni for much of the following information in this section of the *Blue Book of Airguns*.

Shark began in 1975, producing underwater spear guns, using elastic bands or a gas-spring mechanism. The great power and ease of power regulation in the underwater gas-spring guns led to the development of air rifles for use on land. Two years of research resulted in the Shark Model CD 455 (Caño Deslizable de 455mm or "455mm Sliding Barrel") in .22/5.5mm caliber. The barrel of this rifle slides through a bushing when an underlever is activated to move the piston back and compress the gas spring. As with the Theoben gas-spring airguns (sometimes inappropriately referred to as gas ram airguns), independently developed later in England, the mainspring consists of a trapped body of gas. The gas, in this case air, which does not exit with the shots, is supplied from a separate manual air pump. This system was granted Argentina patent number 213,908 (application 22 June 1978, granted 30 March 1979) and USA patent number 4,282,852 (granted 11 August 1981).

To take advantage of the great power, special Shark ogival projectiles of 1.6 grams were developed. With these projectiles, muzzle velocity could be adjusted to more than 300 MPS at various levels suitable for the smallest game at close range or larger game to more than 50 meters.

In 1979, a unique application of this gas-spring mechanism was used in the development of the Shark CQ air rifles which use a conventional barrel cocking system but have a very interesting, special multiple cocking capability. A single barrel-cocking stroke compresses the gas-spring to ordinary power potential; two strokes triples the power.

In 1985, Shark introduced an unusual CO_2 powered rifle/shotgun combination. These were charged from separate CO_2 storage bottles. It features instantly interchangeable .22 cal., (5.5mm) rifle and 13mm shotgun barrels. In the shotgun mode it uses shot charges in plastic or metal cases and is claimed to be effective to 25 meters for hunting of birds and small mammals. In 2003 this model was produced with a horizontally attached buddy-style CO_2 bottle. Caliber .25 (6.35mm) and a rifled 13mm barrel were also made available. This gun has been used, with arrow projectiles, to take water buffalo in Argentina!

In the early 1990s, Shark switched most of its production to a light, handy CO_2 carbine with a Mauser-type bolt in either .22 (5.5mm) or .25 (6.35mm) caliber. Sturdy, handy SP pistols of the same arrangement were also produced in much smaller numbers.

In 1997, Shark began production of a semi-automatic carbine powered by a horizontally attached buddy-style CO_2 bottle. A 17.5mm paintball version was produced for the newly arrived paintball games.

The Shark airguns have been virtually handmade in a small plant which has grown to only ten employees. Because of this extremely limited production and the fact that these guns normally are produced only for Argentina and Chile, they are rarely seen in most countries. Their scarcity and unusually interesting, very well built mechanisms make them highly desirable to collectors. The early, independently developed, complex gas-spring mechanism is especially interesting. Shark guns with the gas spring system now are of special interest to collectors because the factory has decided that they are too expensive to make more of them.

Only a very few of the total production runs of Shark airguns have ever left Argentina. Local specimens may show extremely hard usage.

PISTOLS

MODEL SP 95 STANDARD – .177 or .22 (13mm new 2002) cal., CO_2, quick change barrel. Approx. 700 mfg. 1995 to date.

courtesy Beeman Collection

N/A	$250	$200	$165	$125	$90	$50

MODEL SP 95 MAGNUM – .25 cal., CO_2. Approx. 185 mfg. 2002 to date.

courtesy Beeman Collection

N/A	$250	$200	$165	$125	$90	$50

GRADING	100%	95%	90%	80%	60%	40%	20%

MODEL SP 95 REPEATER – .174/BB cal., spring-fed internal magazine.

courtesy Beeman Collection

| | N/A | $300 | $240 | $195 | $150 | $105 | $60 |

RIFLES

MODEL CD 405 – .22 cal., GS, hand pump, 16 in. barrel. Approx. 519 mfg. 1980-85.

courtesy Beeman Collection

| | N/A | $450 | $350 | $295 | $225 | $160 | $90 |

MODEL CD 455 – .22 or 8mm (shot) cal., GS, hand pump, 17.9 in. barrel. Approx. 1,252 mfg. 1979-85.

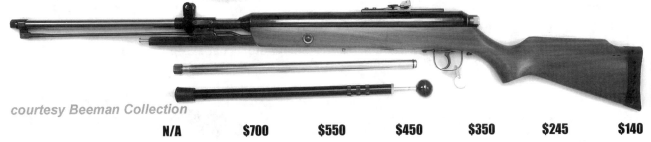

courtesy Beeman Collection

| | N/A | $700 | $550 | $450 | $350 | $245 | $140 |

MODEL CQ-1E – .22 cal., GS, single cocking action with hand pump, identified by rear of receiver being a large flat disc. with a large coin slot, removing the disc exposes the charging valve. Approx. 636 mfg. 1997-2001.

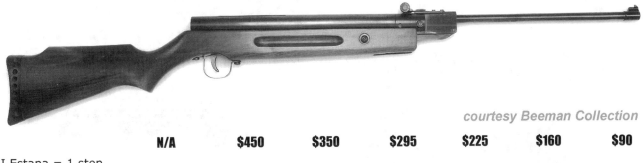

courtesy Beeman Collection

| | N/A | $450 | $350 | $295 | $225 | $160 | $90 |

I Estapa = 1 step

GRADING	100%	95%	90%	80%	60%	40%	20%

MODEL CQ-2E – .22 cal., GS, double cocking action (one cocking action provides standard power, two cocking actions provide maximum power) allowed by the captive charge of the gas spring system, rear end of receiver is conical with visible opening for air charging with hand pump. Approx. 850 mfg. 1982-86.

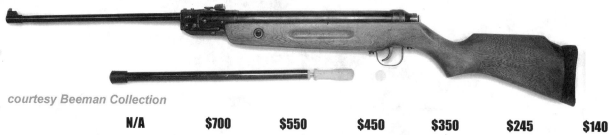

courtesy Beeman Collection

	N/A	$700	$550	$450	$350	$245	$140

2 Estapas = 2 steps

MODEL CARBINE CERROJO – .22 or .25 (new 2002) cal., CO_2, manual slide action. Approx. 8,350 mfg. 1991 to date.

	$275	$235	$195	$160	$125	$80	$55

MODEL REPEATING CARBINE – .22 or 13mm (dart) cal., CO_2, interchangeable barrels, Mauser-style bolt action. Approx. 4,500 mfg. 1993 to date.

	$275	$235	$195	$160	$125	$80	$55

This model was also made in 17.5mm paintball and tranquilizer versions.

MODEL SEMI-AUTOMATIC CARBINE – .22 lead round ball only cal., CO_2, thirty shots. Approx. 650 mfg. 1998-2003.

courtesy Beeman Collection

	$275	$235	$195	$160	$125	$80	$55

MODEL SEMI-AUTO QC – all basic airgun cals., similar to Semi-Auto Model except has quick change barrels, bolt slot RHS of stock, approx. thirty shots. New 2004.

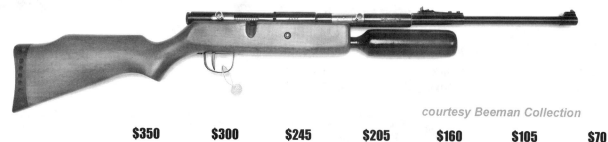

courtesy Beeman Collection

	$350	$300	$245	$205	$160	$105	$70

MODEL BOLT ACTION – .25 cal., BA, CO_2, ambidextrous Monte Carlo stock with rubber recoil pad, sling swivels, scope grooves, no safety, 37.4 in. OAL, 4.8 lbs. New 2004.

courtesy Beeman Collection

	$275	$235	$195	$160	$125	$80	$55

GRADING	100%	95%	90%	80%	60%	40%	20%

SHOTGUNS

MODEL SHOTGUN – .22, .25 (new 2003) pellet or 13mm (shot) cal. CO_2, quick change rifled barrels. Approx. 3,000 mfg. 1989-90. Reintroduced in 2003.

courtesy Beeman Collection

	$650	$600	$575	$550	$500	$475	$450

Add 25% for pre-1990 version.

SHARP

Current tradename of air rifles and pistols manufactured by Sharp Rifle Manufacturing Company, located in Tokyo, Japan. Previously imported by Beeman Precision Airguns, then of San Rafael, CA, and perhaps by others.

Founded by Kensuke Chiba, an airgun marksman and inventor, in 1952 as the Tokyo Rifle Laboratory. Name changed in 1955 to Tokyo Rifle Company and then to Sharp Rifle Manufacturing Company in 1960. Over twenty models of gas and pneumatic guns have been developed by this firm; most of these were produced for Asian markets. This listing shows main Sharp models seen in USA. Other models, to be detailed later, include: Full Mark, Veteran, Victory, Champion, Champion Tiger, Export, Eagle, Pan-Target 700, Ace Hunter, U-SL, Mini- UD-I and II. Research is ongoing with this trademark, and more information will be included both online and in future editions. Ref: AAG - Jan. 1999.

PISTOLS

MODEL U-FP – .177 cal., 545 FPS, CO_2, SS, black finish, hardwood grips, 8 in. BBL, 12 in. OAL. Intro. 1969.

courtesy Beeman Collection

	N/A	$475	$375	$325	$250	$165	$110

Add 10% for factory box.

RIFLES

ACE SPORTER – .177 or .22 cal., swinging forearm pump pneumatic, BA, SS, leaf rear sight, hardwood stock, rubber buttplate with white spacer, 23.9 in. BBL, 920/750 FPS, manual safety catch, 38.4 in. OAL, 6.3 lbs. Mfg. circa 1981-1987. Ref: AR1 (1997): pp. 36-38.

courtesy Beeman Collection

	N/A	$500	$400	$325	$250	$175	$100

Last MSR was $295.

GRADING	100%	95%	90%	80%	60%	40%	20%

ACE TARGET – .177 or .22 cal., SL, BA, SS, SL at 45 degree angle, target stock, adjustable buttplate, and match diopter sights. Mfg. circa 1981-1987. Ref: AR1 (1997): pp. 36-38.

courtesy Howard Collection

N/A	$1,100	$875	$725	$550	$375	$220

Last MSR was $450

GR-75 – .177 cal., CO_2, pump action loading repeater, two 12 gm CO_2 cylinders, 19.6 in. rifled bbl., deep blue steel parts, wood stock, grip cap and buttplate with white line spacers, manual cross bolt safety, 39 in. OAL, 6.7 lbs.

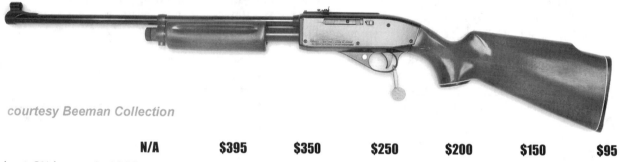

courtesy Beeman Collection

N/A	$395	$350	$250	$200	$150	$95

Highest SN known is 1933.

INNOVA – .177 or .22 cal., swinging forearm pump pneumatic, BA, SS, 20 in. BBL, 920/720 FPS, smooth wood stock and forearm, bolt catch serves as safety, 34.6 in. OAL, 4.3 lbs. Disc. 1988.

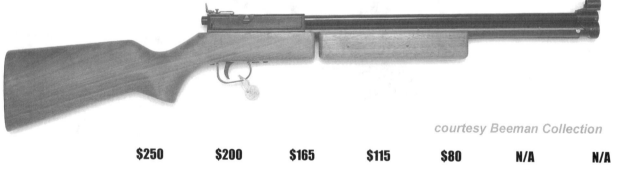

courtesy Beeman Collection

$250	$200	$165	$115	$80	N/A	N/A

Last MSR was $175.

The Innova Special model has side lever pump handle and one-piece stock. New 1985.

PAN TARGET – .177 cal., SL, BA, SS, SL at 90 degree angle, hard wood stock, match diopter sights. Mfg. circa 1981-1987.

courtesy Howard Collection

N/A	$1,000	$825	$750	$575	$350	$225

GRADING	100%	95%	90%	80%	60%	40%	20%

TIGER 500 TARGET – similar to Ace, except has double set trigger, palm rest, special match sights and thumbhole match stock, adj. buttplate, match sling, and fitted case.

courtesy Beeman Collection

Scarcity precludes accurate pricing.

Examples marked "SPORTSMAN" are known.

USL – .177 cal., CO_2, BA, SS, sporter or thumbhole wood stock, approx. 620 FPS, 32 in. OAL. Mfg. beginning 1969.

	100%	95%	90%	80%	60%	40%	20%
	$200	$175	$150	$100	$70	N/A	N/A

SHARPSHOOTER

For information on Sharpshooter airguns, see Bulls Eye in the "B" section.

SHERIDAN PRODUCTS, INC.

Current trademark marketed by Crosman Corp. located in Bloomfield, NY.

In 1994 through 1995, after their purchase by Crosman Air Guns, some of the separate lines of the Benjamin and Sheridan airgun companies were merged into one.

The Sheridan Company of Racine, WI was started in 1945 by E.H. Wackerhagen, who teamed up with fellow airgun enthusiast Robert Kraus, who had engineering skills. He stated that their objective was to best the Benjamin Air Rifle Company by producing what they planned would be the best possible pneumatic air rifle. Mr. Kraus related to Robert Beeman that they felt that because Wackerhagen and Kraus would not be too catchy a name for an air rifle, they named the company after Sheridan Street, a road in Racine which they traversed almost daily as they went between their respective garages during the development of the new gun. Their first model, the Model A, was produced in March 1947. The first paid advertisements evidently appeared about 1948. The perfection of the Model A required a retail price of $56.50 in 1948. Sales were very poor. A less expensive model, the Model B, introduced in October 1948 at a retail price of $42.50, was even less successful. Good sales did not begin until after the introduction of the Model C, which sold for $23.95 in 1949.

See the introduction to the Benjamin section for information on manufacturing locations and the names under which these guns have been marketed in the 1990s.

All Sheridan air rifles and pistols are single shot, bolt action, breech-loading, and .20 (5mm) caliber. Muzzle velocity figures are for Sheridan's standard weight pellets of 14.3 grains.

For more information and current pricing on the Sheridan firearms, please refer to the *Blue Book of Gun Values* by S.P. Fjestad (also available online).

PISTOLS

Values listed below assume good working order with no missing parts. If finish has been removed, and the brass polished, the value is reduced to approximately one half of the 90% value.

MODEL E – .20 cal., 12 gm CO_2 cylinder, 5.85 in. barrel, 400 FPS, high polish nickel finish, walnut grips, special serial range of EOOxxxx. Limited mfg. 1990 only.

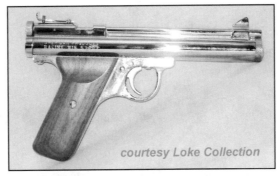

courtesy Loke Collection

	100%	95%	90%	80%	60%	40%	20%
	N/A	$110	$90	$70	$55	$40	$20

Add 25% for box and owner's manual.

GRADING	100%	95%	90%	80%	60%	40%	20%

MODEL EB – .20 cal., 12 gm CO_2 cylinder, 5.85 in. barrel, 400 FPS, matte black finish, brown plastic grips. Mfg. 1977-1989.

courtesy Beeman Collection

	N/A	$100	$80	$65	$50	$35	$20

Add 25% for Sheridan box and owner's manual.

MODEL G DART PISTOL – .50 (13mm) cal., CO_2 or multiple stroke forearm pneumatic, SS, similar to Models EB and HB, except is tranquilizer dart version, matte black finish.

courtesy Beeman Collection

	N/A	$175	$140	$115	$85	$60	$35

This model was previously identified incorrectly as the Model ED Dart Pistol. The only identifying marking on these pistols was the grips since there were no standard factory role marks.

MODEL HB – .20 cal., multiple stroke forearm pneumatic, matte black finish, walnut forearm, brown plastic grips, 8.75 in. barrel, 400 FPS, marked "Sheridan 1982-1990". Mfg. in Racine, WI until 1994, and in E. Bloomfield, NY from 1995 to 1998.

	N/A	$100	$80	$65	$50	$35	$20

Add 20% for Sheridan box and owner's manual.
Add 5% for later box and owner's manual.

This design has been marketed under the Sheridan name, the Benjamin/Sheridan name, and the Benjamin name. Also marketed as the Sheridan HB20, it cannot be distinguished from identical pistols under the Benjamin HB20 heading in the Benjamin section (please refer to names used in the 1990s in the introduction to the Benjamin section).

MODEL H20PB – .20 cal., multiple stroke forearm pneumatic, polished brass plated, 8.75 in. barrel, 400 FPS, commemorates the 50th Anniversary of Sheridan. Mfg. 1998 only.

	N/A	$145	$115	$95	$70	$50	$30

Add 20% for Sheridan box and owner's manual.

This model was marketed only under the Sheridan name.

RIFLES

Values listed below assume good working order with no missing parts. If finish has been removed, and the brass polished, value is reduced by approx. 50%.

MODEL A SUPER GRADE – .20 cal. (first specimen of the Model A may be .22 cal.), multiple stroke forearm pneumatic, blue finish, walnut half stock with raised cheek piece, aluminum receiver, peep sights, 20.15 in. barrel, 700 FPS. Approx. 2,130 mfg. 1947-1953. Ref: AR 1 (1997): pp. 41-42.

courtesy Beeman Collection

	N/A	$1,500	$1,200	$975	$750	$525	$300

GRADING	100%	95%	90%	80%	60%	40%	20%

Add 60% for box and owner's manual.

Add 15% for first production version without serial numbers, Sheridan logo engraved, felt lining in forearm cocking handle.

Serial numbers on this model were not consecutive, up to about no. 4000 have been observed. Early production had a long handle and felt lined forend. Later production had short handle and no felt lining.

MODEL B SPORTER – .20 cal., multiple stroke forearm pneumatic, black painted finish, walnut half stock, soldered, "ventilated" barrel/pump tube construction, heavy aluminum receiver, peep sights, 20.15 in. barrel, 700 FPS, not serial numbered. Approx. 1,051 mfg. 1948-1951.

courtesy Beeman Collection

N/A	$1,600	$1,275	$1,050	$800	$550	$325

Add 60% for box and owner's manual.

MODEL C SILVER STREAK – .20 cal., multiple stroke forearm pneumatic, nickel finish, walnut full stock, open sights, 19.5 in. barrel, 675 FPS, rotating safety. Ref: AR (1997): pp. 22-24.

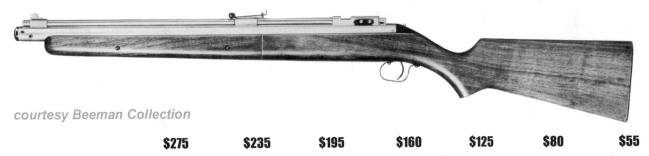

courtesy Beeman Collection

$275	$235	$195	$160	$125	$80	$55

Add $30 for Models CW with Williams peep sight.

Add 20% for Sheridan box and owner's manual.

Add 20% for highly polished original finish, plus 20% for box and owner's manual.

Add 25% for "hold-down" automatic safety models (mfg. 1952-1963 only), and 25% for box and owner's manual.

Subtract 25% for disabled automatic safeties; such guns should be repaired or put into non-firing condition.

Add 150% for early Silver Streaks with knurled windage knobs (mfg. 1949-1952) and 30% for box and owner's manual.

Add 200% for earliest Silver Streak "slab stock" model (mfg. in 1949 only) and 35% for original box and owner's manual.

Add 300% for left-handed models, approx. 400 mfg.

This model was marked "Sheridan" from 1949 to 1990. Serial numbering began in 1972 with #000000. Also marketed later as the Sheridan C9 Silver Streak and the CB9 Blue Streak. (See introduction of Benjamin section for information on manufacturing locations and names used in 1990s.)

MODEL CB BLUE STREAK – .20 cal., multiple stroke forearm pneumatic, black finish, walnut full stock, open sights, 19.5 in. barrel, 675 FPS, rotating safety. Ref: AR (1997): pp. 22-24.

$185	$150	$130	$105	$85	$55	$35

Add $30 for Model CBW with Williams peep sight.

Add 20% for Sheridan box and owner's manual.

Add 20% for highly polished original finish, plus 20% for box and owner's manual.

Add 25% for "hold-down" automatic safety models (mfg. 1952-1963 only), and 25% for box and owner's manual.

Subtract 25% for disabled automatic safeties; such guns should be repaired or put into non-firing condition.

Add 300% for left-handed models, approx. 400 mfg.

This model was marked "Sheridan" from 1949 to 1990. Serial numbering began in 1972 with #000000. (See introduction of Benjamin section for information on manufacturing locations and names used in 1990s.)

GRADING	100%	95%	90%	80%	60%	40%	20%

MODEL CB9 BLUE STREAK – .20 cal. pellet, multi-pump pneumatic, BA, SS, 19.38 in. rifled brass barrel, 675 FPS, black finish, fixed front and fully adj. rear sight, American hardwood Monte Carlo stock and forearm, crossbolt safety, 36.75 in. OAL, 5.5 lbs.

MSR $195	$165	$145	$135	$105	$80	N/A	N/A

Add $100 for Blue Streak CB9 Combo which includes mounted Leapers 4x32 scope, Weaver rings, intermount with Picatinny rail, and Plano rifle case.

MODEL C9PB – .20 cal., multiple stroke forearm pneumatic, 675 FPS, polished brass plating, medallion inset into stock (1998 only) to commemorate the 50th Anniversary of Sheridan. Mfg. 1999-2000.

courtesy Howard Collection

$150	$130	$105	$85	$70	$45	$30

Add 20% for medallion in stock.
Add 20% for box and owner's manual.

This model was marketed only under the Sheridan name.

MODEL C9 SILVER STREAK – .20 cal., multiple stroke forearm pneumatic, BA, SS, 19.38 in. rifled brass barrel, 675 FPS, nickel finish, adj. rear sight, American hardwood stock and forearm, 6 lbs. Disc. 2012.

courtesy Howard Collection

$165	$140	$115	$95	$75	$50	$35

Last MSR was $195.

MODEL F – .20 cal., 12 gm CO_2 cylinder, nickel finish, walnut half stock, open sights, 19.5 in. barrel, 515 FPS, rotating safety. Mfg. 1975-1990.

N/A	$250	$200	$165	$125	$90	$50

Add 30% for early production, highly polished original finish.
Add 20% for Sheridan box and owner's manual.
Add 300% for left-handed models.
Add 30% for Models FW with Williams 5D-SH peep sight.

This model was marked "Sheridan 1975-1990". It was later marketed as the Model F9 under the Benjamin/Sheridan name. (See information on 1990s marketing in the introduction to the Benjamin section.)

GRADING	100%	95%	90%	80%	60%	40%	20%

MODEL FB – .20 cal., 12 gm CO_2 cylinder, black finish, walnut half stock, open sights, 19.5 in. barrel, 515 FPS, rotating safety. Mfg. 1975-1990.

courtesy Howard Collection

	N/A	$200	$160	$130	$100	$70	$40

Add 30% for early production, highly polished original finish.
Add 20% for Sheridan box and owner's manual.
Add 300% for left-handed models.
Add 30% for Models FBW with Williams 5D-SH peep sight.

MODEL FB9 – .20 cal., 12 gm CO_2 cylinder, black finish, walnut half stock, open sights, 19.5 in. barrel, 515 FPS, rotating safety. Mfg. 1991-Disc.

courtesy Howard Collection

	N/A	$200	$160	$130	$100	$70	$40

Add 20% for Sheridan box and owner's manual.

MODEL F9 – .20 cal., 12 gm CO_2 cylinder, nickel finish, walnut half stock, open sights, 19.5 in. barrel, 515 FPS, rotating safety. Mfg. 1991-Disc.

	N/A	$250	$200	$165	$125	$90	$50

Add 20% for Sheridan box and owner's manual.

MODEL G DART RIFLE – .50 (13mm) cal., 12 gm CO_2 or multiple stroke forearm pneumatic, SS, similar to Models CB and FB, except is tranquilizer dart version, matte black finish.

	N/A	$200	$160	$130	$100	$70	$40

There are no standard factory role marks on these rifles.

SHINBISHA AIR RIFLE CO.

Previous Japanese manufacturer.

Shinbisha manufactured break barrel cocking spring piston air rifles and a .22 caliber rimfire rifle. Rifles are marked S.A.R. with a crossed arrows logo.

SHIN SUNG INDUSTRIES CO. LTD.

Current manufacturer located in Korea. Currently imported and distributed by Airguns of Arizona located in Gilbert, AZ. Previously imported by Pyramyd Air located in Warrensville Heights, OH, and RWS Precision Products located in Closter, NJ, also distributed by ARS located in Pine City, NY.

Manufacturer of a wide variety of amazing, usually very large, pre-charged pneumatic airguns, often of great power, ranging from the trumpet look-alike confetti/ribbon-shooting, which advertises that "It is real action for your unforgettable moment" up to large bore rifles, such as Career 707, Ultra, Carbine, Tanker Carbine, and Fire 201 for which the maker claims: "It is a real action to chase the fascinated target" or "Become an explorer in the jungle, run for the freedom with your instinct." The guns are very well built and as interesting as the copy. The shiny brass Celebration trumpet model has a current value above $1,200 in excellent condition. Several simple versions without the trumpet's slide and mouthpieces are known. For more information on these airguns, also see ARS in the "A" section, and RWS in the "R" section.

GRADING	100%	95%	90%	80%	60%	40%	20%

RIFLES

ADVENTURE DB – .22 cal., PCP, removable mag., PG stock, 41.3 in. OAL, 8.2 lbs. Mfg. 1990s.

courtesy Beeman Collection

	100%	95%	90%	80%	60%	40%	20%
	$550	$500	$450	$350	$275	N/A	N/A

VAN STAR 505 – .22 cal., BA, SS, Brocock-type air cartridges (about size of 20 ga. shell), barrel concentric with receiver. 46.2 in. OAL, 6.7 lbs.

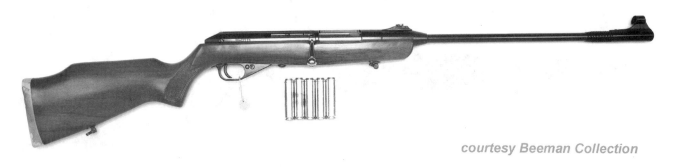

courtesy Beeman Collection

	100%	95%	90%	80%	60%	40%	20%
	$500	$400	$350	$275	$200	N/A	N/A

CAREER 707 9MM ULTRA – 9mm cal., PCP, SS or 6-8 round mag. repeater, lever action w/transverse loading bar, 23.25 in. barrel, adj. power dial, pressure gauge, hand checkered high grade stock, cross bolt manual safety, 41.75 in. OAL, 9.4 lbs.

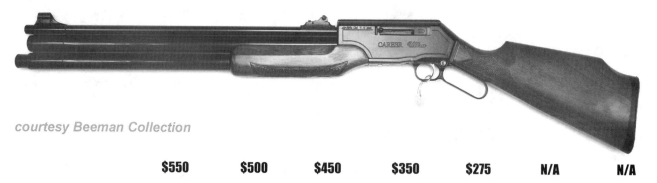

courtesy Beeman Collection

	100%	95%	90%	80%	60%	40%	20%
	$550	$500	$450	$350	$275	N/A	N/A

Last MSR was $655.

CAREER DRAGON SLAYER MODEL – .50 cal., PCP, SS, BA, 20.60 in. rifled barrel, 570 FPS, two stage trigger, checkered PG Monte Carlo hardwood stock, rubber butt pad, 41.30 in. OAL, 8.8 lbs. Mfg. 2004-disc.

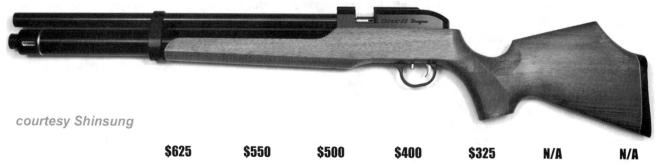

courtesy Shinsung

	100%	95%	90%	80%	60%	40%	20%
	$625	$550	$500	$400	$325	N/A	N/A

Last MSR was $749.

GRADING	100%	95%	90%	80%	60%	40%	20%

CAREER II (CAREER 707) – .22 cal., PCP, six-shot (or side-loading SS) lever action, 22.75 in. blue barrel, 1000 FPS, adj. diopter rear sight, hooded front sight, checkered walnut stock and forearm, 7.75 lbs. Mfg. in Korea 1995-Disc.

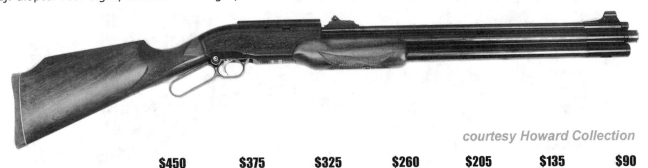

courtesy Howard Collection

	$450	$375	$325	$260	$205	$135	$90

Last MSR was $580.

FIRE 201 – 9mm cal., PCP, SL, smooth bore or rifled barrel, 900 FPS, beech stock. Mfg. in Korea, 2000.

	$450	$375	$325	$260	$205	$135	$90

Last MSR was $595.

CAREERFIRE 202S – 9mm cal., PCP, SS, pull bolt action, 21.50 in. rifled barrel, 900 FPS, two stage trigger, adj. sights, checkered hardwood PG stock and forearm w/rubber butpad, 42 in. OAL, 7.5 lbs.

courtesy Shinsung

	$500	$450	$400	$325	$250	N/A	N/A

Last MSR was $600.

DRAGON – .50 cal., PCP, 22.1 in. barrel, hardwood stock with checkered grip, 40.25 in. OAL, 9.5 lbs. Mfg. in Korea.

MSR $595	$500	$425	$350	$295	$230	$155	$100

INFINITY – 9mm cal., PCP, 26 in. barrel, hardwood thumbhole stock, 43.75 in. OAL, 9.9 lbs. Mfg. in Korea.

MSR $595	$500	$425	$350	$295	$230	$155	$100

FIRE 202 – 9mm cal., PCP, 20.5 in. barrel, hardwood stock with checkered grip, 40 in. OAL, 6.25 lbs. Mfg. in Korea.

MSR $595	$500	$425	$350	$295	$230	$155	$100

SHOTGUNS

CELEBRATION – full-size, trumpet-look-alike PCP shotgun firing several kinds of projectiles including confetti/ribbon. Advertised that "It is real action for your unforgettable moment", high polish brass, several simple versions w/o a trombone-style slide and mouthpiece are known.

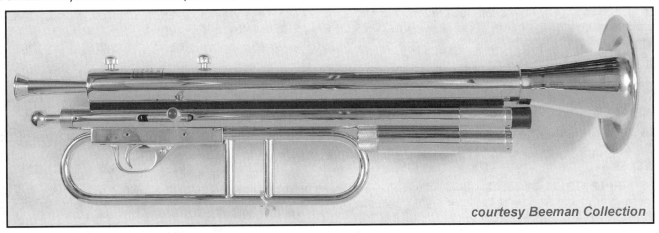

courtesy Beeman Collection

Scarcity precludes accurate pricing.

GRADING	100%	95%	90%	80%	60%	40%	20%

SHOOTING STAR

For information on Shooting Star airguns, see Feltman Products in the "F" section.

courtesy CT Shotgun MFG. Co

SHUE

Previous trademark of Shue High Pressure Air Rifle Company located in Milwaukee, WI circa 1912-14. Ref: AR2:57-60.

RIFLES

SHUE HYPRESURE AIR RIFLE – .173 steel/4.4 lead balls cal., BBC, SP, SS, 423 FPS with steel BB, sheet metal, break action BB gun, 33.4 in. OAL, 2.6 lbs. Ref: AR 2 (1998): pp. 57-60.

courtesy William Gautsch

N/A	$4,000	$3,200	$2,600	$2,000	$1,400	$800

SIBERGUN

Current trademark of airguns and shotguns manufactured by Yazicilarav, located in Trabzon, Turkey. No U.S. importation. Please contact the company directly for U.S. availability and pricing (see Trademark Index).

SIG SAUER

Current airgun trademark manufactured by Kine-Well Toy Industrial Co. Ltd. (KWC) located in Tainan, Taiwan and firearms trademark manufactured by SIG Arms AG (Schweizerische Industrie-Gesellschaft) located in Neuhausen, Switzerland. Airguns are currently imported and distributed by Air Venturi/Pyramyd Air, located in Solon, OH (previously located in Warrensville Hts., OH), and by Palco Sports located in Maple Grove, MN.

For more information and current pricing on both new and used Sig Sauer firearms, please refer to the *Blue Book of Gun Values* by S.P. Fjestad (also available online).

PISTOLS

GSR – .177 cal., CO_2, PCP, semi-auto, 22-shot mag., all black stainless steel slide and comfortable grips, Weaver/Picatinny rail under the barrel, fixed rear sights, 7.75 in. OAL, 2.4 lbs. Mfg. 2012-current.

MSR $100	$85	$70	$60	$50	$40	$25	$15

GSR 1911 – .177 cal., 12g CO_2 cartridge, semi-auto repeater, DA only, 5 in. smoothbore barrel, 20 shot drop-free mag., fixed front and rear sights, manual safety, Weaver accessory rail, black finish, includes laser with momentary remote on/off switch, laser mount, glasses and 250 steel BBs, 8.5 in. OAL, 1.6 lbs.

MSR $50	$40	$35	$30	$25	$20	N/A	N/A

P226 X-FIVE – BB/.177 cal., CO_2, PCP, semi-auto, blowback action, SA/DA, 18-shot mag., black, metal construction, fixed sights, 8.85 in. OAL, 2.55 lbs. Mfg. 2012-current.

MSR $150	$125	$105	$90	$75	$55	$35	$25

P226 X-FIVE OPEN COMBO – BB/.177 cal., CO_2, PCP, semi-auto, blowback action, 18-shot mag., SA/DA, metal construction, fixed front and adj. rear sights, two-stage trigger, manual safety, black, includes X-mount Weaver rail, compensator, and steel BBs, 10.87 in. OAL, 2.86 lbs.

MSR $170	$145	$125	$100	$85	$65	$45	$30

GRADING	100%	95%	90%	80%	60%	40%	20%

SP2022 – BB/.177 cal., PCP, 12g CO$_2$, semi-auto, 23-shot removable mag., silver slide with black frame and grip, or all black, manual safety, fixed rear sights, 7.7 in. OAL, 1.3 lbs. Mfg. 2012-current.

MSR $80	$65	$55	$45	$40	$30	$20	$15

SILVA ARMS

Current manufacturer established 2005, and located in Turkey. No current U.S. importation.

Silva Arms was established by Mr. Cenk Barcin as a Foreign Trade Company in 2005 in Turkey. Since then, the company has been involved in the outdoor and hunting market by selling shotguns, hunting cartridges, blank and rubber ammunitions, blank and traumatic pistols and air rifles.

RIFLES

STRANGER AIR – .177 or .22 cal., 17 in. barrel, advanced polymer stock in Black, Wooden Effect, Greeny or Loft camo finish, 42 in. OAL, 7 lbs.

courtesy Silva Arms

Please contact the company directly for pricing and U.S. availability for this model.

SIMCO

For information on Simco airguns, see Apache in the "A" section.

SKAN AR

Current manufacturer located in Colchester, England 1991 to present.

Current manufacturer of chronographs (chronoscopes) and bullpup PCP air rifles. Owned and operated by Mike Childs. Extruded aluminium frames with small air reservoir in, or forming, the buttstock. Stock parts are usually plastic or rubber, walnut was also offered from 1995.

RIFLES

Skan rifles vary greatly. Older versions will be detailed in later issues of this guide. Models included: Mk 1 with flat 'pipe organ' magazines holding stacked pellets, cocked with side knob. Mk 2 with horizontal, cylindrical magazine with chambers holding about ninety pellets. From 1992 to 1998 cocked with sliding forearm. Forearm cocking was discontinued due to concern that the British government would ban such actions as slide action weapons. Normally set to UK 12 ft./lb. limit. Single stage trigger on all but most recent guns. Black or brushed anodized silver finishes.

R32 MILLENIUM – .177 or .22 cal., PCP, thirty-two-shot mag., Bullpup style, air cylinder in walnut stock, extended forearm with flush fitting bipod, grey anodised aluminium, nickel finished steel components, removable silencer, 33 in. OAL, 7.5 lbs. 10 mfg. 1999.

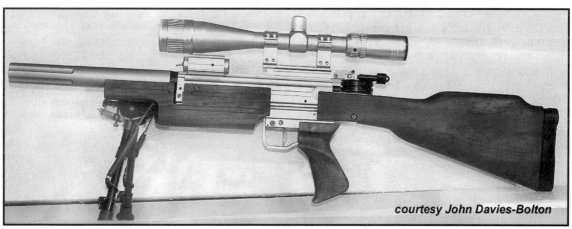

courtesy John Davies-Bolton

MSR $1,800	$1,550	$1,150	$895	$750	$600	N/A	N/A

Add 5% for case.

GRADING	100%	95%	90%	80%	60%	40%	20%

MINI M32 MK3 – .177 or .22 cal., PCP, two vertical drums total thirty-two-shot mag., bullpup style, bottle forms part of buttstock, rubber fittings, two-stage adj. trigger, rear grip slides backwards and forwards to cycle action, built-in sound moderator, bipod, 25 in. OAL, 0.75 lbs.

MSR $1,125	$950	$775	$650	$495	$375	N/A	N/A

Add 15% for laser sight.
Add 5% for case.

R32 ULTRA – .177 or .22 cal., PCP, thirty-two-shot mag., similar to Mini except with walnut fittings, leather cover on bottle, built-in laser, spare magazine slot under buttstock.

MSR $1,350	$1,095	$895	$750	$625	$500	N/A	N/A

Add 5% for case.

SLAVIA

For information on Slavia, see CZ in the "C" section.

courtesy Beeman Collection

SMITH & WESSON

Current manufacturer located in Springfield, MA. Dealer sales. Currently imported and distributed by Umarex USA located in Fort Smith, AR begining 2006.

In 1965, Smith & Wesson was purchased from the Wesson family by the conglomerate Bangor Punta. A major diversification program led to the in-house design of an airgun line. With the aid of a former Crosman engineer, four airgun models were developed: pistol Models 78G, 79G, and rifle Models 77A, 80G ("A" for "air"; "G" for "gas"). The Model 77A was a .22-caliber pump pneumatic pellet rifle with a less-than-sleek wood stock and forearm-pump lever.

The Model 78G was a single-shot .22 caliber pellet pistol designed to resemble the popular Smith & Wesson Model 41 target automatic. The Model 79G is the .177 caliber version. Both had adjustable rear sights and power. Early versions had adjustable triggers; adjustable for sear engagement; later models had non-adjustable trigger mechanisms. A few problems included gas leakage through porous frame castings.

Smith & Wesson's Air Gun Division introduced their fourth and final model in 1972, the Model 80G rifle. It was designed by Roger Curran, formerly with Remington. This autoloader fired .175 caliber BBs from a tubular magazine below the barrel. In 1973 the Air Gun Division moved from Tampa, Florida to Springfield, Massachusetts. Some early Model 80G rifles are marked with the Florida address, as are some Model 77A rifles.

In 1978, the Air Gun Division returned to Florida in a part of the former Westinghouse complex and the Model 77A was dropped. Due to changing from a sprayed paint finish to a baked powder-coat finish, Springfield production pistols have a duller, more uniform finish than earlier production. Also around this time, Curran began to develop a CO_2 pellet revolver, although Smith & Wesson was not destined to complete development of this model.

Around 1980, Bangor Punta decided that Smith & Wesson should concentrate more on its core handgun business. The Air Gun Division was sold to Daisy. Daisy renamed the Smith & Wesson Models 78G and 79G as the Daisy Powerline Models 780 and 790. A nickel-plated model .177 caliber version was introduced as the Power Line Model 41- in honor of the original Smith & Wesson Model 41 firearm.

Smith & Wesson again entered the airgun field in 1999, when they introduced two models made for them by Umarex of Germany: the .177 caliber ten-shot CO_2 pellet revolvers, Models 586 and 686. These were close copies of the .357 Magnum Smith & Wesson revolvers bearing the same numbers.

For more information and current pricing on both new and used Smith & Wesson firearms, please refer to the *Blue Book of Gun Values* by S.P. Fjestad (also available online).

GRADING	100%	95%	90%	80%	60%	40%	20%

PISTOLS

MODEL 78G – .22 cal., CO_2, SS, styled after S&W Model 41 semi-automatic pistol, gun blue finish, brown plastic grips, 8.5 in. barrel, 425 FPS, fully adj. sight, 42 oz. Mfg. 1971-1980.

courtesy Beeman Collection

	$135	$115	$100	$85	$60	N/A	N/A

Last MSR was $53.45.

Add 50% for orig. box with can of S&W pellets and box of CO_2 cylinders.
Add 30% for orig. box with plastic envelope of pellets and CO_2 cylinders.
Add 25% for early pistols with adj. trigger.
Add 10% for Model 78G guns stamped "80G".

MODEL 79G – .177 cal., CO_2, SS, styled after S&W Model 41 semi-automatic pistol, gun blue finish, brown plastic grips, 8.5 in. barrel, 475 FPS, fully adj. sight, 42 oz. Mfg. 1971-80.

	$135	$115	$100	$85	$60	N/A	N/A

Last MSR was $53.45.

Add 50% for orig. box with can of S&W pellets and box of CO_2 cylinders.
Add 30% for orig. box with plastic envelope of pellets and CO_2 cylinders.
Add 25% for early pistols with adj. trigger.

M&P 40 – BB/.177 cal., CO_2, DA, 19-shot drop-out mag., 4.25 in. barrel, 420 FPS, Black or Dark Earth Brown finish synthetic frame and slide, integrated accessory rail, fixed front and rear fiber optic sights, manual safety, 7.5 in. OAL, 1 lb. Mfg. 2008-current.

courtesy Umarex USA

MSR $44	$40	$35	$30	$25	N/A	N/A	N/A

M&P 45 – BB/.177 cal. or pellets, CO_2, SA/DA, 370 FPS, 8-shot, 3.4 in. barrel, fixed front and rear sights, integrated accessory rail, black synthetic frame and slide, manual safety, 8 in. OAL, 1.45 lbs. New 2011.

courtesy Umarex USA

MSR $72	$55	$45	$40	$30	$25	$15	$10

GRADING	100%	95%	90%	80%	60%	40%	20%

REVOLVERS

M&P R8 – BB/.177 cal., CO_2, SA/DA, 410 FPS, 8-shot, 4 or 5.1 (disc.) in. barrel, fixed front and adj. rear sights, integrated accessory rail, black synthetic grip with finger grooves, manual safety, 10.5 in. OAL, 1.35 lbs. New 2011.

courtesy Umarex USA

MSR $78	$60	$50	$40	$35	$25	N/A	N/A

MODEL 327 TRR8 – BB/.177 cal., 12g CO_2 capsule, SA/DA, 400 FPS, features unusual contours, 6-shot rotary mag., 5 1/2 or 6 (disc.) in. metal barrel, swing-out cylinder, manual safety, fixed fiber optic front sight, adj. fiber optic rear sight, integrated Picatinny rails, matte black or nickel plated steel finish, black grip with finger grooves, includes six removable metal casings and speedloader, 12 in. OAL, 2 lbs. New 2012.

courtesy Umarex USA

MSR $109	$90	$75	$65	$50	$40	$25	$20

This model is also available with Kit I which includes a point sight for quick target acquisiton and a tactical forend grip, or Kit II which includes a point sight, and a combined LED/laser module for target illumination.

MODEL 586B4/586B6/586B8 – .177 cal., CO_2, SA/DA, ten-shot cylinder, 400 (4 in.), or 425 (6 in.) FPS, replica of Smith & Wesson Model 586 .357 Mag. revolver, high gloss black finish with black rubber grips, 4, 6, or 8 (disc. 2004) in. interchangeable barrels, adj. micrometer sight, 9.5-11.2 in. OAL, 40-48 oz. New 1999.

courtesy Smith & Wesson

MSR $291	$235	$200	$165	$135	$105	$70	$45

Add $22 for 6 in. barrel (Model 586B6).

Add 15% for 8 in. barrel (Model 586B8), disc. 2004.

GRADING	100%	95%	90%	80%	60%	40%	20%

MODEL 686N4/686N6/686N8 – .177 cal., CO_2, SA and DA, ten-shot cylinder magazine, 425 FPS, replica of Smith & Wesson Model 686 .357 Mag. revolver, 4 (disc. 2004), 6, or 8 (disc. 2004) in. interchangeable barrel, satin nickel finish with checkered black rubber grips, 40-48 oz. New 1999.

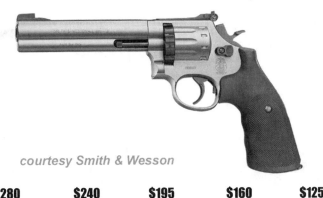

courtesy Smith & Wesson

MSR $336	$280	$240	$195	$160	$125	$85	$55

Add $22 for 8 in. barrel (Model 686N8), disc. 2004.

RIFLES

MODEL 77A – .22 cal., swinging forearm, multi-stroke pump pneumatic, wood buttstock and forearm/pump handle, sliding wedge elev. adj. rear sight, trigger guard drops for loading breech, SS, black oxide blue finish, 22 in. rifled barrel, 6.5 lbs. Mfg. 1971-78.

courtesy Howard Collection

$150	$130	$115	$100	$70	N/A	N/A

Last MSR was $46.50.

Add 10% for Springfield address and scope grooves.

MODEL 80G – BB/.175 cal., CO_2, semi-automatic, brown plastic stock, sliding wedge elev. adj. rear sight, 22 in. barrel. Mfg. 1972-80.

courtesy Beeman Collection

$125	$105	$95	$80	$60	N/A	N/A

Last MSR was $43.50.

Add 10% for Springfield address.

SNIDER AIR PISTOL

For information on Snider airguns, see Hubertus in the "H" section.

SNYDER, RUSS

Current model and tool maker.

Manufactured twelve museum quality firing replicas of the original St. Louis 1899 and 1900 air rifles circa 1997.

RIFLES

In 1997, collector Marv Freund persuaded Russ Snyder, a highly noted model maker and toolmaker, to make only twelve masterpiece replicas - museum quality, firing copies of his original St. Louis 1899 air rifle. On a whim, Snyder also made five double-barrel versions of the airgun - something that had never existed in the historical record. In 2002, Russ Snyder produced just a dozen copies of the St. Louis 1900 model air rifle for the purchasers of the 1899 model reproductions. Ref: AR 2 (1998): 76-78.

GRADING	100%	95%	90%	80%	60%	40%	20%

ST. LOUIS 1899 REPLICA – these replicas are virtually perfect copies of the original, right down to the St. Louis Air Rifle Company logo impressed into the wooden buttstock. Eleven were finished with the original black enamel and nickel plating. One replica was given special decoration, including gold plating. Twelve mfg. circa 1997. Ref: ARZ: 1976-78.

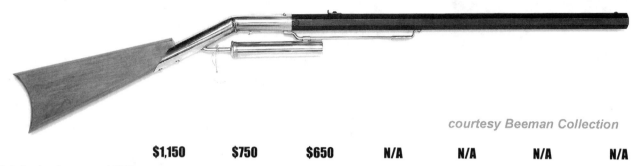

courtesy Beeman Collection

	$1,150	$750	$650	N/A	N/A	N/A	N/A

Original price was $750.

* St. Louis 1899 Replica Double (SxS) – similar to St. Louis 1899 Replica, except double barrel (SxS), no such originals ever existed. Five mfg. circa 1997.

   Scarcity precludes accurate pricing.

ST. LOUIS 1900 REPLICA – .180 in. cal., smoothbore, SS, muzzle-loading barrel under main body tube, 17 3/8 in. barrel, 21 5/8 in. from fwd. end of body tube to base of rear sight blade, (Collectors Note contrast with measurements of original Benjamin/St.Louis 1900), LHS of buttstock with pressed-in lettering: ST.LOUIS AIR RIFLE CO., ST. LOUIS, MO, PAT. JUNE 20 -1899. No mention of OTHER PATENTS PENDING. Serial number from 1 to 12 visible on metal tang only when stock is removed, 33 in. OAL. Twelve mfg. circa 2002.

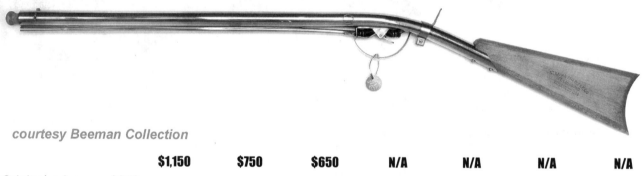

courtesy Beeman Collection

	$1,150	$750	$650	N/A	N/A	N/A	N/A

Original price was $850.

ST. LOUIS 1901 REPEATER REPLICA – .180 in. cal. smoothbore barrel under body tube, 21 3/32 in. length from tip of barrel to center of trigger retaining screw, all major parts, except air seals and trigger tube, are brass. Brass fixed buttstock air reservoir. Marked on top of barrel: "Benjamin Repeating Air Rifle 1901" and serial number from "1 of 10" to "10 of 10". 35 5/16 in. OAL, ten mfg. 2007.

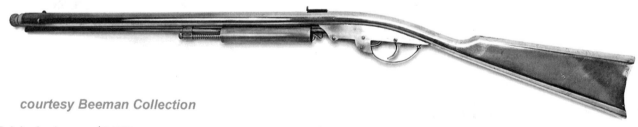

courtesy Beeman Collection

   Original price was $1,900.

SPITFIRE
For information on Spitfire airguns, see Philippine Airguns in the "P" section.

SPLATMASTER
For information on Splatmaster tranquilizer guns, see Palmer Chemical & Equipment Co. in the "P" section.

SPORTSMATCH
Current manufacturer of scope mounts located in Leighton Buzzard, Bedfordshire, UK.

Sportsmatch started around the early 1980s by founder John Ford. Sportsmatch is now run by his son, Matthew Ford.

In its day, the GC2 was probably the most coveted rifle a shooter could own; it was akin to owning a Ferrari. Most were sold for use in UK field target competitions, but some were fitted with sporting stocks. The name was derived from 'Gerald Cardew', the famous airgun engineer who designed the GC2 air regulating mechanism. 'GC1' was a testbed for the regulator and not a production rifle. The GC2 was produced in three marks from 1986 to 1993. In all, around 350 guns were produced, some were sold as 'action only' and were married to custom-built stocks from the likes of John Welham. Weight varies accordingly, but these guns have alloy cylinders and are quite light for their size. The two-stage flat blade trigger is fully adjustable. The Lothar Walther barrel was fitted with a fluted muzzle brake to prevent barrel lift on firing. Most were .177 caliber, although any caliber was available. A bullpup version called the Scimitar was available, although only twelve were made.

The GC2 value is in the $1,750 range with basic walnut stock. Add up to 100% for finest quality custom walnut. The Scimitar value is in the $2,100 range.

courtesy Howard Collection

STANLEY AIR RIFLE COMPANY
Previous manufacturer located in Northville, MI circa 1889.

Merritt Stanley, a former employee of the Markham Air Rifle Company was granted at least three patents for BB guns, starting in 1890. He produced a BB gun under his own name circa 1889 in Northville, Michigan, then moved into the Dubuar Manufacturing Company of Northville which produced the Globe air rifles from the early 1890s. In 1908 Daisy consumed the Stanley and Dubuar BB gun production. Stanley may also have been involved in producing designs used by the Plymouth Air Rifle Company. See the Plymouth, Globe, and Decker sections of this guide.

STARFIRE
For information on Starfire airguns, see Feltman Products in the "F" section.

ST. LOUIS AIR RIFLE CO.
For information on St. Louis Air Rifle Co. air rifles, see Benjamin Air Rifle Co. in the "B" section.

STEINER
Previous trademark for pellet pistols made by a firm presently known only from markings on the guns as BBM located in Italy.

PISTOLS

STEINER-S – .177 cal., BBC, SP, 14 in. OAL, 7.25 in. rifled barrel, SS. Die-cast construction, but sturdily built. Brown plastic grips. Front sight very distinctively placed at forward end of receiver, perhaps in the mistaken notion that consistent sight alignment has any significance if the barrel has irregular positioning. No safety or anti-barrel snap mechanism. Black or bright nickel finish.

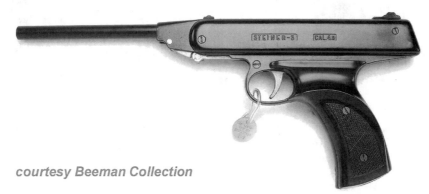

courtesy Beeman Collection

Average original condition specimens on most common (Steiner) models are typically priced in the $35 range for black finish and $40 range for nickel finish.

STELLA
Previous trademark of Kovo AS of Prague, Czechoslovakia.

This firm mainly made spring piston, barrel-cocking air rifles in the early 1950s. The line may have moved into the Slavia brand.

GRADING	100%	95%	90%	80%	60%	40%	20%

PISTOLS

MODEL 551 – .177 cal., smoothbore, BBC, SP, SS, marked with "STELLA" (pierced by an arrow) and "Made in Czechoslovakia" on top of the barrel, 7.9 in. OAL, 1.7 lbs. Mfg. circa 1950.

courtesy Kenth Friberg

Scarcity precludes accurate pricing.

GAT STYLE – .177 cal., smoothbore, push-barrel cocking, folded metal construction, blued, SP, SS. Marked "STELLA" in round logo on grip and "Made in Czechoslovakia" on side of the barrel.

courtesy Beeman Collection

Estimated value about $65 in 90% condition.

RIFLES

CZ/STELLA MODEL Vz-36 – 4.40mm, SP, TL, cocks by swinging lever attached to right side of action up and back, military style stock w/upper hand guards, gravity or spring fed magazine repeater manufactured for the commercial market. Reportedly less than 100 mfg. circa 1936 w/12 specimens known.

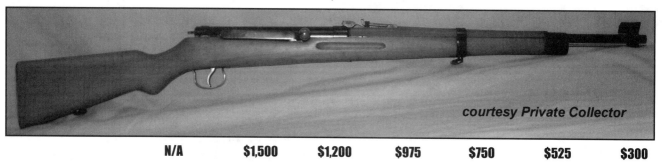

courtesy Private Collector

N/A	$1,500	$1,200	$975	$750	$525	$300

STERLING

Previous trademark manufactured by Sterling in England.

Design and trademark purchased by the Benjamin Air Rifle Company, located in East Bloomfield, NY, in 1994. After Benjamin was purchased by Crosman Air Guns in 1994, the manufacture of the Sterling line was discontinued.

RIFLES

HR 81 – .177, .20, or .22 cal., UL, SP, 700/660 FPS, adj. V-type rear sight, 8.5 lbs.

$295	$250	$200	$155	$115	$80	N/A

Last MSR was $250.

Add $50 for original English markings.
Add $10 for .22 cal.
Add $20 for .20 cal.

GRADING	100%	95%	90%	80%	60%	40%	20%

HR 83 – .177, .20, or .22 cal., UL, SP, 700/660 FPS, adj. Williams (FP) peep sight, walnut stock, 8.5 lbs.

courtesy Howard Collection

	$325	$275	$240	$195	$150	$95	N/A

Last MSR was $300.

Add $50 for original English markings. Add $5 for .22 cal. Add $20 for .20 cal.

STERLING/UPTON

Previous tradename of American Tool Works located in Chicago, IL. Previous manufacturer of BB guns under the Sterling and Upton names circa 1891-1928.

For information on Sterling and Upton, see American Tool Works in the "A" section.

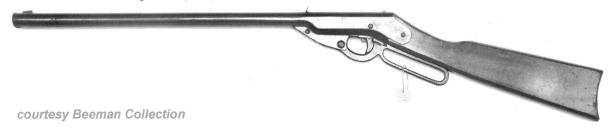

courtesy Beeman Collection

STEYR SPORTWAFFEN GmbH

Current manufacturer located in Ernsthofen, Austria. Currently imported by Pilkington Competition Equipment, LLC, located in Monteagle, TN, and Champion's Choice located in LaVergne, TN. Previously imported and distributed by Nygord Precision Products, located in Prescott, AZ. Dealer or consumer direct sales.

For more information and current pricing on both new and used Steyr firearms, please refer to the *Blue Book of Gun Values* by S.P. Fjestad (also available online).

PISTOLS

LP-1/LP-1P/LP-C – .177 cal., CO_2 or PCP, UIT pistol with compensator, 15.33 in. overall, 2 lbs. 2 oz. Disc. 2002.

	$1,200	$1,025	$850	$700	$550	$350	$240

Last MSR was $995.

Add 10% for colored tank variations (red, blue, green, or silver - marked "LP1-C").
Add 100% for limited edition models.
Subtract 50% for CO_2.

The Limited Edition consists of 250 units, engraved and signed Barbara Mandrell LP-1 USA Shooting Team, in red, white, and blue, and complete with lined walnut presentation case and certificate of authenticity.

LP-2 – .177 cal., CO_2 or PCP, SS, UIT pistol, 9 in. BBL with two-port compensator, 530 FPS, two-stage adj. trigger, adj. sights, adj. Morini grip, 15.3 in. OAL, 2 lbs. New 2003.

courtesy Steyr Collection

MSR $1,650	$1,375	$1,150	$950	$800	$625	$400	$275

Subtract 15% for CO_2.
This model is also available in a compact variation - MSR $1,295 (LP-2 Compact, new 2011).

GRADING	100%	95%	90%	80%	60%	40%	20%

* **LP-2 Junior** – .177 cal., CO_2 or PCP, SS, UIT pistol, similar to LP-2, except 13.2 in. OAL, 1.8 lbs. New 2004.

courtesy Steyr Collection

MSR $1,550	$1,325	$1,150	$1,050	$850	$650	N/A	N/A

Subtract 15% for CO_2.

LP-5/LP-5P/LP5C – .177 cal., CO_2, PCP (LP-5P), match pistol, five-shot semi-auto.

	$1,000	$850	$700	$575	$450	$300	$200

Last MSR was $1,150.

Subtract 15% for CO_2.

LP-10 – .177 cal., CO_2 or PCP, SS, UIT pistol with internal stabilizer, adj. trigger, adj. sights, adj. Morini grip, four ten-gram barrel weights, 15.25 in. OAL, 2 lbs. 2 oz. New 1999.

courtesy Steyr Collection

MSR $2,045	$1,750	$1,525	$1,400	$1,125	$850	N/A	N/A

Subtract 15% for CO_2.

This model is also available in a compact variation - MSR $1,900 (LP-10 Compact, new 2011).

* **LP-10E** – .177 cal., PCP, SS, UIT pistol with internal stabilizer, adj. electronic trigger, adj. sights, adj. Morini grip, four ten-gram barrel weights, 15.25 in. OAL, 2 lbs. 2 oz. Mfg. 2009-current.

MSR $2,575	$2,200	$1,875	$1,525	$1,275	$975	$650	$450

This model is also available in a compact variation - MSR $2,275 (LP-10E Compact, new 2011).

LP-50 – .177 cal., CO_2 or PCP, five-shot semi-automatic, match pistol, similar to LP-5, except LP-10 style BBL shroud with three ports. New 2003.

courtesy Steyr Collection

MSR $2,245	$1,900	$1,600	$1,325	$1,100	$850	$575	$375

Subtract 15% for CO_2

This model is also available in a compact variation - MSR $2,070 (LP-50 Compact, new 2011).

* **LP-50E** – .177 cal., PCP, five-shot semi-automatic, match pistol, similar to LP-50, except electronic trigger and LP-10 style BBL shroud with three ports. Mfg. 2009-current.

MSR $2,775	$2,375	$2,025	$1,650	$1,375	$1,075	$700	$475

This model is also available in a compact variation (LP-50E Compact, new 2011).

GRADING	100%	95%	90%	80%	60%	40%	20%

LP SILHOUETTE – .177 cal., PCP, SS, steel BBL with two-port compensator, two-stage adj. trigger, 11mm top rail for scope or sights, stipled anatomical walnut grip. Mfg. 2009-current.

MSR $2,395	$2,025	$1,725	$1,425	$1,175	$900	$600	$400

RIFLES

LG-1 – .177 cal., SL/SSP, target model, micrometer sight and adj. stock. Disc. 1998.

	$900	$775	$625	$525	$400	$270	$180

Last MSR was $995.

LG-1P – .177 cal., PCP, target model, micrometer sight and adj. stock. Disc. 1998.

	$900	$775	$625	$525	$400	$270	$180

Last MSR was $995.

MODEL LG-10/LG-10P – .177 cal., SL, SSP, target model, micrometer sight, adj. stock, has stabilizer and distinctive anodized red frame. Disc. 2000.

	$1,100	$950	$775	$650	$500	$325	$220

Last MSR was $1,139.

MODEL LG-20 – .177 cal., PCP, SS, radial adj. Alu butt plate and cheek piece, laminated wood stock, Steyr stabilizing system, single stage trigger, dry fire action. Mfg. 2005-2009.

	$1,300	$1,100	$900	$750	$575	$400	$260

Last MSR was $1,785.

MODEL LG-100 – .177 cal., PCP, aluminum two-piece stock, 17 in. barrel, 27 in. steel barrel shroud, 570 FPS, match sight set, 9.5 lbs. Mfg. 2001-06.

	$1,675	$1,425	$1,175	$975	$750	$500	$325

Last MSR was $1,850.

MODEL LG-110 – .177 cal., PCP, match rifle, dry fire cocking lever action, single stage trigger, SS, take down Alu-stock, infinitely adj. butt plate, pistol grip, cheek piece, front and rear sights, Steyr stabilizer system with barrel and stock weights. New 2005.

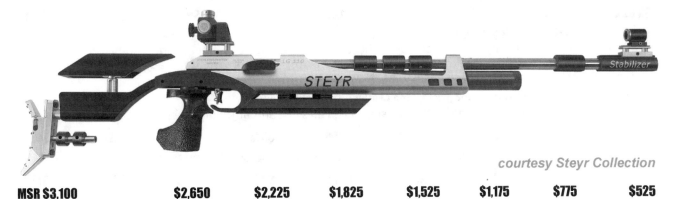

courtesy Steyr Collection

MSR $3,100	$2,650	$2,225	$1,825	$1,525	$1,175	$775	$525

MODEL LG-110 BENCH REST – .177 cal., PCP, 17.7 in. barrel, special longer stock and forearm, lateral stock adjustment, elongated adj. cheek piece, vibration free system, Steyr stabilizer, longer compressed air cylinder, dry-fire, multi-directional adjustment of the grip, single or two-stage adj. trigger, CONNECT (quick takedown buttstock in a 97cm case), 11-12 lbs. New 2011.

Please contact the importer directly for pricing and availability on this model.

MODEL LG-110 LIGHT – .177 cal., PCP, similar to the Model LG-110, except is lighter due to a shorter barrel extension and short buttstock. New 2011.

Please contact the importer directly for pricing and availability on this model.

GRADING	100%	95%	90%	80%	60%	40%	20%

MODEL LG-110 FIELD TARGET – .177 cal., PCP, SS, field target rifle, 17.5 in. nickel-plated barrel, dry fire cocking lever action, single stage trigger, take down Alu-stock, infinitely adj. butt plate, pistol grip, cheek piece, no sights, Steyr stabilizer system, comes with plastic case and without scope and weaver rail, some improvements for 2011 include the CONNECT (quick takedown buttstock in a 97cm case), adj. of the muzzle velocity without dismantling the rifle, multi-directional adjustment of the grip, hook with multiple adjustments, vibration free system, lateral stock adjustment, 37 in. OAL, 10 lbs. New 2005.

courtesy Steyr Collection

MSR $3,195	$2,750	$2,325	$1,900	$1,575	$1,225	$825	$550

MODEL LG-110 HIGH POWER – .177, .20 (new 2010), or .22 cal., PCP, SS, field target rifle, 17.5 in. nickel-plated barrel, available in silver (.177 cal.), or black (.20 and .22 cal.) finish, dry fire cocking lever action, single stage trigger, Alu-stock w/thumbhole polymer butt stock, no sights, Steyr stabilizer system, comes with plastic case and without scope and weaver rail, 34.7 in. OAL, 8.3 lbs. New 2005.

MSR $2,150	$1,825	$1,550	$1,275	$1,050	$825	$550	$375

Add $50 for .22 cal.

* **Model LG-110 HP Black Beauty** – .177 or .22 cal., PCP, SS, field target rifle, similar to Model LG-110 High Power except black finish with black synthetic thumbhole stock. Mfg. 2009-current.

MSR $2,150	$1,825	$1,550	$1,275	$1,050	$825	$550	$375

* **Model LG-110 HP Hunting** – .177, .20 (new 2010), or .22 cal., PCP, SS, field target rifle, nickel-plated barrel, similar to Model LG-110 High Power except black finish with wood synthetic thumbhole stock and adj. cheek piece. Mfg. 2009-current.

MSR $2,495	$2,125	$1,800	$1,475	$1,225	$950	$625	$425

MODEL LG-110 RUNNING TARGET – .177 cal., PCP, 17.7 in. barrel, 2x100 g barrel weights on the elongated barrel case, adj. forearm, mounted sights, lateral stock adjustment, vibration free system, Steyr stabilizer, dry fire, multi-directional adjustment for the grip, adj. trimmer on the buttplate, single or two-stage adj. trigger, CONNECT (quick takedown buttstock in a 97cm case), 9.3-11.9 lbs. New 2011.

Please contact the importer directly for pricing and availability on this model.

MATCH 88 – .177 cal., CO_2, match rifle with precision receiver sight and adj. buttplate. Mfg. 1991-1995.

	$650	$550	$450	$375	$295	$195	$130

MATCH 91 – .177 cal., CO_2, match rifle with precision receiver sight and adj. buttplate. Mfg. 1991-1995.

	$750	$625	$525	$425	$325	$225	$150

Last MSR was $1,400.

Add $50 for left-hand variation.
Add $100 for Running Target.

LGB1 BIATHLON – .177 cal., PCP, five-shot repeater, Fortner-type action, adj. match trigger, adj. snow sights, 40 in. OAL, 9.6 lbs. New 2004.

courtesy Steyr Collection

MSR $2,900	$2,475	$2,175	$1,975	$1,600	$1,225	N/A	N/A

Comes with one-shot and five-shot magazine.

GRADING	100%	95%	90%	80%	60%	40%	20%

STIGA

Previous tradename of Stig Hjelmqvist AB located in Trånas, Sweden.

Makers of firearms, sporting goods, and may be maker or distributor only of a Zenit-style top-lever air pistol. Research is ongoing with this trademark, and more information will be included both online and in future editions.

PISTOLS

ZENIT – 4.5mm cal., TL, SP, SS, 5 in. smooth bore barrel. First variant: wood grips with Stiga shield on left-hand side, the name "Zenit" is stamped on the left side of cocking lever, rear sight incorporated in cocking lever, mfg. 1949-1961. Second variant: uses the Zenit action with brown plastic grips Stiga name molded into bottom of grip on both sides, mfg. 1962-65. Third variant: Stiga action with blue-grey plastic grips with heavy-duty reinforced sheet metal cocking lever with wings for easier grip, rear sight is at the end of the action, 11 in. OAL, approx. 1.5 lbs. Mfg. 1965-69. Ref: AR 2 (1998): pp. 16-20.

courtesy Howard Collection

	$350	$300	$250	$175	$125	$75	N/A

Very similar to Zenit single shot, top lever air pistol patented by Franz Moller, Zella-Mehlis, Germany for Em-Ge (See the "E" section) in 1937 and discontinued in 1939 due to WWII. (Also copied by Milbro Bros. as the British Diana Model 4.)

CADET – 4.5mm cal., SP, SS, push-barrel, similar to Diana Model 2, loaded from rear of action, 7.9 in. OAL, .66 lbs. Mfg. 1949-1969.

	$300	$255	$210	$175	$135	$90	$60

RIFLES

MODEL 99 (JUNIOR) – .177 cal., BBC, SP, SS, rifled bore steel barrel with beech stock, 36 in. OAL. Mfg. 1948-1960.

	$175	$150	$125	$100	$80	$50	$35

MODEL 100 – 4.5mm cal., BBC, SP, SS, 17.4 in. rifled bore solid steel barrel, adj. rear and blade front sights, PG wood stock with Stiga shield on LH side, marked "STIGA TRANAS SWEDEN" on spring tube, 40 in. OAL. Mfg. 1948-1960.

	$275	$235	$195	$160	$125	$80	$55

ORIGINAL – 6 1/3mm cal., trigger guard lever cocking, SP, SS, 20.5 in. smooth bore octagon steel barrel, blue or chrome finish, adj. rear and blade front sights, English style straight grip beech stock with Stiga shield on LH side, marked "STIGA TRANAS SWEDEN" on spring tube, 40 in. OAL. Mfg. 1952-1960.

	$600	$500	$425	$350	$270	$180	$120

Add 20% for blue finish.

STOEGER INDUSTRIES INC.

Current importer/trademark established in 1924, and located in Accokeek, MD. Previously located in Wayne, NJ, until 2000. Stoeger Industries, Inc. was purchased by Beretta Holding of Italy in 2000, and is now a division of Benelli USA. Stoeger introduced the "X" series air rifle line in 2008.

RIFLES

ATAC SUPPRESSOR – .177 or .22 cal., BBC, Gas-Ram Technology (GRT), 1000/800 FPS, 16 1/2 in. barrel with AFC suppressor, two-stage adj. trigger, tactical synthetic stock with integral Picatinny rails attached to both sides of the forend and receiver, Black finish, ambidextrous automatic safety, includes 4-16x40 AO scope, 43 in. OAL, 9 lbs. New 2013.

MSR $299	$245	$210	$170	$140	$110	$75	$50

X3 YOUTH – .177 cal., SP, break action, SS, 550 FPS, 11 3/4 in. barrel, fixed trigger, fiber optic rear sights, hardwood hunter-style stock with non-slip rubber buttpad, 11 3/4 in. LOP, automatic ambidextrous safety, 4.21 lbs. New 2013.

MSR $99	$85	$70	$60	$50	$40	$25	$15

GRADING	100%	95%	90%	80%	60%	40%	20%

X5 – .177 cal., BBC, SP, SS, 640 FPS, 16.5 in. rifled steel barrel, ergonomically designed cocking grip, two stage adj. trigger, fiber optic sights, integral dovetail scope rail, blue finish, Monte Carlo style with pistol grip hardwood or black synthetic (new 2010) stock with full checkering, rubber recoil pad, deeply grooved receiver, automatic ambidextrous safety, 41 in. OAL, 5.7 lbs. Mfg. 2008-current.

courtesy Stoeger Industries Inc.

MSR $109	$90	$75	$65	$50	$40	$25	$20

Add $40 for 4x32mm scope.

X10 – .177 or .22 (new 2011, scope combo only) cal., BBC, SP, SS, 16.5 in. rifled steel barrel, 1000/800 FPS, two stage adj. trigger, fiber optic sights, integral dovetail scope rail, blue finish, hunter straight-style with pistol grip hardwood or black synthetic stock, rubber recoil pad, deeply grooved receiver, automatic ambidextrous safety, 43 in. OAL, 6.8 lbs. Mfg. 2008-current.

courtesy Stoeger Industries Inc.

MSR $139	$115	$100	$80	$65	$50	$35	$25

Add $30 for 4x32mm scope.

X20 – .177 or .22 (new 2011) cal., BBC, SP, SS, 16.5 in. rifled steel barrel, 1000/800 FPS, two-stage adj. trigger, fiber optic sights, integral dovetail scope rail, blue finish, Monte Carlo style with pistol grip hardwood, Advantage Timber HD camo (disc. 2012), or black synthetic stock, checkering on pistol grip and front stock, recoil pad, automatic ambidextrous safety, double cheek piece, 3-9x40 AO scope became standard in 2013, 43 in. OAL, 7 lbs. Mfg. 2008-current.

courtesy Stoeger Industries Inc.

MSR $199	$170	$145	$120	$100	$75	$50	$35

Add $40 for Advantage Timber HD camo stock (disc. 2012).

X20 SUPPRESSOR – .177 or .22 cal., BBC, SP, AFC (air flow control) technology, Dual-Stage Noise Reduction System, 1000/800 FPS, 17.5 in. rifled barrel, blued steel, black synthetic Monte Carlo stock with checkering, double cheek piece, 4x32 illuminated red/green scope and rings, integral dove tail on top of receiver, ergonomic cocking grip, adj. two-stage trigger, non-slip deluxe rubber recoil pad, automatic safety, 43 in. OAL, 7 lbs. New 2011.

MSR $249	$210	$180	$145	$120	$95	$65	$40

GRADING	100%	95%	90%	80%	60%	40%	20%

X50 – .177 or .22 (new 2011) cal., BBC, SP, SS, 19.7 in. rifled steel barrel, 1200/1000 FPS, two stage adj. trigger, fiber optic sights, integral dovetail scope rail, blue finish, ambidextrous hunting-style hardwood (disc. 2011), black synthetic, or Advantage Timber HD camo stock (disc. 2012), raised ambi. cheek piece, checkering on pistol grip and forend, rubber recoil pad, 3-9x40 AO scope became standard in 2013, 50 in. OAL, 8.3 lbs. Mfg. 2008-current.

courtesy Stoeger Industries Inc.

MSR $319	$265	$225	$185	$155	$120	$80	$55

Add $50 for Timber HD camo stock (disc. 2012).

STURM, RUGER & CO., INC.

Current manufacturer with production facilities located in Newport, NH and Prescott, AZ. Currently distributed by Umarex USA, located in Fort Smith, AR. Previously manufactured in Southport, CT 1949-1991 (corporate and administrative offices remain at this location). A second factory was opened in Newport, NH in 1963, and still produces single action revolvers, rifles and shotguns. During 2008 a licensed partnership was formed with Umarex USA Inc. located in Fort Smith, AR to manufacture and market airguns under the Sturm, Ruger & Co. Inc. trademark.

On July 6, 2002, the legendary William B. Ruger, Sr. passed away in his home in Prescott, AZ. He is remembered for his visionary efforts in firearms manufacturing and marketing, exceptional design skills, and his philanthropic donations in support of the firearms industry. For more information and current pricing on both new and used Sturm, Ruger & Co., Inc. firearms, please refer to the *Blue Book of Gun Values* by S.P. Fjestad (now online also). Please refer to the *Blue Book of Modern Black Powder Arms* by John Allen (also online) for more information and prices on Sturm Ruger black powder models.

PISTOLS

MARK I – .177 cal., SP, BBC, 500 FPS, blued receiver, 6.5 in. rifled barrel, blued receiver, fiber optic sights, ergonomic synthetic grip, anti-slam trigger barrel safety system, cocking assist handle included, Black finish, 14.25 in. OAL, 2.8 lbs. New 2012.

courtesy Umarex USA

MSR $78	$60	$50	$40	$35	$25	N/A	N/A

RIFLES

AIR HAWK – .177 cal., BBC, SP, SS, 18.7 in. rifled steel barrel with muzzle brake (disc. 2008), blue finish, 490 or 1000 FPS, adj. rear and fixed front fiber optic sights, 4x32 scope with mounts, adj. two-stage trigger, automatic safety, semi (new 2009) Monte Carlo dark wood stock with PG and rubber recoil pad, 44.8 in. OAL, 8.25 lbs. Mfg. 2008-current.

courtesy Umarex USA

MSR $148	$120	$100	$85	$70	$55	$35	$25

GRADING	100%	95%	90%	80%	60%	40%	20%

* ***Air Hawk Elite*** – .177 cal., BBC, SP, SS, 18.7 in. rifled steel barrel with muzzle brake, blue finish, 1000 FPS, 3-9x40mm scope with mounts, adj. trigger automatic safety, ambidextrous hardwood thumbhole stock with vented rubber recoil pad and checkered forearm, cheek piece on both sides, 44.8 in. OAL, 9 lbs. Mfg. 2008-2012.

courtesy Umarex USA

	$185	$155	$130	$105	$85	$55	$35

Last MSR was $220.

AIR MAGNUM – .177 or .22 (new 2012) cal., BBC, SP, SS, 1200/1000 FPS, 19.5 in. rifled barrel, all-weather black composite stock, blued barrel and receiver, two-stage adj. trigger, adj. fiber optic rear and fixed fiber optic front sights, automatic safety, rubber recoil pad, 4x32 scope with rings, Picatinny scope rail, 48.5 in. OAL, 9.5 lbs. New 2011.

courtesy Umarex USA

MSR $212	$175	$150	$125	$100	$80	$50	$35

BLACKHAWK – .177 cal., BBC, SP, SS, 18.7 in. rifled steel barrel, blue finish, 1000 FPS, two-color adj. rear and fixed front fiber optic sights, 4x32 scope with mounts, automatic safety, ambidextrous black composite stock with PG and rubber recoil pad, adj. two-stage trigger, 44.8 in. OAL, 7.85 lbs. Mfg. 2009-current.

courtesy Umarex USA, Inc.

MSR $137	$110	$95	$75	$65	$50	$35	$20

BLACKHAWK MAGNUM – .177 cal., BBC, SP, 1000 FPS, blued, black synthetic stock with checkering on grip and forearm, fiber optic sight, two-stage adj. trigger, auto safety, 48.2 in. OAL, 8.6 lbs.

While advertised during 2012, this model never went into production.

EXPLORER – .177 cal., BBC, SP, single shot cocking mechanism, 495 FPS, 15 in. rifled barrel, blue receiver, adj. fiber optic rear sight, fixed fiber optic front sight, all-weather black composite ambidextrous thumbhole stock with ambidextrous vent. cheekpiece and rubber recoil pad, Anti-slam trigger-barrel safety system, 12 in. LOP, 37.12 in. OAL, 4.45 lbs. New 2010.

courtesy Umarex USA, Inc.

MSR $84	$65	$55	$45	$40	$30	$20	$15

GRADING	100%	95%	90%	80%	60%	40%	20%

This model is also available with a Starter Kit which includes a pellet trap, targets, dart board with air rifle darts, shooting glasses, and pellets (mfg. 2012 only).

LGR – .177 cal., two 12g CO_2, BA, refillable cylinder, 650 FPS, 21.4 in. rifled barrel, blue finish, ambidextrous wood stock, adj. fiber optic rear and fixed fiber optic front sight, adj. two-stage trigger, auto/manual safety, rubber recoil pad, 39.6 in. OAL, 5.3 lbs. Mfg. 2011-2012.

courtesy Umarex USA

	$125	$105	$90	$75	$55	$35	$25

Last MSR was $150.

TALON – .177 cal., BBC, SP, SS, 1000 FPS, 18.7 in. barrel with SilencAir 5-chamber noise dampener, adj. two-stage trigger, adj. fiber optic rear and fixed fiber optic front sights, automatic safety, blued barrel and receiver, Picatinny scope rail, all-weather synthetic stock with rubber recoil pad, Black finish, 4x32 scope, 44.85 in. OAL, 9.85 lbs. New 2013.

courtesy Umarex USA

MSR $182	$155	$130	$110	$90	$70	$45	$30

TALON HUNTER – .22 cal., BBC, SS, SP, 800 FPS, 18.7 in. barrel with SilencAir 5-chamber noise dampener, blued barrel and receiver, adj. two-stage trigger, adj. fiber optic rear and fixed fiber optic front sights, automatic safety, Picatinny scope rail, sling and swivels for the field, all-weather synthetic stock with rubber recoil pad, Black finish, 3-9x32 scope, 44.85 in. OAL, 9.85 lbs. New 2014.

MSR $211	$175	$150	$125	$100	$80	$50	$35

YUKON – .177 or .22 cal., BBC, ReAxis gas piston, SS, 1050/850 FPS, 18.7 in. barrel with SilencAir 5-chamber noise dampener, adj. two-stage trigger, Picatinny scope rail, fixed fiber optic front and adj. fiber optic rear sights, automatic safety, blued barrel and receiver, hand finished hardwood stock with rubber recoil pad, textured grip and forearm, 3-9x32 scope with mounts, 44.8 in. OAL, 9 lbs. New 2013.

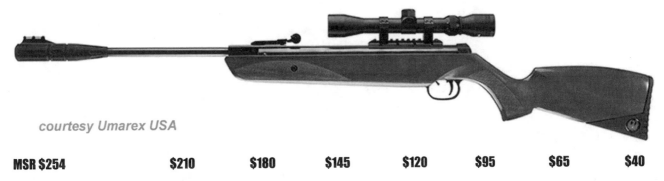

courtesy Umarex USA

MSR $254	$210	$180	$145	$120	$95	$65	$40

SUSSEX ARMORY

For information on Sussex Armory airguns, see Gun Toys SRL in the "G" section.

SUPER TORNADO

For information on Super Tornado airguns, see Relum Limited in the "R" section.

GRADING	100%	95%	90%	80%	60%	40%	20%

SWISS ARMS MANUFACTURE (SAM)

Current manufacturer located in Viganello Lugano, Switzerland. Previously located in Davesco, Switzerland. No current US importation. Previously imported and distributed by Nygord Precision Products, located in Prescott, AZ. Dealer or consumer direct sales.

Please contact the factory directly for more information and current pricing (see Trademark Index).

PISTOLS

MODEL M5 JUNIOR – .177 cal., PCP, similar to Model M10, except shorter and lighter.

	100%	95%	90%	80%	60%	40%	20%
	$600	$500	$425	$350	$270	$180	$120

MODEL M10 – .177 cal., PCP, 492 FPS, 9.50 in. barrel with compensator, adj. trigger, sights and pistol grip, special dry firing mechanism, walnut grips. Mfg. 1998-2000.

	100%	95%	90%	80%	60%	40%	20%
	$700	$600	$500	$400	$325	$210	$140

MODEL SAM K-9 – .177 cal., PCP, 492 FPS, 7.8 in. barrel with compensator, adj. trigger, adj. sights, ergonomic walnut grip, special dry firing mechanism.

MSR N/A	$1,050	$900	$725	$600	$475	$325	$210

MODEL SAM K-11 – .177 cal., PCP, 492 FPS, 9.45 in. barrel with compensator, adj. trigger, sights and pistol grip, two rod counterbalancing system, special dry firing mechanism, walnut grips, 2.34 lbs. New 2000.

MSR N/A	$900	$775	$625	$525	$400	$270	$180

MODEL SAM K-12 – .177 cal., PCP, 492 FPS, 9.45 in. barrel with compensator, adj. trigger, sights and pistol grip, one rod counterbalancing system, special dry firing mechanism, walnut grip, 2.34 lbs. New 2002.

MSR N/A	$850	$725	$600	$500	$375	$255	$170

MODEL SAM K-15 – .177 cal., PCP, 492 FPS, 9.45 in. barrel with compensator, adj. trigger, sights and pistol grip, one rod counterbalancing system, special dry firing mechanism, adj. ergonomic walnut grip, 2.34 lbs. New 2006.

MSR N/A	$1,250	$1,050	$875	$725	$550	$375	$250

SWIVEL MACHINE WORKS, INC.

Current manufacturer of AIRROW trademark CO_2 and PCP powered pellet and arrow firing rifles.

For information on the AIRROW airguns, see AIRROW in the "A" section.

T SECTION

TAHITI

For information on Tahiti airguns, see Dianawerk in the "D" section.

TAIYO JUKI

Current trademark of Miroku Firearms Manufacturing Company (Miroku Taiyo Zuki) located in Kochi, Japan. Airguns manufactured beginning circa 1970s.

For more information and current pricing on both new and used firearms, please refer to the *Blue Book of Gun Values* by S.P. Fjestad (also available online).

GRADING	100%	95%	90%	80%	60%	40%	20%

RIFLES

BOBCAT – .177 or .22 cal., CO_2, SS, similar to Crosman Model 160.

courtesy Beeman Collection

	100%	95%	90%	80%	60%	40%	20%
	$200	$170	$140	$115	$90	$60	$40

DELUXE MODEL – .22 cal., CO_2, BA, five-shot repeater.

courtesy Howard Collection

	100%	95%	90%	80%	60%	40%	20%
	N/A	$450	$350	$295	$225	$160	$90

GRAND SLAM II – .177 or .22 cal., CO_2, BA, five-shot repeater.

courtesy Beeman Collection

	100%	95%	90%	80%	60%	40%	20%
	N/A	$350	$280	$230	$175	$125	$70

JUNIOR – .177 cal., CO_2, similar to Bobcat.

courtesy Beeman Collection

	100%	95%	90%	80%	60%	40%	20%
	$200	$170	$140	$115	$90	$60	$40

GRADING	100%	95%	90%	80%	60%	40%	20%

TANFOGLIO, FRATELLI, S.r.l.

Current manufacturer located in Gardone, Italy. Currently imported and distributed by Air Venturi/Pyramyd Air, located in Solon, OH. Previously located in Warrensville Heights, OH.

For more information and current pricing on both new and used Tanfoglio firearms, please refer to the *Blue Book of Gun Values* by S.P. Fjestad (also available online).

PISTOLS

CUSTOM GOLD – BB/.177 cal., CO_2, 12-gram cylinder, semi-auto, blowback single action only, 5 in. barrel, 330 FPS., 20-shot mag., full metal body with functional slide, top mounted Weaver rail permanently attached, textured grips, blade and ramp front and fixed rear sights, manual safety, 8.6 in. OAL, 1.98 lbs. Mfg. 2013-current.

MSR $200	$170	$150	$135	$110	$85	N/A	N/A

Add $40 for Walther Competition II Top Point Sight.

LIMITED CUSTOM – BB/.177 cal., CO_2, 12-gram cylinder, semi-auto, blowback single action only, 4 in. barrel, 320 FPS., 20-shot mag., full metal body with functional slide, black finish, fixed front adj. rear sights, textured grips, blade and ramp front and fixed rear sights, manual safety, 8.43 in. OAL, 2.67 lbs. Mfg. 2013-current.

MSR $190	$160	$145	$130	$105	$80	N/A	N/A

Add $40 for Walther Competition II Top Point Sight.

WITNESS 1911 BLACK GRIPS – BB/.177 cal., PCP, CO_2, semi-auto, 1911 replica, rifled barrel, single stage trigger, black textured grips, front rail system, 20-shot mag., blade and ramp front and fixed rear sights, manual safety, 7.5 in. OAL, 1.4 lbs. Mfg. 2012-current.

MSR $50	$45	$40	$35	$30	$20	N/A	N/A

WITNESS 1911 BROWN GRIPS – BB/.177 cal., CO_2, semi-auto, blowback action, 1911 replica, full metal body with functional slide, brown textured grips, 18-shot mag., blade and ramp front and fixed rear sights, manual safety, 8.6 in. OAL, 1.98 lbs. Mfg. 2012-current.

MSR $150	$130	$115	$100	$85	$65	N/A	N/A

TARG-AIRE (AND RANCO)

Previously manufactured by Targ-aire Pistol Co., located at 120 S. La Salla St. Chicago, IL.

PISTOLS

TARG-AIRE PISTOL – .177 or .22 cal., BBC, SP, 4.25 in. rifled barrel, 10.5 in. overall, blue finish, Tenite or cast aluminum grips, backstrap cocking lever, "Targ-aire" molded in circle around grip screw, large protruding thumbrest top left side of grip, 2.8 lbs. Mfg. 1946-1947.

courtesy Beeman Collection

	N/A	N/A	$450	$375	$275	$200	$125

Add 40% for factory box.
Add 10% for cast aluminum grips.
Add 25% for Ranco markings.

When Targ-aire production ceased, Randall Tool Co. continued production of identical guns for a short time using existing Targ-aire marked grips and compression tubes. Thus, some Targ-aire marked guns are found in Ranco boxes. Ranco marking began in Nov. 1947. Ranco manufacture ceased in 1951. See Ranco in the "R" section for image.

TAU BRNO, spol. s.r.o.

Current manufacturer located in Brno, Czech Republic. Imported and distributed by Top Gun Air Guns Inc. located in Scottsdale, AZ. Previously imported by Pilkington Competition Equipment, LLC located in Monteagle, TN, and by Airguns of Arizona/Precision Airgun Distribution, located in Gilbert, AZ. Dealer or consumer direct sales.

GRADING	100%	95%	90%	80%	60%	40%	20%

PISTOLS

TAU-7 – .177 cal., CO_2, SS, UIT target model, attaché case, extra seals, and counterweight, 2.3 lbs. Mfg. by Aeron. Disc. circa 1997.

	100%	95%	90%	80%	60%	40%	20%
	$260	$220	$180	$150	$115	$80	$50

TAU-7 JUNIOR – .177 cal., CO_2, SS, 8 in. barrel, 450 FPS, adj. trigger and sights, attaché case, extra seals, and counterweight, 2 lbs. Mfg. 2009-current.

MSR $595	$500	$450	$400	$325	$250	N/A	N/A

TAU-7 MATCH – .177 or .22 cal., CO_2, SS, UIT target model, 10 in. select grade barrel, compensator, adj. trigger, adj. sights, attaché case, extra seals, and counterweight, 2.3 lbs.

MSR $695	$600	$525	$475	$375	$290	N/A	N/A

TAU-7 SILHOUETTE – .177 or .22 cal., CO_2, SS, UIT target model, 12.6 in. select grade barrel, scope mount, compensator, adj. trigger, adj. sights, attaché case, extra seals, and counterweight, 2.3 lbs.

MSR $800	$675	$600	$550	$450	$325	N/A	N/A

TAU-7 SPORT – .177 or .22 cal., CO_2, SS, UIT target model, 10 in. barrel, 426 FPS, adj. trigger and sights, attaché case, extra seals, and counterweight, 2.3 lbs.

MSR $515	$425	$375	$350	$285	$215	N/A	N/A

TAU-7 STANDARD – .177 or .22 cal., CO_2, SS, UIT target model, 10.25 in. barrel, 426 FPS, adj. trigger and sights, attaché case, extra seals, and counterweight, 2.3 lbs. Disc. 2004.

	100%	95%	90%	80%	60%	40%	20%
	$265	$225	$185	$155	$120	$80	$55

Last MSR was $315.

TAU MK8 MATCH – .177 cal., PCP, SS, target model, 8 in. barrel, completely recoilless, adj. trigger and sights, attaché case, extra seals, and counterweight, 17.5 in. OAL, 2 lbs. Mfg. 2010-current.

MSR $1,350	$1,150	$1,000	$925	$750	$575	N/A	N/A

TAU MK8 SHORT – .177 cal., PCP, SS, target model, 10 in. barrel, completely recoilless, adj. trigger and sights, attaché case, extra seals, and counterweight, 15.9 in. OAL, 1.8 lbs. Mfg. 2010-current.

MSR $1,350	$1,150	$1,000	$925	$750	$575	N/A	N/A

RIFLES

TAU-200 – .177 cal., CO_2, SS, UIT target model, synthetic adj. stock. Mfg. by Aeron. Disc. circa 1997.

	100%	95%	90%	80%	60%	40%	20%
	$210	$180	$145	$120	$95	$65	$40

TAU-200 JUNIOR – .177 cal., CO_2, SS, UIT target model, 400 FPS, adj. sights, adj. trigger, adj. laminated stock, 40 in. OAL, 7 lbs.

MSR $660	$550	$500	$450	$375	$275	N/A	N/A

TAU-200 ADULT – .177 cal., CO_2, SS, UIT target model, 512 FPS, adj. sights, adj. trigger, adj. beech stock, 46 in. OAL, 7 lbs.

MSR $695	$600	$525	$475	$375	$290	N/A	N/A

TAU MK300 – .177 cal., PCP, SS, target model, adj. sights, adj. trigger, adj. cheek piece and buttplate, beech or laminate stock. Mfg. 2010-current.

MSR $1,260	$1,075	$925	$750	$625	$475	$325	$215

Add $100 for laminate stock.

TAURUS

For information on Taurus airguns, see Relum Limited in the "R" section.

T. DIANA

Probably an illegal trademark previously used by manufacturer of unauthorized copy of the Dianawerk Model 5 air pistol.

The most interesting feature is the logo stamped in the top of the receiver - it shows Diana, the Goddess of Hunting, holding her bow and arrow. (Over the curved stamping: T. DIANA). The maker used this classical view of Diana instead of Dianawerk's humorous and protected trademark which shows Diana holding her air rifle aloft while discarding her bow and arrow. This switch in logos was done either out of ignorance or as a clever attempt to avoid

GRADING	100%	95%	90%	80%	60%	40%	20%

trademark prosecution. Solidly made, blued, two-step barrel, wooden grip with coarse hand checkering. .177 cal., 13.3 in. OAL, BBC, SP, SS. Value of this novel T. Diana airgun collection item estimated to be about $175.

courtesy Beeman Collection

TECH FORCE

Current trademark manufactured in China. Currently imported and distributed by Air Venturi/Pyramyd Air located in Solon, OH. Previously located in Warrensville Hts., OH. Previously imported and distributed until 2011 by Compasseco, Inc. located in Bardstown, KY.

PISTOLS

TECH FORCE SS2 – .177 cal., SL, SP, 520 FPS, recoilless action, includes carrying case, match adj. trigger, 2.75 lbs. Disc. 2007.

$235	$200	$165	$135	$105	$70	$45

Last MSR was $295.

TECH FORCE S2-1 – .177 cal., BBC, SP, single shot, single stage trigger, fixed front sight, adj. rear sight, rifled barrel, no safety, brown laminated wood stock, 2.6 lbs. Disc. 2013.

$20	$15	$15	$10	N/A	N/A	N/A

Last MSR was $30.

TECH FORCE 8 – .177 cal., BBC, SP, 400 FPS, adj. rear sight, ambidextrous polymer grip, 7.25 in. barrel, 2.6 lbs. Disc. 2004.

$45	$40	$30	$25	$20	$15	N/A

Last MSR was $60.

TECH FORCE 35 – .177 cal., UL, SP, 400 FPS, adj. rear sight, 2.8 lbs. Disc. 2013.

$35	$30	$25	$20	$15	$10	N/A

Last MSR was $40.

RIFLES

BS-4 OLYMPIC – .177 cal., 640 FPS, SL, SP, recoilless, adj. trigger, micro adj. diopter sight, stippled stock, adj. buttplate, case, 43.3 in. OAL, 10.8 lbs. Disc. 2007.

$425	$375	$300	$250	$195	$130	$85

Last MSR was $495.

TECH FORCE 6 – .177 cal., SL, SP, 800/750 FPS, all metal tactical configuration folding stock, adj. rear sight, 35.5 in. OAL, 6 lbs. Importation disc.

$60	$50	$40	$35	$25	$20	$10

TECH FORCE 11 – .177 cal., BBC, SP, 600 FPS, trigger safety, Monte Carlo stock, 38.5 in. OAL, 5.5 lbs. Disc. 2007.

$30	$25	$20	$15	$15	N/A	N/A

Last MSR was $35.

TECH FORCE 12 – .177 cal., BBC, SP, 750 FPS, trigger safety, Monte Carlo stock, 40 in. OAL, 5.7 lbs. Mfg. 2003-2009.

$75	$65	$55	$45	$35	$25	$15

TECH FORCE 15 – .177 cal., BBC, SP, SS, youth dimensions, 18 in. barrel, 650 FPS, adj. rear and hooded ramp front sights, scope stop, hardwood Monte Carlo style PG stock, 38.4 in. OAL, 5.25 lbs. Imported 2008-2013.

$40	$35	$30	$25	$20	$10	N/A

Last MSR was $50.

GRADING	100%	95%	90%	80%	60%	40%	20%

TECH FORCE 20 – .177 or .22 cal., BBC, SP, 1000/750 FPS, dovetail receiver, adj. sights, adj. trigger, trigger safety, Monte Carlo stock, recoil pad, 43 in. OAL, 7.3 lbs. Mfg. 2003-2005.

	100%	95%	90%	80%	60%	40%	20%
	$120	$100	$85	$70	$55	$35	$25

Last MSR was $150.

TECH FORCE 21 – .177 or .22 cal., SL, SP, 1000/750 FPS, dovetail receiver, adj. sights, adj. trigger, trigger safety, Monte Carlo stock, recoil pad, 46 in. OAL, 9.3 lbs. Mfg. 2003-2009.

	100%	95%	90%	80%	60%	40%	20%
	$150	$130	$105	$85	$70	$45	$30

TECH FORCE 22 – .177 or .22 cal., BBC, SP, 700/600 FPS, adj. sights, trigger safety, Monte Carlo stock, 43 in. OAL, 6.4 lbs. Disc. 2007.

	100%	95%	90%	80%	60%	40%	20%
	$30	$25	$20	$15	$15	N/A	N/A

Last MSR was $36.

TECH FORCE 22A – .177 or .22 cal., BBC, SP, 700/600 FPS, ramp front sight, trigger safety, Monte Carlo stock, 43 in. OAL, 6.4 lbs. Disc. 2004.

	100%	95%	90%	80%	60%	40%	20%
	$40	$35	$30	$25	$20	$10	N/A

Last MSR was $46.

TECH FORCE 25 – .177 or .22 cal., BBC, SP, 1000/800 FPS, adj. trigger with safety, Monte Carlo stock, adj. buttplate, 46.2 in. OAL, 7.5 lbs. Disc. 2007.

	100%	95%	90%	80%	60%	40%	20%
	$100	$85	$70	$60	$45	$30	$20

Last MSR was $125.

TECH FORCE B26 – .177 or .22 cal., BBC, SP, SS, 1000/750 FPS, 16 in. rifled steel barrel, dovetail receiver, adj. Truglo fiber optic sights, adj. trigger, trigger safety, Monte Carlo stock, recoil pad, 43 in. OAL, 7.3 lbs. Mfg. 2008-2009.

	100%	95%	90%	80%	60%	40%	20%
	$190	$160	$135	$110	$85	$55	$40

* ***Tech Force B26TH*** – .177 or .22 cal., BBC, SP, SS, 1000/820 FPS, 16 in. rifled steel barrel, dovetail receiver, adj. Truglo fiber optic sights, adj. trigger, trigger safety, thumbhole Monte Carlo style stock, recoil pad, 43 in. OAL, 7.3 lbs. Mfg. 2008-2009.

	100%	95%	90%	80%	60%	40%	20%
	$220	$185	$155	$130	$100	$65	$45

TECH FORCE 31 – .177 cal., SL, SP, 750/550 FPS, adj. rear sight, folding stock, 36 in. OAL, 7 lbs. Disc. 2007.

	100%	95%	90%	80%	60%	40%	20%
	$65	$55	$45	$40	$30	$20	$15

Last MSR was $75.

TECH FORCE 3-1 – .177 or .22 cal., SL, SP, SS, 750/550 FPS, adj. rear sight, folding stock, 36 in. OAL, 7 lbs. Mfg. 2008-2009.

	100%	95%	90%	80%	60%	40%	20%
	$80	$65	$55	$45	$35	$25	$15

TECH FORCE 34 – .177 or .22 cal., UL, SP, 850/650 FPS, trigger safety, Monte Carlo hardwood stock, 41 in. OAL, 7.7 lbs. Mfg. 2004-2009.

	100%	95%	90%	80%	60%	40%	20%
	$55	$45	$40	$30	$25	$15	$10

Add $10 for Tech Force® 34 Scope Combo with a Tech Force® 4x20 scope and rings.

TECH FORCE 36 – .177 cal., UL, SP, 900 FPS, trigger safety, Monte Carlo stock, 7.4 lbs. Disc. 2004.

	100%	95%	90%	80%	60%	40%	20%
	$85	$70	$60	$50	$40	$25	$15

Last MSR was $95.

TECH FORCE 38 – .177 or .22 cal., UL, SP, 850/650 FPS, trigger safety, hardwood stock, 7 lbs. Disc. 2007.

	100%	95%	90%	80%	60%	40%	20%
	$45	$40	$30	$25	$20	$15	N/A

Last MSR was $53.

* ***Tech Force 38D*** – .177 cal., UL, SP, 850/650 FPS, trigger safety, hardwood stock, includes 4x20 scope, 7 lbs. Disc. 2004.

	100%	95%	90%	80%	60%	40%	20%
	$65	$55	$45	$40	$30	$20	$15

Last MSR was $74.

* ***Tech Force 38GD*** – .177 or .22 cal., UL, SP, 850/650 FPS, Monte Carlo stock and lengthened under-lever, trigger safety. Disc. 2002.

	100%	95%	90%	80%	60%	40%	20%
	$45	$40	$30	$25	$20	$15	N/A

Last MSR was $60.

GRADING	100%	95%	90%	80%	60%	40%	20%

TECH FORCE B40 – .177 or .22 cal., UL, SP, SS, 17.5 in. rifled steel BBL, 1050/750 FPS, built-in sound suppressor, blue finish, Monte Carlo hardwood stock with recoil pad, two-stage adj. trigger with safety, 41.25 in. OAL, 8.5 lbs. Mfg. 2005-2009.

	100%	95%	90%	80%	60%	40%	20%
	$295	$250	$205	$170	$135	$90	$60

* **Tech Force 40D** – .177 or .22 cal., BBC, SP, 700/600 FPS, hardwood stock, trigger safety, 43.5 in. OAL, 6.5 lbs. Disc. 2007.

	100%	95%	90%	80%	60%	40%	20%
	$30	$25	$20	$15	$15	N/A	N/A

Last MSR was $40.

TECH FORCE 41 – .177 cal., SL, SP, 800 FPS, hardwood Monte Carlo stock, trigger safety, 40.5 in. OAL, 7.2 lbs.

	100%	95%	90%	80%	60%	40%	20%
	$55	$45	$40	$30	$25	$15	$10

TECH FORCE B50 – .177 or .22 cal., PCP, semi-pistol grip Monte Carlo style wood stock with recoil pad, muzzle brake, manual safety. Mfg. 2005-2009.

	100%	95%	90%	80%	60%	40%	20%
	$350	$300	$245	$205	$160	$105	$70

Add $25 for .22 cal.

TECH FORCE B51 – .177 or .22 cal., PCP, thumbhole Monte Carlo wood stock with recoil pad, muzzle brake, manual safety. Mfg. 2005-2009.

	100%	95%	90%	80%	60%	40%	20%
	$375	$325	$260	$215	$165	$110	$75

Add $25 for .22 cal.

TECH FORCE 51 – .177 cal., BBC, SP, 500 FPS, hardwood/folding stock with pistol grip, automatic safety, adj. sights, 14 in. barrel, 6 lbs. Disc. 2001.

	100%	95%	90%	80%	60%	40%	20%
	$60	$50	$40	$35	$25	$20	$10

Last MSR was $70.

TECH FORCE 5-10 – .177 cal., UL, multi-stroke pneumatic, 300-750 FPS, ten-shot mag., adj. sights, adj. wire stock, 15 in. barrel, 4.5 lbs.

	100%	95%	90%	80%	60%	40%	20%
	$90	$75	$65	$50	$40	$25	$20

TECH FORCE 66 – .177 cal., SL, SP, ten-shot mag., 750 FPS, 18 in. barrel, tactical configuration, includes briefcase and 4x32 scope. Disc. 2002, reintroduced 2005-2009.

	100%	95%	90%	80%	60%	40%	20%
	$100	$85	$70	$60	$45	$30	$20

TECH FORCE 67 – .177 cal., similar to TF 66, except SS, take down, includes briefcase and 4x32 scope. Mfg. 2001-2004, reintroduced 2006-2013.

	100%	95%	90%	80%	60%	40%	20%
	$95	$80	$65	$55	$45	$30	$20

Last MSR was $120.

TECH FORCE 78 – .177 or .22 cal., BA, two CO_2 cartridges, 20 in. barrel, adj. rear and ramp front sights, 750/600 FPS, wood stock, adj. trigger, 40 in. OAL, 6.6 lbs.

	100%	95%	90%	80%	60%	40%	20%
	$90	$75	$65	$50	$40	$25	$20

* **Tech Force 78 Gold Series** – .177 or .22 cal., BA, two CO_2 cartridges, 20 in. barrel, adj. rear and ramp front sights, 750/600 FPS, wood stock, adj. trigger, 40 in. OAL, 6.6 lbs. Importation disc. 2013.

	100%	95%	90%	80%	60%	40%	20%
	$85	$70	$60	$50	$40	$25	$15

Last MSR was $108.

* **Tech Force 78 Gold Series Scope Combo** – .177 or .22 cal., BA, two CO_2 cartridges, 20 in. barrel, adj. rear and ramp front sights, Tech Force® 4x32AR Scope and rings, 750/600 FPS, wood stock, adj. trigger, 40 in. OAL, 6.6 lbs. Importation disc. 2013.

	100%	95%	90%	80%	60%	40%	20%
	$150	$130	$105	$85	$70	$45	$30

* **Tech Force 78T** – .177 or .22 cal., CO_2, BA, 700/600 FPS, built-in bulk fill adaptor for 88g cartridge, 20 in. barrel, wood stock, adj. trigger, 40 in. OAL, 6.6 lbs. Mfg. 2005-2009.

	100%	95%	90%	80%	60%	40%	20%
	$100	$85	$70	$60	$45	$30	$20

TECH FORCE 79 – .177 or .22 cal., CO_2, BA, 20.50 in. barrel, 700/520 FPS, grooved receiver, competition style wood stock, adj. trigger, diopter peep sight, 40 in. OAL, 6.6 lbs. Imported 2001-2013.

	100%	95%	90%	80%	60%	40%	20%
	$175	$150	$125	$100	$80	$50	$35

Last MSR was $216.

GRADING	100%	95%	90%	80%	60%	40%	20%

* ***Tech Force 79T (Tanker)*** – .177 or .22 cal., CO_2, BA, built-in bulk fill adaptor, 700/550 FPS, 20.5 in. barrel, grooved receiver, competition style wood stock, adj. trigger, diopter peep sight, 40 in. OAL, 7.4 lbs. New 2005.

MSR $240	$205	$180	$165	$130	$100	N/A	N/A

* ***Tech Force 79 TH (Thumbhole)*** – .177 or .22 cal., CO_2, BA, 20.5 in. barrel, 700/520 FPS, grooved receiver, thumbhole wood stock, adj. trigger, diopter peep sight, 40 in. OAL, 6.6 lbs. Mfg. 2006-2009, reintroduced 2012-2013.

	$185	$155	$130	$105	$85	$55	$35

Last MSR was $225.

* ***Tech Force 79 Tactical*** – .177 or .22 cal., CO_2, BA, 20.5 in. barrel, 700/520 FPS, grooved receiver, all-weather black tactical thumbhole stock, adj. trigger, diopter peep sight, Tech Force 4x32 AR scope with adjustable objective and target turrets, Tech Force Tactical Flash Light and Laser, 40 in. OAL, 6.6 lbs. Mfg. 2007-2009.

	$280	$240	$195	$160	$125	$85	$55

TECH FORCE 88 – .177 cal., SL, SP, 850 FPS, 19.5 in. barrel, adj. sights, safety, 7.5 lbs. Disc. 2007.

	$85	$70	$60	$50	$40	$25	$15

Last MSR was $95.

TECH FORCE 89 – .177 cal., SL, SP, bullpup configuration, extending buttplate, 600 FPS, 25 in. overall length. Mfg. 1999-2001.

	$80	$70	$55	$45	$35	$25	$15

Last MSR was $110.

TECH FORCE 97 – .177 or .22 cal., UL, SP, 900/700 FPS, 16 in. barrel, adj. sights, grooved receiver for scope mounting, automatic safety, oil finished Monte Carlo stock with recoil pad, 43 in. OAL, 7.4 lbs. Imported 1999-2013.

	$85	$70	$60	$50	$40	$25	$15

Last MSR was $100.

Add $15 for an installed MacCari spring.

* ***Tech Force 97S Scope Combo*** – .177 or .22 cal., UL, SP, 900/700 FPS, 16 in. barrel, adj. sights, grooved receiver for scope mounting, TF 4x32AR scope and rings, automatic safety, oil finished Monte Carlo stock with recoil pad, 43 in. OAL, 7.4 lbs. Mfg. 1999-disc.

	$150	$130	$105	$85	$70	$45	$30

* ***Tech Force 97SC Scope Combo*** – .177 or .22 cal., UL, SP, 900/700 FPS, 16 in. barrel, adj. sights, grooved receiver for scope mounting, TF 2-7x32AR scope and rings, automatic safety, oil finished, Monte Carlo stock with recoil pad, Tech Force® Flat Target Trap, Targets, and 500 rounds of Tech Force Match Pellets, and rifle case, 43 in. OAL, 7.4 lbs. Mfg. 2007-2009.

	$160	$135	$110	$95	$70	$50	$30

* ***Tech Force 97X Scope Combo*** – .177 or .22 cal., UL, SP, 900/700 FPS, 16 in. barrel, adj. sights, grooved receiver for scope mounting, TF 4x32AR scope and rings, automatic safety, oil finished, Monte Carlo stock with recoil pad, Tech Force® Flat Target Trap, Targets, 500 rounds of Tech Force Match Pellets, and rifle case, 43 in. OAL, 7.4 lbs. Mfg. 2007-2009.

	$160	$135	$110	$95	$70	$50	$30

TECH FORCE 99 – .177 or .22 cal., UL, SP, 1000/800 FPS, 19.5 in. barrel, MacCari spring, adj. sights, grooved receiver for scope mounting, automatic safety, oil finished Monte Carlo stock with recoil pad, 7.5 lbs. Mfg. 2000-2007.

	$170	$145	$120	$100	$75	$50	$35

* ***Tech Force 99 Magnum*** – .177 or .22 cal., UL, SP, 1100/900 FPS, 18 in. barrel, adj. sights with front sight inserts, grooved receiver for scope mounting, automatic safety, oil finished Monte Carlo stock with recoil pad, anti-bear trap lock and automatic safety, 44.5 in. OAL, 8 lbs. Mfg. 2007-2009.

	$170	$145	$120	$100	$75	$50	$35

* ***Tech Force 99S Magnum Scope Combo*** – .177 or .22 cal., UL, SP, 1100/900 FPS, 18 in. barrel, adj. sights with front sight inserts, grooved receiver for scope mounting, 2-7x32AR scope with rings, automatic safety, oil finished Monte Carlo stock with recoil pad, anti-bear trap lock and automatic safety, 44.5 in. OAL, 8 lbs. Mfg. 2007-2009.

	$230	$195	$160	$135	$105	$70	$45

* ***Tech Force 99SC Magnum Scope Combo*** – .177 or .22 cal., UL, SP, 1100/900 FPS, 18 in. barrel, adj. sights with front sight inserts, grooved receiver for scope mounting, 3-12x44 AR scope with rings, automatic safety, oil finished Monte Carlo stock with recoil pad, anti-bear trap lock and automatic safety, 44.5 in. OAL, 8 lbs. Mfg. 2007-2009.

	$250	$215	$175	$145	$115	$75	$50

GRADING	100%	95%	90%	80%	60%	40%	20%

* ***Tech Force 99SCC Magnum Scope Combo*** – .177 or .22 cal., UL, SP, 1100/900 FPS, 18 in. barrel, adj. sights with front sight inserts, grooved receiver for scope mounting, 4x32AR scope with rings, automatic safety, oil finished Monte Carlo stock with recoil pad, anti-bear trap lock and automatic safety, 44.5 in. OAL, 8 lbs. Mfg. 2007-2009.

	$240	$205	$170	$140	$110	$70	$50

* ***Tech Force 99 Premier*** – .177 or .22 cal., UL, SP, 1100/900 FPS, 18 in. barrel, adj. sights with front sight inserts, grooved receiver for scope mounting, built-in scope stop, automatic safety, checkered Monte Carlo stock with recoil pad, anti-bear trap lock and automatic safety, 44.5 in. OAL, 8 lbs. Mfg. 2007-2013.

	$145	$125	$100	$85	$65	$45	$30

Add $130 for Nitro Piston model (new 2012). **Last MSR was $170.**

* ***Tech Force 99PC Premier Scope Combo*** – .177 or .22 cal., UL, SP, 1100/900 FPS, 18 in. barrel, adj. sights with front sight inserts, grooved receiver for scope mounting, built-in scope stop, 4x32AR scope and rings, automatic safety, checkered Monte Carlo stock with recoil pad, anti-bear trap lock and automatic safety, 44.5 in. OAL, 8 lbs. Mfg. 2007-2009.

	$240	$205	$170	$140	$110	$70	$50

* ***Tech Force 99PS Premier Scope Combo*** – .177 or .22 cal., UL, SP, 1100/900 FPS, 18 in. barrel, adj. sights with front sight inserts, grooved receiver for scope mounting, built-in scope stop, 2-7x32AR scope and rings, automatic safety, checkered Monte Carlo stock with recoil pad, anti-bear trap lock and automatic safety, 44.5 in. OAL, 8 lbs. Mfg. 2007-2009.

	$250	$215	$175	$145	$115	$75	$50

* ***Tech Force 99PSC Premier Scope Combo*** – .177 or .22 cal., UL, SP, 1100/900 FPS, 18 in. barrel, adj. sights with front sight inserts, grooved receiver for scope mounting, built-in scope stop, 3-12x44AR scope and rings, automatic safety, checkered Monte Carlo stock with recoil pad, anti-bear trap lock and automatic safety, 44.5 in. OAL, 8 lbs. Imported 2007-2013.

	$220	$185	$155	$130	$100	$65	$45

* ***Tech Force 99R5 Scope Combo*** – .177 or .22 cal., UL, SP, 1100/900 FPS, 18 in. barrel, adj. sights with front sight inserts, grooved receiver for scope mounting, automatic safety, oil finished Monte Carlo stock with recoil pad, anti-bear trap lock and automatic safety, 44.5 in. OAL, 8 lbs. Mfg. 2007-2009.

	$170	$145	$120	$100	$75	$50	$35

TECH FORCE M8 – .177 cal., BBC, SP, SS, 9 in. barrel with muzzle brake, ambidextrous Monte Carlo hardwood stock with checkered grip and forearm, rubber buttpad, matte black finish, no sights, automatic safety, with or without 4x32 AO scope and mount, 40 in. OAL, 6.5 lbs.

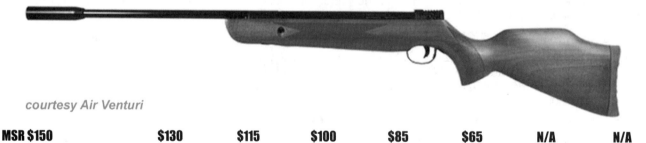

courtesy Air Venturi

MSR $150	$130	$115	$100	$85	$65	N/A	N/A

Add $46 for 4x32 AO scope and mount.

TECH FORCE M12 – .177 or .22 cal., BBC, SP, SS, 1000/700 FPS, 9.25 in. rifled barrel with muzzle brake, SST, ambidextrous Monte Carlo hardwood stock with checkered grip and forearm, rubber buttpad, automatic safety, no sights, 44.25 in. OAL, 6.85 lbs.

courtesy Air Venturi

MSR $200	$170	$150	$135	$110	$85	N/A	N/A

Add $50 for 3-9x32 AO scope.
Add $80 for 4-12x40 AO scope.
Add $100 for 4-12x40 AO/IR scope.

GRADING	100%	95%	90%	80%	60%	40%	20%

TECH FORCE PCP – .177 or .22 cal., BA, PCP, SS, 21.5 in. barrel, adj. rear and ramp front sights, 1200/1050 FPS, wood stock, adj. trigger, manual safety, 40 in. OAL, 6.6 lbs. Disc.

	$220	$185	$155	$130	$100	$65	$45

TECH FORCE TFJET – adj. rear sight, 11mm scope rail, raised right hand cheek piece, beech thumbhole stock with checkered forearm, two-stage trigger, rubber buttpad, 9.8 lbs. Imported 2012-2013.

	$210	$180	$145	$120	$95	$65	$40

Last MSR was $252.

RIFLES: CONTENDER SERIES

MODEL 20 CONTENDER – .177 or .22 cal., BBC, SP, SS, 21.5 in bbl., 600/550 FPS, dovetail receiver, adj. fiber optic sights, adj. trigger, auto-safety, polymer Monte Carlo stock, recoil pad, 40 in. OAL, 5.7 lbs. Mfg. 2010-2011.

	$60	$50	$40	$35	$25	$20	$10

Add $35 for scope combo.

MODEL 39 CONTENDER – .177 cal., BBC, SP, SS, youth dimensions, no sights, 4x20 scope and rings, 18 in. bbl., 650 FPS, hardwood Monte Carlo style PG stock, 38.4 in. OAL, 5.25 lbs. Mfg. 2007-2011.

	$60	$50	$40	$35	$25	$20	$10

Add $3 for TF4x20 scope.
Add $10 for TF3-7x20 scope.

MODEL 49 CONTENDER – .177 or .22 cal., BBC, SP, SS, medium dimensions, 18.8 in. bbl., 800/650 FPS, no sights, 4x20 scope and rings, hardwood Monte Carlo style PG stock, 45 in. OAL, 6 lbs. Mfg. 2007-2011.

	$80	$70	$55	$45	$35	$25	$15

Add $50 for 4x32 scope.
Add $60 for 3-9x50 scope.

MODEL 58 CONTENDER – .177 cal., SLC, SS, 18 in. bbl., 700 FPS, adj. sights, hardwood Monte Carlo style PG stock, 41.5 in. OAL, 6.7 lbs. Mfg. 2010-2011.

	$80	$70	$55	$45	$35	$25	$15

Add $25 for scope combo.

MODEL 59 CONTENDER – .177 or .22 cal., BBC, 17.75 in. bbl., 900/730 FPS, adj. sights or 4x20 scope and rings, hardwood Monte Carlo style PG stock, 42.3 in. OAL, 7 lbs. Mfg. 2007-2011.

	$100	$85	$70	$60	$45	$30	$20

Add $50 for 4x32AR scope.
Add $60 for 3-9x50AR scope.

MODEL 87 CONTENDER – .177 or .22 cal., UL, SP, 1000/800 FPS, 19. in. barrel, MacCari spring, adj. sights, grooved receiver for scope mounting, automatic safety, oil finished Monte Carlo stock with recoil pad, auto-safety, 9 lbs. Imported 2010-2013.

	$210	$180	$145	$120	$95	$65	$40

Last MSR was $250.

Add $60 for scope combo.

MODEL 89 CONTENDER – .177 or .22 (disc.) cal., BBC, SP, SS, 17.9 in. barrel, muzzle brake, 1000/900 FPS, fiber optic sights, scope stop, checkered beechwood Monte Carlo style PG stock with rubber recoil pad, two-stage adj. trigger, 46.1 in. OAL, 7.72 lbs. Mfg. 2007-current.

courtesy Air Venturi

MSR $225	$185	$155	$130	$105	$85	$55	$35

TELL

Previous trademark manufactured by Venuswaffenwerk, located in Zella, Mehlis, Germany.

Venuswaffenwerk was formed by Oskar Will in 1844, and made both air rifles and pistols for nearly one hundred years. The Tell 1 was most likely designed by Will as a companion to his popular rifles. The design of Tell 2 & Tell 3 are very different and more elegant. They were not companions to any rifle and were designed after Wilhelm Foss took over the company about 1919. The company ceased operations in the late 1950s.

GRADING	100%	95%	90%	80%	60%	40%	20%

PISTOLS

TELL 1 – .177 cal., BBC, SP, rifled 9.75 in. blue barrel, 300 FPS (.177 cal.), blue or nickel plated body, rounded wood grips, 21 in. overall, nickel plated trigger guard with finger rest. Its ungainly size and style suggests that it was a pistol version of the original Will-style air rifle. At least two versions: one unmarked, the other marked "TELLOW" - for Tell and the initials of Oskar Will. 2.9 lbs. Mfg. 1912-1930s.

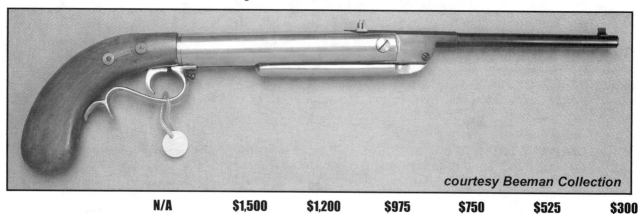

courtesy Beeman Collection

	N/A	$1,500	$1,200	$975	$750	$525	$300

Add 20% for "Tellow" marking.
Add 20% for blue body.

TELL 2 – .177 cal., SP, concentric-piston, 5 in. rifled barrel, 220 FPS (.177 cal.), 5.75 in. overall, blue or nickel finish, grip backstrap folds out to aid cocking which is accomplished by front of trigger guard engaging piston, checkered wood grips, 0.9 lbs. Mfg. 1925-1940.

courtesy Beeman Collection

	N/A	$300	$240	$195	$150	$105	$60

Add 35% for nickel finish (rare).
Add 50% for factory box, pellet tin, and paperwork.

The Tell 2 and the Clarke's Bulldog apparently are the world's smallest spring piston airguns.

TELL 3 – .177 cal., BBC, SP, unique cocking link above air chamber, 5.38 in. rifled barrel, 280 FPS, blue finish, brown checkered Bakelite grips with Tell emblem in center, 10 in. OAL, 2.2 lbs. Approx. fifty mfg. 1936-1940. Ref: AW - June 2003.

courtesy Beeman Collection

	N/A	$750	$600	$475	$375	$265	$150

Add 40% for factory box, accessories, and paperwork.

GRADING	100%	95%	90%	80%	60%	40%	20%

RIFLES

MARS 85 – 4.4mm lead round ball cal., SP, BA, youth sized, full length hardwood stock, gravity-fed mag. loads through gate on barrel sleeve, swinging safety, 34.1 in. OAL, 3.6 lbs.

courtesy Beeman Collection

	N/A	$400	$325	$255	$195	$140	$80

MARS 100 – 4.4mm lead round ball cal., SP, BA, similar to Mars 85, except over-all-length.

	N/A	$400	$325	$255	$195	$140	$80

MARS 115 – 4.4mm round lead ball cal., SP, BA, paramilitary-style trainer based on Schmeisser design of Anschütz Model 275, styled very closely to Mauser 98 paramilitary rifle w/full length stock, top wooden hand guards and side slot in buttstock for leather sling, paramilitary type rear sight marked 6 to 12 meters, repeating mechanism with gravity-fed magazine, Mauser wing-type manual safety, 43 in. OAL, 7.3 lbs.

courtesy Beeman Collection

$425	$350	$300	$245	$190	$125	$85

Produced for German Third Reich Hitlerjuged training. Related military-style models reported: 1935-1940 (perhaps some later during Soviet occupation; these would be much lower quality).

MILITIA MODEL – .177 cal., BBC, SP, SS, milita-style rifle, part-round/part-octagonal BBL, walnut buttstock, blue steel buttplate, 5.4 lbs.

courtesy Beeman Collection

$450	$375	$325	$260	$205	$135	$90

TELLY

For information on Telly airguns, see Relum Limited in the "R" section.

TESRO GmbH & COMPANY KG

Current manufacturer located in Bächingen, Germany. No current U.S. importation.

Tesro manufactures high quality air pistols and air rifles. Please contact the company directly for more information regarding U.S. availability and pricing (see Trademark Index).

TEXAN

For information on Texan airguns, see Apache in the "A" section.

GRADING	100%	95%	90%	80%	60%	40%	20%

THEOBEN LTD (THEOBEN ENGINEERING)

Current manufacturer located in Cambridgeshire, U.K. Currently imported and distributed by Theoben USA located in Minor Hill, TN beginning 2008, previously located in Garden Grove, CA beginning 2004. Previously imported by Beeman Precision Airguns, located in Huntington Beach, CA, beginning 1992, and Air Rifle Specialists located in Pine City, NY. Dealer and consumer direct sales.

Models built for Beeman Precision Airguns can be found in the Beeman section of this text. Please contact Theoben USA directly for more information and prices of their products (see Trademark Index listing).

RIFLES

The U.S. importation of the models listed below was discontinued during 1993 (unless otherwise marked).

Add $150 for Theoben pump applicable for some models listed below.

CRUSADER – .177, .20, .22, or .25 cal., BBC, SS, 16 in. Walther barrel, H.E. Gas Ram System, Evolution trigger, deluxe checkered ambidextrous walnut or laminate sporter PG stock with cheek piece and pad, 48.5 in. OAL, 8 lbs. Mfg. 2009-current.

	100%	95%	90%	80%	60%	40%	20%
MSR $1,014	$850	$750	$700	$550	$425	N/A	N/A

Add $60 for left-hand variation.

This model incorporated an improved barrel design featuring pronounced rifling for the higher velocity pellets.

DUAL MAGNUM – .22 cal., UL, two stroke cocking H.E. Gas Ram System, first stroke produces 24 ft/lbs and second stroke 36 ft/lbs power, Anschütz bbl., 840 FPS, adj. two stage Evolution trigger, checkered hard wood or laminated stock w/vented recoil pad, automatic safety. Approx. 104 mfg. 2001-02.

	100%	95%	90%	80%	60%	40%	20%
	N/A	$2,550	$2,100	$1,750	$1,350	$900	$600

Last MSR was $1,800.

ELIMINATOR – .177 or .22 cal., BBC, 1100/900 FPS, H.E. Gas Ram System, 16 in. choked barrel, two-stage trigger, deluxe checkered walnut thumbhole or laminate stock with cheek piece and pad, 9 1/2 lbs.

	100%	95%	90%	80%	60%	40%	20%
MSR $1,223	$1,050	$925	$825	$675	$525	N/A	N/A

Add $60 for left-hand variation.

This model incorporated an improved barrel design featuring pronounced rifling for the higher velocity pellets.

EVOLUTION – .177, .20 or .22 cal., BBC, H.E. Gas Ram System, SS, 10.5 in. Walther barrel, two-stage trigger with automatic safety, deluxe checkered walnut Beech pistol grip, ambidextrous walnut, or right-hand walnut thumbhole stock with laser cut checkered pistol grip and forend, cheek piece, and vent. recoil pad, 38.5 in. OAL, 7.5 lbs. Mfg. 2009-current.

	100%	95%	90%	80%	60%	40%	20%
MSR $860	$725	$650	$575	$475	$350	N/A	N/A

Add $49 for left-hand variation.
Add $112 for thumbhole stock.

IMPERATOR – .22 cal., UL, SP, 750 FPS, walnut hand checkered stock, automatic safety. Mfg. 1989.

	100%	95%	90%	80%	60%	40%	20%
	$825	$700	$575	$475	$375	$245	$165

Last MSR was $1,500.

IMPERATOR SLR 88 – similar to Imperator, except has a seven-shot magazine. Very limited importation.

	100%	95%	90%	80%	60%	40%	20%
	$1,200	$1,025	$850	$700	$550	$350	$240

Last MSR was $1,680.

MFR – .177, .20, .22, or .25 cal., PCP, BA, SS, 7, 12, or 17 shot mag. (depending on cal.) repeater, 280cc bottle, 16 or 21 in. sleeved barrel, blue finish, adj. two-stage trigger, walnut PG sporter stock, 38.5 or 43.5 in. OAL, 7.2 or 7.6 lbs. Mfg. 2007-current.

	100%	95%	90%	80%	60%	40%	20%
MSR $1,785	$1,525	$1,350	$1,225	$975	$750	N/A	N/A

Add $70 for left-hand variation.
Add $255 for thumbhole stock (MFR CS800 model, right hand only).
Add $87 for tactical variation (new 2012).

RAPID 7 – .22 cal., PCP, 19 in. Anschütz barrel, stippled walnut stock, seven-shot bolt action design, 6 3/4 lbs.

	100%	95%	90%	80%	60%	40%	20%
	$1,000	$850	$700	$575	$450	$300	$200

Last MSR was $1,300.

Add $60 for left-hand variation.
Add $120 for scuba tank adaptor.

RAPID MKII – .177, .20, .22, or .25 cal., PCP, BA, SS, 12 or 17 shot mag. (depending on cal.) repeater, 400cc bottle, 16 or 23.75 in. barrel, blue finish, adj. two-stage trigger, walnut PG sporter or thumbhole stock, 40 or 47.75 in. OAL, 7.2 or 7.6 lbs. Mfg. 2007-current.

	100%	95%	90%	80%	60%	40%	20%
MSR $1,709	$1,450	$1,275	$1,150	$950	$725	N/A	N/A

Add $69 for left-hand variation.

GRADING	100%	95%	90%	80%	60%	40%	20%

Add $152 for ambidextrous thumbhole walnut stock (Rapid Sentinel).

Add $331 for thumbhole stock (MKII CS800).

RAPID XP PRO – .177, .20, .22, or .25 cal., similar to the Rapid MKII model, except has a handmade custom stock with a quick fill installed. New 2011.

MSR $2,300	$1,950	$1,725	$1,575	$1,275	$975	N/A	N/A

SIROCCO CLASSIC – similar to Sirocco Deluxe, except has updated floating inertia system in piston chamber and automatic safety, 900/1100 FPS. Mfg. 1987.

	$750	$625	$525	$425	$325	$225	$150

Last MSR was $830.

Add $60 for left-hand variation.

This model was available with either a choked or unchoked Anschütz barrel as standard equipment.

SIROCCO COUNTRYMAN – .177 or .22 cal., BBC, 1100/800 FPS, pre-charged sealed gas spring, includes scope rings, barrel weight, walnut stained beechwood stock, 7 1/2 lbs. Importation disc. 1987.

	$550	$450	$375	$325	$245	$160	$110

Last MSR was $585.

SIROCCO DELUXE – similar to Sirocco Countryman, except has hand checkered walnut stock. Importation disc. 1987.

	$675	$575	$475	$375	$300	$200	$135

Last MSR was $650.

SIROCCO GRAND PRIX – similar to the Sirocco Classic, except has checkered walnut thumbhole stock.

	$825	$700	$575	$475	$375	$245	$165

Last MSR was $940.

Add $60 for left-hand variation.

Subtract 50% for older models without safety and new piston design.

In 1987, this model was updated with a floating inertia system in piston chamber, automatic safety, and variable power.

This model was available with either a choked or unchoked Anschütz barrel as standard equipment.

SLR (SELF LOADING RIFLE) – .177 or .22 cal., BBC, multi-shot UL, H.E. Gas Ram System, seven shot mag., 13 in. barrel, two-stage trigger with automatic safety, scope mounts, integral underlever silencer, deluxe checkered walnut PG or thumbhole stock with cheek piece and pad, laser-cut checkering on pistol grip and forend, 42 in. OAL, 7.8 lbs. Mfg. 2009-current.

MSR $1,258	$1,075	$950	$850	$700	$525	N/A	N/A

Add $57 for left-hand variation.

Add $177 for thumbhole stock.

S-TYPE – .177, .20, .22, or .25 cal., PCP, BA, SS, 7, 12, or 17 shot mag. (depending on cal.) repeater, 500cc bottle, 19 or 23 in. sleeved barrel, blue finish, adj. two-stage trigger, walnut PG sporter stock w/recessed accessory rail, 38.5 or 46 in. OAL, 9.2 or 9.6 lbs. Mfg. 2007-current.

MSR $1,930	$1,650	$1,450	$1,300	$1,050	$800	N/A	N/A

Add $70 for left-hand variation.

TTR1 – .177, .20, and .22 cal., PCP, BA, 19 in. barrel, adj. ambidextrous black walnut stock with satin finish, integral trigger guard, accessory rail, adj. cheek piece, adj. butt pad, two-stage MKIV trigger, MFR regulator, particle Filter, Vortex silencer, 44 in. OAL, 10 lbs. Mfg. 2010-2011.

	$1,575	$1,350	$1,100	$925	$700	$475	$325

TTR2 – .177, .20, and .22 cal., tactical version of the MFR with a shrouded barrel, same features as the TTR1. Mfg. 2010-2011.

	$1,575	$1,350	$1,100	$925	$700	$475	$325

Last MSR was $1,872.

VANQUISH – .177 or .22, cal., PCP, BA, 12 or 17 shot mag. (depending on cal.) repeater, 180cc bottle, blue finish, adj. two-stage trigger, adj. laminated thumbhole stock. Mfg. 2009-current.

MSR $2,730	$2,325	$2,050	$1,850	$1,500	$1,150	N/A	N/A

THUNDERBOLT

For information on Thunderbolt airguns, see Produsit in the "P" section.

TIGER

For information on Tiger airguns, see F.I.E. in the "F" section.

GRADING	100%	95%	90%	80%	60%	40%	20%

TITAN (CURRENT MFG.)

Current tradename resurrected by a current British airgun maker who seems to have operated under several names and perhaps several ownerships circa 1990 to present.

Products include high quality air rifles and pistols, including PCP and pump pneumatic power plants. Additional research is being done on this maker and their guns. Research is ongoing with this trademark, and more information will be included both online and in future editions. Average original condition specimens on most common Titan models are typically priced in the $400-$1,200 range. See also Beeman and Falcon sections.

courtesy Beeman Collection

TITAN (DISC.)

Previous trademark of air pistols patented and probably manufactured by Frank Clarke located in Birmingham, England circa 1916-1926.

Note that there are a considerable number of variations from these basic models; variations which do not seem to merit model level status at this time. These model numbers have been proposed by noted airgun researcher John Atkins (Airgun Editor, *Airgunner Magazine*) and do not represent model designations of the maker. Numbers on guns probably are not serial numbers. The authors and publisher wish to express their appreciation to John Atkins and Ingvar Alm for their valuable assistance with the following information in this section of the *Blue Book of Airguns*.

PISTOLS

Unless otherwise noted, all air pistols noted below are rear rod-cocking, blue finish steel, with walnut grip plates fitted into the sides of the grip frame.

MARK 1 – .177 cal., SP, SS, BA, 9.25 in barrel, nickel finish, one-piece grip frame and breech block with black hard rubber grip plates, front sight sleeves muzzle, rear sight is a notch on the bolt handle, cocking plunger in front of compression chamber, angled hard rubber grip plates with "FC" for Frank Clark and "B" for Birmingham on the right side, and "Titan" imprinted on the left side, a crown is stamped over "MADE IN ENGLAND" on back of breech block, 10 in. OAL, approx. 1.1 lbs. Mfg. 1916-1917.

courtesy Loke Collection

N/A	$2,000	$1,600	$1,300	$1,000	$700	$400

To aid cocking, a device made of twisted steel wire could be attached to the cocking plunger and then held down by the user's toe.

MARK 2 – .177 cal., SP, SS, similar to Mark 1, except has iron grip frame and air chamber cast in one piece, no grip plates, cocked by plunger rod (apparently removable) from rear, bolt attached to BBL, BBL slides forward to load, nickel plated finish. Mfg. 1917.

Scarcity precludes accurate pricing.

The spring is compressed by means of a plunger and rod operated from the rear of the action.

GRADING	100%	95%	90%	80%	60%	40%	20%

MARK 3 – .177 cal., SP, SS, similar to Mark 1 and Mark 2, except has one-piece cast iron compression tube and vertical grip frame, barrel bands with rear band acting as sight, front sight on barrel, breech block rotated counter-clockwise for loading, cocking rod folds into grooved back strap, three pins mounting trigger guard, black painted finish, cocked by pushing a rod in from the rear. Mfg. 1918.

> **Scarcity precludes accurate pricing.**

Establishes the basic Titan pattern of cocking and loading found in all later Titan air pistols.

MARK 4 – .177 cal., SP, SS, similar to Mark 3, except more streamlined and longer barrel, BBL support lugs cast into body tube, pinned cap at forward end allows forward removal of mainspring, vertical grip frame with checkered wood grip plates inset into frame, 10.5 in. OAL. Mfg. 1919-1923.

courtesy Loke Collection

| | N/A | N/A | N/A | $900 | $650 | $550 | $450 |

MARK 5 – .177 cal., SP, SS, similar to Mark 4, except has 7 in. barrel, mainspring removes from breech end, front sight cast on top of front barrel band, checkered hard rubber grips, roll stamped LH side compression chamber 'THE "TITAN" AIR PISTOL' over 'PATENT 110999/17', approx. 1.9 lbs. Most common model. Mfg. circa 1920.

courtesy Beeman Collection

| | N/A | N/A | N/A | $695 | $550 | $450 | $350 |

MARK 6 – .177 cal., SP, SS, similar to Mark 5, except has trigger sear adj. screw through rear of trigger guard, four pins mounting trigger and guard, roll stamped LH side 'THE "TITAN" AIR PISTOL' over 'PATENT 110999/17', approx. 1.8 lbs. Mfg. circa 1921.

courtesy Loke Collection

| | N/A | N/A | N/A | $695 | $550 | $450 | $350 |

GRADING	100%	95%	90%	80%	60%	40%	20%

MARK 7 – .177 cal., SP, SS, similar to Mark 6, except without trigger sear adj. screw, internal grip safety disengaged when cocking rod is depressed into frame slot, checkered hard rubber grip with "T" inside of a circle molded on top half, roll stamped LH side 'THE "TITAN" AIR PISTOL' over 'PATENT 110999/17', approx. 1.7 lbs. Mfg. circa 1923-1925. Ref: AG July, Aug, Sept 1987, Oct 1988, Oct 1991.

courtesy Loke Collection

N/A	N/A	N/A	$850	$650	$550	$450

Only turning-breech, folding-cocking-rod Titan with slanted grips. Evolved into the Clarke-designed Webley Mk 1 which replaced it.

TOKYO

Previous manufacturer of barrel cocking air rifles in Japan.

Research is ongoing with this trademark, and more information will be included both online and in future editions.

RIFLES

INDIAN JUNIOR – .177 cal., BBC, SP, SS, one-inch dia. receiver tube, copy of BSA barrel cocking air rifle, 17 in. barrel, marked with outline letters "INDIAN" and an Indian head on top of receiver, stamped across receiver: Made by TOKYO. 39.4 in. OAL, 3.7 lbs.

courtesy Beeman Collection

$250	$215	$175	$145	$115	$75	$50

INDIAN SENIOR – .177 cal., BBC, SP, SS, receiver tube, barrel marked with outline letters "INDIAN" and an Indian head on top of receiver, stamped across receiver: Made by TOKYO.

$250	$215	$175	$145	$115	$75	$50

TONG IL

Current trademark manufactured by Ting Il Industrial Co. Ltd. located in Seoul, South Korea.

Relationship to Yewha and National brands are not clear at this time.

RIFLES

GARAND MODEL MT 1 – .177 cal., SS, UL, swinging lever pump pneumatic, parkerized finish, marked "TONG IL MT 1" on top rear of receiver, 28.5 in. round barrel with flash suppressor, 46.7 in. OAL, 9.8 lbs.

courtesy Beeman Collection

N/A	N/A	$1,800	$1,500	$1,000	$650	$300

This model is a slightly oversized replica of the Garand military rifle.

GRADING	100%	95%	90%	80%	60%	40%	20%

MI CARBINE MODEL CT 2 – .177 cal., SP, SS, SL, web sling with oiler sling retainer, some other original M1 parts, parkerized finish, marked "MOD. CT 2." 36.3 in. OAL, 7.3 lbs.

courtesy Beeman Collection

N/A	N/A	$1,600	$1,100	$850	$500	$200

This model is a very realistic replica of the U.S. M1 military carbine, and uses the same bolt action to load and the sidelever is very suggestive to the Feinwerkbau 300 side lever.

TOPGUN

For information on Topgun airguns, see Philippine Airguns in the "P" section.

TORUNARMS

Current manufacturer located in Konya, Turkey. No current U.S. importation.

TorunArms company was organized in 1996 by Kadir Torun in Beysehir/Uzumlu, Turkey. They manufacture a complete line of good quality air rifles. Please contact the company directly for more information on their models, U.S. pricing, and availability (see Trademark Index).

TRIDENT

For information on Trident airguns, see Philippine Airguns in the "P" section.

TSS FORTUNE CO., LTD.

Current manufacturer located in Tianjin, China. No current U.S. importation.

TSS Fortune Co., Ltd. manufactures a wide variety of air rifles and air pistols, as well as paintball guns and miniature replicas of famous firearms configurations. Please contact the company directly for more information on their models, U.S. pricing, and availability (see Trademark Index).

TyROL

Previous brand name of previous manufacturer Tiroler Sportwaffenfabrik und Apparatenbau GmbH ("TyROL Sport Weapon Makers and Apparatus Factory"), located in Kufstein, Austria. Circa 1939 to 1970s.

Many airgun collectors think that non-match CO_2 rifles were made only in the United States. Here are some wonderful exceptions. The rifles below bear the same TyROL brand name (in the same unusual font printed in this unique way), same Austrian eagle logo, and "MADE IN AUSTRIA" marking. Production of these airguns sometimes has been attributed to Tiroler Waffenfabrik ("Tyrol Weapon Makers") Peterlongo, Richard Mahrhold & Sohn, Innsbrück, Austria, founded in 1854 and reportedly still making airguns into the 1970s, but Richard Mahrhold's *Waffenlexikon* (Weapon Dictionary) edition of 1998 notes that they are the product of the firm presently known as Tiroler Sportwaffenfabrik und Apparatebau GmbH ("Tyrol Sport Weapon Makers and Apparatus Factory Inc.") (aka Tiroler Jagd undSportwaffenfabrik or "TyROL Hunting and Sport Weapon Makers") of Kufstein, Austria, a gun maker associated with Voetter & Co. of Vöhrenbach/Schwarzwald ("Black Forest"), Germany. The Tiroler Jagd und Sportwaffenfabrik Company name was established in 1965, but the firm was known as the Tiroler Maschinenbau und Holzindustrie ("TyROL Machine Factory and Wood Works") in the 1950s when the TyROL COmatic and CM1 CO_2 rifles were produced and prior to that as Tiroler Waffenfabrik H. Krieghoff (probably unrelated to H. Krieghoff of Suhl and then Ulm, Germany). These airguns, especially the M1 Carbine-style trainer, may have been supplied to Voetter & Co. who reportedly was the official supplier of arms to the Austrian Army. Voetter also used the well-known brand name of Voere. The M1 Carbine version known officially as the Österreichischen Übungskarabiner KM 1 or "ÜK" is one of the most sought-after military arms among European arms and airgun collectors.

The association of the Austrian TyROL CO_2 rifles and the Italian Armigas "OLYMPIC" CO_2 rifles is a puzzle. While the civilian COmatic version of the TyROL gas rifle and the Armigas "OLYMPIC" appear to be the same, close examination shows that while virtually every part is similar, with almost identical styling, none actually are the same and they certainly are not interchangeable! Perhaps the TyROL CO_2 repeater was the inspiration for the OLYMPIC from Armigas. The TyROL CO-Matic rifle obviously was also the model for Venturini's Golondrina COMatic CO_2 pellet rifle, not surprising, considering the past ties of Germany and Argentina. The Golondrina repeater was in turn the model for the Golondrina repeating CO_2 pistol.

The TyROL COmatic and CM1 rifles may have additional special significance in the historical development of airguns as the maker claimed that they were the first semi-automatic CO_2 rifles to be developed commercially. (Ref: Amer. Rifleman Sept 1959:62-3; DWJ March 1992:401-3).

GRADING	100%	95%	90%	80%	60%	40%	20%

RIFLES

TyROL GAS RIFLE ("COmatic" R MODEL) – .177 cal., CO_2 bulk feed, charging valve by muzzle, semi-automatic, spring-fed removable eighty-shot magazine for lead balls, combination cocking tab/manual safety cannot be reset to safe after cocking, 21.2 in. rifled barrel, blue finish, date stamped LHS, 38 in. OAL, 5.3 lbs. Mfg. 1959.

courtesy Beeman Collection

	N/A	$750	$600	$475	$375	$265	$150

TyROL MODEL CM1 – .177 cal., CO_2 bulk feed, 21 in. barrel, long removable spring-fed magazine for lead balls on right side of barrel, stock similar to U.S. M1 Carbine, complete with web sling retained by oiler tube, military style adj. peep rear and blade protected front sight, LH receiver marked TyROL and with Austrian eagle logo, rear edge of receiver marked 4.5mm DPH, 6 in. OAL, 5.7 lbs. Approx. only 340 mfg. circa 1950s.

courtesy Beeman Collection

	N/A	$1,750	$1,400	$1,125	$875	$600	$350

Subtract 25% if missing accessories.

This model was also supplied with four magazines, gas charging extension tube, cleaning rod and canvas case.

Spring-fed magazine reportedly designed to take approx. the same time to replace as a box magazine of cartridges on the actual U.S. M1 Carbine. Original U.S. M1 carbine magazines fit into the gun in the conventional manner, but did not function. Reportedly used for training of Austrian and Dutch troops who had received large quantities of the U.S. M1 Carbines after WWII, most were destroyed by military authorities. Specimens remaining in Germany usually were modified to a "non-military configuration" by removing the military style sights, regulation sling and oiler, and filling in the sling slot in the stock.

TyROL MODEL 51 – .177 cal., SP, BC, SS, conventional sporter-style stock, open sights, TyROL and eagle logo markings.

$100	$85	$70	$60	$45	$30	$20

TyROL TOURNIER 53 – .177 cal., SP, BC, SS, 17.7 in. rifled barrel, blue finish, precision diopter (match aperture sight), match style stock with carved grip cap, marked on barrel "Tournier 53", "TyROL" plus a large Austrian eagle logo enclosing a large stylized letter "M" on top of receiver, and "MADE IN AUSTRIA" and serial number on LH side of barrel block, no safety, 42 in. OAL, 9.6 lbs.

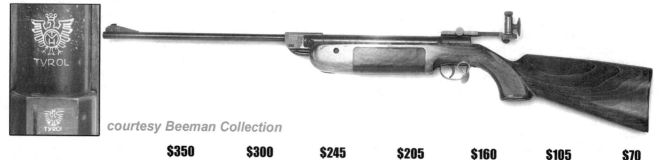

courtesy Beeman Collection

$350	$300	$245	$205	$160	$105	$70

Stylized letter "M" may indicate an association with Richard Mahrholdt.

U SECTION

ULTI-SHOT

Previous trademark of Ultimate Force in England and the manufacturer of the UltiShot air shotgun designed by Luke Cammilleri and Martin McManus of Merseyside, England.

Research is ongoing with this trademark, and more information will be included both online and in future editions.

GRADING	100%	95%	90%	80%	60%	40%	20%

SHOTGUN

ULTISHOT – .38 caliber air shotgun (or .375 lead balls or .38 cal. 110 gr. HP slugs), PCP, 19.3 in. smoothbore barrel, British FAC version produces about 30 ft./lb. ME (9mm rifled barrel version made in at least prototype form), tilting breech block, takes .38 cal. Crosman shot cartridges, checkered walnut straight grip stock, appears to be based on Falcon PCP action, 37.2 in. OAL, 6.9 lbs. Serial numbers to 6 known. Produced in 1996 only.

courtesy Beeman Collection

$1,200	$995	$800	N/A	N/A	N/A	N/A

ULTRA-HI PRODUCTS

Previous Pioneer BB76 BB gun distributor of air rifles made in Japan, located in Hawthorne, NJ.

RIFLES

PIONEER BB76 – 4.4mm cal. lead balls (bore too large for American steel .173 in BBs), SP, 50-shot spring-fed magazine similar to Daisy 25, underlever charging lever, 304 FPS (with 7.8 gr lead balls), 372 FPS (with 5.4 gr Daisy Quick Silver BBs), three stage adj. trigger, hammer is the safety, 45 in. OAL, 4.1 lbs. Manufactured in 1976 only.

courtesy Beeman Collection

$350	$300	$225	$150	$100	N/A	N/A

This model is a copy of a Kentucky rifle for the 1976 US Bicentennial, US Patent 238780. Ref: AR 6:7-10.

UMAREX SPORTWAFFEN GMBH & CO. KG

Current manufacturer of Umarex airguns, in addition to private label airguns sold under the Beretta, Browning, Colt, Hämmerli, Heckler & Koch, Magnum Research Inc., Makarov, RWS, Smith & Wesson, Sturm, Ruger & Co., Inc., Umarex and Walther names, located in Arnsberg, Germany. These airguns are imported and distributed in the United States beginning 2006, by Umarex USA located in Fort Smith, AR.

UMAREX was founded in 1972 as the "UMA Mayer & Ussfeller GmbH" first manufacturing tear-gas and signal pistols and began manufacturing air rifles beginning in 1984. After acquiring Reck Sportwaffen Fabrick Karl Arndt, the company was reorganized under the UMAREX name. UMA was first reorganized as UMARECK and then as UMAREX. The success story began in 1978 with the introduction of the RECK PK 800 tear-gas and signal pistol, a perfect replica of the renowned Walther PPK. Today UMAREX is Europe's largest importer of air rifles, marketing brands such as Crosman, Marksman, and Norica and at the same time is the world's largest maker of replicas. Famous makers such as Smith & Wesson, Colt, Beretta, FN Browning, Magnum Research Inc. and Walther have awarded UMAREX licenses to construct tear-gas/signal guns and CO_2 weapons.

Umarex is the present owner of Walther. Umarex does not sell directly to the general market, and the various private label models produced are listed under their respective trademark names. Please refer to the Beretta, Browning, Colt, Hämmerli, H&K, Magnum Research Inc., Makarov, RWS, Smith & Wesson, Sturm, Ruger & Co., Inc., and Walther listings in this text.

For more information and current pricing on both new and used Umarex firearms, please refer to the *Blue Book of Gun Values* by S.P. Fjestad (also available online).

GRADING	100%	95%	90%	80%	60%	40%	20%

UMAREX USA, INC.

Current importer and distributor of private label airguns sold under the Beretta, Browning, Colt, Hämmerli, H&K, Magnum Research Inc., Makarov, RWS, Smith & Wesson, Sturm, Ruger & Co., Inc., and Walther names, located in Fort Smith, AR.

Umarex USA began with the acquisition of Ruag Ammotec USA, marketers of the RWS trademark (manufactured by Dianawerk) adult airguns. Combined with the world class products from German based Umarex, the parent company of Walther Firearms, Umarex USA has become one of the premier providers of airguns and airgun accessories to North America. Please refer to the Beretta, Browning, Colt, Hämmerli, H&K, Magnum Research Inc., Makarov, RWS, Smith & Wesson, Sturm, Ruger & Co., Inc., and Walther listings in this text.

CARBINES

FUEL – .177 cal., SS, ReAxis gas piston, 1200 FPS, rifled barrel, SilencAir 5-chamber noise dampener, two-stage adj. trigger, metal Picatinny scope rail, automatic safety, fiber optic sights, all-weather synthetic thumbhole stock with rubber recoil pad, Black finish, tactical integrated bipod, 3-9x32 scope, Black finish. New 2014.

MSR $211	$175	$150	$125	$100	$80	$50	$35

FUSION – .177 cal., BA, SS, CO_2, rifled barrel, SilencAir 5-chamber noise dampener, Dovetail rail, automatic safety, ergonomic all-weather synthetic stock with rubber recoil pad, Black finish, includes 4x32 scope. New 2013.

courtesy Umarex USA

MSR $200	$170	$145	$120	$100	$75	$50	$35

OCTANE – .177 or .22 cal. pellet, BBC, SS, ReAxis gas piston, 1250/1050 FPS, 19 1/2 in. rifled barrel, features SilencAir 5-chamber noise dampener, two-stage adj. trigger, fixed fiber optic front and adj. fiber optic rear sights, metal Picatinny scope rail, automatic safety, ambidextrous all-weather synthetic thumbhole stock with rubber recoil pad, Black finish, includes 3-9x40 scope, 14.25 in. LOP, 48.5 in. OAL, 9.5 lbs. New 2013.

courtesy Umarex USA

MSR $263	$220	$185	$155	$130	$100	$65	$45

SURGE – .177 cal. pellet, BBC, SS, SP, 1000 FPS, 18.7 in. rifled barrel with muzzle brake, blued finish, two-stage adj. trigger, automatic safety, Dovetail rail, tactical all-weather synthetic thumbhole stock with sculpted ambidextrous cheekpiece, rubber recoil pad, Black finish, includes 4x32 scope, 14 in. LOP, 44.8 in. OAL, 7.85 lbs. New 2013.

courtesy Umarex USA

MSR $117	$95	$80	$65	$55	$45	$30	$20

GRADING	100%	95%	90%	80%	60%	40%	20%

PISTOLS

C P S – .177 cal., CO_2, DAO, 8-shot rotary mag., 395 FPS, adj. rear sight, manual safety, Weaver rail, black, 7.1 in. OAL, 1.2 lbs. New 2012.

Please contact the company directly for pricing and availability on this model.

EBOS TACTICAL BB – BB/.177 cal., 88g CO_2 capsule, SS semi-auto action with 1, 4 or 8-shot full-auto burst, 9.7 in. barrel, 540 FPS, 24-shot mag., black finish, two sided accessory rail, vertical pistol grip, electronic trigger control, fixed front and windage adj. rear sight, 24.75 in. OAL, 3 lbs. New 2010.

courtesy Umarex USA, Inc.

MSR $155	$130	$110	$90	$75	$60	$40	$25

HPP BB REPEATER – BB/.177 cal., CO_2, DA, blowback action, 3.8 in. barrel, 410 FPS, 15 shot mag., black finish, integrated accessory rail, 7 in. OAL, 1.7 lbs. New 2010.

courtesy Umarex USA, Inc.

MSR $79	$65	$55	$50	$40	$30	N/A	N/A

Add $10 for 15 shot drop-free magazine.

MORPH 3X – BB/.177 cal., CO_2, DA, 380 FPS (pistol) or 600 FPS (rifle), built-in 30-shot mag., 5.1 (pistol) or 9.75 (rifle) in. barrel, black synthetic stock, manual safety, Picatinny rail, fiber optic sights, ambidextrous grip, 11.5 (pistol) or 38.5 (rifle) in. OAL, 1.5 or 2.5 lbs. New 2012.

courtesy Umarex USA

MSR $91	$75	$65	$55	$45	$35	N/A	N/A

This is one model that can convert into three versions: a pistol, shotgun, or rifle, package includes pistol, extra barrel, forearm grip with fiber optic sight and rifle stock.

GRADING	100%	95%	90%	80%	60%	40%	20%

SA177 BB REPEATER – BB/.177 cal., CO_2, DA, blowback action, 4.1 in. barrel, 380 FPS, 19-shot mag., black finish, integrated lower accessory rail, metal slide, fiber optic rear sight, ergonomic grips, 7.25 in. OAL, 2.2 lbs. Mfg. 2010-2012.

courtesy Umarex USA, Inc.

	100%	95%	90%	80%	60%	40%	20%
	$55	$45	$40	$35	$25	N/A	N/A

Last MSR was $62.

PM – BB/.177 cal., CO_2, SA and DA, 2.8 in. barrel, 380 FPS, 16-shot mag., blue finish, fixed sights, brown checkered grips, 6.25 in. OAL, 1.25 lbs. Mfg. 2009-Disc.

	100%	95%	90%	80%	60%	40%	20%
	$60	$50	$40	$35	$25	N/A	N/A

Last MSR was $61.

RACE GUN – .177 cal., CO_2, SA, blowback action, 22-shot drop free mag., 410 FPS, all metal construction, black finish, Picatinny rail, manual safety, replaceable adj. sight with option of fiber optic or standard sight, also features a compensator, longer functional elements, and a jet funnel, an additional Picatinny rail and slide racker, ergonomic grips, skeleton trigger, large magazine release, 10.5 in. OAL, 2.2 lbs. New 2012.

Please contact the company directly for pricing and availability on this model.

This model is also available with a Race Gun Kit which includes a red dot sight.

STEEL FORCE – BB/.177 cal., two 12g CO_2 capsules, SS, semi-auto, 6-shot full auto burst, 430 FPS, 7.5 in. barrel, built-in 30 shot mag., integrated tactical railing, flip-up front and rear sights, collapsible stock, Black finish, 24.4-28.2 in. OAL, 3.37 lbs. New 2013.

courtesy Umarex USA

MSR $132	$105	$90	$75	$60	$45	$30	$20

STEEL STORM TACTICAL – BB/.177 cal., two 12g CO_2 capsules, SS semi-auto action w/6-shot full-auto burst, 7.5 in. barrel, 430 FPS, 30-shot mag., black finish, integrated upper and lower tactical accessory rails, 15 in. OAL, 2.7 lbs. New 2010.

courtesy Umarex USA, Inc.

MSR $115	$95	$80	$65	$55	$45	$30	$20

GRADING	100%	95%	90%	80%	60%	40%	20%

T A C – BB/.177 cal., 12g CO_2, DA, 410 FPS, 4.25 in. barrel, 19 shot drop-free metal mag., fixed front and adj. rear sights, integrated Picatinny rails, foldable stock, removable front grip, easily converts from a pistol to a carbine, Black finish, 14-22.5 in. OAL, 1.85 lbs. New 2013.

courtesy Umarex USA

MSR $62	$50	$45	$35	$30	$25	N/A	N/A

Add $55 for T A C Converter.

T D P 45 – BB/.177 cal., DA, 12g CO_2 capsule, compact design, 410 FPS, 4.25 in. barrel, 19 shot drop-free metal mag., fixed sights, integrated Picatinny rail, Black finish, 6.5 in. OAL, .85 lbs. New 2013.

courtesy Umarex USA

MSR $32	$20	$15	$15	$10	N/A	N/A	N/A

T D P 45 TAC – BB/.177 cal., DA, 12g CO_2 capsule, compact size, 4.25 in. barrel, 19 shot drop-free metal mag., fixed front and rear sights, integrated Picatinny rail and mount, includes red laser sight, 400 steel BBs, two CO_2 cartridges, 12 in. OAL, 1.2 lbs. New 2014.

MSR $55	$45	$40	$30	$25	$20	N/A	N/A

X B G – BB/.177 cal., 12g CO_2, DA, 410 FPS, compact design, 4.25 in. barrel, 19-shot mag., fixed sights, manual safety, integrated Picatinny rail, black finish, 6.75 in. OAL, approx. 0.7 lb. New 2012.

courtesy Umarex USA

MSR $31	$20	$15	$15	$10	N/A	N/A	N/A

UNICA

Previous manufacturer, probably Armas Juaristi in Spain was founded by Francisco Juaristi. Produced Juaristi airguns. Ref. Walter. About circa 1950-1980s.

Details of construction, including cast aluminum receiver, indicate that the one known model is a regular production item.

GRADING	100%	95%	90%	80%	60%	40%	20%

SHOTGUNS

UNICA AIR SHOTGUN – .25 cal., SP, BBC, SS, breech opening, 18.3 in. barrel, appears to be an over/under shotgun, but bottom barrel-like tube is open near barrel pivot, side sling swivels, blued steel and aluminum, rib runs full length of barrel and receiver (serves as scope base on receiver), threaded muzzle ring removes to receive muzzle brake or suppressor, walnut stock, "Unica" in molded type and winged eagle logo on white plastic buttplate, matching grip cap, no safety, 41.5 in. OAL, 6.5 lbs.

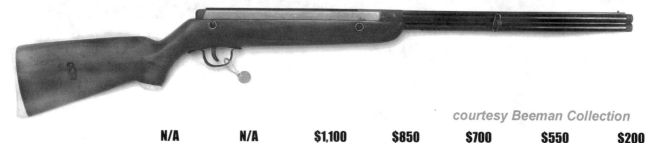

courtesy Beeman Collection

| | | N/A | N/A | $1,100 | $850 | $700 | $550 | $200 |

Information on this gun is actively solicited - please contact guns@bluebookinc.com.

UPTON

For information on Upton airguns, see Sterling/Upton in the "S" section.

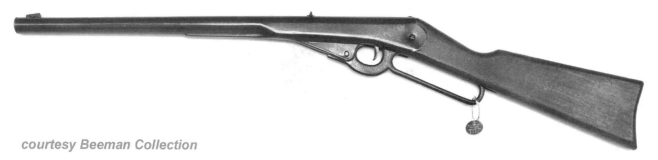

courtesy Beeman Collection

URKO

Previous trade name on Brazilian spring piston air pistols. Research is ongoing.

UZI

Current trademark manufactured by Israel Weapon Industries (IWI, previously called Israel Military Industries). Currently imported and distributed by Umarex USA, located in Fort Smith, AR.

CARBINES

MINI UZI CARBINE – BB/.177 cal., CO_2, DA, blowback action, semi-auto, 390 FPS, 5 in. barrel, removable mock silencer, 28 shot mag., fixed front and fixed flip-up rear sights, grip safety, folding stock, black finish, 23.5 in. OAL, 2.45 lbs. New 2014.

| MSR $109 | $90 | $75 | $65 | $50 | $40 | $25 | $20 |

Add $13 for 28 shot drop-free magazine.

UZI BB CARBINE – BB/.177 cal., CO_2, blowback action, semi-auto, 360 FPS, 5.6 in. barrel, metal parts, 25 shot, grip safety, adj. sights, integrated Picatinny rail and rail covers, grip safety, foldable stock, black finish, 23.5 in. OAL, 4.8 lbs. New 2013.

Please contact the company directly for pricing and availability on this model.

V SECTION

VALESQUEZ

For information on Valesquez airguns, see Philippine Airguns in the "P" section.

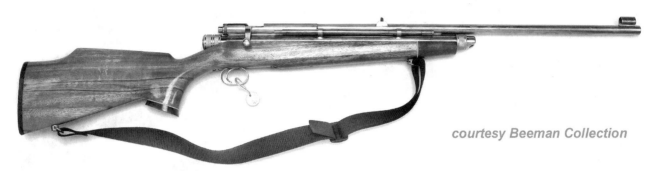

courtesy Beeman Collection

VALIENTE

For information on Valiente airguns, see Philippine Airguns in the "P" section.

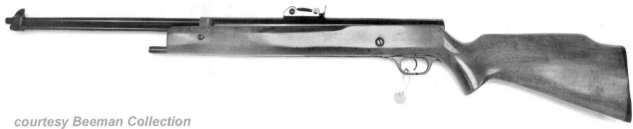

courtesy Beeman Collection

VALMET

Previous tradename of Valmet Oy located in Jyväskylä, Finland. Manufacture of Valmet firearms was replaced by Tikka circa 1989.

Former governmental engineering works, later famous for fine sporting and military firearms, such as the Model 58 Kalashnikov assault rifle. Merged with Sako in 1987 to become Sako-Valmet. Valmet's produced BBC air rifles were of especially high quality. For more information and current values on used firearms, please refer to the *Blue Book of Gun Values* by S.P. Fjestad (also available online).

GRADING	100%	95%	90%	80%	60%	40%	20%

RIFLES

AIRIS – .177 cal., BBC, SP, SS, steel parts, fwd. sling swivel mounted into outside of barrel, blue finish, hardwood stock with finger-grooved forearm, 39.5 in. OAL, 5 lbs.

courtesy Beeman Collection

$425	$350	$300	$245	$190	$125	$85

VALTRO (ITALIAN ARMS SRL)

Previous airgun and current firearms trademark located in Brescia, Italy.

Valtro manufactured a CO_2 air pistol. For more information on Valtro firearms, please refer to the most current edition of the *Blue Book of Gun Values* by S.P. Fjestad, or check online at www.bluebookofgunvalues.com.

GRADING	100%	95%	90%	80%	60%	40%	20%

VENOM ARMS CUSTOM GUNS

Previous manufacturer/customizer located in Birmingham, England. Venom Arms Custom Guns was a division of Webley & Scott. The Custom Shop officially closed December, 2005.

Venom Arms specialized in customizing Weihrauch air rifles which are manufactured in Germany. See also Weihrauch and Webley & Scott in the "W" section. Pricing for Venom Arms Custom Guns models may run 100%-300% over the initial cost of a standard gun.

courtesy Beeman Collection

VENTURINI

Previous airgun manufacturer located in Argentina which produced airguns under the Zamas, Venturini, Rubi, and Golondrina brand names. Circa 1970-1980s.

PISTOLS

GOLONDRINA ("C-O-MATIC") – .177 cal., CO_2 repeater, removable spring-fed magazine along barrel, bulk feed, no safety, unusual pistol version of Golondrina "C-O-matic" rifle.

courtesy Beeman Collection

N/A	$525	$425	$350	$260	$185	$105

RIFLES

GOLONDRINA ("C-O-MATIC") – .177 cal., CO_2 repeater, removable spring-fed magazine along RH length of barrel, bulk feed, almost surely copied from the German Tyrol "C-O-matic" repeater, also similar to the Spanish ArmiGas "Olympic" and Brazilian "Fionda".

courtesy Beeman Collection

N/A	$750	$600	$475	$375	$265	$150

GRADING	100%	95%	90%	80%	60%	40%	20%

RUBI – .177 cal., BBC, SP, SS, birch stock with finger grooved forearm.

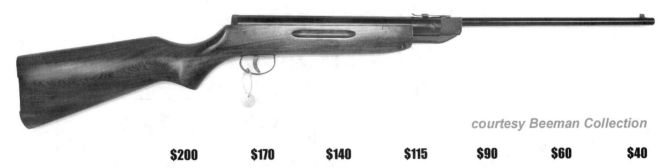

courtesy Beeman Collection

	$200	$170	$140	$115	$90	$60	$40

VENUSWAFFENWERK

For information on Venuswaffenwerk airguns, see Tell in the "T" section.

VINCENT

Previously manufactured by Frank Vincent, located in Hillsdale, MI.

Metal pump lever handle under barrel. Designed to be pumped to high pressure with seventy strokes. Would shoot many times with one fill, but with diminishing power unless pumped about thirty strokes between shots. Original instructions warned to use only "automobile brake fluid" to lubricate pump. Walnut stocks are handcrafted and metal parts are painted black. Mfg. circa 1930s.

Dennis Quackenbush (see the "Q" section of this guide) has recently manufactured some working replicas of the Vincent airguns.

RIFLES

RIFLE – .177 or .22 cal., BA, 700+ FPS, rifled brass barrel, 39.75 in. OAL, 5 lbs.

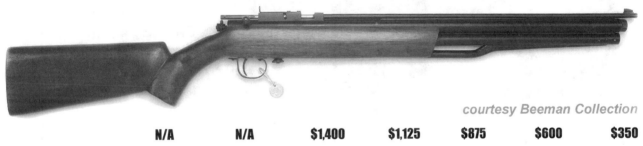

courtesy Beeman Collection

	N/A	N/A	$1,400	$1,125	$875	$600	$350

SHOTGUNS

SHOTGUN – .410 cal., bolt action, smoothbore steel barrel, with brass shot shells, wadcutter, and shell filling tools, 44.6 in. OAL, 6.4 lbs.

courtesy Beeman Collection

	N/A	N/A	$1,550	$1,275	$975	$675	$400

Add 25% for tool kit and spare cartridges.

VINTAGE PNEUMATICS

For information on Vintage Pneumatics airguns, see Feltman Products in the "F" section.

VZ

For information on VZ airguns, see CZ in the "C" section.

W SECTION

WAFFENTECHNIK JONISKEIT

For information on Waffentechnik Joniskeit airguns, see Joniskeit in the "J" section.

WALTHER (CARL WALTHER GmbH SPORTWAFFEN)

Current manufacturer located in Ulm, Germany. Match/Target model airguns are currently imported and distributed by Champion's Choice, located in La Vergne, TN. Sport model airguns imported and distributed by Umarex USA located in Fort Smith, AR. Previously, Sport model airguns imported by Crosman Corp., located in East Bloomfield, NY. Previously imported by Walther USA located in Springfield, MA, and Interarms, located in Alexandria, VA. Dealer or consumer direct sales.

For more information and current pricing on both new and used Walther firearms, please refer to the *Blue Book of Gun Values* by S.P. Fjestad (also available online).

GRADING	100%	95%	90%	80%	60%	40%	20%

PISTOLS

CP 2 – .177 cal., CO_2, 9 in. barrel, adj. sights and trigger, UIT target model, 2.5 lbs. Mfg. 1985-1990.

	100%	95%	90%	80%	60%	40%	20%
	$450	$375	$325	$260	$205	$135	$90

Last MSR was $850.

Subtract 10% for left-hand variation.

CP 3 – .177 cal., CO_2, adj. sights and electronic trigger, UIT target model. Importation 1987-1993.

	100%	95%	90%	80%	60%	40%	20%
	$450	$375	$325	$260	$205	$135	$90

Last MSR was $1,360.

CP 5 – .177 cal., CO_2, target model. Mfg. 1989-1995.

	100%	95%	90%	80%	60%	40%	20%
	$600	$500	$425	$350	$270	$180	$120

Last MSR was $1,650.

This model had engineering and design problems.

CP 88 – .177 cal., CO_2, SA/DA, 3.5 in. rifled barrel, 400 FPS, two 8 shot rotary magazines, polished black or nickel (disc. 2013) finish with black synthetic grips, adj. rear sight, replaceable front sight, manual safety lever, 7 in. OAL, 2.3 lbs. New 1996.

courtesy Umarex USA

MSR $224	100%	95%	90%	80%	60%	40%	20%
	$190	$170	$150	$125	$95	N/A	N/A

Add $29 for nickel finish (disc. 2013). Add $99 for wood grips (disc.).

This model was marked Umarex USA beginning 2006.

* *CP88 Competition* – .177 cal., CO_2, SA/DA, 450 FPS, 8-shot rotary mag., 5.5 (new 2008) or 6 (disc. 2007) in. barrel with compensator, adj. rear sight, replaceable front sight, smooth trigger pull, polished black or nickel (disc. 2013) finish with black synthetic or wood (disc.) grips, 9 in. OAL, 2.5 lbs. New 1996.

courtesy Umarex USA

MSR $240	100%	95%	90%	80%	60%	40%	20%
	$205	$180	$165	$130	$100	N/A	N/A

Add $23 for nickel finish (disc. 2013). Add $99 for wood grips (disc.).

This model was marked Umarex USA beginning 2006.

GRADING	100%	95%	90%	80%	60%	40%	20%

CP88 TACTICAL – .177 cal., CO_2, SA/DA, 450 FPS, 6 in. barrel with compensator, adj. rear sight, 8-shot mag., polished black or nickel finish, black synthetic grips, 7 in. OAL, 2.5 lbs. Mfg. 2005-2008.

	$250	$215	$175	$145	$115	$75	$50

Last MSR was $277.

This model was marked Umarex USA beginning 2006.

CP 99 – .177 cal., CO_2, semi-auto repeater, 8 shot rotary magazine at breech, 360 FPS, 3.3 in. rifled barrel, slide action for first shot or single action firing, single or double action trigger, manual safety and decocking system, black polymer frame and black or nickel (disc. 2013) slide finish, open fixed rear sight, integrated accessory rail, interchangeable backstrap, 7.1 in. OAL, 1.7 lbs. Marked Umarex USA beginning 2006. New 2000.

courtesy Beeman Collection

MSR $205	$175	$155	$140	$115	$85	N/A	N/A

Add $21 for nickel finish slide (disc. 2013). Add 15% for Class III laser (CP99BLS mfg. 2005-06).

The CP99 is designed for police, military and civilian training, where the actual feel, weight, and action of a firearm are necessary. The CO_2 capsule is loaded in a removable cartridge-style magazine.

* **CP 99 Compact** – BB/.177 cal., CO_2, 18-shot mag., 345 FPS, blowback semi-auto, compact version of CP 99, 3.25 in. rifled barrel, slide action for first shot or single action firing, manual safety and decocking system, integrated accessory rail, black polymer frame and black, nickel, or black with fitted laser sight slide finish, fixed front and rear sights, 6.6 in. OAL, 1.7 lbs. Marked Umarex USA. New 2006.

courtesy Umarex USA

MSR $89	$75	$65	$60	$50	$35	N/A	N/A

Add $4 for nickel finish slide. Add $19 for CP99 Compact with Laser (black only), mfg. 2006-current.

* **CP 99 Compact Recon** – .177 cal., CO_2, 17 shot mag., 345 FPS, 3.6 in. rifled barrel, slide action for first shot or single action firing, manual safety and decocking system, black polymer frame and slide finish, bridge mount, Walther Shot Dot green illuminated point sight and compensator, 2.3 lbs. Mfg. 2008-2010.

courtesy Umarex USA

	$95	$80	$65	$55	$45	$30	$20

Last MSR was $110.

GRADING	100%	95%	90%	80%	60%	40%	20%

* **CP 99 Military** – .177 cal., CO_2, 8 shot rotary magazine at breech, 360 FPS, 3.3 in. rifled barrel, slide action for first shot or single action firing, single or double action trigger, manual safety and decocking system, green polymer frame with black slide finish, adj. rear sight, 7 in. OAL, 1.7 lbs. Marked Umarex USA beginning 2006. Mfg. 2001-2013.

courtesy Umarex USA

	$185	$155	$130	$105	$85	$55	$35

Last MSR was $220.

* **CP 99 Trophy** – .177 cal., CO_2, SA/DA, 360 FPS, eight-shot rotary magazine at breech, 3.3 in. rifled barrel, slide action for first shot or single action firing, manual safety and decocking system, black polymer frame and black or nickel slide finish, includes bridge mount, red dot optical sighting system and case, 1.7 lbs. Mfg. 2001-2006.

	$250	$215	$175	$145	$115	$75	$50

Last MSR was $300.

Add 10% for nickel finish slide.

CPM-1 – .177 cal., CO_2, adj. sights and trigger, UIT target model. Mfg. 1992-Disc.

	$500	$425	$350	$290	$225	$150	$100

CP SPORT (CPS) – .177 cal., CO_2, DA, 3.3 in. rifled barrel, 400 FPS, eight-shot mag., black, orange (disc.), or yellow (disc.) polymer frame with blue slide, fixed front sight, adj. rear sight, integrated accessory rail, 7.1 in. OAL, 1.2 lbs. Marked Umarex USA beginning 2006. Mfg. 2001-2011.

courtesy Umarex USA

	$90	$75	$65	$50	$40	$25	$20

Last MSR was $108.

Add $30 for Class III laser (CP Sport Laser available 2005-current).

Add $10 for CP Sport Kit including 2-CO_2 cylinders, tin of 250 RWS Superdome pellets, Hämmerli shooting glasses and 5 targets (Mfg. 2008-2011).

* **CPS Trophy** – .177 cal., CO_2, DA, 400 FPS, eight-shot mag., 3.3 in. rifled barrel, black, orange (disc.), or yellow (disc.) polymer frame with blue slide, fixed front sight, adj. rear sight, integrated accessory rail, red dot scope and mount included, 7.1 in. OAL, 1.2 lbs. Mfg. 2002-Disc.

	$150	$130	$105	$85	$70	$45	$30

LP 2 – .177 cal., SSP using linked lever around trigger and grip. Mfg. 1967-1972.

	N/A	N/A	$450	$350	$300	N/A	N/A

Add 25% for fitted case.

GRADING	100%	95%	90%	80%	60%	40%	20%

LP 3 – .177 cal., SSP, 450 FPS, 2.8-3 lbs. Mfg. 1973-1985.

courtesy Beeman Collection

	N/A	N/A	$450	$375	$275	N/A	N/A

Add 15% for shaped barrel (shown) rather than round.
Add 20% for fitted case.
Add 20% for match grade (adjustable wooden grips).

LP 53 – .177 cal., BBC, with SP system in grip, 9.45 in. rifled barrel, adj. sights with two sets of extra inserts, smooth blue (until circa SN 23,200) black crinkle enamel finish, brown or black plastic grips with Walther logo, wood cocking block, 40.6 oz. Mfg. 1952-1983. Ref: AAG - Oct. 1991.

courtesy Beeman Collection

	N/A	$350	$280	$230	$175	$125	$70

Add 35% for fitted case, blue and gray inside.
Add 25% for fitted case, maroon inside.
Add 10% for original brown factory cardboard box.
Add 30% for original smooth blue finish.
Add 25% for straight back receiver.
Add 15% for barrel weight.
Subtract 5% for missing sight inserts.

Early versions of the fitted case are blue and gray inside; later versions are maroon. Several examples in the 2,750-3,000 S/N range had the model number marking struck hard making the "3" look like an "8". Early versions with a curved receiver back, later versions are straight. This pistol was made famous by appearing in a James Bond poster.

LPM-1 – .177 cal., SSP, 9.15 in. barrel, 2.25 lbs. Mfg. 1990-2004.

	$750	$625	$525	$425	$325	$225	$150

Last MSR was $1,050.

LP 200/CP 200 – .177 cal., PCP (CO_2 on CP 200, disc. March 1996), 450 FPS, 9 1/8 in. barrel, adj. grips, sights, and trigger, UIT target model, 2.5 lbs.

	$800	$675	$550	$475	$350	$240	$160

Last MSR was $1,100.

Subtract 35% for CO_2.

LP 201/CP 201 – .177 cal., PCP (CO_2 on CP201, disc. March 1996), 450 FPS, 9.15 in. barrel, adj. grips, sights, and trigger, UIT target model, 2.5 lbs. New 1990.

	$800	$675	$550	$475	$350	$240	$160

Last MSR was $1,065.

Subtract 35% for CO_2.

GRADING	100%	95%	90%	80%	60%	40%	20%

LP 300 – .177 cal., PCP (integral pressure gauge in cylinder), integrated front sight with three different widths, adj. rear sight, 450 FPS, 9.15 in. barrel, adj. grips and trigger, UIT target model, 2.2 lbs. Mfg. 2001-2008.

	$1,300	$1,100	$900	$750	$575	$400	$260

Last MSR was $1,295.

* **LP 300 Ultra Light** – .177 cal., PCP (integral pressure gauge in cylinder), integrated front sight with three different widths, adj. rear sight, 450 FPS, 8.19 in. barrel, adj. grips and trigger, UIT target model, 1.9 lbs. Mfg. 2004-2011.

	$1,300	$1,100	$900	$750	$575	$400	$260

Last MSR was $1,540.

* **LP 300 XT** – .177 cal., PCP (integral pressure gauge in cylinder), integrated front sight with three different widths, adj. rear sight, 450 FPS, 9.15 in. barrel, adj. grip, adj. trigger, UIT target model, 15.75 in. OAL, 2.2 lbs. Mfg. 2007-2011.

	$1,350	$1,150	$950	$775	$600	$400	$270

Last MSR was $1,595.

NIGHTHAWK – .177 cal., CO_2, DA, semi-automatic, 3.3 (new 2008) or 3.5 (disc. 2007) in. rifled steel barrel, 400 FPS, synthetic body, eight-shot mag., detachable compensator, red dot sight, side mounted tactical Walther flashlight, grip mount light activation switch, Picatinny bridge accessory rail mount, adj. rear sight, black or Military Green (disc. 2012) finish, 9.8 (mfg. 2008-2012) or 11.5 in. OAL, 2.4 lbs. Marked Umarex USA beginning 2006. New 2004.

courtesy Umarex USA

MSR $275	$235	$205	$185	$150	$115	N/A	N/A

SG9000 – BB/.177 cal., CO_2, 88g cylinder, semi-auto, DA, 40-shot mag., 250 (three shot burst) or 480 (single shot) FPS, 12.6 in. barrel, black polymer frame and ergonomic grips, manual 1 or 3 shot safety selector, integrated tactical rails, 22 in. OAL, 2.8 lbs. Mfg. 2009-2012.

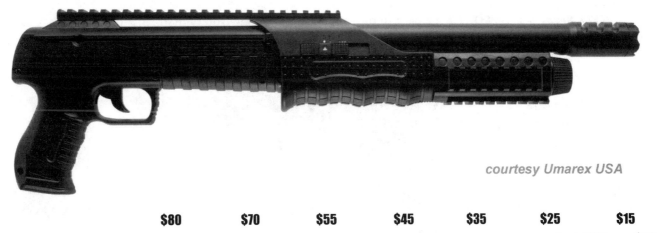

courtesy Umarex USA

	$80	$70	$55	$45	$35	$25	$15

Last MSR was $92.

GRADING	100%	95%	90%	80%	60%	40%	20%

P38 – BB/.177 cal., CO_2, blowback action, SA, 400 FPS, all metal design, 20 shot drop-free mag., 4.75 in. removable barrel, blued, polished, brown grips, fixed sights, 8.6 in. OAL, 1.5 lbs. New 2012.

courtesy Umarex USA

MSR $104	$90	$80	$70	$55	$45	N/A	N/A

PPK/PPK/S/PPK/S LASER – BB/.175 (disc.) or .177 cal., CO_2, SA, semi-auto repeater, blowback action, 3.5 in. smooth bore barrel, 295 FPS, 15-shot mag., heavyweight metal construction, black frame with black or nickel slide, fixed sights, Class III laser (PPK/S Laser new 2005), 6.1 in. OAL, 1.2 lbs. Marked Umarex USA beginning 2006. New 2000.

courtesy Umarex USA

MSR $81	$70	$60	$55	$45	$35	N/A	N/A

Add $9 for nickel finish slide (PPK/S).
Add $18 for PPK/S Laser (mfg. 2005-2013).
Add $13 for Sports Kit including PPK/S pistol (black), shooting glasses, two 12g CO_2 cylinders, 5 targets, and 250 steel BBs (disc. 2012).

PPQ – BB/.177 cal. or pellets, CO_2, DA, semi-auto repeater, 360 FPS, 8-shot rotary mag., 3.3 in. barrel, black synthetic frame, new grip design, adj. rear and fixed front sights, integrated accessory rail, CO_2 compartment in the grip, manual slide lever safety, 7 in. OAL, 1.37 lbs. New 2011.

courtesy Umarex USA

MSR $72	$60	$55	$50	$40	$30	N/A	N/A

PPS – BB/.177 cal., CO_2, blowback action, SA, semi-auto repeater, 350 FPS, 3 in. metal barrel, 18 shot drop-free mag., fixed front and rear sights, heavyweight metal construction, integrated weaver rail, integrated hex tool in the backstrap, remove backstrap to reveal CO_2 compartment, 6.37 in. OAL, 1.2 lbs. New 2014.

MSR $76	$65	$55	$50	$40	$30	N/A	N/A

GRADING	100%	95%	90%	80%	60%	40%	20%

RED HAWK – .177 cal., CO$_2$, DA, semi-auto, eight-shot mag., 3.3 in. rifled steel barrel, 360 FPS, synthetic body, red dot sight, 7.1 in. OAL, 1.39 lbs. Mfg. 2004-2006.

	$145	$125	$100	$85	$65	$45	$30

Last MSR was $170.

RED STORM – .177 cal., CO$_2$, DA, semi-auto, eight-shot mag., 3.3 in. rifled steel BBL, 360 FPS, synthetic body, red dot sight, 7.1 in. OAL, 1.39 lbs. Marked Umarex USA. Mfg. 2007.

	$145	$125	$100	$85	$65	$45	$30

Last MSR was $170.

RED STORM RECON – .177 cal., CO$_2$, DA, semi-auto, eight-shot mag., 3.3 in. rifled steel barrel, 420 FPS, synthetic body, red dot sight and RS compensator, 11.5 in. OAL, 1.5 lbs. Marked Umarex USA. Mfg. 2007-2008.

	$145	$125	$100	$85	$65	$45	$30

Last MSR was $170.

Add $18 for red or blue grips.

RIFLES

During 2006 Walther introduced a new anti-vibration system, absorber, modified pressure reducer, Centra front sight, and MEC Contact III butt plate on all aluminum or carbon stocked match/target air rifles. These changes are indicated by the "XT" (ie. LG 300 XT) added to model names.

1250 DOMINATOR – .177, .22, or .25 (mfg. 2009-disc.) cal., PCP, BA, 1250/1000 FPS, eight-shot rotary mag., 23.62 in. rifled steel barrel, adj. fiber optic sights, synthetic black stock, ambidextrous Monte Carlo cheekpiece, checkering on pistol grip and forearm, two-stage adj. trigger, automatic safety, vented rubber recoil pad, 40.94 in. OAL, 5.73 lbs. Mfg. 2008-2013.

courtesy Umarex USA

	$700	$575	$475	$400	$300	$205	$140

Last MSR was $805.

* **1250 Dominator FT** – .177 or .22 cal., PCP, BA, 1250/1000 FPS, eight-shot rotary mag., 23.62 in. rifled steel BBL with compensator, quick mount adj. bipod, adj. fiber optic sights, 4-16x56mm (disc. 2010), or 8-32x56mm (new 2010) Walther FT scope, synthetic black stock with checkering on pistol grip and forearm, ambidextrous Monte Carlo cheekpiece, vented rubber recoil pad, automatic double safety system, two-stage adj. trigger, 40.94 in. OAL, 5.73 lbs. Mfg. 2008-current.

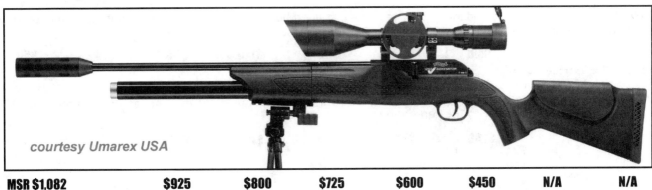

courtesy Umarex USA

MSR $1,082	$925	$800	$725	$600	$450	N/A	N/A

MODEL 30 UNIVERSAL SPECIAL – .177 cal., PCP, manometer, 16.5 in. barrel, ambidextrous aluminum stock, adj. cheek piece, butt pad, adj. chrome-molybdenum steel trigger, precision diopter rear sight, steel cylinder, 42.6 in. OAL, 10.5 lbs. Mfg. 2007-2012.

	$1,050	$900	$725	$600	$475	$325	$210

Last MSR was $1,250.

GRADING	100%	95%	90%	80%	60%	40%	20%

* *Model 30 Universal Special Junior* – .177 cal., PCP, manometer, 16.5 in. barrel, ambidextrous aluminum stock, adj. cheek piece, butt pad, adj. chrome-molybdenum steel trigger, precision diopter rear sight, aluminum cylinder, 42.6 in. OAL, 9.5 lbs. Mfg. 2008-2012.

	$850	$725	$600	$500	$375	$255	$170

Last MSR was $1,000.

CG 90 – .177 cal., CO_2, 18.9 in. barrel, 10 lbs. 2 oz. Mfg. 1989-1996.

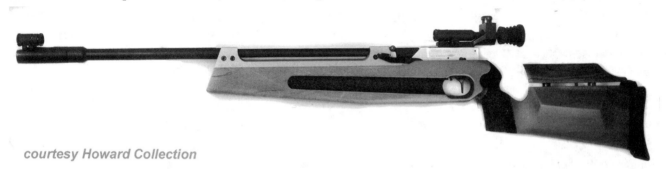

courtesy Howard Collection

	$850	$725	$600	$500	$375	$255	$170

Last MSR was $1,750.

CGM – .177, CO_2, target model, laminated stock, similar to LGM-2. Disc. 1997.

	$850	$725	$600	$500	$375	$255	$170

Last MSR was $1,270.

Add 10% for junior model.
Add 10% for running target model.

FALCON HUNTER EDITION – .22 or .25 (disc. 2010) cal., BBC, SP, SS, 19.75 in. rifled steel BBL with muzzle brake, 1000/800 FPS, black finish, checkered Mossy Oak Break-Up synthetic Monte Carlo stock with adj. rubber recoil pad, raised right-hand cheek piece, automatic safety, single (disc. 2010) or two (new 2011) stage adj. trigger, adj. rear fixed front Truglo fiber optic sights, 3-9x44mm blue illuminated scope, 49 in. OAL, 8.25 lbs. Mfg. 2008-2011.

courtesy Umarex USA

	$265	$225	$185	$155	$120	$80	$55

Last MSR was $309.

JAGUAR – .177 cal., SL, SP, tap loading, 16.4 in. barrel, stained beech adj. stock (for comb, buttplate, and pull), adj. trigger, adj. rear sight, fixed front sight with interchangeable inserts, 7.5 lbs. New 1994.

	$250	$215	$175	$145	$115	$75	$50

Add 25% for aperture sight.
Add 20% for box, accessories, and factory papers.

LEVER ACTION CARBINE – .177 cal., CO_2, eight-shot rotary mag., similar to Lever Action Rifle, except with 15 in. rifled steel barrel, 34.5 in. OAL, 7 lbs. Mfg. 2003.

	$250	$215	$175	$145	$115	$75	$50

Last MSR was $255.

GRADING	100%	95%	90%	80%	60%	40%	20%

LEVER ACTION RIFLE – .177 cal., CO_2, holds 2-12g cylinders (disc. 2010), or one 88g CO_2 (new 2011) in rear of stock, lever action, eight-shot rotary mag., 18.9 in. rifled steel barrel, 630 FPS, elegant hardwood straight stock, blued, black (new 2011), or nickel plated (mfg. 2011-2013) steel finish, adj. rear and hooded front sights, cross bolt safety, 39.2 in. OAL, 6.2 lbs. Marked Umarex USA beginning 2006. New 2002.

courtesy Umarex USA

MSR $517	$450	$375	$350	$285	$215	N/A	N/A

Add $108 for nickel plated, steel finish (mfg. 2011-2013). Last MSR in 2013 was $662.
Add $34 for 4x32mm scope and mount (mfg. 2006-2012).
Add 10% for Wells Fargo Edition with stage coach scene on gold color receiver (mfg. 2006).

LG30 VISION PLUS – .177 cal., CO_2, multi-functional aluminum stock, rotatable grip, adj. cheek piece, adj. buttstock, adj. hand rest, integrated pressure gauge, standard match sight set, 8.7 lbs. Mfg. 2011-2012.

	$1,275	$1,075	$900	$750	$575	$375	$255

Last MSR was $1,500.

Subtract $250 for LG30 Junior Model with Basic sight set, 7.8 lbs. (new 2011).

LG 51 – .177 cal., BBC, SP, 17.75 in. smoothbore barrel, adj. rear sight, blue finish, walnut color beech stock, steel (early) or plastic buttplate, grooved forearm, pistol grip, 5.7 lbs. Mfg. 1951-53.

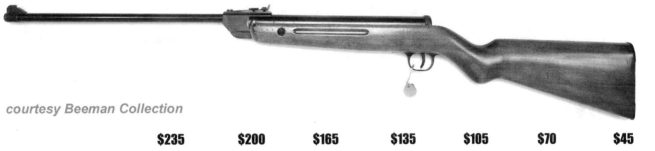

courtesy Beeman Collection

	$235	$200	$165	$135	$105	$70	$45

Approx. 1951 Retail $34.

Add 10% for steel buttplate.
Add 25% for aperture sight.
Add 20% for box, accessories, and factory papers.
Walther's first post-WWII airgun.

* **LG 51 Z** – .177 cal., similar to LG 51, except has rifled barrel. Mfg. 1953 - disc.

	$200	$170	$140	$115	$90	$60	$40

1953 retail was approx. $30.

Add 25% for aperture sight.
Add 20% for box, accessories, and factory papers.

LG 52 – .177 cal., BBC, SP, beech stock, grooved forearm, checkered pistol grip, adj. trigger, 17.75 in. barrel, steel buttplate, 15mm steel post inset in stock behind receiver for optional aperture sight. Mfg. 1953.

	$275	$235	$195	$160	$125	$80	$55

Add 20% for box, accessories, and factory papers.
Add 40% for aperture sight.

LG 53 – .177 cal., similar to Model LG 51, except has plastic buttplate, aperture sight. Mfg. 1952-1976.

	$225	$190	$160	$130	$100	$65	$45

Add 20% for box, accessories, and factory papers.
Add 40% for aperture sight.

GRADING	100%	95%	90%	80%	60%	40%	20%

* **LG 53 M** – .177 cal., similar to Model LG 53, except has match-style stock, front sight with interchangeable inserts, stock and barrel weight. Mfg. 1956-disc.

	$325	$275	$230	$190	$145	$95	$65

Add 20% for box, accessories, and factory papers.
Add 40% for aperture sight.

* **LG 53 ZD** – .177 cal., similar to Model LG 53, 5.7 lbs. Mfg. 1951-53.

	$325	$275	$230	$190	$145	$95	$65

Add 20% for box, accessories, and factory papers.
Add 40% for aperture sight.

LG54 MG – .177 cal. lead balls, similar to Model LG 51, except six-shot rotary magazine for lead balls. Mfg. 1954-disc.

	$575	$500	$400	$325	$260	$170	$115

Add 20% for box, accessories, and factory papers.
Add 25% for aperture sight.
Add 20% for blank magazine for shooting pellets.

LG 55 – .177 cal., BBC, SP, deep leaded forearm, checkered pistol grip, adj. trigger, aperture sight, cresent rubber buttplate. Mfg. 1955-1967 (was available through 1974).

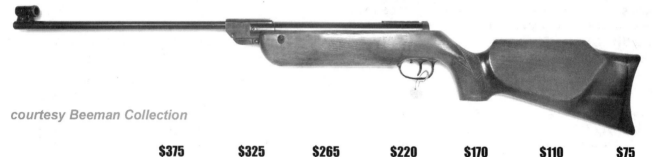

courtesy Beeman Collection

	$375	$325	$265	$220	$170	$110	$75

Add 20% for box, accessories, and factory papers.   Add 10% for barrel weight.
Add 25% for aperture sight.   Add 50% for Tyrolean stock.
Add 20% for walnut stock.   Add 50% for double triggers.

LG 90 – SL, target model, 11 lbs. Mfg. 1989-Disc.

	$850	$725	$600	$500	$375	$255	$170

Last MSR was $1,320.

LGM-1 – .177 cal., SL, 19 in. barrel, approx. 10 lbs. Mfg. 1991-Disc.

	$900	$775	$625	$525	$400	$270	$180

Last MSR was $1,890.

LGM-2 – .177 cal., SL, similar to LGM-1, laminated stock, 10 lbs. Mfg. 1993-98.

	$900	$775	$625	$525	$400	$270	$180

Last MSR was $1,890.

Subtract 15% for Junior model.
Add 10% for Running Target model.

LGR RIFLE – .177 cal., SL, single stroke pneumatic, 580 FPS, target model, 10 lbs. 8 oz. Mfg. 1974-1989.

courtesy Beeman Collection

	N/A	$575	$450	$375	$285	$200	$115

Last MSR was $1,250.

Add 100% for Running Boar Model.
Add 15% for Universal.

GRADING	100%	95%	90%	80%	60%	40%	20%

LGV MATCH RIFLE – .177 cal., BBC, SP, match rifle, barrel latch, heavy barrel sleeve, aperture sight with Walther banner on left, cresent shaped, fixed rubber buttplate, beech stock with cheek piece and stippled grip. Mfg. 1963-1968.

	N/A	$475	$375	$300	$235	$165	$95

Add 20% for box, accessories, and factory papers.
Add 15% for later version with adjustable buttplate, new style aperture sight with Walther banner on top.
Add 15% for walnut stock.

* *LGV Special* – similar to LGV Match Rifle, except more massive beech stock, receiver diameter increased to allow direct milling of aperture sight dovetail, double mainspring system. Mfg. 1968-1972 (was available through 1985).

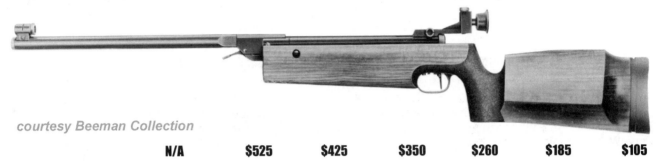

courtesy Beeman Collection

	N/A	$525	$425	$350	$260	$185	$105

Add 10% for box, accessories, and factory papers.
Add 40% for Tyrolean stock.
Add 10% for Junior version.
Add 15% for Junior 3 position version.

LGV CHALLENGER – .177 or .22 cal., BBC, SP, SS, 1000/700 FPS, 15.7 in. blued barrel, super silent technology, features vibration reduction system, ambidextrous black synthetic stock with checkering and rubber recoil pad, HI-GRIP finish on grip and forend, wedge lock with release lever, adj. match trigger, TruGlo fiber optic fixed front and adj. rear sights, automatic trigger safety, 43.1 in. OAL, 8.4 lbs. Mfg. 2012-2013.

courtesy Umarex USA

	$550	$450	$375	$325	$245	$160	$110

Last MSR was $635.

LGV COMPETITION ULTRA – .177 or .22 cal., BBC, SP, SS, 1000/700 FPS, features Super Silent Technology and a Vibration Reduction System, 15.7 in. blued barrel, ambidextrous Beech wood stock with checkering and rubber recoil pad, adj. cheekpiece, two-stage adj. trigger, TruGlo fiber optic front and adj. rear sights, automatic trigger safety, 43.1 in. OAL, 10.1 lbs. New 2013.

courtesy Umarex USA

MSR $844	$725	$625	$575	$475	$350	N/A	N/A

GRADING	100%	95%	90%	80%	60%	40%	20%

LGV MASTER – .177 or .22 cal., BBC, SP, SS, 1000/700 FPS, features Super Silent Technology and a Vibration Reduction System, 15.7 in. blued barrel, ambidextrous wooden stock with checkering and rubber recoil pad, two-stage adj. trigger, adj. rear sight and multiple inserts for front sight, interchangeable fixed post front sight, automatic trigger safety, wedge lock with release lever, 43.1 in. OAL, 9.3 lbs. Mfg. 2012-2013 only.

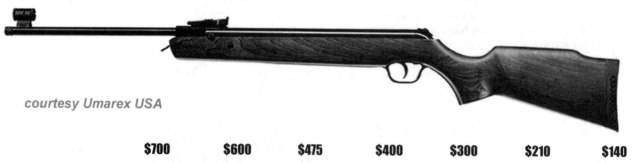

courtesy Umarex USA

	100%	95%	90%	80%	60%	40%	20%
	$700	$600	$475	$400	$300	$210	$140

Last MSR was $811.

LGV MASTER ULTRA – .177 or .22 cal., BBC, SP, SS, 15.7 in. barrel, Vibration Reduction Technology, wedge lock with release lever, adj. match trigger, Super Silent Technology, Beech wood stock w/cheekpiece and rubber recoil pad, adj. open rear sight, interchangeable fixed post front sight, multiple front sight inserts included, automatic trigger safety, Walther tuning trigger, and piston grease, 43.1 in. OAL, 9.45 lbs. New 2013.

courtesy Umarex USA

MSR $793	$675	$600	$550	$425	$325	N/A	N/A

LGV ULTRA – .177 or .22 cal., BBC, SP, SS, 1000/700 FPS, 15.7 in. blued barrel, Super Silent Technology, features Vibration Reduction Technology, ambidextrous black synthetic stock with checkering and rubber recoil pad, HI-GRIP finish on grip and forend, wedge lock with release lever, adj. match trigger, TruGlo fiber optic fixed front and adj. rear sights, automatic trigger safety, 43.1 in. OAL, 8.4 lbs. New 2013.

courtesy Umarex USA

MSR $679	$575	$500	$450	$375	$285	N/A	N/A

LG 210 – .177 cal., SL, pneumatic, 16.5 in. barrel, laminated wood stock with anatomic pistol grip, rubber butt plate, adj. cheek piece, inline compensator, chrome-molybdenum steel trigger, and peep sight with twenty-click-adjustment. 11.5 lbs. Mfg. 1998-2004.

	$1,175	$1,000	$825	$675	$525	$350	$235

Last MSR was $1,393.

Add $85 for fully adj. light metal buttplate.

* **LG 210 Junior** – .177 cal., SL, pneumatic, similar to Model LG 210, except scope rail for the three-position competition and an anatomical metal buttplate, 9.92 lbs. Mfg. 1999-2004.

	$1,150	$975	$800	$675	$525	$350	$230

Last MSR was $1,314.

GRADING	100%	95%	90%	80%	60%	40%	20%

LG300 UNIVERSAL – .177 cal., BA, PCP, SS, 16.5 in. rifled barrel, carbon fiber barrel jacket, post globe front and adj. diopter rear sights, two-stage adj. trigger, ambidextrous grip, removable aluminum air reservoir with integral manometer (air pressure gauge), universal ambidextrous beech stock with adj. rubber buttpad, adj. stock length, and adj. cheekpiece. New 2001.

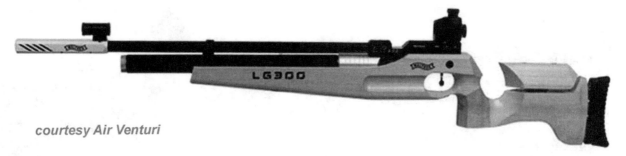

courtesy Air Venturi

MSR $1,540	$1,300	$1,150	$1,050	$850	$650	N/A	N/A

LG 300 XT – .177 cal., PCP (integral pressure gauge in cylinder), carbon fiber barrel jacket and absorber (dampener) system eliminates perceptible recoil, 16.5 in. barrel, laminated wood stock with adj. cheekpiece, adj. and tiltable alloy buttplate, adj. chrome-molybdenum steel trigger, precision diopter rear sight, 9.7 lbs. New 2001.

MSR $1,655	$1,400	$1,250	$1,125	$900	$700	N/A	N/A

* **LG 300 Alutec/LG 300 XT Alutec** – .177 cal., similar to Model LG 300, except has aluminum stock with adj. cheek piece, adj. and tiltable alloy buttplate, interchangeable, adj. pistol grip, adj. forearm, adj. chromolybdenum steel trigger, precision diopter rear sight, 9.7 lbs. Imported 2001-2012.

	$1,650	$1,400	$1,150	$950	$750	$500	$325

Last MSR was $1,945.

* **LG 300 XT Alutec Evolution** – .177 cal., similar to Model LG 300 Alutec, except has all black finish with non-slip film coating, aluminum stock with adj. cheek piece, adj. and tiltable alloy buttplate, interchangable, adj. pistol grip, adj. forearm, adj. chrome-molybdenum steel trigger, precision diopter rear sight, 9.7 lbs. Mfg. 2006-2008.

	$1,875	$1,600	$1,325	$1,100	$850	$575	$375

* **LG 300 FT Dominator (Field Target)** – .177 cal., similar to Model LG 300, except has 19.3 in. barrel and 9.48 lbs. laminated wood stock or 10.7 lbs. aluminum stock. Mfg. 2001-2010.

	$1,675	$1,425	$1,175	$975	$750	$500	$325

Last MSR was $1,975.

Add $280 for aluminum stock.

* **LG 300 XT Anatomic** – .177 cal., similar to Model LG 300, except has 19.3 in. barrel and 9.48 lbs. fully adjustable laminated wood stock. Mfg. 2009-2012.

	$2,400	$2,050	$1,675	$1,400	$1,075	$725	$475

Last MSR was $2,825.

* **LG 300 Hunter/LG 300 XT Hunter** – .177 cal., similar to Model LG 300, except with brown laminated wood stock with adj. cheek piece, no sight, 935 FPS, 7.6 lbs. Mfg. 2004-2009.

	$1,700	$1,450	$1,175	$975	$750	$500	$350

* **LG300 Junior** – .177 cal., similar to Model LG 300, except has beech stock with adj. cheek piece, adj. and tilting alloy buttplate, interchangable, adj. pistol grip, adj. forearm, chrome-molybdenum steel trigger, precision diopter rear sight, 9.7 lbs. Mfg. 2001-2009.

	$1,500	$1,275	$1,050	$875	$675	$450	$300

Add $35 for left-hand variation.

GRADING	100%	95%	90%	80%	60%	40%	20%

* LG 300 XT Junior – .177 cal., PCP, BA, SS, 16.54 in. rifled barrel, carbon fiber barrel jacket, post globe front and adj. diopter rear sights, removable aluminum air reservoir with integral manometer (air pressure gauge), two stage adj. trigger, ambidextrous laminated adj. stock with adj. rubber buttpad and adj. cheekpiece, ambidextrous grip, 39.76 in. OAL, 7.72 lbs. Imported 2001-2009, re-introduced 2013.

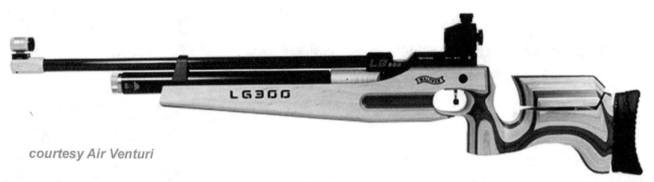

courtesy Air Venturi

MSR $1,595	$1,350	$1,200	$1,075	$875	$675	N/A	N/A

* LG 300 XT Carbontec – .177 cal., similar to Model LG 300, except anti-vibration system, 25.5 in. rifled steel barrel with carbon fiber sleeve, scaled BBL weight, Centra front sight, 41.7 in. OAL, carbon stock, 10.7 lbs. Mfg. 2004-09.

	$3,400	$2,850	$2,350	$1,950	$1,525	$1,000	$675

LG400 ALUTEC BASIC – .177 cal., CO_2, silver aluminum cylinder with pressure gauge, 600 shot, aluminum stock with wide range of settings, Protouch grip, two-stage and dry-firing trigger, Basic competition sights, standard match diopter, standard foresight holder, carbon barrel jacket, ergonomically shaped loading lever, QuickClean air filter, ECO valve technology, light metal buttplate, adj. Protouch wooden forend, includes plastic case, approx. 9 lbs. New 2011.

MSR $2,115	$1,800	$1,575	$1,450	$1,175	$900	N/A	N/A

LG400 ALUTEC BASIC SENIOR – .177 cal., CO_2, similar to the LG400 Alutec Basic, except has MAXI steel cylinder with pressure gauge, 800 shot, approx. 9.4 lbs. New 2011.

Please contact the importer directly for pricing and availability on this model.

LG400 ALUTEC COMPETITION – .177 cal., CO_2, silver aluminum cylinder with pressure gauge, 600 shot, aluminum stock with wide range of settings, 3D grip with memory effect, two-stage and dry-firing trigger, Insight Out match diopter sights, carbon barrel jacket, ergonomically shaped loading lever, QuickClean air filter, equalizer magnet absorber system, ECO valve technology, light metal buttplate, aluminum buttstock with MEC Contact II, Centra Score foresight holder, loading status indicator, adj. Protouch wooden forend, includes plastic case, approx. 9 lbs. 4 oz. New 2011.

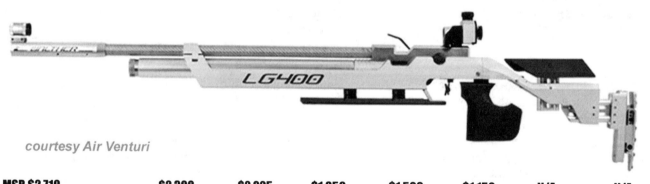

courtesy Air Venturi

MSR $2,710	$2,300	$2,025	$1,850	$1,500	$1,150	N/A	N/A

LG400 ALUTEC COMPETITION SENIOR – .177 cal., CO_2, similar to the LG400 Alutec Competition, except has MAXI steel cylinder with pressure gauge, 800 shot, approx. 11 lbs. 7 oz. New 2011.

Please contact the importer directly for pricing and availability on this model.

LG400 ALUTEC EXPERT – .177 cal., CO_2, silver aluminum cylinder with pressure gauge, 600 shot, aluminum stock with wide range of settings, 3D grip with memory effect, two-stage and dry-firing trigger, Insight Out match diopter sights, carbon barrel jacket, ergonomically shaped loading lever, QuickClean air filter, equalizer magnet absorber system, ECO valve technology, light metal buttplate, aluminum buttstock with MEC Contact II, Centra Score foresight holder, loading status indicator, adj. Protouch wooden forend with double joint, long cheek piece rods, short buttplate rods, Centra raised line of sight Block Club, includes plastic case, approx. 9 lbs. 7 oz. New 2011.

MSR $3,175	$2,700	$2,375	$2,150	$1,750	$1,325	N/A	N/A

GRADING	100%	95%	90%	80%	60%	40%	20%

LG400 ALUTEC EXPERT SENIOR – .177 cal., CO_2, similar to the LG400 Alutec Expert Senior, except has MAXI steel cylinder with pressure gauge, 800 shot, approx. 11 lbs. 10 oz. New 2011.

Please contact the importer directly for pricing and availability on this model.

LG400 ANATOMIC EXPERT – .177 cal., CO_2, aluminum cylinder with pressure gauge, 600 shot, 3D grip with memory effect, two-stage and dry-firing trigger, Insight Out match diopter sights, carbon barrel jacket, ergonomically shaped loading lever, QuickClean air filter, equalizer magnet absorber system, ECO valve technology, blue laminated wood stock, MEC aluminum buttplate Contact III, Centra Score foresight holder, loading status indicator, laminated wood forend with double joint, short cheek piece rods, short buttplate rods, Centra raised line of sight Block Club, includes plastic case, approx. 9 lbs. New 2011.

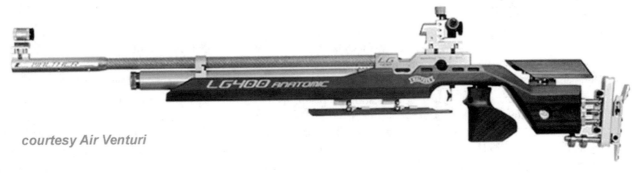

courtesy Air Venturi

MSR $3,530	$3,000	$2,650	$2,400	$1,950	$1,475	N/A	N/A

LG400 ANATOMIC SENIOR – .177 cal., CO_2, similar to the LG400 Anatomic Expert, except has MAXI steel cylinder with pressure gauge, 800 shot, approx. 11 lbs. 7 oz. New 2011.

Please contact the importer directly for pricing and availability on this model.

PANTHER – .177 cal., similar to Jaguar, except barrel cocking. New 1994.

	$225	$190	$160	$130	$100	$65	$45

Add 25% for aperture sight.
Add 20% for box, accessories, and factory papers.

TALON MAGNUM – .177, .22, or .25 (new 2011) cal., BBC, SP, SS, 19.75 in. rifled steel BBL with muzzle brake, 1200/1000 FPS, black finish, checkered black synthetic Monte Carlo stock with adj. rubber recoil pad, checkered grip and forearm, automatic safety, adj. rear and fixed front Truglo fiber optic sights, 3-9x32 scope with mounts, raised cheek piece, 49 in. OAL, 8.25 lbs. Mfg. 2008-2012.

courtesy Umarex USA

	$215	$185	$150	$125	$95	$65	$45

Last MSR was $256.

WARRIOR

For information on Warrior, see Accles & Shelvoke Ltd. in the "A" section.

WEBLEY & SCOTT, LTD.

Current trademark and airgun manufacturer located in Dartmouth, U.K., with headquarters located in Luzern, Switzerland beginning 2010. Previously located in West Midlands, England, with history dating back to 1790, and Birmingham, England. Currently imported by Webley & Scott USA, located in Reno, NV.

Webley & Scott, Ltd. went into receivership late 2005. In March, 2006 the Webley & Scott, Ltd. trademark was purchased by Airgunsport, a leading airgun supplier for the UK. Since the re-organization and re-location Webley has released improved versions of a limited number of models. In June 2010, Webley announced the formation of a wholly-owned US subsidiary company, Webley & Scott, Inc., located in Millbrook, NY. Webley & Scott, Ltd. was previously (2008) exclusively imported/distributed by Legacy Sports International, located in Reno, NV, Airguns of Arizona, located in Gilbert, AZ, by Beeman

Precision Airguns, then located in Huntington Beach, CA, and by Pyramyd Air International, located in Warrensville Hts., OH. Contact the importer (see Trademark Index) for more information.

Webley joined with Venom Arms Company to form the Webley Venom Custom Shop that operated out of the Webley factory until it was closed in December 2005. The Custom Shop partnership opened a host of new design developments and manufacturing capabilities, offering airgun products and services including custom air rifles and tuning accessories. The Webley Venom team claimed that no project in the airgun market could be too daunting.

The authors and publisher wish to thank Gordon Bruce for his valuable assistance with the air pistols section, as well as John Atkins, Peter Colman, and Tim Saunders for their assistance with the rifle section information in this section of the *Blue Book of Airguns*. Bruce's 2001 book, *Webley Air Pistols*, is required reading. Ref: Hannusch, 1988 and AGNR - July 1988, Atkins, AG April, May, & June 1996.

For more information and current pricing on Webley & Scott firearms, please refer to the *Blue Book of Gun Values* by S.P. Fjestad (also available online).

Webley & Scott, LTD. 1790-1932

Webley reports that their roots go back to circa 1790. The name Webley has been associated with a wide variety of firearms, ranging from early percussion pistols and centerfire revolvers to much later military and police self-loading pistols. The current name dates to 1897, when the company amalgamated with shotgun manufacturers W & C Scott and Sons, becoming The Webley and Scott Revolver and Arms Company Ltd of Birmingham. The name was shortened in 1906 to the now familiar name of Webley and Scott Ltd.

Webley's airgun history began in 1910 when an interesting air pistol, with an in-line spring piston and barrel, was designed and patented by William Whiting, then director of Webley & Scott. At least one working example was constructed, but the gun never went into production. The first production Webley airgun was the Mark I air pistol designed by Douglas Johnstone and John Fearn. It was patented and appeared in 1924 and became an immediate success. Like the Webley & Scott firearms, these pistols were built of interchangeable parts of superior quality and the designs were internationally patented. In these new pistols, placing the barrel over the spring chamber allowed a relatively long barrel in a compact gun. The Mark I was soon followed by a target model, the Mark II Deluxe version. A smaller air pistol, the Junior, was introduced in 1929 to give younger shooters a more economical version. It had a smoothbore barrel for firing reusable darts for economy of use. These young users soon were eager to acquire the more advanced Webley models. Shortly after the Junior air pistol had been launched, Webley & Scott brought out the more powerful Senior air pistol which established a basic pattern for future manufacture. Its improved method for cocking the air chamber piston, plus the use of the stirrup barrel latch, now a Webley hallmark, contributed to the enduring popularity of the design.

Success of the Webley air pistols encouraged Webley to introduce the Mark I air rifle, basically an extended version of the Mark II Target air pistol. The Mark I air rifle was well received but was produced in limited numbers only from 1926 to 1929. A much improved, larger version, the Service Air Rifle Mark II, was introduced in 1932. Acknowledged to be the finest of its type, it dominated the British airgun scene for many years. The new model featured an airtight barrel locking collar and an additional safety sear, but its most outstanding feature was a quick-change barrel system.

Webley & Scott, LTD. 1932-1979

A major shift in appearance of the Mark I and Senior air pistols occurred in 1935 when Webley & Scott introduced the "New Model" series. The key difference was an increase in the vertical grip angle from 100 to 120 degrees. This, and a slightly shorter barrel, created a more contemporary look and considerably improved their balance and gave them a much more natural pointing characteristic. The advent of war in 1939 caused a sudden end to commercial manufacture at the Webley plant and created a five-year gap in all commercial manufacture until the production of airguns was resumed in 1946. The New Model pistol styling, but with a grip angle of only 110 degrees, was extended to the Junior air pistol when airgun production resumed.

Post-WWII activities also included new designs for the Webley air rifles. The original barrel-cocking linkage design was replaced in 1947 by an under lever cocking system in the Mark III, Junior, and Jaguar air rifles. These were followed by the introduction of the Ranger air rifle in 1954.

The original Webley factory site at Weaman Street, Birmingham, which had survived two world wars, was vacated during 1958 and the entire operation moved to Park Lane, Handsworth. In 1960, the Senior air pistol was replaced by the Premier. The Premier was virtually identical to its predecessor but featured a series of minor refinements. These series were identified in an alphabetical sequence, starting with model A in 1960 and progressing to model F in 1975. A redesigned version of the Junior air pistol, using new lighter alloy castings, was designated the Junior Mk. II. This was followed by the Premier Mk.II, of similar construction. That model enjoyed only a brief production run.

During the 1970s, Webley introduced the barrel-cocking Hawk, Tomahawk, Victor, Vulcan and Valiant air rifles and the side-lever cocking Osprey and Supertarget air rifles. An improved piston seal development, which helped to reduce piston rebound, was patented in 1979. The improved seal became an important feature of the Vulcan and subsequent rifle models.

To compete with new foreign models, more modern styling was added to the air pistol line in the mid-1970s with the introduction of the Hurricane and its slightly less powerful junior mate, the Typhoon. In 1977, Webley's largest customer at that time, the Beeman Precision Airgun Company in the United States, requested a more compact version. The resulting Tempest, designed by Paul Bednall in the Webley technical department, that more closely followed the size and balance of the more traditional Webley air pistols was introduced in 1979 and soon became the most popular model of the series.

GRADING	100%	95%	90%	80%	60%	40%	20%

Webley & Scott, LTD. 1979-To Date

As noted by Walther (1984 - see "Airgun Literature Review" section in the 3rd edition, *Blue Book of Airguns*), Webley and Beeman mutually benefited by forming additional links in the 1980s. Beeman expanded their Webley offerings and helped design some Webley airguns, most notably the Beeman C1 air rifle. Webley incorporated Beeman Silver Jet pellets and several of their accessories, such as special air pistol grips, into the Webley international promotions. The Beeman/Webley association became even closer as Webley's president, Keith Faulkner, became Beeman's vice president and Harold Resuggan, then Webley's very talented head engineer, moved up to head Webley.

A basic shift in Webley's business base was completed in 1979 when the company discontinued the manufacture of all firearms. The manufacture of Webley airguns continued at Handsworth until 1984, when the company moved to a modern industrial site at Rednal, South Birmingham, England. Various additions to the Webley line of air rifles during the 1980s included the Viscount, Tracker, Omega, Airwolf, and Eclipse models, while manufacture of air pistols was limited to the Hurricane and Tempest. These two pistols continue to feature the same forward-swing barrel-cocking system as those produced more than seventy years earlier, a sound testament to its efficiency. In 1994, Webley expanded into the mass market arena by adding completely fresh designs, the Nemesis, a single-stroke pneumatic air pistol and the Stinger, a spring-piston, repeating BB pistol, in 1996.

The twenty-first century finds Webley rapidly evolving. Air rifles, ranging from conventional barrel-cocking, spring piston models to the latest pre-charged pneumatic and CO_2 guns are now the mainstay of the company. The latest state-of-the-art, computer-driven production stations have replaced the cumbersome networks of separate huge machines powered by noisy forests of immense overhead shafts, wheels, and belts.

PISTOLS

All pistols have rifled barrels, unless otherwise noted. Webley airguns are a large and complex group. It is strongly advised that you consult the *Webley Air Pistols* book mentioned above for additional details and illustrations.

Add 25-40% for original factory box.
Add 50-100% for fitted case.
Add 100-200% for factory cut-away display models with moving parts.
Add 50-100% for factory nickel plating, not offered in all models, unless otherwise noted.
Add 25-75% for factory etching.

ALECTO – .177 or .22 cal., patented technology multi-stroke pneumatic, black finish, right or left hand, 7.13 in. barrel with (Ultra Model) or w/o muzzle brake, accessory rail, adj. trigger, adj. grip, 2.4 lbs. New 2009.

courtesy Webley & Scott, LTD.

MSR $360	$300	$270	$245	$200	$150	N/A	N/A

GnAT – .177 darts, slugs, pellets, or corks, SP, SS, push-barrel cocking, black alloy and plastic, smoothbore barrel, muzzle nut for shooting corks. Mfg. 2004-05.

courtesy Beeman Collection

	N/A	$65	$50	$40	$30	$25	$15

GRADING	100%	95%	90%	80%	60%	40%	20%

HURRICANE – .177 or .22 cal., TL, SP, SS, 420/330 FPS, plastic grips with RH thumbrest, adj. rear sight with replacement adapter for scope mounting, hooded front sight, aluminum grip frame cast around steel body tube, RH manual safety, black epoxy finish, 8 in. button rifled barrel, 11.2 in. OAL, 38 oz.

* ***Hurricane Variant 1*** – forearm marked "HURRICANE", barrel housing (under front sight) 2.75 in. Mfg. 1975-1990.

N/A	$215	$170	$140	$105	$75	$45

Add 5% for simulated wood grips (not available in USA).

Add 10% for wood grips.

Add 15% for finger groove Beeman "combat" wood grips.

Add 20% for Beeman factory markings with San Rafael address.

Add 10% for Beeman factory markings with Santa Rosa address.

Add 10% for lack of F in pentagon mark ("little hut") which indicated lower power for European market.

Add 20% for large deluxe factory box with form fitting depressions, including depression for mounted scope, in hard plastic shell with red flocked surface.

Add 10% for factory box with molded white foam support block.

* ***Hurricane Variant 2*** – forearm marked "WEBLEY HURRICANE", barrel housing 2.187 in. with full length flattop. Mfg. 1990-2005.

N/A	$195	$155	$130	$100	$65	$45

Add 5% for simulated wood grips (not available in USA).

Add 10% for wood grips.

Add 15% for finger groove Beeman "combat" wood grips.

Add 20% for Beeman factory markings with San Rafael address.

Add 10% for lack of F in pentagon mark ("little hut") which indicated lower power for European market.

Add 20% for large deluxe factory box with form fitting depressions, including depression for mounted scope, in hard plastic shell with red flocked surface.

Add 10% for factory box with molded white foam support block.

JUNIOR – .177 cal., TL, SP, SS, metal grips with screw head on RH side, 100-degree grip slant ("straight grip"), fixed rear sight, sliding barrel latch, no safety, 6.5 in. smoothbore barrel for darts, 287 FPS, 7.75 in. OAL, 24 oz. Mfg. 1929-1938.

courtesy Gordon Bruce

N/A	$350	$280	$230	$175	$125	$70

Add 20% for adjustable rear sight.

Add 20-50% for original wood grips with vertical grooves, grip screw head on LH side.

Subtract 5% for final version with 6.25 in. barrel (protrudes beyond body tube).

* ***Junior New Model*** – .177 cal., TL, SP, SS, Bakelite grips, 110-degree grip slant, adj. rear sight, sliding barrel latch, 6.125 in. smoothbore barrel for darts, 290 FPS, blued, no safety, 7.75 in. OAL, 24 oz. Mfg. 1945-1973.

courtesy Gordon Bruce

N/A	$225	$180	$145	$110	$80	$45

Add 5% for early versions with grip plate "spur" that extends about 0.25 inches from the upper forward edge of the Bakelite grip plates.

Add 5% for good condition leather breech seal (barrel joint washer) in pre-1960 production.

GRADING	100%	95%	90%	80%	60%	40%	20%

Subtract 20% for Suncorite 243 paint finish (post-1970).

Add 40% for factory nickel or chrome finish (uncommon on Junior models).

* **Junior Mark II** – .177 cal., TL, SP, SS, aluminum grip frame cast around steel body tube, Bakelite grips, rhombus-shaped logo with "BIRMID" mark and a casting number under grips, stirrup barrel latch, black epoxy coating, adj. rear sight, no safety, 6.125 in. barrel, 290 FPS, 8 in. OAL, 23 oz. Approx. 31,750 mfg. 1973-76.

courtesy Gordon Bruce

	N/A	$175	$140	$115	$85	$60	$35

Add 50% for low rear sight (barrel latch visible thru aperture), caused pre-Sept 1973 pistols to shoot low.

Add 10% for smoothbore (pre-August 1975).

Add 15% for seven-groove broached rifling (special order, pre-August 1975).

This model introduced the massive aluminum grip frame cast around steel body tube characteristic of Webley pistols. BIRMID mark for Birmingham Aluminium Casting Company Ltd.

MARK I – .177 or .22 cal., TL, SP, SS, 367/273 FPS, wood grips, adj. rear sight, 100-degree grip slant ("straight grip"), manual safety, 8.5 in. OAL, 30 oz. Mfg. 1924-1935.

* **Mark I First Series - Variant 1** – single spring clip barrel catch on right side of breech block, no trigger adj. screw on forward edge of trigger guard.

Scarcity precludes accurate pricing.

* **Mark I First Series - Variant 2** – dual spring clip barrel catch on each side of breech block, no trigger adj. screw on forward edge of trigger guard.

Scarcity precludes accurate pricing.

* **Mark I Second Series** – sliding barrel catch on top of breech block, no trigger adj. screw on forward edge of trigger guard.

courtesy Gordon Bruce

	N/A	$425	$325	$270	$205	$145	$85

* **Mark I Third Series** – trigger adj. screw on forward edge of trigger guard.

courtesy Beeman Collection

	N/A	$400	$325	$255	$195	$140	$80

GRADING	100%	95%	90%	80%	60%	40%	20%

* **Mark I Fourth Series** – trigger adj. screw on forward edge of trigger guard, U.S. Patent notice on RS, barrel hinge screw with retainer.

	N/A	$400	$325	$255	$195	$140	$80

* **Mark I Fifth Series** – locking screw on LH side for cone-head trigger adj. screw.

	N/A	$400	$325	$255	$195	$140	$80

* **Mark I Sixth Series** – flanged screw plug at front end of body cylinder provided front end access to mainspring and piston assembly.

	N/A	$400	$325	$255	$195	$140	$80

MARK I NEW MODEL – .177 and .22 cal., TL, SP, SS, 345/293 FPS, Bakelite grips, blued, adj. rear sight, introduced the "New Model" 120-degree angle grip, 8.5 in. OAL, 30 oz. Mfg. 1935-1964.

* **Mark I New Model Pre-WWII** – blued trigger, barrel without thicker section ahead of rear sight.

courtesy Gordon Bruce

	N/A	$295	$235	$190	$145	$105	$60

Add 20% for smooth bore barrel.

Add 5% for diamond knurling on barrel. Late 1939.

Add 10% for unmarked rear breech cap with small retaining screw below sight.

Add 10% for black bakelite grips without Webley name.

* **Mark I New Model Post-WWII** – introduced batch numbers instead of serial numbers (none exceed approx. 6000), barrel with 2.4 in. thicker reinforced section with straight knurling.

	N/A	$215	$170	$140	$105	$75	$45

Add 5% for unmarked rear breech cap.

MARK II TARGET – .177 or .22 cal., TL, SP, SS, 410/325 FPS, vulcanite grips, adj. rear sight, barrel latch secured by screw instead of pin, 100-degree grip slant ("straight grip"), improved piston seal, sliding barrel latch, manual safety, 8.5 in. OAL, 28 oz. Mfg. 1925-1930.

* **Mark II Target - First Pattern** – spring guide recessed into front end of body tube, fillister head trigger adj. screw without locking screw.

courtesy Gordon Bruce

	N/A	$695	$525	$425	$325	$230	$130

Add 100%-200% for special order models made in 1928, chased with scroll engraving, silver plated, mother-of-pearl grips.

* **Mark II Target - Standard Pattern** – spring guide with flange to match diameter of front end of body tube, cone head trigger adj. screw with LH locking screw.

	N/A	$500	$400	$325	$245	$175	$100

Add 100%-200% for special order models made in 1928, chased with scroll engraving, silver plated, mother-of-pearl grips.

GRADING	100%	95%	90%	80%	60%	40%	20%

* *Mark II Target - Final Pattern* – walnut grips, Stoeger address on RH side.

courtesy Howard Collection

	N/A	$695	$525	$425	$325	$230	$130

Add 100%-200% for special order models made in 1928, chased with scroll engraving, silver plated, mother-of-pearl grips.

NEMESIS – .177 or .22 cal. pellets, TL, SP, SS, 385/300 FPS, two-stage adj. trigger, black or brushed chrome finish, manual safety, adj. sights, integral scope rail, 2.2 lbs. Mfg. 1995-2005.

courtesy Gordon Bruce

$175	$140	$115	$95	$75	$50	$35

Add 10% for brushed chrome finish.

PREMIER – .177 or .22 cal., TL, SP, SS, 350/310 FPS, Bakelite grips, blued finish, adj. rear sight, no safety, 8.5 in. OAL, 37 oz. Last of the traditional forged steel blued Webley air pistols. Six variation series were produced, fortunately each series was marked with a capital letter, starting with A and ending with F, stamped on the LH side of the frame, usually near the trigger guard. Mfg. 1964-1975.

courtesy Beeman Collection

	N/A	$295	$235	$190	$145	$105	$60

Subtract 20% for painted finish on series E and F.

Details of each series are given in Bruce (2001). Plated finishes were not provided by the factory during the period of Premier production.

GRADING	100%	95%	90%	80%	60%	40%	20%

* ***Premier MKII*** – .177 or .22 cal., TL, SP, SS, 350/310 FPS, Bakelite grips, blued finish, adj. rear sight, no safety, 8.5 in. OAL, 37 oz. series A through F, production date stamped (LH side of grip frame under grips). Mfg. 1964-1975.

courtesy Beeman Collection

	N/A	$375	$290	$235	$180	$130	$75

Add 25% for barrel forged from one piece of steel (identified by ring-like raised area about 1 in. behind front sight), only 1,700 produced in 1976. Most production had muzzle end of barrel in a 1.48 in. muzzle shroud which incorporates the front sight. Add 20% for Beeman factory markings.

SENIOR – .177 or .22 cal., vulcanite grips, blued, adj. rear sight, stirrup barrel latch, 100-degree grip slant ("straight grip"), no safety, 416/330 FPS, 8.5 in. OAL, 33 oz. Mfg. 1930-35.

The Senior Model introduced the stirrup barrel latch from Webley revolvers to the air pistols.

* ***Senior First Pattern*** – trigger adj. screw at forward end of trigger guard.

courtesy Gordon Bruce

	N/A	$475	$400	$325	$240	$170	$95

Add 25% for A.F. Stoeger marking on RH side of air cylinder with checkered walnut grip.
Add 10% for flat cocking links which obscured hole in top of air cylinder. Replaced by forward link with wings which operated upon wedge-shaped small rear link.

* ***Senior Second Pattern*** – no trigger adj. screw.

courtesy Gordon Bruce

	N/A	$575	$450	$375	$285	$200	$115

Add 25% for A.F. Stoeger marking on RH side of air cylinder with checkered walnut grip.
Add 10% for flat cocking links which obscured hole in top of air cylinder. Replaced by forward link with wings which operated upon wedge-shaped small rear link.

GRADING	100%	95%	90%	80%	60%	40%	20%

* **Senior New Model** – .177 or .22 cal., TL, SP, SS, 416/330 FPS, Bakelite grips, blue finish, adj. rear sight, no safety, 8.5 in overall, 33 oz. Mfg. 1935-1964.

courtesy Gordon Bruce

Judged to be the best of the pre-WWII Webley air pistols. Over the thirty-year production span of this model, there were at least fourteen variations, different finishes, barrels, etc. Consult Bruce (2001) for details.

»**Senior New Model Pre-WWII** – plain exterior of barrel ahead of rear sight - a few 1939 guns had knurled barrels, slim trigger, grips w/o Webley name.

	N/A	$495	$375	$300	$235	$165	$95

Add 30% for original nickel plating.
Add 5% for unmarked rear breech cap.
Add 30% for extra long target barrel.

»**Senior New Model Post-WWII** – cross knurling on barrel, thick trigger, Webley name on grips.

	N/A	$295	$235	$190	$145	$105	$60

Add 30% for original nickel plating.
Add 5% for unmarked rear breech cap.
Add 30% for extra long target barrel.

STINGER – BB/.175 cal., slide action dual-cocking, SP, 220 FPS, forty-five-shot internal mag., smoothbore, fixed sights with integral scope rail, black finish. Mfg. 2001-05.

$60	$50	$40	$35	$25	$20	$10

TEMPEST – .177 or .22 cal., TL, SP, SS, 420/330 FPS, plastic grips with RH thumb rest, adj. rear sight, aluminum grip frame cast around steel body tube, compact version of Hurricane, RH manual safety, 6.87 in. button rifled barrel, black epoxy finish, 9.2 in. OAL, 32 oz.

Tempest bodies were produced by grinding off the rear section of Hurricane castings. Bruce (2001) refers to the Tempest as "the most charismatic of all Webley air pistols." (Webley offered "Beeman Accessories," such as special grips, for the Tempest and Hurricane in their factory leaflets in England and other world markets.)

* **Tempest Variant 1** – forearm marked "TEMPEST". Mfg. 1979-1981.

	N/A	$215	$170	$140	$105	$75	$45

Add 5% for simulated wood grips (not sold in USA).
Add 10% for Beeman wood grips.
Add 15% for finger groove Beeman "combat" wood grips.
Add 20% for Beeman factory markings with San Rafael address (rare).
Add 20% for large factory box 11.6 x 8.6 inches, black with logo.
Add 10% for medium factory box 10.2 x 6.6 inches, black with logo.

* **Tempest Variant 2** – forearm marked "WEBLEY TEMPEST", Beeman versions of this variation marked with Beeman name and address and "TEMPEST". Mfg. 1981-2005.

	N/A	$215	$170	$140	$105	$75	$45

Add 5% for simulated wood grips. (not sold in USA)
Add 10% for Beeman wood grips.
Add 15% for finger groove Beeman "combat" wood grips.
Add 20% for Beeman factory markings with San Rafael address (rare).
Add 10% for Beeman factory markings with Santa Rosa address.
Add 20% for large factory box, 11.6 x 8.6 inches, black with logo.
Add 10% for medium factory box, 10.2 x 6.6 inches, black with logo.

GRADING	100%	95%	90%	80%	60%	40%	20%

TEMPEST (CURRENT MFG.) – .177 or .22 cal., 6.89 in. barrel, black finish, ergonomic grips, 2 lbs. New 2010.

courtesy Webley & Scott, LTD.

MSR $270	$230	$205	$185	$150	$115	N/A	N/A

Add $30 for limited edition Centennial model with wood and leather carrying case and certificate of authenticity.

TYPHOON (DISC.) – .177 or .22 cal., TL, SP, SS, similar to Hurricane, except intended for youth and persons with smaller hands, 360/280 FPS, plastic grips, adj. rear sight, 11.2 in. OAL, 37.5 oz. Approx. 14,214 mfg. 1987-1992.

courtesy Gordon Bruce

	$225	$190	$160	$130	$100	$65	$45

This model is uncommon in the USA, as it was not regularly imported. Warning: early versions could fire upon release of safety; guns should be returned to Webley distributor for correction. Corrected guns have a satin chrome finish on the trigger.

TYPHOON (CURRENT MFG.) – .177 or .22 cal., BBC, SP, SS, 420/330 FPS, synthetic grip frame around steel body tube, 6.87 in. rifled steel BBL, blue finish, 14.5 in. OAL, 3.2 lbs. Mfg. 2008-current.

courtesy Webley

MSR $150	$130	$115	$100	$85	$65	N/A	N/A

RIFLES

AXSOR – .177 or .22 cal., PCP, bolt action loading, eight-shot rotary magazine, 1000/800 FPS, 19.7 in. barrel, walnut or beech Monte Carlo stock, recoil pad, two-stage adj. trigger, integral scope grooves, 39.5 in. overall, 6 lbs. Mfg. 1998-2000.

courtesy Howard Collection

	$550	$475	$375	$325	$250	$165	$110

Add 10% for walnut stock.

Last MSR was $625.

GRADING	100%	95%	90%	80%	60%	40%	20%

BEARCUB – .177 cal., BBC, SP, SS, 915 FPS, 13 in. barrel, single stage adj. trigger, manual safety, beech stock with PG, cheek piece, forearm ends at barrel pivot, threaded muzzle weight, PTFE, nylon Spring Tamer spring guide, 37.8 in. OAL, 7.2 lbs. Mfg. for Beeman 1995-1998.

	$255	$215	$180	$150	$115	$75	$50

Last MSR was $325.

The muzzle weight threaded for silencer on this model (if silencer/sound moderator is present), transfer to qualified buyer requires $200 federal tax in USA.

BLACKHAWK – .177 or .22 cal., checkered brown thumbhole polystock, TruGlo focussed vision sight system, tuned vibration absorber, adj. two-stage trigger, easy-touch thumb rest with quick safety release, Powr-lok mainspring metallurgy and non-slip forend and grip. New 2012.

courtesy Webley & Scott, LTD.

MSR $235	$200	$175	$160	$130	$100	N/A	N/A

Add $15 for 3-9x40 Nikko Stirling scope.

CARBINE C1 – .177 or .22 cal., SP, BBC, SS, 830/660 FPS, slim stock with straight wrist, PTFE, "Spring Tamer" nylon spring guide, rubber buttplate, scope grooves, no safety, 38.2 in. OAL, 6.3 lbs. Mfg. 1981-1996.

courtesy Beeman Collection

	$250	$215	$175	$145	$115	$75	$50

Last MSR was $290.

Subtract 10% for manual safety in later versions.

Designed by Robert Beeman for fast handling in the hunting field. USA serial numbers began at 800,000.

COBRA – .177 or .22 cal., PCP, BA, multi-shot. Mfg. 2009-disc.

	$850	$725	$600	$500	$375	$255	$170

DOMIN8TOR – .177 or .22 cal., BBC, SP, SS 1250/1000 FPS, 17.5 in. barrel, two-stage adj. trigger, integral scope grooves, low-profile sights, checkered wood or TH synthetic Monte Carlo stock with recoil pad, 46.5 in. OAL, 8.2 lbs. Mfg. 2008- 2010.

	$400	$350	$280	$230	$180	$120	$80

Add $90 for wood stock.

ECLIPSE – .177, .22, or .25 cal., SP, UL, SS, fully opening breech loading hatch allows direct seating of pellet in chamber, 975/710/620 FPS MV, deluxe Monte Carlo stock, cut checkering, rubber buttplate and grip cap w/white line spacers, PTFE, muzzle threaded for Beeman Air Tamer or Webley Silencer, automatic safety, 44 in. OAL, 7.9 lbs. Mfg. 1990-96.

	$350	$300	$245	$205	$160	$105	$70

Last MSR was $510.

Add 25% for .25 caliber.
Add 10% for Air Tamer (muzzle unit without baffles).
Add 10% for Webley Silencer.

The muzzle threaded for silencer on this model (if silencer is present), transfer to qualified buyer requires $200 federal tax in USA.

EXCEL – .177 or .22 cal., BBC, 870/660 FPS, 11.37 (carbine) or 17.5 in. barrel, integral scope grooves, open sights, beech stock, 7 lbs. Disc. 2000.

	$175	$150	$125	$100	$80	$50	$35

Last MSR was $215.

GRADING	100%	95%	90%	80%	60%	40%	20%

FALCON – .177 or .22 cal., SP, BBC, SS, 550/500 FPS, SN hidden by cocking arm when closed, scope ramp welded to body tube, all metal parts, Webley medallion inletted into LHS buttstock, no safety, 41 in. OAL, 6 lbs. Mfg. 1960-1970.

	$150	$130	$105	$85	$70	$45	$30

Subtract 10% for no medallion.

FX2000 – .177 or .22 cal., PCP, 1000/800 FPS, bolt action loading, eight-shot magazine, 19.7 in. match quality choked barrel, beech or walnut stock, two-stage adj. trigger, integral pressure gauge, 6.6 lbs. New 2000.

courtesy Howard Collection

	$1,050	$900	$725	$600	$475	$325	$210

Add 15% for walnut stock.

* **FX2000 Field Target** – .22 cal., similar to FX2000, except has Field Target competition black walnut stock with adj. cheek piece and buttplate, 1000 FPS. Mfg. 2002-2004.

	$1,100	$925	$775	$650	$500	$325	$220

* **FX2000 Hunter SK** – .22 cal., similar to FX2000, except threaded for noise suppressor, two-stage adj. trigger, walnut skeleton stock. New 2000.

	$1,100	$925	$775	$650	$500	$325	$220

Add 15% for High-Power model (suppressor requires $200 federal tax in the USA).

HAWK – .177 or .22 cal., BBC, SP, SS, interchangeable barrels, 40-41 in. OAL, approx. 6.5 lbs.

* **Hawk Mk I** – angular stock lines, forearm with forward bulge, interchangeable barrels. Mfg. 1971-74.

	$160	$135	$110	$95	$70	$50	$30

Add 20% for extra interchangeable barrel.

* **Hawk Mk II** – smooth stock lines, interchangeable barrels. Mfg. 1974-77.

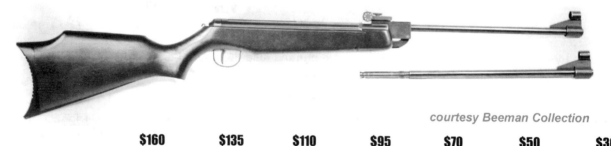

courtesy Beeman Collection

	$160	$135	$110	$95	$70	$50	$30

Add 20% for extra interchangeable barrel.

Most specimens in USA were diverted by Beeman Company from shipments which failed to reach agents of the Shah of Iran.

* **Hawk Mk III** – fixed barrel. Mfg. 1977-79.

	$160	$135	$110	$95	$70	$50	$30

JAGUAR – .177 or .22 cal., SP, BBC, SS, 500 FPS .177, sheetmetal "tinplate construction," sheetmetal barrel shroud, scope ramp (early with dumb-bell shape, later with parallel sides), early versions with finger grooves on forearm, no safety, 36.25 in. (early), 39 in. (later) OAL, 3.75 lbs. Mfg. 1940s to late 1970s.

courtesy Beeman Collection

	$150	$130	$105	$85	$70	$45	$30

GRADING	100%	95%	90%	80%	60%	40%	20%

Subtract 10% for early versions.

Some parts interchangeable with Webley Junior and Milbro Diana 22 air rifles.

JAGUAR (2008) – .177 or .22 cal., SP, BBC, SS, 1000/800 FPS, rifled steel BBL, adj. TruGlo fiber optic sights, anti-bear trap cocking safety, OD green molded synthetic stock with recoil pad, 44 in. OAL, 7.3 lbs. Mfg. 2008-2010.

	100%	95%	90%	80%	60%	40%	20%
	$140	$120	$100	$80	$65	$40	$30

JUNIOR – .177 cal., SP, BBC, SS, smoothbore (early) or rifled brass inner barrel, 405 FPS, sheetmetal barrel shroud, sheetmetal "tinplate construction," blued, no safety, 36.25 in. OAL, 3.25 lbs. Mfg. late 1940s to late 1960s.

	100%	95%	90%	80%	60%	40%	20%
	$150	$130	$105	$85	$70	$45	$30

Subtract 10% for smoothbore.

This model may have been made by Millard Bros.

LONGBOW/LONGBOW DELUXE – .177 or .22 cal., SP, BBC, SS, 850 FPS, short cylinder and barrel version of Tomahawk, scope grooves, no sights, Venom designed removable adj. trigger system, beech or walnut (Longbow Deluxe) checkered PG Monte Carlo stock with vented recoil pad, blue finish, ported muzzle brake. 39 in. OAL, 7.3 lbs. Mfg. 2003-disc.

	100%	95%	90%	80%	60%	40%	20%
	$400	$350	$280	$230	$180	$120	$80

Add 15% for Longbow Deluxe w/Walnut stock.

LONGBOW (2008) – .177 or .22 cal., SP, BBC, SS, 800/600 FPS, short cylinder and barrel version of Tomahawk, scope grooves, no sights, adj. trigger system, beech checkered PG Monte Carlo stock with vented recoil pad, blue finish, ported muzzle brake, 39 in. OAL, 7.3 lbs. Mfg. 2008-2010.

courtesy Webley

	100%	95%	90%	80%	60%	40%	20%
	$350	$300	$245	$205	$160	$105	$70

MARK I – .177 or .22 cal., BBC, SP, SS, a small rifle version of the Webley Mark I air pistol, barrel swings forward over compression chamber for cocking, interchangeable barrels, wood half stock, 34 in. OAL, 5.3 lbs. Approx. 1,500 mfg. 1926-29.

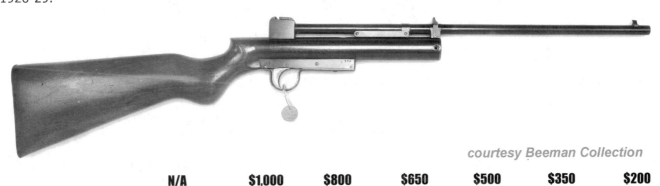

courtesy Beeman Collection

	100%	95%	90%	80%	60%	40%	20%
	N/A	$1,000	$800	$650	$500	$350	$200

Add 30% for .22 cal.

MARK II – .177, .22, or .25 cal., similar to Mark I, except larger, quick change barrels, bolt handle turns to open action and to cam barrel back into airtight connection with air vent, wood half stock, typical size: 43.8 in. OAL, approx. 6.8 lbs.

Important Note: there are many variations of the Webley Mark II rifles, rare versions add to the value. Essential information is available in Atkins, AG April, May, and June 1996.

GRADING	100%	95%	90%	80%	60%	40%	20%

* ***Mark II Version 1*** – .177 or .22 cal., L-shaped aperture sight, dovetail mounted barrel, leaf spring ahead of receiver which secures the barrel. S serial number prefix. Approx. 1,000 mfg. in 1932.

courtesy Beeman Collection

	N/A	$1,100	$875	$725	$550	$375	$220

Add 10% for extra .177 or .22 cal. barrel.
Add 100% for original factory box with inserts.
Add 150% for fitted factory case.

* ***Mark II Version 2*** – .177 or .22 cal., L-shaped aperture sight, side mounted push button for quick release of interchangeable barrels, S serial number prefix. Approx. 1,000 guns mfg. early 1933-34, approx. 2,000 total of version one and two mfg. circa 1935-38.

	N/A	$1,100	$875	$725	$550	$375	$220

Add 10% for extra .177 or .22 cal. barrel.
Add 20% for extra .25 cal. barrel (as added after 1937).
Add 100% for original factory box with inserts.
Add 150% for fitted factory case.

After 1937, Mark II Version 3 .25 cal. barrels were added to some Mark II Version 2 sets.

* ***Mark II Version 3*** – .177, .22, or .25 cal., U-shaped folding aperture sight mounted in center of receiver frame, push button barrel release, S serial number prefix from S2001 forward. Approx. 13,700 mfg. 1934 -1945 (sales ceased during WWII).

courtesy Beeman Collection

	N/A	$850	$675	$550	$425	$300	$170

Add 20% for extra .177 or .22 cal. barrel.
Add 30% for .25 caliber (The Webley "Rook and Rabbit Rifle", only mfg. 1937 and later).
Add 100% for original factory box with inserts.
Add 150% for fitted factory case.

MARK III SERIES – .177 or .22 cal., UL, SP, SS, tap loader. 42.25 to 43.5 in. OAL, 6.8 lbs. Mfg. 1947-1975.

Many British airgun enthusiasts consider the Mark III as one of the finest air rifles ever produced. This model became less complex and detailed as it evolved. Made in great numbers and great variety, this guide can only introduce this model. Fortunately, the basic variations generally can be identified by serial number. Additional info is available in the literature, esp. Hiller (1985).

* ***Mark III Series I*** – SN 1-2500. Standard: straight grooving in forearm, ribbed butt. Deluxe: hand checkered stock, ribbed buttplate. Mfg. 1947-49.

	N/A	$375	$300	$245	$185	$130	$75

Add 50% for Mark III Series I Deluxe.

* ***Mark III Series II*** – SN 2501-6000. Mfg. 1949-1957.

	$350	$300	$250	$210	$160	$110	$70

* ***Mark III Series III*** – SN 6001-42857. Mfg. 1957-1961.

	$325	$280	$230	$190	$150	$100	$65

* ***Mark III Series IV*** – SN 42858-46289. Mfg. 1961-64.

	$300	$255	$210	$175	$135	$90	$60

GRADING	100%	95%	90%	80%	60%	40%	20%

* Mark III Late Model Series – SN 46290 on. Mfg. 1964-1975.

	100%	95%	90%	80%	60%	40%	20%
	$300	$255	$210	$175	$135	$90	$60

MARK III SUPERTARGET (MODEL 2) – .177 or .22 cal., UL, SP, SS, tap loader, similar to Mark III, except fitted with Parker-Hale micrometer aperture sight, stamped "SUPERTARGET" on receiver (body tube, air chamber), 9.4 lbs. Mfg. 1963-1975.

	100%	95%	90%	80%	60%	40%	20%
	$500	$425	$350	$290	$225	$150	$100

NIMBUS – .177 cal., BBC, SP, SS, 570 FPS, beech stock with contoured comb, plastic buttplate, pressed steel trigger guard, adj. sights, scope grooves, push-button manual safety, junior size, economy level air rifle, imported from China. New 2004.

Please contact the importer directly for pricing and availability on this model.

OMEGA – .177 or .22 cal., SP, BBC, SS, PTFE and O-ring piston seal, 830/675 FPS, scope grooves, auto/manual safety, 42 in. OAL, 7.8 lbs. Mfg. 1989-1992.

	100%	95%	90%	80%	60%	40%	20%
	$225	$190	$160	$130	$100	$65	$45

Last MSR was $430

Add 20% for Beeman marking.

OSPREY – .177 or .22 cal., SL, SP, SS, tap loader, manual safety, 43 in. OAL, 7.3 lbs. Mfg. 1975-1990s.

	100%	95%	90%	80%	60%	40%	20%
	$150	$130	$105	$85	$70	$45	$30

Add 20% for Supertarget version with semi-match style stock, heavier.

PARADIGM – .177 or .22 cal., SSP. Mfg. 2010.

	100%	95%	90%	80%	60%	40%	20%
	$975	$825	$700	$575	$450	$295	$195

PATRIOT – .177, .22, or .25 cal., BBC, 1170/920/820 FPS, 17.5 in. barrel, two-stage adj. trigger, integral scope grooves, low-profile sights, walnut Monte Carlo stock with hand-checkered grip, recoil pad, 9 lbs.

	100%	95%	90%	80%	60%	40%	20%
	$575	$475	$400	$325	$255	$170	$115

Add 15% for Venom Edition with black walnut stock and gold plated trigger guard.

PATRIOT (CURRENT MFG.) – .177, .22, or .25 cal., BBC, SP, SS, 1170/920/820 FPS, 17.5 in. precision steel rifled barrel, POWR-LOK mainspring, two-stage adj. trigger, integral scope grooves, low-profile sights, walnut Monte Carlo stock with hand-checkered grip, recoil pad, 45.6 in. OAL, 9.6 lbs. Mfg. 2008-current.

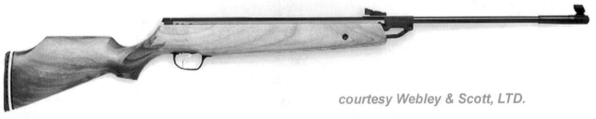

courtesy Webley & Scott, LTD.

MSR $360	100%	95%	90%	80%	60%	40%	20%
	$300	$270	$245	$200	$150	N/A	N/A

Add $15 for 4-12x50 Nikko Stirling scope.

RAIDER – .177 or .22 cal., PCP, 1000/800 FPS, BA, SS or two-shot magazine (.22 cal. only), Venom Custom designed beech or walnut stock, 7 lbs. Mfg. 2000-disc.

courtesy Webley

	100%	95%	90%	80%	60%	40%	20%
	$500	$425	$350	$285	$225	$150	$100

Add 15% for walnut stock.
Add 10% for two-shot version.

GRADING	100%	95%	90%	80%	60%	40%	20%

RAIDER (CURRENT MFG.) – .177 or .22 cal., PCP, BA, precision steel choked rifled barrel, 10 shot detachable mag., 4-way adj. trigger, built-in pressure gauge, uncheckered hardwood stock with cheekpiece and vent. recoil pad, blue finish, 8.5 lbs. New 2010.

courtesy Webley & Scott, LTD.

MSR $400	$350	$300	$270	$220	$170	N/A	N/A

Add $20 for 3-9x40 Nikko Stirling scope.

RANGER – .177 cal., SP, BBC, SS, rifled or smoothbore steel barrel, scope ramp (late versions), full length stock, no safety, blued, 38.25 in. OAL, 3.5 lbs. Mfg. 1950-1970.

	$450	$375	$325	$260	$205	$135	$90

Add 10% for no code or scope ramp.

Variations: four minor changes indicated with code letter stamped LHS barrel: no code = early, A, B, C. Ranger (grip lever cocking). Ranger name also used as a Webley private label version of Erma ELG10 grip lever Winchester-carbine-style pellet rifle: see Erma section.

REBEL – .177 or .22 cal., SS, pump up recoilless mechanism, 20 in. steel rifled barrel, HiViz sights, manual safety, Black synthetic stock, 35.5 in. OAL, 4.4 lbs.

courtesy Webley & Scott, LTD.

MSR $140	$120	$105	$95	$75	$60	N/A	N/A

SIDEWINDER – .177 or .22 cal., PCP, SL, multi-shot. Mfg. 2009-2010.

	$925	$775	$650	$525	$400	$275	$185

SPECTRE – .22 cal., PCP, BA, eight-shot rotary magazine indexed and cocked by RHS cocking lever, neoprene pads inletted into grip and forearm, pressure gauge in synthetic stock, two-stage adj. trigger, free floating barrel, 36.2 in. OAL, 5.5 lbs. Mfg. 2004.

	$900	$775	$625	$525	$400	$270	$180

This model was a joint design with Axelsson of Sweden.

STINGRAY (CURRENT MFG.) – .177 or .22 cal., BBC, SP, SS, 800/600 FPS, two-stage trigger, beech Monte Carlo-style stock, adj. rear sight, hooded front sight, 41.1 in. OAL, 7.3 lbs. Mfg. 2008-current.

courtesy Webley

MSR $280	$240	$210	$190	$155	$120	N/A	N/A

Add $20 for 3-9x40 Nikko Stirling scope.

GRADING	100%	95%	90%	80%	60%	40%	20%

STINGRAY RIFLE – .177 or .22 cal., BBC, 870/660 FPS, two-stage trigger, beech or walnut (Deluxe) Monte Carlo-style stock, adj. rear sight, hooded front sight, 44 in. overall. New 2001.

	$350	$300	$250	$210	$160	$110	$70

Add 15% for checkered walnut stock (Deluxe).

* **Stingray KS (Carbine)** – .177 or .22 cal., similar to Stin

	$295	$250	$205				60

Add 15% for checkered walnut stock (Deluxe).

SPORT – .22 in. cal., BBC, SP, SS. 490 FPS, beech stock, s, scope grooves, no safety, junior size, economy level air rifle, impo

	$235	$200	$165				45

s $235.

TOMAHAWK – .177 or .22 cal., BBC, 845/622 FPS, 15 in. ba vo-stage adj. trigger, automatic safety, beech or walnut (deluxe) sto

	$475	$400	$325				90

Add 15% for checkered walnut stock (Deluxe).

TOMAHAWK (RECENT MFG.) – .177 or .22 cal., BBC, 100 vo-stage adj. trigger, automatic safety, walnut (deluxe) stock with du -2010.

	$350	$300	$245				70

TOMAHAWK (CURRENT MFG.) – .177 or .22 cal., BBC, SP in. rifled steel barrel, automatic resettable safety catch, fully adj. two-stage Quattro trigger, ambidextrous walnut stock, 44.5 in. OAL, 8 lbs.

courtesy Webley & Scott, LTD.

(handwritten note: My Webley VMX .22 is made in Turkey.)

MSR $300	$255	$225	$205	$165	$125	N/A	N/A

TRACKER/CARBINE – .177 or .22 cal., SL 750/600 FPS, 11.37 (carbine) or 17.5 in. barrel with removable muzzle weight, single-stage "hunter" adj. trigger, integral scope grooves, Black Nighthunter, Camo Fieldshooter, or beech Monte Carlo stock with recoil pad, optional stocks, 7.2-7.4 lbs. Disc. 2000.

	$240	$205	$170	$140	$110	$70	$50

Last MSR was $300.

Add 5% for .22 cal. model.
Add 15% for Black Nighthunter or Camo Fieldshooter stocks.

VALUEMAX – .177, .20, or .22 cal., SP, black, green, or Mossy Oak camo synthetic stock with cheek piece, TruGlo sights, rubber buttpad. New 2009.

MSR $160	$135	$120	$110	$90	$65	N/A	N/A

Add $15 for camo.
Add $15 for Nikko Stirling 3-9x40 scope.

VENOM VIPER – .177, .20 or .22 cal., PCP, similar to Raider, except 6.2 lbs. New 2001.

	$775	$675	$550	$450	$350	$235	$155

Add 15% for walnut stock.

VICTOR – .177 or .22 cal., SP, BBC, SS, 720/580 FPS, PTFE and O-ring piston seal, no safety, 40.1 in. OAL, 7 lbs. Mfg. 1981.

	$150	$130	$105	$85	$70	$45	$30

This model was the Junior version of Vulcan II.

GRADING	100%	95%	90%	80%	60%	40%	20%

VISCOUNT/VISCOUNT DELUXE – .177 or .22 cal., SP, SL, SS, tap-loading, 830/650 FPS, PTFE and O-ring piston seal, Italian beech or European walnut (Viscount Deluxe) Monte Carlo full stock, black plastic PG cap, rubber buttplate with white line spacer, manual safety. 43.5-43.8 in. OAL, 7.6-7.7 lbs. Mfg. 1982.

	$300	$255	$210	$175	$135	$90	$60

Add 75% for Viscount Deluxe.

The Viscount Deluxe included oil-finished European walnut stock with hand checkering, sling swivels, and vent. rubber buttplate. Intro. Aug. 1982.

VMX – .177, .20 Webley, or .22 cal., POWR-LOK Mainspring or D-RAM Gas Piston, precision rifled barrel, TruGlo Sight System with micro adj. rear sight, Black, Green, Mossy Oak Camo, Muddy Girl Camo, or Legends Blaze Camo synthetic ambidextrous stock, 43 in. OAL, 6.4 lbs. New 2014.

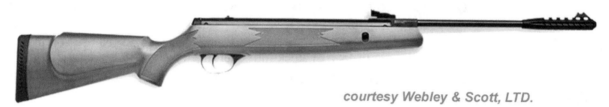

courtesy Webley & Scott, LTD.

MSR $160	$135	$120	$110	$90	$65	N/A	N/A

Add $15 for camo finish.
Add $40 for camo finish with 3-9x40 Nikko Stirling scope.

VULCAN I – .177 or .22 cal., SP, BBC, SS, 810/630 FPS, PTFE and O-ring piston seal, PG beech stock with angular forearm, shallow cheek piece, black rubber buttplate, adj. trigger (to 3 lbs.) with constant sear engagement, manual safety, 40.8 in. OAL, 7.1 lbs. Mfg. 1979-1981.

	$125	$105	$90	$75	$55	$35	$25

Introduced "Webley Power Intensification System" PTFE and O-ring piston seal.

* ***Vulcan I Deluxe*** – similar to Vulcan I, except .177 cal. only, special walnut stock, hand checkered forearm and PG, soft rubber buttplate with white line spacer, gold plated trigger and manual safety, 43.8 in. OAL, 7.65 lbs. Mfg. 1980-81.

	$350	$300	$245	$205	$160	$105	$70

VULCAN II – .177 or .22 cal., SP, BBC, SS, 830/650 FPS, PTFE and O-ring piston seal, PG beech stock with rounded forearm and plastic grip cap, shallow cheek piece, ventilated rubber buttpad with white line spacer, adj. trigger (to 3 lbs.) with constant sear engagement, manual safety, 43.6 in. OAL, 7.65 lbs. Mfg. 1981-1984.

	$175	$150	$125	$100	$80	$50	$35

* ***Vulcan II Deluxe*** – similar to Vulcan II, except special walnut stock, hand cut checkering, sling swivels. Optional: Special Sporter or Tyrolean stocks of select French Walnut, oil finished, 43.8 in. OAL, 7.85 lbs. Mfg. 1981-1984.

	$295	$250	$205	$170	$135	$90	$60

Add 75% for Special Sporter or Tyrolean stocks of select French Walnut, oil finished.

VULCAN III – .177, .22, or .25 (carbine) cal., BBC, 870/660/620 FPS, 11.37 (carbine) or 17.5 in. barrel with threaded muzzle-brake, single-stage "hunter" adj. trigger, integral scope grooves, open sights, beech Monte Carlo stock with recoil pad, 7.6 lbs. Mfg. 1984-2000.

	$225	$190	$160	$130	$100	$65	$45

Last MSR was $300.

Add 10% for .25 cal. model.
Add 5% for Carbine version in .177 and .22 cal.
Add 10% for noise suppressor (requires $200 federal tax in the USA).

* ***Vulcan III Deluxe*** – similar to Vulcan III, except has special walnut stock with hand cut checkering and sling swivels.

	$280	$240	$195	$160	$125	$85	$55

XOCET CARBINE – .177 or .22, cal., similar to Xocet Rifle, except 36 in. overall. New 2001.

	$290	$245	$205	$170	$130	$85	$60

XOCET RIFLE – .177 or .22 cal., SP, BBC, 870/660 FPS, beech Monte Carlo stock, adj. rear sight, hooded front sight, 39 in. overall. New 2001.

	$290	$245	$205	$170	$130	$85	$60

WEIHRAUCH SPORT

Current manufacturer located in Mellrichstadt, Germany. Formerly known as Hans-Hermann Weihrauch. Currently imported and distributed by Air Venturi/Pyramyd Air, located in Solon, OH (previously located in Warrensville Hts., OH), Airguns of Arizona located in Gilbert, AZ and by Air Rifle Headquarters located in Elkton, MD. Previously distributed by Beeman Precision Airguns located in Huntington Beach, CA. Dealer sales.

The authors and publisher wish to thank Mr. Ulrich Eichstädt for the following information in this section of the *Blue Book of Airguns*. The world-wide success of Weihrauch airguns is still based on the motto which the company has used for over a century: "Quality - Made in Germany." International gun expert John Walter noted that "Weihrauch is rightly regarded as one of the last bastions of traditional airgun smithing." It is interesting and instructive to compare the details of their airgun design and quality with any other sporting airguns. Note that guns stamped with an "F" in a pentagon are low velocity versions intended for the German and other markets with strict power limits. Without that mark the guns generally are designed for the English market with its 12 ft./lb. limit for air rifles and 6 ft./lb. limit for air pistols.

Beeman/Weihrauch guns: For those special models and versions of Beeman brand airguns made by Weihrauch, see the Beeman Precision Airguns in the "B" section.

For more information and current pricing on Weihrauch firearms, please refer to the *Blue Book of Gun Values* by S.P. Fjestad (also available online).

HISTORY 1899-1970

The Hermann Weihrauch company was founded in 1899 in Zella-Mehlis, the same small German town where several other famous gun manufacturers such as Walther, Sauer & Sohn, and Anschütz also began. Hermann Weihrauch, Sr. was well-known for making excellent hunting rifles. His three sons, Otto, Werner, and Hermann, Jr., soon joined the family-based company. Several new models were introduced after WWI, including the HWZ 21 smallbore rifle (HWZ stands for Hermann Weihrauch, Zella-Mehlis). This was the first mass-produced German .22 rimfire rifle and soon developed an excellent match record. Double and triple barrel shotguns, over and under shotguns, and large bore hunting rifles rounded out the line and established an excellent reputation for quality.

In 1928, Weihrauch began a large international sale of bicycle parts and mechanical door closers. During WWII, Weihrauch was the only German factory to continue production of spare parts for bicycles. At the end of the war, Zella-Mehlis became part of the Soviet occupation zone. In 1948, the Weihrauchs were forced out of their homes and factories by the communist government.

Otto Weihrauch became a mechanic and later a gunsmith in Zella-Mehlis. Werner went to work at the Jagdwaffenwerk (Hunting Weapon Factory) in nearby Suhl. Hermann Weihrauch, Jr. moved to the little German village of Mellrichstadt in Bavaria. There, with the help of his long-time hunting club friends and former customers, and his son Hans, he started the Weihrauch business all over again in the barracks of a pre-war laundry. Spare parts for bicycles were their first and main products.

When German companies were again allowed to manufacture airguns in the early 1950s, Weihrauch made their first air rifle, the HW Model 50V. This airgun had to have a smooth bore because the Allied Occupation Government would not allow rifled barrels. Finally, after the German Shooting Federation ("Deutscher Schützenbund") was re-established, the allied government allowed the production of rifled barrels. However, because they were not allowed to produce firearms, they put their efforts into making the finest sporting airguns in the world. Even after the firearm manufacturing ban finally was withdrawn, the Hermann Weihrauch KG company continued to produce sporting air rifles of the highest quality. The little HW 25 was slanted towards the youth market while versions of the HW 30 and HW 50 continued as solid mid-market air rifles. The HW 55 was one of Europe's leading barrel-cocking target rifles. The rather uncommon HW 55T version with its ornate Tyrolean-style stock, usually sporting fine walnut of exceptional grain, has always been a favorite among offhand shooters and collectors. The big HW 35 sporting air rifle was their main and most successful model.

After Hermann Weihrauch, Jr. died in 1967, a new era in the company began under the leadership of Hans Weihrauch, Sr. (born in 1926 and the father of today's directors Stefan and Hans-Hermann.) The company celebrated 1970 with the introduction of the HW 70 air pistol.

The company had begun plans, and first production, of a repeating air pistol before WWII, but the war aborted its regular production. Although pre-war HWZ sales literature shows an illustration of that thirty-shot top-lever spring piston air pistol, only one specimen of that HWZ LP-1 air pistol is now known. It had survived both the war and the Russian occupation by having safely gone overseas as a sales sample to the Hy-Score Arms Company in the USA. The Hy-Score president, Steve Laszlo, had given it to his friend, Dr. Robert Beeman. Dr. Beeman surprised Hans, Sr. and Christel Weihrauch, the husband/wife directors of the new HW company, when they were visiting the Beeman home, in San Anselmo, CA, by showing them this Weihrauch airgun which was completely unknown to them!

HISTORY 1970-1990

The close connection between the owners of the Weihrauch company and Beeman Precision Airguns led to one of the first (if not the first) joint ventures between a German-based manufacturer and an American airgun distributor. After a period of importing Weihrauch-designed airguns, the Beemans had decided that they needed to introduce a German-made air rifle with American styling and features. They had determined that their main need, in addition to new styling, was a power level above anything that had been known before in the airgun field. They had been very impressed with the quality of the HW 35, but puzzled by its power, which was lower than that of the Feinwerkbau Model 124. That gun, for which Beeman had developed a large market in the U.S., had a lighter spring and smaller compression chamber.

Based on their computer simulation studies, the Beemans proposed a new air rifle model with the quality of the HW 35. This cooperative development program resulted in the Beeman R1 (sold outside of the USA as the Weihrauch HW 80 in a lower power version with a more European-style stock). The new model quickly became the best-selling adult sporting air rifle; it is credited with bringing the American airgun market into the world of adult airguns. Ironically, due to delivery problems with the longer, more complex R1 stock, the first HW 80 rifles were available some weeks earlier than the R1. This led to the incorrect conclusion made by some that the R1 was a copy of the HW80. Tom Gaylord also has written about that coincidence in his book *The Beeman R1* and pointed out that clearly Dr. Beeman was the main force behind the invention of the R1/HW80 and that Weihrauch did an outstanding job of production engineering and manufacture.

Almost the same thing happened with the introduction of the next Weihrauch air pistol, the very successful Beeman P1 (sold outside of the USA as the Weihrauch HW 45). Although the Beemans provided the full specifications and design features of this pistol, there was an initial misunderstanding about the external appearance. The factory presented a rather bulky, high top, "Desert Eagle-like" design which the Beemans did not think would appeal to the American market. They felt that it should follow the very popular and trim lines of the Colt 1911 automatic pistol. So the Beeman Company quickly made a plaster-of-paris, life-sized 3D model which the Weihrauch technicians used as a model for the final design. Ironically, the Weihrauch engineers were far ahead of their time in a different way because of another misunderstanding: they thought that, because the Beeman plans were blank in the powerplant area, that Beeman had suggested a single-stroke pneumatic air system instead of the desired, more powerful spring-piston action. These pneumatic models came some years later, when the Beeman P2/Weihrauch HW 75 was introduced. The huge commercial success of the P1 design was aided by its many features: high power, accuracy, solid metal construction, three caliber choices, different choices of finish, and especially its great flexibility: the ability to fire at two power levels, integral scope rail, and the availability of a Beeman-designed shoulder stock.

The R1/HW80, and its several variations, gave rise to a lighter, easier to cock model: the R10/HW85. Weihrauch then produced an under-lever spring piston rifle, the HW77. This gun opened fully for loading directly into the breech of the barrel, like a Feinwerkbau match rifle. This was a great improvement over barrel-cocking air rifles which utilized a loading tap from which the pellet had to leap into the barrel. The HW77 and HW77 Carbine, with their rigid barrel and easy cocking and loading, became extremely popular in countries where their lower power was under the legal limit. However, these models had very disappointing sales in the USA, where shooters still preferred the R1/HW80 and R10/HW85 barrel-cockers, by a margin of over 20 to 1, due to their higher power.

The field-style air rifle designs for the American market were a great success because only a very small minority of adult airgun shooters were involved in any competition or group shooting activities. Field target shooting was the most popular of the American group airgun shooting sports, but even that involved much less than one percent of adult airgun shooters. Almost the exact opposite was true of airgun shooters in Germany; there, most such shooters were involved in 10 meter competition. Nevertheless, in 1989, the leading German gun magazine, VISIER, discovered from a survey that a large number of German airgun shooters would be willing to pay more than 500 DM (about 300 U.S. dollars) for an air rifle which was equipped with a sporting-style stock and designed for scope use. Many Germans responding to the poll also submitted useful suggestions for new designs to be added to the many new stock designs being developed by Weihrauch.

The reunification of Germany in 1990 resulted in many changes for every German citizen and manufacturer. Weihrauch began a cooperation with Theoben Engineering in England which resulted in the introduction of the first German/English air rifle design: the Weihrauch HW 90 (the Beeman versions are the RX and RX-1). This was the first Weihrauch rifle using the patented Theoben gas-spring system (sometimes inappropriately called "gas ram"). These new rifles sold very well in Great Britain where field target shooting had originated in the early 1980s and also were well received there and in the USA for small game hunting.

The great optimism of that period of the company's development was dampened by the unexpected death of Hans Weihrauch, Sr. on April 3, 1990 at the age of only 63. His business accomplishments were so admired that he was posthumously decorated with the Federal Cross of Merit. His wife, Christel, and sons, Stefan and Hans-Hermann, took the reins of the company. Fortunately, Christel Weihrauch had shared the management of the firm for decades and the preparation of the two sons for their expected future management roles was well advanced. Both had been involved with the company all of their lives and had nearly finished their engineering and marketing training as well. Director-to-be Hans-Hermann had even spent several months as an apprentice executive in the Beeman Precision Airguns business in America and had polished his English language skills by living with Robert and Toshiko Beeman in their California home during that time.

The fall of the German wall right by their little village of Mellrichstadt suddenly placed them "in the middle of Germany." This opened new markets for their surface engineering branch. They added new machines for electroless nickel plating and bronzing (and made the floors slip-proof with expanded mesh, stainless-steel fencing panels supplied from the nearby fallen "Iron Curtain!").

PISTOLS

MODEL HWZ · LP 1 – .177 lead balls, thirty-shot repeater, TL, SP, walnut single-piece grip, front sight acts as BB magazine retainer, blue finish. Extremely rare. Mfg. 1939.

courtesy Beeman Collection

Scarcity precludes accurate pricing.

GRADING	100%	95%	90%	80%	60%	40%	20%

Weihrauch's first airgun, production was halted by WW II.

MODEL HW 40 PCA – .177 cal., CO$_2$, SSP, contoured and finger grooved polymer frame styled like semi-auto firearm, 6.7 in. BBL, 400-410 FPS, two-stage trigger, black finish, adj. TruGlo fiber optic sights, 9.45 in. OAL, 1.72 lbs.

MSR $272	$230	$205	$185	$150	$115	N/A	N/A

MODEL HW 45 LP – .177, .20, or .22 cal., SP, 6.7 in. barrel, 560/500/425 FPS, adj. fiber optic TruGlo sights, adj. two-stage trigger, blue finish, checkered ambi. walnut grips, 11 in. OAL, 2.54 lbs.

MSR $523	$450	$400	$350	$290	$220	N/A	N/A

Add $35 for .20 cal.
Add 50% for shoulder stock.
Developed from Beeman P1.

* **Model HW 45 STL** – .177 or .22 cal., SP, 6.7 in. barrel, 560/425 FPS, adj. fiber optic sights, adj. 2-stage trigger, Duo Tone matte nickel finish, checkered ambi. black wooden grips, 11 in. OAL, 2.54 lbs.

MSR $610	$525	$450	$425	$325	$255	N/A	N/A

* **Model HW 45 Black Star** – .177 or .22 cal., SP, 6.7 in. barrel, 560/425 FPS, TruGlo adj. fiber optic sights, two-stage adj. trigger, black anodised upper assembly with black/grey laminated grip, 11 in. OAL, 2.6 lbs. New 2010.

MSR $595	$500	$450	$400	$325	$250	N/A	N/A

* **Model HW 45 Silver Star** – .177 or .22 cal., SP, 6.7 in. barrel, 560/425 FPS, TruGlo adj. fiber optic sights, two-stage adj. trigger, black upper assembly with matte nickel (Duo Tone) finish, laminate match grips, 11 in. OAL, 2.6 lbs.

MSR $595	$500	$450	$400	$325	$250	N/A	N/A

MODEL HW 70 – .177 cal., BBC, SP, 440 FPS, two-stage adj. trigger, 6 in. rifled steel barrel, blue/black epoxy or silver (HW 70S, mfg. 1992 only) finish, hooded front and adj. rear (scope grooves added to rear sight base of HW 70A in 1992) sights, one-piece composition grip and forearm. 2.4 lbs. Mfg. in Germany with importation beginning in 1972.

	$155	$130	$110	$90	$70	$45	$30

Last MSR was $170.

Add 30% for chrome.
Subtract 20% for safety.
Add 10% for Santa Rosa address.

Early versions did not have a retainer screw in the side of the rear body plug. The plug may come loose and fly out (recalled).

* **Model HW 70-A** – .177 cal., similar to Model HW 70, except has 6.3 in. barrel, improved rear sight suitable for scope mount, improved trigger and safety, 12.8 in. OAL, 2.4 lbs.

courtesy Beeman Collection

MSR $316	$270	$235	$215	$175	$135	N/A	N/A

Add 10% for stylized black grip and silver finish.
Add 10% for early versions without safety.

MODEL HW 70 BLACK ARROW – .177 cal., BBC, SP, 6.3 in. barrel with muzzle break, prism rail for scope use, black finish, black ambi. grip, new design, especially developed for scope shooting, gold plated trigger, 14.37 in. OAL, 2.6 lbs.

Please contact the importer directly for pricing and availability on this model.

* **Model HW 70 LP** – .177 cal., BBC, 440 FPS, 2.25 lbs.

	$185	$155	$130	$105	$85	$55	$35

GRADING	100%	95%	90%	80%	60%	40%	20%

MODEL HW 75 M – .177 cal., SSP, 6.7 in. BBL, 410 FPS, adj. rear sight, manual safety, checkered walnut target grips, 11 in. OAL, 2.34 lbs.

MSR $524	$450	$400	$350	$290	$220	N/A	N/A

RIFLES

MODEL HW 25 L – .177 cal., BBC, SP, SS, 15.25 in. rifled steel barrel, 590 FPS, TruGlo adj. fiber optic sights, two-stage trigger, walnut stained beech stock, manual safety, 37 in. OAL, 4.4 lbs.

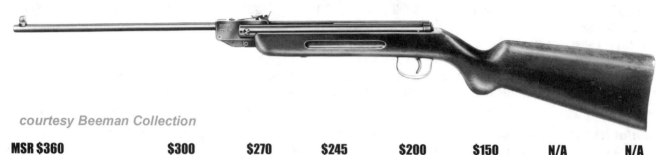

courtesy Beeman Collection

MSR $360	$300	$270	$245	$200	$150	N/A	N/A

MODEL HW 30 – .177 or .20 (disc.) cal., BBC, SP, SS, 675/600 FPS, two-stage non-adj. trigger, plain beech stock with or w/o buttplate, automatic safety, adj. rear sight (early versions all metal), 5.5 lbs. 40 in. OAL. Mfg. in Germany. New 1972.

courtesy Beeman Collection

	$175	$150	$125	$100	$80	$50	$35

Add 10% for no safety.
Add 20% for .20 caliber.
Add 10% for San Rafael or Santa Rosa address.
Add 20% for early M versions - stock with cheekpiece, deep forearm, and rubber buttplate.

* **Model HW 30 M/II** – .177 or .22 cal., BBC, SP, 660/450 FPS, match trigger, automatic safety, 17 in. barrel, 5.3 lbs.

	$210	$180	$145	$120	$95	$65	$40

Add 15% for Monte Carlo cheekpiece.
Add 20% for Beeman factory markings.

* **Model HW 30 S** – .177 or .22 cal., BBC, SP, 15.5 in. rifled steel barrel, 620/425 FPS, Rekord match trigger, tunnel front sight sporter PG beechwood stock, 38.78 in. OAL, 5.5 lbs.

courtesy Beeman Collection

MSR $375	$325	$280	$255	$205	$160	N/A	N/A

GRADING	100%	95%	90%	80%	60%	40%	20%

* *Model HW 30 S Deluxe* – .177 cal., similar to Model HW 30 S, except has upgraded walnut beech stock with four panel checkering, adj. sights.

courtesy Precision Airgun Distribution

MSR $425	$350	$325	$290	$235	$180	N/A	N/A

MODEL HW 35 – .177 or .22 cal., BBC, SP, 790/600 FPS, Rekord match trigger, walnut, beech or stained beech Safari stock, matte blue finish barrel and receiver.

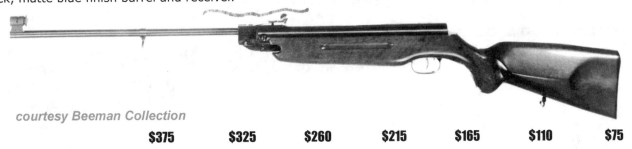

courtesy Beeman Collection

	$375	$325	$260	$215	$165	$110	$75

Add 10% for Safari Model with safari finish stock.
Add 25% for walnut stock.
Add 20% for thumbhole stock.
Add 15% for Safari Model - matte blue, safari finish stock.
Add 20% for Beeman factory markings.

Produced by Weihrauch as Mini-ject Model 18 for Dist-Inject Co. in Weil am Rhein, Germany. Purpose made in 11mm (.433) caliber as a syringe projector. Values generally $400 to $600.

* *Model HW 35 E/ HW 35 EB* – .177 or .22 cal., BBC, SP, 755/660 FPS, 18.5 or 20 (disc.) in. barrel, walnut stock with special cheek piece, fine checkered pistol grip, pistol grip cap and rubber buttplate with ivory colored spacers, two sling swivels, 755/660 FPS, 43.5 in. OAL, 7.8-8 lbs. Disc. 1985. Mfg. 2009-current.

courtesy Precision Airgun Distribution

MSR $735	$625	$550	$500	$400	$300	N/A	N/A

Add 20% for chrome (disc.).

MODEL HW 50 – .177 cal., BBC, SP, SS, 700 FPS, non-adj. trigger, plain beech stock w/o cheek piece or buttplate, automatic safety, heavy machined receiver cap, front sight with interchangeable posts, 43.1 in. OAL, 6.9 lbs. Mfg. in Germany 1972-95.

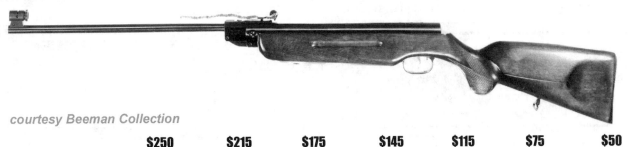

courtesy Beeman Collection

	$250	$215	$175	$145	$115	$75	$50

Subtract 25% for sheet metal receiver cap (post 1994 mfg.).
Add 10% for no safety.
Add 20% for early M versions - stock w/cheekpiece, deep forearm, and rubber buttplate.

GRADING	100%	95%	90%	80%	60%	40%	20%

* **Model HW 50 M/II** – .177 or .22 cal., BBC, SP, 850/620 FPS, 17 in. barrel, beechwood stock with long forearm and cheek piece on both sides, stippled pistol grip and forearm, 6.6 lbs.

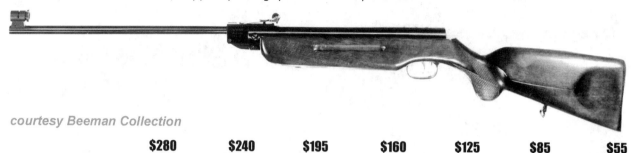

courtesy Beeman Collection

	$280	$240	$195	$160	$125	$85	$55

Add 20% for Beeman factory markings.

* **Model HW 50S** – .177 or .22 cal., BBC, SP, SS, 15.5 in. barrel, 840/600 FPS, beechwood stock, Rekord trigger, adj. sights, rubber buttplate, 40.5 in. OAL, 6.8 lbs. Mfg. 2009-current.

courtesy Precision Airgun Distribution

MSR $440	$375	$325	$300	$240	$185	N/A	N/A

Add 40% for Beeman factory markings with up-grade stock, and rubber buttplate.

* **Model HW 50S Stainless** – .177 or .22 cal., similar to Model HW 50S, except has resistant stainless metal finish action, and black synthetic stock. Mfg. 2009-current.

MSR $617	$525	$450	$425	$350	$260	N/A	N/A

MODEL HW 50V – .177 cal., smoothbore, BBC, SP, SS, beech stock with rounded grip end, grooves across butt, cast trigger guard, knurled and threaded rear end cap, marked "H.W.50" with image of soaring bird over that marking, no safety, 42.1 in. OAL, 5.6 lbs. Mfg. late 1940s.

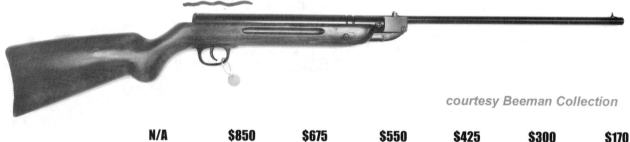

courtesy Beeman Collection

	N/A	$850	$675	$550	$425	$300	$170

This model was Weihrauch's first airgun, smoothbore because the Allied Occupation Government would not allow German civilians to own rifled guns after WWII.

HW BARAKUDA EL 54 – .22 cal., BBC, SP, SS, power augmented by diesel ignition of ether vapors from ether-injection tube affixed to right side of main body tube, 19.7 in. barrel, approx. 600-700 FPS without ether; much higher with ether, early versions with steel trigger guard and simple steel trigger system, later versions with cast aluminum trigger guards and Rekord trigger system, 8.4 lbs. Mfg. 1954-1981.

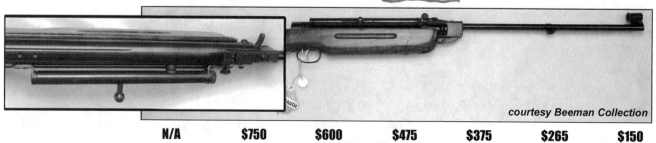

courtesy Beeman Collection

	N/A	$750	$600	$475	$375	$265	$150

Add 25% for Beeman markings. (Factory stamped with RDB for Robert David Beeman serial number.)
Add 30% for high gloss factory chrome plating.

GRADING	100%	95%	90%	80%	60%	40%	20%

Subtract 20% for Standard Model with beech stock.
Ether injection attachment only = $295.

Only a few hundred were made under cooperation of Weihrauch Company and Barakuda Company in Hamburg, Germany. Twenty specially made for Beeman Precision Airguns in 1981 from last remaining parts.

Caution: Specimens are not authentic unless factory stamped "BARAKUDA". Air rifles with ether-injection tubes, but marked HW 35, or with other model numbers, are fakes; compromised specimens of other models. Handle ether with care.

MODEL 55 – .177 cal., BBC, SP, 660-700 FPS, 7.5 lbs.

courtesy Beeman Collection

	100%	95%	90%	80%	60%	40%	20%
	$550	$475	$375	$325	$250	$165	$110

Last MSR was $610.

Add 10% for left-hand variation.
Add 20% for Match (squarish forearm with lower line equal to bottom of trigger guard).
Add 30% for Tyrolean stock.
Add 10% for Beeman factory markings.

The stock variations are MM, SM, T, S, M, SF, MF, CM, and Champ (Jr. version). There are many variations not listed here; HW 55 air rifles are a collecting field in themselves. Serious collectors should contact Mike Driskill at DFHalass@hswp.org for additional information.

* **Model HW55MM** – .177 cal., BBC, SP, 660/700 FPS, match aperture sight, walnut stock with checkered grip, forearm and cheek piece, 43.7 in. OAL, 7.8 lbs.

	$650	$550	$450	$375	$295	$195	$130

* **Model HW55SM** – .177 cal., BBC, SP, 590 FPS, beech stock with checkered pistol grip, adj. match target rear sight, hooded front sight, match trigger.

	$450	$400	$325	$265	$205	$140	$90

* **Model HW55T** – .177 cal., BBC, SP, 660/700 FPS, match aperture sight, deluxe Tyrolean walnut stock with deep dish cheek piece, 43.7 in. OAL, 7.8 lbs.

courtesy Beeman Collection

	$750	$625	$525	$425	$325	$225	$150

Only 25 Beeman specimens were made and imported.

MODEL HW 57 – .177 or .22 cal., UL, SP, 820/570 FPS, 14.2 in. barrel, beech stock, rubber buttplate, Rekord trigger, 7 lbs.

	$295	$250	$205	$170	$135	$90	$60

This model was an economy version of the HW97 with a pop-up loading tap.

GRADING	100%	95%	90%	80%	60%	40%	20%

MODEL HW 77/HW 77 K – .177, .20, .22, or .25 cal., UL, SP, SS, 950/830/755/610 FPS, 11.8 in. fixed barrel, blue finish, automatic safety, two-stage adj. Rekord trigger, beech high comb Monte Carlo hardwood hand cut checkered PG sporter stock, white-lined grip cap and rubber recoil pad, factory stamped with Santa Rosa address, automatic safety, 43.7 in. OAL (carbine version 39.7 in. OAL), 8.7 lbs. Mfg. in Germany 1983-1998.

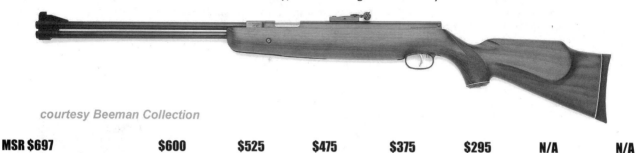

courtesy Beeman Collection

	100%	95%	90%	80%	60%	40%	20%
MSR $697	$600	$525	$475	$375	$295	N/A	N/A

Add $30 for left-hand variation.
Add 10% for deluxe version.
Add $79 for .25 cal.
Add 25% for Tyrolean stock.

Beginning in 1995, the Model HW 77 could have been upgraded to the power of the Model HW 77 Mk II.

* *Model HW 77 MKII Carbine* – .177 cal., SP, UL, SS, 930 FPS, 11.5 in. barrel, blue finish, automatic safety, two-stage adj. Rekord trigger, beech high comb Monte Carlo hardwood hand cut checkered pistol grip sporter stock, white-lined grip cap and rubber recoil pad, factory stamped with Huntington Beach address, 39.7 in. OAL, 8.7 lbs. Mfg. in Germany 1999-Disc.

	100%	95%	90%	80%	60%	40%	20%
	$575	$500	$400	$325	$260	$170	$115

MODEL HW77 SPECIAL EDITION – .177, .20, .22, or .25 cal., UL, SP, SS, 950/830/755/610 FPS, 11.8 in. fixed barrel, blue finish, automatic safety, two-stage adj. Rekord trigger, beech high comb Monte Carlo hardwood hand cut checkered PG sporter stock, white-lined grip cap and rubber recoil pad, also available with red/blue/brown laminated stock, checkering on PG, pistol grip cap and with rubber buttplate (HW 77 Special Edition), factory stamped with Santa Rosa address, automatic safety, 43.7 in. OAL (carbine version 39.7 in. OAL), 8.7 lbs. Mfg. in Germany 1983-1998.

	100%	95%	90%	80%	60%	40%	20%
MSR $822	$700	$625	$550	$450	$350	N/A	N/A

Add $30 for left-hand variation.
Add 10% for deluxe version.
Add $79 for .25 cal.
Add 25% for Tyrolean stock.

Beginning in 1995, the Model HW 77 could have been upgraded to the power of the Model HW 77 Mk II.

MODEL HW 80 – .177, .20, .22, or .25 cal., BBC, SP, SS, 19.7 in. barrel (16.1 in. barrel for Carbine), 1000/765 FPS, Rekord trigger, Monte Carlo beech stock does not cover barrel pivot, adj. sights, checkered pistol grip, rubber buttplate, 45.3 in. OAL, 8.8 lbs.

courtesy Precision Airgun Distribution

	100%	95%	90%	80%	60%	40%	20%
MSR $680	$575	$500	$450	$375	$285	N/A	N/A

Add $15 for .177 or .22 cal.

MODEL HW 85 – .20 or .22 cal., similar to Model HW 80 except 20 in. barrel, plain hardwood stock with walnut finish, 700/685 FPS, TruGlo fiber optic sights, 46 in. OAL, 7.7 lbs. Importation disc. 2011. Imported 2013-current.

courtesy Precision Airgun Distribution

	100%	95%	90%	80%	60%	40%	20%
MSR $582	$500	$425	$400	$325	$245	N/A	N/A

GRADING	100%	95%	90%	80%	60%	40%	20%

Add 15% for Deluxe Model with fine checkered pistol grip with cap and white spacers.

MSR when disc. in 2011 was $495.

MODEL HW 90 – .177, .20, .22, or .25 cal., Theoben gas spring system, 1125/940/860/725 FPS, 20 in. barrel, adj. Elite trigger, extended forearm, high cheek piece, checkering on pistol grip, rubber buttplate, 45.3 in. OAL, 8.8 lbs.

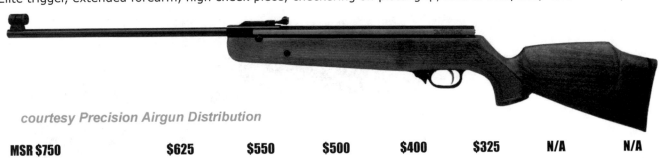

courtesy Precision Airgun Distribution

MSR $750	$625	$550	$500	$400	$325	N/A	N/A

Add $37 for .20 or .25 cal.

MODEL HW 95 – .177, .20, .22, or .25 cal., BBC, SP, SS, 16.14 in. barrel, 965-570 FPS, hardwood stock with walnut finish, contoured forearm, fine checkered pistol grip, rubber buttplate, fixed front sight tunnel, automatic safety, Rekord trigger, 7.8 lbs. New 2005.

MSR $477	$400	$350	$325	$260	$200	N/A	N/A

MODEL HW 95 LUXUS – .177, .20, .22, or .25 cal., BBC, SP, SS, 16.14 in. barrel, 950/800/755/700 FPS, walnut finished hardwood beech stock, adj. Rekord match-grade trigger, globe front and adj. rear sights, cut checkering on pistol grip and forend, raised cheek piece, rubber butt pad, ambidextrous, 42.32 in. OAL, 7.5 lbs.

courtesy Precision Airgun Distribution

MSR $600	$500	$450	$400	$325	$250	N/A	N/A

Add $10 for .20 or .25 cal.

MODEL HW 97 – .177, .20, .22, or .25 cal., UL, SP, 930 FPS in .177 cal., 9 lbs laminated stock, designed for scope use only. Replaced by HW 97K in 2001.

courtesy Beeman Collection

	$475	$400	$325	$270	$210	$140	$95

Add 10% for .20 cal.

Add 20% for .25 cal. in USA.

Note: Director/Owner Hans Weihrauch flatly states that no HW97 rifles were made with a Tyrolean stock. Such stocks were added after sale. Only the HW 55, 77, and 80, plus the Beeman R1 were ever factory produced with a Tyrolean stock.

MODEL HW 97 BLACK LINE – .177, .20, .22. or .25 cal., 11.8 in. barrel, blued system, black or stainless-look (HW 97 Black Line STL) synthetic thumbhole stock, ambidextrous, 40 in. OAL, 9.26 lbs. New 2011.

Please contact the importer directly for pricing and availability on this model.

GRADING	100%	95%	90%	80%	60%	40%	20%

MODEL HW 97 K – .177, .20, .22, or .25 cal., UL, SP, 950/820/755/610 FPS, 11.8 in. barrel with muzzle break, designed for field target and silhouette, blue or stainless, Rekord adj. match-grade trigger, walnut stained beech stock, blue/grey laminated stock, or different thumbhole stocks available, checkered or stippled pistol grip forearm, rubber buttplate, 40.25 in. OAL, 8.8 lbs.

courtesy Precision Airgun Distribution

MSR $730	$625	$550	$500	$400	$300	N/A	N/A

Add $20 for .20 cal. or $30 for .22 cal.
Add $75 for stainless.
Add $140 for blue/grey laminated stock.
Add $275 for thumbhole stock (HW 97 KT).

Add 15% for green laminated stock (disc.).
Add 25% for HW Centennial model, marked "100 Jahre Weihrauch" (Germany) or "100 years Weihrauch" (UK version) in USA.

* **Model HW97 MKI** – .177 or .20 cal., UL, SP. Mfg. 1995-1998.

	$475	$400	$325	$275	$215	$140	$95

Add 5% for .20 cal.
Add 15% for .177 cal. Centennial Model with blue/gray laminate stock.

* **Model HW97 MKII** – .177 or .20 cal., UL, SP, similar to Model HW97 MKI except velocity increased to 930 FPS for .177 and 820 FPS for .20 cal. Mfg. 1999-2001.

	$475	$400	$325	$275	$215	$140	$95

Add 20% for .20 cal. Millennium Model with blue/gray laminate stock.

* **Model HW97 MKIII** – .177 or .20 cal., UL, SP, similar to Model HW97 MKII, except shortened barrel to improve appearance, balance, and lock time, 40.25 in. OAL, 9.2 lbs. Mfg. in Germany, new 2002.

	$575	$500	$400	$325	$260	$170	$115

MODEL HW 98 – .177 or .22 cal., BBC, SP, 950/755 FPS, blued, all steel barrel, stippled forestock and palm swell, brown hardwood stock with long forearm, black highlights of stippling grooves, two-stage Rekord adj. trigger, automatic safety, Field Target Competition model with adj. cheek piece, buttplate, 43.5 in. OAL, 8.6 lbs.

courtesy Precision Airgun Distribution

MSR $797	$675	$600	$550	$450	$325	N/A	N/A

MODEL HW 100 S F.S.B. – .177 or .22 cal., PCP, side lever action, 14-shot rotary mag., 16.25 or 22 (FSB - fully shrouded barrel) in. BBL, 1050/885 FPS, no sights, blue finish, two stage adj. trigger, built-in pressure gauge, walnut sporter or thumbhole target (HW 100 T) stock with stippled grip, 38.6 or 44.3 in. OAL, 7.94-8.6 lbs. New 2004.

courtesy Precision Airgun Distribution

MSR $1,730	$1,475	$1,300	$1,175	$950	$725	N/A	N/A

GRADING	100%	95%	90%	80%	60%	40%	20%

MODEL HWB CHAMP – .177 cal., BBC, SP, 590 FPS, adj. match target rear sight, hooded front sight, youth model.

	$450	$400	$325	$265	$205	$140	$90

WELLS

Previous airgun designer located in Palo Alto, CA.

William Wells may have been one of the greatest airgun innovators of the twentieth century. Born in 1872, he apparently started designing and producing experimental airguns in the 1930s. He became a design consultant to Daisy in 1947. He also produced many dozens of designs, mostly repeating pneumatic rifles, but his work also included air pistols and spring piston airguns. These designs are represented by actual working specimens. Identification may not be easy; the interested reader must refer to Hannusch's paper, cited below. Many are marked "Cde P" on the base of the grip. The base of the stock usually is marked with his favorite .180 caliber (true BB shot), but several other calibers are known, including .187. Several models were produced in the election year 1952 and are marked with a small elephant emblem engraved with the 52 date. Many of Wells' designs are incorporated into Daisy and other brand airguns. William Wells died in October 1968, still very alert at the age of 96. It is not possible to assign values to the wide variety of Wells' experimental airguns, but his industry changing designs are of great value. The specimen shown below has been estimated to have a value over $3,500. Ref: Larry Hannusch, 1999, *Airgun Revue 4*.

courtesy Beeman Collection

WESSON, DAN FIREARMS

Current trademark manufactured under license by ASG (ActionSportGames A/S) located in Humleback, Denmark. Currently imported and distributed by ASG USA located in Simi Valley, CA.

For information and current pricing on both new and used Dan Wesson firearms, please refer to the *Blue Book of Gun Values* by S.P. Fjestad (also available online).

REVOLVERS

DAN WESSON 2.5 INCH – BB/.177 cal., 12 g CO_2 cylinder, DA, 6-shot repeater, 2.5 in. barrel, 318 FPS, silver finish, black textured grips, fixed front and adj. rear sights, manual safety, working ejector rod, 8.27 in. OAL, 1.65 lbs.

MSR $150	$130	$115	$100	$85	$65	N/A	N/A

This model also includes a detachable Weaver rail, speedloader, and six shells. Each shell is loaded with one steel BB. The shells are loaded into the gun's cylinder.

DAN WESSON 2.5 INCH GOLD – BB/.177 cal., 12 g CO_2 cylinder, DA, 6-shot repeater, 2.5 in. barrel, 318 FPS, gold finish, black textured grips, fixed front and adj. rear sights, manual safety, working ejector rod, 8.27 in. OAL, 1.65 lbs. Mfg. 2013-current.

MSR $180	$155	$135	$120	$100	$75	N/A	N/A

This model also includes a detachable Weaver rail, speedloader, and six shells. Each shell is loaded with one steel BB. The shells are loaded into the gun's cylinder.

DAN WESSON 4 INCH – BB/.177 cal., 12 g CO_2 cylinder, DA, 6-shot repeater, 4 in. barrel, 344 FPS, black finish, black textured grips, fixed front and adj. rear sights, manual safety, working ejector rod, 9.84 in. OAL, 1.95 lbs.

MSR $150	$130	$115	$100	$85	$65	N/A	N/A

This model also includes a detachable Weaver rail, speedloader, and six shells. Each shell is loaded with one steel BB. The shells are loaded into the gun's cylinder.

DAN WESSON SIX INCH – BB/.177 cal., 12 g CO_2 cylinder, DA, 6-shot repeater, 6 in. barrel, 426 FPS, silver finish, black textured grips, fixed front and adj. rear sights, manual safety, working ejector rod, 11.73 in. OAL, 2 lbs.

MSR $150	$130	$115	$100	$85	$65	N/A	N/A

This model also includes a detachable Weaver rail, speedloader, and six shells. Each shell is loaded with one steel BB. The shells are loaded into the gun's cylinder.

GRADING	100%	95%	90%	80%	60%	40%	20%

DAN WESSON EIGHT INCH BLACK – BB/.177 cal., 12 g CO_2 cylinder, DA, 6-shot repeater, 8 in. barrel, 426 FPS, black finish, black textured grips, fixed front and adj. rear sights, manual safety, working ejector rod, 13.3 in. OAL, 2.29 lbs.

MSR $150	$130	$115	$100	$85	$65	N/A	N/A

This model also includes a detachable Weaver rail, speedloader, and twelve shells. Each shell is loaded with one steel BB. The shells are loaded into the gun's cylinder.

DAN WESSON EIGHT INCH SILVER – BB/.177 cal., 12 g CO_2 cylinder, DA, 6-shot repeater, 8 in. barrel, 426 FPS, silver finish, black textured grips, fixed front and adj. rear sights, manual safety, working ejector rod, 13.3 in. OAL, 2.29 lbs.

MSR $150	$130	$115	$100	$85	$65	N/A	N/A

This model also includes a detachable Weaver rail, speedloader, and twelve shells. Each shell is loaded with one steel BB. The shells are loaded into the gun's cylinder.

WESTERN AUTO

Catalog sales/retailer which has subcontracted various manufacturers for its private label airguns.

To date, there has been very little interest in collecting Western Auto airguns, regardless of scarcity. Rather than list Western Auto models, a general guideline is that values generally are under those of their "first generation relatives." As a result, prices are ascertained by the shooting value of the airgun, rather than its collector value. See "Store Brand Crossover List" located in the back of this text.

WESTINGER & ALTENBURGER

For information on Westinger & Altenburger, see Feinwerkbau in the "F" section.

WESTLEY RICHARDS & CO. LTD.

Current manufacturer located in Birmingham, England. Previously located in London, England.

Westley Richards previously manufactured the "Highest Possible" air pistols circa 1907 to late 1920s. Airgun production was quite limited; the highest known airgun serial number is 1052. For more information and current pricing on Westley Richards firearms, please refer to the *Blue Book of Gun Values* by S.P. Fjestad (also available online).

PISTOLS

TOP BARREL MODEL – .177 cal., BBC, SP, SS, rifled 9.7 in. barrel on top of compression tube/body tube, marked (WESTLEY RICHARDS "HIGHEST POSSIBLE" AIR PISTOL) on tube, piston moves rearward during firing, horn or bakelite grips, blue or nickel finished, 11.9 in. OAL, 3.1 lbs., patented 1907, marketed Dec. 1909 to late 1914.

* ***Top Barrel Model First Variant*** – some with heart-shaped opening in frame behind trigger, with smooth horn grip plates.

courtesy Howard Collection

	N/A	$1,500	$1,200	$975	$750	$525	$300

Add 25% for nickel finish.
Add 15% for barrel over 10 inches.

GRADING	100%	95%	90%	80%	60%	40%	20%

* ***Top Barrel Model Second Variant*** – vertically curved rear sight screwed to frame, frame behind trigger closed, checkered hard rubber grip plates.

courtesy Howard Collection

	N/A	$1,250	$1,000	$750	$600	$450	$300

Add 10% for horn grips (transitional Model).
Add 25% nickel finish.

CONCENTRIC PISTON MODEL – .177 cal. BBC, SP, SS, piston concentric around central rifled 7.2 in. BBL, piston moves rearward during firing, 9.4 in. OAL, 2.3 lbs, patented 1921, marketed in 1924.

courtesy Beeman Collection

	N/A	$2,500	$2,000	$1,625	$1,250	$875	$500

Designed by Edwin Anson. Blued (two known in nickel). The length of the sleeve ("shoe") covering the rear of the body tube varies. Ref: AG:Dec.1998, May 1999, Dec. 2004.

WHISCOMBE AIR RIFLES

Previous manufacturer of Whiscombe Opposed Piston Air Rifles located in Thatcham, England.

High-end, spring-piston rifles with twin pistons opposing each other rather than moving in opposite directions as in Giss patent airguns manufactured by Dianawerk where one piston is a dummy. The opposing action eliminates almost all recoil and intensifies power. Each piston has a pair of springs, the total of four springs gives up to 650 lbs. loading.

The authors and publisher wish to thank Tim Saunders for his valuable assistance with the following information in this section of the *Blue Book of Airguns*.

RIFLES

MODELS JW50-JW80 – .177, .20, .22 or .25 cal., field target and hunting air rifles with high recoilless power without resorting to precharged gases or pumping. The model numbers, ranging from JW50 to JW80, indicate the piston stroke in millimeters. Smaller stroke guns usually are cocked by two stokes of an underlever. Larger stroke guns (70/80 mm) use three strokes. The large JW80 version, which requires an FAC license in Britain, produces up to 28 ft./lb. ME in .22 caliber and 30 ft/lb. ME in .25 caliber, blued or silverized steel finish, sporter or thumbhole stocks, action design, and standard or match trigger. 15 in. polygonal rifled barrel. About 450 rifles produced, most stocked for field target. Estimated about 2/3 sold into USA. Sporting stock versions about 9.8 lbs; thumbhole versions about

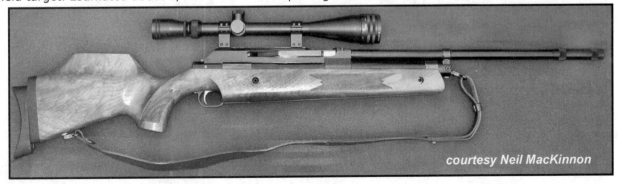

courtesy Neil MacKinnon

GRADING	100%	95%	90%	80%	60%	40%	20%

10.5 lbs. All guns hand built by John Whiscombe. Mfg. 1987-2009.

	100%	95%	90%	80%	60%	40%	20%
	$4,000	$3,400	$2,800	$2,325	$1,800	$1,200	$800

Add 10% for extra barrel.

Last MSR was $2,200-$2,600.

Many upgrades and extras were available.

WILKINS, JOE

Previous custom maker of the Predator PCP repeating air rifle located in England.

Sometimes incorrectly referred to as the Ripley Predator. However, Ripley Rifles, the small firm which produced the Ripley AR-5 rifle, is owned by Steve Wilkens, Joe's son. The Wilkens Predator was discontinued to a large degree because slide action guns are considered politically incorrect in Britain and the maker did not want to stimulate the Home Office into further control of airguns.

RIFLES

PREDATOR – .22 cal., PCP, Field Target rifle, 15 or 16-shot repeater, slide action loads and cocks with a single rapid stroke, power regulator, most set at 12 ft./lb., one at 18 ft./lb., and one at 26 ft./lb. 20. Mfg. 1987-1999.

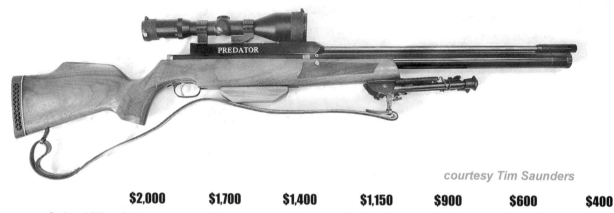

courtesy Tim Saunders

$2,000	$1,700	$1,400	$1,150	$900	$600	$400

One was made in .177 cal.

WILL

Previous tradename of Oskar Will of Zella-Mehlis, Thüringen, Germany, established in 1844.

His son, Oskar Will The Younger, was one of the most famous airgun makers in Germany before 1914. Circa 1923, the company was sold to Wilhelm Foss who operated it as Venuswaffenfabrik until 1945. Especially famous for air rifles, with large diameter central compression chambers, which used the extended trigger guard as a cocking lever ("Bügelspanners") . These guns carried on the tradition of the large receiver gallery airguns made in the USA in the mid-1800s. Such trigger guard lever guns (Bügelspanners) continued to be listed in European gun wholesaler catalogs into the 1960s. (See American Gallery Airguns section in the "A" section.) Actual old specimens of Will and Original Will airguns currently retail in the $500-$750 range, while newer copies, marked "Original", or without markings, retail in the $250-$400 range. Crank style air rifles (Kürbelspanners) from the Wills usually retail in the $650-$1,250 range. Crank style pistols retail in the $1,500-$3,500 range.

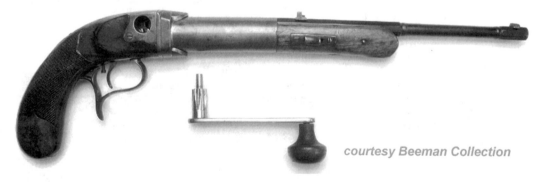

courtesy Beeman Collection

GRADING	100%	95%	90%	80%	60%	40%	20%

WINCHESTER

Current manufacturer located in Morgan, UT. Previously located in New Haven, CT. Sales and service are through Daisy Outdoor Products, located in Rogers, AR.

Beginning 2001, airguns under the Winchester label were imported again; this time from Spain and Turkey.

Between 1969 and 1975 Winchester imported eight rifle models and two pistol models into the United States from Meyer & Grammelspacher located in Germany. A total of 19,259 airguns were imported through 1973. See "STORE BRAND CROSS-OVER LIST" for a table of Winchester airguns made by M&G in Germany.

For more information and current pricing on both new and used Winchester firearms, please refer to the *Blue Book of Gun Values* by S.P. Fjestad (also available online).

PISTOLS

MODEL 11 – BB/.177 cal., CO_2 semi-auto, blowback action, smooth bore steel barrel, brown composite grip, manual trigger block safety, 16-shot clip, blade front and fixed open rear sights, 410 FPS, 8.5 in. OAL, 1.9 lbs. New 2012.

courtesy Daisy

MSR $150	$125	$105	$90	$75	$55	$35	$25

MODEL 11K – BB/.177 cal., CO_2, semi-auto, blowback action, 410 FPS, smooth bore steel barrel, 16 shot, blade front and fixed open rear sights, nickel finish with black checkering on grip plates, manual trigger block safety, includes hard shell case with foam inserts, 8.5 in. OAL, 3.3 lbs.

courtesy Daisy

MSR $150	$125	$105	$90	$75	$55	$35	$25

Add $5 for Model 11K kit with two CO_2 cartridges and tin of 750 Winchester steel BBs.

MODEL 353 – .177 or .22 cal., BBC, SP, SS, 7 in. rifled steel barrel, 378 FPS, blue finish, composition plastic stock, hooded bead front and adj. rear sights, 2.75 lbs.

N/A	$200	$160	$130	$100	$70	$40

1974 retail price was $42.

MODEL 363 – .177 cal., BBC, SP, SS, 7 in. rifled steel barrel, 378 FPS, double piston recoilless design, micrometer rear and interchangeable front sights, fully adj. trigger, match grade composition plastic stock with thumb rest, 16 in. overall, 3 lbs.

N/A	$250	$200	$165	$125	$90	$50

1974 retail price was $64.

GRADING	100%	95%	90%	80%	60%	40%	20%

RIFLES

MODEL 77XS – BB/.177 cal. or pellet, multi-pump pneumatic, 800FPS, rifled steel barrel, Truglo fiber optic front and adj. rear sights, rugged, durable black composite thumbhole stock and forearm, Crossbolt trigger block safety, includes 4x32 scope, 37.6 in. OAL, 3.1 lbs. New 2012.

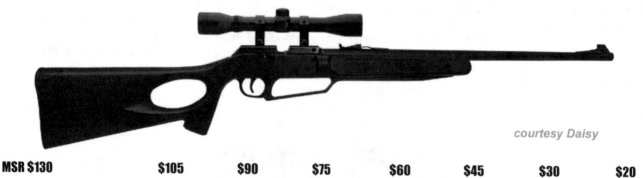

courtesy Daisy

MSR $130	$105	$90	$75	$60	$45	$30	$20

MODEL 333 – .177 cal., BBC, SP, SS, 576 FPS, diopter target sight, fully adj. trigger, double piston recoilless action, checkered and stippled walnut stock, 9.5 lbs.

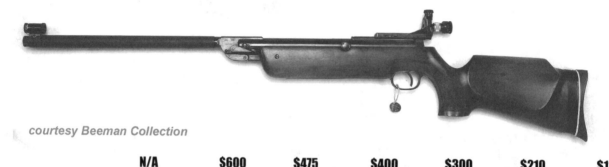

courtesy Beeman Collection

N/A	$600	$475	$400	$300	$210	$120

MODEL 416 – .177 cal., BBC, SP, SS, smooth bore barrel, blue finish, double pull-type trigger, wood stock, 363 FPS, fixed front and adj. rear sights, 33 in. overall, 2.75 lbs.

$50	$45	$35	$30	$25	$15	$10

1974 retail price was $21.

MODEL 422 – .177 cal., BBC, SP, SS, rifled barrel, blue finish, wood stock, double pull-type trigger, 480 FPS, fixed front and adj. rear sights, 36 in. overall, 3.75 lbs.

$65	$55	$45	$40	$30	$20	$15

1974 retail price was $30.

MODEL 423 – .177 cal., similar to Model 422, except fixed ramp front and adj. rear sights, 36 in. overall, 4 lbs.

$85	$70	$60	$50	$40	$25	$15

1974 retail price was $37.

MODEL 425 – .22 cal., similar to Model 423, except with 543 FPS, adj. double-pull type trigger, dovetail base for scope, non-slip composition buttplate, 38 in. overall, 5 lbs.

courtesy Beeman Collection

$125	$105	$90	$75	$55	$35	$25

1974 retail price was $42.

GRADING	100%	95%	90%	80%	60%	40%	20%

MODEL 427 – .22 cal., similar to Model 425, except with 660 FPS, micrometer rear and hooded front sight, 42 in. OAL, 6 lbs.

| | $195 | $165 | $135 | $115 | $90 | $60 | $40 |

1974 retail price was $48.

MODEL 435 – .177 cal., similar to Model 427, except with 693 FPS, micrometer rear and interchangeable front sight, checkered stock and adj. trigger, 44 in. OAL, 6.5 lbs.

| | $225 | $190 | $160 | $130 | $100 | $65 | $45 |

1974 retail price was $70.

MODEL 450 – .177 cal., UL, SP, SS, rifled steel barrel, blue finish, 693 FPS, micrometer rear and interchangeable front sight, dovetail base for scope, checkered Schutzen style stock, rubber buttplate, 44.5 in. OAL, 7.75 lbs.

| | $350 | $300 | $245 | $205 | $160 | $105 | $70 |

1974 retail price was $100.

MODEL 500X – .177 cal., BBC, SP, SS, 490 FPS, rifled steel barrel, micro-adj. rear and hooded front blade and ramp sights, grooved receiver, sporter-style select walnut stock, 5.7 lbs., 45.7 in. OAL. Mfg. in Turkey 2003-2011.

| | $125 | $110 | $100 | $80 | $60 | N/A | N/A |

Last MSR was $147.

* **Model 500XS** – .177 cal., BBC, SP, SS, 490 FPS, rifled steel barrel, solid steel shroud, sporter-style select walnut stock, front blade (disc.) and Truglo fiber optic front sight, Truglo (new 2008) micro-adj. rear and hooded (Disc. 2007) ramp sights, grooved receiver w/Winchester 4x32 AO scope, auto rear button safety, 41.4 in. OAL, 5.9 lbs. Mfg. in Turkey. New 2004.

courtesy Daisy

| MSR $130 | $105 | $90 | $75 | $60 | $45 | $30 | $20 |

MODEL 600X – .177 cal., BBC, SP, SS, 600 FPS, rifled steel barrel, micro-adj. rear sight, hooded front sight with blade and ramp, grooved receiver, sporter-style select walnut stock, 5.9 lbs. Mfg. in Turkey 2001-06.

| | | $85 | $70 | $60 | $50 | $40 | $25 | $15 |

Last MSR was $90.

Add 30% for Model 600XS with 4x32 Winchester scope new 2004.

MODEL 722X – .22 cal., BBC, SP, SS, 700 FPS, rifled steel barrel, micro-adj. rear sight, hooded front sight with blade and ramp, grooved receiver, rear safety button, sporter-style select walnut stock, 6.6 lbs. Mfg. in Turkey 2001-03.

| | $115 | $100 | $80 | $65 | $50 | $35 | $25 |

Last MSR was $170.

MODEL 800X – .177 cal., BBC, SP, SS, 800 FPS, rifled steel barrel, Truglo (new 2008) micro-adj. rear and hooded (Disc. 2007) front blade and ramp sights, grooved receiver, rear safety button, sporter-style select walnut stock, 6.6 lbs., 46.7 in. OAL. Mfg. in Turkey. Mfg. 2001-2011.

| | $140 | $125 | $110 | $90 | $70 | N/A | N/A |

Last MSR was $165.

* **Model 800XS** – .177 cal., BBC, SP, SS, 800 FPS, rifled steel barrel, micro-adj. rear and hooded front blade and ramp sights, grooved receiver w/Winchester 4x32 AO scope, rear safety button, sporter-style select walnut stock, 6.6 lbs., 46.7 in. OAL. Mfg. in Turkey. Mfg. 2004-2011.

| | $170 | $150 | $135 | $110 | $85 | N/A | N/A |

Last MSR was $202.

MODEL 850XS22 – .22 cal., BBC, SP, SS, 850 FPS, rifled steel barrel, Truglo micro-adj. rear and hooded front ramp fiber optic sights, grooved receiver w/Winchester 4x32 AO scope, auto-rear safety button, sporter-style solid hardwood stock, 7.6 lbs., 45 in. OAL. Mfg. in Turkey. Mfg. 2004-2011.

| | $300 | $265 | $240 | $195 | $150 | N/A | N/A |

Last MSR was $355.

GRADING	100%	95%	90%	80%	60%	40%	20%

MODEL 1000B – .177 cal., BBC, SP, SS, 1000 FPS, rifled steel barrel, Truglo fiber optic (new 2008) micro-adj. rear and hooded front ramp sights, grooved receiver, auto rear safety button, black sporter-style composite stock, recoil pad, 44.5 in. OAL, 6.6 lbs. Mfg. 2004-2011.

	100%	95%	90%	80%	60%	40%	20%
	$155	$140	$125	$100	$80	N/A	N/A

Last MSR was $185.

* Model 1000SB – .177 cal., BBC, SP, SS, 1000 FPS, rifled steel barrel, Truglo fiber optic (new 2008) micro-adj. rear and hooded front ramp sights, grooved receiver w/4x32 AO Winchester scope, auto rear safety button, black sporter-style composite stock, recoil pad, 44.5 in. OAL, 6.6 lbs. Mfg. 2004-2011.

	100%	95%	90%	80%	60%	40%	20%
	$195	$175	$160	$130	$95	N/A	N/A

Last MSR was $232.

MODEL 1000C – .177 cal., BBC, SP, SS, 1000 FPS, rifled steel barrel, micro-adj. rear sight, hooded front sight with blade and ramp, grooved receiver, rear safety button, camo sporter-style composite stock, recoil pad, 44.5 in. OAL, 6.6 lbs. Mfg. 2004-2007.

	100%	95%	90%	80%	60%	40%	20%
	$140	$120	$100	$80	$65	$40	$30

Last MSR was $150.

Add 15% for Model 1000SC with 3-9x32 Winchester scope (new 2004).

MODEL 1000X – .177 cal., BBC, SP, SS, 1000 FPS, rifled steel barrel, micro-adj. rear sight, hooded front sight with blade and ramp, grooved receiver, rear safety button, sporter-style select walnut stock, 6.6 lbs. Mfg. 2001-2011.

	100%	95%	90%	80%	60%	40%	20%
	$195	$170	$155	$125	$95	N/A	N/A

Last MSR was $229.

* Model XS – .177 cal., BBC, SP, SS, 1000 FPS, rifled steel barrel, Truglo fiber optic (new 2008) micro-adj. rear sight and hooded (disc. 2007) ramp front sights, grooved receiver with 4x32 AO Winchester scope, auto rear safety button, sporter-style select walnut stock, 46.7 in. OAL, 6.6 lbs. Mfg. 2004-2011.

	100%	95%	90%	80%	60%	40%	20%
	$230	$205	$185	$150	$115	N/A	N/A

Last MSR was $270.

MODEL 1028 WS – .177 cal., BBC, SP, SS, 1000 FPS, rifled steel barrel, solid steel shroud, solid hardwood stock with checkering, TruGlo fiber optic front and micro adj. fiber optic rear sights, 4x32 scope with AO, grooved receiver, auto rear thumb safety, 46.25 in. OAL, 6.6 lbs. Mfg. 2011-2012.

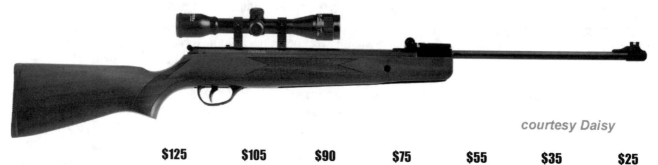

courtesy Daisy

	100%	95%	90%	80%	60%	40%	20%
	$125	$105	$90	$75	$55	$35	$25

Last MSR was $150.

MODEL 1029 – .177 cal., BBC, SP, SS, 1000 FPS, fluted, composite jacketed rifled steel barrel, black composite stock with thumbhole grip, no open sights, grooved receiver, 3-9x32mm scope with AO, auto rear thumb safety, 46.7 in. OAL, 6.6 lbs. Model 2011-2012.

courtesy Daisy

	100%	95%	90%	80%	60%	40%	20%
	$170	$145	$120	$100	$75	$50	$35

Last MSR was $200.

GRADING	100%	95%	90%	80%	60%	40%	20%

MODEL 1100SS – .177 cal., SP, SS, BBC, 1100 FPS, rifled steel barrel with solid steel shroud, micro-adjustable rear sight and white dot front sight, black composite stock, includes 4x32 scope, 46.25 in. OAL, 11.4 lbs.

courtesy Daisy

| MSR $130 | $105 | $90 | $75 | $60 | $45 | $30 | $20 |

MODEL 1100WS – .177 cal., BBC, SP, SS, 1000 FPS, rifled steel barrel with solid steel shroud, micro-adjustable rear sight and white dot front sight, solid hardwood stock, includes 4x32 scope, 46.25 in. OAL, 8.5 lbs.

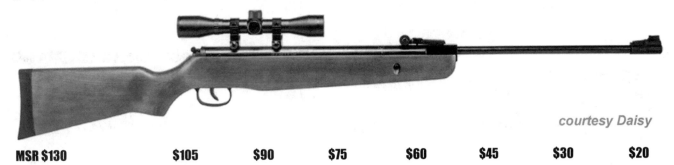

courtesy Daisy

| MSR $130 | $105 | $90 | $75 | $60 | $45 | $30 | $20 |

MODEL 1100XSU – .177 cal., UL, SP, SS, 1100 FPS, rifled steel barrel, sporter-style solid hardwood stock with checkering, Truglo fiber optic micro-adj. rear sight and hooded ramp front sights, grooved receiver w/4x32 AO Winchester scope, auto rear safety button, 46.5 in. OAL, 8.75 lbs. Mfg. 2009-2011.

| | $425 | $375 | $325 | $270 | $210 | N/A | N/A |

Last MSR was $495.

MODEL 1250CS – .177 cal., BBC, SP, SS, 1000 FPS, rifled steel barrel, fiber optic sights, Mossy Oak Break-up Infinity Camo composite stock with thumbhole grip, fold-down bipod legs, web sling, includes 3-9x32 air rifle scope, 46.5 in. OAL, 8.7 lbs.

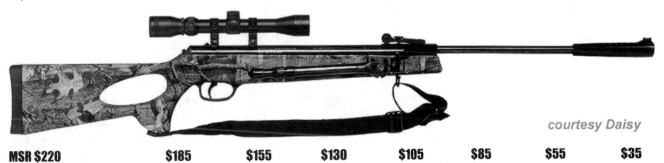

courtesy Daisy

| MSR $220 | $185 | $155 | $130 | $105 | $85 | $55 | $35 |

MODEL 1250SS – .177 cal., BBC, SP, SS, 1000 FPS, fluted, composite jacketed, rifled steel barrel with bull barrel shroud, Black composite stock with thumbhole grip, includes 3-9x 32 scope, 46.7 in. OAL, 9.1 lbs.

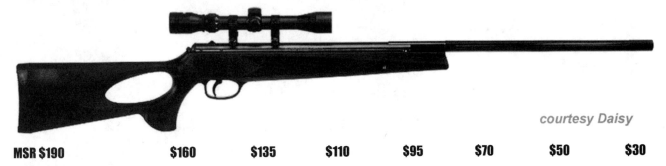

courtesy Daisy

| MSR $190 | $160 | $135 | $110 | $95 | $70 | $50 | $30 |

GRADING	100%	95%	90%	80%	60%	40%	20%

MODEL 1250WS – .177 cal., SP, SS, BBC, 1000 FPS, rifled steel barrel with solid steel shroud, fiber optic front and micro-adj. fiber optic rear sights, hardwood stock with checkered grip, includes 4x32 AO scope, 46.25 in. OAL, 8.5 lbs.

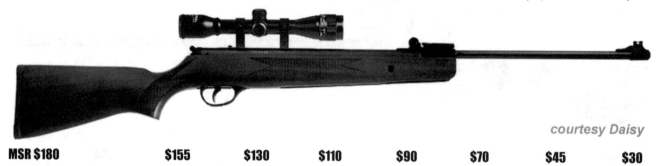

courtesy Daisy

MSR $180	$155	$130	$110	$90	$70	$45	$30

MODEL 1400CS – .177 cal., BBC, SP, SS, up to 1400 FPS, rifled steel barrel with muzzle-mounted sound suppressor, no open sights, Mossy Oak Break-up Infinity Camo composite stock with thumbhole grip, fold-down bipod legs, web sling, includes 3-9x32 break-barrel air rifle scope, 52 in. OAL, 9 lbs.

courtesy Daisy

MSR $230	$195	$165	$135	$115	$90	$60	$40

MODEL 1894 – BB/.174 cal., lever action, SP, 300 FPS, 15-shot mag., smooth bore steel barrel, micro-adj. rear sight, blade and ramp front sight, crossbolt trigger safety, western-style wood stock and forearm, 3.4 lbs. Imported from Turkey. Mfg. 2003-2008.

courtesy Daisy

	$95	$80	$65	$55	$45	$30	$20

Last MSR was $100.

MODEL M14 – .177 cal., CO$_2$, semi-auto, BB or pellet, rifled steel barrel, blade front and adj. rear sights, rugged, durable brown composite stock, trigger lock safety, 16-shot BB or pellet clip, 700 FPS, 44.5 in. OAL, 4.4 lbs. New 2012.

courtesy Daisy

MSR $100	$85	$70	$60	$50	$40	$25	$15

GRADING	100%	95%	90%	80%	60%	40%	20%

MODEL MP4 – .177 cal., BB or pellet, two 12g CO_2 cylinders, semi-auto, 700 FPS, rifled steel barrel, 16 shot, adj. folding sights, trigger lock safety, metal receiver, forearm quad rail with extended top rail and sling swivel, composite collapsible stock, pistol grip, Black finish, 38.5 in. OAL, 5.8 lbs.

courtesy Daisy

MSR $200	$170	$145	$120	$100	$75	$50	$35

WINSEL

Previously manufactured by Winsel Corporation of Rochester, NY.

PISTOLS

JET PISTOL – .22 cal., CO_2, SS, breech loading, brass barrel, 410 FPS, button safety behind trigger, cocked and breech opened by pushing lever at bottom of grip, black plastic grips, aluminum frame, 12 in. overall, with cylinder attached, black crinkle paint finish on receiver and rear of barrel housing, glossy black elsewhere. Supplied with two CO_2 cylinders, one in a slim cardboard "mailing box" for returning cylinders to factory for refill, 2.3 lbs. Mfg. 1948.

courtesy Beeman Collection

	N/A	$1,000	$800	$650	$500	$350	$200

Add 30% for original maroon factory box and papers.
Subtract 20% for each missing cylinder.

Most specimens are without one or both cylinders because the manufacturer went out of business while holding many customers' cylinders. They were destroyed.

WISCHO

For information on Wischo air guns, see B.S.F. in the "B" section.

WRIGHT MFG. CO.

Previous manufacturer located in Burbank, CA.

PISTOLS

WRIGHT TARGET SHOT JR. – .177 cal., SP, SS, rear plunger pulls out to cock, 2.5 in. smoothbore barrel unscrews for rear loading of pellet, shot, or dart. Diecast body includes checkered grip panels. 8.1 in. OAL, 1 lbs.

	N/A	N/A	$45	$40	$35	$30	$25

WYANDOTTE

Previous tradename of American Tool Works located in Chicago, IL.

For information on Wyandotte, see American Tool Works in the "A" section.

Join the Firearms Industry in Promoting Safe and Responsible Firearm Storage

For more than a decade, the firearms industry has worked to encourage the proper storage of firearms through the Project ChildSafe Program. It's part of our commitment to foster firearms safety and help prevent firearms accidents, theft and misuse.

We know safe and secure storage works, and we invite you to join us in spreading this message.

Please visit ProjectChildSafe.org to learn more.

A program of the National Shooting Sports Foundation

X-Y-Z SECTION

XTSG

Previous manufacturer located in Zhejiang Province, China.

XTSG had more than 40 years experience manufacturing airguns and airsoft.

YEWHA

Previous tradename of airguns manufactured in South Korea.

Yewha (Ye-Wha) airguns are reported to have been made by Tong-Il Industrial Co. Ltd. of Seoul, South Korea, but that may be only a trading company. Yewha may be the name of the maker. Distributed in the United States by Beeman Precision Airguns in the 1970s. These airguns were apparently made only in the 1970s. Due to anti-firearm laws in Korea, gun clubs may be equipped only with these guns. Club pictures show huge piles of ringneck pheasants taken with the B3 Dynamite airgun. Ref: AGNR - Oct. 1987, www.beemans.net (see also the "A Shot of Humor" section on the www.beemans.net website).

GRADING	100%	95%	90%	80%	60%	40%	20%

RIFLES/SHOTGUNS

3-B – .25 cal., PP (pump-rod-at-the-muzzle), BA, SS, 28.7 in. rifled bbl., globe front and apature rear sights, parkerized finish, hardwood stock, twenty or more pumps can produce up to 1000 FPS, 41.3 in. OAL, 5.75 lbs.

N/A	$600	$475	$400	$300	$210	$120

B3 DYNAMITE – .25 cal., PP (pump-rod-at-the-muzzle), BA, SS, 28.7 in. smoothbore barrel, parkerized finish, hardwood stock, twenty or more pumps can produce up to 1000 FPS, 41.3 in. OAL, 5.75 lbs.

courtesy Beeman Collection

N/A	$500	$400	$325	$250	$175	$100

Breech loaded with plastic birdshot cartridge or single lead balls.

REVOLVING RIFLE – .177 cal., pump pneumatic (pump-rod-at-the-muzzle), DA, 6-shot revolving cylinder for pellets, 28.7 in. rifled barrel, parkerized finish, hardwood stock, exposed hammer, twenty or more pumps can produce up to 1000 FPS, 41.3 in. OAL, 5.75 lbs.

courtesy Beeman Collection

N/A	$1,000	$800	$650	$500	$350	$200

TARGET RIFLE - PUMP ROD MODEL – .177 cal., pump pneumatic (pump-rod-at-the-muzzle), SS, 6-shot revolving cylinder for pellets, 28.7 in. rifled barrel, parkerized finish, hardwood stock, exposed hammer, twenty or more pumps can produce up to 1000 FPS, 41.3 in. OAL, 5.75 lbs.

courtesy Beeman Collection

N/A	$900	$725	$575	$450	$325	$180

GRADING	100%	95%	90%	80%	60%	40%	20%

TARGET 200 – .177 cal., SL, SP, recoilless match target air rifle.

	N/A	$350	$280	$230	$175	$125	$70

This model was an unauthorized copy of the Feinwerkbau Model 300 of much lower quality and reliability.

ZENITH

Previous trademark manufactured by Nick Murphy of Sileby, Loughborough, England from about 2001 to 2003.

Nick Murphy developed and produced top level Field Target air rifles. All had .177 caliber Walther or Career barrels. All barrels were sleeved and free floating. Most stocks were made by custom stock maker Paul Wilson. All were built with special Zenith regulators. Ripley and Zenith air rifles were among the outstanding field target guns in German and English FT competition during 2003 and 2004. These were produced with a wide variety of features and finishes. Production stopped at a total of sixteen rifles. The most recent sale was for $3,100.

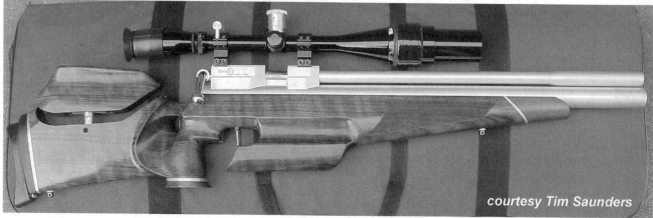

courtesy Tim Saunders

ZORAKI (ATAK SILAH SAN. TIC. LTD. STI.)

Current manufacturer located in Istanbul, Turkey. No current importation.

Zoraki manufactures quality air pistols. Please contact the company directly for more information regarding U.S. availability and pricing (see Trademark Index).

ZOS (NANTONG UNIVERSAL OPTICAL INSTRUMENT CO., LTD)

Current manufacturer located in Nantong, Jiangsu, China. No current U.S. importation.

ZOS manufactures quality air rifles. Please contact the company directly for more information regarding U.S. availability and pricing (see Trademark Index).

TRADEMARK INDEX

The listings below represent the most up-to-date information we have regarding airgun manufacturers (both domestic and international), trademarks, importers, and distributors (when applicable) to assist you in obtaining additional information from these sources. Website and email listings are provided whenever possible – this may be your best way of obtaining up-to-date model and pricing information directly from the manufacturers, importers, and/or distributors. More and more companies are offering online information about their products and it pays to surf the net!

As this edition goes to press, we feel confident that the information listed below is the most up-to-date and accurate listing possible. Remember, things change every day in this industry, and a phone/fax number that is current today could have a new area code or be gone tomorrow. International fax/phone numbers may require additional overseas and country/city coding. If you should require additional assistance in "tracking" any of the current airgun manufacturers, distributors, or importers listed in this publication, please contact us and we will try to help you regarding these specific requests.

ASG (ACTION SPORT GAMES A/S)
Distributor/Importer - ASG, USA
Factory Address:
Bakkegaardsvej 304
Humlebaek, DK-3050 DENMARK
Phone No.:011-45-8928-1888
Fax No.:011-45-4919-3160
Website: www.actionsportgames.com

AERON CZ S.R.O.
Distributor - POMONA AIR GUNS
Distributor/Importer - TOP GUN-AIRGUNS, INC.
Factory Address:
Svitavske Nab. 27
612 00 Brno, CZECH REPUBLIC
Phone No.:011-420-5-4557-3080
Fax No.:011-420-5-4521-0407
Website: www.aeron.cz
Email: info@aeron.cz

AIR ARMS
Factory Address:
Unit 5/6 Hailsham Industrial Park
Diplocks Way, Hailsham, East Sussex
BN27 3JF U.K.
Phone No.:011-44-1323-845853
Fax No.:011-44-1323-440573
Website: www.air-arms.co.uk
Email: sales@air-arms.co.uk

AIRFORCE INTERNATIONAL (AIRFORCE AIRGUNS)
P.O. Box 2478
Fort Worth, TX 76113
Phone No.:817-451-8966
Toll Free: 877-247-4867
Fax No.:817-451-1613
Website: www.airforceairguns.com
Email: staff@airforceairguns.com

AIRGUN EXPRESS, INC.
See Pyramyd Air.

AIR ORDNANCE, LLC
3518 Adams Center Rd.
Fort Wayne, IN 46806 USA
Toll Free: 800-671-1498
Website: www.air-ordnance.com
Email: web@air-ordnance.com

AIRROW
See Swivel Machine Works, Inc.

AIR VENTURI
5135 Naiman Parkway
Solon, OH 44139
Phone No.:216-292-2570
Fax No.:216-373-0086
Website: www.airventuri.com
Email: dealers@airventuri.com

ALFA - PROJ SPOL. S.R.O.
Distributor/Importer - TOP GUN-AIRGUNS, INC.
Factory
Zábrdovická 11
Brno, 615 00 CZECH REPUBLIC
Phone No.:011-420-545-120-667
Fax No.:011-420-545-120-668
Website: www.alfa-proj.cz/en/
Email: info@alfa-proj.cz

ANICS GROUP
Headquarters
7 Vorontsovo Pole Street
Moscow, 105062 RUSSIA
Phone No.:011-495-917-2085
Fax No.:011-495-917-1766
Website: www.anics.com
Email: anics@anics.com

ANSCHÜTZ
Distributor/Importer - CHAMPION SHOOTERS SUPPLY, LLC
Distributor/Importer - CHAMPION'S CHOICE INC.
Daimlerstraße 12
Ulm, D-89079 GERMANY
Phone No.:011-49-731-40-120
Fax No.:011-49-731-40-12700
Website: www.anschuetz-sport.com
Email: JGA-Info@anschuetz-sport.com

ARAL ARMS
ISTOC 4. Ada No. 73
Mahmutbey-Bagcilar
Istanbul, TURKEY
Phone No.:011-90-212-659-4092
Website: www.aralsilah.com.tr

ARES AIRGUNS
1456 Sokak No:83 Kat : 4 / 402
Alsancak, Izmir 35220 TURKEY
Phone No.:011-90-232-464-56-40
Fax No.:011-90-232-464-56-50
Website: www.aresairguns.com
Email: info@aresairguns.com

ARMSCOR
(ARMS CORPORATION OF THE PHILIPPINES)
Armscor Avenue, Fortune
Marikina City, 1800 PHILIPPINES
Phone No.:011-44 -632-941-6243
Fax No.:011-44-632-942-0682
Website: www.armscor.com.ph
Email: info@armscor.com.ph

ATAMAN
DEMYAN LLC
10, the 2nd Donskoy Passway, building 3
Moscow, 119071 RUSSIA
Phone No.:011-7-495-984-7629
Website: www.ataman-guns.com
Email: info@bvgindustrial.ru

BAM (BEST AIRGUN MANUFACTURER IN CHINA)
Distributor/Importer - XISICO USA, INC.
No. 517 Datong Road Binhu District
Wuxi, Jiangsu Province 214024 CHINA
Phone No.:011-86-510-8025-8706
Fax No.:011-86-510-8025-8767
Website: www.china-bam.com
Email: van.yang@china-bam.com

BSA GUNS (U.K.), LTD.
Distributor/Importer - BSA GUNS USA (A division of Gamo Outdoor USA, Inc.)
Factory Address:
Armoury Road
Small Heath, Birmingham B11 2PP U.K.
Phone No.:011-44-121-772-8543
Fax No.:011-44-121-773-0845
Website: www.bsaguns.co.uk
Email: export@gamo.com

BAIKAL

Distributor/Importer - AIRGUNS OF ARIZONA

(Izhevsky Mekhanichesky Zavod)
8, Promyshlennaya str.
Izhevsk, 426063 RUSSIA
Fax No.:011-007-3412-665830
Website: www.baikalinc.ru
Email: worldlinks@baikalinc.ru

BARNES PNEUMATIC

Gary Barnes
P.O. Box 138
New Windsor, MD 21776
Website: www.glbarnes.com
Email: mail@glbarnes.com

BEEMAN PRECISION AIRGUNS

10652 Bloomfield Ave.
Santa Fe Springs, CA 90670
Phone No.:562-968-5891
Toll Free: 800-227-2744
Fax No.:562-968-5823
Website: www.beeman.com

BENELLI ARMI S.P.A.

Distributor/Importer - LARRY'S GUNS

Via della Stazione, 50
Urbino, PU 61029 ITALY
Phone No.:011-0722-307-1
Fax No.:011-0722-307-207
Website: www.benelli.it

BENJAMIN AIR RIFLE COMPANY (BENJAMIN)

See Crosman Corp. listing

BERETTA, PIETRO

Distributor/Importer - UMAREX USA, INC.

Fabbrica D'Armi Pietro Beretta S.p.A.
Via Pietro Beretta, 18
Gardone Val Trompia, Brescia 25063
ITALY
Phone No.:011-39-30-8341-1
Fax No.:011-39-30-8341-399
Website: www.beretta.it

BERETTA, PIETRO

Beretta U.S.A. Corp
17601 Beretta Drive
Accokeek, MD 20607
Toll Free: 800-237-3882
Website: www.berettausa.com

BOWKETT, JOHN

Website: www.johnbowkett.net

BROCOCK

Distributor/Importer - AIRGUNS OF ARIZONA

Unit 32 Heming Road, Washford
Industrial Estate
Redditch, Worcestershire B98 0DH U.K.
Phone No.:011-44-1527-527800
Fax No.:011-44-1527-527850
Website: www.brocock.co.uk
Email: sales@brocock.co.uk

BROWNING

Distributor/Importer - UMAREX USA, INC.

Administrative Headquarters:
One Browning Place
Morgan, UT 84050-9326
Phone No.:801-876-2711
Toll Free: 800-333-3288
Fax No.:801-876-3331
Website: www.browning.com

CZ (CESKA ZBROJOVKA)

Distributor/Importer - TOP GUN-AIRGUNS, INC.

Svatopluka Cecha 1283
Uhersky Brod, CZ 68827
CZECH REPUBLIC
Phone No.:011-420-572-651-111
Fax No.:011-420-572-633-665
Website: www.czub.cz
Email: info@czub.cz

COLT'S MANUFACTURING COMPANY, INC.

Distributor/Importer - UMAREX USA, INC.

Factory Address:
545 New Park Avenue
West Hartford, CT 06110
Phone No.:860-236-6311
Fax No.:860-244-1442
Website: www.coltsmfg.com

COMETA

Distributor/Importer - AIRFORCE INTERNATIONAL

Carbinas Cometa S.A.
C/Txonta, 26 Apdo, P.O. Box 310
Eibar, 20600 SPAIN
Phone No.:011-34-943-120-116
Fax No.:011-34-943-120-316
Website: www.cometaairgun.com
Email: cometa@cometaairgun.com

COMMANDO ARMS

Pasaalani MH 225 Sokak No. 2A/1
10040 Balikesir, TURKEY
Phone No.:011-90-266-266-2660
Website: www.commando-arms.com
Email: info@commando-arms.com

CROSMAN CORP.

7629 Routes 5 & 20
Bloomfield, NY 14469
Toll Free: 800-7Airgun (724-7486)
Fax No.:716-657-5405
Website: www.crosman.com
Email: info@crosman.com

CYBER GUN

Z.I. Les Bordes 9-11
rue henri Dunant, 91070 Bondoufle
FRANCE
Phone No.:011-33-(0)169-117-100
Fax No.:011-33-(0)169-117-101
Website: www.cybergun.com
Email: infos@cybergun.com

DAISY OUTDOOR PRODUCTS

P.O. Box 220
Rogers, AR 72757-0220
Phone No.:479-636-1200
Toll Free: 800-643-3458
Fax No.:479-636-1601
Website: www.daisy.com
Email: info@daisy.com

DAYSTATE LTD

Distributor/Importer - AIRGUNS OF ARIZONA

Birch House Lane
Cotes, Swynnerton Nr. Stone,
Staffordshire ST15 0QQ U.K.
Phone No.:011-44(0)-1782-791755
Fax No.:011-44(0)-1782-791617
Website: www.daystate.com
Email: sales@daystate.co.uk

DIANA (DIANAWERK) MAYER & GRAMMELSPACHER GMBH & CO. KG

Distributor/Importer - UMAREX USA, INC.

Factory Address:
Karlstraße 34
Rastatt, D-76437 GERMANY
Phone No.:011-49-7222-762-0
Fax No.:011-49-7222-762-78
Website: www.diana-airguns.de
Email: info@diana-airguns.de

DRULOV

Distributor/Importer - TOP GUN-AIRGUNS, INC.

výrobní družstvo
Smetanovo nám. 81
Litomyšl, 570 01 CZECH REPUBLIC
Phone No.:011-420-461-615-451
Fax No.:011-420-461-615-451

DRUMMEN CUSTOM GUNS

Maurice Drummen BV
Valkenburgerweg 49
6361 EB Nuth, THE NETHERLANDS
Phone No.:011-31-45-565-0040
Fax No.:011-31-45-565-0032
Website: www.dillonprecisioneurope.nl

EDGUN

Website: www.edgun.ru

EUN JIN

KOREA

EVANIX (MECA EVANIX CORPORATION)

Kumho Bldg, 123-25, Karak-Dong
Seoul, Songpa-Gu 138-160
SOUTH KOREA
Phone No.:011-82-2-430-9975-6
Fax No.:011-82-2-430-9974
Website: www.evanix.com
Email: evanix@evanix.com

FAS

Distributor/Importer - AIRGUNS OF ARIZONA

FX AIRGUNS AB
Distributor/Importer - AIRGUNS OF ARIZONA
Vasterangsvagen 10
SE-54235 Mariestad, SWEDEN
Website: www.fxairguns.com
Email: info@fxairguns.com

FALCON AIRGUNS
Hailsham Industrial Park Unit 5-6
Diplocks Way, Hailsham, East Sussex
BN27 3JF U.K.
Phone No.:011-1323-844-760
Email: sales@falcon-airguns.co.uk

FEINWERKBAU WESTINGER & ALTENBURGER GMBH
Distributor/Importer - BRENZOVICH FIREARMS & TRAINING CENTER
Distributor/Importer - CHAMPION'S CHOICE INC.
Neckarstraße 43
Oberndorf, Neckar 78727 GERMANY
Phone No.:011-49-7423-814-0
Fax No.:011-49-7423-814-200
Website: www.feinwerkbau.de
Email: info@feinwerkbau.de

GAMO PRECISION AIRGUNS (INDUSTRIAS EL GAMO, S.A.U.)
Distributor/Importer - GAMO OUTDOOR USA, INC.
Factory Address:
P.O. BOX16Sant Boi de Llobregat
Barcelona, 08830 SPAIN
Phone No.:011-34-93-640-72-48
Website: www.gamo.com/portal/es/home
Email: export@gamo.com

GERMAN SPORT GUNS GMBH (GSG)
Oesterweg 21
Ense-Höingen, D-59469 GERMANY
Phone No.:011-49-2938-97839-0
Fax No.:011-49-2938-97837-130
Website: www.germansportguns.de
Email: info@germansportguns.de

GUNPOWER LIMITED
P.O. Box 567
Ashford, Kent TN23 5FP U.K.
Phone No.:011-44-1233-642357
Fax No.:011-44-1233-613899
Website: www.gunpower.net
Email: sales@gunpower.net

GUN TOYS SRL
10, Via Misano
Calvenzano, (BG) Calvenzano 24040
ITALY

HAENEL
Spare Parts and Repairs
WTS Waffentechnik
Lauter 40
Suhl, 98528 GERMANY
Fax No.:011-49-3681-80-5766
Website: www.gunmaker.org
Email: info@gunmaker.org

HÄMMERLI AG
Distributor/Importer - LARRY'S GUNS
Also see Walther listing.
Factory Address:
Industrielplatz
Neuhausen, CH-8212 SWITZERLAND
Fax No.:011-41-52-674-6418
Website: www.hammerli.ch
Email: info@hammerli.ch

HATSAN ARMS CO.
Distributor/Importer - HATSAN USA, INC.
Ankara Karayolu 28. km. No. 289
Kemalpasa, Izmir 35170 TURKEY
Phone No.:011-90-232-878-91-00
Fax No.:011-90-232-878-91-02
Website: www.hatsan.com.tr
Email: info@hatsan.com.tr

HECKLER & KOCH GMBH
Distributor/Importer - UMAREX USA, INC.
Corporate Headquarters
Postfach 1329
Oberndorf, Neckar D-78722 GERMANY
Phone No.:011-49-74-23-79
Fax No.:011-49-74-23-79-2350
Website: www.heckler-koch.com
Email: hkinfoboard@heckler-koch-de.com

HEGMANS, THEO
Dorfstrasse 108
Kerken, D-47647 GERMANY
Website: www.hegmans.de
Email: theo@hegmans.de

INDUSTRY BRAND
Shanghai Air Gun Factory
9F, Zhongcheng Building, No. 2159
South Pudong Road
Pudong, Shanghai, PR 200127 CHINA
Phone No.:011-86-21-50941989
Fax No.:011-86-21-50941983
Website: www.airrifle-china.com
Email: SAG@airrifle-china.com

ISRAEL WEAPON INDUSTRIES (I.W.I.)
Factory - Israel

JONES, TIM
412 Church Street
Hawley, PA 18428

JONISKEIT
P.O. Box 7
Allmersbach im Tal, 71571 GERMANY
Phone No.:011-07191-53276
Fax No.:011-07181-53856
Website: www.joniskeit.de
Email: tannerconsult@arcor.de

KWC (KIEN WELL TOY INDUSTRIAL CO. LTD)
Distributor/Importer - AIR VENTURI/PYRAMYD AIR
Importer - PALCO SPORTS
Factory Address:
No. 5, Lane 209, Sec. 2, Zih Yo Rd.
Tainan, TAIWAN
Phone No.:886-6-2691815 #105
Fax No.:886-6-2698364
Website: www.kwcgun.com
Email: sales@mail.kwcgun.com

KALIBRGUN
Distributor/Importer - AIRGUNS OF ARIZONA
Distributor/Importer - TOP GUN-AIRGUNS, INC.
VALDY EU LTD.
Na louži 940/3
Praha 10, Vrsovice 101 00 CZECH REPUBLIC
Phone No.:011-420 267 314 622
Website: www.kalibrgun.com
Email: kalibrgun@gmail.com

KRAL
Fatih Mah Beysehir Caddesi
Uzumlu Kasabasi Beysehir, Konya
TURKEY
Phone No.:011-90-332-524-6628
Fax No.:011-90-332-524-6871
Website: www.kralav.com
Email: info@kralav.com

KÜNG (KUENG) AIRGUNS
Danv Kueng Fuerstensteinerst 47
Basel, CH 4053 SWITZERLAND
Phone No.:011-41-61-331-2822
Fax No.:011-41-61-331-2822
Website: www.blueline-studios.com/kuengairguns.com
Email: feedback@blueline-studios.com

MAC-1 AIRGUN DISTRIBUTORS
13974 Van Ness Ave
Gardena, CA 90249
Phone No.:310-327-3582
Fax No.:310-327-0238
Website: www.mac1airgun.com
Email: mac1airgun@gmail.com

MAGNUM RESEARCH, INC.
Distributor/Importer - UMAREX USA, INC.
Website: www.magnumresearch.com

MAGTECH
CBC - COMPANHIA BRASILEIRA DE CARTUCHOS
Av. Humbertos de Campos, 3220
Ribeirão Pires, SP, 09426-900 BRAZIL
Phone No.:011-55-11-2139-8374
Fax No.:011-55-2139-8323
Website: www.cbc.com.br
Email: export@cbc.com.br

MAKAROV

Distributor/Importer - UMAREX USA, INC.

MÄNNEL SPORT SHOOTING GMBH

Haupstrabe 78
Kronstorf, 4484 AUSTRIA
Phone No.:011-43-7225-21-1100
Fax No.:011-43-125-33-033-4879
Website: www.maennel.at
Email: office@maennel.at

MARKSMAN PRODUCTS

10652 Bloomfield Ave.
Santa Fe Springs, CA 90670
Phone No.:562-968-5892
Toll Free: 800-822-8005
Website: www.marksman.com

MARLIN

P.O. Box 1781
Madison, NC 27025
Phone No.:203-239-5621
Website: www.marlinfirearms.com

MAROCCHI

Distributor/Importer - AIRGUNS OF ARIZONA
MAROCCHI/CD EUROPE S.r.l.
Società Unipersonale, Via Galilei, 6
Sarezzo, 25068 ITALY
Phone No.:011-39-030-80-10-14
Fax No.:011-39-030-89-00-370
Website: www.marocchiarms.com
Email: info@marocchiarms.com

MATCHGUNS SRL

Via Fornari Giulio 17A
Vigatto, Parma 43124 ITALY
Phone No.:011-39-0521-632020
Fax No.:011-39-0521-631973
Website: www.matchguns.com
Email: info@matchguns.com

MAUSER

Zeigelstadel 1
Isny, D-88316 GERMANY
Fax No.:011-4190-368-4750794
Website: www.mauserwaffen.de
Email: info@mauserwaffen.de

MENALDI

Cassafouth 1574
Barrio Providencia, Cordoba CP 5000
ARGENTINA
Phone No.:011-54-351-4726872
Website: www.menaldi.com.ar
Email: info@menaldi.com.ar

MENDOZA S.A. DE C.V.

Distributor/Importer - AIR VENTURI/PYRAMYD AIR
Prolongacion Constitucion No. 57
Xochimilco, 16210 MEXICO
Phone No.:011-5255-1084-1122
Fax No.:011-5255-1084-1155
Website: www.pmendoza.com.mx

MOLOT

Vyatskie Polyany Machine-Building Plant
135 Lenin Street Vyatskie Polyany, Kirov
Region 612960 RUSSIA
Phone No.:011-007-83334-62870
Fax No.:011-007-83334-62199
Website: www.molot.biz
Email: molot_ves@list.ru

MORINI COMPETITION ARM SA

Distributor/Importer - CHAMPION'S CHOICE INC.
Distributor/Importer - PILKINGTON COMPETITION EQUIPMENT LLC
Via Ai Gelsi 11
Bedano, CH 6930 SWITZERLAND
Phone No.:011-41-91-935-2230
Fax No.:011-41-91-935-2231
Website: www.morini.ch
Email: morini@morini.ch

NATIONAL RIFLES LTD. (INDIA)

Indian Hume Pipe Co.
INDIA
Website: www.indianhumepipe.com
Email: info@indianhumepipe.com

NORICA LAURONA

Avda. Otaola, 16
Eibar, Guipuzcoa 26000 SPAIN
Fax No.:011-34-943-207-449
Website: www.norica.es
Email: farmi@norica.es

OTTOMANGUNS

Yayalar Mah. Yayalar Card. No: 6 Kat: 5/6
Pendik, Istanbul TURKEY
Phone No.:011-90-216-627-0627
Fax No.:011-90-627-0282
Website: www.ottomanguns.com

PALCO SPORTS

8555 Revere Lane N.
Maple Grove, MN 55369 USA
Toll Free: 800-882-4656
Fax No.:763-559-2286
Website: www.palcosports.com/index.cfm
Email: info@palcosports.com

PALMER CHEMICAL AND EQUIPMENT CO.

P.O. Box 867 Palmer Village
Douglasville, GA 30133
Phone No.:928-717-2315
Fax No.:928-717-2198

PARDINI, ARMI S.R.L.

Distributor/Importer - PARDINI USA LLC.
Via Italica 154/a
Lido Di Camaiore, LU 55041 ITALY
Phone No.:011-39-0584-90121
Fax No.:011-39-0584-90122
Website: www.pardini.it
Email: info@pardini.it

PARDUS

PARDUS SILAH LTD. STI.
Dudullu OSB Imes Sanayi SitesiB-Blok,
205 Sokak, No. 22
Umraniye, Istanbul, TURKEY
Phone No.:011-90-216-642-2353
Fax No.:011-90-216-642-2360
Website: www.pardusarms.com
Email: info@pardusarms.com

PARK RIFLE COMPANY

Unit 68A, Dartford Trade Park
Powder Mill Lane, Dartford, Kent DA1
1NX U.K.
Phone No.:011-44-1322-292238

PIPER

Distributor - X-CALIBER TACTICAL
Piper Precision Products
Box 95
Lamposa, TX 76550 USA
Website: www.pipersprecisionproducts. com

PNEU-DART, INC.

15223 Route 87 Hwy.
Williamsport, PA 17701
Phone No.:570-323-2710
Toll Free: 866-299-3278
Fax No.:570-323-2712
Website: www.pneudart.com
Email: info@pneudart.com

PYRAMYD AIR INTERNATIONAL

5135 Naiman Parkway
Solon, OH 44139
Toll Free: 888-262-4867
Fax No.:216-896-0896
Website: www.pyramydair.com
Email: sales@pyramydair.com

QUACKENBUSH, DENNIS

Quackenbush Air Guns
2203 Hwy. AC
Urbana, MO 65767
Phone No.:417-993-5262
Website: www.quackenbushairguns.com

RWS PRECISION PRODUCTS

Distributor/Importer - UMAREX USA, INC.
See Umarex USA listing.

REAMES, MIKE

Email: reames@wcoil.com

REMINGTON ARMS COMPANY, INC.

Corporate Headquarters
870 Remington Drive, P.O. Box 700
Madison, NC 27025-0700
Toll Free: 800-243-9700
Fax No.:336-548-7801
Website: www.remington.com
Email: info@remington.com

RETAY ARMS CORP.
F. Cakmak Mah No. 10728 Sk.
No. 5, Konya 42050 TURKEY
Phone No.:011-90-332-342-6513
Fax No.:011-332-342-6514
Website: www.retayarms.com
Email: info@retayarms.com

RIPLEY AIR RIFLES
Distributor/Importer - AIRGUNS OF ARIZONA
Factory Address:
P.O. Box 8640, Market Harborough
Leicestershire LE16 0DB U.K.
Phone No.:011-44-1858-410-683
Fax No.:011-44-1857-341-111
Website: www.hoganfirearms.co.uk
Email: sales@hoganfirearms.co.uk

RIPLEY RIFLES
42 Fletcher Street
Ripley, Derbyshire, DE5 3LP
UNITED KINGDOM
Phone No.:011-017-737-48353

RÖHM GMBH
Postfach 1161
Sontheim, Benz D-89565 GERMANY
Phone No.:011-49-73-25-160
Fax No.:011-49-73-25-16-492
Website: www.roehm.rg.de
Email: inforg@roehm.rg.de

RUTTEN AIRGUNS SA
RUTTEN HERSTAL
Parc Industriel des Hauts-Sarts
Premiere Avenue, 7-9, Herstal B-4040
BELGIUM
Fax No.:011-32-41-64-8589

SAG (SHANGHAI AIR GUN FACTORY)
9F, Zhongcheng Bldg.
No. 2159 South Pudong Road, Shanghai
200127 CHINA
Phone No.:011-86-21-5094-1990
Fax No.:011-86-21-50941-983
Website: www.airrifle-china.com
Email: SAG@airrifle-china.com

SAM YANG PRECISION IND. CO.
75-1 Nae-dong Ojung-ku
Bucheon-si, Gyeonggi-do
SOUTH KOREA
Phone No.:82-32-6771795
Website: www.sygun.en.ec21.com

SAULS, RON
P.O. Box 5772
Anderson, SC 29623
Phone No.:864-261-6810
Website: www.bryanandac.com
Email: bryanandac@aol.com

SHARK MANUFACTURING CO.
Buenos Aires, ARGENTINA

SHERIDAN PRODUCTS, INC.
See Crosman Corp. listing.

SHIN SUNG INDUSTRIES CO. LTD.
Distributor/Importer - AIRGUNS OF ARIZONA
201-6, Samjung-Dong, Ohjeong-Ku,
Buchon-City, Kyungki-Do KOREA

SIBERGUN
Yazicilar Av Malzemeleri Tic. Ltd. Sti
Yesiltepe Mah. Yavuz Selim Bulvari Can
SitesiB Blok 351/B
Trabzon, TURKEY
Phone No.:011-90-462-230-5616
Fax No.:011-90-462-224-1859
Website: www.yazicilarav.com
Email: info@yazicilarav.com

SIG SAUER
Distributor/Importer - AIR VENTURI/PYRAMYD AIR
Importer - PALCO SPORTS
See also Kine Well Toy Industrial Co. Ltd.
18 Industrial Park Drive
Exeter, NH 03833 USA
Phone No.:603-772-2302
Fax No.:603-772-9082
Website: www.sigarms.com

SIG SAUER
Factory Address:
Schweizerische Industrie-Gesellschaft
Industrielplatz
Neuhausen am Rheinfall CH-8212
SWITZERLAND
Fax No.:011-41-153-216-601

SILVA ARMS
Giyimkent Orug Reis Mah.
Vadi Cad 240-A Esenler
Istanbul, TURKEY
Website: www.silvaarms.com

SKAN AR
P.O. Box 3342
White Colne, Colchester CO62RA U.K.

SMITH & WESSON
Distributor/Importer - UMAREX USA, INC.
Factory Address:
2100 Roosevelt Avenue
Springfield, MA 01104
Phone No.:413-781-8300
Toll Free: 800-331-0852
Fax No.:413-747-3317
Website: www.smith-wesson.com
Email: ga@smith-wesson.com

STEYR SPORTWAFFEN GMBH
Distributor/Importer - CHAMPION'S CHOICE INC.
Olympiastraße 1
Ernsthofen, A-4432 AUSTRIA
Phone No.:011-43-7435-202-59-0
Fax No.:011-43-7435-202-59-99
Website: www.steyr-sport.com
Email: office@steyr-sport.com

STOEGER INDUSTRIES INC.
17603 Indian Head Hwy
Accokeek, MD 20607
Phone No.:301-283-6300
Toll Free: 800-264-4962
Fax No.:301-283-6988
Website: www.stoegerairguns.com
Email: benusa1@aol.com

STURM, RUGER & CO., INC.
1 Lacey Place
Southport, CT 06890
Fax No.:203-256-3367
Website: www.ruger.com

SWISS ARMS MANUFACTURE (SAM)
Via alla Roggia 9a
Viganello Lugano, CH-6962
SWITZERLAND
Fax No.:011-41-91-9721213
Website: www.samarms.ch
Email: marco@dolina.ch

SWIVEL MACHINE WORKS, INC.
11 Monitor Hill Road
Newtown, CT 06470
Phone No.:203-270-6343
Website: www.swivelmachine.com
Email: swivelmachine@swivelmachine.com

TAIYO JUKI
Miroku Firearms Mfg. Co. 537-1
Shinohara
Nangoku City, Kochi-Pref JAPAN
Phone No.:011-81-88-863-3317

TANFOGLIO, FRATELLI, S.R.L.
Factory Address:
Via Valtrompia 39/41
Gardone, V.T. (BS) - 25063 ITALY
Phone No.:01139 030.8910623
Fax No.:01139 030.8910183
Website: www.tanfoglio.it
Email: info@tanfoglio.it

TAU BRNO, SPOL. S R.O.
Distributor/Importer - TOP GUN-AIRGUNS, INC.
Stará 8
Brno, 602 00 CZECH REPUBLIC
Phone No.:011-420-545-212-323
Fax No.:011-420-545-212-323
Website: www.taubrno.com
Email: taubrno@tiscali.cz

TECH FORCE
Distributor/Importer - AIR VENTURI/PYRAMYD AIR

TESRO GMBH & COMPANY KG
Seehofstraße 14 / b
Bächingen, D-89431 GERMANY
Phone No.:011-49-7325-919382
Fax No.:011-49-7325-919384
Website: www.tesro.de
Email: info@tesro.de

THEOBEN LTD (THEOBEN ENGINEERING)
Distributor/Importer - THEOBEN USA
Factory Address:
Sterling Place, Elean Business Park
Sutton, Cambridgeshire CB6 2QE U.K.
Phone No.:011-44-1353-777861
Fax No.:011-44-1353-777508
Website: www.theoben.co.uk
Email: customerservices@theoben.co.uk

TORUNARMS
Üzümlü-Beysehir, Konya TURKEY
Phone No.:011-90-332-524-7064
Fax No.:011-90-332-524-7065
Website: www.torunarms.com
Email: bilgi@torunsilah.com

TSS FORTUNE CO., LTD.
Add: No. 8 You Yi Road
Tianjin, 300074 CHINA
Phone No.:011-86-22-28136598
Fax No.:011-86-22-28131342
Website: www.tss-cn.com
Email: wang_shaohui@tss-cn.com

UMAREX SPORTWAFFEN GMBH & CO. KG
P.O. Box 27 20
Arnsberg, D-59717 GERMANY
Phone No.:011-49 (0) 29-32 - 638-01
Fax No.:011-49 (0) 29-32 - 638-222
Website: www.umarex.de
Email: sales@umarex.de

UMAREX USA, INC.
7700 Chad Colley Blvd.
Fort Smith, AR 72916
Phone No.:479-646-4210
Fax No.:479-646-4206
Website: www.umarexusa.com

UZI
Importer - Umarex

WALTHER (CARL WALTHER GMBH SPORTWAFFEN)
Distributor/Importer - CHAMPION'S CHOICE INC.
Distributor/Importer - UMAREX USA, INC.
P.O.Box 2740
Arnsberg, D-59717 GERMANY
Phone No.:011-49-29-32/6-38-100
Fax No.:011-49-29-32/6-38-149
Website: www.carl-walther.de
Email: sales@carl-walther.de

WEBLEY & SCOTT, LTD.
Distributor/Importer - WEBLEY & SCOTT, USA
P.O. Box 75
Dartmouth, TQ6 9AL U.K.
Website: www.webley.co.uk
Email: sales@webley.co.uk

WEIHRAUCH SPORT
Distributor/Importer - AIR RIFLE HEADQUARTERS
Distributor/Importer - AIRGUNS OF ARIZONA
Industriestraße 13
Mellrichstadt, D-97638 GERMANY
Phone No.:011-49-9776-8122-0
Fax No.:011-49-9776-8122-81
Website: www.weihrauch-sport.de
Email: info@weihrauch-sport.de

WESSON, DAN FIREARMS
Distributor/Importer - ASG, USA
Headquarters/Factory
(ASG A/S)
Bakkegaardsvej 304
Humlebaek, DK - 3050 DENMARK
Phone No.:011-45- 89-28-1888
Fax No.:011-45-49-3160
Website: www.actionsportgames.com
Email: sales@actionsportgames.com

WINCHESTER
Administrative Offices - Firearms only
275 Winchester Ave
Morgan, UT 84050
Toll Free: 800-945-1392
Fax No.:801-876-3737
Website: www.winchester-guns.com

WINCHESTER
Umarea
Winchester Air Rifles
P.O. Box 220
Rogers, AR 72757-0220
Toll Free: 800-643-3458
Website: www.winchesterairrifles.com
Email: info@winchesterairrifles.com

ZORAKI (ATAK SILAH SAN. TIC. LTD. STI.)
Imes San. Sit. A Blok 107 Sk. No:70
Istanbul, Yukari Dudullu, Ümraniye 34775
TURKEY
Phone No.:011-90-216-420-39-96
Fax No.:011-90-216-420-39-98
Website: www.zoraki.com

ZOS (NANTONG UNIVERSAL OPTICAL INSTRUMENT CO., LTD)
No. 1 Pingchao Industrial Garden
Nantong, Jangsu 226361 CHINA
Phone No.:011-86-513-86726888
Fax No.:011-86-513-86718158
Website: www.zoscn.com
Email: sale@zoscn.com

AIR RIFLE HEADQUARTERS

3054 Maccari
Elkton, MD 21921
Phone No.:206-495-0764
Fax No.:206-495-0764
Website: www.airrifleheadquarters.com
Email: contactarh@yahoo.com
Distributor/Importer - WEIHRAUCH SPORT

AIR VENTURI/PYRAMYD AIR

5135 Naiman Parkway
Solon, OH 44139
Phone No.:216-292-2570 Air Venturi
Toll Free: 888-262-4867 Pyramyd Air
Fax No.:216-373-0086/216-896-0896
**Website: www.airventuri.com or www.
pyramydair.com**
**Email: dealers@airventuri.com or sales@
pyramydair.com**
*Distributor/Importer - KWC (KIEN WELL TOY INDUSTRIAL CO.
Ltd)*
Distributor/Importer - MENDOZA S.A. de C.V.
Distributor/Importer - SIG SAUER
Distributor/Importer - TECH FORCE

AIRFORCE INTERNATIONAL

P.O. Box 2478
Fort Worth, TX 76113
Toll Free: 877-247-4867
Website: www.cometausa.com
Distributor/Importer - COMETA

AIRGUNS OF ARIZONA

1970 W. Elliot Road, Suite 109
Gilbert, AZ 85233
Phone No.:480-461-1113
Fax No.:480-461-3928
Website: www.airgunsofarizona.com
Email: mail@airgunsofarizona.com
Distributor/Importer - BAIKAL
Distributor/Importer - BROCOCK
Distributor/Importer - DAYSTATE LTD
Distributor/Importer - FAS
Distributor/Importer - FX AIRGUNS AB
Distributor/Importer - KALIBRGUN
Distributor/Importer - MAROCCHI
Distributor/Importer - RIPLEY AIR RIFLES
Distributor/Importer - SHIN SUNG INDUSTRIES CO. LTD.
Distributor/Importer - WEIHRAUCH SPORT

ASG, USA

3355 Cochran Street Ste. 203
Simi Valley, CA 93063
Website: www.actionsportgames.com
Email: sales@actionsportgames.com
Distributor/Importer - ASG (ACTION SPORT GAMES A/S)
Distributor/Importer - WESSON, DAN FIREARMS

BRENZOVICH FIREARMS & TRAINING CENTER

22301 Texas Hwy 20
Ft. Hancock, TX 79839
Toll Free: 877-585-3775
Website: www.brenzovich.com
*Distributor/Importer - FEINWERKBAU WESTINGER &
ALTENBURGER GmbH*

BSA GUNS USA (A DIVISION OF GAMO OUTDOOR USA, INC.)

3911 SW 47th Ave, Suite 914
Ft. Lauderdale, FL 33314 USA
Phone No.:954-581-2144
Website: www.bsagunsusa.com
Email: export@gamo.com
Distributor/Importer - BSA GUNS (U.K.), LTD.

CHAMPION SHOOTERS SUPPLY, LLC

11018 Camp Ohio Road
Utica, OH 43080 USA
Phone No.:800-821-4867
Fax No.:740-745-1274
Website: www.championshooters.com
Distributor/Importer ANSCHÜTZ

CHAMPION'S CHOICE INC.

201 International Blvd.
La Vergne, TN 37086
Phone No.:615-793-4066
Toll Free: 800-345-7179
Fax No.:615-793-4070
Website: www.champchoice.com
Email: sales@champchoice.com
Distributor/Importer ANSCHÜTZ
*Distributor/Importer - FEINWERKBAU WESTINGER &
ALTENBURGER GmbH*
Distributor/Importer - MORINI COMPETITION ARM SA
Distributor/Importer - STEYR SPORTWAFFEN GmbH
*Distributor/Importer - WALTHER (CARL WALTHER GmbH
SPORTWAFFEN)*

CROSMAN CORP.

7629 Routes 5 & 20
Bloomfield, NY 14443
Toll Free: 800-7-AIRGUN
Fax No.:716-657-5405
Website: www.crosman.com
Email: info@crosman.com

GAMO OUTDOOR USA, INC.

3911 SW 47th Ave. Suite 914
Ft. Lauderdale, FL 33314
Phone No.:954-581-5822
Toll Free: 888-872-4266
Fax No.:954-581-3165
Website: www.gamousa.com
Email: info@gamousa.com
*Distributor/Importer - GAMO PRECISION AIRGUNS (INDUSTRIAS
EL GAMO, S.A.U.)*

HATSAN USA, INC.

P.O. Box 576
Bentonville, AR 72712
Phone No.:479-273-5629
Fax No.:918-517-3040
Website: www.hatsanusa.com
Distributor/Importer - HATSAN ARMS CO.

LARRY'S GUNS

56 West Gray Road
Gray, ME 04039
Phone No.:207-657-4559
Fax No.:207-657-3429
Website: www.larrysguns.com
Email: info@larrysguns.com
Distributor/Importer - BENELLI ARMI S.P.A.
Distributor/Importer - HÄMMERLI AG

PALCO SPORTS

8555 Revere Lane N.
Maple Grove, MN 55369 USA
Toll Free: 800-882-4656
Fax No.:763-559-2286
Website: www.palcosports.com/index.cfm
Email: info@palcosports.com
Importer - KWC (KIEN WELL TOY INDUSTRIAL CO. Ltd)
Importer - SIG SAUER

PARDINI USA LLC.

7811 North Dale Mabry Hwy.
Tampa, FL 33614 USA
Phone No.:813-748-3378
Fax No.:813-899-9696
Website: www.PardiniGuns.com
Email: info@PardiniGuns.com
Distributor/Importer - PARDINI, ARMI S.r.l.

PILKINGTON COMPETITION EQUIPMENT LLC

354 Little Trees Ramble, P.O. Box 97
Monteagle, TN 37356
Phone No.:931-924 3400
Fax No.:931-924 3489
Website: www.pilkguns.com
Email: info@pilkguns.com
Distributor/Importer - MORINI COMPETITION ARM SA

POMONA AIR GUNS

15555 Main Street, Ste. D-4 #496
Hesperia, CA 92345
Phone No.:760-244-8271
Fax No.:760-244-4484
Website: www.pomona-airguns.com
Distributor - AERON CZ s.r.o.

PRECISION AIRGUNS AND SUPPLIES

5213 Bordman
Dryden, MI 48428 USA
Phone No.:248-969-0377
Website: recisionairgunsandsupplies.com
Email: precisionairguns@gmail.com

STRAIGHT SHOOTERS PRECISION AIRGUNS
2000 Prairie Hill Road
St. Cloud, MN 56301
Phone No.:320-240-9062
Fax No.:320-259-0759
Website: www.straightshooters.com
Email: shooters@straightshooters.com

THEOBEN USA
13264 Minor Hill Hwy
Minor Hill, TN 38473
Phone No.:931-565-4841
Website: www.theobenusa.com
Email: airgunwerk@aol.com
Distributor/Importer - THEOBEN LTD (THEOBEN ENGINEERING)

TOP GUN-AIRGUNS, INC.
8442 E. Hackamore Dr.
Scottsdale, AZ 85255
Phone No.:480-513-3778
Website: www.topgun-airguns.com
Email: sales@topgunsairguns
Distributor/Importer - AERON CZ s.r.o.
Distributor/Importer - ALFA - PROJ spol. s.r.o.
Distributor/Importer - CZ (CESKA ZBROJOVKA)
Distributor/Importer - DRULOV
Distributor/Importer - KALIBRGUN
Distributor/Importer - TAU BRNO, spol. s r.o.

UMAREX USA, INC.
7700 Chad Colley Blvd.
Fort Smith, AR 72916
Phone No.:479-646-4210
Fax No.:479-646-4206
Website: www.umarexusa.com
Distributor/Importer - BERETTA, PIETRO
Distributor/Importer - BROWNING
Distributor/Importer - COLT'S MANUFACTURING COMPANY, INC.
Distributor/Importer - DIANA (DIANAWERK) MAYER & GRAMMELSPACHER GmbH & CO. KG
Distributor/Importer - HECKLER & KOCH GmbH
Distributor/Importer - MAGNUM RESEARCH, INC.
Distributor/Importer - MAKAROV
Distributor/Importer - RWS PRECISION PRODUCTS
Distributor/Importer - SMITH & WESSON
Distributor/Importer - UZI
Distributor/Importer - WALTHER (CARL WALTHER GmbH SPORTWAFFEN)

WEBLEY & SCOTT, USA
4750 Longley Lane, Ste. 208
Reno, NV 89502
Phone No.:775-825-9835
Fax No.:775-825-9329
Website: www.webleyandscott.com
Distributor/Importer - WEBLEY & SCOTT, LTD.

X-CALIBER TACTICAL
Round Rock, TX USA
Website: www.xcalibertactical.com
Email: contact@xcalibertactical.com
Distributor - PIPER

XISICO USA, INC.
16802 Barker Springs Rd, Suite 550
Houston, TX 77084
Phone No.:281-647-9130
Fax No.:208-979-2848
Website: www.xisicousa.com
Email: Info@xisicousa.com
Distributor/Importer - BAM (BEST AIRGUN MANUFACTURER IN CHINA)

STORE BRAND CROSS-OVER LIST

Many companies sell airguns under their own name but which have been made by others. In many cases all of the models sold under a given brand may be made by another company and it may be impossible or difficult to know who is the actual maker. In other cases a known maker will produce "private label" or "store brand" models for various sellers based on models which they produce under their own name. Only rarely will the private label version be "just the same as" the original base model. The value of comparable models may differ, even hugely, from the base models. Rarely the private label will be a lesser grade version of the base model, but in many cases the private label gun will be an improved version and/or have different cosmetic features. In some cases the private label model will be almost an entirely different gun, only using many of the parts of the base model. Values may differ due to different features and variations, including power levels (higher or lower depending on regulations and demand in the selling area), stock designs, stock material and quality, calibers, sights, trigger mechanisms, etc. In some cases quality control will be higher on the private labels, simply because when the maker sells the guns under their own name returns will come back one by one, but when they make them in huge groups for another company, they may get returns of entire production runs, even thousands of guns, if there is a problem.

This table lists the actual manufacturer and the manufacturer's model that comes closest to the private label brand name and model numbers which will be found on the airgun. Once the name and model of the base model is determined, the reader should find the description of the base model to gather possible information on parts interchangeability, base specifications, and an idea of value range.

(NOTE: These tables are not complete; more information will be added in future editions. Readers are encouraged to submit information on known comparable models not yet listed.)

MONTGOMERY WARDS STORES; HAWTHORN BRAND

Wards number	Actual Manufacturer	Equivalent model	Notes
1414A	Crosman	V350	
M180	Crosman	180	
1415	Crosman	99	
1412	Crosman	140	
1447	Crosman	38C	
1448	Crosman	38T	
1435	Crosman	MK I	
1445	Crosman	45	
1434	Crosman	760	
1438	Crosman	130	

J. C. PENNEY STORES; PENNEY'S BRAND

Penney number	Actual Manufacturer	Equivalent model	Notes
7236	Daisy	1894	Wood stock and forearm

SEARS STORES; J. C. HIGGINS, SEARS, AND TED WILLIAMS BRANDS

Sears number	Actual Manufacturer	Equivalent model	Notes
126.10294	Crosman	V350	
126.1930	Crosman	140/1400	
126.1931	Crosman	180	
126.1932	Crosman	400	
126.1933	Crosman	166	
126.1934	Crosman	130	
126.1935	Crosman	150	
126.1936	Crosman	600	
126.1937	Crosman	45	
126.1938	Crosman	SA6	
126.1909	Crosman	150	
126.1910	Crosman	160	
126.294	Crosman	V350	
126.1923	Crosman	760	
126.2831	Crosman	180	
126.10349	Crosman	38C	
126.10350	Crosman	38T	
126.19041	Crosman	V350	

Sears Stores; J. C. Higgins, Sears, and Ted Williams Brands, cont.

Sears number	Actual Manufacturer	Equivalent model	Notes
126.19131	Crosman	45	
126.19141	Crosman	166	
126.19151	Crosman	180	
126.19161	Crosman	400	
126.19171	Crosman	160	
126.19181	Crosman	SA6	
126.19191	Crosman	150	
126.19201	Crosman	600	
123.19211	Crosman	130	
126.19241	Crosman	140	
126.19221	Crosman	38C	
126.19231	Crosman	38T	
126.19391	Crosman	M1	
126.19331	Crosman	760	
799.10276	Daisy	25	
799.19020	Daisy	111	
799.19025	Daisy	177	
799.19052	Daisy	1894	Octagon barrel "Crafted by Daisy"
799.19054	Daisy	1894	
799.19062	Daisy	300	
799.19072	Daisy	880	
799.1912	Daisy	1894	Black, round barrel, no scope rail
799.203	Daisy	94	
799.9009	Daisy	105	
799.9012	Daisy	111	
799.9045	Daisy	25	
799.9048	Daisy	1938	
799.9051	Daisy	1894	With scope bracket
799.9052	Daisy	1894	
799.9054	Daisy	1894	
799.9057	Daisy	1914	
799.9061	Daisy	572	
799.9062	Daisy	300	

Sears Stores; J. C. Higgins, Sears, and Ted Williams Brands, cont.

Sears number	Actual Manufacturer	Equivalent model	Notes
799.9068	Daisy	840	
799.9072	Daisy	880	
799.9073	Daisy	1938	
799.9076	Daisy	822	
799.9078	Daisy	922	
799.9079	Daisy	922	
799.9082	Daisy	880	
799.9083	Daisy	880	
799.9085	Daisy	850	
799.9093	Daisy	880	
799.9113	Daisy	900	
799.9115	Daisy	130	
799.9166	Daisy	95	
799.9215	Daisy	545	
799.9224	Daisy	7800	
799.924	Daisy	111	
799.9306	Daisy	557	
799.9313	Daisy	40	
799.9323	Daisy	562	
799.9355	Daisy	1880	
799.9382	Daisy	1880	
799.9393	Daisy	1880	
799.9478	Daisy	1922	
799.9498	Daisy	499	
799.9499	Daisy	499	
799.19083C	Daisy	880	Gold Receiver
799.19383C	Daisy	880	Gold Receiver and scope
799.19385C	Daisy	850	With scope
799.19478C	Daisy	922	
79919085C	Daisy	850	

WESTERN AUTO STORES; REVELATION BRAND

Revelation number	Actual Manufacturer	Equivalent model	Notes
GC3376	Crosman	760	First variation
GC3370	Crosman	73	
GC3375	Crosman	788	
GC3377	Crosman	766	
GC3360	Crosman	V350	
GC3367	Crosman	99	
GC3379	Crosman	140	
GC3416	Crosman	45	
GC3412	Crosman	38T	
GC3375	Crosman	166	

DIANAWERK COMPARABLE MODEL NUMBERS

Only airguns made by Dianawerk of Rastatt, Germany are considered here. The Diana brand name was taken to Scotland as war reparations after WWII. Scottish Dianas were made by Milbro. Some were exported to the USA as economy airguns under the Daisy label. Important note: Comparable models often have different values due to different demand by collectors, different levels of rarity, and, because distributors of private label guns often specified different power levels (for different markets, and not just mainspring differences) Stock design, stock material and quality, calibers, sights, trigger mechanisms, etc. may differ from the basic manufacturer´s model. Beeman-marked and pre-1970 Winchester-marked guns generally sell for a premium. Early models of the same number may differ from more recent model.

Diana, RWS Original* Geco, Peerless	Beeman	Hy-Score	Winchester	Crosman
1				
2		814		
5*		815T	353	
5G	700	825T		
6*		816M	363	
6G	800	826M		
6M	850	827M		
10	900	819SM		
15		808		
16		805	416	
22		806	422	
23 w/receiver rails		813 Mark1		
25 / 25D		801	425	
27*	100	807	427	
35*	200	809	435	
45	250	828		Challenger 6100
50			450	
60		810M		
65		810SM	333	
66		811SM		
75	400, 400 Univ.	820SM		

* Also produced as Beeman´s "Original" series under the same model number.

AIRGUN LITERATURE
AN ANNOTATED PARTIAL REFERENCE LIST
By Dr. Robert D. Beeman

Largely limited to separate publications such as books, periodicals, and booklets, rather than individual airgun articles. (For a large listing of airgun articles prior to 1990 see Groenewold [1990]). For more information and a detailed analysis of the references listed below, see the Literature Review section of www.Beemans.net and a less up-to-date analysis in the Second Edition of the *Blue Book of Airguns*.

PERIODICALS:

The latest contact and subscription information is available on www.Google.com. Older issues sometimes available at secondary book markets, eBay, Doug Law (dlaw1940@yahoo.com, PO Box 42, Sidney, NE 69162); FSI at 906-482-1685; gunshows; etc.

Airgun Ads. Box 1534, Hamilton, Montana 59840, airgunads@brvmontana.com. Small monthly, only ads for airguns and accessories.

Addictive Airgunning. Jan. to Oct. 2004. Online format allowed large articles and color pictures. For both collectors and shooters.

Airgun Hobby (www.airgunhobby.com). October 2004 to date. Now America's only airgun periodical. Quarterly, published by airgun enthusiasts Ron Sauls and Jim Giles. Less glitzy than some previous airgun periodicals, but far superior in reporting airgun events and info on airgun collecting and use.

Airgun Illustrated. August 2002 to January 2004. The first five issues, with Tom Gaylord's input, were truly wonderful.

Airgun Journal (Beeman Precision Airguns). Published only 1979 to 1984. Edited by Robert Beeman. Many articles valuable to airgun shooters and collectors. One of the rarest of all airgun publications. Less than 500 copies of each of the six issues were printed. Beautifully printed on heavy, textured deep tan paper with green and brown masthead; extremely difficult to scan or photocopy because of the dark paper. Back issues available at www.Beemans.net.

Airgun Letter. Monthly newsletter of 12-16 pages, plus Airgun Revue 1-6 of about 100 pages each, perhaps the world's best reference material on adult airguns. Closed August 2002 when editor Tom Gaylord moved to *Airgun Illustrated*.

Airgun News & Report (later as *American Airgunner*). Valuable articles, out of print.

Airgun World and Airgunner. Both by Romsey Publishing Co., 4 The Courtyard, Denmark St., Workingham, Berkshire RG402AZ, England. British monthlies. *Airgun World* articles of Roy Valentine (under pen name "Harvey" in 1970s) and later, those of John Atkins in *Airgunner* and Tim Saunders in *Airgun World*, are especially valuable to collectors.

Guns Review. British gun magazine formerly carried excellent articles on airguns; especially the pioneer research of John Walter and the late Dennis Commins around 1970s.

New Zealand Airgun Magazine. Pub. by Trevor Adams from February 1986 to April 1988.

Philippine Airgun Shooter. Only four quarterly issues, plus an annual, in 1989.

Shotgun News. Newspaper format, mainly firearm ads, but also airgun ads and America's only airgun column - by outstanding airgun writer Tom Gaylord.

U.S. Airgun (last issue as *Rimfire and Airgun*). Valuable articles for airgun shooters and collectors, out of print.

VISIER, Das Internationale Waffen-Magazin. Lavishly illustrated, prestigious slick German language magazine. Basically a firearm publication, but contains some of the best written, best illustrated airgun articles ever. VISIER Specials, such as 1996 Special Number 4, may have only airgun articles.

Other gun periodicals sometimes have airgun articles: *Precision Shooting* and *The Accurate Rifle*, perhaps the best shooting magazines in the English language, frequently present excellent articles on airguns. *The Rifle* and *Guns* previously featured airgun columns. Most American gun magazines such as *American Rifleman, Arms and the Man, Guns and Ammo, Sports Afield*, etc. only have occasional airgun articles.

REFERENCES:

Adler, Dennis. 2001. (Edited by Dr. Robert D. Beeman and S.P. Fjestad). *Blue Book of Airguns*, First Edition. 160 pp. Blue Book Publications, Inc., Minneapolis, Minnesota. Now rare collectors' item (hardbounds sell for $100+).

Atkinson, R. Valentine. 1992. *Air Looms. Gray's Sporting Journal*. Sept. 1992: 35-41. Beautifully illustrated report on some of the Beeman collection. Some garbled information.

Baker, Geoffery and Colin Currie. 2002, 2003, 2006. Vol. 1: Revised 2nd Ed., *The Construction and Operation of the Austrian Army Repeating Air Rifle*, 102 pp.; Vol. 2, The Walking Stick Air Gun 79 pp., info and direct from geoffrey.baker@virgin.net. Detailed photos, full-scale drawings, and measurements. Everyone even slightly interested in these amazing airguns and certainly anyone who contemplates opening one should have these guides. More guides in planning.

Beeman, Robert D. 1977. *Air Gun Digest*. 256 pp. DBI Books, Northfield, IL. Airgun collection, selection, use, ballistics, care, etc. When I did this volume way back in the 20th century, when the field of adult airgunning hardly existed, I never dreamed that someday it would be called a classic collectible, but I'm not going to fight it.

Beeman, Robert D. 1977. *Four Centuries of Airguns*, pp. 14-26. *The Basics of Airgun Collecting*. Pp. 218-235 (Later reprinted together as *The Art of Airgun Collecting* by Beeman Precision Arms in 1986, 23 pp.). Considered as the first guide to airgun collecting. A key work. Should be teamed with the "Rare Air" airgun collecting article by R. Beeman in the First Edition of the *Blue Book of Airguns*.

Beeman, Robert and M.J. Banosky, John W. Ford, Randy Pitney, Joel Sexton. 1991. *Air Guns, A Guide to Air Pistols and Rifles*. National Rifle Association, Washington, D.C. Abbreviates and revises the original Beeman manuscript, but very useful introduction to airgun shooting and programs.

Beeman, Robert D. 1995. *The Odyssey of the Beeman* R1. Chapter in *The Beeman R1 - Supermagnum Air Rifle*, pp. 1-9. GAPP. The real story of the gun that brought America into the adult airgun world - and gave rise to the HW 80.

Beeman, Robert D. and John Allen. 2002-2011. *Blue Book of Airguns*, Second through Ninth Editions. Blue Book Publications, Inc., Minneapolis, Minnesota. Price is not the primary purpose of these guides. Model ID and information are. From 19th century to latest guns. Valuable to all airgunners. Every volume has valuable articles; serious airgunners should have a complete set of all editions!

Beeman, Robert D. 2006. Meriwether *Lewis's Wonder Gun. We Proceeded On* May 2005: 29-34. Lewis and Clark Trail Heritage Association. On the Beeman Girardoni: *"this rifle, in fact, was the one carried on the expedition."*

Beeman, Robert D. 2012. *The Lewis and Clark Airgun – Key to the American West*. In Press. Basic story of "The most important individual gun in American history" and availability info at www.beemans.net.

Behling, Larry. 2006. *Air Machine Guns*. 324 pp. Pub. by L. Behling. rte6larry@alltel.net. Huge, wonderfully illustrated on a group of airguns that previously were very poorly known and understood by most airgun collectors. A must.

Bruce, Gordon. 2000. *Webley Air Pistols*. 224 pp. Robert Hale, London. The bible on Webley air pistols.

Brukner, Bruno, 2000. *Der Luftpistole*. Second edition, 230 pp. Journal Verland Schwend. Outstanding book on air pistols. All air pistol fans, not just those reading German, should have it. Just the diagrams are worth the price of admission.

Brychta, Frank S. 1994 a. *FSI Airgun Ballistic Tables*. 88 pp. 1994b. FSI *Advanced Airgun Ballistics*. 52 pp. Firearms & Supplies, 514 Quincy St., Hancock, MI 49930. Absolutely essential pair of books for all who are interested in airgun ballistics, field target shooting, and airgun hunting ballistics. Many very useful tables.

Cardew, G.V. & G.M. Cardew, E.R. Elsom. 1976. *The Air Gun from Trigger to Muzzle*. 96 pp. Martin Brothers, Birmingham, England. Highly technical. The best guide to internal airgun ballistics.

Cardew, G.V. & G.M. Cardew. 1995. *The Airgun from Trigger to Target*. 235 pp. Privately published. ISBN 0 9505108 2 3. Extension of Cardew's pioneer book to include external ballistics. Reveals how much and how little we know about airgun ballistics.

Chapman, Jim. 2003. *The American Airgun Hunter.* 234 pp. Chapman, Jim and Randy Mitchell, 2003. *The Airgunners Guide to Squirrel Hunting.* 128 pp. Jaeger Press, 67 Sentinel, Alviso Viejo, CA. www.geocites.com/echochap/airgun_hunter.html. The "American" book actually covers airgun hunting in several countries. Entertaining gab mixed into an essential guide - these fellows are most interested in results while I would lean more towards the quality of the gun. Great.

Churchill, Bob & Granville Davies. 1981. *Modern Airweapon Shooting.* 196 pp. David & Charles, Devon, England. Authors should be shot for using the word "weapon." Excellent introduction to formal airgun target shooting.

Darling, John. 1988. *Air Rifle Hunting.* 160 pp. Crowood Press, Wilshire, England. Excellent, but now rather dated w/o good coverage of PCP guns, night lights, etc.

Dieter, Ernst. 2002. *Luftgewehre und Luftpistolen nach 1945 aus Suhl und Zella-Mehlis.* 143 pp. WTS Waffentechnik in Suhl GmbH, Lauter 40, 98528 Suhl, Germany. Writing under a pseudonym, a former top engineer at Haenel presents invaluable information on almost 60 models - some not previously known to collectors.

Dunathan, Arni T. 1971. *The American BB Gun: A Collector's Guide.* 154 pp. A.S. Barnes and Co., Cranbury, New Jersey. The pioneer work on BB gun collecting. Now badly out of date, but forever essential! The 1970 prices will bring tears to your eyes!

Eichstädt, Ulrich 2007. *Corpus delicti, Die Suche nach der Lewis & Clark Windbüchse.* (Body of Evidence -The Search for the Lewis & Clark Airgun), VISIER Jan.2007:135-143. Europe's leading airgun historian and author says: "*the puzzle about the legendary airgun carried by Captains Meriwether Lewis and William Clark from 1803 to 1806 appears to have been solved.*".

Elbe, Ronald E. 1992. *Know Your Sheridan Rifles & Pistols.* 79 pp. Blacksmith Corp. The best review of the Sheridan guns.

Fletcher, Dean. 1996-98. *The Crosman Arms Handbooks,* 259 pp.; and *The Crosman Rifle 1923-1950,* 265 pp., *The Crosman Arms Model "160" Pellgun,* 144 pp., *75 Years of Crosman Airguns,* 223 pp., *Crosman Arms Library* (CD). Pub. by D.T. Fletcher, 6720 NE Rodney Ave, Portland, Oregon 97211. (For more Crosman info see Eichstädt, Ulrich and Dean Fletcher. 1999. *Eine Unbekannte Größe. Visier,* Feb. 1999:52-57 and Oakleaf, Jon B. 1979. *Vintage Crosmans. The Airgun Journal* 1(1): 1-3, 1980. *Vintage Crosmans II. The Airgun Journal* 1(2):1-7.)

Fletcher, Dean. Undated. *The Crosman Arms Library.* CD with 888 full color scans of Crosman literature. 1998c. *The Chronology of Daisy Air Guns 1900 - 1981 and Daisy Toy and Metal Squirt Guns.* 18 pp.; 1999. *The St. Louis and Benjamin Air Rifle Companies,* 305 pp. Pub. by D.T. Fletcher.

Friberg, Av Kenth. 2001. *Luftvapen.* 191 pp. Karlshamn\Göteborg, Sweden. (K. Friberg, Ekbacken 3, 37450 Asarum, Sweden). In Swedish; one of several guides to some airguns not generally known to Americans.

Galan, Jess I. 1988. *Airgun Digest,* 2nd Edition; 1995. *Airgun Digest.* 3rd Edition. 288 pp. DBI Books, Northbrook, IL. Classic books, all aspects of airgunning. Outstanding author.

Garber, Gary. 2007. *An Encyclopedia of Daisy Plymouth Guns.* 8.5 in. x 11 in., 414 pp. Published by author at BBgunBook@aol.com. Finally, the much-waited, huge "bible" on Daisy airguns made at Plymouth, MI from late 1880s to 1958 and a few latter ones from Rogers, AK.

Gaylord, Tom. 1995. *The Beeman R1- Supermagnum Air Rifle.* 174 pp. GAPP. One of the classic, best books on airguns. Highly recommended by many airgun writers. Includes a chapter by R. Beeman on the Beeman R1 as the precursor of the HW 80. The most useful book on the market for understanding the function and use of ANY spring piston airgun.

Griffiths, John. 2008. *The Encyclopedia of Spring Air Pistols,* 390 pp. Ashlea Publications, Leeds, England. J.Griffiths@leeds.ac.uk. Covers over 500 models plus targets, boxes, etc. Monumental book, simply one of the best and most necessary airgun references ever published. Essential as a companion to *Blue Book of Airguns* editions.

Groenewold, John. 1990. *Bibliography of Technical Periodical Airgun Literature.* 28 pp. Pub. by John Groenewold, Box 830, Mundelein, IL 60060. A great listing. John promises to go beyond 1990 "someday"!

Groenewold, John. 2000. *Quackenbush Guns.* 266 pages. Pub. by John Groenewold, Box 830, Mundelein, IL 60060-0830. Phone 847- 566.2365. The definitive guide to the wonderful antique Quackenbush guns.

Hannusch, Larry. 2001. *Pneumatic Reflections.* 280 pages. Self published by L. Hannusch, 5521-B, Mitchelldale, Houston, TX 77092 or lhannusch@netscape.net. Compilation of last twenty years of interesting and valuable articles on airgun collecting by one of the world's leading authorities.

Herridge, Les. 1987. *Airgun Shooting.* 96 pp. A & C Black, London. Herridge, 1994. *Airgun Shooting Handbook.,* 80 pp. Herridge, Les and Ian Law. 1989. *Airgun Field Target Shooting.* 100pp. Peter Andrew Publishing Co. Basic introductions to British field target airgun shooting.

Hiller, Dennis E. 1982. *The Collector's Guide to Air Pistols,* Revised Second Edition. 187 pp. Published by Dennis Hiller. Rather dated, depressed values, but invaluable model info - mainly European models. An almost essential item to pair with *Blue Book of Airguns,* but sadly out of print.

Hiller, Dennis E. 1985. *The Collectors' Guide to Air Rifles,* Enlarged Third Edition. 276 pp. Published by Dennis Hiller. See above note. Again, lots of invaluable information.

Hoff, Arne. 1972. *Air Guns and Other Pneumatic Arms.* 99 pp. Barrie and Jenkins, London. A classic that everyone interested in the history of airguns simply must have!

Hoff, Arne, 1977. *Windbüchsen und andere Druckluftwaffen.* 105 pp. Parey, Berlin. Updated version of above; in German.

Holzel, Tom. 1991. *The Air Rifle Hunter's Guide.* 159 pp. Velocity Press, 52 Lang St., Concord, MA 01742. Simply the best book on hunting with an air rifle. Presents crow hunting as philosophically similar to fly fishing. The "Killing as a Sport" chapter is one of the best ever presentations on the morality and ethics of hunting. Includes outstanding, practical material on field ballistics of airguns.

Hough, Cass S. 1976. *It's A Daisy!* 336 pp. Daisy Division, Victor Comptometer Corp., Rogers, Arkansas. Delightful history of the Daisy Company by one of its longest term executives. Rare, a very desirable collectors' item - softbound.

House, James E. 2002. *American Air Rifles.* 208 pp., 179 black and white illus. 2003. *CO2 Pistols & Rifles.* Krause (www.krause.com). Both softbound books press the theme that pellet guns from Daisy, Crosman, etc. should be seriously considered by adults also. Some of the best ballistic info available for airguns of this level.

Hughes, D.R. 1973. *An original handbook for the model 35D, 27, 35 & 50 air rifles.* 77 pp. Pub. by D.R. Hughes, England. (Original brand = Diana, RWS, Gecado, some Winchester, some Beeman, some HyScore). Delightful guide to assembly, etc.

Hughes, D.R. 1981. *HW 35. A Handbook for Owners and Users of the HW35 Series Air Rifles.* 65 pp. Optima Leisure Products, 75 Foxley Lane, Purley, Surrey, England. Another delightful Hughes tour through a famous airgun.

Janich, Michael D. 1993, *Blowguns, The Breath of Death.* 81 pp. Paladin Press, Boulder, Colorado. Basic info on the most basic of airguns.

Johnson, Bill 2003. *Bailey and Columbian Air Rifles.* 38 pp. Book plus CD. Bill Johnson, PO Box 97B, Tehachapi, CA 93581. The definitive work on some of America's most interesting and solid airguns (formerly known as Heilprin airguns). 1/4 and 1/2 scale detailed drawings.

Kishi, Takenobu. 1999. *The Magnum,* 303 pp. Printed in Japan. ISBN 4- 7733-6563-3 C0075. In Japanese. Detailed info on airgun ballistics.

Kersten, Manfred. 2001. *Walther - A German Legend.* 400 pp. Safari Press, 15621 Chemical Lane B, Huntington Beach, CA 92649-1506 USA. This gorgeous masterpiece covers all Walther guns, including excellent coverage of the airguns. Also available in German.

Knibbs, John. 1986. *B.S.A. and Lincoln Jeffries Air Rifles.* 160 pp. Published by John Knibbs Publications, Birmingham. Another classic British work on the history and models of a leading airgun maker.

Kolyer, John M. 1969. *Compilation of Air Arm Articles and Data* 130 pp. John Kolyer, 55 Chimney Ridge Drive, Convent, New Jersey 07961. Primarily older airgun ballistic material. Pioneer work.

Kolyer, John M. & Ron Rushworth. 1988. *Airgun Performance.* 157 pp. Sangreal Press, Newport Beach, California. Updated version of Kolyer's 1969 work. Even includes blowgun and slingshot data.

Law, Robert. 1969. *The Weihrauch Handbook.* 44 pp. Air Rifle Monthly, Grantsville, West Virginia. One of a series of how-to-do-it airgun maintenance and tuning booklets by one of America's early adult airgun hobbyists. Verbose but very useful. Last supply available in Sale section www.Beemans.net.

Lawrence, Andrew. 1969. *Development of the Hy-Score Air Pistol.* Engineering Case Library No. 134. Department of Mechanical Engineering. Leland Stanford Jr. University. Extremely rare paper on the origin of the American HyScore concentric piston air pistols.

Marchington, James. 1988. *Field Airgun Shooting.* 200 pp. Pelham Books/London (Penguin). Basic guide to British field target shooting.

Middleton, Richard. 2007. *The Practical Guide to Man-Powered Weapons and Ammunition: Experiments with Catapults, Musketballs, Stonebows, Blowpipes, Big Airguns, and Bulletbows.* Skyhorse Publishing. 224 pp. A lively, most unusual, very personal book.

Moore, Warren, 1963. *Guns, the Development of Firearms, Air Guns, and Cartridges.* 104 pp., Grosset and Dunlap, New York, N.Y. Contains a wonderful, well-illustrated section on antique airguns.

Munson, H. Lee. 1992. *The Mortimer Gunmakers, 1753-1923.* 320 pp. Andrew Mowbray, Lincoln, Rhode Island. Includes excellent material on the elegant large bore airguns made by the Mortimer family, 1700s to early 1900s.

Nonte, George C. 1970, *Complete Book of the Air Gun.* Stackpole, Harrisburg, PA. Somewhat lightweight and dated, but very useful.

Oscar Will-Catalogue *Venus Waffenwerk Reprint of 1902/03 catalog.* 94 pp. Journal-Verlang in Schwäbish Hall.

Parks, Michael R. 1992, 1994. *Pneumatic Arms & Oddities,* Vol. 1 and Vol. 2. 245 and 211 pp. Southwest Sports, 1710 Longhill Road, Benton, AR 72015. Fascinating collection of older American airgun patents.

Punchard, Neal. 2002. *Daisy Air Rifles & BB Guns, The First 100 Years.* 156 pp., 300 color illustrations, MBI Publishing. Not really a guide, but a beautiful celebration of Daisy air guns!

Reno, Brett. 2004. *Airgun Index and Value Guide.* 13th edition, 150+ unnumbered pages in three-ring binder. Brett Reno, RR2 Box 63, Heyworth, IL 61745. No illustrations, descriptions, history, model details, etc. but invaluable for its literature references!

Robinson, Ron. 1998. *The Manic Compressive* 125 pp.; (2001) *Airgun Hunting and Sport,* 138 pp.; (2003) *A Sporting Proposition,* 126 pp. Ron Robinson, 4225 E. Highway 290, Dripping Springs, Texas 78620. Three thoroughly Texan tomes on airgun hunting. Loves hunting with airguns, from his favorite Beeman R1 to latest oriental big bore airguns. A real hunter, real character, real ego! Every airgun hunter should have all three.

Saunders, Tim. 2006. *History Maker, Airgun World* Oct. 2006, pp. 47-59. British report on the Beeman Girardoni: *"The weight of new evidence is such that few doubt that it is indeed the actual Lewis and Clark rifle."*

Schreier, Philip 2006. *The Airgun of Meriwether Lewis and the Corps of Discovery. American Rifleman* Oct.2006: pp. 66-69, 86, 97-99. Senior Arms Curator at the prestigious National Firearms Museum of the NRA reports on the Beeman Girardoni as the Lewis airgun: *"the circumstantial evidence is overwhelming".*

Skanaker, Ragnar and Laslo Antal. 2001. *Sportliches Pistolen-schießen.* (Competitive Pistol Shooting). In German. 194 pp. Motorbuch Verlang, Postbox 103743, Stuttgart 70032, Germany. Includes a chapter on air pistol target shooting.

Shepherd, Arthur. 1987. *Guide to Airgun Hunting.* 123 pp. Argus Books, London. Very interesting, but severely British.

Smith, W.H.G. 1957. *Smith's Standard Encyclopedia of Gas, Air, and Spring Guns of the World.* 279 pp. Arms and Armour Press, London and Melbourne. The initial bible of airguns, badly dated and with many errors, but absolutely indispensable.

Stöckel, Johan F. 1978-82. Revision edited by Eugene Heer: *Heer der Neue Stöckel. Internationales Lexikon der Büchsenmacher, Feurwaffenfabrikanten und Armbrustmacher von 1400-1900.* 2287 pp. Journal-Verlang, Schwend GmbH, Schwäbish Hall, Germany. Extremely expensive, extremely useful three volume guide to virtually all gun makers from 1400 to 1900. In German, but that is not much of a handicap for those speaking other tongues when looking up names and dates.

Thomas, James F., 2000. *The BB Gun Book - A Collectors Guide.* 75 pp. Self-published. (Basically a brief update of the classic 1971 Dunathan book).

Townshend, R.B. 1907. *The Complete Air-Gunner.* 88 pp. I. Upcott Gill, London and Chas. Scribner's Sons, New York. (reprinted). Delightful insight to airgunning at the beginning of the 20th century.

Traister, Robert J. 1981. *All About Airguns.* 306 pp. Tab Books, Blue Ridge Summit, PA. Pot-boiler, largely derived from 1980 Beeman catalog.

Tyler, Jim. 1988. *Vermin Control with an Air Rifle.* Andrew Publishing Company, Ltd. Controlling what Americans call "varmints" or pests.

Wade, Mike. 1984. *The Weihrauch HW 80 and Beeman R1 Air Rifle, A User's Guide to Higher Performance.* 19 pp. Techpress, Mike Wade Engineering, 87 Elgin Rd., Seven Kings, Ilford, Essex, England. Technical, excellent.

Walter, John. 1981. *The Airgun Book.* 146 pp. Arms and Armour Press, London. British based register of then current airguns. Excellent.

Walter, John. 1984. *The Airgun Book,* 3rd Edition. 176 pp. Arms and Armour Press, London. Contains best ever survey of airgun manufacturing history from 1900 to 1984.

Walter, John. 1985, *Airgun Shooting, Performance Directory and Index of Suppliers from A to Z.* 96 pp. Lyon Press Ltd., West Hampstead, London. Sized to fit the vest pocket.

Walter, John. 1987. *The Airgun Book,* 4th Edition. Arms and Armour Press, London. Broadened the scope of this series. The last of an excellent series.

Walter, John. 2002, *Greenhill Dictionary of Guns and Gunmakers.* 576 pp. Greenhill Books, London and Stackpole Books, PA. Indispensable guide includes amazing amount of airgun information. Covers 1836 to 2000.

Wesley, L. and G.V. Cardew. 1979, *Air-Guns and Air-Pistols.* 208 pp. Cassell, London. Updated revision of a British classic on all aspects of airgunning and airguns.

Wolff, Eldon G. 1958. *Air Guns.* 198 pp., Milwaukee Public Museum Publications in History 1, Milwaukee, WI. A classic work on antique airguns. Try to find an original museum edition!

Wolff, Eldon G. 1963. *Air Gun Batteries.* 28 pp. Milwaukee Public Museum Publications in History 5, Milwaukee, Wisconsin. Concise guide to how airgun mechanisms, from early to modern, work. Rare, valuable. Photocopies available in Sale section of www.Beemans.net.

Wolff, Eldon G. 1967. *The Scheiffel and Kunitomo Air Guns.* 54 pp. Milwaukee Public Museum Publications in History 8, Milwaukee, WI. A rare booklet on an unusual pair of antique airguns. Rare collectors' item.

OTHER LITERATURE:

In addition to following the current airgun periodicals and latest books, one cannot remain current, or develop understanding of older models, without consulting the latest and old catalogs from Beeman Precision Airguns, Dynamit-Nobel (RWS), Air Rifle Specialties, etc. There is a wealth of information in factory bulletins and ads. Beeman Precision Airguns was especially productive: look for pre- 1993 *Beeman Technical Bulletins,* and the early *Beeman Precision Airgun Guide/ Catalogs,* starting with Edition One (only 500 were printed!) in 1974, and *Beeman's Shooter's News,* basically a sales bulletin to its retail customers. Especially interesting to airgun collectors are the Beeman Used Gun Lists (the "UGL") published in the 1970s to 1990s. They hold a wealth of information on the large numbers of vintage and antique airguns sold by the company over that period. The former prices of the collectors' items will make today's collectors pale. Old Crosman manuals are also highly collectible.

Finding and Collecting Airgun Literature: Astute collectors, most notably Dean Fletcher and Doug Law, have realized that airgun literature itself has become a key field of collecting. Unlike the airguns themselves, the literature, especially the airgun company literature, generally is quickly lost. Thus the literature becomes both a challenge to collect and a vital link to the special history of the field, which, like so many histories, soon becomes very hazy. As every year passes, this literature becomes harder to find and more valuable in several ways. Many readers will find that many of the references mentioned here have been printed in only limited editions and can be purchased "not for love nor money." Try gunshows and the special order desks of Barnes and Noble and Brothers book stores, and the search services of their websites and those of www.Amazon.com, www.Alibris.com, and especially www.AddALL. com for used and out of print books. Generally these books are not going to be easy to find, so act fast if you do find any. Some airgun literature is available in the "Sale and Wanted" section of www.Beemans.net. Doug Law dlaw1940@ yahoo.com (PO Box 42, Sidney, NE 69162) specializes in the sale of airgun literature. (The *Blue Books of Airguns* themselves have become a very collectible series. Hardbound editions are the most sought. They can sell for up to 100 dollars and more.)

INDEX